ENGLISH HISTORICAL DOCUMENTS

General Editor

DAVID C. DOUGLAS

M.A., D.Litt., F.B.A.

ENGLISH HISTORICAL DOCUMENTS

General Editor: DAVID C. DOUGLAS, M.A., D.LITT., F.B.A.

VOLUMES

ANTIQUITY TO EARLY MEDIEVAL

I *c.* 500–1042 DOROTHY WHITELOCK
II 1042–1189 DAVID C. DOUGLAS AND GEORGE W. GREENAWAY
III 1189–1327 HARRY ROTHWELL

LATE MEDIEVAL

IV 1327–1485 A. R. MYERS
V 1485–1558 C. H. WILLIAMS

EARLY MODERN

VI 1660–1714 ANDREW BROWNING
VII 1714–1783 D. B. HORN AND MARY RANSOME

MODERN

VIII 1783–1832 A. ASPINALL AND E. ANTHONY SMITH
IX 1833–1874 G. M. YOUNG AND W. D. HANDCOCK
X 1874–1914 W. D. HANDCOCK

GENERAL PREFACE

ENGLISH HISTORICAL DOCUMENTS is a work designed to meet a present need. Its purpose is to make generally accessible a wide selection of the fundamental sources of English history.

During the past half-century there has been an immense accumulation of historical material, but only a fraction of this has been made readily available to the majority of those who teach or who study history. The transcendent importance of the original authorities is recognized, but direct approach to them remains difficult, and even some of the basic texts (which are frequently quoted) are hard to consult. A gulf has thus opened between the work of the specialist scholar and those students, both at schools and universities, who best can profit by his labours. Historical studies tend too often today to consist of a commentary on documents which are not included in the available books; and, in the absence of any representative and accessible collection of the sources, the formation of opinion proceeds without that direct study of the evidence which alone can give validity to historical judgment.

The editors of these volumes consider that this situation now calls for a remedy. They have striven to supply one by providing what they hope can be regarded as an authoritative work of primary reference.

An enterprise of this nature could only be effective if planned on a large scale. In scope and content, therefore, these volumes differ materially from the conventional 'source-books' which usually contain only a restricted number of selected extracts. Here, within much wider limits, the editors have sought to produce a comprehensive *corpus* of evidence relating generally to the period with which they deal. Their aim, in each case, has been to present the material with scholarly accuracy, and without bias. Editorial comment has thus been directed, in the main, towards making the evidence intelligible, and not to drawing conclusions from it. Full account has been taken of modern textual criticism to compile a reliable collection of authentic testimony, but the reader has in general been left to pass his own judgment upon this, and to appraise for himself the value of current historical verdicts. A general introduction to each volume seeks to portray the character of the period under review, and critical bibliographies have been added to assist further investigation.

The material to be included in each volume naturally varies according to the needs of each period as assessed by the editors. The present book attempts to document the main trends in English history during the central years of the eighteenth century. Thus the constitutional problems of the age are displayed in the operation of the Legislature, and in the relations of Parliament with the Crown on the one hand, and with the people on the other. Legal Administration and Public Finance are illustrated, and particular attention has been paid to the economic and social state of the nation at this period. Separate sections have been devoted to Scotland and Ireland, and the concluding portion of the book is concerned with the documentation of foreign policy. In general, this book can be regarded as, in some sense, forming a sequel to Vol. VIII of this Series, which was devoted to the later Stuart period, and the arrangement of these two volumes is similar. Both of them, moreover, stand in direct relation to Vol. IX in the Series, where American colonial development before 1776 has been specifically documented.

All concerned in this Series are fully aware of the magnitude of the undertaking to which they have addressed themselves. They are conscious of the hazards of selecting from the inexhaustible store of historical material. They realize also the difficulties involved in editing so large a mass of very varied texts in accordance with the exigent demands of modern scholarship. They believe, however, that the essential prerequisite for the healthy development of English historical studies is wider acquaintance with the original authorities for English history. And they are content that their work should be judged by the degree to which they have succeeded in promoting this object.

DAVID DOUGLAS

VOLUME VII

ENGLISH HISTORICAL DOCUMENTS
1714–1783

ENGLISH HISTORICAL DOCUMENTS

1714–1783

Edited by

D. B. HORN

M.A., D.LITT.

and

MARY RANSOME

M.A.

London and New York

First published in 1957 by Eyre & Spottiswoode Ltd

Reissued in 1996 by Routledge
11 New Fetter Lane
London EC4P 4EE

Reprinted 1998

Simultaneously published in the USA and Canada
by Routledge
29 West 35th Street
New York, NY 10001

Printed and bound in Great Britain by
Antony Rowe Ltd, Chippenham, Wiltshire

British Library Cataloguing in Publication Data
A catalogue record for this book is available from the British Library

Library of Congress Cataloguing in Publication Data
A catalogue record for this book is available from the Library of Congress

ISBN 0-415-14372-1

Complete set	0-415-14361-6	Vol.I	0-415-14366-7
		Vol.II	0-415-14367-5
		Vol.III	0-415-14368-3
Boxed set 1	0-415-14362-4	Vol.IV	0-415-14369-1
Boxed set 2	0-415-14363-2	Vol.V	0-415-14370-5
Boxed set 3	0-415-14364-0	Vol.VI	0-415-14371-3
Boxed set 4	0-415-14365-9	Vol.VII	0-415-14372-1
		Vol.VIII	0-415-14373-X
		Vol.IX	0-415-14374-8
		Vol.X	0-415-14375-6

ACKNOWLEDGEMENTS

THE editors wish to express their thanks to Professor Richard Pares, who spared the time to read the General Introduction in typescript and to give them the benefit, which they much appreciate, of his advice and constructive criticism; to the General Editor of the series, Professor David Douglas, for his encouragement and his helpful criticism of the Volume as a whole; to Mr. R. Mackworth-Young of the Royal Archives, Windsor, who kindly undertook to check extracts from the *Correspondence of George III* against the original letters; to the Librarians and staff of the Edinburgh and Birmingham University Libraries, whose efficient and cheerful help has lightened the labour of collecting the material used in the preparation of this Volume; and to the Librarian and staff of the National Library of Scotland for help in checking the bibliographical sections.

Permission has been generously granted to include extracts from many works still under copyright. The editors have to acknowledge the gracious permission of Her Majesty the Queen to make use of material from the Royal Archives, Windsor. Their grateful thanks are also due to the Comptroller of H.M. Stationery Office for permission to make extensive use of its publications; and to the following owners of copyright: the Marquess of Bute (*Letters of George III to Lord Bute*); Mr. Romney Sedgwick (editor of those *Letters* and of *Lord Hervey's Memoirs*); Professor Bonamy Dobrée (*Lord Chesterfield's Letters*); Mr. Philip Yorke (P. C. Yorke, *Life and Correspondence of Lord Hardwicke*); the Royal College of Physicians, Edinburgh (letter of James Lind in their possession); the Catholic Record Society (two extracts on the Yorkshire Catholics); the Navy Records Society (*Letters of Samuel Hood*, the *Sandwich Papers* and Julian S. Corbett, *Signals and Instructions, 1776–94*); the Old Edinburgh Club ('The New Town of Edinburgh'); the Royal Historical Society (*Private Correspondence of Chesterfield and Newcastle*); the Scottish History Society (*The Lyon in Mourning*); the Yorkshire Archaeological Society (*Archbishop Herring's Visitation Returns, 1743*); G. Bell & Sons (*Correspondence of Jonathan Swift*, and *Early Diary of Frances Burney*); Basil Blackwell (*Prose Works of Jonathan Swift*, ed. H. Davis); the Cambridge University Press (genealogical table from the *Cambridge Modern History*); the Clarendon Press (*Genealogical Tables illustrative of Modern History* and C. P. Moritz, *Travels through England*); Constable & Company (*The Blecheley Diary of William Cole*); Hugh Hopkins, Glasgow (Faujas de Saint Fond, *Journey through England and Scotland*); Jackson, Son & Co. (H. M. Cadell, *The Story of the Forth*, and *Scottish Historical Review*);

William Kimber & Co. Ltd. (*Journal of Augustus Hervey*, ed. David Erskine); the University of London Press (Lillian M. Penson, *Colonial Agents of the British West Indies*, now out of print); Longmans, Green & Co. (D. O. Dykes, *Source Book of Constitutional History*, and *English Historical Review*); The Macmillan Company of New York (*Correspondence of William Shirley*, and *Correspondence of William Pitt with Colonial Governors*); the Manchester University Press (document from T. S. Ashton, *Iron and Steel in the Industrial Revolution*); and Methuen & Co. (*The Diary of Dudley Ryder*). The editors would like to take this opportunity of thanking the publishers to whom they addressed enquiries about copyright (those mentioned above and others) for their invariable courtesy and helpfulness.

D. B. Horn
Mary Ransome

NOTE ON DATES

The Old Style of reckoning was still used in England until 1752, when the New Style of the Gregorian Calendar, in general use on the Continent, was also adopted in England. The Old Style began the year on 25 March, and in the eighteenth century was eleven days behind the New Style. In this volume all dates prior to 1752 mentioned in the text, whether of events at home or of events abroad, are given according to the Old Style, but the year is taken as beginning on 1 January, not on 25 March. Dates mentioned in documents are given as they appear in these documents, but where confusion may thus be caused a note is appended.

CONTENTS

F. THE MOVEMENT FOR PARLIAMENTARY REFORM

PART III. THE LAW AND ITS ADMINISTRATION

A. THE LAW

(a) *Statutes*

(b) *Judicial Proceedings*

B. CENTRAL ADMINISTRATION AND THE KEEPING OF ORDER

C. LOCAL GOVERNMENT

PART IV. PUBLIC FINANCE

A. REVENUE AND EXPENDITURE

B. CUSTOMS AND EXCISE

C. DIRECT TAXES

D. FINANCIAL ADMINISTRATION

E. THE NATIONAL DEBT

Part V. THE CHURCHES

A. CHURCH AND STATE

B. THE CONDITION OF THE CHURCH OF ENGLAND

(a) *Ecclesiastical Revenues*

(b) *The Work of the Clergy*

C. THE METHODISTS

D. NONCONFORMITY

(a) *The Protestant Dissenters*

(b) The Catholics

PART VI. THE STATE OF THE NATION: ECONOMIC

A. AGRICULTURE

B. INDUSTRY

(a) Textiles

(*b*) *The Midland Industries*

(*c*) *Mines*

C. COMBINATIONS OF WORKMEN

D. TRADE

E. SOME POPULATION STATISTICS

Part VII. THE STATE OF THE NATION: SOCIAL

Part VIII. THE ARMED FORCES

(b) Administration

B. THE HIGHLANDS AND THE RISINGS OF 1715 AND 1745

C. SCOTLAND AFTER 1745

PART X. IRELAND

A. RELATIONS WITH ENGLAND

B. RELIGION

C. ECONOMIC AND SOCIAL CONDITIONS

PART XI. THE COLONIES

A. EIGHTEENTH-CENTURY VIEWS ON COLONIES

B. COLONIAL TRADE

C. GENERAL ORGANIZATION

D. AMERICA

(*a*) *The Thirteen Colonies*

(b) *The West Indies*

(c) *Canada*

(d) *Nova Scotia and Newfoundland*

E. INDIA

F. AFRICA

Part XII. FOREIGN POLICY AND WARS

C. TREATIES

APPENDICES

DIAGRAMS

MAPS

INDEX TO TEXTS

ENGLAND AND WAL

[Based on the map in E. and A. G.
are tak

DURHAM Boroughs with 1,000 voters or more
BERWICK Boroughs with 500-999 voters
Morpeth Boroughs with 200-499 voters
SEAFORD Boroughs with 50-199 voters
Appleby Boroughs with under 50 voters
WICK
Morpeth
EWCASTLE
DURHAM
DURHAM
hmond
Northallerton
THIRSK
Scarborough
RIPON
BOROUGHBRIDGE
Malton
ALDBOROUGH
YORK
YORKSHIRE
BEVERLEY
HULL
HEDON
Pontefract
GRIMSBY
LINCS
E. RETFORD
NOTTS
LINCOLN
DERBY
NEWARK
NOTTINGHAM
Boston
DERBY
Grantham
Castle Rising
King's Lynn
LEICS
STAMFORD
RUT-LAND
YARMOUTH
LEICESTER
PETERBOROUGH
NORFOLK
NORWICH
OVENTRY
NORTHANTS
HUNTS
CAMBS
Thetford
HIGHAM FERRERS
Huntingdon
Eye
WARWICK
Cambridge & U.
Bury St. Edmunds
Dunwich
NORTHAMPTON
SUFFOLK
Aldeburgh
BEDFORD
SUDBURY
Orford
Banbury
Brackley
IPSWICH
Buckingham
OXON
BUCKS
BEDS
HERTS
COLCHESTER
Harwich
WOODSTOCK
AYLESBURY
HERTFORD
OXFORD & U.
WENDOVER
ST. ALBANS
MALDON
AGMONDESHAM
ABINGDON
WYCOMBE
ESSEX
WALLINGFORD
Marlow
MIDDLESEX
WESTMINSTER
LONDON
Windsor
SOUTHWARK
QUEENBOROUGH
Marlborough
BEDWIN
BERKS
READING
ROCHESTER
SURREY
Gatton
Sandwich
LUDGERSHALL
BLETCHINGLEY
KENT
WHITCHURCH
Reigate
MAIDSTONE
CANTERBURY
Andover
GUILDFORD
HASLEMERE
STOCKBRIDGE
E. Grinstead
HYTHE
DOVER
SALISBURY
WINCHESTER
Horsham
New Romney
PETERSFIELD
SUSSEX
Midhurst
Bramber
Rye
SOUTHAMPTON
STEYNING
Winchelsea
Lewes
LYMINGTON
Hastings
SEAFORD
CHICHESTER
ARUNDEL
NEW SHOREHAM
PORTSMOUTH
Newport
YARMOUTH
NEWTOWN
I. OF WIGHT

G THE PARLIAMENTARY BOROUGHS

ned House of Commons, 1909, Vol. I. The numbers of voters
History of the Boroughs, 1792.]

GENERAL INTRODUCTION

GENERAL INTRODUCTION

WHEN historians speak of the eighteenth century they usually mean the years covered by this volume and not the years 1701 to 1800. The reign of Anne is best regarded as a period of transition between the seventeenth and eighteenth centuries. The eighties and nineties saw the irrevocable triumph of the French Revolution and the Industrial Revolution, which between them were to determine the character and content of the nineteenth century. The years from 1714 to 1783 therefore present the quintessence of the eighteenth century when at its highest point of development and least modified by residuary traces of its predecessor or the coming shadow of its successor.

The traditional tendency has been to regard this era as a rather dull interlude between the romantic, epoch-making struggles of the seventeenth century and the tremendous moral and material progress which the Victorians prided themselves had been accomplished in their own age. They spoke of it as the age of reason or the age of common sense: literary historians talked of the peace of the Augustans. Politics had ceased to be a life-and-death struggle and become a game played for their own advantage alike by Whig magnate and Tory squire, who paid at best lip service to the voice of the people they claimed to represent. The fierce, spiritual exaltation of Anglican and Puritan had sunk after Anne's death into a tolerant Deism; religious enthusiasm had become bad form, and the bishops were content to take their orders from the masters of the State. Even Professor Basil Williams, with reservations on the period after 1760, wrote of the first half of the century as "an age of stability in politics, in religion, in literature and in social observances, a stability needed to enable the nation to recover its poise after more than a century of excitement".[1]

Yet underneath this appearance of stability changes no less fundamental than those of the seventeenth century were going on. Revolutions usually raise as many questions as they settle and the Revolution of 1688 was no exception. It doubtless determined that in the last resort Parliament was to be the supreme authority in England and, in Locke's interpretation at least, Parliament was, again in the last resort, responsible to the people. But fortunately last resorts do not happen every day, and the Revolution failed to make provision for the daily routine of administration and the active participation of the people in politics.

Some slight progress in the former respect had been made before 1714, but the really effective steps were taken in our period. The casual and inchoate meetings of ministers of 1714 had become an essential and fully recognized part

[1] *The Whig Supremacy*, 1714–60, p. 1.

of the constitution before 1783. It was agreed that while the king had the right to appoint any ministers he pleased, they could hold office only so long as they were acceptable to a majority of the House of Commons.[1] A great step towards a more rational organization of government was taken when the Secretariat of State was organized on a functional basis with the appointment of Lord Hillsborough in 1768 as Secretary of State for the Colonies and the creation in 1782 of the Home and Foreign Offices instead of the anomalous distribution of duties between secretaries of state for the Northern and Southern Departments.[2]

Even more important was the tendency towards the recognition of one man in each ministry as the leading minister. This is traditionally linked with the failure of George I and his successors to attend meetings of the most prominent ministers for the discussion of policy and the taking of executive decisions, which is supposed to have necessitated the appointment of a chairman of the meeting and a reporter to the king of views held and decisions taken. Undoubtedly the political insufficiency of George II and the long tenure of power by Sir Robert Walpole contributed to acclimatize in England the idea of a first minister. It is true that even Walpole did not succeed in establishing entire control over his cabinet, and that in the next few ministries it is often hard to say who was prime minister. Though the mantle (but not the office) of Walpole fell on Henry Pelham, he did not at first enjoy a superintending authority and, even after he succeeded in getting rid of Carteret, he shared power to a considerable extent with his brother, the duke of Newcastle. On Pelham's death, Newcastle after a brief two years of unquestioned ascendancy had in his turn to share power with Pitt from 1757 to 1761. The weak, short-lived ministries which held sway from 1761 to 1770 were rather imperfect coalitions of party leaders than governments with an unquestioned head. Lord North had the opportunity but lacked the will to discharge effectively the duties of a prime minister, so it was not really until the era of the younger Pitt that the office of Prime Minister became in fact an accepted part of the British constitution. This is beyond our period, but it is beyond argument that the idea of a leading minister, with special responsibilities both towards the king and the House of Commons, became current in English political life in the decades between Walpole and the younger Pitt.[3]

It may be suggested that the essential reason for the development of such an office was at least as much in the relationship between ministers and the House of Commons as between ministers and the Crown. Once it had been accepted that ministries must enjoy the support of the House of Commons, the minister whose job it was to secure and retain this indispensable prop of eighteenth-century governments occupied a special position in a cabinet which consisted almost entirely of peers. It was usually an easy matter to replace one or two

[1] Nos. 9–18. [2] Nos. 70 and 227. [3] Nos. 19–27.

unsatisfactory or discontented peers without affecting the stability of the ministry, but men who could manage the House of Commons, even with government patronage behind them, were rare.

The point is illustrated by the predicament in which the duke of Newcastle found himself when he became First Lord of the Treasury in 1754. He offered Henry Fox the post of Secretary of State with the leadership of the House of Commons, but stipulated that he himself should retain the 'management' of the House. Fox declined on the ground that "he should not know how to talk to members of Parliament, when some might have received *gratifications*, others not". Newcastle then secured the appointment of an obscure diplomatist, Sir Thomas Robinson, on his own terms. When Robinson's incapacity to lead the House became apparent, Newcastle reluctantly paid Fox's price, and Fox became Secretary of State "with a notification to be divulged, that he had power with the King to help or hurt in the House of Commons". When Lord Chesterfield heard of the new arrangement he remarked, "The duke of Newcastle had turned out everybody else, and now he has turned out himself." This proved to be an exaggeration, but has the merit of stating forcefully that the management of the House of Commons was so important that the minister who controlled it would in the normal course of events become the leading minister. This is not to imply that the prime ministers of the eighteenth century necessarily sat in the House of Commons, but the system worked much better when they did.

Another marked development during the eighteenth century was the expansion in numbers and importance of the civil service. This was due partly to the extension of the sphere of government and the steadily increasing burden of taxation, but also to the casualness of many eighteenth-century political heads of government departments. This threw responsibility and power upon their under-secretaries or deputies. While he was Secretary of State the duke of Bedford was notorious for his long week-end absences at Woburn, and Lord North's aversion to business made possible the rôle of the Secretary to the Treasury, John Robinson, in the politics of George III's reign. In fact, the continual parliamentary complaints about 'secret influence' under George III[1] were partly at least due to the increased importance of these civil servants in their several departments.

It would, however, be easy to exaggerate the significance of this development since the whole framework of administration was almost as medieval in organization in 1783 as it had been in 1714.[2] Sinecures abounded and many offices which still had duties to perform were held by influential politicians or their relations and the duties discharged by deputy. Payment was still largely by fees, gratuities and casual windfalls. Appointments were often made not

[1] No. 25. [2] No. 68.

for administrative efficiency but to increase government influence in the House of Commons. Once appointed, there was very little supervision and many opportunities for private profit: one Lord Chancellor in our period was found guilty of corruption–Lord Macclesfield in 1725. But the appointment in 1780 of a body of commissioners to examine into the public accounts marked the beginning of a new era. In a series of reports the commissioners presented to Parliament a clear view of the defects of the existing system of spending and accounting for public money.[1] Most of their recommendations were adopted by the younger Pitt.

The slowness with which the eighteenth century worked towards a centralized and efficient administration was partly due to the anomalous position of the fighting services.[2] Since there was no such parliamentary jealousy of the navy as there was, until almost the end of our period, of the army, it is customary to regard naval organization as simple and even rational. Nevertheless the secretaries of state usually had more responsibility for the conduct of naval operations than the Admiralty. The fleets during the war of the Austrian Succession were controlled mainly by the duke of Newcastle and directed in the Seven Years War by Pitt, while Lord George Germain, the colonial secretary, exercised almost as much power over naval operations in the next war. The essential task of the Admiralty was naval administration,[3] not the conduct of operations. In this sphere it was supreme and almost independent of external control. The details of organization were divided amongst different boards, the Navy Board, which was responsible for most supplies, the Victualling Board, the Sick and Hurt Board, while there were even separate boards of commissioners for each royal dockyard. By 1782 there were thirteen different departments, administered on thirteen different sites, responsible for different aspects of naval administration. Over these semi-autonomous departments the Board of Admiralty, while theoretically supreme, had in practice a somewhat imperfect control.

The lowest point in naval administration was reached under Walpole. That the system worked as well as it did subsequently was due largely to the reforms of Anson, who served on the Admiralty Board from 1744 to 1762, and later Sir Charles Middleton, who was comptroller of the navy from 1779 to 1790. Anson introduced the principle of retirement, the abandonment of promotion in strict seniority and the wearing of uniform by naval officers, remodelled the code of naval discipline, adopted a more logical classification of ships, reorganized the corps of marines and struggled to free naval tactics from the dead weight of the traditional *Fighting Instructions*. His work in this last respect had little result until it was taken up and developed by the great admirals of the

[1] No. 89. [2] Nos. 161–182. [3] Nos. 166–169.

succeeding age, Kempenfelt and Howe, who, by adopting a numerary system of signals, gave to their successors a freedom of action and flexibility of manœuvre which made possible the rôle of the British navy in the wars of the French Revolution and Empire.[1]

While naval administration was complicated and defective enough, the army was in much a worse case. The Hanoverian kings took a particular interest in military matters and guarded jealously the royal prerogative of supreme command over all the military forces. These included the militia, which was reorganized in 1757 and in which Gibbon served as a captain with consequent improvement to the *Decline and Fall*, but the standing army was the main thing. Until the middle of the century, in peace-time nearly half the army was on the Irish establishment and maintained from the Irish revenues. Royal control of the militia and the regular army was usually exercised through the secretaries of state, who were responsible equally for the general strategy of a war, the movement of troops, the provision of adequate supplies of ammunition, arrangements for home defence and a dozen other duties. But the secretary at war, who first appeared in the preceding century as the personal secretary of the commander-in-chief, had an ill-defined though certainly subordinate share in the administration of the army throughout the eighteenth century. He issued marching orders to regimental officers and beating orders for recruitment,[2] made arrangements for billeting troops[3] and often presented to Parliament estimates for military expenditure on specific objects. A further complication was introduced at times when the Crown delegated part of its supreme authority to a commander-in-chief such as the duke of Cumberland in 1746. In addition there was the paymaster of the forces, responsible for paying officers and men, widows and pensioners as well as the subsidies paid to foreign rulers for the hire of troops, and the Board of General Officers which was mainly concerned with army clothing. It should also be remembered that the Board of Ordnance, which exercised a co-ordinate authority both with the army and the navy and had direct access to Parliament, was responsible for supplying arms and stores needed by both services. In fact, the determination of the Hanoverian kings to retain as far as possible their personal control over the army, coupled with parliamentary suspicion of a permanent military organization, prevented during our period the establishment of a single War Ministry, the duties of which were divided to an almost incredible degree amongst various officials and departments.

Nevertheless it was precisely at this time that a standing army, though it can hardly be said to have become an integral part of the constitution, was at least grafted on to it. The number of soldiers authorized in the annual Mutiny Acts increased rapidly in time of war, but the peace-time establishment remained

[1] No. 171. [2] Nos. 172 and 173. [3] Nos. 180 and 181.

almost stationary until the accession of George III, after which there was a notable increase. But clearly the contemporary hopes entertained by the opposition Peers in 1717 that the regular army of old soldiers, if they did not die would at any rate fade away, had proved illusory. In 1715 and 1717 Acts of Parliament recognized and increased the statutory powers of the Crown to maintain discipline in the army by issuing articles of war and the soldier, without abandoning his rights and duties as a citizen, became subject to a special code of military law.

Probably had the royal authority been greater the army would have been more efficient and the administration would certainly have been simpler. George I would gladly have ended the practice of purchasing commissions and did at least stop the worst abuses of the system, while George II took a personal interest in army uniforms[1] and equipment and introduced the use of official numbers and titles for the regiments which had hitherto been customarily referred to as Colonel So-and-so's regiment. More important was the formation of permanent artillery companies which became in 1727 the Royal Regiment of Artillery while in 1741 Woolwich Academy was founded to train artillery officers. A corps of engineer officers dates from 1717. George III shared the interests of his predecessors, tried to limit the evils of patronage and purchase of commissions and insisted on the need for experienced and capable staff and field officers during the war of American Independence. It must in fairness be added that his efforts do not appear to have had much practical result.

If on the whole the eighteenth century did little to provide for the effective administration of the fighting services, it had certainly witnessed substantial progress towards the establishment of our modern system of civil government. While the responsibility of the monarchy for administration remained unquestioned, the actual exercise of power was passing into the hands of a group of ministers, assisted by the departmental civil servants for whose conduct they were responsible to the House of Commons.

It cannot be argued that nearly so much progress had been made before 1783 to settle the other problem raised by the Revolution of 1688, that is, to make provision for the effective participation of the people in politics. This was mainly because contemporaries did not regard this as a problem at all; though Locke himself had pointed out that the system of representation was anachronistic. As the eighteenth century went on, it became more and more unsatisfactory from the standpoint of a modern democrat. The rise of industry in some areas and its decline in others led to appreciable movements of population in the latter years of the century, which had no counterpart in the representative system. Even more important, new sectional interests organized themselves,

[1] No. 177.

West Indian planters and East Indian nabobs, and competed vigorously with the older groups for seats in the House of Commons.

Even so, in most constituencies the result of a poll was a foregone conclusion and actual contests were few in comparison with unopposed returns. Sir Lewis Namier has calculated that only forty-eight constituencies finally went to the polls in the general election of 1761. In fact, Rousseau's gibe about the English people being free only during a general election shows a misunderstanding of the functions of general elections in eighteenth-century England. With the possible exception of that held in 1741, "no government", Sir David Keir informs us, "ever lost a general election, nor did any government, until the ill-success of that of Lord North in the American War caused its overthrow in 1782, ever fail to sway Parliament so long as it possessed the King's confidence".

Nevertheless it is easy to trace in this period the pressure of public opinion at times of crisis upon the government and the tentative beginnings of nineteenth-century democracy. It is significant that the exceptional cases in 1741 and 1782 both occurred in times of unsuccessful war, when patriotic feeling rose high and swept a government, discredited by failure, out of office. To them may be added the hurried abdication of the duke of Newcastle in 1756 and the firm establishment of Pitt as war minister in the following year without the necessity of a general election. In each case the will of the people made itself felt with effect in spite of the admitted inadequacy of the representative system.

Further progress was made in the first part of George III's reign when the main body of Whigs, led by Rockingham and inspired by Burke, began to transform itself from a Hanoverian Court party, foremost in advocating the vested interests of the landed and moneyed oligarchy, into a party which unequivocally asserted the sovereignty of the people. Amongst the measures which they demanded at this time were reforms designed to bring the legislature and the people into closer contact, purification of administration, reduction of royal 'influence' in the Commons, and the rights of electors to choose their representatives freely and keep themselves informed of the conduct of those representatives by the publication of division lists and reports of debates. Admittedly they had not carried out much of this programme before 1783, but a beginning had been made.[1]

Probably more important in the long run than the first faltering steps of the official Whig party along the road that was to lead them to the Reform Bill of 1832 and all that followed from it was the appearance of a much more radical party under the leadership of John Wilkes. The agitation over the Middlesex election of 1768[2] marks the effective entry into English political life of the democratic forces which were to triumph in the following century. 'Junius' had already called attention to Locke's statement that it was the duty

[1] Nos. 33 and 34. [2] No. 39.

and right of the sovereign people to remodel a corrupt legislature; but it was Wilkes who gave practical effect to the academic theory by defying the House of Commons and demonstrating that he had support not only from the London mob but from respectable freeholders throughout England.

It is characteristic of English political life that Wilkes and his supporters tried to throw the cloak of conservatism over their revolutionary proposals. The political society which was organized to support him in 1769 called itself the Society of Supporters of the Bill of Rights, but its objects included not only the already familiar demand for the exclusion of placemen from the House of Commons[1] but a radical programme of parliamentary reorganization, including electoral reform, annual parliaments and the recognition of the duty of members of Parliament to pay heed to the views and instructions of their constituents.

This new Radical party, in an uneasy alliance with the Rockingham Whigs, brought about the constitutional crisis of 1779–1780. Though they secured a snap victory in the House of Commons when Dunning's celebrated motion that "the power of the Crown has increased, is increasing and ought to be diminished" was carried by a majority in 1780, their Whig allies were half-hearted and failed to drive home their victory. The Radicals themselves did not succeed in establishing a permanent national organization which they had at one time hoped would be able to act as a counterpoise to Parliament itself. Lord North's government continued to govern by influence for another two years, and the threatened overthrow of the traditional eighteenth-century system was averted. Nevertheless from this period onwards the Radical party has had a continuous influence and existence, and it originates in the late sixties and seventies of the eighteenth century.[2]

When we turn from the central government and national politics to local administration, the description of the eighteenth century as an age of stability is seen to be much more applicable. In essentials the system had not been altered since the reign of Elizabeth, except in so far as the overthrow of the House of Stuart, and the triumph of the country gentry class in the constitutional struggles of the seventeenth century, had all but ended supervision of local government by central authorities except in times of disturbance and civil war. The main units of local administration, the parish, the borough and the county with their respective officials, some of whom were appointed by the Crown while others were, in theory at least, elected, did from time to time have new tasks assigned to them by statute, but neither Parliament nor the central government took the trouble to supervise effectively the local authorities in the discharge of their new or even of their old customary duties.

Much the most important of the local officials were the justices of the peace,

[1] No. 32. [2] Nos. 52–57.

who were appointed by the Crown and possessed very wide powers, which were constantly being added to in our period. Apart from their judicial powers, they fixed rates for various local purposes,[1] including poor relief and upkeep of bridges, jails and houses of correction, appointed the overseers of the poor, the surveyors of highways and often the parish constables, licensed trades and dealt with disorderly houses. In rural districts the justices were drawn from the same class as the members of Parliament and formed a close oligarchy, especially when legislation in George II's reign raised the property qualification of justices from an estate of £20 per annum to one of £100. Combining as they did judicial and administrative powers and practically unsupervised in their exercise of them by any superior authority, they tended to become local tyrants. Many of them exercised their powers benevolently for what they considered to be the public good; but even of them the saying probably holds good that all power corrupts and absolute power corrupts absolutely. Others used their power quite arbitrarily and unscrupulously in their own interests to punish poachers, revenge private injuries or fancied slights, and intimidate their servants and humble neighbours.

In urban areas the results were probably still less satisfactory. Burke described the Middlesex magistrates as the scum of the earth, and the Webbs after an elaborate inquiry into the activities of the 'trading justices' who flourished there more or less endorse his condemnation. Undoubtedly many of these trading justices were men of bad character, who contrived to make a living out of an unpaid magistracy. Bribery and corruption flourished, while drunkenness, prostitution, theft and highway robbery were unrepressed. Yet even here the eighteenth century can point to the unremitting activity of the two Fieldings at Bow Street to restore public well-being and security, which anticipated in essentials the work of the stipendiary magistrates of the nineteenth century.[2]

In the sphere of local government, then, the most obvious characteristic is local diversity and the absence of uniformity and system. It is true that the whole structure was based on the general acceptance of the principle that there was an obligation on all citizens when called upon to undertake administrative, judicial and executive duties without payment. The extraordinary thing is not that a system based on this principle worked so badly, but that it continued to function at all. It is clear that eighteenth-century society was no longer content with the traditional framework of local government which it had inherited, any more than with a central government founded on royal influence over an oligarchic parliament. Professor Holdsworth in his great *History of English Law* has shown how the existing authorities sometimes added to their customary duties additional statutory powers for such purposes as paving and lighting streets or regulating markets. Even more frequently in response to local

[1] No. 74. [2] No. 73.

petitions Parliament sanctioned the establishment of new authorities to meet new needs, notably the turnpike trusts. Anyone who turns over the pages of the *Journals of the House of Commons* in the second half of the eighteenth century cannot fail to be impressed by the numerous schemes for local improvements due to individual initiative or a strong feeling of corporate interest.

Little need be said about the judiciary in the eighteenth century. Its separation from the legislative and executive power was regarded by contemporary publicists as an essential basis of English liberty and had for all practical purposes been secured by the Act of Settlement. George III on his accession removed the last remnant of executive control over the judiciary by securing the passage of an Act which made the tenure of office by the judges independent of the demise of the Crown.[1]

In the main the complex legal system inherited from previous ages was passed on without substantial modification by the great lawyers of this century to their successors. Such reforms as were made were often secured in the teeth of opposition by the lawyers. The substitution of English for Latin in legal proceedings in 1731[2] was still regretted by Blackstone a generation later. More important was Hardwicke's reform of the law of marriage by the famous Act of 1753.[3] In 1736 witchcraft ceased to be a crime; but eighteenth-century Parliaments were constantly creating new felonies and prescribing the death penalty without benefit of clergy for such offences as cutting down cherry trees and stealing sheep. The intention was undoubtedly to deter criminals by severity of punishment, but such laws defeated their own end. The eighteenth-century police force was quite unable to arrest more than a fraction of such offenders, and even those who were brought to book frequently escaped punishment owing to the reluctance of witnesses to give evidence against them and of juries to convict them. A considerable percentage even of those who were convicted were in fact pardoned either unconditionally or subject to transportation for a term of years. Thus certainty of punishment was completely lacking.

Sir John Fielding's experiments in the metropolitan area indicated the line which reform was to take in the nineteenth century, but they were not immediately followed up. Nevertheless it is possible to trace before the end of our period a growing aversion to the haphazard brutality of the eighteenth-century criminal law. Burke wrote of criminals that "they are the diseased and infirm part of our country, which we must treat with sharpness indeed, but with all the tenderness in our power. They are under cure; and that is a state which calls for tenderness, and diligence, and great consideration. We are in a great hospital, and it ill becomes us to be angry with our patients." The modern psychiatrist could not say more.

[1] No. 63. [2] No. 60. [3] No. 62.

On the whole the judges of the eighteenth century seem to have been upright and competent in discharging their professional duties. Lord Chancellor Macclesfield was certainly an exception and not a type, though there were no doubt other cases where the distinction between a legitimate perquisite and an actual bribe was not drawn as clearly as it might have been. But the charges usually brought against them concern their private rather than their professional lives, the drunkenness of Lord Chancellor Northington, the lechery of Sir John Willes, Chief Justice of the Common Pleas, and the insolent brutality of Lord Chancellor Thurlow.

At least two judges of our period left a permanent impression on the English legal system. In the opinion of Sir William Holdsworth, Lord Hardwicke, who held the office of Chancellor for nearly twenty years, "laid the foundations and erected a large part of the edifice of modern Equity", while Lord Mansfield, Chief Justice of the Common Pleas for thirty years, reformed and developed the common law and "settled the main principles of our modern system of commercial and maritime law". Sir William Holdsworth concludes that, "The fact that English law was able to adapt its principles to the needs of the new age of reform and yet remained a stable and steadying influence in the life of the nation, was due principally to the influence of Mansfield's work." Yet Mansfield was the best-hated man of his time, universally regarded as an upholder of prerogative and, after Bute, the secret and irresponsible counsellor of the king in tyrannical courses.

Contemporaries do not trouble to explain how this sinister ogre of the political backstairs was also the judge who reversed the sentence of outlawry on John Wilkes and declared general warrants illegal, extended the protection afforded to Protestant Dissenters by his famous dictum that nonconformity was no longer a crime, strained the law in favour of Roman Catholics with the result that his house was destroyed in the Gordon Riots, and declared that the state of slavery was "so odious that nothing can be suffered to support it, but positive law", and since it was not allowed or approved by the law of England the power of a master over his slave ended as soon as the slave landed on English soil.[1]

To these great names may perhaps be added that of Chief Justice Pratt, Lord Camden, who is remembered for his judgments on general warrants which stripped the secretaries of state of the discretionary powers which they had gradually assumed in the course of the preceding centuries.[2]

The English financial system of the eighteenth century was as chaotic as the general administration. Such superintending and co-ordinating work as was accomplished was discharged by the Treasury Board, but its authority over naval and military expenditure was incomplete. Estimates for such naval and

[1] Nos. 65 (*d*); 108; 66. [2] No. 65 (*c*) and (*e*).

military expenditure as could be foreseen were regularly presented to the House of Commons, usually by the secretary at war or the treasurer of the navy, but frequently the money was spent first and then subsequently authorized.

Expenditure on civil government was not regularly estimated, since it was defrayed from the Civil List which was voted to the king at the beginning of his reign. This sum was supposed to cover the personal expenses of the king and his family, the cost of the royal court, the payment of the ministers and civil service, including the judges and foreign ministers, and a heterogeneous mass of wages, pensions, annuities and charities. In practice it was never adequate, and from time to time on a royal appeal to Parliament the amount was increased and the civil list debts discharged. Under George II the Crown refused to submit accounts of the expenditure of the civil list to Parliament, but under George III accounts from 1752 to 1770 were submitted and may be examined in the *Journals of the House of Commons*.[1]

But down to the closing years of our period, if not beyond it, the Crown maintained that expenditure from the civil list was no concern of Parliament, and since there was no real accountability to Parliament and the other spending ministries did not admit the superiority of the Treasury, Treasury control was inevitably lax and in some spheres non-existent. This explains what strikes the student at first sight as an extraordinary anomaly that there are no contemporary official statements of the national revenue and expenditure, though unofficial budgets were prepared by economists such as Postlethwayt. The inquirer who wishes to examine the national balance-sheets from 1714 to 1783 must have recourse to a compilation made in the following century on the initiative of Mr. Gladstone and published officially in *Parliamentary Papers, House of Commons, 1868–69*, vol. 35.

Little need be said about taxation in our period. The outline of the system had been determined in the previous reigns and was not appreciably modified before 1783. Apart from gradual changes in contemporary opinions about taxation, the only significant development was the steady increase in the amount raised by the various taxes.[2]

The national income and expenditure of the first and last years of our period may reasonably be selected for purposes of comparison.[3] Both came at the end of long and costly wars. It is true that the regnal year 23 George III was a year when the war of American Independence was still being carried on, whereas the Spanish Succession War had been concluded before the accession of George I. On the other hand, Anne had left behind her an exceptional burden of current debt–for example, the salaries of her diplomatic agents were months and in some cases several years in arrears–and this threw an exceptional burden of expenditure on the new government.

[1] Vol. XXXII, pp. 466–603. [2] Nos. 82–87. [3] No. 77.

In the regnal year 1 and 2 George I, if we ignore a few comparatively trifling items such as stamps £142,207, the Customs produced £1,684,661, the Excise duties £2,302,807 and the Land Tax, etc., £1,128,669. The corresponding figures for the regnal year 23 George III are Customs £2,949,374, Excise £5,479,975 and Land Tax, etc., £2,595,639. The amount raised in customs duties had almost doubled and excise duties and land tax, etc., more than doubled, while the yield from stamps now reached the respectable total of £855,025. In both years the amount raised by taxation was quite inadequate to meet the annual expenditure. It has been reckoned that in 1 and 2 George I £3,025,333 was raised by the creation of debt and in 23 George III the corresponding figure was £17,379,392.

Turning to expenditure the main items in 1 and 2 George I were various payments connected with the National Debt which amounted to £3,275,683, to which must be added £2,220,542 applied to the reduction of debt. The expenses of civil government amounted to £733,669 while the army, navy and ordnance services required £2,218,997. By 23 George III the interest and management of the public debt had risen to £8,054,141, to which must be added £5,927,447 applied in reduction of debt, the total cost of civil government to £1,788,531, and the army, navy and ordnance services to £13,667,041. Thus debt charges rose from approximately 2½ millions to 14 millions; civil government expenditure more than doubled; and the army, navy and ordnance costs rose from 2½ millions to 13½ millions.

Contemporaries were well aware that these spectacular increases were due to the protracted wars in which Britain at this time was repeatedly engaged, and they were particularly apprehensive at the accumulating burden of debt. Another war, it seemed to them, would ruin us for ever. It is true that since England prospered the revenue displayed a certain elasticity which rejoiced the stony hearts of chancellors of the exchequer. Sir John Sinclair calculated that at the Revolution of 1688 the income of England was usually reckoned at 43 millions and the maximum amount which could be raised in taxes, without completely ruining the country, was placed at 2 millions. A century later the national income, Sinclair asserted, could not be less than 120 millions of which 15 millions were paid in taxation, "and any popular clamour that is heard, is more owing to the manner in which our taxes are laid on, than to the quantum which is levied". This he attributes largely to the fact that only about 2 millions were raised in taxation on property, whereas 13 millions were levied upon consumption and the consumer in a luxurious age "confounding the duty and the price together, furnishes, without reluctance, to the public treasury a sum which by any other means could hardly have been exacted".[1]

The changes in taxation made in successive sessions of Parliament from 1714

[1] No. 78.

to 1783 show that substantial increases were made again and again in the rates of duty payable in customs and excise and that desperate attempts were made to find new sources of revenue from luxury expenditure.[1] Thus Pelham in 1748, after employing his thoughts for some months on devising a tax "which will be most easily raised by those that are subjected to the payment of it, and which will be least burthensome to the people in general, especially of the poorer sort", could only propose "a new impost of poundage upon all goods imported". This he justifies on the ground that it will not affect the poor who subsist on home-produced articles and the trifling increase in the price of imported goods "will hardly be felt by the better sort of people". It may be noted in passing that successive increases of this sort made our customs duties by the end of the period a trackless labyrinth. Only a few clerks at the Customs House, with years of experience behind them, were capable of calculating correctly the duties payable on most imported goods.[2]

Few aspects of eighteenth-century life have been more severely and universally censured than its attitude to religion.[3] Not only did Deism hold sway in high places, but the Established Church and the old Dissenting congregations vied with each other in complacency and lethargy. The temper of the age was so secular as to be easily confused with complete indifference to religion: its practice was so completely Erastian that bishops often received their offices as a reward for political services to the government such as writing pamphlets in support of its policy or, in one extreme case, deciphering the intercepted dispatches of foreign diplomatists. Since the income of the various sees ranged from Canterbury at £7,000 a year to Bristol at £360, most holders of the poorly endowed bishoprics were eager to secure translation to a better paid see and in the meantime had to supplement their incomes by holding deaneries and other ecclesiastical benefices *in commendam*. Thus the higher clergy of the Hanoverian age spent a large part of their energies in a perpetual scramble for preferment and many of them were not too particular about the methods they used to curry favour with the dispensers of patronage. Nothing endeared a bishop or indeed a would-be bishop more to the duke of Newcastle than effective assistance in winning a hard-fought electoral contest. Quite apart from this, it was the duty of a bishop to reside in London during the parliamentary session in order that his vote in the House of Lords would be at the disposal of the government, so that for some months in the year the bishop was necessarily absent from his diocese.

In these circumstances the three essential duties of the episcopate were on the whole inadequately performed. There is evidence of great laxity in ordination – the episcopal register of Bangor suggests that there were no ordinations there

[1] No. 83. [2] Nos. 79 and 81. [3] Nos. 91–101.

between 1713 and 1723, and frequently candidates for ordination were required to travel long distances. Similar laxity in visitation of the clergy and confirmation of the laity over considerable periods is clearly established, but there is also proof that many bishops exerted themselves to discharge these duties with efficiency and success. In this connexion the enormous extent of some eighteenth-century sees, the advanced age of some of the bishops in an era which made no provision for retirement, and the state of the roads should be taken into account.

Apart from the bishoprics, there were many other preferments in the Church which yielded substantial incomes and had far fewer responsibilities, deaneries and prebends, canonries and archdeaconries. Many of these were set aside to supplement the inadequate incomes of the less well-endowed bishops: others were awarded to royal chaplains and cadets of the peerage, less often to a nobleman's tutor or government pamphleteer.

These were rich prizes in a kind of government lottery which tempted young men of birth or exceptional ability to enter the Church. Many of them drew blanks and had to content themselves as parish clergymen for the rest of their days; some of the latter remained as curates for the greater part or even the whole of their clerical careers. At the beginning of our period it was estimated that nearly 4,000 out of the 10,000 benefices of the Church of England were worth less than £50 a year, while more than half of the 4,000 benefices under £50 were of less than £30 annual value. Goldsmith's clergyman who was "passing rich on £40 a year" must have been a very common type: the average remuneration paid to curates in the first half of the eighteenth century was £30–£40 a year, and many of them only made up this income by undertaking extra duties such as that of village schoolmaster. Professor Sykes has characterized the curatical status as one of inadequate remuneration, inferiority of status and uncertainty of tenure. Not until the great rise in prices during the French revolutionary wars was there an appreciable rise in these wage rates. Just as the less well-endowed bishop required something *in commendam* to make ends meet, so the poorer parish clergy could only exist by pluralism and non-residence.[1]

The social status of the clergymen in eighteenth-century England has been much debated and this analysis of the various ranks in the clerical order should at least make clear the dangers of generalization. Possibly the writer at the middle of the century who suggested that the clergy were looked down on by the aristocracy, largely ignored by the lower orders and really influential only with the middle class was not far from the truth.[2] It is unquestionable that many of them neglected their duties or performed them perfunctorily. Most of them had little conception of a spiritual calling. Others were ill-educated or even

[1] No. 95. [2] No. 97.

illiterate, such as "the parcel of strolling curates" in South Wales who are accused in 1720 of being ready to marry anybody under a hedge for a crown or at most for a guinea. More commonly such parsons were to be found among the riff-raff of the capital where, until their trade was stopped by Hardwicke's Marriage Act, they were responsible for the national scandal of Fleet marriages. Such black sheep have probably attracted more attention than they deserve.

The evidence offered in *Archbishop Herring's Visitation Returns* for the diocese of York suggests that the parish clergy were on the whole reasonably conscientious and diligent in discharging their duties.[1] Parson Woodforde, also, a few years later, may be accepted as typical of the better class of the eighteenth-century parish clergyman. His piety is sincere, his charity extensive and generous, his concern for the sick and dying and consolation of the bereaved a prominent feature of his ministry. On the other hand, the amount of space given in his diary to purely secular concerns, and above all to eating and drinking, shows clearly that there was no trace of asceticism or mysticism in his make-up. There is little sign either of theological learning or scholarship. Even in the better type of Hanoverian divine the exercise of religious duties was somewhat superficial and religion tended to become a system of morality. Their strength lay in practical Christianity: the defence of the Church from Deism and atheism they left to a handful of bishops and scholars who, though some of them fell into error on the way, on the whole discharged this task with success. The age of Butler and Berkeley, Warburton and Paley does not require defence against a charge of lacking great theologians.

It has already been suggested that the Protestant dissenters, especially the Presbyterians, Independents and Baptists, were almost as lethargic as the Established Church. They were in the main satisfied with the modest privileges accorded to them by the Toleration Act, though they remained excluded from office under the Crown, could not hold a commission in the army or take a degree at a university. There is even doubt whether they could be members of a corporation unless they became 'occasional conformers'.[2] The refusal of the Quakers to pay tithes constantly brought them into conflict with the law, and there is occasional evidence of local attempts at persecution of other Protestant Dissenters, usually thwarted by the 'Dissenting Deputies'–an unofficial body which kept a close watch over their interests.[3] Many Protestant dissenters, however, voluntarily returned to the Church of England. A more dangerous threat to their organization was the tendency to Arianism, which appeared in their ranks as early as the Salters' Hall controversy under George I, and the later growth of Unitarianism and Methodism. Their best work during the century was done in education, and several prominent bishops, especially Butler and Secker, graduated from the Dissenting academies.

[1] Nos. 99–101. [2] No. 106. [3] No. 107.

The legal restrictions imposed on the Protestant nonconformists were mild compared with those affecting the Roman Catholics which still remained in force in 1714.[1] While registered meeting houses of Protestant dissenters (not Unitarians, however) were tolerated and protected by law, public worship according to Roman Catholic rites was forbidden. Most of the savage penalties of the Elizabethan laws against popish recusants were still in force, while additional restrictions had been imposed on them by later legislation mostly dating from the reign of Charles II. Even after 1714 a new penalty was applied, and Roman Catholic landlords had to pay double the normal land tax on their estates on the specious plea that their support of Jacobitism had involved Protestant tax-payers in large expenditure. As the century went on, these penal statutes were more and more laxly enforced, and we hear of a curious incident in Lancashire when a young woman became a convert to the Roman Catholic Church. Instead of invoking the law, a public debate between Roman Catholic and Protestant spokesmen was arranged for the benefit of the young woman, who, as might be expected, remained of the same opinion still in spite of all the eloquence lavished upon her. Nevertheless Protestant bigotry was never far from the surface of eighteenth-century England, as was proved when the legislature passed Catholic Relief Acts in favour both of English and Irish Catholics.[2] The result was the outbreak of the Gordon Riots, probably the most formidable of all the outbursts of mob violence during the century.

It seems likely that the Roman Catholics, like the old Protestant nonconformists, and for much the same reasons, declined in numbers and influence during our period.[3] This remark applies even more to the extreme Anglican right-wing party, the Non-Jurors, which in 1714 was still strong in influence and refused to recognize the Protestant succession. Its numbers never exceeded 20,000. When its leaders, such as William Law, author of *A Serious Call to a Devout and Holy Life*, and Charles Leslie died, the movement soon ceased to count for anything in the national life.

Just as the attempt to improve the legal position of the Roman Catholics provoked a popular outcry, so the earlier effort supported by Henry Pelham, to grant certain privileges to Jews, was seized upon and exploited by the opposition. Though the Jews had enjoyed since the preceding century a tacit toleration, they could not hold offices nor, with rare exceptions, own land. Nor could they become naturalized Englishmen unless they abandoned their religion. This last restriction was removed in 1753, but anti-Semitism was so violent and widespread in the country that the Pelham administration thought it wiser to restore the *status quo* in the following year. Hardwicke's Marriage Act of 1753,[4] however, made special arrangements for Jewish marriages. In spite of legal restrictions more severe than those imposed on Roman Catholics, the Jews prospered in

[1] Nos. 109 and 110. [2] Nos. 112 and 216. [3] No. 113. [4] No. 62.

this century and many of the less fortunate adherents of this religion in other countries made their way to England in the reign of George III and indeed embarrassed the more prosperous Jews already settled there. Samson Gideon, the Jewish financial adviser to Henry Pelham, made a large fortune and his son established his position amongst the county families of England.

It remains to consider the Methodist movement,[1] which is the outstanding feature of the religious life of our period, and the importance of which in the political, economic and social life of the following age has been so well appreciated by M. Halévy. The immediate success of John and Charles Wesley and their younger contemporary, George Whitefield, shows that Hanoverian England was not so dead to spiritual things as it appeared to be. The three leaders were brought up in the Established Church and received episcopal ordination. John Wesley indeed until his death remained a member of the Church and steadfastly refused to allow the organization he had built up to break the last links with the Church of England. Whitefield, on the other hand, soon adopted the cardinal tenets of Calvinistic predestination and became estranged from the Established Church. While Whitefield's influence was probably greater in the early stages of the movement in England and has always been powerful in America, the preaching of the Wesleys has had in the long run more effect in England.

It is not difficult to understand the mixture of contempt and resentment which most, though by no means all, clergymen of the Established Church felt for Methodism. The casual wandering of Methodist preachers from diocese to diocese, the great crowds attracted to their out-of-door services when they were debarred from the parish churches, the wild enthusiasm and mass hysteria induced in many of their hearers by their flights of eloquence, their firm conviction that they must follow the dictates of their conscience even if they were thereby brought into conflict with Church and State–all threatened the propriety and decorum of the eighteenth-century Church. Their enemies, of course, not content with such well-founded charges, put about all sorts of incredible stories such as the one mentioned by Egmont in conversation with Whitefield that he allowed women to preach, or the even commoner and mutually contradictory slanders that Methodists were Roman Catholics or Communists.

In an age which emphasized strongly the outward manifestation of religion in conduct and good works, the Wesleys adhered to the Arminian doctrine of justification by faith in Jesus Christ. When their preaching and missionary activities brought them many thousands of converts, they lost no time in building up a compact organization. John Wesley indeed was a prince of organizers, and until his death in 1791 retained effective control of the movement he and his brother had originated and developed. A declaration of conversion

[1] Nos. 102–104 and No. 156.

was only the first step: the convert was expected to prove the sincerity of his conversion by the daily tenor of his life and also by active participation in the movement as lay preacher, band or class leader or at least by regular attendance at class meetings and love feasts, together with such financial contributions as his circumstances allowed. Much of the strength of the movement depended on the lay preachers, whose circuits were arranged for them by John Wesley and soon covered the whole country. The rank and file met regularly in classes and bands and at longer intervals love feasts were held.

For fifty years John Wesley travelled from end to end of England and frequently in Wales, Scotland and Ireland and his visitations, in the eyes of his followers, partook of something of the solemnity of the day of judgment. Confirmed backsliders were ignominiously drummed out; those whose reformation was still thought probable were reprimanded and admonished; the waverers were confirmed in faith and adjured to greater exertions in the cause; while the stalwart soldiers of Methodism rejoiced in the Master's words, "Well done thou good and faithful servant." As early as 1744 Wesley had set up a central organization which developed into the Methodist conference, but as long as he lived his personal visits had probably more effect in holding his followers together.

While it is true that Methodism affected members of all classes in town and country from Selina, countess of Huntingdon, and the good earl of Dartmouth –'one who wears a coronet and prays'–to the prisoners in the jails, it was most influential in the lower middle and working classes, many of whom probably had never been inside their parish churches. Others no doubt may have been passive attenders at church where a bored and beneficed parson gabbled through the services. It is significant that the movement caught on rapidly amongst the colliers and tinners as well as amongst the rural population of Wales, whose spiritual needs had long been ignored by the Established Church. Later when the Industrial Revolution created a large class of factory workers in the towns, the Church did little to meet new conditions and it was left to Methodism to cheer the lot of the depressed classes, enable them to retain their self-respect and in course of time help to make them the pious and contented backbone of Victorian England. In the opinion of one authority on the following era, Methodism in this way saved England from political and social revolution. Even within the Established Church it contributed to the evangelical revival,[1] which borrowed largely from Methodism in its methods of preaching the Gospel and was greatly influenced by Whitefield in the unbending Calvinism of its doctrines. Thus the outstanding ecclesiastical movement of our period led to denigration of the eighteenth-century Church by enthusiastic evangelicals, themselves a product of the revival which had taken place during the century.

[1] No. 101.

The evangelical revival may be regarded as a typical product of the century in the part played in it by the laity. Wilberforce and Cowper were as important as Grimshaw and Newton. Professor Sykes indeed insists that the outstanding ecclesiastical tendency of our period was not the secularization of the Church, but the steady and progressive laicization of religion. For the first time "the laity not only deemed themselves a proper and necessary part of the organization of the Christian Church but acted upon that persuasion with vigour and conviction".[1]

The comparative political stability of the eighteenth century may be contrasted with the economic changes which began in the second half of the century to transform England from a country of yeomen and small farmers into the workshop of the world. It is true that the earliest economic historians exaggerated both the magnitude and the rapidity of the changes and it is now agreed that the most catastrophic period of transformation came after 1783. In fact, one authority, Professor Nef, has argued[2] that the English Industrial Revolution began not in 1760, the traditional date, but in 1780. Up to 1780 England and France were developing economically in the same direction and at approximately the same rate; after 1780, England shot ahead on a line of development peculiar to herself at the time though it has subsequently been followed elsewhere. By destroying eighteenth-century cosmopolitanism and promoting aggressive economic nationalism supported by industrialization on a large scale, it has brought the world into its present sorry state.

From another point of view the economic historians, by a more detailed examination of the available evidence, have shown that many features, which it used to be assumed were introduced into England by the Industrial Revolution, notably the factory system and other methods of large-scale production, had in fact been long present in certain industries. Attention has also been paid to the predisposing factors which made an industrial revolution possible. Commercial expansion preceded and perhaps determined industrial development. Extensive foreign trade and exploitation of a colonial empire provided the capital required. Liverpool became an important port before Lancashire really developed its industries. Was the growth of population within England and possibly a demand for a higher standard of living responsible in part for the improvements in industrial techniques or did the need for labour to man the factories and work the newly invented machines bring about a rise in the birth-rate? Thus if the real beginnings of a large-scale revolution are now placed at the very end of our century the whole period has acquired additional importance as a formative era during which capital was being accumulated, labour was becoming more plentiful and more mobile, transport more rapid and capable of dealing with

[1] *Church and State in England*, p. 379. [2] *Journal of Economic History*, III (1943), pp. 1–32.

increased burdens and technical improvements of all sorts were being made. From the economic point of view stability is certainly not the keynote of the eighteenth century.

Contemporaries were, however, more impressed by and interested in the agrarian than the industrial revolution.[1] The improving landlord is one of the best-known eighteenth-century types. His improvements took various forms – the cultivation of root crops, the working out of rotations, regular manuring and better methods of cultivating the soil, improvement of the breeds of cattle, sheep and pigs, and sometimes even an interest in forestry. All these required the application of capital as well as specialized knowledge. Agriculture ceased to be an innocent and pleasant occupation for a country gentleman's leisure and became a competitive, industrial process. The new techniques were adopted because they increased the yield or diminished the cost of production or eliminated wasteful fallowing of the land. It came to be recognized that you cannot take more out of the soil than you have put in.

The main barrier to the adoption of this new agriculture was the survival over a large part of England of the open field system. It is now recognized that the enclosure of these fields was a long-drawn-out process. The amalgamation of strips may be traced back to the fourteenth century at least and the process had continued partly by agreement, partly, in spite of many spirited protests and the resolute intervention of the Tudor Government, by *force majeure*, throughout the fifteenth and sixteenth centuries. After a time of comparative inactivity in the seventeenth century, the enclosure movement got under way again in our century and continued until all the available land had been enclosed. Since the landlord class now ruled the State, the new generation of enclosers could count on the support of the government and the distinguishing feature of the new enclosure movement is that it was mainly carried out by commissioners under the authority of an Act of Parliament.[2] Between 1721 and 1740 there were 67 such Acts and between 1741 and 1760, 205. In the following years, 1761–1780, no less than 4,039 enclosure Acts were passed, followed by 900 for the years from 1781 to 1800.

The result was to make England in the next century the foremost agricultural country as well as to make it possible to feed the growing urban populations required to make her the leading industrial power. There were, however, obvious drawbacks to the new system. In spite of Arthur Young's statistical demonstration that a large farm employed more labour than several small farms aggregating the same acreage,[3] contemporaries blamed enclosures for rural depopulation. The remark attributed to one of the greatest improvers, Coke of Holkham, that "it is a sad thing for a man to be alone in the district of his residence: I look around, and can see no other house than mine. I am like the

[1] Nos. 114–119. [2] No. 116. [3] No. 117.

ogre in the tale, and have eaten up all my neighbours" expressed an indubitable truth. The yeoman class, so long regarded as the backbone of the country, had virtually disappeared by 1800 and the pattern of English rural life had consequently altered. The typical village no longer contained representatives of every class from the lord of the manor to the pauper, but tended to social stratification. The lord of the manor remained at the top, the middle tier was occupied by a small ring of tenant-farmers, and the great bulk of the population of the village was composed of landless labourers whose condition for long was indistinguishable from that of the pauper.

Two considerations largely explain why enclosure proved so disastrous to the yeoman and the cottar classes. Even if their legal rights were fully safeguarded by the commissioners, they lost their rights of pasturage and wood-cutting on the common land of the village which were economically essential to them.

"If to some common's fenceless limits strayed
He drives his flocks to pick the scanty blade,
Those fenceless fields the sons of wealth divide,
And e'en the bare-worn common is denied."

Secondly, the cost of enclosure per acre, especially when fencing costs were added, was high and most yeomen had no surplus capital from which they could pay their share. Such men had no option but to sell their rights for what they would fetch and try to obtain employment from a more prosperous neighbour or else to seek their fortunes in the growing industrial towns. In this as in other ways the agrarian revolution prepared the ground for the industrial revolution by creating a mobilel abour force. Left-wing historians tend therefore to represent the expropriation of the yeomen and cottars as part of a deliberate Machiavellian policy pursued by an unholy alliance of greedy landlords and rich merchants.

Nevertheless agriculture was still the leading industry at the end of our period; probably it still gave employment directly to at least half the total population. Its nearest rival was the woollen industry,[1] largely localized in the south-western counties, Norfolk, especially at Norwich, and the West Riding of Yorkshire. The last-named district grew in relative importance during the eighteenth century, but did not eclipse the others until after 1783. Other textile industries were still more localized, notably the Lancashire manufacture of cotton goods which became the manufacture *par excellence* of the Industrial Revolution, and the silk-weaving of Spitalfields and Macclesfield.[2] The linen industry, except in so far as linen was mixed with cotton, England left to Scotland and Ireland.

[1] Nos. 120–123. [2] Nos. 124–126.

For long too much attention was probably given by historians to the rôle of the textiles in the Industrial Revolution. Equally important developments were taking place in the metal-working trades, especially the old-established iron industry.[1] Lack of timber led to a marked decline of the old centres of production in Sussex and the Forest of Dean, but the first Abraham Darby's success in smelting iron in a coke furnace, apparently as early as 1709, linked iron and coal in a partnership which revolutionized modern industrial development.[2] This process was improved by the second Abraham Darby, but does not seem to have been generally adopted until the closing years of our period, though in Wales and the Midlands great ironworks had already been established. The progressive improvements effected by James Watt on the steam-engine, which required iron for its construction and coal for its motive power, linked coal and iron still more closely. The improved engine could be used to drive the machinery on which all other industries were becoming more and more dependent. By 1781 Watt's partner, Matthew Boulton, could write that "the people in London, Manchester and Birmingham are steam-mill mad". The total output of English pig-iron trebled between 1714 and 1783, but expansion was much more rapid in the following years.

Also notable for its development in our period was the pottery trade of Staffordshire under the enterprising leadership of Josiah Wedgwood, who turned out with equal readiness elaborate dinner services for the enlightened despots on the Continent and cheap pottery for working-class homes in England. Watt's early patron, Dr. John Roebuck, contributed to the expansion of the infant British chemical industry. By using lead containers instead of glass globes he reduced the price of sulphuric acid from 2*s.* a pound to 4½*d.*

It has already been suggested that commercial expansion preceded and perhaps determined industrial development. Mercantile theorists emphasized the importance of foreign trade[3] in the national economy and the Customs House statistics of exports and imports were often appealed to. Dr. G. N. Clark has shown reason to treat these with scepticism if not with contempt, but they do show a fairly steady and continuous increase between 1714 and 1783. Even if they are quantitatively unreliable it seems probable that they show correctly a general trend and they certainly confirm the impression of some contemporaries that each war led to a marked drop in commercial activity followed by a new high level when the war was over.[4] But we must discount carefully the tendency of the theorists to exaggerate the foreign trade of the country and ignore what must have been quantitatively the much larger internal trade.

Most of this foreign trade was concentrated in the port of London. Bristol at the beginning of the century, thanks to its pre-eminence in the wine and slave trades and to its exports of goods from its midland and south-western

[1] Nos. 127–132. [2] No. 127. [3] Nos. 136–139. [4] No. 139 (*a*).

hinterland, was second to London in importance, though a long way after it. Before the middle of the century Bristol had dropped far behind Liverpool, whose rapid rise amazed contemporaries and led Defoe to call it "one of the wonders of Britain".[1] Newcastle was important chiefly for the coal trade, mostly to London in small boats which provided a reserve of seamen for the press-gang in time of war. Many other small ports which have long ceased to have any commercial significance flourished in the eighteenth century, when, owing to the impossibility of transporting heavy goods by land, a swarm of coasting-vessels plied from harbour to harbour. The industrial developments already outlined contributed at first to increase the prosperity of the coasting trade, until the construction of canals and the adaptation of the road system to meet the needs of an industrial age led to a decline in its relative importance.

Defoe realized more clearly than most of his contemporaries the place of internal trade in the national economy, though later on Arthur Young was so impressed by the importance of the London market for food products of all sorts that he attempted to show that the price of standard foodstuffs such as meat, eggs and cheese varied with the distance from London.[2] The nearer to London the higher the price. He did, however, admit local exceptions to this rule–for example, in proximity to the populous rising industrial areas of Lancashire and the West Riding.

We get glimpses of this internal trade in the pages both of Defoe and Young, of the enormous herds of cattle which were driven every year from the Highlands of Scotland and Wales to the London markets, of the droves of geese and turkeys which came from East Anglia, of the butter and cheese which often was brought from distant counties by packhorse and coasting-vessel, of the fruits and vegetables which were increasingly produced in the Home Counties, of the Newcastle coal required to warm the London populace and the grain which was needed to supply them with their daily bread. In addition huge quantities of raw materials were now needed to provide work for the skilled craftsmen of the metropolis, the silk-weavers and tailors, the milliners and dressmakers, the printers, builders and watchmakers, and all those engaged in the luxury trades which flourished in the eighteenth century. Similar though much less important and more local markets existed in the leading provincial towns, Bristol and Liverpool, Birmingham and Manchester, Norwich and Leeds. The medieval fairs at Stourbridge and Winchester, Boston and Beverley still played a part in the exchange of commodities and helped to iron out some of the differences of price in the various more local markets.

Compared with continental States, England was fortunate in the complete absence of local customs barriers within the country, but at the beginning of the eighteenth century the difficulty and cost of transporting heavy or bulky goods

[1] No. 139 (*b*). [2] No. 119.

by land was almost as effective in cutting off the various local markets from each other. As late as the middle of the century, in the opinion of Professor Mantoux, the universal means of conveying goods inside the country was by packhorse. Even the Great North Road between London and Grantham was described by a traveller in 1735 as "a narrow causeway, with an unmade soft road on each side of it". Along this route travelled strings of packhorses, from thirty to forty in a gang. The leading horse was provided with a bell to warn travellers to get off the causeway and make use of the side road, out of which they often found it difficult to get back to the causeway.

As early as the reign of Charles II attempts had been made to alter the medieval system by which the upkeep of roads was the duty of the parish in which the road lay. When Parliament passed the first Turnpike Act authorizing the collection of tolls from the users of a particular stretch of road, it adopted an entirely new principle, viz., that those who used the road should pay for its maintenance. But this principle was put into practice very slowly, and it was so unpopular that there were numerous turnpike riots in the first half of the century. Also the management of the turnpike trusts was as lax and inefficient as anyone acquainted with local administration would expect. Turnpikes were frequently no better than the ordinary roads kept up by parish labour and rates, but after the middle of the century they became more general,[1] their administration was improved and in Yorkshire and Lancashire John Metcalf (1717–1810) set an example to other road engineers which was soon to be followed and improved upon by Telford and MacAdam.

This improvement made possible a great development in coaching. In the first half of the century there were comparatively few coaches, and it took a week to travel from London to York, while a journey even from London to Oxford might well occupy two days. Once the roads were improved 'flying coaches' were introduced and the time taken progressively reduced. By 1766 it was already possible to travel from London to Lancashire in under three days, though there were sometimes complaints that the pioneers of speedy travel promised more in their advertisements than they were able to perform on the road. The apotheosis of the stage-coach under the reign of William Palmer falls in the years immediately after our period.

Perhaps even more important at the time than the development of an adequate road system were the improvements in water-transport. These included the development of the coastal trade and the deepening and widening of river channels at the end of the seventeenth century: there were already well over a thousand miles of navigable rivers in England by 1727. The first canal, constructed by James Brindley for the duke of Bridgewater, to carry to Manchester coal from the duke's colliery at Worsley, was completed in 1761,

[1] Nos. 149 and 150.

and the price of coal in Manchester at once fell to half of what it had been.[1] Others soon followed, notably the Trent–Mersey canal, which was completed in 1777 to link the Irish to the North Sea. Soon after 1783 the whole of England was covered with a network of canals which made possible the transport of heavy goods which the road system still could not handle, and greatly reduced the cost of carrying the goods. Whereas earlier in the century it had cost £2 to transport a ton of merchandise from Liverpool to Manchester by road, the carriage by canal soon dropped to 6*s*.

Any study of the population[2] of England in the eighteenth century must begin with the first official census of 1801 and the subsequent statistical inquiries of John Rickman. Contemporary estimates of population are not much removed from guess-work, as may be seen from the two methods most commonly used. Some contemporaries tried to work from the official returns of inhabited houses, but these did not purport to include all houses, merely those liable to assessment for duty. Thus an estimate had to be made of the number of houses omitted by accident or design from the admittedly incomplete official lists and this conjectural total number of houses was then multiplied by what the calculator considered the most likely number of persons who, on an average, lived in a house. There was a further difficulty in that more than one family sometimes occupied the same house, and contemporaries were in some doubt whether the official returns of houses meant houses or households. Using this method, Dr. Richard Price in his celebrated *Essay on the Population of England and Wales* (1780) had no difficulty in proving to his own satisfaction that there had been a noticeable decline of population in our period.

Price's conclusions were at once attacked by Howlett and Wales, who themselves used though they appreciated the weaknesses of Price's methods, but also sought to substitute actual enumerations of sample districts and statistical tables of burials and baptisms in selected parishes. Professor Gonner, whose article on "The Population of England in the Eighteenth Century"[3] remains the best treatment of this subject, accepts the proof thus offered that the population was increasing, but holds that the numerical insufficiency of the samples prevents any calculation from them of the rate of increase.

This controversy left its mark on subsequent discussion, so much so that the official title of the Act under which the first census was taken was "An Act for taking an Account of the Population of Great Britain, and the Increase or Diminution thereof". Rickman in his *Observations* on this Act worked from the 1801 census figure of 9,168,000 and the average medium number of baptisms during the previous five years. If a population of 9,168,000 produced 255,426

[1] No. 151. [2] Nos. 140 and 141.
[3] *Journal of the Royal Statistical Society*, vol. LXXVI (1912/1913).

baptisms, from what population would 152,540 (the number of baptisms recorded in 1700) be produced? The answer to this simple sum in proportion gave the estimated population 5,475,000 for 1700. By this method he calculated the population for every tenth year down to 1780 and every fifth year from 1780 to 1800.[1] Rickman himself was not satisfied with these figures and spent the next forty years in further inquiries and calculations which were published in later census returns. The most obvious weakness is the assumption of a fixed birth-rate, that of 1795–1800, throughout the century, and there is also the difficulty that the registration of births and marriages was by no means so accurate and complete in the eighteenth century as it was to become in the nineteenth. Professor Gonner and Mr. Griffith, who has examined this problem more recently, agree in estimating the population in 1700 at approximately 5,800,000 and in 1750 at approximately 6,300,000. After 1750 the increase becomes rapid, and the rate of increase between 1775 and 1800 is substantially higher than that achieved between 1750 and 1775. By 1783 the population was not less than 7½ millions and *may* have approached 8 millions.

Rickman breaks down the figures he gives for 1700, 1750 and 1801 into totals for each county. This enables us to calculate the relative density of population in the various counties at each date and of each county at the three selected dates. If Middlesex and Surrey are excluded owing to their connexion with London, the counties with the greatest density of population in 1700 are Worcester, Somerset, Devonshire, Lancashire and Gloucester. By 1750 Lancashire has moved up to first place and is followed by Gloucester, Warwick, Somerset and Durham. In 1801 the industrial areas have finally triumphed; Lancashire is now followed at the top of the table by Warwick, West Riding (which had been 27th in 1700 and 15th in 1750), Stafford and Gloucester. In contrast to these areas we may take agricultural counties such as Northampton, where the density of population rose from 115 to 122 in the first half and from 122 to 134 in the second half of the century, and early manufacturing areas such as Norfolk, where the density at the same dates fell from 116 to 112 and then rose only to 129. In Lancashire, on the other hand, the density rose from 127 to 179 in 1750 and 253 in 1801. Thus in these three counties where the density was roughly equal in 1700, Lancashire doubled its figure in a hundred years, and the other two increased theirs by less than 10 per cent.

These figures—for what they are worth—confirm the customary generalization about the drift of population from the south-eastern lowland plain to the hilly regions of the north-west, which went on steadily in this period and entirely altered the balance of power between the northern and the southern halves of England. By 1801 the population north of the Trent was substantially in excess of the southern counties, if we leave London out of account. This

[1] No. 141.

movement of population also helps to explain the discrepancy between the contemporary estimates made by Price and his critic Howlett, who drew a considerable part of his statistical samples from Yorkshire. It should, however, be emphasized that even between 1700 and 1750 Rickman's figures show an absolute decline of population only in Cambridge (5 per cent), Huntingdon (6 per cent), Lincoln (11 per cent), Rutland (2 per cent) and the East Riding (11 per cent).

Much the most effective analysis of the standard of life of the eighteenth-century Englishman is that made by Mrs. Elizabeth W. Gilboy in her work on *Wages in Eighteenth Century England.* Mrs. Gilboy begins by dividing England into three main regions: London, the West and the North. She estimates that the annual wages of a labourer in London rose from £25 in 1700 to £27 10*s.* in 1725 and £30 in 1750, where they remained until 1790, whereas in the West the corresponding figure of £17 10*s.* in 1700 remained unaltered until 1750, and then rose only to £18 15*s.* in 1775 and £20 in 1790. In the North, on the other hand, the estimated wage of £11 5*s.* in 1700–less than half of the London rate–rose steadily to £15 in 1750, increased by 50 per cent in the next twenty-five years to £22 10*s.* and by 1790 had substantially exceeded the rate of wages paid in the West, and come within measurable distance of what had been in the first half of the century the much higher London rate.

Even this does not tell the whole story. Additional earnings by women and children can almost be disregarded in London, but in the North right through the century and in the West until the decline of the woollen industry set in, the total family income may be estimated at almost double the above rates and in addition most labourers outside of the London area enjoyed valuable perquisites. As in addition employment was probably less regular and prices were undoubtedly higher in London, the advantage suggested by higher nominal wages for the London labourer was quite unreal. Nevertheless Mrs. Gilboy concludes that the position of the London working classes was better at the end than at the beginning of this period, whereas the low standard of living of the western labourers in 1700 did not rise and may even have deteriorated. In the North the standard of living of the working classes was improving steadily and their demand for articles which had been beyond their reach in 1700 may well have been a factor in bringing about the Industrial Revolution.

The wages of skilled craftsmen, especially in London, were of course much higher. As early as 1720 3*s.* a day was commonly paid in London when 1*s.* 6*d.* to 2*s.* was normal in other areas. About the middle of the century the Newcastle colliers are said to have earned 15*s.* a week, but this was considerably in excess of the normal rates paid to other industrial workers in the textile, pottery and hardware trades.

It is difficult to arrive at any reliable estimate of the national trend of real wages, since there are so many uncertain factors. Apart from those already indicated, Sir William Ashley showed that the grain used for baking bread differed in the various regions of England. Wheaten bread in the earlier part of the century at least was almost unknown except in south-eastern England. Rye and oat bread and various mixtures were regularly used in the north and west and even in some south-eastern areas. Similarly tea, which was a luxury even for the upper classes at the beginning of the century, became before its end the standard beverage of the poor, displacing (to the great indignation of social workers) the home-brewed beer of their ancestors. It must suffice to repeat here the generally accepted conclusion that on the whole the standard of living of the working class rose in our period. On the other hand, the increasing tendency to subsidize agricultural wages out of the poor rates throws some doubt on its validity.

The eighteenth century inherited the basic principles of its system of poor relief from its predecessor and transmitted it without fundamental change to the following age. Nevertheless the state of the poor was one of the standard topics of eighteenth-century economists and social reformers. Attempts were continually being made by public-spirited individuals, usually with parliamentary sanction, to improve the poor law administration. Contemporaries usually approached the problem from the standpoint that it was a national disgrace that so many idle and disorderly persons should contribute nothing to the wealth of the nation. Consequently in 1722 Parliament passed the Workhouse Act[1] and authorized the institution of reformed workhouses for the able-bodied poor where they would be set to work on productive labour under strict supervision. But everything depended on the initiative of the local authorities and the efficiency of their management. In spite of local and temporary successes failure was inevitable. Other Acts followed, each recording the failure of its predecessor, notably the Act of 1782[2] which authorized the formation of unions of parishes in which specially appointed Guardians of the Poor would control the poor law administration. This Act pointed the way to better administration but had little practical effect.

Partly because they were a political danger from their proximity to each other and to the seat of government, the London poor attracted much attention. In Henry Fielding's graphic words–"They starve, and freeze, and rot among themselves; but they beg, and steal, and rob among their Betters." The London mortality rates were so heavy that its population was maintained only by continuous recruitment of young men and women who believed that the streets of London were paved with gold and found out their mistake too late. The seasonal nature of many London trades contributed to their disappointment, and they were continually tempted to spend any money they had earned in luxuries or expensive entertainments. Worst of all, in the first half of the

[1] No. 75. [2] No. 76.

century and especially in the middle years of George II's reign, there was an outbreak of gin-drinking on a scale which dismayed contemporary observers and finally forced Parliament to take effective measures for its suppression.[1] But from 1730 to 1750 there were thousands of dram-shops in London, some of them displaying the enticing notice, "Drunk for a penny, dead drunk for twopence." Some authorities believe that this orgy of cheap gin-drinking was responsible for a decline in population during these years: this too was the opinion of Henry Fielding, the Bow Street magistrate, who was in the best position to judge its effects.

The treatment of pauper children,[2] not only in London but throughout the country, must also have diminished the natural increase of the population. Some children were sent to the workhouses, but most of them were boarded out with parish nurses, who received quite inadequate payment. Comparatively few pauper children, in London at least, survived more than a year or two of this treatment. Those who did were apprenticed to anyone who would take them for a small premium and no real supervision was exercised over their masters and mistresses. Notorious cases of ill-treatment occasionally reached the courts and the newspapers and were undoubtedly far too common.

It must be admitted that this brutality was characteristic of the century. We have already noticed the readiness of Parliament to inflict the death penalty for trifling offences. It appears also in the whipping and branding currently practised, the frequent use of the pillory and the stocks, the treatment meted out to mothers of illegitimate children, above all, perhaps in the ritual of public executions at Tyburn. The state of the prisons was notorious and the best-meant efforts of contemporaries such as Oglethorpe and Hanway produced little change. Not until John Howard began his single-minded crusade in the closing years of the century did a real improvement take place.[3] But callous if not calculated brutality was not confined to the poor law administration and the legal system. It is equally apparent in the press-gang and the savage punishments inflicted under military and naval law. The eighteenth-century Englishman could not even amuse himself without causing pain: present-day blood sports such as fox-hunting flourished along with prize-fighting, bull-baiting, cock-fighting and others which have long been virtually extinct.

Spasmodic attempts were made from time to time by local working-class organizations to improve the condition of their members. The assessment of wages by the justices of the peace had largely fallen into disuse, and where it survived there is little evidence that the rates fixed were the rates actually paid. Associations of workmen[4] to raise wages or improve conditions of labour were not uncommon in some areas, especially in London, where the Spitalfields silk-weavers and journeymen tailors earned a certain notoriety, but also in the

[1] No. 153. [2] No. 154. [3] No. 155. [4] Nos. 133–135.

woollen industries of the south-west and amongst the Newcastle colliers. There was as yet no general condemnation and prohibition of such organizations by the legislature, but there were several statutes prohibiting them in individual trades,[1] ordering strict adherence by master and man to the legal rate of wages and imposing severe penalties on men who left their employment or engaged in malpractices. Apart from these occasional and ineffective anticipations of the militant trade-unionism of the nineteenth century, it appears that the eighteenth century witnessed a marked increase, again especially in London, of trade clubs and friendly societies.

The general level of education was undoubtedly low in this period. The great public schools, in particular Eton and Westminster, still produced classical scholars, but their curriculum was practically limited to Greek and Latin authors with a smattering of French and mathematics. The universities were at a low ebb.[2] Idleness and lethargy were the characteristic features of "the monks of Christ Church" and the other colleges both at Oxford and Cambridge. In spite of the protest of George III professors rarely lectured and tutors treated their appointments as sinecures. Such regular instruction as there was did not extend much beyond classics and theology, and both universities had become little more than training colleges for teachers and clergymen. If the sons of the upper classes continued to resort to them, they came mostly to lead lives of dissipation and not to improve their minds. Partly for this reason parents often preferred to send their sons on the Grand Tour under the charge of a tutor,[3] instead of leaving them to their own devices at the university. Oxford had indeed been prominent in the scientific renaissance of the seventeenth century, but the impulse had soon spent itself and such scientific and mathematical study as the universities fostered in the eighteenth century was mainly carried on at Cambridge, partly no doubt as a legacy from Isaac Newton. Neither university contributed appreciably to the intellectual life of our period.

Much more important were the Dissenting academies,[4] which had been established to cater for Nonconformists excluded from Oxford and Cambridge. Their curriculum was, if anything, too wide, including as it did theology, classical and modern languages, literature and history, logic, metaphysics and moral philosophy, various branches of science and sometimes even medical subjects such as anatomy. This curriculum illustrates the survival into the eighteenth century of the Baconian ideal that a student should occupy himself with the whole field of knowledge, but even in the twelve- or fourteen-hour day which was customary in these seminaries, few students can really have mastered so many branches of learning. From these academies many able students, aided by a special bursary fund, proceeded to the universities of Edinburgh and

[1] No. 134. [2] No. 159. [3] No. 158. [4] No. 157.

Glasgow, Leyden and Utrecht, to complete their education. It is pleasant to record that some of the links thus forged in the eighteenth century still survive in the twentieth when the conditions which brought about the original connexion have long since passed away.

But the universities, even supplemented by a handful of public schools and Dissenting academies, hardly touched the fringe of the problem of educating the children of the upper and middle classes. Much more was still done by the grammar schools, many of them already ancient foundations, though Miss M. G. Jones has calculated that 128 were actually founded in the eighteenth century. As one would expect, their curriculum and efficiency varied greatly, but many grammar school pupils reached the highest positions in the State, and some of them testified to the excellence of their old schools. One headmaster of Lichfield Grammar School boasted that he had flogged seven judges. In addition there were numerous private schools both for boys and girls, and the upper and upper middle classes often employed tutors at home.

There was, of course, no national system of elementary education nor was its absence much felt. Working-class children were expected to contribute to the family exchequer from a tender age. "Hardly anything above four years old, but its hands are sufficient to itself," Defoe commented of the West Riding early in the century. Towards its end the younger Pitt spoke approvingly of the weight which the support of children "by their own labours took off the country, and the addition which, by the fruits of their toil, and the habits to which they were formed, was made to its internal opulence". Since this was the prevalent attitude, there can have been little effective demand for the services of the village schoolmasters whose

> ". . . words of learned length, and thundering sound
> Amaz'd the gazing rustics rang'd around;
> And still they gaz'd, and still the wonder grew
> That one small head could carry all he knew."

Nevertheless the charity schools which had been instituted by the Society for Promoting Christian Knowledge at the end of the seventeenth century continued to develop and increase in numbers in the early years of our period. A network of over 1,300 of these schools financed by local subscriptions and managed by local committees was set up all over England, but chiefly in the towns. The basis of the curriculum was religious instruction combined with useful knowledge, such as arithmetic for the boys and needlework for the girls. Reading and spelling were taught primarily in order that the pupils could read and, it was hoped, understand the New Testament. Some schools attempted also to teach writing and grammar. After a short period of instruction the charity school children went out into the world as servants and apprentices armed with a Bible, Book of Common Prayer and the *Whole Duty of Man*. In fact, the aim of these schools in England was not to educate, but to inculcate morality and religious duties along with a respect for 'their Betters'.[1]

In Wales they were differently organized, thanks mainly to Griffith Jones. Schools were not established at fixed centres but circulated from place to place, according to the demand. Adults frequently attended after doing their day's work, mostly to learn to read the Bible in their native tongue. The duty of catechizing, neglected by the non-resident and pluralist clergy, was often undertaken by the charity school masters. These schools helped to bring together the Welsh people from their scattered hamlets, provide opportunities for discussion of religious and political affairs, and thus contributed essentially to the national revival which began in Wales during the eighteenth century.

One educational improvement may be assigned to our period. It was coming to be recognized that special books were required for the instruction of children and Newbery's Little Books for Children represented an advance on anything of this kind which had previously appeared in England. Here again the object was the inculcation of morality rather than the acquisition of knowledge, as may be indicated by the contemporary advertisement for Mother Bunch's Fairy Tales which was "intended for the Amusement of all those little Masters and Misses, who, by Duty to their Parents, Obedience to their Superiors, and Affability to their Inferiors, aim at becoming Lords and Ladies".

As yet there was little, apart from the decaying apprentice system, in the way of specialized training for particular occupations. The Inns of Court were no better than the universities. The keeping of terms and eating dinners were practically all that was required of law students. More than one contemporary deplored the absence of education for the diplomatic service, and George I tried to remedy it by establishing professorships of modern history with special provision for the teaching of modern languages. It is notable, however, that some progress was made in the education of doctors and surgeons, though as late as the middle of the century ambitious students were advised to complete their training abroad. The institution of the great London hospitals and the work of the two Hunters in our period helped to make this unnecessary.

If middle-class ascendancy was to culminate in the nineteenth, the stage was already set in the eighteenth century. The squirearchy ruled unchallenged in the country districts while the prosperous merchant and rising industrialist between them dominated the towns. Arthur Young[2] reckoned the income of the clergy at over £5,000,000 a year and estimated that as much accrued every year to the lawyers, physicians, artists and writers, out of a total income of £122,000,000. Since the landlord's rent amounted to £16,000,000 and the

[1] No. 160. [2] No. 114.

tenant's profit to over £18,000,000, professional men between them possibly earned between one-half and two-thirds of the income of all the landlords or all the tenant-farmers in England.

The middle classes both in town and country tended to stay at home. The habit of annual holidays as an essential part of middle-class life had not yet begun. Many prosperous merchants and professional men travelled no farther than the neighbouring county town. In fact, England was still divided up into local regions with local capitals, to which the many middle-class families who spent summer in the depths of the country flocked in the winter months for the sake of company and diversion. Such towns as York and Ipswich were, however, beginning to suffer from the competition of the more fashionable spas and watering-places, notably Bath, Scarborough and Tunbridge Wells, while the craze for sea-bathing in the last quarter of the century increased the competition still further.[1]

Travel was still expensive and, as we have already remarked, slow and difficult. In addition highway robbery was a flourishing industry in the eighteenth century, especially on the main roads leading out of London. In order to save paying his fare by coach from London to Edinburgh, on one occasion the Reverend Mr. Somerville of Jedburgh agreed to take charge of a valuable parcel. When it proved to contain 8,000 to 10,000 gold guineas consigned to the Bank of Scotland in Edinburgh he bitterly rued his bargain, even although the bank considerately supplied him with a guard for the first and most dangerous forty miles of the journey. Even short journeys could be unpleasant enough, especially in winter, and Defoe tells of an elderly lady who was habitually conveyed to church in her coach drawn by a team of oxen. In the country districts in winter evening engagements were regularly arranged to coincide as far as possible with the season of the full moon.

No doubt the tone of this middle-class society was largely determined by imitation and emulation of the small group of titled families who were, until the advent of George III at least, not only the unquestioned rulers of England but the accepted arbiters of taste and fashion. Disraeli's quip that in our century the displeasure of a peer of England was equivalent to a sentence of death contains a fundamental truth. Not only the authors, artists, sculptors and architects but the engineers, doctors, surgeons and even the lawyers depended largely on the patronage of individual peers. Even here, however, things were changing. Dr. Johnson made a successful literary career for himself, though Chesterfield refused him his patronage until it was too late to be of service.

The rapid development of circulating libraries is only one indication of the growth of a reading public in the eighteenth century. Newspapers increased greatly in number and size if not in quality, and in the profusion of monthly

[1] No. 145.

magazines eighteenth-century journalism was seen at its best, especially in the acknowledged leaders, *The Gentleman's Magazine* and *The London Magazine*. In the first half of the century the writing of plays had been the most profitable branch of literature for the unfortunate inhabitants of Grub Street, but the development of the English novel during the century opened another avenue to fame and fortune. Whereas Johnson's friend, Richard Savage, considered the £100 he made in the twenties from a play a very substantial sum, Fielding received £1,000 for *Amelia*. The very fact that pirated editions of popular works such as Cook's *Journals* became common shows that many more people were now buying books. The steady stream of eighteenth-century libraries which has appeared in the sale-rooms in recent years tells the same story.

Apart from poems and plays, essays and novels, the eighteenth century had an insatiable taste for historical works and travel books of all sorts. The Reverend Mr. Somerville, then a completely unknown author, received £500 in 1792 for his *History of Political Transactions and of Parties from the Restoration of King Charles II to the Death of King William III*, provided only that the 700 copies of the first edition were sold. Principal William Robertson, the historian, received £3,500 for the first edition of his *History of the Reign of Charles V*. This too is the great age of the makers of dictionaries and encyclopaedias, beginning with Ephraim Chambers's *Cyclopaedia or Universal Dictionary of Arts and Sciences*, published in 1728 and frequently reissued with a steadily increasing number of volumes. This pioneer work influenced Johnson in compiling his famous *Dictionary* later in George II's reign and is said to have suggested to the French encyclopaedists, d'Alembert and Diderot, the form to be given to their own compilation. Soon specialized dictionaries such as Malachy Postlethwayt's *Universal Dictionary of Trade and Commerce* (1751–1755) and William Falconer's *Universal Dictionary of the Marine* (1780) were being published to assuage the thirst of the middle classes for up-to-date knowledge on the many subjects which interested them.

The emancipation of the artist from dependence on individual patronage was slower and less certain than that of the author. It is true that the Industrial Revolution with the consequent development of roads and the great canal age gave obvious opportunities to engineers while the widespread rage for building and landscape-gardening among the upper and middle classes helped to create an architectural profession.[1] Whereas Colin Campbell and Isaac Ware owed their careers to Lord Burlington, the Adam brothers had a much wider basis of support amongst the middle classes. Brindley and Metcalf were dependent on ducal patronage, but McAdam and Telford derived their incomes from official positions and Government contracts. The professions of architect and engineer

[1] Nos. 146–148.

which had hardly existed at the beginning of the century were both, before it closed, well established on a basis of public support.

In painting and sculpture progress was slower in spite of the fact that the eighteenth century witnesses the appearance for the first time in England of a genuine national school, whose works, in painting at least, have never been surpassed and not often equalled. Part of the credit for this must be assigned to the foundation by Sir Godfrey Kneller, himself the leading painter of his day, of an academy at which young artists could receive training. This was a great improvement on the older system by which the would-be artist was apprenticed to a master. Equally valuable also was the regular practice of travel abroad and study at first hand of the masterpieces of Italian art. One of the objects of the select Dilettanti Society (1734) was to aid artists in this way. Some idea of the importance of patronage to the eighteenth-century painter is offered by the paintings from the collection of the duke of Bedford exhibited some years ago when the fifty-four pictures shown included portraits and landscapes by Gainsborough, a whole series of portraits by Reynolds and two views of Russell Mansions by Richard Wilson, nearly all apparently purchased directly from the painters.

As yet there were no public exhibitions of painting and sculpture even in London, though Sir Hans Sloane and some other collectors allowed the public access to their private collections. For a time under George II exhibitions of contemporary art were arranged at the Foundling Hospital and soon became fashionable. In the early years of George III a more extensive exhibition was also arranged by the Society of Arts and finally, under royal patronage, the Royal Academy was instituted in 1768. This combined the function of teaching students previously undertaken by private academies and of holding annual exhibitions of contemporary art. The painter and, to a less extent, the sculptor, now had a recognized place in society, a means of professional training and access to the middle-class public on which he was to depend in the following century. Sir Joshua Reynolds, the first president of the Academy, kept the new institution well in the public eye by the *Discourses* which he delivered to its students and later published.

The spacious and comfortable Georgian houses in town and country did not merely need pictures and statuary for their adornment and books to occupy the leisure hours of their inhabitants. The earlier architects of the time, especially Kent, were also largely occupied with the furniture and interior decoration of the houses they built, and even Robert Adam later designed fireplaces, mantelpieces and other accessories. In the second half of the century, with the rise of Chippendale and his successors, the designing of furniture came to be a distinct and specialized occupation. Line-engravings and mezzotints were produced on an extensive scale: reproductions of Hogarth's satires may have had more effect than many sermons of the clergy in raising contemporary standards of morality.

There was an insatiable demand for china and although much was still imported–envoys to the Saxon court were expected to supply their friends with a Meissen dinner service–the English factories recently established at Chelsea and Bow, Worcester and Derby were now producing graceful and serviceable pieces for middle-class homes. The opening of Wedgwood's pottery works at Burslem in 1759 led to further expansion on an unprecedented scale.

Just as in painting and sculpture the foreign practitioners of the early Georgian age gave way to native artists, so in music a similar tendency showed itself, though the glory of the eighteenth-century visual arts finds only a pale reflection in the history of music. If George II had little use for poetry and painting he showed his musical taste by patronizing Handel's operas and oratorios. Almost the only other large work of this period to survive is *The Beggar's Opera*, written by John Gay, with its pointed allusions to the politics and social life of the day, but Thomas Arne and some others wrote music for patriotic and sentimental songs which have been sung ever since. Maurice Greene and William Boyce collected and made notable additions to our Church music, and many hymns which are still used were composed by Isaac Watts, John and Charles Wesley and first sung by Methodist congregations. The duke of Chandos had a private orchestra, and the earl of Holdernesse directed operas and masquerades; a Noblemen's and Gentlemen's Catch Club was founded in George II's reign, and harpsichords were being introduced into upper middle-class homes. In 1782 a journalist attributed to the earl of Sandwich an interest in ancient music, while the earl of Abingdon engaged in flute-playing and Lord Malden performed on the violoncello. The simultaneous publication in the early years of George III's reign of two histories of music by the great Dr. Burney and Sir John Hawkins is sufficient testimony to the growth of a substantial public with musical tastes. Concerts and other musical entertainments took a prominent place in the programmes of the Ranelagh and Vauxhall pleasure-gardens, which were for long the popular resort of the Londoners in the evenings.

In spite of the fact that our period produced no great playwright–Congreve is too early and Sheridan appears only at the very end–the theatre was probably the most consistently popular form of entertainment in London, and the first theatres outside of London were being built. The actor and even the actress were gradually taking their places among the professional classes and ceasing to be grouped with rogues and vagabonds. The Whig aristocrat, Horace Walpole, was on the best of terms with his neighbour at Twickenham, Kitty Clive. Garrick was on a friendly footing with the leading authors and artists and even some of the politicians of his day. The first thing Fanny Burney's well-brought-up, not to say priggish heroine, Evelina, did on visiting London was to rush to the theatre to see Garrick before she had even been equipped with clothes suitable for the occasion. To Evelina and her contemporaries the play was definitely not the thing–it was the actor who mattered, and this helps to explain the cavalier manner in which Shakespeare's plays were treated in the eighteenth century. Here Garrick himself was one of the worst offenders. The eighteenth-century player went to see Garrick, Foote or Mrs. Siddons as the twentieth-century cinema-goer follows the fortunes of his favourite stars in any film in which they choose to appear. The power of the Press had already grown so far that the successful London actor or actress was a national figure, sure of a rapturous welcome when he undertook a provincial tour.

Before passing from the eighteenth-century social scene with all its superficial brilliance and solid achievement, I must say something about its scholarship and particularly its contributions to scientific progress. An age which produced Bishop Butler, author of *The Analogy of Religion*, and William Law, author of the *Serious Call* which had a decisive influence at one stage on the Wesleys and Whitefield and a more permanent one on the evangelical revival within the Church, amongst its theologians; Bishop Berkeley and David Hume amongst its philosophers; Adam Smith amongst its economists, and Hume, Gibbon and Robertson amongst its historians needs no defence in these directions.

It is true that with the exception of Richard Bentley, whose best work had been done before our period begins, classical scholarship is almost a blank, but there were still many scholars of the second and third rank who did useful work in other fields and particularly in English history and antiquities. Madox, *History and Antiquities of the Exchequer*, had been published in 1711; Wilkins, *Concilia Magnae Britanniae*, followed in 1737; Thomas Hearne published what were for long the only editions of various medieval chronicles; and several other scholars made industrious researches into the state of Roman Britain. More important in the long run than these individualistic efforts were the revival of the Society of Antiquaries in 1717 and the foundation of the British Museum in 1753.

Dr. G. N. Clark ends his stimulating survey of *Science and Social Welfare in the Age of Newton* with a few disparaging remarks on the achievement of the following age. "The central eighteenth century", he writes, "was not like the seventeenth, a time of cardinal scientific discoveries" and this is explained partly by the "general administrative torpor of England in the eighteenth century". Professor Butterfield in his recent work on *The Origins of Modern Science 1300–1800* would seem by implication at least to share this view of the unimportance of the eighteenth century, which is discussed only in two chapters on biology and chemistry. While one is ready to agree that the method and theoretical bases of modern science had been largely determined in the brilliant early days of the Royal Society, it may be suggested that their practical working out was hardly less important and that this was the task which was in the main successfully performed in the eighteenth century. This was conspicuously so in technology: there is no need to list here the long series of inventions and improved processes which made possible the Industrial Revolution. In navigation John Harrison produced chronometers of extraordinary accuracy for the calculation of longitude which were of assistance to Captain Cook in his great voyages, while John Smeaton effected similar improvements on the mariner's compass, and Captain Campbell transformed the quadrant into the sextant by extending its arc.

It is hardly less true in the experimental sciences. James Bradley, who was astronomer royal from 1742 to 1762, improved the instruments available for observations at Greenwich Observatory and has been described as "the founder of modern observational astronomy". In physics the main advances were in electricity. They include John Smeaton's perfecting of the Leyden Jar for storing electrical current and Franklin's famous kite experiment, which proved that the familiar thunderstorm was an electrical discharge and led to the general adoption of the lightning-conductor. In addition great improvements were made in the accuracy of thermometers, and aneroid barometers came into regular use for calculating the heights of hills as well as barometric pressure on the level. The eighteenth century may fairly be described as the golden age of the English precision instrument maker.

In chemistry the main names are the two Josephs, Joseph Black and Joseph Priestley, the former professor of chemistry at Edinburgh University, the latter the well-known Nonconformist divine. Both are remembered chiefly for their experiments in oxidization in which Black anticipated in essentials the later work of the great French chemist, Lavoisier. In addition Black was the discoverer of-latent as distinct from specific heat and played some part in developing the infant British chemical industry.

Even more significant work was being done in the natural sciences. In botany Stephen Hales published his important study of *Vegetable Staticks* and made valuable discoveries in animal and plant physiology. Equally remarkable in geology was the work of James Hutton later in the century. The system of classification devised by the Swedish naturalist Linnæus had been adopted in England by the 1760's and facilitated the practical work of the field naturalists, amongst whom White of Selborne still enjoys a deservedly great reputation. Thomas Pennant, the famous traveller, was as much interested in natural science as in scenery and antiquities, and his works contain much information on zoology and botany. Others approached botany from the utilitarian angle of its usefulness in medicine. They included many old-fashioned herbalists as well as the fashionable physician, Sir Hans Sloane, who presented a Physic Garden to the Society of Apothecaries.

In no direction is the practicality of the century more clearly demonstrated than in the advances made in medical and surgical practice. Here again epoch-making discoveries were few, but an all-round general advance was made between 1714 and 1783. The final separation of the surgeons from the barbers in 1745 was an important step: henceforth the surgeons were to be linked with the physicians, who had up to then enjoyed a definitely higher social status and usually more generous financial rewards. Subsequently John Hunter transformed surgery from a form of butchery to a branch of scientific medicine and founded a school which exerted influence for good long after its founder's death.

It is not too much to say that medical education in Great Britain was revolutionized in our period largely through the example and influence of the newly founded Edinburgh medical school. Students received a thorough training in Anatomy from Alexander Monro, and after 1754 from his son, Alexander Monro *secundus*. From the middle of the century increasing emphasis was laid on clinical instruction. This contributed to and was made possible by the foundation of hospitals and dispensaries. Most of the great London general hospitals were founded under the first two Georges[1] and specialized hospitals were already coming into existence. Amongst the latter were several lying-in hospitals which facilitated the emergence of the 'man midwife', or obstetrical surgeon, to take the place of the untrained women who had formerly officiated at births. Here, too, the work of William Hunter, brother of the surgeon, must be mentioned. Under George III additional hospitals were founded both in London and the provinces, and a new type of institution, the medical dispensary, supplemented extensively the provision made by hospitals for the treatment of disease.

Attention was also being paid to preventive medicine. Lady Mary Wortley Montagu's introduction from the East of the practice of inoculation for smallpox is well known. Some experts have thrown doubt on its advantages, especially under the conditions in which it was practised in the eighteenth century, but it seems probable that it contributed to the decline of the disease, which was marked even before the introduction by Jenner of the present-day method of vaccination. In calculations of the London death-rate from various diseases in 1780 consumption heads the list, followed by fevers and then smallpox. Consumption was responsible for as many deaths as fevers and smallpox put together. Attention was also given to jail fever which caused many deaths not only amongst the unfortunate prisoners but also amongst judges, jurors and other people who came into contact with them. It came to be realized that the disease could be prevented by improved hygiene and sanitation, and strenuous attempts were made by various reformers to ensure control of this and other diseases endemic in eighteenth-century jails.

[1] No. 152.

Similar conditions existed in the navy, where men were packed together in close proximity with inadequate ventilation and monotonous if not bad food, often for long periods under tropical conditions. James Lind, a member of a noted family of Edinburgh physicians, as early as the middle of the century conducted a series of experiments which proved that fresh fruit and vegetables were a cure for scurvy,[1] but it was not until after the end of our period that Sir Gilbert Blane persuaded the Admiralty to adopt this simple remedy. In the meantime Captain Cook had insisted rather on hygiene and cleanliness as the best prophylactic against this dread disease,[2] and had personally demonstrated their effectiveness during his famous voyages. The foundation of the naval hospital at Haslar is also a landmark in naval medical history. In the army, Sir John Pringle made the first scientific investigation of the causes of disease during the war of the Austrian Succession.[3]

Authorities are pretty well agreed that the great rise in population in the second half of the century was fundamentally due to a marked reduction of the death-rate. Professor H. J. Habakkuk, however, in an article in the *Economic History Review* (1953) has recently expressed some doubts about this and has suggested that the alternative theory that it was caused by a substantial increase in the birth-rate deserves more consideration than it has received. Miss Buer believes that the birth-rate for England and Wales in our period was under 40 per 1,000 and did not appreciably alter. Mr. Griffith takes the view that there were appreciable changes and in particular a rise from 30·5 per 1,000 of population in 1720 to 35·44 in 1790, but they agree that it was the reduction in the death-rate, and particularly the spectacular drop in infant mortality, which caused the steep rise of the population curve under George III. For this much greater expectation of life the newly born children of the seventies and eighties had to thank the advance in medical skill and knowledge during our period. Incidentally, Abraham de Moivre, Richard Price and Joshua Milne developed Newtonian mathematics and constructed tables of expectation of life which made life insurance a practicable business instead of a wild gamble: on their work rests the world-wide reputation and imposing fabric of the British insurance industry.

If we turn from England to the sister kingdoms of Scotland and Ireland the generalization about the period from 1714 to 1783 as an age of stability between two periods of rapid development does not have even a superficial plausibility. It may be argued that our period was decisive in the creation both of modern Scotland and Ireland. While the union of the Parliaments of England and Scotland had occurred a few years before the accession of George I, everything depended on how this voluntary partnership of two proud and independent

[1] No. 163. [2] No. 164. [3] Nos. 165 and 178.

peoples would work in practice. There was no precedent for it at the time, and it has remained unique in modern history. In the first part of the century it was subjected to almost unbearable strains and stresses: by 1783 it had been universally accepted in both countries. Beginning as an unpopular political expedient, it had been transformed into a genuine partnership, in which both peoples found economic advantage and social betterment.

These changes, as one would expect, were more apparent in the smaller and poorer country. The fierce single-minded Calvinism of the national Church was transformed into a cultivated 'Moderatism'.[1] The end of Jacobitism and the clan system made possible the reconciliation of the Highlands and Lowlands and their fusion for the first time in a single Scottish nation. If unfortunately it also led to the Highland clearances, even this had compensations in strengthening and developing the Scottish contribution to the British Empire. The Canadian emigrants soon attained a standard of life which their native land could never have afforded them and yet many of their descendants retain to this day their Scottish nationality.[2]

It is a moot point whether the literary and artistic renaissance of eighteenth-century Scotland can safely be attributed to the union. The correlation, if any, between political factors and intellectual and artistic greatness is one of the most difficult questions a historian is ever called upon to decide. What is unquestioned is the magnitude of Scotland's contribution to European culture in our period.[3] Equally impressive is its distribution over wide groups of subjects ranging from metaphysics to poetry and fiction, moral philosophy to medicine and surgery, and history to chemistry and geology. Just as markedly as in England a native school of painters arose, which was to culminate after the end of our period in Raeburn. Wonder of wonders, a Scottish clergyman, the Reverend John Home, wrote a play, *Douglas*, which caused a furore in Edinburgh in 1756. The Scottish universities, particularly Edinburgh and Glasgow which had hardly been heard of beyond their own country in the seventeenth century, now came to the forefront of European scholarship and in spite of Dr. Johnson's gibe that learning in Scotland was like bread in a beleaguered city, have retained that reputation in some degree ever since.

It is possible to establish a much closer relationship between the union of the Parliaments and the economic advance of Scotland in the following age. Glasgow grew from a small town of perhaps 12,000 inhabitants to a great mercantile city between 1714 and 1783, and this development was based on its participation in the American colonial trade thrown open to Glasgow merchants by the Act of Union.[4] At the beginning of our period Glasgow had less than 2,000 tons of shipping: by 1783 the figure had risen to over 22,000. Again as in England the accumulated profits of this trade were used to finance the

[1] No. 184. [2] No. 191. [3] No. 196. [4] No. 194.

Industrial Revolution, which affected Lowland Scotland almost as early as England, and at first in a very similar way. The foundation of the Carron Iron Works[1] pointed to the acclimatization of the heavy industries in Scotland and established a one-sided trend which even now worries Scottish economists and is not proving easy to reverse. Notable too is the influence of the Glasgow tobacco lords on Adam Smith during his formative years, which went far to shape the characteristic outlook of the *Wealth of Nations.*

While the wealth of the newly enriched merchants of Glasgow must also have influenced the attitude to the land, it would seem that the agrarian revolution in the Lothians and Aberdeenshire was directed mainly by an improving landlord class with a similar outlook to their counterparts in England. Sir Archibald Grant of Monymusk in Aberdeenshire and Lord Kames in East Lothian are among the best-known leaders of the Scottish agrarian revolution, which virtually eliminated 'run-rig' cultivation in the Lowlands.[2]

The economic and social revolution was even more catastrophic in the Highlands after the '45, because there the need for change was greater. At the opening of our period the Highlands had hardly altered since the early Middle Ages: everywhere the clan chiefs ruled their clansmen with unchallenged if usually paternal despotism. Not only did some of them possess the power of life and death over the clansmen but also the right to demand military service from their tenants. This meant that even after 1714 the Hanoverian Government had little effective power, and the great duke of Argyll was better known in the Highlands than the nominal king. The first real steps to change this state of affairs were taken by General Wade, who, between the two Jacobite risings, raised independent companies of Highlanders, officered by Campbells and allied clan chiefs and their relations. The companies were used partly to protect the loyal clans from broken men such as the notorious Rob Roy MacGregor, partly to disarm their hereditary Jacobite enemies and partly to construct 250 miles of military roads. These roads linked the main centres of Hanoverian strength at Perth, Inverness, Fort Augustus and Fort William.

After the '45 the chiefs lost their medieval powers, but received considerable sums in cash by way of compensation.[3] The proceeds of the confiscated estates were on the whole wisely spent in promoting the woollen and especially the linen industry and greatly extending the network of Highland roads. Many of the Highland roads popularly referred to as 'Wade roads' were in fact built much later in the century. Equally valuable was the establishment of elementary schools in the Highlands. This had begun in 1709 under the auspices of the Scottish Society for Promoting Christian Knowledge and now grew considerably. Part of the proceeds of the forfeited estates was spent on elementary and technical education and a royal bounty was utilized to appoint missionaries and

[1] No. 192. [2] No. 193. [3] No. 189.

catechists in isolated parts of the Highlands and Islands.[1] Instruction was always given in English, and to this Dr. Johnson largely attributed the gratifying improvement in the manners and customs of the Highlanders.

The agrarian revolution now spread to the Highlands. The black cattle which had fed to the highest summits of Glencoe were replaced by sheep, under the charge of shepherds from the Lowland counties, and subsequently the hills were often transformed into deer forests. Before our period ends we read of Sir William Howe and other officers of distinction renting Braemar Castle as a hunting-lodge while the neighbouring castle of Corgarff, reputed to be the scene of the ballad 'Edom of Gordon', was also used as a lodge by gentlemen who "delighted to wander o'er the higher hills to enjoy the recreations of the field". At the same time Colonel Thornton was performing on Speyside those prodigies of sportsmanship which he meticulously recorded in his *Sporting Tour*. The shooting tenant was soon to take the place of the clan chief as the uncrowned king of the Highlands.

Summing up what has been said about Scotland, this period must be regarded as the climax of Scottish history. It is true that there was complete political stagnation: the beginning of the movement for parliamentary reform was later in Scotland than in England. It is equally true that some unfortunate tendencies made their effective entry into Scottish history during the eighteenth century, as I have tried to show, but they had not yet made much impression. The upper class had not yet become anglicized and to all intents and purposes divorced from the national life: when the privileges of the Scottish capital were threatened by the English Government after the Porteous Riots the Scottish members of Parliament rallied *en bloc* to their defence. Religious bigotry declined while the Church continued to produce able men of affairs such as Principal Robertson, scholars such as the Reverend James Stuart of Killin and his son, the Reverend John Stuart, the minister of Luss, who between them translated the Bible into Gaelic, devotional writers such as the Reverend Thomas Boston, minister of Ettrick, whose works enjoyed immense popularity during his life and were read for a century after his death, and cultivated and conscientious parish ministers such as 'Jupiter' Carlyle and the Reverend Thomas Somerville of Jedburgh. The middle-class laity experienced unprecedented prosperity and increased greatly in numbers. Not only did their material standard of life rise in the century but their canons of taste, their intellectual interests and their power to express themselves gave them an influence on the national life which they had not previously had. It was the solid, disinterested patriotism of this class typified perhaps in Sir Walter Scott in the next generation which was to preserve the Scottish nation from the danger of complete absorption in England in the following century.

[1] No. 190.

With the exception of Webster's work, mentioned later in this paragraph, estimates of the population and vital statistics of Scotland in the eighteenth century are even less reliable than those for England, since parish registers were much less regularly kept and preserved. On a basis of registers relating to about one-tenth of the parishes Rickman estimated in 1801 that the population rose from 1,048,000 in 1700 to 1,390,000 in 1720, fell slightly during the next two decades and in 1750 barely exceeded the figure for 1720, again dropped in the following decade, rose somewhat in the 1760's and remained practically stationary in the 1770's. On these figures it increased by less than 200,000 between 1710 and 1780 and by the same amount between 1780 and 1800. Rickman himself suggests that these figures probably state the increase higher than it would have appeared if all the registers had been available. Actually the figures he gives for 1750–1760 agree remarkably well with the contemporary calculation made by the Reverend Dr. Alexander Webster for 1755, which showed a total population of 1,265,380. It is notable that the great bulk of this population lived in rural areas. In 1700 the population of Edinburgh is estimated at 25,000 and that of Glasgow eight years later at 12,000. In 1750 Edinburgh's population may have reached 50,000 and doubled again in the next fifty years, while even including the suburbs Glasgow barely exeeeded 40,000 in 1780.

While the eighteenth century proved that the Act of Union between England and Scotland would benefit and be acceptable to both, it indicated as clearly that the system of English political and economic domination of Ireland, which had been worked out in the seventeenth century and confirmed by the formal assertion in 1719 of the legislative dependence of Ireland upon the imperial Parliament,[1] would break down. The main interest in Irish history therefore is political and constitutional, whereas in Scotland economic and social development almost monopolize attention.

At first there was little disposition to challenge English domination, but the authorization given in 1722 to William Wood to flood Ireland with a copper coinage provoked Swift to write *The Drapier's Letters*, and the resulting crisis ended in 1725 with the withdrawal of Wood's patent.[2] More serious was the conflict of 1753–1756 over the disposal of the Irish revenues and the passage of the Octennial Act in 1767,[3] while even clearer indication of the growth of national resentment is seen in the proposal to tax the revenues of absentee landlords. Political grievances were aggravated by the oppression of both Roman Catholic and Presbyterian by the small Episcopalian minority, although some tentative steps were taken in the seventies to modify the penal laws against Papists.[4] Ireland also was subjected to the full rigour of the mercantilist system, and the economic distress which resulted from further restrictions by the

[1] No. 197. [2] Nos. 198 and 199. [3] No. 200. [4] Nos. 213, 215 and 216.

English Government on Irish trade at the opening of the war of American Independence contributed essentially to the great political crisis of 1779–1782.[1]

The English Government, beset with difficulties on every side and itself weak and unstable, yielded to half-veiled threats of force from Grattan and the Volunteers.[2] A settlement was reached by which the British Parliament renounced for ever any claim to legislate for Ireland,[3] but the imperial Government retained control over the Irish executive. For the time being this satisfied both parties, but the existence side by side of two sovereign legislatures created a position of unstable equilibrium between England and Ireland. Within Ireland the settlement did nothing to solve the fundamental religious, economic and social problems which were now coming to the front.

This was due partly to the rapid increase of population in Ireland in the closing years of the eighteenth century, for reasons which still baffle the experts. Mr. K. H. Connell, indeed, considers that the increase was less marked than the traditional estimates indicate.[4] According to his revised figures the total population of Ireland rose from 2,791,000 in 1712 to just over 3,000,000 in 1726, reached nearly 3,500,000 in 1767 and exceeded 4,000,000 in 1781. The traditional estimates are much lower throughout our period, varying from just over 2,000,000 in 1712 to 2,500,000 in 1767 and 2,845,932 in 1785, after which the sensational increase occurs. Contemporary estimates of the population are, if anything, more numerous than in England and agree remarkably well with each other. There was no fierce controversy such as reigned in England between Price, Howlett and Wales. On the other hand, Ireland was not included in the census of 1801, and there are no reliable figures for an enumeration until 1821.

Even before the great increase of population, the bulk of the people were on the margin of subsistence: from time to time and especially in the reign of George II famines occurred on a national scale in which hundreds of thousands of peasants are said to have died of starvation. In the early years of George III there was a marked improvement and Arthur Young considered the lot of the Irish peasantry in some districts at least more prosperous than that of the English agricultural labourer, though this is perhaps less impressive than it sounds.[5] Such education as the peasantry received was due to 'hedge schools' organized by the Catholic clergy: for Protestant children there were the charity schools organized by the Society for Promoting Christian Knowledge and later supplemented by schools, subsidized by the Crown and the Irish Parliament, intended primarily to convert Roman Catholic orphans 'into good Christians'.

Anglo-Irish society centred in Dublin, the political capital, the seat of the law courts and of the only Irish university, and the chief port and commercial centre. Some public buildings and private houses of this period still survive

[1] Nos. 201–204. [2] No. 205. [3] Nos. 206–212.
[4] *Economic History Review*, vol. XVI (1946). [5] No. 221.

amongst the notable architectural features of present-day Dublin. Most of them were designed by English architects, though at least one Irishman, Thomas Ivory, made a name for himself. Similarly the Smock Alley Theatre gained a reputation by its production of Shakespearean plays and depended on visits from the leading English actors as well as on native talent, while the highlights of Dublin musical history in the period were the visits of Handel and Arne. The Dublin publishers regularly made money from pirated editions of English classics and best-sellers.

Swift and Berkeley in the early part of our period, Goldsmith and Burke in the later, reinforced at the very end by Sheridan, are better proofs of the variety and vitality of Irish culture in our period. All were educated, in part at least, at Trinity College, Dublin, and made a deep and characteristic impression on English civilization. It must be remembered that they were drawn from the ranks of the Protestant minority, though some of them retained their sympathies for the Roman Catholic majority. All roads to self-advancement in Ireland and England were still closed to Roman Catholics, who had perforce to seek fame and fortune abroad–some by emigrating to America, but many more by military service in the armies of the European continent. Most of them served in the Irish Brigade of Louis XV or in the Irish regiments in the pay of the Spanish Bourbons, but others went even farther afield. Two of Maria Theresa's best generals, Browne and Lacy, were Irishmen.

The history of eighteenth-century Wales has been much less studied than that of Scotland and Ireland. Here too the upper classes had been to a large extent anglicized and divorced in interest and outlook from the bulk of their countrymen, while the middle class was comparatively small and exerted little influence either politically or socially. Just as in Ireland, though for different reasons, the Established Church had lost its hold on the mass of the Welsh people. The higher clergy, especially the holders of Welsh bishoprics, were in the main non-resident pluralists whose chief interest was to obtain a more lucrative and congenial bishopric in England. From 1706 to 1820 the bishops of Llandaff were absentees from their see, and of twenty-seven bishops appointed by George I and George II twenty-one were translated to England. The parish clergy were miserably paid, often no better educated than their parishioners and quite inadequately supervised. In some parts, according to a contemporary observer, the very fabric of the churches was in decay, and the churches "do only serve for the solitary habitations of owls and jackdaws". In one case the same authority alleges that the parish church had been rented to a neighbouring congregation of Dissenters. Even where such extremes had been avoided, there is ample evidence of the low moral and intellectual level of the parish clergymen and the widespread neglect of their most essential duties.

The breach between the anglicized upper-class laity and clergy and the great proportion of the Welsh people was accentuated by difference in language. No official statistics of the languages spoken in Wales seem to exist before the census of 1891, but it is generally agreed that in the eighteenth century, except along the English border and in a few other localities, Welsh was the only language spoken by the peasantry, who formed the great majority of the population. The first printing press in the Principality was set up in 1719, and during our period there was a great increase in the number of books and periodicals published in Welsh.

This is one aspect of the renaissance of Wales in our period, which took the form primarily of a religious revival. It was instituted by Griffith Jones and established by Howell Harris and others in close association with the English leaders of Methodism. "In 1730", write the authors of the standard work *The Welsh People*, "the Welsh-speaking people were probably as a whole the least religious and most intellectually backward in England and Wales. By 1830 they had become the most earnest and religious people in the whole kingdom, and in the course of their development had created powerful Nonconformist bodies stronger than those to be found in any other part of the country, while the adherents of the Church had in the Welsh districts dwindled down to a comparatively small class."[1] The same authorities summarize the results of the national rebirth as the preservation of the Welsh language, increased literary activity, a remarkable rise in the education both of clergy and laity, and the general acceptance of an improved morality.

As in other parts of the British Isles the initiative in the educational movement was provided by the Society for Promoting Christian Knowledge, but the really effective work was done by the Reverend Griffith Jones, who between 1730 and his death in 1761 had organized thousands of circulating schools attended both by children and by adults. In one year ten thousand men, women and children are supposed to have learned to read their native tongue at these schools. No corresponding advance was made in our period in secondary education, though one or two Dissenting academies on the English pattern existed from time to time at various towns in Wales.

English travellers in Wales, with a few striking exceptions such as John Wesley, do not write of the Welsh as fellow citizens but as natives. Their works abound with descriptions of the badness of the roads and the economic backwardness of the country. Both in North and in South Wales the agrarian revolution was only beginning in the closing years of our period. The foundation of the Brecknockshire Agricultural Society in 1755, partly by the efforts of Howell Harris, may be taken as an important landmark. Common lands were enclosed and 'spirited proprietors' adopted the same methods of improved cultivation as had already brought advantage in England. Even in 1800, however, it is probable that South Wales was affected by the agrarian revolution to

[1] John Rhys and David Brynmor-Jones, *The Welsh People* (London, 1909), p. 472.

a lesser extent than England, while in North Wales the enclosure of common lands was rare before 1775 and gained momentum slowly thereafter.

The importance of the coasting trade led to notable development of many small ports both in North and South Wales, while Swansea enjoyed as well a considerable foreign trade. It was claimed a few years after the end of our period that the tonnage entering the port of Swansea was more than double that making use of Bristol. The trade of the South Wales ports developed still further when canals opened up their hinterland, but this is almost entirely after our period, though canals are mentioned at Neath in 1700 and Llanelly before 1770. From the early years of George III's reign turnpike trusts were established in Wales and did much to improve the roads before 1800.

The woollen industry was widespread in eighteenth-century Wales, but continued to be organized on the domestic system and declined in the second half of the century. Not until the nineties and the early nineteenth century were the improved machinery and the factory system extensively adopted. On the other hand, there was a marked growth of mining and the metallurgical industries largely owing to immigrant adventurers from England and even farther afield. John Wilkinson's works at Bersham, the Dowlais works under John Guest, the original Guest in the present-day firm of Guest, Keen and Nettlefolds, and the Cyfarthfa works of Anthony Bacon all became famous and indicated what would be the major line of Welsh industrial development in the following century. With the iron foundries and forges came a consequential expansion of coal-mining in South Wales.

These developments were to introduce into South Wales the evils attendant on the Industrial Revolution, but it should not be thought that the old system of society which they transformed was an ideal one. Eminent authorities believe that there had been little change in Welsh social conditions from the time of William the Conqueror. One reason why English capitalists established the heavy industries in Wales was the abundant labour supply and the low rates of wages which prevailed. Professor Dodd's conclusion that to represent the Industrial Revolution "as reducing to misery a land of prosperous and contented peasants would be the merest travesty of the truth" seems to be as applicable to South as to North Wales.

We must now turn our attention from the home countries to the colonial empire overseas. Here again the age is dynamic and not static. It opens with the Utrecht settlement which greatly increased Britain's responsibilities and opportunities as a colonial power. As Sir John Seeley wrote long ago, with exaggeration pardonable in the hey-day of the British Empire, Britain had become a world Venice with the seas for streets. She held in Gibraltar and Minorca the keys of the Mediterranean. Her East India Company, newly reunited and strengthened after a period of conflict between the old and new companies, was undoubtedly the leading trading power in India, judged by the number and importance of its factories, which, with the exception of Bombay, were leased from native rulers. But the centre of gravity of the Empire lay in North America, where the Utrecht settlement had increased our possessions. Newfoundland with its valuable fisheries, the Hudson's Bay territory and Nova Scotia had been added to an Empire which already included nearly the whole eastern seaboard south of the St. Lawrence. A few years later the southern limit of British power was extended by the foundation of the colony of Georgia. Less extensive but more valuable were our West Indian colonies, which already included Jamaica, the Bermudas and Bahamas and some of the Leeward and Windward islands.[1]

No important territorial changes occurred until the Seven Years War. In the war of the Austrian Succession we did indeed lose Madras and conquer Cape Breton Island, but the peace of Aix-la-Chapelle[2] restored the *status quo ante bellum*. Controversy raged at the time and has more or less ever since on the adequacy of the Treaty of Paris which closed the Seven Years War,[3] the most successful Britain ever fought. Canada and Florida and indeed all North America as far as the Mississippi were added to the Empire along with a few West Indian islands and Senegal in Africa. France, however, retained her Newfoundland fishing rights and her trading settlements in India. Twenty years later everything which Britain had gained on the North American continent, except Canada, was surrendered by the Treaty of Versailles[4] at the end of the war of American Independence, while Britain's position in the Mediterranean was weakened by the final loss of Minorca. Thus during our period Britain had lost the great bulk of her American empire, both old and new. She did retain and consolidate her gains from the earlier Treaty of Utrecht, and Canada had been acquired, while she had at least maintained her position in the West Indies. In imperial history, however, the outstanding achievement of the period was the firm establishment of British military, political and economic mastery of India, though only a small part of the vast sub-continent had actually been annexed to the Empire.

Clearly diversity was already the dominant characteristic of the eighteenth-century British Empire. This is especially obvious when the methods of governing the various territories are examined. In 1714 and long after there were still remains of proprietary government in certain colonies, including Pennsylvania and the two Carolinas, though these became less and less obvious as time went on. Rhode Island and Connecticut retained archaic charters and have been described as "republics owning only a vague allegiance to the British crown". But apart from these exceptional survivals from a bygone age there were differences and anomalies even in the colonies controlled directly by the Crown.

[1] Nos. 234–240. [2] No. 280. [3] Nos. 239 and 283. [4] No. 285.

There was, for example, a distinction between colonies originally established by English emigrants and those conquered from other powers. The latter were held to be completely under royal control and were sometimes left for a time under military rule.

Nevertheless in Nova Scotia and Newfoundland, conquered from France in 1713, the Crown gradually restricted its absolute powers. Nova Scotia secured an elected legislative assembly in 1758, and about the same time when the all-the-year-round population of Newfoundland substantially increased, a permanent council of settlers was established there.[1] Similarly in Canada the Crown by proclamation in 1763 declared its intention of setting up representative institutions. Ultimately the Quebec Act[2] placed the government in the hands of a governor, who retained control of the military forces while a nominated council was set up with the power of legislating for the colony but not of taxing the inhabitants. The well-known case *Campbell* v. *Hall* in 1774 established the principle that once the Crown had set up a representative legislature in a conquered territory its prerogative power of taxation lapsed.[3]

In the early part of the century no one questioned the legislative sovereignty of the imperial Parliament over this diversified collection of territories. In practice it was used mainly to enforce mercantilist regulations. The best known of these Acts in the early part of the century during which, it has been said, Walpole treated the colonies with a wise and salutary neglect, was the Molasses Act of 1733. This imposed prohibitive duties on the importation into the colonies of foreign sugar, molasses and rum. Other Acts regulated the carrying on of certain manufactures, including the making of pig-iron and beaver hats in the colonies. Already conflict between imperial and colonial legislation was not uncommon. Colonial Acts were frequently disallowed and colonial assemblies showed their irritation by adopting ingenious devices intended not to challenge but to evade in practice imperial control.

Over colonial administration control from the mother country was even less effective, partly because of the number of departments of the home government which dealt directly with the colonies and had their own agents there. Such were the Treasury, the Customs, the Admiralty which dealt with offences committed at sea and evasions of mercantile regulations in special Admiralty courts, and the secretary at war. Chief responsibility, however, rested with the secretary of state for the Southern Department, aided by the (advisory) Board of Trade and Plantations. The latter body had been active under George I and was revitalized by Halifax on his appointment as its president in 1748, but after the appointment of a third secretary of state for the colonies in 1768 it ceased to perform any useful function.[4] It was abolished as part of Burke's scheme of economic reform in 1782.

[1] Nos. 244–246. [2] No. 242. [3] No. 228. [4] Nos. 226 and 227.

Every royal province, except some chartered colonies, had a governor appointed by the Crown, usually on the recommendation of the Southern secretary. Normally the governors were assisted by a nominated council which combined executive, legislative and judicial functions; but in most colonies the dominant power was the popularly elected assembly, which had the control of the purse and used it without hesitation or scruple to reduce to subservience the royal governor, whose own salary usually depended in part on its grants. Thus Sir D. L. Keir concludes that "the executive power of the Crown tended in colonies where elective assemblies existed to become something of a figment. In its place emerged the *de facto* sovereignty of the assemblies themselves."

No doubt this picture of the disorganization and the internal strains and stresses of the old colonial system is based primarily on the mainland colonies of North America, which were soon to break away completely from the Empire. The West Indian assemblies were more tractable, but, even there, long-drawn-out conflicts occurred between royal governors and local assemblies,[1] notably in Jamaica in the years down to 1729. Nevertheless this analysis reveals that the political factors which were to lead to the break-up of the first British Empire were already in existence in the first half of the century.

When the economic aspects of the old colonial system are considered a similar conclusion is easily reached. English imperialism in the eighteenth century was nakedly and unashamedly economic. Writers on the plantations solemnly prepared balance-sheets to show how much profit the mother country drew annually from the Bahamas or West Africa as the case might be.[2] The whole basis of mercantilism was to make this profit as large as possible, and the end was to be attained in two obvious ways. The colonies must buy everything that they required from within the Empire, and everything which the colonies produced and which would be useful to her must be sold to the mother country. Thus the Molasses Act of 1733 imposed prohibitive duties on the importation of foreign sugar by the American colonists in the interests of the British planters in the West Indies, while attempts were made throughout the century to stimulate American production of timber, iron ore, tar and other naval stores, in order to reduce British dependence on the Baltic countries. Restrictions were imposed on the manufacture by the colonists of certain finished goods for inter-colonial trade. The classic example is that of beaver hats. The skins had to be exported to Britain, made up into hats and then returned for sale to the American colonists.

On the other hand, even the most advanced colonies were only now reaching the stage where the manufacture of finished goods becomes practicable and profitable. Also it was an essential part of the system that such staple American products as tobacco and sugar enjoyed a monopoly of the home country's

[1] No. 237. [2] No. 225.

market and certain American products for which there was little demand at home could be exported directly to southern Europe. Moreover, colonial ships were entitled to participate in imperial trade on the same conditions as English ships, and this contributed to a noticeable development of shipbuilding in our period on the North American coastline.

It should be remembered too that many of the restrictions existed only on paper: smuggling has been described as the national industry of the New England colonies. Pitt at the crisis of the Seven Years War protested bitterly but unavailingly at the persistence of the colonists in trading with the enemy. It has been calculated that the yield of the duties imposed by the Molasses Act between 1734 and 1765 in America averaged a mere £250 a year. Any attempt to tighten up the administration and enforce the trade laws would have immediate repercussions in North America.

The Seven Years War showed clearly the need for a radical reorganization of the whole structure of the colonial empire. By removing the threat from France to the mainland colonies, it made certain that the colonists would be less inclined than ever to submit to effective imperial control over their political and economic interests. Hitherto the colonies had made very little contribution to imperial defence, which was generally regarded as the responsibility of the mother country. This resulted partly from the weakness of individual colonies and still more, perhaps, from their jealousy of their neighbours. This defeated several attempts by the imperial authorities to organize the American colonies in a closer bond of union. Benjamin Franklin, representing Pennsylvania at the Albany Conference in 1754, failed to secure the acceptance by the other colonies of the plan he proposed for this purpose. It became clear that union would have to come, if at all, through intervention of the imperial government.

If the expulsion of the French eased the problem of defence, real danger from the Indians remained as was shown by Pontiac's rebellion in 1763. Since the colonists could not agree on a common Indian policy the imperial Government, after the Albany Conference, had appointed its own agents for political discussions with the Indians. By the royal proclamation of 1763 it now added to its responsibilities control over westward expansion and trade with the Indians. Since the colonies failed also to make any effective contribution to the cost of their own defence the Stamp Act was passed in 1765 to secure by internal taxation a moderate revenue towards the British Government's military expenditure on their protection. The hurried withdrawal of the Stamp Act in the face of combined colonial resistance to internal taxation by the imperial Parliament was followed by Charles Townshend's import duties. These nominally fell into the category of measures for the regulation of commerce, but were deliberately intended to provide a permanent revenue for the maintenance of the civil administration and law courts in the colonies. Since they were accompanied by greatly increased efficiency in their collection they produced a still more violent American reaction. In 1770 all these duties, except one on tea, were withdrawn in their turn. The Quebec Act added to the weight of what was now an organized separatist movement by assigning to Canada the western lands coveted by the New England colonists and establishing a non-representative system of government, a Roman Catholic Church and the French legal system in Canada.

Punitive measures increased the agitation in America while opinion at home was now strongly divided.[1] Probably a majority supported the king in his determined policy of repression; but the opposition was equally resolute, far more vocal and divided against itself on fundamental issues. Chatham believed as firmly as George III that the legislative sovereignty of the imperial Parliament must be maintained, but drew a quite illogical distinction between the power to legislate and the power to tax–the latter power he attributed to the colonial assemblies. Burke also maintained the principle of imperial sovereignty, but qualified its practical applications by his customary insistence on the liberties of Englishmen and considerations of expediency. Neither had a policy which could have averted for long the loss of the first British Empire once the colonists had passed, as they did in the Declaration of Independence, from claiming their legal to asserting natural rights. Concessions were subsequently made by the home Government, but they came too late. The peace terms offered in 1778, however, foreshadowed the outstanding characteristics of the constitutional history of the British Empire in the following centuries in their readiness to circumscribe the control of the imperial Government over legislation, taxation, administration and economic development of the colonies.

In the eighteenth century, British interest in Africa was almost limited to the slave trade, which was largely controlled in the first half of the century by the Royal African Company. In face of keen competition from the Dutch and the French, Parliament had to subsidize the Company by contributing to the upkeep of its forts on the Gold Coast.[2] The hopes entertained that the *Asiento* secured by the Treaty of Utrecht would lead to an enormous increase of this trade to satisfy the requirements of the Spanish colonies were not in fact realized. Protests that the monopolistic practices of the Royal African Company helped to prevent this development led to its reorganization in 1750 as the Company of Merchants Trading to Africa.[3] Mixed cargoes were exported from Bristol or Liverpool to West Africa and used to purchase slaves, which were then shipped to the West Indies and the southern mainland colonies of America. There they were sold to planters and the slave ships returned to their home ports with cargoes of sugar, rum and tobacco.

If the eighteenth century witnessed the disruption of our American empire

[1] Nos. 229–233. [2] Nos. 253 and 254. [3] No. 255.

and the absence of any marked progress in Africa, it saw an extraordinary expansion of British influence in India. This is the more remarkable since it was achieved, almost unaided, by the most important of the chartered companies which have played such a prominent part in building up the British Empire – the East India Company. In our period the Company was transformed from a trading corporation into a sovereign power ruling over extensive tracts of Indian territory. This process began as early as the grant of Bombay to the Company by Charles II, but had not proceeded far in 1714.

In the first half of the century the Company continued to lend money to the Government, and secured in exchange successive prolongations of its exclusive trading rights. In the generation after 1714 its exports and imports practically doubled and every year it paid its shareholders a substantial dividend. At the same time renewals of its charter gave it extended political powers such as the right to coin money, administer justice and acquire territory. The break-up of the Mogul Empire and the resulting anarchy in India, as well as the spirited competition of the French, compelled it to exercise these powers, and ultimately, after a period of confused rivalry between French and English companies and their native protégés, allowed it to inherit the political ascendancy of the Mogul emperors. This was secured by the 'heaven born general', Robert Clive, whose sensational victories between 1757 and 1760 established English control of Bengal, Bihar and Orissa, while Eyre Coote and Forde simultaneously cleared the French out of the Carnatic and the northern Sarkars. Clive's suggestion in 1759[1] that the Crown should assume direct responsibility for the government of these provinces and the collection of their revenues was not adopted: the East India Company was allowed to add to its trading functions the political control of enormous tracts of India.

Even at the beginning of this period there had been numerous complaints about the incapacity of the board of directors at home to control effectively the behaviour of the Company's servants in India. The inadequate salaries paid by the Company to its clerks and factors compelled them to engage in private trade, and many of them exploited their position in other ways. Bribery and corruption flourished on a gigantic scale, and after a few years in India the more successful racketeers returned home with huge fortunes. The intervention of these nabobs in English politics incidentally was usually blamed for increasing the corruption of English political life under George III and particularly for the rise in the market price of safe parliamentary seats.

To such men the addition of political to commercial power merely meant greater opportunities of gaining wealth for themselves with even more rapidity and ease. They cared as little for the welfare of their Indian subjects as for the prosperity of the Company whose servants they were. At home the Company's

[1] No. 247.

financial position rapidly deteriorated, owing to the burden of military and political responsibilities which it had assumed, while the Company's servants in India, by corruption and extortion, were sucking dry the provinces committed to their care.

After prolonged parliamentary inquiries[1] the first attempt was made to remedy these scandals by Lord North's Regulating Act of 1773,[2] which not only remodelled the organization of the Company at home and introduced more effective barriers to the evil practices of its servants abroad, but created an entirely new form of government in India. In place of the three autonomous presidencies at Bombay, Calcutta and Madras, the Act established a governor-general and council at Calcutta. It is true that the powers of the governor-general and council over the other presidencies were little more than nominal, while they were bound to take their orders from the board of directors and submit to the jurisdiction of the Court of King's Bench at London. The Act also established a regular hierarchy of courts with a supreme court at Calcutta exercising a carefully limited jurisdiction over the three north-eastern provinces and itself subject to the right of appeal to the Court of King's Bench. The board of directors in London were expressly brought under the supervision of the secretary of state, and the whole system rested on the principle that the territories and revenues acquired by the Company were not its own property but belonged to the Crown, whose agent the Company was in India.

The defects of this first attempt of a British parliament to legislate for India are only too apparent. Warren Hastings, the first governor-general, stated some of them, with characteristic moderation, in the *Memoirs* of his own rule in India which he wrote on the voyage home.[3] Not only was he expected to control the other presidencies by personal influence instead of being given effective power over them. If anything, his relations with his council were even more unsatisfactory. He was bound to act by the decisions of a majority, yet he had no say in the appointment of members of his council and could neither get rid of nor ignore them. Most of them in the early years were his personal enemies. In addition serious difficulties were implicit in the position of the supreme court in the new constitution.

Yet between the years 1773 and 1784 Hastings laid the true foundations of British administration in India. During the critical years of the war of American Independence he frustrated, with inadequate resources, a series of powerful attempts to overthrow British rule. He dealt firmly with the old question of private trade and restored the financial stability of the Company. Native participation in the collection of revenue was ended and local collectors became pillars of strength in their districts. The beginnings of centralized control over revenue and administration may also be discerned. Hastings took a keen interest

[1] Nos. 248 and 249. [2] No. 250. [3] No. 251.

in the judicial system, including such subjects as the codification and application of native laws. No doubt he acted arbitrarily towards the native potentates, but few proconsuls have been placed under such burdensome and dangerous restrictions at a time of crisis and none did more for our Indian empire.

Before Hastings had returned to England and impeachment, a second attempt had been made in Fox's India Bill of 1783 to remodel the government of India.[1] In principle this measure was sound in its attempt to draw a dividing-line between the political and commercial functions of the Company, but the commissioners to whom the political business was to be transferred would also have distributed the whole patronage of the Indian empire without any adequate supervision by Parliament. George III made use of the Bill to get rid of the Fox-North coalition and appoint his own nominee William Pitt as prime minister.[2] The first task of the new government, successfully achieved by Pitt's India Act of 1784, was to set up the system of Indian administration which survived essentially unchanged until the Indian Mutiny.

The foreign policy of this period may be considered from two distinct points of view; that is to say, the geographical extension of British interests, and the basic ideas according to which the policy was directed. In 1714 Britain's primary objective was still defence. Internal disunion and the insecurity of a newly settled dynasty made this traditional basis of the country's foreign relations more prominent than ever. The dominant factor was fear of a Jacobite restoration engineered by France or some other continental power, and for the next thirty years home and foreign policy were inextricably interwoven.

At the same time commercial ambitions played a much larger part than in the history of English diplomacy in the seventeenth century. This was perhaps most obvious in the Mediterranean, where military garrisons were now maintained at Gibraltar and Port Mahon, naval squadrons were regularly seen, the Barbary pirates were overawed or bribed, and the merchant navy, aided by a network of consulates, did a brisk trade. Similarly, in the Baltic there was a great expansion of British mercantile activity. A consulate was established at Elsinore to keep watch on ships entering the Sound as well as at Riga and St. Petersburg. During the Northern war the British Government did not hesitate to send fleets into the Baltic, mainly to try and impose a settlement upon Peter the Great but also to defend the extending commercial activity of its subjects, who were–for once–asserting the rights of neutrals in a maritime war.

In two other areas British commercial and political interests were closely linked. Portugal was not only a valuable market for woollen exports and a source of bullion imports, but its ports were useful in time of war to British warships and merchant vessels. If necessary, as it was in the closing stages of the Seven Years War, the British Government was prepared to undertake

[1] No. 252. [2] No. 18.

military measures for the defence of 'our oldest ally'. The British Parliament voted £100,000 for the relief of distress after the Lisbon tidal wave of 1755. An even keener interest was taken in the Low Countries, the defence of which was entrusted to our allies the Austrians and the Dutch by the Barrier Treaty of 1715.[1] When Austria betrayed the trust reposed in her by seeking to revive the commercial prosperity of the Netherlands, the two countries came within measurable distance of war over the Ostend Company.

British interest in the remaining areas of Europe was much less close and active. As yet she had no political preoccupations in the Eastern Question, being intent merely on her trade with the Ottoman Empire, which in fact markedly declined in the early eighteenth century. It is significant that the Treaties of Carlowitz and Passarowitz between Austria and Turkey were mediated by the maritime powers, who objected to their ally Austria involving herself in a Balkan war when they wished her to keep her hands free to assist them in western Europe. Even in Germany comparatively little interest was taken, provided that British merchants were allowed to sell their goods freely and that Protestant fanaticism was not aroused by Roman Catholic proselytism or persecution. Beyond Europe, Britain already had commercial and colonial interests in America, Africa and India, but, apart from embittering relations with Spain, these exerted little influence on foreign policy for nearly a generation after 1714.

Such was the geographical extension of the system at the opening of our period and surprisingly little change took place before 1783. Undoubtedly the main alteration was the much greater importance attached to extra-European problems. This manifested itself clearly in the causes of the Anglo-Spanish war of 1739 and the Seven Years War–the first large-scale war in which British participation is to be explained primarily by colonial ambitions.[2] In western Europe the primary centres of interest were still the Low Countries and Portugal, though in both areas there had been a decline of British influence. Britain was still vitally concerned in the Mediterranean and the Baltic, though in the former, the alliance of France and Spain, and in the latter, the first Armed Neutrality, both during the war of American Independence, had weakened her position. Even earlier Russian determination to exploit her political ascendancy in the Baltic was shown by the markedly less favourable terms secured for British merchants in the commercial treaty of 1766 as compared with those gained in the previous commercial treaty of 1734.

On the other hand, there had been some extension of interest in central and eastern Europe. In Germany during the middle years of the century Britain had subsidized a number of the princes in the hope of organizing an anti-French league or at least of securing military aid in war against France. When after 1783

[1] No. 277. [2] Nos. 262–270.

national revival came, Britain was to emerge from isolation by alliance with Prussia. For a time too, in close conjunction with the ambitious power of Sardinia, Britain had played a part in Italian politics and wars, but the Treaty of Aranjuez in 1752 ended this activity and Italy remained at peace in the following generation. Even with Poland in the fifties and early sixties there had been a certain tendency to closer ties, seen, for example, in the proposal of the Czartoryski party to place Ferdinand of Brunswick on the Polish throne. But when the news of the First Partition of Poland broke upon an astonished world the British Government washed its hands publicly of the whole transaction on the avowed ground that Poland lay beyond the British sphere of interest and that it had no means of intervening effectively in Poland. Similarly, until the time of the Triple Alliance of 1788 the British Government dissociated itself from the Eastern Question. British politicians at the most privately avowed an academic sympathy with the Russians against the Turks either on humanitarian and religious grounds (Burke) or because British interests required an understanding with Russia (Chatham).

If one asks what were the factors which shaped British foreign policy in the century, a variety of answers are offered. Foremost amongst them were, of course, commercial and colonial expansion on the one hand and the balance of power on the other. It is easy to show that neither of these was dominant throughout the period. The former was probably most influential in the middle section, but was comparatively weak in the early years when the main factor was probably fear of Jacobitism, and weak again in the later years when Britain on the whole regarded herself as a satiated State.

Similarly, although the secretaries of state continually wrote of the need to preserve "the Protestant cause and the liberties of Europe" they hardly lived up to this policy. Within two years of the accession of the House of Hanover Britain was in close alliance with France, undoubtedly, in spite of her recent defeats, the strongest Power in Europe. For the next twenty years this alliance was maintained by Townshend and Walpole until too late Walpole realized that by continuing the French alliance too long and failing to intervene in the Polish Succession War he had made France the arbiter of Europe. Alike to Carteret and Pitt and even to Newcastle, the maintenance of the liberties of Europe meant antagonism to France, if not to the whole House of Bourbon. Carteret and Newcastle struggled in vain to find an effective counterpoise. Pitt was luckier as well as abler; and the failure of his successors to maintain his system was responsible for the worst disasters of the concluding years of our period. So far from being able to act as the balancing power of Europe after 1763, Britain virtually dropped out of European politics. A continental league was ultimately organized against her by France. The wheel had turned full circle since 1714, and the dominating idea until the closing years was again self-defence, complicated now by a great extension of the area to be defended and by a massive and final breach within the Empire itself.

The nearest approach to a single dominant idea will probably be found in hostility to France, which was detested by the average Englishman throughout the century. It was not merely that France was our most dangerous commercial and colonial rival beyond Europe. From her proximity, her much larger population and her alliance with other Bourbon States she was a standing threat to the security of Britain. France was detested equally as the patron of the Pretenders and the leading Roman Catholic power in Europe. Contemporary Englishmen, proud of the free institutions bequeathed to them by their ancestors, affected to despise–and certainly hated–the absolutism which Louis XIV had established in France and propagated in Europe. Only in the days of the Armada did internal security, religious zeal, political prejudice and economic advantage designate so clearly a natural and national enemy. The more one considers these truths the more one must be impressed by the willingness of the government to sign the Triple Alliance with France in 1717[1] and to make the Tory peace settlement of 1713–1714 the basis of Whig foreign policy for two decades.

What made it possible was the long survival of the tradition that foreign policy was a mystery of State with which Parliament, let alone the common man, had no right to meddle and about which it had almost as little right to be informed. In the days of the Stuarts, Parliament had vainly asserted claims to control of foreign policy, but the victory of Parliament over the Monarchy at the Revolution was not followed by any sensational advance in this direction. William III was notoriously his own foreign minister, and even after 1714 the powers of the executive were at their widest and were least supervised when dealing with foreign relations.

At the end, as at the beginning, of the period Parliament was entitled to debate and demand information on foreign policy and its approval was normally sought for important treaties, particularly for treaties of peace or subsidy which required financial supply. By these methods it had secured some measure of control over foreign affairs; but it was spasmodic and often indirect and the actual direction of policy was still in the hands of the executive. In the debate on the Treaty of Aix-la-Chapelle, Pelham informed the House of Commons that "the power of making peace and war is by our constitution most wisely lodged solely in the Crown, because in both it is absolutely necessary to keep our designs secret, till the moment of their execution". In the same speech he warned the House that if it "should once begin to enquire into our foreign treaties and negotiations, I am persuaded the consequence would be such that no foreign prince or minister would ever have anything to do with us".

[1] No. 278.

This is not to say that eighteenth-century governments were free to follow any policy they chose and abandon it when they felt inclined. Walpole was forced into war with Spain contrary to his own wishes; Carteret came into power as the advocate of a more determined anti-Bourbon policy and paid for its failure with the loss of his office; the collapse of his foreign policy drove Newcastle from power and brought in Pitt, with the backing of powerful interests outside Parliament, as the self-designated saviour of his country; above all, perhaps the failure of Lord North during the war of American Independence undermined his apparently impregnable parliamentary position and brought the peace party into office in 1782. Governments were judged not so much on abstract *a priori* grounds as on the manifest success or failure with which they carried out an agreed policy.

Once the Jacobite menace was scotched, Englishmen did not differ much on the fundamentals of foreign policy. It was means rather than ends which were fiercely disputed. Ought Britain to concentrate on commerce and colonies and allow the Continent to take care of itself? Or would this policy defeat its own ends by allowing France, as Walpole did, to dominate Europe?[1] If so, British interests required the building up of a continental league against France such as Newcastle vainly tried to secure between 1748 and 1756, and the firm adoption of the balance of power on the Continent as an essential condition of British maritime and extra-European ascendancy. Newcastle's failure helped to discourage his successors from attempting this line of policy in the years after 1763. Britain virtually abdicated the position she had gained in the councils of Europe. The simultaneous decline of French power and prestige left the field clear to the three autocrats of eastern Europe. That intervention against their activities would be impossible and futile except in co-operation with France was generally regarded as demanding a policy of non-intervention since France was the natural enemy of England.

If the king's speeches at the opening of Parliament seldom have much to say about foreign affairs and parliamentary debates are comparatively rare, there is other evidence of a growth of public interest in this sphere. Newspapers devoted a surprising amount of space to 'foreign intelligence', and the leading magazines contain many references to the personalities and problems of foreign policy. French works on international law, diplomatic etiquette, the politics and economic resources of the leading States, and the recent diplomatic history of Europe were read in England, and many of them were translated into English. John Campbell's *Present State of Europe* went through five editions between 1750 and 1757. The newly founded *Annual Register* regularly devoted an appreciable part of its space to European politics.

[1] Nos. 256–259.

In this introductory survey the political, administrative and judicial framework within which the English people lived was first considered. Then the ecclesiastical organization, the economic development and social condition of the people were discussed. After a brief glance at Scotland, Ireland and Wales, whose fate was inextricably bound up with that of England, the position of the British Empire beyond the seas was reviewed. Finally the relationship of the British people to the rest of the world and particularly to the continent of Europe was examined. While remarkable advances were made in some directions between 1714 and 1783, in others progress was comparatively slow. In one or two, contemporaries thought they detected deterioration instead of improvement; but even here a larger view and a better perspective suggest that they were suffering from an optical illusion common to all contemporary observers. The position of the British people in 1783 was indeed like that of a patient recovering from a severe operation complicated by shock. Thanks to the soundness of his constitution and the skill of the family doctor, the younger Pitt, the patient recovered with remarkable rapidity and was soon even more robust than he had been before.

Certainly the century has less than its predecessor or its successor to offer the political historian. Here its main function was to consolidate the gains of the seventeenth century and transmit them with some improvements to the nineteenth. It saw the transference of a large part of the powers exercised by William III and even Anne to a group of ministers whose retention of office, if not their original appointment, depended on the will of the House of Commons. It witnessed the emergence of one of these ministers to a position of pre-eminence less exalted than in later ages but not much less effective. It gave these ministers in their several departments a numerous and important cadre of civil servants and introduced the process of organizing the Secretariat of State on a functional basis which was to be carried much further as new needs developed in the nineteenth and twentieth centuries.

Perhaps most important of all, the political system established by the Revolution of 1688 was still largely indeterminate in 1714. There were possibilities of development towards anarchy, and this was indeed implicit in the contemporary emphasis on the division of powers without any superintending and co-ordinating authority. Down to 1775 at least the governments of the eighteenth century found the obtaining and retaining of political power in itself nearly a full-time occupation. On the other hand, the revolutionary system might have produced a return to despotism of the patriot king type. Eighteenth-century politicians are a much maligned race, but they deserve some credit for avoiding either extreme. The solution they necessarily found in patronage and influence – equally abhorrent to the nineteenth and twentieth centuries with their highly organized parties and elaborate political programmes.

Eighteenth-century radicals, however, were already advocating the replacement of influence and patronage by other ties. And the most recent students of eighteenth-century politics play down the importance of influence and exalt the role of the independent country gentleman!

Scotland probably developed more rapidly in these years than in any other period of her history. In Wales there was a powerful educational and religious revival which made possible the re-emergence of an articulate Welsh nation in the following century. In Ireland the forces which were to end by driving Eire out of the British Commonwealth of Nations were already in existence and steadily gaining strength. Beyond the seas the thirteen colonies had proclaimed their independence, but in India the foundations of the British Raj had been securely built.

In foreign policy Britain, in spite of a set-back at the end of our period, had firmly established her position as one of the leading powers of Europe, so much so that a recent French historian, writing from a European point of view, has described the eighteenth century as the century of England. In 1714 England had been merely one of three roughly equal powers leagued against France and, in the eyes of contemporaries, almost certainly not the most important of the three. For half a century, if we except the Polish Succession War, Britain took a leading part in the affairs of Europe, and no major crisis was settled without her participation and concurrence. The magnitude of this achievement is revealed clearly when it is contrasted with the normal weakness and futility of English foreign policy in the preceding century and the non-interventionist line often followed by British statesmen in the second half of the nineteenth century. Even the humiliating crisis of 1776–1783 was in itself a tribute to the place which Britain had held in general estimation – the States of Europe would not have sunk their differences in order to combine against a second-rate power. The resurrection of her naval supremacy in the last year of this war provided the essential basis for the rapid recovery which followed in the next decade.

Lastly, what of the condition of the English people in our period? So far as the upper classes are concerned they retained their political ascendancy unchallenged and increased in economic prosperity. The tradition of unpaid public service was consolidated and perpetuated, and they also had a virtual monopoly of many honourable and lucrative offices. For example, John Bright's gibe that the diplomatic service was a gigantic system of outdoor poor relief for the upper classes is at least as applicable to our century as to the one which followed. To all this many of them added a cultivated taste, which left abiding marks on the literature, arts and scholarship of the age. They were no Venetian oligarchy but were constantly recruited from the ranks of the prosperous middle class below – mostly successful merchants, nabobs and planters, but also as the century went on, leaders in the various professions and representatives of the 'new powerful rich class' of industrial magnates.

It is equally clear that the middles classes prospered, increased in numbers, and were beginning to claim a political influence corresponding to their economic importance. There was a particularly marked rise both in the personal status and economic position of the professional classes, while economic development did not merely affect merchants and industrialists but gave opportunities to bankers and brokers, inventors and engineers. The houses they built for themselves in many English towns survive as a proof of their standard of living and their good taste. Against these developments must be set the decline of the yeoman class in the country, though even here the agrarian revolution gave opportunities to agricultural experts, farm managers and tenant-farmers, while many dispossessed yeomen found new careers in the rapidly growing towns.

It is not possible to be so dogmatic when we consider the mass of the people. It was not unknown for men who started life with no advantages of birth or education to become prosperous or even eminent citizens, but these cases are undoubtedly much rarer than at the present day. Similarly, the novels of the time record many cases where, either by misfortune or their own fault, people of gentle birth and formerly prosperous members of the middle classes were to be found living in penury and degradation in the slums or jails of London. Possibly social historians are inclined to attach too much importance to conditions in London where overcrowding, irregular employment, gin-drinking, knavery and prostitution were at their worst.

Almost nine-tenths of the population lived in the country or in towns which we would now regard as large villages rather than towns. While no one would describe their living conditions as satisfactory their lot was certainly much better than that of the London poor. They were not exposed to the same temptations, employment was more regular, while their money wages were often supplemented by food and valuable perquisites. Wages were low, but so were prices, as harvests were usually good in this period. Though there were occasional local scarcities corn was plentiful and until the closing years was exported in large quantities under the bounty system. Nevertheless the wages of unskilled labour in town and country were at best on the margin of subsistence. From quite early in the century they were frequently subsidized out of the poor rates, and in times of dearth supplemented by private charity. The figures supplied by Arthur Young suggest that it would be almost impossible for an agricultural labourer with a family to make ends meet in the seventies when grain prices were beginning to rise substantially. But the traditional view that the first fifty years of our period was an era of agricultural prosperity in which all classes benefited may be accepted with some reservations.

The eighteenth century has suffered both from the attacks of its enemies and the ill-advised eulogies of its friends. Nineteenth-century Liberals inveighed against the corruption of its politics, the sordid realism of its statesmen and the absence of political idealism. Evangelical parsons condemned its lack of religious enthusiasm and its easy-going Erastianism. The Romantic poets and artists of the next age revolted against its artificial wit and formal styles. The nineteenth-century social historian was repelled and sickened by the brutality of its manners and customs, and often neglected to observe the powerful beginnings of a humanitarian reaction against them. On the other hand, drum and trumpet historians stressed unduly the achievements – great though they were – of Clive and Wolfe, Hawke and Rodney. Dilettante critics with a taste for literature and gossip skimmed the cream of its society and claimed that here was the quintessence of the century.

Even when the emphasis gradually shifted to economics, it became customary to attribute to the eighteenth century, with its agrarian and industrial revolutions, the destruction of 'Merry England' and the substitution of the sordid conditions and grasping capitalism of the early nineteenth century. This showed a fundamental misconception. Long hours of work, unhealthy and insanitary conditions, low wages, capitalistic exploitation of labour, abuses connected with the employment of children were not the creation of the eighteenth century. They had existed long before. In fact, there had been appreciable and widespread improvement in some of these respects during the period we have studied. In others the worst abuses became more widespread in and were more characteristic of the succeeding era. It must, however, be admitted that the decay of the yeomanry, 'their country's pride', had gone so far by 1783 that the process could hardly be reversed, and that the technical inventions of the period, taken with the prevailing attitude of the government, clearly foreshadowed what was to come. But without the increased productivity of agriculture and the flying start in industrialization which the eighteenth century gave to her, Great Britain would never have played the part she did in the history of Europe and of the world.

GENERAL BIBLIOGRAPHY

I. MODERN REFERENCE WORKS

(*a*) BIBLIOGRAPHIES AND LIBRARY CATALOGUES

The standard bibliography is the *Bibliography of British History, the Eighteenth Century, 1714–1789*, edited by Stanley Pargellis and D. J. Medley and published under the direction of the Royal Historical Society and the American Historical Association (Oxford, 1951). The preceding volume, *Bibliography of British History, Stuart Period, 1603–1714*, edited by G. Davies (Oxford, 1928), also lists many works of value for the earlier part of the Hanoverian era. This is also true of W. T. Morgan, *A Bibliography of British History, 1700–1715, with special reference to the reign of Queen Anne*, 5 vols. (Bloomington, Indiana, 1934–1942). The admirable work of C. L. Grose, *A Select Bibliography of British History, 1660–1760* (Chicago, 1939), with the same author's supplementary "Studies of 1931–40 on British History, 1660–1760" in the *Journal of Modern History*, XII (1940), pp. 515–534, may still be used for the period from 1714 to 1760. The short commentary on the authorities at the end of Basil Williams, *The Whig Supremacy, 1714–60* (Oxford, 1939), makes a judicious selection from an unwieldy mass of material. Of guides to the most recent publications, *Writings on British History* compiled by A. T. Milne for the Royal Historical Society is the most complete; but the volumes which have appeared (1937, 1939, 1940, 1951 and 1953) deal only with the publications of the years 1934–1939. Until it can be brought up to date, therefore, other publications must be consulted. These include L. B. Frewer, *Bibliography of Historical Writings published in Great Britain and the Empire, 1940–45* (Oxford, 1947); the *Annual Bulletin of Historical Literature*, published by the Historical Association; and the lists of articles printed each year in the July number of the *English Historical Review*. The *International Bibliography of Historical Sciences*, issued under the auspices of the International Committee of Historical Sciences, lists the publications of the years from 1926 to 1948 (excepting 1940–1946 inclusive) (16 vols., Paris, etc., 1930–1950). There are also numerous special bibliographies, such as Dorothy A. Guthrie and C. L. Grose, "Forty Years of Jacobite Bibliography" in the *Journal of Modern History*, XI (1939), pp. 49–60, and Jane E. Norton, *Guide to the National and Provincial Directories of England and Wales, excluding London, published before 1856* (Royal Historical Society Guides and Handbooks, No. 5, London, 1950), useful for the period after 1760. Many of these will be mentioned later in the lists of books appended to the Sectional Introductions. The *Local History Handlist*, published by the Historical Association (London, 1947), provides an up-to-date list of books on every conceivable aspect of local history, and many of them are equally useful to anyone interested in national but non-political history. Reference should be made to *A World Bibliography of Bibliographies*, edited by T. Besterman (3 vols., London, revised edition, 1947–1949).

The catalogues of the British Museum provide the most complete lists of books published in the eighteenth century. They include *The British Museum Catalogue of Printed Books* with supplement (London, 1881–1905), new edition, which has reached letter DEZ (51 vols., London, 1931–1949), and *Subject Index of the Modern Works added to the Library of the British Museum*, London (16 vols., 1886–1953). More manageable and more readily accessible are the similar publications of the London Library, the *Subject Index* (4 vols., London, 1909, 1923, 1938, 1955) and the *Author Catalogues* (5 vols., London, 1913–1914, 1920, 1929, 1953).

(*b*) GUIDES TO MANUSCRIPT SOURCES

The printed sources are a mere fragment of the unpublished materials available to the student at the Public Record Office, British Museum, official local repositories and private collections. The British Museum alone possesses 522 volumes of the duke of Newcastle's correspondence which dovetail into that other great collection in its custody, the Hardwicke Papers, and several smaller collections whose importance is primarily for diplomatic history. The Liverpool Papers are almost as important for the following period, and they too are supplemented by smaller collections such as the Auckland Papers. Every aspect of the national life is covered by the official documents preserved at the Public Record Office, which also holds some unofficial documents, notably the Chatham Manuscripts, being the correspondence of the elder Pitt. The local public repositories have even now by no means been thoroughly exploited by historical students. They are particularly valuable for economic, social and legal history. Every year or two important discoveries are made of manuscripts in private custody which have escaped destruction by a succession of miracles until seen by someone who understands their value.

Hubert Hall, *Repertory of British Archives, Part I: England*, published by the Royal Historical Society (London, 1920), provides a survey of the central and local repositories of public records. The most important of these, the Public Record Office, is dealt with by the standard guide, M. S. Guiseppi, *Guide to the Manuscripts Preserved in the Public Record Office* (2 vols., London, 1923–1924), supplemented by various official publications, notably numbers 43 and 52 of *Lists and Indexes*, which give respectively a *List of Volumes of State Papers Relating to Great Britain and Ireland* [1509–1837] (1914), and a *List of Foreign Office Records to 1878* (1929). The manuscript collections of the other great national repository, the British Museum, have been much more fully catalogued and indexed. Separate guides exist to *inter alia* the Harleian Manuscripts (4 vols., 1808–1812); Lansdowne Manuscripts (1819), Stowe Manuscripts (2 vols., 1895–1896), and Sloane Manuscripts (1904), while all additional manuscripts acquired since 1836, along with Egerton Manuscripts 607–3030, are included in *British Museum Catalogue of Additions to the Manuscripts* (15 vols., London, 1843–1933). Indispensable for serious study of British foreign policy, and particularly Franco-British relations, is the official *Inventaire Sommaire des Archives . . . des Affaires Étrangères I . . . Angleterre* (Paris, 1903). The great bulk of manuscript records remain in private hands and in local public repositories, but many of the collections most important for this period have been examined and selections from them published by the Historical Manuscripts Commission in their *Reports and Appendices* (London, 1870). See *infra.*

(*c*) ENCYCLOPAEDIAS, DICTIONARIES AND OTHER REFERENCE WORKS

Useful articles on many subjects will be found in the standard encyclopaedias, notably the various editions of the *Encyclopaedia Britannica*, the new edition of *Chambers's Encyclopaedia* (London, 1950), and the *Encyclopaedia of the Social Sciences* (15 vols., London, 1930–1935, reissued 1948). *The Dictionary of National Biography* (2nd edition, 22 vols., London, 1908–1909) with supplements is particularly strong on the eighteenth century. *The Concise Dictionary of National Biography* (London, 1939) is a useful epitome and periodical lists of additions and corrections appear in *The Bulletin of the Institute of Historical Research*. *The Dictionary of American Biography* (edited by A. Johnson and D. Malone for the American Council of Learned Societies, 20 vols. and supplement 1 vol., New York, 1928–1937 and 1944) includes lives of some Britons who came to America as well as of some Americans who played a part in British history. *The Handbook of British Chronology*, edited by F. M. Powicke for the Royal Historical Society (London, 1939), gives useful details about the royal family, officers of State, bishops, regnal years, etc., and on pp. 373–378 explains clearly and authoritatively the old and new styles of calculating dates which often puzzle students of this period. For the enormous and valuable pamphlet literature, S. Halkett and J. Laing, *Dictionary of Anonymous and Pseudonymous English Literature* (7 vols., new edition by J. Kennedy, W. A. Smith and A. F. Johnson, Edinburgh, 1926–1934), is indispensable.

Genealogical tables of the royal and ex-royal families of Hanover and Stuart will be found in H. B. George, *Genealogical Tables illustrative of Modern History*, edited by J. R. H. Weaver (Oxford, 1930), and in the *Cambridge Modern History*, vol. XIII (Cambridge, 1911). On the peerage, G. E. C[okayne], *The Complete Peerage*, edited by Hon. V. Gibbs and others (12 vols. London, 1910–1953), is authoritative and complete to Towton. G.E.C. was also responsible for *The Complete Baronetage* (6 vols., Exeter, 1900–1909), while W. A. Shaw listed *Knights of England: a complete record from the earliest times to the present day* (2 vols., London, 1906). *Alumni Cantabrigienses*, edited by J. and J. A. Venn, part i to 1751 (Cambridge, 4 vols., 1922–1927) and part ii, 1752–1900 (6 vols., 1940–1954), is another useful compilation. *Alumni Oxonienses 1715–1886*, edited by J. Foster (4 vols., Oxford, 1887–1888), covers the period from 1715 to 1783. H. Raven-Hart and Marjorie Johnston, "Bibliography of the Registers (Printed) of the Universities, Inns of Court, Colleges and Schools of Great Britain and Ireland" in the *Bulletin of the Institute of Historical Research*, IX (1931–1932), pp. 19–30, 65–83, 154–170, and X (1932–1933), pp. 109–113, is a useful guide to these sources. T. R. Thomson, *Catalogue of British Family Histories* (London, 1928), and H. G. Harrison, *Select Bibliography of English Genealogy with brief Lists for Wales, Scotland and Ireland* (London, 1937), are also sometimes useful. R. S. Crane and F. B. Kaye, *Census of British Newspapers and Periodicals, 1620–1800* (University of North Carolina, Chapel Hill, 1927), G. A. Cranfield, *Hand-list of English Provincial Newspapers and Periodicals, 1700–1760* (Cambridge, 1952), and R. T. Milford and D. M. Sutherland, *Catalogue of English Newspapers and Periodicals in the Bodleian Library, 1622–1800* (Oxford, 1936), provide exhaustive references to contemporary periodicals. The *Catalogue of Prints and Drawings in the British Museum Division I Political and Personal Satires*, prepared by F. G. Stephens, vols. 2–4, cover the period from 1689 to *circa* 1700 (London, 1873–1883). This invaluable publication was continued by Mary Dorothy George under the title *Catalogue of Political and Personal Satires* (London, 1935–1954), vol. 5 of which (London, 1935) carries the survey down to 1783.

Portraits of leading eighteenth-century statesmen, ecclesiastics, soldiers, sailors, diplomatists, civil servants, authors and artists and of many eighteenth-century men and women with no particular claim to distinction abound in public and private collections. They form a splendid introduction to the period. W. G. Constable, *Collections of Historical Portraits and other Forms of Iconography in Great Britain*, Leaflet No. 96 of the Historical Association (London, 1934), is an invaluable guide. F. M. O'Donoghue and H. M. Hake, *Catalogue of Engraved British Portraits preserved in the British Museum* (6 vols., London, 1908–1925), gives some idea of the richness and variety of these sources. In addition the National Portrait Gallery has indexes of portraits, which are readily made available to serious students.

(*d*) LISTS OF MAPS, ETC.

The British Museum, *Catalogue of the printed maps, plans and charts* (2 vols., London, 1885), must be supplemented by Sir G. Fordham, *Some Notable Surveyors and Map-makers of the 16th, 17th and 18th Centuries* (Cambridge, 1929); E. Lynam, *British Maps and Map-makers, 1250–1931* (London, 1944), and R. V. Tooley, *Maps and Map-makers* (London, 1949), which are both useful guides. H. C. Darby (editor), *Historical Geography of England before 1800* (Cambridge, 1936), is a standard work. Useful maps are also included in the *Cambridge Modern History Atlas* (Cambridge, 1912); R. L. Poole, *Historical Atlas of Modern Europe* (Oxford, 1896–1902); Muir's

Historical Atlas, 7th edition, edited by G. Goodall (London, 1947); and W. R. Shepherd, *Historical Atlas* (New York, 1929).

II. CONTEMPORARY PRINTED SOURCES

(*a*) NEWSPAPERS AND MAGAZINES

Official announcements were published in the *London Gazette*, "the oldest existing European newspaper", and it was one of the duties of diplomatic and consular agents abroad to supply material for it. Reference has been made in the preceding volume of this series to *The Tatler* and *The Spectator*, but in the early Hanoverian era much the best-known periodical was *The Craftsman*, founded by Pulteney and Bolingbroke to attack Walpole, and edited by N. Amhurst, which appeared from 1726 to 1736. A new stage in journalism opened with the first number of *The Gentleman's Magazine*, edited by Edward Cave, which appeared monthly from 1731, and its imitator and chief rival from 1732 *The London Magazine*. Newspapers were even more numerous than magazines in the eighteenth century, but were often short-lived. There is a good survey of *English literary periodicals* by W. J. Graham (New York, 1930). G. S. Marr discusses *Periodical essayists of the eighteenth century with illustrative extracts from the rarer periodicals* (London, 1923), and L. Hanson treats with equal skill and knowledge the thorny problem of *Government and the Press, 1695–1763* (London, 1936). K. G. Burton, *The Early Newspaper Press in Berkshire, 1723–1855* (Reading, 1954), is a useful study of the provincial Press, as are the articles on "Wiltshire Newspapers" by J. J. Slade and by Mrs. Richardson in *Wiltshire Archaeological Magazine*, XL (1917–1919), pp. 37–74, 129–141, 318–351; and XLI (1920–1922), pp. 53–69. The development of the newspaper in this period on which S. Morison, *English Newspaper* (Cambridge, 1932), is authoritative, rendered newsletters, which had been important in the seventeenth century, almost obsolete, although examples are still occasionally found. Bibliographical lists of periodicals are mentioned in Section I (*c*).

(*b*) PAMPHLETS

The pamphlet literature of the period is most extensive and, unlike that of the preceding period, has never been collected in convenient form. The British Museum, however, and many other important libraries have bound series of Political Tracts. Extracts from some notable pamphlets have been printed in the text of this volume and reference made to others in the sectional bibliographies. Swift's pamphlets are included in the *Prose Works of Jonathan Swift*, edited by Temple Scott (12 vols., 1897–1908); and in the new definitive text of the *Prose Works*, edited by Herbert Davis (Oxford, 1939), to be complete in fourteen volumes, of which vols. 1–3 and 6–12 have so far appeared. Those of Defoe are listed by H. C. Hutchins in the *Cambridge Bibliography of English Literature*, II, pp. 495–514 (Cambridge, 1940). The once celebrated *Letters of Junius* have been reprinted from time to time; the latest edition is edited by C. W. Everett (London, 1927).

(*c*) REFERENCE WORKS

A mass of information of the most miscellaneous character, including lists of officials, information about the court, Parliament, law courts, army and navy, universities, etc., will be found in two unofficial publications, John Chamberlayne, *Magnae Britanniae Notitia*, editions of which appeared at frequent intervals from 1708 to 1755, and Guy Miège, *Present State of Great Britain*, which was published less frequently. There is a bibliographical note on *Magnae Britanniae Notitia* by Muriel M. S. Arnett in the *Bulletin of the Institute of Historical Research*, XV (1937–1938), pp. 24–30. M. Jolliffe contributed a short note on the *Present State of Great Britain* to *ibid.*, XVII

(1939–1940), pp. 130–138. Later compilations of this kind include "The Court and City Register" and "The Royal Kalendar" on which the bibliographical article by Alizon M. Mathews in *ibid.*, XIX (1942–1943), pp. 9–24, should be consulted. Of more general use is R. Beatson, *Political Index* (3 parts in one volume, Edinburgh, 1786), dedicated to Adam Smith, which was later re-edited by J. Haydn as *Beatson's Political Index Modernised* (London, 1851) and later editions.

Another class of publications tried to record the outstanding events of the time. These include the *Historical Register* which was issued by the Sun Fire Office Company from 1716 to 1738 to its clients and Abel Boyer's *Political State of Great Britain* (London, 1711–1740), which gives the text of letters, addresses, speeches, memorials, etc., relating to public affairs. After 1758 there appeared regularly *The Annual Register, or a view of the history, politics and literature for the year,* which was founded by Robert Dodsley with the assistance of Edmund Burke in 1758 and still appears annually.

(*d*) PRINTED CALENDARS OF OFFICIAL DOCUMENTS

Hardly any documents relating to our period have been published or even calendared in official publications. The main exceptions are the *Calendar of Treasury Papers*, edited by J. Redington [1714–1728] (2 vols., London, 1883–1889); the *Calendar of Treasury Books and Papers*, edited by W. A. Shaw [1729–1745] (5 vols., London, 1898–1903); the *Calendar of Home Office Papers*, edited by J. Redington and R. A. Roberts [1760–1775] (4 vols., London, 1878–1899); and the *Journals of the Board of Trade and Plantations* [1704–1782] (14 vols., London, 1920–1938), and other collections relating to the colonies (see sectional bibliography on the colonies).

(*e*) PUBLICATIONS OF THE HISTORICAL MANUSCRIPTS COMMISSION

These form much the largest and most important collection of printed sources for the eighteenth century. Some attempt has been made to indicate their variety and usefulness in the text of this volume. The *Calendar of the Stuart Papers* (7 vols. to 1718, 1902–1923) and several less important collections, especially *Lindley Wood Manuscripts, Report on Manuscripts in Various Collections*, vol. VIII (1913), *Hodgkin Manuscripts* (1897) and *Fitzherbert Manuscripts* (1893), are invaluable for Jacobite activities. The *Portland Manuscripts* (vols. 5–7, 1899–1901) include Harley's papers for the early years of the Hanoverian era and interesting 'tours' by the second earl of Oxford and his countess. *The Diary of the First Earl of Egmont* [1730–1747] (3 vols., 1920–1923) is of outstanding interest for political and social history and in particular for references to the foundation of Georgia and the origins of Wesleyanism. The *Onslow Manuscripts, Report XIV, App. 9* (1895) include the papers of Arthur Onslow, who was Speaker of the House of Commons throughout the reign of George II. The *Rutland Manuscripts*, vol. 2, *Report XII, App. 5*, and vol. 3, *Report XIV, App. 1* (1889, 1894), include the papers of the Marquess of Granby and give information about the continental side of the Seven Years War. The *Eyre Matcham Manuscripts, Report on Manuscripts in Various Collections*, vi (1909), supplement Bubb Dodington's *Diary* (*infra*, p. 74) and throw valuable light on the 'reversionary interest' and its political importance. The *Carlisle Manuscripts* (1897) contain a mass of private correspondence of political and social interest, including many letters from George Selwyn. Similar collections are the *Denbigh Manuscripts, Part V* [1735–1787] (1911); *Hare Manuscripts, Report XIV, App. 9* (1895); *Ailesbury Manuscripts, Report XV, App. 7* (1898); *Hastings Manuscripts*, vol. 3 (1934) (mostly correspondence of the ninth and tenth earls of Huntingdon); and *Manuscripts of the Earl of Donoughmore* [1760–1795], *Report XII, App. 9* (1891). The *Fortescue Manuscripts*, vol. 1 (1892), contain family and occasional political correspondence of the Pitt family. The *Abergavenny Manuscripts* (1887) include a calendar of some of the papers of that notorious civil servant, John Robinson. More important are the *Knox Manuscripts, Report on Manuscripts in Various Collections*, vol. VI (1909), which contain the papers of another of George III's civil servants and are particularly but not exclusively valuable for American affairs before and during the war of American Independence. This period is also illuminated by the *Dartmouth Manuscripts*, vol. I, *Report XI, App. 5*, and vol. II, *Report XVI, App. 10* (1887, 1895), and vol. III, *Report XIV, App. 1* (1896) (chiefly the private papers and some official correspondence of "the good earl of Dartmouth"), and the *Stopford Sackville Manuscripts*, vols. 1–2 (1904–1910). The *Palk Manuscripts* (1922) are mainly of interest to students of Indian history after 1763. References to other collections of particular interest for Scottish, Irish, diplomatic, naval or military history will be found *infra* in these sectional bibliographies. Even with these additions the list is not exhaustive, but an attempt has been made to include all those likely to interest the general reader.

Reference to this enormous mass of material is facilitated by the 22nd Report (1946), which lists alphabetically the collections examined and indicates the approximate period covered by each. It also gives details of past and present owners and places of deposit and, where known, present location. *The Bulletin of the Institute of Historical Research* regularly prints notes on migrations of these and other manuscripts (particularly Eleanor S. Upton's article in vol. XV (1937), pp. 73–78, dealing with the location of the manuscripts covered by the first nine (folio) reports). There is also up to 1911 a topographical index and an index of persons edited by F. Bickley (2 vols., London, 1935 and 1938); continuations of both guides up to 1946 are in preparation. Miss Frances G. Davenport listed *Materials for English Diplomatic History* (1509–1783), based on the Historical Manuscripts Commission publications and the British Museum Manuscript Collections, both in 18th and 19th Reports (1917 and 1926).

(*f*) GENERAL HISTORIES

Fortunately or otherwise the great historians of the eighteenth century did not essay contemporary history in an age when the writing of history had become fashionable and even profitable. What the historian of the decline and fall of the Roman Empire would have made of the decline and fall of the Whig oligarchy must remain a barren speculation. David Hume's *Essays* (London, 1741–1742) and many later editions give some indication of his outlook on his own age, but are merely detached fragments. The civil and ecclesiastical statesmen of the period, the Walpoles and the Pitts, the Gibsons and the Hoadlys, made no attempt to rival Clarendon's *History of the Great Rebellion* or Burnet's *History of My Own Time*. The contemporary scene was therefore left to industrious compilers and literary hacks. Among their works may be mentioned the continuations by N. Tindal of Rapin-Thoyras, *History of England* (various editions down to 1763), and by Tobias Smollett of David Hume's once celebrated *History of Great Britain* [to 1688]. Rapin is chiefly valuable as a contemporary recorder of events, while Smollett occasionally makes an illuminating comment on the facts.

(*g*) MEMOIRS, DIARIES, ETC.

Here again it must be confessed that no work of this class relating to our period has become a literary classic rivalling the *Diaries* of Samuel Pepys and John Evelyn. But there is no lack of contemporary chroniclers of the political scene, most of them, it must be admitted, intent on their own justification. In a class by himself stands Horace Walpole. While still a young man, he set out to present to posterity a picture of his own age. In the main he has succeeded in imposing his views on later writers in spite of their protestations against his bias, which is undeniable. His memoirs are contained in three separate works, *Memoirs of the Reign of King George the Second* [1751–1760], edited by Lord Holland (3 vols., 2nd edition, London, 1847); *Memoirs of the Reign of King George the Third* [1760–1770], edited by G. F. Russell Barker (4 vols., London, 1894); and *Journal of the Reign of King George the Third* [1771–1783], edited by Dr. Doran (2 vols., London, 1859). Taken together these volumes provide a continuous narrative of the last thirty-three years of our period. Walpole was not an active politician, but he sat in the House of Commons from 1754 until 1767 and gives valuable reports at first hand of its proceedings at a time when outside reporting was a task of some difficulty and even danger. Throughout the second half of our period he had the *entrée* to the inner governing circles of the Whig aristocracy, whose point of view he faithfully reflects. Walpole's numerous other writings are listed by A. T. Hazen, *A Bibliography of Horace Walpole* (New Haven, 1948).

Second only to Walpole, but much more circumscribed in his interests and in the period which he covers, 1727 to 1737, is the work of Lord Hervey, *Some Materials towards Memoirs of the Reign of King George II*, edited by R. Sedgwick (3 vols., London, 1931). This presents an unforgettable picture of the court and nobility. A slighter and less highly coloured account of court life under George I will be found in the *Diary of Mary, Countess Cowper* [1714–1720], edited by C. S. Cowper (London, 1864). The *Diary* [1749–1761] of G. Bubb Dodington, edited by H. P. Wyndham (Salisbury, 1784 and later editions), provides a frank, first-hand account of the borough-mongering, place-hunting activities of a third-rate politician, who none the less in the end obtained the peerage he coveted. The *Memoirs of a Celebrated Literary and Political Character* [Richard Glover] (London, 1813) extend from 1742 to 1757 and are especially valuable for the careers of Carteret and Pitt. Lord Waldegrave, *Memoirs from 1754 to 1758* (London, 1821), gives instructive 'characters' of his contemporaries and sketches from his inside knowledge the ministerial negotiations of these vital years. George Grenville's diary, which he himself characteristically calls "Some Account of the Memorable Transactions since the Death of Lord Egremont", is published with the other *Grenville Papers*, edited by W. J. Smith (4 vols., London, 1852–1853). The *Autobiography of the Duke of Grafton*, edited by Sir W. R. Anson (London, 1898), although it was written long after the events in which the author played a prominent part, is useful, while Sir N. W. Wraxall, Bt., in his *Historical and Posthumous Memoirs* [1772–1789], edited by H. B. Wheatley (5 vols., London, 1884), gives a lively, gossipy account of the leading politicians of the seventies and eighties, which it is unwise to accept without corroboration. *British Diaries* [1442–1942] compiled by William Matthews (Berkeley, California, 1950) provides an annotated list of diaries, published and unpublished.

(*h*) COLLECTIONS OF CORRESPONDENCE, ETC.

The eighteenth century is, *par excellence*, the age of the great letter-writers. Even novelists such as Smollett and pamphleteers such as Junius often presented their works to the public in the epistolary form. Among the letter-writers proper three stand out as supreme practitioners of the art, Lady Mary Wortley Montagu, Horace Walpole and Lord Chesterfield. The *Letters and Works of Lady Mary Wortley Montagu*, edited by Lord Wharncliffe, appeared in 3 vols. (London, 1837), and there are later editions as well as numerous editions of selections from her letters. Lewis Gibbs, *The Admirable Lady Mary* (London, 1949), and the *Life* by Robert Halsband (Oxford, 1956) are useful biographies. The standard edition of the *Letters of Horace Walpole*, edited by Mrs. P. J. Toynbee (16 vols., Oxford, 1903–1905), is completed by three supplementary volumes, edited by P. J. Toynbee (Oxford, 1918–1925). The sumptuous Yale Edition of Horace Walpole's Correspondence under the general editorship of W. S. Lewis (London, 1937—) is making slow progress. Unlike the Toynbee edition, it is arranged according to Walpole's correspondents including letters addressed to as well as those written by him. So far twenty-one volumes of correspondence between Walpole and the Reverend William Cole, Madame du Deffand, George Montagu, the Misses Berry and Miss Seton, Thomas Gray, Richard West, Thomas Ashton, Horace Mann and others have appeared in this edition. R. W. Ketton-Cremer, *Horace Walpole, a biography* (London, 1940, new edition, 1946), is perhaps the best modern commentary on Horace Walpole. Chesterfield's *Letters* should be read in the six-volume edition by Bonamy Dobrée (London, 1932), which has a good account of Chesterfield's political career. The plan of this edition required the omission of Chesterfield's famous 'characters' of most of the contemporary politicians, which may, however, conveniently be read in the third volume of J. Bradshaw's edition of the *Letters* (London, 1892). The commentary in S. Shellabarger, *Lord Chesterfield* (London, 1935), is highly recommended. These three collections are indispensable both for the political and the social historian. Equally indispensable are the numerous selections which have been published from the correspondence and other papers of the leading statesmen, though few of these have much literary merit. For the first half of the century the student owes a great debt to the extensive researches amongst the family papers of the leading politicians conducted by Archdeacon William Coxe. His *Memoirs of Sir Robert Walpole* (3 vols., London, 1798) contain a massive appendix of letters relating to Walpole's administration. Equally valuable for the following period is the illustrative correspondence printed in his *Memoirs of Henry Pelham* (2 vols., London, 1829). Extensive collections of George III's letters and papers are mentioned in the sectional bibliography on the monarchy. Some idea of Pitt's personality and policy may be obtained from *Chatham Correspondence*, edited by W. S. Taylor and J. H. Pringle (4 vols., London, 1838–1840). A number of Pitt's letters to Bute, complementary to Bute's letters to Pitt included in the *Chatham Correspondence*, have been printed by Romney Sedgwick in "Letters from William Pitt to Lord Bute: 1755–1758" in *Essays Presented to Sir Lewis Namier* (London, 1956). The letters from Edmund Burke printed in his *Works and Correspondence* (8 vols., London, 1852) contain many interesting comments on affairs. Other collections of value mainly for political history include *Annals and Correspondence of the Earls of Stair*, edited by J. M. Graham (2 vols., London, 1875), Franco-British relations after the Spanish Succession War and episodes in the war of the Austrian Succession; *A selection from the Papers of the Earls of Marchmont*, edited by Sir G. Rose (3 vols., London, 1831), chiefly useful for the opposition to Walpole; *Letters to and from Henrietta, Countess of Suffolk*, edited by J. M. Croker (2 vols., London, 1824), on court life and politics under George II; *Private Correspondence of Chesterfield and Newcastle*, edited by Sir R. Lodge for the Royal Historical Society (London, 1930), on domestic and foreign affairs, 1744–1746. Three collections essential to any study of politics during the middle years of the century are *Correspondence of John, 4th Duke of Bedford*, edited by Lord John Russell (3 vols., London, 1842–1846); *Memoirs and Correspondence of George Lyttelton*, edited by R. J. Phillimore (2 vols., London, 1845); *Grenville Papers* [of Earl Temple and George Grenville], edited by W. J. Smith (4 vols., London, 1852–1853); earl of Albemarle, *Memoirs of the Marquis of Rockingham* (2 vols., London, 1852); *Memorials and Correspondence of Charles James Fox*, edited by Lord John Russell (4 vols., London, 1853–1857); and *Jenkinson Papers, 1760–66*, edited by Ninetta S. Jucker (London, 1949), are indispensable for political transactions in the reign of George III. A few letters of interest for Bute's official career are printed in *A Prime Minister and his Son*, edited by Hon. Mrs. E. Stuart Wortley (London, 1925), and some of Lord North's by Professor E. Hughes in "Lord North's Correspondence, 1766–83" in the *English Historical Review*, LXII (1947), pp. 218–238. The *Correspondence of the late John Wilkes*, edited by John Almon (5 vols., London, 1805), is also of some interest. Other collections mentioned in the sectional bibliography on social history contain occasional references to politics.

III. LATER WORKS

(a) PERIODICALS

For long the publications of the Camden Society, 1838–, and the *Transactions of the Royal Historical Society*, both indexed by Hubert Hall, *List and Index* [1840–1897] (London, 1925), were almost the only periodical publications of value to the historian of the eighteenth century in Britain, apart from reviews in foreign languages. The foundation of the *English Historical Review* in 1886 was an epoch-making event and was followed almost immediately in 1895 by the *American Historical Review* and in 1903 by the *Scottish Historical Review*. The first number of *History* appeared in 1912, and this more popular review soon became the official journal of the newly founded Historical Association, whose long series of pamphlets and guides also include much valuable material for the eighteenth century. Then came the *Bulletin of the Institute of Historical Research* in 1923, which specializes in the more technical aspects of historical studies, publishing bibliographical aids for advanced students, notes on archives and migrations of manuscripts, summaries of theses, etc. More recently reviews have been founded to specialize in one period or aspect of history, notably the *Journal of Modern History* (Chicago, 1929), *Economic History* (*A Supplement to the Economic Journal*) (London, 1926), the *Economic History Review* (London, 1927), *Irish Historical Studies* (Dublin, 1928), the *Journal of the History of Ideas* (New York, 1940), the *Journal of Economic History* (New York, 1941), and the *Agricultural History Review* (Reading, 1953–). Another tendency is for individual institutions of university rank to publish their own historical review, the best known of these being the *Cambridge Historical Journal* (Cambridge, 1923–) and the revived *Scottish Historical Review* (Edinburgh, 1947–), which is subsidized by the four Scottish universities. There are indexes to the *English Historical Review* up to 1935 (4 vols., London, 1906–1937) and to the *Scottish Historical Review* (2 vols., Glasgow, 1918 and 1933), but the difficulty of tracing an article on a particular subject is almost insuperable. It must also be remembered that many articles of historical interest appear in non-historical periodicals such as the *Proceedings of the British Academy*, the *Economic Journal*, etc., and also in the publications of the numerous local societies of antiquarians, etc. For information on all publications of this kind the *Union Catalogue of the Periodical Publications in the University Libraries of the British Isles* (London, 1937) should be consulted.

(b) GENERAL HISTORIES

There is no modern history covering the whole period 1714 to 1783. Two eminent Victorian historians, however, covered the whole field, and their works may still be read with enjoyment and profit. Lord Mahon (later fifth Earl Stanhope) published at London between 1836 and 1854 a seven-volume *History of England* [1713–1783] which went through various later editions. Based largely on the original sources, it is outspokenly Whig in sympathy and is particularly strong on military, political and imperial history. An interesting contrast is provided by the later and rather fuller and more comprehensive work of W. E. Lecky, *History of England in the Eighteenth Century* (8 vols., London, 1878–1890) and later editions. Lecky shows little acquaintance with the primary materials and is particularly weak on diplomatic history. He accepts in the main uncritically the views current in his own day on English political and constitutional development in the eighteenth century. As one would expect from his other works, his strength lies in depicting English society, appreciating its institutions and explaining the significance of the intellectual and religious movements of the century. On Lecky as a historian the recent work of a sympathetic fellow countryman may be consulted: J. J. Auchmuty, *Lecky* (Dublin, 1945). On the last twenty years of the period W. N. Massey, *History of England during the Reign of*

George III (4 vols., London, 1855–1863), though hardly a classic, still deserves mention; but the nearest approach to a standard modern history of the first half of George III's reign is Sir G. O. Trevelyan, *The American Revolution* (6 vols., London, 1905–1916). T. B. Macaulay's once celebrated contributions to *The Edinburgh Review*, reprinted in three volumes (London, 1843) and many later editions, include essays on the elder Pitt and the younger Horace Walpole, as well as on the two great Indian proconsuls, Clive and Warren Hastings. In them Macaulay sketches the course of domestic and imperial politics from Walpole to the end of our period, and they may be read with pleasure and profit by anyone sufficiently acquainted with the eighteenth century to discount Macaulay's partisanship and over-emphasis.

Basil Williams, *The Whig Supremacy, 1714–60* (Oxford, 1939) and later reprints, is undoubtedly the standard work on that period. It presents an admirable picture of English central and local government, legal system, religion and the Churches, social and economic life, and then gives a reasonably detailed narrative of the political history of the period, concluding with chapters on Scotland and Ireland, the colonies and India, science and historical research, the arts and literature. Unfortunately the volume in the Oxford History on the following period, 1760–1815, is not yet published. Meanwhile reference may be made to the relevant volumes of *The Political History of England*, edited by W. Hunt and R. L. Poole, vol. IX by I. S. Leadam from 1702–1760 (London, 1909), and vol. X by W. Hunt from 1760–1801 (London, 1905). More readable and at least as valuable, though less detailed, is Sir C. Grant Robertson, *England under the Hanoverians* (London, 1911), being the sixth volume of *A History of England*, edited by Sir C. Oman. Some of the chapters in the *Cambridge Modern History*, vol. VI (Cambridge, 1909), are still serviceable. Professor W. Michael's *Englische Geschichte im 18ten Jahrhundert* (5 vols., Hamburg, Leipzig and Basel, 1896–1955) stops at 1743, but is a remarkable achievement, based on lifelong study of continental as well as of British public archives and private collections of manuscripts. The first two volumes have fortunately been translated, under the supervision of Sir Lewis Namier, with the title *England under George I* (2 vols., London, 1936, 1939). Naturally strong on foreign policy, this work also throws much and occasionally unexpected light on English domestic affairs, chiefly from the reports of the Austrian, German and French diplomatic agents to their governments. Sir Lewis Namier's own notable work on the politics of the period is included in the sectional bibliography on Parliament. H. Butterfield, *The Englishman and His History* (Cambridge, 1944), is a brilliant essay on Whig interpretation of history and the influence of tradition in English life.

Part I

THE MONARCHY

THE MONARCHY

Introduction

THE Revolution of 1688 and its final confirmation by the accession of the House of Hanover in 1714 established, both in theory and in practice, the constitutional monarchy which was the essence of the eighteenth-century constitution. The theory of this constitution was expounded and praised in the mid-eighteenth century by many English and foreign writers, and some examples are collected in the first group of documents in this section.[1] Most of these writers regarded the English Constitution as something perfect and permanent, and all of them stressed its 'mixed' nature and the equilibrium produced by the nice balance of the various parts.

In practice, fundamental changes in the position of the monarchy were taking place between 1714 and 1783. This was to some extent due to the characters of the Hanoverian kings, and especially George I and George II. Lady Mary Wortley Montagu's description of George I,[2] while perhaps under-estimating his ability, shows how he was handicapped by his ignorance of England and the English language. George II, though he could speak English, also disliked England and took little interest in English affairs;[3] and though Lord Waldegrave shows that he was not the fool described by Chesterfield and Hervey, he admits that the king lacked political courage.[4] Both George I and George II were notoriously on bad terms with their heirs, though this was perhaps due as much to political circumstances as to family idiosyncrasy. Ambitious politicians tended to gather round the heir apparent, both in order to obtain the support of the considerable patronage of the Prince of Wales, and in the hope of royal favour in the next reign. These family quarrels reappeared in the reign of George III, and one of their abiding results was the Royal Marriage Act of 1772.[5] George III had the great advantage of being born and bred in England, and was both in character and political ability an improvement upon his predecessors. Nevertheless his character was obstinate rather than strong, and the best that Wraxall, in a sympathetic portrait, could say of him was that he had all the domestic virtues and inspired the affection of his people.[6]

Under the Revolution Settlement the king was still the head of the executive and retained considerable powers. Theoretically he had complete freedom to choose ministers acceptable to himself, and not to choose others who might be more acceptable to Parliament; but the fact that the House of Commons now had complete control of finance meant that ministers in fact had to be acceptable to it; and that they owed a double responsibility, to the king on the one hand and to Parliament on the other. For some years after 1688 their responsibility to the king was the more important, but the eighteenth century shows a slow but steady shifting of the balance. The first two Hanoverians were, of course, further limited in their choice of ministers by the fact that they owed their thrones to the Whigs; and politicians were coming to realize the value of combining together against the king. There were, therefore,

[1] Nos. 1–3. [2] No. 4. [3] No. 5. [4] No. 6. [5] No. 8. [6] No. 7.

considerable limitations in practice upon the king's right to choose his own ministers; and there was a growing tendency for executive power to pass out of the hands of the king and into those of his ministers.

The documents in the next group have been chosen from political correspondence and memoirs to illustrate this process. By combining against him, the leading Whig politicians forced George II in 1746 to retain, and in 1757 to accept, ministers whom he disliked,[1] because he could find no alternative ministers with any hope of support in the House of Commons. George III's position at his accession was much stronger than that of his predecessors. The king was English and young, with no heir apparent around whom an opposition could gather; the Hanoverian monarchy was now firmly established and Jacobitism dead; and there was growing resentment of the long concentration of political power in the hands of a few Whig families. George III thus had a much wider field for the choice of ministers, and it is not surprising that he attempted to exploit this favourable situation by emerging from the political prison in which the Whigs had confined George II. Even Horace Walpole, who perhaps did more than any other contemporary to spread the idea of George III as a would-be tyrant, admitted that the king was humbling the aristocracy rather than invading liberty, and George III's own view was that he was reasserting rights and powers left to the Crown in 1688 which his predecessors had allowed to slip into the hands of ministers. He held that the king had the right to the services of all his subjects, and that therefore politicians ought not to make conditions, before accepting office, about the measures to be pursued or the men with whom they would or would not serve. These views, and the difficulties he encountered in the early years of his reign in putting them into practice, emerge clearly from George III's review of his dealings with the Grenville Ministry.[2] Although he was obliged to keep the obnoxious Grenville longer than he wanted,[3] and had for a short time to accept the still more obnoxious Rockingham,[4] George III did not have to put up with ministers he disliked for any length of time during these early years, and he was never in the hands of the politicians in the way George II had been. In Lord North he at length found what he was seeking–a minister ready to be in the fullest sense the king's minister, and at the same time capable of managing the House of Commons. The king was the senior partner in this arrangement,[5] and can be said during this period to have ruled as well as reigned in a sense never true of George II. This happy state of affairs was brought to an end by the disasters of the American War, which succeeded in bringing into existence a united opposition to the government in Parliament. They succeeded in forcing the resignations of the entire ministry except the Lord Chancellor, against the king's wishes, a striking assertion of the responsibility of ministers to Parliament, of which North himself was well aware.[6] During the next year, although many people felt that it was wrong to force upon the king ministers who were distasteful to him,[7] George III was obliged to accept ministries whose composition and policy he strongly disliked, on their own terms: first the Rockingham Ministry, and later the Fox-North Coalition under the nominal leadership of the duke of Portland.[8] With the fall of North and the ending of the war, however, the opposition had once more fallen apart into factions, and George III was able to take advantage of this and get rid of the Coalition government and replace it by a ministry under Pitt.[9] This, while demonstrating that the king was still a force in politics, was perhaps not quite the

[1] Nos. 9, 10. [2] No. 12. [3] No. 11. [4] No. 13. [5] No. 14.
[6] No. 16. [7] No. 15. [8] No. 17. [9] No. 18.

resounding triumph that it appeared. Pitt owed his position as much to the unpopularity of the Coalition as to the support of the king, to whom he was not prepared to be entirely subservient; and it is perhaps significant that George III felt unable either to veto Fox's India Bill or to dismiss the ministry until he had, by indirect means, brought about its defeat in at least one House of Parliament. George III had in fact done no more than retard for a short time the process whereby power was passing from the Crown to ministers whose main responsibility was to Parliament.

The gradual emergence during this period of a Cabinet beginning to develop a sense of collective responsibility, and of a 'Prime Minister' as its leader, was an important part of this process. To illustrate this a number of extracts have been collected from the speeches and letters of leading politicians; most of these also illustrate the relationship between ministers and the Crown. The attacks on Walpole as a 'Prime Minister'[1] show how far the politicians of the period were from any conception of a Prime Minister at the head of a united administration obedient to him, and for whose actions he was responsible. Walpole was accused of keeping all patronage in his own hands and dispensing it only to those who would support him; of dismissing from office all those who ceased to support him; and of domineering over his colleagues and interfering in their departments. Walpole's position was largely due to his own dominating personality, and no first minister after him till the younger Pitt had the same degree of control over his colleagues. But his insistence on the necessity of patronage being dispensed only by the first minister was followed by Newcastle[2] and by Grenville;[3] and the need for a first minister to superintend and hold together all the rest was stressed by Lord North in a letter to George III printed earlier in this section.[4] Walpole's practice of increasing the solidarity of the 'inner cabinet' by means of meetings at his house to discuss business to be laid later before the whole Cabinet was also followed by Newcastle[5] and by Grenville.[6] But the distrust with which dictatorial first ministers were still regarded can be seen from the duke of Grafton's indignation in 1782, when Shelburne added a new member to his Cabinet without consultation with the other ministers.[7] The idea of the collective responsibility of ministers was evolving slowly, as can be seen by comparing Newcastle's defence of Walpole in 1741 on the grounds that "very few of the transactions" condemned by Parliament "fell under the particular inspection" of Walpole,[8] with Lord North's assertion in 1778 that faults committed in the Cabinet "were imputable to the whole body, and not to a single individual who composed it".[9] Speaker Onslow's views are particularly interesting because of his long experience as Speaker under George II.[10] Under George III, and particularly during the later part of North's ministry, the value of cabinet government was the more appreciated because it was feared that it was being superseded by a cabal of 'secret advisers', not ministers and therefore not responsible to Parliament.[11] Exaggerated as these fears were, some colour was given to them during these years by North's apathy and the absolute necessity for government to be carried on through such officials as the Secretary to the Treasury, who acted as a channel of communication between North and the king. Finally, Shelburne in a speech in the House of Lords in 1779 stated fully the constitutional doctrine that the king could only act through ministers responsible to Parliament, and that these ministers were "separately and conjunctly responsible for every measure that they carried into execution through their respective departments".[12]

[1] No. 19A and B. [2] No. 21. [3] No. 22. [4] No. 14. [5] No. 20. [6] No. 22.
[7] No. 26. [8] No. 23A. [9] No. 23B. [10] No. 24. [11] No. 25. [12] No. 27.

BIBLIOGRAPHY

I. THE THEORY OF THE CONSTITUTION

The theoretical basis of the eighteenth-century constitution had been expounded once and for all by John Locke in his *Two Treatises on Government* (London, 1690), which was frequently reprinted and constantly appealed to as authoritative. Sir Frederick Pollock's contribution on "Locke's Theory of the State" in the *Proceedings of the British Academy* (1903–1904) and J. W. Gough, *John Locke's Political Philosophy* (Oxford, 1950) are the best modern commentaries. Locke's first treatise was an answer to Sir Robert Filmer, *Patriarcha, or the natural power of Kings* (London, 1680). This work does not seem to have been reprinted between 1685 and 1884, but it no doubt continued to be read by High Tories and Jacobites. Bolingbroke made an attempt to bring Tory views on government up to date, especially in his *Dissertation on Parties,* which first appeared in *The Craftsman* (1733–1734) and the *Idea of a Patriot King*, which seems to have been printed without the author's permission as early as 1743, and is still popularly believed to have inspired George III's determined effort to recover control of the royal prerogative in the early years of his reign. W. S. Sichel, *Bolingbroke and his Times* (2 vols., London, 1901–1902), offers a sympathetic Tory interpretation of its hero. Other authorities are discussed by Sir. C. Grant Robertson in *Bolingbroke* (Historical Association Pamphlet G5, London, 1947) and include Professor H. N. Fieldhouse's "Historical Revision" on "Bolingbroke and the idea of non-party government" in *History,* XXIII (1938–1939), pp. 41–56. Bolingbroke's own *Works* were published in collected editions, the first being in five vols. (London, 1754).

Much more lasting has been the influence of Edmund Burke, both on constitutional theory and parliamentary practice. The *Works and Correspondence of Edmund Burke* (8 vols., London, 1852, and later editions) is a rich quarry not only for the political philosopher but for the political and constitutional historian. Especially notable for our period are his *Thoughts on the Cause of the Present Discontents* (1770) in which he attacks George III's attempts to control Parliament through "the King's friends" and maintains the Whig view of the constitutional rights of the magnates. His addresses to the electors of Bristol are also constantly quoted to show the classic conception of the relations which exist or ought to exist between a member of Parliament and his constituents.

From the numerous lives of Burke, J. Morley, *Edmund Burke* (London, 1867), R. H. Murray, *Edmund Burke* (Oxford, 1931), and Sir P. M. Magnus, *Edmund Burke* (London, 1939), may be selected for mention. A. P. I. Samuels, *Early Life of Edmund Burke* (Cambridge, 1923), D. Wecter, *Edmund Burke and his Kinsmen* (Boulder, Colorado, 1939), A. Cobban, *Edmund Burke and the Revolt against the Eighteenth Century* (London, 1929), D. C. Bryant, *Edmund Burke and his Literary Friends* (Saint Louis, 1939), and T. W. Copeland, *Edmund Burke: Six Essays* (London, 1950), are useful monographs.

The outstanding foreign commentator on the constitution is the Baron de Montesquieu in his celebrated work, *The Spirit of the Laws,* translated into English by T. Nugent (1st edition, 2 vols., London, 1750, and later editions). His brief but eulogistic reference may be supplemented by the elaborate commentary by Jean L. de Lolme, *Constitution of England* (English translation, 2 vols., 1st edition, London, 1775, and many later editions). F. T. H. Fletcher, *Montesquieu and English Politics* (London, 1939), traces Montesquieu's connexion with and influence on England down to 1800.

II. WORKS ON CONSTITUTIONAL HISTORY

The place of the monarchy in the constitution is discussed in the standard works on constitutional history. Henry Hallam, *The Constitutional History of England from the Accession of Henry VII to the Death of George II* (2 vols., London, 1827), and many editions later, revised and continued to the death of George III, was for long the standard work and helped to carry forward into the nineteenth century the Whiggish interpretations of the eighteenth century already popularized by Burke and Horace Walpole. It was, however, a work of solid research, though now completely antiquated. F. W. Maitland, *The Constitutional History of England* (Cambridge, 1908), includes a brief but brilliant review of eighteenth-century constitutional changes. T. P. Taswell-Langmead, *English Constitutional History*, should be used only in the 10th edition by T. F. T. Plucknett (London, 1946). A. V. Dicey, *Introduction to the Law of the Constitution* (9th edition by E. C. S. Wade, London, 1939), is still useful for its lucid exposition of fundamental principles. Sir William R. Anson, *Law and Custom of the Constitution*, vol. I, *Parliament*, edited by Sir M. L. Gwyer (Oxford, 1922), vol. II, *The Crown*, 4th edition, by A. B. Keith (London, 1935), are useful for their historical references. D. L. Keir, *The Constitutional History of Modern Britain, 1485–1937* (3rd edition, London, 1946), contains an admirable chapter on "The Classical Age of the Constitution, 1714–1782", and Mark A. Thomson, *A Constitutional History of England, 1642–1801* (London, 1938), is also excellent on the eighteenth-century constitution. C. S. Emden, *The People and the Constitution* (Oxford, 1933), is illuminating and authoritative. E. R. Turner's article on "Parliament and Foreign Affairs, 1603–1760" in the *English Historical Review*, XXXIV (1919), pp. 172–197, is almost the only discussion of this important aspect of parliamentary activity.

Collections of documents illustrative of eighteenth-century constitutional development include the classic work of Sir. C. Grant Robertson, *Select Statutes, Cases and Documents* [1660–1832] (London, 1904, and later editions); D. O. Dykes, *Source Book of Constitutional History from 1660* (London, 1930); D. L. Keir and F. H. Lawson, *Cases in Constitutional Law* (3rd edition, London, 1948), more severely technical than the others; C. Stephenson and F. G. Marcham, *Sources of English Constitutional History* (New York, 1937), which is widely used in American colleges; and W. C. Costin and J. Steven Watson, *The Law and Working of the Constitution: Documents*, vol. I, 1660–1783 (London, 1952). All royal proclamations issued from 1714 to 1910 are listed, with an analytical index, in *Bibliotheca Lindesiana*, vol. III (Wigan, 1913).

III. THE HANOVERIAN KINGS

The Hanoverian royal family has attracted numerous biographers; the latest biographical study is J. H. Plumb's *First Four Georges* (London, 1956). Sir H. M. Imbert-Terry, *A Constitutional King, George I* (London, 1927), and the study of George II by J. D. Griffith Davies, *A King in Toils* (London, 1938), are the best accounts of the first two Hanoverian sovereigns. Frederick, Prince of Wales, is the subject of two biographies, Sir George Young, *Poor Fred* (London, 1937), and Averyl Edwards, *Frederick Louis Prince of Wales* (London, 1947); both seek to whitewash 'the people's prince'. On George II's queen, W. H. Wilkins, *Caroline the Illustrious* (2 vols., London, 1901), has been superseded by more outspoken and up-to-date lives, Mrs. R. L. Arkell, *Caroline of Ansbach* (Oxford, 1939), and P. Quennell, *Caroline of England* (London, 1939).

While there are few documents of their own composition available in print for George I and George II, primary sources of this kind abound for George III. For long *The Correspondence of George III with Lord North*, edited by Donne (2 vols., London, 1867), was the essential source. It must now be supplemented by *The Correspondence of King George III* [1760–1783], edited by Sir J. W. Fortescue (6 vols., London, 1927–1928). Unfortunately this indispensable collection is badly edited (see L. B. Namier, *Additions and Corrections to Vol. I*, Manchester, 1937). *Letters from George III to Lord Bute*, edited by R. Sedgwick (London, 1939), is essential for the opening of the reign and has a valuable introduction on the 'reversionary interest'. Bonamy Dobrée in his introduction to a selection of George III's *Letters* (London, 1935) offers an interesting reassessment of that monarch as a politician, which wisely stops short of the uncritical adulation of his latest biographer, G. M. Boustead, *Lone Monarch* (London, 1940). The best of the recent lives is by J. D. G. Davies, *George the Third* (London, 1936). There is a brilliant study of

George III in Sir Lewis Namier's *Personalities and Powers* (London, 1955); and H. Butterfield, *George III, Lord North and the People* (London, 1949), begins with a brief but judicious account of the king's character, motives and political activities. Richard Pares, *King George III and the Politicians* (Oxford, 1953), is authoritative. Some information on George III's queen and other Hanoverian princesses may be obtained from Agnes Strickland, *Lives of the Queens of England* (12 vols., London, 1840–1848; Bohn edition, 6 vols., London, 1884–1889); Alice D. Greenwood, *Lives of the Hanoverian Queens of England* (2 vols., London, 1909–1911); and Dorothy Stuart, *The Daughters of George III* (London, 1939).

The king's relations with his ministers can best be studied in the works on those ministers, given in the next section. To these may be added E. R. Turner and G. Megaro, "The Importance of Access to the King's Closet in the 18th Century" in the *American Historical Review*, XLV (1939–1940), pp. 760–776; Carl Becker, "Horace Walpole's Memoirs of the Reign of George III" (which concludes that Walpole's charges of despotism against the king were not made until after the American War) in *ibid.*, XVI (1910–1911), pp. 255–272, 496–507; and A. S. Foord, "The Waning of 'the Influence of the Crown'" in the *English Historical Review*, LXII (1947), pp. 484–507.

IV. THE KING'S MINISTERS AND THEIR POLICIES

Miss L. S. Sutherland's article on "The East India Company in eighteenth-century Politics" in *Economic History Review*, XVII (1947–1948), pp. 16–26, sketches in a few pages the administrative and political problems which faced every eighteenth-century minister. Basil Williams, *Stanhope* (London, 1932), is authoritative on that dimly remembered statesman, who nevertheless helped to establish the Hanoverian succession and to make Britain a Mediterranean power. There is no modern biography of Townshend, but he inevitably appears in the numerous works on his brother-in-law and colleague, Sir Robert Walpole. These include G. R. Stirling Taylor, *Robert Walpole: and his Age* (London, 1931), and on a much larger scale, F. S. Oliver, *Endless Adventure* (3 vols., London, 1930–1935), which is mainly concerned with Walpole as a practising politician. These and all other works on Walpole draw largely on the sources collected in Coxe's *Memoirs of Sir Robert Walpole*, and also on the similar study of Sir Robert's brother and assistant, by Archdeacon Coxe, *Memoirs of Horatio, Lord Walpole* (2 vols., London, 2nd edition, 1808). The first volume of a new standard life of Walpole by J. H. Plumb, *Sir Robert Walpole: the making of a Statesman* (London, 1956), covers Walpole's early life and political career up to 1722, and is based on an exhaustive study of manuscript material. Aspects or periods of Walpole's administration are studied in Professor Vaucher's standard works on *Robert Walpole et la politique de Fleury* [1731–1742] (Paris, 1924) and *La Crise du Ministère Walpole* [1733–1734] (Paris, 1924); and in the works of two American scholars, C. B. Realey, *Early Opposition to Sir Robert Walpole 1720–27* (Philadelphia, 1931), and A. J. Henderson, *London and the National Government* (Durham, North Carolina, 1945). There is an interesting leading article on some of the constitutional aspects of Walpole's administration in *The Times Literary Supplement* for 24 March 1945; and J. B. Owen, *The Rise of the Pelhams* (London, 1956), is valuable for Walpole's fall as well as for the period which followed. S. H. Nulle has examined the early political career of the duke of Newcastle to 1724 in *Thomas Pelham-Holles, Duke of Newcastle* (Philadelphia, 1931). Basil Williams's *Carteret and Newcastle* (Cambridge, 1943) contrasts the characters and careers of these two contemporaries. There are two full-length biographies of Carteret, A. Ballantyne, *Lord Carteret* (London, 1887), and W. B. Pemberton, *Carteret: the Brilliant Failure of the Eighteenth Century* (London, 1936), the latter better than its journalistic title would suggest. On the Pelham brothers during their period of supremacy Coxe's *Memoirs of Henry Pelham* remains unsuperseded, but must be supplemented by a modern work in the Coxe tradition, P. C. Yorke, *Life and Correspondence of the Earl of Hardwicke* (3 vols., Cambridge, 1913). T. W. Riker's article "The Politics behind Braddock's expedition" in the *American Historical Review*, XIII (1907–1908), pp. 742–752, is a useful sketch of ministerial policies and manœuvring for position from

1748 to 1754. R. J. Lucas, *George II and his Ministers* (London, 1910), is still worth reading. The dominating figure of William Pitt, earl of Chatham, has attracted, perhaps, even more attention than he strictly deserves, because of the contrast between his administration and that of the incompetent muddlers who preceded him and the divided and distracted ministries which followed each other in rapid succession in the seventeen-sixties. J. Almon, *Anecdotes of the Life of Pitt* (2 vols., London, 1792, and later editions), may almost be described as the 'official' life. Also eulogistic is the Reverend F. Thackeray, *History of the Right Honourable William Pitt* (2 vols., London, 1827). Of the modern works Lord Rosebery's brilliant essay, *Chatham, his Early Life and Connections* (London, 1910), is still worth reading, but the standard biography is Basil Williams, *Life of William Pitt, Earl of Chatham* (2 vols., London, 1913). There is also an excellent one-volume life, Brian Tunstall, *William Pitt, Earl of Chatham* (London, 1938); a good short biography by J. H. Plumb, *Chatham* (London, 1953); a brief estimate of the importance of his career in Sir C. Grant Robertson, *Chatham and the British Empire* (London, 1946), and a popular sketch of both Pitts in Sir T. Lever, *The House of Pitt* (London, 1947). It is worth remarking that almost the only biography of Pitt which takes an unfavourable view of its subject is A. von Ruville, *William Pitt, Graf von Chatham* (English translation, 3 vols., London, 1907). E. Eyck, *Pitt versus Fox, Father and Son* (London, 1950), sketches the careers of both the Pitts and of Henry and Charles James Fox against the political background.

Lives of minor politicians who held office under George II include T. W. Riker, *Henry Fox, First Lord Holland* (2 vols., Oxford, 1911); Lord Ilchester, *Henry Fox, First Lord Holland* (London, 1920); Lord Ilchester and Mrs. Langford-Brooke, *Life of Sir Charles Hanbury Williams* (London, 1929), and L. C. Sanders, *Patron and Place-Hunter: a Study of Lord Melcombe* (London, 1919); John Carswell, *The Old Cause* (London, 1954), contains studies of Dodington and of Charles Fox. Sir Lewis Namier contributed to the *English Historical Review*, XLII (1927), pp. 408–413, an article on "Three Eighteenth Century Politicians", including Pelham's secretary, John Roberts, whose career is further elucidated by J. E. Tyler's note on "John Roberts M.P. and the first Rockingham administration" in the *English Historical Review*, LXVII (1952), pp. 547–560. Basil Williams in "The Eclipse of the Yorkes", *Transactions of the Royal Historical Society*, 3rd Series, II (1908), pp. 129–151, describes the downfall of this once powerful family in the sixties.

For the reign of George III various collections of correspondence of George III, already mentioned (*supra*, p. 85), are essential to any understanding of ministerial policies as are also the primary sources listed for this period in the General Bibliography (*supra*, pp. 74–75) and the works of Sir Lewis Namier and H. Butterfield (*infra*, pp. 147–148). The best account of the politics of the first twelve years of the reign is still to be found in two works by D. A. Winstanley, *Personal and Party Government* [1760–1766] and *Lord Chatham and the Whig Opposition* [1766–1772] (Cambridge, 1910, 1912). Miss L. S. Sutherland surveys the problems and estimates the significance of the first Rockingham Ministry in "Edmund Burke and the First Rockingham Ministry" in the *English Historical Review*, XLVII (1932), pp. 46–72. G. H. Guttridge, *The Early Career of Lord Rockingham, 1730–1765* (Berkeley, 1952), says all that can be said about that rather colourless figure. J. A. Lovat-Fraser, *John Stuart, Earl of Bute* (Cambridge, 1912), is useful. There are two full-dress biographies of Lord North, W. B. Pemberton, *Lord North* (London, 1938), and R. Lucas, *Lord North* (London, 1913), the latter an attempt to rehabilitate North against the attacks of Whig historians. Lord E. Fitzmaurice, *Life of Shelburne* (2nd edition, 2 vols., London, 1912), is still the standard work but should be supplemented by important articles: (1) by Lucy S. Sutherland on "Lord Shelburne and East India Company Politics 1766–9" in the *English Historical Review*, XLIX (1934), pp. 450–486; (2) by R. A. Humphreys on "Lord Shelburne and the Proclamation of 1763" and "Lord Shelburne and British Colonial Policy 1766–8" in *ibid.*, XLIX (1934), pp. 241–264, and *ibid.*, L (1935), pp. 257–277 respectively; and (3) by C. W. Alvord on "Lord Shelburne and the Founding of British-American Goodwill" in the *Proceedings of the British Academy* (1925). The views of his own time on Charles James Fox are stated in J. B. Trotter, *Memoirs of the latter years of Charles James Fox* (3rd edition, London,

1811), and in W. S. Landor, *Charles James Fox: a Commentary on his Life and Character*, edited by S. Wheeler (London, 1907). More recent biographies include J. L. le B. Hammond, *Charles James Fox: a Political Study* (London, 1903); J. Drinkwater, *Charles James Fox* (London, 1928); C. Hobhouse, *Fox* (London, 1934, new edition, 1948); and, the best, E. Lascelles, *The Life of Charles James Fox* (London, 1936). Works on Burke have already been listed in the section on the theory of the constitution. The account given of the career of the second Viscount Barrington, who held office after office in uninterrupted succession for thirty-three years, by his brother, Shute Barrington, in *Political Life of Viscount Barrington* (London, 1815), is instructive and should be supplemented by *The Barrington-Bernard Correspondence*, edited by E. Channing and A. C. Coolidge (Cambridge, Mass., 1912). George H. Guttridge writes on "Lord George Germain in Office 1775–82" in the *American Historical Review*, XXXIII (1927–1928), pp. 23–43, and there is an unconvincing attempt to whitewash that singularly unsuccessful minister in L. Marlow, *Sackville of Drayton* (London, 1948).

V. THE DEVELOPMENT OF CABINET GOVERNMENT

There is still no satisfactory account of the development of the cabinet system of government, which may be regarded as the central problem of eighteenth-century political and administrative history. E. R. Turner in his *Privy Council of England* [1607–1784] (2 vols., Baltimore, 1927–1928) and *Cabinet Council of England* [1622–1784] (2 vols., Baltimore, 1930–1932) provides a great mass of material on this and other problems of government, but does little to interpret them adequately. W. T. M. Torrens, *History of Cabinets* (2 vols., London, 1894), is still a useful chronological survey, though rendered in some respects out of date by Turner's work and by review articles by H. W. V. Temperley in the *English Historical Review*, XXVII (1912), pp. 682–699, and XXXI (1916), pp. 291–296, Sir W. R. Anson in *ibid.*, XXIX (1914), pp. 56–78 and 325–327, R. R. Sedgwick in *ibid.*, XXXIV (1919), pp. 290–302, and E. T. Williams in *History*, XXII (1937–1938), pp. 240–252, the last being a "Historical Revision" and, qualified by the supplementary note, *ibid.*, XXII (1937–1938), pp. 332–334, perhaps the best available introduction to an extremely complicated subject.

Essentially connected with cabinet government was the emergence of the office of prime minister. The eighteenth-century attitude towards this office is clearly illustrated in R. Beatson, *Political Index* (Edinburgh, 1786), which gives on pp. 7–9 a single list of "Prime Ministers and Favourites from the Accession of Henry VIII to the present time". According to Beatson the only time between 1714 and 1786 when there was one prime minister was from 1721 to 1742. At all other times he names two, three, four or even more prime ministers, or at least indicates the existence of rivals as in 1770–1782, when his entry runs "Lord North etc". Léon Cahen in *Studies in Anglo-French History*, edited by A. Coville and H. W. V. Temperley (Cambridge, 1935), compared the English and French prime ministers of the eighteenth century. Interesting letters on the use of the terms Prime Minister and Premier appeared in *The Times Literary Supplement* between 27 February and 20 March 1930. C. Bigham, *Prime Ministers of Britain 1721–1921* (London, 1922), gives popular accounts of holders of office.

A. THE THEORY OF THE CONSTITUTION

1. Sir William Blackstone on the mixed nature of the Constitution, 1765

(William Blackstone, *Commentaries on the Laws of England*, 7th ed., I (1775), pp. 154, 155; 160–162; 170–172; 178–179.)

Blackstone, the famous jurist and judge, was born in 1723. So influential were his *Commentaries* that no less than eight editions appeared before their author's death in 1780. See also No. 105.

It is highly necessary for preserving the ballance of the Constitution, that the executive power should be a branch, though not the whole, of the legislature. The total union of them, we have seen, would be productive of tyranny; the total disjoint of them, for the present, would in the end produce the same effects, by causing that union against which it seems to provide. The legislature would soon become tyrannical, by making continual encroachments, and gradually assuming to itself the rights of the executive power. Thus the long parliament of Charles the first, while it acted in a constitutional manner, with the royal concurrence, redressed many heavy grievances and established many salutary laws. But when the two houses assumed the power of legislation, in exclusion of the royal authority, they soon after assumed likewise the reins of administration; and, in consequence of these united powers, overturned both church and state, and established a worse oppression than any they pretended to remedy. To hinder therefore any such encroachments, the king is himself a part of the parliament: and, as this is the reason of his being so, very properly therefore the share of legislation, which the constitution has placed in the crown, consists in the power of *rejecting*, rather than *resolving*; this being sufficient to answer the end proposed. For we may apply to the royal negative, in this instance, what Cicero observes of the negative of the Roman tribunes, that the crown has not any power of *doing* wrong, but merely of *preventing* wrong from being done.[1] The crown cannot begin of itself any alterations in the present established law; but it may approve or disapprove of the alterations suggested and consented to by the two houses. The legislative therefore cannot abridge the executive power of any rights which it now has by law, without its own consent; since the law must perpetually stand as it now does, unless all the powers will agree to alter it. And herein indeed consists the true excellence of the English government, that all the parts of it form a mutual check upon each other. In the legislature, the people are a check upon the nobility, the nobility a check upon the people; by the mutual privilege of rejecting what the other has resolved: while the king is a check upon both, which preserves the executive power from encroachments. And this very executive power is again checked and kept within due bounds by the two houses, through the privilege they have of enquiring into, impeaching, and punishing the conduct (not indeed of the king, which would destroy his constitutional independence; but, which is more beneficial to the public) of his evil and pernicious counsellors. Thus every branch of our civil polity supports and is supported, regulates

[1] Note omitted.

and is regulated by, the rest: for the two houses naturally drawing in two directions of opposite interest, and the prerogative in another still different from them both, they mutually keep each other from exceeding their proper limits; while the whole is prevented from separation, and artificially connected together by the mixed nature of the crown, which is part of the legislative, and the sole executive magistrate. Like three distinct powers in mechanics, they jointly impel the machine of government in a direction different from what either, acting by itself, would have done; but at the same time in a direction partaking of each, and formed out of all; a direction which constitutes the true line of the liberty and happiness of the community.

... The power and jurisdiction of parliament, says sir Edward Coke,[1] is so transcendent and absolute, that it cannot be confined, either for causes or persons, within any bounds. And of this high court he adds, it may be truly said, "*si antiquitatem spectes, est vetustissima; si dignitatem, est honoratissima; si jurisdictionem, est capacissima.*" It hath sovereign and uncontrolable authority in making, confirming, enlarging, restraining, abrogating, repealing, reviving, and expounding of laws, concerning matters of all possible denominations, ecclesiastical, or temporal, civil, military, maritime, or criminal: this being the place where that absolute despotic power, which must in all governments reside somewhere, is entrusted by the constitution of these kingdoms. All mischiefs and grievances, operations and remedies, that transcend the ordinary course of the laws, are within the reach of this extraordinary tribunal. It can regulate or new model the succession to the crown; as was done in the reign of Henry VIII and William III. It can alter the established religion of the land; as was done in a variety of instances, in the reigns of king Henry VIII and his three children. It can change and create afresh even the constitution of the kingdom and of parliament themselves; as was done by the act of union, and the several statutes for triennial and septennial elections. It can, in short, do every thing that is not naturally impossible; and therefore some have not scrupled to call it's power, by a figure rather too bold, the omnipotence of parliament. True it is, that what the parliament doth, no authority upon earth can undo. So that it is a matter most essential to the liberties of this kingdom, that such members be delegated to this important trust, as are most eminent for their probity, their fortitude, and their knowledge; for it was a known apothegm of the great lord treasurer Burleigh, "that England could never be ruined but by a parliament:" and, as sir Matthew Hale observes,[2] this being the highest and greatest court, over which none other can have jurisdiction in the kingdom, if by any means a misgovernment should any way fall upon it, the subjects of this kingdom are left without all manner of remedy. To the same purpose the president Montesquieu, though I trust too hastily, presages;[3] that as Rome, Sparta, and Carthage have lost their liberty and perished, so the constitution of England will in time lose it's liberty, will perish: it will perish, whenever the legislative power shall become more corrupt than the executive.

It must be owned that Mr. Locke,[4] and other theoretical writers, have held, that "there remains still inherent in the people a supreme power to remove or alter the legislative, when they find the legislative act contrary to the trust reposed in them: for, when such trust is abused, it is thereby forfeited, and devolves to those who gave it."

[1] 4 Inst. 36. [2] of parliaments. 49. [3] Sp. L. II. 6. [4] on Gov. p. 2. §. 149. 227.

But however just this conclusion may be in theory, we cannot adopt it, nor argue from it, under any dispensation of government at present actually existing. For this devolution of power, to the people at large, includes in it a dissolution of the whole form of government established by that people; reduces all the members to their original state of equality; and, by annihilating the sovereign power, repeals all positive laws whatsoever before enacted. No human laws will therefore suppose a case, which at once must destroy all law, and compel men to build afresh upon a new foundation; nor will they make provision for so desperate an event, as must render all legal provisions ineffectual. So long therefore as the English constitution lasts, we may venture to affirm, that the power of parliament is absolute and without control.

. . . NEXT with regard to the elections of knights, citizens and burgesses; we may observe, that herein consists the exercise of the democratical part of our constitution: for in a democracy there can be no exercise of sovereignty but by suffrage, which is the declaration of the people's will. In all democracies therefore it is of the utmost importance to regulate by whom, and in what manner, the suffrages are to be given. And the Athenians were so justly jealous of this prerogative, that a stranger, who interfered in the assemblies of the people, was punished by their laws with death: because such a man was esteemed guilty of high treason, by usurping those rights of sovereignty, to which he had no title. In England, where the people do not debate in a collective body but by representation, the exercise of this sovereignty consists in the choice of representatives. The laws have therefore very strictly guarded against usurpation or abuse of this power, by many salutary provisions.

. . . The true reason of requiring any qualification, with regard to property, in voters, is to exclude such persons as are in so mean a situation that they are esteemed to have no will of their own. If these persons had votes, they would be tempted to dispose of them under some undue influence or other. This would give a great, an artful, or a wealthy man, a larger share in elections than is consistent with general liberty. If it were probable that every man would give his vote freely, and without influence of any kind, then, upon the true theory and genuine principles of liberty, every member of the community, however poor, should have a vote in electing those delegates, to whose charge is committed the disposal of his property, his liberty, and his life. But, since that can hardly be expected in persons of indigent fortunes, or such as are under the immediate dominion of others, all popular states have been obliged to establish certain qualifications; whereby some, who are suspected to have no will of their own, are excluded from voting, in order to set other individuals, whose wills may be supposed independent, more thoroughly upon a level with each other.

And this constitution of suffrages is framed upon a wiser principle, with us, than either of the methods of voting, by centuries or by tribes, among the Romans. In the method by centuries, instituted by Servius Tullius, it was principally property, and not numbers, that turned the scale: in the method by tribes, gradually introduced by the tribunes of the people, numbers only were regarded, and property entirely overlooked. Hence the laws passed by the former method had usually too great a tendency to aggrandize the patricians or rich nobles; and those by the latter had too much of a levelling principle. Our constitution steers between the two extremes. Only such are entirely excluded, as can have no will of their own: there is hardly a free agent to be found, but what is entitled to a vote in some place or other in the kingdom. Nor is comparative wealth, or property, entirely disregarded in elections; for though the richest man has only one vote at one place, yet, if his property be at all diffused, he has probably a right to vote at more places than one, and therefore has many representatives. This is the spirit of our constitution: not that I assert it is in fact quite so perfect as I have here endeavoured to describe it; for, if any alteration might be wished or suggested in the present frame of parliaments, it should be in favour of a more complete representation of the people. . . .

And, as it is essential to the very being of parliament that elections should be absolutely free, therefore all undue influences upon the electors are illegal, and strongly prohibited. For Mr. Locke[1] ranks it among those breaches of trust in the executive magistrate, which according to his notions amount to a dissolution of the government, "if he employs the force, treasure, and offices of the society to corrupt the representatives, or openly to preingage the electors, and prescribe what manner of persons shall be chosen. For thus to regulate candidates and electors, and new model the ways of election, what is it, says he, but to cut up the government by the roots, and poison the very fountain of public security?" As soon therefore as the time and place of election, either in counties or boroughs, are fixed, all soldiers quartered in the place are to remove, at least one day before the election, to the distance of two miles or more; and not to return till one day after the poll is ended. Riots likewise have been frequently determined to make an election void. By vote also of the house of commons, to whom alone belongs the power of determining contested elections, no lord of parliament, or lord lieutenant of a county, hath any right to interfere in the election of commoners; and, by statute, the lord warden of the cinque ports shall not recommend any members there. If any officer of the excise, customs, stamps, or certain other branches of the revenue, presumes to intermeddle in elections, by persuading any voter or dissuading him, he forfeits 100*l.*, and is disabled to hold any office.

Thus are the electors of one branch of the legislature secured from any undue influence from either of the other two, and from all external violence and compulsion. But the greatest danger is that in which themselves co-operate, by the infamous practice of bribery and corruption. To prevent which it is enacted that no candidate shall, after the date (usually called the *teste*) of the writs, or after the vacancy, give any money or entertainment to his electors, or promise to give any, either to particular persons, or to the place in general, in order to his being elected: on pain of being incapable to serve for that place in parliament. And if any money, gift, office, employment, or reward be given or promised to be given to any voter, at any time, in order to influence him to give or withhold his vote, as well he that takes as he that offers such bribe forfeits 500*l.*, and is for ever disabled from voting and holding any office in any corporation; unless, before conviction, he will discover some other offender of the same kind, and then he is indemnified for his own offence.[2] The first instance that occurs, of election bribery, was so early as 13 Eliz. . . . But, as this practice hath since

[1] on Gov. p. 2. §. 222.

[2] In like manner the Julian law *de ambitu* inflicted fines and infamy upon all who were guilty of corruption at elections; but, if the person guilty convicted another offender, he was restored to his credit again. Ff. 48. 14. 1.

taken much deeper and more universal root, it hath occasioned the making of these wholesome statutes; to complete the efficacy of which, there is nothing wanting but resolution and integrity to put them in strict execution.

2. Jean Louis De Lolme's view of the stability of the English Constitution and the reasons for that stability, 1775

(Jean Louis De Lolme, *The Constitution of England* (1775), pp. 176–190.)

Jean Louis De Lolme (1740–1806), a Swiss lawyer, lived some years in England, returning to his native Geneva in 1775. His *Constitution de l'Angleterre* was published in Amsterdam in 1771.

[After speaking of civil war and the lack of stability which results from it, he continues]

The English Constitution has prevented the possibility of misfortunes of this kind. Not only, by diminishing the power, or rather the actual exercise of the power, of the people,[1] and making them share in the Legislature only by their representatives, the irresistible violence has been avoided of those numerous and general Assemblies, which, on whatever side they throw their weight, bear down every thing. Besides, as the power of the people, when they have any power and know how to use it, is at all times really formidable, the Constitution has set a counterpoise to it; and the Royal authority is this counterpoise.

In order to render it equal to such a task, the Constitution has, in the first place, conferred on the King, as we have seen before, the exclusive prerogative of calling and dismissing the legislative Bodies, and of putting a negative on their resolutions.

Secondly, it has also placed on the side of the King the whole Executive power in the Nation.

Lastly, in order to effect still nearer an equilibrium, the Constitution has invested the Man whom it has made the sole Head of the State, with all the personal privileges, all the pomp, all the majesty, of which human dignities are capable. In the language of the law, the King is Sovereign Lord, and the people are his subjects;–he is universal proprietor of the whole Kingdom;–he bestows all the dignities and places;–and he is not to be addressed but with the expressions and outward ceremony of almost oriental humility. Besides, his person is sacred and inviolable; and any attempt whatsoever against it, is, in the eye of the law, a crime equal to that of an attack against the whole State.

In a word, since to have too exactly compleated the equilibrium between the power of the People, and that of the Crown, would have been to sacrifice the end to the means, that is, to have endangered liberty with a view to strengthen the Government, the deficiency which ought to remain on the side of the latter, has at least been in appearance made up, by conferring on the King all that sort of strength that may result from the opinion and reverence of the people; and amidst the agitations which are the unavoidable attendants of liberty, the Royal power, like an anchor which

[1] We shall see in the sequel, that this diminution of the exercise of the power of the people, has been attended with a great increase of their liberty.

resists both by its weight and the depth of its hold, insures a salutary steadiness to the vessel of the State.

The greatness of the prerogative of the King, by its thus procuring a great degree of stability to the State in general, has much lessened the possibility of the evils we have described before; it has even totally prevented them, by rendering it impossible for any Citizen ever to rise to any dangerous greatness.

And to begin with an advantage by which the people easily suffer themselves to be influenced, I mean that of birth, it is impossible for it ever to produce in England effects in any degree dangerous: for though there are Lords who, besides their wealth, may also boast of an illustrious descent, yet that advantage, being exposed to a continual comparison with the splendor of the Throne, dwindles almost to nothing; and in the gradation universally received of dignities and titles, that of Sovereign Prince and King places him who is invested with it, out of all degree of proportion.

The ceremonial of the Court of England is even formed upon that principle; those persons who are related to the King, have the title of Princes of the blood, and, in that quality, an undisputed pre-eminence over all other persons.[1] Nay, the first Men in the Nation think it an honourable distinction to themselves to hold the different menial offices in his Household. If we therefore were to set aside the extensive and real power of the King, as well as the numerous means he possesses of satisfying the ambition and hopes of individuals, and were to consider only the Majesty of his title, and that strength, founded on public opinion, which results from it, we should find that advantage so considerable, that to attempt to enter into a competition with it, with the bare advantage of high birth, which itself has no other foundation than public opinion, and that too in a very subordinate degree, would be an attempt compleatly extravagant.

If this difference is so great as to be thoroughly submitted to, even by those persons whose situation might incline them to disown it, much more does it influence the minds of the people. And if, notwithstanding the value which every Englishman ought to put upon himself as a Man, and a free Man, there were any whose eyes are so tender as to be dazzled by the appearance and the arms of a Lord, they would be totally blinded when they came to turn them towards Royal Majesty.

The only Man therefore, who, to those who are unacquainted with the Government of England, might appear in a condition to put the Government in danger, would be a Man who, by the greatness of his abilities, and public services, had acquired in a high degree the love of the people, and obtained a great influence in the House of Commons.

But how great soever this enthusiasm of the public may be, barren applause is the only fruit which he whom they favour can expect from it. He can hope neither for a Dictatorship, nor a Consulship, nor in general for any power under the shelter of which he may at once safely unmask that ambition with which we might suppose him to have been actuated; or, if we suppose him to have been hitherto free from any, grow insensibly corrupt. The only door which the Constitution leaves open to his

[1] This, by Stat. of the 3d of Hen. VIII. extends to the sons, grandsons, brothers, uncles, and nephews, of the reigning King.

ambition, of whatever kind it may be, is a place in the administration during the pleasure of the King. If, by the continuance of his services, and the preservation of his influence, he becomes able to aim still higher, the only door which again opens to him, is that of the House of Lords.

But this advance of the favourite of the people towards the establishment of his greatness, is at the same time a great step towards the loss of that power which might render him formidable.

In the first place, the people seeing that he is become much less dependant on their favour, begin, from that very moment, to lessen their attachment to him. Seeing him moreover distinguished by privileges which are the object of their jealousy, I mean their political jealousy, and member of a body, whose interests are frequently opposite to theirs, they immediately conclude, that this great and new dignity cannot have been acquired but through a secret agreement to betray them. Their favourite, thus suddenly transformed, is going, they entertain no doubt, to adopt a conduct intirely opposite to that which hitherto has been the cause of his advancement and high reputation, and in the compass of a few hours, compleatly renounce those principles which he has so long and so loudly professed. In this certainty the people are mistaken; but yet they would not be wrong, if they feared that a zeal hitherto so warm, so constant, I will even add, so sincere, when it concurred with his private interest, would, by being thenceforth often in opposition to it, be gradually much abated.

Nor is this all; the favourite of the people does not even find in his new-acquired dignity, all the increase of greatness and eclat, that might at first be imagined.

Hitherto he was, it is true, only a private individual; but then he was the object in which the whole Nation interested themselves; his actions and discourses were set forth in all the public prints; and he every where met with applause and acclamation.

All these tokens of public favour are, I know, sometimes acquired very lightly; but they never last long, whatever people may say, unless real services are performed. Now, the title of Benefactor of the Nation, when deserved, and universally bestowed, is certainly a very fine title, and which does nowise require the assistance of outward pomp to set it off. Besides, though he was only a Member of the inferior body of the Legislature, we must observe, he was the first; and the word *first* is always a word of very great moment.

But now that he is made a Lord, all his greatness, which hitherto was indeterminate, becomes defined.–By granting him privileges established and fixed by known laws, that uncertainty is taken from his lustre which is so precious in those things which depend on imagination; and his price falls, just because it is ascertained.

Besides, he is a Lord; but then there are several Men who possess but small abilities, and few estimable qualifications, who also are Lords: his lot is, nevertheless, to sit among them: the law places him exactly on the same level with them; and all that is real in his greatness, is thus lost in a crowd of dignities, hereditary and conventional.

And these are not the only losses which the favourite of the people has to suffer. Independantly of those great changes which he descries at a distance, he feels around him alterations no less visible, and still more painful.

Seated formerly in the Assembly of the Representatives of the People, his talents and continual success had soon raised him above the level of his fellow Members; and, carried on by the vivacity and warmth of the public favour, those who might have been tempted to set up as his competitors, were reduced to silence, or even became his supporters.

Admitted now into an Assembly of persons invested with a perpetual and hereditary title, he finds Men hitherto his superiors,–Men who see with a jealous eye the superior talents of the *homo novus*; and who are firmly resolved, that after having been the leading Man in the House of Commons, he shall not be the first in theirs.

In a word, the successes of the favourite of the people were brilliant, and even formidable; but the Constitution, in the very reward it prepares for him, makes him find a kind of Ostracism. His advances were sudden, and his course rapid; he was, if you please, like a torrent ready to bear down every thing before it; but then this torrent is compelled, by the general arrangement of things, finally to throw itself into a vast reservoir, where it mingles, and loses its direction and force.

I know it may be said, that, in order to avoid the fatal step which is to deprive him of so many advantages, the favourite of the people ought to refuse the new dignity which is offered to him, and wait for more important successes from his eloquence in the House of Commons, and his influence over the people.

But those who give him this counsel, have not sufficiently examined it. Without doubt, there are Men in England, who in their present pursuit of a project which they think essential to the public good, would be capable of refusing for a while a place which would deprive their virtue of opportunities of exerting itself, or might more or less endanger it. But woe to him who would persist in such a refusal, with any pernicious design! and who, in a Government where liberty is established on so solid and extensive a basis, would make the people believe that their fate depends on the persevering virtue of a single Citizen. His ambitious views, being at last discovered, (nor could it be long before they were so) his obstinate resolution to move out of the ordinary course of things, would indicate aims, on his part, of such an extraordinary nature, that all Men whatever, who have any regard for their Country, would instantly rise up from all parts to oppose him; and he must fall, overwhelmed with so much ridicule, that it would be better for him to fall from the Tarpeian rock.[1]

In fine, even though we were to suppose, that the new Lord might, after his exaltation, have preserved all his interest with the people, or, what would be no less difficult, that any Lord whatever could, by dint of his wealth and high birth, rival the splendor of the Crown itself, all these advantages, how great soever we may suppose them, as they would not be able of themselves to confer on him the least executive authority, must for ever remain mere showy unsubstantial advantages. Finding all the active powers in the State confined in that very seat of power, which

[1] The Reader will perhaps object, that no Man in England can possibly entertain such views as those I have supposed here: this is precisely what I intended to prove. The essential advantage of the English Government above all those that have been called *free*, and which in fact were but apparently so, is, that no person in England can entertain so much as a thought of his ever rising to the level of the Power charged with the execution of the Laws. All Men in the State, whatever may be their rank, wealth, or influence, are thoroughly convinced, that they shall (in reality as well as in name) continue for ever to be *Subjects*; and are thus compelled really to love, to defend, and to promote those laws which secure the liberty of the Subject. This observation will be more amply insisted upon afterwards.

we suppose him inclined to attack, and there secured by the most formidable provisions, his influence must always evaporate in ineffectual words; and after having advanced himself, as we suppose, to the very foot of the Throne, finding no branch of independant power which he might appropriate to himself, and thus give at last a reality to his political importance, he would soon see it, however great it might have at first appeared, decline and die away.

God forbid, however, that I should mean that the people of England are so fatally tied down to inaction, by the nature of their Government, that they cannot, in times of oppression, find means of appointing a Leader. No; I only meant to say, that the laws of England open no door to those accumulations of power, which have been the ruin of so many Republics: that they offer to the ambitious no possible means of taking advantage of the inadvertence, or even the gratitude, of the People, to make themselves their Tyrants: and that the public power, of which the King has been made the exclusive depositary, must remain unshaken in his hands, as long as things continue to keep in their legal order, which, it may be observed, is a most strong inducement to him constantly to endeavour to maintain it.[1]

3. David Hume on "Whether the British Government inclines more to Absolute Monarchy, or to a Republic", *circa* 1740

(David Hume, *Essays Moral, Political, and Literary*, ed. T. H. Green and T. H. Grose, I (1875), pp. 122–126.)

Hume's *Essays* were first published in Edinburgh in 1741–1742.

. . . Those[2] who assert, that the balance of our government inclines towards absolute monarchy, may support their opinion by the following reasons. That property has a great influence on power cannot possibly be denied; but yet the general maxim, *that the balance of one depends on the balance of the other*, must be received with several limitations. It is evident, that much less property in a single hand will be able to counterbalance a greater property in several; not only because it is difficult to make many persons combine in the same views and measures; but because property, when united, causes much greater dependence, than the same property, when dispersed. A hundred persons, of 1000*l*. a year a-piece, can consume all their income, and no body shall ever be the better for them, except their servants and tradesmen, who justly regard their profits as the product of their own labour. But a man possessed of 100,000*l*. a year, if he has either any generosity or any cunning, may create a great dependence by obligations, and still a greater by expectations. Hence we may observe, that, in all free governments, any subject exorbitantly rich has always created jealousy, even though his riches bore no proportion to those of the state. CRASSUS's fortune, if I remember well, amounted only to about two millions and a half of money; yet we find, that, though his genius was nothing extraordinary, he was able, by means of his riches alone, to counterbalance, during his lifetime, the power of POMPEY as well as that of CAESAR, who afterwards became master of the world. The wealth of the MEDICI

[1] Note omitted.

[2] Notes have been omitted.

made them masters of FLORENCE; though, it is probable, it was not considerable, compared to the united property of that opulent republic.

These considerations are apt to make one entertain a magnificent idea of the BRITISH spirit and love of liberty; since we could maintain our free government, during so many centuries, against our sovereigns, who, besides the power and dignity and majesty of the crown, have always been possessed of much more property than any subject has ever enjoyed in any commonwealth. But it may be said, that this spirit, however great, will never be able to support itself against that immense property, which is now lodged in the king, and which is still encreasing. Upon a moderate computation, there are near three millions a year at the disposal of the crown. The civil list amounts to near a million; the collection of all taxes to another; and the employments in the army and navy, together with ecclesiastical preferments, to above a third million: An enormous sum, and what may fairly be computed to be more than a thirtieth part of the whole income and labour of the kingdom. When we add to this great property, the encreasing luxury of the nation, our proneness to corruption, together with the great power and prerogatives of the crown, and the command of military force, there is no one but must despair of being able, without extraordinary efforts, to support our free government much longer under these disadvantages.

On the other hand, those who maintain, that the byass of the BRITISH government leans towards a republic, may support their opinion by specious arguments. It may be said, that, though this immense property in the crown, be joined to the dignity of first magistrate, and to many other legal powers and prerogatives, which should naturally give it greater influence; yet it really becomes less dangerous to liberty upon that very account. Were ENGLAND a republic, and were any private man possessed of a revenue, a third, or even a tenth part as large as that of the crown, he would very justly excite jealousy; because he would infallibly have great authority, in the government: And such irregular authority, not avowed by the laws, is always more dangerous than a much greater authority, derived from them. A man, possessed of usurped power, can set no bounds to his pretensions: His partizans have liberty to hope for every thing in his favour: His enemies provoke his ambition, with his fears, by the violence of their opposition: And the government being thrown into a ferment, every corrupted humour in the state naturally gathers to him. On the contrary, a legal authority, though great, has always some bounds, which terminate both the hopes and pretensions of the person possessed of it: The laws must have provided a remedy against its excesses: Such an eminent magistrate has much to fear, and little to hope from his usurpations: And as his legal authority is quietly submitted to, he has small temptation and small opportunity of extending it farther.

. . . It may farther be said, that, though men be much governed by interest; yet even interest itself, and all human affairs, are entirely governed by *opinion*. Now, there has been a sudden and sensible change in the opinions of men within these last fifty years, by the progress of learning and of liberty. Most people, in this island, have divested themselves of all superstitious reverence to names and authority: The clergy have much lost their credit: Their pretensions and doctrines have been ridiculed; and even religion can scarcely support itself in the world. The mere name of *king* commands little respect; and to talk of a king as GOD's vice regent on earth, or to give him any of those magnificent titles, which formerly dazzled mankind, would but excite laughter in every one. Though the crown, by means of its large revenue, may maintain its authority in times of tranquillity, upon private interest and influence; yet, as the least shock or convulsion must break all these interests to pieces, the royal power, being no longer supported by the settled principles and opinions of men, will immediately dissolve. Had men been in the same disposition at the *revolution*, as they are at present, monarchy would have run a great risque of being entirely lost in this island.

Durst I venture to deliver my own sentiments amidst these opposite arguments, I would assert, that, unless there happen some extraordinary convulsion, the power of the crown, by means of its large revenue, is rather upon the encrease; though, at the same time I own, that its progress seems very slow, and almost insensible. The tide has run long, and with some rapidity, to the side of popular government, and is just beginning to turn towards monarchy.

It is well known, that every government must come to a period, and that death is unavoidable to the political as well as to the animal body. But, as one kind of death may be preferable to another, it may be enquired, whether it be more desirable for the BRITISH constitution to terminate in a popular government, or in absolute monarchy? Here I would frankly declare, that, though liberty be preferable to slavery, in almost every case; yet I should rather wish to see an absolute monarch than a republic in this island. For, let us consider, what kind of republic we have reason to expect. The question is not concerning any fine imaginary republic, of which a man may form a plan in his closet. There is no doubt, but a popular goverment may be imagined more perfect than absolute monarchy, or even than our present constitution. But what reason have we to expect that any such government will ever be established in GREAT BRITAIN, upon the dissolution of our monarchy? If any single person acquire power enough to take our constitution to pieces, and put it up a-new, he is really an absolute monarch; and we have already had an instance of this kind, sufficient to convince us, that such a person will never resign his power, or establish any free government. Matters, therefore, must be trusted to their natural progress and operation; and the house of commons, according to its present constitution, must be the only legislature in such a popular government. The inconveniences attending such a situation of affairs, present themselves by thousands. If the house of commons, in such a case, ever dissolve itself, which is not to be expected, we may look for a civil war every election. If it continue itself, we shall suffer all the tyranny of a faction, subdivided into new factions. And, as such a violent government cannot long subsist, we shall, at last, after many convulsions, and civil wars, find repose in absolute monarchy, which it would have been happier for us to have established peaceably from the beginning. Absolute monarchy, therefore, is the easiest death, the true *Euthanasia* of the BRITISH constitution.

Thus, if we have reason to be more jealous of monarchy, because the danger is more imminent from that quarter; we have also reason to be more jealous of popular government, because that danger is more terrible. This may teach us a lesson of moderation in all our political controversies.

B. THE ROYAL FAMILY

4. Lady Mary Wortley Montagu on the Character of George I

(Lady Mary Wortley Montagu's "Account of the Court of George I" in her *Letters and Works*, ed. Lord Wharncliffe, I (1837), pp. 107–108.)

Lady Mary Wortley Montagu (1689–1762) was the daughter of the first duke of Kingston. Her husband, Edward Wortley Montagu, was a Commissioner of the Treasury in the first months of George I's reign, and was said to be the only member of the board who could talk to the king in French, which he understood.

. . . The King's character may be comprised in very few words. In private life he would have been called an honest blockhead; and Fortune, that made him a king, added nothing to his happiness, only prejudiced his honesty, and shortened his days. No man was ever more free from ambition; he loved money, but loved to keep his own, without being rapacious of other men's. He would have grown rich by saving, but was incapable of laying schemes for getting; he was more properly dull than lazy, and would have been so well contented to have remained in his little town of Hanover, that if the ambition of those about him had not been greater than his own, we should never have seen him in England; and the natural honesty of his temper, joined with the narrow notions of a low education, made him look upon his acceptance of the crown as an act of usurpation, which was always uneasy to him. But he was carried by the stream of the people about him, in that, as in every act of his life. He could speak no English, and was past the age of learning it. Our customs and laws were all mysteries to him, which he neither tried to understand, nor was capable of understanding if he had endeavoured it. He was passively good-natured, and wished all mankind enjoyed quiet, if they would let him do so. . . .

5. George II and Queen Caroline on England and the English, 1735

(John, Lord Hervey, *Some Materials towards Memoirs of the Reign of King George II*, ed. R. Sedgwick, II (1931), pp. 485–488.)

John, Lord Hervey (1696–1743) was Vice-Chamberlain of the Household, 1730–1740, and the confidant of Queen Caroline, who referred to him as "her child, her pupil and her charge".

[1735] Whilst the late King lived, everybody imagined this Prince loved England and hated Germany; but from the time of his first journey, after he was King, to Hanover, people began to find, if they had not been deceived in their former opinion, at least they would be so in their expectations; and that his thoughts, whatever they might have been, were no longer turned either with contempt or dislike to his Electoral dominions. But after this last journey Hanover had so completed the conquest of his affections that there was nothing English ever commended in his presence that he did not always show, or pretend to show, was surpassed by something of the same kind in Germany. No English or even French cook could dress a dinner; no English confectioner set out a dessert; no English player could act; no English coachman could drive, or English jockey ride, nor were any English horses fit to be drove or fit to be ridden; no Englishman knew how to come into a room, nor any Englishwoman how to dress herself, nor were there any diversions in England, public or private, nor any man or woman in England whose conversation was to be borne–the one, as he said, talking of nothing but their dull politics, and the others of nothing but their ugly clothes. Whereas at Hanover all these things were in the utmost perfection. The men were patterns of politeness, bravery, and gallantry; the women of beauty, wit, and entertainment; his troops there were the bravest in the world, his counsellors the wisest, his manufacturers the most ingenious, his subjects the happiest; and at Hanover, in short, plenty reigned, magnificence resided, arts flourished, diversions abounded, riches flowed, and everything was in the utmost perfection that contributes to make a prince great or a people blessed.

Forced from that magnificent delightful dwelling to return again to this mean dull island, it was no wonder, since these were his notions of them, that he felt as great a change in his humour as in his enjoyments; and that frowns should take the place of smiles upon his countenance, when regret had taken that of pleasure in his heart. But as everybody who came near him, in any calling (except just that of a common courtier in his public circle at the levee or the drawing-room), had some share of his bilious temper at this time, so what everybody knew and everybody felt, everybody talked of and everybody confessed; for, by a practice very uncommon in courts, people, instead of hiding with shame the snubs they received from their master, bragged of them in mirth; and, by finding these distinctions so general, revealed in sport those affronts which, had they been more particular, the objects of them would have concealed in sorrow.

In truth he hated the English, looked upon them all as king-killers and republicans, grudged them their riches as well as their liberty, thought them all overpaid, and said to Lady Sundon one day as she was waiting at dinner, just after he returned from Germany, that he was forced to distribute his favours here very differently from the manner in which he bestowed them at Hanover; that there he rewarded people for doing their duty and serving him well, but that here he was obliged to enrich people for being rascals, and buy them not to cut his throat.

The Queen did not always think in a different style of the English, though she kept her thoughts more to herself than the King, as being more prudent, more sensible, and more mistress of her passions; yet even she could not entirely disguise these sentiments to the observation of those who were perpetually about her, and put her upon subjects that betrayed her into revealing them.

I have heard her at different times speak with great indignation against assertors of the people's rights; have heard her call the King, not without some despite, the humble servant of the Parliament, the pensioner of his people and a puppet of sovereignty, that was forced to go to them for every shilling he wanted, that was obliged to court those who were always abusing him, and could do nothing of himself. And once added, that a good deal of that liberty that made them so insolent, if she could do it, should be much abridged; nor was it possible for the best prince in the world to be very solicitous to procure benefits for subjects that never cared to trust him. At other times she was more upon her guard: I have heard her say she wondered how the English could imagine that any sensible prince would take away their liberty if he could. "My God!" she cried, "what a figure would this poor island make in Europe if it were not for its government! It is its excellent free government that makes all its inhabitants industrious, as they know that what they get nobody can take from them; it is its free government, too, that makes foreigners send their money hither, because they know it is secure, and that the prince cannot touch it; and since it is its freedom to which this kingdom owes everything that makes it great, what prince, who had his senses, and knew that his own greatness depended on the greatness of the country over which he reigned, would wish to take away what made both him and them considerable? I had as lief," added she, "be Elector of Hanover as King of England, if the government was the same. Who the devil would take you all, or think you worth having, that had anything else, if you had not liberties? Your island might be a very pretty thing in that case for Bridgeman and Kent to cut out into gardens; but, for the figure it would make in Europe, it would be of no more consequence here in the West than Madagascar is in the East: and for this reason, your princes, if they are sensible, as impudent and as insolent as you all are with your troublesome liberty, will rather bear with your impertinences than cure them, a way that would lessen their influence in Europe full as much as it would increase their power at home."

But, at the very moment Her Majesty was uttering these truths, the love of rule, the thirst of dominion, and the jealousy of prerogative were so strongly implanted in her, the German and the Queen so rooted in her mind, that the King himself had not more at heart all the trappings and pageantry of sovereignty than she the essential parts of it; nor could she more easily brook any checks to the authority of the Crown than he any contradiction to his opinion.

6. Lord Waldegrave on the Character of George II and of George III as Prince of Wales, 1758.

(James, Earl Waldegrave, *Memoirs from 1754 to 1758* (1821), pp. 4–7; 8–10.)

James, second Earl Waldegrave (1715–1763), was Lord of the Bedchamber to George II, and his close friend. His sympathetic portrait of the king is in strong contrast to the better known portraits by Hervey and Chesterfield. Waldegrave was Governor to the Prince of Wales, 1752–1756.

[1758] The King is in his 75th year; but temperance and an excellent constitution have hitherto preserved him from many of the infirmities of old age.

He has a good understanding, though not of the first class; and has a clear insight into men and things, within a certain compass.

He is accused by his ministers of being hasty and passionate when any measure is proposed which he does not approve of; though, within the compass of my own observation, I have known few persons of high rank who could bear contradiction better, provided the intention was apparently good, and the manner decent.

When any thing disagreeable passes in the closet, when any of his ministers happen to displease him, it cannot long remain a secret; for his countenance can never dissemble: but to those servants who attend his person, and do not disturb him with frequent solicitations, he is ever gracious and affable.

Even in the early part of life he was fond of business; at present, it is become almost his only amusement.

He has more knowledge of foreign affairs than most of his ministers, and has good general notions of the constitution, strength, and interest of this country: but being past thirty when the Hanover succession took place, and having since experienced the violence of party, the injustice of popular clamor, the corruption of parliaments, and the selfish motives of pretended patriots, it is not surprising that he should have contracted some prejudices in favor of those governments where the royal authority is under less restraint.

Yet prudence has so far prevailed over these prejudices, that they have never influenced his conduct. On the contrary, many laws have been enacted in favor of public liberty; and in the course of a long reign, there has not been a single attempt to extend the prerogative of the crown beyond its proper limits.

He has as much personal bravery as any man, though his political courage seems somewhat problematical: however, it is a fault on the right side; for had he always been as firm and undaunted in the closet as he shewed himself at Oudenarde and Dettingen, he might not have proved quite so good a king in this limited monarchy.

In the drawing-room, he is gracious and polite to the ladies, and remarkably cheerful and familiar with those who are handsome, or with the few of his old acquaintance who were beauties in his younger days.

His conversation is very proper for a tête-à-tête: he then talks freely on most subjects, and very much to the purpose; but he cannot discourse with the same ease, nor has he the faculty of laying aside the king in a larger company; not even in those parties of pleasure which are composed of his most intimate acquaintance.

His servants are never disturbed with any unnecessary waiting; for he is regular in all his motions to the greatest exactness, except on particular occasions, when he outruns his own orders, and expects those who are to attend him before the time of his appointment. This may easily be accounted for: he has a restless mind, which requires constant exercise; his affairs are not sufficient to fill up the day; his amusements are without variety, and have lost their relish; he becomes fretful and uneasy, merely for want of employment; and presses forward to meet the succeeding hour before it arrives.

Too great attention to money seems to be his capital failing; however, he is always just, and sometimes charitable, though seldom generous: but when we consider how rarely the liberality of princes is directed to the proper object, being usually bestowed on a rapacious mistress or an unworthy favorite, want of generosity, though it still continues a blot, ceases, at least, to be a vice of the first magnitude.

Upon the whole, he has some qualities of a great prince, many of a good one, none which are essentially bad; and I am thoroughly convinced that hereafter, when time shall have wore away those specks and blemishes which sully the brightest characters, and from which no man is totally exempt, he will be numbered amongst those patriot kings, under whose government the people have enjoyed the greatest happiness. . . . The Prince of Wales is entering into his 21st year, and it would be unfair to decide upon his character in the early stages of life, when there is so much time for improvement.

His parts, though not excellent, will be found very tolerable, if ever they are properly exercised.

He is strictly honest, but wants that frank and open behaviour which makes honesty appear amiable.

When he had a very scanty allowance, it was one of his favorite maxims that men should be just before they are generous: his income is now very considerably augmented, but his generosity has not increased in equal proportion.

His religion is free from all hypocrisy, but is not of the most charitable sort; he has rather too much attention to the sins of his neighbour.

He has spirit, but not of the active kind; and does not want resolution, but it is mixed with too much obstinacy.

He has great command of his passions, and will seldom do wrong, except when he mistakes wrong for right; but as often as this shall happen, it will be difficult to undeceive him, because he is uncommonly indolent, and has strong prejudices.

His want of application and aversion to business would be far less dangerous, was he eager in the pursuit of pleasure; for the transition from pleasure to business is both shorter and easier than from a state of total inaction.

He has a kind of unhappiness in his temper, which, if it be not conquered before it has taken too deep a root, will be a source of frequent anxiety. Whenever he is displeased, his anger does not break out with heat and violence; but he becomes sullen and silent, and retires to his closet; not to compose his mind by study or contemplation, but merely to indulge the melancholy enjoyment of his own ill humor. Even when the fit is ended, unfavorable symptoms very frequently return, which indicate that on certain occasions his Royal Highness has too correct a memory.

Though I have mentioned his good and bad qualities, without flattery, and without aggravation, allowances should still be made on account of his youth, and his bad education: for though the Bishop of Peterborough, now Bishop of Salisbury,[1] the preceptor; Mr. Stone,[2] the sub-governor; and Mr. Scott,[3] the sub-preceptor, were men of sense, men of learning, and worthy, good men, they had but little weight and influence. The mother and the nursery always prevailed.

During the course of the last year, there has, indeed, been some alteration; the authority of the nursery has gradually declined, and the Earl of Bute, by the assistance of the mother, has now the intire confidence. But whether this change will be greatly to his Royal Highness's advantage, is a nice question, which cannot hitherto be determined with any certainty.

[1] Dr. John Thomas (1691–1766).

[2] Andrew Stone (1703–1773), M.P. for Hastings and Commissioner of Trade, 1749–1761.

[3] George Lewis Scott (1708–1780), mathematician.

7. Nathaniel Wraxall on the Character of George III

(Sir Nathaniel William Wraxall, *Historical and Posthumous Memoirs*, ed. H.B. Wheatley, I (1884), pp. 280–285.)

Nathaniel Wraxall (1751–1831) was for a time in the service of the East India Company. He returned to England in 1772 and was a member of Parliament from 1780 to 1794. His character sketches are the most valuable part of his *Historical Memoirs*, which first appeared in 1815 and created much indignation.

In the King's countenance a physiognomist would have distinguished two principal characteristics; firmness, or, as his enemies denominated it, obstinancy, tempered with benignity. The former expression was, however, indisputably more marked and prominent than the latter sentiment.... The King seemed to have a tendency to become corpulent, if he had not repressed it by systematic and unremitting temperance. On this subject I shall relate a fact which was communicated to me by a friend, Sir John Macpherson, who received it from the great Earl of Mansfield, to whom the King himself mentioned it, forcibly demonstrating that strength of mind, renunciation of all excesses, and dominion over his appetites, which have characterized George III at every period of his life. Conversing with William, Duke of Cumberland, his uncle, not long before that Prince's death in 1765, his Majesty observed that it was with concern he remarked the Duke's augmenting corpulency. "I lament it not less, sir," replied he, "but it is constitutional, and I am much mistaken if your Majesty will not become as large as myself, before you attain to my age." "It arises from your not using sufficient exercise," answered the King. "I use, nevertheless," said the Duke, "constant and severe exercise of every kind. But there is another effort requisite in order to repress this tendency which is much more difficult to practise, and without which no exercise, however violent, will suffice. I mean great renunciation and temperance. Nothing else can prevent your Majesty from growing to my size." The King made little reply, but the Duke's words sunk deep and produced a lasting impression on his mind. From that day he formed the resolution, as he assured Lord Mansfield, of checking his constitutional inclination to corpulency by unremitting restraint upon his appetite, a determination which he carried into complete effect in defiance of every temptation.

Perhaps no sovereign of whom history, ancient or modern, makes mention in any age of the earth, has exceeded him in the practice of this virtue. It is a fact that during many years of his life, after coming up from Kew or from Windsor, often on horseback and sometimes in heavy rain, to the Queen's House, he has gone in a sedan-chair to St. James's, dressed himself, held a levée, passed through all the forms of that long and tedious ceremony, for such it was in the way that he performed it, without leaving any individual in the circle unnoticed, and has afterwards assisted at a Privy Council, or given audience to his Cabinet Ministers and others, till five, and even sometimes till six o'clock. After so much fatigue of body and of mind, the only refreshment or sustenance that he usually took consisted of a few slices of bread and butter and a dish of tea, which he sometimes swallowed as he walked up and down, previous to getting into his carriage in order to return into the country. His understanding, solid and sedate, qualified him admirably for business, though it was neither of a brilliant, lively, nor imposing description. But his manner did injustice to the endowments of his intellect, and unfortunately, it was in public that these minute personal defects or imperfections became more conspicuous. Dr Johnson, indeed, thought otherwise on the subject; for after the conversation with which his Majesty was pleased to honour that great literary character in the library of the Queen's house in February 1767, he passed the highest encomiums on the elegant manners of the sovereign. Boswell, in Johnson's Life, speaking of this circumstance, adds, "He said to Mr Barnard, the librarian, 'Sir, they may talk of the King as they will, but he is the finest gentleman I have ever seen.' And he afterwards observed to Mr Langton, 'Sir, his manners are those of as fine a gentleman as we may suppose Louis XIV. or Charles II.'"

Independent of the effect necessarily produced on Johnson's mind by so unexpected and flattering a mark of royal condescension, which may well be imagined to have operated most favourably on the opinions of the moralist, he was perhaps of all men the least capable of estimating personal elegance of deportment. His vast intellectual powers lay in another line of discrimination. Had Johnson been now living, he might indeed witness the finest model of grace, dignity, ease, and affability which the world has ever beheld united in the same person. In *him* are really blended the majesty of Louis XIV. with the amenity of Charles II.[1] But George III. was altogether destitute of these ornamental and adventitious endowments. The oscillations of his body, the precipitation of his questions, none of which, it was said, would wait for an answer, and the hurry of his articulation afforded, on the contrary, to little minds, or to malicious observers, who only saw him at a drawing room, (or, as the Duchess of Chandos called it, the *drawling* room), occasion for calling in question the soundness of his judgment, or the strength of his faculties. None of his Ministers, however, and Mr Fox, if possible, less than any other, entertained such an opinion. His whole reign forms, indeed, the best answer to the imputation. That he committed many errors, nourished many prejudices, formed many erroneous estimates, and frequently adhered too pertinaciously to his determinations, where he conceived, perhaps falsely, that they were founded in reason, or in justice–all these allegations may be admitted. Nor can the injurious effects to himself and to his people, necessarily flowing in various instances from such defects of character and of administration, be altogether denied. But these infirmities, from which no man is exempt, cannot impugn his right to the affectionate veneration of posterity for the inflexible uprightness of his public conduct; and as little can they deprive him of the suffrages of the wise and good of every age, who will bear testimony to the expansion of his mind and the invariable rectitude of his intentions.

It would indeed be difficult for history to produce an instance of any prince who has united and displayed on the throne during near half a century, so many personal and private virtues. In the flower of youth, unmarried, endowed with a vigorous constitution, and surrounded with temptations to pleasure or indulgence of every kind when he succeeded to the crown, he never yielded to these seductions. Not less affectionately attached to the Queen than Charles I was to his consort Henrietta Maria, he remained, nevertheless, altogether exempt from the uxoriousness which characterised his unfortunate predecessor, and which operated so fatally in the course of his reign.

[1] The Prince Regent, later George IV.

8. The Royal Marriage Act, 1772

(*Statutes at Large*,[1] XXIX, Part II, pp. 11–12. 12 Geo. III, cap. 11.)

This Act was occasioned by the marriages of the king's two brothers, the dukes of Cumberland and Gloucester, to English commoners. It met with strong opposition in Parliament, which insisted on the insertion of Clause II, not originally included. The Act was described by one member as "giving leave to the Princes of the Blood to lie with our wives, and forbidding them to marry our daughters".

An act for the better regulating the future marriages of the royal family.

MOST GRACIOUS SOVEREIGN,

WHEREAS *your Majesty, from your paternal affection to your own family, and from your royal concern for the future welfare of your people, and the honour and dignity of your crown, was graciously pleased to recommend to your parliament to take into serious consideration, whether it might not be wise and expedient to supply the defect of the laws now in being; and, by some new provision, more effectually to guard the descendants of His late majesty King* George *the Second, (other than the issue of princesses who have married, or may hereafter marry, into foreign families) from marrying without the approbation of your Majesty, your heirs, or successors, first had and obtained; we have taken this weighty matter into our serious consideration; and, being sensible that marriages in the royal family are of the highest importance to the state, and that therefore the Kings of this realm have ever been entrusted with the care and approbation thereof; and, being thoroughly convinced of the wisdom and expediency of what your Majesty has thought fit to recommend, upon this occasion, we, your Majesty's most dutiful and loyal subjects the lords spiritual and temporal, and commons, in this present parliament assembled, do humbly beseech your Majesty that it may be enacted:* and be it enacted by the King's most excellent majesty, by and with the advice and consent of the lords spiritual and temporal, and commons, in this present parliament assembled, and by the authority of the same, That no descendant of the body of his late majesty King *George* the Second, male or female, (other than the issue of princesses who have married, or may hereafter marry, into foreign families) shall be capable of contracting matrimony without the previous consent of his Majesty, his heirs, or successors, signified under the great seal, and declared in council, (which consent, to preserve the memory thereof, is hereby directed to be set out in the licence and register of marriage, and to be entered in the books of the privy council); and that every marriage, or matrimonal contract, of any such descendant, without such consent first had and obtained, shall be null and void, to all intents and purposes whatsoever.

II. Provided always, and be it enacted by the authority aforesaid, That in case any such descendant of the body of his late majesty King *George* the Second, being above the age of twenty-five years, shall persist in his or her resolution to contract a marriage disapproved of, or dissented from, by the King, his heirs, or successors; that then such descendant, upon giving notice to the King's privy council, which notice is hereby directed to be entered in the books thereof, may, at any time from the expiration of twelve calendar months after such notice given to the privy council as aforesaid, contract such marriage; and his or her marriage with the person before proposed, and rejected, may be duly solemnized, without the previous consent of his Majesty,

[1] Danby Pickering's edition of the *Statutes at Large* has been used throughout this volume.

his heirs, or successors; and such marriage shall be good, as if this act had never been made, unless both houses of parliament shall, before the expiration of the said twelve months, expressly declare their disapprobation of such intended marriage.

III. And be it further enacted by the authority aforesaid, That every person who shall knowingly or wilfully presume to solemnize, or to assist, or to be present at the celebration of any marriage with any such descendant, or at his or her making any matrimonial contract, without such consent as aforesaid first had and obtained, except in the case above-mentioned, shall, being duly convicted thereof, incur and suffer the pains and penalties ordained and provided by the statute of provision and premunire made in the sixteenth year of the reign of *Richard* the Second.

C. THE CROWN AND ITS MINISTERS

(*a*) RELATIONS BETWEEN KING AND MINISTERS

9. Letter from the duke of Newcastle to Lord Chesterfield on the ministerial crisis of 1746, 18 February 1746

(*Private Correspondence of Chesterfield and Newcastle*, ed. R. Lodge (1930), pp. 108–111.)

Early in 1746 the Pelhams wished to strengthen their ministry by taking in Pitt and some of his friends. George II, who disliked the Pelhams and would have liked a ministry under Lords Bath and Granville, made difficulties, and the ministers resigned in a body. Bath and Granville could not form a ministry with support in the House of Commons, and the king was obliged to take back the former ministers on their own terms, though he was able to prevent Pitt becoming Secretary at War. Constitutionally the episode is important as the first mass-resignation of this kind on a matter of policy.

The Duke of Newcastle to Lord Chesterfield, then Lord-Lieutenant of Ireland

Newcastle House, Feb. 18th 1745/6.

Private.

My Dear Lord,

I am now to give you an account of the most surprising scene that ever happened in this country, or, I believe, in any other. And, that you may have as perfect an idea of it as I can give you, you shall have a short account of every thing that has any immediate relation to it.

Some few days before the meeting of Parliament after Christmass Mr Pitt, (who had for some time before had no commerce upon business with any of us) went to the Duke of Bedford, expressed an inclination to know our foreign scheme, shewed a disposition to come into it, and wished that some of us would go and talk with Lord Cobham,[1] into whose hands they had now entirely committed themselves.

I went accordingly the next day to Lord Cobham, and opened our whole scheme to him, which he owned was much more reasonable than he imagined we could have made it, and that, if we would support the continent at all, it could not be in a better or cheaper manner.[2] He seemed very desirous to come into us, and to bring in his Boys, as he called them, exclusively, (as he expressly said) of the Tories, for whom he had nothing to say. The terms were Mr Pitt to be Secretary at War, Lord Barrington in the Admiralty and Mr James Grenville[3] to have an employment of £1,000 a year. He flung out Lord Denbigh, the Duke of Queensberry, and some Scotch Politicks, but not as points absolutely to be insisted upon.

Upon this, I soon opened the budget to the King, which was better received than I expected; and the only objection was, to the giving Mr Pitt this particular office of Secretary at War. For any other His Majesty was willing he should have. We had,

[1] Richard Temple, Viscount Cobham (1669?–1749).

[2] The Pelham Ministry, scared by the 1745 Jacobite Rising, were now in favour of cutting down their continental commitments in the war of the Austrian Succession, and insisting on the Dutch undertaking more in the defence of their territory against the French.

[3] Brother of George Grenville and brother-in-law of Pitt.

all of us, several conferences with His Majesty upon it the King insisting for some time that he would not make him Secretary at War; afterwards, that he would use him ill, if he had it; and at last that he would give him the office, but would not admit him into his presence to do the business of it.

You may easily imagine we shewed His Majesty that the giving the office in the two last instances would not be doing the thing. We represented to him how necessary the making Mr Pitt Secretary at War was for the service of his affairs and for enabling his administration to carry them on with success.

The King grew very uneasy, and complained extremely of being forced. But, when the difficulty seemed in a way of being removed, my Lord Bath got to the King, represented against the behaviour of his ministers in forcing him in such a manner to take a disagreeable man into a particular office and thereby dishonouring him both at home and abroad and encouraging the King to resist it by offering him, I suppose, the support of his friends in so doing. This strengthened the King in his dislike of the measure, and encouraged, I conclude, His Majesty to think, that he had a party behind the curtain who would either force his ministers to do what he liked or, if they did not do it, would be able to support his affairs without them.

Tho' Lord Bath[1] was, luckily for us and for the publick, the open transactor of this affair, it is not to be imagined but that my Lord Granville[2] was in the secret.

Mr Pitt, very decently and honourably, authorised us immediately to renounce all his pretensions to the office of Secretary at War. But it was thought proper, at the same time, to suggest to the King that, after so public an éclat, as my Lord Bath had made of this affair, it was thought absolutely necessary that His Majesty should give some publick mark of his resolution to support and place confidence in his then administration; or otherwise we should be at the mercy of our enemies, whenever they should be able to take any advantage of us, without having it in our power to do the King or the publick any service.

His Majesty was extremely irritated, loudly complaining of our conduct both at home and abroad, unwilling to give us any satisfaction or assurance of his countenance or support and plainly shewing a most determined predilection for the other party.

Upon this, we thought, in duty to the King and in justice to ourselves, the wisest and honestest part that we could take was to desire leave to resign our employments. And we determined that Lord Harrington[3] should go first, myself next, then my Brother, and afterwards my Lord Chancellor.[4] Accordingly my Lord Harrington went (as you know), on Monday the 10th, and resigned the seals. My Lord Bath went into the Closet after him, and I after my Lord Bath. My Lord Pembroke, my Brother, the Duke of Bedford, and my Lord Gower resigned the next day. The Chancellor was prevented from going till the Friday following by the King's going to the House of Lords.[5] The interview with Lord Harrington, I believe, was pretty warm. With me it was otherwise, very civil, kind enough; and we parted very good friends.

The next day it began to be seen how this thing would be taken in the world; and

[1] Formerly William Pulteney (1684–1764).
[2] Formerly John, Lord Carteret (1690–1763).
[3] William, first earl of Harrington (1690–1756), Secretary of State with Newcastle.
[4] Lord Hardwicke.
[5] On Thursday, 13 February.

great resentment was shewed in my Brother's audience on Tuesday. It was soon evident that the resignations would have been almost universal, tho' without any concert or any endeavours used of any kind for that purpose. This struck such a terror upon the new ministers that Lord Bath went on Wednesday to declare to the King that he could not undertake it, and the King sent Mr Winnington[1] to us that day to desire that we would return to court and to our old employments.

We represented to His Majesty, that it would be necessary for him to make some publick declaration of his design to make us his ministers if we were to return to his service. We then considered that, on that condition, as the publick had declared so strongly in our favour, if we refused to serve the King and the publick when called upon, the torrent would turn against us, especially as it was plain that they could not carry on government without us.

We immediately desired that the court might be purged of all their friends and dependents; that Lord Bath might be out of the Cabinet Council; the Duke of Bolton, Lord Berkeley of Stratton, Mr William Finch, the Vice-Chamberlain, Mr Edward Finch, the Groom of the Bedchamber,[2] Mr Boone,[3] and the Advocate of Scotland[4] (which were all that were left of that sort) should be removed. We were told that all should be done, except what related to the Bedchamber, and accordingly we returned to court on Friday last.

My Brother had a long conference on Saturday evening, wherein the chief resentment was shewed to Lord Harrington, and that in the strongest and bitterest manner, and hints flung out that if we would give him up, every thing else should be done. But my Brother saw Lord H.'s chief fault was his having stuck to us. You may easily imagine we had more honor than to give in to any thing of that kind; and that conference, which began tolerably well, ended very unsuccessfully, with strong declarations against making some of the alterations proposed.

The Duke of Grafton had a long conversation on Monday morning, which certainly had a good effect. I went in alone that day, was very graciously received, and got every thing done that was wanted except the removal of the Vice-Chamberlain, which the King begged us not to insist upon in such a manner and said he should take it so kindly if we did not do it, that in the opinion of every body it would have been indecent to have pressed it.

As to Ned Finch, we all thought the Bedchamber could not be attacked. And indeed, considering the part we found ourselves under the necessity of acting, and the publick declaration there was in our favour, we did apprehend that the insisting too strongly upon a particular point, which the King appeared to have so much at heart, would have been universally blamed....[5]

[1] Thomas Winnington (1696–1746), M.P. for Worcester and Paymaster of the Forces.

[2] William Finch (1690–1766), M.P. for Cockermouth; Edward Finch (1697–1771), M.P. for Cambridge University, sons of the seventh earl of Winchilsea.

[3] Daniel Boone (1710–1770), M.P. for Grampound, Commissary General of Musters.

[4] Robert Craigie of Glendoich (1685–1760).

[5] Pitt became Vice-Treasurer of Ireland in the restored ministry till the following April, when he became Paymaster-General.

10. Letters from Lord Hardwicke describing the ministerial crisis of 1757, June 1757

(P. C. Yorke, *Life and Correspondence of Philip Yorke, Earl of Hardwicke*, II (1913), pp. 399–400, 403–404.)

The king wished to exclude Pitt, but Newcastle would not serve without him, and no ministry could succeed which had the support of neither of them. George II was therefore obliged to accept Pitt.

Earl of Hardwicke to Lord Royston.[1]

POWIS HOUSE, *June 12th*, 1757.

DEAR ROYSTON,

This is a season fertile of new events and extraordinary motions, whether owing to the approach of the comet or not, I can't tell. . . . [Lord Mansfield] attended yesterday noon at Kensington, by order, to deliver up the Exchequer Seal, and Mr Fox was there to receive it, as were the Duke of Bedford, Lord Gower, the Duke of Devonshire, the Duke of Marlboro', Lord Winchilsea, etc. to grace the ceremony. Upon his coming into the Closet, the King unexpectedly talked to him of the present melancholy situation, and bid his Lordship tell him what he thought of it. Lord Mansfield told the King 'twas an affair quite out of his province, but if his Majesty commanded him, he would tell his opinion very sincerely and would not deceive him, unless he was deceived himself. He then told the King very plainly that he was of opinion that the scheme he was going upon would not do, could not carry on his affairs but would end in greater confusion. The result was that the King ordered his Lordship to carry the Seal back again with him and speak to the Duke of Newcastle and to me. Mr Fox went into the Closet immediately afterwards, and was surprised to be told this in a whisper as he passed along to the Closet door; and the good Company attending in the antechamber were amazed as, you may easily imagine, the whole court was. This new *remora* stopt (as it ought) the Marquis of Rockingham's and the Duke of Rutland's resignations, who were all attending for that purpose, and the Duke of Bedford went to Woburn yesterday evening, in wrath, as I am told. The King complained and lamented much, and appeared greatly embarrass'd, but spoke well of your humble servant. I went today to the Drawing-room at Kensington, where his Majesty (though grave) was very civil to me. . . . What all this will end in, I cannot foresee. . . .

Earl of Hardwicke to Lord Anson.[2]

POWIS HOUSE, *June 18th*, 1757.
Saturday night, 11. o'clock.

MY DEAR LORD,

. . . You have heard how the administration, projected under Mr Fox, failed this day sev'nnight, in the very moment it was to have been carried into execution, and he was just going into the Closet to receive the Exchequer Seal. On Tuesday night the King, by the Duke of Devonshire, ordered me to attend him on Wednesday morning. I have since had the honour of several audiences of His Majesty, some of them most uneasy and painful ones, though without any anger towards me. My first

[1] Hardwicke's son.

[2] Hardwicke's son-in-law.

orders were for the Duke of Newcastle and myself to negotiate some settlement of an Administration with Mr Pitt and his friends under certain restrictions, from which His Majesty declared he would never depart. In the course of my audience, I told His Majesty that I could take no part at all, unless some honourable regard was shewn to your Lordship,[1] though I could not just then point out the particular thing; that I had told the gentlemen with whom we had conferred the same thing and had formerly humbly conveyed it to His Majesty. . . . Some minutes afterwards the King read over my list in heat, objected to Mr Legge being made a Peer and first Lord of the Admiralty, was determined not to do two great things for one man at the same time, and in this he was peremptory. I then threw your Lordship in his way, but that I was far from knowing what the other persons would say to it. His Majesty answered quick, "I shall like it extremely."

. . . I have been negotiating ever since upon other points and have led a most fatiguing life. However, at last the whole was settled and I carried the King the plan in writing this day at noon. The three things which the King had made his sine qua nons were 1. That he would perform his promise to make Mr Fox Paymaster. 2. That there should be no change in the Secretary at War. 3. That Lord Anson should be at the head of the Admiralty. When I told His Majesty that we had carried all this for him and that all those points were most dutifully yielded up to his pleasure, I never saw such a change in man. He said at once, with a gracious smile, "Then this thing is done; and, my Lord, I thank you heartily." . . .

11. The Grenville Ministry state the terms upon which they are prepared to remain in office, 22 May 1765

(*The Grenville Papers*, ed. W. J. Smith, III (1852), p. 41.)

George III, wishing to rid himself of the Grenville Ministry, negotiated, through the duke of Cumberland, with Pitt. This failed, and he was obliged to ask the Grenville Ministry to remain in office. (See also No. 12.) It was suspected that Lord Bute was behind these negotiations.

At a Meeting at Mr. Grenville's in Downing Street
Wednesday May 22, 1765

Present:

Lord Chancellor[2] — Lord Sandwich
Duke of Bedford — Mr. Grenville
Lord Halifax

The points agreed upon by all His Majesty's servants present at this meeting to be humbly offered to His Majesty by Mr. Grenville, in consequence of the orders which the King gave to him last night, to know their sentiments with regard to their continuing in his Government, were as follows, and Mr. Grenville was desired to lay them before His Majesty as indispensably necessary in their opinion for carrying on the public business, viz.

[1] Anson had been First Lord of the Admiralty, 1751–1756, *i.e.* at the time of Byng's failure at Minorca. He had been removed from the Admiralty during the brief ministry of the duke of Devonshire and Pitt in 1756.

[2] Lord Northington.

1st. That the King's Ministers should be authorized to declare that Lord Bute is to have nothing to do in His Majesty's Councils or Government, in any manner or shape whatever.

2nd. That Mr. Stewart Mackenzie[1] be removed from his office of Lord Privy Seal of Scotland, and from the authority and influence which has been given to him in that kingdom.

3rd. That Lord Holland be removed from the office of Paymaster General, and that office disposed of as has been usual in the House of Commons.

4th. That Lord Granby be appointed Commander in Chief of the Army.

5th. That the King would be pleased to settle the Government of Ireland with his Ministers.

12. George III's view of the Grenville Ministry's behaviour to him, 1765

(*Correspondence of King George III*, ed. Sir John Fortescue, I (1927), pp. 169–173.)

George III strongly opposed the idea that ministers could impose conditions upon the king before consenting to take office and could dictate to him the men with whom they would or would not serve.

No. 141. *Memorandum by the King.*[2]

To state with perspicuity the various causes that occasion'd the change of Ministry in July last,[3] it will be necessary to begin the Account from the unhappy Epoch when the Earl of Bute from an ill state of Health chose to retire from Public Affairs; He shew'd on this occasion a most uncommon moderation by declining any Post of Dignity; the very great affection & confidence I place in him, which His tallents & high notions of honour added to the long series of Years I have known him, make him very worthy of, inclin'd me to consult how I could best form my Ministry; with his advice I brought Mr. Greenville from Head of the board of Admiralty, to that of Treasury, who in conjunction with the Earls of Halifax & Egremont the two Secretarys of State was to take the lead in all State affairs; the Earl of Bute then went to Harrowgate for the benefit of that effecacious Water, till which time these Ministers sought his advice; but on his return their minds were already fill'd with jealousys against him, nay they even began to be insolent to Me; for on the Earl of Granville's death, I thought the late Earl of Hardwycke from his Character & Abilitys the best suited for the Presidency of the Council; tho' they at first appear'd to relish it, yet soon shew'd marks of apprehension least it should lessen their personal weight, from feeling his Superiority over them; their ill humour encreas'd to such an height in August that the Earl of Egremont parted from Me the day preceeding his sudden death not very amicably; which event encourag'd Me to attempt a coalition of partys, I saw Mr. Pitt twice but could not come to any agreement; I therefore offer'd Mr. Greenville cordial Support provided he acted firmly & with that defferance He ow'd Me; to my utmost astonishment He press'd for the Earl of Sandwich as Successor to the Earl of Egremont,

[1] Bute's brother.

[2] The Memorandum is undated, but Sir Lewis Namier has shown that it was probably written some time in November or December 1765. L. B. Namier, *Additions and corrections to Sir John Fortescue's Edition of the Correspondence of King George III, Vol.* I (1937,) p. 38.

[3] The replacement of the Grenville by the first Rockingham Ministry.

as my having appointed him to the Head of the board of Admiralty in May was at the time alledg'd as one of the first causes of dissatisfaction; this Earl instantly persuaded the Duke of Bedford to accept the Presidency of the Council, who but a fortnight before had declar'd to Me the Kingdom ruin'd if Mr. Pitt did not come into Office, nay even advis'd the giving him Carte blanche; yet now he termed Mr. Pitt's propositions, insolent, & that it was the duty of every honest Man to stand forth to prevent his ever coming into Administration.

The Earl of Bute that the World might see the truth that He meant no more to meddle in Ministerial affairs, pass'd the greatest part of the Winter in Luton; on his return in March the Ministry, but most particularly the Duke of Bedford, declar'd that a breach of the agreement at his entering Office; whenever Opposition allarm'd them they were very attentive to Me; but when releas'd from that their sole ideas were rested on ye. best method of getting sole possession of the Closet; no Office fell vacant of ever so little value, or in any other department, that they did not claim it, & declar'd that if not comply'd with they could not serve;

To prove the hight of Mr. Greenvilles insolence it may not be improper to mention his language to Mr. Worstley[1] on My determination of curtailing the Office of painter; When the Surveyor reported to him my intentions; He say'd if People presum'd to speak to Me on business without his previous consent, he would not serve an hour; had I given way to my feelings on receiving this account, He would have been instantly dismiss'd; but I thought it detrimental to the business of the Nation to make any alteration during the sitting of Parliament. Mr. G. conduct on ye. death of ye. late Primate of I. was not less extraordinary, for tho way was given to his desire of offering y^{t} great Pref^{t} to two Eng; Bish: yet on their declining it, He was much nettl'd at it's being conferr'd on a very worthy Irish Bish. as He wish'd to hawk it about till He could by it have made a vacancy on ye. Eng. Bench; the Earl of Northumberland very honorably threw out a doubt whether he should be by his health permitted to return there;[2] within a day or two the Duke of Bedford came & drop'd to Me the necessity of early fixing on a proper subject to fill that Office, & nam'd Lord Weymouth, I instantly gave reasons why I disapprov'd of the idea, He ended with saying He recommended my examining the list of the Peerage, & that He knew I should fix on the most proper person thus He left it quite at large; illness soon follow'd, after which the two Secretarys in a slight manner recommended Lord Weymouth for the Lieutenancy of Ireland; on my objecting to it they were silent; Mr. Greenville soon after press'd it with eagerness for the same person, I cooly ask'd him if He was thoroughly acquainted with the Lord whose cause he so warmly espous'd, He said no, I then gave him weighty reasons why that Lord was not calculated for the Office propos'd, to which He gave the most extraordinary reply, that ever was avow'd by a Man who pretended to make the advantage of the State his only rule of action that as the Duke of Bedford wish'd it, He must support it. On maturely reflecting on the confusion that would arise if it should please God to put a period to my life during the Nonage of the Successor to my Crown; there being no provision for the administration of Government in such a case; I resolv'd not to end the Session

[1] Thomas Worsley, M.P. for Oxford. [2] Northumberland was Lord-Lieutenant of Ireland.

till that salutary measure was effected; knowing that Mr. Greenville would be but too ready to take the merit of it to himself, I open'd my idea to the Chancellor & Duke of Bedford previously to him; who both in the warmest & most unaffected manner express'd their gratitude & approbation of the measure; Mr. Greenville on the contrary seem'd grave & thoughtful when acquainted with it; & the next interview loudly complain'd of want of confidence, because not spoke to before any of his Collegues; this I treated as absurd, & declar'd that tho in affairs of State He might have more colour, tho no reason for claiming more ample confidence than the other Ministers, yet in an affair of so delicate a nature as this, & which could only take rise from my own feelings for my Children & Subjects, it would have been improper; during all the Stages of this affair through Parliament He & his Collegues lost no opportunity to thwart it as much as they could;

Lord Northumberland having express'd to Me the Duke of Cumberland's wishes to be an instrument of obtaining Me a more efficient Ministry; the conduct of my Ministers made me with joy to embrace this offer, for added to the very improper conduct they on so many occasion shew'd Me, the American affairs & indeed every other except those which Mr. Greenville thought tended to his acquiring Popularity were neglected; for the complaints of the most serious kind came from the new Conquer'd province of Canada against their Chief Justice, I never could get the affair examin'd into; & Mr. Greenville's great system of Finances, was the starving of the different Services of the State in short ruining the fleet, that He might have the popularity of raising but small supplys; these weighty reasons I repeat made me empower the Duke to sound Mr. Pitt, who declin'd, & no other Persons being willing to engage; I was from necessity, & the joint opinions of the Duke of Cumberland the Chancellor, & the Earl of Egmont obliged to continue that Ministry I with so much reason was anxious to displace they demanded terms before they would consent to continue which were

1°. That Ld Bute should not be consulted either as to Men or measures.

2°. That Mr. Mackenzie should not only be dismissed from the Scotch Patronage but also from his Employment, tho they knew I had promiss'd him y[t] tho it should ever be convenient for my affairs to alter the patronage, that the office I never would take from him.

3°. Ld. Holland to be remov'd & succeeded by Mr. Townshend.

4°. Ld. Weymouth to be Ld Lieutenant of Ireland.

Tho unable to remove them, I could not be so wanting to myself as to omit every time I saw them shewing them by the coldness of my manner the real dislike I bore of them; this drove the D. of Bedford to take the most improper step of coming to Me a day or two before his going to Wooburn, & taking a paper out of His pocket which he read to the following effect; that the very visible distance he & his friends met with, & the regard shewn to Men he dislik'd had occasion'd Him & his Collegues resolving to retire when He return'd to Town; if they were not treated with cordiality & those with frowns who they thought their Enemys; nothing but stone could have bore this fresh insolence, I therefore by the advice of the D. of Cumberland sent for Mr. Pitt with whom I had two very satisfactory conversations, who was ready to have taken

Office had not Lord Temple declin'd accompanying him, which in his opinion disabl'd him from accepting; then the D. of Cumberland persuaded the present Gentlemen[1] to accept.

On dismissing the late Ministers justice to my much injur'd friend Lord Bute made me assure Mr. Greenville that He had no personal share in the Change of the Ministry & that he had not interfer'd during the course of that Administration either as to Persons or Measures; I express'd the Same to the D. of Cumberland, Lord Talbot, Ld. Litchfield & others at different times, & at the formation of this Ministry I produc'd the very handsome letter Ld Bute wrote me wherein He freed Me in his own & Brother's Name from the promise I had given Mr. Mackenzie not to remove him to the late D. of Cumberland, the Chancellor, Ld. Rockingham & others.

All the advantage I expect from this account of What has pass'd, is that honest Men will feel for Me & will see that it was impossible for me either as a King or Man to bear any longer the Usage I met with, & that necessity not choise has made Me take several Steps that cut Me to the Soul.

13. Letter from George III to Lord Bute on the 'King's Friends' and the Rockingham Ministry, 10 January 1766

(*Letters from George III to Lord Bute*, ed. Romney Sedgwick (1939), pp. 241–242, 245–246.)

This letter illustrates the peculiar relationship between George III and the first Rockingham Ministry, which he had accepted purely in order to get rid of the Grenville Ministry, and whose ideas were opposed to his own, particularly on the question of the repeal of the Stamp Act. While feeling bound in honour to support them as his ministers, he makes an ominous distinction between "my friends" and "those whom I employ".

Friday. [10 January 1766.]

My Dear Friend,

You cannot feel more strongly than I do the situation of those men who have invariably stood by you, and those few besides whose personal conduct to me have made them dear to you; what I now learn from you, concerning the treatment they meet with from the present Ministers does not surprise, though it grieves me; for I knew too well from the many cruel scenes I underwent during the formation of them how very personal they are against the men they got remov'd, and their diffidence of those that remain'd; as to their being wrong represented to me that shall never affect me in my opinion; for as I am apprised of the passions that influence those who may try to hurt them with me, they may throw dirt but none of it will stick. . . .

As to the tallents or experience necessary to carry on the business of this nation, we I should imagine, look on the present set with the same eyes; but I owne I should think I had great reason to complain if those of my friends that are still in office try'd to overturn those I employ; for then they would be acting towards me the very part I have met with from all, that is making disturbance that they may profit by it; that conduct alone could make me think myself at liberty as a man of honour to be for ever detach'd from them; as to my friends differing from Ministers where they think their honour and conscience requires it, that I not only think right, but am of opinion

[1] The first Rockingham Ministry.

it is their duty to act so; nay I think that it is also incumbent on my Dear Friend to act entirely so also.[1]

I will now open my ideas with regard to this Ministry undoubtedly their still imbibing those strange ideas in government, that they addopted whilst in opposition, cannot make me anxious for their continuance; but when I receiv'd them into my service I promis'd them ample support, this I am as a man of honour oblig'd and will punctually act up to, for they have not rose in any one term that they made at first accepting; but should they find themselves unable to go on then they quit me not I them; I feel the more the necessity of this conduct because every set that have retired have ever said I drove them to it, and laid the principle blame on you; nay Mr Pitt in the last negotiation frequently hinted at that....

When I look at the length of my epistle, I am quite asham'd but can't conclude without mentioning a few words, as I think my D. Friend seems hurt I did not see him when he offered it; as to that I own I see it just in the light I then did; if my D. Friend had continu'd coming to me during this Ministry I should have been happy, but as he at the time declared he could not come till after the first sessions I saw that at so critical a moment doing that anew might cause speculations that would have not pleas'd my D. Friend; besides Ministers might have pretended schemes were hatching for their dismission and have made that a reason for retiring whilst now if they quit they cannot say I have in the least been the cause of it; my D. Friend cannot easily form to himself how I felt grieved at thinking I owd'd it to him (as well as to myself) to decline at that time; on the whole I mean to support these men if they can go on if not I am free to do what I should think best, and from the fate of the first day am inclin'd out of my true friends to form an Administration without again entreating Mr Pitt, which I think would for ever stain my name, pray believe me incapable of ever thinking of you but with the greatest love and friendship, and keep my friends from personal opposition and when they from opinion differ let them be as civil in their expressions as the occasion will permit; as to the Peace it is not named in the Speech.

14. Letters between George III and Lord North, June–November 1778

(*Correspondence of King George III*, ed. Sir John Fortescue, IV (1928), pp. 162–163, 213, 215–217, 220–221.)

The following letters illustrate the relations between the king and Lord North as Prime Minister during the later years of the North administration.

No. 2639. *The King to Lord North.*

Kew, June 2nd, 1778. 52 min. pt. 7 p.m.

Lord North–In consequence of Your repeated Solicitations to quit Your present Employment I have seriously attempted to release You; but am convinced still more than at any other period how detrimental it would be to the Public as well as to me whose interests can never be separated if I consented to it at present; indeed Your language for the last ten days is the more encouraging, as it manifestly has tended to Shew a desire in You to continue; I therefore trust that the same attachment that

[1] *i.e.* Bute's friends holding offices might vote against the repeal of the Stamp Act, without forfeiting their offices.

prompts You not to put me under difficulties, will also prevent Your being swayed by the unfortunate events which at the beginning of the War may naturally be expected to arise in Some of the Wide possessions of this Great Empire, to take the same idea of retiring perhaps at an hour still more inconvenient if possible than the present, I also trust the Summer's repose will enable You to rouse Your mind with Vigour to take the lead again in the House of Commons, and not let every absurd idea be adopted as has too recently appeared.

I know you complain the House does not attend to Your wishes, but Your own candour must also convince You that it is impossible Your ideas can be followed, whilst You have not Yourself decided the path You mean to take; the moment You will decide, the love and esteem most of the House have for You, will appear conspicuously, and a little attention on Your part to the most efficient Men will restore due order.

I cannot help touching on another delicate point, but at this hour it would neither be right to myself nor friendly towards You, to conceal a single idea, the greatest part of Your difficulties arise from entering too far with others in plans of business but particularly arrangements of Employments, without fairly stating Your sentiments unto Me; if on the contrary You sounded my opinion first You would save much trouble and vexation to both of us, and where can you repose Your undigested thoughts more safely than in the breast of one who has ever treated You more as his friend than Minister, and who would perhaps frequently put You on Your guard against things which if consented to from Your being hampered disgrace my service, or if refused distress your mind. . . .

No. 2444. *The King to Lord North.*

KEW, Nov. 2nd. 1778.

Lord North Cannot be surprised that at an hour when this Country is cirrounded with impending evils, I should think myself highly culpable if I did not to the utmost of my ability prepare against them; on that account I the last Week insisted on Your forthwith preparing a Plan on Paper for procuring an handsome Attendance on the Opening of the Session, and a continuance of it during the Sitting of Parliament; this You promised to draw up; yet the Week has elapsed without Your producing it, and Your aversion to decide would lead You to postpone it till too late, unless forced by me to what I look upon not only as essential to the conducting public affairs with credit, but as necessary for Your own ease of mind; I therefore must insist on Your laying Your thoughts on that Subject before the Cabinet at Your meeting on Thursday, and I have just wrote to the two Secretaries of State to acquaint them You have my directions for that purpose. Indeed, my Dear Lord, though the present Scene is not very clear, yet with activity, decision and zeal, things may soon wear a very different appearance.

No. 2446. *Lord North to the King.*

. . . There are two points, which Lord North has the honour of submitting to his Majesty's consideration, & which he conceives very important for the government of this country.

The first is, That the Public business can never go on as it ought, while the Principal & most efficient offices are in the hands of persons who are either indifferent to, or actually dislike their situation.

The second is, That in critical times, it is necessary that there should be one directing Minister, who should plan the whole of the operations of government, & controul all the other departments of administration so far as to make them co-operate zealously & actively with his designs even tho contrary to their own.

Lord North conceives these two rules to be wise & true, & therefore, thinks it his duty to submit the expediency of his Majesty's removing him as soon as he can, because he is certainly not capable of being such a minister as he has described, & he can never like a situation which he has most perfectly disliked even in much better and easier times....

...Lord North hopes that his Majesty will have the goodness to pardon the length, & inaccuracy of this note, which is much more tedious than Lord North expected when he begun it, but flows from a heart truly zealous for his service, which he should never wish to quit, unless he were convinced that he is not equal to a station of such consequence as that where his Majesty's goodness has done him the honour to place him.

BUSHEY PARK, Novr. 10, 1778.
55 m. pt 12.p.m.

No. 2451. *The King to Lord North.*

KEW, *Nov.* 14th. 1778. 1 m pt 1 p.m.

It has ever been a certain position with Me that firmness is the Characteristick of an Englishman, that consequently when a Minister will shew resolution boldly to advance that He will meet with support, consequently Lord North's report that the Gentlemen who attended the meeting in Downing Street last night will cordialy support during the next Session is what I expected, and if on the opening of the Session the Speech from the Throne is penned with firmness, and shews no other end is sought but benevolence to all the branches provided the Empire is kept Entire, and invite all who will cordially unite in that point and in a resolution to withstand the natural Enemies of the Country, and the Ministers in their Speeches shew that they will never consent to the Independency of America and that the assistance of every man will be accepted on that ground I am certain the cry will be strong in their favour.

I should have concluded here, had not the letter contained the following expression that Lord North *is conscious and certain that he neither has the Authority nor Abilities requisite for the conduct of Affairs at this time*, the word *authority* puzzles me, for from the hour of Lord North's so handsomely devoting himself on the retreat of the D. of Grafton, I have never had a political thought which I have not communicated unto him, have accepted of persons highly disagreeable to me, because he thought they would be of advantage to his conducting public Affairs, and have yielded to measures my own opinion did not quite approve; therefore I must desire to have an explanation in writing on what is meant to be conveyed by that word, as also that *a change might be made to the benefit of my service without having recourse to the Opposition*; this is quite a new thought, and till Lord North explains what that means, the idea is quite incomprehensible to me.

If Lord North can see with the same degree of enthusiasm I do, the beauty, excellence, and perfection of the British Constitution as by Law Established, and consider that if any one branch of the Empire is alowed to cast off its dependency, that the others will infalably follow the Example, that consequently though an arduous struggle that is worth going through any difficulty to preserve to latest Posterity what the Wisdom of our Ancestors have carefully transmitted to us; he will not allow despondency to find a place in his breast, but resolve not merely out of Duty to fill his post, but will resolve with Vigour to meet every obstacle that may arise he shall meet with most cordial Support from me; but the times require Vigour or the State will be ruined.

15. Letters from George Selwyn on the ministerial negotiations of March 1782

(*Hist. MSS. Comm., Carlisle MSS.*, pp. 581, 594.)

George Selwyn (1719–1791), the famous wit, was M.P. for Ludgershall and a supporter of Lord North. His views illustrate the convention, widely held in the eighteenth century, that it was wrong to force upon the king ministers whom he disliked. He is writing during the last weeks of Lord North's ministry, when the king was desperately trying to avoid having to accept a ministry composed of the Rockingham Whigs.

[George Selwyn to Lord Carlisle.]

[1782, Feb. 19?] Tuesday night, 8 o'clock.–. . . .

I hear from one quarter that a change of some sort in Administration is determined upon, and that the Chancellor[1] has the task of composing those jarring atoms to prevent the King's Cabinet from being stormed. That Lord Shelbourne will be taken in, *de quelque manière ou d'autre*. Storming the Cabinet is a phrase coined in my time, to express what I cannot pretend to say that I do not understand, but how the fact is practicable, *invite rege*, will be for ever a mystery to me, and if it happens with his consent I am yet to learn how the Cabinet is storm[ed]. I will never believe but if a prince very early in his reign had a mind to set a mark upon those who distinguish themselves in Opposition with that view, he would never have the thin[g] attempted. It may be necessary to change measures and men, but why it is necessary that particular men must be fixed upon you, whether you will [or] not, I do not conceive, nor will ever admit as [a] possibility while the Laws and Constitution remain as they are; so with this I wish you a good night. . . .

[Same to Same.]

[1782,] March 16, Saturday morning, 10 o'clock.–

. . . But good God! what a Government is this! if the King has not the power of choosing his own Ministers. It is enough, when he has chosen them, that they are amenable to Parl[iamen]t for their conduct. But if it is in the power of any man, on account of his Parl[iamen]t[ary] talents, to force himself upon the King and into Government, when his private character would exclude him from ever[y] other station, or society, I wish for my part not to belong to that Government in any shape

[1] Lord Thurlow, through whom George III approached various politicians in his attempts to form a ministry to replace North's.

whatever; and it would satisfy my mind infinitely more, that, while things remained upon that foot, that neither of us were in any kind of employment whatsoever. But I do not presume to dictate to you. You can see and feel for yourself, with as much discernment and sensibility as another. . . .

16. Letter from Lord North to George III insisting on resignation now that his ministry has lost the support of the House of Commons, 18 March 1782

(*Correspondence of King George III*, ed. Sir John Fortescue, v (1928), pp. 394–396.)

The forcing of the resignation of North and almost all his colleagues was an unprecedented triumph for the House of Commons. North's attitude should be compared with Walpole's in 1741. (No. 19C.)

No. 3566. *Lord North to the King.* [18 March 1782.]

. . . When I had the honour of an audience of Your Majesty this morning, I humbly endeavoured to state to Your Majesty my reasons for thinking that the fate of the present Ministry is absolutely and irrevocably decided; The votes of the Minorities on Friday sevennight, and on Friday last[1] contained, I believe, the genuine sense of the House of Commons, and, I really think, of the Nation at large; Not that I suppose the minds of men in general exasperated against the individuals, who compose the Administration, but they are tired of the Administration collectively taken, and wish at all events to see it alter'd. The torrent is too strong to be resisted; Your Majesty is well apprized that, in this country, the Prince on the throne, cannot with prudence, oppose the deliberate resolution of the House of Commons: Your Royal Predecessors (particularly King William the Third and his late Majesty) were obliged to yield to it much against their wish in more instances than one: They consented to changes in their Ministry which they disapproved because they found it necessary to sacrifice their private wishes, and even their opinions to the preservation of public order, and the prevention of these terrible mischiefs, which are the natural consequence of the clashing of two branches of the Sovereign Power in the State. The concessions they made were never deemed dishonourable, but were considered as marks of their wisdom, and of their parental affection for their people. Your Majesty has graciously and steadily supported the servants you approve, as long as they could be supported: Your Majesty has firmly and resolutely maintained what appeared to you essential to the welfare and dignity of this Country, as long as this Country itself thought proper to maintain it. The Parliament have altered their sentiments, and as their sentiments whether just or erroneous, must ultimately prevail, Your Majesty having persevered, as long as possible, in what you thought right, can lose no honour if you yield at length, as some of the most renowned and most glorious of your Predecessors have done, to the opinion and wishes of the House of Commons.

Your Majesty's desire is, I know, to form a Ministry on a broad bottom, and such an arrangement would certainly be the best, but, in the present moment, it is I fear, not attainable. In consequence of the disposition of the Ho. of Commons, a change in the Ministry is become absolutely necessary: There are no persons capable and willing

[1] On 8 March resolutions of censure on the ministers moved by Lord John Cavendish were defeated by 226–216; on 15 March Sir John Rous's motion to withdraw the confidence of Parliament from ministers was defeated by 236–227.

to form a new administration, except Lord Rockingham and Lord Shelburne with their parties, and They will not act with any of the present Ministry but the Chancellor.[1] It follows then that the present Cabinet must be removed, and either one or both of the before-mentioned parties must compose the new administration; or, that there will be no Ministry and the greatest confusion, with the most pernicious consequences, will prevail in every part of the Government. It is with great reluctance that I presume to advise your Majesty to send either for Lord Rockingham or Lord Shelburne, but I should not be an honest man or a friend to my Country if I did not advise even that step rather than that Your Majesty, being no longer able to retain your present Ministers, should run the risk of leaving the Nation at this time, without any administration, at the mercy of all the evils and all the dangers which are naturally to be apprehended in such an unsettled state of affairs. Your Majesty's goodness encourages me to lay my poor but honest advice before you, and to submit whether it will not be for your Majesty's welfare, and, even, glory, to sacrifice, at this moment, former opinions, displeasures and apprehensions (though never so well founded) to that great object (which is always the uppermost in your Majesty's heart, and which is at present in a degree of peril,) The Public Safety.

Your Majesty's future Administration will be strong with respect to all the great measures of government, to the obtaining of supplies, to the conduct of War, and the conclusion of Peace; But, if Your New Ministers should attempt any dangerous innovations in the constitution, they will, I believe, meet with a powerful and I hope, a successful opposition. . . .

17. Memoranda by George III on the negotiations ending in his unwilling acceptance of the coalition of North and Fox, 30 March–1 April 1783

(*Correspondence of King George III*, ed. Sir John Fortescue, VI (1928), pp. 325–327, 328–329.)

The acceptance of this ministry, under the nominal leadership of the duke of Portland, on their own terms, insisted upon in advance was a defeat for George III's view of the proper relationship between the king and his ministers. He had already suffered a similar defeat the previous year, when Rockingham had insisted on the acceptance by the king of a particular policy before he would agree to take office.

No. 4268. *Memorandum by the King.*

. . . The next day Friday March 21st, . . . as soon as I returned from St. James's I saw the Duke of Portland, who said his object in wishing to see Me was to acquaint that the cause of difference between his friends and Lord North no longer existed, they having withdrawn their objection to Lord Stormont; that He the Duke of Portland could now therefore shew me the names of the proposed Cabinet Ministers; I declined seeing it, referring to the letter of March 18th which I had written to Lord North, and which had been communicated to Him, by which I had declared that I must see and examine the whole Plan of Arrangements before I could give any opinion on particular parts of it. He, to my astonishment said this was want of confidence in him for that the Cabinet once laid before Me, he expected that on his coming to the head of the Treasury, I should rely on his making no propositions but such as He thought

[1] Lord Thurlow. He was the only member of North's ministry to remain in office under Rockingham.

necessary for my affairs and consequently that I should acquiesce in them. This unexpected idea, I fortunately did not treat with the warmth it deserved, but on finding that [the] Duke would not see the singularity of the proposition and that on discussing it he began to grow warm, said I must have time to consider of a proposition I thought so novel.

Therefore the next morning I sent for Lord North and did not disguise from him the indecency of the proposal; but pretended to immagine it was not meant, and insisted on his going to the Duke of Portland, and on their joint plan of Arrangement being sent to Me in the course of the Evening.

Hearing nothing from Lord North, on Sunday morning, March 23rd, I sent for him to know why the Plan of Arrangements had not been transmitted to Me the night before; He said he wondered the Duke of Portland had not either by letter or in person conveyed to Me that morning the Plan: I therefore directed him instantly to go and acquaint that Duke that I must have it as soon as I returned from St. James's.

After the drawing [Room] the Duke of Portland asked an Audience, when he said he came in consequence of the intimation through Lord North, that he had drawn up no Plan, but was ready to shew Me the list of Efficient Cabinet Ministers; I answered I was sorry to return to what past on Friday; the only alteration in his language was to press much for my looking at that list, which I desired to decline from an intention which I avowed again of not entering into parts of the Plan till he had enabled Me to examine the whole; but he pressed so much for my looking at his Paper that I so far complied, and then returned it to Him. He then complained of my not saying I approved of the Names; this I told him I had before declined doing, and repeated my words. He upon that said he could not think of forming any Plan, and that he thought I might trust the Seven Persons mentioned could not propose anything but what it would be right for me to Acquiesce in. This I replied was asking more than any Man above forty could engage to do, and insisted he should in the evening send either his Plan or a refusal of doing it. . . .

In the evening I received the Duke of Portland's letter.[1] . . . Thus ended this Strange Negotiation. . . . March 30th 1783.

Some days since elapsed in attempting again to persuade Mr Pitt to continue at the head of the Treasury, but he declined much to my sorrow; since when I have attempted again to call forth Mr Thos. Pitt[2] to the first efficienct Office in the House of Commons; on that not succeeding I have taken the last step that could occur to Me, the sending again for Lord North and seeing whether he had no seeds of gratitude that might make him from a knowledge of my distress form a Plan, in which I have also not succeeded.

No. 4271. *Memorandum by the King*

[1 April 1783]

The total stagnation of Public Business by no Administration in reality subsisting at a time when the Definitive Treaties ought to be prosecuted, the Navy and the

[1] Refusing to form a ministry on the king's terms.

[2] Thomas Pitt (1737–1793) later Lord Camelford; Chatham's nephew.

Army reduced to a state of Peace and Taxes laid for defraying the Expenses of the State and for settling the unpaid Debt obliged Me no longer to defer submitting to the erection of an Administration whose conduct as individuals does not promise to deserve collectively my confidence.

I therefore on Tuesday evening, April 1st 1783, sent for Ld. North and enquired if the Seven Persons named by the D. of Portland and him were ready to accept the Employments proposed, on his answering in the affirmative I authorized him to acquaint them they might receive them the next day, after which the D. of Portland and He should plan the arrangements of Employments.

They accordingly were appointed the next day and that Duke and Ld. North desired to arrange the various Employments they chose to vacat; but to my great surprise another day nearly elapsed before they would arrange the Board of Treasury and advanced no farther. The Duke proposed a Dukedom for the E. of Hertford[1] and a Marquisate for the E. of Fitzwilliams,[2] but I declined entering on that subject.

18A–C. Documents illustrating the fall of the Coalition government, December 1783

Fox's India Bill, by providing that the territories and patronage of the East India Company should be controlled by commissioners named in the Bill and holding office for four years unless either House of Parliament addressed the king for their removal, struck at the executive power of the Crown. The king's intervention, through Lord Temple, to bring about its defeat in the House of Lords was defended on these grounds.

18A. Lord Temple's Memorandum, 1 December 1783[3]

(The duke of Buckingham and Chandos, *Memoirs of the Court and Cabinets of George III*, I (1853), pp. 288–289.)

George Nugent-Temple (1753–1813), later first marquis of Buckingham, was the second son of George Grenville. He held no office in 1783.

To begin with stating to His Majesty our sentiments upon the extent of the Bill, viz: We profess to wish to know whether this Bill appear to His Majesty in this light: a plan to take more than half the royal power, and by that means disable [the King] for the rest of the reign. There is nothing else in it which ought to call for this interposition.

Whether any means can be thought of, short of changing his Ministers, to avoid this evil.

The refusing the Bill, if it passes the Houses, is a violent means. The changing his Ministers after the last vote of the Commons, in a less degree might be liable to the same sort of construction.

An easier way of changing his Government would be by taking some opportunity of doing it, when, in the progress of it, it shall have received more discountenance than hitherto.

[1] Francis Seymour Conway (1719–1794), earl of Hertford, brother to General Conway.

[2] William, second Earl Fitzwilliam (1748–1833), nephew and heir to Lord Rockingham.

[3] Partly in Lord Temple's handwriting but mainly in a hand scarcely legible and believed to be that of Lord Thurlow.

This must be expected to happen in the Lords in a greater degree than can be hoped for in the Commons.

But a sufficient degree of it may not occur in the Lords if those whose duty to His Majesty would excite them to appear are not acquainted with his wishes, and that in a manner which would make it impossible to pretend a doubt of it, in case they were so disposed.

By these means the discountenance might be hoped to raise difficulties so high as to throw it [out], and leave His Majesty at perfect liberty to choose whether he will change them or not.

This is the situation which it is wished His Majesty should find himself in.

Delivered by Lord Thurlow, Dec. 1st, 1783.

NUGENT TEMPLE.

18B. Letter from Richard Fitzpatrick to Lord Ossory, 15 December 1783

(*Memorials and Correspondence of Charles James Fox*, ed. Lord John Russell, II (1853), p. 220.)

Richard Fitzpatrick (1747–1813), a life-long friend of Fox, was Secretary for War in the Coalition government. Lord Ossory was his brother.

Monday, December 15th, 1783.

Lord Temple had a long audience on Thursday last, and is said to have come out declaring himself authorised to say that the King disapproved of the Bill, as unconstitutional, and subversive of the rights of the Crown, and that he should consider all who voted for it as his enemies. Lord Temple has not dared to avow this, but continues to insinuate it. The Bishops waver, and *the Thanes fly from us*; in my opinion, the Bill will not pass; the Lords are now sitting, and the debate will certainly be too late to send you an account of the division; the proxies of the King's friends are arrived against the Bill. The public is full of alarm and astonishment at the treachery as well as the imprudence of this unconstitutional interference. No body guesses what will be the consequence of a conduct that is generally compared to that of Charles the First in 1641. I hope you will come to town, for it will be certainly impossible to send you satisfactory accounts, and some measures must, of course, be immediately taken in the House of Commons. I consider the Ministry as over.

Yours affectionately,

R. F.

18C. Letters from the duke of Portland to the King and from the King to Lord North, 17–18 December 1783

(*Correspondence of King George III*, ed. Sir John Fortescue, VI (1928), pp. 475, 476.)

Portland was the official head of the administration; North and Fox Secretaries of State.

The Duke of Portland to the King.

The Duke of Portland must humbly beg permission to acquaint Your Majesty that the Commitment of the East India Bill has been negatived by a Majority, Proxies included, of 19. The Contents were 57, Proxies 19; the Not Contents 75, Proxies 20 & the Bill was afterwards rejected without a Division.

DOWNING STREET, *Wednesday, 17 Decr.* 1783 *at midnight.*

The King to Lord North.

Lord North Is by this required to send Me the Seals of His Department, and to acquaint Mr Fox to send those of the Foreign Department. Mr Frazer or Mr Nepean[1] will be the proper Channel of delivering them to Me this Night; I choose this method as Audiences on such occasions must be unpleasant.

QUEEN'S HOUSE. *Dec. 18th*, 1783. m. 43 past 10 p.m.

(*b*) THE DEVELOPMENT OF THE CABINET AND THE OFFICE OF PRIME MINISTER

19A–C. Sir Robert Walpole as 'Prime Minister'.

19A. Lord Egmont in his Diary criticizes Walpole as first minister, 25 March 1730

(*Hist. MSS. Comm. MSS. of the Earl of Egmont; Diary of Viscount Perceval, afterwards first Earl of Egmont*, I, pp. 85–86.)

John, first earl of Egmont (1683–1748), was M.P. for Harwich and one of the trustees for the founding of the colony of Georgia. Relations between him and Walpole later became strained, but at the time when the following criticism was written they were on cordial terms. Egmont's Diary is of great value for accounts of parliamentary debates.

Wednesday, 25 March, 1730.–Today I heard the House sat on Sir Thomas Aston's election[2] till eleven last night, when Brereton's friends perceiving it would go against him, moved to adjourn the debate, but Sir Thomas's friends carried it for proceeding, one hundred and twenty against ninety-nine. Upon this the adverse party crowded away, and the main question that Sir Thomas was duly elected passed without opposition. Sir Robert Walpole stayed till the division was over, in order to influence the House for Brereton, but he found there are certain occasions where he cannot carry points; it is this meanness of his (the prostitution of the character of a first Minister in assisting and strenuously supporting the defence of dunghill worms, let their cause be ever so unjust, against men of honour, birth, and fortune, and that in person too), that gains him so much ill-will; formerly, when the first Minister appeared in any matter, he did it with gravity, and the honour and service of the Crown appeared to be concerned, but Sir Robert, like the altars of refuge in old times, is the asylum of little unworthy wretches who, submitting to dirty work, endear themselves to him, and get his protection first, and then his favour, which as he is first Minister, is sure to draw after it the countenance of the Court; in the meantime, the world, who know the insignificancy, to say no worse, of these sort of tools, are in indignation to see them preferred and cherished beyond men of character and fortune, and set off in a better light to the King, and this with men of small experience, which are the bulk of a nation, occasions hard thoughts of the Crown itself; whereas in very deed the

[1] Under-Secretaries.

[2] A by-election at Liverpool, May 1729, when one of the former members, Thomas Brereton, sought re-election after accepting an office of profit under the Crown.

King can seldom know the merits and character of private persons but from the first Minister, who we see has no so great regard for any as for these little pickthanks and scrubs, for whom he risks his character, and the character of his high station, in opposition to the old gentry of the kingdom, and that in matters of right and wrong, in the face of his country, namely, in Parliament. . . .

19B. Speech by Samuel Sandys in the House of Commons on the motion for the removal of Sir Robert Walpole, 13 February 1741

(*Parl. Hist.*, XI, pp. 1232–1233.)

Samuel Sandys (1695?–1770), later first Baron Sandys, was M.P. for Worcester and a leading member of the opposition to Walpole in the House of Commons.

. . . I know, Sir, it will be objected, that as every material step in the late conduct of our public affairs, either at home or abroad, has been authorized or approved of by parliament, what I have said must be looked on as a general charge against his majesty's counsels and our parliaments, rather than a personal charge against any one minister; but this, upon a due consideration, becomes the most heavy, and the most evident charge against the minister I aim at. According to our constitution, we can have no sole and prime minister: we ought always to have several prime ministers or officers of state: every such officer has his own proper department; and no officer ought to meddle in the affairs belonging to the department of another. But it is publicly known, that this minister, having obtained a sole influence over all our public counsels, has not only assumed the sole direction of all public affairs, but has got every officer of state removed that would not follow his direction, even in the affairs belonging to his own proper department. By this means he hath monopolized all the favours of the crown, and engrossed the sole disposal of all places, pensions, titles, and ribbons, as well as of all preferments, civil, military, or ecclesiastical.

This, Sir, is of itself a most heinous offence against our constitution: but he has greatly aggravated the heinousness of his crime; for, having thus monopolized all the favours of the crown, he has made a blind submission to his direction at elections and in parliament, the only ground to hope for any honours or preferments, and the only tenure by which any gentleman could preserve what he had. This is so notoriously known, that it can stand in need of no proof. Have not many deserving gentlemen been disappointed in the preferment they had a just title to, upon the bare suspicion of not being blindly devoted to his personal interest? Have not some persons of the highest rank and most illustrious characters been displaced, for no other reason than because they disdained to sacrifice their honour and conscience to his direction in parliament. . . . Nay, has not this minister himself not only confessed it, but boasted of it? Has he not said, and in this House too, that he would be a pitiful fellow of a minister who did not displace any officer that opposed his measures in parliament? . . .

19C. Speech by Sir Robert Walpole in the House of Commons on the motion for his removal, 13 February 1741

(*Parl. Hist.*, XI, p. 1296.)

The following extract is the conclusion of Walpole's speech, and illustrates his own view of his position as first minister. It should be compared with Lord North's view. (No. 16.)

. . . But while I unequivocally deny that I am sole and prime minister, and that to my influence and direction all the measures of government must be attributed, yet I will not shrink from the responsibility which attaches to the post I have the honour to hold; and should, during the long period in which I have sat upon this bench, any one step taken by government be proved to be either disgraceful or disadvantageous to the nation, I am ready to hold myself accountable.

To conclude, Sir, though I shall always be proud of the honour of any trust or confidence from his majesty, yet I shall always be ready to remove from his counsels and presence, when he thinks fit; and therefore I should think myself very little concerned in the event of the present question, if it were not for the encroachment that will thereby be made upon the prerogatives of the crown. But I must think, that an address to his majesty to remove one of his servants, without so much as alleging any particular crime against him, is one of the greatest encroachments that was ever made upon the prerogatives of the crown; and therefore, for the sake of my master, without any regard for my own, I hope all those that have a due regard for our constitution, and for the rights and prerogatives of the crown, without which our constitution cannot be preserved, will be against this motion.

20. The duke of Newcastle's proposals for increased solidarity amongst the members of the 'inner cabinet', 19 January 1745

(William Coxe, *Memoirs of the Administration of Henry Pelham*, I (1829), pp. 205–206.)

This letter marked the reconciliation after one of the misunderstandings between the Pelham brothers, due to Newcastle's fear that his brother might be led "into Lord Orford's old method, of being the first person upon all occasions".

Newcastle House, Jan, 19th, 1744/5

DEAR BROTHER,

I cannot forbear taking the first opportunity to express to you, the great satisfaction I had, in the confidential conversation we had last night together, so necessary and proper for our respective stations, and so agreeable to that true love and affection, which I know in reality there is between us.

I shall not touch upon any disagreeable incidents, that may have occasioned a contrary behaviour; but only just mention what, I am persuaded, will, with ease and satisfaction to us both, improve and confirm the mutual disposition at present in us, to do what is so right and necessary for ourselves and our friends, who, I find, begin to think themselves concerned, in any possible difference or coolness between us. I know my own present situation at court, as well as any body. I can bear a good deal; but cannot bear, that any of my colleagues, especially those who are become considerable only by the measure,[1] should take advantage of the ill will and resentment, that I have drawn upon myself by it. This you, and you alone, can prevent. I am sure you will not think unreasonable what I now propose: that every thing, as far as possible, should be first talked over by you and me, before it is either flung out in the closet, or communicated to *any* of our brethren; I always except the chancellor,[2] who, I know, is a third brother: that we shall have no reserve, either *public* or *private* with each other: and, that in our transactions with the other ministers, and other persons, who may be to be negotiated with, we should always let it be understood, that we speak in the name of both, or in the name of neither. This conduct, once established, will grow easy and natural, and effectually prevent any jealousies, on one side, or disagreeable warmth, occasioned by them, on the other.

In order to make this practicable, I will call every morning, as regularly at your house, as I once did at Sir Robert's. There the scheme of the day shall be settled, to be handed out to others afterwards, as shall be necessary; and a frequent intercourse with ease, at each other's houses, and at all hours and times, will also make this very easy to us.

I have only one thing to add, which relates to the closet. You must take an opportunity to let the king see, that I feel his behaviour; that I don't deserve it; and that I am and must be always a principal part of this present scheme; and indeed it would be very unjust, that I should be the object of the resentment of all our enemies, and be destroyed by my own bull.* You see I write in good humour; I do so most sincerely. I beg you would attend to it. Indeed it is in your power to make yourself, and every body easy, as far as relates to *ourselves*. If you think so, I am sure you will do it. I am, with the same real affection and inclination I ever was, my dearest brother, &c.

21. Letters between the duke of Newcastle and Lord Hardwicke about George II's view that the First Lord of the Treasury should confine his activities to his own department, 3 and 4 January 1755

(P. C. Yorke, *Life and Correspondence of Philip Yorke, Earl of Hardwicke*, II (1913), pp. 224–227.)

George II, like George III later, was in favour of 'departmental' ministries. He resented Newcastle's view that the First Lord of the Treasury should control all patronage.

Lord Chancellor Hardwicke to the Duke of Newcastle.

POWIS HOUSE, *Jan. 3rd.*, 1755. At night.

. . . I . . . said that I thought it my duty to mention to His Majesty that, though I had not seen your Grace, I had received a letter from you last night, by which I found you were under the greatest concern that His Majesty should interpret the opinion you gave him for suspending the disposition of the Groom of the Stole for

[1] The removal of Granville from office, which the king resented and which he attributed to Newcastle.
[2] Lord Hardwicke.
* Alluding to the brazen bull formed for the tyrant Phalaris, by Perillus, who was the first victim of his own cruel invention.

the present, as proceeding from any other motive than the real one, a desire that it might be further considered by His Majesty. The King grew warm, and said, "The Duke of Newcastle meddles in things he has nothing to do with. He would dispose of my Bedchamber, which is a personal service about myself, and I won't suffer anybody to meddle in. I know what he wanted; he wanted to recommend my Lord Lincoln or his brother-in-law".

. . . His Majesty then talked of his Father's having been in the right in resolving to have no Groom of the Stole, and of Sunderland's having forced him to make him etc.; that the Treasury was the Duke of Newcastle's department, and that was business enough etc.; that your Grace had begun at the wrong end, and proposed Lords of the Bedchamber to him before there was any vacancy there. To this I said that the head of his Treasury was indeed an employment of great business, very extensive, which always went beyond the bare management of the revenue; that it extended through both Houses of Parliament, the members of which were naturally to look thither; that there must be some principal person to receive applications, to hear the wants and the wishes and the requests of mankind, with the reasons of them, in order to lay them before His Majesty for his determination; that it was impossible for the King to be troubled with all this himself. This he in part admitted, but there were some things nobody should meddle in etc. I said it was only a method of laying things before him, and the absolute final decision was in *him*; that it had been always the usage in this Country, and I supposed was so in others; that without it no administration could be enabled to serve him, that ministers bore all the blame and resentment of disappointed persons, and they could never carry on his affairs without having some weight in the disposition of favours. The King said, he had seen too much of that in this Country already, and it was time to change it in some degree. I then asked his pardon for presuming so far; that I only thought it my duty and a point of justice. The King said the thing was over, and he had determined it; "But I know how you are connected (I am not sure whether he did not say linked) together." I answered that it was far from my intention to argue for altering *the thing*, but only to shew him the reasons why a suspension had been proposed; that as to connections I had none, but what were very consistent with his service and tended to the real support of it; and here my audience ended. One thing I forgot that, in the course of what I said, I let him know that such things would materially create appearances and interpretations in the world that, by weakening his administration, might give rise to disturbance in Parliament, and alter that state of ease and quiet, which His Majesty and his servants under him had been endeavouring to bring about; that people would be looking different ways, and every question upon an election might become a contest between different sides of the Court. But the King seemed to despise such fears at present. . . .

The Duke of Newcastle to the Lord Chancellor.

CLAREMONT, *Jan. 4th*, 1755.

MY DEAREST LORD,

I have read over twice, with the greatest attention, your most kind letter, and cannot delay one moment returning your Lordship my most sincere thanks for the very proper and friendly manner, in which you talked to the King upon my subject, though it had not the desired effect. . . . The principle of *confining me to the Treasury* and, I suppose, all of us to our respective offices, seems now avowed; and . . . I adhere to my opinion that, if Mr Fox had not been admitted into favour, his Majesty would not have ventured to avow that principle in the manner he has done, and own to your Lordship *that it was time to change it in some degree*. . . . I shall take no rash resolution, but do as you shall advise. Humility, submission, obeying and feeding we have seen (though attended with all imaginable success), will not do; there must be a mixture of something else which may *donne à penser*, strike some fear. The branch of foreign affairs has the greatest weight with us. . . . Nothing seems to me so natural as for me to tell Munchausen[1] that, as his Majesty is pleased to confine me to the Treasury, I could not meddle in any foreign affair. It would be contrary to his Majesty's intention, and dangerous for me to attempt . . . and at once wash my hands of Hessian Convention, Russian treaty and the Saxon and Bavarian subsidies. . . .

HOLLES NEWCASTLE.

P.S. It is impossible for us to do the King's business if things remain as they are. We must, in justice to ourselves, tell the King so. . . .

22. Extracts from the Diary of George Grenville, 1763–1764

(*The Grenville Papers*, ed. W. J. Smith, II (1852–1853), pp. 211–212.)

The extracts show Grenville's determination, as first minister, to keep patronage under his own control. They also illustrate the practice of the more important ministers meeting informally to discuss business before it was considered by the whole Cabinet.

Tuesday, 11th. [October, 1763.] Lord Sandwich came to Mr. Grenville, and said that he understood from Lord Halifax, and hoped to find from Mr. Grenville, that he was to stand exactly in the same situation as Lord Egremont had done.[2]

Mr. Grenville told him that no man could stand to him in the degree of nearness and dearness of friendship that Lord Egremont had, but that he had every degree of regard and good will to his Lordship. Lord Sandwich said he supposed the disposition of offices was to be in partition between them three, Lord Halifax, himself and Mr. Grenville, and that Lord Halifax intended to mention it to the King. Mr. Grenville said that as to that he could say nothing, the King must take such determination upon it as he pleased, but that he must observe to his Lordship that the Duke of Bedford was not likely to be pleased with that partition, and that for his own part he would never consent that any of the House of Commons' offices should go through any channel but his own; that he would be glad to receive the recommendations of his friends, and to forward them when it was in his power, but that people must speak to him himself; that he did not do this from the thirst of power or patronage, but from knowing it to be essentially necessary whilst he held that station in Government. . . .

[1] The Hanoverian minister.

[2] Lord Egremont, who was Grenville's brother-in-law, died on 21 August 1763 and was succeeded as Secretary of State by Lord Sandwich, Lord Halifax being the other Secretary.

Saturday, November 12th. [1763] Mr. Stanley[1] came to Mr. Grenville in the evening, had a long conversation with him. Mr. Grenville again repeated to him his determined resolution to have the sole disposal of the offices belonging to the House of Commons, and of giving them to such persons only as would shew themselves to be his friends; that though he had great regard for Lord Halifax and Lord Sandwich, he could not, in this instance, look upon them as his colleagues, because, whilst he was understood to manage the King's business in the House of Commons, he could acknowledge no colleague there.

Mr. Stanley was much more explicit than in the former conversation, and declared fully that he meant to support the King's Government, and to show his personal regard to Mr. Grenville. . . .

Saturday, 28th [January, 1764]. . . .

A scheme was proposed, chiefly by Lord Sandwich (at this time), for the two Secretaries of State, the Duke of Bedford, and Mr Grenville, to dine together once a week to talk upon business; to this Mr Grenville agreed, as often as the business of the House of Commons would allow of his coming to it. Lord Sandwich named it to the King, who when he saw Mr Grenville asked him about it, and advised him to treat of nothing there but public business only, and not to come upon the arrangements for offices, in which he would be overpowered by the other three. Mr Grenville assured his Majesty that it was his intention to do so, knowing that the Duke of Bedford and Lord Sandwich would always join upon that head against him. The King said he thought he would do well to join the Chancellor into this weekly meeting.

23A–B. Two views of the collective responsibility of ministers, 1741 and 1778

23A. Speech by the duke of Newcastle in the House of Lords against the motion to remove Sir Robert Walpole, 13 February 1741

(*Parl. Hist.*, XI, p. 1182.)

Newcastle's view of the position of the First Lord of the Treasury does not altogether agree with Walpole's at the same date (see No. 19c.), nor with his own in 1755 (see No. 21.).

. . . I mention the ministry, my lords, because I am unacquainted with any man who either claims or possesses the power or title of sole minister. I own in my province no superior but his majesty, and am willing and ready to answer any charge which relates to that part of the public business which I have had the honour to transact or direct.

A great part of what I have now offered was therefore no otherwise necessary on the present occasion, than because silence might have appeared like a consciousness of misconduct, and have afforded a new subject of airy triumph to the enemies of the administration; for very few of the transactions which have been so severely censured, fell under the particular inspection of the right honourable gentleman against whom the motion is levelled; he was not otherwise concerned in counselling or in ratifying,

[1] Hans Stanley (1720?–1780), M.P. for Southampton and a Lord of the Admiralty.

than as one of his majesty's privy council; and therefore, though they should be defective, I do not see how it is reasonable or just, that he should be singled out from the rest for disgrace or punishment. . . .

23B. Speech by Lord North in the House of Commons in the debate on the army estimates, 14 December 1778

(*Parl. Hist.*, XX, p. 89.)

The opposition turned this debate into an attack on the conduct of the American War, and particularly upon Lord George Germain, the Secretary of State for the Colonies.

. . . Several gentlemen had likewise called for an inquiry into the conduct of ministers; and some had pointed their censure directly at the noble lord near him (G. Germain) as the principal author of all our miscarriages. An inquiry into the conduct of ministers, no person in that House more ardently wished for; for he was conscious, whenever that event should happen, that it would be found he had discharged his duty to the best of his abilities. It had been insinuated that ministers recommended measures not their own; and that in the day of examination they would endeavour to shelter themselves under a certain great authority. He now disclaimed any intention of resorting to any such subterfuge. The measures pursued were his measures, in concert with the rest of the King's servants. He assisted in advising them, and looked upon himself responsible, in every possible view, as far as any minister can be responsible, for the measures he advised. If they were founded in propriety, justice, and sound policy, he expected to share the merit; if they were weak and pernicious, he wished to partake of the blame or censure attending them. As to the personal attacks made on the noble lord near him, relative to the measures respecting the war, there, if censure was due, he laid his claim for part; they were measures of state, originating in the King's counsels, and were of course no more the noble lord's measures than they were of any other member of the cabinet: the crimes or faults, or errors committed there, were imputable to the whole body, and not to a single individual who composed it.

24. Speaker Onslow on the collective responsibility of ministers, *circa.* 1765

(*Hist. MSS. Comm. 14th Report, App. Part IX, Onslow MSS.*, pp. 460–461.)

This document–an essay "On Opposition"–is undated, but it refers to Sir John Barnard, who died in 1764, as "lately dead", and Onslow himself died in 1768. Arthur Onslow (1691–1768) was Speaker of the House of Commons from 1728 to 1761.

. . . And I must also here say a few things to you on another particular I have mentioned of Mr Craggs–the defending and supporting in public what he was really against and opposed in private–I know it is the common practice among Ministers.

I know it is said that Ministers cannot otherwise be kept together or the business of a Government be otherwise carried on, and that one man's scruples ought to yield to the judgment of the many, and he to suppose himself in the wrong. I know also that this practice has been sanctified by very good men conforming to it, and particularly by the example of that great and excellent Minister my Lord Chancellor Clarendon (except in one remarkable instance, which however contributed to his ruin. See the history of his life, pages 246, 247, 248, 249), than whom a wiser or a more virtuous man never was in power. I know likewise that the not doing this, brings upon a man the disagreeable imputation of intractableness and obstinacy and of being impracticable in business, and draws often not only odium but contempt on those who do it not. Yet what shall a man say where conscience is concerned, or what will he be able to say when he is to answer for every action of his, not by the conscience of others but by his own, and how miserable is all worldly business, take it for a course of time, that is not carried on by men who make a conscience of what they do in it? And is there anything so likely to make men lose all conscience at last as to be deluded out of it in some perhaps very few particulars at first by the speciousness of worldly wisdom, convenience and complaisance? I don't say nor would I be thought to contend for this strictness in trifles, they are not subjects of conscience, nor where the matter is doubtful, though where I doubt I would rather not do. But I mean it in points of great importance, where conviction is clear and where the error may be dangerous. In such cases, advised as I am, I think he cannot be an honest man that does not use all the talents and means he is master of everywhere to oppose and prevent the thing he even singly disapproves of, be his station and bindings with others what they will. How much evil to the public may not one just man properly situated be able to stop by his resolution and perseverance? If he cannot do it in private consultations, he may in public councils and thither he ought to follow it.

The Cabinet, the Privy Council, and the Parliament are all of them the King's Councils, and I can see no reason why a man's conscience is to govern him in one or two and not in all; why he may be allowed to differ with his fellow ministers in the Cabinet and not in Parliament; why difference of opinion there should break Ministerial union more than in the other, provided decency and proper deference be observed in the one place as well as the other. But Ministers seldom love Parliaments; never bring business there for counsel, but to carry points that must have the authority of the Legislature; and in order to carry such points must previously strengthen themselves there by collecting all the force they can for it. This polity I own requires the firmest connexion among the Ministers; but then it is a polity that I have ever found to produce far more evil to the State than good, and to the Crown too.

The Crown and Ministers also have been always most safe and strong when they have had the free and fair determinations of Parliament for their direction, and I know nothing is so likely to procure this and all that a Court almost can wish to have done there, as to let the Parliament see the Ministers are not in a combination to force things upon them, and nothing can demonstrate that more than Ministers allowing one another the leave to differ in their actings there according to the real difference of their opinions. If the difference of opinion be not real, it is faction, and the Crown ought, in a proper way, to check that among the Ministers; but that is not what I am speaking of. I mean the conscientious difference of sentiment that may happen among honest men, and when it is among such only, it will not be so frequent as to confound or disturb business. The general difference among Ministers is not from this, but from envy, emulation, jealousy and lust of superiority, and from thence arises disorder and confusion in counsels often fatal to the Government. . . .

25. Speech by Alderman Oliver in the House of Commons on 'responsible' and 'secret' advisers, 27 November 1775

(*Parl. Hist.*, XVIII, pp. 1005–1007.)

Richard Oliver (1734–1784) was M.P. for the City of London and an energetic member of the opposition to Lord North's ministry. This speech was made on moving to address the king to impart to the House who were the authors and advisers of the measures against America. The allegations about 'secret advisers' which formed such a prominent part of opposition attacks on the government were a veiled method of attacking what was felt to be the king's personal policy. For Oliver, see also No. 240.

Mr. *Alderman Oliver* said, that the motion which he had then to make, related to the advising and counselling the King in matters of great national concern; an object of no small importance; it had ever been considered as such in this nation, and in all monarchies where the interest of the whole employed the attention of the individual; and must especially be considered so by those (amongst whom he ranked himself) who were most warmly attached to the rights and dignity of the crown, and most personally affectionate to the present monarch. The wisdom of our constitution had never at any moment, from its first establishment, neglected this most important province. The great council of the nation, the hereditary counsellors of the crown, the privy council, were all names with which we were constitutionally acquainted; and the oath appointed for the last made any arguments from him unnecessary to shew the superlative importance of the office. To these his motion had not any reference. Modern times, he said, had presented us with novel institutions, and we now talked familiarly of a cabinet council. Very modern times had brought us acquainted with something farther; and the present House of Commons would know (which preceding Houses did not) what was meant by an efficient[1] cabinet council. Whether these were blemishes or improvements in our system of government, it belonged not to him to pronounce; for to these likewise his motion had not any reference. His motion went to those, who, not as members of any of the councils he had mentioned, but as something still more efficient, have the undoubted merit or demerit of counselling and advising to his Majesty the late measures concerning America, before those measures were brought forward in parliament. That there were such counsellors and advisers, he took to be an undoubted fact; and he must be permitted to entertain his own private opinion of the veracity and integrity of any intelligent person who should seriously and solemnly declare that he believed there was none of this description. He presumed it would not be denied that the unanimous opinion of an ostensible prime minister, a chancellor, and a responsible secretary of state, composing even this efficient cabinet council, had been over-ruled by this something still more efficient. There was one measure, and a measure which he conceived to be the most important and uncommon that ever was produced in an English parliament; the establishment of absolute despotism in Canada; the author and adviser of which remained to this moment unknown. Though approved, and admired, and adopted, as it had been, by parliament; yet no privy counsellor, no cabinet, no efficient cabinet counsellor, had ever yet assumed its merit; but all to whom it has been imputed, had invariably disavowed it. The unanimous complaint of all those who had been in administration

[1] *i.e.* effective. The word is used in this sense throughout the speech.

during the present reign, as well as the frequent mortification and distressing embarrassment, self-contradiction, tergiversation, apparent inconsistency, and seemingly intended imposition on parliament, of those who were now in administration, all proved the existence of these unknown counsellors. He did not mean to charge the present administration with any real inconsistency in their opinions, or with any intention themselves of imposing on parliament; he entirely acquitted them of both. He believed them innocent of these charges, for they were obliged to give way to an efficiency they could not counteract, and in which they had not the smallest share. Now these super-efficient counsellors, for he knew not what other name to give them, were the sole objects of his present inquiry. Upon these the attention of the House should fix; as that of the nation had long been fixed. These he desired to have declared to that House authentically; and he desired it now, when they would enjoy the full popularity to which those measures entitled them, which the sense of the nation was said to approve.

26. The duke of Grafton disapproves of Lord Shelburne's "views of becoming *Prime* Minister", 16 February 1783

(*Autobiography and Political Correspondence of Augustus Henry Third Duke of Grafton*, ed. W. R. Anson (1898), pp. 359–361.)

Grafton was Lord Privy Seal in both the second Rockingham and the Shelburne ministries. Lord Camden was Lord President of the Council.

The following day [16 February, 1783] it was said, though unknown to, and disbelieved by Lord Camden and myself, that the Duke of Rutland having the Lord Steward's wand, was to have a seat at the Cabinet.

Under this conception, I went early the next morning, to ascertain the fact, from Mr Secretary Townshend[1] himself; when to my greatest astonishment, I found that the Duke of Rutland was actually of the Cabinet. I started so much on this information, that he said 'Surely it was within etiquette, that a Cabinet might be changed or added to, without the concurrence of the other members of it.' I replied that I could not admit this position; for I was confident, that it ought to be otherwise: and I was sorry to add moreover, that this measure was decisive of my situation. However as a friend to the Duke of Rutland, I wished to express to him that the bare appearance of any objection to his Grace was the only point that could give me embarrassment in the business: for that the duke was a man whom I not only valued highly but was one to whom I had some obligations.

From Mr Townshend's I walked up to Lord Camden's, in order to relate to his lordship, what had passed. We agreed in thinking, that I should immediately go to inform Lord Shelburne of my determination. On finding the last mentioned lord at home, I began with expressing my surprize at the information which Mr Townshend had just given me: and I complained that such a proceeding little agreed with that confidence which I had been assured, I should find from his lordship when we both embarked in the Ministry; and which had been repeated on the death of Lord

[1] Thomas Townshend (1733–1800), later Viscount Sydney.

Rockingham. I then plainly declared to Lord Shelburne that no consideration should induce me to act so insignificant a part, or submit to be so little considered, under any Administration whatsoever. His lordship first wished to excuse himself, by saying, that he had no opportunity to impart to me his intention: but on my reminding him of the particular conversation I had with him on Friday morning last, his lordship replied, that the king's pleasure had not at that time been taken. Lord Shelburne then said, that as much as he should be sorry to be deprived of any one's assistance, he would deprecate no man (be his consequence what it would) from taking the part, which he thought to be becoming his station: however he added in a milder tone that he did not know whether it was actually done; that he must write to Mr. Pitt, to enquire how the matter stood: and how it was understood by the Duke of Rutland himself; and that he would let me know.

He observed, that Mr. Townshend was new in office; and happened to say, 'was one of the Cabinet'; when he rather ought to have said 'that it was intended that his Grace should be called to it.'

Lord Shelburne's language so thoroughly convinced me, that he expected to be the sole adviser to the king, of measures of this sort, that I became, if possible more determined to quit my office. With a declaration to this effect I left his house saying also, that as the part I should take was known fully to him, I was ready to resign at such moment as His Majesty should approve. However, on reviewing in my mind what had passed in this conversation, I was not quite satisfied with the footing on which my decision was left; I therefore turned back to Lord Shelburne's fully determined, that whatever was the answer of Mr. Pitt, concerning what had been said to the Duke of Rutland, it would not keep me in my situation; for it was a demonstration that it would be, as abetting Lord Shelburne's views of becoming *Prime* Minister, which were so apparent: whereas I would never consider his lordship but as holding the principal office in the Cabinet. I told him that on considering again, that the king's pleasure was taken, that it was known to the duke himself, by which the matter was in fact determined, and no longer open to consideration, these circumstances together with the whole tenor of his lordship's discourse determined me to take the earliest opportunity of desiring the king to allow me to retire from my office: but that I should leave His Majesty to decide when it suited best with his affairs. I acquainted Lord Shelburne likewise that I should no longer attend any Cabinet.

27. Speech by Lord Shelburne in the House of Lords censuring ministers for their conduct towards Ireland, 1 December 1779

(*Parl. Hist.*, XX, pp. 1166–1168.)

Shelburne here expounds the doctrine of ministerial responsibility.

Lord Shelburne. . . . His lordship next took a view of the state of the empire and its various dependencies, and a retrospect of the last summer campaign, in the course of which he dwelt on the language of ministers out of that House, which amounted exactly to this: that the King was his own general, for it was actually reported with confidence, and he believed was universally understood to be true, that his Majesty, had the enemy attempted a landing, meant to take the command of the army. It was said likewise, that the King was his own secretary; his own first commissioner of the Admiralty, &c. This was a most preposterous idea, and a language totally unknown to the constitution. The King might be as well his own chief justice and dispense law on the bench in Westminster-hall, as be his own general. He could not act but through the medium of his ministers in their several departments. Those ministers who would permit his Majesty to head his army would take the risk upon themselves and deserve impeachment. The constitution held a very different language, and was precise on the subject. Every one of his Majesty's servants were separately and conjunctly responsible for every measure that they carried into execution through their respective departments; and as a committee of council, for the measures decided there, and passing under the idea of an act of state, or the resolution of the crown, previously advised to it by his constitutional counsellors. It was upon this clear doctrine of constitutional law that the well-known maxim "the King can do no wrong" was founded. Why so? Because the King, in contemplation of law, can do nothing without previous consultation and advice. He allowed, however, that a king in some cases might so far abuse his trust as to do wrong, by usurping upon the powers which the constitution had placed in other hands. What happened more than once before, might again happen. The conduct of Edward 2, and Richard 2, exhibited two melancholy instances how far a prince, under the influence of secret advice, may be tempted to mistake his own dignity, and the mutual rights and interests of himself and his subjects, which, when properly supported and wisely pursued, are for ever inseparable. It was true, that the civility of the law lays down as a maxim, what it presumes, out of respect to the person of the King, will never happen; that is, that by a breach of every duty, moral and political, he will act merely on his own judgment; farther the maxim that "the king can do no wrong" was to the last degree blasphemous, ridiculous and absurd; he therefore was of opinion, that a prince above all things should be ever attentive to these two considerations; namely, the exact relation he stood in with respect to his subjects, the ground of their obedience, and his own power; and the very particular station in which the laws and constitution had placed him as an individual, most certainly at the head of government, but nevertheless bound by every motive of religion and regard to the laws, with the meanest subject in the empire; and, he was free to say, that any king of this country, who should venture hereafter to depart from those sound maxims of law and policy, would sooner or later experience the fatal consequences of exercising in his own person those active powers placed by the constitution in his ministers and advisers, for the due and faithful discharge of which they were, from the nature of the trust reposed in them, personally responsible.

He could not help observing, that, however improbable it might be, that our present sovereign would ever depart from those sentiments of justice and good faith so deeply engraven on his heart, many matters had lately happened which afforded cause of just alarm to the friends of the constitution. The servants of the crown, by the aid of the dangerous influence which it carried with it, had departed from that system of government which had borne us through four most heavy and expensive wars, and had raised at length the glory of this country to the highest pinnacle of fame, accompanied with an accession of national prosperity hitherto unequalled. This system had been gradually giving way since the commencement of the present reign, till one of a very different tendency was now established in its place; a system planned in secret advice and supported by corruption. This double influence was now become in a great measure irresistible indeed: the wisest could not well see where it might end, though he was perfectly satisfied that it pointed and would lead to some fatal issue.

Part II
PARLIAMENT

PARLIAMENT

Introduction

AT no period in English history did the reputation of Parliament stand higher than in the first half of the eighteenth century. The 'Glorious Revolution' had established it firmly as the supreme power in the State; and it spent the next half-century in steadily adding to its effective control over the machinery of government. The importance attached to Parliament by the first Hanoverian king may be illustrated from George I's Proclamation for summoning a new Parliament in 1715.[1]

There was at this time a close approximation of Whig and Tory views on the place of Parliament in the constitution. Bolingbroke, the Tory spokesman, in fact out-Whigs the Whigs in his insistence on the need for free and frequent elections. Once in power, however, the Whigs lost no time in abandoning their previous attitude when they took advantage of the Jacobite Rising of 1715 to pass the Septennial Act.[2] There was a brisk debate on this measure in the House of Lords,[3] and Tory arguments against it were recapitulated in the protest of the minority peers.

By 1714 the House of Commons was clearly the more important of the two Houses, and it steadily consolidated its dominant position. Yet there is an almost complete absence of open conflicts between the two Houses in our period, largely due to the predominant Whiggism of both; and after the refusal of the House of Commons to pass the Peerage Bill,[4] the rights and privileges of the House of Lords were not in question. As individuals, the political importance of the peers can hardly be over-estimated, and their extensive patronage gave them a measure of control over the composition of the House of Commons through their influence in elections.[5] The number of 'placemen' in the House of Commons, in spite of the measures taken against them in Anne's reign, was the subject of denunciation by opposition speakers throughout the period, and the policy of excluding specific types of placemen was continued. An Act of this kind was passed in 1743[6] by those who had long denounced the corruption of Walpole's administration. In 1782 the Rockingham Whigs, on coming into power, set about putting into practice the principles of economical reform which they had been advocating in opposition. The Contractors' Act declared all government contractors incapable of sitting in the House of Commons;[7] and the Act generally known as Crewe's Act disqualified various categories of placemen from voting at parliamentary elections.[8]

The *Journals of the House of Commons* afford a very clear view of the proceedings of the House. An extract from them relating to the opening of George I's Parliament in 1714[9] shows the characteristic activities of the House at the opening of a session. Members were busily taking the statutory oaths; the Grand Committees were being organized; arrangements were being made to determine disputed elections; the standing orders were being restated, and a mass of heterogeneous instructions were

[1] No. 28. [2] No. 29. [3] No. 30. [4] No. 31. [5] No. 44 B.
[6] No. 32. [7] No. 33. [8] No. 34. [9] No. 35.

being given to various officials, intended to facilitate the smooth conduct of the business of the House. Horace Walpole, for some years himself a member, is a valuable source of information about proceedings in the House of Commons at this period. His account of the different types of parliamentary oratory in the last years of George II's reign,[1] and the description by the German Carl Philipp Moritz of a visit to the gallery of the House in 1782,[2] give a more intimate picture than can be found in the formal accounts in the *Journals*.

The next group of documents illustrates the important cases of privilege which arose during this period. Two of these cases concerned John Wilkes, and show the House of Commons less interested in privilege than in supporting the government of the day against one of its sharpest and most radical critics. In the case of Wilkes's arrest on a general warrant in 1763, the House of Commons took a narrower view of its privilege than did the Court of Common Pleas;[3] while over the Middlesex Election in 1769[4] the House drew down upon itself the strictures of a minority of the Lords, as well as the denunciations of Junius, by its disregard of the rights of electors. The House treated publication of its debates as a breach of privilege almost until the end of our period. Extracts are given from an interesting debate on this subject in 1738,[5] when the leaders of the opposition, Wyndham and Pulteney, agreed with the government spokesmen that such publication, during the parliamentary session at least, was a notorious breach of the privileges of the Commons. After the case of Brass Crosby in 1771,[6] though the Commons affirmed their previous practice by a large majority, attempts to prevent the publication of debates were in fact abandoned. Towards the end of the period many members, of whom Burke is the most notable, were coming to feel that the electors should be allowed more information about the conduct of their members in Parliament, so that they might be better qualified to elect good members at elections.

The actual conduct of eighteenth-century elections is illustrated by an example of very moderate election expenses in the early part of the century;[7] by an extract from the *Diary* of that ardent electioneer, George Bubb Dodington,[8] who had considerable influence in Dorset; and by Carl Philipp Moritz's description of the Westminster election of 1782.[9] During the first half of the century, election petitions were dealt with by the House of Commons in a partisan spirit, as can be seen from the Windsor election of 1738.[10] The passing of the Grenville Act in 1770[11] was an attempt to bring about a more judicial attitude in the deciding of controverted elections.

Political parties in anything like the modern sense had not yet come into existence, and in this period the terms Whig and Tory meant very little. The Whigs managed to convince both George I and George II that they were the only true friends of the House of Hanover;[12] and for the next half-century they maintained themselves in power and became the Court party, while the Tories were stigmatized as Jacobites and relegated to the political wilderness. The opposition to Walpole consisted not only of Tories but of groups of discontented Whigs, differing little from Walpole in political principles and disunited among themselves.[13] The same could be said of the opposition to Lord North[14] until the disasters of the American War temporarily united the various opposition groups. During the greater part of the period, party was identified with 'faction',[15] and most people would have agreed with George III

[1] No. 36. [2] No. 37. [3] No. 38. [4] No. 39. [5] No. 40.
[6] No. 41. [7] No. 42. [8] No. 43. [9] No. 46. [10] No. 44.
[11] No. 45. [12] No. 47. [13] No. 48. [14] No. 50. [15] No. 49.

and with Chatham that government should be by the best men from all political groups. While this attitude prevailed, the development of parties was impossible. The idea of party as based not on connexion but on principles, enunciated by Burke in the *Thoughts on the Cause of the Present Discontents* in 1770, is too well known to warrant inclusion here. Evolved as a new political method for the Whigs, who had seen their old methods turned against them by George III, this was an important first step towards making party respectable.

During the last thirty years of the century an important movement for parliamentary reform began to develop, and the last group of documents in this section illustrates the views of the reformers and of some of the leading politicians on the subject. The speeches of the two Pitts[1] contain the generally prevailing views on the corruption of the essentially perfect constitution, more especially in the boroughs, and prescribe an increase of the more independent county members. Major John Cartwright went much farther than this and was much less respectful in his attitude to the Revolution of 1688 and the constitution it had set up.[2] The famous Yorkshire Association of 1779–1780, model for many other county associations, began as a movement for economy in public expenditure and developed into a movement for parliamentary reform.[3] Both the county associations and Cartwright's Society for Constitutional Information[4] were very respectable in their membership and were anxious to restrain their more radical members, lest reform should be defeated by fear of revolution. Rockingham, at first a supporter of the Yorkshire movement, disliked its radical side;[5] but Shelburne was more sympathetic;[6] and the duke of Richmond advocated universal male suffrage as the best way of restraining the mob, which, he held, would always be guided by the better-educated aristocracy.[7] The speech of Edmund Burke in opposition to Pitt's proposed reform in 1782[8] typifies his whole attitude towards attacks, based on theories of natural rights, upon a constitution based on prescription and tradition, and foreshadows his attitude to the French Revolution.

[1] Nos. 57 and 58. [2] No. 52. [3] No. 53. [4] No. 57.
[5] No. 54. [6] No. 55. [7] No. 56. [8] No. 59.

BIBLIOGRAPHY

Reference should also be made to the general works on constitutional history in the sectional bibliography on the Monarchy.

I. MEMBERSHIP, PROCEDURE AND DEBATES: BOTH HOUSES

On membership the official "Return of the names of every member in each parliament" (*Parliamentary Papers*, House of Commons, 1878, vol. LXII, part ii, London, 1878) supersedes older compilations. *The Parliamentary Papers of John Robinson 1774–84*, edited by W. T. Laprade, Camden Series (London, 1922), gives a clear picture of the House of Commons at the end of our period. The formal activities of the members are officially recorded in the *Journals of the House of Lords* and the *Journals of the House of Commons*. These *Journals* include many reports of committees, but should be supplemented by two useful collections, *Reports from Committees of the House of Commons* (4 vols., London, 1773) and the later collection with the additional volumes covering *inter alia* the years from 1772 to 1783 (16 vols., London, 1803). The latter includes a useful index to reports (whether included in the collection or previously printed in the *Journals*) covering the years from 1696 to 1800. Reference should also be made to the "Catalogue of Parliamentary Reports and a breviate of their Contents, 1696–1834" (*Parliamentary Papers*, 1834 [626], vol. LI, London, 1834), which includes bills, accounts and papers as well as reports of committees. The Protests of the Lords have been edited by J. E. Thorold Rogers, from the *Journals* (3 vols., Oxford, 1815). The useful contemporary work of John Hatsell, *Precedents of Proceedings in the House of Commons* (4 vols., London, 1781, new edition, 1818), was based on the *Journals*. A mid-eighteenth-century manual on the procedure of the House of Commons, *The Liverpool Tractate*, has been printed by Catherine Strateman (New York, 1937).

Contemporary publication of statutes was made in *Statutes at Large*, of which several editions appeared in the eighteenth century, each based on its predecessor and adding later statutes. In cases of difficulty the official *Chronological Table of and Index to the Statutes* (London, 1870), which is frequently reissued, may be consulted.

There is an account of "Division Lists of the House of Commons 1715–60" by Mary Ransome in the *Bulletin of the Institute of Historical Research*, XIX (1942–1943), pp. 1–8. Other helpful bibliographical aids include H. H. Bellot and E. S. de Beer, "Parliamentary Printing 1660–1837" in *ibid.*, XI (1933–1934), pp. 85–98, and C. G. Parsloe and W. G. Bassett, "British Parliamentary Papers: Catalogues and Indexes" in *ibid.*, XI (1933–1934), pp. 24–30. The standard work on procedure is T. Erskine May, *Treatise on the Law, Privileges, Proceedings and Usage of Parliament* (1844 and many later editions: new edition by Sir Gilbert Campion, London, 1946). Sir Gilbert Campion, *Introduction to Procedure of the House of Commons* (London, new edition, 1947), has a valuable introduction on the historical development of parliamentary procedure. There is a full account of eighteenth-century private bill procedure in O. C. Williams, *Historical Development of Private Bill Procedure* (2 vols., London, 1948–1949).

Until the celebrated case of Brass Crosby (*infra*, p. 178), Parliaments from time to time vigorously enforced their view that it was a breach of privilege to publish, at least during the session, and in the case of the House of Lords at any time, reports of the debates in either House. Enterprising journalists frequently circumvented or defied this rule, sometimes with the help of the speakers but more frequently to their great annoyance. There was an insistent demand for reports of this kind which at first the *Political State of Great Britain* and subsequently *The Gentleman's Magazine* and *The London Magazine* did their best to satisfy. From time to time also there appeared collections of debates over a long period in many volumed editions by Torbuck, Timberland, Chandler, Almon and others, which are listed by H. H. Bellot *et al.* in "General

Collections of Reports of Parliamentary Debates for the Period since 1660" in the *Bulletin of the Institute of Historical Research*, x (1932–1933), pp. 171–177. The general reader will find his needs amply met in W. Cobbett, *Parliamentary History of England*, vols. 7–24 (London, 1811–1815). Many members kept notes of parliamentary proceedings for their own use, *e.g.* Archbishop Secker and Lord Chancellor Hardwicke in the House of Lords, while Lord Egmont's and Horace Walpole's valuable accounts of debates in the Commons were based on notes taken by themselves while members of the House. The notes taken by a private member of "the unreported Parliament" which sat from 1768 to 1774 are now in the British Museum, and the part relating to 1768–1771 was published by J. Wright as *Sir Henry Cavendish's Debates of the House of Commons* (2 vols., London, 1841–1843). P. J. Mantoux in "French Reports of British Parliamentary Debates" in the *American Historical Review*, XII (1907), pp. 244–269, and *Comptes Rendus des Séances du Parlement Anglais* (Paris, 1906) drew attention to the elaborate reports of parliamentary debates transmitted by French diplomatic agents to their government. Useful, too, is L. F. Stock, *Proceedings and Debates of the British Parliaments respecting North America* (5 vols. (in progress), Washington, 1924–1942). There is a discussion of "The Reliability of Contemporary Reporting of the Debates of the House of Commons, 1727–41" by Mary Ransome in the *Bulletin of the Institute of Historical Research*, XIX (1942–1943), pp. 67–79; an essay on "The Reporting and Publishing of the House of Commons' Debates 1771–1834" by A. Aspinall in *Essays Presented to Sir Lewis Namier* (London, 1956); and a more general examination of the whole question of parliamentary reporting in M. Macdonagh, *The Reporters' Gallery* (London, 1913). M. Macdonagh also gives a brief account of the Speakers of the eighteenth century in *The Speaker of the House* (London, 1914).

II. HOUSE OF LORDS: LATER WORKS

A. S. Turberville, *The House of Lords in the Eighteenth Century* (Oxford, 1927), is the standard, indeed the only account of the Upper House in our period. There is an important review of Professor Turberville's work by Sir W. S. Holdsworth in the *Law Quarterly Review*, XLV (1929), pp. 307–342, 432–458. On "The Peerage Bill of 1719" E. R. Turner's article in the *English Historical Review*, XXVIII (1913), pp. 243–259, should be consulted. O. C. Lease, "The Septennial Act of 1716" in the *Journal of Modern History*, XXII (1950), pp. 42–47, adds little to our knowledge.

III. HOUSE OF COMMONS: LATER WORKS

On the House of Commons the general conclusions reached by L. B. Namier, *Structure of Politics at the Accession of George III* (2 vols., London, 1929), on membership and parliamentary elections in 1760 are valid in essentials for the whole period. Confirmation of this for later years has been provided by Sir Lewis Namier himself in his *England in the Age of the American Revolution* (London, 1930), which is continued by John Brooke, *The Chatham Administration, 1766–1768* (London, 1956). Gerritt P. Judd, *Members of Parliament, 1734–1832* (London, 1955), is an elaborate and not always wholly reliable analysis of the social status, occupation, etc., of the members during these years. It also contains useful lists of members, with dates of birth and death, the constituencies for which they sat, and the sources of biographical information about them. T. H. B. Oldfield, *Representative History of Great Britain and Ireland* (6 vols., London, 1816), gives the fullest account of the many peculiar borough franchises, but the general reader will find all that he requires in E. and A. G. Porritt, *The Unreformed House of Commons* (2 vols., Cambridge, 1903). The detailed working of the electoral system is illustrated by several articles in the *English Historical Review*; Basil Williams, "The Duke of Newcastle and the Election of 1734", XII (1897), pp. 448–488; H. S. Toy, "Eighteenth Century Elections of Freemen and Aldermen at Helston, Cornwall", *ibid.*, XLVI (1931), pp. 452–457, which shows the extremely close nature of many eighteenth-century corporations; R. C. Jasper, "Edward Eliot and the

Acquisition of Grampound", *ibid.*, LVIII (1943), pp. 475–481, which explains how the voters of a 'freeman' borough could sometimes control their patron; and Ian R. Christie, "Private Patronage versus Government Influence: John Buller and the contest for control of Parliamentary Elections at Saltash, 1780–90", *ibid.*, LXXI (1956), pp. 249–255; D. Cook's unpublished thesis on "The Representative history of the county, town and University of Cambridge 1698–1832" in the *Bulletin of the Institute of Historical Research*, XV (1937–1938), pp. 42–44; C. Perkins's article on "Electioneering in Eighteenth century England" in *Quarterly Journal of the University of North Dakota*, XIII (1923), pp. 103–124; Professor S. H. Nulle's "Duke of Newcastle and the Election of 1727" in *Journal of Modern History*, IX (1937), pp. 1–22; R. J. Robson, *The Oxfordshire Election of 1754* (Oxford, 1949), and Eric G. Forrester, *Northamptonshire County Elections and Electioneering, 1695–1832* (Oxford, 1941), all reach some conclusions of general interest. The essay by Betty Kemp, "The Stewardship of the Chiltern Hundreds" in *Essays Presented to Sir Lewis Namier* (London, 1956), is partly concerned with the eighteenth century.

On political groups, parties and 'interests', there is K. G. Feiling, *The Second Tory Party, 1714–1832* (London, 1938). Unfortunately there is no such work on the Whigs, and one must fall back on the antiquated and unsatisfactory *History of Party* by G. W. Cooke (3 vols., London, 1836–1837). There is an article by G. H. Guttridge on "The Whig Opposition in England during the American Revolution" in *Journal of Modern History*, VI (1934), pp. 1–13, an introduction to the same author's *English Whiggism and the American Revolution* (Berkeley, 1942). Some light is thrown on the various groups in opposition to Lord North by Ian R. Christie's "The Marquis of Rockingham and Lord North's offer of a coalition, June–July, 1780", *English Historical Review*, LXIX (1954), pp. 388–407. Sir Lewis Namier analyses the role of the independent country gentleman in "Monarchy and the Party System" and "Country Gentlemen in Parliament, 1750–1785", both in *Personalities and Powers* (London, 1955). On merchant interests there is Lucy Sutherland, "The City of London in Eighteenth Century Politics" in *Essays Presented to Sir Lewis Namier* (London, 1956). Works on the East and West Indian interests are included in the appropriate section of the bibliography for the Colonies. There is an interesting study of a 'non-party' civil servant in politics by I. R. Christie, "The Political allegiance of John Robinson, 1770–1784" in *Bulletin of the Institute of Historical Research*, XXIX (1956), pp. 108–122.

On the origins of the movement for parliamentary reform, G. S. Veitch, *The Genesis of Parliamentary Reform* (London, 1913), is still the best general account. H. Butterfield's *George III, Lord North and the People* (London, 1949) and the same author's "Yorkshire Association and the Crisis of 1779–80", *Transactions of the Royal Historical Society*, 4th Series, XXIX (1947), pp. 69–91, are authoritative on the events of 1779–1780. Gwen Whale discussed "The Influence of the Industrial Revolution on the Demand for Parliamentary Reform 1760–90" in *ibid.*, V (1922), pp. 101–131. D. S. Reid, "An Analysis of British Parliamentary Opinion" [*circa* 1782], in *Journal of Modern History*, XVIII (1946), pp. 202–221, deals with the relations of M.P.s to their constituencies, local groups and political parties, but requires to be corrected by M. Dorothy George's paper on "Fox's Martyrs: the General Election of 1784" in *Transactions of the Royal Historical Society*, 4th Series, XXI (1939), pp. 133–168. The effect of the Whig measures of 'economical reform' have been studied by Betty Kemp, "Crewe's Act", in *English Historical Review*, LXVIII (1953), pp. 258–263, and by Ian R. Christie, "Economical Reform and 'The Influence of the Crown', 1780", in *Cambridge Historical Journal*, XII (1956), pp. 144–154. S. Maccoby, *English Radicalism, 1762–1785* (London, 1955), analyses the changes in public opinion, especially as it is reflected in contemporary newspapers. Recent lives of the most famous radical politician of the period, John Wilkes, are by O. A. Sherrard, *Life of John Wilkes* (London, 1930), and R. W. Postgate, *That Devil Wilkes* (London, 1939), but H. Bleackley, *Life of John Wilkes* (London, 1917), is still the best. G. Nobbe, *The North Briton* (New York, 1939), and Sir W. P. Treloar, *Wilkes and the City* (London, 1917), are useful monographs on special aspects of Wilkes's career.

A. SUMMONS, DURATION AND COMPOSITION

28. Proclamation summoning the first Parliament of George I, 15 January 1715

(*Journals of the House of Commons*, XVIII, p. 14.)

This Proclamation is a piece of Whig election propaganda.

By the KING.

A PROCLAMATION

For Calling a new Parliament.

GEORGE R.

It having pleased Almighty GOD, by most remarkable Steps of his Providence, to bring Us in Safety to the Crown of this Kingdom, notwithstanding the Designs of evil Men, who shewed themselves disaffected to Our Succession, and who have since, with the utmost Degree of Malice, misrepresented Our firm Resolution, and uniform Endeavours, to preserve and defend Our most excellent Constitution both in Church and State; and attempted, by many false Suggestions, to render Us suspected to Our People; We cannot omit, on this Occasion, of First summoning our Parliament of *Great Britain* (in Justice to Ourselves, and that the Miscarriages of others may not be imputed to Us, at a Time when false Impressions may do the greatest and irrecoverable Hurt before they can be cleared up), to signify to Our whole Kingdom, That We were very much concerned, on Our Accession to the Crown, to find the publick Affairs of Our Kingdoms under the greatest Difficulties, as well in respect of Our Trade, and the Interruption of Our Navigation, as of the great Debts of the Nation, which We were surprized to observe, had been very much increased since the Conclusion of the last War: We do not, therefore, doubt, that if the ensuing Elections shall be made by Our loving Subjects with that Safety and Freedom which, by Law, they are intitled to, and We are firmly resolved to maintain to them, they will send up to Parliament the fittest Persons to redress the present Disorders, and to provide for the Peace and Happiness of Our Kingdoms, and the Ease of Our People for the future; and therein will have a particular Regard to such as shewed a Firmness to the Protestant Succession when it was most in Danger: We have, therefore, found it necessary, as well for the Causes aforesaid, as for other weighty Considerations concerning Us and Our Kingdoms, to call a new Parliament; and We do accordingly declare, That, with the Advice of Our Privy Council, We have this Day given Order to Our Chancellor of *Great Britain*, to issue out Writs, in due Form, for the Calling a new Parliament; which Writs are to bear *Teste* on *Monday* the Seventeenth Day of this instant *January*, and to be returnable on *Thursday* the Seventeenth Day of *March* next following.

Given at our Court at *St. James*'s, the Fifteenth Day of *January* 1714,[1] in the First Year of Our Reign.

GOD save the KING.

[1] 1715 New Style.

29. The Septennial Act, 1716

(*Statutes at Large*, XIII, p. 282, 1 Geo. I, Stat. 2, cap. 38.)

Under the Triennial Act a general election was due in 1718. In view of the disturbed state of the country after the 1715 Rising, this was considered unwise.

An act for enlarging the time of continuance of parliaments, appointed by an act made in the sixth year of the reign of King William *and Queen* Mary, *intituled,* An act for the frequent meeting and calling of parliaments.

WHEREAS *in and by an act of parliament made in the sixth year of the reign of their late Majesties King* William *and Queen* Mary *(of ever blessed memory) intituled* An act for the frequent meeting and calling of parliaments: *it was, among other things enacted, That from thence forth no parliament whatsoever, that should at any time then after be called, assembled or held, should have any continuance longer than for three years only at the farthest, to be accounted from the day on which by the writ of summons the said parliament should be appointed to meet: and whereas it has been found by experience, that the said clause hath proved very grievous and burthensome, by occasioning much greater and more continued expences in order to elections of members to serve in parliament, and more violent and lasting heats and animosities among the subjects of this realm, than were ever known before the said clause was enacted; and the said provision, if it should continue, may probably at this juncture, when a restless and popish faction are designing and endeavouring to renew the rebellion within this kingdom, and an invasion from abroad, be destructive to the peace and security of the government;* be it enacted by the King's most excellent majesty, by and with the advice and consent of the lords spiritual and temporal, and commons, in parliament assembled, and by the authority of the same, That this present parliament, and all parliaments that shall at any time hereafter be called, assembled or held, shall and may respectively have continuance for seven years, and no longer, to be accounted from the day on which by the writ of summons this present parliament hath been, or any future parliament shall be appointed to meet, unless this present, or any such parliament hereafter to be summoned, shall be sooner dissolved by his Majesty, his heirs or successors.

30. Arguments for and against the Septennial Act, 1716

(*Diary of Dudley Ryder, 1715–16*, ed. W. Matthews (1939), pp. 219–221.)

Dudley Ryder (1691–1756) later became successively Solicitor-General, Attorney-General and Lord Chief Justice of the King's Bench. He was a supporter of Walpole.

Sunday, April 15. [1716.] . . .

Cousin Robert Billio[1] was at the House of Lords last Saturday when the Bill for the repeal of the Triennial Act and establishing a septennial Parliament was devised in the House of Lords upon the second reading. The chief speakers on the side of the Whigs who were for the Bill were Lord Cowper, Parker, Islay, and on the side of the Tories against the Bill were Nottingham, Anglesey, Aylesford, Peterborough. Some of the chief arguments that were used against the Bill were that it was a taking away the liberty of the subject, destroying our constitution, giving too much prerogative to the crown; the people chose their present representatives only for three years and

[1] Reverend Robert Billio, later vicar of Lutterworth and Swepstone, Leicestershire.

they would be no longer the Parliament chose by the people if they are continued longer without their consent, and their mind and will ought always to be consulted in matters wherein the constitution is to be altered. That formerly by the ancient custom of the Kingdom the Parliament used to be chose every year and the Triennial Act gave the crown a greater prerogative in this matter than it had before by the custom of Parliaments, since he might now continue one three years. That this will alienate the mind of the people from the King and if they are now disposed to rebel will encourage that disposition. That we ought not for a present little necessity or conveniency alter the fundamental laws of the nation and give up the liberty of the subject, nor put a power into the hands of the crown which some future evil prince or counsellors or ministry may make use of to the quite destroying the liberty of the subject. That it is therefore a matter of the greatest consequence, at least to posterity, to have this Triennial Act kept in being, and besides the very same reasons that are now urged for making this a Septennial Parliament may be used at the end of the seven years to continue it still further, so that we don't see where this will end.

The arguments that were made use of chiefly for the Bill were: that the present necessity of our affairs require it; that there is a strong disposition in the people to rebel and the enemies of the government were waiting for such an opportunity as the choice of a new parliament would give them to rebel again when the nation is all in a ferment and disturbances and mobs and tumults were raised through the Kingdom and the people assembled; that the Triennial Act had been a great prejudice to the people as it had been the means and would be so still of keeping up the spirit of faction and disaffection in the nation, setting people's minds against one another and destroying all society and good neighbourhood; that it ruined the estates of country gentlemen who could not bear the expense of so frequent elections. And besides this present Triennial Act is but of twenty years' standing and therefore to take it away can be no breach of our constitution unless the making it had been one. That there had been a Triennial Parliament enacted in the year 1640 but was repealed presently after the accession of Charles II to the throne for much the same reason that it is to be repealed now, viz. it being just a rebellion in order to strengthen the hands of the prince against his rebel subjects. And as to the ancient custom of calling Parliaments every year that was for the convenience of the subjects themselves who wanted to be at their own houses in the country.

31. The Peerage Bill, 1719

(D. O. Dykes, *Source Book of Constitutional History from 1660* (1930), pp. 185–188; printed from the Records of the House of Lords.)

The Peerage Bill was introduced by the Stanhope Ministry. The Prince of Wales favoured the Walpole section of the Whigs, now in opposition, and the ministry feared for their majority in the House of Lords when he became king; hence their attempt to limit the number of new peerages which could be created. Walpole played the leading part in the Bill's defeat.

WHEREAS by the Articles for an Union of the two Kingdoms of England and Scotland, Sixteen of the Peers of Scotland at the time of the Union was declared to be the number to sit and vote in the House of Lords, the same being then considered as a just and necessary proportion of the said Peers of Scotland in the House of

Parliament, And whereas the number of the other Peers of Great Britain has been greatly increased since that time, and whereas the Election of the Peers of Scotland to sit and vote in the House of Lords is attended with many bad consequences, and is inconsistent with the true Constitution of Parliament, and whereas it will greatly conduce to the establishing and perpetuating the Freedom of Parliament, and thereby the Rights and Liberties of all his Majesty's Subjects, that the number of the House of Lords may not be arbitrarily increased in a manner detrimental and dangerous to the whole Legislature, To the end therefore that the Peers of Scotland by the enlarging the number of them who are to sit and vote in the House of Lords, and the establishing them on an Independent Foundation, more advantageous to the Peerage of Scotland, and to that part of Great Britain, as well as to the whole United Kingdom, may be in a great measure relieved from the difficulties and disadvantages they now lye under, and that the Freedom and Constitution of Parliament by his Majesty's most gracious indulgence to his People may now receive a lasting Sanction and Security, Be it enacted by the King's most excellent Majesty, by and with the advice and consent of the Lords Spiritual and Temporal, and Commons, in this present Parliament assembled, and by the Authority of the same, That instead of the Sixteen elective Peers of Scotland, there shall be Twenty five of the Peers of Scotland at the time of the Union, and of their Successors to their Peerage, who shall have hereditary Seats and Votes in Parliament on the part of the Peerage of Scotland, to be appointed and have continuance and succession and in case of failure supplyd out of the remaining Peers of Scotland, in manner as is herein after contained (that is to say) that such twenty five Peers of Scotland at the time of the Union or of their successors as his Majesty, his Heirs and Successors shall think fit, shall be nominated declared and appointed by his Majesty, his Heirs and Successors, before the next Session of Parliament, by one or more Instrument or Instruments under the great Seal of Great Britain, to have hereditary seats and votes in Parliament, and that Nine of the said twenty five so to be declared (not being of the number of the Sixteen Peers now sitting in Parliament on the part of the Peerage of Scotland) shall in such Instrument or some one or more of such Instruments (in case there be more than one) be appointed to have immediate right to such hereditary seats and votes in Parliament; and such Twenty five Peers so declared and appointed and their heirs and successors in their Peerage, according to the limitations hereinafter contained, shall have and enjoy hereditary seats and votes in Parliament according to such declaration or declarations, appointment or appointments, and all other such Rights and Privileges as the Sixteen elective Peers on the part of the Peerage of Scotland were intituled to by the said Act of Union, subject nevertheless to the qualifications required of other Lords of Parliament by the Laws in being. Provided nevertheless, and it is hereby Enacted and Declared that none of the Sixteen Peers the remaining part of the said Twenty five Peers so to be declared as aforesaid, over and above such Nine Peers to be appointed to have immediate right to seats in Parliament nor their Heirs, shall by virtue of such Declaration or appointment be admitted to have seat or vote in Parliament, till after the determination of this present Parliament, except such of them as are already of the number of the Sixteen Peers now sitting in Parliament on the part of the Peerage of Scotland and their

Heirs, And to the end that the extent and continuance of the hereditary seat and vote in Parliament, so to be declared and appointed to such Twenty five Peers of the Peers of Scotland, may be plainly and clearly ascertained, Be it enacted by the Authority aforesaid, That such Declaration or Appointment, and such hereditary right shall extend only to Males, succeeding to the Peerage of the Peer to whom such Declaration and Appointment is made, and that all Females and all persons claiming through such Females as shall hereafter succeed, or in case they should be living at the time of such claim would succeed to such Peerage, shall be excluded from the succession to the right of such hereditary seat in Parliament, and whenever any such Peerage shall descend or come to a female, or to the descendants of such female as aforesaid (in which case the hereditary seat in Parliament thereunto belonging shall be deemed and adjudged to cease and determine) or shall be utterly extinct then and in every such case the King's Majesty, his Heirs and Successors, shall make a new Declaration and Appointment, under the Great Seal of Great Britain, of some other Peer of Scotland at the time of the Union, or of his Successor in such Peerage to have hereditary Seat and Vote in Parliament, and so from time to time as often as any Peerage of Scotland having hereditary seat in Parliament shall be extinct, or the right of such Seat shall cease, and such Peers so from time to time Declared and Appointed to have hereditary seat and vote in Parliament, and their heirs and successors, shall hold and enjoy the same accordingly, subject to the restriction and limitation therein contained; That so long as there shall be a sufficient number remaining of the Peers of Scotland at the time of the Union or of their successors, there may instead of the Sixteen elective Peers, be Twenty five Peers of such Peers, and of their successors, who as Peers on the [part] of the Peerage of Scotland may have hereditary seats and votes in the Parliament of Great Britain in manner and forms aforesaid.

And be it further Enacted by the Authority aforesaid that the number of the Peers of Great Britain to sitt in Parliament on the part of England, shall not at any time hereafter be enlarged (without preceedent right) beyond the number of Six, over and above what they are at Present, but that as any of the Present Peerages or of the Six new Peerages in case they shall be created, or such of them as shall be created shall fail and be extinct, the King's Majesty, his Heirs and Successors, may supply such vacancies or failures by creating new Peers out of Commoners of Great Britain born within the Kingdoms of Great Britain or Ireland or any of the Dominions thereunto belonging or born of British parents, and in case such new Peerage shall afterward fail or be extinct, the King's Majesty, his Heirs and Successors, may Resupply such Vacancies in like manner, and so Toties Quoties as any such failure or vacancy shall happen. And be it further enacted by the Authority aforesaid That whensoever any Peer now living, who so far hath been called up the House of Lords by Writ, shall depart this life, That then and in such case the King's Majesty, his Heirs and Successors, may in the roome of every such Peer so dying, make and Create a new Peer out of such Commoners aforesaid, And on the failure or extinction of such new Peerage, may make and Create another Peer out of the persons so as aforesaid described, and so in like manner as often as any other such extinction or failure shall happen to be, And to the intent and purpose That in all future Grants the Dignity of the Peerage may be confined to the persons meriting and obtaining the same, and to the Issue male of their Bodys, Be it also Enacted by the authority aforesaid That from and after the . . . day of . . . in the year of our Lord . . . all Creation of Peers shall be by Letters Patent only, and not by Writ, and that no Peerage shall be thereafter granted by any Letters Patent for any longer or greater Estate than to the new respective Grantees and the heirs male of their bodys begotten And that all Grants of Peerages or Creation of Peers that shall be at any time thereafter made contrary to this Act shall be null and void to all intents and purposes Provided always nevertheless, that no thing in this Act contained shall be taken or construed to lay any restraint upon the King's Majesty, his Heirs or Successors, from advancing or promoting any Peer, having Vote and Seat in Parliament to any higher Rank or Degree of Dignity or Nobility, nor from creating or making any of the Princes of the Blood Peers of Great Britain or Lords of Parliament, and such Princes of the Blood so created shall not be esteemed to be any part of the number to which the Peers of Great Britain are by this Act restrained.

32. A Place Act, 1743

(*Statutes at Large*, XVIII, pp. 36–37, 15 Geo. II, cap. 22.)

One of several eighteenth-century Acts to exclude certain specific officer-holders from the House of Commons.

An act to exclude certain officers from being members of the house of commons.

For further limiting or reducing the number of officers capable of sitting in the house of commons, be it enacted by the King's most excellent majesty, by and with the advice and consent of the lords spiritual and temporal, and commons, in this present parliament assembled, and by the authority of the same, That from and after the dissolution, or other determination of this present parliament, no person who shall be commissioner of the revenue in *Ireland*, or commissioner of the navy or victualling offices, nor any deputies or clerks in any of the said offices, or in any of the several offices following; that is to say, The office of lord high treasurer, or the commissioners of the treasury, or of the auditor of the receipt of his Majesty's exchequer, or of the tellers of the exchequer, or of the chancellor of the exchequer, or of the lord high admiral, or of the commissioners of the admiralty, or of the paymasters of the army, or of the navy, or of his Majesty's principal secretaries of state, or of the commissioners of the salt, or of the commissioners of the stamps, or of the commissioners of appeals, or the commissioners of wine licences, or of the commissioners of hackney coaches, or of the commissioners of hawkers and pedlars, nor any persons having any office, civil or military, within the island of *Minorca*, or in *Gibraltar*, other than officers having commissions in any regiment there only, shall be capable of being elected, or of sitting or voting as a member of the house of commons, in any parliament which shall be hereafter summoned and holden.

II. And be it further enacted by the authority aforesaid, That if any person hereby disabled or declared to be incapable to sit or vote in any parliament hereafter to be holden, shall nevertheless be returned as a member to serve for any county, stewartry, city, borough, town, cinque port, or place in parliament, such election and return are hereby enacted and declared to be void to all intents and purposes whatsoever: and if any person disabled, and declared incapable by this act to be elected, shall, after the dissolution, or other determination of this present parliament, presume to sit or vote as a member of the house of commons in any parliament to be hereafter summoned, such person so sitting or voting, shall forfeit the sum of twenty pounds for every day in which he shall sit or vote in the said house of commons, to such person or persons who shall sue for the same in any of his Majesty's courts at *Westminster*; and the money so forfeited shall be recovered by the persons so suing, with full costs of suit, in any of the said courts, by action of debt, bill, plaint or information, in which no essoin, privilege, protection, or wager of law shall be allowed, and only one imparlance, and shall from thenceforth be incapable of taking, holding, or enjoying any office of honour or profit under his Majesty, his heirs or successors.

III. Provided always, and it is hereby enacted and declared by the authority aforesaid, That nothing in this act shall extend or be construed to extend, or relate to, or exclude the treasurer or comptroller of the navy, the secretaries of the treasury, the secretary to the chancellor of the exchequer, or secretaries of the admiralty, the under secretary to any of his Majesty's principal secretaries of state, or the deputy paymaster of the army, or to exclude any person having or holding any office or employment for life, or for so long as he shall behave himself well in his office; any thing herein contained to the contrary notwithstanding.

33. A Place Act (Members), 1782

(*Statutes at Large*, XXXIV, pp. 56–58, 22 Geo. III, cap. 45.)

Generally known as the Contractors Act. With No. 34, it was part of the Rockingham Ministry's programme of Economical Reform.

An act for restraining any person concerned in any contract, commission, or agreement, made for the public service, from being elected, or sitting and voting as a member of the house of commons.

FOR *further securing the freedom and independence of parliament*, be it enacted by the King's most excellent majesty, by and with the advice and consent of the lords spiritual and temporal, and commons, in this present parliament assembled, and by the authority of the same, That, from and after the end of this present session of parliament, any person who shall, directly or indirectly, himself, or by any person whatsoever in trust for him, or for his use or benefit, or on his account, undertake, execute, hold, or enjoy, in the whole or in part, any contract, agreement, or commission, made or entered into with, under, or from the commissioners of his Majesty's treasury, or of the navy or victualling office, or with the master general or board of ordnance, or with any one or more of such commissioners, or with any other person or persons whatsoever, for or on account of the publick service; or shall knowingly and willingly furnish or provide, in pursuance of any such agreement, contract, or commission, which he or they shall have made or entered into as aforesaid, any money to be remitted abroad, or any wares or merchandize to be used or employed in the service of the publick, shall be incapable of being elected, or of sitting or voting as a member of the house of commons, during the time that he shall execute, hold, or enjoy, any such contract, agreement, or commission, or any part or share thereof, or any benefit or emolument arising from the same.

II. And be it further enacted by the authority aforesaid, That if any person, being a member of the house of commons, shall directly or indirectly, himself, or by any other person whatsoever in trust for him, or for his use or benefit, or on his account, enter into, accept of, agree for, undertake, or execute, in the whole or in part, any such contract, agreement, or commission, as aforesaid; or if any person, being a member of the house of commons, and having already entered into any such contract, agreement, or commission, or part or share of any such contract, agreement, or commission, by himself, or by any other person whatsoever in trust for him, or for his use or benefit, or upon his account, shall, after the commencement of the next session of parliament, continue to hold, execute, or enjoy the same, or any part thereof, the seat of every such person in the house of commons shall be, and is hereby declared to be void. . . .

X. And be it enacted, That in every such contract, agreement, or commission, to be made, entered into, or accepted, as aforesaid, there shall be inserted an express condition, that no member of the house of commons be admitted to any share or part of such contract, agreement, or commission, or to any benefit to arise therefrom: and that in case any person or persons who hath or have entered into or accepted, or who shall enter into or accept, any such contract, agreement, or commission, shall admit any member or members of the house of commons to any part or share thereof, or to receive any benefit thereby, all and every such person and persons shall, for every such offence, forfeit and pay the sum of five hundred pounds;

XI. Provided also, and be it enacted, That no person shall be liable to any forfeiture or penalty inflicted by this act, unless a prosecution shall be commenced within twelve calendar months after such penalty or forfeiture shall be incurred.

34. A Place Act (Electors), 1782

(*Statutes at Large*, XXXIV, pp. 48–50, 22 Geo. III, cap. 41.)

This is generally known as Crewe's Act, after John Crewe, M.P. for Cheshire, who introduced it. It differs from Nos. 32 and 33 in that it disabled certain office-holders, not from sitting in the House of Commons, but from voting at elections. For a discussion of the practical effects of this Act, see Betty Kemp, "Crewe's Act", *Eng. Hist. Rev.*, LXVIII (1953), pp. 258–263.

An act for better securing the freedom of elections of members to serve in parliament, by disabling certain officers, employed in the collection or management of his Majesty's revenues, from giving their votes at such elections.

FOR *the better securing the freedom of elections of members to serve in parliament*, be it enacted by the King's most excellent majesty, by and with the advice and consent of the lords spiritual and temporal, and commons, in this present parliament assembled, and by the authority of the same, That, from and after the first day of *August*, one thousand seven hundred and eighty-two, no commissioner, collector, supervisor, gauger, or other officer or person whatsoever, concerned or employed in the charging, collecting, levying, or managing the duties of excise, or any branch or part thereof; nor any commissioner, collector, comptroller, searcher, or other officer or person whatsoever, concerned or employed in the charging, collecting, levying, or managing the customs, or any branch or part thereof; nor any commissioner, officer, or other person concerned or employed in collecting, receiving, or managing, any of the duties on stamped vellum, parchment, and paper, nor any person appointed by the commissioners for distributing of stamps; nor any commissioner, officer, or other person employed in collecting, levying, or managing, any of the duties on salt; nor any surveyor, collector, comptroller, inspector, officer, or other person employed in collecting, managing, or receiving, the duties on windows or houses; nor any postmaster, postmasters general, or his or their deputy or deputies, or any person employed by or under him or them in receiving, collecting, or managing, the revenue of the post-office, or any part thereof, nor any captain, master, or mate, of any ship, packet, or other vessel, employed by or under the postmaster or postmasters general in conveying the mail to and from foreign ports, shall be capable of giving his vote for the election of any knight of the shire, commissioner, citizen, burgess, or baron, to serve in parliament for any county, stewartry, city, borough, or cinque port, or for chusing any delegate in whom the right of electing members to serve in parliament, for that part of *Great Britain* called *Scotland*, is vested: and if any person, hereby made incapable of voting as aforesaid, shall nevertheless presume to give his vote, during the time he shall hold, or within twelve calendar months after he shall cease to hold or execute any of the offices aforesaid, contrary to the true intent and meaning of this act, such votes so given shall be held null and void to all intents and purposes whatsoever, and every person so offending shall forfeit the sum of one hundred pounds, one moiety thereof to the informer, and the other moiety thereof to be immediately paid into the hands of the treasurer of the county, riding, or division, within which such offence shall have been committed, in that part of *Great Britain* called *England*; and into the hands of the clerk of the justices of the peace of the counties or stewartries, in that part of *Great Britain* called *Scotland*, to be applied and disposed of to such purposes as the justices at the next general quarter session of the peace to be held for such county, stewartry, riding, or division, shall think fit; to be recovered by any person that shall sue for the same, by action of debt, bill, plaint, or information, in any of his Majesty's courts of record at *Westminster*, in which no essoin, protection, privilege, or wager of law, or more than one imparlance, shall be allowed; or by summary complaint before the court of session in *Scotland*; and the person convicted on any such suit shall thereby become disabled and incapable of ever bearing or executing any office or place of trust whatsoever under his Majesty, his heirs and successors.

II. Provided always, and be it enacted, That nothing in this act contained shall extend, or be construed to extend, to any person or persons for or by reason of his or their being a commissioner or commissioners of the land tax, or for or by reason of his or their acting by or under the appointment of such commissioners of the land tax, for the purpose of assessing, levying, collecting, receiving, or managing the land tax, or any other rates or duties already granted or imposed, or which shall hereafter be granted or imposed, by authority of parliament.

III. Provided also, and be it further enacted, That nothing in this act contained shall extend, or be construed to extend, to any office now held, or usually granted to be held, by letters patent for any estate of inheritance or freehold.

IV. Provided always, and be it enacted by the authority aforesaid, That nothing herein contained shall extend to any person who shall resign his office or employment on or before the said first day of *August*, one thousand seven hundred and eighty-two.

V. Provided also, and be it enacted, That no person shall be liable to any forfeiture or penalty by this act laid or imposed, unless prosecution be commenced within twelve months after such penalty or forfeiture shall be incurred.

B. PROCEEDINGS

35. Formal business in the House of Commons at the beginning of a session, 6 August 1714

(*Journals of the House of Commons*, XVIII, pp. 4–6.)

Queen Anne died on 1 August. Parliament met that day, but adjourned till 5 August, owing to the absence of the Speaker, Sir Thomas Hanmer, in Wales.

Veneris, 6° die Augusti;

Anno I° Georgii Regis, 1714.

PRAYERS.

Several other Members present took the Oaths, and made and subscribed the Declaration, and took and subscribed the Oath of Abjuration, according to the Act, of the Sixth Year of her late Majesty's Reign, intituled, An Act for the Security of her Majesty's Person and Government, and of the Succession of the Crown of *Great Britain* in the Protestant Line.

Ordered, That the Grand Committee for Religion do sit every *Tuesday* in the Afternoon, in the House.

Ordered, That the Grand Committee for Grievances do sit every *Thursday* in the Afternoon, in the House.

Ordered, That the Grand Committee for Courts of Justice do sit every *Saturday* in the Afternoon, in the House.

Ordered, That the Grand Committee for Trade do sit every *Friday* in the Afternoon, in the House.

Ordered, That a Committee of Privileges and Elections be appointed, [Names of Members follow]. And they are to meet upon *Monday* Sevennight at Five a Clock in the Afternoon, in the Speaker's Chamber; and to sit every *Wednesday*, *Friday*, and *Monday*, in the Afternoon: And all that come are to have Voices: And they are to take into Consideration all such Matters as shall or may come in Question touching Returns, Elections, and Privileges; and to proceed upon Double Returns in the first Place; and to report their Proceedings, with their Opinion therein, to the House, from time to time: And all Persons that will question any new Returns, are to do it in Fourteen Days next after such Returns shall be brought in: And the Committee are to have Power to send for Persons, Papers, and Records, for their Information: And all Members who are returned for Two or more Places, are to make their Elections, within Fourteen Days next, for which of the Places they will serve, provided there be no Question upon the Return for that Place: And if any thing shall come in Question touching the Return, Election, or Matter of Privilege, of any Member, he is to withdraw during the time the Matter is in Debate: And that all Members returned upon Double Returns do withdraw till their Returns are determined.

Resolved, That no Peer of this Realm hath any Right to give his Vote in the Election of any Member to serve in Parliament.

Resolved, That where the House shall judge any Petition, touching Elections, to be frivolous and vexatious, the House will order Satisfaction to be made to the Persons petitioned against.

Resolved, That in case it shall appear any Person hath procured himself to be elected, or returned, as a Member of this House, or endeavoured so to be, by bribery, or any other corrupt Practice, this House will proceed with the utmost Severity against such Person.

Resolved, That if it shall appear that any Person hath been tampering with any Witness, in respect of his Evidence to be given to this House, or any Committee thereof; or directly, or indirectly, hath endeavoured to deter or hinder any Person from appearing, or giving Evidence; the same is declared to be a high Crime and Misdemeanour; and this House will proceed with the utmost Severity against such Offender.

Resolved, That if it shall appear, that any Person hath given false Evidence, in any Case, before the House, or any Committee thereof, this House will proceed with the utmost Severity against such Offender.

Resolved, That it is a high Infringement of the Liberties and Privileges of the Commons of *Great Britain*, for any Lord of Parliament, or any Lord Lieutenant of any County, to concern themselves in the Elections of Members to serve for the Commons in Parliament.

Ordered, That the Serjeant at Arms attending this House do, from time to time, take into his Custody any Stranger, or Strangers, that he shall see, or be informed of, to be in the House, or Gallery, while the House, or any Committee of the whole House, is sitting.

Ordered, That the Back-door of the Speaker's Chamber be locked up every Morning at the Sitting of the House, and the Key delivered to the Clerk, to be locked up by him; and that he do not presume to deliver the same to any Person whatsoever, without Order of the House: And that the Serjeant at Arms attending this House do take care to clear the Speaker's Chamber every Day, before the Door is locked up.

Ordered, That no Member of this House do presume to bring any Stranger, or Strangers, into the House, or Gallery thereof, while the House is sitting.

Ordered, That the Constables and other Officers of *Middlesex* and *Westminster* do take care, That, from Nine of the Clock in the Morning to Three in the Afternoon, during this Session of Parliament, the Passages through the Streets, between *Temple bar* and *Westminster-hall*, be kept free and open; and that no Obstruction be made by Cars, Drays, Carts, or otherwise, to hinder the Passage of the Members to and from this House: And that the Serjeant at Arms attending this House do give Notice of this Order to the Officers aforesaid.

Ordered, That the Constables in Waiting do take care, there be no Gaming, or other Disorders, in *Westminster-hall*, or Passages leading to the House, during the Sitting of Parliament; and that there be no Annoyance by Chairmen, Footmen, or otherwise, therein, or thereabouts.

Ordered, That the said Orders be sent to the High-Bailiff of *Westminster*: And that he do see the same put in Execution.

Ordered, That the Serjeant at Arms attending this House do take care, that no Footmen be permitted to be within the Lobby of the House, or upon the Stairs leading thereto.

Mr. Secretary *Bromley* reported from the Committee appointed Yesterday to draw up an humble Address, to be presented to his Majesty, That they had drawn up an Address accordingly; which they had directed him to report to the House; and he read the same in his Place; and afterwards delivered it in at the Clerk's Table: Where it was read; and is as followeth; *viz.*

Most Gracious Sovereign,

We, your Majesty's most dutiful and loyal Subjects, the Commons of *Great Britain* in Parliament assembled, having a just Sense of the great Loss the Nation has sustained by the Death of our late Sovereign Lady Queen *Anne*, of blessed Memory, humbly crave Leave to condole with Your Majesty on this sad Occasion.

It would but aggravate our Sorrow, particularly to enumerate the Virtues of that pious and most excellent Princess: The Duty we owe to Your Majesty, and to our Country, oblige us to moderate our Grief, and heartily to congratulate Your Majesty's Accession to the Throne; whose Princely Virtues give us a certain Prospect of future Happiness, in the Security of our Religion, Laws, and Liberties; and engage us to assure Your Majesty, That we will, to our utmost, support Your undoubted Right to the Imperial Crown of this Realm, against the Pretender, and all other Persons whatsoever.

Your faithful Commons cannot but express their impatient Desire for Your Majesty's safe Arrival and Presence in *Great Britain.*

In the mean time, we humbly lay before Your Majesty the unanimous Resolution of this House, to maintain the publick Credit of the Nation; and effectually to make good all Funds which have been granted by Parliament, for the Security of any Money which has been, or shall be, advanced for the publick Service; and to endeavour, by every thing in our Power, to make Your Majesty's Reign happy and glorious.

The said Address being read a Second time;

Resolved, Nemine contradicente, That the House doth agree with the Committee in the said Address.

Ordered, That such Members of this House as are of his Majesty's most Honourable Privy-Council, do present the said Address to the Lords Justices, with the Desire of this House, That they do transmit the same to his Majesty with all convenient Speed.

The Order of the Day being read, for taking into Consideration the Lords Justices Speech to both Houses of Parliament;

The same was read again by Mr. Speaker.

And a Motion being made, That a Supply be granted to his Majesty, for the better Support of his Majesty's Household, and of the Honour and Dignity of the Crown;

Resolved, Nemine contradicente, That this House will, To-morrow Morning, resolve itself into a Committee of the whole House, to consider of that Motion.

And then the House adjourned till To-morrow Morning,

Nine of the Clock.

36. Horace Walpole's account of the different styles of oratory in the House of Commons, *circa* 1755

(Horace Walpole, *Memoirs of the Reign of King George the Second*, ed. Lord Holland, 2nd edition, II (1847), pp. 143–149.)

Horace Walpole was himself a member of the House of Commons from 1741 to 1767.

1755.

. . . After so long a dose of genius, there at once appeared[1] near thirty men, of whom one was undoubtedly a real orator, a few were most masterly, many very able, not one was a despicable speaker. Pitt, Fox, Murray, Hume Campbell, Charles Townshend, Lord George Sackville, Henry Conway, Legge, Sir George Lyttelton, Oswald, George Grenville, Lord Egmont, Nugent, Doddington, the Lord Advocate of Scotland, Lord Strange, Beckford, Elliot, Lord Barrington, Sir George Lee, Martin, Dr. Hay, Northey, Potter, Ellis, Lord Hilsborough, Lord Duplin, and Sir Francis Dashwood, these men, perhaps, in their several degrees, comprehended all the various powers of eloquence, art, reasoning, satire, learning, persuasion, wit, business, spirit, and plain common sense. Eloquence as an art was but little studied by Pitt: the beauties of language were a little, and but a little more cultivated, except by him and his family. Yet the grace and force of words were so natural to him, that when he avoided them, he almost lost all excellence. As set speeches were no longer in vogue, except on introductory or very solemn occasions, the pomp and artful resources of oratory were in a great measure banished; and the inconveniences attending long and unpremeditated discourses, must (as I have delivered them faithfully,) take off from, though they ought to add to, their merit. Let those who hear me extol, and at the same time find Mr. Pitt's orations not answer to my encomiums, reflect how bright his talents would shine, if we saw none of his, but which, like the productions of ancient great masters, had been prepared for his audience, and had been polished by himself for the admiration of ages! Similes, and quotations, and metaphors were fallen into disrepute, deservedly: even the parallels from old story, which, during the virulence against Sir Robert Walpole, had been so much encouraged, were exhausted and disregarded. It was not the same case with invectives; in that respect, eloquence was little more chastened. Debates, where no personalities broke out, engaged too little attention. Yet, upon the whole, the style that prevailed was plain, manly, argumentive; and the liberty of discussing all topics in a government so free, and the very newspapers and pamphlets that skimmed or expatiated on all those subjects, and which the most idle and most illiterate could not avoid perusing, gave an air of knowledge and information to the most trifling speakers.

I shall not enter into a detail of all the various talents of the men I have mentioned; the genius and characters of many of them have been marked already in different parts of this work. Most of them were more or less imperfect; I pretend to consider the whole number but as different shades of oratory. Northey saw clearly, but it was for a very little way. Lord Strange was the most absurd man that ever existed with a very clear head: his distinctions were seized as rapidly as others advance positions. Nugent's assertions would have made everybody angry, if they had not made everybody laugh; but he had a debonnaire jollity that pleased, and though a bombast

[1] In the House of Commons.

speaker, was rather extravagant from his vociferation, than from his arguments, which were often very solid. Dr. Hay's manner and voice resembled Lord Granville's, not his matter; Lord Granville was novelty itself; Dr. Hay seldom said anything new; his speeches were fair editions of the thoughts of other men: he should always have opened a Debate! Oswald overflowed with a torrent of sense and logic: Doddington was always searching for wit; and what was surprising, generally found it. Oswald hurried argument along with him; Doddington teased it to accompany him. Sir George Lyttelton and Legge were as opposite in their manners; the latter concise and pointed; the former, diffuse and majestic. Legge's speeches seemed the heads of chapters to Sir George Lyttelton's dissertations. Lord Duplin aimed at nothing but understanding business and explaining it. Sir Francis Dashwood, who loved to know, and who cultivated a roughness of speech, affected to know no more than what he had learned from an unadorned understanding. George Grenville and Hume Campbell were tragic speakers of very different kinds; the latter far the superior. Grenville's were tautologous lamentations; Campbell's bold reprehensions. Had they been engaged in a conspiracy, Grenville, like Brutus, would have struck and wept; Campbell would have rated him for weeping. The six other chief speakers may, from their ages and rank in the House, be properly thrown into two classes.

Mr. Conway soothed and persuaded; Lord George Sackville informed and convinced; Charles Townshend astonished; but was too severe to persuade, and too bold to convince. Conway seemed to speak only because he thought his opinion might be of service; Lord George because he knew that others misled, or were misled; Charles Townshend, neither caring whether himself or others were in the right, only spoke to show how well he could adorn a bad cause, or demolish a good one. It was frequent with him, as soon as he had done speaking, to run to the opposite side of the House, and laugh with those he had attacked, at those who had defended. One loved the first, one feared the second, one admired the last without the least mixture of esteem. Mr. Conway had a cold reserve, which seemed only to veil goodness: Lord George, with a frankness in his speech, had a mystery in his conduct, which was far from inviting. Charles Townshend had such openness in all his behaviour, that he seemed to think duplicity the simplest conduct: he made the innocence of others look like art. But what superiority does integrity contract, when even uniformity of acting could exalt so many men above the most conspicuous talents that appeared in so rhetorical an age! Mr. Townshend was perhaps the only man who had ever genius enough to preserve reason and argument in a torrent of epigrams, satire, and antithesis!

The other parliamentary chiefs were as variously distinguished by their abilities. Pitt, illustrious as he was in the House of Commons, would have shone still more in an assembly of inferior capacity: his talents for dazzling were exposed to whoever did not fear his sword and abuse, or could detect the weakness of his arguments. Fox was ready for both. Murray, who, at the beginning of the session, was awed by Pitt, finding himself supported by Fox, surmounted his fears, and convinced the House, and Pitt too, of his superior abilities: he grew most uneasy to the latter. Pitt could only attack, Murray only defend: Fox, the boldest and ablest champion, was still more formed to worry: but the keenness of his sabre was blunted by the difficulty with which he drew it from the scabbard; I mean, the hesitation and ungracefulness of his delivery took off from the force of his arguments. Murray, the brightest genius of the three, had too much and too little of the lawyer: he refined too much, and could wrangle too little for a popular assembly. Pitt's figure was commanding; Murray's engaging from a decent openness; Fox's dark and troubled—yet the latter was the only agreeable man: Pitt could not unbend; Murray in private was inelegant; Fox was cheerful, social, communicative. In conversation, none of them had wit; Murray never had: Fox had in his speeches from clearness of head and asperity of argument: Pitt's wit was genuine, not tortured into the service, like the quaintnesses of my Lord Chesterfield.

37. Carl Philipp Moritz's description of the House of Commons, 1782

(Carl Philipp Moritz, *Travels, chiefly on foot, through several parts of England in 1782*, ed. P. E. Matheson (1924), pp. 51–60.)

Moritz (1756–1793) was a friend of Goethe. His *Travels* were published in Berlin in 1783, and the first English translation in 1795. He was a shrewd observer. For his account of an election see No. 46.

London, 13th. June 1782.

Westminster Hall is an enormous gothic building, whose vaulted roof is supported not by pillars, but instead of these there are on each side, large unnatural heads of angels carved in wood, which seem to support the roof.

When you have passed through this long hall, you ascend a few steps at the end, and are led through a dark passage into the House of Commons; which, below, has a large double door; and above, there is a small stair-case, by which you go to the gallery, the place allotted for strangers.

The first time I went up this small stair-case and had reached the rails, I saw a very genteel man in black, standing there. I accosted him, without any introduction, and I asked him whether I might be allowed to go into the gallery. He told me, that I must be introduced by a member, or else I could not get admission there. Now as I had not the honour to be acquainted with a member, I was under the mortifying necessity of retreating, and again going down the stairs; as I did, much chagrined. And now, as I was sullenly marching back, I heard something said about a bottle of wine, which seemed to be addressed to me. I could not conceive what it could mean, till I got home, when my obliging landlady told me, I should have given the well-dressed man, half-a crown, or a couple of shillings, for a bottle of wine. Happy in this information, I went again the next day; when the same man, who before had sent me away, after I had given him only two shillings, very politely opened the door for me, and himself recommended me to a good seat in the gallery.

And thus I now, for the first time, saw the whole of the British nation assembled in its representatives, in rather a mean-looking building, that not a little resembles a chapel. The Speaker, an elderly man, with an enormous wig, with two knotted kind of tresses, or curls, behind, in a black cloak, his hat on his head, sat opposite to me on a lofty chair; which was not unlike a small pulpit, save only that in the front of this there was no reading desk. Before the Speaker's chair stands a table, which looks like an altar; and at this there sit two men, called clerks, dressed in black, with black cloaks.

On the table, by the side of the great parchment acts, lies an huge gilt sceptre, which is always taken away and placed in a conservatory under the table, as soon as ever the Speaker quits the chair; which he does as often as the house resolves itself into a committee. A committee means nothing more than that the house puts itself into a situation freely to discuss and debate any point of difficulty and moment, and, while it lasts, the Speaker partly lays aside his power as a legislator. As soon as this is over, some one tells the Speaker, that he may now again be seated! and immediately on the Speaker's being again in the chair the sceptre is also replaced on the table before him.

All round on the sides of the house under the gallery, are benches for the members, covered with green cloth, always one above the other, like our choirs in churches; in order that he who is speaking, may see over those who sit before him. The seats in the gallery are on the same plan. The Members of Parliament keep their hats on, but the spectators in the gallery are uncovered.

The Members of the House of Commons have nothing particular in their dress; they even come into the house in their great coats, and with boots and spurs. It is not at all uncommon to see a member lying stretched out on one of the benches, while others are debating. Some crack nuts, others eat oranges, or whatever else is in season. There is no end to their going in and out; and as often as any one wishes to go out, he places himself before the Speaker, and makes him his bow, as if, like a schoolboy, he asked his tutor's permission.

Those who speak, seem to deliver themselves with but little, perhaps not always with even a decorous, gravity. All that is necessary, is to stand up in your place, take off your hat, turn to the Speaker, (to whom all the speeches are addressed;) to hold your hat and stick in one hand, and with the other hand to make any such motions as you fancy necessary to accompany your speech.

If it happens, that a member rises, who is but a bad speaker; or if what he says is generally deemed not sufficiently interesting, so much noise is made, and such bursts of laughter are raised, that the member who is speaking can scarcely distinguish his own words. This must needs be a distressing situation; and it seems then to be particularly laughable, when the Speaker in his chair, like a tutor in a school, again and again endeavours to restore order, which he does by calling out *to order, to order*; apparently often without much attention being paid to it.

On the contrary, when a favourite member, and one who speaks well and to the purpose, rises, the most perfect silence reigns: and his friends and admirers, one after another, make their approbation known by calling out, *hear him*; which is often repeated by the whole house at once; and in this way so much noise is often made that the speaker is frequently interrupted by this same emphatic *hear him*. Notwithstanding which, this calling out is always regarded as a great encouragement; and I have often observed, that one who began with some diffidence, and even somewhat inauspiciously, has in the end been so animated, that he has spoken with a torrent of eloquence.

As all speeches are directed to the Speaker, all the members always preface their speeches with, *sir*; and he, on being thus addressed, generally moves his hat a little, but immediately puts it on again. This *sir* is often introduced in the course of their speeches, and serves to connect what is said: it seems also to stand the speaker in some stead, when any one's memory fails him, or he is otherwise at a loss for matter. For while he is saying, *sir*, and has thus obtained a little pause, he recollects what is to follow. Yet I have sometimes seen some members draw a kind of memorandum out of their pockets, like a candidate who is at a loss in his sermon: this is the only instance in which a member of the British parliament seems to read his speeches.

The first day that I was at the House of Commons, an English gentleman, who sat next to me in the gallery, very obligingly pointed out to me the principal members, such as *Fox*, *Burke*, *Rigby*, &c. all of whom I heard speak. The debate happened to be whether, besides being made a peer, any other specific reward should be bestowed by the nation on their gallant admiral Rodney. . . .

Fox was sitting to the right of the Speaker, not far from the table on which the gilt sceptre lay. He now took his place so near it that he could reach it with his hand, and, thus placed, he gave it many a violent and hearty thump, either to aid, or to shew, the energy with which he spoke. . . . It is impossible for me to describe, with what fire, and persuasive eloquence he spoke, and how the Speaker in the chair incessantly nodded approbation from beneath his solemn wig; and innumerable voices incessantly called out, *hear him*! *hear him*! and when there was the least sign that he intended to leave off speaking, they no less vociferously exclaimed, *go on*; and so he continued to speak in this manner for nearly two hours: Mr Rigby in reply, made a short but humourous speech, in which he mentioned of how little consequence the title *lord* and *lady* was without money to support it, and finished with the latin proverb "infelix paupertas,–quia ridiculos miseros fecit." After having first very judiciously observed, that previous enquiry should be made whether Admiral Rodney had made any rich prizes or captures; because, if that should be the case, he would not stand in need of further reward in money. I have since been almost every day at the parliament house, and prefer the entertainment I there meet with, to most other amusements.

Fox is still much beloved by the people, notwithstanding that they are, (and certainly with good reason) displeased at his being the cause of Admiral Rodney's recall; though even I have heard him again and again, almost extravagant in his encomiums on this noble admiral. This same celebrated Charles Fox is a short, fat, and gross man, with a swarthy complexion and dark; and in general he is badly dressed. There certainly is something Jewish in his looks. But upon the whole, he is not an ill made nor an ill looking man: and there are many strong marks of sagacity and fire in his eyes. I have frequently heard the people here say, that this same Mr. Fox is as cunning as a Fox. Burke is a well-made, tall, upright man, but looks elderly and broken. Rigby is excessively corpulent, and has a jolly rubicund face.

The little less than downright open abuse, and the many really rude things, which the members said to each other, struck me much. For example, when one has finished, another rises, and immediately taxes with absurdity all that *the right honourable gentleman*, (for with this title the members of the House of Commons always honour each other) had just advanced. It would indeed be contrary to the rules of the house, flatly to tell each other, that what they have spoken, is *false*, or even *foolish*: instead of this, they turn themselves, as usual, to the Speaker, and so, whilst their address is directed to him, they fancy they violate neither the rules of parliament, nor those of good breeding and decorum, whilst they utter the most cutting personal sarcasms against the member, or the measure they oppose.

It is quite laughable to see, as one sometimes does, one member speaking, and another accompanying the speech with his action. This I remarked more than once in a worthy old citizen, who was fearful of speaking himself, but when his neighbour spoke, he accompanied every energetic sentence with a suitable gesticulation, by which means, his whole body was sometimes in motion.

It often happens that the jett, or principal point, in the debate, is lost in these personal contests, and bickerings between each other. When they last so long as to become quite tedious and tiresome, and likely to do harm rather than good, the house takes upon itself to express its disapprobation; and then there arises a general cry, of *the question*! *the question*! This must sometimes be frequently repeated, as the contending members are both anxious to have the last word. At length however the question is put, and the votes taken; when the Speaker says: "those who are for the question, are to say *aye*, and those who are against it, *no*!" You then hear a confused cry of *aye* and *no*: but, at length, the Speaker says: "I think there are more *ayes* than *noes*; or more *noes* than *ayes*. The *ayes* have it; or the *noes* have it;" as the case may be. But all the spectators must then retire from the gallery: for then, and not till then, the voting really commences. And now the members call aloud to the gallery, *withdraw*! *withdraw*! On this the strangers withdraw; and are shut up in a small room, at the foot of the stairs, till the voting is over, when they are again permitted to take their places in the gallery. Here I could not help wondering at the impatience even of polished Englishmen; it is astonishing with what violence, and even rudeness, they push and jostle one another, as soon as the room door is again opened; eager to gain the first and best seats in the gallery. In this manner we, the strangers, have sometimes been sent away two or three times, in the course of one day, or rather evening; afterwards again permitted to return. Among these spectators are people of all ranks; and even, not infrequently, ladies. Two short-hand writers have sat sometimes not far distant from me, who, (though it is rather by stealth) endeavour to take down, the words of the speaker; and thus all that is very remarkable in what is said in parliament, may generally be read *in print*, the next day. The short-hand writers, whom I noticed, are supposed to be employed and paid by the editors of the different newspapers. There are it seems some few persons who are constant attendants on the parliament; and so they pay the door-keeper beforehand a guinea for a whole session. I have now and then seen some of the members bring their sons, whilst quite little boys, and carry them to their seats along with themselves.

A proposal was once made to erect a gallery in the house of peers also, for the accomodation of spectators. But this never was carried into effect. There appears to be much more politeness and more courteous behaviour in the members of the upper house. But he who wishes to observe mankind, and to contemplate the leading traits of the different characters, most strongly marked, will do well to attend frequently the lower, rather than the other house.

C. PRIVILEGE

38A–B. John Wilkes and *The North Briton*, 1763[1]

38A. Proceedings in the Court of Common Pleas, 3 May 1763

(*State Trials*, XIX, pp. 989–990.)

Wilkes was arrested on a general warrant after publication of No. 45 of *The North Briton* and then committed to the Tower. The Court of Common Pleas granted a writ of *habeas corpus*, and Wilkes's counsel argued (i) that the warrant was technically defective, and (ii) that as a member of Parliament Wilkes was privileged from arrest except for treason, felony or breach of the peace. Lord Chief Justice Pratt repelled the technical objections, but decided that a member of Parliament should not be arrested on a charge of seditious libel.

Pratt, L. C. J., said . . . The third matter insisted upon for Mr Wilkes, is that he is a member of parliament, (which has been admitted by the king's serjeants) and intitled to privilege to be free from arrests in all cases except treason, felony, and actual breach of the peace; and therefore ought to be discharged from imprisonment without bail; and we are all of opinion that he is intitled to that privilege, and must be discharged without bail. In the case of the Seven Bishops, the Court took notice of the privilege of parliament, and thought the bishops would have been intitled to it, if they had not judged them to have been guilty of a breach of the peace; for three of them, Wright, Holloway, and Allybone, deemed a seditious libel to be an actual breach of the peace, and therefore they were ousted of their privilege most unjustly. If Mr Wilkes had been described as a member of parliament in the return, we must have taken notice of the law of privilege of parliament, otherwise the members would be without remedy, where they are wrongfully arrested against the law of parliament. We are bound to take notice of their privileges as being part of the law of the land. 4 Inst. 25, says, the privilege of parliament holds unless it be in three cases, viz. treason, felony, and the peace: these are the words of Coke. In the trial of the Seven Bishops, the word 'peace' in this case of privilege is explained to mean where surety of the peace is required. Privilege of parliament holds in informations for the king, unless in the cases before excepted. . . . We are all of opinion that a libel is not a breach of the peace. It tends to the breach of the peace, and that is the utmost, . . . But that which only tends to the breach of the peace cannot be a breach of the peace. Suppose a libel be a breach of the peace, yet I think it cannot exclude privilege; because I cannot find that a libeller is bound to find surety of the peace, in any book whatever, nor ever was, in any case, except one, viz. the case of the Seven Bishops, where three judges said, that surety of the peace was required in the case of a libel. Judge Powell, the only honest man of the four judges, dissented; and I am bold to be of his opinion, and to say, that case is not law. But it shews the miserable condition of the state at that time. Upon the whole, it is absurd to require surety of the peace or bail in the case of a libeller, and therefore Mr Wilkes must be discharged from his imprisonment.

[1] See also No. 65A–B.

38B. Proceedings in the House of Commons, November 1763

(*Journals of the House of Commons*, XXIX, pp. 667–668, 675.)

Wilkes's arrest had taken place during the recess.

[15 November 1763]

Mr. Chancellor of the Exchequer informed the House, that he was commanded by the King to acquaint the House, that His Majesty having received Information that *John Wilkes* Esquire, a Member of this House, was the Author of a most seditious and dangerous Libel, published since the last Session of Parliament; He had caused the said *John Wilkes* Esquire to be apprehended, and secured, in order to his being tried for the same by due Course of Law: And Mr. *Wilkes* having been discharged out of Custody by the Court of *Common Pleas*, upon Account of his Privilege as a Member of this House; and having, when called upon by the legal Process of the Court of *King's Bench*, stood out, and declined to appear, and answer to an Information which has since been exhibited against him by His Majesty's Attorney General for the same Offence: In this Situation, His Majesty being desirous to shew all possible Attention to the Privileges of the House of Commons, in every Instance wherein they can be supposed to be concerned; and at the same Time thinking it of the utmost Importance not to suffer the Public Justice of the Kingdom to be eluded, has chosen to direct the said Libel, and also Copies of the Examinations upon which Mr. *Wilkes* was apprehended and secured, to be laid before this House for their Consideration: And Mr. Chancellor of the Exchequer delivered the said Papers in at the Table.

Resolved, Nemine contradicente, That an humble Address be presented to His Majesty, to return His Majesty the Thanks of this House for His most gracious Message, and for the tender Regard therein expressed for the Privileges of this House; and to assure His Majesty that this House will forthwith take into their most serious Consideration, the very important Matter communicated by His Majesty's Message. . . .

[24 November 1763]

Then the Question being put, That Privilege of Parliament does not extend to the Case of writing and publishing seditious Libels, nor ought to be allowed to obstruct the ordinary Course of the Laws, in the speedy and effectual Prosecution of so heinous and dangerous an Offence;

The House divided.

The Yeas went forth.

Tellers for the Yeas,	Mr. *Morton*, Mr. *Oswald*:	258.
Tellers for the Noes,	Mr. *Onslow*, Mr. *Hussey*.	133.

So it was resolved in the Affirmative.

The House was moved, that the Resolutions of the House, of the 15th Day of this Instant *November*, relating to the Paper, intituled "The *North Briton* N° 45," might be read.

And the same were read accordingly; and are as followeth; *viz.*

"*Resolved*, That the Paper, intituled the *North Briton*, N° 45, is a false, scandalous, and seditious Libel, containing Expressions of the most unexampled Insolence and Contumely towards His Majesty, the grossest Aspersions upon both Houses of Parliament, and the most audacious Defiance of the Authority of the whole Legislature; and most manifestly tending to alienate the Affections of the People from His Majesty, to withdraw them from their Obedience to the Laws of the Realm, and to excite them to traitorous Insurrections against His Majesty's Government."

"*Resolved*, That the said Paper be burnt by the Hands of the common Hangman."

39A–B. John Wilkes and the Middlesex Election, 1769

39A. Proceedings in the House of Commons, February–May 1769

(*Journals of the House of Commons*, XXXII, pp. 178–179, 228–229, 386–387, 447, 451.)

The following extracts show the action of the Commons in three stages: 3 February, the expulsion of Wilkes after his first election; 17 February, the resolution, after his second election, that his expulsion rendered him incapable of being elected; 15 and 29 April and 8 May, the decision, after his third election, that his opponent, Colonel Luttrell, ought to have been, and therefore was elected, and the reaffirming of this decision after hearing a petition from the Middlesex freeholders against it. All these resolutions were expunged from the *Journals* on 3 May 1782.

[3 February 1769]

And a Motion being made, and the Question being put, That *John Wilkes*, Esquire, a Member of this House, who hath at the Bar of this House, confessed himself the Author and Publisher of what this House has resolved to be an insolent, scandalous, and seditious Libel; and who has been convicted in the Court of King's Bench, of having printed and published a seditious Libel, and Three obscene and impious Libels; and, by the Judgment of the said Court, has been sentenced to undergo Twenty-two Months Imprisonment, and is now in Execution under the said Judgment; be expelled this House;

The House divided.

The Yeas went forth

Tellers for the Yeas { Lord Frederick Campbell, Mr Stevens; } 219

Tellers for the Noes, { Lord John Cavendish, Mr Montagu, } 137

So it was resolved in the Affirmative.

Ordered, That Mr Speaker do issue his Warrant to the Clerk of the Crown, to make out a new Writ for the Electing of a Knight of the Shire to serve in this present Parliament for the County of *Middlesex*, in the room of *John Wilkes*, Esquire, expelled this House. . . .

[17 February 1769]

Ordered, That the Deputy Clerk of the Crown do attend this House immediately, with the Return to the Writ for electing a Knight of the Shire to serve in this present

Parliament for the County of *Middlesex*, in the room of *John Wilkes*, Esquire, expelled this House.

And the Deputy Clerk of the Crown attending, according to Order;

The said Writ and Return were read.

A Motion was made, and the Question being proposed, That *John Wilkes*, Esquire, having been, in this Session of Parliament, expelled this House, was, and is, incapable of being elected a Member to serve in this present Parliament;

The House was moved, That the Entry in the Journal of the House, of the 6th Day of *March*, 1711, in relation to the Proceedings of the House, upon the Return of a Burgess to serve in Parliament for the Borough of *King's Lynn* in the County of *Norfolk*, in the room of *Robert Walpole*, Esquire, expelled the House, might be read.

And the same was read accordingly.

The House was also moved, that the Resolution of the House, of *Friday* the 3rd Day of this Instant *February*, relating to the Expulsion of *John Wilkes*, Esquire, then a Member of this House, might be read.

And the same being read accordingly;

An Amendment was proposed to be made to the Question, by inserting after the Word "House" these Words, "for having been the Author and Publisher of what this House hath resolved to be an insolent, scandalous, and seditious Libel; and for having been convicted in the Court of King's Bench, of having printed and published a seditious Libel, and Three obscene and impious Libels; and having, by the Judgment of the said Court, been sentenced to undergo Twenty-two months Imprisonment, and being in Execution under the said Judgment."

And the Question being put, That those Words be there inserted;

The House divided . . . [102–228.]

So it passed in the Negative.

Then the Main Question being put, That *John Wilkes*, Esquire, having been, in this Session of Parliament, expelled this House, was, and is, incapable of being elected a Member to serve in this present Parliament;

The House divided. . . . [235–89.]

So it was resolved in the Affirmative.

A Motion being made, That the late Election of a Knight of the Shire to serve in this present Parliament for the County of *Middlesex*, is a void Election;

A Member in his Place, informed the House, that he was present at the last Election of a Knight of the Shire to serve in this present Parliament for the said County; that there was no other Candidate than the said Mr. *Wilkes*; that there was no Poll demanded for any other Person, nor any Kind of Opposition to the Election of the said Mr. *Wilkes*.

Resolved, That the late Election of a Knight of the Shire to serve in this present Parliament for the County of *Middlesex*, is a void Election.

Ordered, That Mr. Speaker do issue his Warrant to the Clerk of the Crown, to make out a new Writ for the Electing of a Knight of the Shire to serve in this present Parliament for the County of *Middlesex*, in the room of *John Wilkes*, Esquire, who is adjudged incapable of being elected a Member to serve in this present Parliament, and whose Election for the said County has been declared void. . . .

[15 April 1769]

The Orders of the Day, for taking into Consideration the Poll taken at the last Election of a Knight of the Shire to serve in this present Parliament for the County of *Middlesex*; and for the Attendance of the Sheriffs of the said County; being read;

And the Sheriffs of the said County attending according to Order; they were called in; and, at the Bar, produced the original Poll Books.

And then they were directed to withdraw.

And the Paper produced Yesterday by the said Sheriffs, containing the Numbers of Votes for each Candidate upon the Poll, was read. . . .

Then the Question being put, That *Henry Lawes Luttrell*, Esquire, ought to have been returned a Knight of the Shire to serve in this present Parliament for the County of *Middlesex*;

The House divided.

The Yeas went forth.

Tellers for the Yeas, { Mr. *Onslow*, Mr. *Edmondstone*: } 197.

Tellers for the Noes, { Mr. *Thomas Townshend*, Junior, Mr. *Montagu*. } 143.

So it was resolved in the Affirmative.

Ordered, That the Deputy Clerk of the Crown do amend the Return for the County of *Middlesex*, by rasing out the Name of *John Wilkes*, Esquire, and inserting the Name of *Henry Lawes Luttrell*, Esquire, instead thereof.

And the Deputy Clerk of the Crown, attending according to Order, amended the said Return accordingly.

Ordered, That Leave be given to petition this House, touching the Election of *Henry Lawes Luttrell*, Esquire, within Fourteen Days next.

Ordered, That the Sheriffs of the County of *Middlesex* be again called in; and that the Poll Books be re-delivered to them.

They were accordingly called in, to the Bar; and the said Poll Books were re-delivered to them accordingly.

And then they were again directed to withdraw. . . .

[29 April 1769]

A Petition of the Freeholders of the County of *Middlesex*, was presented to the House, and read; Setting forth, That the Petitioners being informed by the Votes of the House, that the Return for the said County hath been amended by raising out the Name of *John Wilkes*, Esquire, and inserting the Name of *Henry Lawes Luttrell*, Esquire, instead thereof, and that Leave was given to petition this House, . . . and representing to the House, that the said *Henry Lawes Luttrell* had not the Majority of legal Votes at the said Election, nor did the Majority of the Freeholders, when they voted for *John Wilkes*, Esquire, mean thereby to throw away their Votes, or to waive their Right of Representation, nor would they by any Means have chosen to be represented by the said *Henry Lawes Luttrell*, Esquire; the Petitioners therefore apprehend he cannot sit as the Representative of the said County in Parliament, without manifest Infringement of the Rights and Privileges of the Freeholders thereof: . . . *Ordered* That the Matter of the said Petition, so far as the same relates to the Election of *Henry Lawes Luttrell*, Esquire, be heard at the Bar of this House upon Monday Sevennight, the 8th Day of *May* next. . . .

[8 May 1769]

The House proceeded to the Hearing of the Matter of the Petition of the Freeholders of the County of *Middlesex*.

And the Counsel were called in.

And the said Petition was read. . . .

And the Counsel for the Petitioners were heard; and having proposed to produce Evidence, to shew that the Numbers upon the Poll were for Mr. *Wilkes* 1143, and for Mr. *Luttrell* 296;

The same was admitted by the Counsel for the Sitting Member. . . .

And a Motion being made, and the Question being put, That *Henry Lawes Luttrell*, Esquire, is duly elected a Knight of the Shire to serve in this present Parliament for the County of *Middlesex*;

The House divided. [221–152]. . . .

So it was resolved in the Affirmative.

39B. Proceedings in the House of Lords, 2 February 1770

(*Journals of the House of Lords*, XXXII, pp. 417–418.)

The arguments of the dissentient peers are much the same as those put forward by Junius and other writers who attacked the government's behaviour over the Middlesex election.

[2 February 1770]

Then it was moved,[1] "To resolve, That the House of Commons, in the Exercise of its Judicature in Matters of Election, is bound to judge according to the Law of the Land, and the known and established Laws and Custom of Parliament, which is Part thereof."

It was resolved in the Negative.

DISSENTIENT

1st, Because the Resolution proposed was in our Judgment highly necessary to lay the Foundation of a Proceeding, which might tend to quiet the Minds of the People, by doing them Justice, at a Time when a Decision of the other House, which appears to us inconsistent with the Principles of the Constitution, and irreconcileable to the Law of the Land, has spread so universal an Alarm, and produced so general a Discontent, throughout the Kingdom.

2ndly, Because, although we do not deny that the Determination on the Right to a Seat in the House of Commons is competent to the Jurisdiction of that House

[1] By Lord Rockingham.

alone, yet when to this it is added, that whatever they, in the Exercise of that Jurisdiction, think fit to declare to be Law, is therefore to be so considered, because there lies no Appeal, we conceive ourselves called upon to give that Proposition the strongest Negative; for, if admitted, the Law of the Land (by which all Courts of Judicature, without Exception, are equally bound to proceed) is at once overturned, and resolved into the Will and Pleasure of a Majority of One House of Parliament, who, in assuming it, assume a Power to over-rule at Pleasure the fundamental Right of Election, which the Constitution has placed in other Hands, those of their Constituents: and if ever this pretended Power should come to be exercised to the full Extent of the Principle, the House will be no longer a Representative of the People, but a separate Body, altogether independent of them, self-existing and self-elected.

3rdly, Because, when we are told that Expulsion implies Incapacity; and the Proof insisted upon is, that the People have acquiesced in the Principle, by not re-electing Persons who have been expelled; we equally deny the Position as false, and reject the Proof offered, as in no Way supporting the Position to which it is applied; we are sure the Doctrine is not to be found in any Statute or Law-Book, nor in the Journals of the House of Commons, neither is it consonant with any just or known Analogy of Law; and as not re-electing would, at most, but infer a Supposition of the Electors Approbation of the Grounds of the Expulsion, and by no Means their Acquiescence in the Conclusion of an implied Incapacity; so, were there not One Instance of a Re-election after Expulsion but Mr *Woolaston's,*[1] that alone demonstrates that neither did the Constituents admit, nor the House of Commons maintain, Incapacity to be the Consequence of Expulsion; even the Case of Mr *Walpole*[2] shews, by the first Re-election, the Sense of the People, that Expulsion did not infer Incapacity; and that Precedent too, (which is the only One of an Incapacity), produced as it was under the Influence of Party Violence in the latter Days of Queen *Anne*, in so far as it relates to the Introduction of a Candidate having a Minority of Votes, decides expressly against the Proceedings of the House of Commons, in the late *Middlesex* Election.

4thly, Because as the Constitution hath been once already destroyed by the Assumption and Exercise of the very Power which is now claimed, the Day may come again when Freedom of Speech may be criminal in that House, and every Member who shall have Virtue enough to withstand the Usurpations of the Time, and assert the Rights of the People, will for that Offence be expelled, by a factious and corrupt Majority, and by that Expulsion rendered incapable of serving the Public: in which Case the Electors will find themselves reduced to the miserable Alternative of giving up altogether their Right of Election, or of choosing only such as are Enemies of their Country, and will be passive at least, if not active, in subverting the Constitution.

5thly, Because, although it has been objected in the Debate, that it is unusual and irregular in either House of Parliament to examine into the judicial Proceedings of the other, whose Decisions, as they cannot be drawn into Question by Appeal, are, it is said, to be submitted to without Examination of the Principles of them elsewhere; we conceive the Argument goes directly to establish the exploded Doctrine of Passive

[1] Expelled 20 February 1699 because he was a receiver of taxes.
[2] Expelled for corruption, 17 January 1712.

Obedience and Non-resistance, which, as applied to the Acts of any Branch of the Supreme Power, we hold to be equally dangerous: and though it is generally true, that neither House ought lightly and wantonly to interpose, even an Opinion, upon Matters which the Constitution hath entrusted to the Jurisdiction of the other, we conceive it to be no less true, that where, under Colour of a judicial Proceeding, either House arrogates to itself the Powers of the whole Legislature, and makes the Law which it professes to declare, the other not only may, but ought to assert its own Right and those of the People: That this House has done so in former Instances, particularly in the famous Case of *Ashby* and *White*, in which the First Resolution of the Lords declares, "That neither House of Parliament hath any Power, by any Vote or Declaration, to create to themselves any new Privilege that is not warranted by the known Laws and Custom of Parliament;" we ought to interfere at this Time, the rather as our Silence on so important and alarming an Occasion, might be interpretated into an Approbation of the Measure, and be a Means of losing that Confidence of the People, which is so essential to the Public Welfare that this House, the hereditary Guardians of their Rights, should at all Times endeavour to maintain.

6thly, Because, upon the Whole, we deem the Power which the House of Commons have assumed to themselves, of creating an Incapacity, unknown to the Law, and thereby depriving, in Effect, all the Electors of *Great Britain* of their valuable Right of Free Election, confirmed to them by so many solemn Statutes, a flagrant Usurpation, as highly repugnant to every essential Principle of the Constitution as the Claim of Ship-money by King *Charles* the First, or that of suspending and dispensing Power by King *James* the Second; this being, indeed, in our Opinion, a suspending and dispensing Power assumed and exercised by the House of Commons against the ancient and fundamental Liberties of the Kingdom.

[Signatures of 42 Peers.]

40. Speeches by Sir William Windham and William Pulteney on the reporting of debates, 13 April 1738

(*Parl. Hist.*, x, pp. 800–801, 802–804, 806–808, 811–812.)

These two speeches illustrate two different views about the public's wish to know more about proceedings in the House of Commons. Both speakers were leading members of the opposition to Walpole's government.

[13 April 1738]

. . . the *Speaker* informed the House, that it was with some concern he saw a practice prevailing, which a little reflected upon the dignity of that House: what he meant was the inserting an Account of their Proceedings in the printed News Papers, by which means the Proceedings of the House were liable to very great misrepresentations. That he had in his hands a printed News Paper, which contained his Majesty's Answer to their late Address, before the same had been reported from the Chair, the only way of communicating it to the public. That he thought it his duty to inform the House of these practices, the rather because he had observed them of late to have run into very great abuses; and therefore he hoped that gentlemen would propose some method of stopping it. . . .

Sir *William Windham* spoke next:

Sir: No gentleman can be more jealous and tender than I have always been of the rights and privileges of this House, nor more ready to concur with any measure for putting a stop to any abuses which may affect either of them. But at the same time, Sir, I own, I think we ought to be very cautious how we form a Resolution upon this head; and yet I think it is absolutely necessary that some question should be formed. I say, Sir, we ought to be very cautious in what manner we form a Resolution; for it is a question so nearly connected with the Liberty of the Press, that it will require a great deal of tenderness to form a Resolution which may preserve gentlemen from having their sense misrepresented to the public, and at the same time guard against all encroachments upon the Liberty of the Press. On the other hand, Sir, I am sensible that there is a necessity of putting a stop to this practice of printing, what are called the Speeches of this House, because I know that gentlemen's words in this House have been mistaken and misrepresented: I do not know, Sir, but I have some reason of complaint myself upon that head. I have, indeed, seen many speeches of gentlemen in this House that were fairly and accurately taken; and no gentleman, when that is the case, ought to be ashamed that the world should know every word he speaks in this House: for my own part, I never shall, for I hope never to act or speak in this House, any thing that I shall be ashamed to own to all the world. But of late, Sir, I have seen such monstrous mistakes in some gentlemen's speeches, as they have been printed in our news-papers, that it is no wonder if gentlemen think it high time to have a stop put to such a practice.

Yet still, Sir, there are two considerations, which I own weigh very much with me upon this occasion. That this House has a right to prohibit the publication of any of its proceedings during the time we are sitting, is past all doubt, and there is no question, but that, by the Resolutions that now stand upon our Votes, and are renewed every session, the printers of the papers you have in your hand are liable to the censure of this House. But I am not at all so clear as to the right we may have of preventing any of our proceedings from being printed during our recess; at least, Sir, I am pretty sure that people without doors are strongly possessed with that notion, and therefore I should be against our inflicting any censure at present, for what is past of that kind. If gentlemen are of opinion, which I do own I am not, that we have a power to prevent any account of our Proceedings and Debates from being communicated to the public, even during our recess, then, as this affair has been mentioned, they will no doubt think it very proper to come to a Resolution against that practice, and to punish it with a very severe penalty; but, if we have no such power, Sir, I own I do not see how you can form any Resolution upon this head, that will not be liable to very great censure.

The other consideration, that weighs very much, Sir, with me upon this occasion, is the prejudice which the public will think they sustain, by being deprived of all knowledge of what passes in this House, otherwise than by the printed Votes, which are very lame and imperfect, for satisfying their curiosity of knowing in what manner their representatives act within doors. They have been long used to be indulged in this, and they may possibly think it a hardship to be deprived of it now. Nay, Sir,

I must go farther: I do not know but they may have a right to know somewhat more of the proceedings of this House than what appears upon your Votes; and if I were sure that the sentiments of gentlemen were not misrepresented, I should be against our coming to any Resolution that could deprive them of a knowledge that is so necessary for their being able to judge of the merits of their representatives within doors. If gentlemen, however, are of opinion that they can frame a Resolution, which will put a stop to all impositions, and yet leave the public some room for having just information of what passes within these walls, I shall be extremely glad to give it my concurrence. But I am absolutely against our stretching our power farther than it will go consistently with the just rights of Parliament; such stretches rather weaken than give any strength to the constitution; and I am sure no gentleman will care to do what may not only look like our claiming powers unknown to our constitution, but what, in its consequences, may greatly affect the liberty of the press. If we shall extend this Resolution to the recess of parliament, all political writing, if the authors shall touch upon any thing that past in the preceding session, may be affected by it; for I do not know that any body would venture to publish any thing that might bring upon them the censure of this House.

In the mean time, Sir, I am as willing as any gentleman in this House, that a stop should be put to the practice you have taken notice of from the Chair. It has grown to such a pitch, that I remember some time ago there was a public dispute in the news-papers, betwixt two printers or booksellers of two pamphlets, which of them contained the true copy of a certain hon. gentleman's speech in this House. It is therefore high time for gentlemen to think of somewhat to be done for that purpose, and I make no doubt but that any Resolution this House shall think fit to come to, will put an effectual stop to it. . . .

Mr. *Pulteney* said:

Sir: I agree entirely with the gentleman who has already spoken, that it is absolutely necessary a stop should be put to the practice which has been so justly complained of: I think no appeals should be made to the public with regard to what is said in this assembly, and to print or publish the Speeches of gentlemen in this House, even though they were not misrepresented, looks very like making them accountable without doors for what they say within. Besides, Sir, we know very well that no man can be so guarded in his expressions, as to wish to see every thing he says in this House in print. I remember the time when this House was so jealous, so cautious of doing any thing that might look like an appeal to their constituents, that not even the Votes were printed without leave. A gentleman every day rose in his place, and desired the Chair to ask leave of the House, that their Votes for that day should be printed. How this custom came to be dropped I cannot so well account for, but I think it high time for us to prevent any farther encroachment upon our privileges; and I hope gentlemen will enter into a proper Resolution for the purpose.

But, though I am as much as any gentleman can be for putting a stop to this scandalous practice, I should be very tender of doing it in such a manner, as may either affect the Liberty of the Press, or make it seem as if we claim a privilege to which we have no title. An honourable gentleman near me was pleased to mention the powers which the other House had of calling printers to an account for printing their Protests. It is very true, Sir, they have such a power, and they have exercised it very lately; but we have no such power: they may punish a printer for printing any part of the Proceedings of their House, for twenty, thirty, or forty years back; but then, gentlemen are to consider that the House of Peers is a Court of Record, and as such, its rights and privileges never die. Whereas, this House never pretended to be a Court of Record; our privileges expire at the end of every parliament; and the next House of Commons is quite different from the last. As to the question whether we have a right to punish any printer, who shall publish our proceedings, or any part of them, during our recess, which I take to be the only question at present, it may be worthy consideration: for my own part, I am apt to think that we may; because our privileges as a House of Parliament exist during the whole continuance of parliament; and our not sitting never makes any violation of these privileges committed during a recess less liable to censure, the next time we meet as a House. However, Sir, as it has been long the practice to print some account of our proceedings during our recess, I am against punishing any person for what is past, because very possibly they did not know they were doing amiss; and if gentlemen think fit to enter into any Resolution for the time to come, I dare say it will be sufficient to deter all offenders in that way. But that Resolution, Sir, cannot affect any person, who shall print an account of your proceedings when this Parliament shall be dissolved. . . .

Then the Speaker having drawn up the question, it was unanimously resolved:

"That it is an high indignity to, and a notorious breach of the Privilege of, this House, for any News-Writer, in Letters or other Papers, (as Minutes, or under any other denomination) or for any printer or publisher of any printed News-Paper of any denomination, to presume to insert in the said Letters or Papers, or to give therein any Account of the Debates, or other Proceedings of this House, or any Committee thereof, as well during the Recess, as the sitting of Parliament; and that this House will proceed with the utmost severity against such offenders."

41A–B. The Case of Brass Crosby, 1771

In this case a city printer, taken into custody by order of the House of Commons for printing reports of its debates, was discharged by the Lord Mayor, who was also a member of Parliament. The House successfully asserted its right to imprison the Lord Mayor for breach of privilege, but took no further action against the printer. Attempts to prevent the reporting of debates were largely abandoned after 1771.

41A. Proceedings in the House of Commons, 27 March 1771

(*Journals of the House of Commons*, XXXIII, p. 289.)

Then the Question being put;

Resolved, That *Brass Crosby*, Esquire, Lord Mayor of the City of *London*, having discharged out of the Custody of One of the Messengers of this House, *J. Miller* (for whom the News-paper, intituled, "*The London Evening Post*, from *Thursday*, *March* 7, to *Saturday*, *March* 9, 1771," purports to be printed, and of which a Complaint was made in the House of Commons, on the 12th Day of this Instant

March, and who, for his Contempt, in not obeying the Order of this House, for his Attendance on this House upon *Thursday* the 14th Day of this Instant *March*, was ordered to be taken into the Custody of the Serjeant at Arms, or his Deputy, attending this House, and who, by virtue of the Speaker's Warrant, issued under the said Order, had been taken into the Custody of the said Messenger) and having signed a Warrant against the said Messenger, for having executed the said Warrant of the Speaker, and having held the said Messenger to Bail for the same, is guilty of a Breach of the Privilege of this House.

A Motion was made, and the Question being proposed, That *Brass Crosby*, Esquire, Lord Mayor of the City of *London*, and a Member of this House, be, for his said Offence, committed to the Custody of the Serjeant at Arms attending this House;

The Lord Mayor was heard in his Place.

And then he again withdrew.

Then an Amendment was proposed to be made to the Question, by leaving out the Words "Custody of the Serjeant at Arms attending this House," and inserting the Words "Tower of *London*" instead thereof.

And the Question being put, That the Words "Custody of the Serjeant at Arms attending this House," stand Part of the Question:

It passed in the Negative.

And the Question being put, That the Words "Tower of *London*" be inserted instead thereof;

It was resolved in the Affirmative.

Then the main Question, so amended, being put, That *Brass Crosby*, Esquire, Lord Mayor of the City of *London*, and a Member of this House, be, for his said Offence, committed to the Tower of *London*;

The House divided.

The Yeas went forth.

Tellers for the Yeas,	Lord *Burghersh*, Mr. *Gascoyne*:	202.
Tellers for the Noes,	Colonel *Jennings*, Mr. *Whitworth*:	39.

So it was resolved in the Affirmative.

Ordered, That Mr. Speaker do issue his Warrants accordingly.

41B. Lord Chief Justice de Grey's judgment in the Court of Common Pleas, 22 April 1771

(*State Trials*, XIX, pp. 1146–1152.)

If either myself or any of my brothers on the bench, had any doubt in this case, we should certainly have taken some time to consider, before we had given our opinions; but the case seems so very clear to us all, that we have no reason for delay.

The writ by which the lord mayor is now brought before us, is a Habeas Corpus at common law, for it is not signed *per statutum*. It is called a prerogative writ for the king; or a remedial writ: and this writ was properly advised by the counsel for his lordship because all the judges (including Holt) agreed, that such a writ as the present case required, is not within the statute. This is a writ by which the subject has a right of remedy to be discharged out of custody, if he hath been committed, and is detained contrary to law; therefore the Court must consider, whether the authority committing, is a legal authority. If the commitment is made by those who have authority to commit, this Court cannot discharge or bail the party committed; nor can this Court admit to bail, one charged or committed in execution. Whether the authority committing the lord mayor, is a legal authority or not, must be adjudged by the return of the writ now before the Court. The return states the commitment to be by the House of Commons, for a breach of privilege, which is also stated in the return; and this breach of privilege or contempt is, as the counsel has truly described it, threefold; discharging a printer in custody of a messenger by order of the House of Commons; signing a warrant for the commitment of the messenger, and holding him to bail; that is, treating a messenger of the House of Commons as acting criminally in the execution of the orders of that House. In order to see whether that House has authority to commit, see Co. 4 Inst. 23. Such an assembly must certainly have such authority; and it is legal, because necessary. Lord Coke says they have a judicial power; each member has a judicial seat in the House: he speaks of matters of judicature of the House of Commons, 4 Inst. 23. The House of Commons, without doubt, have power to commit persons examined at their bar touching elections, when they prevaricate or speak falsely; so they have for breaches of privilege; so they have in many other cases. . . . This power of committing must be inherent in the House of Commons, from the very nature of its institution, and therefore is part of the law of the land. They certainly always could commit in many cases. In matters of elections, they can commit sheriffs, mayors, officers, witnesses, &c. and it is now agreed that they can commit generally for all contempts. All contempts are either punishable in the Court contemned, or in some higher court. Now the parliament has no superior court; therefore the contempts against either house can only be punished by themselves. . . .

. . . The House of Commons therefore having an authority to commit, and that commitment being an execution, the question is, what can this court do? It can do nothing when a person is in execution by the judgment of a court having a competent jurisdiction: in such case, this court is not a court of appeal.

. . . How then can we do any thing in the present case, when the law by which the lord-mayor is committed, is different from the law by which he seeks to be relieved? He is committed by the law of parliament, and yet he would have redress from the common law. The law of parliament is only known to parliament-men, by experience in the House. Lord Coke says, every man looks for it, but few can find it. The House of Commons only know how to act within their own limits. We are not a court of appeal. We do not know certainly the jurisdiction of the House of Commons. We cannot judge of the laws and privileges of the House, because we have no knowledge of those laws and privileges. We cannot judge of the contempts thereof: we cannot judge of the punishment thereof.

I wish we had some code of the law of parliament; but till we have such a code, it is impossible we should be able to judge of it. Perhaps a contempt in the House of Commons, in the Chancery, in this court, and in the court of Durham, may be very different; therefore we cannot judge of it, but every court must be sole judge of its own contempts. Besides, as the court cannot go out of the return of this writ, how can we inquire into the truth of the fact, as to the nature of the contempt? We have no means of trying whether the lord-mayor did right or wrong. This court cannot summon a jury to try the matter. We cannot examine into the fact. Here are no parties in litigation before the court. We cannot call in any body. We cannot hear any witnesses, or depositions of witnesses. We cannot issue any process. We are even now hearing *ex parte*, and without any counsel on the contrary side. Again, if we could determine upon the contempts of any other court, so might the other courts of Westminster-hall; and what confusion would then ensue! none of us knowing the law by which persons are committed by the House of Commons. If three persons were committed for the same breach of privilege, and applied severally to different courts, one court perhaps would bail, another court discharge, a third re-commit.

. . . Courts of justice have no cognizance of the acts of the houses of parliament, because they belong 'ad aliud examen.' I have the most perfect satisfaction in my own mind in that determination. . . . I am therefore clearly and with full satisfaction of opinion, that the lord-mayor must be remanded.

D. ELECTIONS

42. Expenses of Sir Robert Kemp, Bart., in his son's election at Orford, 1730

(Brit. Mus. Add. MSS. 19, 185, ff. 99–103.)

Sir Robert Kemp of Ubbeston, Suffolk, was M.P. for Dunwich, 1700–1715, and for Suffolk, 1727–1735. His son Robert was elected for Orford at a by-election in February 1730, caused by the death of Dudley North.

(a)	A memorandum of charges in relation to the Election att Orford.			
	Paid a messenger who Mr Colman sent from Ipswich, to give me an account of Mr North's death,	0:	7:	6.
	Feb: the 23: 1729/30. Being the Election Day, Paid Bills for my son att Orford the sum off	[40:	19:	0.][1]
the 24: ditto	Given Ipswich musick		0:	5.
	Given Mr Devereux' Servts.	1:	5:	0.
	Given a poor man	0:	0:	2.
	Paid to Craggs and Skoulding att Orford	109:	5:	8.
	Spent besides on the account of the Orford Election	1:	13:	0.
	paid Sewell for carrying a letter to Mr Twiss in Beccles	0:	2:	6.
	[Endorsed] In all spent about the Orford Election	152:	6:	6.
		[153.	13.	3.]

(b)	Feb: the 14: 1729.			
	Skoldings Bill is 21 L: 0s: 4d:			
	Feb. the 23rd the Election Day,			
	His Bill is 36L 0: 1:			
	In all to Skoulding. 57. 0: 5.			
	Feb. the 15: 1729/30; Craggs Bill is	9:	12:	0.
	Feb. the 23rd Craggs Bill the Election day is	42:	13:	3.
	In all to Craggs	52:	5:	3.
		57:	0:	5.
	Both come to	109:	5:	8.

[1] Blank in MS., but see the son's separate account, (d) p. 183.

29
(c) March ye 4th 1730
Recd. then of Sir Robert Kemp by the hand of Mr William Clouthing. the sum of fifty & two pounds & five shillings being in full payment for Eatting & Liquor had at the Electing Mr Kemp at Orford.

Recd. by me
Sam^el Cragg.

March 4d 1729/30.
Recd. then of Sr Robt. Kemp the Sum of fifty & Seven pds: Two Shillings & five pence: for wine & Eating at the day of Election & befor. Being in full of all Demands.

£57: 2: 5. Recd. by me Wm Scolding.

(d) Money laid out by me[1]

	£	s	d
gave ye town clerk	03	03	0
gave men who carried ye chair	10	10	0
gave ye ringers	04	04	0
gave Mr Norton who wrote ye letters	05	05	0
gave Mr Spooner, Mr Devereux's gen:	02	02	0
gave ye housekeeper	01	01	0
gave ye servt 2 moidores who went for ye writ	02	14	0
gave a livery servt	00	10	6
gave 3 maid servts	01	11	6
gave Mr Stephens	05	05	0
gave Ipswich musick	01	17	6
gave ye Bramford musick	01	01	6
pd. for being sworn before I went into ye House	01	12	6
pd. for being sworn in ye house	00	02	0
In all	£40	19	0

43. Extracts from the Diary of George Bubb Dodington, 1753–1754

(*Diary of the late George Bubb Dodington, . . . 1749 to . . . 1761*, ed. Henry Penruddock Wyndham (1784), pp. 247–249, 256, 273–275, 285–288.)

Dodington (1691–1762) had influence at Weymouth and at Bridgewater. The following extracts from his diary illustrate his electioneering activities at the general election of 1754.

Aug: 11 [1753.] I was at Bridgewater, and with Mr Balch, canvassed near half the town. The people did not chuse to speak out, though very few declared they were engaged to Lord Egmont.[2]

[1] Robert Kemp, the son.
[2] John, second earl of Egmont (1711–1770), at this time a leading member of the opposition.

18. We returned home to Eastbury. The excessive badness of the roads and weather, with the nature of the business, made it much the most disagreeable journey, and the most fatiguing week I ever passed. All this trouble, vexation and expence, as well as that to come, flows from a set of low, worthless fellows, who finding they shall not be bribed without an opposition, have prevailed on Lord Egmont to lend his name, to whom they will give one vote, that they may be able to sell the other. And, notwithstanding, as things now appear, his Lordship has no chance of making his election. This he does not see, nor that the Tories (though partly for other reasons) make his greatest strength; so that he is setting up an interest, which, if it should succeed, he could never sit in quiet in that place. But though, I think, he has no chance at present, yet the uneasiness and expence will be the same to me, as if he was sure of success. . . .

Dec. 11 I saw the Duke of Newcastle, and convinced him, that my trouble and expence at Bridgewater, was only to keep out a man, who opposed those to whom I attached myself:[1] that my own seat was not concerned in it: that the maintaining the interest there was, to me, nothing, having nobody to bequeath it to. I then told him that, in these matters, those who would take money, I would pay, and not bring him a bill: those, that would not take, he must pay, and I recommended my two parsons of Bridgewater and Weymouth, Burroughs and Franklin: he entered into it very cordially, and assured me that they should have the first Crown livings that should be vacant in their parts, if we would look out and send him the first intelligence. . . .

21 Mar. [1754.] Went to the Duke of Newcastle's . . . to repeat my readiness to comply with the engagements I had taken with his brother,[2] which I understood to be with him, and supposed he would continue to approve: but that, what had happened, made it necessary to recapitulate them, though he knew them: that the engagements on my side were, to give him all the little interest I had, towards the electing the new Parliament–I did it in the county of Dorset, as far as they pleased to push it–I engaged also, specifically, to chuse two members for Weymouth, which he desired might be a son of the Duke of Devonshire, and Mr Ellis, of the Admiralty–I supposed he would confirm that nomination, but that was nothing to me: I was to chuse two, of his nomination, which now was fallen to *him*; so he might name whom he pleased: that I was also engaged to exclude Lord Egmont from Bridgewater, if I could, of which I should give him a farther account, when I knew his pleasure upon this first part: because there might be mention made of that transaction in the closet, and there were some particularities attending it, that 'twas probable, he might not be acquainted with.[3] He assured me of his friendship and affection, in a solemn and dejected manner; knew his brother was sincere to me; knew all our engagements, and looked upon himself as party to them; would do every thing in his power to comply with them, and agreed to his brother's nomination of Lord J. Cavendish and Ellis, and hoped they would be agreeable to me. . . .

[1] *i.e.* the Pelhams.

[2] Henry Pelham had died on 6 March.

[3] Pelham had promised to try and overcome the king's personal objection to Dodington's admission to office, in return for Dodington's help at the election.

April 11. Dr Sharpe and I set out from Eastbury at four o'clock in the morning, for Bridgewater, where, as I expected, I found things very disagreeably framed.

12. Lord Egmont came, with trumpets, noise, &c.

13. He and we walked the town: we found nothing unexpected, as far as we went.

14.–16. Spent in the infamous and disagreeable compliance with the low habits of venal wretches.

17. Came on the election, which I lost by the injustice of the Returning Officer. The numbers were for Lord Egmont 119, for Mr Balch 114, for me 105. Of my good votes, 15 were rejected: 8 bad votes for Lord Egmont were received.

18. Left Bridgewater–for ever. Arrived at Eastbury in the evening.

24. Arrived at Hammersmith in the evening.

26. I went to the Duke of Newcastle's. Received with much seeming affection: thanks for Weymouth, where I had succeeded: sorrow for Bridgewater, where I had not. I told him, that I would give him a detail of that whole transaction, in as clear and short a manner as was possible, if he was then at leisure to receive it: but if not, and he thought it worth mentioning to the King, I would only give him the heads of it, and he might say, that I was to acquaint him with the proofs of those heads, at a meeting which he had appointed on purpose. Accordingly, I began by telling him, that I had done all that was in the power of money and labour, and shewed him two bills for money remitted thither, before I went down, one of 1000l. one of 500l. besides all the money then in my steward's hands, so that the election would cost me about 2,500l. In the next place, if this election stood, the borough was for ever in Tory hands: that all this was occasioned by want of proper support from the Court, and from the behaviour of the servants of the Crown. Upon Mr Pelham's death, seeing the multitude of promotions in which no notice was taken of me, and Lord Poulett acting openly against me, with all his might; seeing no check given to him, or encouragement to me, they so strongly concluded the Government to be indifferent, that five out of the Custom-house officers gave single votes for Lord Egmont. The next head was–that, in spite of all, I had a fair majority of legal votes, for that the Mayor had admitted eight bad votes for Lord Egmont, and refused fifteen good ones for me; so that it was entirely in their own hands, to retrieve the borough, and get rid of a troublesome opponent, if they pleased: that if the King required this piece of service, it was to be done, and the borough put into Whig hands, and under his influence, without any stretch of power; for the cause was so clear and indisputable, that, instead of wanting their power to support it, nothing but their power could withstand it: that, if it was expected, I would lend my name, and my assistance here and in the country, to rescue the borough, and deliver it into such hands as the King should approve of; but that I, on my own account, would have nothing more to do with it. . . .

44A–B. Election petitions, March 1738

44A. Petitions on a double return at Windsor, 14 March 1738

(*Journals of the House of Commons*, XXIII, pp. 88–89.)

This and No. 44B illustrate both election methods and the partisan spirit in which election petitions were dealt with by the House of Commons.

[14 March 1737/8]

A Petition of the Right honourable *Vere Beauclerk* Esquire, commonly called Lord *Vere Beauclerk*, was presented to the House and read; setting forth, That the Petitioner and *Richard Oldfield* Esquire stood Candidates at the last Election of Burgesses to serve in this present Parliament for the Borough of *New Windsor*, in the County of *Berks*: That the said *Richard Oldfield*, and his Agents, by Threats and Menaces, and other illegal and unwarrantable Practices, procured several Persons to vote for him, some of whom had no Right so to do: And that Mr *Buller*, the Mayor of the said Town, who is the Returning Officer, hath returned the said *Richard Oldfield*, together with the Petitioner, notwithstanding the Petitioner had a Majority of legal Votes, and was duly elected: And therefore praying the House to take the Premises into Consideration, and that the Petitioner may have such Relief therein, as to the House shall seem meet.

And also:

A Petition of *Richard Oldfield* Esquire was presented to the House and read; setting forth, That a new Writ having issued for electing a Burgess to serve in this present Parliament for the Borough of *New Windsor*, in the County of *Berks*, in the room of the Right honourable *Vere Beauclerk* Esquire, commonly called Lord *Vere Beauclerk*,[1] the said Election came on the 7th of March 1737, when the said Lord *Vere Beauclerk* and the Petitioner stood Candidates: That there polled for the Petitioner and Lord *Vere Beauclerk* 133 Votes each, which made an Equality; whereupon the Mayor hath made a Return of the said Lord *Vere Beauclerk* as [well as] the Petitioner: That the said Mayor admitted several Persons to poll for the said Lord *Vere Beauclerk*, who had no Right to vote at the said Election, and refused the Votes of many Persons who had a Right to vote, and offered to poll for the Petitioner; and many other indirect and unwarrantable Practices were made use of, before and at the said Election, in order to procure the said Lord *Vere Beauclerk* to be elected and returned a Burgess for the said Borough; And therefore praying the House to take the Premises into Consideration, and to give the Petitioner such Relief therein as to the House shall seem meet.

Ordered, That the Matter of the said Double Return, and the Matters of the said Petitions, be heard at the Bar of this House upon *Thursday* Sevennight.

[1] Who had recently been made a Commissioner of the Admiralty, and therefore had to seek re-election.

44B. Sarah, duchess of Marlborough's account of the hearing of the Windsor election petition, March 1738

(*Private Correspondence of Sarah Duchess of Marlborough*, II (1838), pp. 225–229.)

This extract also illustrates the part often played by peers in the election of members of the House of Commons.

March 19, 1737–8. Disputed election at Windsor will be heard at the bar of the House on Thursday next; in which the Duke of Marlborough assisted a country gentleman with a very good estate. They tell me, it is the strongest election that ever came into that House. The opposer is my Lord Vere, Nell Gwyn's grandson,[1] and of the family of the idiots, who I dare say will carry it; because they will always vote as they are ordered by the minister, let him be ever so bad. Nothing illegal or wrong has been done on the Duke of Marlborough's side; for people out of power can neither turn any one in nor out. But on t'other side all manner of infamous practices were used. Notwithstanding which, the mayor was forced to return both candidates, the votes being equal. His Majesty was pleased to say publicly in the drawing room, when the account was given him of it, "But we have the returning officer." The members in constant pay will be assisted by some of the patriots, so it will only be a trouble to no purpose. One of the patriots, who is Mr. Grenville, my Lord Cobham's heir and nephew, has declared already, that he is extremely sorry he can't be on the right side, to which he wishes success: but he has married a relation of Lord Vere's wife. A poor soldier, whose arm was shot off under the Duke of Marlborough, and who had a pension from Chelsea College, was ordered to give his vote for Lord Vere, having a house at Windsor, and a right to do it, and told if he did not, his pension should be taken away. To which he answered, "I will venture starving rather than it shall be said, that I voted against the Duke of Marlborough's grandson, after having followed his grandfather so many hundred leagues." And accordingly he voted against Lord Vere. I don't know whether they have taken away his pension, but I hope they will, for I have sent him word, if they do take it away, I will settle the same upon him for his life.

March 27, 1738. The Windsor election ended last night. And after it was demonstrated, that the side the Duke of Marlborough was of had a clear majority all ways they could possibly turn it, without pretending to argue on Lord Vere's side, because they had nothing in the world to say, they put the question, and carried it, "That Lord Vere was legally chose by 240 to 160." There was nobody that shined so much in the debate as my Lord Polwarth, his brother, and Mr. Plumer. The two first I have heard some say are *too warm*; but I own I love those that are so, and never saw much good in those that are not. But if we had a thousand speakers, it had been the same thing. For the facts were so strongly proved on our side, as to be enough for anything but corruption, had nothing been said at all. One that is a very good observer, gave me an account, that he had time to examine the faces of the voters on Sir Robert's[2] side, and he said, some of them looked angry, others grieved, and others laughed. Nothing so detestable as the behaviour of some of the patriots. My Lord Cobham's heir, Mr. Grenville, said, he wished Mr. Oldfield might succeed, for it was right, but

[1] Lord Vere Beauclerk was a son of the first duke of St. Alban's, elder son of Charles II and Nell Gwyn.
[2] Sir Robert Walpole.

he had married Lady Vere's sister, and therefore must be for Lord Vere. It is impossible for anybody to believe, that my Lord Cobham could not have hindered his heir from giving a vote so shameful to his nephew and self, as he professes being such a patriot. Mr. Berkley had another reason for being on that side, for he is Lady Betty Germaine's[1] relation, and hopes to get some of her riches when she dies. My Lord Scarborough persuaded his brother, Sir William (Thomas) Sanderson, to vote contrary to his promise and his reason, for it was said, that his brother had desired him to do it because he lived so much with Lady Betty Germaine. My Lord Townshend writ out of the country, to command his son to be for Lord Vere, right or wrong, and he obeyed his father's commands, contrary to his promise and his known inclination. Two of the three admirals voted for Lord Vere, though they owned they had been wronged, by bringing him over their head. The third admiral, Steward, staid away. A gentleman who has the most profitable place in the Prince's family, voted for them or stayed away, I don't know which. And the reason for that I think was the best of any, that the St. Alban's family had voted in a cause of his, as bad as this of Lord Vere's; which I allow was a great obligation, but such a one as he never could have had from me. Another of the patriots, I don't remember his name, voted for Lord Vere, because he had been his school-fellow. And Mr. Compton, my Lord Wilmington's nephew, voted against the Marlborough interest, who had not been in the House, if the Duke of Marlborough and John Spencer had not chose him in Northamptonshire, which I hope they'll remember, if this country subsists so long as to have another election. My Lord Wilmington has been a great manager in this affair, and governed the Mayor of Windsor in all his proceedings. And the Duke of Dorset commanded one of his sons to break his word, which he did with a great deal of trouble. The Master of the Rolls sent me word he would be sure to attend the cause, if it was heard at the bar of the House, supposing then it would not be heard there; but when he found it was, he pretended to be sick. This strange woman (Lady Betty Germaine) has had a great influence over many, even upon Mr. Sandys, who would have been an useful man in the House of Commons, but could not be prevailed on to take any part in this affair. But it was too infamous for him to vote in such a cause for Lord Vere, and he sat silent all but his vote. And his — wife, and he too, are often at court. His Majesty declared publicly at his levee, before the election was decided, that Lord Vere should have the seat in Parliament, for Windsor was his borough.

45. The Grenville Act, 1770

(*Statutes at Large*, XXVIII, pp. 287–293, 10 Geo. III, cap. 16.)

This Act, introduced by George Grenville, was an attempt to bring about a more impartial consideration of election petitions. It was made permanent in 1774.

An act to regulate the trials of controverted elections, or returns of members to serve in parliament.

WHEREAS *the present mode of decision upon petitions, complaining of undue elections or returns of members to serve in parliament, frequently obstructs publick business; occasions much expence, trouble, and delay to the parties; is defective, for want of those sanctions and solemnities which are established by law in other trials; and is attended with*

[1] Widow of Sir John Germain. It was at one time thought that she might marry Lord Sidney Beauclerk, Lord Vere's brother.

many other inconveniences: for remedy thereof, be it enacted by the King's most excellent majesty, by and with the advice and consent of the lords spiritual and temporal, and commons, in this present parliament assembled, and by the authority of the same, That after the end of the present session of parliament, whenever a petition, complaining of an undue election or return of a member or members to serve in parliament, shall be presented to the house of commons, a day and hour shall by the said house be appointed for taking the same into consideration; and notice thereof in writing shall be forthwith given, by the speaker, to the petitioners and the sitting members, or their respective agents, accompanied with an order to them to attend the house, at the time appointed, by themselves, their counsel, or agents. . . .

IV. And be it further enacted, That the time appointed for taking such petition into consideration, and previous to the reading the order of the day for that purpose, the serjeant at arms shall be directed to go with the mace to the places adjacent, and require the immediate attendance of the members on the business of the house; and that after his return the house shall be counted, and if there be less than one hundred members present, the order for taking such petition into consideration shall be immediately adjourned to a particular hour on the following day (*Sunday* and *Christmas* day always excepted); and the house shall then adjourn to the said day; and the proceedings of all committees, subsequent to such notice from the said serjeant, shall be void: and, on the said following day, the house shall proceed in the same manner; and so, from day to day, till there be an attendance of one hundred members at the reading the order of the day, to take such petition into consideration.

V. And be it further enacted, That if after summoning the members, and counting the house as aforesaid, one hundred members shall be found to be present; the petitioners by themselves, their counsel or agents, and the counsel or agents of the sitting members, shall be ordered to attend at the bar; and then the door of the house shall be locked, and no member shall be suffered to enter into or depart from the house, until the petitioners, their counsel, or agents, and the counsel or agents for the sitting members, shall be directed to withdraw as herein after is mentioned: and when the door shall be locked as aforesaid, the order of the day shall be read, and the names of all the members of the house, written or printed on distinct pieces of parchment or paper, being all as near as may be of equal size, and rolled up in the same manner, shall be put in equal numbers into six boxes or glasses, to be placed on the table for that purpose, and shall there be shaken together; and then the clerk or clerk assistant attending the house shall publickly draw out of the said six boxes or glasses alternately the said pieces of parchment or paper, and deliver the same to the speaker, to be by him read to the house; and so shall continue to do, until forty-nine names of the members then present be drawn.

VI. Provided always, That if the name of any member who shall have given his vote at the election so complained of as aforesaid, or who shall be a petitioner complaining of an undue election or return, or against whose return a petition shall be then depending, or whose return shall not have been brought in fourteen days, shall be drawn; his name shall be set aside, with the names of those who are absent from the house.

VII. Provided also, That if the name of any member of sixty years of age or upwards be drawn, he shall be excused from serving on the select committee, to be appointed as herein after is mentioned, if he require it, and verify the cause of such requisition upon oath.

VIII. Provided also, That if the name of any member who has served in such select committee during the same session be drawn, he shall, if he requires it, be excused from serving again in any such select committee, unless the house shall, before the day appointed for taking the said petition into consideration, have resolved, that the number of members who have not served on such select committee, in the same session, is insufficient to fulfil the purposes of this act, respecting the choice of such select committee. . . .

XI. And be it further enacted, That instead of the members so set aside and excused, the names of other members shall be drawn; who may, in like manner, be set aside or excused, and others drawn to supply their places, until the whole number of forty-nine members, not liable to be so set aside or excused, shall be complete; and the petitioners or their agents shall then name one, and the sitting members, or their agents, another, from among the members then present, whose names shall not have been drawn, to be added to those who shall have been so chosen by lot. . . .

XIII. And be it further enacted, That as soon as the said forty-nine members shall have been so chosen by lot, and the two members to be added thereunto shall have been so nominated as aforesaid, the door of the house shall be opened, and the house may proceed upon any other business; and lists of the forty-nine members so chosen by lot shall then be given to the petitioners, their counsel, or agents, and the counsel or agents for the sitting members, who shall immediately withdraw, together with the clerk appointed to attend the said select committee; and the said petitioners and sitting members, their counsel or agents, beginning on the part of the petitioners, shall alternately strike off one of the said forty-nine members, until the said number shall be reduced to thirteen; and the said clerk, within one hour at farthest from the time of the parties withdrawing from the house, shall deliver in to the house the names of the thirteen members then remaining; and the said thirteen members, together with the two members nominated as aforesaid, shall be sworn at the table, well and truly to try the matter of the petition referred to them, and a true judgment to give according to the evidence; and shall be a select committee to try and determine the merits of the return or election appointed by the house to be that day taken into consideration; and the house shall order the said select committee to meet at a certain time to be fixed by the house, which time shall be within twenty-four hours of the appointment of the said select committee, unless a *Sunday* or *Christmas* day shall intervene; and the place of their meeting and sitting shall be some convenient room or place adjacent to the house of commons or court of requests, properly prepared for that purpose. . . .

XVIII. And be it further enacted, That the said select committee shall have power to send for persons, papers and records; and shall examine all the witnesses who come before them upon oath; and shall try the merits of the return, or election, or both; and shall determine, by a majority of voices of the said select committee, whether the petitioners or the sitting members, or either of them, be duly returned or elected, or whether the election be void; which determination shall be final between the parties to all intents and purposes: and the house, on being informed thereof by the chairman of the said select committee, shall order the same to be entered in their journals, and give the necessary directions for confirming or altering the return, or for the issuing a new writ for a new election, or for carrying the said determination into execution, as the case may require. . . .

XXV. And be it further enacted, That if the said select committee shall come to any resolution other than the determination above mentioned, they shall, if they think proper, report the same to the house for their opinion, at the same time that the chairman of the said select committee shall inform the house of such determination; and the house may confirm or disagree with such resolution, and make such orders thereon, as to them shall seem proper. . . .

XXVIII. Provided always, That no such determination as aforesaid shall be made, nor any question be proposed, unless thirteen members shall be present; and no member shall have a vote on such determination, or any other question or resolution, who has not attended during every sitting of the said select committee. . . .

XXX. And be it further enacted, That this act shall continue in force seven years, and till the end of the session of parliament next after the expiration of the said seven years, and no longer.

46. Carl Philipp Moritz's description of an election, 1782

(Carl Philipp Moritz, *Travels, chiefly on foot, through several parts of England in 1782*, ed. P. E. Matheson (1924), pp. 61–64.)

An account of the by-election at Westminster in 1782. For Moritz, see note to No. 37.

[*London*, 13*th June*, 1782.]

The cities of London and Westminster send, the one four, and the other two members to parliament. Mr Fox is one of the two members for Westminster; one seat was vacant; and that vacancy was now to be filled. And the same Sir Cecil Wray, whom Fox had before opposed to Lord Hood, was now publicly chosen. They tell me, that at these elections when there is a strong opposition-party, there is often bloody work; but this election was, in the electioneering phrase, an *hollow thing*, i.e. quite sure; as those who had voted for Admiral Hood now withdrew, without standing a poll; as being convinced beforehand, their chance to succeed was desperate.

The election was held in Covent-Garden, a large market-place, in the open air. There was a scaffold erected just before the door of a very handsome church, which also is called *St. Paul's*; but which however is not to be compared to the cathedral.

A temporary edifice, formed only of boards and wood nailed together, was erected on the occasion. It was called *the hustings*: and filled with benches; and at one end of it, where the benches ended, mats were laid; on which those, who spoke to the people, stood. In the area before the hustings, immense multitudes of people were assembled; of whom the greatest part seemed to be of the lowest order. To this tumultous crowd, however, the speakers often bowed very low, and always addressed them by the title of *gentlemen.* Sir Cecil Wray was obliged to step forward and promise these same *gentlemen,* with hand and heart, that he would faithfully fulfil his duties, as their representative. He also made an apology, because, on account of his journey and ill-health, he had not been able to wait on them, as became him, at their respective houses. The moment that he began to speak even this rude rabble became all as quiet as the raging sea after a storm; only every now and then rending the air with the parliamentary cry of *hear him! hear him!* and as soon as he had done speaking, they again vociferated a loud and universal huzza, every one at the same time waving his hat.

And now, being formally declared to have been legally chosen, he again bowed most profoundly, and returned thanks for the great honour done him: when a well-dressed man, whose name I could not learn, stepped forward, and in a well indited speech congratulated both the chosen and the chusers. "Upon my word," said a gruff carter, who stood near me, "that man speaks well."

Even little boys clambered up and hung on the rails and on the lamp-posts; and as if the speech had also been addressed to them, they too listened with the utmost attention: and they too testified their approbation of it, by joining lustily in the three cheers, and waving their hats.

All the enthusiasm of my earliest years, kindled by the patriotism of the illustrious heroes of Rome, Coriolanus, Julius Caesar, and Antony, were now revived in my mind: and though all I had just seen and heard, be, in fact, but the semblance of liberty, and that too tribunitial liberty, yet at that moment, I thought it charming, and it warmed my heart. Yes, depend on it, my friend, when you here see how in this happy country, the lowest and meanest member of society thus unequivocally testifies the interest which he takes in every thing of a public nature; when you see, how even women and children bear a part in the great concerns of their country; in short, how high and low, rich and poor, all concur in declaring their feelings and their convictions, that a carter, a common tar, or a scavenger, is still a man, nay, an Englishman; and as such has his rights and privileges defined and known as exactly and as well as his king, or as his king's minister–take my word for it, you will feel yourself very differently affected from what you are, when staring at our soldiers in their exercises at Berlin.

When Fox, who was among the voters, arrived at the beginning of the election, he too was received with an universal shout of joy. At length when it was nearly over, the people took it into their heads to hear him speak, and every one called out *Fox! Fox!* I know not why; but I seemed to catch some of the spirit of the place and time; and so I also bawled, *Fox! Fox!* and he was obliged to come forward and speak: for no other reason that I could find, but that the people wished to hear him speak. In this speech, he again confirmed, in the presence of the people, his former declaration in parliament, that he by no means had any influence as minister of state in this election, but only and merely as a private person.

When the whole was over, the rampant spirit of liberty, and the wild impatience of a genuine English mob were exhibited in perfection. In a very few minutes the whole scaffolding, benches, and chairs, and every thing else, was completely destroyed;

and the mat with which it had been covered torn into ten thousand long strips or pieces, or strings; with which they *encircled* or enclosed multitudes of people of all ranks. These they hurried along with them and every thing else that came in their way, as trophies of joy: and thus, in the midst of exultation and triumph, they paraded through many of the most populous streets of London.

E. POLITICAL PARTIES

47. An account of political parties at the accession of George I, 1714

(John, Lord Campbell, *Lives of the Lord Chancellors*, IV (1846), pp. 421–429. Appendix to Life of Lord Cowper.)

William, first Earl Cowper, (d. 1723), the author of the following document, was Lord Chancellor, 1707–1710 and 1714–1718.

An Impartial History of Parties.

May it please your Majesty,

It being probable that many of those who have had the honour of serving you as Lords Justices during your Majesty's absence, will think themselves obliged, on your Majesty's arrival in your kingdom, severally to offer their thoughts, concerning the first settlement of your government, as that upon which not only the security, but also the tranquillity and comfort of your Majesty's whole reign, will entirely depend, I humbly beg leave (not being sufficiently master of the French tongue to explain myself fully, by speaking on a matter of so great consequence) to offer to your Majesty's judgment, in this manner, the best information I can, together with a few thoughts on that important subject; which is done with an entire resignation to your wisdom, and a most cordial disinterested zeal for your Majesty's service.

Nothing can sooner conduce to your Majesty's entering on right measures, at this juncture, than the giving a true idea of the parties into which, to our great misfortune, your people are divided. When that is once done, none is so well able from thence to make proper inferences, and form the most useful rules of government, as your Majesty; whose wisdom, experience, application, and success in that particular, are known and admired by all Europe.

That part of your people which consists of Papists and nonjurors, who manifest their disaffection to your Majesty's government by denying to give those assurances which the laws require, are, in England, but few in proportion to the rest of your Majesty's subjects; but I choose to mention these first, because all that need be suggested concerning them is in a very narrow compass. There are several penal laws in force contrived to curb and restrain them as there is occasion; and accordingly, those laws have been used to be put in execution with more or less rigour, as they who are obnoxious to them have behaved themselves with more or less duty and submission to the government, and sometimes with respect to the usage the Protestants meet with in the countries of Roman Catholic princes or states; and there is no question but your Majesty will be advised to deal with them in the same manner.

The residue of your Majesty's subjects, who take the oaths, and give all the assurances the laws require, are, notwithstanding, divided into two parties with respect to the government.

These parties began to form themselves and give names to each other about the time the Bill of Exclusion was set on foot, in the reign of King Charles II., though some affect to carry their beginning so far back as the civil wars, which is part of the scandal one of them is pleased to fling upon the other, without the least ground of truth, since, to do them right, both are sincerely for the Monarchy of Great Britain and the Church of England (excepting as to the Church the Protestant Dissenters, who range themselves with those called Whigs, as the Papists do with those called Tories, almost in all state controversies whatsoever).

The Tories accuse the others of being inclined to set up a commonwealth, and the Whigs them of a design to introduce Popery, or at least to bring the Church of England nearer to that of Rome. Whereas, on one side, there are hardly ten in the whole kingdom that may be justly suspected of being for a commonwealth; and, on the other side, whenever the danger has been near and imminent, have shown themselves firm against Popery; and they among them who are projecting a union with the Gallican Church, are either Nonjurors or as few in number and as inconsiderable as the commonwealth men have been said to be on the other side. . . .

Your Majesty may be told, and it has been often said, that the only difference is about the places; but this is either a superficial judgment, or a desire to hinder the true causes from being discerned. For if that was true, then the struggle would only be between individuals, and not between two set parties of men, which can only be kept up by some diversity of opinion upon fundamentals, at least points of consequence; and experience shows that many who have no design on preferment either for themselves or friends, but live retired on their estates, are yet as hot or hotter than any in these distinctions: and therefore I take those before stated to be the true causes which divide them, and which I beg leave to recapitulate in a few words,–that as the Whigs always contended for the toleration of the Protestant Dissenters and exclusion of the Popish line from the Crown to be established by law, the Tories did always as earnestly and publicly oppose them till they were enacted. The former are rejoiced at their success in these great points, the latter more or less discontented to see their principles discountenanced, and those of their adversaries succeed. Both, therefore, keep and improve their strength as much as they can–the one to defend their acquisitions, the other to retake them and get rid of both the laws as soon as they safely can. Not that I would have it believed that many of the Tories are not perfectly against restoring the Pretender, by force at least, or that some few of them did not make it appear, by their actions the last year, they would not have concurred to the bringing him in even in a parliamentary way; but the true reason was, they believed their religion and liberties could not be secured if they should; and their consciences not accusing them of having done any thing towards the Protestant settlement, they were well contented to enjoy the security arising from the act of others, which, though very useful, had something of unjust in it.

I have sat continually in one or other House of Parliament now about twenty-four years, and observed with as much deligence and indifference as I could, the inclinations and motions of both parties, and I will venture to assure your Majesty as what I am very certain of, that the Whigs would venture all to support the Protestant succession in your Majesty's family; on the other hand, that many of the Tories would rejoice to see Pretender restored, as they call it, even by a French power, much more if by any safer means; that the best of them would hazard nothing to keep him out, though probably do nothing hazardous to bring him in; but that if ever he should declare himself a Protestant, with proper circumstances to make his conversion probable (as after the death of the French King and his mother, it is not unlikely he may do), they would greedily swallow the cheat, and endeavour by all possible means to put in practice again their old notions of divine, hereditary, and indefeazible right, by a restoration of the person in whom by their opinion that right is lodged. . . .

It is an old scandal now almost worn out, thrown out by their adversaries on the Whigs, that they are against the prerogative of the crown, which I should not have thought worth mentioning, but that 'tis generally believed to have made some impression on King William in the beginning of his reign, to the irrecoverable detriment of his affairs; but he afterwards found that the Tories, not liking the hand which held the prerogative, were more inclined to straighten it, and the Whigs for the contrary reason to support it. And this false suggestion will certainly have the less weight with your Majesty, when you shall be informed, as the truth is, that the only ground for it was, the Whigs being so zealous for setting aside the Popish line in favour of the Protestant, which the Tories thought an high violation of the rights of Monarchy, and of what they erroneously called the prerogative of the Crown, the descent of which they held to be unalterable by any power on earth, and thence took the liberty of branding all of a contrary opinion as Anti-monarchical, or enemies to the prerogative. But in all other respects the Whigs are as zealous to support the prerogative as the Tories can be, and rather more they are under a government founded on the Revolution.

Having thus stated to your Majesty the practices and dispositions of the parties, I shall only add, that 'tis not to be doubted but your Majesty's known goodness and experienced wisdom will necessarily incline you to such moderate counsels as will render you King of all your divided people. But I humbly conceive it not possible so to distribute your royal favours, but that one or other of the parties will appear to have a superior degree of trust reposed in them: and if such a perfect equality was possible to be observed, perhaps it would follow that an equal degree of power, tending at the same time different ways, would render the operations of the government slow and heavy, if not altogether impracticable.

It remains therefore, in my humble opinion, for your Majesty to determine which of these shall have the chief share in your Majesty's confidence, as most likely to support your title to the Crown with the greatest zeal and most untainted affection to it. For as to their power to do it, give me leave to assure your Majesty, on repeated experience, that the parties are so near an equality, and the generality of the world so much in love with the advantages a King of Great Britain has to bestow, without the least exceeding the bounds of law, that 'tis wholly in your Majesty's power, by showing your favour in due time (before the elections) to one or other of them, to give which of them you please a clear majority in all succeeding parliaments.

It is needless to suggest to your Majesty, but, for method's sake, it ought just to be touched upon, that whichsoever party shall have the lower degree of your Majesty's trust, it ought nevertheless to be used by those in power with very great tenderness and affection while obedient to your Majesty and the laws, and as a father would a child whom he dearly loves, though he does not totally approve, and, to be more particular, should, in my humble opinion, be admitted to a fair share of such places and employments of trust, according to their several qualifications, as are during the pleasure of the Crown, and not attended with the chief dependences. . . .

I have but one thing more humbly to represent to your Majesty, as the only, and, if I mistake not, a sure means to extinguish the being and the very name of party amongst us, that your Majesty would be pleased to use the utmost caution not to prefer any of those ecclesiastics whose known principles lead them to scruple the validity of a limitation of the right to the Crown by act of parliament. There is a sufficient number of the clergy of the Church of England, of the most learned and best livers, out of whom your Majesty may choose for all preferments that shall fall vacant, who are not the least tainted with those notions which, while they continue, will ever find matter for discontents and divisions in your Majesty's kingdoms. But when once it is discerned that, by a steady and uninterrupted administration, no man who is known to hold opinions inconsistent with the very foundation of your Majesty's government can get into any of the Crown preferments in the Church, they who find themselves troubled with these inconvenient scruples will soon apply their thoughts and studies in good earnest to satisfy themselves, and then others, of the weakness of those errors, which will afterwards, in a little time, be confined to a few melancholy Nonjurors, who are the less dangerous for being known; and when the clergy are brought to be of one mind as to your Majesty's title, all differences in opinion among the laity on that head will soon vanish. But that part of the clergy who have always violently contended against excluding the next successor, though a Papist, will never own themselves to have been in the wrong while they find they have a fair chance for the best of the Church preferments without disavowing those errors, otherwise than by taking the oaths in form.

I have nothing further to importune your Majesty with, nor that good Providence which so visibly has placed you on the throne with any thing so earnestly as my hearty prayers that your reign may be long and glorious, and that your posterity to the end of time may rule over an happy and dutiful, and, if it is not too much to ask, an unanimous people.

48. Letter from Lord Chesterfield to George Bubb Dodington on the disunity of the opposition to Sir Robert Walpole's government, August 1741

(*Letters of Philip Dormer Stanhope, 4th Earl of Chesterfield,* ed. Bonamy Dobrée, II (1932), pp. 467–470.)

Dodington (for whom see also No. 43) was at this time full of plans for the organization of the opposition, which had won considerable successes in the general election of 1741.

Lord Chesterfield to G. Bubb Dodington Esq.

Spa, August 8, 1741.[1]

Sir,

Having at last found a safe way of sending you this letter, I shall, without the least reserve, give you my thoughts upon the contents of yours of the 30th. of May. O.S.[2]

[1] Dated September; corrected to August by the editor of the *Letters.*

[2] The letter to which this is an answer is printed in Coxe, *Memoirs of Sir Robert Walpole,* III, p. 565.

By the best judgment I can form of the list of this present Parliament, and I have examined it very carefully, we appear to be so strong, that I think we can but just be called the minority, and I am very sure that such a minority, well united and well conducted, might soon be a majority. But, *Hoc opus hic labor est.*

It will neither be united nor well conducted. Those who should lead it will make it their business to break and divide it; and they will succeed; I mean Carteret and Pulteney. Their behaviour for these few years has, in my mind, plainly shown their views and their negotiations with the Court: but, surely, their conduct at the end of last Session puts that matter out of all dispute. They feared even the success of that minority, and took care to render it as insignificant as possible. Will they then not be much more apprehensive of the success of this: and will not both their merit and their reward be much the greater for defeating it? If you tell me that they ought rather to avail themselves of these numbers, and, at the head of them, force their way where they are so impatient to go, I will agree with you, that in prudence they ought; but the fact is, they reason quite differently, desire to get in with a few, by negotiation, and not by victory with numbers, who, they fear, might presume upon their strength, and grow troublesome to their generals.

On the other hand, Sir Robert must be alarmed at our numbers, and must resolve to reduce them before they are brought into the field. He knows by experience where and how to apply for that purpose; with this difference only, that the numbers will have raised the price, which he must come up to. And this is all the fruit I expect from this strong minority. You will possibly ask me, whether all this is in the power of Carteret and Pulteney? I answer, yes–in the power of Pulteney alone. He has a personal influence over many, and an interested influence over more. The silly, half-witted, zealous Whigs consider him as the only support of Whigism; and look upon us as running headlong into Bolingbroke and the Tories. The interested Whigs, as Sandys, Rushout and Gibbon,[1] with many others, are as impatient to come into Court as he can be; and, persuaded that he has opened that door a little, will hold fast by him to squeeze in with him, and think they can justify their conduct to the public, by following their old leader, under the colours (though false ones) of Whigism.

What then, is nothing to be done? Are we to give it up tamely, when the prospect seems so fair? No; I am for acting, let our numbers be what they will. I am for discriminating, and making people speak out; though our numbers should, as I am convinced they will, lessen considerably by it. Let what will happen, we cannot be in a worse situation than that we have been in for these last three or four years. Nay, I am for acting at the very beginning of the Session, and bringing our numbers the first week; and points for that purpose, I am sure, are not wanting. Some occur to me now, many more will, I dare say, occur to others; and many will, by that time, present themselves.

For example, the Court generally proposes some servile and shameless tool of theirs to be Chairman of the Committee of Privileges and Elections. Why should not we, therefore, pick out some Whig of a fair character, and with personal

[1] Samuel Sandys, M.P. for Worcester, Sir John Rushout, M.P. for Evesham, Phillips Gibbon, M.P. for Rye. They became junior Lords of the Treasury on the fall of Walpole, Sandys becoming Chancellor of the Exchequer.

connections, to set up in opposition? I think we should be pretty strong upon this point. But as for opposition to their Speaker, if it be Onslow, we shall be but weak; he having, by a certain decency of behaviour, made himself many personal friends in the minority. The affair of Carthagena[1] will, of course, be mentioned; and there, in my opinion, a question, and a trying one, too, of censure, lies very fair, that the delaying of that expedition so late last year was the principal cause of our disappointment. An Address to the King, desiring him to make no peace with Spain, unless our undoubted right of navigation in the West Indies, without molestation or search, be clearly, and in express words, stipulated; and till we have acquired some valuable possession there, as a pledge of the performance of such stipulation: such a question would surely be a popular one, and distressful enough to the Ministry.

I entirely agree with you, that we ought to have meetings to concert measures some time before the meeting of the Parliament; but that, I likewise know, will not happen. I have been these seven years endeavouring to bring it about, and have not been able; fox-hunting, gardening, planting, or indifference having always kept our people in the country, till the very day before the meeting of the Parliament. Besides, would it be easy to settle who should be at those meetings? If Pulteney and his people were to be chosen, it would only be informing them beforehand, what they should either oppose or defeat; and if they were not there, their own exclusion would in some degree justify, or at least colour, their conduct. As to our most flagitious house, I believe you agree there is nothing to be done in it; and for such a minority to struggle with such a majority, would be much like the late King of Sweden's attacking the Ottoman army at Bender, at the head of his cook and his butler.

These are difficulties, the insurmountable difficulties, that I foresee; and which make me absolutely despair of seeing any good done. However, I am entirely at the service of you and the rest of my friends who mean the public good. I will either fight or run away, as you shall determine. If the Duke of Argyle sounds to battle, I will follow my leader; if he stays in Oxfordshire, I'll stay in Grosvenor Square. I think it is all one which we do as to our House; yours must be the scene of action, if action there be; and action, I think, there should be, at least for a time, let your numbers be what they will.

I leave this place to-morrow, and set out for France; a country which, in my conscience, I think as free as our own: they have not the form of freedom, as we have. I know no other difference. I shall pass a couple of months in rambling through the Southern Provinces, and then return to England, to receive what commands you may leave for, etc.

[1] *i.e.* the failure of the expedition to Cartagena in November 1740.

ENGLAND AND WALES

SHOWING THE DISTRIBUTION OF THE OPPONENTS OF THE EXCISE BILL IN 1733 AND THE CONVENTION OF THE PARDO IN 1739

(Based on the division lists in *The Gentleman's Magazine*, November 1733 and June 1739)

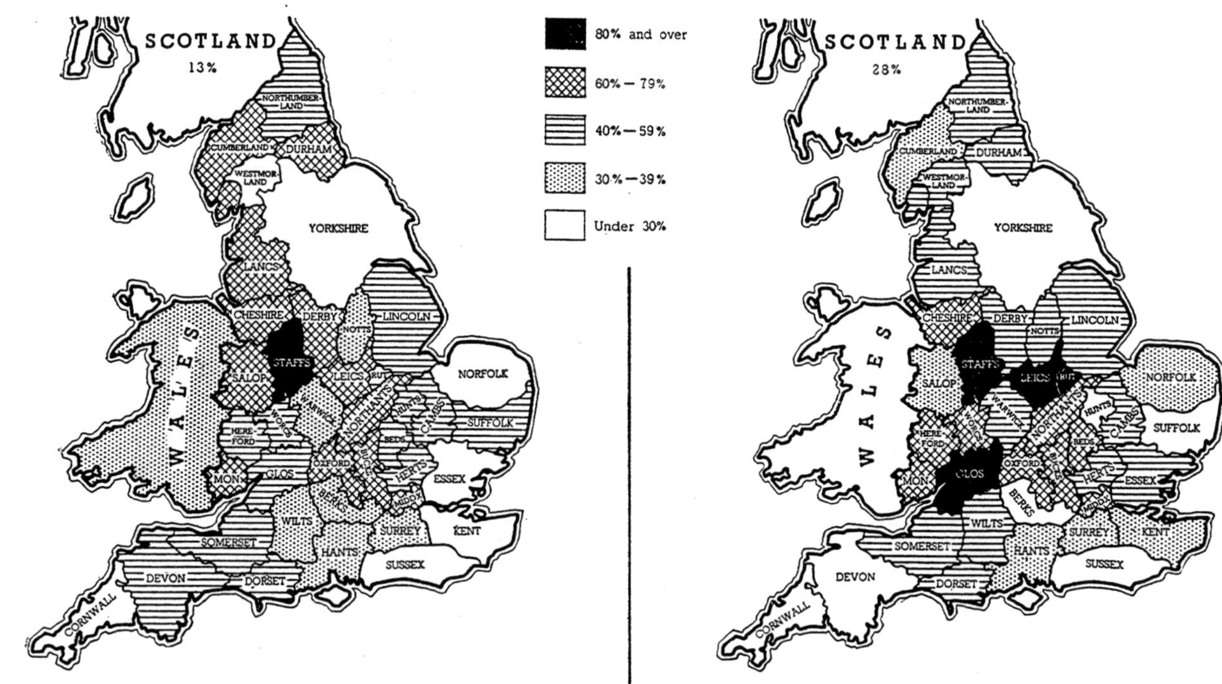

A. *Members of the Commons who voted against the Excise Bill, 1733*

B. *Members of the Commons who voted against the Convention of the Pardo, 1739*

49. A pamphlet on the wickedness of 'faction', 1761

(*Seasonable Hints from an Honest Man on the Present Important Crisis of a New Reign and a New Parliament* (1761), pp. 19–34.)

The author of this pamphlet was probably John Douglas (1721–1807), later bishop of Salisbury, who had been tutor to the son of William Pulteney, earl of Bath, under whose direction he wrote this and several other political pamphlets. It was attributed by Horace Walpole to Pulteney himself. The view of party here expressed was very generally accepted at the time, and is the complete opposite of Burke's well-known definition of party as "a body of men united for promoting by their joint endeavours the national interest upon some particular principle in which they are all agreed".

. . . Though the plan of fettering majesty in the chains of party, was at least coeval with the *accession* of the royal family; ministers, at first, could not guess how far they might venture to push their usurped influence. Our history, since the times of the *barons*, had furnished few or no instances of *oligarchical* restraint put upon the crown; it required time and experience, therefore, to model this new system of modern politics. And surely nothing but experience could have proved it to be possible, that a time should ever happen, when the dignity of the king could be trampled upon without regard to decency; and when ministers might presume to carry their insolence so far as to set their master at defiance, and to govern in spite of him.–I need not enter into many particulars, to enable my readers to guess, to what period of our history I now allude. . . .

What should we think of soldiers who threaten their general to abandon his standards, when the enemy is in sight, mutinying not for want of pay, but in hopes to extort from him unreasonable gratifications? What opinion could we have of a crew of sailors who, when their ship was in danger of sinking, should refuse to stand to the pump, and threaten to go off in the long-boat, unless the master should submit to be put in irons, and allow them to divide the cargo? or to use an illustration perhaps still more similar to the transaction now alluded to, what notion could we have of the characters of a set of domestics, who, in order to force an indulgent master to submit to them, should insist on his dismissing every friend from his house; require him to take into his family some of their own dependents, who had personally used him ill, and whose presence might be necessary to assist them in enslaving him; and finding him averse to compliance, should take occasion, when they saw his house on fire, to threaten, in a body, they would abandon him, at that dangerous conjuncture, unless he yielded immediately to all their insolent demands?–The questions I now state, but faintly describe the odious circumstances of an *association* of ministers, within the memory of many, but exactly when, I won't say,[1] who finding that, though they had forced their sovereign to submit to many mortifying indignities and galling concessions, he had too delicate a sense of honor not to make resistance against some of their demands, had recourse to an act of factious insolence, of which no preceding part of our history furnished an example. For, at a time when every honest subject ought to have had full employment in soothing the distresses of majesty, and in defending the tottering throne; when faction should have suspended its ambitious intrigues, to oppose daring disaffection, and too successful rebellion; at that very instant, the nation saw with amazement a *formal confederacy* entered into by the king's

[1] February 1746. See No. 9.

servants, associating to resign, in a body, in hopes that their unhappy sovereign, alarmed to be abandoned, at such a crisis of public danger, might be induced to comply with every demand of their insolent ambition, which, hitherto, he had refused to gratify.

. . . The transaction above referred to is pregnant with so many odious circumstances, that I should have been glad, for the honor of our country, to have drawn a veil over it. But my argument naturally led me to take notice of it; and every candid reader must admit that I have touched the wound with the gentlest hand; and with the single and honest intention of warning every future confederacy of party leaders, to avoid such personal insults on the sovereign, as *history* must relate with severe animadversion, *patriotism* read with indignation, and *candor* itself can scarcely endeavour to extenuate. It was the fashion of the times we have been speaking of, to use such factious methods of acquiring and preserving power; and much is to be said to lessen the guilt of those who are linked with a party, and bound, as it were, in honor, (at least thinking themselves so) to attempt things as an aggregate body, which, as individuals, they perhaps disapproved of, at the very time, and which, certainly, they could not but condemn, as soon as the violence of party zeal subsided, and cool reflexion was permitted to operate on probity and good sense.

If ministerial combinations to engross power, and to invade the closet, have produced such personal insults on the *king*, the consequences of such attempts, with regard to the public, were equally odious. For truth obliges me to confess, that however favorable to national freedom the true genuine principles of *whiggism* be, some individuals of that denomination, (who, in times happily at an end, got possession of the royal family) were the great promoters, if not the first introducers of such a plan of wicked policy, as had a natural tendency to sap the firm foundation, of British liberty, and to destroy the independence of the constitution.

The charge I now bring may seem severe; but the facts, on which it is built, are notorious.–Such is the happy distribution of supreme power in this country, that the sovereign finds it his interest to pursue no measures but such as are agreeable to the representatives of the people; and the necessity of obtaining parliamentary concurrence has increased since the revolution; from which period, by separating the civil list from the other charges of government, annual sessions must be held, and annual supplies granted. Ministers, therefore, who wanted to force themselves into employments at court, saw that they should gain their point, if they could convince the sovereign that they had the power over parliament. But how could any particular set of men acquire such a power? It was impossible that the whole body of the people, in this great country, should concur in enslaving their sovereign and themselves, to any junto of their fellow-subjects; and it was obvious that a parliament *chosen freely*, and composed of gentlemen of real property, whose inclination it would be to *vote freely*, were not likely to act the despicable part of tools to a narrow party-cabal of ambitious courtiers.

In this situation, therefore, there was no alternative; the scheme of putting the sovereign into the leading-strings of party must be abandoned, or else such methods put in practice, as might check the freedom of election, and procure such a parliament as might support a particular set of ministers. The real disaffection that existed at the accession of George the First, furnished those who then got possession of the closet, with a specious pretence to employ secretly the court influence upon certain important occasions; and having once prevailed upon the king to look upon such *secret* influence, as necessary for the security of his family, they knew it would answer a more immediate purpose to themselves, by giving them the means of perpetuating their own power; a point, in their opinion, not too dearly purchased, by a most enormous expence of public money,[1] and by establishing venality and corruption into a system, as necessary engines of government.

To consider the English constitution in theory, its stability would be supposed to arise from parliament. But parliaments, when once they become appendages of administration, must open the widest door to slavery. In this case, they became a mere *state engine* in the hands of the ministers, to *stamp* a value on the basest metal, and to give every bad measure the sanction of national consent. And no chains are so heavy as those which we put on ourselves; for we shall bear from our representatives, what prerogative, openly exerted, never will venture to put in practice. . . .

Here then let me congratulate my fellow-subjects, on the pleasing prospects which already open to our view. In this infancy of his majesty's government, he hath conducted himself, in such a manner, as gives us just grounds to form the highest ideas, both of his good disposition and of his abilities; to expect that this will be a reign of dignity and importance, a reign in which ministers will depend on the crown, not the crown on the ministers; in short, a reign in which the hateful and worn-out distinctions of party will be abolished, and government carried on, without having recourse to the mischievous arts of corruption, and without reviving the odious tyranny of ministerial dictators. . . .

But it is not merely from this circumstance, that we may hope for a new *aera*; for we see that his majesty is resolved to put himself at the head of all his subjects, by abolishing all distinctions of party, by accepting with paternal affection the assistance of *every honest man*, to support the throne; and, as a mark of his royal confidence, placing in the most honorable stations, near his own person, some, who have not surely owed their places to ministerial importunity, because they have always opposed ministerial influence. . . .

But, has not this very measure given an alarm? Has it not been thought a hardship on those who have been enriched with all the rewards of government, these fifty years, to have so much as one employment given away, from their party? . . .

When the private interest of a few individuals is affected, we frequently see that they have art enough to get their cause to be looked upon as the cause of a whole party. I should be sorry if this happened to be the case at present; and yet, we have been told, that, because a few *tories* have got places, attempts have been made to induce the *whigs* to consider this as an attack on their whole body: but if the *whigs* can be so far deluded as to believe this, it will give us a remarkable proof, that *party is the madness of the many, for the gain of the few*. For does any candid and intelligent man seriously believe, that at this time of day, there subsists any party distinction amongst us, that is

[1] Note omitted.

not merely nominal? Are not the *tories* friends of the *royal family*? Have they not long ago laid aside their aversion to the dissenters? Do they not think the toleration and establishment, both necessary parts of the constitution? And can a *whig* distinguish these from his own principles? Must not, therefore, every honest man see and confess, that the cry against widening the bottom of government, is propagated by some, who, finding their own views of ambition or gain affected by this measure, endeavour to render it odious amongst the body of the party, who otherwise would have seen no reason to be alarmed, even in point of private interest? For all that the *tories* possibly can hope for, or expect, is that a few marks of confidence may be given them at present, as a proof, that the *proscription* is at an end, and as an earnest that in the future disposal of court favors, when there are vacancies by deaths and not by removals, they will stand an equal chance of being taken notice of, with the rest of his majesty's good subjects. And here I may ask, has so much as a single *whig* been displaced, to make room for a *tory* successor? Have not the few places conferred on the formerly excluded party, been such as his majesty has created, in his own bed-chamber, by increasing the number of his servants? Why therefore should there be complaints, where there is so little foundation? Indeed, the thing speaks for itself. The ground of the uneasiness is not that any *whig* has been displaced, but that a nation of *whigs*, as we may now justly be called, must cease for the future to be governed by the narrow maxims of faction.

50. Speech by Lord Sandwich in the House of Lords on the duke of Richmond's motion on the seizure of the Falkland Islands, 22 November 1770

(*Parl. Hist.*, XVI, pp. 1116–1119.)

Sandwich here attacks the lack of principles shown by the Opposition to Lord North's government.

[22 November 1770]

Lord *Sandwich*: My lords; I am heartily for the previous question, and thoroughly convinced with respect to the injustice of the accusations, which in the course of the debate have been urged against his Majesty's ministers. Their proceedings have, in the general, been pronounced weak and wicked; the terms folly and treachery have been very plentifully poured upon their conduct, and if the voice of popularity is to be credited, they ought to be instantly sacrificed to the just resentment of the kingdom. It is not a little unfortunate however, for the open rivals of administration, the declared candidates for office, that the legal judges of ministerial rectitude or delinquency, are quite of a contrary opinion; that no period of the British history can shew an administration, more powerfully supported; more heartily approved by both houses of parliament than the present; notwithstanding the universal detestation in which they are held, notwithstanding the outcry industriously fomented against them in every quarter of the kingdom, still the only constitutional tribunal at which their actions can be tried, bears testimony to their worth, and applauds their integrity; it has deemed the charges, urged by their enemies, too despicable, too rancorous even to be heard: it has dismissed them with insuperable contempt, and declared that its own honour, even in the most atrocious allegations of criminality, was immediately connected with the honour of his Majesty's ministers.

The noble lords will undoubtedly say, that the parliamentary majority, which has thus supported the measures, pursued by the servants of the crown, is a corrupt majority of court dependants, composed of placemen and place-hunters, pensioners, contractors, officers in the army, and practitioners at the bar, who have continual favours either to solicit or expect from administration. Who, however, let me ask, are the pillars of the opposition? discarded courtiers with their hungry retainers; men rendered implacable by dismission, and desperate through necessity; men who are maddened at having lost their places, and who would do any thing to recover them: they will not, I hope, be offended at this imputation of venality; they deal very largely in imputations of venality themselves, and must not be astonished at recrimination: it is moreover as natural for them to violate the principles of honesty to gain, as it is for the objects of their envy to be corrupt, through a desire of keeping possession of their employments; besides, my lords, let me ask when the patriots themselves were in power, if they did not make use of the very placemen and pensioners, whom they now treat with so much contempt, and declare to be utterly unfit for the confidence of the kingdom; when they were in the great departments of government no complaint whatever was made of places or pensions; nay these mirrors of political virtue were the first to stipulate for them; were the first to encrease the burdens of their miserable country by personal appointments and reversions in case of dismission, to their families. The present prostitute administration, as they are pleased to call it, has done nothing like this; the members of it have come in without condition, if they go out to-morrow, they will go out without condition, and leave the plunder of their country to its immaculate deliverers.

The noble lords who have spoken in support of the motion, seem to think, that if the present administration is bellowed out of office, unanimity will be immediately restored at home, and that they will be able to take a quiet possession of all the great employments in the state. In this, however, they must be miserably disappointed; they are all patriots now while out of place, but the different leaders of opposition are as adverse to each other as they are inimical to administration; they differ besides as much in their political creed, as they affect to differ from the principles of government. One party declares impressing for the sea service utterly repugnant to the constitution; another party is for calling the abettors of this dangerous doctrine to immediate punishment. One party is for governing by an aristocracy of the great families; another thinks such a measure injurious to the privileges of the people. Some are for remonstrating only; others are for impeachments: in short down to Wilkes and Edridge they are divided among themselves; so that if a new arrangement was instantly to take place, we must only expect a fresh flame of discord raging through the kingdom. At present, opposition is in a manner annihilated; change hands however, and you furnish a new opportunity for complaining; the leaders of our different parties aspire each, to take the lead in office; each refuses to admit the superiority of the other; what therefore are we to gain by a change? Let the opposition itself answer; and let them, if they can, say, that all would not be as the poet says, "anarchy and uproar".

Having delivered my sentiments thus freely, my lords, give me leave to take some notice of what a noble earl [Chatham] has been pleased to say, with respect to the propriety of an hereditary gratitude in the crown to the great Whig families; his lordship talks much of the merit which these families had in bringing in the House of Hanover, and it is a merit I am very ready to acknowledge; but will the noble earl say, that because they served their country, and consequently themselves, in bringing in the House of Brunswick, that they are therefore to make a perpetual monopoly of the royal favour? If bringing in that line was not a national good, they are traitors to the community; if it was a national good, the present reigning family, instead of being obliged, conferred an actual obligation. Besides, my lords, is the booby descendant of a Whig, to be employed in the first departments of the state, because his ancestor was a man of abilities; or is the deserving offspring of a Tory to be overlooked, because his father's principles were obnoxious? If principles, my lords, are hereditary, we must be all attached to the House of Stuart; nay, we brought in his Majesty's great grandfather because he was the nearest Protestant relation to that House.

It is not to the House, my lords, we ever objected, but to the Papists of the House. In the moments of our warmest indignation against the bigot James the second, we loved his family, we placed his daughter on the throne, and, as I before observed, it was our love for the Protestant part of his family, that led us to apply to the electress Sophia in the settlement of the regal succession. The noble lord wishes, he tell us, to abolish all party distinctions, yet he is greatly offended that the distinction of Whig and Tory is not inflexibly kept up; the King must govern by a faction to please his lordship, he must not be the common father of his people, but only the monarch of the Whigs; at a time that these destructive distinctions are happily hastening to oblivion, they must be revived by a judicious sovereign, and to conciliate the affections of all to the government of a Brunswick prince, the unoffending posterity of the Tories must be held in a state of eternal proscription! What weight, what regard, my lords, is due to the reasonings of such wretched politicians; these mountebanks in government, who prescribe the revival of parties as the means of restoring domestic peace, and when they paint us on the brink of ruin, declaim on the necessity of our commencing an immediate war! To your lordships I submit the debate, and desire the previous question may now decide the force of our respective arguments.

F. THE MOVEMENT FOR PARLIAMENTARY REFORM

51. Speech by Lord Chatham in the House of Lords on parliamentary reform, 22 January 1770

(*Parl. Hist.*, XVI, pp. 751–755.)

These views were expressed in Chatham's speech during the debate on the state of the nation. They should be compared with those of his son in 1782, No. 58.

[22 January 1770]

. . . I feel myself compelled, my lords, to return to that subject, which occupies and interests me most; I mean the internal disorder of the constitution, and the remedy it demands. . . . For some years past, there has been an influx of wealth into this country, which has been attended with many fatal consequences, because it has not been the regular, natural produce of labour and industry. The riches of Asia have been poured in upon us, and have brought with them not only Asiatic luxury, but, I fear, Asiatic principles of government. Without connections, without any natural interest in the soil, the importers of foreign gold have forced their way into parliament, by such a torrent of private corruption, as no private hereditary fortune could resist. My lords, I say nothing but what is within the knowledge of us all; the corruption of the people is the great original cause of the discontents of the people themselves, of the enterprise of the crown, and the notorious decay of the internal vigour of the constitution. For this great evil some immediate remedy must be provided; and I confess, my lords, I did hope, that his Majesty's servants would not have suffered so many years of peace to elapse, without paying some attention to an object, which ought to engage and interest us all. I flattered myself I should see some barriers thrown up in defence of the constitution, some impediment formed to stop the rapid progress of corruption. I doubt not we all agree that something must be done. I shall offer my thoughts, such as they are, to the consideration of the House, and I wish that every noble lord who hears me would be as ready as I am to contribute his opinion to this important service. I will not call my own sentiments crude and indigested; it would be unfit for me to offer any thing to your lordships, which I had not well considered; and this subject, I own, has long occupied my thoughts. I will now give them to your lordships without reserve.

Whoever understands the theory of the English constitution, and will compare it with the fact, must see at once how widely they differ. We must reconcile them to each other, if we wish to save the liberties of this country; we must reduce our political practice, as nearly as possible, to our principles. The constitution intended that there should be a permanent relation between the constituent and representative body of the people. Will any man affirm, that, as the House of Commons is now formed, that relation is in any degree preserved? My lords, it is not preserved, it is destroyed. Let us be cautious, however, how we have recourse to violent expedients.

The boroughs of this country have properly enough been called the rotten parts of the constitution. I have lived in Cornwall, and, without entering into any invidious particularity, have seen enough to justify the appellation. But in my judgment, my lords, these boroughs, corrupt as they are, must be considered as the natural infirmity of the constitution. Like the infirmities of the body, we must bear them with patience, and submit to carry them about with us. The limb is mortified, but amputation might be death.

Let us try, my lords, whether some gentler remedies may not be discovered. Since we cannot cure the disorder, let us endeavour to infuse such a portion of new health into the constitution, as may enable it to support its most inveterate diseases.

The representation of the counties is, I think, still preserved pure and uncorrupted. That of the great cities is on a footing equally respectable; and there are many of the larger trading towns, which still preserve their independence. The infusion of health, which I now allude to, would be to permit every county to elect one member more, in addition to their present representation. The knights of the shires approach nearest to the constitutional representation of the country, because they represent the soil. It is not in the little dependent boroughs, it is in the great cities and counties that the strength and vigour of the constitution resides, and by them alone, if an unhappy question should ever arise, will the constitution be honestly and firmly defended. I would increase that strength, because I think it is the only security we have against the profligacy of the times, the corruption of the people, and the ambition of the crown.

I think I have weighed every possible objection that can be raised against a plan of this nature; and I confess I see but one, which, to me, carries any appearances of solidity. It may be said, perhaps, that when the act passed for uniting the two kingdoms, the number of persons who were to represent the whole nation in parliament was proportioned and fixed on for ever – That this limitation is a fundamental article, and cannot be altered without hazarding a dissolution of the Union.

My lords, no man who hears me can have a greater reverence for that wise and important act, than I have. I revere the memory of that great prince who first formed the plan, and of those illustrious patriots who carried it into execution. As a contract, every article of it should be inviolable; as the common basis of the strength and happiness of two nations, every article of it should be sacred. I hope I cannot be suspected of conceiving a thought so detestable, as to propose an advantage to one of the contracting parties at the expence of the other. No, my lords, I mean that the benefit should be universal, and the consent to receive it unanimous. Nothing less than a most urgent and important occasion should persuade me to vary even from the letter of the act; but there is no occasion, however urgent, however important, that should ever induce me to depart from the spirit of it. Let that spirit be religiously preserved. Let us follow the principle on which the representation of the two countries was proportioned at the Union; and when we increase the number of representatives for the English counties, let the shires of Scotland be allowed an equal privilege. On these terms, and while the proportion limited by the Union is preserved by the two nations, I apprehend that no man who is a friend to either, will object to an alteration, so necessary for the security of both. I do not speak of the authority of the legislature to carry such a measure into effect, because I imagine no man will dispute it. But I would not wish the legislature to interpose by an exertion of its power alone, without the cheerful concurrence of all parties. My object is the happiness and security of the two nations, and I would not wish to obtain it without their mutual consent. . . .

52. Major John Cartwright on the evils of long parliaments, 1776

(*Take Your Choice* (1776), pp. ix–xi, xxi–xxv.)

This extract from Cartwright's famous pamphlet illustrates, among other things, the new, critical attitude to the 1688 Revolution that was emerging in the later eighteenth century. The pamphlet expressed the views of the Radical reformers.

TAKE YOUR CHOICE!

Representation and Respect:	Imposition and Contempt.
Annual Parliaments and Liberty:	Long Parliaments and Slavery.

INTRODUCTION

Having proposed to urge upon you, my country men! a reformation, both as to the length, and as to the constituting of your parliaments; it seems but proper, previously to state some of the inconveniences and evils, which I apprehend to be the necessary consequences of, and inseparable from, our present rotten parliamentary system.

All men will grant, that the lower house of parliament is elected by only a handful of the commons, instead of the whole; and this, chiefly by bribery and undue influence. Men who will employ such means are villains; and those who dupe their constituents by lying promises, are far from honest men. An assembley of such men is *founded* on *iniquity*: consequently, the fountain of legislation is poisoned. Every stream, how much soever mixed, as it flows with justice and patriotism, will still have poison in its composition.

Nor will it be denied me, that, in consequence of the long duration of a parliament, the members, as soon as seated, feel themselves too independent on the opinion and good will of their constituents, even where their suffrages have not been extorted nor bought; and that, of course, they despise them.

From the first of these data, it will follow, that we are subject to have the House of Commons filled by men of every bad description that can be thought of, and that strict integrity, which ought to be the strongest of all recommendations, amounts to a positive exclusion; except it happen indeed to be united with a capital fortune and great county connections.

From the first and second jointly; our respresentatives, who are in fact our deputed servants, are taught to assume the carriage and haughtiness of despotic masters; to think themselves unaccountable for their conduct; and to neglect their duty.

Whether, indeed, the house of commons be in a great measure filled with idle school-boys, insignificant coxcombs, led-captains and toad-eaters, profligates, gamblers, bankrupts, beggars, contractors, commissaries, public plunderers, ministerial dependants, hirelings, and wretches, that would sell their country, or deny their God for a guinea, let every one judge for himself. And whether the kind of business very often brought before the house, and the usual manner of conducting it, do not bespeak this to be the case; I likewise leave every man to form his own opinion: particularly that independent and noble-minded few, who experience the constant mortification of voting and speaking without even a hope of being able thereby to serve their country.

But without insisting on these things as fact, and only admitting the possibility of them from the combined causes already assigned, of long parliaments, undue influence and bribery, it is natural to expect, as indeed all experience shews it must happen, that a country, whose affairs are *subject to fall* into such hands must be ruined, sooner or later, by those very men who shall be in the office of its guardians and preservers; except it shall make an alteration in this particular. . . .

So ruinous a system needs must, in its progress, grow worse. The chariot of corruption, (if I may be allowed a new metaphor) under the guidance of rotten whigs would soon enough have arrived, without the whip, at the goal of despotism: but now, that furious tories have seized the reins, 'tis lashed onward with impetuous haste; nor do they seem sensible to their danger, though its axles are already on fire with its rapidity. The ministers of the present reign have daringly struck at your most sacred rights, have aimed through the sides of America a deadly blow at the life of your constitution, and have shewn themselves hostile, not only to the being, but to the very name of liberty. The word itself has been proscribed the court; and for any one who dared to utter it, the gentlest appellations have been Wilkite, republican and disturber of the peace. Facts recent in every one's memory I have no need to repeat. I will only therefore just mention the atrocious violation of the first principle of the constitution in the never-to-be-forgotten business of the Middlesex election. An enumeration of all their crimes would shew them to be deserving of the highest punishments. And yet, the sum of all the evils they have brought upon us, added to all those which former ministers had intailed upon the nation, are light and trivial in comparison of the ONE GREAT EVIL OF A LONG PARLIAMENT. Feast the fowls of the air with such ministers, but leave your legislature unreformed; and you will only add a few inglorious days to the period of your expiring liberties. Succeeding ministers might be more circumspect; but with the aid of a prostitute parliament, they would at last succeed. . . . It is downright quixotism to imagine, that so long as your parliament remains corrupt, you can ever have a patriot minister: and, except parliament be reformed, 'tis a matter of very great indifference who are *in* and who are *out*. I will not utterly deny the possibility of your having a patriot minister prior to a parliamentary reformation; but I do not myself conceive *how* such a man is to arrive at such a station. One of that stamp could not go through thick and thin, and wade through all the miry paths that lead to it: nor have I any great expectation of a miraculous conversion of anyone, who hath once passed through those ways to the seat of power. Neither do I see the prudence of waiting for so rare a phenomenon as a patriot minister, to do that for you which you can do for yourselves; and thereby put things in such a state, that a patriot minister will no longer be a phenomenon, but a natural and common appearance.

The revolution which expelled the tyrant James from the throne, glorious as it was to the character, and essential to the safety of this nation, was yet a very defective proceeding. It was effected in too anxious a moment, and in too precipitate a manner, to lay a lasting foundation for the security of public freedom and property. *William* the deliverer was but half the friend to liberty which he pretended to be. Had he been a truly patriot prince, his share in the expulsion of a tyrant would have been his smallest merit; and he would have embraced the opportunity afforded him by his own success and the tide of reformation being set in, to have guarded the constitution against every conceivable danger towards which it had any tendency to be exposed in process of time. When the immortal and blessed *Alfred* had overthrown the oppressors of his country, he thought the work of a king only begun; and devoted the rest of his reign to the correcting abuses, the establishing of justice, and laying the broad foundations of liberty and happiness.[1] But history shews *William* to have been a cold-hearted Dutchman, ungrateful to a people who had given him a crown, and more fond of power than of squaring his government with the principles of the constitution. And this was one of the best of our kings. Then put not your trust in princes: neither have confidence in ministers! Whether they covet inordinate power for its own sake, or for the sake of lucre, they will have it if possible. And when one lusts for gold, the other for dominion, they will be reciprocally the pimps to each others passion. The prince will invade the people's property, in order to enrich his minister; the minister will violate their liberties, in order to render his master absolute. For one *Alfred*, there are a thousand *Charles's*; for one *Falkland*, a thousand *Walpoles*. Trust not, I say, in princes nor in ministers; but trust in YOURSELVES, and in representatives chosen by YOURSELVES alone!

53. Petition and Resolutions of the Yorkshire Association, 1779–1780

(*Political Papers . . . collected by the Rev. Christopher Wyvill*, I (1794), pp. 7–9, 143–147.)

The Yorkshire petition and the form of association and committee of correspondence set up to support it, were the models copied by many other counties in the early months of 1780. These petitions were considered by a committee of the whole House of Commons on 6 April 1780, when they were the occasion of Dunning's famous motion that "the influence of the Crown has increased, is increasing and ought to be diminished", carried in one of the fullest Houses of the eighteenth century by 233–215; a sufficiently striking example of the limits of the "influence of the Crown". The House followed this up by carrying without a division a resolution of its competence to

[1] Note omitted.

examine and correct abuses in public expenditure, including that of the Civil List. The Yorkshire movement thus coincided very conveniently with the Rockingham Whigs' programme of Economical Reform; in fact, that programme was probably hurried on in order to get the advantage of this support outside Parliament. The Yorkshire movement had, however, from the beginning its more radical side, pressing for parliamentary, not merely economical reform. This element soon became dominant, and caused the Rockingham Whigs to withdraw their support, though Fox and Shelburne were more sympathetic.

PETITION agreed to at the Meeting of the County of York, held the 30th day of December, 1779, which having been afterwards circulated through the County, was signed by near nine thousand Freeholders, and presented by Sir George Savile[1] to the House of Commons, on the 8th day of February, 1780.

To the Honourable the Commons *of* Great-Britain,
in Parliament *assembled,*
The Petition of the Gentlemen, Clergy, and Free-holders of the County of York,

Sheweth,

That this nation hath been engaged for several years in a most expensive and unfortunate war; that many of our valuable colonies, having actually declared themselves independent, have formed a strict confederacy with France and Spain, the dangerous and inveterate enemies of Great-Britain; that the consequence of these combined misfortunes hath been a large addition to the national debt; a heavy accumulation of taxes; a rapid decline of the trade, manufactures, and land-rents of the kingdom.

Alarmed at the diminished resources and growing burthens of this country, and convinced that rigid frugality is now indispensably necessary in every department of the State, your petitioners observe with grief, that, notwithstanding the calamitous and impoverished condition of the nation, much public money has been improvidently squandered, and that many individuals enjoy sinecure places, efficient places with exorbitant emoluments, and pensions unmerited by public service, to a large and still increasing amount; whence the crown has acquired a great and unconstitutional influence, which, if not check'd, may soon prove fatal to the liberties of this country.

Your petitioners conceiving that the true end of every legitimate government is not the emolument of ANY INDIVIDUAL, but the welfare of the community; and considering that, by the constitution of this realm, the national purse is intrusted in a peculiar manner to the custody of this Honourable House, beg leave farther to represent, that, until effectual measures be taken to redress the oppressive grievances herein stated, the grant of any additional sum of public money, beyond the produce of the present taxes, will be injurious to the rights and property of the people, and derogatory from the honour and dignity of Parliament.

Your petitioners therefore appealing to the justice of this Honourable House, do most earnestly request that, before any new burthens are laid upon this country,

[1] Sir George Savile, Bart. (1726–1784), M.P. for Yorkshire and an active member of the opposition.

effectual measures may be taken by this House, to inquire into and correct the gross abuses in the expenditure of public money; to reduce all exorbitant emoluments; to rescind and abolish all sinecure places and unmerited pensions; and to appropriate the produce to the necessities of the State, in such manner as to the wisdom of Parliament shall seem meet. . . .

Resolutions *at a* Meeting *of the* Committee *of the* County *of* York, *held by adjournment in the evening of the 27th of March,* 1780.

The Committee appointed to form, and report to this Committee, a proper plan of Association, to be presented to the General Meeting of this county on the 28th of March instant, having laid before this Committee the following Form of Association, viz.

FORM of ASSOCIATION agreed to by the Committee of sixty-one, to be recommended to the General Meeting of the County of York, held on the 28th day of March, 1780.

WHEREAS during the present expensive and unfortunate war, the trade, manufactures, and land rents, of this kingdom, have been greatly diminished; the public burthens grievously augmented by the annual imposition of new and additional taxes; the national debt enormously increased, and the undue influence of the Crown extended, to an alarming degree, by these very circumstances which threaten the utter impoverishment of this country. And whereas, in these times of national difficulty and distress, a just redress of grievances can only be expected from a free and uncorrupted Parliament; and measures tending in a legal and peaceful way to restore the freedom of Parliament, cannot effectually be supported but by a general union of independent men throughout the kingdom.

"We whose names are here-under written considering an economical reformation in the expenditure of public money to be a most essential and necessary measure for restoring the freedom of Parliament:—

"And considering also that the representation of the people in Parliament is become extremely unequal, insomuch that a great majority of Members is returned by decayed and indigent Boroughs, which are either at the command of the Crown and a few great families, or else open to general venality, whence support in Parliament may be obtained for the measures of any Administration, however ruinous they may be to the great landed and commercial interests of this kingdom, contrary to the true intent and use of the institution of Parliament; which unequitable distribution of the right to elect Representatives in Parliament is now a principal cause of our numerous public evils, to which no radical cure is likely to be applied till a more adequate Representation of the People hath been established by law.

"And considering further, that when the fund of corruption hath been in some competent degree reduced, and a more equal Representation of the People obtained, more frequent elections might be restored, not only to the great content of the people, but with certain advantage to the honour and integrity of Parliament itself, without the mischievous consequence of exposing independent gentlemen to vexatious contests with the dependents of any Administration." We do declare our assent to,

1. The economical reform requested by the petitions of the people; that plan of strict and rigid frugality now indispensably necessary in every department of the State; that most important regulation for reducing the unconstitutional influence of the Crown.
2. The proposition for obtaining a more equal Representation in Parliament, by the addition of at least one hundred Knights, to be chosen in a due proportion, by the several counties of the kingdom of Great-Britain.
3. The proposition for Members of the House of Commons to be elected to serve in Parliament for a term not exceeding three years.

And in order more effectually to promote this laudable plan of Public Reformation, by our joint assistance in a pacific way, we do associate for that express purpose, and we do testify the same by our signatures respectively. And we do resolve jointly and separately to support these regulations to the utmost of our power, by every measure that may be perfectly agreeable to law and the constitution. More particularly we do resolve, and do mutually and most solemnly engage, that until a reasonable reform in the expenditure of public money hath been obtained, and until regulations for returning at least one hundred additional County Members to Parliament, and for shortening the duration of Parliament to a term not exceeding three years, have been established by law, we will support with our votes and interest no Candidate whatsoever at the next General Election, or at any future election, to represent this county, or any other county or place in Parliament, from whose known integrity and attachment to our free constitution, and his assent to these constitutional improvements, declared by signing this Association, or in such other mode as to each Candidate may seem most eligible, we shall not be first fully satisfied that he will give his utmost support in Parliament to the following propositions, or to such part of the reform, proposed thereby, as shall not then be accomplished, viz.

1. For one or more bills to correct profusion in the expenditure of public money; to regulate the manner of making all public contracts, and the mode of keeping and passing public accounts; to reduce exorbitant emoluments of office, and to reform the abuses of sinecure places and pensions, unmerited by public service.

2. For a bill to establish greater equality in the Representation of the People in Parliament, by allowing the several counties of the kingdom of Great-Britain to elect, in due proportion, one hundred Knights at least, in addition to the present number.

3. For a bill to shorten the duration of Parliaments to a term not exceeding three years.

Resolved, (with only one dissentient voice) That the above Form of Association be offered to the General Meeting of this county on the 28th of March.

Resolved, That this Committee do adjourn.

C. WYVILL.[1]

[1] Reverend Christopher Wyvill (1740–1822), Secretary and afterwards Chairman of the Association.

54. Letter from Lord Rockingham to Pemberton Milnes on parliamentary reform, 28 February 1780

(George Thomas, earl of Albemarle, *Memoirs of the Marquis of Rockingham and his Contemporaries*, II (1852), pp. 395–400.)

Pemberton Milnes, a prominent Yorkshire Dissenter, was one of the leaders of the Yorkshire reformers. This letter is typical of the attitude of the Rockingham Whigs.

THE MARQUIS OF ROCKINGHAM TO MR. PEMBERTON MILNES.

Grosvenor Square, *February 28th*, 1780.

I rejoice very much in the spirit which now seems rising in all parts of this country. *Yorkshire* has done itself great honour in taking the lead, and I am happy that so much *sense* and *discretion* prevailed in the outset of the business at the meeting of York.

It behoves Yorkshire, not only for its own honour, but also for the infinite general good of the whole nation, that when the county *proceeds again*, the mode and the objects of the measures proposed and adopted should be well considered. My mind, I confess, is by no means at ease in regard to *certain rumours* respecting some vague and crude propositions, which I am *told* are likely to be brought forth. I don't like the idea of *tests*, and especially on vague and unexplicit propositions. The being elected a representative, *if it implies a trust*, is most highly honourable, but if it is to lock up your reasoning faculties of deliberating and judging, and is to tie you up beforehand, and preclude you from acting according to your conscience at the moment, I think it would be a disgraceful bondage, and what *many men* of the nicest sense of honour cannot submit to. How much more too must it weigh if the *tests* which you are called upon to take, are to *propositions* which are *loosely and generally worded.*

It seems to me that the fair conclusion to be drawn (when the men *who are eager for shortening the duration of Parliament*, cannot as yet agree amongst themselves whether annual, triennial, and quintennial Parliaments, *should be substituted*), is that the matter is by no means ripe for them to call upon a candidate for a declaration. It seems to me that the idea of calling for a declaration of support for a *non-equal representation* is also, as yet, very premature; for I am sure there are *many* which have been thought of, yet the one *peculiarly preferable* is by no means a fixed and decided opinion.

Some persons, I know, by the expression of a *more equal representation*, mean *little more* than the abolishing *what are called the rotten boroughs*; some of these persons think that these boroughs should be taken away from their possessors, *without any compensation* (as being unconstitutional); some allow that the possessors should be compensated. Some persons think, that the seats for these boroughs should be filled up by additional members from their respective counties; others think, that like *Shoreham*, the seats should be filled up by the voices of the persons resident within certain neighbouring districts. Others think, that many of the great, important towns of trade and manufactures, who have not at present their respective local representatives, should fill up the parliamentary vacant seats. It is endless, indeed, to state the variety of ideas, which are now, as it were, afloat on these points.

There is still *one* speculation on the proposition of a *more equal representation*, which from its magnitude is indeed a most grave, solemn, and important subject of consideration. The proposition, I mean, is that as matters now are, *the people*, as they are called, are *not represented.* It is held, that retaining the right of voting to *freeholders* in a county, is an arbitrary and *unconstitutional* assumption of power. The same opinions are held in regard to the now settled rights of voting in towns and boroughs. The assertion is, that *all men* (the whole people) *should give their votes.*

What a situation will every honest, conscientious candidate be in, when he is called upon to declare most solemnly upon his honour, that he will be for *shortening the duration of Parliament*, and for a *more equal representation*, when he cannot form a guess, what specific proposition it is on either of these points, which *those persons* mean, who require the declaration from him.

What a situation will an honest man be in, if after the making of the declaration, the proposition *moved* in a future Parliament on either of these points, should be a proposition to which his conscience revolted. You will observe that I do not argue as thinking that the duration of Parliament (septennial) might not be altered. I confess I have no idea of anything but confusion and weakness from *annual* parliaments. I by no means disagree to the idea of equitable reform, in regard to what are called rotten boroughs, &c.

The grievances we feel, and the cause of our misfortune, arise from the *corruption of men when chosen into Parliament.* Cut off the ways and means of corruption, and the effect must and will naturally cease. Mr. Burke's plan cuts off thirty-nine offices tenable and now held by members of the House of Commons. It also cuts off eleven now held by Peers in the House of Lords. This, indeed, is *striking* in *earnest* at the influence of the Crown over persons in Parliament. The effect is certain and immediate, and it also has a most beneficial and salutary operation in future, and which may not occur to many people's thoughts on the first view.

The *great number* of offices of more or less emolument, which are now tenable by parties sitting in Parliament, really operate like *prizes* in a *lottery*. An *interested* man purchases a seat, upon the same principle as a person buys a *lottery* ticket. The value of the ticket depends upon the quantum of prizes in the *wheel.* I think, therefore, if there are less chances of emolument, the value of seats in Parliament *will fall* (though the situations will become much more honourable).

If these happy consequences should ensue, how much more respectable will the House of Commons become. *Interested men* will lay out their money in some other way of *lucrative* advantages, while on the other hand the honest, distinterested, and well-intentioned gentlemen of fortune, rank, or abilities, will be able to serve their country in Parliament, without (what is too generally the case) ruining themselves and their families, by the enormous expenses of elections.

I really feel more solid grounds of hope that the constitution, the liberty and happiness of this country *may revive*, than I ever expected to have done, for many years past. I think most seriously that if this county of York, at their next proceedings, adheres to the *great objects* of enforcing frugal expenditure, and striking at the root of corruption, by reducing the ways and means of influence in the Crown, success will attend their endeavours; but if various speculations are gone into, even though they might be partly well founded in principles, I fear, nay, indeed, *I am certain*, that there are so many visionary schemes and expedients *by way of reforms on float*, that a *general* confusion and disagreement will ensue. . . .

Ever dear Mr. Milnes,
Your most obedient and very affectionate
humble servant,
ROCKINGHAM.

55. Letter from Lord Shelburne to the chairman of the Wiltshire Committee of Correspondence, 26 March 1780

(*Copies of the Proceedings of the General Meetings of the County of Wilts.* . . . (1780), pp. 54–58.)

This letter, apologizing for his inability to attend the forthcoming county meeting, illustrates Shelburne's views on parliamentary reform, which were more radical than those of the Rockingham Whigs.

Berkley Square, March 26, 1780.

. . . But I am sensible, that it must occur to our County, as it has already done to others, to consider what Steps can be taken to obtain that Reform of which our present Parliament gives so little Hope, acting even under all its present Circumstances, or what Security can be had for preserving in future what we may have the good Fortune to obtain in this Moment of Exigence. . . .

Two Measures have offered themselves for Consideration, which, inasmuch as they affect the House of Commons merely, come unquestionably within the Province of our County Meeting, and cannot by any Misrepresentation be construed to arise from improper Motives:–The one is to shorten the Duration of Parliaments; the other, to equalize the Representation, which at present confessedly bears no Proportion, either to the Number of People, the Quantum of Property, or the Proportion of public Contribution; nor does it hold to any Rank or Description whatever; but is the mere Child of Accident or Intrigue.

The People of England, I conceive, have, and always had, a clear, unalienable, indefeasible Right, both to the one and the other, in their fullest Extent, upon a stronger Ground than that of any Act or Acts of Parliament. That "the House of Commons must be free in every Circumstance of its Constitution", is the Foundation Stone of all our Government. The same Right which the People had formerly, and, through the Blessing of God, exerted so happily for us, their Posterity, to have Parliaments frequently *holden*, when they were aggrieved by the Crown's with-holding them, now goes to have them *frequently* and *equally chosen*, when it appears, through the Length of the Duration, and the Inequality of the Representation, that they are still more aggrieved than they were formerly, by the total Want of them–And if this should appear to be the Sense of a fair Majority of the People, collected together, either in County Meetings or in any other constitutional Mode, there can be no Doubt, but that proper Laws will be immediately enacted to restore the Constitution to its first Principles in these Particulars: For it is not to be presumed, that the present defective Representation would venture to oppose the manifest Sense of those from whom they derive all their Authority; much less that the House of Lords, constituted as it is, or the Crown, could be so ill-advised as to deny their Concurrence and Assent to so salutary a Reform, in a Part of the Constitution, which more particularly belongs to the Democracy.–These Principles are so unalterably engraven in my Mind, that I should hold myself criminal in the Suppression of them when called for. It will be for the County to judge, whether they will proceed to declaratory Resolutions on the Subject of them, and then wait till the Sense of the rest of the Kingdom is so far known; or whether they will be contented finally, without pushing the Right of the People to its utmost Extent, by insisting upon an annual Election, and a total Change of the Representation. There are Men, of whose Integrity there is but one Voice, and whose Judgment deserves every Attention throughout England, who foresee more Inconvenience than I confess I do in the *whole* Extent of these Propositions. Besides, the Consequences of great Changes have been, in all Times, so uncertain, that it may be most prudent to avoid them; especially as, in the present Instance, I am free to own, that, so far as I am capable of judging, every End may be obtained by the Repeal of the septennial Act, and a reasonable Addition of County Members, chosen by Districts, or under some Regulation, which might preclude all Necessity of Expence. But I shall most willingly subscribe to the Discretion and Wisdom of the Meeting in this and every other Consideration of Expediency, and I dare rely upon the Generosity and Candor of the County and Committee, that they will put a just Interpretation upon the Liberty I take, meaning to assume no more than what might become any other Freeholder; submitting my unreserved Sentiments, in Time of Distress, to their better Judgment, as I cannot have the Honor of attending in Person, when I might explain myself more particularly upon each Part, as Occasion, might require.–I have nothing so much at Heart as to prove the Sincerity and Consistency of my Conduct upon all Occasions, but most of all in the County of my Residence, and among a Neighbourhood whose good Opinion must in the End make the Comfort and Honor of my Life.

I have the Honor to be, with great Respect and Consideration, SIR,

Your most obedient

and humble Servant,

SHELBURNE.

To John Awdry, Esq, Chairman of the Wiltshire Committee.

56. The duke of Richmond's plan for parliamentary reform, 3 June 1780

(*Parl. Hist.*, XXI, pp. 686–688.)

At Richmond's request the Bill was given a first reading in the House of Lords, so that it might be recorded in the *Journals*. He then agreed to its withdrawal. Richmond did not fear universal male suffrage, as the aristocracy would always have the advantage over the masses of education, and would be able to lead them more easily if the people had the franchise and no longer felt defrauded of it.

[3 June, 1780]

The Duke of *Richmond* presented to the House a Bill intitled "An Act for declaring and restoring the natural, unalienable and equal right of all the Commons of Great Britain (infants, persons of insane mind and criminals incapacitated by law only excepted) to vote in the election of their representatives in parliament; for regulating the mode and manner of such elections; for restoring annual parliaments, for giving an hereditary seat to the sixteen peers which shall be elected for Scotland, and for establishing more equitable regulations concerning the peerage of Scotland." He said that as it was growing late, he would be as concise as possible in explaining to their lordships the plan of reformation which he had that day intended to submit to their consideration. The boroughs in this country, he said, were, according to their present constitutions, dangerous to liberty, and the great engine in the hands of ministers to enforce measures the most opposite to the real interests of the state. They were the very sink of corruption; corrupt themselves, they enabled the ministry to corrupt others, and to buy and sell the dignity and honour of the nation. Some of these boroughs, which might perhaps have been formerly considerable, were now so sunk, that scarcely the traces of a house could be found in them. In one borough in particular, Midhurst, he had often remarked several stones marked 1, 2, 3, 4, &c. in the park wall of a noble lord then in his eye (lord Montague); having asked what was the meaning of them, he had been told that they were votes! and returned members to parliament. He immediately perceived that they were very valuable stones, and that the noble lord would not part with them for a great deal of money.–The right of election was taken from all males of the community, in whom it ought naturally to rest; and was placed in the hands of a very small number indeed. Thus, not more than 6,000 men returned a clear majority of members to the House of Commons. The number of males in England and Wales he computed at 1,625,000, and yet the right of voting was confined to 210,000. This surely, he insisted, called loudly for reformation.–His grace spoke of the constitution of this country in the most rapturous expressions of admiration and delight. He explained what the parliament could do; what it could not do; and at last came to open his plan of reformation. He drew a Bill from his pocket, which contained his plan, and which it took him an hour and a half to read: the following were the heads: "The parliament in future to last but one year–the number of members to continue as at present, at 558.–Every man born a subject of Great Britain to be entitled to a vote at the age of 21 years.–A list to be taken in every parish of the number of men of that description, and returns to be made of them to the Lord Chancellor.–The numbers to be tolled up, and divided by 558; and then the quotient to be the number by which one member of parliament is to be elected. Every county to be divided into as many districts as they contain quotients of this nature, and these districts to be called boroughs.–The sixteen peers of Scotland to have the representation of the Scots peerage hereditary in their families; the other peers of Scotland to be made capable of being created peers of England, and their eldest sons to be eligible to seats in parliament for boroughs in Scotland." There were a number of regulations contained in the Bill; and after his grace had read the whole, he moved for leave to bring it in.

57. Prospectus and List of Members of the Society for Constitutional Information, 1780

(*Society for Constitutional Information* (n.d., ? 1780).)

The Society was founded in April 1780 by Major John Cartwright (1740–1824) and other Radical parliamentary reformers. It will be noticed that its membership was very respectable.

SOCIETY

FOR

CONSTITUTIONAL INFORMATION.

The design of this Society is to diffuse throughout the kingdom, as universally as possible, a knowledge of the great principles of Constitutional Freedom, particularly such as respect the election and duration of the representative body. With this view Constitutional Tracts, intended for the extension of this knowledge, and to communicate it to persons of all ranks, are printed and distributed GRATIS, at the expence of the Society. Essays, and extracts from various authors, calculated to promote the same design, are also published under the direction of the Society, in several of the News-papers: and it is the wish of the Society to extend this knowledge throughout every part of the united kingdoms, and to convince men of all ranks, that it is their interest, as well as their duty, to support a free constitution, and to maintain and assert those common rights, which are essential to the dignity, and to the happiness of human nature.

To procure short parliaments, and a more equal representation of the people, are the primary objects of the attention of this Society, and they wish to disseminate that knowledge among their Countrymen, which may lead them to a general sense of the importance of these objects, and which may induce them to contend for their rights, as men, and as citizens, with ardour and with firmness.

The communication of sound political knowledge to the people at large must be of great national advantage; as nothing but ignorance of their natural rights, or inattention to the consequence of those rights to their interest and happiness, can induce the majority of the inhabitants of any country to submit to any species of civil tyranny. Public Freedom is the source of national dignity, and of national felicity; and it is the duty of every friend to virtue and mankind to exert himself in the promotion of it.

By the laws of the Constitutional Society it is unlimited in its numbers. All questions in the Society are determined by ballot; and all ballots are taken by the President, or presiding Member. Gentlemen desirous of becoming Members are to be admitted by ballot, and to subscribe from One to Five Guineas per Annum; and those who wish to contribute otherwise to the support of this Institution, will please remit their contributions for this purpose to *Edward Bridgen, Esq. in Pater-noster Row, London*; signifying, that what they order is to be paid into the Hands of the *Treasurer of the Society for Constitutional Information.*

LIST OF THE MEMBERS

JAMES MARTIN, Esq. *President.*

B.

BARWIS Jackson, Esq.
Batley Jeremiah, Esq.
Bellas George, Esq.
Bennett the Rev. Thomas
Bott Edmund, Esq.
Boyes John, Esq.
Bridgen Edward, Esq. *Treasurer.*
Brocklesby Dr. Richard
Bromley the Rev. Mr.
Brown Joseph, Esq.
Budgen John Smith, Esq.
Bull Mr. Alderman
Buller Mr. William

C.

Canning Stratford, Esq.
Carter Sir John, Knt.
Carter John, Esq.
Carter Edward, Esq.
Cartwright Major John
Chancey Philip, Esq.
Chaplin Mr. Amos
Churchill John, Esq. *Vice President*
Cooksey Richard, Esq.
Crosby Mr. Alderman

D.

Day Thomas, Esq.
Dehany Philip, Esq.
Dilly Mr. Charles

E.

Eaton Mr.
Effingham the Right Hon. Earl of

F.

Finch John, Esq.
Fitzpatrick the Hon. Col.
Foy Sidney Hollis, Esq.
Frost Mr. John
Fytche Lewis Disney, Esq.

G.

Gibson Mr. Henry

H.

Hall Edward, Esq.
Hamilton Charles, Esq.
Hartley James, Esq.
Hodges Thomas Hallet, Esq.
Hodgson William, Esq.
Hollis Thomas Brand, Esq.
Horton Sir Watts Bart.
Huthwaite William, Esq.

J.

Jackson George, Esq.
Jebb Dr. John
Jervois Jervois Clark, Esq.
Jones William, Esq.

K.

Keene Mr. Henry
Kinnaird the Right Hon. Lord
Kippis the Rev. Dr.
Kirkby Capt. John
Kirkpatrick Lieut. Col.
Knowlys Newman, Esq.

L.

Lawrence French, Esq.
Lewes Sir Watkin, Knt.
Lloyd Gamaliel, Esq.
Lofft Capel, Esq.

M.

Mawbey Sir Joseph, Bart.
Metcalfe Benjamin, Esq.

N.

Nash Mr.
Norcliffe Sir James, Bart.
Northcote the Rev. Thomas

O.

O'Hara John Hamilton, Esq.
Oldfield Mr.

P.

Paradise John, Esq.
Parker Joseph, Esq.
Pickett Mr. Alderman
Plummer William, Esq.
Powlett the Rev. Charles
Price the Rev. Dr.

R.

Redman John, Esq.
Reynolds Richard, Esq.
Richards John, Esq.
Robinson the Rev. Robert
Rogers Thomas, Esq.
Rollestone Launcelot, Esq.

S.

Sawbridge Mr. Alderman
Sharp Mr. Richard
Sherbrooke William, Esq.
Sheridan Richard Brinsley, Esq.
Shore Samuel, Esq.
Shove Alured Henry, Esq. *Vice President*
Sinclair John, Esq.
Stamford Thomas, Esq.
Sturche Mr. William

T.

Temple Richard Goodman, Esq.
Tooke William, Esq.
Tooke John Horne, Esq.
Towers the Rev. Dr.
Towgood Mathew, Esq.
Townsend Mr. Alderman
Trecothick James, Esq. *Vice President*
Turner Mr Alderman

V.

Vardy John, Esq.
Vaughan Samuel, Esq.
Vaughan Benjamin, Esq.
Vaughan William, Esq.

W.

Walker Adam, Esq.
Walker the Rev. George
Webber Mr. James
White Dr.
Williams Mr. Thomas
Winter John, Esq.
Wood Thomas, Esq.

Y.

Yeates Mr. Thomas

Thomas Yeates jun. *Secretary.*

Joseph Keys, Messenger.

N.B. Letters of Communication to the Society to be directed to Mr. Thomas Yeates, *Attorney,* No. 2, *New Inn, London.*

58. Speech by William Pitt in the House of Commons on parliamentary reform, 7 May 1782

(*Parl. Hist.*, XII, pp. 1416–1422.)

This should be compared with Lord Chatham's views on the subject (No. 51).

. . . Upon these occasions,[1] they were unsuccessful in their efforts, on account of that corrupt influence of which he had spoken; but at last, he thanked God, the voice of the people had happily prevailed, and we were now blessed with a ministry,[2] whose

[1] *i.e.* previous attempts at parliamentary reform. [2] The second Rockingham Ministry.

wishes went along with those of the people, for a moderate reform of the errors which had intruded themselves into the constitution; and he was happy to see that there was a spirit of unanimity prevalent in every part of the kingdom, and also in every part of that House, which made the present day the fittest for undertaking this great task. The ministers had declared their virtuous resolution of supporting the King's government by means more honourable as well as more permanent than corruption; and the nation had confidence in the declarations of men who had so invariably proved themselves the friends of freedom, and the animated supporters of an equal and fair system of representation. That the frame of our constitution had undergone material alterations, by which the Commons' House of parliament had received an improper and dangerous bias, and by which, indeed, it had fallen so greatly from that direction and effect which it was intended, and ought to have in the constitution, he believed it would be idle for him to attempt to prove. It was a fact so plain and palpable, that every man's reason, if not his experience, must point it out to him. He had only to examine the quality and nature of that branch of the constitution as originally established, and compare it with its present state and condition. That beautiful frame of government which had made us the envy and admiration of mankind, in which the people were entitled to hold so distinguished a share, was so far dwindled and had so far departed from its original purity, as that the representatives ceased, in a great degree, to be connected with the people. It was of the essence of the constitution, that the people should have a share in the government by the means of representation; and its excellence and permanency was calculated to consist in this representation, having been designed to be equal, easy, practicable, and complete. When it ceased to be so; when the representative ceased to have connection with the constituent, and was either dependent on the crown or the aristocracy, there was a defect in the frame of representation, and it was not innovation, but recovery of constitution, to repair it.

He would not, in the present instance, call to their view, or endeavour to discuss the question, whether this species of reform, or that; whether this suggestion, or that, was the best; and which would most completely tally and square with the original frame of the constitution: it was simply his purpose to move for the institution of an inquiry, composed of such men as the House should, in their wisdom, select as the most proper and the best qualified for investigating this subject, and making a report to the House of the best means of carrying into execution a moderate and substantial reform of the representation of the people. Though he would not press upon their consideration any proposition whatever, he should still think it his duty to state some facts and circumstances, which, in his idea, made this object of reform essentially necessary. He believed, however, that even this was unnecessary, for there was not a gentleman in the House who would not acknowledge, with him, that the representation, as it now stood, was incomplete. It was perfectly understood, that there were some boroughs absolutely governed by the Treasury, and others totally possessed by them. It required no experience to say that such boroughs had no one quality of representation in them; they had no share nor substance in the general interests of the country; and they had in fact no stake for which to appoint their guardians in the popular assembly. The influence of the Treasury in some boroughs was contested, not by the electors of these boroughs, but by some one or other powerful man, who assumed or pretended to an hereditary property of what ought only to be the rights and privileges of the electors. The interests of the Treasury were considered as well as the interests of the great man, the lord or the commoner who had connection with the borough; but the interests of the people, the rights of the electors, were the only things that never were attended to, nor taken into the account. Would any man say, that in this case, there was the most distant idea or principle of representation? There were other boroughs which had now, in fact, no actual existence, but in the return of members to the House. They had no existence in property, in population, in trade, in weight. There were hardly any men in the borough who had a right to vote; and they were the slaves and subjects of a person who claimed the property of the borough, and who in fact made the return. This also was no representation, nor any thing like it. Another set of boroughs and towns, in the lofty possession of English freedom, claimed to themselves the right of bringing their votes to market. They had no other market, no other property, and no other stake in the country, than the property and price which they procured for their votes. Such boroughs were the most dangerous of all others. So far from consulting the interests of their country in the choice which they made, they held out their borough to the best purchaser, and, in fact, they belonged more to the nabob of Arcot than they did to the people of Great Britain. They were cities and boroughs more within the jurisdiction of the Carnatic than the limits of the empire of Great Britain; and it was a fact pretty well known, and generally understood, that the nabob of Arcot had no less than seven or eight members in that House. Such boroughs, then, were sources of corruption; they gave rise to an inundation of corrupt wealth, and corrupt members, who had no regard nor connection, either for or with the people of this kingdom. It had always been considered, in all nations, as the greatest source of danger to a kingdom, when a foreign influence was suffered to creep into the national councils. The fact was clear, that the influence of the nabobs of India was great; why then might not their imaginations point out to them another most probable circumstance that might occur, the danger of which would be evident, as soon as mentioned? Might not a foreign state in enmity with this country, by means of these boroughs, procure a party of men to act for them under the mask and character of members of that House?

It had been thought by some, that the best means of effecting a more near relation between the representatives and the people, was to take from the decayed and corrupt boroughs a part of their members, and add them to those places which had more interest and stake in the country. Another mode of making the connection between the representative and constitution more lively and intimate, was to bring the former more frequently before the electors, by shortening the duration of parliament. But all these propositions he would beg leave, for the present, to omit entirely, and to deliver the matter to the committee to be chosen free from all suggestions whatever, that they might exercise their own judgment, and collect, from the lights which they would receive, full and complete information on the subject. . . . He concluded with moving, "That a committee be appointed to enquire into the present State of the

Representation of the Commons of Great Britain in parliament, to report the same to the House, and likewise what steps in their opinion it may be proper for parliament to take concerning the same."[1]

59. Speech by Edmund Burke in the House of Commons against Pitt's proposal for a committee to consider parliamentary reform, 7 May 1782

(*Works and Correspondence of Edmund Burke*, VI (1852), pp. 129–131, 136.)

This speech is interesting not only as an illustration of Burke's views on parliamentary reform, but because it foreshadows the doctrine he put forward later in the *Reflections on the Revolution in France*.

. . . On the other side, there are two parties who proceed on two grounds, in my opinion, as they state them, utterly irreconcilable. The one is juridicial, the other political. The one is in the nature of a claim of right, on the supposed rights of man as man; this party desire the decision of a suit. The other ground, as far as I can divine what it directly means, is, that the representation is not so politically framed as to answer the theory of its institution. . . . The language of the first party is plain and intelligible; they who plead an absolute right cannot be satisfied with any thing short of personal representation, because all *natural* rights must be the rights of individuals; as by *nature* there is no such thing as politic or corporate personality; all these ideas are mere fictions of law, they are creatures of voluntary institution; men as men are individuals, and nothing else. They, therefore, who reject the principle of natural and personal representation, are essentially and eternally at variance with those who claim it. As to the first sort of reformers, it is ridiculous to talk to them of the British constitution upon any or upon all of its bases; for they lay it down that every man ought to govern himself, and that where he cannot go himself he must send his representative; that all other government is usurpation; and is so far from having a claim to our obedience, it is not only our right, but our duty, to resist it. Nine-tenths of the reformers argue thus, that is, on the natural right. It is impossible not to make some reflection on the nature of this claim, or avoid a comparison between the extent of the principle and the present object of the demand. If this claim be founded, it is clear to what it goes. The House of Commons, in that light, undoubtedly is no representative of the people, as a collection of individuals. Nobody pretends it, nobody can justify such an assertion. When you come to examine into this claim of right, founded on the right of self-government in each individual, you find the thing demanded infinitely short of the principle of the demand. What! one *third* only of the legislature, and of the government no share at all? What sort of treaty of partition is this for those who have an inherent right to the whole? Give them all they ask, and your grant is still a cheat; for how comes only a third to be their younger children's fortune in this settlement? How came they neither to have the choice of kings, or lords, or judges, or generals, or admirals, or bishops, or priests, or ministers, or justices of peace? Why, what have you to answer in favour of the prior rights of the crown and peerage but this–our constitution is a prescriptive constitution; it is a constitution whose sole authority is that it has existed time out of mind. It is settled in these *two* portions

[1] Pitt's motion was rejected by 161 to 141.

against one, legislatively; and in the whole of the judicature, the whole of the federal capacity, of the executive, the prudential, and the financial administration, in one alone. Nor was your House of Lords and the prerogatives of the crown settled on any adjudication in favour of natural rights, for they could never be so partitioned. Your king, your lords, your judges, your juries, grand and little, are all prescriptive; and what proves it is the disputes not yet concluded, and never near becoming so, when any of them first originated. Prescription is the most solid of all titles, not only to property, but, which is to secure that property, to government. They harmonize with each other, and give mutual aid to one another. It is accompanied with another ground of authority in the constitution of the human mind,–presumption. It is a presumption in favour of any settled scheme of government against any untried project, that a nation has long existed and flourished under it. It is a better presumption even of the *choice* of a nation, far better than any sudden and temporary arrangement by actual election. Because a nation is not an idea only of local extent, and individual momentary aggregation; but it is an idea of continuity, which extends in time as well as in numbers and in space. And this is a choice not of one day, or one set of people, not a tumultuary and giddy choice; it is a deliberate election of ages and of generations; it is a constitution made by what is ten thousand times better than choice, it is made by the peculiar circumstances, occasions, tempers, dispositions, and moral, civil, and social habitudes of the people, which disclose themselves only in a long space of time. It is a vestment, which accommodates itself to the body. Nor is prescription of government formed upon blind, unmeaning prejudices–for man is a most unwise and a most wise being. The individual is foolish. The multitude, for the moment, is foolish, when they act without deliberation; but the species is wise, and, when time is given to it, as a species it always acts right.

The reason for the crown as it is, for the lords as they are, is my reason for the commons as they are, the electors as they are. Now, if the Crown, and the Lords, and the Judicatures, are all prescriptive, so is the House of Commons of the very same origin and of no other. We and our electors have their powers and privileges both made and circumscribed by prescription, as much to the full as the other parts; and as such we have always claimed them, and on no other title. The House of Commons is a legislative body corporate by prescription, not made upon any given theory, but existing prescriptively–just like the rest. This prescription has made it essentially what it is,–an aggregate collection of three parts, knights, citizens, burgesses. The question is whether this has been always so, since the House of Commons has taken its present shape and circumstances, and has been an essential operative part of the constitution; which, I take it, it has been for at least five hundred years.

This I resolve to myself in the affirmative: and then another question arises, whether this House stands firm upon its ancient foundations, and is not, by time and accidents, so declined from its perpendicular, as to want the hand of the wise and experienced architects of the day to set it upright again, and to prop and buttress it up for duration;–whether it continues true to the principles upon which it has hitherto stood;–whether this be *de facto* the constitution of the House of Commons, as it has been since the time that the House of Commons has, without dispute, become a necessary and an efficient part of the British constitution? To ask whether a thing which has always been the same stands to its usual principle, seems to me to be perfectly absurd; for how do you know the principles but from the construction? and if that remains the same, the principles remain the same. It is true, that to say your constitution is what it has been is no sufficient defence for those who say it is a bad constitution. It is an answer to those who say that it is a degenerate constitution. To those who say it is a bad one I answer, look to its effects. In all moral machinery the moral results are its test.

On what grounds do we go to restore our constitution to what it has been at some given period, or to reform and reconstruct it upon principles more conformable to a sound theory of government? A prescriptive government, such as ours, never was the work of any legislator, never was made upon any foregone theory. It seems to me a preposterous way of reasoning, and a perfect confusion of ideas, to take the theories which learned and speculative men have made from that government, and then, supposing it made on those theories which were made from it, to accuse the government as not corresponding with them. . . .

. . . It is to this humour, and it is to the measures growing out of it, that I set myself (I hope not alone) in the most determined opposition. Never before did we at any time in this country meet upon the theory of our frame of government, to sit in judgment on the constitution of our country, to call it as a delinquent before us, and to accuse it of every defect and every vice; to see whether it, an object of our veneration, even our adoration, did or did not accord with a pre-conceived scheme in the minds of certain gentlemen. Cast your eyes on the journals of parliament. It is for fear of losing the inestimable treasure we have, that I do not venture to game it out of my hands for the vain hope of improving it. I look with filial reverence on the constitution of my country, and never will cut it in pieces, and put it into the kettle of any magician, in order to boil it, with the puddle of their compounds, into youth and vigour. On the contrary, I will drive away such pretenders; I will nurse its venerable age, and with lenient arts extend a parent's breath.

Part III

THE LAW AND ITS ADMINISTRATION

THE LAW AND ITS ADMINISTRATION

Introduction

A NUMBER of important changes in the law occurred between 1714 and 1783, many of them connected with the two great eighteenth-century lawyers, Lords Hardwicke and Mansfield. In 1731 English was ordered to be used in place of Latin in all legal proceedings;[1] the Calendar was reformed in 1751, bringing Great Britain into line with the Continent;[2] and in 1760 the judges were given complete security of tenure during good behaviour by an Act providing that their commissions should not terminate with a demise of the Crown.[3] Hardwicke's Marriage Act of 1753[4] introduced for the first time the principle that marriage, formerly regarded as the concern of ecclesiastical law, was a civil contract in which the State was concerned; and was directed against a great social evil of the day, the clandestine marriages of minors without the consent of their parents.

A number of important judicial decisions also fall within this period. The eighteenth century was a vital period in the development of the freedom of the Press. Since the lapsing of the Licensing Act in 1696, writers could publish what they liked, subject to the law of seditious libel, which was strictly interpreted by the judges, the jury in these cases having only the power to decide on the fact of publication, not upon the question whether or not the work under consideration was a seditious libel. This is illustrated by the trial of Richard Francklin, printer of *The Craftsman*, in 1731.[5] A growing public opinion regarded this state of affairs as inequitable, and a few years after the end of our period Fox's Libel Act of 1792 gave the jury the right to decide upon the question of law as well as that of fact. More important for the freedom of the Press was the abolition, as a result of the case of John Wilkes and *The North Briton* in 1763, of the general warrants which the Secretaries of State had for many years used widely as a means of arresting writers, printers and publishers of anonymous works.[6] In the case of the Negro Somersett in 1772, Lord Mansfield decided, against previous high authority, that slavery was not recognized by the law of England;[7] and the trial of Lord George Gordon in 1781 was the occasion of a lucid exposition by Mansfield of the law of treason.[8]

The central government in the eighteenth century had, according to modern ideas of the proper sphere of governmental action, a very limited conception of its duties; and the principal officers of State were, by modern standards, provided with a very small staff of civil servants.[9] Even in fields where its intervention was accepted the local authorities of the parishes, boroughs and counties did nearly all the work. The central administration as a rule contented itself with seeing that suitable persons were appointed and laying down general rules for their conduct. The Secretaries of State were the only ministers with much responsibility for the internal condition of England. They had special duties in connexion with the maintenance of order and

[1] No. 60. [2] No. 61. [3] No. 63. [4] No. 62. [5] No. 64.
[6] No. 65. [7] No. 66. [8] No. 67. [9] No. 68.

the arresting of political offenders. They were also the normal channel by which royal commands were communicated to the king's subjects. Until 1782 these duties, both foreign and domestic, were divided between the Secretaries of the Southern and Northern Departments.[1] In 1771 George III had suggested the more practical arrangement of giving all foreign business to one secretary and all domestic business to the other, and this was adopted, by informal arrangement, on the formation of the second Rockingham Ministry in March 1782.[2]

Eighteenth-century governments were poorly equipped for maintaining order. They trusted for the preservation of internal security mainly to the activity of the local magistrates, and the troubles experienced by them in controlling Jacobite mobs led to the passing in 1715 of the Riot Act.[3] Much later than this it was not hard to rouse the London mob; for example, in 1768 it demonstrated its enthusiasm for "Wilkes and Liberty", and its antipathy to Papists a few years later in the Gordon Riots. When exhortation failed to disperse the rioters, the civil authorities called on the army. If the disturbances took place in London the guards could be used; otherwise the nearest troops were summoned; but according to the Secretary at War in 1772, the number of troops available for this purpose in the whole of England did not exceed 5,000. The necessity for co-operation between civil and military bodies often led to difficulties, and both Secretaries of State and magistrates were subjected to much criticism. The Gordon Riots were in fact suppressed only after orders had been issued to all commanding officers instructing them "to act without waiting for directions from the Civil Magistrates and to use force for dispersing the illegal and tumultuous assemblies of the people".[4] Apart from these outbreaks of rioting, the day-to-day keeping of order, especially in London, was a constant source of anxiety and difficulty throughout the century. Parliament continually increased the number of crimes punishable by death in the hope that severity would be a real deterrent. Sir John Fielding, the Bow Street magistrate, realized that what was required was a sound police system, and his patrols did effect some temporary improvement in preventing and detecting crimes of violence in the London area.[5]

The general structure and working of local administration remained the same as in the preceding century. The justices of the peace were still much the most important officials of local government, and throughout the eighteenth century new tasks were continually imposed on them by statute. As the century advanced, it became increasingly clear that the existing machinery of local government was inadequate for all the work it now had to do, and some attempts at co-ordination were made. Two general Acts dealing with Poor Relief were passed,[6] and the County Rates Act of 1739 substituted one general county rate for the various rates formerly levied by the justices.[7] In many towns street and improvement commissioners were set up by statute to deal with the increasing urban problems, such as drainage and the paving and lighting of the streets. Fundamental reorganization of the machinery of both central and local government had, however, to wait till after the end of our period.

[1] No. 69. [2] No. 70. [3] No. 71. [4] No. 72.
[5] No. 73. [6] Nos. 75 and 76. [7] No. 74.

BIBLIOGRAPHY

I. THE LEGAL SYSTEM

Sir William Blackstone's contemporary exposition, *Commentaries on the Laws of England* (4 vols., Oxford, 1765–1769), became at once and has remained ever since a classic. There are lives of Blackstone by L. C. Warden (Charlottesville, Va., 1938) and D. A. Lockmuller (Chapel Hill, N.C., 1938). The monumental *History of English Law* by Sir William Holdsworth (12 vols., London, 1922–1938), the last three volumes of which deal systematically with the eighteenth century, is the standard modern work. Sir F. D. Mackinnon's chapter on "Law and the Lawyers" in *Johnson's England*, II (Oxford, 1933), pp. 287–309, is a useful introduction. L. Radzinowicz, *A History of the English Criminal Law and its Administration from 1750*, vol. I (London, 1948), approaches the subject from the historical angle. The standard reference books for the eminent lawyers of the eighteenth century are still John (Lord) Campbell, *Lives of the Lord Chancellors* (8 vols., London, 1845–1869) and *Lives of the Chief Justices* (3 vols., London, 1849–1857), and E. Foss, *Judges of England* (9 vols., London, 1848–1864). The work of the greatest chancellor of the period is surveyed and eulogized in P. C. Yorke, *Life and Correspondence of Hardwicke*, II, pp. 413–555. There is also a modern life of Lord Mansfield by C. H. S. Fifoot (Oxford, 1936), but John Holliday, *Life of Mansfield* (London, 1797), is still of use. For Lord Camden, H. S. Eeles, *Lord Chancellor Camden and his Family* (London, 1934), should be consulted. Books on the various Inns of Court throw light on legal education, *e.g.* W. Herbert, *Antiquities of Inns of Court and Chancery* (London, 1804), and W. J. Loftie, *Inns of Court and Chancery* (2nd edition, London, 1895). Reports of cases, usually made by lawyers for their own use, are abundant but not reliable, though there was a great improvement towards the end of our period, in which Burrow's reports of cases decided in the King's Bench deserve honourable mention. The historian is most likely to want to refer to the well-known series of *State Trials*, vols. 15–21 [1710–1784], edited by T. B. Howell (London, 1812–1814). They have sometimes been criticized for inaccuracy but provide valuable material not only for legal history but for social conditions, since they include reports of many trials which were not State trials except in the sense that they attracted widespread attention at the time. The second part of this comment is also applicable to Sir A. D. McNair, *Dr. Johnson and the Law* (Cambridge, 1948).

Some specialized studies contributed to historical periodicals may also be listed. These include three in the *American Historical Review*: (1) A. H. Carpenter, "Naturalization in England and the American Colonies", IX (1903–1904), pp. 288–303; (2) A. L. Cross, "The English Criminal Law and Benefit of Clergy", XXII (1916–1917), pp. 544–565; and (3) C. Kirkby, "The English Game Law System", XXXVIII (1932–1933), pp. 240–262. Equally valuable are the articles by Miss L. S. Sutherland on "The Law Merchant in England in the Seventeenth and Eighteenth Centuries" and by Miss Sybil Campbell on "Economic and Social Effect of the Usury Laws in the Eighteenth Century" in the *Transactions of the Royal Historical Society*, 4th Series, XVII (1934), pp. 149–176, and XVI (1933), pp. 197–210, respectively. "Marriage Settlements in the 18th century" by H. J. Habakkuk in *ibid.*, XXXII (1950), pp. 15–30, is equally valuable for social as for strictly legal history.

On the enforcement of law and order, R. Leslie-Melville, *Life and Work of Sir John Fielding* (London, 1935), is a sound study of crime and punishment in London; Patrick Pringle, *Hue and Cry* (London, 1955), is an entertaining account of the work of the Bow Street police; while Sir A. P. Herbert, *Mr. Gay's London* (London, 1948), based on the proceedings at the London sessions, provides a cross-section of the criminal classes of the period. C. Reith, *The Police Idea, its History and Evolution in England in the Eighteenth century and After* (Oxford, 1938), is a helpful survey. On the Gordon Riots, J. P. de Castro, *The Gordon Riots* (London, 1926), should be supplemented by George F. E. Rudé, "The Gordon Riots: a study of the Rioters and their

Victims", an interesting analysis of the social status of the rioters, in *Transactions of the Royal Historical Society*, 5th Series, VI (1956), pp. 93–114. *The Official Diary of Lieutenant-General Adam Williamson*, edited by J. C. Fox, Camden Society (London, 1912), has details on the use of the Tower of London as a State prison, especially for Jacobite prisoners: the works of John Howard, notably *State of the Prisons in England and Wales* (Warrington, 1777), and other philanthropists on the ordinary prisons are well known. E. W. Pettifer, *Punishments of Former Days* (Bradford, 1939), is also useful.

II. HISTORY OF THE DEPARTMENTS OF ADMINISTRATION

Recently more attention has at last been given to this branch of institutional history. The most valuable of the resulting studies are M. A. Thomson, *The Secretaries of State 1681–1782* (Oxford, 1932), and Margaret M. Spector, *The American Department of the British Government 1768–1782* (New York, 1940). Basil Williams compared the English and French holders of the office of Secretary of State in *Studies in Anglo-French History*, edited by A. Coville and H. W. V. Temperley (Cambridge, 1935). Unfortunately there is no study of the Treasury comparable to that of Professor Thomson on the office of the Secretaries of State. Some help is obtainable, however, from the official *Calendars*; from the works on taxation cited in the sectional bibliography on Public Finance; and from Dora M. Clark's article on "The Office of Secretary to the Treasury in the Eighteenth Century" in the *American Historical Review*, XLII (1936–1937), pp. 22–45. The recently published *Jenkinson Papers 1760–66*, edited by Ninetta S. Jucker (London, 1949), throw much light on the problems of administration and patronage presented to a secretary to the Treasury in the eighteenth century. The scholarly work of E. Hughes, *Studies in Administration and Finance* (Manchester, 1934), though chiefly concerned with the duties on salt, is also helpful on administrative developments. O. M. Dickerson, *American Colonial Government 1696–1765: a Study of the British Board of Trade* (Cleveland, 1912), A. H. Basye, *Lords Commissioners of Trade and Plantations* [1748–1782] (New Haven, 1925), Mary P. Clarke, "Board of Trade at Work" in the *American Historical Review*, XVII (1911–1912), pp. 17–43, and D. B. Horn, "The Board of Trade and Consular Reports 1696–1782", in the *English Historical Review*, LIV (1939), pp. 476–480, help to explain the origins, functions and place of the board in the central administrative system.

Some miscellaneous articles may be grouped together here. E. R. Turner wrote on "The Lords Justices of England" in the *English Historical Review*, XXIX (1914), pp. 453–476. G. F. James gave a detailed account of the internal organization of the Admiralty in "The Admiralty Establishment 1759" in the *Bulletin of the Institute of Historical Research*, XVI (1938–1939), pp. 24–27. E. J. Parry's article on "Undersecretaries of State for Foreign Affairs 1782–1855" in the *English Historical Review*, XLIX (1934), pp. 308–320, opens with a brief but suggestive retrospect. A. V. Judges in "Government Personnel in the Eighteenth Century" in the *Bulletin of the Institute of Historical Research*, XVII (1939–1940), pp. 67–68, mentions some of the available sources of information on this little explored subject. A. L. Cross, *Eighteenth Century Documents relating to the Royal Forests, the Sheriffs and Smuggling* (New York, 1928), has information on miscellaneous administrative problems, and Sir John Craig, *Newton at the Mint* (Cambridge, 1946), discusses the organization of this department in the early part of the eighteenth century.

On administrative reform generally, there is an important article by D. L. Keir in the *Law Quarterly Review*, L (1934), pp. 368–385, "Economical Reform, 1779–87", which draws attention to the epoch-making reports of the Commission on the Public Accounts, 1780–1786, which "provide an unrivalled picture of the English administrative system of the pre-Reform era".

III. LOCAL GOVERNMENT

The selective *Local History Handlist* published by the Historical Association (London, 1947) is invaluable to anyone interested in local history and is expressly designed to help the "untrained worker". The earlier leaflets of the Historical Association, No. 66, *Parish History and Records*, and No. 72, *Short Bibliography of Local History*, may also be consulted. W. E. Tate, *The Parish Chest: A Study of the Records of Parochial Administration in England* (Cambridge, 1946), provides an admirable introduction to the classes of record which may be of use to the parish historian. More elaborate guides include C. Gross, *Bibliography of British Municipal History* (New York, 1897), and A. L. Humphreys, *A Handbook to County Bibliography* (London, 1917). These must be supplemented for more recent work by G. L. Gomme, *Index of Archeological Papers* (London, 1907), with supplements, and by Guy and Zirphie Parsloe and others, *Guide to the Historical Publications of the Societies of England and Wales*, which appeared in the form of an annual supplement to the *Bulletin of the Institute of Historical Research*, Nos. 1–13 (London, 1930–1948). The *Victoria History of the Counties of England* contributes notably to the history of the localities which have now been included in it, but it is still far from complete and some volumes are already obsolescent. Many of the works listed in the sectional bibliography on Social Life are of value for local conditions.

The main features of eighteenth-century local government were the wide powers exercised locally by the justices of the peace, with very little supervision by the central government. Much information about their activities may be gleaned from R. Burn, *Justice of the Peace and Parish Officer* (2 vols., London, 1755), which was constantly reprinted and remained the standard authority until well on in the nineteenth century. Sidney and Beatrice Webb, *English Local Government from the Revolution to the Municipal Corporations Act* (9 vols., London, 1906–1929), provides an authoritative account, at once comprehensive and exact, of the whole complicated system. In conclusion, a few specialized studies may be mentioned, especially E. Cannon, *History of Local Rates in England* (2nd (enlarged) edition, London, 1912); J. Toulmin Smith, *The Parish* (London, 1854); E. G. Dowdell, *Hundred Years of Quarter Sessions* [1660–1760] (Cambridge, 1932), which deals with Middlesex only; and an unpublished thesis on "The Middlesex Magistrate 1760–1820" by Iris Forrester, mentioned in the *Bulletin of the Institute of Historical Research*, XIII (1935–1936), pp. 50–52.

A. THE LAW

(*a*) STATUTES

60. Act providing that all proceedings in the Law Courts shall be in English, 1731

(*Statutes at Large*, XVI, pp. 248–249, 4 Geo. II, cap. 26.)

This substitution of English for Latin in indictments was opposed by many lawyers and was deplored by Blackstone.

An act that all proceedings in courts of justice within that part of Great Britain *called* England, *and in the court of exchequer in* Scotland, *shall be in the* English *language.*

WHEREAS *many and great mischiefs do frequently happen to the subjects of this kingdom, from the proceedings in courts of justice being in an unknown language, those who are summoned and impleaded having no knowledge or understanding of what is alledged for or against them in the pleadings of their lawyers and attornies, who use a character not legible to any but persons practising the law*: To remedy these great mischiefs, and to protect the lives and fortunes of the subjects of that part of *Great Britain* called *England*, more effectually than heretofore, from the peril of being ensnared or brought in danger by forms and proceedings in courts of justice, in an unknown language, be it enacted by the King's most excellent majesty, by and with the advice and consent of the lords spiritual and temporal, and commons, of *Great Britain* in parliament assembled, and by the authority of the same, That from and after the twenty-fifth day of *March* one thousand seven hundred and thirty-three, all writs, process and returns thereof, and proceedings thereon, and all pleadings, rules, orders, indictments, informations, inquisitions, presentments, verdicts, prohibitions, certificates, and all patents, charters, pardons, commissions, records, judgments, statutes, recognizances, bonds, rolls, entries, fines and recoveries, and all proceedings relating thereunto, and all proceedings of courts leet, courts baron and customary courts, and all copies thereof, and all proceedings whatsoever in any courts of justice within that part of *Great Britain* called *England*, and in the court of exchequer in *Scotland*, and which concern the law and administration of justice, shall be in the *English* tongue and language only, and not in *Latin* or *French*, or any other tongue or language whatsoever, and shall be written in such a common legible hand and character, as the acts of parliament are usually ingrossed in, and the lines and words of the same to be written at least as close as the said acts usually are, and not in any hand commonly called *court hand*, and in words at length and not abbreviated; any law, custom or usage heretofore to the contrary thereof notwithstanding: and all and every person or persons offending against this act, shall for every such offence forfeit and pay the sum of fifty pounds to any person who shall sue for the same by action of debt, bill, plaint or information in any of his Majesty's courts of record in *Westminster* hall, or court of exchequer in *Scotland* respectively, wherein no essoin, protection or wager of law, or more than one imparlance shall be allowed.

II. And be it further enacted by the authority aforesaid, That mistranslation, variation in form by reason of translation, mispelling or mistake in clerkship, or pleadings or proceedings begun or to be begun before the said twenty-fifth day of *March* one thousand seven hundred and thirty-three, being part in *Latin* and part in *English*, shall be no error, nor make void any proceedings by reason thereof; but that all manner of mistranslation, errors in form, mispellings, mistakes in clerkship, may at any time be amended, whether in paper or on record or otherwise, before or after judgment, upon payment of reasonable costs only.

III. Provided always, That nothing in this act, nor any thing herein contained, shall extend to certifying beyond the seas any case or proceedings in the court of admiralty; but that in such cases the commissions and proceedings may be certified in *Latin* as formerly they have been.

IV. *And whereas several good and profitable laws have been enacted, to the intent that the parties in all manner of actions and demands might not be delayed and hindred from obtaining the effect of their suits, after issue tried and judgment given, by reason of any subtile, ignorant or defective pleadings, nor for any defect in form, commonly called* jeofails; it is hereby enacted and declared, That all and every statute and statutes for the reformation and amending the delays arising from any *Jeofails* whatsoever, shall and may extend to all and every form and forms, and to all proceedings in courts of justice (except in criminal cases) when the forms and proceedings are in *English*; and that all and every error and mistake whatsoever, which would or might be amended and remedied by any statute of *Jeofails*, if the proceedings had been in *Latin*, all such errors and mistakes of the same and like nature, when the forms are in *English*, shall be deemed, and are hereby declared to be amended and remedied by the statutes now in force for the amendment of any *Jeofails*; and this clause shall be taken and construed in all courts of justice in the most ample and beneficial manner, for the ease and benefit of the parties, and to prevent frivolous and vexatious delays.

61. Act substituting the Gregorian for the Julian Calendar, 1751

(*Statutes at Large*, xx, pp. 186–192, 24 Geo. II, cap. 23.)

This Act brought the English calendar into line with that used on the Continent. It met with much opposition, and the suppression of the eleven days between 2 and 14 September led to the popular demand, "Give us back our eleven days!"

An act for regulating the commencement of the year; and for correcting the calendar now in use.

WHEREAS *the legal supputation of the year of our Lord in that part of* Great Britain *called* England, *according to which the year beginneth on the twenty-fifth day of March, hath been found by experience to be attended with divers inconveniences, not only as it differs from the usage of neighbouring nations, but also from the legal method of computation in that part of* Great Britain *called* Scotland, *and from the common usage throughout the whole kingdom, and thereby frequent mistakes are occasioned in the dates of deeds, and other writings, and disputes arise therefrom: and whereas the calendar now in use throughout all his Majesty's* British *dominions, commonly called* The Julian Calendar, *hath been discovered to be erroneous, by means whereof the vernal or spring equinox, which at the time of the general council of* Nice *in the year of our Lord three hundred and twenty-five, happened on or about the twenty-first day of* March, *now happens on the ninth or tenth day of the same month; and the said error is still increasing, and if not remedied, would, in process of time, occasion the several equinoxes and solstices to fall at very different times in the civil year from what they formerly did, which might tend to mislead persons ignorant of the said alteration: and whereas a method of correcting the calendar in such manner, as that the equinoxes and solstices may for the future fall nearly on the same nominal days, on which the same happened at the time of the said general council, hath been received and established, and is now generally practised by almost all other nations of* Europe: *and whereas it will be of general convenience to merchants, and other persons corresponding with other nations and countries, and tend to prevent mistakes and disputes in or concerning the dates of letters, and accounts, if the like correction be received and established in his Majesty's dominions:* may it therefore please your Majesty, that it may be enacted, and be it enacted by the King's most excellent majesty, by and with the advice and consent of the lords spiritual and temporal, and commons, in this present parliament assembled, and by the authority of the same, That in and throughout all his Majesty's dominions and countries in *Europe, Asia, Africa* and *America*, belonging or subject to the crown of *Great Britain*, the said supputation, according to which the year of our Lord beginneth on the twenty-fifth day of *March*, shall not be made use of from and after the last day of *December* one thousand seven hundred and fifty-one; and that the first day of *January* next following the said last day of *December* shall be reckoned, taken, deemed and accounted to be the first day of the year of our Lord one thousand seven hundred and fifty-two; and the first day of *January*, which shall happen next after the said first day of *January* one thousand seven hundred and fifty-two, shall be reckoned, taken, deemed and accounted to be the first day of the year of our Lord one thousand seven hundred and fifty-three; and so on, from time to time, the first day of *January* in every year, which shall happen in time to come, shall be reckoned, taken, deemed and accounted to be the first day of the year; and that each new year shall accordingly commence, and begin to be reckoned, from the first day of every such month of *January* next preceding the twenty-fifth day of *March*, on which such year would, according to the present supputation, have begun or commenced: and that from and after the said first day of *January* one thousand seven hundred and fifty-two, the several days of each month shall go on, and be reckoned and numbered in the same order; and the feast of *Easter*, and other moveable feasts thereon depending, shall be ascertained according to the same method, as they now are, until the second day of *September* in the said year one thousand seven hundred and fifty-two inclusive; and that the natural day next immediately following the said second day of *September*, shall be called, reckoned and accounted to be the fourteenth day of *September*, omitting for that time only the eleven intermediate nominal days of the common calendar; and that the several natural days, which shall follow and succeed next after the said fourteenth day of *September*, shall be respectively called, reckoned and numbered forwards in numerical order from the said fourteenth day of *September*, according to the order and succession of days now used in the present calendar; and that all acts, deeds, writings, notes and other instruments of what nature or kind soever, whether ecclesiastical or civil, publick or private, which shall be made, executed or signed, upon or after the said first day of *January* one thousand seven hundred and fifty-two shall bear date according to the said new method of supputation, and that the two fixed terms of Saint *Hilary* and Saint *Michael*, in that part of *Great Britain* called *England*, and the courts of great sessions in the counties palatine, and in *Wales*, and also the courts of general quarter-sessions and general sessions of the peace, and all other courts of what nature or kind soever, whether civil, criminal or ecclesiastical, and all meetings and assemblies of any bodies politick or corporate, either for the election of any officers or members thereof, or for any such officers entering upon the execution of their respective offices, or for any other purpose whatsoever, which by any law, statute, charter, custom or usage within this kingdom, or within any other the dominions or countries subject or belonging to the crown of *Great Britain*, are to be holden and kept on any fixed or certain day of any month, or on any day depending upon the beginning, or any certain day of any month (except such courts as are usually holden or kept with any fairs or marts) shall, from time to time, from and after the said second day of *September*, be holden and kept upon or according to the same respective nominal days and times, whereon or according to which the same are now to be holden, but which shall be computed according to the said new method of numbering and reckoning the days of the calendar as aforesaid; that is to say eleven days sooner than the respective days whereon the same are now holden and kept; any law, statute, charter, custom or usage, to the contrary thereof in any wise notwithstanding.

II. And for the continuing and preserving the calendar or method of reckoning, and computing the days of the year in the same regular course, as near as may be, in all times coming; be it further enacted by the authority aforesaid, That the several years of our Lord, one thousand eight hundred, one thousand nine hundred, two thousand one hundred, two thousand two hundred, two thousand three hundred, or any other hundredth years of our Lord, which shall happen in time to come, except only every fourth hundredth year of our Lord, whereof the year of our Lord two thousand shall be the first, shall not be esteemed or taken to be bissextile or leap years, but shall be taken to be common years, consisting of three hundred and sixty-five days, and no more; and that the years of our Lord two thousand, two thousand four hundred, two thousand eight hundred, and every other fourth hundred year of our Lord, from the said year of our Lord two thousand inclusive, and also all other years of our Lord, which by the present supputation are esteemed to be bissextile or leap years, shall for the future, and in all times to come, be esteemed and taken to be bissextile or leap years, consisting of three hundred and sixty-six days, in the same sort and manner as is now used with respect to every fourth year of our Lord.

III. [Easter and the other moveable Feasts, to be observed according to the new Calendar, Tables and Rules. Feasts and Fasts, &c. to be according to the new Calendar.]

IV. [Courts of Session and Exchequer in Scotland, and Markets, Fairs and Marts to be held upon the same natural Days.]

V. [The Times for opening and inclosing of Commons, not altered.]

VI. Provided also, and it is hereby further declared and enacted, That nothing in this present act contained shall extend, or be construed to extend, to accelerate or anticipate the time of payment of any rent or rents, annuity or annuities, or sum or sums of money whatsoever, which shall become payable by virtue or in consequence of any custom, usage, lease, deed, writing, bond, note, contract or other agreement whatsoever, now subsisting, or which shall be made, signed, sealed or entered into, at any time before the said fourteenth day of *September*, or which shall become payable by virtue of any act or acts of parliament now in force, or which shall be made before the said fourteenth day of *September*, or the time of doing any matter or thing directed or required by any such act or acts of parliament to be done in relation thereto; or to accelerate the payment of, or increase the interest of, any such sum of money which shall become payable as aforesaid; or to accelerate the time of the delivery of any goods, chattels, wares, merchandize or other things whatsoever; or the time of the commencement, expiration or determination of any lease or demise of any lands, tenements or hereditaments, or of any other contract or agreement whatsoever; or of the accepting, surrendering or delivering up the possession of any such lands, tenements or hereditaments; or the commencement, expiration or determination of any annuity or rent; or of any grant for any term of years, of what nature or kind soever, by virtue or in consequence of any such deed, writing, contract or agreement; or the time of the attaining the age of one and twenty years, or any other age requisite by any law, custom or usage, deed, will or writing whatsoever, for the doing any act, or for any other purpose whatsoever, by any person or persons now born, or who shall be born before the said fourteenth day of *September*; or the time of the expiration or determination of any apprenticeship or other service, by virtue of any indenture, or of any articles under seal, or by reason of any simple contract or hiring whatsoever; but that all and every such rent and rents, annuity and annuities, sum and sums of money, and the interest thereof, shall remain and continue to be due and payable; and the delivery of such goods and chattels, wares and merchandize, shall be made; and the said leases and demises of all such lands, tenements and hereditaments, and the said contracts and agreements, shall be deemed to commence, expire and determine; and the said lands, tenements and hereditaments shall be accepted, surrendered and delivered up; and the said rents and annuities, and grants for any term of years, shall commence, cease and determine, at and upon the same respective natural days and times, as the same should and ought to have been payable or made, or would have happened, in case this act had not been made; and that no further or other sum shall be paid or payable for the interest of any sum of money whatsoever, than such interest shall amount unto, for the true number of natural days for which the principal sum bearing such interest shall continue due and unpaid; and that no person or persons whatsoever shall be deemed or taken to have attained the said age of one and twenty years, or any other such age as aforesaid, or to have completed the time of any such service as aforesaid, until the full number of years and days shall be elapsed on which such person or persons respectively would have attained such age, or would have completed the time of such service as aforesaid, in case this act had not been made; any thing herein before contained to the contrary thereof in any wise notwithstanding.

62. Lord Hardwicke's Marriage Act, 1753

(*Statutes at Large*, XXI, pp. 124–130, 26 Geo. II, cap. 33.)

This important Act introduced for the first time the principle that marriage was a civil contract in which the State as well as the Church was concerned. The Church had previously required the publishing of banns, but Hardwicke's Act for the first time provided that omission to do so invalidated the marriage.

An act for the better preventing of clandestine marriages.

WHEREAS *great mischiefs and inconveniences have arisen from clandestine marriages;* for preventing thereof for the future, be it enacted by the King's most excellent majesty, by and with the advice and consent of the lords spiritual and temporal, and commons, in this present parliament assembled, and by the authority of the same, That from and after the twenty-fifth day of *March* in the year of our Lord one thousand seven hundred and fifty-four, all banns of matrimony shall be published in an audible manner in the parish church, or in some publick chapel, in which publick chapel banns of matrimony have been usually published, of or belonging to such parish or chapelry wherein the persons to be married shall dwell, according to the form of words prescribed by the rubrick prefixed to the office of matrimony in the book of common prayer, upon three *Sundays* preceding the solemnization of marriage, during the time of morning service, or of evening service (if there be no morning service in such church or chapel upon any of those *Sundays*) immediately after the second lesson: and whensoever it shall happen that the persons to be married shall dwell in divers parishes or chapelries, the banns shall in like manner be published in the church or chapel belonging to such parish or chapelry wherein each of the said persons shall dwell; and where both or either of the persons to be married shall dwell in any extraparochial place, (having no church or chapel wherein banns have been usually published) then the banns shall in like manner be published in the parish church or chapel belonging to some parish or chapelry adjoining to such extraparochial place: and where banns shall be published in any church or chapel belonging to any parish adjoining to such extraparochial place, the parson, vicar, minister or curate, publishing such banns, shall, in writing under his hand, certify the publication thereof in such manner as if either of the persons to be married dwelt in such adjoining parish; and that all other the rules prescribed by the said rubrick concerning the publication of banns, and the solemnization of matrimony, and not hereby altered, shall be duly observed; and that in all cases where banns shall have been published, the marriage shall be solemnized in one of the parish churches or chapels where such banns have been published, and in no other place whatsoever.

II. Provided always, and it is hereby further enacted, That no parson, vicar, minister or curate shall be obliged to publish the banns of matrimony between any persons whatsoever, unless the persons to be married shall, seven days at the least before the time required for the first publication of such banns respectively, deliver or cause to be delivered to such parson, vicar, minister or curate, a notice in writing of their true christian and surnames, and of the house or houses of their respective abodes within such parish, chapelry or extraparochial place as aforesaid, and of the time during which they have dwelt, inhabited or lodged in such house or houses respectively.

III. Provided always, and be it enacted by the authority aforesaid, That no parson, minister, vicar or curate solemnizing marriages after the twenty-fifth day of *March* one thousand seven hundred and fifty-four, between persons, both or one of whom shall be under the age of twenty-one years, after banns published, shall be punishable by ecclesiastical censures for solemnizing such marriages without consent of parents or guardians, whose consent is required by law, unless such parson, minister, vicar or curate shall have notice of the dissent of such parents or guardians; and in case such parents or guardians, or one of them, shall openly and publickly, or cause to be declared in the church or chapel where the banns shall be so published, at the time of such publication, his, her or their dissent to such marriage, such publication of banns shall be absolutely void.

IV. And it is hereby further enacted, That no licence of marriage shall, from and after the said twenty-fifth day of *March* in the year one thousand seven hundred and fifty-four, be granted by any archbishop, bishop, or other ordinary or person having authority to grant such licences, to solemnize any marriage in any other church or chapel, than in the parish church or publick chapel of or belonging to the parish or chapelry, within which the usual place of abode of one of the persons to be married shall have been for the space of four weeks immediately before the granting of such licence; or where both or either of the parties to be married shall dwell in any extraparochial place, having no church or chapel wherein banns have been usually published, then in the parish church or chapel belonging to some parish or chapelry adjoining to such extraparochial place, and in no other place whatsoever.

V. Provided always, and be it enacted by the authority aforesaid, That all parishes where there shall be no parish church or chapel belonging thereto, or none wherein divine service shall be usually celebrated every *Sunday*, may be deemed extraparochial places for the purposes of this act, but not for any other purpose.

VI. Provided always, That nothing herein before contained shall be construed to extend to deprive the archbishop of *Canterbury* and his successors, and his and their proper officers, of the right which hath thitherto been used, in virtue of a certain statute made in the twenty-fifth year of the reign of the late King *Henry* the eighth, intituled, *An Act concerning* Peter Pence *and dispensations*; of granting special licences to marry at any convenient time or place.

VII. Provided always, and be it enacted, That from and after the twenty-fifth day of *March* in the year one thousand seven hundred and fifty-four, no surrogate deputed by any ecclesiastical judge, who hath power to grant licences of marriage, shall grant any such licence before he hath taken an oath before the said judge faithfully to execute his office, according to law, to the best of his knowledge, and hath given security by his bond in the sum of one hundred pounds to the bishop of the diocese, for the due and faithful execution of his said office.

VIII. *And whereas many persons do solemnize matrimony in prisons and other places without publication of banns, or licence of marriage first had and obtained;* therefore, for the prevention thereof, be it enacted, That if any person shall, from and after the said twenty-fifth day of *March* in the year one thousand seven hundred and fifty-four, solemnize matrimony in any other place than a church or publick chapel, where banns have been usually published, unless by special licence from the archbishop of *Canterbury*; or shall solemnize matrimony without publication of banns, unless licence of marriage be first had and obtained from some person or persons having authority to grant the same, every person knowingly and wilfully so offending, and being lawfully convicted thereof, shall be deemed and adjudged to be guilty of felony, and shall be transported to some of his Majesty's plantations in *America* for the space of fourteen years, according to the laws in force for transportation of felons; and all marriages solemnized from and after the twenty-fifth day of *March* in the year one thousand seven hundred and fifty-four, in any other place than a church or such publick chapel, unless by special licence as aforesaid, or that shall be solemnized without publication of banns, or licence of marriage from a person or persons having authority to grant the same first had and obtained, shall be null and void to all intents and purposes whatsoever.

IX. Provided, That all prosecutions for such felony shall be commenced within the space of three years after the offence committed.

X. Provided always, That after the solemnization of any marriage, under a publication of banns, it shall not be necessary in support of such marriage, to give any proof of the actual dwelling of the parties in the respective parishes or chapelries wherein the banns of matrimony were published; or where the marriage is by licence, it shall not be necessary to give any proof that the usual place of abode of one of the parties, for the space of four weeks as aforesaid, was in the parish or chapelry where the marriage was solemnized; nor shall any evidence in either of the said cases be received to prove the contrary in any suit touching the validity of such marriage.

XI. And it is hereby further enacted, That all marriages solemnized by licence, after the said twenty-fifth day of March one thousand seven hundred and fifty-four, where either of the parties, not being a widower or widow, shall be under the age of twenty-one years, which shall be had without the consent of the father of such of the parties, so under age (if then living) first had and obtained, or if dead, of the guardian or guardians of the person of the party so under age, lawfully appointed, or one of them; and in case there shall be no such guardian or guardians, then of the mother (if living and unmarried) or if there shall be no mother living and unmarried, then of a guardian or guardians of the person appointed by the court of *Chancery*; shall be absolutely null and void to all intents and purposes whatsoever.

XII. *And whereas it may happen, that the guardian or guardians, mother or mothers, of the parties to be married, or one of them, so under age as aforesaid, may be* Non compos mentis, *or may be in parts beyond the seas, or may be induced unreasonably, and by undue motives to abuse the trust reposed in him, her or them, by refusing or with-holding his, her or their consent to a proper marriage;* be it therefore enacted, That in case any such guardian or guardians, mother or mothers, or any of them whose consent is made necessary as aforesaid, shall be *Non compos mentis*, or in parts beyond the seas, or shall refuse or with-hold his, her or their consent to the marriage of any person, it shall and may be lawful for any person desirous of marrying, in any of the before-mentioned cases, to apply by petition to the lord chancellor, lord keeper, or the lords commissioners of the great seal of *Great Britain* for the time being, who is and are hereby impowered to proceed upon such petition, in a summary way; and in case the marriage proposed, shall upon examination appear to be proper, the said lord chancellor, lord keeper, or lords commissioners of the great seal for the time being, shall judicially declare the same to be so by an order of court, and such order shall be deemed and taken to be as good and effectual to all intents and purposes, as if the guardian or guardians, or mother of the person so petitioning, had consented to such marriage.

XIII. And it is hereby further enacted, That in no case whatsoever shall any suit or proceeding be had in any ecclesiastical court, in order to compel a celebration of any marriage *in facie ecclesiae*, by reason of any contract of matrimony whatsoever, whether *per verba de praesenti*, or *per verba de futuro*, which shall be entered into after the twenty-fifth day of *March* in the year one thousand seven hundred and fifty-four; any law or usage to the contrary notwithstanding.

XIV. And for preventing undue entries and abuses in registers of marriages; be it enacted by the authority aforesaid, That on or before the twenty-fifth day of *March* in the year one thousand seven hundred and fifty-four, and from time to time afterwards as there shall be occasion, the church-wardens and chapel-wardens of every parish or chapelry shall provide proper books of vellum, or good and durable paper, in which all marriages and banns of marriage respectively, there published or solemnized, shall be registered, and every page thereof shall be marked at the top, with the figure of the number of every such page, beginning at the second leaf with number one; and every leaf or page so numbered, shall be ruled with lines at proper and equal distances from each other, or as near as may be; and all banns and marriages published or celebrated in any church or chapel, or within any such parish or chapelry, shall be respectively entered, registered, printed, or written upon or as near as conveniently may be to such ruled lines, and shall be signed by the parson, vicar, minister or curate, or by some other person in his presence, and by his direction; and such entries shall be made as aforesaid, on or near such lines in successive order, where the paper is not damaged or decayed, by accident or length of time, until a new book shall be thought proper or necessary to be provided for the same purposes, and then the directions aforesaid shall be observed in every such new book; and all books provided as aforesaid shall be deemed to belong to every such parish or chapelry respectively, and shall be carefully kept and preserved for publick use.

XV. And in order to preserve the evidence of marriages, and to make the proof thereof more certain and easy, and for the direction of ministers in the celebration of marriages and registering thereof, be it enacted, That from and after the twenty-fifth day of *March* in the year one thousand seven hundred and fifty-four, all marriages shall be solemnized in the presence of two or more credible witnesses, besides the minister who shall celebrate the same; and that immediately after the celebration of every marriage, an entry thereof shall be made in such register to be kept as aforesaid; in which entry or register it shall be expressed, That the said marriage was celebrated by banns or licence; and if both or either of the parties married by licence, be under age, with consent of the parents or guardians, as the case shall be; and shall be signed by the minister with his proper addition, and also by the parties married, and attested by such two witnesses; which entry shall be made in the form or to the effect following; that is to say,

A. B. of [the / this] Parish

and *C. D.* of [the / this] Parish

were married in this [Church / Chapel] by [Banns / Licence] with Consent of [Parents / Guardians]

this Day of in the Year

by me *J. J.* [Rector / Vicar / Curate]

This marriage was solemnized between us *A. B.* in the Presence of *E. F.*
C. D. in the Presence of *G. H.*

XVI. And be it further enacted by the authority aforesaid, That if any person shall, from and after the twenty-fifth day of *March* in the year one thousand seven hundred and fifty-four, with intent to elude the force of this act, knowingly and wilfully insert, or cause to be inserted in the register book of such parish or chapelry as aforesaid, any false entry of any matter or thing relating to any marriage; or falsely make, alter, forge or counterfeit, or cause or procure to be falsely made, altered, forged or counterfeited, or act or assist in falsely making, altering, forging or counterfeiting any such entry in such register; or falsely make, alter, forge or counterfeit, or cause or procure to be falsely made, altered, forged or counterfeited, or assist in falsely making, altering, forging, or counterfeiting any such licence of marriage as aforesaid; or utter or publish as true any such false, altered, forged or counterfeited register as aforesaid, or a copy thereof, or any such false, altered, forged or counterfeited licence of marriage, knowing such register or licence of marriage respectively, to be false, altered, forged or counterfeited; or if any person shall, from and after the said twenty-fifth day of *March*, wilfully destroy or cause or procure to be destroyed, any register book of marriages, or any part of such register book with intent to avoid any marriage, or to subject any person to any of the penalties of this act; every person so offending, and being thereof lawfully convicted, shall be deemed and adjudged to be guilty of felony, and shall suffer death as a felon, without benefit of clergy.

XVII. Provided always, That this act, or any thing therein contained, shall not extend to the marriages of any of the royal family.

XVIII. Provided likewise, That nothing in this act contained shall extend to that part of *Great Britain* called *Scotland*, nor to any marriages amongst the people called *Quakers*, or amongst the persons professing the *Jewish* religion, where both the parties to any such marriage shall be of the people called *Quakers*, or persons professing the *Jewish* religion respectively, nor to any marriages solemnized beyond the seas.

XIX. And be it further enacted by the authority aforesaid, That this act shall be publickly read in all parish churches and publick chapels, by the parson, vicar, minister or curate of the respective parishes or chapelries, on some *Sunday* immediately after morning prayer, or immediately after evening prayer, if there shall be no morning service on that day, in each of the Months of *September*, *October*, *November* and *December*, in the year of our Lord one thousand seven hundred and fifty-three, and afterwards at the same times, on four several *Sundays* in each year, (that is to say,) the *Sundays* next before the twenty-fifth day of *March*, twenty-fourth day of *June*, twenty-ninth day of *September*, and twenty-fifth day of *December* respectively, for two years, to be computed from and immediately after the first day of *January* in the said year one thousand seven hundred and fifty-four.

63. Judges and the demise of the Crown, 1760

(*Statutes at Large*, XXIII, pp. 305–306, 1 Geo. III, cap. 23.)

This Act provided for the continuance of the judges' commissions on the death of the king.

An act for rendering more effectual the provisions in an act made in the twelfth and thirteenth years of the reign of his late majesty King William *the Third (intituled,* An act for the further limitation of the crown, and better securing the rights and liberties of the subject) *relating to the commissions and salaries of judges.*

WHEREAS *by an act passed in the twelfth and thirteenth years of the reign of his late majesty King* William *the Third, intituled,* An Act for the further limitation of the crown, and better securing the rights and liberties of the subject; *it was enacted, That after the limitation of the crown thereby made should take effect, judges commissions be made* quamdiu se bene gesserint, *and their salaries ascertained and established; but upon the address of both houses of parliament, it might be lawful to remove them: and whereas your Majesty has been graciously pleased to declare from the throne to both houses of parliament, that you look upon the independency and uprightness of judges, as essential to the impartial administration of justice, as one of the best securities to the rights and liberties of your loving subjects, and as most conducive to the honour of your crown; and in consequence thereof, your Majesty has recommended it to the consideration of your parliament, to make further provision for continuing judges in the enjoyment of their offices during their good behaviour, notwithstanding the demise of your Majesty, or any of your heirs and successors: and your Majesty has also desired your faithful commons, that you may be enabled to secure the salaries of judges, during the continuance of their commissions; and whereas in return for this paternal goodness, and in the justest sense of your tender concern for the religion, laws, and liberties, of your people, we have taken this important work into our consideration, and have resolved to enable your Majesty to effectuate the wise, just, and generous purposes, of your royal heart:* may it therefore please your Majesty that it may be enacted; and be it enacted by the King's most excellent majesty, by and with the advice and consent of the lords spiritual and temporal, and commons, in this present parliament assembled, and by the authority of the same, That the commissions of judges for the time being, shall be, continue, and remain, in full force, during their good behaviour, notwithstanding the demise of his Majesty (whom God long preserve) or of any of his heirs and successors; any law, usage, or practice, to the contrary thereof in any wise notwithstanding.

II. Provided always, and be it enacted by the authority aforesaid, That it may be lawful for his Majesty, his heirs and successors, to remove any judge or judges upon the address of both houses of parliament.

III. And be it enacted by the authority aforesaid, That such salaries as are settled upon judges for the time being, or any of them, by act of parliament, and also such salaries as have been or shall be granted by his Majesty, his heirs, and successors, to any judge or judges, shall, in all time coming, be paid and payable to every such judge and judges for the time being, so long as the patents or commissions of them, or any of them respectively, shall continue and remain in force.

IV. And be it further enacted by the authority aforesaid, That such salaries of judges as are now or shall become payable out of the annual rent or sum granted for the support of his Majesty's household, and of the honour and dignity of the crown, shall, from time to time, after the demise of his Majesty, or any of his heirs and successors, be charged upon, and paid and payable out of, such of the duties or revenues granted for the uses of the civil government of his Majesty, his heirs, and successors, as shall be subsisting after every such demise respectively, until some further or other provision be made by parliament for the expences of the civil government; and from and immediately after the making of such provision, and during the continuance thereof, such salaries shall be paid and payable out of all or any of the monies which shall be applicable to such uses and expences as aforesaid.

(*b*) JUDICIAL PROCEEDINGS

64A–B. The trial of Richard Francklin for seditious libel, 3 December 1731

64A. *The Craftsman*, No. 235, 2 January 1731

(*The Country Journal, or The Craftsman*, Saturday, 2 January 1730.)[1]

Francklin was prosecuted for printing the "Extract of a private letter from the Hague" which formed part of this number of *The Craftsman*, probably written by Bolingbroke. The resignation of Townshend in 1730 led to the abandonment of his policy of alliance with Spain in the Treaty of Seville, of 1729, and its replacement by Walpole's policy of an alliance with the Emperor, achieved in the Treaty of Vienna of March 1731. (See No. 279.) *The Craftsman* is prophesying this change of policy.

FOREIGN AFFAIRS.

Extract of a private letter from the Hague.

"A Rumour hath been for some Time privately spread about and begins to gain "Credit here, that a Misunderstanding will soon discover itself between the Allies of

[1] 1731 in the New Style.

"*Seville*;[1] and that *certain Ministers* having at length found out that too close an Union "with *France*, and a War upon the Foot of the *Treaty of Seville* are quite against the "Grain of the People, are endeavouring to bring about an Accommodation with the "*Emperor*, and to undo every Thing They have been doing for these *five Years past*. If "This should prove true, it will certainly redound very much to the Honour of *those* "*Gentlemen*, who have so vigorously opposed the *late Measures*; and the *Ministers*, who "have not only concerted and pursued *these Measures*, but loaded all Opposition to "Them with the foulest Imputations, will be obliged to *take a great deal of Shame to* "*Themselves*; for what can be a stronger Condemnation of their own *past Conduct*, or "the Conduct of *Those* whom They have employed to write in their Cause, than to see "Them wheel about all on a sudden and pursue Measures directly opposite, which have "been pointed out to them, for several Years together, by their *Adversaries*; and for "which They have represented *those Gentlemen*, in the most opprobrious Colours, as "*factious Incendiaries, Germanized Patriots*, and *Enemies to* their Country? What can be "more ridiculous than to see Them desert *one Ally*, whose *good Faith, Sincerity*, and even "*Cordiality of Friendship* they have so often extoll'd; and at last run into the Arms of "*another*, whom they have so industriously set forth as the most *dishonourable, ungrateful*, "and *perfidious Prince*? They must have alter'd their Opinion of *this Prince* very much "(if this Report is true) and seem to rely upon his *good Nature*, putting Themselves "thus absolutely in his Power; for if He should refuse to deal with Them, after the "*Usage* He hath received, They will be broke with all the Courts of *Europe*; and He "cannot be insensible of their Perfidy to *others*, at the same Time that He is treating "with Them. How will they be able to justify those *vast Expences*, which they have "already brought upon their Country, by an obstinate Perseverance in *other Measures*, "till the last Extremity, as well as those *farther Expences* and *Hazards*, in which such a "precipitate Alteration of Counsels, in the present Circumstances of Europe, will "certainly involve it? For though the *Measure*, which is now said to be secretly carrying "on, was certainly the most eligible, whilst They remained unembarrass'd with En-"gagements of another Kind; and though it must be confess'd to be very desirable at "present; yet it seems to be attended with very fatal Consequences, and almost insu-"perable Difficulties. The People, of whom I am speaking, had their Hands at Liberty, "*five Years* ago; and might have enter'd into what Measures They pleas'd with the "*Emperor*, without giving Umbrage, or any just Reason of Complaint, to *other Courts*; "but at present They cannot do it, without an Infraction of *solemn Treaties*, and drawing "upon their Country the Resentments, which usually attend *Violations of Faith*. One "immediate Effect of this Resentment may be the Interruption of *Trade* and the Seizure "of that *vast Pledge*, which *Spain* hath at this Time in her *Hands*; so that the only "pretended good Effect of their *former Conduct* may be absolutely defeated by their "*present Scheme*. Another necessary Effect (for so I think I may call it) of *such a Measure*, "at present, will be a Conjunction of *France* and *Spain*; and a *certain Court* may have the "Mortification to see those *two Crowns* united against Them more strongly than ever, "by their extraordinary Management, after they have spent so many Millions to "prevent it. I am far from designing to insinuate from hence, that an Accommodation

[1] England, France, and Spain.

"with the *Emperor* is a wrong Measure. On the contrary, I wish it had been thought a "right Measure long ago. My only Intention is to shew how difficult, in my Appre-"hension, the Conduct of *some Ministers* hath rendered it to their *Country*, as well as "dishonourable to *Themselves*, by carrying along with it the severest Censure of their "*own Conduct*, and the strongest Justification of their *Adversaries*, against all the "Aspersions which have been cast upon them.–I cannot take upon me to justify the "Truth of this Report; but as it hath been pretty confidently buzz'd about, I though "proper to let you know what is said upon it; and if it should appear to have any "Foundation, you may expect to hear farther from me on the same Subject."

64B. Lord Chief Justice Raymond's charge to the jury, 3 December 1731

(*State Trials*, XVII, pp. 671–675.)

This illustrates the limited function of the jury in libel cases before Fox's Libel Act of 1792. It is made clear to the jury that what they have to decide is *fact*: whether Francklin published this number of *The Craftsman*; and whether the passages complained of refer to the king and his ministers. Whether these passages constitute a seditious libel is a matter of *law*, to be decided not by the jury but by the judge.

L.C.J. [Raymond.] Gentlemen of the jury, this is an information, wherein the king is plaintiff, and Mr Francklin defendant, for printing and publishing the Country Journal or Craftsman, the 2d of January 1730, wherein is inserted an extract of a private letter from the Hague, reflecting on his majesty and his principal officers and ministers of state. In this information or libel, there are three things to be considered, whereof two by you the jury, and one by the Court. The first thing under your consideration is, Whether the defendant, Mr Francklin, is guilty of the publication of this Craftsman or not? The second is, Whether the expressions in that letter refer to his present majesty and his principal officers and ministers of state, and are applicable to them or not? This is the chief thing in the information; for if you think that these defamatory expressions are not applicable to them, then the defendant is not guilty of what is charged upon him; but if you think that they are applicable to them, then the defendant is guilty thereof; upon this supposition, that you find him to be the publisher of that paper. These are the two matters of fact that come under your consideration; and of which you are proper judges. But then there is a third thing, to wit, Whether these defamatory expressions amount to a libel or not? This does not belong to the office of the jury, but to the office of the Court; because it is a matter of law, and not of fact; and of which the Court are the only proper judges; and there is redress to be had in another place, if either of the parties are not satisfied; for we are not to invade one another's province, as is now of late a notion among some people who ought to know better; for matters of law and matters of fact are never to be confounded. . . .

So, gentlemen, you are to consider whether or not you are satisfied with the evidence produced to prove the defendant to be the publisher of that Craftsman of 2d of January last. The next thing which you are to consider is, whether the expressions in that Hague letter, refer to his present majesty and his principal officers and ministers of state, and are applicable to them as in the information or not; for when people's names are not set down at length, but pointed at by circumlocution, or pieces of words, or by initial letters, &c. the law always allows innuendos in informations, which explain and tell what the defendant meant by them; and the law likewise allows juries to give their verdict on oath, whether they think that these dark, defamatory speeches have the same meaning as mentioned in the information or not. The counsel for the king have gone on and explained and applied these defamatory expressions exactly as in the information; and they have given their arguments and reasons for so doing; drawn from the several parts of that letter, which I shall not trouble you with, because they have been so often repeated in your hearing. . . . The counsel for the defendant said, that these scandalous expressions could not be understood to refer to his majesty or his ministers; but they did not tell to whom they referred; I should have been glad to have heard them do so; so that you are to consider of whom these defamatory expressions are meant, or to whom they are applicable; and as to the rule and manner of understanding them, you are to do it, on oath, after the same manner and way as you do privately by yourselves, taking all the parts of the letter together. . . . There was one thing more mentioned by the defendant's counsel which was, that there is no room to think that letter libellous; because there could be no malice supposed by inserting it in the Craftsman, being only designed as a piece of foreign news; and that the latter part of the letter qualifies it, by saying that the letter-writer does not take upon him to justify the truth of that report; but that will not do; for the injury is the same to the persons scandalized, whether the letter was inserted out of malice or not; besides, there is no knowing or proving particular malice, otherwise than from the act itself; and therefore if the act imports as much, it is sufficient; nor is he to take the liberty to print what he pleases; for the liberty of the press is only a legal liberty, such as the law allows; and not a licentious liberty. Gentlemen, I tell you again, that I have designedly shortened things, because it hath been so fully again and again laid before you. But if there is any thing afterwards that you want to know, after you have considered these things, I desire you would acquaint me. So, gentlemen, if you are sensible, and convinced that the defendant published that Craftsman of 2d of January last; and that the defamatory expressions in the letter refer to the ministers of Great Britain; then you ought to find the defendant guilty; but if you think otherwise, then you ought not to find him guilty.

The Jury found the defendant guilty of publishing the said libel.

65A–E. General Warrants, 1763–1765

65A. *The North Briton*, No. 45, 23 April 1763

(*The North Briton from No. I to No. XLVI inclusive*, collected edition (1763), pp. 302–305.)

NUMB. XLV.[x] SATURDAY, APRIL 23, 1763.

Genus ORATIONIS *atrox, & vehemens*, cui opponitur *lenitatis & mansuetudinis*. CICERO.

"The *King's Speech* has always been considered by the legislature, and by the public at large, as the *Speech of the Ministers*.[y] It has regularly, at the beginning of "every session of parliament, been referred by both houses to the consideration of a "committee, and has been generally canvassed with the utmost freedom, when the "minister of the crown has been obnoxious to the nation. The ministers of this free "country, conscious of the undoubted privileges of so spirited a people, and with the "terrors of parliament before their eyes, have ever been cautious, no less with regard "to the matter, than to the expressions of *speeches*, which they have advised the sove-"reign to make from the throne, at the *opening* of each session. They well knew that an* "honest house of parliament, true to their trust, could not fail to detect the fallacious "arts, or to remonstrate against the daring acts of violence committed by any minister. "The speech at the *close* of the session has ever been considered as the most *secure* method "of promulgating the favourite court-creed among the vulgar; because the parliament, "which is the constitutional guardian of the liberties of the people, has in this case no "opportunity of remonstrating, or of impeaching any wicked servant of the crown."

"This week has given the public the most abandonned instance of ministerial "effrontery ever attempted to be imposed on mankind. The *minister's speech* of last "Tuesday is not to be paraleled [sic] in the annals of this country. I am in doubt, whether "the imposition is greater on the sovereign, or on the nation. Every friend of his "country must lament that a prince of so many great and amiable qualities, whom "England truly reveres, can be brought to give the sanction of his sacred name to the

[x] The passages included within the inverted commas are the *only* passages to which any objection is made in the INFORMATION filed in the *King's-Bench* by the *Attorney-General*. against the publisher, Mr. *George Kearsly*.

[y] Anno 14 G.II. 1740. Duke of Argyle.

The King's Speech is always, in this House, considered as the Speech of the Ministers.—LORDS Debates, vol. 7, p. 413.

Lord Carteret.

When we take his Majesty's Speech into consideration, though we have heard it from his own mouth, yet we do not consider it as his Majesty's Speech, but as the speech of his Ministers. p. 425.

Anno 7 G.II. 1733. Mr. Shippen.

I believe it has always been granted, that the speeches from the Throne are the compositions of ministers of state; upon that supposition we have always thought ourselves at liberty to examine every proposition contained in them; even without doors people are pretty free in their marks upon them. I believe no Gentleman here is ignorant of the reception the speech from the throne, at the close of last session, met with from the nation in general.—COMMONS Debates. vol. 8, p. 5.

Anno 13 G.II. 1739. Mr. Pulteney, now Earl of Bath.

His Majesty mentions heats and animosities. Sir, I do not know who drew up this speech; but whoever he was, he should have spared that expression: I wish he had drawn a veil over the heats and animosities that must be owned ONCE *subsisted upon this head;* for I AM SURE NONE NOW SUBSIST. Vol. II, p. 96.

* The House of Commons in 1715 exhibited *Articles of impeachment of high treason, and other high crimes and misdemeanours against* Robert *Earl of* OXFORD, *and Earl* MORTIMER. Article 15 is *for having corrupted the sacred fountain of truth, and put falshoods into the mouth of Majesty, in several speeches made to parliament.* See the Journal of the House of Commons, Vol. XVIII, Page 224.

"most odious measures, and to the most unjustifiable, public declarations, from a "throne ever renowned for truth, honour, and unsullied virtue." I am sure all foreigners, especially the king of Prussia, will hold the minister in contempt and abhorrence. He has made our sovereign declare, *My expectations have been fully answered by the happy effects which the several allies of my crown have derived from this salutary measure* of the definitive Treaty. *The powers at war with my good brother, the king of Prussia, have been induced to agree to such terms of accomodation, as that great prince has approved; and the success which has attended my negotiation, has necessarily and immediately difused* [sic] *the blessings of peace through every part of Europe.* The infamous fallacy of this whole sentence is apparent to all mankind: for it is known, that the king of Prussia did not barely *approve*, but absolutely *dictated*, as conqueror, every article of the terms of peace. No advantage of any kind has accrued to that magnanimous prince from *our negotiation*, but he was basely deserted by the *Scottish* prime minister of *England*. He was known by every court in Europe to be scarcely on better terms of friendship *here*, than at *Vienna*; and he was betrayed by us in the *treaty of peace.*[1] What a strain of insolence, therefore, is it in a minister to lay claim to what he is conscious all his efforts tended to prevent, and meanly to arrogate to himself a share in the fame and glory of one of the greatest princes the world has ever seen. The king of *Prussia*, however, has gloriously kept *all* his former *conquests*, and stipulated security for his allies, even for the *elector of Hanover*. I know in what light this great prince is considered in Europe, and in what manner he has been treated here; among other reasons perhaps, for some contemptuous expressions he may have used of the *Scot*: expressions which are every day echoed by the whole body of *Englishmen* through the southern part of this island.

The *Preliminary Articles of Peace* were such as have drawn the contempt of mankind on our wretched negotiators. All our most valuable conquests were agreed to be restored, and the *East-India company* would have been infallibly ruined by a single article of this falacious and baneful negotiation. No hireling of the minister has been hardy enough to dispute this; yet the minister himself has made our sovereign declare, *the satisfaction which he felt at the approaching re-establishment of peace upon conditions so honourable to his crown, and so beneficial to his people.* As to the *entire approbation* of parliament, which is so vainly boasted of, the world knows how that was obtained. The large debt on the *Civil List*, already above half a year in arrear, shews pretty clear the transactions of the winter. It is, however, remarkable, that the minister's speech dwells on the *entire approbation* given by parliament to the *Preliminary Articles*, which I will venture to say, he must by this time be ashamed of; for he has been brought to confess the total want of that knowledge, accuracy and precision, by which such immense advantages, both of trade and territory, were sacrificed to our inveterate enemies. These gross blunders, are, indeed, in some measure set right by the *Definitive Treaty*; yet the most important articles, relative to *cessions, commerce*, and the FISHERY, remain as they were, with respect to the *French*. The proud and feeble *Spaniard* too does not RENOUNCE, but only DESISTS *from all pretensions, which he may have formed, to the right of Fishing* . . . where? Only *about the island of* NEWFOUNDLAND . . . till a favourable opportunity arises of *insisting* on it, *there, as well as elsewhere.*

[1] The Treaty of Paris (1763). See No. 283.

"The minister cannot forbear, even in the *King's Speech*, insulting us with a dull "repetition of the word *œconomy*. I did not expect so soon to hear that word again, "after it had been so lately exploded, and more than once by a most numerous audience, "*hissed* off the stage of our *English* theatres. It is held in derision by the *voice of the people*, "and every tongue loudly proclaims the universal contempt, in which these empty "professions are held by *this* nation. Let the public be informed of a single instance of "*œconomy*, except indeed in the household." Is a regiment, which was completed as to its compliment of officers on the *Tuesday*, and broke on the *Thursday*, a proof of *œconomy*? Is the pay of the *Scottish Master Elliot* to be voted by an *English* parliament, under the head of *œconomy*? Is this, among a thousand others, one of the convincing proofs of a *firm resolution to form government on a plan of strict œconomy*? Is it not notorious, that in the reduction of the army, not the least attention has been paid to it? Many unnecessary expences have been incurred, only to increase the power of the crown, that is, to create more lucrative jobs for the creatures of the minister? The *staff* indeed is broke, but the discerning part of mankind immediately comprehended the mean subterfuge, and resented the indignity put upon so brave an officer as marshal *Ligonier*. That step was taken to give the whole power of the army to the crown, that is, to the minister. Lord *Ligonier* is now no longer at the head of the army; but lord *Bute* in effect is; I mean that every preferment given by the crown will be found still to be obtained by *his* enormous influence, and to be bestowed only on the creatures of the *Scottish* faction. The nation is still in the same deplorable state, while *he* governs, and can make the tools of *his* power pursue the same odious measures. Such a retreat, as he intends, can only mean the personal indemnity, which, I hope, guilt will never find from an injured nation. The negotiations of the late inglorious *peace* and the *excise*,[1] will haunt him wherever he goes, and the terrors of the just resentment which he must be sure to meet from a brave and insulted people, and which must finally crush him, will be for ever before his eyes.

"In vain will such a minister, or the foul dregs of his power, the tools of corruption "and despotism, preach up in *the speech that spirit of concord, and that obedience to the laws,* "*which is essential to good order*. They have sent the *spirit of discord* through the land, and "I will prophecy, that it will never be extinguished, but by the extinction of their "power. Is the *spirit of concord* to go hand in hand with the PEACE and EXCISE, through "this nation? Is it to be expected between an insolent EXCISEMAN, and *a peer, gentleman,* "*freeholder*, or *farmer*, whose private houses are now made liable to be entered and "searched at pleasure? *Gloucestershire, Herefordshire*, and in general all the *cyder* counties, "are not surely the *several counties* which are alluded to in the *speech*. The *spirit of* "*concord* hath not gone forth among them, but the *spirit of liberty* has, and a noble "opposition has been given to the wicked instruments of oppression. A nation as "sensible as the *English*, will see that a *spirit of concord* when they are oppressed, means a "tame submission to injury, and that a *spirit of liberty* ought then to arise, and I am sure "ever will, in proportion to the weight of the grievance they feel. *Every* legal *attempt* "*of a contrary tendency* to the *spirit of concord* will be deemed a justifiable resistance, "warranted by the *spirit of the English constitution*.

[1] *i.e.*, the Cider Tax.

"A despotic minister will always endeavour to dazzle his prince with high-flown "ideas of the *prerogative* and *honour* of the *crown*, which the minister will make a "parade of *firmly maintaining*. I wish as much as any man in the kingdom to see "*the honour of the crown* maintained in a manner truly becoming *Royalty*. I lament "to see it sunk even to prostitution. What a shame was it to see the security of this "country in point of military force, complimented away, contrary to the opinion of "Royalty itself, and sacrificed to the prejudices and to the ignorance of a set of people, "the most unfit, from every consideration, to be consulted on a matter relative to the "security of the house of *Hanover*." I wish to see the honour of the *crown* religiously asserted with regard to our allies, and the dignity of it scrupulously maintained with regard to foreign princes. Is it possible such an indignity can have happened, such a sacrifice of *the honour of the crown of England*, as that a minister should already have kissed his majesty's hand on being appointed to the most insolent and ungrateful court in the world, without a previous assurance of that reciprocal nomination which the meanest court in Europe would insist upon, before she proceeded to an act otherwise so derogatory to her honour? But *Electoral Policy* has ever been obsequious to the court of *Vienna*, and forgets the insolence with which *Count Colloredo* left England. Upon a principle of *dignity* and *œconomy*, lord *Stormont*, a *Scottish* peer of the loyal house of *Murray*, kissed his majesty's hand, I think, on Wednesday in the *Easter* week; but this ignominious act has not yet disgraced the nation in the *London Gazette*. The ministry are not ashamed of doing the thing in private; they are only afraid of the publication. Was it a tender regard for the honour of the late king, or of his present majesty, that invited to court *lord George Sackville, in these first days of peace*, to share in the general satisfaction, which all good courtiers received in the indignity offered to Lord *Ligonier*, and on the advancement of - - - ? Was this to shew *princely* gratitude to the eminent services of the accomplished general of the house of *Brunswic*, who has had so great a share in rescuing *Europe* from the yoke of *France*; and whose nephew we hope soon to see made happy in the possession of the most amiable princess in the world? Or is it meant to assert the honour of the *crown* only against the united wishes of a loyal and affectionate people, founded in a happy experience of the talents, ability, integrity, and virtue of those, who have had the glory of redeeming their country from bondage and ruin, in order to support, by every art of corruption and intimidation, a weak, disjointed, incapable set of - - - I will call them any thing but *ministers* - - - by whom the *Favourite* still meditates to rule this kingdom with a rod of iron.

The *Stuart* line has ever been intoxicated with the slavish doctrines of the *absolute, independent, unlimited* power of the crown. Some of that line were so weakly advised, as to endeavour to reduce them into practice: but the *English* nation was too spirited to suffer the least encroachment on the antient liberties of this kingdom. "The *King of* "*England* is only the first magistrate* of this country; but is invested by the law with "the whole executive power. He is, however, responsible to his people for the due "execution of the royal functions, in the choice of ministers, &c. equal with the "meanest of his subjects in his particular duty." The personal character of our present

* In the first speech of JAMES I to his *English parliament*, March 22, 1603, are the following words, *That I am a* SERVANT *is most true . . . I will never be ashamed to confess it My principal honour, to be the* GREAT SERVANT *of the commonwealth*. Journal of the House of Commons, Vol. I, Page 145.

amiable sovereign makes us easy and happy that so great a power is lodged in such hands; but the *favourite* has given too just cause for him to escape the general odium. The *prerogative* of the crown is to exert the constitutional powers entrusted to it in a way not of blind favour and partiality, but of wisdom and judgment. This is the spirit of our constitution. The people too have their *prerogative*, and I hope the fine words of DRYDEN will be engraven on our hearts.

Freedom *is the English Subject's* Prerogative.

65B. The general warrant on which John Wilkes was arrested, 30 April 1763

(*State Trials*, XIX, p. 981.)

General warrants were of two kinds: (i) for the arrest of persons unnamed; (ii) for the arrest of a person named, and the general seizure of all his papers. The warrant on which Wilkes was arrested was a combination of the two types, but as the author of No. 45 of *The North Briton* (No. 65A) Wilkes was in fact covered by the description in the warrant of the persons to be arrested. In the cases to which the following extracts relate, *Wilkes* v. *Wood* and *Entick* v. *Carrington* were concerned with the second type of general warrant; *Leach* v. *Money* with the first type.

"George Montague Dunk, earl of Halifax, viscount Sunbury and baron Halifax, one of the lords of his majesty's most honourable privy council; lieutenant "general of his majesty's forces, and principal secretary of state: these are in his majesty's "name to authorize and require you (taking a constable to your assistance) to make "strict and diligent search for the authors, printers and publishers of a seditious and "treasonable paper, intitled, The North Briton, No. 45, Saturday April 23, 1763, "printed for G. Kearsley in Ludgate-street, London, and them, or any of them, having "found to apprehend and seize, together with their papers, and to bring in safe custody "before me, to be examined concerning the premisses, and further dealt with according "to law: and in due execution thereof, all mayors, sheriffs, justices of the peace, "constables, and all other his majesty's officers civil and military, and loving subjects "whom it may concern, are to be aiding and assisting to you, as there shall be occasion; "and for so doing this shall be your warrant. Given at St. James's the 26th day of April, "in the third year of his majesty's reign. DUNK HALIFAX."

"To Nathan Carrington, John Money, James Watson, and Robert Blackmore, "four of his majesty's messengers in ordinary."

65C. *Wilkes* v. *Wood*; Lord Chief Justice Pratt's judgment, 6 December 1763

(*State Trials*, XIX, pp. 1166–1168.)

Wilkes brought an action for trespass in the Court of Common Pleas against Robert Wood, an Under-Secretary of State. Wood had superintended the execution of the general warrant printed above.

The Chief Justice then summed up the evidence of the whole. . . .

. . . As to Mr. Wood, he was described on one side as very active in the affair, and on the other side as quite inoffensive. Aiders and abettors are always esteemed parties; but if a person present remains only a spectator, he cannot be affected. The evidence on the one side had been positive, and on the other side only negative. Mr. Wood might have said and done as represented on the one side, when the evidences on the other side were not present: if upon the whole they should be of opinion, that Mr. Wood was active in the affair, they must find a verdict for the plaintiff with damages. His lordship then went upon the warrant, which he declared was a point of the greatest consequence he had ever met with in his whole practice. The defendants claimed a right, under precedents, to force persons' houses, break open escrutores, seize their papers, &c. upon a general warrant, where no inventory is made of the things thus taken away, and where no offenders' names are specified in the warrant, and therefore a discretionary power given to messengers to search wherever their suspicions may chance to fall. If such a power is truly invested in a secretary of state, and he can delegate this power, it certainly may affect the person and property of every man in this kingdom, and is totally subversive of the liberty of the subject.

And as for the precedents, will that be esteemed law in a secretary of state which is not law in any other magistrate of this kingdom? If they should be found to be legal, they are certainly of the most dangerous consequences; if not legal, must aggravate damages. Notwithstanding what Mr. Solicitor General has said, I have formerly delivered it as my opinion on another occasion, and I still continue of the same mind, that a jury have it in their power to give damages for more than the injury received. Damages are designed not only as a satisfaction to the injured person, but likewise as a punishment to the guilty, to deter from any such proceeding for the future, and as a proof of the detestation of the jury to the action itself.

As to the proof of what papers were taken away, the plaintiff could have no account of them; and those who were able to have given an account (which might have been an extenuation of their guilt) have produced none. It lays upon the jury to allow what weight they think proper to that part of the evidence. It is my opinion the office precedents, which had been produced since the Revolution, are no justification of a practice in itself illegal, and contrary to the fundamental principles of the constitution; though its having been the constant practice of the office, might fairly be pleaded in mitigation of damages. . . .

The Jury, after withdrawing for near half an hour, returned, and found a general verdict upon both issues for the plaintiff, with a thousand pounds damages.

65D. *Leach* v. *Money*; opinions on general warrants expressed by the judges, 18 June 1765

(*State Trials*, XIX, pp. 1026–1027.)

Dryden Leach, printer of earlier numbers of *The North Briton*, brought an action for trespass in the Court of Common Pleas against the king's messengers who arrested him on the same general warrant as Wilkes. The part of the warrant relating to the seizure of papers was never executed and was therefore not in question in this case. It was proved that Leach was not the printer of No. 45, and he was awarded damages of £400. In 1765, when the case came into the King's Bench on a writ of error, the judges all expressed opinions against general warrants, and the case was not pursued by the Attorney-General, probably to avoid a judicial decision against the validity of general warrants of this type.

Lord *Mansfield*–. . . .

At present–as to the validity of the warrant, upon the single objection of the incertainty of the person, being neither named nor described–the common law, in many cases, gives authority to arrest without warrant; more especially, where taken in the very act: and there are many cases where particular acts of parliament have given authority to apprehend, under general warrants; as in the case of writs of assistance, or warrants to take up loose, idle, and disorderly people. But here, it is not contended, that the common law gave the officer authority to apprehend; nor that there is any act of parliament which warrants this case.

Therefore it must stand upon principles of common law.

It is not fit, that the receiving or judging of the information should be left to the discretion of the officer. The magistrate ought to judge; and should give certain directions to the officer. This is so, upon reason and convenience.

Then as to authorities–Hale and all others hold such an uncertain warrant void: and there is no case or book to the contrary.

It is said, 'that the usage has been so; and that many such have been issued, since the Revolution, down to this time.'

But a usage, to grow into law, ought to be a general usage, *communiter usitata et approbata*; and which, after a long continuance, it would be mischievous to overturn.

This is only the usage of a particular office, and contrary to the usage of all other justices and conservators of the peace.

There is the less reason for regarding this usage; because the form of the warrant probably took its rise from a positive statute; and the former precedents were inadvertently followed, after that law was expired.[1]

Mr. Justice *Wilmot* declared, that he had no doubt, nor ever had, upon these warrants: he thought them illegal and void.

Neither had the two other judges, Mr. Justice Yates, and Mr. Justice Aston, any doubt (upon this first argument) of the illegality of them: for no degree of antiquity can give sanction to a usage bad in itself. And they esteemed this usage to be so. They were clear and unanimous in opinion, that this warrant was illegal and bad.

65E. *Entick* v. *Carrington*; the warrant, and Lord Chief Justice Camden's judgment in the Court of Common Pleas, 1765

(*State Trials*, XIX, pp. 1034, 1063–1074.)

John Entick, chief writer of the anti-government paper *The Monitor*, had been arrested, and his papers seized under a general search warrant in 1762. Encouraged by Wilkes's success, he brought an action against the king's messengers who had executed the warrant.

(i) *The warrant.*

"George Montagu Dunk, earl of Halifax, viscount Sunbury, and baron Halifax, "one of the lords of his majesty's honourable privy council, lieutenant general of his "majesty's forces, lord lieutenant general and general governor of the kingdom of "Ireland, and principal secretary of state, &c. these are in his majesty's name to authorize "and require you, taking a constable to your assistance, to make strict and diligent "search for John Entick, the author, or one concerned in writing of several weekly

[1] The Licensing Act, which finally expired in 1696.

"very seditious papers, intitled the Monitor, or British Freeholder, No. 357, 358, 360, "373, 376, 378, 379, and 380, London, printed for J. Wilson and J. Fell in Pater Noster "Row, which contain gross and scandalous reflections and invectives upon his majesty's "government, and upon both houses of parliament; and him, having found you are "to seize and apprehend, and to bring, together with his books and papers, in safe "custody before me to be examined concerning the premisses, and further dealt with "according to law; in the due execution whereof all mayors, sheriffs, justices of the "peace, constables, and other his majesty's officers civil and military, and loving subjects "whom it may concern, are to be aiding and assisting to you as there shall be occasion; "and for so doing this shall be your warrant. Given at St. James's the 6th day of "November 1762, in the third year of his majesty's reign, Dunk Halifax.

"To Nathan Carrington, James Watson, Thomas Ardran and Robert Blackmore, "four of his majesty's messengers in ordinary."

(ii) *Lord Chief Justice Camden's judgment.*

L.C.J. . . .

I come in the last place to the point, which is made by the justification; for the defendants, having failed in the attempt made to protect themselves by the statute of the 24th of Geo. 2, are under a necessity to maintain the legality of the warrants, under which they have acted, and to shew that the secretary of state in the instance now before us, had a jurisdiction to seize the plaintiff's papers. If he had no such jurisdiction, the law is clear, that the officers are as much responsible for the trespass as their superior.

This, though it is not the most difficult, is the most interesting question in the cause; because if this point should be determined in favour of the jurisdiction, the secret cabinets and bureaus of every subject in this kingdom will be thrown open to the search and inspection of a messenger, whenever the secretary of state shall think fit to charge, or even to suspect, a person to be the author, printer, or publisher of a seditious libel.

The messenger, under this warrant, is commanded to seize the person described, and to bring him with his papers to be examined before the secretary of state. In consequence of this, the house must be searched; the lock and doors of every room, box, or trunk must be broken open; all the papers and books without exception, if the warrant be executed according to its tenor, must be seized and carried away; for it is observable, that nothing is left either to the discretion or to the humanity of the officer.

This power so assumed by the secretary of state is an execution upon all the party's papers, in the first instance. His house is rifled; his most valuable secrets are taken out of his possession, before the paper for which he is charged is found to be criminal by any competent jurisdiction, and before he is convicted either of writing, publishing, or being concerned in the paper.

This power, so claimed by the secretary of state, is not supported by one single citation from any law book extant. It is claimed by no other magistrate in this kingdom but himself: the great executive hand of criminal justice, the lord chief justice of the court of King's-bench, chief justice Scroggs excepted, never having assumed this authority.

The arguments, which the defendants' counsel have thought fit to urge in support of this practice, are of this kind.

That such warrants have issued frequently since the Revolution, which practice has been found by the special verdict; though I must observe, that the defendants have no right to avail themselves of that finding, because no such practice is averred in their justification.

That the case of the warrants bears a resemblance to the case of search for stolen goods.

They say too, that they have been executed without resistance upon many printers, booksellers, and authors, who have quietly submitted to the authority; that no action hath hitherto been brought to try the right; and that although they have been often read upon the returns of Habeas Corpus, yet no court of justice has ever declared them illegal.

And it is further insisted, that this power is essential to government, and the only means of quieting clamours and sedition.

These arguments, if they can be called arguments, shall be all taken notice of; because upon this question I am desirous of removing every colour or plausibility.

Before I state the question, it will be necessary to describe the power claimed by this warrant in its full extent.

If honestly exerted, it is a power to seize that man's papers, who is charged upon oath to be the author or publisher of a seditious libel; if oppressively, it acts against every man, who is so described in the warrant, though he be innocent.

It is executed against the party, before he is heard or even summoned; and the information, as well as the informers, is unknown.

It is executed by messengers with or without a constable (for it can never be pretended, that such is necessary in point of law) in the presence or the absence of the party, as the messengers shall think fit, and without a witness to testify what passes at the time of the transaction; so that when the papers are gone, as the only witnesses are the trespassers, the party injured is left without proof.

If this injury falls upon an innocent person, he is as destitute of remedy as the guilty: and the whole transaction is so guarded against discovery, that if the officer should be disposed to carry off a bank-bill, he may do it with impunity, since there is no man capable of proving either the taker or the thing taken.

It must not be here forgot, that no subject whatsoever is privileged from this search; because both Houses of Parliament have resolved, that there is no privilege in the case of a seditious libel.

Nor is there pretence to say, that the word 'papers' here mentioned ought in point of law to be restrained to the libellous papers only. The word is general, and there is nothing in the warrant to confine it; nay, I am able to affirm, that it has been upon a late occasion executed in its utmost latitude: for in the case of Wilkes against Wood, when the messengers hesitated about taking all the manuscripts, and sent to the secretary of state for more express orders for that purpose, the answer was, "that all must be taken, manuscripts and all." Accordingly, all was taken, and Mr. Wilkes's private pocket-book filled up the mouth of the sack.

I was likewise told in the same cause by one of the most experienced messengers, that he held himself bound by his oath to pay an implicit obedience to the commands of the secretary of state; that in common cases he was contented to seize the printed impressions of the papers mentioned in the warrant; but when he received directions to search further, or to make a more general seizure, his rule was to sweep all. The practice has been correspondent to the warrant.

Such is the power, and therefore one should naturally expect that the law to warrant it should be clear in proportion as the power is exorbitant.

If it is law, it will be found in our books. If it is not to be found there, it is not law.

The great end, for which men entered into society, was to secure their property. That right is preserved sacred and incommunicable in all instances, where it has not been taken away or abridged by some public law for the good of the whole. The cases where this right of property is set aside by positive law, are various. Distresses, executions, forfeitures, taxes, &c. are all of this description; wherein every man by common consent gives up that right, for the sake of justice and the general good. By the laws of England, every invasion of private property, be it ever so minute, is a trespass. No man can set his foot upon my ground without my licence, but he is liable to an action, though the damage be nothing; which is proved by every declaration in trespass, where the defendant is called upon to answer for bruising the grass and even treading upon the soil. If he admits the fact, he is bound to shew by way of justification, that some positive law has empowered or excused him. The justification is submitted to the judges, who are to look into the books; and if such a justification can be maintained by the text of the statute law, or by the principles of common law. If no such excuse can be found or produced, the silence of the books is an authority against the defendant, and the plaintiff must have judgment.

According to this reasoning, it is now incumbent upon the defendants to shew the law, by which this seizure is warranted. If that cannot be done, it is a trespass.

Papers are the owner's goods and chattels: they are his dearest property; and are so far from enduring a seizure, that they will hardly bear an inspection; and though the eye cannot by the laws of England be guilty of a trespass, yet where private papers are removed and carried away, the secret nature of those goods will be an aggravation of the trespass, and demand more considerable damages in that respect. Where is the written law that gives any magistrate such a power? I can safely answer, there is none; and therefore it is too much for us without such authority to pronounce a practice legal, which would be subversive of all the comforts of society. . . .

I come now to the practice since the Revolution, which has been strongly urged, with this emphatical addition, that an usage tolerated from the æra of liberty, and continued downwards to this time through the best ages of the constitution, must necessarily have a legal commencement. Now, though that pretence can have no place in the question made by this plea, because no such practice is there alleged; yet I will permit the defendant for the present to borrow a fact from the special verdict, for the sake of giving it an answer.

If the practice began then, it began too late to be law now. If it was more ancient, the Revolution is not to answer for it; and I could have wished, that upon this occasion the Revolution had not been considered as the only basis of our liberty.

The Revolution restored this constitution to its first principles. It did no more. It did not enlarge the liberty of the subject; but gave it a better security. It neither widened nor contracted the foundation, but repaired, and perhaps added a buttress or two to the fabric; and if any minister of state has since deviated from the principles at that time recognized, all that I can say is, that, so far from being sanctified, they are condemned by the Revolution.

With respect to the practice itself, if it goes no higher, every lawyer will tell you, it is much too modern to be evidence of the common law; and if it should be added, that these warrants ought to acquire some strength by the silence of those courts, which have heard them read so often upon returns without censure or animadversion, I am able to borrow my answer to that pretence from the Court of King's-bench, which lately declared with great unanimity in the Case of General Warrants, that as no objection was taken to them upon the returns, and the matter passed *sub silentio*, the precedents were of no weight. I most heartily concur in that opinion; and the reason is more pertinent here, because the Court had no authority in the present case to determine against the seizure of papers, which was not before them; whereas in the other they might, if they had thought fit, have declared the warrant void, and discharged the prisoner *ex officio*.

This is the first instance I have met with, where the ancient immemorable law of the land, in a public matter, was attempted to be proved by the practice of a private office.

The names and rights of public magistrates, their power and forms of proceeding as they are settled by law, have been long since written, and are to be found in books and records. Private customs indeed are still to be sought from private tradition. But whoever conceived a notion, that any part of the public law could be buried in the obscure practice of a particular person?

To search, seize, and carry away all the papers of the subject upon the first warrant: that such a right should have existed from the time whereof the memory of man runneth not to the contrary, and never yet have found a place in any book of law; is incredible. But if so strange a thing could be supposed, I do not see, how we could declare the law upon such evidence.

But still it is insisted, that there has been a general submission, and no action brought to try the right.

I answer, there has been a submission of guilt and poverty to power and the terror of punishment. But it would be strange doctrine to assert that all the people of this land are bound to acknowledge that to be universal law, which a few criminal booksellers have been afraid to dispute. . . .

It is then said, that it is necessary for the ends of government to lodge such a power with a state officer; and that it is better to prevent the publication before than to punish the offender afterwards. I answer, if the legislature be of that opinion, they will revive the Licensing Act. But if they have not done that, I conceive they are not of that opinion. And with respect to the argument of state necessity, or a distinction that has been aimed at between state offences and others, the common law does not understand that kind of reasoning, nor do our books take notice of any such distinctions.

Serjeant Ashley was committed to the Tower in the 3d of Charles 1st, by the House of Lords only for asserting in argument, that there was a 'law of state' different from the common law; and the Ship-Money judges were impeached for holding, first, that state-necessity would justify the raising money without consent of parliament; and secondly, that the king was judge of that necessity.

If the king himself has no power to declare when the law ought to be violated for reason of state, I am sure we his judges have no such prerogative.

Lastly, it is urged as an argument of utility, that such a search is a means of detecting offenders by discovering evidence. I wish some cases had been shewn, where the law forceth evidence out of the owner's custody by process. There is no process against papers in civil causes. It has been often tried, but never prevailed. Nay, where the adversary has by force or fraud got possession of your own proper evidence, there is no way to get it back but by action.

In the criminal law such a proceeding was never heard of; and yet there are some crimes, such for instance as murder, rape, robbery, and house-breaking, to say nothing of forgery and perjury, that are more atrocious than libelling. But our law has provided no paper-search in these cases to help forward the conviction. . . .

I have now taken notice of every thing that has been urged upon the present point; and upon the whole we are all of opinion, that the warrant to seize and carry away the party's papers in the case of a seditious libel, is illegal and void.

66. Somersett's Case; Lord Mansfield's judgment, 22 June 1772

(*State Trials*, XX, pp. 80–82.)

This important case, of which the main facts are recited in Lord Mansfield's judgment, decided that the state of slavery was not known in English law. The Court of Session in Scotland on 15 January 1778 delivered a similar judgment in the case of *Knight* v. *Wedderburn*.

Trinity Term, June 22, 1772.

Lord *Mansfield*.–On the part of Somersett, the case which we gave notice should be decided this day, the Court now proceeds to give its opinion. I shall recite the return to the writ of Habeas Corpus, as the ground of our determination; omitting only words of form. The captain of the ship on board of which the negro was taken, makes his return to the writ in terms signifying that there have been, and still are, slaves to a great number in Africa; and that the trade in them is authorized by the laws and opinions of Virginia and Jamaica; that they are goods and chattels; and, as such, saleable and sold. That James Somersett is a negro of Africa, and long before the return of the king's writ was brought to be sold, and was sold to Charles Steuart, esq. then in Jamaica, and has not been manumitted since; that Mr. Steuart, having occasion to transact business, came over hither, with an intention to return; and brought Somersett to attend and abide with him, and to carry him back as soon as the business should be transacted. That such intention has been, and still continues; and that the negro did remain till the time of his departure in the service of his master Mr. Steuart, and quitted it without his consent; and thereupon, before the return of the king's writ, the said Charles Steuart did commit the slave on board the Anne and Mary, to safe custody, to be kept till he should set sail, and then to be taken with him to Jamaica, and there sold as a slave. And this is the cause why he, captain Knowles, who was then and now is, commander of the above vessel, then and now lying in the river of Thames, did the said negro, committed to his custody, detain; and on which he now renders him to the orders of the Court. We pay all due attention to the opinion of sir Philip Yorke, and lord chancellor Talbot, whereby they pledged themselves to the British planters, for all the legal consequences of slaves coming over to this kingdom or being baptized, recognized by lord Hardwicke, sitting as chancellor on the 19th of October, 1749, that trover would lie: that a notion had prevailed, if a negro came over, or became a Christian, he was emancipated, but no ground in law: that he and lord Talbot, when attorney and solicitor-general, were of opinion, that no such claim for freedom was valid; that though the statute of tenures had abolished villeins regardant to a manor, yet he did not conceive but that a man might still become a villein in gross, by confessing himself such in open court. We are so well agreed, that we think there is no occasion of having it argued (as I intimated an intention at first,) before all the judges, as is usual, for obvious reasons, on a return to a Habeas Corpus. The only question before us is, whether the cause on the return is sufficient? If it is, the negro must be remanded; if it is not, he must be discharged. Accordingly, the return states, that the slave departed and refused to serve; whereupon he was kept, to be sold abroad. So high an act of dominion must be recognized by the law of the country where it is used. The power of a master over his slave has been extremely different, in different countries. The state of slavery is of such a nature, that it is incapable of being introduced on any reasons, moral or political, but only by positive law, which preserves its force long after the reasons, occasion, and time itself from whence it was created, is erased from memory. It is so odious, that nothing can be suffered to support it, but positive law. Whatever inconveniences, therefore, may follow from the decision, I cannot say this case is allowed or approved by the law of England; and therefore the black must be discharged.

67. Lord Mansfield on the law of treason, 1781

(*State Trials*, XXI, pp. 644–645.)

In the trial in the Court of King's Bench of Lord George Gordon on a charge of high treason arising out of the anti-popery riots in London in June 1780, Lord Mansfield began his summing-up with a lucid exposition of the law of treason.

Lord *Mansfield*:

Gentlemen of the Jury; the prisoner at the bar is indicted for that species of high treason which is called levying war against the king, and therefore it is necessary you should first be informed what is in law levying war against the king, so as to constitute the crime of high treason, within the statute of Edward 3, and perhaps according to the legal signification of the term before that statute. There are two kinds of levying war:–one against the person of the king; to imprison, to dethrone, or to kill him; or to make him change measures, or remove counsellors:–the other, which is said to be levied against the majesty of the king, or, in other words, against him in his regal capacity; as when a multitude rise and assemble to attain by force and violence any object of a general public nature; that is levying war against the majesty of the king; and most reasonably so held, because it tends to dissolve all the bonds of society, to destroy property, and to overturn government; and by force of arms, to restrain the king from reigning according to law.

Insurrections, by force and violence, to raise the price of wages, to open all prisons, to destroy meeting-houses, nay, to destroy all brothels, to resist the execution of militia laws, to throw down all inclosures, to alter the established law, or change religion, to redress grievances real or pretended, have all been held levying war. Many other instances might be put. Lord chief justice Holt, in sir John Friend's case, says "if persons do assemble themselves and act with force in opposition to some law which they think inconvenient, and hope thereby to get it repealed, this is a levying war and treason." In the present case, it don't rest upon an implication that they hoped by opposition to a law to get it repealed, but the prosecution proceeds upon the direct ground, that the object was, by force and violence, to compel the legislature to repeal a law; and therefore, without any doubt, I tell you the joint opinion of us all, that, if this multitude assembled with intent, by acts of force and violence, to compel the legislature to repeal a law, it is high treason.

Though the form of an indictment for this species of treason mentions drums, trumpets, arms, swords, fifes, and guns, yet none of these circumstances are essential. The question always is, whether the intent is, by force and violence, to attain an object of a general and public nature, by any instruments, or by dint of their numbers. Whoever incites, advises, encourages, or is any way aiding to such a multitude so assembled with such intent, though he does not personally appear among them, or with his own hands commit any violence whatsoever, yet he is equally a principal with those who act, and guilty of high treason.

B. CENTRAL ADMINISTRATION AND THE KEEPING OF ORDER

68. The staffs of some of the offices of State, 1741

(John Chamberlayne, *Magnae Britanniae Notitia: or, the Present State of Great Britain*, Part II (1741), pp. 47–48, 55, 82–83.)

This work was started by Edward Chamberlayne as *Angliae Notitia* in 1669, changing its name as above after the Union with Scotland in 1707. It continued to appear at intervals till 1755.

NUMBER XII.

Secretaries *of* STATE, *and their Officers.*

The most Noble *Thomas*, Duke of *Newcastle*, Secretary of State for the *Southern Province.*

John Couraud, *Andrew Stone*,	Esqrs. Under-Secretaries.
Daniel Preverau, Esq.	First Clerk.
Mr *Edmund Maskelyne*, Mr *Joseph Stepney*, Mr *Francis Hutcheson*, Mr *Thomas Ramsden*, Mr *Thomas Gage*,	Clerks.
Mr *Alexander Ward*, Mr *Joseph Noble*,	Chamber-Keepers.
Mrs *Mary Bickford*,	Office-Cleaner.

The Right Honourable the Lord *Harrington*, Secretary of State for the *Northern Province.*

Edward Weston, The Hon. *Thomas Stanhope*,	Esqrs; Under-Secretaries.
John Wace, Esq;	First Clerk.
Mr *James Payzant*, Mr *Joseph Richardson*, Mr *John Larpent*, Mr *George Brown*, Mr *George Hucksley*, Mr *William Houghton*,	Clerks.
Mr *William Quin*, Mr *John Somers*,	Chamber-Keepers.
Mrs *Elizabeth Smart*,	Office-Cleaner.

Clerks of the Signet.

Joseph Moyle, Esq; acts for himself,

<table>
<tr><td>Gantlet Fry,
Charles Delafaye,
Edward Weston,</td><td>Esqrs.</td></tr>
<tr><td>Mr Edmund Maskelyne,
Mr Haines,
Mr Richardson,</td><td>Deputies.</td></tr>
</table>

Mr *Thomas Richardson*, Office-Keeper.

John Couraud, Esq; Keeper of the Papers and Records of State.

John Wace, Esq; Deputy.

Decypherers.

The Reverend Dr. *Edward Willes*, Dean of *Lincoln*.

Anthony Corbier, Esq;

Sir *Thomas Brand*, Embellisher.

Writer of the *Gazette*.

Samuel Buckley Esq; 300L. *per Annum*.

John Couraud, Esq; *Latin* Secretary, 200L. *per Annum*.

. . .

NUMBER XXI.

Lords Commissioners for Trade *and* Plantations.

<table>
<tr><td>John, Lord Monson,
Martin Bladen, Esq;
Edward Ashe, Esq;
James Brudenell, Esq;
Richard Plummer, Esq;
The Hon. Robert Herbert, Esq;
Benjamin Keene, Esq;
Thomas Pelham, jun. Esq;</td><td>each 1000L. per Annum.</td></tr>
</table>

Thomas Hill, Esq; Secretary . . . 500L. *per Annum*.

Samuel Gillibrand, Esq; Deputy-Secretary.

William Popple, Esq; Clerk of the Reports.

<table>
<tr><td>Mr Israel Hudson,
Mr Richard Rogers,
Mr George Bradley,
Mr William Campion,
Mr Gabriel Mathias,
Mr John Tutté,
Mr Edmund Sedgwick,</td><td>Clerks.</td></tr>
</table>

Mr *Samuel Simpson,* Chamber-Keeper and Assistant-Messenger.

Mr *John Wilson,* Messenger, and Assistant-Chamber-Keeper.

Mr *Giles Griffin,* Porter.

Mrs *Bridget Griffin,* Necessary-Woman.

. . .

NUMBER XXVI.

A LIST *of the Officers belonging to his Majesty's General Letter-Office in* Lombard-Street.

THE Right Honourable *Thomas* Lord *Lovell,* and the Honourable Sir *John Eyles,* Bart. Post-masters General.

George Stone, Esq; Receiver-General.

John Searle, Esq; Accomptant General.

Mr *Thomas Horne,* Deputy-Accomptant.

Mr *Thomas Pitches,* Accomptant-General's Clerk.

John Jesse, Esq; Cashire.

Joseph Bell, Esq; Comptroller of the Inland Post, and Deputy.

John-David Barbut, Esq; Secretary to the Postmasters-General.

John Jesse, Esq; Chief Clerk to the Post-masters-General.

Mr *Thomas Strickland,* Clerk.

Clerks of the Roads, etc.

Chester Road, — Mr *Robert Giddings.*
Mr *Henry Potts,* his Assistant.

North Road, — Mr *Christopher Harris.*
Mr *Robert Saxby,* his Assistant.

West-Road, — Mr *Richard Dickerson.*
Mr *Joshua Baker,* jun. his Assistant.

Bristol Road, — Mr *John Sawtell.*
Mr *Anthony English,* his Assistant.

Yarmouth Road, — Mr *John Jackson.*
Mr *William Boulton.*

Kent Road, — Mr *Samuel Potts.*
Mr *Thomas Smith,* his Assistant.

Clerk of the By-Nights, Mr *John Stobbs,* jun.

Windowman, Mr *Joseph Archer.*

Mr *Robert Parsons,* and Mr *John Barber,* to overlook the Franks and mis-sent Letters.

Mr *Savil Leigh,* Windowman for the By-Days.

Mr *James Watson,* Chamber-Keeper to the Commissioners.

Dennis Bond, Esq; Court Post.

Mrs *Dinis Chapman*, House-keeper.

Mr *Matthew Waring* and Mr *John Wakelin*, Mail-makers.

SORTERS.

Mr *Edward Cave*	Mr *John Green*
Mr *Thomas Ravenhill*	Mr *James-Samuel Redmaine*
Mr *Richard Lloyd*	Mr *John Silvester*
Mr *William Cotsford*	Mr *Thomas Clarke*
Mr *David Brown*	Mr *Jacob Jackson*

Sixty-nine Inland Letter-Carriers, to distribute the Letters, at 11s. *per week*; One of which takes care of the unknown and uncertain Letters, and has an Addition to his Salary.

Eight Foreign Letter-Carriers, One of which takes care of the unknown and uncertain Letters, and has an Addition to his Salary. Supervisor, Mr *John Stobbs*, sen.

Four Porters.

John Wrighte	*Thomas Pearce*
William Burleigh	*Henry Brown*

Watchman, *Robert Collins.*

Foreign Office.

Comptroller, *John Daye*, Esq;

Foreign Secretary, *John le Febure*, Esq;

Alphabet-keeper, Mr *Edmund Jones.*

CLERKS.

Mr *George Hindmas*	Mr *Joseph Bell*, jun.
Mr *Francis Morant*	Mr *John Calcott.*
Mr *Charles Lee.*	Mr *Anthony Todd.*

Mr *William van Almond*, Manager of the Pacquet-boats at the *Brill.*

Sollicitor to the Post-Office, *Matthew Lamb*, Esq;

69. A contemporary account of the office of Secretary of State, 1735

(John Chamberlayne, *Magnae Britanniae Notitia: or the Present State of Great Britain*, Part I (1735), pp. 83–85.)

In addition to the lists of offices and their holders, given in Part II of each number, the *Present State of Great Britain* also, in Part I of each number, gave a general description of England and its government. The following account of the office of Secretary of State omits to mention the Secretaries' powers as magistrates.

SECRETARIES OF STATE. The King of *England* had anciently but one Secretary of State, until about the End of *Henry* the Eighth's Reign, it was thought fit, that weighty and important Office should be discharged by two Persons, both of equal Authority, and both stiled *Principal Secretaries of State*. In those Days, and some while after, they sat not at the Council-Board, but having prepared their Business in a Room adjoining to the Council-Chamber, they came in, and stood on either Hand of the King; and nothing was debated at the Table until the Secretaries had gone through with their Proposals. But Queen *Elizabeth* seldom coming to the Council, that Method was altered, and the Secretaries took their Places as Privy-Counsellors, which Dignity they have retained and enjoyed ever since; and a Council is seldom or never held without the Presence of one of them at the least.

Their Employment being of extraordinary Trust and Multiplicity, renders them most considerable in the Eyes of the King, upon whom they attend every Day, as Occasion requires; and of the Subject also, whose Requests and Desires are for the Manner if he hath no other Qualification; but if above the Degree of a *Baron*, then he most Part lodged in their Hands, to be represented to the King, and always to make Dispatches thereupon, according to his Majesty's Answers and Directions.

The Correspondence with all Parts of *Great-Britain* is, without Distinction, managed by either of the Secretaries, relating to the Church, the Army, the Militia, Grants, Pardons, Dispensations, &c. But as for foreign Affairs, all the Nations which have Intercourse of Business with *Great-Britain*, are by them divided into two Provinces the *Northern* and *Southern*; of which the *Northern* is usually under the Junior Secretary, and contains *Scandinavia*, &c. The *Southern* under the Senior, and contains *Flanders*, *France*, &c.

They have this special Honour, that if either of them be a *Baron*, he taketh Place, and hath the Precedence of all other Persons of the same Degree, tho' otherwise by their Creation some of them might have Right to precede him; and a *Knight* in like Manner, if he hath no other Qualification; but if above the Degree of a *Baron*, then he takes Place only according to the Seniority of his Creation.

They have their several Lodgings appointed them in all the King's Houses, as well for their own Accommodation, as for their Office, and those that attend upon it. They have also Board-Wages.

Their settled Allowance from the King, in Salary and Pension, is 2000l. *Sterling per Annum* to each of them.

The Secretaries and Clerks, whom they employ under them, are wholly at their own Choice, and have no Dependance upon any other Power or Persons besides themselves.

The Secretaries of State have the Custody of that Seal of the King, which is properly called the *Signet*; the Use and Application whereof gives Denomination to an Office, constantly attending the Court, called the *Signet-Office*, wherein there are 4 Clerks, who wait alternately by Months, and prepare such Things as are to pass the *Signet*, in order to the *Privy-Seal*, or *Great-Seal*. . . .

Moreover, depending on the Secretaries of State is an ancient Office called the *Paper-Office*, the Keeper whereof hath in his Charge all the publick Papers, Writings, Matters of State, and Council; all Letters, Intelligences, Negotiations of the King's publick Ministers abroad, and generally all the Papers and Dispatches that pass through the Offices of the two Secretaries of State, which are, or ought to be from Time to Time transmitted into this Office, and here remain, disposed by way of a Library, within his Majesty's Palace of *White-Hall*.

70. Circular letter from Charles James Fox to British representatives at foreign courts that they should address their letters to him as Foreign Secretary, 29 March 1782

(Public Record Office, State Papers Domestic, Entry Book 416, p. 102: quoted in W. R. Anson, *Law and Custom of the Constitution*, 4th ed., II (1935), Part I, p. 180.)

This appears to be the only official document announcing the reorganization of the Secretaryships of State in 1782. The former arrangement of two Secretaries, one for the Southern and one for the Northern Department, each dealing with both domestic and foreign affairs, was now changed to the modern practice of having a Foreign Secretary and a Home Secretary. George III had suggested this in 1771, and it seems to have taken place in 1782 by agreement between the king and the Rockingham Ministry.

[29 March 1782]

The King having, on the resignation of the Lord Viscount Stormont, been pleased to appoint me to be one of His Principal Secretaries of State, and at the same time *to make a new arrangement in the Departments by conferring that for Domestic Affairs and Colonies on the Earl of Shelburne, and entrusting me with the sole direction of the Department for Foreign Affairs,* I am to desire that you will for the future address your letters to me.

71. The Riot Act, 1715

(*Statutes at Large*, XIII, pp. 142–146, 1 Geo. I, Stat. 2, cap. 5.)

The Act increased the power of the justices of the peace to deal with "tumults and riotous assemblies", and was passed as a result of the disturbances in many parts of the country in the first half of 1715.

An act for preventing tumults and riotous assemblies, and for the more speedy and effectual punishing the rioters.

I. WHEREAS *of late many rebellious riots and tumults have been in divers parts of this kingdom, to the disturbance of the publick peace, and the endangering of his Majesty's person and government, and the same are yet continued and fomented by persons disaffected to his Majesty, presuming so to do, for that the punishments provided by the laws now in being are not adequate to such heinous offences; and by such rioters his Majesty and his administration have been most maliciously and falsely traduced, with an intent to raise divisions, and to alienate the affections of the people from his Majesty: therefore for the preventing and suppressing of such riots and tumults, and for the more speedy and effectual punishing the offenders therein;* be it enacted by the King's most excellent majesty, by and with the advice and consent of the lords spiritual and temporal and of the commons, in this present parliament assembled, and by the authority of the same, That if any persons to the number of twelve or more, being unlawfully, riotously, and tumultuously assembled together, to the disturbance of the publick peace, at any time after the last day of *July* in the year of our Lord one thousand seven hundred and fifteen, and being required or commanded by any one or more justice or justices of the peace, or by the sheriff of the county, or his under-sheriff, or by the mayor, bailiff or bailiffs, or other head-officer, or justice of the peace of any city or town-corporate, where such assembly shall be, by proclamation to be made in the King's name, in the form herein after directed, to disperse themselves, and peaceably to depart to their habitations, or to their lawful business, shall, to the number of twelve or more (notwithstanding such proclamation made) unlawfully, riotously, and tumultuously remain or continue together by the space of one hour after such command or request made by proclamation, that then such continuing together to the number of twelve or more, after such command or request made by proclamation, shall be adjudged felony without benefit of clergy, and the offenders therein shall be adjudged felons, and shall suffer death as in case of felony without benefit of clergy.

II. And be it further enacted by the authority aforesaid, That the order and form of the proclamations that shall be made by the authority of this act, shall be as hereafter followeth (that is to say) the justice of the peace, or other person authorized by this act to make the said proclamation shall, among the said rioters, or as near to them as he can safely come, with a loud voice command, or cause to be commanded silence to be, while proclamation is making, and after that, shall openly and with loud voice make or cause to be made proclamation in these words, or like in effect:

Our sovereign Lord the King chargeth and commandeth all persons, being assembled, immediately to disperse themselves, and peaceably to depart to their habitations, or to their lawful business, upon the pains contained in the act made in the first year of King George, *for preventing tumults and riotous assemblies.*

God save the King.

And every such justice and justices of the peace, sheriff, under-sheriff, mayor, bailiff, and other head-officer, aforesaid, within the limits of their respective jurisdictions, are hereby authorized, impowered and required, on notice or knowledge of any such unlawful, riotous and tumultuous assembly, to resort to the place where such unlawful, riotous, and tumultuous assemblies shall be, of persons to the number of twelve or more, and there to make or cause to be made proclamation in manner aforesaid.

III. And be it further enacted by the authority aforesaid, That if such persons so unlawfully, riotously, and tumultuously assembled, or twelve or more of them, after proclamation made in manner aforesaid, shall continue together and not disperse themselves within one hour, That then it shall and may be lawful to and for every justice of the peace, sheriff, or under-sheriff of the county where such assembly shall be, and also to and for every high or petty-constable, and other peace-officer within such county, and also to and for every mayor, justice of the peace, sheriff, bailiff, and other head-officer, high or petty-constable, and other peace-officer of any city or town-corporate where such assembly shall be, and to and for such other person and persons as shall be commanded to be assisting unto any such justice of the peace, sheriff, or under-sheriff, mayor, bailiff, or other head-officer aforesaid (who are hereby authorized and impowered to command all his Majesty's subjects of age and ability to be assisting to them therein) to seize and apprehend, and they are hereby required to seize and apprehend such persons so unlawfully, riotously and tumultuously continuing together after proclamation made, as aforesaid, and forthwith to carry the persons so apprehended before one or more of his Majesty's justices of the peace of the county or place where such persons shall be so apprehended, in order to their being proceeded against for such their offences according to law; and that if the persons so unlawfully, riotously and tumultuously assembled, or any of them, shall happen to be killed, maimed or hurt, in the dispersing, seizing or apprehending, or endeavouring to disperse, seize or apprehend them, by reason of their resisting the persons so dispersing, seizing or apprehending, or endeavouring to disperse, seize or apprehend them, that then every such justice of the peace, sheriff, under-sheriff, mayor, bailiff, head-officer, high or petty-constable, or other peace-officer, and all and singular persons, being aiding and assisting to them, or any of them, shall be free, discharged and indemnified, as well against the King's Majesty, his heirs and successors, as against all and every other person and persons, of, for, or concerning the killing, maiming, or hurting of any such person or persons so unlawfully, riotously and tumultuously assembled, that shall happen to be so killed, maimed or hurt, as aforesaid.

IV. And be it further enacted by the authority aforesaid, That if any persons unlawfully, riotously and tumultuously assembled together, to the disturbance of the publick peace, shall unlawfully, and with force demolish or pull down, or begin to demolish or pull down any church or chapel, or any building for religious worship certified and registered according to the statute made in the first year of the reign of the late King *William* and Queen *Mary*, intituled, *An act for exempting their Majesty's protestant subjects dissenting from the church of* England *from the penalties of certain laws*, or any dwelling-house, barn, stable, or other out-house, that then every such demolishing, or pulling down, or beginning to demolish, or pull down, shall be adjudged felony without benefit of clergy, and the offenders therein shall be adjudged felons, and shall suffer death as in case of felony without benefit of clergy.

V. Provided always, and be it further enacted by the authority aforesaid, That if any person or persons do, or shall, with force and arms, wilfully and knowingly oppose, obstruct, or in any manner wilfully and knowingly let, hinder, or hurt any person or persons that shall begin to proclaim, or go to proclaim according to the proclamation hereby directed to be made, whereby such proclamation shall not be made, that then every such opposing, obstructing, letting, hindering or hurting such person or persons, so beginning or going to make such proclamation, as aforesaid, shall be adjudged felony without benefit of clergy, and the offenders therein shall be adjudged felons, and shall suffer death as in case of felony, without benefit of clergy; and that also every such person or persons so being unlawfully, riotously and tumultuously assembled, to the number of twelve, as aforesaid, or more, to whom proclamation should or ought to have been made if the same had not been hindered, as aforesaid, shall likewise, in case they or any of them, to the number of twelve or more, shall continue together, and not disperse themselves within one hour after such lett or hindrance so made, having knowledge of such lett or hindrance so made, shall be adjudged felons, and shall suffer death as in case of felony, without benefit of clergy.

VI. And be it further enacted by the authority aforesaid, That if after the said last day of *July* one thousand seven hundred and fifteen, any such church or chapel, or any such building for religious worship, or any such dwelling-house, barn, stable, or other out-house, shall be demolished or pulled down wholly, or in part, by any persons so unlawfully, riotously and tumultuously assembled, that then, in case such church, chapel, building for religious worship, dwelling-house, barn, stable or out-house, shall be out of any city or town, that is either a county of itself, or is not within any hundred, that then the inhabitants of the hundred in which such damage shall be done, shall be liable to yield damages to the person or persons injured and damnified by such demolishing or pulling down wholly or in part; and such damages shall and may be recovered by action to be brought in any of his Majesty's courts of record at *Westminster*, (wherein no essoin, protection, or wager of law, or any imparlance shall be allowed) by the person or persons damnified thereby, against any two or more of the inhabitants of such hundred, such action for damages to any church or chapel to be brought in the name of the rector, vicar or curate of such church or chapel that shall be so damnified, in trust for applying the damages to be recovered in rebuilding or repairing such church or chapel; and that judgment being given for the plaintiff or plaintiffs in such action, the damages so to be recovered shall, at the request of such plaintiff or plaintiffs, his or their executors or administrators, be raised and levied on the inhabitants of such hundred, and paid to such plaintiff or plaintiffs, in such manner and form, and by such ways and means, as are provided by the statute made in the seven and twentieth year of the reign of Queen *Elizabeth*, for reimbursing the person or persons on whom any money recovered against any hundred by any party robbed, shall be levied: and in case any such church, chapel, building for religious worship, dwelling-house, barn, stable, or out-house so damnified, shall be in any city or town that is either a county of itself, or is not within any hundred, that then such damages shall and may be recovered by action to be brought in manner aforesaid (wherein no essoin, protection or wager of law, or any imparlance shall be allowed) against two or more inhabitants of such city or town; and judgment being given for the plaintiff or plaintiffs in such action, the damages so to be recovered shall, at the request of such plaintiff or plaintiffs, his or their executors or administrators, made to the justices of the peace of such city or town, at any quarter-sessions to be holden for the said city or town, be raised and levied on the inhabitants of such city or town, and paid to such plaintiff or plaintiffs, in such manner and form, and by such ways and means, as are provided by the said statute made in the seven and twentieth year of the reign of Queen *Elizabeth*, for reimbursing the person or persons on whom any money recovered against any hundred by any party robbed, shall be levied.

VII. And be it further enacted by the authority aforesaid, That this act shall be openly read at every quarter-session, and at every leet or law day.

VIII. Provided always, That no person or persons shall be prosecuted by virtue of this act, for any offence or offences committed contrary to the same, unless such prosecution be commenced within twelve months after the offence committed.

IX. And be it further enacted by the authority aforesaid, That the sheriffs and their deputies, stewards and their deputies, bailies of regalities and their deputies, magistrates of royal boroughs, and all other inferior judges and magistrates, and also all high and petty-constables, or other peace-officers of any county, stewartry, city, or town, within that part of *Great Britain* called *Scotland*, shall have the same powers and authority for putting this present act in execution within *Scotland*, as the justices of the peace and other magistrates aforesaid, respectively have by virtue of this act, within and for the other parts of this kingdom; and that all and every person and persons who shall at any time be convicted of any the offences aforementioned, within that part of *Great Britain* called *Scotland*, shall for every such offence incur and suffer the pain of death, and confiscation of moveables: and also that all prosecutions for repairing the damages of any church or chapel, or any building for religious worship, or any dwelling-house, barn, stable, or out-house, which shall be demolished or pulled down in whole or in part, within *Scotland*, by any persons unlawfully, riotously or tumultuously assembled, shall and may be recovered by summary action, at the instance of the party aggrieved, his or her heirs, or executors, against the county, stewartry, city or borough respectively, where such disorders shall happen, the magistrates being summoned in the ordinary form, and the several counties and stewartries called by edictal citation at the market-cross of the head-borough of such county or stewartry respectively, and that in general, without mentioning their names and designations.

X. Provided, and it is hereby declared, That this act shall extend to all places for religious worship, in that part of *Great Britain* called *Scotland*, which are tolerated by law, and where his majesty King *George*, the prince and princess of *Wales*, and their issue are prayed for in express words.

72A–B. The use of troops to quell civil disorder

72A. The riots in St. George's Fields on 10 May 1768

(*Sir Henry Cavendish's Debates of the House of Commons, 1768–71*, I (1841), pp. 307–311, 334.)

This debate illustrates the criticism which the Secretaries of State had to face in carrying out their duty of maintaining order; and the procedure followed in using troops for this purpose.

Wednesday, March 8, [1769]

In pursuance of the notice he had given, that he would move for the appointment of a committee, to inquire into the conduct of the magistrates and the employment of the military power, in the suppressing of the riots and tumults in St. George's Fields, on the 10th May last,

Mr *Edmund Burke* rose, and addressed the House as follows.–It now becomes my task, Sir, under the double obligation of my promise and my duty, to lay before the House, for their consideration, a statement of the proceedings and conduct of his Majesty's administration, under colour of the riots and disturbances which took place in the metropolis in the course of the months of April and May last. . . .

In order, Sir, to keep this important question from being overloaded by what is bad; by what does not belong to it; I shall beg leave to state what I disclaim doing. The first thing I will say is, that any one thing whatever upon which the judges' determination has passed, I do not intend to agitate: whatever has the sacred seal of judgment impressed upon it, I shall leave untouched. I will not touch the sacred ark that rests upon the table of our laws. God forbid we should suspect any thing wrong there! In the next place, I do not propose to deprive government of any one power or authority it has in the world; to take from it its judicial or executive power; to take from it any civil or military power whatever. In the third and last place, I heartily and totally disclaim all ideas of a lax and faint execution of justice; any thing that tends to weaken the springs of the executive power of this government. Peace and order are to be preserved at any price; if the voice of the magistrate cannot do it, the constable must do it: if the constable cannot do it, the sword of the soldier must do it: if it cannot be purchased without blood, it must be purchased by blood. Liberty ought not to exist in a country where peace and order are not observed. I appeal to the sense of the House, how far I have ever been from entertaining any violent notions upon the subject of liberty. My ideas upon that head have been kept a little below level. Not that I think that that good principle ought to be checked, but I rather chose to fit it to my own knowledge and abilities. I would choose that I should stick by my principles, and they by me, to the end, for ever. I am by opinion, by principle, by constitution, an enemy to all violence whatever. There is an innovation from above as well as from below: power can innovate as well as be innovated upon. I premise this, because such an innovation has been, as I conceive, attempted in this country: an innovation, tending to subvert, first its liberty, next its order; and to introduce, instead of order and decorum, confusion into this country. Depend upon it, Sir, this country will not let go its liberty without a struggle. An attempt has been made to introduce into the administration of our justice a martial police, upon a principle, as I understand, acknowleged, avowed, supported, winked at, by the greatest lawyers in the kingdom. Some of the great men in place, those in authority, may declare otherwise: but I say, they have expressed a desire and a design of incorporating the military with the civil constitution of this country: they teach the magistrate to look to the military power as his first instrument, and not as the final and desperate resource in cases of necessity. If such an opinion shall prevail, it will, Sir, be an innovation well worth the attention of the House. The matters I am now about to bring before you are so many overt acts, teaching and tending to bring it into practice, under circumstances which have already happened, and which may happen again. . . .

The first thing, Sir, is the letter addressed by Lord Weymouth, the secretary of state, to the chairman of the quarter-sessions at Lambeth. . . . In speaking of this letter, I shall consider what it really and truly is, and no more. It is, Sir, a strong recommendation of a military police, when it is said, that it can "never be employed to a more constitutional purpose, than in the support of the authority and dignity of the magistracy." . . . This sentence, Sir, is altogether at variance with the spirit of the constitution. The military power cannot be employed to any constitutional purpose whatever. What the danger of the country's falling to pieces would justify, I cannot say; but I will say, that the position laid down in this letter is a false and dangerous position, tending alike to corrupt the civil magistrates and to ruin the constitution. The consequence of it is this–that, under the authority of it, there is not a trading justice in the metropolis but would find it convenient to call for a military guard–there is not one of those magistrates who may not walk out with a military guard about him, for the preservation of his authority and dignity. . . .

Lord *Barrington*.[1]–I think I can throw some light on the question before the House, which no other individual can give. As my conduct made up a part of the speech which introduced this motion, I have a right to be the last speaker. It is said,

[1] William, second Viscount Barrington (1717–1793), Secretary at War.

that the introduction of the military in cases of riot is a novel practice. Sir, the standing army itself is novel: it is but eighty years old: the practice is very old compared with the existence of the army. In the war-office books there is no copy of orders given previous to the year 1715, because, before that time, the books were imperfectly kept. Several persons now alive, and some who are dead, have assured me, that they themselves saw the troops employed in the latter part of the reign of Queen Anne. Troops were employed at the time of Sacheverell's case:[1] at the accession of the present royal family they were employed, not only in cases of rebellion, but in riots and suspicions of riots. Troops were employed at Oxford, by the advice of some of the most able persons of the law. Troops have been employed for many years, exactly in the manner they now are. The directions given to troops ordered to assist the civil magistrate run in the same words as they did fifty years ago. They have varied a little, more or less, according to circumstances. I have always selected the most cautious words; and from the numerous requisitions of the magistrates for assistance, I have had a good deal of practice. From beginning to end I have invariably cautioned them not to call for troops, except in cases of absolute necessity. In some instances, I have refused troops, and have said, "It is your fears that induce you to call for them; I will not send them." In the course of ten years' experience, I do not recollect any instance of riots of magnitude being quelled without, but some hundred by, a military force. In Northumberland sixty persons were killed in a riot, and yet no inquiry was made with regard to those sixty persons. In the city of London, since the peace, I have been told that, in one instance, the troops called in to suppress a riotous assembly were compelled to fire, and twelve men were killed; and in another instance, nine, yet no observations were made; it was done in the discharge of their duty. . . . I do not wish the civil magistrate to resort to the use of the troops, but when he thinks the use of them necessary for the public safety, I wish them to be ready for him. . . . When I have not spirit and nerve enough to perform the duties of my office, I shall wish to be no longer in it. I will leave it to others, who desire the emolument of it without the labour. . . .

72B. The Gordon Riots, June 1780

(Charles M. Clode, *The Military Forces of the Crown*, II (1869), pp. 635–637, 660. Appendix of documents.)

As the magistrates on this occasion refused to order the troops to fire on the mob, and the belief that it was illegal to do so without an order from the civil magistrate was widely held at the time, it was decided at a meeting of the Privy Council on 7 June (at which leading members of the opposition were present) to take the unusual step of ordering the officers commanding the troops to act without waiting for orders from the magistrates.

Secretary at War's Order to the Guards to assist the Civil Power at Lord George Gordon's riots.

War Office, 5th June 1780.

SIR,

One of His Majesty's Principal Secretaries of State having transmitted to me information that numbers of people are assembled in the City of London in a tumultuous manner, and are actually committing great outrages there, and desiring that

[1] 1710.

immediate orders may be given to the Commanding Officer at the Tower to afford the Civil Magistrate such assistance as he shall think proper to demand for restoring the public tranquillity, I do hereby signify to you His Majesty's pleasure that you hold yourself and the Troops under your command in readiness to assist the Civil Magistrate in case he shall require it, and that upon his requisition, and under his authority, you do order, from time to time, such of the said Troops as shall be thought necessary for the purpose before mentioned, to march to the place or places which the Civil Magistrate shall point out.

I am, Sir, etc.

C. JENKINSON

Officer Commanding the Foot Guards at the Tower.

Letter from Secretary at War to the Secretary of State as to conduct of the Magistrates at Lord George Gordon's riots.

War Office, 6th June, 1780.

MY LORD,

In the course of last night, I was honoured with your Lordship's letter, dated the 5th at midnight. Before the receipt of this, every possible order had been given for Troops to be in readiness, and a very large Military Force has continued to assemble through the whole of yesterday and last night, ready to assist the Civil Magistrates at their requisition in preserving the public peace.

I can further add, it appears to me by reports made to me from the Officers Commanding those Troops, that except in two instances that happened in the Tower (and, by sending a larger Force into that Garrison, this defect was remedied yesterday evening), there has always been a number of Foot Guards ready to assist the Civil Magistrate, and more than he has called for or appeared to want.

I have further to acquaint your Lordship that I have, with Lord Amherst's concurrence, sent a special messenger with an order for a Regiment of Dragoons to march without delay from Canterbury to the neighbourhood of London.

I have now the honour to enclose to your Lordship a Copy of a Letter and Report transmitted to be [me] by Major-General Winyard, the Field Officer in Staff Waiting for the Foot Guards, of what happened in the course of yesterday and last night, and must beg in the most serious manner to call your Lordship's attention to some parts of that Letter and Report, wherein it appears that in one instance the Civil Magistrate, having called for the Troops, was not ready to attend them; that in another instance, the Troops having been called out, were left by the Magistrates exposed to the fury of the populace, when the party, as I am informed was insulted in a most extraordinary manner; and that in two other instances, after the Troops had marched to the places appointed for them, several of the Magistrates refused to act.

It is the duty of the Troops, my Lord, to act only under the authority and by the direction of the Civil Magistrate. For this reason they are under greater restraints than any other of His Majesty's subjects, and when insulted are obliged to be more cautious even in defending themselves. If, therefore, the Civil Magistrate, after having called upon them, is not ready to attend them, or abandons them before they return to their

Quarters, or after they arrive at the places to which they have been ordered, he refuses to act, I leave it to your Lordship to judge in how defenceless and how disgraceful a situation the Military are left, and how much such a conduct as this tends even to encourage riots, and to bring matters to the last fatal extremity; and how much the Public Service as well as the Troops must suffer by it.

I am forced to urge this matter the more strongly to your Lordship, as what I have now laid before you are not the first instances that have come to my knowledge of a conduct of the like kind in the Civil Magistrates.

I have the honour to be
My Lord, &c.,
C. JENKINSON.

Lord Viscount Stormont, &c., &c., &c.

General Orders.

Adjutant-General's Office, June 7, 1780.

In obedience to an Order of the King in Council, the Military to act without waiting for directions from the Civil Magistrates, and to use force for dispersing the illegal and tumultuous assemblies of the people.

WM. AMHERST, *Adjutant-General.*

73. Letter from Sir John Fielding on highway robberies in London, 28 June 1764

(*Grenville Papers*, ed. W. J. Smith, II (1852), pp. 366–368.)

Sir John Fielding (d. 1780), the blind magistrate, was half-brother to Henry Fielding, the novelist. Charles Jenkinson was at this time Secretary to the Treasury.

Sir John Fielding to Mr. Jenkinson.

Bow Street, June 28, 1764.

Sir John Fielding presents his respectful compliments to Mr. Jenkinson; thought it his indispensable duty to his country to transmit to him the enclosed account of robberies committed since Monday night last, and to acquaint him that in consequence of these repeated informations, he last night sent a foot patrole consisting of a peace officer and three assistants, into the fields near Tyburn and Tottenham Court Roads, to search the ditches where footpads have lately infested, that before they got out of the coach which carried them to the spot, they narrowly escaped being murdered, by three footpads, who without giving them the least notice fired two pistols immediately into the coach, but thank God without effect; two of them were afterwards taken, though not before one of them was dangerously wounded; all which circumstances might, I am convinced, have been prevented. There is nothing I so sincerely lament as the want of an opportunity of convincing Mr. Grenville[1] of the amazing importance of the police to Government; for notwithstanding his most laudable resolution not to lay any permanent expense on the Crown that can be avoided, yet I am sure that he will never spare any necessary expense where public good is the object. For my part I can only propose and inform, which I shall always do most faithfully; but,

[1] First Lord of the Treasury.

in justice to myself, cannot conclude this letter without assuring you that your manner of behaviour to me the other morning gave me much real concern, it being totally different from any that I have ever received from any person, in any department whatever, on whom I have been obliged to attend, in consequence of my miserable employ. However, I still hope, that time will convince you how little I deserve the most distant diffidence. Your sincere friend and the public's faithful servant,

JOHN FIELDING.

Account of Robberies committed–

1. Christopher Pratt, driver of Mr. Stanton's waggon of Market Harborough, with the Bedford and Huntingdon waggoners robbed on Finchley Common on Friday night by two footpads, who beat and wounded them much.

2. Francis Walker, master coachman, of Nag's Head Yard, Oxford Road, drives No. 325, robbed on Tuesday night by two or three footpads near Paddington, of his own watch and money; and two ladies of their purses.

3. Mr. Taylor of King Street, Golden Square, brewer, in company with another gentleman, robbed the same night near Gunnersbury House, by a single highwayman.

4. The Honourable Mrs. Grey, robbed the same night near Sion House, by a highwayman.

5. Mr. Kearr, whipmaker of the Mews, with three other gentlemen in post-chaises, all robbed the same night near Turnham Green, by a highwayman.

6. Mr. Jackson, of Great Queen Street, robbed in one of the Hampstead stages, near Kentish Town, by a single highwayman, on Monday night.

7. The Bath and Bristol coaches on Hounslow Heath, Tuesday night.

8. Mr. Rosser, near Islington, last night, of his gold watch, by two footpads.

C. LOCAL GOVERNMENT

74. The County Rates Act, 1739

(*Statutes at Large*, XVII, pp. 316–328, 12 Geo. II, cap. 29.)

This Act consolidated into one general rate the various levies formerly made by the justices of the peace.

An act for the more easy assessing, collecting and levying of county rates.

[The Preamble recites the various Acts authorising justices of the peace in Quarter Sessions to assess and levy rates for repair of bridges, building and repair of gaols and houses of correction, the relief of poor prisoners, and conveying or maintaining rogues and vagabonds.]

. . . *and whereas many and great doubts, difficulties and inconveniences have arisen in making and collecting other of the said rates;* therefore that the good ends and purposes of the said several statutes may be answered, and the several sums of money thereby intended to be raised may effectually be collected, with as much ease and certainty, and as little expence as can be to the parties obliged by the said laws to pay the same; be it therefore enacted by the King's most excellent majesty, by and with the advice and consent of the lords spiritual and temporal, and commons, in this present parliament assembled, and by the authority of the same, That from and after the first day of *September*, one thousand seven hundred and thirty nine, the justices of the peace in that part of *Great Britain* called *England*, within the respective limits of their commissions, at their general or quarter sessions, or the greater part of them then and there assembled, shall have full power and authority, from time to time, to make one general rate or assessment for such sum or sums of money as they in their discretions shall think sufficient to answer all and every the ends and purposes of the before recited acts, instead and in lieu of the several separate and distinct rates directed thereby to be made, levied and collected; which rate shall be assessed upon every town, parish or place within the respective limits of their commissions, in such proportions as any of the rates heretofore made in pursuance of the said several acts have been usually assessed; and the several and respective sums so assessed upon each and every town, parish or place within the respective limits of their commissions, shall be collected by the high constables of the respective hundreds and divisions, in which any town, parish or place doth lie, in such manner, and at such times, as is herein after directed.

II. And, that the respective sum or sums so to be assessed and collected may be well and truly paid to the respective high constables, be it further enacted by the authority aforesaid, That the church-wardens and overseers of the poor for the time being of each and every parish and place within the respective counties, cities and liberties, in which they respectively lie, shall and they are hereby required, out of the money collected or to be collected for the relief of the poor of such parish or place, pay to the high constables of the respective hundreds or divisions of the said counties, cities and liberties, the respective sum or sums of money so rated and assessed upon such parish or place, within the space of thirty days after demand thereof made in writing, to be given to the said churchwardens or overseers of the poor, or any of them, or left at their or either of their dwelling-house or houses, or affixed on any of the church doors of such parish or place to which such officer shall belong, by the said high constable or high constables of the respective hundreds or divisions; which demand the respective high constable or high constables is and are hereby required to make, at such times as the said justices of the peace, or the greater part of them, shall by their order in sessions direct; and the receipt or receipts of such high constable or high constables shall be a full and sufficient discharge to such churchwardens and overseers of the poor, or other person paying the same, and shall be allowed in their accounts as such by the justices of the peace before whom such accounts shall be passed: and in case such churchwardens and overseers of the poor or any of them, shall neglect or refuse to pay any sum or sums of money hereby assessed, after demand made as aforesaid; such high constable or high constables shall and they are hereby impowered to levy the same by distress and sale of the goods and chattels of such churchwardens and overseers or either of them so refusing or neglecting to pay the same as aforesaid, by warrant under the hands and seals of two or more justices of the peace of the county, riding, division, city, town-corporate, liberty, or place, residing in or near such parish or place; rendering the overplus, if any there shall be, after deducting the money assessed, and the charges of the distress and sale, to the owner or owners thereof.

[III. & IV. In any place where no rate for the relief of the poor is made, and in the counties of York, Derby, Durham, Lancaster, Chester, Westmorland, Cumberland and Northumberland, where it will be inconvenient to pay it out of the rate for relief of the poor, the county rate to be levied and paid by the petty constables to the high constable.]

[V. Justices in Quarter Sessions to fix the proportion of the county rate to be paid by places or persons liable to only one or more, and not all, of the rates which the general rate is replacing.]

VI. And be it further enacted by the authority aforesaid, That the respective high constables shall, and they are hereby required, at or before the next general or quarter sessions respectively after they or any of them shall have received such sum or sums of money, to pay the same into the hands of such person or persons (being resident in any such county, riding, division, city, liberty, or place, where such rates shall be respectively made) whom the said justices shall at their respective general or quarter sessions, or the greater part of them then and there assembled, appoint to be the treasurer or treasurers (which treasurer or treasurers they are hereby authorized and impowered to nominate and appoint) such treasurer or treasurers first giving sufficient security in such sums as shall be approved of by the said justices at their respective general or quarter sessions, or the greater part of them then and there assembled, to be accountable for the several and respective sums of money which shall be respectively paid to them in pursuance of this act, and to pay such sum or sums of money as shall be ordered to be paid by the justices in their general or quarter sessions, and for the due and faithful execution of the trusts reposed in him or them. . . .

[VII. Treasurers required to keep books of entries of the sums received and paid by them in pursuance of the Act; and to deliver accounts on oath (which the justices are empowered to administer) to the justices at quarter sessions.] . . .

X. And be it further enacted by the authority aforesaid, That no new rates shall be made until it shall appear to the said justices, . . . by the accounts of their respective treasurer or treasurers or otherwise, that three fourths of the money collected by virtue of the preceding rate have been expended for the uses and purposes aforesaid.

[XI. Treasurers to be continued or removed at the will of the Justices in Quarter Sessions, who may allow treasurers a sum not exceeding £20 for their care in executing such trust.]

[XII. Churchwardens of any parish who believe the parish is over-rated can appeal to the Justices in Quarter Sessions, who have power finally to determine such cases.] . . .

75. The Workhouse Act, 1722

(*Statutes at Large*, XV, pp. 28–33, 9 Geo. I, cap. 7.)

This Act provided for the setting up of workhouses in each parish and the provision of poor relief in these workhouses only.

An act for amending the laws relating to the settlement, imployment and relief of the poor.

I. WHEREAS *by an act of parliament made and passed in the third and fourth years of the reign of their late majesties King* William *and Queen* Mary, *it was provided, That in every parish a book or books should be kept, wherein the names of all persons who did or might receive collections should be registered, with the time when they were first admitted to such relief, and the occasion which brought them under that necessity; and that no such person should be allowed to have or receive collection at the charge of the parish, but by authority or under the hand of one justice of peace residing in such parish, or if none there dwelling in the parts near or next adjoining, or by order of the justices at their quarter-sessions, except in case of pestilential diseases, plague or small-pox: and whereas under colour of the proviso in the said act, many persons have applied to some justices of peace, without the knowledge of any officers of the parish, and thereby upon untrue suggestions, and sometimes upon false or frivolous pretences have obtained relief, which hath greatly contributed to the increase of the parish-rates:* for remedy whereof, be it enacted by the King's most excellent Majesty, by and with the advice and consent of the lords spiritual and temporal, and commons, in this present parliament assembled, and by the authority of the same, That from and after the twenty-fifth day of *March* which shall be in the year of our Lord one thousand seven hundred and twenty-three, no justice of peace shall order relief to any poor person dwelling in any parish, until oath be made before such justice of some matter which he shall judge to be a reasonable cause or ground for having such relief, and that the same person had by himself, herself or some other, applied for relief to the parishioners of the parish, at some vestry or other publick meeting of the said parishioners, or to two of the overseers of the poor of such parish, and was by them refused to be relieved, and until such justice hath summoned two of the overseers of the poor to shew cause why such relief should not be given, and the person so summoned hath been heard or made default to appear before such justice; any thing in the said proviso, or any law to the contrary notwithstanding. . . .

IV. And for the greater ease of parishes in the relief of the poor, be it further enacted by the authority aforesaid, That it shall and may be lawful for the churchwardens and overseers of the poor in any parish, town, township or place, with the consent of the major part of the parishioners or inhabitants of the same parish, town, township or place, in vestry, or other parish or publick meeting for that purpose assembled, or of so many of them as shall be so assembled, upon usual notice thereof first given, to purchase or hire any house or houses in the same parish, township or place, and to contract with any person or persons for the lodging, keeping, maintaining and employing any or all such poor in their respective parishes, townships or places, as shall desire to receive relief or collection from the same parish, and there to keep, maintain and employ all such poor persons, and take the benefit of the work, labour and service of any such poor person or persons, who shall be kept or maintained in any such house or houses, for the better maintenance and relief of such poor person or persons, who shall be there kept or maintained; and in case any poor person or persons of any parish, town, township or place where such house or houses shall be so purchased or hired, shall refuse to be lodged, kept or maintained in such house or houses, such poor person or persons so refusing shall be put out of the book or books where the names of the persons, who ought to receive collection in the said parish, town, township or place, are to be registered, and shall not be entitled to ask or receive collection or relief from the churchwardens and overseers of the poor of the same parish, town or township; and where any parish, town or township shall be too small to purchase or hire such house or houses for the poor of their own parish only, it shall and may be lawful for two or more such parishes, towns or townships or places, with the consent of the major part of the parishioners or inhabitants of their respective parishes, town, township or places, in vestry or other parish or publick meeting for that purpose assembled, or of so many of them as shall be so assembled, upon usual notice thereof first given, and with the approbation of any justice of peace dwelling in or near any such parish, town or place, signified under his hand and seal, to unite in purchasing, hiring, or taking such house, for the lodging, keeping and maintaining of the poor of the several parishes, townships or places so uniting, and there to keep, maintain and employ the poor of the respective parishes so uniting, and to take and have the benefit of the work, labour or service of any poor there kept and maintained, for the better maintenance and relief of the poor there kept, maintained and employed; and that if any poor person or persons in the respective parishes, townships or places so uniting, shall refuse to be lodged, kept and maintained in the house, hired or taken for such uniting parishes, townships or places, he, she or they so refusing, shall be put out of the collection-book, where his, her or their names were registered, and shall not be entitled to ask or demand relief or collection from the churchwardens and overseers of the poor in their respective parishes, townships or places; and that it shall and may be lawful for the churchwardens and overseers of the poor of any parish, township or place, with the consent of the major part of the parishioners or inhabitants of the said parish, township or place where such house or houses is, are, or shall be purchased or hired for the purposes aforesaid, in vestry, or other parish or publick meeting, for that purpose assembled, or of so many of them as shall be so assembled, upon usual notice thereof first given, to contract with the churchwardens and overseers of the poor of any other parish, township or place, for the lodging, maintaining or employing of any poor person or persons of such other parish, township or place, as to them shall seem meet; and in case any poor person or persons of such other parish, township or place, shall refuse to be lodged, maintained and employed in such house or houses, he, she or they so refusing shall be put out of the collection-book of such other parish, township or place, where his, her or their names were registred, and shall not be entitled to ask, demand or receive any relief or collection from the churchwardens and overseers of the poor of his, her or their respective parish, township or place: provided always, that no poor person or persons, his, her or their apprentice, child or children, shall acquire a settlement in the parish, town or place, to which he, she or they are removed by virtue of this act, but that his, her or their settlement, shall be and remain in such parish, town or place, as it was before such removal; any thing in this act to the contrary notwithstanding.

V. And be it further enacted by the authority aforesaid, That from and after the twenty-fifth day of *March* which shall be in the year of our Lord one thousand seven hundred and twenty-three, no person or persons shall be deemed, adjudged or taken, to acquire or gain any settlement in any parish or place, for or by virtue of any purchase of any estate or interest in such parish or place, whereof the consideration for such purchase doth not amount to the sum of thirty pounds, *bona fide* paid, for any longer or further time than such person or persons shall inhabit in such estate, and shall then be liable to be removed to such parish or place where such person or persons were last legally settled, before the said purchase and inhabitancy therein.

VI. And be it further enacted by the authority aforesaid, That no person or persons whatsoever, who from and after the twenty-fifth day of *March* in the year of our Lord one thousand seven hundred and twenty-three, shall be taxed, rated or assessed to the scavenger or repairs of the highway, and shall duly pay the same, shall be deemed or taken to have any legal settlement in any city, parish, town or hamlet, for or by reason of his, her or their paying to such scavenger's rate or repairs of the highway as aforesaid; any law to the contrary in any wise notwithstanding.

76. Gilbert's Act, 1782

(*Statutes at Large*, XXXIV, pp. 155–186, 22 Geo. III, cap. 83.)

This Act in effect abolished the "workhouse test" imposed by the Act of 1722 (No. 75). The optional clauses permitting the grouping of parishes into unions were not widely applied. The Act's chief promoter, after whom it is named, was Thomas Gilbert (1720–1798), M.P. for Lichfield.

An act for the better relief and employment of the poor.

WHEREAS *notwithstanding the many laws now in being for the relief and employment of the poor, and the great sums of money raised for those purposes, their sufferings and distresses are nevertheless very grievous; and, by the incapacity, negligence, or misconduct of overseers, the money raised for the relief of the poor is frequently misapplied, and sometimes expended in defraying the charges of litigations about settlements indiscreetly and unadvisedly carried on; and whereas, by a clause in an act, passed in the ninth year of the reign of King* George *the First, intituled,* An act for the amendment of the laws relating to the settlement, employment, and relief of the poor, *power is given to the churchwardens and overseers, in the manner therein mentioned, to purchase or hire houses, and contract with any person for the lodging, keeping, maintaining, and employing the poor, and taking the benefit of their work, labour, and service, for their maintenance; and, where any parish, town, or township, shall be found too small, to unite two or more for those purposes, with the consent of the major part of the parishioners or inhabitants, and the approbation of a justice of peace; which provisions, from the want of proper regulations and management in the poor houses or workhouses that have been purchased or hired under the authority of the said act, and for want of due inspection and controul over the persons who have engaged in those contracts, have not had the desired effect, but the poor, in many places, instead of finding protection and relief, have been much oppressed thereby:* for remedy of these grievances and inconveniences, and in order to make better and more effectual provision for the relief and employment of the poor, and to introduce a prudent oeconomy in the expenditure of the parish money; may it please your Majesty that it may be enacted; and be it enacted by the King's most excellent majesty, by and with the advice and consent of the lords spiritual and temporal, and commons, in this present parliament assembled, and by the authority of the same, That from and after the twenty-fifth day of *March*, which shall be in the year of our Lord one thousand seven hundred and eighty-three, so much of the said clause as respects the maintaining or hiring out the labour of the poor by contract, within any parish, township, or place, which shall adopt the provisions of this act, shall be, and is hereby repealed, and every contract or agreement made in pursuance thereof, for either of those purposes, shall become, and is hereby declared to be, null and void. . . .

VII. And be it further enacted, That it shall and may be lawful for two justices of the peace of the limit where such poor house shall be, or be so agreed to be situated, and they are hereby required, as soon as conveniently may be after such agreement shall have been made as aforesaid, upon application to them by two or more of the persons who shall have signed such agreement, and upon producing the same to them, to appoint one of the persons so recommended to be guardian of the poor for each of such parishes, townships, and places, in the form contained in the said schedule, N°. VII; or to that or the like effect; and every such guardian shall attend the monthly meetings hereby directed to be holden, and execute the several powers and authorities given to guardians by this act, and shall have, and is hereby invested with, all the powers and authorities given to overseers of the poor by any other act or acts of parliament, . . .

XVII. And be it further enacted, That the guardians of the poor of the several parishes, townships, and places, which shall adopt the provisions of this act, shall provide a suitable and convenient house or houses, with proper buildings and accommodations thereto, when wanted, either by erecting new ones on land to be purchased or rented by them for that purpose, altering old ones, or hiring buildings for the purpose; and shall fit up and dispose the same, with the advice and approbation of the visitor,[1] if any, in such manner as shall be most conducive to the general

[1] A person "respectable in character and Fortune" appointed, on the recommendation of the guardians, by the justices to superintend the poor house.

purposes of this act, at the expence of such parish or township, or parishes, townships, and places respectively, in the proportions herein-after mentioned; and shall provide such utensils and materials as they shall think necessary for their employment, according to the true intent and meaning of this act. . . .

XXVIII. And be it further enacted, That every person or persons, to be sent to any house or houses to be provided under the authority of this act, shall, at the time of his or her entering such house, deliver, or cause to be delivered to the governor thereof, or to his assistant, if any, an order, signed by one of the guardians of the poor of the parish, township, or place, from which such person shall come, for the admission of such person or persons, in the form or to the effect contained in the said schedule, N° XII; which order shall be carefully kept by the governor, and entered by him in a book to be provided for that purpose.

XXIX. *And, to render the provisions of this act more practicable and beneficial,* be it further enacted, That no person shall be sent to such poor house or houses, except such as are become indigent by old age, sickness, or infirmities, and are unable to acquire a maintenance by their labour; and except such orphan children as shall be sent thither by order of the guardian or guardians of the poor, with the approbation of the visitor; and except such children as shall necessarily go with their mothers thither for sustenance.

XXX. And be it further enacted, That all infant children of tender years, and who, from accident or misfortune, shall become chargeable to the parish or place to which they belong, may either be sent to such poor House as aforesaid, or be placed by the guardian or guardians of the poor, with the approbation of the visitor, with some reputable person or persons in or near the parish, township, or place, to which they belong, at such weekly allowance as shall be agreed upon between the parish officers and such person or persons, with the approbation of the visitor, until such child or children shall be of sufficient age to be put into service, or bound apprentice to husbandry, or some trade or occupation; and a list of the names of every child so placed out, and by whom and where kept, shall be given to the visitor; who shall see that they are properly treated, or cause them to be removed, and placed under the care of some other person or persons, if he finds just cause so to do; and when every such child shall attain such age, he or she shall be so placed out, at the expence of the parish, township, or place, to which he or she shall belong, according to the laws in being: provided nevertheless, That if the parents or relations of any poor child sent to such house, or so placed out as aforesaid, or any other responsible person, shall desire to receive and provide for any such poor child or children, and signify the same to the guardians at their monthly meeting, the guardians shall, and are hereby required to dismiss, or cause to be dismissed, such child or children from the poor house, or from the care of such person or persons as aforesaid, and deliver him, her, or them, to the parent, relation, or other person so applying as aforesaid: provided also, That nothing herein contained shall give any power to separate any child or children, under the age of seven years, from his, her, or their parent or parents, without the consent of such parent or parents.

XXXI. And be it further enacted, That all idle or disorderly persons, who are able, but unwilling, to work or maintain themselves and their families, shall be prosecuted by the guardians of the poor of the several parishes, townships, and places, wherein they reside, and punished in such manner as idle and disorderly persons are directed to be by the statute made in the seventeenth year of the reign of his late majesty King *George* the Second; and if any guardian shall neglect to make complaint thereof, against every such person or persons, to some neighbouring justice of the peace, within ten days after it shall come to his knowledge, he shall, for every such neglect, forfeit a sum not exceeding five pounds, nor less than twenty shillings, one moiety whereof, when recovered, shall be paid to the informer, and the other moiety to be disposed of as the other forfeitures are herein-after directed to be applied.

XXXII. And be it further enacted, That where there shall be, in any parish, township, or place, any poor person or persons who shall be able and willing to work, but who cannot get employment, it shall and may be lawful for the guardian of the poor of such parish, township, or place, and he is hereby required, on application made to him by or on behalf of such poor person, to agree for the labour of such poor person or persons, at any work or employment suited to his or her strength and capacity, in any parish, township, or place, near the place of his or her residence, and to maintain, or cause such person or persons to be properly maintained, lodged, and provided for, until such employment shall be procured, and during the time of such work, and to receive the money to be earned by such work or labour, and apply it in such maintenance, as far as the same will go, and make up the deficiency, if any; and if the same shall happen to exceed the money expended in such maintenance, to account for the surplus, which shall afterwards, within one calendar month, be given to such poor person or persons who shall have earned such money, if no further expences shall be then incurred on his or her account to exhaust the same. And in case such poor person or persons shall refuse to work, or run away from such work or employment, complaint shall be made thereof by the guardian to some justice or justices of the peace in or near the said parish, township, or place; who shall enquire into the same upon oath, and on conviction punish such offender or offenders, by committing him, her, or them, to the house of correction, there to be kept to hard labour for any time not exceeding three calendar months, nor less than one calendar month.

XXXIII. And be it further enacted, That the guardian of the poor for any parish, township, or place, adopting the provisions of this act as aforesaid, shall provide, at the expence of such parish, township, or place, suitable and necessary clothing for the persons sent by him to such poor house as aforesaid; . . .

XLI. *And whereas it frequently happens that poor children, pregnant women, or poor persons afflicted with sickness, or some bodily infirmity, are enticed, taken, or conveyed by parish officers, or other persons, from one parish or place to another, without any legal order of removal, in order to ease the one parish or place, and to burthen the other with such poor persons:* for remedy whereof, be it further enacted, That when any guardian, or other person or persons, shall so entice, take, convey, or remove, or cause or procure to be so enticed, taken, conveyed, or removed, any such poor person or persons from one parish or place to another, which shall adopt the provisions of this act, without an order of removal from two justices of the peace for that purpose, every person or persons so offending shall, for every such offence, forfeit a sum not exceeding twenty pounds, nor less than five pounds. . . .

XLIV. Provided always, and be it further enacted, That nothing in this act contained shall extend to or affect, or be deemed, construed, or adjudged to extend or to affect, any parish, township, or place, which shall not agree to adopt the provisions herein contained, in the manner hereby directed and prescribed; any thing herein contained to the contrary thereof notwithstanding. . . .

RULES, ORDERS, BYE LAWS, and REGULATIONS, to be observed and enforced at every POOR HOUSE to be provided and established under the authority of the act of the twenty-second year of King *George* the Third.

First. THAT *the several persons who shall be sent to any such poor house, who are capable of doing any work, shall be employed by the governor in some labour which may be best suited to their strength and capacity.*

Second. *That the governor shall take particular care to keep the said house, and the several apartments therein, and also the several persons who shall inhabit the same, clean and wholesome; and for that purpose he shall employ such of the said poor persons who shall be sent thither, whom he shall think most able and best qualified for the offices, to assist him therein, and also in the providing and dressing victuals for the use of such poor persons; and if any such poor person shall refuse or neglect to perform the work or labour in which he or she shall be so employed, or shall be directed to do by the governor, every such person shall be punished by confinement, or alteration of diet, in such manner as the governor shall direct; and for a second offence of the like sort, complaint thereof shall be made to some justice of the peace for the limit, who, on conviction, shall commit such person to the house of correction for any time not exceeding two calendar months, nor less than one calendar month.*

Third. *That the apartments in the house or houses to be provided as aforesaid, shall be adapted so as to accommodate the poor who shall be sent thither in the best manner they are capable.–That the governor shall place in the best apartments such poor persons who, having been creditable housekeepers, are reduced by misfortune, in preference to those who are become poor by vice and idleness; and that separate apartments shall be provided for the reception of the sick and distempered poor, and an apothecary or surgeon to be sent for to attend them when there shall appear necessity for it, at the expence of the parish or place to which such poor persons belong.*

Fourth. *That such poor persons who are able to work, shall be called up by ring of bell, and set to work by six in the morning from* Lady-day *to* Michaelmas, *and by eight from* Michaelmas *to* Lady-day; *and continue until four in the afternoon from* Michaelmas *to* Lady-day, *and from* Lady-day *to* Michaelmas *till six in the afternoon (meal times and times for reasonable recreation excepted); and if any such poor person shall refuse or neglect to do such work as shall be allotted him or her, or wilfully spoil the same, or depart from such house without leave from the governor, or shall be guilty of any disorder or disobedience to these rules and orders, the governor shall reprove such person for the same, and punish him or her by confinement or alteration of diet, as the said governor shall think fit; and if such person shall be guilty of the like offence a second time, the governor shall complain thereof to the visitor of such house, who is hereby authorised to order the punishment of confinement to be increased to such degree as he shall think fit.*

Fifth. *That the governor shall enter in a book to be kept by him, an account of the household goods, linen, furniture, and utensils provided for the said house; and also an account of the materials bought for manufacture, and of the goods manufactured there; which shall be laid before the guardians at their monthly meetings, and before the visitor whenever he comes to such house.*

Sixth. *That the governor shall visit the several persons maintained in such house or houses, and their apartments, once at least in every day; and shall take care that there is no waste of fire, candles, or provisions; and shall see that the fires and candles are put out at the hours fixed for such persons going to bed, which shall be at eight of the clock between* Michaelmas *and* Lady-day, *and nine between* Lady-day *and* Michaelmas.

Seventh. *That when any person shall die in the house, the governor shall take care that the body of such person be immediately removed into some separate apartment, and be decently buried, as soon as conveniently may be; and also take care of the cloaths and goods of such person, and deliver them to the guardian of the poor of the parish or place to which such person did belong, who is to pay the charges of the funeral of such poor person.*

Eighth. *That no poor person be permitted to go out of the poor house, nor any person permitted to come into such house or houses, except the persons maintained and employed there, without the permission of the governor; and that no spirituous liquors be permitted to be drank in such house or houses; and that no other liquors shall be brought thither, without the permission of the said governor.*

Ninth. *That the rules, orders, and bye-laws shall be publickly read by the governor to all the poor persons kept in such house or houses, once at least in every month.*

Tenth. *That all the poor persons able to go to church, shall attend divine service every* Sunday.

Eleventh. *That the governor shall dismiss from the poor house, or workhouse, every person who shall, in the opinion of the guardian or guardians, be thought improper to continue longer there, and upon an order from him or them for that purpose.*

Part IV
PUBLIC FINANCE

PUBLIC FINANCE

Introduction

LITTLE change took place either in financial administration or methods of taxation in the period 1714–1783, although fundamental changes were introduced by Pitt in the years immediately following. Public finance was not well organized in this period. Such superintendence and co-ordination as existed was exercised by the Treasury, but its superiority was not fully accepted by the other spending departments, and its control was therefore partial and weak. The expenses of civil government were paid out of the Civil List, and to the end of the period the Crown attempted, though not always with success, to maintain that expenditure from the Civil List was not the concern of Parliament. It is for this reason that no complete statements of the national revenue and expenditure were presented to Parliament during this period, though approximate figures were sometimes given, both officially and unofficially. Thanks to Mr. Gladstone, however, full and accurate statements based on the official contemporary records were drawn up and presented to Parliament in the session 1868–1869. The statements for the years 1715 and 1783,[1] when compared, show a big increase in the yield of taxation, but a far bigger increase in expenditure.

The next two groups of documents have been chosen to illustrate the ways in which the public revenue was raised in this period. There were no startling new methods, and on the whole, apart from a regular grumble about the land tax from the squires, there were few controversies about taxation in the eighteenth century. Much the most notable arose over Walpole's proposed excise scheme in 1733, which gave rise to animated argument in the House of Commons and even fiercer polemics in the country as a whole. Walpole himself led the defence of his scheme, not only in the House but in the pamphlet war outside, and his general principles of taxation emerge to some extent in the course of his pamphlet.[2] At the end of the war of the Austrian Succession, in a debate in the House of Commons, Henry Pelham expounded views on taxation which were widely held throughout the eighteenth century; and in the same debate Henry Fox reviewed the various taxes which might conceivably be levied or increased and brought out the comparative inelasticity of the national system of taxation, apart from customs duties.[3] In war-time the line of least resistance was to place additional duties on imports. This helps to explain the extraordinarily complicated system of customs duties which grew up within the century. Some idea of the number of these duties can be gathered from the Table of Contents of a manual for the guidance of customs officers and merchants written by an official of the Customs House in London.[4]

Of the direct taxes, the land tax remained the chief stand-by. The window tax was reorganized by Henry Pelham in 1747, and a new method of assessment introduced, in the hope of increasing the revenue from it;[5] and the rates were subsequently

[1] No. 77. [2] No. 80. [3] No. 81. [4] No. 79. [5] No. 82.

raised several times. The expense of the American War led to the imposition of a number of new taxes, mostly on luxuries, by Lord North, including one on male servants in 1777,[1] and a new tax on inhabited houses in 1778.[2] An idea of the annual yield of some of these taxes can be gathered from the Reports from the Select Committee on Public Income and Expenditure in 1786;[3] and the incidence of the house taxes upon different parts of the country can be estimated from George Chalmers's compilation from the records of the Tax Office.[4]

In raising money to meet the greatly increasing public expenditure, largely due to the expensive wars in which Great Britain engaged in these years, eighteenth-century statesmen were much hampered by the abuses of the system (if system it can be called) of financial administration. The reorganization of the window tax, for example, was the result of a long series of complaints from the Commissioners of Taxes about abuses and inefficiency in the collection of the tax.[5] The abuses of the Pay Office, the dilatoriness of the Receivers of the Land Tax, and the general inefficiency and wastefulness of the whole financial administration, were laid bare by the Commissioners of Public Accounts, appointed by Lord North in 1780, whose reports were to be the basis of the reforms later instituted by the younger Pitt.[6]

The most salient feature of eighteenth-century public finance was the great increase in the National Debt, illustrated by the table at the end of this section.[7] The statements of Public Income and Expenditure already referred to show that debt charges rose from about 2½ millions to about 14 millions during the period 1715–1783.[8] This accumulated burden of debt was a recurring source of alarm to contemporaries, since it appeared that another war must bring about the country's ruin. Sir John Sinclair, in his *History of the Public Revenue of the British Empire*, published in 1790, struck a more cheerful note, stressing the great increase in national wealth since 1689, and expounding the reasons why the country was able to bear a greatly increased burden of taxation since that date.[9]

[1] No. 83. [2] No. 84. [3] Nos. 86 and 87. [4] No. 85. [5] No. 88.
[6] No. 89. [7] p. 338. [8] No. 90. [9] No. 78.

BIBLIOGRAPHY

Various contemporary works are mentioned in the sectional bibliography on the Economic State of the Nation. Full and authoritative accounts for each year will be found in *Accounts of the Net Public Income and Expenditure of Great Britain* [1688–1801] in *Parliamentary Papers, House of Commons*, vol. xxxv (1868–1869). Part ii, Appendix 6, deals with eighteenth-century sinking funds; Appendix 12 with the National Debt, while Appendix 13 gives valuable historical accounts of the several heads of public income and expenditure in this period. Further information on the National Debt will be found in *Parliamentary Papers*, House of Commons, vol. 33 (1857–1858), pp. 2–105, and vol. 52 (1898) [C. 9010], which gives elaborate analyses of the amount of the various categories of the public debt year by year. The official *Calendars of Treasury Books and Papers* are also of value.

Modern works are not numerous. H. E. Fisk, *English Public Finance from 1688* (London, 1921), is a mere primer. E. L. Hargreaves, *The National Debt* (London, 1930), gives a very brief survey of our period. Miss L. S. Sutherland writes on "Samson Gideon and the Reduction of Interest 1749–50" in the *Economic History Review*, xvi (1946), pp. 15–29. Alice Carter, "Analyses of Public Indebtedness in Eighteenth Century England" in *Bulletin of the Institute of Historical Research*, xxiv (1951), pp. 173–181, gives elaborate analyses of the distribution of the capital of some of the funds making up the National Debt in the latter part of 1760. S. Dowell, *History of Taxation in England* (4 vols., London, 1884), is readable but in some ways out of date, while W. Kennedy, *English Taxation 1640–1799* (London, 1913), is correctly described by its author as "an essay on policy and opinion". Studies of individual taxes have been made by W. R. Ward in *The English Land Tax in the Eighteenth Century* (Oxford, 1953), and "The administration of the window and assessed taxes, 1696–1798" in *English Historical Review*, lxvii (1952), pp. 522–542. The same author has also written on tax administration in "The Office for Taxes, 1666–1798", *Bulletin of the Institute of Historical Research*, xxv (1952), pp. 204–212; and "Some Eighteenth Century Civil Servants; The English Revenue Commissioners", *English Historical Review*, lxx (1955), pp. 25–54. H. Hall, *History of the Custom-Revenue in England–to 1827* (2 vols., London, 1885); E. E. Hoon, *Organization of the English Customs System 1696–1786* (New York, 1938); B. R. Leftwich, "The Later History and Administration of the Customs Revenue in England" in the *Transactions of the Royal Historical Society*, 4th Series, xiii (1930), pp. 187–203, which explains the not altogether simple distinction between Customs and Excise duties; E. A. Hughes, *Studies in Administration and Finance 1558–1825* (Manchester, 1934), dealing mainly with the salt duties, and the same author's "English Stamp Duties 1664–1764" in the *English Historical Review*, lvi (1941), pp. 234–264; A. Aspinall, "Statistical Accounts of the London Newspapers in the Eighteenth Century" in *English History Review*, lxiii (1948), pp. 201–232, dealing with the newspaper stamp duties; and E. R. Turner, "The Excise Scheme of 1733", which is based on contemporary pamphlets and newspaper articles, in the *English Historical Review*, xlii (1927), pp. 34–57, are valuable studies of particular problems. The article in *English Historical Review*, lxx (1955), pp. 229–257, by L. S. Sutherland and J. Binney, "Henry Fox as Paymaster-General of the Forces", is an interesting study of eighteenth-century financial administration in one of its most notorious aspects.

There are accounts of the *South Sea Bubble* by Lewis Melville (London, 1921) and Viscount Erleigh (London, 1933), and R. D. Richards examined the relations between "the Bank of England and the South Sea Company" in the first half of the eighteenth century in *Economic History*, ii (1930–1933), pp. 348–374. Other articles by R. D. Richards include "The Lottery in the History of English Government Finance", *ibid.*, iii, No. 9 (1934), pp. 57–76, and "The Exchequer Bill in the History of English Government Finance" in *ibid.*, iii, No. 11 (1936), pp. 193–211.

A. REVENUE AND EXPENDITURE

77. Net Public Income and Expenditure of Great Britain in 1715 and 1783 respectively

(*Accounts of the Net Public Income and Expenditure of Great Britain*, II, pp. 52–53, 188–189; *Parliamentary Papers*, XXXV, 1868–1869.)

(I.) (1 & 2 Geo. I.) NET PUBLIC INCOME and EXPENDITURE of *Great Britain*, and of other Receipts into and Issues from the Exchequer, &c., in the Year ended 29th September 1715. (1 & 2 Geo. I.)

	£	s.	d.	£	s.	d.	£	s.	d.
BALANCES in the Exchequer on 29th September 1714 .							1,066,689	15	5
Net Receipts of Public Income, deducting Drawbacks, &c., and Charges of Collection and Management, *viz.*:									
Customs				1,684,661	11	5			
Excise				2,302,807	9	0			
Stamps				142,207	10	11			
Land and Assessed Taxes, and Duties on Pensions, Offices, Personal Estates, &c.				1,128,669	8	10			
Post Office				95,263	3	0			
Crown Lands (including Sales of Tin, 151,000*l.*) .				158,976	3	0			
Miscellaneous, *viz.*:									
First Fruits and Tenths . .	11,544	15	9						
Other small Branches of the Hereditary Revenue . .	7,498	16	0						
Imprest Money repaid, &c. .	15,789	17	0						
				34,833	8	9			
TOTAL NET INCOME							5,547,418	14	11
Other Receipts, *viz.*:									
Raised to complete 1,400,000*l.*, Contributions to Lottery Loan, Anno 1714, per 12 Anne, stat. 2, c. 9				570,000	0	0			
Raised in part of 1,079,000*l.*, by Contributions for 5 per cent. Annuities, from Michaelmas 1715, per 1 Geo. I, stat. 2, cc. 19 & 21				137,000	0	0			
Raised by Loan of Additional Capital Stock of South Sea Company, at 6 per cent., from 24th June 1715, per 1 Geo. I, stat. 2, c. 21 . .				822,032	4	8*			
* *Note.*—The following Amounts of Public Receipt and Expenditure, in the year ended 29th September 1715, are included in this Account, but did not pass through the Exchequer: Raised by further Debt bearing interest at 6 per cent. per annum, incurred to the South Sea Company, per Act 1 Geo. I, stat. 2, c. 21				822,032	4	8			

	£ s. d.	£ s. d.
To be applied as follows:		
For half a year's Interest at 6 per cent. to South Sea Company, on 9,177,964*l.* 15*s.* 4*d.*, to 24th June 1715	275,339 0 8	
For half a year's Interest at 6 per cent. to South Sea Company, on 10,000,000*l.*, to 25th December 1715	300,000 0 0	
For one year's Management to ditto ditto	8,000 0 0	
For Navy Services	238,693 4 0	
	822,032 4 8	
Raised by Loans in anticipation of Duties, &c.: £ s. d.		
In Tallies 473,379 0 5		
In Money 1,022,922 0 3	1,496,301 0 8	
Total raised by Creation of Debt . . .		3,025,333 5 4
	£	9,639,441 15 8

	£ s. d.	£ s. d.
PAYMENTS for INTEREST and MANAGEMENT of the Public Debt, *viz.*:		
To Bank of England	201,501 13 5	
To East India Company	134,695 13 8	
To South Sea Company, on 608,000*l.* at 6*l.* per cent., including Management, 8,000*l.*	861,678 1 4	
Bankers' Annuities	38,681 3 2	
TOTAL Funded Debt		1,236,556 11 7
Exchequer Life and Terminable Annuities, including Management, £ s. d.	777,151 15 4	
ment, ... 5,250 0 0		
Lottery Annuities–ditto . . . 2,907 2 7	762,619 1 8	
TOTAL Terminable Annuities. . . .		1,539,770 17 0
Interest on Debentures for the Sufferers at Nevis and St. Christopher	10,907 7 7	
Interest and circulation of Exchequer Bills . .	294,718 19 9	
Interest on Loans in anticipation of Duties, &c. .	186,142 4 2	
TOTAL Unfunded Debt.		491,768 11 6
Discount for prompt Payment and for receiving Loans		7,587 4 0
TOTAL INTEREST, &c. of PUBLIC DEBT .		3,275,683 4 1

	£	s.	d.	£	s.	d.	£	s.	d.
Civil government, *viz.*:									
H.M.'s Household				221,086	3	4			
Works				28,580	14	5			
Civil List Pensions and Annuities, *viz.*:									
The Prince of Wales . .	35,000	0	0						
Other Pensions (including 39,062*l.* 19*s.* paid out of Gross Revenues) . .	68,989	13	2						
H.M.'s Charities and Pensions	63,920	8	1						
				167,910	1	3			
Royal Bounty				16,529	12	4			
Secret Service				17,677	7	11			
Fees and Salaries				78,026	7	4			
British Ministers Abroad				62,220	11	8			
Tin Affair				21,000	0	0			
Civil Government of Scotland				29,558	12	1			
Other Contingent and Miscellaneous Charges, Civil List				50,295	8	9			
Total Civil List				692,884	19	1			
Mint Expenses				11,558	17	10			
Salaries in West India Islands, &c., out of 4½*l.* per cent. Duty				1,896	5	6			
Queen Anne's Bounty for Augmentation of Poor Livings				2,300	0	0			
Expenses of Exchequer Bills				1,029	9	5			
Towards building 50 new Churches . . .				24,000	0	0			
Total civil government . . .							733,669	11	10
Army services (Balance of Tallies undisposed of, 15,501*l.* 0*s.* 5*d.*)				923,625	17	10			
Navy services–ditto . . . 313,168*l.* 0*s.* 5*d.*				1,205,269	1	2			
Ordnance services				90,102	7	2			
							2,218,997	6	2
Total expenditure							6,228,350	2	1
Issued to pay off Exchequer Bills				115,787	10	0			
„ Loans on anticipation of . . . Duties, &c.				2,104,755	7	6			
Total applied to Reduction of Debt .							2,220,542	17	6
Balances in the Exchequer on 29th September 1715 .							1,190,548	16	1
						£	9,639,441	15	8

(2.) (23 Geo. III.) NET PUBLIC INCOME and EXPENDITURE of *Great Britain*, and of other Receipts into and Issues from the Exchequer, &c., in the Year ended 10th October 1783. (23 Geo. III.)

	£	£	s.	d.	£	s.	d.	£	s.	d.
BALANCES in the Exchequer on 10th October 1782								3,757,230	16	0
NET RECEIPTS of Public Income, deducting Drawbacks, &c., and Charges of Collection and Management, *viz.*:										
Customs					2,949,374	13	4			
Excise					5,479,975	5	9			
Stamps					855,025	16	2			
Land and Assessed Taxes, and Duties on Pensions, Offices, and Personal Estates					2,595,639	13	5			
Post Office					165,600	0	0			
Crown Lands					1,066	13	4			
Miscellaneous, *viz.*:										
First Fruits and Tenths		5,095	16	1						
Other Small Branches of the Hereditary Revenue		6,487	5	6						
Imprest Money repaid, including 20,083*l.* 14*s.* 6*d.*, Balances of Army and Navy Grants repaid into the Exchequer, per 21 Geo. 3, c. 48		84,716	13	0						
Money received from the Sale of French Prizes taken before declaration of the late War		5,377	8	11						
Lottery, 1782, to complete 405,000*l.*, per 22 Geo. 3, c. 8	61,000									
Lottery, 1783, in part of 480,000*l.*, per 23 Geo. 3, c. 35	468,000									
		529,000	0	0						
					630,677	3	6			
TOTAL NET INCOME								12,677,359	5	6
OTHER RECEIPTS, *viz.*:										
Raised by Contributions to Annuities, with a Lottery, to complete 13,500,000*l.*, anno 1782, per 22 Geo. 3, c. 8.					1,200,000	0	0			
Raised by Contributions to Annuities, in part of 12,000,000*l.*, per 23 Geo. 3, c. 35					9,700,000	0	0			
TOTAL raised by CREATION of FUNDED DEBT					10,900,000	0	0			

	£ s. d.	£ s. d.	£ s. d.
Raised by Issue of Exchequer Bills (Supply), *viz.*:			
For Exchange . . .	500,000 0 0		
For Public Services . .	3,229,392 1 6		
Raised by Issue of Exchequer Bills in anticipation of Malt Duty and Land Tax . . .	2,750,000 0 0		
		6,479,392 1 6	
TOTAL raised by CREATION of FUNDED and UNFUNDED DEBT . . .			17,379,392 1 6
		£	33,813,982 3 0

	£ s. d.	£ s. d.
PAYMENTS for INTEREST and MANAGEMENT of the PUBLIC DEBT, *viz.*:		
Interest of the Funded Debt.		6,313,962 12 9
Long Annuities and Annuities for Lives and Terms of Years		1,245,178 11 2
Management of Funded Debt		132,584 15 1
Interest and Circulation of Exchequer Bills (Supply)	97,251 11 11	
Interest and Circulation of Exchequer Bills on Malt Duty and Land Tax	178,242 8 9	
		275,494 0 8
Discount for prompt Payment and Receiving Charges of Loan, 1782		86,921 8 11
TOTAL INTEREST, &c. of PUBLIC DEBT .		8,054,141 8 7
CIVIL GOVERNMENT, *viz.*:		
H.M.'s Privy Purse	60,000 0 0	
H.M.'s Household	240,998 11 8	
Works	16,107 16 0	
Annuities and Pensions out of Civil List, *viz.*:		
The Queen . . . . £.50,000 0 0		
Prince of Wales . . . 20,204 12 7		
Princes William Henry and Edward 11,000 0 0		
Duke of Cumberland . . 9,000 0 0	297,625 17 1	
Princess Amalie . . . 12,000 0 0		
Other Civil List Pensions paid at Exchequer . . . 148,057 7 7		
Paid by Paymaster of Pensions 47,363 16 11		

	£	s.	d.	£	s.	d.
Royal Bounty				6,024	1	3
Secret Service				38,942	5	0
Fees and Salaries				140,486	8	6
British Ministers Abroad				95,487	7	5
Contingent and Miscellaneous Charges Civil List				235,803	4	4
TOTAL Civil List, exclusive of 50,000*l.*, applied to pay off Exchequer Bills charged on Civil List				1,131,475	11	3
Pensions granted by Parliament, *viz.*:						
Duke of Gloucester, per 7 Geo. 3, c. 19	£.8,000	0	0			
Duke of Cumberland, per 7 Geo 3, c. 19	8,000	0	0			
Representatives of A. Onslow, Esq., per 2 Geo. 3, c. 33	3,000	0	0			
Earl of Chatham, per 18 Geo. 3, c. 65	4,000	0	0			
Late Officers for Wine Licenses, per 30 Geo. 2, c. 19	151	4	2			
				23,151	4	2
Salaries and Allowances:						
Mint	£.14,403	0	10			
Bank of England, for passing their Accounts of Annuities	14,209	10	0			
				28,612	10	10
Courts of Justice:						
Sheriffs of England and Wales, for passing their Accounts	£.4,000	0	0			
Clerk of the Hanaper in the Court of Chancery	1,500	0	0			
Augmentation of the Salaries of the Judges	8,950	0	0			
				14,450	0	0
Queen Anne's Bounty for Augmentation of Poor Livings				14,854	12	0
Ancient Pensions, &c., paid out of Excise and Post Office Hereditary Revenues				29,200	0	0
Bounties for the Encouragement of the Growth of Hemp and Flax in Scotland				2,870	17	2
Salaries in West India Islands, &c., including the Duke of Gloucester's Pension, 9,000*l.*, out of 4½ per cent Duty				13,812	10	0
Lottery, 1782–Discount and receiving Charges, 1,222*l.* 1*s.* 4*d.*; Prizes, 405,000*l.*				406,222	1	4
Expenses of Exchequer Bills				2,141	15	8

				£	s.	d.	£	s.	d.
Miscellaneous Supply Grants:									
Maintenance of British Forts on Coast of Africa	£.13,000	0	0						
Civil Establishment of–									
Georgia	3,340	0	0						
Nova Scotia	5,943	9	5						
East Florida	4,120	4	1						
West Florida	4,800	0	0						
Senegambia	2,450	0	0						
Levant Company	5,000	0	0						
Damages during the Riots, 1782	1,006	15	0	121,739	19	0			
Roads and Bridges in Scotland	5,829	10	6						
Buildings at Somerset House	20,000	0	0						
Paving and Lighting Westminster	800	0	0						
Prince of Wales's Household	35,000	0	0						
Commissioners of Public Accounts	7,700	0	0						
Expenses of managing Lottery	12,750	0	0						
TOTAL CIVIL GOVERNMENT							1,788,531	1	5
ARMY SERVICES				5,331,677	18	0			
NAVY SERVICES				6,994,326	4	2			
ORDNANCE SERVICES				1,341,036	19	5			
							13,667,041	1	7
TOTAL EXPENDITURE							23,509,713	11	7
Advance by way of Loan to the East India Company in Exchequer Bills, per 23 Geo. 3, c. 83							300,000	0	0
Issued to pay off Principal of Exchequer Bills (Supply), *viz.*:									
In Exchange	£. 500,000	0	0						
In Money	2,950,000	0	0						
				3,450,000	0	0			
Issued to pay off Principal of Exchequer Bills in anticipation of Malt Duty and Land Tax				2,477,447	1	4			
TOTAL applied to REDUCTION of DEBT							5,927,447	1	4
BALANCES in the Exchequer on 10th October 1783							4,076,821	10	1
						£	33,831,982	3	0

78. Sir John Sinclair on the great increases of the Public Revenue during the eighteenth century, 1790

(Sir John Sinclair, Bart., *History of the Public Revenue of the British Empire*, Part III (1790), pp. 1–5.)

Sir John Sinclair (1754–1835) was President of the Board of Agriculture, 1793–1798 and 1806–1813 and a Commissioner of Excise, 1811. He wrote a number of works on agriculture and currency questions.

CHAP. I.

Of the Progress of the national Income since the Revolution.

Among the various political problems which it would be not a little desirable to have satisfactorily explained, there is none more curious in itself, or more truly interesting to this country, than a statement of the means which have enabled it to bear its progressive weight of taxes, but more particularly the heavy burdens to which it is now subject. A century has scarcely elapsed, since a revenue of about two millions was supposed to be fully equal to its utmost ability; nor since D'Avenant, the most intelligent writer of his time on public questions, openly asserted, that the commerce and manufactures of England would sink under a heavier load. [Works, vol. ii. p. 283.] Whereas now, England alone supplies the public treasury with above *fifteen millions*; and any popular clamour that is heard, is more owing to the manner in which our taxes are laid on, than to the quantum which is levied.

In endeavouring to account for this singular political phenomenon, it is natural to consider as the most efficient cause, the great addition that has been made to the general wealth and capital of the kingdom. The income of England at the revolution was usually calculated at forty-three millions. On that sum the inhabitants of this country lived; and, besides furnishing themselves with every article necessary for the sustenance and comfort of life, supplied the public treasury with two millions *per annum*. Whereas at present, in consequence of the various improvements which have taken place in *agriculture*, *manufactures*, and *commerce*, the general revenue of the whole island cannot be less than 120 millions; and hence it is enabled to contribute so much greater a sum than heretofore to the coffers of the public.

Agriculture in particular, that best and surest source of national wealth, in no country perhaps of equal extent has been carried to such perfection. By improvements in that art, not only the fields have been made more productive, but lands, formerly waste and uncultivated, have been rendered fertile: nay, independently of other products of the earth, grain alone, to the value of nearly forty millions of pounds, has been sent to other countries. Indeed, during the space of only five years, from 1743 to 1749, no less a quantity than 3,768,440 quarters of corn of different kinds, the value of which, at the medium price of from forty to forty-five shillings, could not be less than *eight millions*, were actually exported.

Formerly England was obliged to supply itself with various important articles from other countries, and sent hardly any commodity of considerable value abroad, woollens only excepted. But, since the revolution, the case has been greatly altered: valuable manufactories of silk and cotton have been established. With the assistance of

Ireland, it is now almost able to supply itself with the important article of linen; and, instead of importing, it actually exports glass, paper, earthen-ware, and many other commodities which formerly rendered the balance of trade, in particular with France, rather unfavourable to this country.

The general commerce of the nation has also been materially augmented. *Anno* 1697 the imports amounted to 3,482,586*l.* 10*s.* 5*d.* the exports to 3,525,906*l.* 18*s.* 6*d.* and the balance in our favour only to 43,320*l.* 8*s.* 1*d.* Whereas *anno* 1787 the imports, including those of Scotland, amounted to 17,804,824*l.* 16*s.* 1*d.* the exports to 18,296,166*l.* 12*s.* 11*d.* and the balance to 492,141*l.* 16*s.* 10*d.*[b] This is partly to be attributed to the increased industry and commercial exertions of the nation, and partly to the great value and opulence of our colonial possessions, which, notwithstanding the independence of North America, still continue of immense importance. Our commerce and settlements in the East, in particular, cannot be the means of importing into this country less than *five millions and a half per annum.*[c]

At first sight, it is natural to wonder how 120 millions of annual income can yield a public revenue of above fifteen millions *per annum*, when forty-three millions only produced two. But it should be considered that it is from superfluous wealth alone, that a large revenue can be drawn. At the revolution, the people of England required the greater part of their income to purchase merely the necessaries and conveniencies of life: and four shillings in the pound must be less felt, and less liable to complaint, from the additional wealth that has been acquired since, than one shilling in the pound, taken from an income that was little more than sufficient for the sustenance of the people.

Besides, the financial, like every other art, requires much experience before it can be brought to perfection. The ingenuity of able men must be exercised, to counteract the various artifices of those who may be desirous of evading the taxes to which they are subject; and in no country can the public revenue be brought to the highest standard of which it is capable, until many have made it the sole, or at least the principal object of their study and attention; nor indeed until the people have been accustomed to taxes. For, however obnoxious they may be when originally imposed, yet, in process of time, when they become familiar to the public, they are paid with less reluctance, and consequently become more productive. Hence, if the general income of England had still remained at only forty-three millions *per annum*, a much larger portion of that sum would probably have been at present paid, than at first could have been expected.

The advantages resulting to a public revenue from an easy circulation, and from credit being fully established in a country, from an abundance of money (whether paper or specie is of little consequence where paper is received by the exchequer), and also from the establishment of public debts themselves, have already been taken notice of. But there are two important circumstances, namely, the enormous size of

[b] The apparent balance is not so considerable at present, as in former years, particularly *anno* 1750, when it amounted to 7,359,964*l.* 10*s.* 8*d.* But the commercial prosperity of a nation depends less upon the balance in the books of the Custom-house than upon other circumstances, to be afterwards explained.

[c] That is the sum at which the sales of the company, the property of private traders, and the effects of British subjects, remitted through foreign companies, may be estimated. The particulars will be detailed in the account that will be given of the East India Company (chap. VI).

the capital, and the luxurious manners of the people, which have not as yet been considered. Wherever great multitudes are assembled together, there much wealth must be concentered; and the government of a country finds it much less difficult to draw a considerable revenue from those who are immediately under its eye, and live contiguous to each other, than from such as reside at a distance, and are scattered over the whole face of the country. Nor is it perhaps an exaggerated calculation, that the inhabitants of London and its neighbourhood, in proportion to their number, pay as much again to the public, as those who dwell at a distance from that metropolis.[d]

Lastly, the luxurious manner in which the inhabitants of this country live, is not a little favourable to an increase of revenue. Where private œconomy reigns, no productive impost can be laid, but on property alone. That resource, however, is very limited: for few can bear that the public should share very largely in their wealth, or should openly demand too great a portion of their income. But in luxurious ages a considerable revenue may be raised without hurting the feelings of the people. Taxes on consumption become efficient and productive, and the consumer, confounding the duty and the price together, furnishes, without reluctance, to the public treasury a sum which by any other means could hardly have been exacted.[e]

These circumstances tend to elucidate the astonishing increase of the revenue within the present century.

[d] Note omitted.

[e] Of the many millions raised in this country, only about two millions and a half are imposed upon property: whereas thirteen millions are levied upon consumption.

B. CUSTOMS AND EXCISE

79. Customs and Excise duties payable in 1724

(Henry Crouch, of the Custom-house, London, *A Complete View of the British Customs*, (1724), Table of Contents.)

This book was a guide for Customs officials and merchants, giving all the rates of merchandise. It was brought up to date by Samuel Baldwin, also of the Custom-house, London, in his *Survey of the British Customs* (1770). In his Preface, Baldwin remarked, "It were to be wished, that the whole of our Imposts had been framed upon a more uniform Plan, and that they had preserved both the Convenience and Beauty of System."

PARTITION THE FIRST.

The several Branches of the Revenue, at present payable to His MAJESTY, *in* Great-Britain, *upon Goods and Merchandizes, Imported, Exported, and carried Coastwise, are as follows,* viz.

No. 1. Customs
2. New Subsidy
3. One Third Subsidys
4. Two Third Subsidy
5. Impost on Wines and Vinegar
6. Impost on Tobacco
7. Impost 1690
8. Impost 1692/3
9. New Duty on Whale-fins
10. Fifteen *per Cent.* on Muslins
11. New Duty on Coffee, Tea, Chocolate, Cocoa-Nuts, Cocoa-Paste, Spicery, and Pictures
12. Additional New Duty on Coffee, Tea, Chocolate, Cocoa-Nuts, Cocoa-Paste, Spicery, and Pictures. And New Duty on Drugs, White Callicoes, and *China* Ware.
13. Second 25 *per Cent.* on *French* Goods.
14. Coinage
15. Prizage
16. Butlerage
17. New Duty on Pepper, Raisins, and Snuff. And a further New Duty on Spicery.
18. New Duty on Candles, imported
19. New Duty on Coals, Culm, and Cynders
20. Subsidy Outwards, One *per Cent.* Outwards, Duty on Leather exported, Duty on White Woollen Broad-Cloth exported; Additional new Duty on Coals, Culm, and Cynders; And Additional new Duty on Candles, imported
21. New Duty on Hops imported

22. New Duty on Hides, Skins, Parchment, Vellom, Cards, and Dice, imported: And Rock-Salt exported to *Ireland*
23. Additional New Duty on Hides, Skins, Parchment, and Vellom; A further New Duty on Coffee, Tea, and Drugs; And New Duty on Starch, and Gilt-Silver Wire imported
24. New Duty on Sope, Paper, Mill-boards, Paste-boards, Scale-boards, and Linnen chequer'd, strip'd &c. imported
25. Additional New Duty on Sope, Paper, Mill-boards, Paste-boards, Scale-boards, and Linnen chequer'd, Strip'd &c., and Starch, imported; And New Duty on Coals exported
26. New Duty on Sail-cloth, imported
27. New Duty on Wrought Plate, imported
28. New Duty on Apples, imported.
29. Excise on Salt, imported
30. Excise on Liquors, imported.

NOTE. *Tho' the Branch of Customs comprehends other Duties, besides the Old Subsidy, yet that only is meant by No.* 1 *in the above Scheme; and the rest are distinguish'd by the following Numbers,* viz.

No. 31. Additional Duty
32. Petty Custom
33. Double Petty-Custom
34. One *per Cent.*
35. Double Old Subsidy.

80. Sir Robert Walpole's defence of his Excise Bill, 1733

(*A Letter from a Member of Parliament to his Friends in the Country, concerning the Duties on Wine and Tobacco* (1733), pp. 10–13, 16, 19–20, 22–23, 26–27, 30–33.)

In this pamphlet Walpole defended the Excise Bill in detail against the attacks upon it in the opposition Press. It is a good example of his clear, straightforward style, and an illustration of his general principles of taxation.

Magna est VERITAS et PRAEVALEBIT

. . . *Taxes* are absolutely necessary to the *very being of all governments*, and therefore ought not, as such, to be esteemed grievances. The chief care of the legislature ought therefore to consist, in imposing such as may be *easiest borne* by the whole body of the people, and in taking the best care they can that they be equally and effectually collected. Let us apply these maxims, which I believe will remain uncontroverted, to our present case.

It has been the unavoidable fate of this nation, to be engaged in a long and expensive war in defence and support of our *liberties* and *religion*. Those invaluable blessings, restored to us at the *Revolution*, and since very providentially secured by the peaceable accession of his *late Majesty*, and the success of his arms against his *rebellious subjects*. This has occasion'd many Taxes, which now stand engaged for the payments of principal and interest, to such persons, or their representatives, who contributed to support the publick expenses. Other Taxes are, and must ever be, necessary, for the annual charges and current supply of the government.

THE first of these branches have been so managed, by constant care and application, and by an inviolable preservation of *publick credit*, that they are at present more than sufficient to answer the annual interest, and to discharge yearly, *one million* of the principal: and the only contest among the creditors of the publick, is, who shall be the *last* to receive their proportion of the surplus.

THIS being the case of that branch of the publick revenue, it became the duty of every member of the house of commons, to turn his thoughts how to render the *annual supplies* as *easy* as possible to those he represents. With this view, the most grievous and most unequal of all our Taxes, has been happily and gradually reduced, from *four* shillings to *one* shilling in the pound; a situation, which I am persuaded no freeholder in the kingdom was sanguine enough, a few years ago, to flatter himself with the hopes of. If then it shall be found practicable, to continue this seasonable *ease to the landed interest*, from a burden so long and so grievously borne by a small proportion of the whole collective body of the nation, is it not highly desirable? If the *annual exigencies of the government* may be supplied; if the *growing interest* may be duly paid to the creditors of the publick; if a *million per annum* may be applied to the discharge of *publick debts*: If, I say, all this may be done, without burdening the *land*, without laying any *new* Duty on *any* commodity whatsoever, or *any additional* Duty on *any* commodity already taxed; is not *such a proposition* highly worthy the mature deliberation of parliament?

BUT if *all* This will follow from doing our duty, by putting a stop to the *notorious frauds*, and undoubted *impositions* of a few persons, to the apparent loss of the *publick*, and of every *individual*, not concern'd in the unlawful *gain*; are we not under the strictest obligation to endeavour to effect it? And this, I am confident, may be done, by an *alteration* of the *present method* of *collecting* the publick *revenues*, as to those two commodities of *Wine and Tobacco*.

IN order to prove this, it is necessary in the first place to lay it down as a truth, That great and monstrous *frauds* are *committed*, in the importation and exportation of those *two commodities*. If I should say, that *no Duty* is paid for *one half*, or perhaps *two thirds*, of them consumed at home, the *whole* of which *ought* to pay, I am fully persuaded it would be short of the truth: nay, I believe it is so notorious a fact, that the most zealous advocates against the proposed alteration, as they have not yet, so I fancy they will not venture to deny it. If they should, it will not be difficult to produce proofs to confirm it.

It is unnecessary therefore, till then, to enter minutely into the several methods by which these frauds are committed, any farther than to shew in general, how the alteration proposed will probably prevent them for the future. First then,

If an *unfair trader* has a mind to defraud the publick, there is but one opportunity at present of his being detected; if by any artifice he can get his goods landed without the inspection of a *Custom-house* officer, his business is done, there is no farther check upon him (without a particular information) and his *unrighteous gains* are in his *pocket*. But if, in the next place, he be inclined to go a safer way to work, and not to run the hazard of a seizure, such is the nature of these trades, that 'tis well worth while to blind the officer with a large bribe, make him a partner in his wickedness at once, and he is, and must be, his slave for ever. By this means the publick is liable, and has been *doubly defrauded* by false weights, and false measures. Small weights at importation, by which the Duty is paid; large weights on exportation, by which the Duty is drawn back. . . .

AS to the *frauds* in the *Wine Trade*, they are allow'd on all hands to be *equally notorious*, and are so generally known, that it seems unnecessary, and I am sure would be too tedious, to enter into particulars. That a great deal is *clandestinely run* is very well known, that for the *greatest part* of what is sold in publick houses is nothing but a *poisonous composition* of unknown materials, is an *undeniable truth*; I shall therefore say no more on this head, but that the *poor consumer* is here again saddled with a price as if the Duty were *really paid*, and which he would with cheerfulness contribute for the good of the *whole*, but which in *reality* goes solely into the pockets of the *artful and fraudulent brewers of wine*. . . .

FROM what has been said, I am persuaded, THE PEOPLE will not be of opinion that these frauds ought to be continued and connived at: it is therefore to be considered in the *next place*, whether the *remedy* proposed is such as will *prevent* this *grievance* for the future. This, I believe, will not be much controverted, and *hinc illae lachrymae*. This is the great foundation of the present opposition; these are the dreadful apprehensions, that alarm the persons concerned; were the remedy weak or insufficient, the terror would be less, and heaven and earth would not be mov'd in the outrageous manner as has been attempted, to prevent the success.

BUT lest this should be disputed, I will only acquaint you with a matter of fact which I am well informed of. The *same* Duties on *Tea*, *Coffee* and *Chocolate*, which were formerly paid at the *Custom-house*, have been now collected for eight years past by way of Excise, excepting a small reservation of customs on entry. Now it appears by a compare of these *eight* years with the *eight* years immediately preceding, that considerably above a *million of money* has been paid into the *Exchequer* MORE in the last eight years, than in the former, notwithstanding the great quantity of Tea which may have been run, and notwithstanding the great quantity now remaining in the *East-India Ware-house*, by their having postponed the *publick sales* of that commodity, on account of the great importations into other parts of *Europe*, and which pays no *Excise* till after *such sale*. From hence it follows, that a *million* MORE of the publick debt has been discharged out of the Duties on these three commodities *only*, than would have been discharg'd, had not *that alteration* been made *in the then method of collecting these revenues*. Whether *any* inconvenience has arisen from that alteration, and if *any*, whether in the least degree adequate to the *vast benefit* which has accrued to the publick, I leave it to you, Gentlemen, and to every *impartial*, and *disinterested* person to consider. This is all I shall say as to the probability of the proposed alteration being attended with success.

HAVING therefore, I think, demonstrated, that it is an insufferable grievance to allow the abominable frauds and impositions to go on with impunity; and that the method intended to be proposed will in all human probability remedy the evil; it only remains to be consider'd, whether that *remedy* be *worse* than the *disease*. And in order to prove that it is so, the three following objections are made; first, That it will be *prejudicial* to *trade*, and *burdensome* on the *merchant*; secondly, That it is *injurious* to *English liberty*; and thirdly, That it will greatly encrease the *number of officers*. I shall briefly consider these three objections, and so conclude. . . .

As the law now stands, the merchant . . . must, on importation, pay down the full Duty for the commodity he imports; which Duty amounts, in *one* of the instances before us, to at least *equal* to the *prime cost*; in the *other* instance, to at least *five times the value*. Let any man now consider, whether this burthen on the merchant does not deprive him of the benefit of employing one half, or five parts in six, of his substance in trade, for his own advantage, and that of the community: Since so much must actually be deposited and lock'd up till he can find a vent for what he has imported, either to the consumer at home, or to some foreign market, whereby he may again receive a re-imbursement by way of drawback: And for this, in one of these commodities, three whole years is supposed to be necessary, and consequently so long time is allow'd before he is excluded the benefit of the drawback. But, in case the proposed alteration should take place, the merchant will either be entirely freed from this burthen, or at least will have a very inconsiderable sum to deposit on importation, and even that will be drawn back on re-exportation. In *that case* the *bulk* of the Duties will *never* be paid at all, and in the other, not sooner, than when the commodity is *actually* sold to the retailer or consumer.

LET any fair reader then say, whether this is not a very material difference to the *advantage* of the merchant, and consequently of trade: more especially to young beginners with small stocks, who will now be at liberty to employ their whole fortunes in commerce, to the greater enriching, not only of themselves, but of their native country; a consideration well worthy a *British* parliament, were there no prospect of advantage to the publick revenue. . . .

THE instances in which it is said to be *injurious* [to liberty] are, the being *subject* to be *survey'd* by an *Exciseman*, and the *method of tryal*, by the commissioners of Excise in town, or by two justices of the peace in the country, instead of being try'd in the court of *Exchequer*, and *by a jury*. I have said before, that Taxes are necessary for the support, and Laws for the regulation of all governments: in consequence of which, officers are necessary to gather Taxes, and to prevent the evasion of Laws for that purpose: for these ends *Custom-house* officers are appointed for collecting Duties on importation, officers of *Excise* for collecting *inland Duties*: But the *power* of the *latter* extends not farther, nor is more absolute, within the different districts to which they are confined, than the *power* of the *former*. The *Custom-house* officer has power to examine, to search, to rummage every locker, hole, and corner of the ship to which he is appointed; not a bundle or packet must be carried from thence, but he has a power to search and to inspect. By the laws of Excise, whoever deals in Excisable commodities, must enter himself as a dealer in such commodity; and must set apart some certain place, as a warehouse, cellar, or shop, where all that species of commodity is to be kept. Over *this place*, so *set apart*, the Excise officer has the same power to visit, search, and examine, as the *Custom-house* officer has over the ship to which he is appointed: the retailer of Excisable Goods is liable to great penalties on *false accounts*; the merchant is liable to as great penalties on *false entries*. The *ship* is the *warehouse* of the *merchant*: the *shop* or *cellar*, of the *retailer and Tobacco factor*. . . .

AS to the different *methods* of *tryal*, I will say but a few words; that the greatest privilege of an *Englishman*, is a *fair* and *impartial* tryal, and in most cases *by a jury*, is an undoubted *truth*, and which, I hope, I shall ever *support*, while I have a *seat* in *parliament* or any *share* of *property* in my country. But that it has been thought *reasonable* by the legislature, time out of mind, in *many instances* of taxes, and *other levies*, for the *ease and benefit* of the *parties themselves*, to *vary* from the ordinary method, and to direct disputes to be determined in a *less expensive*, a more *summary way*, is an *undeniable truth*; and the *advantage* of it is as *undeniable*. I have no books by me, so shall mention only those few instances I can recollect. The proportions of the Land-Tax and Window-Tax, by which one estate is loaded in favour of another; disputes about parish rates to church and poor; the repair of high-ways and bridges; the payment of servants and manufacturers wages; disputes between the clergy and their parishioners about small tythes; and a hundred other instances, with which every justice of the peace is acquainted; are directed by law to be adjudged and determined, either by particular commissioners for that purpose, or by neighbouring justices of peace, either in their private capacity, or at the quarter session, and *without a jury*. And in *whose favour* are these particular instances, and the others not named, directed to be *thus determined*? In one of these cases there is an *option* of a different method of proceeding; let us see the consequence of that and then judge. In the case of *small tythes* the *vicar* may, if he pleases, sue in the *Exchequer*; and I remember, since I sat in parliament, I heard on a certain occasion a complaint from the bar, that in a very few years there had been no less than 1200 suits commenced in the *Exchequer* on this head: And how did they end? The parishioners were all glad to submit, rather than bear the expence of such a tryal. Which method then, think you, was most favourable to the people? That, where the expence was so great, that they yielded without redress; or, That where they might have had redress, without any expence? . . .

As to the *dangers* insinuated from the encrease of the *number of officers*, I have enquired into that matter, and am *credibly inform'd* that there are so *few additional* places to be survey'd, which are not *already* under survey for some *Exciseable commodity*, that the number will not be considerable enough to create even a murmur. The *additional* officers on Coffee, Tea, and Chocolate, were *no more* than *eighty*, excepting clerks and persons employ'd solely in writing; and I am told the *present proposed encrease* will not be 150 *in all England*, besides *some Warehouse-keepers* in *this* Town of *London*, whose sole business will be to keep a key jointly with the *merchant*, and the *number* of them must depend on what *number of warehouses the merchants* shall desire. . . .

I THINK I have gone through the *material objections* to the *intended proposal*; but I cannot help mentioning *one* more, *ludicrous* as it seems to be, since I have heard it mention'd very seriously by persons who zealously oppose this alteration. And it is this, That if this goes on, the necessary *annual supplies* may be raised by the *parliament* with *great ease*, and without any *burthen* being *felt* by the *people*. If this be *true*, as in my conscience I believe it is, all their *other* objections, as to the *burdensomeness* and *grievousness* of this alteration, fall to the ground at *once*; and if *they* will be so kind to maintain *this proposition*, we can have *no debate*, but whether *this last* be an objection? And upon that subject I have but this to say, It will be time enough for *those gentlemen* who maintain *that maxim*, That *Taxes* ought to be as *grievous* as possible, when *they* shall have *more* power and *more* influence, to endeavour to put their maxim in execution; let *them* have all the merit, and all the advantages of the *experiment*: for my self, I shall think it *my duty*, as long as I have a seat in *parliament*, to make all necessary *impositions*, as *light* and *easy* to my *fellow subjects* as possible. . . .

81. A debate in the House of Commons on Supply, 8 February 1748

(*Parl. Hist.*, XIV, pp. 152–157.)

The advantages of Customs duties as a form of taxation is illustrated by this extract from the debate in the House of Commons on 8 February 1748, on the Bill "granting to his Majesty a Subsidy of Poundage upon all Goods and Merchandize to be imported into this kingdom", to raise money for carrying on the war of the Austrian Succession.

Mr. *Pelham*:

. . . I need not say any thing in justification of the war we are now engaged in, nor do I believe there is a man in the kingdom, who wishes the continuance of our present happy establishment, that will begrudge the expence. And I have the more reason to be of this opinion, because we so unanimously agreed to the Resolution of the Committee of Supply, for granting to his majesty the sum of 6,300,000*l*. to be raised by transferable annuities, after the rate of 4 per cent. per ann. together with a premium of 10*l*. per cent. to the subscribers who should engage to advance the money.

This, I say, Sir, was a proof of the zeal of parliament for supporting the present war, and the people shewed so much zeal for the same cause, and so much confidence in the wisdom and justice of parliament, that the whole, indeed a great deal more than the whole money was subscribed in a few hours, though they knew nothing of the fund that was to be provided for their payment, which shews, that we are not as yet under any difficulty as to the borrowing of money for the support of the war; but I must confess, it is not so easy to find a sufficient fund for securing the repayment. To establish a fund for this purpose without laying some new tax upon the people, is impossible, and there is nothing I have so great an aversion to as that of proposing any new imposition; but something of this sort must be done, and therefore all we can do is, to fix upon that tax which will be most easily raised by those that are subjected to the payment of it, and which will be least burthensome to the people in general, especially those of the poorer sort. This has employed my thoughts for some months, and many schemes have been offered to me, but of all I have thought or heard of, that of a new impost of Poundage upon all goods imported, with a drawback in case of exportation, is, in my opinion, the best, because it may be easily paid by those that are to be subjected to the payment of it; because it will not be burthensome to any, and indeed will no way affect the poorer sort of our people; because we may be sure that it will produce a sum sufficient for paying the interest annually, with a surplus for paying off part of the principal; and because it can be attended with no bad consequences to our trade, as it is to be wholly drawn back, in case the goods be afterwards exported.

With regard to those who are to be subjected to the payment of this tax, it will be the merchant importers only; and as they are all men of considerable fortunes and extensive credit, they can be under no difficulty in advancing 5 per cent. or a shilling in the pound, upon the importation of their goods; and with regard to the rest of the people, as in this nation we have the good fortune to want nothing from abroad that is absolutely necessary for the subsistence of the poor, they cannot be in the least affected by this tax, because they consume none of these goods that are to be made subject to it, the price of which will, I shall grant, be a little enhanced by it, but it will be a mere trifle, which will hardly be felt by the better sort of people.

A third advantage is, Sir, because we may before-hand with some certainty judge of the amount of the produce, by considering the produce of taxes of the same kind long since imposed and still subsisting; and from these we may almost certainly conclude, that it will produce annually a sum sufficient for paying the annuities to be now established, with a surplus for paying off part of the principal yearly, in case the parliament should think fit to apply it that way; for this, I think, we ought not at present to determine, but leave it to the discretion of future parliaments, because we cannot foresee what future exigencies may require.

And a fourth advantage attending this tax is, because it cannot, I think, Sir, any way injure or obstruct our foreign commerce, as it is proposed to be wholly drawn back upon exportation; to which I may add, that it will be levied without any new expence, and without increasing the number of officers now employed in collecting the customs: at least I may venture to say, that no new tax can be thought of, which will occasion less expence to the public, or less trouble to those made liable to it, or a less increase of officers.

This tax, Sir, as I have already hinted, is proposed to be 5 per cent. or 1*s.* in the pound, upon all goods and merchandizes, now liable to any subsidy on importation, that shall be imported into this kingdom, or any of his majesty's dominions to the same belonging, at any time after the 1st day of March, to be paid before the landing thereof, according to the rates or values as they are now rated in the two books of rates referred to by the acts of the 12th of Charles 2, and 11th of George I, or in case of their not being rated in either of these books, according to the value they shall be rated at by the importer upon oath; and as we have already several subsidies now payable in the same way, this new subsidy can create no new trouble to the merchant or the collector, except that of adding a new article to the account of the duties payable upon exportation. . . .

[Special arrangements for certain goods from China and the East Indies, tea, sugar, and prize goods.]

This scheme, I know, Sir, may be liable to many objections, as schemes of this nature must always be. It is impossible to contrive a tax but what must be productive of some inconveniencies, and suggestions of this kind are but too much attended to, the imagination of mankind being a sort of microscope, that magnifies every danger dreaded as well as every pleasure expected. I shall not therefore pretend to answer every objection that may be made to this scheme: all I can say is, it is the best I could think of; and if any gentleman can suggest a better, I shall be most ready and willing to give up my scheme.

But after having made this declaration, Sir, I must observe, that, in our present circumstances, no gentleman ought, I think, to start objections against what I have proposed without proposing or suggesting something he thinks better. Neither of the wars we are now engaged in, can with any justice or reason be objected to; but if it were otherwise, now we are in, we must get out: we must get out with our arms in our hand; for I trust in God! this nation will never be forced to fall upon its knees, and cry for mercy to any earthly power. To get out with our arms in our hand, we must have money: we must have money sufficient for the purpose; and money cannot be had without a sufficient security. Therefore, to start objections and suggest inconveniences against the security now proposed, without offering any other, can answer no end but that of alarming the people, which must give a great advantage to our enemies, and may be of the most fatal consequence in this dangerous conjuncture. For this reason I expect to see the proposition I have made unanimously agreed to, or a much better offered in its stead, the last of which would to me be the most agreeable, because I should always chuse to be an approver, rather than the author of any scheme for taxing the people.

Mr *Henry Fox*: . . . before I sit down, I must make some observations upon two other maxims, which the hon. gentleman[1] was pleased to favour us with. The first was, Sir, that as we are a trading nation, we ought not to supply the public expence by taxes which affect our commerce or manufactures. So far do I approve of this maxim, that I could wish with all my heart, if it were possible, to see every port in the kingdom made a free port, that is to say, to have no customs or duties payable upon the importation or exportation of goods at any port in the kingdom. But is this possible, Sir? Money must be had some way or other for supporting our government; and no money can be had but by taxes of some kind or other. Those taxes must either be by way of land-tax, poll-tax, hearth-money, window-tax, or taxes upon consumption; and these last must be raised either by way of custom or excise. As to the land tax, we know how difficult it was to get the parliament to consent to it at the time of the Revolution, and how many frauds were made use of for concealing the true value of estates, though the country was then in so much danger, and the new government in such distress for money. We know what heart-burnings were raised by the tax called hearth-money in the reigns of Charles and James 2: we know what discontents were raised in king William's time by the poll-tax; and we know what a combustion was lately raised in this kingdom, by an attempt to raise the duties on tobacco and wines by way of excise: therefore, if money be raised by taxes upon consumption, and those taxes levied by way of customs upon the importation of goods, it is not the fault of the government but the fault of the people, who will not submit to any other methods for raising money. Such taxes, I shall grant, affect in some measure our commerce and manufactures; but as the duties paid upon importation are mostly drawn back upon re-exportation, I believe, there is no country in the

[1] Mr. Velters Cornwall.

world where their commerce and manufactures are less affected by their customs or taxes than in this; and it must be allowed, that since the Revolution, and especially since the accession of the present royal family, both our commerce and manufactures have been considerably eased by the laws made for freeing almost all sorts of goods from the payment of any duties upon exportation, except those sorts which we ought not to allow to be exported at all, or at least not without enhancing the price by a duty upon exportation.

Now, Sir, as to the other maxim the hon. gentleman was pleased to impart to us, which was, that even in time of war we ought to raise as much money within the year as shall be necessary for answering the current service of that year; I shall grant, that this ought to be done, if it be possible, but there are two reasons which may, and do often, render it impossible. In the first place, those who pay the taxes must subsist, as well as those who subsist by them; how can the former subsist but by the income of their estates, trade, or business, clear of all taxes? Now a war may become so heavy and expensive, that if we were to raise the whole necessary expence within the year, we should not leave enough for the subsistence of those who pay the taxes; and in such a case we must necessarily run in debt. The other reason, which often renders it necessary for a government to run in debt is this: all governments must have a regard not only to what the people are able to pay, but what they are willing to pay, and the manner in which they are willing to pay, without being provoked to a rebellion. This often makes it necessary for a government to run in debt, as well as to raise money for the public service, in the most improper manner, especially when they are engaged in a war for preventing a remote danger; for as the people in general are not sensible of remote dangers, they are extremely unwilling to contribute a great deal out of their yearly income, towards preventing such dangers. . . . We are now engaged as principals in a land war, and we must go on with it till we can obtain a safe and honourable peace, otherwise, as I have shewn, we shall bring inevitable destruction upon ourselves: we must now in time of war run in debt yearly; for without doing so, we can carry on no war, not even a naval war: and we must increase that branch of the public revenue, called the customs, as a security for that new debt; because, I believe, no minister will dare to propose increasing either the land tax, the window tax, or the number of our excises; and as little will any minister dare to propose renewing either the poll-tax, or the tax called hearth-money.

C. DIRECT TAXES

82. Act imposing Window Tax, 1747

(*Statutes at Large*, XIX, pp. 2, 4–5, 16, 18, 20 Geo. II, cap. 3.)

The original Window Tax of 1696 (see vol. VIII of these *Documents*, No. 111) imposed a basic charge of 2*s*. a house, plus a charge of 4*s*. for all houses having 10–20 windows, and 8*s*. for those having 20 windows or more. An Act of 1710 imposed charges of 10*s*. for houses having 20–30 windows and 20*s*. for those with 30 windows or more. The Act of 1747, the work of Henry Pelham, laid down a new method of assessment; houses having 10–14 windows being charged 6*d*. a window, those having 15–19 windows, 9*d*. a window, and those with 20 or more windows 1*s*. a window. Two amending and explanatory Acts, in 1747 and 1748, were needed to make the new method work satisfactorily. The rates were raised by Acts of 1758, 1761 and 1766.

An act for repealing the several rates and duties upon houses, windows, and lights; and for granting to his Majesty other rates and duties upon houses, windows, or lights; and for raising the sum of four millions four hundred thousand pounds by annuities, to be charged on the said rates or duties.

[Preamble recites the previous Acts, *i.e.* 7 and 8 Wm. III, cap. 18; 8 and 9 Wm. III, cap. 20; 1 Anne, St. 1, cap. 13; 5 Anne, cap. 13; 8 Anne, cap. 4; 5 Geo. I, cap. 19.]

. . . *and whereas the revenue arising by the said several and respective rates and duties upon houses hath for some years past greatly decreased, and the same is still likely to diminish,* we your Majesty's most dutiful and loyal subjects, the commons of *Great Britain*, in parliament assembled, think it will be for the advantage of the publick to repeal the present rates and duties upon houses, and in lieu thereof to grant unto your Majesty the several new rates and duties herein after mentioned, as well for securing a certain fund for payment of such incumbrances as are now charged upon the said rates and duties upon houses, as to enable your Majesty to raise a certain sum of money towards the supply for the service of the year one thousand seven hundred and forty seven; and therefore do most humbly beseech your Majesty that it may be enacted, and be it enacted by the King's most excellent majesty, by and with the advice and consent of the lords spiritual and temporal, and commons, in this present parliament assembled, and by the authority of the same, That from and after the twenty fifth day of *March*, which shall be in the year of our Lord one thousand seven hundred and forty seven, all the rates and duties, and additional rates and duties upon houses, granted, continued, and made perpetual by the several acts of parliament herein before recited, shall cease, determine, and be no longer paid or payable; and that then and from thenceforth all the powers and authorities given or granted by the said several acts, so far as the same relate to levying, securing, collecting, or recovering the said rates and duties upon houses, and all penalties and forfeitures relating thereto, shall also cease, determine, and not be put in execution; save only and except in all cases relating to the recovering any arrears, which may at that time remain unpaid, of the said rates and duties upon houses, or to any penalties or forfeitures in respect thereof which shall have arisen or grown due and payable to his Majesty, or may have been incurred, upon or at any time before the said twenty fifth day of *March*, one thousand seven hundred and forty seven; any thing herein before contained to the contrary notwithstanding.

II. And be it further enacted by the authority aforesaid, That from and after the said twenty fifth day of *March* one thousand seven hundred and forty seven, there shall be charged, raised, levied, and paid unto his Majesty, his heirs and successors, the several rates and duties upon houses, windows, or lights, herein after mentioned; that is to say,

For and upon every dwelling house inhabited, which now is, or hereafter shall be erected within that part of *Great Britain* called *England*, the yearly sum of two shillings.

And for every window or light, in every dwelling-house within and throughout the whole kingdom of *Great Britain*, which shall contain ten, eleven, twelve, thirteen, or fourteen windows or lights, the yearly sum of six pence for every window or light in such house.

And for every window or light, in every dwelling house as aforesaid, which shall contain fifteen, sixteen, seventeen, eighteen, or nineteen windows or lights, the yearly sum of nine pence for each window or light in such house.

And for every window or light, in every such dwelling house as aforesaid, which shall contain twenty windows or lights, and upwards, the yearly sum of one shilling for each window or light in such house as aforesaid.

III. Provided nevertheless, and it is the true intent and meaning of this act, that the said several and respective yearly sums before charged upon every window or light, contained in every dwelling-house in *England* as aforesaid, shall be paid over and above the said duty of two shillings upon houses before mentioned; . . .

IV. And be it further enacted by the authority aforesaid, That the said rates and duties by this act granted as aforesaid, shall be paid quarterly, at the four most usual feasts or days of payment in the year; that is to say, the feasts of the nativity of Saint *John* the Baptist, Saint *Michael* the Archangel, the birth of our Lord Christ; the annunciation of the blessed virgin *Mary*, by even and equal portions, the first payment thereupon to be made at the feast of the nativity of Saint *John* the Baptist, which shall be in the year of our Lord one thousand seven hundred and forty seven.

V. And be it further enacted by the authority aforesaid, That the rates and duties by this act granted aforesaid, shall be charged only upon the inhabitants or occupiers for the time being of the respective dwelling-houses, in which such windows or lights are contained, his, her, or their executors or administrators respectively, and not on the landlord who lett or demised the same, except in such case as is in this act hereafter mentioned. . . .

XXIX. Provided always, and be it further enacted and declared, That such dwelling-houses only where the occupier or occupiers thereof, by reason of his, her, or their poverty only is or are exempted from the usual taxes, payments, and contributions towards the church and poor, shall be construed or understood to be excepted out of this act, or discharged of the rates and duties hereby granted, and that only in such cases where the dwelling-houses so occupied are cottages, not containing above nine windows or lights in the whole; any thing herein contained to the contrary notwithstanding. . . .

XXXV. And be it enacted and declared by the authority aforesaid, That where any dwelling-house is or shall be lett in different apartments, to several persons, and the landlord of such house pays other taxes and parish rates for the same, such landlord shall be deemed and taken to be the occupier of such dwelling-house, and be charged with, and liable to pay the said rates and duties for the same, as one entire house. . . .

83. Act imposing Tax upon Male Servants, 1777

(*Statutes at Large*, XXXI, pp. 372–373, 375–376, 378–379, 17 Geo. III, cap. 39.)

This was one of the new taxes introduced by Lord North's government in order to finance the American War. Other new taxes were those on carriages, cards, and dice, and on inhabited houses (see No. 84). It will be noted that the bulk of these taxes were of a sumptuary character.

An act for granting to his Majesty a duty upon all servants retained or employed in the several capacities therein mentioned; . . . [also for repealing duties on glass and granting new ones and repealing duty on silver plate.]

Most Gracious Sovereign

We your Majesty's most dutiful and loyal subjects, the commons of Great Britain, *in parliament assembled, towards raising the necessary supplies, which we have chearfully granted to your Majesty in this session of parliament, have resolved to give and grant to your Majesty the several rates and duties herein-after mentioned;* and do therefore most humbly beseech your Majesty that it may be enacted; and be it enacted by the King's most excellent Majesty, by and with the advice and consent of the lords spiritual and temporal, and commons, in this present parliament assembled, and by the authority of the same, That, from and after the fifth day of *July*, one thousand seven hundred and seventy-seven, there shall be charged, raised, levied, and paid unto his Majesty, his heirs and successors, after the rate of twenty-one shillings *per annum* for every male servant, within the kingdom of *Great Britain*, who shall then have been, or shall afterwards be, retained or employed in the following capacities; (that is to say) of maitre d'hotel, house-steward, master of the horse, groom of the chamber, valet de chambre, butler, under-butler, clerk of the kitchen, confectioner, cook, house-porter, footman, running-footman, coachman, groom, postillion, stable-boy, and the respective helpers in the stables of such coachman, groom, or postillion, or in the capacity of gardener (not being a day-labourer), park-keeper, game-keeper, huntsman, whipper-in, whether such male servants shall have been or shall be retained and employed in one or more of the said capacities, or in any other business jointly with one or more of the said capacities of a servant; which said sum of twenty-one shillings *per annum* shall be charged and paid in manner herein-after mentioned; that is to say, every such master or mistress shall be charged fifteen shillings for every such servant so retained or employed within the time which shall elapse between the fifth day of *July*, one thousand seven hundred and seventy-seven, and the twenty-fifth day of *March*, one thousand seven hundred and seventy-eight; and every such master or mistress shall be charged the sum of twenty-one shillings for every such servant which shall be so retained or employed within every subsequent year, ending on the twenty-fifth day of *March*; and the said several sums herein-before mentioned shall be levied and paid in every year, within six months subsequent to the twenty-fifth day of March, on which such charges are hereby directed to be made.

II. Provided always, That this act shall not extend to any servant who shall be retained or employed *bona fide*, for the purposes of husbandry or manufactures, or of any trade or calling by which the master or mistress of such servant earn a livelihood or profit.

III. Provided also, That the duty hereby granted for every coachman, groom, postillion, or helper, let out to hire by way of jobb, shall be paid by the master or mistress for whose use, and in whose service, such coachman, groom, postillion, or helper, shall be employed respectively; and that the duty hereby granted for every gardener, retained or employed by any person or persons who shall contract for the keeping of any garden or gardens, shall be paid by the person or persons for whose use and in whose garden such gardener shall be employed.

IV. Provided also, That nothing in this act contained shall extend, or be construed to extend, to exempt any person or persons from payment of the duty imposed by this act, in respect of any servant retained or employed in any of the capacities aforesaid, on account or under pretence that such servant is or shall be bound as an apprentice to such person or persons; save and except such apprentices as are or shall be imposed upon any master or mistress, under and by virtue of the powers given to magistrates and parish officers by any act of parliament, so as the number of such apprentices so imposed upon any master or mistress does not exceed two.

V. Provided also, That this act, or any thing herein contained, shall not extend, or be construed to extend, to charge with the duty hereby granted, the butler or butlers, manciple, cook or cooks, gardener or gardeners, porter or porters, of any college or hall within either of the universities of *Oxford* or *Cambridge*, or the universities of *Edinburgh, Glasgow, Aberdeen*, or *Saint Andrews in Scotland*, or of the several colleges of *Westminster, Eaton*, or *Winchester*, or to the servants of his Majesty, or any of the royal family, or of any ambassador or foreign minister residing in the kingdom of *Great Britain*.

VI. Provided always, and be it enacted, That nothing hereby contained shall extend to charge with the duty herein granted, any of the royal hospitals of *Christ, Saint Bartholomew, Bridewell, Bethlehem, Saint Thomas* in the city of *London* and borough of *Southwark*, or *Guy's*, or the *Foundling Hospital*.

[VII. Provides that the duties are to be collected and paid into the Exchequer by the same people appointed for the duties on houses and windows.] . . .

X. And be it further enacted by the authority aforesaid, That such persons to be appointed assessors as aforesaid, shall, within fourteen days after such their appointment yearly, give or leave notice or warning in writing, to or for the master or mistress of every servant on whom a duty is imposed by this act, within the limits of the places for which such assessors are to act, at his or her dwelling house, to prepare and produce, within the space of fourteen days then next ensuing, a list in writing of his or her servants retained or employed within the said parish or district, describing the number by him or her retained or employed, the christian and surname of each servant, and the office or capacity in or for which each servant is retained or employed; every such list to contain the greatest number of servants at any one time retained and employed in the course of the year, ending on the twenty-fifth day of *March* in each preceding year; and that every such master or mistress do and shall, after such notice so given or left, make out a list of his or her servants accordingly, and sign the same with his or her own hand, and deliver the same, or cause the same to be delivered, to such assessor or assessors. [Where the master neglects to make this return, the assessor shall make an assessment on the best information he can obtain, this assessment to be final; unless the master can prove he was not at his dwelling-house at any time between the delivering of the notice and the time when the assessment was due, or prove such other excuse as the Commissioners shall think sufficient.] . . .

XVI. *And to the end that every master and mistress may deliver, or cause to be delivered, to the assessor or assessors, a true list of their respective servants, according to the intent of this act,* be it further enacted by the authority aforesaid, That in all cases where any assessor or surveyor shall make a surcharge upon any master or mistress, for or in respect of any servant or servants omitted to be inserted in any such list, such surcharge shall be made after the rate of two pounds two shillings an head for every such servant so omitted; and the assessor or surveyor so making such surcharge shall be, and is hereby intitled to, and shall have and receive, to and for his own use, one pound one shilling of every such surcharge which shall be justly made upon any such list. . . .

84. Act imposing Tax on Inhabited Houses, 1778

(*Statutes at Large*, XXXII, pp. 27–30, 37, 18 Geo. III, cap. 26.)

This tax, like the preceding one (No. 83), was imposed by the North government in order to finance the American War. An Act of the following year (19 Geo. III, cap. 59) slightly increased the rates and made warehouses attached to dwelling-houses chargeable with the dwelling-house.

An act for granting to his Majesty certain duties upon all inhabited houses within the kingdom of Great Britain.

Most gracious Sovereign.

We, your Majesty's most dutiful and loyal subjects, the commons of *Great Britain*, in parliament assembled, towards raising the necessary supplies, which we have freely granted to your Majesty in this session of parliament, have resolved to give and grant to your Majesty the several new rates and duties herein-after mentioned; and do therefore most humbly beseech your Majesty that it may be enacted; and be it enacted by the King's most excellent Majesty, by and with the advice and consent of the lords spiritual and temporal, and commons, in this present parliament assembled, and by the authority of the same, That, from and after the fifth day of *July*, one thousand seven hundred and seventy-eight, the several duties upon houses with their appurtenances herein-after mentioned, shall be charged, raised, levied, and paid unto his Majesty, his heirs and successors, by the occupiers thereof respectively; (that is to say,) Upon and for every dwelling-house inhabited, together with the household offices therewith occupied, which now are, or shall hereafter be erected within the kingdom of *Great Britain*, and which are, or for the time being shall be worth the yearly rent of five pounds and upwards, and under the yearly rent of fifty pounds, the yearly sum of sixpence in the pound; and upon and for every dwelling-house inhabited, together with the household offices therewith occupied, which now are, or hereafter shall be, erected within the kingdom of *Great Britain*, and which are, or for the time being shall be, worth a yearly rent of fifty pounds and upwards, the yearly sum of one shilling in the pound, to be estimated and ascertained in manner herein-after expressed.

II. Provided nevertheless, and it is the true intent and meaning of this act, that the said several yearly sums of sixpence and one shilling in the pound, hereby respectively charged as aforesaid, shall be paid over and above, and in addition to, the respective duties charged upon houses, by virtue of an act, made in the sixth year of the reign of his present Majesty, intituled, *An act for repealing the several duties upon houses, windows, and lights; and for granting to his Majesty other duties upon houses, windows, and lights.*

III. And be it further enacted by the authority aforesaid, That the said several duties by this act granted as aforesaid, shall, in that part of *Great Britain* called *England*, and in *Wales*, be paid quarterly, on the four most usual days of payment in the year; (that is to say,) the fifth day of *January*, the fifth day of *April*, the fifth day of *July*, and the tenth day of *October*, in every year, by equal portions, the first payment thereupon to be made on the tenth day of *October* next: and in that part of *Great Britain* called *Scotland*, on or before the twenty-ninth day of September yearly, for the half year betwixt *Whitsunday* and *Martinmas-day*; and on or before the twenty-fifth day of *March* yearly, for the half year betwixt *Martinmas-day* and *Whitsunday*.

IV. And be it further enacted by the authority aforesaid, That the said duties granted by this act, as aforesaid, shall be charged only upon the inhabitants or occupiers for the time being of the houses or tenements hereby charged, his, her, or their respective executors or administrators, and not onthe landlord or landlords who let or demised the same.

V. *And whereas several manufactures, trades, occupations, and callings, necessarily require warehouses and buildings requisite for carrying them on, by reason whereof the persons concerned therein are obliged to pay large rents, or have laid out considerable sums thereon, and it may be a great hardship upon such persons to be rated to the full extent of their respective rents, or of the value of the premises abovementioned;* be it further enacted and declared That such premises shall not be liable to the duty imposed by this act, but the assessment shall be made on the dwelling-house only, with the household offices belonging to it.

VI. Provided always, and it is hereby enacted by the authority aforesaid, That no duty shall be imposed, assessed, or levied, by virtue of this act, for or in respect of any dwelling-house, cottage, or tenement, whereof the occupier or occupiers, by reason of his, her, or their poverty only, is or are exempted from the actual payment of usual taxes, assessments, and contributions, towards the church and poor. . . .

[VII enacts that the duties shall be assessed and collected in the same way as the window tax.] . . .

[XXIX exempts the king, the royal family and foreign ministers resident in Great Britain from the duties.] . . .

XXXI. And be it further enacted by the authority aforesaid, That no dwelling-house, or other such premises as aforesaid therewith occupied, chargeable by this act as aforesaid, shall be estimated or rated at any less value yearly than that at which the same stands legally rated and assessed to the publick rates, taxes, and assessments, or any of them now subsisting, where such premises are charged by a pound rate, according to the full annual value thereof respectively; and when such premises as aforesaid are charged by a pound rate, according to any proportionate part of the real annual value thereof respectively, the same shall not be estimated or rated, for the purposes of this act, at less than the full annual value, upon which such proportions have been computed and taken as aforesaid.

XXXII. Provided always, and it is hereby further enacted and declared, That no farm-house shall be assessed or rated as aforesaid for the purpose of raising the duty herein mentioned.

XXXIII. *And, for the better understanding what is hereby meant as a farm-house,* it is further declared, That all houses *bona fide* used or occupied for the purpose of husbandry only, shall be deemed and taken to be farm-houses, and no other.

XXXIV. Provided always, That no such farm-house, which shall be occupied by the owner thereof, shall be intitled to such exemption, which shall be valued under this act at more than ten pounds *per annum,* distinct from the land therewith occupied. . . .

85. Incidence of the House Taxes, 1750 and 1781

(G. Chalmers, *An Estimate of the Comparative Strength of Great Britain* (1804 ed.), p. 216.)

George Chalmers (1742–1825) was a Scot who emigrated for a time to Baltimore, and settled in London in 1775. He wrote a number of biographies and several pamphlets on the American colonies. *An Estimate of the Comparative Strength of Great Britain* was first published in 1782, but the list given below appeared only in the later enlarged edition. In the following tables the figures for 1750 and 1781 have been extracted from Chalmers's *View*. For his figures for 1690 and 1708, see vol. VIII of these *Documents*, No. 112.

A COMPARATIVE VIEW of the Number of HOUSES, in each County of England and Wales, as they appeared in the Hearth-books of Lady-day 1690; as they were made up at the Tax-office, in 1708–1750–1781; and, as they appear from the enumeration of 1801

Counties	*No. of Houses charged and chargeable,* 1750	*No. of Houses charged and chargeable,* 1781
Bedfordshire	6,802	5,360
Berks	9,762	8,277
Bucks	10,687	8,670
Cambridge	9,334	9,088
Chester	16,006	17,201
Cornwall	14,520	15,274
Cumberland	11,914	13,419
Derby	13,912	14,046
Devon	30,049	28,612
Dorset	11,711	11,132
Durham	10,475	12,418
York	70,816	76,224
Essex	19,057	18,389
Gloucester	16,251	14,950

Counties	*No. of Houses charged and chargeable,* 1750	*No. of Houses charged and chargeable,* 1781
Hereford	8,771	8,092
Hertford	9,251	8,628
Huntingdon	4,363	3,847
Kent	30,029	30,975
Lancashire	33,273	30,956
Leicester	12,957	12,545
Lincoln	24,999	24,591
London, etc.	71,977	74,704
Norfolk	20,697	20,056
Northampton	12,464	10,350
Northumberland	10,453	12,431
Nottingham	11,001	10,872
Oxford	10,362	8,698
Rutland	1,873	1,445
Salop	13,332	12,895
Somerset	27,822	26,407
Southampton, etc.	18,045	15,828
Stafford	15,917	16,483
Suffolk	18,834	19,589
Surrey, etc.	20,037	19,381
Sussex	11,170	10,574
Warwick	12,759	13,276
Westmoreland	4,937	6,144
Wilts	14,303	12,856
Worcester	9,967	8,791
Anglesea	1,334	2,264
Brecon	3,234	3,407
Cardigan	2,542	2,444
Carmarthen	5,020	5,126
Carnarvon	2,366	2,675
Denbigh	6,091	5,678
Flint	3,520	2,990
Glamorgan	6,290	5,146
Merioneth	2,664	2,972
Monmouth	4,980	4,454
Montgomery	4,890	5,421
Pembroke	2,803	3,224
Radnor	2,425	2,076
	729,048	721,351

86. Produce of the House and Window Taxes, 1775–1785

(*Reports from Committees of the House of Commons, 1715–1801*, XI, p. 51; Report from the Select Committee on the Public Income and Expenditure, 21 March 1786.)

AN ACCOUNT of the Sums annually paid into the Exchequer on the Duties on Houses and Windows under the Act of the 6th of His present Majesty, for ten years, ending at Michaelmas 1785: distinguishing the Amount in each Year, and how much of the same was remitted from North Britain.

	England			*Scotland*			*Total*		
	£	s.	d.	£	s.	d.	£	s.	d.
From Michas. 1775 to Michas. 1776	395,874	14	2	8,000	0	0	403,874	14	2
- - 1776 to Michas. 1777	429,038	16	11½	5,500	0	0	434,538	16	11½
- - 1777 to Michas. 1778	448,285	7	6	3,700	0	0	451,985	7	6
- - 1778 to Michas. 1779	396,378	0	1	2,000	0	0	398,378	0	1
- - 1779 to Michas. 1780	405,661	8	3½	1,950	0	0	407,611	8	3½
- - 1780 to Michas. 1781	401,098	2	3	1,000	0	0	402,098	2	3
- - 1781 to Michas. 1782	436,810	10	1¼	18,150	0	0	454,960	10	1¼
- - 1782 to Michas. 1783	389,939	12	3¼	13,600	0	0	403,539	12	3¼
- - 1783 to Michas. 1784	391,152	10	9	1,700	0	0	392,852	10	9
- - 1784 to Michas. 1785	432,017	1	7	3,110	19	8	435,128	1	3
£	4,126,256	3	11½	58,710	19	8	4,184,967	3	7½

Exchequer
the 3d day of March 1786

John Hughson

87. The annual produce of the Land Tax, 1774–1785

(*Reports from Committees of the House of Commons, 1715–1801*, XI, pp. 64–65; Report from the Select Committee on the Public Income and Expenditure. 21 March 1786.)

AN ACCOUNT of the Net Produce of the LAND TAX, imposed in the years 1774, 1775, 1776, 1777, 1778, 1779, 1780, 1781, 1782 and 1783

	From Lady Day 1774 to Lady Day 1775	*From Lady Day 1775 to Lady Day 1776*	*From Lady Day 1776 to Lady Day 1777*	*From Lady Day 1777 to Lady Day 1778*	*From Lady Day 1778 to Lady Day 1779*	*From Lady Day 1779 to Lady Day 1780*
	£ *s.* *d.*	£ *s.* *d.*	£ *s.* *d.*	£ *s.* *d.*	£ *s.* *d.*	£ *s.* *d.*
21st. . 3s. Aid–A° 1774.	276,600 0 0	670,157 12 10	308,560 4 4¼	22,884 3 2¼	135 3 3½	84 19 9
22nd. . 3s. Aid–A° 1775.		236,550 0 0	822,687 17 8½	235,197 11 11	4,253 1 8	3,341 8 5
40th. . 4s. Aid–A° 1776.			404,900 0 0	1,237,618 11 6¼	193,865 1 5½	10,145 19 6½
41st. . 4s. Aid–A° 1777.				422,455 0 0	1,246,968 16 8¾	160,947 10 6
42nd. . 4s. Aid–A° 1778.					488,800 0 0	1,209,895 4 1
43rd. . 4s. Aid–A° 1779.						496,220 0 0
44th. . 4s. Aid–A° 1780.						
45th. . 4s. Aid–A° 1781.						
46th. . 4s. Aid–A° 1782.						
47th. . 4s. Aid–A° 1783.						
£	276,600 0 0	906,707 12 10	1,536,148 2 0¾	1,918,155 6 7½	1,934,022 3 1¾	1,880,635 2 3½

	From Lady Day 1780 to Lady Day 1781			From Lady Day 1781 to Lady Day 1782			From Lady Day 1782 to Lady Day 1783			From Lady Day 1783 to Lady Day 1784			From Lady Day 1784 to Lady Day 1785			TOTALS of each Tax		
	£	s.	d.	£	s.	d.	£	s.	d.	£	s.	d.	£	s.	d.	£	s.	d.
21st..3s. Aid–A° 1774.	54	12	4½													1,278,476	15	9½
22nd..3s. Aid–A° 1775.	2,311	8	10½	9,800	0	0	304	14	4							1,314,446	2	11
40th..4s. Aid–A° 1776.	5,136	1	5½	1,211	10	10½	28	7	8	84	6	6	1,511	17	4¾	1,854,501	16	5
41st..4s. Aid–A° 1777.	26,654	18	7	3,938	5	3¼	230	10	2	14	7	10	250	13	4	1,861,460	2	5
42nd..4s. Aid–A° 1778.	162,249	4	5¼	23,258	18	7¾	2,396	7	9¾	710	1	11	130	9	6½	1,887,435	6	5¼
43rd..4s. Aid–A° 1779.	1,261,350	19	7¾	154,227	19	8½	21,473	15	8	1,615	16	9	685	17	7½	1,935,574	9	4¾
44th..4s. Aid–A° 1780.	533,130	0	0	1,201,846	10	5¾	143,888	16	0½	21,577	8	2½	8,502	18	9½	1,908,945	13	6¼
45th..4s. Aid–A° 1781.				530,878	11	2	1,267,418	6	9	169,847	3	5¼	7,540	12	9¾	1,975,684	14	2
46th..4s. Aid–A° 1782.							522,700	0	0	1,238,725	1	8¼	195,575	17	2¾	1,957,000	18	11
47th..4s. Aid–A° 1783.										495,300	0	0	1,168,673	13	9½	1,663,973	13	9½
£	1,990,887	5	4½	1,925,156	16	1¾	1,958,440	18	5¼	1,927,874	6	4	1,382,872	0	6¼	17,637,499	13	9¼
				[1,925,161	16	1¾]												

Exchequer, the 3d day of March 1786

John Hughson

Memorandum–From Lady Day 1785 (the time to which the Land Tax Account is made up) to the 5th day of January 1786, there has been paid into the Exchequer, upon the 47th 4s. Aid, A° 1783, the sum of £205,222 18s. 3½*d*.

D. FINANCIAL ADMINISTRATION

88. Representations from the Commissioners of Taxes on the unsatisfactory administration of the Window Tax, 1739–1743

(*Calendar of Treasury Books and Papers*, IV (1739–1741), pp. 30–31; V (1742–1745), pp. 277–278.)

The following representations from the Commissioners of Taxes show the extent to which the negligence of the surveyors was resulting in loss of revenue. A general reorganization of the house duties was undertaken by Henry Pelham, the new Window Tax of 1747 being one of the results (see No. 82).

June 14 [1739] 87. Representation to the Treasury from the Taxes Commissioners, dated Office for Taxes, concerning the decrease in the yield of the duties on houses. Unless some means be used for the better ascertaining the powers of charging and collecting the said duties, and greater checks had upon the officers employed in the surveys, the two duties will in time raise little more than one formerly did. In 1711, the first year of the New Duties, the yield of the Old was 113,092*l.* 14*s.* 6*d.*, and of the New 41,336*l.* 5*s.* 4*d.*, in all 154,428*l.* 19*s.* 10*d.* In 1737 the yield of the Old Duties was only 107,202*l.* 9*s.* 6*d.* and of the New 32,905*l.* 6*s.* 6*d.*, in all 140,108*l.* 6*s.* 0*d.*, representing a decrease of 14,320*l.* 13*s.* 10*d.*[*sic.*] "The cause of this is not only to be attributed to the stopping up lights, the building houses upon old and new foundations, either under 10, 20, or 30 windows, and the partiality which the justices, who are the Commissioners for these duties, show to their friends and neighbours in arbitrarily excusing them without administering an oath either to the officer or appellant, and excusing shop windows, cellars and offices adjoining. But there is also another and indeed greater inconvenience attends these duties, and that even from the officers themselves, who are almost become a burden instead of a support to them, by their negligence or incapacity. . . . Our General Surveyors are 4 in number, one is stationed in and about Wales, another in the North, neither of which send us any account of their surveys or their officers, though they have been frequently required by us so to do, a third is confined to London and the adjacent counties so that we have been obliged to employ the fourth in all the other counties even in those which are the proper districts of the two first." Pray directions on the whole and for power in future to examine into the age and ability of those who shall be hereafter appointed. . . .

May 18 [1743] 105. Report to the Treasury from the Taxes Commissioners on the state of the duties on houses and the conduct of the surveyors of said duties; same being made upon a Treasury order of 1742–3, March 17, requiring said Commissioners to reconsider their former reports thereon of dates, 1740, June 12[1] and 1739, June 14. The reasons put forward in said reports for the decrease of this revenue still subsist. As a remedy, propose to employ 2 surveyors to be *pro tempore* general surveyors to inspect the proceedings of officers in parts where regular surveys have not been made.

[1] Copy appended, "Similarly detailing the incapacity and negligence of particular surveyors."

The present general surveyors are 4 in number, Mr. Saunderson for London, Westminster and Middlesex; Mr. Stainforth for the northern district (an entirely negligent officer, who does not even answer the letters of the Commissioners exhorting him to his duty); Mr. Underwood for the rest of England; Mr. Lewis for Wales. Detail certain extracts from the Journals and Surveys of these four officers in proof of the negligence and incapacity of 37 officers, detailed, *e.g. inter al.*, Fra. Roberts (Middlesex, 12th division) surveys his division but once in the year, which ought to be done twice, viz. after Lady Day and Michaelmas: Barthw. Lynch (Middlesex 9th division), he is so taken up in another employment that he has no leisure to perform any part of the surveyor's duty; he neither attends at appeals the signing of the rates, nor the making up or setling the collectors' accounts, which occasions backwardness in the payment of the duties, the money not being collected till near 2 years after the same became due, in which time many of the inhabitants die, break or remove; his books are crowded with errors, and from his frequent employment of a deputy many inconveniences may arise, for the deputies not having a proper commission, the inhabitants may refuse them the liberty of inspecting their houses, collectors may refuse them the examination of their rates and assessments, and the Justices often disallow their charges and proceedings by reason they are not lawfully authorised: Tho. Life (Cambridge) keeps no books, neither does it appear that he ever made a survey; he is by profession a surgeon: Robt. Obbinson (Lincoln), this officer is a rich farmer, and has abundance of business, which makes him neglect his duty as surveyor; in Wales the officers look upon their duty as a sinecure, for the most part they keep no books and those who do have no method: there is a great decrease everywhere in these duties and that not so much from the above negligence and incapacity as from the partial and arbitrary proceedings of the Justices in those parts, who will not admit of any surcharges where a regular survey has been made in order to advance the duties, but on the contrary strike them off without examination, as they did lately in Ludlow, Salop, as also in Brecon town, though it appeared that many of the houses had from 30 to 70 lights, and that no appeal was made, they alleging it would be a bad example for one to pay 30 shillings, whilst others in the same circumstances paid but 20 shillings: John Sesse, one of the surveyors of Devon, is incapable of his duty, but the officer lays the blame upon the Justices of the Peace, who suffer the people to come and appeal at any time, and they are taken off without the knowledge of the officer who should be present to defend his charge, for which the clerks to the said Justices receive a fee. In conclusion propose certain qualifications to be demanded in future of persons for this service (being the same proposals which had been made in the previous report of 1740, June 12.)

89. Extracts from the reports of the Commissioners of Public Accounts, 1780–1782

(*Journals of the House of Commons*, XXXVIII, pp. 74–76, 380–382, 577, 714.)

Six Commissioners to "Examine, Take, and State the Public Accounts of the Kingdom" were appointed by Lord North in the summer of 1780, chiefly in order to cut the ground from under the opposition's campaign for 'economical reform'. The Commissioners made fifteen long reports to the House of Commons during the years 1780 to 1787, and these reports furnish much valuable information about the working of the financial side of the eighteenth-century civil service.

[27 November 1780][1]

To the honourable the Knights, Citizens and Burgesses, in Parliament assembled.

A Report of the Commissioners appointed to examine, take, and state, the Public Accounts of the Kingdom. . . .

The Public Accountants may be distinguished into Three Classes.

1st. Those who receive Public Money from the Subject, to be paid into the Exchequer.

2dly. Those who receive Public Money out of the Exchequer, by Way of Imprest, and upon Account.

3dly. Those who receive Public Money from certain of this last Class of Accountants, Subject to Account, and who may be called Sub-Accountants.

We began our Inquiries in the First Class, and of that Class, with the Receivers General of the Land Tax. To come at a Knowledge of their Names, and of the Balances of Public Money in their Hands, we procured from the Tax Office the last Certificate of the Remains of the Land Tax. By that Certificate it appeared that of the Land Tax, Window, and House Tax, to *Lady-Day* last, the Arrears in the Hands of the Receivers General, upon the 14th of *July* last, amounted to the Sum of Three hundred and Ninety-eight thousand Seven hundred and Forty-eight Pounds Nine Shillings and Five Pence Halfpenny. . . .

As the Receiver General is required by the Land Tax Act, within Twenty Days at farthest after he has received Money for that Duty, and by the Acts which grant the Duties on Houses, Windows, Servants, and inhabited Houses, within Forty Days after he has received those Duties, to pay the same into the Exchequer; it became necessary for us to enquire upon what Grounds and for what Purposes, the Receivers General retained in their Hands so considerable a Part of these Duties, so long after the same ought, according to the Directions of the several Acts above mentioned, to have been paid into the Exchequer. . . .

. . . Two Reasons are assigned for this Detention of the Public Money; one is, the Difficulty of procuring Remittances to *London* especially from the distant Counties; the other is, the Insufficiency of the Salary of Two Pence in the Pound, allowed the Receiver by the Land Tax and other Acts, upon the Sums paid by him into the Exchequer, to answer the Trouble, Risk, and Expence, attending his Office, to supply which, and to render the Employment worth having, he has been accustomed to retain in his Hands a considerable Part of these Duties, for the Purpose of his own Advantage.

As an Examination into the Manner and Charge of collecting and remitting, in an Office of Receipt, similar in its Circumstances, might enable us to form some Judgment upon the Validity of these Reasons; we directed our Inquiries to the Collection and Remittance of the Duties of Excise. . . .

[1] First Report.

From these last Examinations we learn, that each Collector of Excise goes his Rounds Eight Times in the Year; that he remits the Whole of his Nett Collection in every Round to the Excise Office, chiefly by Bills at Twenty-one Days after Date, in the Counties near *London*; at Thirty Days, in the more remote Counties; and at Fifty or Sixty Days in the most distant, and none at a longer Date; that he is continually remitting during his Round; and within a Week after it is finished, sends up by a Balance Bill all that remains of the Duties collected by him in that Round; that he finds no Difficulty in procuring Bills; could return more Money by the Same Method; and is never suffered to keep any Money in his Hands.

Each Collector is paid a Salary of One Hundred and Twenty Pounds a Year, subject to Deductions amounting to One Shilling and Nine Pence in the Pound; and is allowed Perquisites to about One hundred Pounds a Year more; and gives Security for Five thousand Pounds.

We endeavoured to form some Computation of the Loss, sustained by the Public, from the Detention of the Money by the Receivers General; and for that Purpose, we called for an Account of the Quarterly Returns made by them to the Tax Office; from whence it appears, that the Average Sum in their Hands, from the 5th of *July* 1778 (when the Mode was adopted of transmitting the Accounts on Oath) to the 7th of July last, amounted to Three hundred Thirty-four thousand and Sixty-one Pounds, the Interest of which, at Four *per Cent.* being Thirteen thousand Three hundred Sixty-two Pounds a Year, we conceive the Public have been obliged to pay, for want of the Use of their own Money. . . .

From this comparative View of the Modes of collecting and remitting these different Duties, and of the Advantages accruing to the Receiver and Collector from their several Employments, we are induced to think, that the Receiver General of the Land Tax is not warranted in his Detention of the Public Money, either by the Difficulty of procuring Bills, or by the Insufficiency of his Salary.

Supposing, however, the Difficulty of procuring Bills really to exist, though it might occasion some Delay in the Remittance, it yet is no Justification of the Receiver for constantly keeping a large Balance in his Hands; and, admitting the Poundage not to be an Equivalent for his Pains, yet we are of Opinion, that the present Mode of supplying the Deficiency, by permitting him to withold the Duties, is injurious to the Public, and ought to be discontinued.

The Revenue should come from the Pocket of the Subject directly into the Exchequer; but to permit Receivers to retain it in their Hands, expressly for their own Advantage, is to furnish them with the strongest Motive for witholding it. A private Interest is created, in direct Opposition to that of the Public; Government is compelled to have Recourse to expensive Loans; and the Revenue itself is finally endangered. . . .

[9 April, 1781][1]

Proceeding in our Inquiries into Balances in the Hands of those Accountants who appear upon the Certificate of Accounts depending in the Office of the Auditor of the

[1] Fourth Report.

Imprest, we find therein, next to the Treasurers of the Navy,[1] the Names of Several Persons whose Accounts have not been prosecuted for upwards of Seventy Years. We could have no Expectation of profiting by a Pursuit of Claims arising at so remote a Period; and therefore, passing on to the next Class, namely, the Paymasters of the Forces. . . .

Having issued our Precepts to *John Powell*, Esquire, the only acting Executor of *Henry* Lord *Holland*; to Lady *Greenwich*, Administratrix to the Right honourable *Charles Townshend*, late Paymasters of the Forces; to Lord *North*, and to the Right honourable *Thomas Townshend*, late Paymasters of the Forces, each jointly with *George Cooke*, Esquire, deceased, for an Account of the Public Money in their respective Hands, Custody or Power; we received Returns thereto, which we have set forth in the Appendix with their several Dates and Sums; the Total of which amounts to Three hundred Seventy-seven Thousand Seven hundred Eighty-eight Pounds Five Shillings and Seven Pence.

Having thus obtained a Knowledge of the Balances, our next Step was to examine whether they were liable to any such Services, or subject to any such Payments, in the Hands of these Accountants, as rendered it necessary to permit them, or any Part of them, to remain longer in their Possession. For this Purpose we examined *John Powell*, Esquire, the Cashier, and *Charles Bembridge*, Esquire, the Accountant to the Paymaster General of the Forces; by whom we are informed, that the Money in the Hands of the Paymasters General of the Forces, after they are out of Office, continues as long as their Accounts are kept open, liable to the Payment of any Claims of the Staff or Hospital Officers, or of any Warrants for Contingencies and Extraordinaries, which were voted during the Time they were respectively in Office, and have not been claimed. After the final Accounts are closed, such Claimants must apply for Payment, either to the Treasury or the War Office, according to the Nature of the Claim. These Sums remaining in their Hands are likewise subject to the Payment of Fees of divers Natures, and of Fees for passing their Accounts and obtaining their Quietus, together with the Payment of a Gratuity to the Officers and Clerks of the Pay Office; who, at the Same Time that they transact the Business of the Paymaster in Office, carry on also, make up, and finally close, the Accounts of the Paymasters after they are out of Office; but, having no Salary or Reward whatever for this extra Business, it has been customary for them, when the final Account is ready to be passed, to present a Memorial to the Lords of the Treasury, praying them to procure the King's Warrant to the Auditors of the Imprest, to allow them a certain Sum for their Trouble, payable out of the Balance remaining in the Hands of that Paymaster.

The Sums now in the Hands of these late Paymasters of the Forces, or of the Representatives of those who are dead, are still liable to Claims that may be made upon them under various Heads of Services, and subject likewise to the Payment of sundry Fees, and of the Customary Gratuities; but neither these Claims, Fees, or Gratuities, do, in our Opinion, furnish any Objection to the Payment of these Balances into the Exchequer.

Lord *Holland* resigned this Office in 1765; Mr. *Charles Townshend*, in 1766; Lord

[1] Dealt with in the Third Report, 7 March, 1781.

North and Mr. *Cooke*, in 1767; Mr. *Cooke* and Mr. *Thomas Townshend*, in 1768; since which, sufficient Time has elapsed for all the Claimants upon these Paymasters to have made their Applications for Payment. The Public are not to be kept out of Possession of large Sums of their own Money, nor Public Accounts to be kept open, because Persons may have for so long a Time neglected their own Business: Not that these Claimants are without Remedy after these Accounts are closed; by applying either to the Treasury, or to the War Office, as the Case may require, their Demands may be inquired into and satisfied by proper Warrants upon the Paymaster in Office. . . .

During the Course of this Enquiry, Two Circumstances engaged our Observation.

First, The Injury sustained by the Public from not having the Use of the Money remaining in the Hands of the Paymasters of the Forces after they have quitted the Office. We procured from the Pay Office, Accounts of the Balances and Sums received and paid every Year, by each of these Paymasters, since they severally went out of Office. A Computation of Interest, at *Four per Cent. per Annum*, upon these Balances every Year, from Six Months after they severally resigned the Office, proves that the Loss by the Money left in the Hands of Lord *Holland* amounts, at Simple Interest, to Two hundred Forty-eight thousand Three hundred Ninety-four Pounds Thirteen Shillings; of Mr. *Charles Townshend*, to Twenty-four thousand Two hundred Forty-seven Pounds Three Shillings; of Lord *North* and Mr. *Cooke*, to Eighteen thousand Seven hundred and Seventy-five Pounds Three Shillings; of Mr. *Cooke* and Mr. *Thomas Townshend*, to Three thousand Four hundred and Nineteen Pounds Fifteen Shillings; Total, Two hundred Ninety-four thousand, Eight hundred Thirty-six Pounds Fourteen Shillings.

Such has been the Loss sustained by the Public. Much does it behove them to guard against the Possibility of the like Evil for the future. If there exists in Government no Power to compel an Accountant to disclose his Balance, and to deliver back to the Public what their Service does not require he should detain, it is Time such a Power was created. If it does exist, the Public Good requires it should be constantly exerted, within a reasonable limited Time after an Accountant has quitted his Office.

Secondly, The other Circumstance that claimed our Attention is, the Delay in passing the Accounts of the Paymasters of the Forces.

The making up and passing these Accounts is the Concern of Three different Parties; the Paymaster, whose Accounts they are; the Pay Office, where they are made up; and the Auditors Office, where they are passed. The first Step must be taken by the Pay Office; there the Accounts must be made up, and from thence sent with the Vouchers to the Auditors Office, before they can be examined. Near Forty-six Millions were issued to Lord *Holland*; his final Account was not delivered into the Auditors Office until Seven Years after his Resignation. Above Two Millions were issued to Mr. *Charles Townshend*; his final Account was not delivered until Eleven Years after his Resignation. Near Two Millions were issued to Lord *North* and Mr. *Cooke*; their final Account was not delivered until Twelve Years after their Resignation. Five hundred and Seventy thousand Pounds were issued to Mr. *Cooke* and Mr. *Thomas Townshend*; their only Account was not delivered until Eleven Years after their Resignation.

In the Office of the Auditors of the Imprest, the Custom of not passing the Accounts of a Successor, until the Predecessors are completed, is a Cause of Delay. A dispute with a Deputy stops Lord *Hollands* Accounts; but that can be no Reason for delaying one Moment the Accounts of his Successors; they depend not upon, nor are connected with, each other. It is regular to examine and pass Accounts in order of Time; but in the Case of the Paymaster's Accounts, Convenience, both public and private, will warrant a Deviation from this Rule. Every Accountant has a material Interest that his Accounts should be passed with Dispatch; the Quiet of himself, his Family, and Fortune. It is not unreasonable to presume, that taking from an Accountant his Balance, may be a Means of expediting the passing of his Accounts; whilst he holds a large Sum in his Hands, he may be less anxious to come to a final Adjustment, less eager to procure a Quietus; the Condition of which is the depriving himself of that Balance. . . .

[28 November 1781][1]

. . . In Public Trusts, the Possibility of a Loss should be guarded against, as much as the Nature of the Trusts will admit, without any Respect to Persons, or placing any more Confidence in any Man than can be helped. The Sums that appear to have been intrusted to Paymasters General, are of a Magnitude that implies Danger to the Public; for who can give, or find Security for the Payment of them? . . . It has been the Practice of the Paymasters General, when they went out of Office, to take with them the Books and Papers that relate to their Accounts, as their own private Property; but as the Paymaster General is an Officer appointed to a Public Trust his Office created for the Use of, and supported by, the Public, and his Books contain Accounts of the Receipt and Expenditure of Public Money; we are of Opinion, that all these Official Books and Papers are, and should be considered as the Property of the Public, and as such, left and deposited in the Pay Office, for the Use and Information of Posterity.

The Regulations hitherto suggested, are upon a Supposition that the Constitution of this Office continues in its present Form; but there is a Modification, which, if it can be adopted, will effectually remove the Power, and therefore the Possibility, of Loss or Abuse; that is, by taking away from the Paymaster General of the Forces the Custody of the Public Cash, and placing it in the Bank of *England*; this Treasury will then be converted into an Office of mere Account, and the Paymaster General, instead of being the Banker of the Army, will be the Instrument only, through whom the Army Services are paid, without having the Power of applying the Public Money to any other Purposes whatever. . . .

We are well aware of the Difficulties that must for ever attend the introducing Novelty of Form into ancient Offices, framed by the Wisdom of our Ancestors, and established by the Experience of Ages; they are considered as incapable of Improvement; the Officers educated in, and accustomed to the Forms in Use, are insensible of their Defects, or, if they feel them, have no leisure, often no Ability, seldom any Inclination, to correct them; alarmed at the Idea of Innovation, they resist the Proposal

[1] Fifth Report.

of a Regulation, because it is a Change, though from a perplexed and intricate, to a more simple and intelligible System. . . .

[11 February 1782][1]

. . . Having thus stated the Mischiefs attending the present Establishment, both to the Public and Individuals, and the Reasons for abolishing the multifarious Emoluments, by which these Offices are now supported, it remains for us to propose such a Regulation as appears best calculated to avoid the like Mischiefs, and most beneficial to the Public Service.

We are of Opinion, that in the Place of all these Salaries, Fees and Gratuities, there should be substituted and annexed to each of these Offices, of whatever Rank or Denomination, One certain Salary, paid to the Officer by the Public Quarterly, and free of all Deductions; this Salary should be an ample Compensation for the Service required; and the Quantum estimated by the various Qualifications and Circumstances necessary for the Execution, and which together form the Title to the Reward.

By this Regulation, the Officer will know his Income, the Public will know their Expence; and Uniformity and Equality will be introduced in the Provisions for Officers of equal Rank and Station in similar Offices. The Industry of some Persons requires the Spur of Profits continually flowing in, or the Hope of Increase; others prefer the Certainty of a known, sure Income, paid at stated Times: No Arrangement can suit the Dispositions or Occasions of all Men; but Time and Usage will soon reconcile one reasonable Rule, extended through these Departments of Government.

Notwithstanding this Regulation throws upon the Public the whole Expence of these Offices, which are at present supported in Part by Individuals, yet, by adopting it, that whole Expence will become less than the Sum it now costs the Public; for that Sum is so great, as to afford every liberal Salary, and yet leave no inconsiderable Saving; Not that this is the only Saving proposed by the Regulation; the Public at present bear a much greater Share of the Burthen than is obvious at the First View: Besides Fees and Gratuities paid by Public Offices, and refunded to them out of Public Money, many Payments, though made by Individuals, are charged by them ultimately to the Account of the Public. For Instance, the Contractor, when he calculates the Terms upon which he may safely engage with Government, must estimate every Article of Profit and Loss, consequential to his Bargain; to the Account of the latter he places all his Charges, and amongst them, the long Catalogue of Fees, certain and uncertain; the first he knows, the last he will calculate not to his own Disadvantage; and if, by them, he can procure Credit, or Preference, or Expedition, he will charge them to Government at their full Price: If this Head of various Expences was blotted out of his Column of Charges, by so much would the Terms of his Contract be more favourable to the Public. . . .

Instances are not wanting, in all these Offices, to warrant this Regulation of Payment by a Salary: The Treasurer of the Navy, and his Paymaster, the Paymaster General of the Forces, the Paymasters of Exchequer Bills, and their Officers, are all paid by Salaries only; and why the Same Rule may not be extended to the rest no

[1] Sixth Report, mainly concerned with the Exchequer.

sufficient Reason has hitherto occurred to us. It might seem too sanguine, to suggest how far this Rule may be applied to other Offices, without a previous Examination into their peculiar Circumstances; and yet the Advantage it holds out to the Public, its Simplicity and Aptitude to be accommodated to all Offices, however distinguished, afford great Reason to believe it may be applied to every Department of Government.

The Principle of Economy, by which we have been guided, has led us to the Conclusions we have formed, and the Regulations we have submitted to the Wisdom of Parliament; Conclusions strictly deduced from that Principle; and Regulations made necessary by the pressing Exigencies of the Times. . . .

E. THE NATIONAL DEBT

90. Total funded and unfunded debt, 1715–1783

(*Accounts of the Net Public Income and Expenditure of Great Britain*, II, pp. 298–304; *Parliamentary Papers*, 1868–1869, XXXV.)

Ireland is included from 1717 onwards. For the total debt, 1691–1714, see vol. VIII of these *Documents*, No. 133.

Funded and unfunded debt at the close of each financial year.

	£		£
1715	37,432,234	1750	76,859,810
1716	37,918,468	1751	77,197,026
1717	40,308,257	1752	76,431,683
1718	40,379,684	1753	75,034,815
1719	41,872,241	1754	72,128,282
1720	53,979,708	1755	72,505,572
1721	54,405,108	1756	74,575,025
1722	54,202,366	1757	77,825,397
1723	52,996,990	1758	83,128,009
1724	53,323,570	1759	91,273,459
1725	52,239,077	1760	102,014,018
1726	52,850,797	1761	114,294,987
1727	52,523,923	1762	126,794,937
1728	51,960,576	1763	132,716,049
1729	51,541,220	1764	133,287,940
1730	50,830,310	1765	131,816,173
1731	50,738,786	1766	131,636,931
1732	49,836,638	1767	132,110,822
1733	48,728,097	1768	132,587,404
1734	48,821,416	1769	130,313,280
1735	48,948,089	1770	129,197,633
1736	50,424,651	1771	128,986,012
1737	47,231,299	1772	128,036,533
1738	46,497,500	1773	128,871,497
1739	46,613,883	1774	127,162,413
1740	47,122,579	1775	126,842,811
1741	48,382,439	1776	131,237,283
1742	51,847,323	1777	136,776,637
1743	53,200,989	1778	143,052,634
1744	56,742,418	1779	153,574,350
1745	59,717,817	1780	167,460,982
1746	64,617,844	1781	189,258,681
1747	69,115,414	1782	214,729,586
1748	75,812,132	1783	231,843,631
1749	77,488,940		

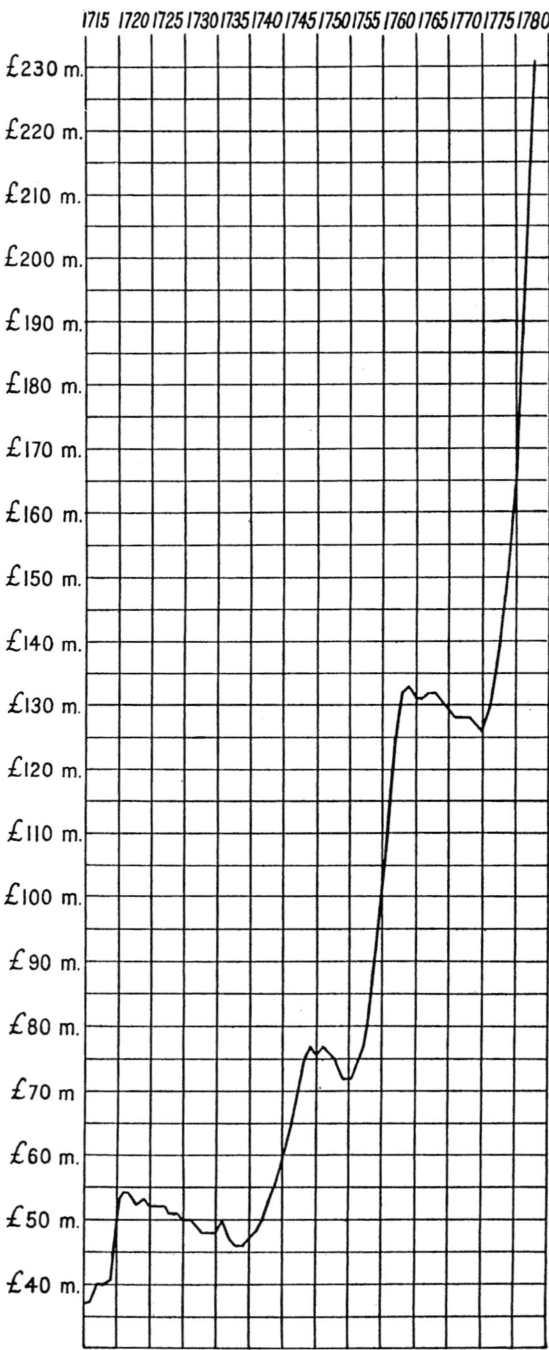

Diagram I

GROWTH OF THE NATIONAL DEBT, 1715–1783

Part V

THE CHURCHES

THE CHURCHES

Introduction

THE dominant secularism and rationalism of the eighteenth century involved a radical change in the position of the English Church. No longer, as in the previous century, did ecclesiastical factions seek to settle their quarrels by gaining control of the machinery of the State. The great bulk of the Whig party was now as loyal to the establishment as its erstwhile champions, the Tories. Both parties were now truly political parties and regarded the still great influence of the Church chiefly as a valuable asset in their political warfare. Since the Whigs were masters of the State from 1714 to 1760, they were able to control the Church also and use its aid to buttress their political position.

In these circumstances contemporaries naturally devoted a great deal of attention to the relations between Church and State. Edmund Gibson laid down the classical doctrine on this point in his *Codex Juris Ecclesiastici Anglicani*,[1] which was soon challenged by the extreme Whig controversialist, Benjamin Hoadly, in his famous sermon on the text, "My Kingdom is not of this World".[2] Hoadly's subversion of the authority of the visible Church provoked a fierce protest from the Lower House of Convocation,[3] and the Whig leaders gladly seized the opportunity to muzzle their opponents by suspending indefinitely the meeting of Convocation. The last word on this topic was said by William Warburton in his *Alliance between Church and State*, published in 1741. Warburton started from an essentially High Church or Tory view of Church and State as distinct entities, but reached the Whig conclusion that the Church should be established, protected and in the last resort governed by the State.[4]

A fundamental weakness of the eighteenth-century Church was the great variation in the values of sees, deaneries and benefices, leading inevitably to constant intrigues for promotion; and the gulf between the highly paid bishops and deans and the great mass of the clergy, who were, on the whole, inadequately paid.[5] Richard Watson, bishop of Llandaff, clearly expounded the evils of the existing system of patronage, and proposed a plan of radical reform which had, however, no chance of acceptance.[6]

Contemporary criticisms of the character and behaviour of the clergy abound;[7] but there is considerable evidence that both higher and lower clergy were on the whole worthy and conscientious, if not particularly spiritually-minded people, doing their best, often in difficult circumstances, to carry out what they conceived to be their duties. Valuable evidence of the conditions of the parish clergy and their performance of their duties is provided by the charges delivered by the bishops to their clergy,[8] and by Visitation returns.[9] Perhaps the best evidence of all is that provided by the parish clergy themselves in their diaries; for example, that of the Reverend William Cole,[10] here chosen in preference to the better known *Diary of a Country Parson* of James Woodforde. The stirring of a new spirit within the Church which was to lead

[1] No. 91. [2] No. 92. [3] No. 93. [4] No. 94. [5] No. 95.
[6] No. 96. [7] No. 97. [8] No. 98. [9] No. 99. [10] No. 100.

to the evangelical revival appears clearly in the letters addressed by the Reverend John Newton to the earl of Dartmouth.[1]

The same spirit inspired Methodism, which during this period was still a movement within the Church. John Wesley's *Plain Account of the People called Methodists* gives an admirably clear description of the origins and aims of the movement.[2] The opposition and persecution encountered by Methodism in its early days are described by both the Wesleys in their Journals; here an extract from Charles Wesley's *Journal* is chosen,[3] as less well known and accessible than the *Journal* of John Wesley. The Methodist enthusiasm ran counter to the dominant trend of eighteenth-century thought and practice, and Methodism was strenuously attacked in many pamphlets and lampoons. The most cogent criticism, because of its studious moderation, came from Edmund Gibson.[4]

The Presbyterians and Independents who had overthrown the Church of England in the seventeenth century were as much affected as the National Church by the secularism of the eighteenth century. Their legal position was now secure,[5] and was strengthened by Lord Mansfield's famous decision in 1767 that nonconformity was no longer a crime.[6] The Test and Corporation Acts remained unrepealed, but acts of indemnity[7] made it in practice no longer essential for holders of municipal offices to take communion according to the rites of the Church of England; although such officers were forbidden to attend Dissenting services in their official robes. Local and sporadic attempts were still made to harass the Protestant dissenters, but in the Dissenting Deputies they now had an organization ready to defend and fully capable of defending their civil rights.[8] Politically they maintained the old alliance with the Whigs, but their importance steadily declined.

It appears that the Catholics were also declining in number and influence during this period,[9] though a revival began in the latter part of the century. In law they were still subject to severe disabilities and to penal taxation;[10] but opinion was turning against strict enforcement of these laws. The Catholics' position, like that of the Protestant dissenters, was in practice a good deal better than it was in theory, and they enjoyed considerable religious freedom, occasionally threatened by public alarm at the time of the Jacobite Risings.[11] This more liberal attitude finally found expression in Sir George Savile's Catholic Relief Act, which was passed in 1778, virtually without opposition.[12] Unfortunately this law was in advance of public opinion, and the result was the celebrated Gordon Riots, which made any further steps towards complete toleration for Catholics unlikely for the rest of the century.

[1] No. 101. [2] No. 102. [3] No. 103. [4] No. 104. [5] No. 105. [6] No. 108.
[7] No. 106. [8] No. 107. [9] No. 113. [10] No. 109. [11] No. 110. [12] Nos. 111 and 112.

BIBLIOGRAPHY

No one since J. Stoughton, whose *History of Religion in England* began to appear in 1867 and was reissued in eight volumes (London, 1901), has tried to cover the whole religious life of the eighteenth century. Leslie Stephen, however, in his *History of English Thought in the 18th Century* (2 vols., London, 1876, and later editions), deals fully with most of the religious controversies of the age. J. M. Creed and J. S. Boyes Smith in *Religious Thought in the 18th Century* (Cambridge, 1934) print an excellent selection of extracts from writings on theological and ecclesiastical subjects.

The works of some outstanding theologians and controversialists may be briefly listed. There is a four-volume annotated edition of Berkeley's *Works* by A. C. Fraser (Oxford, 1871), several more recent studies of his philosophical ideas and the standard *Life of Bishop Berkeley* by A. A. Luce (London, 1949); the editions of Bishop Butler's works include one by W. E. Gladstone (2 vols., Oxford, 1896). There is a good short study of Butler by A. E. Duncan-Jones, *Butler's Moral Philosophy* (Pelican Series, 1952). William Law's *Works* are best edited by G. B. Morgan (9 vols., Brockenhurst, 1892–1893). S. Hobhouse, *William Law: Select Mystical Writings* (London, 1938, new edition, 1948), adds much to our knowledge and understanding of a divine who influenced men of such divergent characters as John Wesley and Dr. Johnson. The only edition of Hoadly's *Works* is that edited by his son (3 vols., London, 1773). William Warburton's *Works* were originally edited by R. Hurd (7 vols., London, 1788–1794, and reissued in 1811): the controversies with which he was connected are reviewed in A. W. Evans, *Warburton and the Warburtonians* (Oxford, 1932). Printed sermons of the period abound, but there is no study of them comparable to W. F. Mitchell's *English Pulpit Oratory* on the seventeenth century. The work of the religious societies which were so important in the first half of the century is the theme of an excellent monograph, *Caritas Anglicana* (London, 1912) by G. V. Portus, while there is a study of the S.P.C.K. by W. O. B. Allen and E. McClure, entitled *Two Hundred Years: the history of the Society for Promoting Christian Knowledge* (London, 1898).

I. THE CHURCH OF ENGLAND

A Dictionary of English Church History by S. L. Ollard and others (3rd revised edition, 1948) has many valuable articles. C. J. Abbey, *The English Church and its Bishops 1700–1800* (London, 1887), and C. J. Abbey and J. H. Overton, *English Church in the 18th Century* (2 vols., London, 1878) are antiquated but still sometimes useful. More recent surveys include J. H. Overton and H. F. Relton, *English Church* [1714–1800] (London, 1906), A. Plummer, *Church of England in the 18th Century* (London, 1910), and J. Wickham Legg, *English Church Life from the Restoration to the Tractarian Movement* (London, 1914). Much the best general account will, however, be found in N. Sykes, *Church and State in England in the 18th Century* (Cambridge, 1934). Alan Savidge, *The Foundation and Early Years of Queen Anne's Bounty* [to 1736] (London, 1955), is useful. Detailed accounts of Church services, devotional literature, sacraments and the lives of the clergy are given in W. K. L. Clarke, *Eighteenth Century Piety* (London, 1944). N. Boston writes in *Archaeological Journal*, xcix (1942), pp. 53–66, on "Music of the 18th century village church". F. Makower, *Constitutional History of the Church of England* (London, 1895), may still be used, and H. H. Henson, *Relation of the Church of England to the other Reformed Churches* (Edinburgh, 1911), gives a clear account of this interesting topic. The ecclesiastical administration of the duke of Newcastle has been studied by Mary Bateson in *English Historical Review*, vii (1892), pp. 685–696, by N. Sykes in *English Historical Review*, lvii (1942), pp. 59–84, and by D. G. Barnes in *Pacific Historical Review*, iii, pp. 164–191. Professor Sykes has also written on "Archbishop Wake and the Whig Party" in *Cambridge Historical Journal*, VIII (1945), pp. 93–116. E. B. Greene in "The Anglican Outlook on the American Colonies" discusses in *American Historical Review*, XX (1914–1915), pp. 64–85, the part played there by the Society for the Propagation of the Gospel.

The dignitaries of the Church are listed in J. le Neve, *Fasti ecclesiae Anglicanae*, edited by T. D. Hardy (3 vols., Oxford, 1854). Few have attracted modern biographers. An exception is Bishop Atterbury, whose *Memoirs and Correspondence* (2 vols., London, 1869) were reprinted by R. F. Williams, and a life of whom was written by H. C. Beeching (London, 1909). Two notable biographies by Professor N. Sykes are *Edmund Gibson, Bishop of London* (Oxford, 1926) and *William Wake, Archbishop of Canterbury* (2 vols., Cambridge, 1957). There is also Edward Carpenter, *Thomas Sherlock* (London, 1936). Other bishops wrote autobiographies, the best known of these being *Anecdotes of the Life of Richard Watson, Bishop of Landaff* (London, 1817). W. F. Hook, *Lives of the Archbishops of Canterbury* (12 vols., London, 1860–1876), A. W. Rowden, *Primates of the Four Georges* (London, 1916), and of course *The Dictionary of National Biography* may be consulted for the lives of other eminent clergymen. A. P. Davis, *Isaac Watts* (London, 1948), gives an account of one of the influential hymn-writers of the century.

On the lives of the parish clergy the most accessible and in many ways the best evidence is provided by their own diaries and correspondence, notably the *Diary of a Country Parson* [Woodforde], edited by J. Beresford (5 vols., London, 1924–1931). Less well known but equally valuable are *The Blecheley Diary of the Rev. William Cole*, edited by F. G. Stokes, (London, 1931); the *Diary of the Revd. William Jones*, edited by O. F. Christie (London, 1929), which, however, does not begin until 1777; and E. Pyle, *Memoirs of a Royal Chaplain*, edited by A. Hartshorne (London, 1905). These autobiographical samples may be checked by eighteenth-century official surveys of individual dioceses, notably the *Archbishop Herring's Visitation Returns* [1743] relating to the diocese of York, edited by Ollard and Walker, Yorkshire Archaeological Society (5 vols., Wakefield, 1928–1931), and *Speculum Dioeceseos Lincolniensis sub Episcopis Gul: Wake et Edm: Gibson A. D. 1705–1723*, edited by R. E. G. Cole for the Lincoln Record Society (London, 1913); and also by secondary accounts such as A. I. Pryce, *The Diocese of Bangor during three Centuries* (Cardiff, 1929), and P. J. Dunn, "The Political and Ecclesiastical Activities of William Nicholson, Bishop of Carlisle 1702–18" in *Bulletin of the Institute of Historical Research*, IX (1931–1932), pp. 196–199. Several well-known eighteenth-century novels give lifelike portraits of various types of parish clergy and help to make clear the prevalent attitude towards the Established Church. Margaret H. Watt, *History of the Parson's Wife* (London, 1943), is a popular work which brings together some good material.

II. THE EVANGELICAL REVIVAL

J. H. Overton, *Evangelical Revival in 18th Century* (London, 1886), gives a brief account of this important movement. G. C. B. Davies, *The Early Cornish Evangelicals, 1735–1760* (London, 1951), is a useful local study. Other useful works are J. Newton, *Memoirs of Grimshaw* (London, 1799, and later editions); R. S. Hardy, *William Grimshaw* (London, 1860); and two recent biographies by G. G. Cragg, *Grimshaw of Haworth* (London, 1947), and B. Martin, *John Newton* (London, 1950).

III. NON-JURORS

The rapid decline of this sect after Anne's reign may be studied in two works by J. H. Overton, *Law, Nonjuror and Mystic* (London, 1881), and *The Nonjurors: their Lives, Principles and Writings* (London, 1902). There is a later treatment by H. Broxap in *Later Nonjurors* (Cambridge, 1924), and Lucy M. Hawkins, *Allegiance in Church and State* (London, 1928), has a useful chapter on Charles Leslie. The Cheetham Society published in four volumes (Manchester, 1854–1857) the *Private Journal and Literary Remains* [1707–1763] of a prominent Hanoverian Non-Juror, J. Byrom.

IV. PROTESTANT NONCONFORMISTS

For long the pioneer works of D. Bogue and J. Bennett, *History of Dissenters* (2 vols., 2nd edition, 1833), and H. S. Skeats, *History of the Free Churches* (London, 1868, and later editions), held the field. They are now superseded by H. W. Clark, *History of English Nonconformity* (2 vols., London, 1911–1913), J. H. Colligan, *18th Century Nonconformity* (London, 1915), and a group of more recent works, E. D. Bebb, *Nonconformity and Social and Economic Life 1660–1800* (London, 1935), A. H. Lincoln, *Some Political and Social Ideas of English Dissent, 1763–1800* (Cambridge, 1938), D. Coomer, *English Dissent under the Early Hanoverians* (London, 1946), and B. L. Manning, *The Protestant Dissenting Deputies* (Cambridge, 1952). In addition there are numerous studies of the various Nonconformist sects in the eighteenth century. Each of these sects, as well as Roman Catholics, Wesleyans and Jews, maintains a large specialized library. Some have published useful bibliographies: others publish a journal devoted wholly or in part to their history. Details of these activities will be found in C. L. Grose, *Select Bibliography* (Chicago, 1939), Section IX. The early work of A. H. Drysdale, *History of Presbyterians in England* (London, 1889), passed lightly over the eighteenth century, but this period is well treated in Olive M. Griffiths, *Religion and Learning: a Study in English Presbyterian Thought* (Cambridge, 1935). The famous Salters's Hall controversy is explained by Alexander Gordon in *Addresses Biographical and Historical* (London, 1922). John Waddington, *Congregational History 1700–1800* (London, 1876), and R. W. Dale, *History of English Congregationalism* (London, 1907), require to be supplemented and corrected by such detailed studies as W. H. Burgess, *Story of Dean Row Chapel, Cheshire* (Hull, 1924). There are histories of the Baptists by W. T. Whitley, *History of British Baptists* (London, 1923) and A. C. Underwood, *A History of the English Baptists* (London, 1947). J. H. Colligan, *Arian Movement* (Manchester, 1913), and H. McLachlan, *Unitarian Movement* (London, 1934), are both valuable. A good contemporary exposition of the Unitarian viewpoint will be found in T. Lindsey, *Historical View of Unitarian Doctrine and Worship* (London, 1783). Valuable information on Protestant nonconformity will also be found in the works of three eminent Dissenters, Edmund Calamy, *Historical Account of my own Life*, edited by J. T. Rutt (2 vols., London, 1829–1830); Philip Doddridge, *Correspondence and Diary*, edited by J. D. Humphreys (5 vols., London, 1829–1831); and *Letters to Dissenting Ministers from Rev. Mr. Job Orton* (2 vols., London, 1806). There are good short lives of two prominent Dissenters in the second half of the century, *A Life of Joseph Priestley* by Anne Holt (London, 1931), and *Richard Price* by R. Thomas (London, 1924). C. F. Mullett contributed to the *Virginian Law Review*, XXIII (1937), pp. 389–418, an article on "Legal Position of English Protestant Dissenters, 1689–1767".

V. QUAKERS

Contemporary works, notably the *Life of Thomas Story* (Newcastle upon Tyne, 1747) and the *Journal* of John Woolman (best edition, London, 1922, by Amelia M. Gummere), which were reprinted at intervals, and J. Gough, *History of the People called Quakers* (4 vols., Dublin, 1789–1790), provide valuable primary material. Story was an indefatigable traveller and his work is interesting for social conditions as well as for eighteenth-century Quakerism. There is a recent study of him under the title *Travelling with Thomas Story*, edited by Emily E. Moore (Letchworth, 1948). R. M. Jones, *Later Periods of Quakerism* (2 vols., London, 1921), is useful on the eighteenth century. E. Russell, *History of Quakerism* (London, 1942), is also recommended. A. Lloyd, *Quaker Social History 1669–1738* (London, 1950), is a mine of detailed information but the emphasis is on the seventeenth century.

VI. METHODISM

Methodism is best studied in the works of its founders. The editions of John Wesley's *Journal*, edited by N. Curnock (8 vols., London, 1909–1916) and of his *Letters*, edited by J. Telford (8 vols., London, 1931), are standard. Less important but valuable are the similar editions of Charles Wesley's *Journal*, edited by T. Jackson (2 vols., London, 1849), and his *Early Journal 1736–39*, edited by J. Telford (London, 1909). *Whitefield's Journals* are best read in W. Wale's edition (London, 1905), but there is no modern edition of his letters. The *Egmont Diaries* amongst the publications of the Historical Manuscripts Commission give the contemporary views of a detached but on the whole sympathetic observer of the movement. L. Tyerman wrote what are still in some ways the standard lives of John Wesley and George Whitefield, *Life and Times of the Rev. John Wesley* (3 vols., London, 1870–1871) and *Life of the Rev. George Whitefield* (2 vols., London, 1876–1877). Recent works on John Wesley include M. L. Edwards, *John Wesley and the 18th Century* (London, 1933); M. Piette, *John Wesley in the Evolution of Protestantism* (London, 1937); and Elizabeth K. Nottingham, *Making of an Evangelist* (London, 1938). There are lives of Charles Wesley by J. Telford (London, 1886) and F. L. Wiseman (New York, 1932). The best modern life of Whitefield, is A. D. Belden, *George Whitefield* (Nashville, Tenn., 1930). There are biographies of the countess of Huntingdon; *Life and Times of Selina, Countess of Huntingdon* (2 vols., London, 1839) by a member of the houses of Shirley and Hastings [A. C. H. Seymour], and Sarah Tytler, *The Countess of Huntingdon and her Circle* (London, 1907). On the movement generally the works of J. S. Simon, especially *Revival of Religion in England in the 18th Century* (London, 1907), and *John Wesley and the Methodist Societies* (London, 1923), are useful, as is L. F. Church, *The Early Methodist People* (London, 1948), and its sequel, *More about the Early Methodist People* (London, 1950). The connexion between the Moravian Church and Methodism is examined by J. E. Hutton, "Moravian contributions to the evangelical revival in England, 1742 to 1755" in *Historical essays by members of the Owens College*, edited by T. F. Tout and J. Tait, pp. 423–452 (Manchester, 1902), and there are many contributions to eighteenth-century Wesleyan history in the *Proceedings* (and publications) *of the Wesley Historical Society* (Burnley and London, 1898–1934).

VII. ROMAN CATHOLICS

J. Gillow, *Literary and Biographical History or Bibliographical Dictionary of the English Catholics* (5 vols., London, 1885–1902), and *The Catholic Encyclopaedia* (15 vols., ?London, 1907–1914) and J. H. Pollen, *Sources for the History of Roman Catholics*, S.P.C.K. *Helps for the student of history* (London, 1921), are useful reference books. The Catholic Record Society and several local societies have published valuable material, *e.g.* the recent volume of the Record Society of Lancashire and Cheshire, *Registers of Estates of Lancashire Papists 1717–88*, edited by R. S. France (Preston, 1946), which is as useful for social as for religious history. J. Berington, *The State and Behaviour of English Catholics* (London, 1780), is a polemical but still useful contemporary source. D. Mathew, *Catholicism in England 1535–1935* (London, 1936, new edition, 1949), is very slight on the eighteenth century. B. N. Ward, *Dawn of the Catholic Revival 1781–1803* (2 vols., London, 1909), and P. Hughes, *Catholic Question 1688–1829* (London, 1929), can be recommended. R. C. Wilton has written in the *Catholic Historical Review*, New Series IV (1925), pp. 367–387, on "Early 18th Century Catholics in England", and P. Purcell in *English Historical Review*, XLIV (1929), pp. 418–432, on "The Jacobite Rising of 1715 and the English Catholics". The abortive negotiation between the Catholic leaders and the government is the subject of S. Baldwin's monograph, *The Catholic Negotiation of 1717–19* (Washington, 1926). Other useful works include E. L. Taunton, *History of the Jesuits in England* (London, 1901); Maude Petre, *Ninth Lord Petre* (London, 1928); and *Richard Challoner 1691–1781*, edited by D. Gwynn

(London, 1946), a volume of essays by various hands on this eminent Roman Catholic dignitary and scholar, which, however, does not supersede E. H. Burton, *Life and Times of Bishop Challoner* (2 vols., London, 1909).

VIII. JEWS

The standard history is still A. M. Hyamson, *History of the Jews in Great Britain* (2 vols., 1908, 2nd edition, 1928). Cecil Roth, *A Short History of the Jewish People* (enlarged edition, London, 1948), is much slighter but useful. There is also S. W. Baron, *A Social and Religious History of the Jews* (3 vols., New York, 1937), with an imposing bibliography. Not much attention was directed to the Jews in the eighteenth century except during the controversy on the Jew Naturalization Act of 1753, on which there are good accounts by A. M. Hyamson, "The Jew Bill of 1753" in *Transactions of the Jewish Historical Society*, VI (1912), pp. 156–188, and by G. B. Hertz in *British Imperialism in the 18th Century* (London, 1908). A. M. Hyamson, *The Sephardim of England* (London, 1951), has several interesting chapters on the eighteenth century.

A. CHURCH AND STATE

91. Edmund Gibson on the legal authority of the Church, 1713

(*Codex Juris Ecclesiastici Anglicani* (1713), p. xxix.)

Edmund Gibson (1669–1748) was bishop of London, 1720–1748, and Walpole's adviser on Church affairs. The extract is taken from the "introductory discourse concerning the present state of the Power, Discipline and Laws of the Church of England", for which Gibson was bitterly attacked in the 1730's. Though a Whig, he was in the moderate High Church tradition, and denied that the Church was subordinate to the State.

We have already observed, that *England* is governed by two distinct Administrations: one *Spiritual*, for matters of a Spiritual nature; and the other *Temporal*, for matters of a Temporal nature. And for the same ends, hath it two *Legislatures*, the one consisting of persons *Spiritual*, and the other of persons *Temporal*; whose business it is, to frame Laws for the Government of Church and State: and these Laws being Enacted and Confirmed by the Prince as *Sovereign*, and *Supreme Head*, become obligatory to the People, and Rules for the Administration of Justice in Spiritual and Temporal Matters. Before the Reformation, such Canons and Constitutions as were made in Provincial Synods, received their *last* Confirmation from the Metropolitan; who also had full power to publish and promulge them. And tho' it was provided by a Statute, in the 25th of *Henry* the Eighth, that no Constitutions should be thenceforth *enacted*, or *promulged*, without the King's Royal *Assent* and *Licence*; yet did not that Statute alter the Ecclesiastical Legislature in *other* respects, but, on the contrary, *supposed* the *legal* and *ancient* Authority of the Church, in that point. Altho' therefore this Statute is a *Recognition* and *Affirmance* of the Legislative Power of the Church, yet may not the authority of Canons and Constitutions be *solely* founded upon it, as some of the Books of Common Law do; since the ancient Ecclesiastical Power was not thereby *extinguished*, or *laid aside*, but only subjected to greater *Restraints* than it had been before.

92. A sermon by Benjamin Hoadly, bishop of Bangor, expressing the extreme Latitudinarian view of the Church, 1717

(*The Nature of the Kingdom, or Church of Christ. A Sermon preached before the King, at the Royal Chapel at St. James's, on Sunday, March 31, 1717. (Published by His Majesty's Special Command.) John xviii. 36. Jesus answered, My Kingdom is not of this World. Works of Benjamin Hoadly, D.D.*, II (1773), pp. 402–409.)

Benjamin Hoadly (1676–1761) was successively bishop of Bangor, Hereford, Salisbury and Winchester. This is the sermon which started the Bangorian controversy. In his pamphlet, *A Preservative against the Principles and Practices of the Non-Jurors* (1716), Hoadly had attacked the Non-Jurors' view that theirs was the only true Church, completely independent of the State. In his sermon he carried this argument still further, virtually demolishing the idea of a 'visible Church' altogether.

... 1. From what hath been said it is very plain, in general, that the Grossest Mistakes in Judgment, about the Nature of *Christ's Kingdom*, or *Church*, have arisen from hence, that Men have argued from Other visible *Societies*, and Other Visible *Kingdoms of this World*, to what ought to be Visible, and Sensible, in *His Kingdom*; Constantly leaving out of their *Notion*, the most Essential Part of it, that *Christ* is *King* in his own *Kingdom*; forgetting this *King* himself, because He is not now seen by mortal Eyes; and substituting *Others* in his Place, as *Law-givers* and *Judges*, in the same Points, in which *He* must either *Alone*, or not at all, be *Law-giver* and *Judge*; not contented with such a *Kingdom* as He established, and desires to reign in; but urging and contending, that *His Kingdom* must be like *Other Kingdoms*. Whereas He hath positively warned them against any such Arguings, by assuring Them that this *Kingdom* is *His Kingdom*, and that it is *not of this World*; and therefore that No *one* of *His Subjects* is *Law-giver* and *Judge* over *Others* of them, in matters relating to *Salvation*, but *He* alone; and that We must not Frame our Ideas from the *Kingdoms of this World*, of what ought to be, in a visible and sensible manner, in *His Kingdom*.

2. From what hath been said it appears that the *Kingdom* of *Christ*, which is the *Church* of *Christ*, is the *Number* of Persons who are Sincerely, and Willingly, *Subjects* to *Him*, as *Law-giver* and *Judge*, in all matters truly relating to Conscience, or Eternal Salvation. And the more close and immediate this Regard to *Him* is, the more certainly and the more evidently true it is, that They are of his *Kingdom*. This may appear fully to their own Satisfaction, if They have recourse to *Him* himself, in the *Gospel*; if They think it a sufficient Authority that He hath declared the *Conditions* of their *Salvation*, and that No Man upon Earth hath any Authority to declare any other, or to add one tittle to them; if They resolve to perform what They see, He laith a stress upon; and if They trust no mortal, with the absolute direction of their *Consciences*, the pardon of their Sins, or the determining of their Interest in God's favour; but wait for their *Judge*, who alone can bring to light *the hidden things of darkness*.

If They feel themselves disposed and resolved to receive the Words of *Eternal Life* from *Himself*; to take their *Faith* from what He himself *once delivered*, who knew better than All the rest of the World what he required of his own Subjects; to direct their *Worship* by his Rule, and their whole practice by the General Law which He laid down: If They feel themselves in this disposition, They may be very certain that They are truly his *Subjects*, and Members of his *Kingdom*. Nor need They envy the Happiness of *Others*, who may think it a much more evident Mark of their belonging to the *Kingdom* of *Christ*, that They have *other* Law-givers, and Judges, in *Christ's Religion*, besides *Jesus Christ*; that They have recourse not to *his own* Words, but to the Words of *Others* who profess to interpret them; that They are ready to Submit to this *Interpretation*, let it be what it will; that They have set up to Themselves the *Idol* of an unintelligible *Authority*, both in *Belief*, and *Worship*, and *Practice*; in Words, *under* Jesus Christ, but in deed and in truth *over* Him; as it removes the minds of his *Subjects* from *Himself*, to Weak, and passionate Men; and as it claims the same Rule and Power in *his Kingdom*, which He himself *alone* can have. But,

3. This will be *Another observation*, that it evidently destroys the *Rule* and *Authority* of *Jesus Christ*, as *King*, to set up any Other *Authority* in *His Kingdom*, to which His Subjects are indispensably and absolutely obliged to Submit their Consciences, or their Conduct, in what is properly called Religion. There are *some* Professed Christians, who contend openly for such an *Authority*, as indispensably obliges All around Them

to *Unity* of Profession; that is, to Profess even what They do not, what They cannot, believe to be true. This sounds so grossly, that *Others*, who think They act a glorious part in opposing such an Enormity, are very willing, for their own sakes, to retain such an *Authority* as shall oblige Men, whatever They themselves think, though not to profess what They do not believe, yet, to forbear the *profession* and *publication* of what They do believe, let them believe it of never so great Importance.

Both these *Pretensions* are founded upon the mistaken *Notion* of the *Peace*, as well as *Authority*, of the *Kingdom*, that is the *Church*, of *Christ*. Which of them is the most insupportable to an honest and a Christian mind, I am not able to say: because They both equally found the *Authority* of the *Church* of *Christ*, upon the ruines of Sincerity and Common Honesty; and mistake *Stupidity* and *Sleep*, for *Peace*; because They would both equally have prevented *All Reformation* where it hath been, and will for ever prevent it where it is not already; and, in a word, because both equally devest *Jesus Christ* of his *Empire* in *his own* Kingdom; set the obedience of his *Subjects* loose from *Himself*; and teach them to prostitute their Consciences at the feet of *Others*, who have no right in such a manner to trample upon them.

The *Peace* of *Christ's Kingdom* is a manly and Reasonable *Peace*; built upon Charity, and Love, and mutual forbearance, and receiving one another, as God receives us. As for any other *Peace*; founded upon a Submission of our *Honesty*, as well as our *Understandings*; it is falsely so called. It is not the *Peace* of the *Kingdom* of *Christ*; but the *Lethargy* of it: and a *Sleep unto Death*, when his *Subjects* shall throw off their relation to *Him*; fix their Subjection to *Others*, and even in Cases, where They have a right to see, and where They think They see, his Will otherwise, shall shut their Eyes and go blindfold at the Command of *Others*; because those *Others* are not pleased with their Enquiries into the Will of their great Lord and Judge.

To conclude, The *Church of Christ* is the *Kingdom of Christ*. He is *King* in his own Kingdom. He is Sole *Law-giver* to his Subjects, and Sole *Judge*, in matters relating to Salvation. His *Laws* and *Sanctions* are plainly fixed: and relate to the Favour of God; and not at all to the Rewards, or Penalties, of *this World*. All his Subjects are *equally* his Subjects; and, as such, *equally* without Authority to alter, to add to, or to *interpret*, his *Laws* so, as to claim the absolute Submission of *Others* to such *Interpretation*. And All are *His Subjects*, and in his Kingdom, who are ruled and governed by *Him*. Their *Faith* was *once* delivered by *Him*. The Conditions of their Happiness were *once* laid down by *Him*. The Nature of *God's Worship* was *once* declared by *Him*. And it is easy to judge, whether of the Two is most becoming a *Subject* of the *Kingdom* of *Christ*, that is, a Member of his *Church*; to seek all these particulars in those plain and short Declarations of their *King* and *Law-giver* himself: or to hunt after Them through the infinite contradictions, the numberless perplexities, the endless disputes, of *Weak Men*, in several Ages, till the Enquirer himself is lost in the Labyrinth, and perhaps sits down in Despair, or Infidelity. If *Christ* be our *King*; let us shew ourselves *Subjects* to *Him* alone, in the great affair of Conscience and Eternal Salvation: and, without fear of Man's judgment, live and act as becomes Those who wait for the appearance of an All-knowing and Impartial Judge; even *that King*, whose *Kingdom is not of this World*.

93. Representation of the Lower House of Convocation against Hoadly's doctrines and positions, 1717

(*Report of the Committee of the Lower House of Convocation . . . Concerning several Dangerous Positions and Doctrines, contained in the Bishop of Bangor's Preservative, and his Sermon preach'd March 31, 1717.* Reprinted Edinburgh (1717), pp. 3–6, 24–27.)

This attack by the predominantly High Church Lower House of Convocation upon Hoadly was the culmination of a long series of dissensions between the two Houses. It led to the suspension of Convocation until 1852.

To his Grace the Lord Archbishop of CANTERBURY,
And to the LORDS the
Bishops of the Province of Canterbury, in Convocation Assembled.

This Representation *from the* CLERGY *of the* Lower House *of* CONVOCATION, Humbly Sheweth,

THAT, with much Grief of Heart, we have observ'd, what, in all dutiful Manner, we now represent to your Grace and your Lordships, That the Right Reverend the Lord Bishop of Bangor, hath given great and grievous Offence, by certain Doctrines and Positions, by him lately published; partly in a Sermon, Intitled, *The Nature of the Kingdom or Church of* CHRIST: And partly in a Book, Intitled, *A Preservative against the Principles and Practices of the Non-jurors both in Church and State.*

The Tendency of the Doctrines and Positions contain'd in the said Sermon and Book, is conceiv'd to be,

(1) *First,* To subvert all Government and Discipline in the Church of *Christ* and to reduce his Kingdom to a State of *Anarchy* and *Confusion.*

(2) *Secondly,* To impugn and impeach the Regal Supremacy in Causes Ecclesiastical, and the Authority of the Legislature, to inforce Obedience in Matters of Religion, by Civil Sanctions.

The Passages in the Sermon and Book aforesaid, which are conceiv'd to carry the evil Tendency express'd under the First Article, are, principally, these that follow: SERMON, At *Page* 11. *Octavo Edit.*

His Lordship affirms–"As the Church of *Christ* is the Kingdom of *Christ,* he him- "self is King: And in this it is implied, That he is himself the sole Lawgiver to his "Subjects, and himself the sole Judge of their Behaviour, in the Affairs of Conscience "and eternal Salvation: And, in this Sense therefore, his Kingdom is not of this World; "That he hath, in those Points, left behind him no visible humane Authority, no "Vicegerents, who can be said, properly, to supply his Place; no Interpreters upon "whom his Subjects are absolutely to depend; no Judges over the Consciences or "Religion of his People." This Passage seems to deny all Authority to the Church, and, under Pretence of exalting the Kingdom of *Christ,* to leave it without any visible humane Authority to judge, censure, or punish Offenders, in the Affairs of Conscience and eternal Salvation. . . .

Your Lordships have now seen, under the *First Head,* That the Church hath no Governours, no Censures, no Authority over the Conduct of Men, in Matters of *Conscience* and *Religion.* You have seen under the *Second Head,* That the Temporal

Powers are excluded from any Right to encourage true Religion, or to discourage the contrary.

But to do Justice to his Lordship's Scheme, and to set it before you in its full Light, we must observe, That he further asserts, that *Christ* himself (the only Power not yet excluded) *never doth Inter*pose (*sic*) in the Direction of his Kingdom here, After observing, *Page* 13 *Sermon*. That Temporal Lawgivers do often Interpose to Interpret their own Laws, He adds . . . *But it is otherwise in Religion or the Kingdom of Christ. He himself never Interposeth, since his first Promulgation of his Law, either to convey Infallibility to such as pretend to handle it over again; Or to assert the true Interpretation of it, amidst the various and Contradictory Opinions of Men about it. To the same purpose he speaks at Page* 15 *in the Passage before cited.*

Since then there are, in the Church no Governours left: In the State none, who may intermeddle in the Affairs of Religion; and since *Jesus Christ* Himself never doth interpose; We leave it to your Grace, and your Lordships to judge, whether the Church and Kingdom of Christ be not reduced to a meer State of Anarchy and Confusion, in which every Man is left to do what is Right in his own Eyes.

And we beg leave to close these Observations in the Words of the Thirty Fourth Article of our Church, *Whosoever through his private Judgement, willingly and purposely doth openly break* (much more teach and encourage others to break) *The Traditions and Ceremonies of the Church, which be not repugnant to the Word of God, and be ordained and approved by common Authority ought to be rebuked openly* (*that others may fear to do the Like*) *as one that offendeth against the common Order of the Church, and hurteth the Authority of the Magistrate, and woundeth the Consciences of weak Brethren.*

Having thus laid before your Grace and your Lordships the several Passages upon which this our humble Representation is grounded together with our Observations on them; We must Profess our selves to be equally surprised and concerned, that Doctrines of so Evil a Tendency should be advanced by a Bishop of this establish'd Church, and that too in a Manner so very Remarkable. . . . That the Supremacy of the King should be openly impeach'd in a Sermon delivered in the Royal audience; and that the Constitution of the Church should be dangerously undermined in a Book professedly Written against the Principles and Practices of some who had departed from it.

But, so it hath happened, this right Reverend Bishop, in his extream Opposition to certain unwarrantable pretensions to extravagant degrees of Church Power, seems to have been so far Transported, beyond his Temper and his Argument, as not only to condemn the abuse, but even to deny the Use, and to destroy the being of these Powers, without which the Church, as a Society, cannot subsist, and by which our National Constitution, next under Christ, is chiefly supported.

Under these Apprehensions, We could not but hold our selves obliged to represent our own Sense, with that of our Brethren of the Clergy, to your Lordships; and to submit the Whole to your much Weightier Judgment, which we do, as with the most unfeigned Sorrow for the unhappy Occasion, and all becoming deference to our Superiours, so with the most sincere and dissinterested Zeal, and with no other View in the World, but to give Check to the Propagation of these Erroneous Opinions; so destructive of all Government and Discipline in the *Church*, and so derogatory to the Regal Supremacy and Legislative Authority, as we presume may have been sufficiently evinced. Of which our honest and loyal Intentions, we doubt not but your Lordships, in your known Goodness, will favourably apprize his Majesty, if it shall be thought needful or expedient, in order to set this Matter, together with our Proceedings thereupon, in a true and proper Light. . . .

94. William Warburton on the position of an established Church, 1736

(*The Alliance between Church and State: or the necessity and equity of an established religion*, 2nd ed. (1741), pp. 53–56, 67–69, 113–115.)

William Warburton (1698–1779) was bishop of Gloucester, 1759–1779. He represents the point of view of the 'Church-Whigs'.

BOOK II.

Of an Established Church.

SECT. I.

HAVING now dispatched the first Part of this Enquiry, and shewn,

I. The Origin of Civil Society,–the natural Deficiency of its Plan,–and how the Influence of Religion only can supply that Defect:

II. How all natural and moral Goods, and consequently *this* of Religion to the State, may be improved by human Art and Contrivance, together with the Necessity there is of *seeking* this Improvement: And,

III. As this depends on an exact Knowledge of a Civil and of a Religious Society, how to judge of their *distinct* Natures and Ends:

We are at length enabled to shew how this Improvement is to be brought about.

For having by a diligent Enquiry found,

I. First, *That the Care of the State extends only to the Body and its Concerns, and the Care of the Church only to the Soul;* it necessarily follows, that the Civil Magistrate, if he will improve this natural Influence of Religion by human Art and Contrivance, must seek some UNION OR ALLIANCE with the Church. For his Office not extending to the Care of Souls, he has not in himself Power to inforce the Influence of Religion: And the Church's Province not extending to the Body, and consequently without coercive Power; she has not, in herself *alone*, a Power of applying that Influence to Civil Purposes. The Consequence is, that their joint Powers must be employed thus to inforce and apply the Influence of Religion.–But they can never act conjointly but in Union and Alliance.

II. *Secondly*, Having found that *each Society is Sovereign, and independent on the other*, it as necessarily follows, that such Union can be produced *only* by FREE CONVENTION AND MUTUAL COMPACT: Because whatever is *sovereign* and *independent* can be brought to no Act without its own Consent: But nothing can give Birth to *a free Convention*, but a Sense of mutual Wants that may be supplied; or a View of mutual Benefits that may be gained by it. *Such*, then, is the Nature of that Union which produces a CHURCH BY LAW ESTABLISHED, and which is indeed no other than a *politic League and Alliance for mutual Support and Defence.* For the State not having *the Care of Souls,* cannot, itself, inforce the Influence of Religion; and therefore seeks the concurring *Aid of the Church*; and the Church having *no coercive Power,* (the Consequence of its Care not extending to Bodies,) as naturally flies *for Protection to the State.* This being of that Kind of *Alliance* which *Grotius* calls, FOEDUS INÆQUALE.–*Inæquale fœdus,* (says he,) *hic intelligo quod ex ipsa vi pactionis* manentem prælationem *quandam alteri donat: Hoc est ubi quis tenetur alterius imperium ac majestatem conservare*–UT POTENTIORI PLUS HONORIS, INFERIORI PLUS AUXILII DEFERATUR.[q]

From whence it appears, that were those common Notions true, which we have been at so much Pains to confute, concerning the Nature of a *Church* and *State,* there could be neither *Room* nor *Motive* for this *Alliance.* Were they not *independent on each other,* there would be no *Room*; because *Freedom of Will,* the very Essence of this Alliance, would be wanting on one Part: And had the *State the Care of Souls, or the Church the Care of Bodies,* there could be no mutual Motive; for, in such Case, the State might apply Religion, by its own Authority, to Civil Purposes; or the Church, having, in Consequence of the Care of Bodies, an inherent coercive Power, might *alone* provide for its own Security.

An *Alliance* then, by *free Convention,* being in its Nature *such* that each Party must have its Motives for compacting; our next Enquiry will be,

I. What those Motives were, which the State had of *seeking,* and the Church of *accepting* the Offers of an *Union.* And,

II. The mutual Benefits and Advantages thereby gained.

By the *first* Part of which Enquiry, we hope to make it appear, THAT THIS ALLIANCE WAS INDISPENSABLY NECESSARY FOR SECURING THE WELL BEING AND HAPPINESS OF CIVIL SOCIETY: And by the *second,* THAT NO COMMON RIGHT OF MAN, CIVIL OR RELIGIOUS, IS IMPEACHED BY IT. To demonstrate *which* is the principal End of this Discourse.

SECT. II.

THE Motives the State had to *seek* this Alliance were of three Kinds.

I. To preserve the Essence and Purity of Religion.

II. To improve its Usefulness, and apply its Influence in the best Manner.

III. To prevent the Mischief that, in its natural independent State, it might occasion to Civil Society.

. . . .

Having now delivered the principal Motives that engaged the State to *seek* an *Alliance* with the Church:

We come, in the next Place, to consider the Motives the Church had to *accept* it. For this being, as we observed, a FREE CONVENTION, unless the Church, as well as State, had its Views of Advantage, no *Alliance* could possibly have been formed. To discover these Motives we must recollect what has been said of the Nature and End of a *Religious Society*; for the Advantage adapted to that Nature and End, can only be her legitimate View; consequently then this Advantage can be no other than SECURITY FROM ALL OUTWARD VIOLENCE. The State indeed could not justly offer any to it, had

[q] *De Jure Bell. & Pac.* lib. i. cap. iii. § 21.

this Alliance never been made. But this is no Reason why the Church should not think it for its Interest to secure this its natural Right by *Compact*, any more than that one State should not bind another, in the same manner, not to do it Violence, tho' *that other* was under prior Obligations, by the Law of Nature and Nations to the same Purpose.

But by this Alliance between the two Societies the State does more; it not only promises not to injure the Church, but to serve it; that is, protect it from the Injuries of other Religious Societies, which exist or *may* arise in the same State. How one Religious Society may be injuriously affected by another, we have shewn just before: How great these Injuries may prove, we shall shew hereafter. It must needs then be the first Care of a Church, and *a reasonable Care*, to preserve itself by all lawful ways, from outward Violence. A State then, as we have said, to induce the Church to accept its Offers of *Alliance*, must propose some Benefit to her by it; and because this is the only *legitimate* Benefit the Church can receive, it must propose *this*; which therefore being considerable, will be the Church's *Motive for Alliance.*

There are but two other Considerations that can be thought *Motives*: The one, *To engage the State to propagate the Established Religion by Civil Force*: And the other, *To bestow Honours, Riches, and Powers upon it.* Now on recurring to the Nature and End of a Church and State, the *first* Motive will be found *unjust*, and the *second, impertinent.* It is *unjust* in the Church to require this Engagement; because the performing it would be violating the natural Right every Man has of worshipping God according to his own Conscience: It is *unjust* in the State to engage in it; because, as we have shewn, its Jurisdiction extends not to Opinions: It is *impertinent* in a Church to aim at Riches, Honours, Powers; because these are Things which, as a Church, she can neither use nor receive Profit from.–To imagine these fit Accomodations for a Church, as such, is as idle a Fancy as that of them who were for building sumptuous Tabernacles for the three Great Messengers of God at the Transfiguration. It is very true, that these Things (which, for the sake of the State, followed this Alliance) might be *in the private Views* of ambitious Churchmen, when an Alliance was projected; and might not a little help forward the Completion of it. But what Motives the *Clergy* of a Church might have, is nothing to the Purpose of our Enquiry; we are only to consider what the *Church* had, which, as a Religious Society, consists of the whole Body of the Community, both Laity and Clergy; and her Motive, we say, could not be Riches, Honours, and Power, because they have no natural Tendency to promote the *ultimate* End of this Society, *Salvation of Souls*; or the *immediate* End, *Purity of Worship.* We conclude therefore, that *the only legitimate Motive she could have, was Security and Protection from outward Violence.* This the Reader would do well to keep in Mind, because *much* will be found to depend on it in the Sequel of this Discourse.

On these mutual Motives then, was formed this FREE ALLIANCE; which gave Birth to a CHURCH BY LAW ESTABLISHED; and these being so forceable and strong, we are not to wonder that all States, of all Times, had an ESTABLISHED RELIGION; which was under the more immediate Protection of the Civil Magistrate, in Contradistinction to those that were only TOLERATED. . . .

Hitherto we have considered that Alliance, between Church and State, which produces an *Establishment*, only under its most simple Form, *i.e.* where there is but *one* Religion in the State. But it may so happen, that either at the Time of Convention, or afterwards, there may be *more than one*.

I. If there be *more than one at the Time of Convention*, the *Alliance* is made by the State with the *largest* of the Religious Societies. It is *fit* it should be so, because the larger the Religious Society is, where there is an Equality in other Points, the better enabled it will be to answer the Ends of the *Alliance*. As having the greatest Number under its Influence. It is *scarce possible* it should be otherwise, because the two Societies being composed of the same Individuals, the greatly prevailing Religion must have a Majority of its Members in the Assemblies of State: Who will naturally prefer their own Religion to all others.

With *this* is the Alliance made. And a full Toleration given to all the rest. Yet under the Restriction of a TEST-LAW to keep them from injuring that which is *established*.

Hence we may see,

1. The Reason and Equity of the *Episcopal Church*'s being the *Established* Church, in *England*, and the *Presbyterian*, the *Established* Church in *Scotland*: An Absurdity, *in Point of Right*, which our Adversaries imagined the Friends of an Establishment could never get clear of.

2. Hence we may see the Duration of this *Alliance*. It is *perpetual*, but not *irrevocable*, *i.e.* it subsists so long as the Church, thereby *Established*, maintains its Superiority of Extent; which, when it loses to any considerable Degree, the Union is dissolved. For the united Church being then no longer able to perform its Part of the *Convention*, which is formed on reciprocal Conditions, the State becomes disengaged. And a new Alliance is, of Necessity, entered into with the *now* prevailing Church, for the Reasons before given. Thus, of old, the Alliance between the *Pagan Church* and the Empire of *Rome* was dissolved, and the *Christian* united to the State in its Place: And again, in these later Times the Alliance between the *Popish Church* and the Kingdom of *England* was broken, and another made with the *Protestant Church* in its stead.

II. If these different Religions arise *after* the Alliance hath been formed, whenever they become considerable, *then* is a *Test-Law* necessary for the Security of the *Established Church*. For when there are Diversities of Religions in a State, each of which thinks itself the only *true*, or, at least, the most *pure*, every one aims at advancing itself on the Ruins of the rest: Which it calls, *bringing into Conformity* with itself; and, when Reason fails, will attempt to do it by the Civil Aid. Which can be only brought about by the Attempter's getting into the public Administration. But when it happens that one of these Religions is the *Established*, and all the rest under a *Toleration*, then it is that these *latter*, still more inflamed, as stimulated with Envy at the Advantages the Established Church enjoys, act in concert, and proceed with joint Attacks to disturb its Quiet. In this imminent Danger, the *Established Church* demands the promised Aid of the State; which gives her a TEST-LAW for her Security. Whereby the Entrance into the Administration, (the only Way, that Mischief to the Established Church is effected) is shut to all but the Members of that Church. So when the *Sectaries*, in the Time of *Charles* the First, had, for want of *this Law*, destroyed the

Established Church; as soon as the Government of *England* was restored on its old Foundations, the Legislature thought fit to make a *Test-Law* (tho' with the latest) to prevent a Repetition of the like Disasters.

Thus a *Test-Law* took its Birth; whether at, or after the Time of Alliance. And from this Moment is the Justice and Equity of an *Established Church* called in question. But that the State is under the highest Obligations of Justice to provide this Security, we shall now shew.

B. THE CONDITION OF THE CHURCH OF ENGLAND

(a) ECCLESIASTICAL REVENUES

95. Values and Patrons of Benefices, *circa* 1780

(Rev. John Lloyd, *Thesaurus Ecclesiasticus: an improved edition of the Liber Valorum* (1788), pp. 241–242, 249, 277–278, 310–311.)

The *Liber Valorum* was compiled in 1711 by John Ecton, an official in the office of Queen Anne's Bounty, and many editions appeared during the eighteenth century. Extracts have been chosen from the dioceses of London, Norwich and Salisbury because the real value of livings is given more often in these dioceses than in others.

THE PREFACE.

The Editor had long ago formed a design of giving the Public a New Edition of Ecton's Thesaurus; the former ones having become very defective, as well by the exchange of property in private Patronages, as by the improved value of almost all the Livings in the kingdom. And, in order to render such a publication as compleat as possible, he has spared no pains to procure on both these points the best information that could be had. Many of the Clergy have been applied to, and have been so good as to favour him with satisfactory accounts of the livings in their respective neighbourhoods; and he has taken such further advantages as the best and latest editions have afforded. Yet it was impossible, after all his labour, to come at the real value of every living: wherever he has aimed at it, he begs it to be in general understood, that it has been his rule to undervalue, rather than to overrate them. . . .

In the livings *remaining in charge*, where their real value can with any degree of precision be ascertained, an asterisk is prefixed to the figures in the first column; which, so distinguished, denote, not their valuation in the King's Book, but their real value; and, in such case the tenths, in the last column, multiplied by *ten*, will always shew their valuation in the King's Book. . . . So likewise the tenths of the livings, *discharged from first fruits*, multiplied by *ten*, will shew the value of those livings, as they stood in the King's Book before the Act of Parliament for their discharge. . . .

London Dioces.

HERTF' D. SANCTI ALBANI.

LIVINGS REMAINING IN CHARGE.

K.B.			BENEFICES.	PATRONS.	*Yearly Tenths.*		
*300	0	0	Bushey, R.	*Exeter Coll. Oxon.*	1	6	2½
*300	0	0	Barnett, R.	*The* KING.	2	4	3¼
*130	0	0	Petri Sti. V.	*Bp. of Ely.*	0	18	1
*140	0	0	Rickmansworth, V.	*The Bishop.*	1	12	0
*120	0	0	Sarett, V.	*Arn. Duncomb.*	0	18	0
*120	0	0	Shephall, V.	*The* KING.	0	18	7
*250	0	0	Watford, V.	*Ld. Essex.*	2	3	2½
* 70	0	0	Walden Abbots, V.	*D. and Ch. of St. Paul's.*	1	0	0

LIVINGS DISCHARGED.

Clear Yearly Value.			BENEFICES.	PATRONS.	Yearly Tenths.		
100	0	0	Albani Sti., V.	*Corpor. of St. Alban's.*	1	0	0
80	0	0	Codicote, V.	*Bishop of Ely.*	0	14	7
20	0	0	Hexton, V.	*Fr. Hawkins.*	0	15	4
160	0	0	Elstree, R.	*The* KING.	0	16	0
90	0	0	Langley Abbotts, V.	*B. Filmer.*	1	10	0
100	0	0	Mich. Sti. V. in Vil.	*Ld. Grimston.*	1	0	1½
30	0	0	Notton, V.	*Ro. Haslefoot.*	0	10	8
30	0	0	Newenham, V.	*Ph. Yorke.*	0	10	0
40	0	0	Rydge, V.	*Ph. Yorke.*	0	13	4
70	0	0	Redburne, V.	*Ld. Grimston.*	1	12	6
110	0	0	Steph. Sti. V. in Vil.	*Ca. Lomax.*	1	10	0
70	0	0	Sandridge, V.	*Ld. Spencer.*	0	16	0

. . .

Norwicen' Dioces.

NORF'

D. BRECKLES.

LIV:NGS REMAINING IN CHARGE.

K.B.							
*130	0	0	Ashill, R.	*Th. Watts.*	1	19	4¼
* 90	0	0	Caston, R.	*Ja. Tyllyard.*	1	3	11
*130	0	0	Sayham Tonye, R.	*Winchester Coll.*	2	3	5¾

LIVINGS DISCHARGED.

Clear Yearly Value.							
13	9	8	Breckles, V.	*Sir Ro. Gardiner.*	0	15	9½
10	11	11	Carbrooke, V.	*Ld. Howard de Walden.*	0	15	3
140	0	0	Elingham parva, R.	*T. Bond.*	0	14	2¼
50	0	0	Griston, V.	*Bp. of Ely.*	0	14	10½
60	0	0	Merton, R.	*Ld. Walsingham.*	0	12	0½
60	0	0	Ovington, R.	*Th. Wright.*	0	14	4¼
70	0	0	Stow Bedon, V.	*Ja. Smith.*	0	9	11¼
8	0	0	Scoulton, R.	*Jn. Weyland.*	1	0	5
70	0	0	Threxton, R.	*Bp. of Norwich.*	0	14	5¾
20	0	0	Tottington, V.	*Gov. of Chigwell School*	0	13	5¾
60	0	0	Watton, V.	*Fr. Hicks.*	0	14	0½
20	0	0	Thompson, Cur.	*Mr Coleman.*	–	–	–

SUFF'

D. ORFORD.

LIVINGS REMAINING IN CHARGE.

K.B.			BENEFICES.	PATRONS.	Yearly Tenths.		
20	0	0	Blaxall, R.	*Mrs Jackson.*	2	0	0
* 70	0	0	Glenham parva, R.	*Mrs Herbert.*	0	12	0
*300	0	0	Sudbourn, R.	*The* KING.	3	6	8
9	2	8½	Sweftling, R.	*Mrs Copland.*	0	18	3¼
* 80	0	0	Sternefield, R.	*Ch. Long.*	0	17	5¼

LIVINGS DISCHARGED.

Clear Yearly Value.							
60	0	0	Aldburghe, V.	*Ld. Strafford.*	3	6	8
35	0	0	Benhall, V.	*Jn. Rush.*	0	14	1½
50	0	0	Cransford, V.	*Jer. Pemberton.*	0	13	4
40	0	0	Chesilford, R.	*G. Bitton.*	0	10	4
50	0	0	Eken, R.	*Chr. Jeafferson.*	0	13	4
50	0	0	Freston, V. cum Snape, V.	*Ld. Strafford.*	0 0	10 10	0 6¾
70	0	0	Stratford Sti. Andr., R.	*The* KING.	0	10	0
60	0	0	Saxmundham, R.	*Ch. Long.*	0	17	7
50	0	0	Tunstall, R.	*Chr. Jeafferson.*	1	13	0½
15	0	0	Farnham, Don.	*Ch. Long.*			
20	0	0	Glenham, Don.	*Mrs Herbert.*			
40	0	0	Rendham, V.	*W. Barnet.*			

. . .

Sarum Dioces.

WILTS'

D. AVEBURY.

LIVINGS REMAINING IN CHARGE.

K.B.							
*300	0	0	Alcannings, R.	*J. Fullerton.*	3	3	8¼
*200	0	0	Alton Barnes, R.	*New Coll. Oxon.*	0	13	10¾
*400	0	0	Bremhill, V.	*The Bishop.*	1	10	6
*200	0	0	Bromeham, R.	*E. B. Rolt.*	1	5	7½
*120	0	0	Bechingstoke, R.	*J. W. Heneage.*	0	14	3½
*120	0	0	Cannings Episcopi, V.	*D. and Chap.*	1	11	11
*200	0	0	Compton Bassett, R.	*The Bishop.*	1	6	8¼
8	5	0	Calne, V.	*Treasurer of Sarum.*	0	16	6
*100	0	0	Cleve Pepper, V.	*Edw. Goddard.*	0	18	0

K.B.			BENEFICES.	PATRONS.	*Yearly*	*Tenths.*	
*150	0	0	Helmerton, V.	*The* KING.	2	0	8
* 80	0	0	Hedington, R.	*Fr. Rogers*	0	17	5¼
* 80	0	0	Henton Magna, V.	*Lady W. Glanville.*	1	9	10¾
2	15	7½	Newenton, P.	*The Bishop.*	0	5	6¾
* 40	0	0	Newenton, R.	*Ld. Pembroke.*	0	14	1½
*140	0	0	Overton, R.	*Duke of Marlborough.*	2	6	0½
*100	0	0	Stanton, P.	*Ld. Pembroke.*	1	5	1¾
*100	0	0	Tokenham, R.	*The* KING.	0	13	4
*160	0	0	Wooton Bassett, V.	*Ld. Clarendon.*	1	4	0
*300	0	0	Winterborne Bassett, R.	*Magd. Coll. Oxon.*	1	16	11½
*160	0	0	Woodborrow, R.	*Ch. Gibbs.*	1	0	0
*120	0	0	Yatesbury, R.	*Mrs Ernley.*	1	14	4

LIVINGS DISCHARGED.

Clear Yearly Value.							
140	0	0	Avebury, V.	*The* KING.	0	18	0
39	0	0	Blakeland, R.	*Th. Smyth and others.*	0	7	1
46	0	0	Caleston, R.	*Th. Ducket.*	0	9	4
40	0	0	Mownton, V.	*The* KING.	0	10	0
50	0	0	Round, V.	*Sir Edw. Bayntun.*	0	13	0¼
80	0	0	Stanton Bernard, V.	*Ld. Pembroke.*	0	14	0

96. Richard Watson's proposals for the reform of the whole system of ecclesiastical patronage, 1783

(Richard Watson, *A Letter to his Grace the Archbishop of Canterbury* (1783), pp. 6–11, 19–22, 25–28.)

Richard Watson (1737–1816) was successively Professor of Chemistry and of Divinity at Cambridge; archdeacon of Ely, 1779; bishop of Llandaff, 1782–1816.

To keep your Grace no longer in suspense as to the meaning of this address, I have two proposals to make to you; one respects the Revenues of the Bishops; the other those of the inferior Clergy; both of them tending to the same end;–not a parity of preferments, but a better apportioned distribution of what the State allows for the maintenance of the established clergy.

... Whatever was the primary occasion of it, the fact is certain–that the Revenues of the Bishopricks are very unequal in value, and that there is a great inequality also in the Patronage appertaining to the different Sees. The first proposal which I humbly submit to your Grace's deliberation, is the utility of bringing a Bill into Parliament–to render the Bishopricks more equal to each other, both with respect to income and patronage, by annexing part of the Estates, and part of the preferments of the richer Bishopricks, *as they become vacant*, to the poorer. ...

1. By a Bill of this kind, the poorer Bishops would be freed from the necessity of holding Ecclesiastical preferments *in commendam* with their Bishopricks; a practice

which bears hard upon the rights and expectations of the rest of the Clergy; which is disagreeable to the Bishops themselves; which exposes them to much, perhaps, undeserved obloquy, but which certainly had better not subsist in the Church. I do not take upon me to fix the precise sum which would enable a Bishop not to pollute Gospel Humility with the Pomp of Prelacy, not to emulate the Noble and Opulent in such luxurious and expensive levities as become neither Churchmen nor Christians; but to maintain such a decent establishment in the world as would give weight to his example, and authority to his admonition; to make such a moderate provision for his children, as their father's mode of living would give them some little right to expect; and to recommend his religion by works of charity, to the serious examination of unbelievers of every denomination. The Sum requisite for these purposes admits of great latitude; some would think that it ought to be more, others that it ought to be less than the Salaries of the Judges; but the revenues of the Bishopricks, if more equally divided, would, probably, be sufficient to afford to each Bishop a sum, not much different from a Judge's salary; and they would do this even supposing that it should be thought right, to make no defalcation from the present incomes of the two Archbishopricks. But whether the Incomes of the Bishops should, by the proposed alteration, be made a little greater or a little less than those of the Judges, still would they be sufficient for the purpose of rendering *Commendams* wholly unnecessary.

2. A second consequence of the Bill proposed, would be a greater independence of the Bishops in the House of Lords.–I know that many will be startled, I beg them not to be offended, at the Surmise of the Bishops not being independent in the House of Lords; and it would be easy enough to weave a logical cobweb, large enough and strong enough to cover and protect the conduct of the Right Reverend Bench from the attacks of those who dislike Episcopacy. This I say would be an easy task, but it is far above my ability to eradicate from the minds of others, (who are, notwithstanding, as well attached to the Church Establishment as ourselves), a suspicion, that the prospect of being translated influences the minds of the Bishops too powerfully, and induces them to pay too great an attention to the beck of a Minister. I am far from saying or thinking, that the Bishops of the present age are more obsequious in their attention to Ministers than their Predecessors have been, or that the Spiritual Lords are the only Lords who are liable to this suspicion, or that Lords in general, are the only persons on whom expectation has an influence; but the suspicion, whether well or ill founded, is disreputable to our order; and, what is of worse consequence, it hinders us from doing that good which we otherwise might do; for the Laity, whilst they entertain such a suspicion concerning us, will accuse us of Avarice and Ambition, of making a gain of Godliness, of bartering the dignity of our Office for the chance of a translation, in one word of–Secularity–; and against that Accusation they are very backward in allowing the Bishops or the Clergy in general, such kind of defence as they would readily allow to any other class of Men, any other denomination of Christians, under the similar circumstances, of large families and small fortunes. . . .

3. A third probable effect, of the proposed plan, would be a longer residence of the Bishops in their respective Dioceses; from which the best consequences might be expected. When the temptations to wish for translations were in a great measure

removed, it would be natural for the Bishops, in general, to consider themselves as settled for life, in the Sees to which they should be first appointed; this consideration would induce them to render their places of residence more comfortable and commodious; and an opportunity of living more comfortably, would beget an inclination to live more constantly in them. Being wedded as it were to a particular Diocese, they would think it expedient to become, and they would of course become better acquainted with their Clergy; and by being better acquainted with the situations, prospects, tempers, and talents of their Clergy, they would be better able to co-operate with them, in the great work of amending the Morals of his Majesty's subjects, and of feeding the flock of Christ. It is the duty of Christian Pastors in general, and of the principal Shepherds particularly, *to strengthen that member of the flock which is diseased, to heal that which is sick, to bind up that which is broken, to bring again that which is driven away, and seek that which is lost*: that these and other parts of the pastoral office can never be so well performed, as when the Shepherd is resident in the midst of his flock, can admit of no question. The manners of the English Bishops are (I trust I speak rightly–I am certain I mean not to speak flatteringly) as pure and irreprehensible as those of any other Prelates in Europe; and as the world in general lives more according to fashion than reason, it is not easy to conceive what beneficial influence the Examples of the Bishops, residing in their Dioceses, and letting their light shine before men who would be disposed to observe it, would have on the lives and conversations of both Clergy and Laity.

I have long considered the Clergy who are dispersed through the kingdom, as a little leaven preserving, from extreme corruption, the whole mass; and the great kindness and respect, with which the whole order is treated by the best and most enlightened part of the Laity, is a proof that they consider them in the same light. Your Grace's candour and moderation will excuse me, if in this commendation I include the Dissenting Clergy, whom I cannot look upon as inferior to the Clergy of the Establishment, either in learning or morals. It is owing principally to the teaching and example of the Clergy in general, that there is not more infidelity in the highest, more immorality in the lowest classes of the community; but there would, probably, be less of both, if we were all of us, in the words of Bishop Burnet addressed to George I, "obliged to live and to labour more suitably to our profession." It may be urged, that the attendance of the Bishops in the House of Lords, is inconsistent with the residence here spoken of–in no wise–; a longer residence does not imply a continual residence; in the course of the year opportunity enough may be found to let the State have, on important occasions, the benefit of their Advice; and their Dioceses, on most occasions, the benefit of their inspection; and they will be best able to judge for themselves where, at any particular time, their presence will be of most use. . . .

The second thing which I have to recommend to your Grace's attention is the introduction of a Bill into Parliament–For appropriating, *as they become vacant*, one third or some other definite part, of the Income of every Deanery, Prebend or Canonry, of the Churches of Westminster, Windsor, Christchurch, Canterbury, Worcester, Durham, Norwich, Ely, Peterborough, Carlisle, &c. to the same purposes, *mutatis mutandis*, as the First Fruits and Tenths were appropriated by the Act passed in the fifth of Queen Anne. Dignities which after this deduction would not yield one hundred a year, should not I think be meddled with.–If any one, in the outset of this inquiry, should be forward to object; that many of these Preferments, being in the Patronage of the Crown, ought not be to lessened without his Majesty's especial consent; let such an one know, that there is no wish to lessen them without that consent; but this consent, we are certain, will not be withheld if the proposal shall appear to his Majesty to be for the credit of the Church, and the good of his Subjects; and God prevent its taking effect if it will not be for both.

This proposal will, I am sensible, be very differently received by different sorts of men: some will consider it as an attack upon the Hierarchy, as tending to lower the Church Establishment; others will think that it does not go far enough, they will prefer levelling to lowering, the abolition of Deans and Chapters to their reduction. So much may reasonably be said on both sides, that I cannot, on this occasion, stop to say any thing on either side; and my business indeed, is not so much with Deans and Chapters, as with a very useful, with what some will not scruple to call the most useful part of the Clergy–the Parochial Clergy. The general provision for this class of men, is so exceedingly scanty and mean, that there surely can be no impropriety in wishing, that it may be increased; especially when the increase is proposed to be made, without either reclaiming any part of the Church Property, which was by strange means enough conveyed into Lay hands; or imposing any new burdens on the community in general; or taking from any one of the Clergy the least part of what he is at present possessed of.

The Revenue of the Church of England is not, I think, well understood in general; at least I have met with a great many very sensible men, of all professions and ranks, who did not understand it. They have expressed a surprise, bordering on disbelief, when I have ventured to assure them, that the whole income of the Church, including Bishopricks, Deans and Chapters, Rectories, Vicarages, Dignities and Benefices of all kinds, and even the two Universities with their respective Colleges, which being Lay Corporations ought not to be taken into the account, did not amount, upon the most liberal calculation, to 1500000L. a year. I will not trouble your Grace with the manner of making this calculation, but I have good reason to believe it to be near the truth, it is certainly near enough for the inference which I wish to draw from it, which is simply this,–that if we had no Bishops to inspect and govern the Church; no Deaneries, Prebends, or Canonries to stimulate the Clergy to excel in literary attainments; no Universities or Colleges (which with all their faults are the best Seminaries of Education in Europe) to instruct our youth; nothing but Parochial Clergy, and all of these provided for by an equal partition, notwithstanding the great inequality of their merits, of the present Ecclesiastical Revenues, there would not be, estimating the number of the Clergy at ten thousand, above 150L. a year for each individual. I would not be understood to affect a mathematical precision in this matter, the subject would admit it, but the present *data* are not sufficient to enable any person to make it; but whether we suppose an officiating Minister to have 120L. or 150L. a year, it is a sum not much to be envied him. Apothecaries and Attornies, in very moderate practice, make as much by their respective professions; without having been at the same expences with the Clergy in their Educations, and without being, like them, prohibited by the laws of their Country, from bettering their circumstances, by uniting to the Emoluments of their professions, the profits resulting from farming or any kind of trade.

(*b*) THE WORK OF THE CLERGY

97. John Brown's view of the clergy, 1757–1758

(John Brown, *An Estimate of the Manners and Principles of the Times* (1757–1758), I, pp. 82–86; II, pp. 117–118.)

John Brown (1715–1766) was rector of Great Horkesley, Essex, and later of St. Nicholas, Newcastle upon Tyne. Macaulay attributed the great success of the *Estimate* to the fact that its denunciations of the degeneracy of the times exactly fitted the "state of angry and sullen despondency" of the nation at this time.

THERE is another *Profession*, which, under this Article of the *national Capacity*, the vulgar Reader will naturally expect to find considered. I mean, that of the *Clergy*. But the general Defect of religious Principle among the higher Ranks, hath rendered this Order of Men altogether useless, except among those in *middle Life*, where they still maintain a certain Degree of Estimation. The Contempt with which not *they*, but their *Profession* is treated by the *Ignorant* and *Profligate*, is equally common indeed to *high* and *low* Life. . . .

AND although the present fashionable Contempt that is thrown upon their *Profession*, preclude the Clergy from the *Opportunity*, had they the *Will*, to practice that Christian Duty of "overcoming Evil with Good;" yet they need not blush to find, that they have *fallen* with the *Fame*, the *Manners*, and *Principles*, of their Country: Nor can the worthy Part of them, sure, aspire to *truer Glory*, than to have become the *Contempt of* EUROPE.

BUT while I defend and *honour* the *Profession*, I mean not to flatter the *Professors*. As far, therefore, as the Influence of *their* Conduct and Knowledge can be supposed to affect the *national Capacity*; so far, they seem falling into the same unmanly and effeminate Peculiarities, by which their Contemporaries are distinguished: Such of them, I mean, as have Opportunity of conversing with what is called *the World*, and are supposed to make a Part of it. In their Conduct they *curb not*, but *promote* and encourage the trifling Manners of the Times: It is grown a fashionable thing, among these Gentlemen, to despise the Duties of their Parish; to wander about, as the various Seasons invite, to every Scene of false Gaiety; to *frequent* and *shine* in all *public* Places, their own *Pulpits* excepted.

OR if their Age and Situation sets them above these puerile Amusements, are we not to lament, that, instead of a manly and rational Regard to the Welfare of Mankind, the chief Employment of many a clerical Life is, to slumber in a *Stall*, haunt *Levees*, or follow the gainful Trade of *Election-jobbing*?

IF false Pleasure and Self-Interest thus take Possession of the Heart, how can we expect that a Regard for Religion and Christianity should find a *Place* there?

IN Consequence of these ruling Habits, must we not farther lament, that a general Neglect of *Letters* is now creeping even upon this Profession, which ought to maintain and support them? Instead of launching into the *Deeps* of Learning, the fashionable *Divine* hardly ventures on the *Shallows*. The great Works of *Antiquity*, the Monuments of ancient Honour and Wisdom, are seldom *opened* or *explored*: and even mere *modern* Books are now generally read at *second Hand*, through the false Mediums of bald *Translations* or sorry *Abstracts*.

THIS seems to be the real State of the *clerical* Profession, so far as it hath Influence on the *national Capacity*. . . .

. . . The Truth is, the Clergy are neither better nor worse than other Men, but are naturally carried along in the general Stream of Manners. And hence, it must be owned and lamented, that Religion cannot possibly have that Influence in the luxurious and effeminate Period, which it hath in simpler Times; on Account of that ruling System of Manners in which its Ministers will naturally be involved. . . .

AT the same Time it must be confessed (or, if you please, it shall be maintained) that the Idea of a proper clerical Conduct is carried higher in *Speculation*, than human Nature will in Reality admit. The Laity seem to forget that the Clergy are Men of like Passions with themselves. From this Archetype of *ideal* Perfection, it comes to pass, that any *Ridicule* in this Order of Men is *doubly ridiculous*; any *Crime*, doubly *criminal*. Yet, with all their Defects and Frailties, the Writer is of Opinion, that, among the middle Ranks of this Profession, there is more Regard to Duty, more open and undesigning Hospitality, more unaffected Generosity, as well as Charity and Piety, than in any other Order of Men now in Being. . . .

98. Archbishop Secker's charge to the clergy in the diocese of Canterbury, 1762

(Thomas Secker, late Lord Archbishop of Canterbury, *Eight Charges delivered to the Clergy of the Dioceses of Oxford and Canterbury* (1769), pp. 245, 250–255.)

Thomas Secker (1693–1768) was bishop of Bristol, 1734–1737; of Oxford, 1737–1758; and archbishop of Canterbury, 1758–1768.

Reverend Brethren,

It having pleased God that I should live to come amongst you a second Time, I think it my Duty to proceed with the same Kind of Exhortations, which I gave you at first. For though many Subjects of Instruction might be proper, there is a peculiar Propriety in those, which relate more immediately to your Conduct: . . .

Too possibly a great Part of our People may like the lukewarm amongst us the better for resembling themselves, and giving them no Uneasiness on Comparison, but seeming to authorize their Indifference. But then, such of us can do them no Good. Our Example can teach them nothing beyond a little decent Regularity, in which they will fancy they need not quite come up to us neither. Our Sermons, and reading of Prayers, they will consider only as Matters of Form: and finding in us hardly any Thing at other Times of what we express at these, they will presume, that our inward Regard to it is not very great, and that they are not bound to have more. Therefore, if they are pleased with us, if they esteem us, while we continue to be of this Turn, it must be for something foreign from our Office, something of a middle, or it may be a blamable Nature, not as Teachers of the Gospel: a Character which they take us to lay aside as much as we well can. And so the better they think of Us, the more lightly they will think of our Ministry; till at length they join with those avowed Infidels, who boldly affirm, though often against their own Consciences, that we believe not what we preach, else it would have more Influence upon us.

Then, at the same Time, the right Dispositions of well inclined Persons will languish and decay, for Want of that Countenance and Assistance in serious Piety, which they should receive from their Pastors. For if the Tokens of our Piety be confined to the Church, they will be of little Service either out of it, or in it. Or if some good People suffer no Harm themselves from our Defects, they will see with great Sorrow, that others do: all of them will be much readier to think the Clerical Order in general careless and light, if those are so, of whom they see most: their Ears will be open to the Invectives, which artful or heated Men are daily pouring forth against us: they will easily be led to undervalue and misconstrue the best Instructions of those, with whom they are disgusted; and run after any Teachers, who have the powerful Recommendation, for it will always, and no Wonder, be a very powerful one, of seeming more in earnest. The Irregularities and Divisions which have prevailed so lamentably in our Church of late, are greatly owing to an Opinion, that we are usually indifferent about vital inward Religion. It is true, the Spreaders of this Imputation, which hath been monstrously exaggerated, will have much to answer for: but so shall we also, unless we take the only Way to silence it, by cutting off hereafter all Occasion for it.

Now the first necessary Step to seem good is to be so; for mere Pretence will be seen through: and the next is, to *let your Light shine before Men*, in the faithful and laborious Exercise of your Function. Living amongst your Parishioners, or as near them as may be: inquiring frequently and personally concerning the Welfare and Behaviour of those, with whom you cannot be statedly present; reverent and judicious Reading of the Prayers and Lessons in your Churches, instructive and affecting Sermons delivered with discreet Warmth, Readiness to take extraordinary Pains for the occasional Assistance of your Brethren, Diligence in forming the Youth to a Sense of their Christian Duty, in bringing your People to the holy Communion, and where it can be, to Week-Day Prayers: all these Things will tend very much both to your Usefulness and your Credit. Relieving or obtaining Relief for such as are distressed in their Circumstances: hearing your People willingly and patiently, though perhaps low in Rank or weak in Understanding, when they would consult you upon any Difficulty, and answering them with Consideration and Tenderness: disposing them to be visited when sick, praying by them with Fervency, exhorting and comforting them with Fidelity, Compassion and Prudence; and reminding them strongly, yet mildly, after their Recovery, of their good Thoughts and Purposes during their Illness; will be further Proofs, very beneficial and very engaging ones, of your Seriousness: which however you must complete by going through every other Office of Religion with Dignity. I will specify two.

One is that of Baptism: which, especially when administered in private Houses without Necessity, is too often treated, even during the Administration, rather as an idle Ceremony than a Christian Sacrament: or however that be, is commonly close followed by very unsuitable, if not otherwise also indecent Levity and Jollity. Now in these Circumstances it is highly requisite, that the Minister should by a due Mixture of Gravity and Judgment support the Solemnity of the Ordinance; and either prevent Improprieties in the Sequel, or if it be doubtful whether he can, excuse himself with a civil Intimation of the Unfitness of them, from being present. The other Instance is, that of saying Grace over our daily Food: which many, if not most, of the Laity have, with a Profaneness more than heathenish, laid aside: and I am sorry to add, that some of the Clergy hurry it over so irreverently, in a Mutter or a Whisper, scarce, if at all, intelligible, that one might question, whether they had not better lay it aside too, which yet God forbid, than make it thus insignificant; and expose to Contempt an Act of Devotion, and themselves along with it, as doing what they are ashamed of.

99. Archbishop Herring's primary visitation of the diocese of York, 1743

(*Archbishop Herring's Visitation Returns, 1743*, ed. S. L. Ollard and P. C. Walker, Yorks. Arch. Soc., Records Series (1928–1931), I, pp. 2–3; II, pp. 31–33; IV, pp. 81–83 131–132.)

Thomas Herring (1693–1757) was bishop of Bangor, 1737–1743; archbishop of York, 1743–1747; and archbishop of Canterbury, 1747–1757.

The Letter from the Archbishop to the Clergy.

Good Brother,

Being by God's Providence call'd to a new Diocese, with the Circumstances whereof I am very much unacquainted, I shall hold myself extreamly oblig'd to You for your Assistance in the Administration of it. To render that more effectual, I send to you and the rest of my Clergy the following Paper of Questions; a clear and satisfactory return to which under the Hand of every several Minister and delivered to my Secretary, or the Register, at the Time of my Visitation, will make me much better acquainted with the Circumstances of this large Diocese, than I cou'd be by any other way, save that of a Parochial Visitation, which it is out of my power to take.

You will therefore be so good as to gratify my request herein, and as this is the only design of my sending these Enquiries to You, You may rest perfectly assured, that no other use shall be made of them, but for my own Information; and for that reason I will hope that You will deal very freely and plainly with me in your Answers to the several Questions.

To God's Favour and Blessing I heartily commend yourself, and your Labours in His Church, and remain,

Reverend Sir,

Your very affectionate Brother,

Tho. Ebor.

Kensington,

2, May 1743.

To the Minister of ....

in the Deanry of ....

QUESTIONS.

I. What Number of Families have you in your Parish? Of these, how many are Dissenters? And of what Sort are they?

II. Have you any Licens'd or other Meeting House in your Parish? How many? Of what Sort? How often do they assemble? In what Numbers? Who teaches in them?

III. Is there any public or Charity School, endow'd, or otherwise maintain'd in your Parish? What Number of Children are taught in it? And what Care is taken to instruct them in the Principles of the Christian Religion, according to the Doctrine of the Church of England; and to bring them duly to Church, as the Canon requires?

IV. Is there in your Parish, any Alms-House, Hospital, or other Charitable Endowment? Have any Lands or Tenements been left for the Repair of your Church; or to any other pious Use? Who has the Direction of such Benefactions? How are they managed? Do you know, or have you heard of any Abuses or Frauds committed in the Management of them?

V. Do you reside Personally upon your Cure, and in your Parsonage House? If not, where do you reside? And what is the Reason of your Non-Residence?

VI. Have you a Residing Curate? Is he duly qualified according to the Canons in that Behalf? Does he live in your Parsonage House? What allowance do you make him?

VII. Do you know of any who come to Church in your Parish that are not Baptized? Or that being Baptized, and of a competent Age, are not confirmed?

VIII. How often is the public Service read in your Church? Is it duly perform'd twice every Lord's-Day? If not how often, and at what Times is it perform'd? And how comes it not to be twice done, as the Act of Uniformity and Canons of the Church require?

IX. How often and at what Times do you Catechise in your Church? Do your Parishioners duly send their Children and Servants who have not learned their Catechism, to be instructed by you?

X. How often is the Sacrament of the Lord's Supper administer'd in your Church? What Number of Communicants have you in your Parish? How many of them usually receive? Particularly, how many did communicate at Easter last?

XI. Do you give open, and timely Warning of the Sacrament before it is administered? Do your Parishioners send in their Names to you as required? Have you refused the Sacrament to anyone? For what Reason? And how has the Person so refused behaved himself since that Time?

If you have met with any particular Difficulties in the Discharge of your Duty;

If you have observed any particular Defects in the present Canons or Discipline, of the Church;

If you have discover'd any Abuses or Corruptions in any Ecclesiastical Officers, or others concern'd in the Execution of the same;

If you have any Advices to give, or Proposals to make, by which the Glory of God, and the Honour and Interest of our establish'd Church may be promoted, or the Government of this Diocese be better ordered.

I desire you freely to communicate your Thoughts to me; and be assur'd, that a proper Use shall be made of your Suggestions, in order to the Attainment of the End propos'd by them.

[Specimen returns]
Halifax,
Pontefract.

(Not written on the printed Form).

Answers to the Lord Archbishop of York's Qus.; by George Legh L.LD. (*sic*) Vicar of Halifax.

20. Ju. 1743.

To 1st Qu. In the Vicarage of Halifax are 26 Townships; 6200 Householders. Of these about 1000 in Halifax-Town.–In the Vicarage 300 Presbyterian Families; scarce any Baptists or Independents; 60 Quaker-Families;–Very few Papists.

2d. In ye Vicarage are 7 Presbyterian Meeting-houses. Their Situation, Teachers, & Numbers of Worshippers are these; viz.

At Halifax,	Mr Eli Dawson,	250.
Eland,	Mr. Tho. Farrar,	100.
Mixenden,	Mr. Jon. Smith,	400.
Warley,	Mr. Wm. Gream,	100.
Sowerby,	Mr. Wm. Dodge,	250.
North Owram,	Mr. Tho: Dickinson,	300.
Stansfield,	Mr. Hesketh,	100
	Totl.	1500

There are I think, but 3 Quaker-Meeting Houses in ye Vicarage. (About 200 resort to them). A new one is now building at Halifax.

At Lightcliff (ye Revd. Mr. Fisher's Chapelry within 2 Miles of Halifax) One Mrs. Holmes's House is resorted to as a Meeting-house by some few Moravians, who are join'd by several vagrant Enthusiasts, concerning wm̃ the sd. Mr. Fisher has given a fuller Acct. They lose Ground daily. And, if not persecuted, are likely to dwindle away, their chief Teachers Mr Spangenberg & Mr. Ingham having left 'em.–All these Protestant Dissenters meet Weekly at their respective Conventicles on Sundays; Ye last Sort at Hours not interfering with those of the Established Church.–Many Stories are told of 'em: Most of 'em [(?) 'false'. corner torn off.]

The Papists (abt. 10 in Number) Meet Monthly at one George Addison's (a Plaisterer) in Halifax. One Mr. Brown from Mr. Townley's in Lancashire, is their Priest.

To Qu. 3. At Halifax there is a Public School, founded by Qu. Elisabeth; Ye Endowmt. near 50li p. añ̃ for a Master & Usher. New Statutes were made for it (pursuant to ye Charter) by the late Archbp. of York. But I fear ye Governors don't observe 'em. Abt. 70 Children are there taught and fitted for ye Universities. The Head-Master, ye Revd. Mr. Holdsworth takes care to instruct 'em in ye Xn. Religion. & to bring 'em to Church frequently.

—— 4. In ye Parish are several Alms-houses & charitable Endowments under the Direction of Trustees. Some of these Trusts are wel (*sic*) executed; some *not*. No Lands are left for ye Repairs of ye Church. In the Vicarage are 12 Chapels; (7 of wch. contribute to ye sd. Repairs;) viz. The Chapel of Eland (this is a great Sufferer by ye Curate's non-residence, which, if continu'd, wil raise a great deal of Clamor).

p. Aññ by Endowmt.	50 li
—— Ripponden, p. añ by Endowmt. & Contribution	100.
—— Rastrick	40.
—— Heptonstall	40.
—— Illingworth	80.
—— Sowerby	60.
—— Sowerby-bridge	50.
—— Luddenden	32.
—— Coley	35.
—— Lightcliffe	22.
—— Crostone	25.
—— St. Anne's in ye Grove	20.

There is a distinct Curate to each of ye sd. Chapels, who has all ye Profits of it, and who is Nominated by ye Vicar; Licens'd by the Lord Archbishop of York.
To Qu. 5, 6. I Reside personally in my Parsonage-House. I have a Residing Curate duly Qualify'd according to ye Canons. He lives in a House near My Own & near the Church. The Allowance I make to him is ye same wch. was allow'd by my Predecessor to his Curate, 32 li: 2ss: Od p. annum: Over & above which he has by

Perquisities	8 : 0 : 0 p. aññ;
& by Contributions above–	10 : 0 : 0 p. aññ;
so that his Curacy exceeds	50 : 0 : 0 Yearly.

—— Q. 7. I know of no Pson in ye parish who comes to Church & is Unbaptiz'd; But there some (*sic*) yt being Baptiz'd & of a competent Age for Confirmn., are Unconfirm'd.
—— 8. The Public Prayers are read in my Church twice every Day: 2 Sermons added to 'em every Lord's Day; ye Latter of ye 2 by ye Lecturer, ye sd. Mr. Holdsworth. Public Prayers are read at Ealand-Chapel afsd every Morning. And in *each* of ye sd. 12 Chapels ye Morning & Evening Prayers are read every Sunday wth. 2 Sermons, There being a greater Congregation in an After Noon than in a Morning at every Place of Worship throughout ye Vicarage.
9. I Catechize in Church, in each Summer Season; No Servts. but only Children are sent.
To Qu. 10. The Sacramt. of ye Lord's Supper is administer'd in my Church 18 or 20 times in ye year. In ye Vicarage are about 15150 Communicants; (i.e. psons of 16 Years of Age & upwards:) about 160 usually Communicate at Halifax-Church. Phaps 260 on one of ye great Festivals, particularly at Easter last.

11. Open & timely Warning of ye Sacramt. is given. The Parishioners do not send in their Names. I have not refus'd ye Sacramt. to any one.

Kirkby in Ashfield,
Nottingham.

(Not written on the printed Form).
Kirkby September the 17th. 1743

To

The Most Reverend Father in God Thomas by Divine Providence Lord Arch-Bishop of York Primate of England and Metropolitan–

The Answers of John Brailsford Rector of Kirkby in Ashfield in the County of Nottingham and in the Province and Diocese of York aforesaid to certain Questions sent by His Grace the said Arch-Bishop to the said Mr: Brailsford dated Kensington. May. 2. 1743.

1. I have about Sixscore Families in my Parish. Seven of them are Protestant Dissenters,–Presbyterians or Independents. There is besides One Family of Quakers in my Parish. And there are an uncertain Number of Persons that run up and down after the Methodist-Teachers.

2d. There is no licens'd or other Meeting House in my Parish. Only sundry Persons have sometimes met in Houses or Outhouses not licens'd in my Parish, to hear a Methodist-Teacher or Teachers; and particularly (as I am inform'd) there was on Monday ye: 12th of this Instant September a Meeting of People to hear one Stephen Dixon a Lay-Methodist-Teacher at the home of one William Burroughs in my Parish, which house, I believe, not to be licens'd: And the said Stephen Dixon was by the Church-Wardens of this Parish presented at Your Grace's primary Visitation at Nottingham for preaching in a Barn in this Parish that was not licens'd, the said Stephen Dixon having not qualified himself according to Law to teach: But I have not heard of any Process against the said Stephen.

3d. There are none but petty Schools in my Parish, the Children's Schooling pay'd for by those that send them to School; And Care is taken that the Children in the said Schools be instructed in the Principles of the Christian Religion, according to the Doctrine of the Church of England, and that they be brought duly to Church, as the Canon requires.

4. There is nothing in my Parish that makes an Answer requisite: Only there is about the Sum of 30 Pounds left for the Use of the Poor under the Management of the Minister and Overseers of the Poor, the Interest of which is duly applied.

5. I do reside personally upon my Cure and in my Parsonage-House.

6. I personally residing on my Cure have no Curate.

7. I do not know of any that come to Church in my Parish that are not baptis'd. I believe there may be some baptis'd and of a competent Age, that are not confirm'd; But I think there are but few such, there having been upwards of 40 of my Parish confirm'd the last Confirmation but one.

8. Publick Service is generally read in my Church Wednesday & Fridays in Lent, and on all Holy Days, and is duly perform'd twice every Lord's Day.

9. I do Catechise in my Church Wednesdays & Fridays in Lent, and frequently on Sunday Afternoons after the Second Lesson, when there is no Sermon: And my Parishioners of the Church of England do for the most Part duly send their Children & Servants to be instructed by Me.

10. The Sacrament is administer'd in my Church ten times in the Year, that is to say, thrice at Easter, thrice at Christmass, twice at Whitsuntide, and twice at St. Luke's Tide, which is ye Season of our Wakes, or Dedication of our Church. I cannot certainly say what Number of Communicants I have in my Parish, or how many of them do usually receive, nor how many did communicate at Easter last, by Reason, though call'd upon by me So to-do, they have not sent in their Names before receiving the Sacrament; But I do believe there may be about Sixty Communicants in my Parish, that about thirty or forty of them do usually receive, and particularly that about forty might receive last Easter.

11th. I do give open and timely Warning of the Sacrament before it is administer'd. My Parishioners do not send in their Names to me as requir'd. I have not refus'd the Sacrament to any one.

With my Most hearty Prayers to God for His special Favour and Blessing on Your Grace in the Discharge of Your Grace's High Office, I am, Your Grace's Most Dutiful Son & Most humble Servant

JOHN BRAILSFORD.

I Beg Your Grace's Direction concerning those that offer themselves to be Partakers of the Sacrament, and have not sent in their Names, as also in the like Case those who follow the Methodists.

There is one Mary Gilbert a Poor Woman in my Parish stands excommunicated for Contumacy, having been presented for Fornication, who would have submitted to the Court, had it not been for her Father, an unworthy Man, whom having found Clarke at my coming into this Parish, I continued, 'till, for his Misbehaviour in this and other Respects, I found myself oblig'd to displace him. Would Your Grace be pleas'd to give Directions that the said Mary's Submission might be accepted without Charge, I believe She might be brought to submit. Otherwise it may please Your Grace to consider whether it might not be proper for Your Grace to give Directions for the Prosecution of the said Excommunicate, for the Prevention of such obstinate Contumacy.

As Ecclesiastical Processes are pro merâ salute animarum, ought they not to be carried on against Rich & Poor–without Respect of Persons, against the former without Commutations, against the latter ex Officio?

Could not Application be some way successfully made that no Denomination of Christians in these Realms should receive into their Communion or admit into their Congregations any that are Excommunicate, or any way under Process according to the Forms of Discipline of another Perswasion for any scandalous Immorality?

Could not Application be made with hopes of Success for a Proclamation, to put in force against the Methodists the Laws in being against Protestant Dissenting Teachers not qualifying themselves according to these Laws?

I am most humbly of Opinion that a particular Exhortation from Your Grace to the Members of the Church of England in Your Grace's Province to receive the Sacrament three times in the Year of which Easter to be one, and to send in their Names to the Ministers of their respective Parishes before their receiving, would be a happy Means to remedy that Neglect, which I am afraid is but too general in those Respects.

Stanford, [Stanford-on-Soar.]
Bingham.

. . .

V. It is not in my power to keep A Canonical Residence as usual. The Curate constantly Resides in ye Parsonage House & being A marreid (*sic*) Man having A child Every year & now Six Living there is not convenience for me to make use of A Room & Furniture wch I reservd. for yt purpose, but twice in ye Year at two of ye Greatr Festivals I administr. ye Sacrament & often lie in ye parsonage House. And once Every year I togethr wth my Wife & part of Family go (for three weeks or a Month) to A chief Farmers House & I officiate & discharge all ye duties of ye Parish whilst I stay & preah (*sic*) occasionally several Sundays in ye year.

VI. I have A Curate duly qualified who constantly Resides in ye Parsonage House & is allowd thirty Pds: A Year & all Surplice dues.

. . .

On this letter the Archbishop noted "Minister can't reside because his Curate who lives in the Vicarage has filled it with Children."

100. Extracts from the Diary of the Rev. William Cole, 1766–1767

(*The Blecheley Diary of the Rev. William Cole*, ed. F. G. Stokes (1931), pp. 109–112, 149, 178.)

William Cole (1714–1782), the Cambridge antiquary and friend and correspondent of Horace Walpole, was rector of Bletchley, Bucks., from 1755 to 1768.

Tuesday, 2. [September 1766.] Windy & some Rain. When I met Mr Watson[1] at Mr Pitt's on Saturday, he shewed me the Bps's Letter to him, telling him that Dr Samuel Chandler of London, the Cheif Dissenting Teacher, & lately dead, had wrote to him, complaining of his, Mr Watson's making the Dissenting Teacher at Newport uneasy, who, according to Dr Chandler's Account, was a quiet, innocent & inoffensive man: & advised him, Mr Watson, to a moderate way with those People, who are never gained by Persecution. Mr Watson shewed me his Answer to the Bp which was, That he was of his Lordship's Opinion, & ever acted accordingly; that Mr Bull, when he first came to Newport, called on him, & told him, that he hoped, if he taught Latin & Greek to half a Dozen of his own sort of People, it would give no offence: Mr Watson told him, That in Case he should ever keep a Curate, if that Curate was desirous of keeping Schole, he should naturally prefer him: but as he had no such Thoughts at present, he should give no Disturbance to him in his Design: accordingly

[1] Vicar of Newport Pagnell.

an House was fitted up, & a Sort of Academy instituted, of which Mr Watson never took the least Notice, 'till Mr Foster, (a very sensible & reputable Apothecary), told Mr Watson, that Mr Bull insisted upon a young Man of the Church of England, whose Parents lived at Stony Stratford, who was under his Care, & who was desirous of attending the Service of the Church, going with him to the Meeting. When Mr Watson heard this, he said, with some Warmth, that he would complain to the Bp or Archdeacon at their next Visitation about it: but never said more, or acted more. But, upon this, Mr Bull, or some of the Dissenters, wrote to the leading Man amongst them to make their Complaints. The Bp told Mr Watson, that when he had sent for Dr Chandler, & shewn him his Mr Watson's Answer, that Dr Chandler could not help saying, That Mr Watson had acted very properly in his Station, & that he was well assured that Mr Bull was an impertinent Coxcomb. And this Description answered indeed very fully to the Appearance of the Man when I saw him at Newport going to the Church at the Bp's Visitation: a tall, thin, pale-faced Man, with a starched & formal Gait, a white wig combed into nice Ringlets, with a large cocked Hat, & a Cane in his Hand. I could not help taking Notice of one Thing in Mr Watson's Answer to the Bp's Letter: before he concluded it, he took Notice to his Lordship of the great Hardships which Vicars in large Market-Towns are exposed to, in their vast Duty, 2 Sermons on a Sunday, besides the Liturgy, & Prayers on Litany and Saints' Days, with a constant visiting the Sick & Funerals; & all this for a very slender Endowment; & if this was attended with a large Family, (as was his Case, having a Wife & 5 Children), it was as much as he could do to make a Provision to support it. This was an almost sure Method to hear no more from his Lordship, as Mr Watson backed all this with a modest Request, that he would be so kind as to consider his Case when he had an opportunity. Accordingly, the Bp as he had wrote first, & made the Complaint, could not but take Notice of it when he came his Visitation, tho' he had not been so civil as to answer his Letter: neither could he omit giving some Kind of Answer to the Request: accordingly he told Mr Watson, That he had not forgot the Conclusion of his Letter; but would take some opportunity of augmenting his Income, when it was convenient for him to do so. If he does it, it will be more than I expect: however, I hope I may be deceived. This was what Mr Watson congratulated himself & me upon in his Letter to me last Friday. He is a worthy man, of Yorkshire, educated in St John's College, was Curate to Mr De[e]ring when he was Vicar of Burley, & on Mr Banks, Vicar of Newport's, Death, the Parish was very desirous to have their Curate to be their Vicar, a lively young man, but of no Character; & applied for it to my Lord Winchelsea[1] to get him to beg it of the Crown for him: but his Lordship having promised to provide for Mr Watson, asked for it for him, & forgot the Parish: with which they were so exasperated, that for a Time they made it very uneasy to Mr Watson, & curtailed his appointment. I forgot one Circumstance in his Letter to the Bp which was this: that as the Dissenters had made the first Complaint, he could not but acquaint his Lordship of one Thing which gave him much Concern: that under Pretence of frequenting Mr Bull's nocturnal Exercises, & Psalm-singing, he was well assured, that many of his younger Parishioners made that a Pretence of

[1] The eighth earl, *ob.* 1769.

going out on Nights, & frequenting Ale-Houses & Places of Ill Fame. And the Reason assigned yesterday at Mr Shann's, why he was not there at Dinner, was, that it was supposed, that he was attending the Meeting of the Justices at Newport, in order to prevent 2 or 3 Houses of notorious ill Fame from being licensed. . . .

Mond: 10. [November 1766.] Very fine Day & frosty. Frank Norris junr of Walton came on the Morn: to go a-shooting with Tom:[1] he brought Charles Fox of Fenny-Stratford with him. Lent Joe Holdom my Horse to go to Plow with. Wrote to Mr Cartwright for some new Books. Wrote an excuse to Mr Eyles for not dining with him to morrow, having forgot my Engagement. They shot only a Leveret & a Partridge–the Leveret I sent to Mr Cartwright & Mr Rowley in London, & wrote to Mr Cartwright to buy me some new Books; wrote to Mr Draper the Grocer to send Sugars, Spices &c. & to Mr Marshall the Carrier about a large Lump of Sugar of 22 lb weight which my Housekeeper says was never delivered in June last, as charged in Mr Draper's last Bill. Wrote to Mr Matthews, my London Barber, to take his money of Mr Marshall. Lent Frank Norris my little Horse to ride Home on, he being ill of a Fever. . . .

Sat: 24. [January 1767.] Fine Day & Frost. In the *Whitehall Evening Post* of 22nd is this bold Advertisement at length:–

"The Archbishops & Bishops are requested to lay an Account of the State of Popery in their respective Dioceses before the Public, that means may be thought of more effectually thereby to check the Growth of Popery in this Kingdom."

By this & such like In[n]uendoes, almost in every Paper, one may see the restless & indefatigable Rage & Disposition of the Fanatics of all sorts, united with their good Friends & allies the Deists & Atheists of the Age, who are out of Measure uneasy at the undisturbed Quiet which they themselves & the Catholics enjoy under a mild & moderate Administration. That Catholics increase is not my Beleif: yet if they should, considering the present System among us, I should not wonder. The great Enquiry, which is never thought of, should be after the Enemies of the Established Church, under every Denomination of Presbyterian, Independant, Quaker, Deist, Atheist, &c, &c, &c, all in League to overturn the Establishment, & rather than that [attempt] should fail, Christianity itself. Thaw & Rain in the Afternoon. The same Advertisement in the next Paper.

101. The Evangelical Revival as illustrated in the activities of the Rev. John Newton, 1765–1774

(*Hist. MSS. Comm.*, *Dartmouth MSS.*, III, pp. 175–176, 190–191, 209–210.)

John Newton (1725–1807) was curate of Olney, Bucks., a living in the gift of the evangelical earl of Dartmouth, 1764–1780, when he became rector of St. Mary Woolnooth, Lombard Street. He was much influenced by Whitefield and the Wesleys and became one of the leading London evangelicals.

The Reverend JOHN NEWTON to the EARL OF DARTMOUTH.

1765, February 11. Olney.–I must confess that the work[2] your Lordship is pleased to enquire after has been suspended for almost a twelve month. I thought my change of

[1] Servant to the diarist. [2] Newton's *Review of Ecclesiastical History*, published in 1770.

situation would have afforded me more leisure; but it is otherwise. On my first coming here I hoped to resume it soon but one thing or other constrained me to postpone it from time to time. Before I made the essay, I had expected to preach extempore but though I use no notes in the pulpit, I have found considerable advantage from writing on my subjects beforehand: this takes up some of my mornings, and my afternoons are generally spent in visiting the people, 3 or 4 families of a day; . . .

The parish is large, the prospect pleasing and demands close attendance. Besides, every day brings something unforeseen of its own. . . .

My thanks are due for your Lordship's approbation of my proposal for a new gallery and for your promised assistance. I hope when it is carried into execution it will not be found unnecessary. The roads all round are now extremely dirty and yesterday was inclining to rain, some of our most distant out-hearers could not come, yet I think every seat and bench in the church was filled and some crowded.

I find great pleasure and form many hopes in my new attempts to instruct the children. The number at my first meeting was 89; it is now increased to 162 and will probably amount to near 200, for some new ones are offered to me every day. Some come from most of the parishes next adjoining, but the bulk of them are our own, and amongst these perhaps 20 or more of the Dissenters' children for I receive all that come with their parents' knowledge and consent. Many of them are very serious and hopeful; all in general behave well. About a hundred of them come constantly to Church and sit in a body before the pulpit. I endeavour to win their attention and affection by books and little rewards and I began to consider this, as one of the most important parts of my service. . . . Too many of the parents need instruction, no less than their children; but either come not to Church, or, if they do, but to little purpose. But the children go home and repeat what I have been saying to them and shew their books. Perhaps some of these artless preachers may be heard where I should not.

1769. Aug. 9. Olney.–I hope the Lord has graciously smiled upon our removal to the large room in the great house;[1] it has given me opportunity of receiving several persons into our society for whom we could not find room before and I have laid the meeting on Sunday evenings more generally open and many of the congregation who knew not well how to improve their time on Sunday evenings now attend with us. . . . The simplicity and happy ignorance of those who live in a country place is a great advantage to a minister; they are out of the reach of many temptations and avocations which distract and divide the attention of many professors. (sic)

A few months ago I heard that some of them in their prayers at home had been much engaged for the welfare of Mr Wilkes. As the whole town of Olney is remarkably loyal and peaceable with regard to the government, I was rather surprised that gentleman should have partisans amongst our serious people. Upon inquiry I found they had just heard of his name and that he was in prison; comparing the imperfect account they had of him with what they read in their Bibles they took it for granted that a person so treated must of necessity be a minister of the Gospel and under that character they prayed earnestly that he might be supported and enlarged.–Your

[1] Belonging to Lord Dartmouth, to which the prayer-meeting had removed from the church for greater space.

Lordship will perhaps be surprised that in this time of general ferment the whole story of Mr Wilkes should be utterly unknown to many people in a market town within 60 miles of London. But this is the fact!

1774, June 29. Olney.–This is our fair-day, a day of great importance to the children in town. . . . On the evening of our fair-days I usually preach, which I call opening my booth. Sometimes I invite them to buy the truth or to come and see; sometimes I depreciate the wares and objects of the fair, and endeavour to convince them that all is vanity and vexation of spirit in comparison to what is set forth to view and to sale, without money or price, in the ordinances of the Gospel; but alas, I have the fewest spectators and the fewest buyers. A mountebank or a dancing dog can gather a crowd, but there are only here or there, one who have leisure or desire to attend to the things which belong to their peace. But a few there are, and usually amongst them some strangers whom the novelty of preaching at such a time, induces to come and hear what the man has to say. For the sake of such, and with a hope of being possibly useful to some poor soul, if but one, I began this custom upon my first coming to Olney. . . .

C. THE METHODISTS

102. John Wesley on the aims and organization of the Methodist Societies, 1749

(John Wesley, *A Plain Account of the People called Methodists* (1749), pp. 4–26.)

. . . I. 1. Above Ten Years ago, my Brother and I were desired, to preach in many Parts of *London*. We had no View therein, but so far as we were able (and we knew GOD *cou'd* work by whomsoever it pleased Him) To *convince* those who wou'd hear, What True Christianity was, and to *persuade* them to embrace it.

2. The Points we chiefly insisted upon were Four: First, That *Orthodoxy* or *Right Opinions* is, at best, but a very slender *Part* of Religion, if it can be allowed to be any Part of it at all: That neither does Religion consist in *Negatives*, in bare Harmlessness of any Kind; nor merely in *Externals*, in doing Good or using the Means of Grace, in Works of Piety (so called) or of Charity: That it is nothing short of or different from *The Mind that was in* CHRIST, The *Image of* GOD stampt upon the Heart, Inward *Righteousness*, attended with the *Peace* of GOD, and *Joy in the Holy Ghost*. Secondly, That the only Way under Heaven to this Religion, is To *repent and believe the Gospel*, or (as the Apostle words it) *Repentance towards* GOD, *and Faith in our* LORD JESUS CHRIST: Thirdly, That by this Faith, *He that worketh not, but believeth on Him that justifieth the Ungodly*, is justified *freely by his Grace, thro' the Redemption which is in* JESUS CHRIST: And Lastly, That *being justified by Faith*, we taste of the Heaven to which we are going: We are Holy and Happy: We tread down Sin and Fear, and *sit in Heavenly Places with* CHRIST JESUS.

3. Many of those who heard this, began to cry out, That we brought *Strange Things to their Ears*: That this was Doctrine which they never heard before, or, at least, never regarded. They *searched the Scriptures, whether these Things were so*, and acknowledged *the Truth as it is in* JESUS. Their Hearts also were influenced as well as their Understandings, and they determined to follow JESUS CHRIST *and Him crucified.*

4. Immediately they were surrounded with Difficulties: All the World rose up against them: Neighbours, Strangers, Acquaintance, Relations, Friends, began to cry out amain: "*Be not righteous overmuch: Why shouldst thou destroy thyself?* Let not *much Religion make thee mad.*"

5. One and another and another came to Us, asking, What they should do? Being distress'd on every Side, as every one strove to weaken, and none to strengthen their Hands in GOD. We advised them, "Strengthen you one another. Talk together as often as you can. And pray earnestly, with and for one another, That you may *endure to the End and be saved.*" Against this Advice we presumed there could be no Objection; as being grounded on the plainest Reason, and on so many Scriptures, both of the Old Testament and the New, that it wou'd be tedious to recite them.

6. They said, "But we want *You* likewise to talk with us often, to direct and quicken us in our Way, to give us the Advices which you well know we need, and to pray with us, as well as for us." I ask'd, Which of you desires this? Let me know your

Names and Places of Abode. They did so. But I soon found, they were too many for me to talk with severally so often as they wanted it. So I told them, "If you will all of you come together, every *Thursday*, in the Evening, I will gladly spend some Time with you in Prayer, and give you the best Advice I can."

7. Thus arose, without any previous Design on either Side, what was afterwards called *A Society*: A very Innocent Name, and very Common in *London*, for any Number of People, *associating* themselves together. The Thing proposed in their associating themselves together, was obvious to every one. They wanted to *flee from the Wrath to come*, and to assist each other in so doing. They therefore united themselves "in order to pray together, to receive the Word of Exhortation, and to watch over one another in Love, that they might help each other to work out their Salvation."

8. "There is One only Condition previously required, in those who desire Admission into this Society, *A Desire to flee from the Wrath to come, and to be saved from their Sins*. But wherever this Desire is fixt in the Soul, it will be shewn by its Fruits. It is therefore expected of all who continue therein, that they should continue to evidence their Desire of Salvation.

"First, By doing no Harm, by avoiding Evil in every kind; especially that which is most generally practised.

("Such as, The taking the Name of GOD in vain; The profaning the Day of the LORD; Drunkenness; Fighting, Quarrelling, Brawling; The Buying or Selling *uncustom'd* Goods; The doing to others as we would not they should do unto us; Uncharitable or Unprofitable Conversation, particularly, Speaking evil of Magistrates or Ministers:)

"Secondly, By doing Good, by being in every kind merciful after their Power; As they have Opportunity, doing Good of every possible Sort, and as far as it is possible to all Men:

"By all possible *Diligence* and *Frugality*, that the Gospel be not blamed:

"By submitting to bear the Reproach of CHRIST to be as *the Filth and Off-scouring* of the World, and looking that Men should *say all manner of Evil of them falsely* for their LORD's Sake:

"Thirdly, By attending upon all the Ordinances of GOD:

"Such as, The Publick Worship of GOD, The Supper of the LORD, Private Prayer, Searching the Scriptures, and Fasting or Abstinence."

They now likewise agreed, That as many of them as had Opportunity, wou'd meet together every *Friday*, and spend the Dinner Hour in crying to GOD, both for each other and for all Mankind.

9. It quickly appear'd, That their thus uniting together, answer'd the End proposed therein. In a few Months the far greater Part of those who had begun to *fear* GOD *and work Righteousness*, but were not united together, grew faint in their Minds, and fell back into what they were before. Mean while the far greater Part of those, who were thus united together, continued *striving to enter in at the strait Gate*, and to *lay hold on Eternal Life*. . . .

II. 1. But as much as we endeavour'd to watch over each other, we soon found some who did not *live the Gospel*. I do not know, that any Hypocrites were crept in;

for indeed there was no Temptation. But several grew cold, and gave Way to the Sins which had long easily beset them. We quickly perceiv'd, there were many ill Consequences of suffering these to remain among us. It was dangerous to others; inasmuch as all Sin is of an infectious Nature. It brought such a Scandal on their Brethren, as exposed them to what was not properly The Reproach of CHRIST. It laid a Stumbling-block in the Way of Others, and caused the Truth to be evil-spoken of.

2. We groaned under these Inconveniences long, before a Remedy could be found. The People were scattered so wide in all Part of the Town, from *Wapping* to *Westminster*, that I cou'd not easily see, what the Behaviour of each Person in his own Neighbourhood was. So that several disorderly Walkers did much Hurt, before I was apprized of it.

3. At Length, while we were thinking of quite another Thing, we struck upon a Method for which we have Cause to bless GOD ever since. I was talking with several of the Society in *Bristol*, concerning the Means of paying the Debts there; when one stood up and said, "Let every Member of the Society give a *Penny* a Week 'till all are paid." Another answered, "But many of them are poor, and cannot afford to do it." "Then said he, Put Eleven of the Poorest with me, and if they can give any Thing, well. I will call on them weekly, and if they can give Nothing, I will give for them as well as for myself. And each of you, call on Eleven of your Neighbours weekly: Receive what they give, and make up what is wanting." It was done. In a While some of these inform'd me, "They found, such and such an one did not live as he ought." It struck me immediately. "This is the Thing: The very Thing we have wanted so long." I call'd together all the *Leaders* of the *Classes*, (so we used to term them and their Companies) and desired That each wou'd make a particular Enquiry, into the Behaviour of those whom he saw weekly. They did so. Many disorderly Walkers were detected. Some turned from the Evil of their Ways. Some were put away from us. Many saw it with Fear, and rejoiced unto GOD with Reverence.

4. As soon as possible the same Method was used in *London* and all other Places. Evil Men were detected, and reproved. They were borne with for a Season. If they forsook their Sins, we receiv'd them gladly: If they obstinately persisted therein, it was openly declared, That they were not of us. The rest mourn'd and pray'd for them, and yet rejoiced, That as far as in us lay, the Scandal was roll'd away from the Society.

5. It is the Business of a Leader

I. To see each Person in his Class, once a Week at the least: In order,
To enquire how their Souls prosper?
To advise, reprove, comfort or exhort, as Occasion may require;
To receive what they are willing to give, toward the Relief of the Poor.

II. To meet the Minister and the Stewards of the Society, in order
To inform the Minister of any that are Sick, or of any that are disorderly and will not be reproved;
To pay to the Stewards what they have receiv'd of their several Classes in the Week preceding.

6. At first they visited each Person at his own House: But this was soon found not so expedient. And that on many Accounts. 1. It took up more Time, than most of the

Leaders had to spare. 2. Many Persons lived with Masters, Mistresses or Relations, who would not suffer them to be thus visited. 3. At the Houses of those who were not so averse, they had often no Opportunity of speaking to them but in Company. And this did not at all answer the End proposed, of exhorting, comforting or reproving. 4. It frequently happen'd, That one affirm'd what another denied. And this cou'd not be clear'd, without seeing them both together: 5. Little Misunderstandings and Quarrels of various Kinds, frequently arose among Relations or Neighbours: Effectually to remove which it was needful to see them all Face to Face. Upon all these Considerations it was agreed, That those of each Class should meet all together. And by this Means, a more full Enquiry was made, into the Behaviour of every Person. Those who cou'd not be visited at Home, or no otherwise than in Company, had the same Advantage with others. Advice or Reproof was given as need required; Quarrels made up, Misunderstandings removed. And after an Hour or two spent in this Labour of Love, they concluded with Prayer and Thanksgiving.

7. It can scarce be conceiv'd, what Advantages have been reap'd from this little Prudential Regulation. . . .

III. 1. About this Time, I was inform'd, That several Persons in *Kingswood*, frequently met together at the School, and (when they cou'd spare the Time) spent the greater Part of the Night, in Prayer and Praise and Thanksgiving. Some advised me to put an End to this: But upon weighing the Thing throughly, and comparing it with the Practice of the Antient Christians, I could see no Cause to forbid it. Rather, I believ'd, it might be made of more General Use. So I sent them Word, "I design'd to watch with them, on the *Friday* nearest the Full-Moon, that we might have Light thither and back again." I gave publick Notice of this, the *Sunday* before, and withall, That I intended to preach: Desiring, They and they only would meet me there, who could do it without Prejudice to their Business or Families. On *Friday* abundance of People came. I began Preaching between *Eight* and *Nine*; and we continued 'till a little beyond the Noon of Night, Singing Praying and Praising GOD.

2. This we have continued to do once a Month ever since, in *Bristol*, *London* and *Newcastle* as well as *Kingswood*. And exceeding great are the Blessings we have found therein: It has generally been an extremely Solemn Season; when the Word of GOD sunk deep into the Heart, even of those who 'till then knew Him not. If it be said, "This was only owing to the Novelty of the Thing, (the Circumstance which still draws such Multitudes together at those Seasons) or perhaps to the awful Silence of the Night," I am not careful to answer in this Matter. Be it so: However, the Impression then made on many Souls, has never since been effaced. Now allowing, that GOD did make Use either of the Novelty or any other indifferent Circumstance, in order to bring Sinners to Repentance, yet they are brought. And herein let us rejoice together.

3. Nay, May I not put the Case farther yet? If I can probably conjecture, That either by the Novelty of this *Antient* Custom, or by any other indifferent Circumstance, it is in my Power to *save a Soul from Death, and hide a Multitude of Sins*: Am I clear before GOD if I do it not? If I do not snatch that Brand out of the Burning?

IV. 1. As the Society increased, I found it requir'd still greater Care, to separate the precious from the vile. In order to this, I determin'd, at least once in three Months, to talk with every Member myself, and to inquire at their own Mouths, as well as of their Leaders and Neighbours, Whether they grew in Grace and in the Knowledge of our LORD JESUS CHRIST? At these Seasons I likewise particularly enquire, Whether there be any Mis-understandings or Differences among them? That every Hindrance of Peace and brotherly Love, may be taken out of the Way.

2. To each of those, of whose Seriousness and Good Conversation, I found no Reason to Doubt, I gave a Testimony under my own Hand, by writing their Name on a *Ticket* prepared for that Purpose: Every Ticket implying as strong a Recommendation of the Person to whom it was given, as if I had wrote at length, "I believe the Bearer hereof to be one that fears GOD and works Righteousness."

3. Those who bore these Tickets (these *Σύμβολα* or *Tesserae*, as the Antients term'd them; being of just the same Force with the *ἐπιστολαὶ συσατικαὶ*, *Commendatory Letters* mention'd by the Apostle) where-ever they came, were acknowledg'd by their Brethren, and received with all Chearfulness. These were likewise of Use in other Respects. By these it was easily distinguish'd when the Society were to meet a-part, who were Members of it and who not. These also supplied us with a quiet and inoffensive Method, of removing any Disorderly Member. He has no New Ticket, at the Quarterly Visitation; (for so often the Tickets are changed) and hereby it is immediately known, That he is no longer of this Community.

V. The Thing which I was greatly afraid of all this Time, and which I resolved to use every possible Method of preventing, was, A Narrowness of Spirit, a Party-Zeal, a being straiten'd in our own Bowels; That miserable Bigotry, which makes many so unready to believe, That there is any Work of GOD but among themselves. I thought it might be a Help against this, frequently to read, to all who were willing to hear, The Accounts I receiv'd from Time to Time, of the Work which GOD is carrying on in the Earth, both in our own and other Countries, not among us alone, but among those of various Opinions and Denominations. For this I allotted One Evening in every Month. And I find no Cause to repent my Labour. It is generally a Time of strong Consolation to those who love GOD, and all Mankind for his Sake: As well as of breaking down the Partition Walls, which either the Craft of the Devil, or the Folly of Men has built up: And of encouraging every Child of GOD to say, (O when shall it once be?) *Whosoever doth the Will of my Father which is in Heaven, the same is my Brother and Sister and Mother.*

VI. 1. By the Blessing of GOD upon their Endeavours to help one another, many found the Pearl of great Price. Being justified by Faith, they had *Peace with* GOD, *thro' our* LORD JESUS CHRIST. These felt a more tender Affection than before, to those who were Partakers of like precious Faith: And hence arose such a Confidence in each other, that they pour'd out their Souls into each other's Bosom. Indeed they had great Need so to do: For the War was not over, as they had supposed. But they had still to wrestle both with Flesh and Blood, and with Principalities and Powers: So that Temptations were on every Side: And often Temptations of such a Kind, as they knew not how to speak in a Class; in which Persons of every Sort, young and old, Men and Women met together.

2. These therefore wanted some Means of closer Union: They wanted to pour out their Hearts without Reserve; particularly with Regard to the Sin which did still *easily beset* them, and the Temptations which were most apt to prevail over them. And they were the more desirous of this, when they observ'd, it was the Express Advice of an inspired Writer, *Confess your Faults one to another, and pray one for another that ye may be healed.*

3. In Compliance with their Desire, I divided them into smaller Companies; putting Married or Single Men, and Married or Single Women together. The chief Rules of these *Bands,* (*i.e.* Little Companies; so that Old *English* Word signifies) run thus:

In order to *confess our Faults one to another and* pray one for another that we may be healed, we intend,

"1. To meet once a Week, at the least;
2. To come punctually at the Hour appointed;
3. To begin with Singing or Prayer;
4. To speak each of us in Order, freely and plainly, the true State of our Soul, with the Faults we have committed in Thought, Word or Deed, and the Temptations we have felt since our last Meeting:
5. To desire some Person among us (thence called a *Leader*) to speak *his* own State first, and then to ask the rest in order, as many and as searching Questions as may be, concerning their State, Sins and Temptations."

4. That their Design in meeting might be the more effectually answered, I desired all the Men-*Bands* to meet me together every *Wednesday* Evening, and the Women on *Sunday*; That they might receive such Particular Instructions, and such Exhortations, as from Time to Time, might appear to be most needful for them: That such Prayers might be offer'd up to GOD, as their Necessities should require: And Praise return'd to the Giver of every Good Gift, for whatever Mercies they had receiv'd.

5. In order to increase in them a grateful Sense of all his Mercies, I desired that One Evening in a Quarter, all the Men; on a Second, all the Women wou'd meet; and on a Third, both Men and Women together; That we might together *eat Bread* (as the Antient Christians did) *with Gladness and Singleness of Heart.* At these *Love-Feasts* (so we term'd them, retaining the Name, as well as the Thing, which was in Use from the Beginning) our Food is only a little plain Cake and Water. But we seldom return from them, without being fed not only with *the Meat which perisheth,* but with *that which endureth to everlasting Life.*

6. Great and many are the Advantages which have ever since flow'd, from this closer Union of the Believers with each other. They pray'd for one another, That they might be healed of the Faults they had confest: And it was so. The Chains were broken: The Bands were burst in sunder, and Sin had no more Dominion over them. Many were deliver'd from the Temptations, out of which 'till then they found no Way to escape. They were built up in our most holy Faith. They rejoiced in the LORD more abundantly. They were strengthen'd in Love, and more effectually provoked to abound in every Good Work.

7. But it was soon objected to the *Bands* (as to the *Classes* before) "These were not at first. There is no Scripture for them. These are Man's Works, Man's Building, Man's Invention." I reply, as before, these are also Prudential Helps, grounded on Reason and Experience, in order to apply the General Rules given in Scripture, according to Particular Circumstances.

8. An Objection much more boldly and frequently urged, is That "all these Bands are mere *Popery*." I hope, I need not pass a harder Censure on those, (most of them at least) who affirm this, than that they talk of they know not what, that they betray in themselves the most gross and shameful Ignorance. Do not they yet know, That the only *Popish* Confession is, the Confession made by a single Person to a Priest? (And this itself is in no wise condemn'd by our Church; nay, she recommends it in some Cases) whereas that *we* practise is, The Confession of several Persons conjointly, not to a Priest, but to each other. Consequently, it has no Analogy at all to *Popish* Confession. But the Truth is, This is a stale Objection, which many People make against any Thing they do not like. It is all *Popery* out of Hand. . . .

IX. 1. This is the Plainest and Clearest Account I can give of The *People*, commonly call'd *Methodists*. It remains only, to give you a short Account, of those who *serve* their Brethren in Love. There are *Leaders* of Classes and Bands (spoken of before) *Assistants, Stewards, Visitors* of the Sick, and *School-masters*.

2. In the Third Part of the *Appeal*, I have mention'd, How we are led to accept of *Lay-Assistants*. Their Office is, in the Absence of the Minister,

1. To expound every Morning and Evening:
2. To meet the United Society, the Bands, the Select Society, and the Penitents once a Week.
3. To visit the Classes (*London* and *Bristol excepted*) once a Month:
4. To hear and decide all Differences:
5. To put the Disorderly back on Trial, and to receive on Trial for the Bands or Society:
6. To see that the Stewards, the Leaders, and the School-masters faithfully discharge their several Offices:
7. To meet the Leaders of the Bands and Classes weekly, and the Stewards, and to over-look their Accounts.

3. I think, he must be no Fool, who has *Gifts* sufficient for these Things: As neither can he be void of the *Grace* of GOD, who is able to observe the Rules of an Assistant, which are these that follow:

"1. Be diligent. Never be unemploy'd a Moment. Never be triflingly employ'd. Never *while away* Time. Neither spend any more Time at any Place than is strictly necessary.

2. Be Serious. Let your Motto be, Holiness to the LORD. Avoid all Lightness, as you wou'd avoid Hell-fire.

3. Believe Evil of no one. If you *see* it done, well: Else take Heed how you credit it. Put the best Construction on every Thing. You know, the Judge is always supposed to be on the Prisoner's Side.

4. Speak Evil of no one. Else *your* Word especially wou'd eat as doth a Canker. Keep your Thoughts within your own Breast, 'till you come to the Person concern'd.
5. Tell every one what you think wrong in him and that plainly and as soon as may be. Else it will fester in your Heart. Make all Haste to cast the Fire out of your Bosom.
6. Do nothing as a Gentleman. You have no more to do with this Character than with that of a Dancing-master. You are the Servant of all. Therefore
7. Be ashamed of nothing but Sin; Not of hewing Wood, if Time permit, or drawing Water.
8. Take no Money of any one. If they give you Food when you are hungry, or Cloaths when you need them, it is Good: But not Silver or Gold. Let there be no Pretence to say, We grow rich by the Gospel.
9. Be Punctual. Do every Thing exactly at the Time.
10. Act in all Things, not according to your own Will, but as *a Son in the Gospel*."

4. In order to try these, before we can receive them as *Assistants*, we enquire,

First, Do they know in whom they have believed? Have they the Love of GOD in their Hearts? Do they desire to seek nothing but GOD? And are they Holy, in all Manner of Conversation?

Secondly, Have they *Gifts*, as well as *Grace*, for the Work? Have they (in some tolerable Degree) a clear, sound Understanding? Have they a Right Judgment in the Things of GOD? Have they a just Conception of Salvation by Faith? And has GOD given them any Degree of Utterance? Can they express themselves justly, readily, clearly?

Thirdly, Have they *Success*? Do they not only so speak (where Trial was made) as to convince and affect the Hearers? But have any received Remission of Sins by their Means? A clear and lasting Sense of the Love of GOD?

5. Those in whom these Three Marks undeniably concur, we gladly receive to assist us in the Work. And these we advise, 1. Always to rise at Four. 2. From Four to Five in the Morning, and from Five to Six in the Evening, partly to use Meditation and Private Prayer; partly to read the Scripture; partly some close Practical Book of Divinity: Such as, The Life of GOD in the Soul of Man, The Christian Pattern, Bishop *Beverege's* Private Thoughts, Mr. *Law*'s Practical Works, Dr. *Heylin's* Devotional Tracts, The Life of Mr. *Halyburton* and of Mr. *de Renty*. 3. From Six in the Morning till Twelve, to read, in order, slowly, and with much Prayer, Bp. *Pearson* on the Creed, Bp. *Fell* on the Epistles, Mr. *Boehm's* and Mr. *Nalson*'s Sermons, Mr. *Pascal's* Thoughts, *Cave*'s and *Fleury*'s Primitive Christianity, and *Echard*'s Ecclesiastical History.

And we believe they who thro'ly digest only these few Books, will *know* enough to save both their own Souls and those that hear them. . . .

[In the rest of the pamphlet Wesley deals similarly with the Stewards, Visitors of the Sick and Schoolmasters.]

103. Charles Wesley describes the trials of the Sheffield Methodists, 1743

(*Journal of the Rev. Charles Wesley*, ed. Thomas Jackson, I (1849), pp. 309–310.)

A typical example of the opposition encountered by Methodism in its early days.

Wed. May 25th. [1743.] . . . In the afternoon I came to the flock in Sheffield, who are as sheep in the midst of wolves; the Ministers having so stirred up the people, that they are ready to tear them in pieces. Most of them have passed through the fire of *stillness*, which came to try them, as soon as they tasted the grace of the Lord.

At six I went to the Society-house, next door to our brother Bennet's. Hell from beneath was moved to oppose us. As soon as I was in the desk with David Taylor, the floods began to lift up their voice. An officer (Ensign Garden) contradicted and blasphemed. I took no notice of him, and sung on. The stones flew thick, hitting the desk and people. To save them and the house, I gave notice I would preach out, and look the enemy in the face.

The whole army of the aliens followed me. The Captain laid hold on me, and began reviling. I gave him for answer, "A Word in Season; or, Advice to a Soldier;" then prayed, particularly for His Majesty King George, and preached the Gospel with much contention. The stones often struck me in the face. After sermon I prayed for sinners, as servants of their master, the devil; upon which the Captain ran at me with great fury, threatening revenge for my abusing, as he called it, "the King his master." He forced his way through the brethren, drew his sword, and presented it to my breast. My breast was immediately steeled. I threw it open, and, fixing mine eye on his, smiled in his face, and calmly said, "I fear God, and honour the King." His countenance fell in a moment, he fetched a deep sigh, put up his sword, and quietly left the place.

To one of the company, who afterwards informed me, he had said, "You shall see, if I do but hold my sword to his breast, he will faint away." So perhaps I should, had I had only his principles to trust to; but if at that time I was not afraid, no thanks to my natural courage.

We returned to our brother Bennet's, and gave ourselves unto prayer. The rioters followed, and exceeded in their outrage all I have seen before. Those of Moorfields, Cardiff, and Walsal, were lambs to these. As there is no King in Israel, (no Magistrate, I mean, in Sheffield,) every man does as seems good in his own eyes. Satan now put it into their hearts to pull down the Society-house, and they set to their work, while we were praying and praising God. It was a glorious time with us. Every word of exhortation sunk deep, every prayer was sealed, and many found the Spirit of glory resting on them.

One sent for the Constable, who came up, and desired me to leave the town, "since I was the occasion of all this disturbance." I thanked him for his advice, withal assuring him "I should not go a moment sooner for this uproar; was sorry for *their* sakes that they had no law or justice among them: as for myself, I had my protection, and knew my business, as I supposed he did his." In proof whereof, he went from us, and encouraged the mob.

They pressed hard to break open the door. I would have gone out to them, but the brethren would not suffer me. They laboured all night for their master, and by morning had pulled down one end of the house. I could compare them to nothing but the men of Sodom, or those coming out of the tombs exceeding fierce. Their outcries often waked me in the night; yet I believe I got more sleep than any of my neighbours.

Thur., May 26th. . . . I took David Taylor, and walked through the open street to our brother Bennet's, with the multitude at my heels. We passed by the spot where the house stood: they had not left one stone upon another. Nevertheless, the foundation standeth sure, as I told one of them, and our house not made with hands, eternal in the heavens. . . .

104. A criticism of the Methodists, probably by Edmund Gibson, bishop of London, *circa* 1740

(*Observations upon the Conduct and Behaviour of a Certain Sect, Usually distinguished by the Name of Methodists*, by Edmund Gibson (1740?), pp. 9–10, 11, 12.)

One of the more moderate of the many pamphlets at this time attacking the Methodists.

BESIDES the many *Irregularities* which are justly charged upon these Itinerant Preachers, as Violations of the Laws of Church and State; it may be proper to enquire, Whether the Doctrins they teach, and those Lengths they run, *beyond* what is practised among our *Religious Societies*, or in any other Christian Church; be a Service or a Disservice to Religion? To which Purpose, the following Queries are submitted to Consideration.

Query 1. WHETHER Notions in Religion may not be heighten'd to such *Extremes*, as to lead *some* into a Disregard of Religion itself, through Despair of attaining such exalted Heights? And whether *others*, who have imbib'd those Notions, may not be led by them into a Disregard and Disesteem of the *common* Duties and Offices of Life; to such a Degree at least, as is inconsistent with that Attention to them, and that Diligence in them, which Providence has made necessary to the well-being of private Families and publick Societies, and which Christianity does not only require in all Stations and in all Conditions, but declares at the same Time, (*Col.* iii.22. *Ephes.* v.6.) that the Performance even of the lowest Offices in Life, *as unto God*, (whose Providence has plac'd People in their several Stations,) is truly a *Serving of Christ*, and will not fail of its Reward in the next World?

Qu. 2. Whether the Enemy of Mankind may not find his Account in their carrying Christianity, which was design'd for a Rule to *all* Stations and *all* Conditions; to such *Heights* as make it fairly practicable by *a very few* in Comparison, or rather by *none*?

Qu. 3. Whether, in particular, the carrying the Doctrin of *Justification by Faith alone* to such a Heighth, as not to allow, that a careful and sincere Observance of *Moral Duties* is so much as a *Condition* of our Acceptance with God, and of our being justified in his Sight; Whether this, I say, does not naturally lead People to a *Disregard* of those Duties, and a low Esteem of them; or rather to think them no Part of the Christian Religion?[1]

[1] Note omitted.

Qu. 4. Whether a due and regular Attendance on the publick Offices of Religion, paid by good Men in a serious and composed Way, does not better answer the true Ends of Devotion, and is not a better Evidence of the Co-operation of the Holy Spirit, than those sudden Agonies, Roarings and Screamings, Tremblings, Droppings-down, Ravings and Madnesses;[1] into which their Hearers have been cast; according to the Relations given of them in the Journals referr'd to? . . .

Qu. 8. Whether, in a Christian Nation, where the Instruction and Edification of the People is provided-for, by placing Ministers in *certain Districts*, to whom the Care of the Souls within those Districts is regularly committed; It can be for the Service of Religion, that Itinerant Preachers run up and down from Place to Place, and from County to County, drawing after them confused Multitudes of People, and leading them into a *Disesteem* of their own Pastors, as[1] less willing or less able to instruct them in the Way of Salvation: . . .

Qu. 9. Whether it does not savour of Self-sufficiency and Presumption, when a few young Heads, without any Colour of a Divine Commission, set up their own Schemes, as the great Standard of Christianity: And, How it can be reconciled to Christian Humility, Prudence, or Charity, to indulge their own Notions to such a Degree, as to perplex, unhinge, terrify and distract the Minds of Multitudes of People, who have lived from their Infancy under a Gospel Ministry, and in the regular Exercise of a Gospel Worship; and all this, by persuading them, that they have never yet heard the true[1] Gospel, nor been instructed in the true Way of Salvation before; and that they neither are, nor can be true Christians, but by adhering to *their* Doctrins and Disciplin, and embracing Christianity upon *their* Schemes: All the while, for the Sake of those Schemes, and in Pursuance of them, violating the wholsom Rules, which the Powers Spiritual and Temporal have wisely and piously established, for the Preservation of Peace and Order in the Church.

[1] Note omitted.

D. NONCONFORMITY

105. Sir William Blackstone on the legal position of Protestant nonconformists and Papists

(William Blackstone, *Commentaries on the Laws of England*, IV (1775 ed.), pp. 52–58.)

Blackstone's view of the legal position of the Protestant dissenters since the Toleration Act should be compared with that of Lord Mansfield (No. 108). See also on this point Sir William Holdsworth, *History of English Law*, XII, p. 714.

Non-conformists are of two sorts: first, such as absent themselves from divine worship in the established church, through total irreligion, and attend the service of no other persuasion. . . .

The second species of non-conformists are those who offend through a mistaken or perverse zeal. Such were esteemed by our laws, enacted since the time of the reformation, to be papists and protestant dissenters: both of which were supposed to be equally schismatics in not communicating with the national church; with this difference, that the papists divided from it upon material, though erroneous, reasons; but many of the dissenters, upon matters of indifference, or, in other words, upon no reason at all. Yet certainly our ancestors were mistaken in their plans of compulsion and intolerance. The sin of schism, as such, is by no means the object of temporal coercion and punishment. If through weakness of intellect, through misdirected piety, through perverseness and acerbity of temper, or (which is often the case) through a prospect of secular advantage in herding with a party, men quarrel with the ecclesiastical establishment, the civil magistrate has nothing to do with it; unless their tenets and practice are such as threaten ruin or disturbance to the state. He is bound indeed to protect the established church: and, if this can be better effected, by admitting none but it's genuine members to offices of trust and emolument, he is certainly at liberty so to do; the disposal of offices being matter of favour and discretion. But, this point being once secured, all persecution for diversity of opinions, however ridiculous or absurd they may be, is contrary to every principle of sound policy and civil freedom. The names and subordination of the clergy, the posture of devotion, the materials and colour of the minister's garment, the joining in a known or an unknown form of prayer, and other matters of the same kind, must be left to the option of every man's private judgment.

With regard therefore to *protestant dissenters*, although the experience of their turbulent disposition in former times occasioned several disabilities and restrictions (which I shall not undertake to justify) to be laid upon them by abundance of statutes,* yet at length the legislature, with a spirit of true magnanimity, extended that indulgence to these sectaries, which they themselves, when in power, had held to be countenancing schism, and denied to the church of England[y]. The penalties are

* 23 Eliz., c. 1, 29 Eliz., c. 6, 35 Eliz., c. 1, 22 Car. II, c. 1.

[y] The ordinance of 1645 (before-cited) inflicted imprisonment for a year on the third offence, and pecuniary penalties on the former two, in case of using the book of common-prayer, not only in a place of public worship, but also in any private family.

conditionally suspended by the statute I W. & M. st. I. c. 18. "for exempting their majesties protestant subjects, dissenting from the church of England, from the penalties of certain laws," commonly called the toleration act; . . . Thus, though the crime of non-conformity is by no means universally abrogated, it is suspended and ceases to exist with regard to these protestant dissenters, during their compliance with the conditions imposed by the act of toleration: and, under these conditions, all persons, who will approve themselves no papists or oppugners of the trinity, are left at full liberty to act as their consciences shall direct them, in the matter of religious worship. And, if any person shall wilfully, maliciously, or contemptuously disturb any congregation, assembled in any church or permitted meeting-house, or shall misuse any preacher or teacher there, he shall (by virtue of the same statute) be bound over to the sessions of the peace, and forfeit twenty pounds. But by statute 5 Geo. I. c. 4. no mayor or principal magistrate, must appear at any dissenting meeting with the ensigns of his office[a], on pain of disability to hold that or any other office: the legislature judging it a matter of propriety, that a mode of worship, set up in opposition to the national, when allowed to be exercised in peace, should be exercised also with decency, gratitude, and humility. Neither doth the act of toleration extend to enervate those clauses of the statutes 13 & 14 Car. II. c. 4. & 17 Car. II. c. 2. which prohibit (upon pain of fine and imprisonment) all persons from teaching school unless they be licensed by the ordinary, and subscribe a declaration of conformity to the liturgy of the church, and reverently frequent divine service *established* by the laws of this kingdom.

As to *papists*, what has been said of the protestant dissenters would hold equally strong for a general toleration of them; provided their separation was founded only upon difference of opinion in religion, and their principles did not also extend to a subversion of the civil government. If once they could be brought to renounce the supremacy of the pope, they might quietly enjoy their seven sacraments, their purgatory, and auricular confession; their worship of reliques and images; nay even their transubstantiation. But while they acknowledge a foreign power, superior to the sovereignty of the kingdom, they cannot complain if the laws of that kingdom will not treat them upon the footing of good subjects.

Let us therefore now take a view of the laws in force against the papists; who may be divided into three classes, persons professing popery, popish recusants convict, and popish priests. 1. Persons professing the popish religion, besides the former penalties for not frequenting their parish church, are disabled from taking any lands either by descent or purchase, after eighteen years of age, until they renounce their errors; they must at the age of twenty-one register their estates before acquired, and all future conveyances and wills relating to them; they are incapable of presenting to any advowson, or granting to any other person any avoidance of the same; they may not keep or teach any school under pain of perpetual imprisonment; and, if they willingly say or hear mass, they forfeit the one two hundred, the other one hundred marks, and each shall suffer a year's imprisonment. Thus much for persons, who, from the

[a] Sir Humphrey Edwin, a lord mayor of London, had the imprudence soon after the Toleration Act to go to a Presbyterian meeting-house in his formalities: which is alluded to by dean Swift, in his *tale of a tub*, under the allegory of *Jack* getting on a grey horse, and eating custard.

misfortune of family prejudices or otherwise, have conceived an unhappy attachment to the Romish church from their infancy, and publicly profess it's errors. But if any evil industry is used to rivet these errors upon them, if any person sends another abroad to be educated in the popish religion, or to reside in any religious house abroad for that purpose, or contributes to their maintenance when there; both the sender, the sent, and the contributor, are disabled to sue in law or equity, to be executor or administrator to any person, to take any legacy or deed of gift, and to bear any office in the realm, and shall forfeit all their goods and chattels, and likewise all their real estate for life. And where these errors are also aggravated by apostacy, or perversion, where a person is reconciled to the see of Rome or procures others to be reconciled, the offence amounts to high treason. 2. Popish recusants, convicted in a court of law of not attending the service of the church of England, are subject to the following disabilities, penalties, and forfeitures, over and above those before-mentioned. They are considered as persons excommunicated; they can hold no office or employment; they must not keep arms in their houses, but the same may be seised by the justices of the peace; they may not come within ten miles of London, on pain of 100*l*; they can bring no action at law, or suit in equity; they are not permitted to travel above five miles from home, unless by license, upon pain of forfeiting all their goods; and they may not come to court under pain of 100*l*. No marriage or burial of such recusant, or baptism of his child, shall be had otherwise than by the ministers of the church of England, under other severe penalties. A married woman, when recusant, shall forfeit two thirds of her dower or jointure, may not be executrix or administratrix to her husband, nor have any part of his goods; and during the coverture may be kept in prison, unless her husband redeems her at the rate of 10*l*. a month, or the third part of all his lands. And, lastly, as a feme-covert recusant may be imprisoned, so all others must, within three months after conviction, either submit and renounce their errors, or, if required so to do by four justices, must abjure and renounce the realm: and if they do not depart, or if they return without the king's license, they shall be guilty of felony, and suffer death as felons without benefit of clergy. There is also an inferior species of recusancy, (refusing to make the declaration against popery enjoined by statute 30 Car. II. st. 2. when tendered by the proper magistrate) which, if the party resides within ten miles of London, makes him an absolute recusant convict; or, if at a greater distance, suspends him from having any seat in parliament, keeping arms in his house, or any horse above the value of five pounds. This is the state, by the laws now in being[b], of a lay papist. But, 3. The remaining species or degree, *viz.* popish priests, are in a still more dangerous condition. By statute 11 & 12 W. III. c. 4. popish priests or bishops, celebrating mass or exercising any part of their functions in England, except in the houses of embassadors, are liable to perpetual imprisonment. And by the statute 27 Eliz. c. 2. any popish priest, born in the dominions of the crown of England, who shall come over hither from beyond sea, (unless driven by stress of weather and tarrying only a reasonable time[c]) or shall be in England three days

[b] Stat. 23 Eliz., c. 1. 27 Eliz., c. 2. 29 Eliz., c. 6. 35 Eliz., c. 2. 1 Jac. I, c. 4. 3 Jac. I, c. 4 & 5. 7 Jac. I, c. 6. 3 Car. I, c. 3. 25 Car. II, c. 2. 30 Car. II, st. 2. 1 W. & M., c. 9, 15 & 26. 11 & 12 W. III, c. 4. 12 Ann. st. 2, c. 14. 1 Geo. I, st. 2, c. 55. 3 Geo. I, c. 18. 11 Geo. II, c. 17.

[c] Raym., 377. Latch., 1.

without conforming and taking the oaths, is guilty of high treason: and all persons harbouring him are guilty of felony without the benefit of clergy.

This is a short summary of the laws against the papists, under their three several classes, of persons professing the popish religion, popish recusants convict, and popish priests. Of which the president Montesquieu observes[d], that they are so rigorous, though not professedly of the sanguinary kind, that they do all the hurt that can possibly be done in cold blood. But in answer to this it may be observed, (what foreigners who only judge from our statute book are not fully apprized of) that these laws are seldom exerted to their utmost rigor: and indeed, if they were, it would be very difficult to excuse them. For they are rather to be accounted for from their history, and the urgency of the times which produced them, than to be approved (upon a cool review) as a standing system of law. The restless machinations of the jesuits during the reign of Elizabeth, the turbulence and uneasiness of the papists under the new religious establishment, and the boldness of their hopes and wishes for the succession of the queen of Scots, obliged the parliament to counteract so dangerous a spirit by laws of a great, and then perhaps necessary severity. The powder-treason, in the succeeding reign, struck a panic into James I, which operated in different ways: it occasioned the enacting of new laws against the papists; but deterred him from putting them in execution. The intrigues of queen Henrietta in the reign of Charles I, the prospect of a popish successor in that of Charles II, the assassination-plot in the reign of king William, and the avowed claim of a popish pretender to the crown in subsequent reigns, will account for the extension of these penalties at those several periods of our history. But if a time should ever arrive, and perhaps it is not very distant, when all fears of a pretender shall have vanished, and the power and influence of the pope shall become feeble, ridiculous, and despicable, not only in England but in every kingdom of Europe; it probably would not then be amiss to review and soften these rigorous edicts; at least till the *civil* principles of the roman catholics called again upon the legislature to renew them: for it ought not to be left in the breast of every merciless bigot, to drag down the vengeance of these occasional laws upon inoffensive, though mistaken, subjects; in opposition to the lenient inclinations of the civil magistrate. and to the destruction of every principle of toleration and religious liberty.

(*a*) THE PROTESTANT DISSENTERS

106. An Act of Indemnity for Dissenters holding municipal offices, 1718

(*Statutes at Large*, XIV, pp. 16–17, 5 Geo. I, cap. 6.)

Although the Dissenters in the eighteenth century failed to achieve the total repeal of the Test and Corporation Acts, many of them in fact held municipal offices and were covered by annual Acts of Indemnity.

An act for quieting and establishing corporations.

I. [Indemnity to persons required to take the non-resistance oath and the declaration against the Solemn League and Covenant prescribed by the Corporation Act of 1661.]

[d] *Sp. L.*, b. 19. c. 27.

II. And be it also further enacted by the authority aforesaid, That so much of the said Statute as requires the taking of the said oath, and subscribing the said declaration, shall be and is hereby repealed; and that neither the said oath or declaration shall be required for the future.

III. *And whereas by the said recited act made in the thirteenth year of King* Charles *the Second, it is enacted, That no person or persons shall be placed, elected or chosen, in or to any of the offices or places relating to or concerning the government of any city, corporation, borough, cinque-port and their members, and other port-towns, or any other offices in the said recited act mentioned or expressed, that shall not have, within one year next before such election or choice, taken the sacrament of the Lord's supper, according to the rites of the church of England, and that in default thereof every such placing, election and choice shall be void:* be it further enacted by the authority aforesaid, That all and every the now member and members of any corporation within this kingdom, and all and every person and persons now in actual possession of any office, that were required by the said above recited act to take the sacrament of the Lord's supper according to the rites of the church of *England* within one year next before his election or choice into such office, shall be and are hereby confirmed in their several and respective offices and places, notwithstanding their omission to take the sacrament of the Lord's supper as aforesaid, and shall be indemnified, freed and discharged, of and from all incapacities, disabilities, forfeitures and penalties arising from such omission; and that none of their acts, nor the acts not yet avoided, of any who have been members of any corporation, or in actual possession of such offices, shall be questioned or avoided for or by reason of such omission; but that all such acts shall be and are hereby declared and enacted to be as good and effectual as if all and every such person and persons had taken the sacrament of the Lord's supper in manner as aforesaid; nor shall any person or persons, who shall be hereafter placed, elected or chosen, in or to any the offices aforesaid, be removed by the corporation, or otherwise prosecuted for or by reason of such omission; nor shall any incapacity, disability, forfeiture or penalty, be incurred by reason of the same, unless such person be so removed, or such prosecution be commenced, within six months after such person's being placed or elected into his respective office, as aforesaid, and that in case of a prosecution the same be carried on without wilful delay.

107. Extracts from the proceedings of the Dissenting Deputies, 1739–1768

(*A Short Account of Some of the Proceedings of the Deputies and Committee, appointed to take Care of the Civil Affairs of the Dissenters* (1768), pp. 4–7, 10–12, 16, 24–25, 28.)

The Dissenting Deputies (two members from each Presbyterian, Independent and Baptist congregation within ten miles of London) were formed in 1732 to protect the civil rights of the Dissenters. These extracts are from one of the several accounts of their proceedings which they published during the eighteenth century. They show attempts at petty prosecution of Protestant dissenters which continued in the early eighteenth century.

1739. . . . THE Justices of the Peace in *Montgomeryshire* refusing to license and record some Houses designed for dissenting Meeting-Places, the COMMITTEE hereupon procured the Attorney General's Opinion on the Case; who declared the Refusal illegal, and directed to proper Means of Redress: On the Sight of which the Justices thought fit to Comply.

1740. . . . THIS Year, at the Request of the Parties concerned, they undertook the Defence of a Baptist-Minister, who had been illegally and maliciously appointed Church-Warden of the Parish where he resided. On the Parishioners being made acquainted with this Resolution, they thought fit to desist from their Appointment of him, and chose another to that Office in his room. . . .

1742. THEY established a Register of the Births of the Children of Protestant Dissenters of the Three Denominations; and of the Baptism of such of their Children as should be baptized in their Infancy. . . .

ON Application made to them, they advised some Protestant Dissenters in the Country not to comply with the Demands of a Clergyman, who claimed his customary Fees for churching their Wives, though the Women had never been at Church; for marrying of their Men, though they were married in another Parish, and by another Minister; and for burying their Dead, though buried in their own burying Ground, and no Service had been read over them: And on the Promise of the COMMITTEE to defend them, if they were prosecuted for not complying, these illegal unreasonable Claims have not been repeated. . . .

1743. . . . THE same Year the COMMITTEE interposed in Behalf of their Brethren in *Anglesea*, disturbed and abused by a riotous Mob; and obtained an Information against several of the Rioters, which has restored the Peace of that Place.

AND about the same Time they obtained a Clause to be inserted in the Act for the better lighting the City of *London*, by which the dissenting Meeting-Houses are kept from being assessed at the Discretion of the Alderman and Common Council of their respective Wards; and are henceforth set on the same Foot with all other Buildings of a like Nature. . . .

1746. . . . A PROSECUTION in the Spiritual Court was commenced against one *Greenwood*, for living in Fornication with his own Wife; because he had not been married according to the Rites of the Church of *England*, but in the Congregation of Protestant Dissenters, of which he was a Member; and this he pleaded was a Matter of Conscience with him. This Prosecution, if carried on, must have ended in the utter Ruin of the Man. The COMMITTEE could not think the Man had acted prudently or legally in this Matter; but yet, in Compassion to him, they thought fit so far to interpose, as to endeavour to engage the Prosecutor to drop his Suit; and were so happy as to prevail with him to put an End to all Proceedings against the poor Man in the Spiritual Court. . . .

1747. TWO School-Masters in *Suffolk* had been cited into the Spiritual Court, for keeping a School without a Licence, and applied to the COMMITTEE for Advice how to act; who thereupon sent them such Instructions and Advices, as, having been followed, prevented the Continuance, or Renewal, of any such vexatious Prosecutions. . . .

1748. . . . SEVERAL Dissenters of *Watesfield* in *Suffolk*, whose Children had been refused Burial there, on Account of their not having been baptized according to the Rites of the Church of England, sent up Complaints on that Head to the COMMITTEE. Upon Application to the Bishop of *Norwich*, he wrote to the particular Clergyman concerned, and hoped there would be no Occasion for such Complaints in future. . . .

1752. . . . UPON Complaint from *Hitchin* of an Order of the Trustees of a Free-School there, excluding Protestant Dissenters Children from the said School; the Attorney

General's Opinion was taken about the Validity of such Order: and upon that Opinion the COMMITTEE have used their Endeavours to have the said Order revoked. And the same has been suspended; and the Dissenters there have been assured it shall not be executed. . . .

1767. SOME Congregations applied to the COMMITTEE to determine disputed Elections, in the Choice of Ministers. . . . The COMMITTEE . . . declined meddling with such Matters, but came to the following Resolutions:

THAT Differences of this Nature, weaken the Dissenting Interest, and tend to bring Dissenters into Contempt. Providence has in several Instances favoured the Attempts of the DEPUTATION and COMMITTEE, to defend the legal civil Rights of the Dissenters against Oppression. This is their proper Business, and not to settle Disputes and Controversies in particular Churches, which should always be adjusted, with a Spirit of Meekness and Humility, by the Congregations themselves, or their Friends, and Neighbours. . . .

THE Dissenters at *Werenford* in *Northumberland,* applied to the COMMITTEE for Relief against the Trustees of *Belford* Turnpike Road, who by putting up a Bar, obliged them to pay Toll as they went to Publick Worship, which seemed to be excepted in the Act. The COMMITTEE finding upon Enquiry, that this was not an Imposition upon Dissenters, as such, came to a Resolution, That it is not consistent with the Institution of this DEPUTATION to intermeddle therewith. . . .

108. Speech by Lord Mansfield in the House of Lords in the case of the Chamberlain of London against Allen Evans, Esq., 4 February 1767

(*Parl. Hist.*, XVI, pp. 319–320.)

In this case the City of London held that Dissenters elected sheriffs could not avoid the fines imposed by a by-law of 1748 on all refusing this office by pleading their disability as Nonconformists under the Corporation Act, because Nonconformity was in itself a crime. The House of Lords decided against the City, a decision of great importance for the Dissenters. The speech was first published, with Mansfield's approval, by Dr. Philip Furneaux in his *Letters to Mr Justice Blackstone*, 2nd edition (1771).

. . . But the case is quite altered since the Act of Toleration: it is now no crime for a man, who is within the description of that act, to say he is a dissenter; nor is it any crime for him not to take the sacrament according to the rites of the church of England: nay, the crime is, if he does it contrary to the dictates of his conscience.

If it is a crime not to take the sacrament at church, it must be a crime by some law; which must be either common or statute law, the canon law inforcing it depending wholly upon the statute law. Now the statute law is repealed as to persons capable of pleading that they are so and so qualified; and therefore the canon law is repealed with regard to those persons. If it is a crime by common law, it must be so either by usage or principle. There is no usage or custom, independent of positive law, which makes nonconformity a crime.

The eternal principles of natural religion are part of the common law: the essential principles of revealed religion are part of the common law; so that any person reviling, subverting, or ridiculing them, may be prosecuted at common law. But it cannot be shewn from the principles of natural or revealed religion, that, independent of positive law, temporal punishments ought to be inflicted for mere opinions with respect to particular modes of worship.

Persecution for a sincere, though erroneous, conscience, is not to be deduced from reason or the fitness of things; it can only stand upon positive law.

. . . The Toleration Act renders that which was illegal before, now legal; the Dissenters' way of worship is permitted and allowed by this act; it is not only exempted from punishment, but rendered innocent and lawful; it is established; it is put under the protection, and is not merely under the connivance, of the law. . . .

Now there cannot be plainer position, than that the law protects nothing, in that very respect in which it is in the eye of the law, at the same time, a crime. Dissenters, within the description of the Toleration Act, are restored to a legal consideration and capacity; and a hundred consequences will from thence follow which are not mentioned in the Act. For instance, previous to the Toleration Act, it was unlawful to devise any legacy for the support of dissenting congregations, or for the benefit of dissenting ministers; for the law knew no such assemblies, and no such persons; and such a devise was absolutely void, being left to what the law called superstitious purposes. But will it be said in any court in England, that such a devise is not a good and valid one now? And yet there is nothing said of this in the Toleration Act. By that Act the Dissenters are freed, not only from the pains and penalties of the laws therein particularly specified, but from all ecclesiastical censures, and from all penalty and punishment whatsoever on account of their nonconformity; which is allowed and protected by this act, and is therefore in the eye of the law no longer a crime. Now if the defendant may say he is a Dissenter; if the law doth not stop his mouth; if he may declare, that he hath not taken the sacrament according to the rites of the church of England without being considered as criminal; if, I say, his mouth is not stopped by the law, he may then plead his not having taken the sacrament according to the rites of the church of England, in bar of this action. It is such a disability as doth not leave him liable to any action, or to any penalty or punishment whatsoever. . . .

(*b*) THE CATHOLICS

109. Proposed penal taxation of Catholics, 1722

(*Hist. MSS. Comm., Polwarth MSS.*, III, pp. 202–203.)

The proposed levy on Catholics' lands was proposed on the pretext of Catholic participation in Layer's and Atterbury's plot in 1722. Carteret, then Secretary of State, was careful to explain this to Dubois, who complained about the proposed tax, and to stress that it was not imposed on religious grounds; and he takes the same line in the letter printed below. Lord Polwarth, later second earl of Marchmont (1675–1740) and Lord Whitworth (1675–1725), were the English plenipotentiaries at the Congress of Cambrai. The letter gives some idea of the landed wealth of the Catholics in the early eighteenth century.

Lord Carteret to Lords Polwarth and Whitworth.

1722, Nov. 19. Whitehall.–You have seen by my despatch of the 10th some of the reasons which members of Parliament give for imposing this year an extraordinary tax upon the lands of those who have fomented here several rebellions as well as the last conspiracy, and who, under pretext of being Papists, stubbornly refuse to recognise the government of the King. This matter being now more fully arranged, his Majesty directs me to write this letter so that you may be able to reply to any objections which may be made through ignorance of the case and the nature of our laws. I shall first tell you that such of the Papists as have not actually taken up arms against the government or been legally convicted of high treason have been treated with less rigour during his Majesty's reign than such were in the time of any of his predecessors. In this the King has acted from his own inclination and out of regard to his allies, the heads of the Catholic world. And we are persuaded that the reasons for this tax, when seen in their true light, will not be regarded as persecution of the Catholics on account of their religion or as including the innocent with the guilty but rather as a very just amends, very light in comparison with what Parliament in virtue of the existing laws has a right to demand, for the part which they have had in the late conspiracy. To put the matter clearly I should tell you that the King in the first year of his reign sent a message to the House of Commons that he was to give up the two thirds of the lands of the Papists which he had the right to seize.[1] A prince less generous would never have made such a renunciation and a Parliament less benevolent would never have allowed such a opportunity of paying the great expenses caused by the late rebellion from the possessions of those who promoted it to escape them. And yet, notwithstanding of the provocation given on the part of the Papists, they proceeded no further than to make an act naming certain commissioners to value the lands of certain traitors and Papists of which the two thirds were liable to confiscation. That same year an act was made obliging all Papists to register their names and the value of their lands under certain penalties in case they were not registered before a certain time. In 1719 that register was presented to the House of Commons by which it appears that the annual rental of the Papists who had registered amounted to 384,950*l.* sterling, it being understood that those registered contained only the lands farmed out, without reckoning the value of parks, woods and policies which the proprietors did not farm out, nor the profits of liferents drawn by the proprietors, which were more considerable than the reserved rents upon the said lands, and it was only the reserved rent which was registered. It is therefore evident that if all the lands of the Catholics had been comprised in this register, which they are not, as several have not obeyed the law for registration, the revenue could never have been less than 400,000*l.* sterling yearly; and without exaggerating, we could easily add one third more to that sum, because if the rents of the lands of the whole kingdom had been similarly registered, the sum would not rise to two thirds of the value of what the whole lands of the kingdom bear. But to show that the tax of 100,000*l.* which the Parliament is imposing for this year is not so unsupportable and ruinous to the Catholics as they pretend, that charge is no greater than it was during the time of the late war. When the nation was paying 4s. per pound, the Catholics had to pay 8s. Reckoning then their lands at 400,000*l.* yearly, the 100,000*l.* which they are to pay this year is at the rate of 5s. per pound, which, joined to the double tax, which is 4s. per pound, if they pay exactly, which they do not, will make their taxes this year 9s. per pound. That is their own

[1] Under the Recusancy Laws.

calculation and it is greatly exaggerated, but the true amount, after the most exact examination, which they will have to pay is about 6s. 6d. per pound, and so they will be this year just about in the same position as they were during the last war. And is it either unjust or unreasonable to place them for a year in this situation when they have endeavoured in every way possible, both by solicitations without and by conspiracies within their country, to throw it into war with all its consequences? And this is what the great majority of the House of Commons think, notwithstanding what is said to the contrary. And, besides, in order to lessen the rigour of this act, the King has decided to remit all penalties and confiscations which have been incurred up till now for which as well as for the arrears of their double tax they were liable to be distressed and even ruined by the ordinary course of law, which the justices of peace in the provinces might lawfully put in execution against them. This gracious act of the King actually changes the impost of the Parliament to an act of clemency by granting an advantageous composition, which the wisest and richest among the Catholics will not fail to regard as a favour when they see that they will thereby escape certain penalties which they feared and which were certain to fall upon them some time or other.

110A–B. The Yorkshire Catholics, *circa* 1730–1746

110A. Archbishop Blackburne's inquiry about the numbers of Catholics in the diocese of York, 1735

(*Catholic Record Society*, XXXII, pp. 205–206, 233–235, 284, 319.)

Lancelot Blackburne (1658–1743), archbishop of York, 1724–1743, annoyed at the conversion of one of his parish clergy to Catholicism, issued inquiries as to the exact numbers of Catholics in the diocese at the archdeacons' visitations in 1733 and 1735.

Enquiries.

1. What numbers of papists or supposed papists have you in your parish, Men, Women and Children above the age of thirteen years: return their Names, Titles, Distinctions, or Trades in pursuance of the 114th Canon.
2. Is there any popish priest, or any persons supposed to be such, who constantly Dwell in your parish, or are Sojourners there and return their Names.
3. Is there any House or place in your parish in which Mass is understood to be performed, and to which there is a resort of papists on the Lord's Day, or at any other time.
4. Is there any popish School within your parish for persons of Either Sex and by whom Kept.
5. Hath any Visitation or Confirmation been understood to have been held by any popish Bishop within your parish.
6. Doe you know of Any persons who have been perverted to the popish Religion, and by whome and when.

His Grace the Lord Arch-Bishop of York desires and expects that every Clergyman make an exact and particular Return in writing signed by him to the Enquiries above mentioned, on or before Michaelmas Day next, at the Registers, Mr Braithwait's office in York.

John Dealtary, Curate of Bugthorp.

. . .

[Specimen returns]

Coxwold Bulmer A List of all the Papists in the Parish of Coxwold in answer to the Enquiries given at the Arch-Deacon's Visitation held at Thirsk June 25th 1735.

1. Coxwold: James Wood, farmer–Ann, his wife, & Elizabeth Wood, their daughter –John Taylor, a taylor–Alice, his wife (Art. 6) perverted upon her marriage about thirteen years agoe–William Mawlam, taylor–Ann, his wife–Benjamin Dale, butcher–Catharine Dale, his sister–Edmund Dale, his apprentice–Thamar Rose, wife of John Rose, servant to the Lord Fauconberg, (Art. 6.) perverted after marriage about fourteen yeares agoe–Jane, their daughter–Lucy Grey, wife of Matthew Grey, carpenter–Joseph Ratcliff, carpenter & farmer–Mary, his wife (Art. 6.) perverted upon marriage about ten yeares agoe–Mary Foster, wife of Robert Foster, taylor–Barbara Smirk, a poor widow–Ann Burgess, wife of Thomas Burgess, weaver & farmer–Dinah Dale, widow & inn-holder–Sarah Dale, her daughter–Mary Barwick, wife of George Barwick, farmer–John Coates, apprentice to Joseph Ratcliff–Thomas Shovell, labourer.

Newbrough: The Right Honourable Thomas Lord Viscount Fauconberg–Catherine, his lady–the hon[ble] Rowland Belasyse esqr.–Mrs Penelope Belasyse–Charles More, (Art. 2.) a priest has been long resident–upper servants: Dinah More, Mary Capps, Mary Fenwick, Elizabeth Gosling, Roger Ormondy, John Cross, Peter Kersey, James Wood–under servants: Jane Wingell, Ann Wardell, Ann Duffin, Elizabeth Wood, Mary Ward, Elizabeth Kirk, Mary Ratcliff, Mary Cramer, Elizabeth Verden, John Rose, Matthew Fetherston, (Art. 6.) perverted about ten yeares agoe, George Turner, John Harrison, John Farrington, Thomas Worrilow, Philip Gosling, Christopher Kirke, Robert Coopland–Henry Gostling, park keeper–Ann Gosling, his wife,–William Gosling & Margaret Gostling, their children–Mrs Margaret Mitchel, widow, mother of Mr Thomas Mitchel steward to Lord Fauconberg–Ann, his wife–Christopher Scarlet, mason and farmer, (Art. 6.) perverted upon his marriage about ten yeares agoe–Ellen, his wife–Ellen Dale & Ann Dale, her daughters–Adam Dale, butcher & farmer.

Yearsley: William Lees, Farmer (Art. 6.) perverted about seven yeares agoe–Thomas Harrison, farmer–Mary, his wife (Art. 6.) perverted upon marriage about five yeares agoe–Robert Goodrick, farmer–Ann, his wife–Thomas Holding, labourer–Mary, his wife, (Art. 6.) perverted upon marriage about two yeares agoe–George Hardwick, father of–Jane Watson, widow & farmer–Mary Watson, Elizabeth Watson, Jane Watson, her daughters.

Oulston: Anthony Smith, farmer–Mary, his wife–Ann Oliver, their servant–Thomas Smith, farmer–Cicely Smith, widow, the mother–Mary Smith, Susanna Smith, the sisters–Alice Harrison, a poor widow.

Angram: Mr Thomas Moor, gent:–Mr Thomas Moor, gent.; his nephew–Elizabeth

Watters, servant–Ralph Hall, farmer–Mary, his wife–John Hall, their son–Ursula Hall, Ann Hall, Ellen Hall, their daughters–Thomas Rose, farmer–his wife (Art. 6) soon after marriage, & maid servant lately perverted about two or three months agoe.

3. There is an apartment at Newbrough in which Mass is understood to be performed, & to which there is a Resort of Papists on the Lord's Day, & at other times.

4. No Popish School.

5. No Visitation, or Confirmation, that I have heard of.

Henry Thomson, Minister of Coxwold.
September 25, 1735.

. . .

Lyth Cleveland. An Acct of all Papists or Supposed Papists we have within the Parish of Lyth, Egton Chappelry excepted, of Men, Women, and Children above the age of thirteen Years.

1. Richard Smith, gent., and Mary his wife–Thomas and Richard, his sons–Robert Wood and Grace his wife–Wm. Keld and Katherine his wife–Wm. Unthank, shoemaker–Elizabeth, wife of Mathew Wilson–Thomas Hogard, batchelor, butcher–Mary, the wife of John Reah–Wm. Stephenson, labourer–Ellis Hill, widow, and Ann, her daughter–Margaret, wife of Thomas Robinson–Ann Peirson, widow–Thomas, her son–George Peirson and Hellenor his wife–Richard Lyth, Isabel his wife, John his son, Hellenor his daughter–John Holehon, widower–Francis Jowsey–John Atkinson–Elizabeth Atkinson–Thomas Garbut–Jane his wife–Francis Wedgewood–Elizabeth Hodgson, widow–Robt Stephenson, mariner, and Dorothy his wife–John Dale, butcher–Martin Adamson, Jane his wife–Ann Hodgson, widow–Christopher Simpson, Margaret his wife–Elizabeth wife of Wm. Mires–Frances Thompson–Wm. Atkinson and Elizabeth his wife–John Atkinson and Katharine his wife–Mary Atkinson, widow–Robt. her son, and Elizabeth her daughter–Luke Gallon and Dorothy his wife–Thomas his son.
2. John Revet, a Popish Priest residing at Ugthorp.[1]
3. The said John Revet occupies a House or place in Ugthorp above named wherein he reads Mass on Sundays and other Holy days.
4. The said John Revet keeps a School at Ugthorp aforesaid and educates young people.
5. We have had no Visitation nor Conformation (sic) held within the Parish of Lyth by any Popish Bishop that I know off.
6. The afore named Robert Wood is perverted to the Romish Religion by Grace, his wife, about two years since. Katharine perverted to the Romish Religion by her husband, Wm. Keld about 8 years since. Wm. Atkinson perverted his wife Elizabeth to the Romish Religion about seven years since. The afore named John Atkinson perverted his wife Katharine to the Romish Religion about 18 years since. Luke Gallon perverted his wife Dorothy to the Romish Religion about 15 years since.

[1] See p. 404, note 1.

The Exact and particular Account of the Enquiries of Popish Recusants in the Parish of Lyth delivered to me at the Arch Deacon's last Visitation.
Witness my hand this 23[d] day of September 1735,

Ralph Bateman, Ministr. de Lyth.

. .

Stokesley Cleveland. An exact & particular Return to the within-mentioned Enquiries.

1. The Number of Papists or supposed Papists in my Parish &c. viz. Mr Bradshaw Peirson, Lord of the Mannour–John Catton, Dennis Kerney, Dennis Kelley, his servants–Clement Sympson, shopkeeper, & Mary, his wife–Elizabeth, the wife of Wm. Robinson, glover, & John, his son–Christopher Newborn, weaver, & Eliz:, his wife, & Isabel, his mother–John Armsom, weaver, & Dorothy, his wife–George Craven, gardener–George Harrison, plaisterer, & Rachel, his wife–Margaret, the wife of James Bartram, weaver–Eliz. Lane, glover–John Sigsworth, farmer, & Elizth: his wife.
2. There is no Popish Priest who constantly dwells in my Parish, but a person suspected to be such, who goes by the name of Gordon & resides at Osmotherley, does as I am inform'd, attend the Papists in it.[1]
3. There is a House in my Parish, in which Mass is understood to be perform'd & to which there is a Resort of Papists in the Lord's Day once a Month, viz. the above-mentioned Chris[r] Newborn's.

4–6 None.

Hen: Cooke, Rec[r] of Stokesley.
September the 15th 1735.

110B. Thomas Fletcher's information against five Yorkshire priests, 1746

(*Catholic Record Society*, XIV, pp. 387–388.)

This is an example of a number of informations laid against Catholics, following the Jacobite Rising of 1745.

North Riding of the County of York } The Information of Thomas Fletcher of Stoxley in the said Riding. Taken before Cholmley Turner, Timothy Mauleverer, Ralph Robinson and Thomas Skottowe Esquires, Justices of the peace for the said Riding y[e] 9th Day of July 1746.

This Informant upon his Oath Saith that when he was about Nine years of age, his Mother marrying a Roman Catholick, brought [him] up afterwards in that Communion, And that he Continued a papist till about Michaelmas last, during which time he went to hear Mass at Several Chappels, And said that he has heard one Mr Anderson Say Mass at a Chappel in Stockton in y[e] County of Durham about five years agoe, and he observ'd at the said Time that he held up a wafer with both his hands, And immediately after a Cup in the same manner, saying something at that instant in a Language unknown to this Informant, And further saith that he had on at

[1] See No. 110B.

the same time a Surplice, And a Red Stole about his Neck, hanging down before, with a Cross wrought in it at Each End. And that the said Mr Anderson did then Eat of the wafer and Drank of the Cup, and after gave the Sacrament to a man and a woman in ye said Chappel. This informant saith that he has been at a Popish Chappel in Craythorn in this Riding Several times and has heard the said Mr Anderson say Mass in the like manner, only at Certain times when there are prayers for the Dead, he had on a black Vestment and Stole upon ye Surplice, He further Saith that he did hear one Mr Rivit[1] say Mass on a Latter Lady Day about Nine years agoe in a Popish Chappel at Osmotherly in this Riding after the same manner and form as Mr Anderson did, And that he had with him several young Gentlemen, said to be Scholars and Boarders with him, And he Saith that the said Mr Rivit came that night to his Fathers, who lived in a House in Stoxley made use of as a Chappel till Mr Pierson[2] built his, And said Mass to his Mother and him and ye family. This Informant likewise upon his Oath saith that he knows one Mr Collingdrige a Popish Priest and has heard him say Mass in a Chappel at Silton in this Riding once, And at diverse times at Stoxley in Mr. Pierson's Chappel, where he Constantly Attended Once a Month for Two or three years last past, And that he perform'd the said Service in the form and after the Same manner as above described, He further Saith that he has heard one Mr Siddell a Popish Priest Say Mass in a Room in Mr Mayes House at Yarm (whilest the Chappel there was building) after the Same manner & in the form as Mr Anderson did as above mention'd, And further That he has heard One Mr Gordon late of osmotherly a Popish Priest say Mass at Osmotherly afors^d, and that he has heard him say he was a Scotch Man & that ye Duke of Gordon was his Unkle–

Taken & Sworn the day & year aboves^d before us–

Cho: Turner
Tim^o Mauleverer
Ra. Robinson
Thos Skottowe.

The Mark of
Thomas + Fletcher

[Endorsed] 9th July 1746. Thomas Fletchers Informac'on ag^t Anderson & Rivett.

111. Speeches of Sir George Savile and John Dunning in the House of Commons, moving and seconding the Bill for Catholic Relief, 14 May 1778

(*The Annual Register for the Year 1778*, pp. 190–191.)

Sir George Savile (1726–1784) was M.P. for Yorkshire, and John Dunning (1731–1783) later first Baron Ashburton, for Calne.

May 14th. Sir George Saville moved accordingly for leave to bring in a bill for the repeal of certain penalties and disabilities provided in an act of the 10th and 11th of William the Third, entituled, An act to prevent the further growth of popery. He stated, that one of his principal views in proposing this repeal was, to vindicate

[1] The *alias* of the Reverend Monoux Hervey, one of the most active of the Yorkshire priests. (See the preceding extract.) After two years imprisonment in York Castle, he was released, on condition that he left Yorkshire.

[2] Lord of the manor of Stokesley.

the honour, and to assert the principles of the Protestant religion, to which all persecution was, or ought to be, wholly adverse. That this pure religion ought not to have had an existence, if persecution had been lawful; and it ill became us to practise that with which we reproached others. That he did not meddle with the vast body of that penal code: but selected that act, on which he found most of the prosecutions had been formed, and which gave the greatest scope to the base views of interested relations, and of informers for reward. The act had not indeed been regularly put in execution, but sometimes it had; and he understood that several lived under great terror, and some under actual contribution, in consequence of the powers given by it. As an inducement to the repeal of those penalties, which were directed with such a violence of severity against Papists, he stated the peaceable and loyal behaviour of that part of the people under a government, which, though not rigorous in enforcing, yet suffered such intolerable penalties and disqualifications to stand against them on the statutes. A late loyal and excellent address which they had presented to the throne, stood high among the instances which Sir George pointed out, of the safety, and the good consequences, which were likely to attend this liberal procedure of Parliament. He observed, that in that address, they not only expressed their obedience to the government under which they lived, but their attachment to the constitution upon which the civil rights of this country have been established by the Revolution, and which placed the present family upon the throne of these kingdoms. As a further guard and security, however, against any possible consequence of the measure, he proposed that a sufficient test might be formed, by which they should bind themselves to the support of the civil government by law established.

The motion was seconded by Mr. Dunning, who, with his well-known ability and knowledge in such subjects, went into a legal discussion of the principle, objects, and past operation, of the bill which was intended to be repealed. The following he stated as the great and grievous penalties.–The punishment of Popish priests or Jesuits, who should be found to teach or officiate in the services of that church; which acts were felony in foreigners, and high treason in the natives of this kingdom.–The forfeitures of Popish heirs, who had received their education abroad, and whose estates went to the next Protestant heir.–The power given to the son or other nearest relation, being a Protestant, to take possession of the father, or other relation's estate, during the life of the real proprietor.–And, the depriving of Papists from the power of acquiring any legal property by purchase; a word, which in its legal meaning carried a much greater latitude, than was understood (and that perhaps happily) in its ordinary acceptation; for it applied to all legal property acquired by any other means than that of descent.

These, he said, were the objects of the proposed repeal. Some of them had now ceased to be necessary, and others were at all times a disgrace to humanity. The imprisonment of a Popish priest for life, only for officiating in the services of his religion, was horrible in its nature; and must, to an Englishman, be ever held as infinitely worse than death. Such a law, in times of so great liberality as the present, and when so little was to be apprehended from these people, called loudly for repeal; and he begged to remind the House, that even then they would not be left at liberty to exercise their functions; but would still, under the restriction of former laws, be liable to a year's imprisonment, and to the punishment of a heavy fine.

And although, he observed, the mildness of government had hitherto softened the rigour of the law in the practice, it was to be remembered, that the Roman catholic priest constantly lay at the mercy of the basest and most abandoned of mankind; of common informers; for on the evidence of any of these wretches, the magisterial and judicial powers were of necessity bound to enforce all the shameful penalties of the act. Others of these penalties, held out the most powerful temptations for the commission of acts of depravity, at the very thought of which our nature recoils with horror. They seem calculated to loosen all the bands of society; to dissolve all civil, moral, and religious obligations and duties; to poison the sources of domestic felicity; and to annihilate every principle of honour. The encouragement given to children to lay their hands upon the estates of their parents, and the restriction which debars any man from the honest acquisition of property, need, said he, only to be mentioned, to excite the utmost indignation of the House.

The motion was received with universal approbation, and a bill was accordingly brought in and passed without a single negative, by which a considerable body of our fellow-citizens were relieved from the pressure, of some of the most intolerable of those grievances under which they had long laboured.

112. Sir George Savile's Act for Relief of Roman Catholics, 1778

(*Statutes at Large*, XXXII, pp. 152–154, 18 Geo. III, cap. 60.)

This Act abolished the prosecution of priests and their imprisonment for life on information from common informers, and permitted Catholics to hold and inherit land. An oath of allegiance was prescribed.

An act for relieving his Majesty's subjects professing the popish religion from certain penalties and disabilities imposed on them by an act, made in the eleventh and twelfth years of the reign of King William *the Third, intituled,* An act for the further preventing the growth of popery.

WHEREAS *it is expedient to repeal certain provisions in an act of the eleventh and twelfth years of the reign of King* William *the Third, intituled,* An act for the further preventing the growth of popery, *whereby certain penalties and disabilities are imposed on persons professing the popish religion*; may it please your Majesty that it may be enacted; and be it enacted by the King's most excellent majesty, by and with the advice and consent of the lords spiritual and temporal, and commons, in this present parliament assembled, and by the authority of the same, That so much of the said act as relates to the apprehending, taking, or prosecuting, of popish bishops, priests, or jesuits; and also so much of the said act as subjects popish bishops, priests, or jesuits, and papists, or persons professing the popish religion, and keeping school, or taking upon themselves the education or government or boarding of youth, within this realm, or the dominions thereto belonging, to perpetual imprisonment; and also so much of the said act as disables persons educated in the popish religion, or professing the same, under the circumstances therein mentioned, to inherit or take by descent, devise, or limitation, in possession, reversion, or remainder, any lands, tenements, or hereditaments, within the kingdom of *England*, dominion of *Wales*, and town of *Berwick upon Tweed*, and gives to the next of kin, being a protestant, a right to have and enjoy such lands, tenements, and hereditaments; and also so much of the said act as disables papists, or persons professing the popish religion, to purchase any manors, lands, profits out of lands, tenements, rents, terms, or hereditments, within the kingdom of *England*, dominion of *Wales*, or town of *Berwick upon Tweed*, and makes void all and singular estates, terms, and other interests or profits whatsoever out of lands, to be made, suffered, or done, from and after the day therein mentioned, to or for the use or behoof of any such person or persons, or upon any trust or confidence, mediately or immediately, for the relief of any such person or persons; shall be, and the same, and every clause and matter and thing herein-before mentioned, is and are hereby repealed. . . .

IV. Provided also, That nothing herein contained shall extend, or be construed to extend, to any person or persons but such who shall, within the space of six calendar months after the passing of this act, or of accruing of his, her, or their title, being of the age of twenty-one years, or who, being under the age of twenty-one years, shall, within six months after he or she shall attain the age of twenty-one years, or being of unsound mind, or in prison, or beyond the seas, then within six months after such disability removed, take and subscribe an oath in the words following: I A.B. *do sincerely promise and swear, That I will be faithful and bear true allegiance to his majesty King* George *the Third, and him will defend, to the utmost of my power, against all conspiracies and attempts whatever that shall be made against his person, crown, or dignity; and I will do my utmost endeavour to disclose and make known to his Majesty, his heirs and successors, all treasons and traiterous conspiracies which may be formed against him or them; and I do faithfully promise to maintain, support, and defend, to the utmost of my power, the succession of the crown in his Majesty's family, against any person or persons whatsoever; hereby utterly renouncing and abjuring any obedience or allegiance unto the person taking upon himself the stile and title of* Prince of Wales, *in the lifetime of his father, and who, since his death, is said to have assumed the stile and title of* King of Great Britain, *by the name of* Charles the Third, *and to any other person claiming or pretending a right to the crown of these realms; and I do swear, that I do reject and detest, as an unchristian and impious position, That it is lawful to murder or destroy any person or persons whatsoever, for or under pretence of their being heretics; and also that unchristian and impious principle, that no faith is to be kept with heretics: I further declare, that it is no article of my faith, and that I do renounce, reject, and abjure, the opinion, that princes excommunicated by the pope and council, or by any authority of the see of* Rome, *or by any authority whatsoever, may be deposed or murdered by their subjects, or any person whatsoever: and I do declare, that I do not believe that the pope of* Rome, *or any other foreign prince, prelate, state, or potentate, hath, or ought to have, any temporal or civil jurisdiction, power, superiority, or pre-eminence, directly or indirectly, within this realm. And I do solemnly, in the presence of God, profess, testify, and declare, that I do make this declaration, and every part thereof, in the plain and ordinary sense of the words of this oath; without any evasion, equivocation, or mental reservation whatever, and without any dispensation already granted by the pope, or any authority of the see of* Rome, *or any person whatever; and without thinking that I am or can be acquitted before God or man, or absolved of this declaration, or any part thereof, although the pope, or any other persons or authority whatsoever, shall dispense with or annul the same, or declare that it was null or void.*

[Clause V omitted.]

113. Joseph Berington's view of the decline of Catholicism during the eighteenth century

(J. Berington, *The State and Behaviour of English Catholics, from the Reformation to the Year 1780* (1780), pp. 114–117, 120–121.)

Joseph Berington (1746–1827) was a Catholic priest, in Staffordshire and later in London.

The few Catholics, I have mentioned, are also dispersed in the different counties. In many, particularly in the West, in South-Wales, and in some of the midland counties, there is scarcely a Catholic to be found. This is easily known from the residence of Priests. After London, by far the greatest number is in Lancashire. In Staffordshire are a good many, as also in the northern counties of York, Durham, and Northumberland. Some of the manufacturing and trading towns, as Norwich, Manchester, Liverpool, Wolverhampton, and Newcastle-upon-Tyne, have Chapels, which are rather crowded, but these constitute the greatest part of the number I have just given to their respective counties. In a few towns, particularly at Coventry, their number, I find, is increased; but this by no means in proportion of the general increase of population in the same places. Excepting in the towns, and out of Lancashire, the chief situation of Catholics is in the neighbourhood of the old families of that persuasion. They are the servants, or the children of servants, who have married from those families, and who chuse to remain round the old mansion, for the conveniency of prayers, and because they hope to receive favour and assistance from their former masters.

Many laws have been enacted to prevent the growth of Popery; and it now is, and always has been, the popular cry, that Papists are daily increasing. One might almost fancy, from the frequency of these reports, that they sprang up, like mushrooms, by instantaneous vegetation. Had there been truth in such reports, how very different, at this day, would be the list of Catholic names, from what it really is. More than one half, if not the whole English nation, must have been long ago subjected to the See of Rome. The truth is, within the present century we have most rapidly decreased. Many congregations have intirely disappeared in different parts; and in one district alone, with which I am acquainted, eight out of thirteen are come to nothing; nor have any new ones risen to make up, in any proportion, their loss. These are facts of certain notoriety.–In the nature of things, it could not possibly be otherwise. Where one cause can be discovered tending to their increase, there will be twenty found to work their diminution. Among these the principal are, the loss of families by death, or by conforming to the established Church; the marrying with Protestants; and that general indifference about religion, which gains so perceptibly on all ranks of Christians.–When a family of distinction fails, as there seldom continues any conveniency either for prayers or instruction, the neighbouring Catholics soon fall away: And when a Priest is still maintained, the example of the Lord is wanting to encourage the lower class, particularly to the practice of their religion. I recollect the names of at least ten noble families that, within these sixty years, have either conformed, or are extinct; besides many Commoners of distinction and fortune.–The marrying with Protestants, which is now very usual, will necessarily produce the same effect. All, or half the children are, in this case, generally educated Protestants; and when this is not done, example or persuasion often proves equally efficacious.–I need not insist on the operation of the third cause I mentioned.–When we add to these the whole pressure of the penal laws, we have discovered an agent almost sufficiently powerful to shake the faith of martyrs. . . .

We have, at this day, but eight Peers, nineteen Baronets, and about a hundred and fifty Gentlemen of landed property.–Among the first, the Duke of Norfolk, the Earl of Shrewsbury, and the Lords Arundel and Petre, are in possession of considerable estates. But the Earl of Surrey, the eldest and only son to the Duke, having lately conformed, the large possessions of that noble and ancient family will soon fall into Protestant hands. The eldest son of Lord Teynham has also left the religion of his father.–Among the Baronets are not more than three great estates: Sir Thomas Gascoigne has this year also taken the oaths. Of the remaining Commoners, with an exception of four or five, the greatest part have not, on an average, more than one thousand pounds per annum, in landed property. Within this year alone, we have lost more by the defection of the two mentioned Gentlemen, than we have gained by Proselytes since the Revolution.

In trade very few fortunes have been made; and at this hour, there are not more than two Catholics of any note who are even engaged in mercantile business. The eldest sons of our Gentry never think of trade; and the younger children have seldom a sufficient fortune, on which to ground any prospect of success. They therefore generally chuse to remain useless and dependent Beings among their relations and friends, or to eat a hardly-earned and scanty bread in the service of some foreign Prince. England, like a cruel stepmother, refuses to give them nourishment.

Part VI

THE STATE OF THE NATION: ECONOMIC

THE STATE OF THE NATION: ECONOMIC

Introduction

ENGLAND in 1714 was an agricultural country. Arthur Young's estimate in 1770 that nearly half the population (exclusive of landlords, clergy, parochial poor and manufacturers) made their livelihood directly from agriculture, and his deduction that £66,000,000 of the national income was derived from the soil as against £37,000,000 from commerce and manufactures,[1] while it should not be accepted as accurate, does demonstrate that in 1783 the basic industry of the country was still agriculture. The agrarian revolution, which is the main feature of the rural history of the eighteenth century, transformed large parts of England and had repercussions throughout the whole country. It may be said to have begun with the introduction on a large scale of new crops, notably turnips and clover and other artificial grasses. Equally important was the influence of Jethro Tull, with his insistence on tillage and his invention of new or much improved agricultural machinery.[2] All this made possible and remunerative the introduction of elaborate rotations of crops, as in Norfolk, and led to improvements in breeds of cattle and sheep. Finally, Arthur Young's *Tours* are not only a most valuable source of information to the historian, but were also of great importance in the eighteenth century. They popularized many of the new ideas and established what the farming conditions actually were in the various parts of the country; and by emphasizing the need to combine practical agriculture with scientific method they made possible further advances.[3] Young also calculated, from information collected on his tours, the average prices of provisions, workmen's tools, and labour in the different parts of the country.[4]

Land ownership came to be valued at least as much for economic reasons as for social prestige and political rights. Landowners were, therefore, eager to get rid of burdensome medieval restrictions such as the strip system of cultivation and rights of common, which prevented them from making the most profitable use of their land. A great deal was done by private bargaining, and if this failed a landlord could always apply to Parliament to pass an enclosure Act[5] which would give him undisputed control of a consolidated piece of land free from rights of common. The process is described at length by Arthur Young and its advantages and disadvantages carefully weighed against each other.[6] It was widely believed at the time that enclosures led to rural depopulation, though this has been challenged by some competent modern authorities, and Young insisted that large farms were most advantageous to population.

The most important industry, after agriculture, was still the wool manufacture. This was largely localized in three areas–the south-western counties of Wiltshire, Somerset, Gloucester and Devon; Norfolk, with its headquarters at Norwich; and the West Riding of Yorkshire. The organization of the Yorkshire industry early in the century was described by Defoe in one of the most frequently quoted passages of

[1] No. 114. [2] No. 115. [3] No. 118. [4] No. 119. [5] No. 116. [6] No. 117.

his *Tour.*[1] Yorkshire was rapidly becoming the most prominent of the three areas, and the west-country trade was declining.[2] A table of the exports of woollen goods and the prices of wool in England, compiled in 1782, gives some indication of the state of this industry throughout the period.[3] The Calico Act[4] shows the importance contemporaries attached to both the woollen and the silk industries. The Act prohibited the home consumption of all prints on pure cotton material, since these would compete with wool and silk goods, both for clothing and household furnishings.

The silk industry early developed a factory system, in which young children were employed with general approval, and is a good illustration of the fact that many features of the industrial system of the early nineteenth century really existed much earlier. Lombe's famous silk mill at Derby is described by William Hutton, the historian of Birmingham, once an apprentice in the mill.[5] The expiration of Lombe's patent in 1732 led to the expansion of the silk industry to Stockport and Macclesfield. This period also saw the rise of the Lancashire cotton industry. Arthur Young visited Manchester during his tour of the northern counties in 1770, and collected information about the wages paid to men, women and children in the various branches of the industry.[6] Looking back on the period which ended in 1783, the outstanding feature of industrial history is the improvement in technique brought about by the great inventions, though this had in fact insufficient time to make much change in industrial organization until after 1783. Machinery had, however, been introduced into the Manchester cotton industry by that date, and the effect is described by James Ogden, a Manchester schoolmaster.[7]

Important developments in this period also took place in other industries besides textiles. One of the earliest and most important of the inventions was the process of smelting iron with coke, thus freeing the iron industry from its dependence upon wood for charcoal. The consequent developments in the ironworks at Coalbrookdale are described by the widow of the second Abraham Darby in a letter written about 1775.[8] Birmingham and its many industries were developing rapidly in the eighteenth century and are described by Lord and Lady Shelburne, who visited the town in 1766, and by a distinguished French geologist who went there in 1784.[9] James Watt's "very capable improvements" in the steam-engine and their usefulness are emphasized by his partner, Matthew Boulton, again a Birmingham manufacturer, in a letter to Lord Dartmouth urging the extension of Watt's patent.[10] The Tyneside industries especially the collieries, are described at the beginning and end of the period.[11] Dr. Richard Pococke, travelling through Cornwall in 1750, was much interested in and described in detail the methods of the Cornish tin-mines.[12]

Industrial unrest was not uncommon in the eighteenth century, and combinations of workmen were frequently formed to raise wages and improve conditions. Such combinations often led to rioting, as among the cloth workers of the south-western counties in 1726, and were a source of alarm to the government. The House of Commons, after a close inquiry into the riots of 1726, ordered a Bill to be introduced for preventing unlawful combinations of weavers and other workers, and for securing better payment of their wages by forbidding truck, etc.[13] The resulting Act is typical of a number of such Acts passed at various times in our period in respect of different

[1] No. 120. [2] No. 121. No. 122. [4] No. 123. [5] No. 124.
[6] No. 125. [7] No. 126. [8] No. 127. [9] No. 128. [10] No. 129.
[11] Nos. 130 and 131. [12] No. 132. [13] No. 133.

industries.[1] In spite of the intervention of Parliament, complaints continued, and two pamphlets published in 1739 were occasioned by further riots in Wiltshire in that year. They discuss the grievances of both masters and men and throw light on conditions in the Wiltshire woollen industry.[2]

Contemporaries were more interested in foreign than in domestic trade. The merchant *par excellence* was an exporter and/or importer of goods, and eighteenth-century journalists regarded him as a national hero, and detailed with some complacency the various branches of British trade with foreign countries.[3] All writers agreed that certain trades were more beneficial than others and that some were definitely disadvantageous to the nation. There was some difference of opinion when it came to assigning trade with a particular country to one or other category, but the views expressed in *The British Merchant* may be taken as fairly representative.[4] The idea of the general balance of trade was still universally accepted, and is implicit in the contemporary statistics of foreign trade and the comments made upon them in George Chalmers's *An Estimate of the Comparative Strength of Great Britain.*[5] At the end of the period Adam Smith was undermining the whole system of mercantilism by his analysis of its economic effects, but his views were not yet widely accepted by economists or statesmen.

This section ends with a few population statistics. The absence of reliable figures before the 1801 census has already been discussed in the General Introduction. Some examples of the Carlisle tables prepared by Dr. Heysham of Carlisle from the Bills of Mortality are included.[6] Finally, John Rickman's calculations from the 1801 census of the total population of England and Wales at ten-year intervals throughout the eighteenth century are included,[7] in the absence of a strictly contemporary estimate giving any idea of the increase of population during this period.

[1] No. 134. [2] No. 135. [3] No. 137. [4] No. 136.
[5] No. 139. [6] p. 140. [7] No. 141.

BIBLIOGRAPHY

I. BIBLIOGRAPHICAL AIDS

The student of economic history is well catered for by the specialized bibliographies which are a regular feature of the *Economic History Review*, especially the commentary on the secondary authorities by T. S. Ashton, "The Industrial Revolution" in v (1934–1935), pp. 104–119. Judith B. Williams, *Guide to the Printed Materials for English Social and Economic History, 1750–1850* (2 vols., New York, 1926), is exhaustive up to that date. More recent but more limited in scope is H. Higgs, *Bibliography of Economics* (Cambridge, 1935), which lists by title 7,000 works with some bearing on economics published between 1751 and 1775. Another volume to cover the years 1701–1750 is to appear shortly. P. W. Buck, *The Politics of Mercantilism* (New York, 1942), discusses the mercantilist authors of the seventeenth and eighteenth centuries and gives extracts from their works. G. N. Clark, *Guide to English Commercial Statistics 1696–1782*, Royal Historical Society (London, 1938), is indispensable and there are many useful articles in the edition of R. H. I. Palgrave, *Dictionary of Political Economy*, edited by H. Higgs (London, 1923–1926). In the United States the *Journal of Economic History* began publication in 1941 and the Business Historical Society, founded in 1925, published *The Journal of Economic and Business History* between 1929 and 1932.

II. CONTEMPORARY WORKS

Contemporaries were particularly interested in this subject. A few had the dispassionate interests of a twentieth-century scholar, but most had practical objects in view. Thus the notable collection of papers, originally inspired by the controversy over the commercial clauses of the Utrecht settlement, *The British Merchant*, was reprinted in three volumes, in 1721. Equally influential was John Smith's collection of documents bearing on the wool trade, *Chronicon rusticum-commerciale: or Memoirs of Wool* (2 vols., London, 1747). Other writers rushed into print because they believed some section of trade or industry was threatened with ruin and could only be saved by the adoption of some nostrum or other. Some writers, either out of disinterested patriotism or to curry favour with the government of the day, set out to show how Britain was developing commercially and industrially, or to call attention to dangerous tendencies which must be corrected if progress was to continue. From this voluminous literature a few outstanding works must be named–Joshua Gee, *Trade and Navigation of Great Britain Considered* (London, 1729, and later editions); James Postlethwayt, *History of the Public Revenue* (London, 1759), and Sir John Sinclair, *History of the Public Revenue* (3 parts, London, 1785–1790); Malachy Postlethwayt, *Universal Dictionary of Trade and Commerce* (2 vols., London, 1751–1755, and later editions), on which an article by Elspet Fraser on "Some Sources of Postlethwayt's Dictionary" in *Economic History*, IV (1938), pp. 25–32, should be consulted, and *Britain's Commercial Interest* (2 vols., London, 1757); Adam Anderson, *Historical and Chronological Deduction of the Origin of Commerce* (2 vols., London, 1764); T. Cunningham, *History of Taxes* (London, 3rd edition, 1778), which lists all taxes in force at the death of Queen Anne and then analyses and abbreviates parliamentary statutes which modified them session by session; George Chalmers, *An Estimate of the Comparative Strength of Great Britain since the Revolution* (London, 1782), and Sir Charles Whitworth, *State of the Trade of Great Britain* (London, 1776). In a class by itself stands Adam Smith's *Wealth of Nations* (2 vols., London, 1776, best modern edition by E. Cannan, London, 1904, reprinted 1950), based on a wide survey of existing commercial and industrial conditions. The standard life of Adam Smith is still John Rae, *Life of Adam Smith* (London, 1895), supplemented by the pious work of W. R. Scott, *Adam Smith as Student and Professor* (Glasgow, 1937). The brief pamphlet on Adam Smith written for the Historical Association by Sir Alexander Gray and numbered G.10 (London, 1948) is an admirable introduction. Much information may also be obtained from the *Journals of the Commissioners for Trade and Plantations 1704–82* (14 vols., London, 1924–1938), and from the numerous 'Tours' by Defoe and his successors which are indicated in the sectional bibliography on Social History.

III. GENERAL HISTORIES

Two volumes in the Home University Library, G. N. Clark, *The Wealth of England* [1496–1760] (London, 1946), and T. S. Ashton, *Industrial Revolution 1760–1830* (London, 1948), between them provide an excellent introductory survey. The standard histories, W. Cunningham, *Growth of English Industry and Commerce, Pt. ii Modern Times*, vols. 2 and 3 (6th edition, Cambridge, 1921), and E. Lipson, *Economic History of England*, vols. 2 and 3, *Age of Mercantilism* (London, 1931, 3rd edition, 1943), deal more fully with the period. E. Lipson, *The Growth of English Society* (London, 1949), includes a brief survey of economic developments, and Sir John Clapham, *A Concise Economic History of Britain* [to 1750] (Cambridge, 1949), is often illuminating in its discussion of the fundamental economic problems in our period. It has been continued by W. H. B. Court, *Concise Economic History of Britain from 1750 to Recent Times* (Cambridge, 1954). T. S. Ashton, *An Economic History of England, The Eighteenth Century* (London, 1955), is intended "to supplement and extend, rather than to supplant existing well-known treatises". There is an interesting article by A. H. John, "War and the English Economy" in *Economic History Review*, Second Series, VII (1955), pp. 329–344. The theory and practice of mercantilism is authoritatively set forth in E. F. Heckshe r, *Mercantilism* (2 vols., London, 1935). L. W. Moffit, *England on the Eve of the Industrial Revolution* (London, 1925), deals with the preliminaries, while the standard work on the Revolution itself is still P. Mantoux, *Industrial Revolution in the Eighteenth Century* (revised edition in English, London, 1928, new edition, 1947). There is a brief "Historical Revision" on the "Industrial Revolution" by H. L. Beales in *History*, XIV (1929–1930), pp. 125–129. N. A. Brisco, *Economic Policy of Walpole* (New York, 1907), provides a useful economic survey of the first half while C. R. Fay, *Great Britain from Adam Smith to the Present Day* (London, 1928), paints a vivid picture of social and economic England in the second half of the eighteenth century. S. and B. Webb, *English Local Government* (9 vols., London, 1906–1929), is a monumental work packed with economic and social material of all kinds. Also indispensable are the works of J. L. and B. Hammond, *The Village Labourer* (London, 4th edition, 1927, reprinted 1948); *The Town Labourer* (London, new edition, 1925); *The Skilled Labourer* (London, 1919); and *The Rise of Modern Industry* (London, 1925).

IV. POPULATION

This was a subject which greatly interested contemporaries in the second half of the century. Various attempts were made to arrive at a satisfactory estimate from the defective evidence of the bills of mortality or the inhabited house duty. The calculators differed widely from each other, and it was the uncertainty whether population was increasing or decreasing which led to the taking of the first census in 1801. This was accompanied by elaborate calculations of the population in each decade of the eighteenth century based on the number of baptisms recorded in the parish registers. More recent statisticians, notably E. C. K. Gonner, "The Population of England in the Eighteenth Century", in the *Journal of the Royal Statistical Society*, LXXVI (1912–1913), pp. 261–296, have criticized these estimates. G. Talbot Griffith, *Population Problems of the Age of Malthus* (Cambridge, 1926), made a bold attempt to substitute a new estimate. His conclusions have, however, been vigorously attacked for the period after 1780 by T. H. Marshall, "The Population Problem during the Industrial Revolution", in *Economic History*, I (1926–1929), pp. 429–456. Miss M. C. Buer also discussed population problems in *Health*,

Wealth and Population in the Early Days of the Industrial Revolution (London, 1926), and her main conclusion that the increase was due to a great fall in the death-rate and not to a rise in the birth-rate has till recently been generally accepted. K. H. Connell, "Some unsettled problems in English and Irish Population History", in *Irish Historical Studies*, VII (1950–1951), pp. 225–234, expresses some doubts; and H. J. Habakkuk in "English Population in the Eighteenth Century", *Economic History Review*, Second Series, VI (1953), pp. 117–133, suggests that sufficient consideration has not been given to the view of contemporary writers that the main cause of the increase was in fact a rising birth-rate.

V. AGRICULTURE

Outstanding amongst the numerous contemporary works are those of Arthur Young, especially his *A Six Months Tour through the North of England* (4 vols., London, 1770). J. G. Gazley gives an account of Young's activities in his article, "Arthur Young and the Society of Arts", in the *Journal of Economic History*, I (1941), pp. 129–152, and the edition of Young's *Tour in Ireland*, edited by A. W. Hutton (London, 1892), includes in vol. II, pp. 349–374 a good "Bibliography of Arthur Young". G. D. Amery's bibliography of Young's writings in *Journal of the Royal Agricultural Society of England*, LXXXV (1924), pp. 175–205, may also be consulted. *The Library Catalogue of Printed Books on Agriculture* [1471–1840], edited by Mary S. Aslin, published by the Rothamstead Experimental Station (2nd edition, Aberdeen, 1940), and the bibliographical surveys of G. E. Fussell (*infra*, p. 419) are useful. The pioneer modern work is R. E. Prothero [Lord Ernle], *English Farming Past and Present* (London, 1888, and later editions), chapters 7 to 9 of which are devoted to our century. Subsequent works have dealt extensively with the enclosure problem and include W. Hasbach, *History of the English Agricultural Labourer* (London, 1908); H. Levy, *Large and Small Holdings* (English translation, Cambridge, 1911); G. Slater, *The English Peasantry and Enclosure of Common Fields* (London, 1907); E. C. K. Gonner, *Common Land and Inclosure* (London, 1912); A. H. Johnson, *Disappearance of the Small Landowner* (Oxford, 1909); and W. H. R. Curtler, *Enclosure and Redistribution of our Land* (Oxford, 1920). W. E. Tate has adduced additional evidence on enclosures in the *English Historical Review*, LVII (1942), pp. 250–263, and LIX (1944), pp. 392–403, and also in his *Parliamentary Land Enclosures, in the county of Nottingham*, published by the Thoroton Society (Nottingham, 1935); and "The Cost of Parliamentary Enclosure in England (with special reference to the County of Oxford)" in *Economic History Review*, Second Series, V (1952–1953), pp. 258–265. J. D. Chambers, "Enclosure and Labour Supply in the Industrial Revolution", *ibid.*, pp. 319–343, deals mainly with the period after 1783. M. W. Beresford, "Commissioners of Enclosure" in the *Economic History Review*, XVI (1946), pp. 130–140, shows that some of the enclosure commissioners might almost be described as professionals. J. L. and B. Hammond, *The English Village Labourer*, is essential and may be supplemented by G. E. Fussell, *The English Rural Labourer* (London, 1949). A. G. Ruston and D. Witney, *Hooton Pagnell* (London, 1934), provides an elaborate inquiry into the agricultural evolution of a single Yorkshire village. Sir W. J. Ashley, *Bread of our Forefathers* (Oxford, 1928), discusses the distribution of various grain crops in eighteenth-century England, and shows that rye, barley and other grains largely made up the food supply of the English agricultural labourer of this time. The impact of the potato on eighteenth-century Britain is discussed in R. N. Salaman, *History and Social Influence of the Potato* (Cambridge, 1949). On the Corn Laws D. G. Barnes, *History of the English Corn Laws* (London, 1930), and C. R. Fay, *The Corn Laws and Social England* (Cambridge, 1932), should be consulted. The earlier pre-eighteenth-century development of the grain trade is explained by N. S. B. Gras, *Evolution of the English Corn Market* (Cambridge, Mass., 1915). Principles and practice are discussed by T. H. Marshall in the *Economic History Review*, II (1929–1930), pp. 41–60, "Jethro Tull and the 'New Husbandry' of the Eighteenth Century". J. H. Plumb, "Sir Robert Walpole and Norfolk Husbandry" in *ibid.*, Second Series, V (1952–1953), pp. 86–89, shows that the 'new husbandry' was being practised on the Walpole estates well before 1700. G. E. Fussell writes in *Economic*

History, II (1930–1933), pp. 521–535, on "Farmers' Calendars from Tusser to Arthur Young" and in the *Economic History Review*, VI (1935–1936), pp. 214–222, on "English Agriculture from Arthur Young to William Cobbett". The same author's *Old English Farming Books* (London, 1947) and *More Old English Farming Books* (London, 1950) cover much the same ground. He also contributed three articles to *Agricultural History*, III (1929), pp. 160–181, and XI (1937), pp. 96–116 and 189–214, on "Animal Husbandry in Eighteenth Century England", and along with Constance Goodman an article on "Eighteenth Century Estimates of British Sheep and Wool Production" to *ibid.*, IV (1930), pp. 131–151. M. K. Bennett in *Economic History*, III (1935), No. 10, pp. 12–29, studied "British Wheat Yield Per Acre for Seven Centuries", including the eighteenth. E. Hughes's essay on the eighteenth-century estate agent in *Essays in British and Irish History*, edited by H. A. Cronne, T. W. Moody and D. B. Quinn (London, 1949), is interesting. Some articles based on local studies are helpful in completing and checking the general picture, *e.g.* H. J. Habakkuk, "English Landownership 1680–1740" (based on Northamptonshire and Bedfordshire), in the *Economic History Review*, X (1940), pp. 2–17; W. G. Hoskins, "The Reclamation of the Waste in Devon 1550–1800", in *ibid.*, XIII (1943), pp. 80–92; M. W. Beresford, "Lot Acres" (the exceptional Midland township of Sutton Coldfield), in *ibid.*, XIII (1943), pp. 74–79, and G. E. Mingay, "The Agricultural Depression, 1730–1750", in *ibid.*, Second Series, VIII (1956), pp. 323–338, based on the accounts of the second duke of Kingston's estates in six counties. On the sale of agricultural products three articles in *Economic History* should be consulted: (1) by G. E. Fussell on "The London Cheesemongers of the Eighteenth Century" in I (1926–1929), pp. 394–398; (2) by G. E. Fussell and Constance Goodman on "Eighteenth Century Traffic in Live-Stock", *ibid.*, III (1934–1937), No. 11, pp. 214–236; and (3) by the same authors on "Eighteenth Century Traffic in Milk Products", *ibid.*, III (1934–1937), No. 11, pp. 380–387. Peter Mathias writes on "Agriculture and the Brewing and Distilling Industries in the Eighteenth Century" in *Economic History Review*, Second Series, V (1952–1953), pp. 249–257.

VI. INDUSTRIAL DEVELOPMENT

Professor A. P. Usher in his *History of Mechanical Inventions* (New York, 1929) describes the various inventions which made industrial development possible, while G. Unwin's articles on "The transition to the Factory System" in the *English Historical Review*, XXXVII (1922), pp. 206–218, 383–397, directed attention to this particular aspect of the Industrial Revolution. Maurice Dobb, *Studies in the Development of Capitalism* (London, 1946), is excellent on the rise of industrial capitalism and related subjects. Biographies of industrial pioneers include H. W. Dickinson's lives of *James Watt* (Cambridge, 1936) and *Matthew Boulton* (Cambridge, 1937), which must, however, be supplemented by the conclusion of J. E. Cule, writing in *Economic History*, IV (1940), pp. 319–325, on "Finance and Industry in the Eighteenth Century: the firm of Boulton and Watt", that it was Boulton's association with Watt in the engine trade which saved Boulton from certain ruin in 1778; G. Unwin, *Samuel Oldknow and the Arkwrights* (Manchester, 1924); and G. F. French, *Life and Times of Samuel Crompton* (Manchester, 1859). L. Jewitt, *The Wedgwoods* (London, 1865), and Eliza Meteyard, *Life of Josiah Wedgwood* (2 vols., London, 1865–1866), should be supplemented by R. M. Hower, "The Wedgwoods", in the *Journal of Economic and Business History*, IV (1932), pp. 281–313. W. Bowden, *Industrial Society in England towards the End of the Eighteenth Century* (New York, 1925), discusses the outlook of the capitalists. Our own generation has produced elaborate studies of the important industries of the eighteenth century. Sir J. H. Clapham, *The Woollen and Worsted Industries* (London, 1907), and E. Lipson, *History of the Woollen and Worsted Industries* (London, 1921), may be supplemented by more specialized studies of this basic industry, such as H. Heaton, *The Yorkshire Woollen and Worsted Industries* (Oxford, 1920); W. G. Hoskins, *Industry Trade and People in Exeter with Special Reference to the Serge Industry* (Manchester, 1935); J. Morris's unpublished thesis on

"West of England Woollen Industry 1750–1840", referred to in the *Bulletin of the Institute of Historical Research*, XIII (1935–1936), pp. 106–110; and, with reference to the period after 1780, *The Leeds Woollen Industry*, edited by W. B. Crump (Publications of the Thoresby Society (Leeds, 1931)). The cotton industry has been studied by G. W. Daniels in his *Early English Cotton Industry* (Manchester, 1920) and more elaborately by A. P. Wadsworth and Julia Mann in their *Cotton Trade and Industrial Lancashire 1600–1780* (Manchester, 1931), while P. J. Thomas wrote on "The Beginnings of Calico Printing in England" in the *English Historical Review*, XXXIX (1924), pp. 206–216, and discussed the state of the cotton industry under George I in his *Mercantilism and the East India Trade* (London, 1926). F. Warner, *The Silk Industry of the United Kingdom* (London, 1921), G. B. Hertz on "The English Silk Industry in the Eighteenth Century" in the *English Historical Review*, XXIV (1909), pp. 710–727, and W. M. Jordan's unpublished thesis on "The Silk Industry in London, 1760–1830", noticed in the *Bulletin of the Institute of Historical Research*, X (1932–1933), pp. 50–53, are all of interest. J. U. Nef, *Rise of the British Coal Industry* (2 vols., London, 1932), explains its processes and internal organization at the beginning of our period: later developments are the theme of T. S. Ashton and J. Sykes, *Coal Industry of the Eighteenth Century* (Manchester, 1929). The metallurgical industries are surveyed in T. S. Ashton, *Iron and Steel in the Industrial Revolution* (Manchester, 1924); and *An Eighteenth Century Industrialist* [Peter Stubs, filemaker, of Warrington] (Manchester, 1939); *The Walker Family, Iron Founders and Lead Manufacturers, 1741–93*, edited by A. H. John (Council for the Preservation of Business Archives, 1951); Arthur Raistrick, *Dynasty of Ironfounders: The Darbys and Coalbrookdale* (London, 1953); H. Hamilton, *English Brass and Copper Industries to 1800* (London, 1926); W. H. B. Court, *Rise of the Midland Industries* (London, 1938); G. I. H. Lloyd, *The Cutlery Trades* (London, 1913); G. R. Lewis, *The Stannaries: a Study of the English Tin Miner* (Boston, 1908); A. K. H. Jenkin, *The Cornish Miner* (London, 1927); and John Rowe, *Cornwall in the Age of the Industrial Revolution* (Liverpool, 1953), a useful regional study. E. W. Hulme's article on "Statistical History of the Iron Trade 1717–50" in the *Transactions of the Newcomen Society*, IX (1928–1929), pp. 12–35, is valuable. H. W. Dickinson, *Short History of the Steam Engine* (Cambridge, 1939), concisely summarizes what is known on this important subject, and J. Lord, *Capital and Steam Power* (London, 1923), uses the letter-books of Boulton and Watt to show the extent to which the steam-engine was employed in our period. E. Roll, *An Early Experiment in Industrial Organisation* (London, 1930), is also based on the records of the firm. T. C. Barker and J. R. Harris, *A Merseyside Town in the Industrial Revolution–St Helen's 1750–1900* (Liverpool, 1954), is an interesting regional study. A. and Nan Clow on "Lord Dundonald" in the *Economic History Review*, XII (1942), pp. 47–58, on "Vitriol in the Industrial Revolution" in *ibid.*, XV (1945), pp. 44–55 and *The Chemical Revolution* (London, 1952), throw light on the development of the chemical industry. V.W. Bladen's article in *Economic History*, I (1926–1929), pp. 116–130, on "The Potteries in the Industrial Revolution" is based on the surviving papers of Josiah Wedgwood. There is an unpublished thesis by J. Thomas on "Economic Development of the North Staffordshire Potteries" mentioned in the *Bulletin of the Institute of Historical Research*, XIII (1935–1936), pp. 177–179, some of the conclusions being summarized in "The Pottery Industry and the Industrial Revolution" in *Economic History*, III (1934–1937), pp. 399–414.

In conclusion, a few special works deserve mention. R. B. Westerfield's study of "Middlemen in English Business" [1660–1760] in the *Transactions of the Connecticut Academy of Arts and Sciences*, XIX (1915), pp. 111–445, is still useful though the author is too ready to accept the statistical guesses of the eighteenth century as fact. Ivy Pinchbeck, *Women Workers and the Industrial Revolution* (London, 1930), is a sound treatment. Works on the relation between Nonconformity and industry include Isabel Grubb, *Quakerism and Industry before 1800* (London, 1930); A. Raistrick, *Quakers in Science and Industry* (London, 1950); W. J. Warner, *Wesleyan Movement in the Industrial Revolution* (London, 1930), and E. D. Bebb, *Nonconformity and Social and Economic Life 1660–1800* (London, 1935). Last but by no means least must be mentioned the introductory chapter on the eighteenth century in S. and B. Webb, *History of Trade Unionism* (London, revised edition, 1920).

VII. WAGES AND PRICES

The works of Arthur Young are the most valuable of many attempts by contemporaries to collect information on this subject, though he is mainly concerned with agricultural wages and prices. R. Campbell, *The London Tradesman* (London, 1747), estimates the wages paid to workmen in a great variety of trades. A modern writer, J. J. Hecht, *The Domestic Servant Class in Eighteenth Century England* (London, 1956), gives the wages of different types of domestic servants, collected from advertisements in contemporary newspapers. Defoe and other pamphleteers such as Jonas Hanway are very ready to make generalizations about wages and prices, but their estimates should be accepted with caution. The Civil List expenditure from 1752 to 1770 is detailed in *Journals of the House of Commons*, XXXII, pp. 466–603, and deductions can be made as to salaries and pensions paid to the king's ministers, court officials, judges, diplomatists and other royal servants, though the figures given may be misleading in view of the importance of perquisites and casual windfalls to the official classes. A systematic study of such sources as Parson Woodforde's *Diary*, *James Beattie's Day-Book*, edited by R. S. Walker (Aberdeen, 1949), the account books on which Gladys Scott Thomson's work, *The Russells in Bloomsbury* (London, 1940), were based, and miscellaneous materials in the publications of the Historical Manuscripts Commission, etc., might yield valuable results.

The pioneer modern works are J. E. Thorold Rogers, *Six Centuries of Work and Wages* (2 vols., London, 1884, sixteenth impression, 1949), and the seventh volume of his *History of Agriculture and Prices in England* (Oxford, 1886–1902), which includes stock-exchange quotations for three leading securities. These works may now be supplemented by the figures given in Sir W. Beveridge and others, *Prices and Wages in England from the 12th to 19th Century*, vol. I (London, 1939). The standard work, however, on the eighteenth century is Elizabeth W. Gilboy, *Wages in Eighteenth Century England* (Cambridge, Mass., 1934). Mrs. Gilboy concludes that there were significant regional variations both in money and real wages. T. S. Willan's "Some Bedfordshire and Huntingdonshire Wage Rates 1697–1730" in the *English Historical Review*, LXI (1946), pp. 244–249, gives information about carpenters and labourers. E. Hughes, *Studies in Administration and Finance*, especially pp. 217–221, gives examples of wages and salaries paid to civil service clerks, cleaners, etc. For the closing years of our period (1779–1783) Professor N. J. Silberling's index numbers of wholesale prices "British Prices and Business Cycles" in the *Review of Economic Statistics* (Cambridge, Mass.), preliminary volume 5, supplement 2, are of value for various purposes. Two articles in the *English Historical Review*, XLIII (1928), pp. 398–408, and LVII (1946), pp. 115–119, the first on "Some New Evidence on Wage Assessments" by Elizabeth L. Waterman, and the second on "A Century of Wage Assessment in Herefordshire" [1662–1762] by R. K. Kelsall, combine statistics with some discussion of the problems involved in wage assessments. The coinage of the period is dealt with by Sir C. W. C. Oman, *Coinage of England* (Oxford, 1931), and G. C. Brooke, *English Coins from 7th Century to the Present Day* (London, 1932, 3rd revised edition, 1950); R. Dalton and S. H. Hamer discuss *Provincial Token Coinage of the Eighteenth Century*, parts 1–14 (London, 1910–1918).

VIII. TRANSPORT

John Owen, *Britannia Depicta or Ogilby Improv'd* (London, 1720), describes the English road system at the beginning of our period. The best general works are S. and B. Webb, *The Story of the King's Highway* (London, 1913), W. T. Jackman, *Development of Transportation in Modern England* (2 vols., Cambridge, 1916), and J. W. Gregory, *The Story of the Road* (London, 1931). Sir H. G. Fordham, *Road Books and Itineraries 1570–1850* (Cambridge, 1924), is a useful bibliography of these works. T. S. Willan, *River Navigation in England 1600–1750* (Oxford, 1936), and *Navigation of the River Weaver* (Cheetham Society, 1951) bring out the importance of inland waterways before the canal age. The same author's *The English Coasting Trade 1600–1750*

(Manchester, 1939) is also a useful survey. Joan Parkes's scholarly work, *Travel in England in the Seventeenth Century* (London, 1925), is largely applicable to at least the first half of the eighteenth century. C. G. Harper, *Stage-coach and Mail in Days of Yore* (2 vols., London, 1903), is better than its title would suggest. The most up-to-date account of the post office is H. Robinson, *The British Post Office* (Princeton, N.J., 1948).

IX. TRADE

Some interesting points concerning both the theory and practice of foreign trade emerged from the discussion between C. Wilson and Professor Heckscher in the *Economic History Review*, Second Series, II (1949–1950), pp. 152–161, III (1950–1951), pp. 219–228, and IV (1951–1952), pp. 231–242. W. R. Scott, *Constitution and Finance of English, Scottish and Irish Joint-Stock Companies to 1720* (Cambridge, 1910–1912), is the standard work on trading companies. A. B. Dubois, *The English Business Company after the Bubble Act 1720–1800* (New York, 1938), covers this period. Most of the other works dealing with internal trade have been included in earlier parts of this sectional bibliography. J. Viner discussed "English Theories of Foreign Trade before Adam Smith" in the *Journal of Political Economy*, XXXVIII (1930), pp. 249–301 and 404–457, and Sir J. F. Rees, "Phases of British Commercial Policy in the Eighteenth Century", in *Economica*, V (1925), pp. 130–150. L. A. Harper, *English Navigation Laws* (New York, 1939), can be recommended. Miss L. S. Sutherland's pioneer work on *A London Merchant 1695–1774* (London, 1933) sketches the activities of a London merchant with many interests. Sir Lewis Namier has studied the careers of some notable merchants and their contacts with the government. His articles include "Anthony Bacon, M.P." in the *Journal of Economic and Business History*, vol. II, No. 1; "Brice Fisher, M.P., a mid-eighteenth century Merchant and his Connexions", in the *English Historical Review*, XLII (1927), pp. 514–532 and 662; and "Charles Garth" in *ibid.*, LIV (1939), pp. 443–469 and 632–652. H. R. Fox Bourne, *English Merchants* (2 vols., London, 1866), includes a memoir of Sir John Barnard; and Miss L. S. Sutherland's article on "Samson Gideon and the Reduction of Interest 1749–50" in *Economic History Review*, XVI (1946), pp. 15–29, throws light on the career of another important financier. There are two modern works of importance on the ports, Sir D. J. Owen, *Origin and Development of the Ports of the United Kingdom* (London, 1939), and C. N. Parkinson, *Rise of the Port of Liverpool* (Liverpool, 1952). Rupert C. Jarvis, *Customs Letter-Books of the Port of Liverpool 1711–1813* (Manchester, 1956), is a selection of the correspondence from the letter-books. There is an article by F. E. Hyde, B. B Parkinson and Sheila Marriner on "The Nature and Profitability of the Liverpool Slave Trade" based on the Davenport papers, in *Economic History Review*, Second Series, V (1952–1953), pp. 368–377; and an article by J. E. Williams, "Whitehaven in the Eighteenth Century", in *Economic History Review*, Second Series, VIII (1956), pp. 393–404, describes the brief period of Whitehaven's national importance as a port. Apart from works on the South Sea Bubble given in the bibliography on Public Finance, the South Sea Company's activities have attracted many historians. Vera L. Brown writes on "The South Sea Company and Contraband Trade" in the *American Historical Review*, XXXI (1925–1926), pp. 662–678; and G. H. Nelson's article on "Contraband Trade under the Assiento 1730–39" in *ibid.*, LI (1945–1946), pp. 55–67, reaches the conclusion that such trade was a real threat to Spanish mercantilism and gives useful references to other periodical literature, which includes an unpublished thesis by Lucy F. Horsfall, "British Relations with the Spanish Colonies in the Caribbean 1713–39", in the *Bulletin of the Institute of Historical Research*, XV (1937–1938), p. 44; Elizabeth Donnan, "The Early Days of the South Sea Company 1711–18", in *Journal of Economic and Business History*, II (1930), pp. 419–451; and Lilian E. M. Batchelor, "The South Sea Company and the Assiento", in the *Bulletin of the Institute of Historical Research*, III (1925–1926), pp. 128–130. C. M. Andrews's articles in the *American Historical Review*, XX (1914–1915), pp. 43–63 and 761–780, on "Colonial Commerce" and "Anglo-French Commercial Rivalry 1700–1750" respectively are of more general interest.

E. C. Burnett printed "Observations of the London merchants on American Trade, 1783" in the *American Historical Review*, XVIII (1912–1913), pp. 769–780. Other books and articles of importance for colonial trade, including that with India and the Far East, will be found in the sectional bibliography on the Colonies. Some useful works on trade with particular countries are listed in the bibliography on Foreign Affairs. To these may be added Annie B. W. Chapman "Commercial Relations of England and Portugal 1487–1807", in the *Transactions of the Royal Historical Society*, Third Series, I (1907), pp. 157–179, supplemented by Sir Richard Lodge, "English Factory at Lisbon", in *ibid.*, Fourth Series, XVI (1923), pp. 211–242; G. B. Hertz, "England and the Ostend Company", in the *English Historical Review*, XXII (1907), pp. 255–279; W. E. Lingelbach, "The Merchant Adventurers at Hamburg", in the *American Historical Review*, IX (1903–1904), pp. 265–287; H. S. K. Kent, "The Anglo-Norwegian Timber Trade in the Eighteenth Century", in the *Economic History Review*, Second Series, VIII (1956), pp. 62–74; and G. Ambrose, "English Traders at Aleppo", in the *Economic History Review*, III (1931–1932), pp. 246–267, which illustrate the organization of English factories at foreign ports; A. Christelow "Great Britain and the Trades from Cadiz and Lisbon to Spanish America and Brazil", in *Hispanic American Historical Review*, XXVII (1947), pp. 2–29; and two articles by A. Rive on "The Consumption of Tobacco since 1600" and "A Short History of Tobacco Smuggling" in *Economic History*, I (1926–1929), pp. 57–75 and 554–559.

X. BANKING AND INSURANCE

There are histories of various banks and insurance companies which operated in the eighteenth century, especially Sir J. H. Clapham, *The Bank of England* (2 vols., Cambridge, 1944), and W. M. Acres, *Bank of England from Within* (2 vols., London, 1931). The more general works on banking include R. D. Richards, *Early History of Banking in England* (London, 1929); an article by the same author on "Evolution of Paper Money in England" in *Quarterly Journal of Economics*, XLI (1927), pp. 361–404; another by F. G. James on "Charity Endowments as sources of Local Credit" in *The Journal of Economic History*, VIII (1948), pp. 153–170; and W. R. Bisschop, *Rise of the London Money Market* (London, 1910). L. S. Pressnell, "Public Monies and the Development of English Banking", in *Economic History Review*, Second Series, V (1952–1953), pp. 378–397, covers the period 1750–1826. There is an article by D. M. Joslin in *ibid.*, Second Series, VII (1954–1955), pp. 167–186, on "London Private Bankers, 1720–1785".

F. B. Relton, *Account of the Fire Insurance Companies* [17th and 18th centuries] (London, 1893), E. A. Davies, *An Account of the Formation and Early Years of the Westminster Fire Office* (London, 1952), and C. Wright and C. E. Fayle, *History of Lloyd's* (London, 1928), deal with the development of insurance in this period.

A. AGRICULTURE

114. Arthur Young's estimate of the state of the nation in 1770

(Arthur Young, *A Six Months Tour Through the North of England*, IV (1770), pp. 493, 515–516, 517–520, 543–547.)

Young arrived at these figures by "proportioning the particulars of this Tour to the whole kingdom". Though they should not be taken as accurate in detail, they give a general idea of the extent to which the English economy in 1770 was still mainly agricultural.

STATE, RENTAL, *and* VALUE OF THE SOIL. [England, excluding Wales]

Acres in all,	32,000,000
Ditto of arable land,	16,000,000
Ditto of grass,	16,000,000
Number of farms,	111,498
Rental*,	£.16,000,000
Value of the soil at 33½ years purchase,	£.536,000,000

. . .

INCOME *of the* SOIL.

The preceding calculations give us the income of the following ranks of the people.

Landlords,
Tenants,
Parochial clergy,
The industrious poor employed by the soil,
The non-industrious poor.

The landlord's rent was found to be	£.16,000,000
The tenant's profit,	18,237,691
The clergy,	5,500,000
The industrious poor (being the amount of labour)	14,596,937
The non-industrious poor, (being the amount of rates)	866,666
Interest of money	4,400,000
Total of these several incomes arising from the soil,	59,601,294

It is, however, to be remarked, that these incomes are exclusive of those very considerable receipts which manufacturers draw from all these classes, amounting perhaps to half the total.

. . .

* The exact rent is 9*s.* 11*d.* but I call it here 10*s.*

POPULATION.

Number of men servants, ...	222,996
Maid ditto, ...	167,247
Boy ditto, ...	111,498
Labourers, ...	334,494
Men servants and labourers, ...	557,490
Farmers, ...	111,498
Number of souls according to the average of fifteen *per* 100*l.* a year, exclusive of extra labour,	2,400,000
The extra labour I before calculated as a third of the labourers, according to which it amounts to of souls	557,490
Total, ...	2,957,490
[Deduct on account of the maids and boys being part of them children of the labourers]	157,490
This will reduce the total to	2,800,000 souls:

And this is about eleven acres and a half *per* head; and 51.15s. rental.

This amount is exclusive of a vast number of people as much dependent on, and maintained by agriculture, as the very plough-man who cultivates the soil; for instance, the whole tribe of landlords; a vast body, branching into a wonderful variety; all those manufacturers who work for the farmer alone; and for the landlord in his rural capacity alone; such as wheel-wrights, blacksmiths, collar-makers, carpenters, brick-makers, masons, thatchers, glaziers, *&c. &c.* And in another path, all those that *cloath* these numerous bodies of people, furnish their houses, and administer to their luxuries. Besides, there are a vast portion of the clergy, and the parochial poor: all together most undoubtedly form a number, which bears a great proportion to the sum total of the kingdom's population.

RECAPITULATION.

Rental, ...	£.16,000,000
Value, ...	536,000,000
Supposed rental houses included, . . .	21,000,000
Value of total	636,000,000
Stock in husbandry, ...	110,000,000
Product of the soil in husbandry, excepting woods, parks, chaces, *&c.*	83,237,691
Expenditure of husbandry, ...	65,000,000
Profit of husbandry, ...	£.18,237,691
Income arising from the soil, exclusive of manufacturers,	59,601,294
The population of agriculture; exclusive of landlords, clergy, parochial poor, and manufacturers,	*Souls* 2,800,000

This little table may be called that part of THE STATE OF THE NATION which depends on rural oeconomics. . . .

But let us, for a moment, enlarge the sphere of our discourse, and take a transient view of the *whole* kingdom.

AGRICULTURE.

The income we have from products specified amount to	60,000,000
Suppose woods, timber, inland fisheries, parks, mines of all sorts, yield a product of	6,000,000
	66,000,000

MANUFACTURES.

The average of five accounts now before me, makes the value of the labour added to our wool to amount to	£.7,000,000
The labour bestowed on leather, exclusive of the consumption in the article wear and tear in husbandry, consisting of shoes, breeches, coaches, chairs, harness, *&c. &c. &c.* Suppose	4,000,000
The manufactures of lead, tin, iron, copper, *&c.* is one of the first, if not the greatest in the kingdom. Suppose the labour is	6,000,000
Flax and hemp, glass, paper, and porcelaine. Suppose	2,000,000
Silk and cotton must be considerably more than	1,500,000
	20,500,000
Besides these articles there are all the earnings of the whole body of artisans that are scattered, (except in the hard-ware way) such as carpenters, masons, cabinet-makers, upholsterers, glaziers, *&c. &c.* with an infinite number of shopkeepers: The whole aggregate of labour, exclusive of the preceding manufacturers, must be prodigiously great: However, that we may not exaggerate, let us suppose it, including all trades, not before specified, at	£.6,500,000
	27,000,000

COMMERCE.

The amount of the income arising from commerce, can only be conjectured: But when we consider that it includes that, not only of the merchants, but also of all the numerous bodies employed by them, such as sailors, ship-builders, boatmen, writers, porters, servants, with a vast number of *& cetera's*, it must certainly be very considerable, suppose	10,000,000
The public revenue, exclusive of the interest paid to foreigners	9,000,000
The interest of the savings in agriculture, manufactures, and commerce, exclusive of the public funds, which are included in the last article; and the sums borrowed by farmers; such as mortgages, bond-debts, *&c. &c. &c.* Suppose	5,000,000
Law, physic, the fine arts, literature, *&c. &c.* cannot create an income of less than	5,000,000

RECAPITULATION.

The soil,	66,000,000
Manufactures,	27,000,000
Commerce,	10,000,000
Publick revenue,	9,000,000
Sums at interest,	5,000,000
Law, physic, *&c.*	5,000,000
Total income of *England*,	122,000,000

Now the most inattentive eye must be able, at the slightest glance, to specify abundance of various kinds of income omitted in this table; but I by no means aim at an accuracy in a matter that requires it not: All I would endeavour to show, is, that the income of the whole people is a very great sum, compared to all public wants! and that it, in all probability, amounts to considerably more than an hundred millions. . . .

From this review of the agriculture, &c. of this kingdom, I apprehend there is no slight reason to conclude, that *England* is, at present, in a most rich and flourishing situation; that her agriculture is, upon the whole, good and spirited, and every day improving; that her industrious poor are well fed, cloathed, and lodged, and at reasonable rates of expence; the prices of all the necessaries of life being moderate; that our population is consequently increasing; that the price of labour is in general high; of itself one of the strongest symptoms of political health; but at the same time not so high as to leave any reason to fear those ill effects which have been prognosticated concerning it; that the wealth of all other ranks of people appear to be very great, from the almost universal manner in which the kingdom is adorned with stately as well as useful buildings, ornamented parks, lawns, plantations, waters, &c. which all speak a wealth and happiness not easily mistaken: That all kinds of public works shew the public to be rich; witness the navigations, roads, and public edifices. If these circumstances do not combine to prove a kingdom to be flourishing, I must confess myself totally in the dark.

This conclusion, I am sensible, will by no means render my undertaking popular. The generality of readers are seldom so well pleased, as when an author lays before them a melancholy picture of accumulated evils under which a nation groans: This is not to be wondered at; it is human nature. But I conceive it a duty incumbent on one, who engages in such a journey as this, to lay a fair and genuine account of all these matters before the public. I have, it is true, offered some reflections on them; perhaps it was an error, and I should have dealt only in facts; but these reflections do not alter those facts, which may be viewed naked, and applied to any use more penetrating minds can make of them. . . .

115. Jethro Tull and the New Husbandry, 1733

Jethro Tull, *The Horse-Hoeing Husbandry*, ed. W. Cobbett (1822), pp. 60–61, 67–68, 111–114.)

Jethro Tull (1674–1741) was a lawyer and a Berkshire farmer. His book, the most famous of the many eighteenth-century treatises on husbandry, first appeared in 1733. These extracts are chosen to illustrate the two main points of the New Husbandry–pulverization of the soil and sowing by Tull's newly invented drill–and their special application to turnip-growing. For the effects of Tull's theories, see T. H. Marshall, "Jethro Tull and the 'New Husbandry' ", *Econ. Hist. Review*, II, pp. 41–60.

[1]Hoeing is the breaking or dividing the soil by tillage, whilst the corn or other plants are growing thereon.

It differs from common tillage (which is always performed before the corn or plants are sown or planted) in the times of performing it; it is much more beneficial, and it is performed by different instruments.

Land that is before sowing tilled never so much (though the more it is tilled the more it will produce) will have some weeds, and they will come in along with the crop for a share of the benefit of the tillage, greater or less, according to their number, and what species they are of.

But what is most to be regarded is, that as soon as the ploughman has done his work of ploughing and harrowing, the soil begins to undo it, inclining towards, and endeavouring to regain its natural specific gravity; the broken parts by little and little coalesce, unite, and lose some of their surfaces, many of the pores or interstices

[1] Notes omitted.

close up during the seed's incubation, and hatching in the ground; and, as the plants grow up, they require an increase of food, proportionable to their increasing bulk; but on the contrary, instead thereof, that internal superficies, which is their artificial pasture, gradually decreases.

The earth is so unjust to plants, her own offspring, as to shut up her stores in proportion to their wants; that is, to give them less nourishment when they have need of more; therefore man, for whose use they are chiefly designed, ought to bring in his reasonable aid for their relief, and force open her magazines with the hoe, which will thence procure them at all times provisions in abundance, and also free them from intruders; I mean, their spurious kindred, the weeds, that robbed them of their too scanty allowance.

There is no doubt, but that one-third part of the nourishment raised by dung and tillage, given to plants or corn at many proper seasons, and apportioned to the different times of their exigencies, will be of more benefit to a crop, than the whole applied as it commonly is, only at the time of sowing. This old method is almost as unreasonable as if treble the full stock of leaves, necessary to maintain silk-worms until they had finished their spinning, should be given them before they are hatched, and no more afterwards. . . .

The highest and lowest vineyards are hoed by the plough; first the high vineyards, where the vines grow, almost like ivy, upon great trees, such as elms, maples, cherry-trees &c.; these are constantly kept in tillage, and produce good crops of corn, besides what the trees do yield; and also these great and constant products of the vines are owing to this sort of hoe-tillage; because neither in meadow or pasture grounds can vines be made to prosper; though the lands be much richer, and yet have a less quantity of grass taken off it than arable has corn carried from that.

The vines of low vineyards, hoed by the plough, have their heads just above the ground, standing all in a most regular order, and are constantly ploughed in the proper season; these have no other assistance but by hoeing, because their heads and roots are so near together, that dung would spoil the taste of the wine they produce, in hot countries.

From these I took my vineyard scheme, observing that indifferent land produces an annual crop of grapes and wood without dung; and though there is annually carried off from an acre of vineyard as much in substance as is carried off in the crop of an acre of corn produced on land of equal goodness, yet the vineyard soil is never impoverished unless the hoeing culture be denied it: but a few annual crops of wheat, without dung, in the common management will impoverish and emaciate the soil.

I cannot find either in theory or practice any other good reason for this difference, except that the vineyard soil is more pulverised by hoeing; and not exhausted by so much more than a competent quantity of plants, as the cornfields in the common management are: . . .

As far as I can be informed, it is but of late years that turnips have been introduced as an improvement in the field.

All sorts of land, when made fine by tillage, or by manure and tillage, will serve to produce turnips, but not equally: for chalky land is generally too dry (a turnip being a thirsty plant), and they are so long in such dry poor land before they get into rough leaf, that the fly is very apt to destroy them there; yet I have known them succeed on such land, though rarely.

Sand and gravel are the most proper soil for turnips; because that is easily pulverised, and its warmth causeth the turnips to grow faster, and so they get the sooner out of danger of the fly; and such a soil, when well tilled, and horse-hoed, never wants a sufficient moisture, even in the driest weather, and the turnips being drilled, will come up without rain, and prosper very well with the sole moisture of the dews, which are admitted as deep as the pulveration reacheth; and if that be to five or six inches, the hottest sun cannot exhale the dews thence in the climate of England: I have known turnips thrive well in a very dry summer, by repeated horse-hoeings, both in sand, and in land which is neither sandy nor gravelly.

When I sowed turnips by hand, and hoed them with a hand hoe, the expence was great, and the operation not half performed, by the deceitfulness of the hoers, who left half the land unhoed, and covered it with the earth from the part they did hoe, and then the grass and weeds grew the faster: besides in this manner a great quantity of land could not be managed in the proper season.

When I drilled upon the level, at three feet intervals, a trial was made between those turnips and a field of the next neighbour's, sown at the same time, whereof its hand-hoeing cost ten shillings per acre, and had not quite half the crop of the drilled, both being measured by the bushel, on purpose to find the difference.

In the new method they are more certain to come up quickly; because in every row half the seed is planted about four inches deep, and the other half is planted exactly over that, at the depth of half an inch, falling in after the earth has covered the first half. Thus planted, let the weather be never so dry, the deeper seed will come up; but if it raineth (immediately after planting) the shallow will come up first; we also make it come up four times, by mixing our seed, half new and half old (the new coming a day quicker than the old); these four comings up give it so many chances for escaping the fly, it being often seen that the seed sown over night will be destroyed by the fly, when that sown the next morning will escape; and *vice versa*; or you may hoe-plough them when you see the fly is like to devour them; this will bury the greatest part of those enemies; or else you may drill in another row, without new ploughing the land.

This method has also another advantage of escaping the fly, the most certain of any other, and infallable, if the land be made fine as it ought to be; this is to roll it with a heavy roller across the ridges after it is drilled, which closing up the cavities of the earth, prevents the fly's entrance and exit, to lay the eggs, hatch, or bring forth the young ones to prey upon the turnips, which they might entirely devour if the fly came before they had more than the first two leaves, which being formed of the very seed itself, are very sweet; but the next leaves are rough and bitter, which the fly does not love. I have always found the rolling disappoint the fly, but very often it disappoints the owner also, who sows at random; for it makes the ground so hard that the turnips cannot thrive, but look yellow, dwindle, and grow to no perfection, unless they have a good hoeing soon after the leaves appear; for when they stand long without it, they will be so poor and stunted, that the hand-hoe does not go deep enough to recover them; and it is seldom that these rolled turnips can be hand-hoed at the critical time; because the earth is then become so hard, that the hoe will not enter it, without great difficulty, unless it be very moist, and very often the rain does not come to soak it until it be too late; but the drilled turnips being in single rows, with six-feet intervals, may be rolled without danger: for be the ground never so hard, the hand-hoe will easily single them out, at the price of sixpence per acre or less (if not in harvest), and the horse-hoe will in those wide intervals, plough at any time, wet or dry; and though the turnips should have been neglected till stunted, will go deep enough to recover them to a flourishing condition.

Drilled turnips, by being nowhere but in the rows, may be more easily seen than those which come up at random, and may therefore be sooner singled out by the hand-hoe; which is another advantage; because the sooner they are so set out, the better they will thrive.

Drilled turnips coming all up nearly in a mathematical line, it is very rarely that a charlock or other weed comes up in the same line amongst them, unless it be drilled in with the turnip-seed, of which weeds our horse-hoed seed never has any; there being no charlock in the rows, nor any turnip in the intervals; we know that whatever comes up in the interval is not a turnip, though so like it, that at first coming up, if promiscuously, it cannot easily be distinguished by the eye, until after the turnips, &c. attain the rough leaf, and even then before they are of a considerable bigness, they are so hard to be distinguished by those people, who are not well experienced, that a company of hand-hoers cut out the turnips by mistake, and left the charlock for a crop, of a large field of sown turnips. Such a misfortune can never happen to drilled turnips unless wilfully done, be they set out ever so young.

Young turnips will enjoy the more of the pasture made by the ploughing, and by that little pulveration of the hand-hoe, without being robbed of any pasture by their own supernumerary plants.

Three or four ounces of seed is the usual quantity to drill; but at random, three or four pounds is commonly sown, which coming thick all over the ground, must exhaust the land more than the other, especially since the sown must stand longer, before the hoers can see to set them out. . . .

116. Parliamentary proceedings on an Enclosure Bill, 1769

(*Journals of the House of Commons*, XXXII, pp. 150, 227, 239, 253, 326–327, 331, 350.)

An example of the many enclosures by Act of Parliament. It should be read in conjunction with No. 117.

[26 January 1769]

A Petition of *Thomas Gibbs*, *George Filsly*, *Edward Witts*, *Joseph Walker*, *William Willcox*, *Groves Wheeler*, *Henry Dawkins*, Esquire, *Samuel Huckvale*, *William Meads*, *John Rook*, *Joseph Newton*, and several other Persons whose Names are thereunder written, Proprietors of Common Fields, Lands, Grounds, and Tithes, in the Parishes of *Chipping Norton* and *Salford*, in the County of *Oxford*, was presented to the House, and read; Setting forth, That there are, within the said Parishes, several Open and Common Fields and Commonable Lands, which lie greatly intermixed, and are of small Advantage to the Proprietors, and, in their present Situation, incapable of Improvement; and that, if the same were divided and inclosed and specific Shares thereof allotted to the several Proprietors, it would be a considerable Improvement to their respective Estates: And therefore praying, That Leave may be given to bring in a Bill for inclosing and dividing the said Common Fields and Commonable Lands, in such Manner, and under such Regulations, as to the House shall seem meet.

Ordered, That Leave be given to bring in a Bill, pursuant to the Prayer of the said Petition: And that Lord *Charles Spencer* and Lord *Robert Spencer*,[1] do prepare, and bring in the same.

[17 February]

Lord *Charles Spencer* presented to the House, according to Order, a Bill for dividing and inclosing certain Open and Common Fields, and Commonable Lands, in the Parishes of *Chipping Norton* and *Salford*, in the County of *Oxford*: And the same was received, and read the First Time:

Resolved, That the Bill be read a Second Time.

[23 February]

A Bill dividing and inclosing certain Open and Common Fields, and Commonable Lands, in the Parishes of *Chipping Norton* and *Salford*, in the County of *Oxford*, was read a Second Time.

Resolved, That the Bill be committed to Lord *Charles Spencer*, Mr. *Harbord*, &c.: And they are to meet this Afternoon, at Five of the Clock, in the Speaker's Chamber.

A Petition of *Henry Dimock*, Vicar of *Chipping Norton*, in the County of *Oxford*, was presented to the House and read; Setting forth, That the Petitioner observes, a Bill is depending for dividing and inclosing certain Open and Common Fields, Commonable Lands, and Waste Grounds in the Parishes of *Chipping Norton* and *Salford*, in the County of *Oxford*; and that the Petitioner conceives it is reasonable that his Income, as Vicar of the said Parish, should be improved by the said Inclosure, in some Proportion with other Estates within the said Parishes; but that no Provision is made in the said Bill for any such Purpose: And therefore praying the House to take the Premises into Consideration, and grant the Petitioner such Relief as shall seem meet.

Ordered, That the said Petition be referred to the Consideration of the Committee, to whom the said Bill is committed.

Ordered, That the said Committee have Power to send for Persons, Papers, and Records.

[28 February]

A Petition of the Bailiffs and Burgesses of *Chipping Norton*, in the County of *Oxford*, and of divers other Persons, whose Names are thereunto subscribed, was

[1] M.P.s respectively for Oxfordshire and Woodstock.

presented to the House, and read; Setting forth, That in the Reign of King *Richard* the First, the Lord of the Manor of *Chipping Norton* granted to the Ville of *Chipping Norton* aforesaid certain Pasture Grounds, called by the several Names of *The Great Common below the Town, Over Norton, Verne Hill, The Heath,* and *South Come*; and that the Owners and Occupiers of Lands and Tenements there have Time immemorial enjoyed the said Ground called *The Verne Hill,* as their separate Common; and that *The Great Common* and *South Come* have been ever since exclusively enjoyed in Common, by the Owners or Occupiers of the Messuages and Lands in the Town, Hamlet, or Division, of *Chipping Norton*; and that such Owners and Occupiers have also Right of Common in *The Heath,* the Open Fields, and all other the Commonable Lands, in the said Division; and that the Petitioners observe, a Bill is depending before the House, for dividing and inclosing the Open and Common Fields, and Commonable Lands, in the Parishes of *Chipping Norton* and *Salford,* in the County of *Oxford,* which, the Petitioners are informed, is intended to include all the Premises granted as aforesaid; and that some of the said Grounds furnish the Poor of the said Town, which are very numerous, with Fuel, a very scarce Commodity, which will be an extreme Hardship upon the Parties interested therein; and that the Petitioners likewise apprehend, That some other Parts of the said Bill, as it now stands, may prejudice them and others: And therefore praying, That so much of the said Bill as tends to the Inclosure of the said Grounds, called *The Great Common, The Heath,* and *South Come,* may not pass into a Law; and that the Petitioners may be heard, by their Counsel, against the same, and such other Parts of the said Bill as may affect them; and that the Petitioners may have such Relief in the Premises as shall seem meet.

Ordered, That the said Petition be referred to the Consideration of the Committee to whom the Bill for dividing and inclosing certain Open and Common Fields, and Commonable Lands, in the Parishes of *Chipping Norton* and *Salford,* in the County of *Oxford,* is committed; and that the Petitioners be heard, by their Counsel, before the said Committee, upon the said Petition, if they think fit.

Ordered, That it be an Instruction to the said Committee, that they do admit Counsel to be heard at the same Time, in favour of the said Bill, against the said Petition.

[20 March]

Lord *Charles Spencer* reported from the Committee, to whom the Bill for dividing and inclosing certain Open and Common Fields, and Commonable Lands, in the Parishes of *Chipping Norton* and *Salford,* in the County of *Oxford,* was committed, That the Committee had considered the Petition of the Bailiffs and Burgesses of *Chipping Norton,* in the County of *Oxford,* and of divers other Persons whose Names are subscribed: and also the Petition of *Henry Dimock,* Vicar of *Chipping Norton,* in the County of *Oxford*; and had heard the First mentioned Petitioners by their Counsel, and had also heard Counsel for the Bill; and that the Committee had examined the Allegations of the Bill, and found the same to be true; and that the Parties concerned had given their Consent to the Bill, to the Satisfaction of the Committee; (except the Proprietors of 16 Yard Lands and a Quarter of a Yard Land, and 24 Acres and a

Quarter, who refused to sign the Bill; and that the whole of the Lands intended to be inclosed consists of 185 Yard Lands and an Half, and about 342 Acres;) and that the Committee had gone through the Bill, and made several Amendments thereunto; which they had directed him to report to the House; and he read the Report in his Place; and afterwards delivered the Bill, with the Amendments, in at the Clerk's Table: Where the Amendments were Once read throughout; and then a Second Time, One by One; and upon the Question severally put thereupon, were agreed to by the House.

And the House being informed that some other Amendments are necessary to be made to the said Bill;

Resolved, That the said Bill be re-committed.

Resolved, That the said Bill be re-committed to the Committee, to whom the same was committed.

[21 March. These further Amendments were reported and accepted by the House, and the Bill, with Amendments, ordered to be ingrossed.]

[4 April]

An ingrossed Bill for dividing and inclosing certain Open and Common Fields, and Commonable Lands, in the Parishes of *Chipping Norton* and *Salford*, in the County of *Oxford*, was read the Third Time.

Resolved, That the Bill do pass: And that the Title be, An Act for dividing and inclosing certain Open and Common Fields, and Commonable Lands, in the Parishes of *Chipping Norton* and *Salford*, in the County of *Oxford*.

Ordered, That Lord *Charles Spencer* do carry the Bill to the Lords, and desire their Concurrence.

117. Arthur Young on enclosures, 1770

(Arthur Young, *A Six Months Tour Through the North of England* (1770), I, pp. 252–264; IV, pp. 40–43.)

In the first of these extracts Young points out that the high cost of enclosure by Act of Parliament frequently makes enclosure much less profitable than is often supposed. In the second, he rebuts the general belief that the formation of large farms leads to rural depopulation.

(*a*) Lastly, let me offer some remarks on the great improvement carrying on of inclosures; but this will require a more diffusive examination. There is scarcely any point in rural œconomics more generally acknowledged, than the great benefits of inclosing open lands: some authors, it is true, have attacked them as suppositious, and asserted them to be a national disadvantage, of trivial use to the proprietors, but very mischievous to the poor. My residence in this part of *Yorkshire* brought (at first accidentally) to my knowledge some particulars respecting the merits of inclosing, and the means commonly pursued in the execution, which are not to be found in the *face* of any *acts* whatever; but which are certainly of importance in weighing and deciding the advantages of the measure. To give you a tolerable idea of these circumstances, it will be necessary to sketch the progress of an inclosure, as it generally is conducted, without any eye to legal forms, or the letter of the act.

First, The proprietors of large estates generally agree upon the measure, adjust the principal points among themselves, and fix upon their attorney before they appoint any general meeting of *all* the proprietors. The small proprietor, whose property in the township is perhaps his all, has little or no weight in regulating the clauses of the Act of Parliament, has seldom if ever an opportunity of putting a single one in the bill favourable to his rights, and has as little influence in the choice of commissioners; and of consequence, they have seldom any great inducement to be attentive to his interest; some recent instances of which I have heard of.

II. Any proprietor possessing a fifth of the manor, parish, lordship, *&c.* to be inclosed, has the right of a negative upon the measure, consequently the poorer proprietors are often obliged to assent to unreasonable clauses, rather than give up all the advantages they hope from the inclosure.

III. The attorney delivers his bill to the commissioners, who pay him and themselves without producing any account, and in what manner they please. Is it therefore any wonder, that the expences previous to the actual inclosing the ground are very frequently (unless where the township is very small) from 1800*l*. to 2000*l*. all which is levied and expended by the commissioners absolutely, and without controul*? To this extravagant expence add, that attending the inclosure itself, the making the ditches; the posts and railing; buying and setting the quickwood, *&c.* this, added to the former expence, must surely run away with great part of the profits expected from the inclosure, even if it was absolutely unavoidably. But what must we think of the indolence of the proprietors, who will thus unnecessarily neglect the great improvement of their estates to advance the private interests of the commissioners, *&c.*

IV. The division and distribution of the lands are totally in their breasts, and as the quality of the soil as well as the number of acres is considered, the business is extremely intricate, and requires uncommon attention; but on the contrary is often

* For a proof of this, see the following extract from an Act which gives an *absolute* and UNLIMITED power to the commissioners to raise *whatever sums* they please, and to assess them *in the proportions* and *in such manner* as they think proper.

"And be it further enacted, That the reasonable costs and charges incident to, and attending the obtaining and passing this Act, and of the surveying, dividing and allotting the said lands and grounds hereby directed to be inclosed, and the preparing and inrolling the said award or instrument, and all other necessary charges and expences relating to the said divisions and inclosures, and to the fencing, hedging, and ditching, the same shall, from time to time, as such costs, charges, and expences shall accrue, be borne, paid and defrayed by the several parties to whom any part of the said lands and grounds shall be allotted, in proportion to the value of their respective shares or interests therein, *such proportions to be adjusted and settled from time to time, by the said commissioners or any two of them*; and in case any person or persons shall refuse or neglect to pay his, her, or their proportion or proportions so to be from time to time adjusted and ascertained, of such charges or expences within the time to be limited by the said commissioners, or any two of them, to such person or persons as they, or any two of them shall appoint to receive the same, then the said commissioners, or any two of them, shall and may raise, and levy the same, by distress and sale of the goods and chattels of the person or persons so neglecting or refusing to pay the same, rendering the overplus (if any) on demand to the owner or owners of such goods and chattels, after deducting the costs and charges of taking and making such distress and sale, or otherwise it shall and may be lawful to and for the said commissioners or any two of them, from time to time, to enter into and upon the premises, so to be allotted to such person or persons refusing or neglecting to pay as aforesaid, and to take the rents and profits thereof respectively, until thereby, or therewith, or otherwise, the share or shares, proportion or proportions of the said costs and charges so to be from time to time directed, awarded or appointed by the said commissioners to be paid by such person or persons as aforesaid, and also all costs, charges, and expences occasioned by or attending such entry upon and receipt of the rents and profits of the same premises shall respectively be fully paid and satisfied."

A most precious piece of delegated despotism.

executed in an inaccurate and blundering manner. Nor is there any appeal but to the commissioners themselves, from their allotments, however carelessly or partially made. Thus is the property of the proprietors, and especially the poor ones, entirely at their mercy; every passion of resentment, prejudice, &c. may be gratified without controul; for they are vested with a despotic power known in no other branch of business in this free country.

V. Justice as well as common sense requires that after the *survey* and *division*, the *award* of the commissioners should be directly published, it being the record which proves the respective properties: and likewise that their accounts should, upon the conclusion of the business, be regularly arranged under each distinct head attended by every corresponding voucher, and made public to the inspection of every proprietor, but unfortunately this is far from being the case, the time of publishing the award, is greatly procrastinated, and as to accounts they seldom show any, all the particulars of that sort remain for ever a profound secret, save the particular sum demanded from each proprietor. That indeed if they chuse it, they may communicate to each other and be able to form some judgment of the inequality of particular assessments, but as there lies no appeal from the award they are generally induced to sit down quietly, though the disproportion of the allotments and assessments should be glaringly conspicuous. . . .

VII. There is no remedy against the impositions or blunders of the commissioners, but that which, perhaps, is as bad as the disease, *viz.* filing a bill in chancery; a remedy, which in all probability, one or two persons must support for the good of *the whole*, but without the assistance of *half.*

VIII. And if I am not greatly mistaken, even this means of redress is more limited than in most other cases: it may compel the commissioners to deliver in their accounts, but how can it rectify any unjust management of the land? It lies in the breast of the commissioners when to make their award, and I do not imagine, that till they have signed it, it would be prudent to file the bill against them. It might possibly be two or three years before a decree could be obtained, and when any proprietor has been at the expence of inclosing his share, cultivating the ground, and raising the fences, how is it possible that even the power of the court of chancery, extensive as it is, can in this case redress the injury, whether it arises from the particular situation of the allotment, the quantity, or the quality of the soil. Need I say any thing further, to point out the real necessity of the proprietors of land exerting themselves to retrench this enormous power, vested in the commissioners. The advantages resulting from inclosures, are not to be looked upon as merely beneficial to the individual, they are of the most extensive national advantage. The improvements in agriculture, that source of all our power, must be trifling without them; surely therefore, every measure that can promote them should be adopted, every difficulty attending them *smoothed*, and every injury redressed.

It appears clearly from the above circumstances that the proprietors of a lordship to be inclosed, give to the commissioners for executing the act, an unlimited power of taxing their estates, and including that unheard of power of being party, judge, and jury in the whole affair of paying themselves. If a proprietor is offended at their proceedings, and refuses to pay the sums levied on him, they are entrusted by the act, with powers immediately to distrain. Such immense confidence in the commissioners, might be attended with few inconveniences, if they were universally men of considerable property, and known integrity; but when the hacknied sons of *business*, are employed (which is the case nine times out of ten) the proprietors have just reason to tremble at the situation of their purses. It is very natural to conclude, that such causes must be attended with a very striking effect, and this accordingly is the case; for impositions, and the inaccuracy of commissioners have arose to such a height, that many proprietors who were eager for inclosures, on a sanguine prospect of benefit, have found the measure highly injurious and totally owing to the immense expences. There is a very false idea current, that rents are doubled by inclosing; a measure may be vastly advantageous without possessing such uncommon merit. This notion hurries numbers to inclosing, who afterwards find the expences to run away with great part of the profit. But even where the expences do not exceed the profit, it is very often the case, that the proprietor is not repaid in six or seven years, perhaps more; and when it is considered, how little able some proprietors, even in good circumstances, are to wait so long before they are reimbursed their expences; how often they are disabled (by advancing their proportions necessary for an inclosure) to provide for the settlement of their children in the world, how often they are prevented cultivating their new inclosure to any advantage, by being drained of their ready money–I think it will incontestibly appear, that the advantages resulting from this extravagant method, are trivial to the majority of proprietors in comparison to what they might reasonably have expected, from a more equal management.

You will not think this surprizing, when you are informed the immediate rise of rent in many inclosures in this neighbourhood, has not amounted to above five or six shillings an acre, and in some to no more than eighteen pence and two shillings an acre. In strong rich lands where they have some meadow lands, the rise is higher. But indeed the smallness of the rise is, in some measure, owing to their want of better husbandry; for with very few meadows, they know scarce any thing of clover and ray-grass or turnips; consequently the value of an inclosure is comparatively small to them.

But whatever cause the fact is owing to, it remains equally surprizing that the proprietors should not be more attentive to their interest, a rise of rent sufficient to pay the expences of the inclosure under the management of honest, able, and careful conductors, *may* vanish into nothing upon the mention of those who have neither integrity, abilities, or attention; and it must be strange supineness indeed, that can suffer the gentlemen of a county to be duped in so flagrant a manner, as to allow even in idea, the trains of imposition which are now common in the business of inclosures. It is wonderful they do not exert themselves to introduce common sense and honesty, in an affair hitherto under the cognizance of ignorance, knavery, and self-interest.

For this purpose, it seems requisite, that the following clauses should be added to the acts for inclosure.

I. That the small proprietors should have a share in the nomination of commissioners; either by a union of votes or otherwise, as might be determined.

II. That the attorney and commissioners should, before the passing the act, agree upon their several rewards, and on no account whatever be suffered to pay themselves one shilling.

III. That the commissioners proceed immediately to the survey, distribution, and assignment, and the building or forming public works.

IV. That in case any man thinks himself injured, he may be at liberty (but totally at his own expence, in case he is in the wrong) to summons a jury immediately, to view and decide the affair.

V. That as soon as the abovementioned business is concluded, the commissioners do give in their account of all sums received and expended, in the most regular manner, and with all the vouchers for payment; and that they immediately publish their award.

VI. That an action at common law be had against the commissioners for false, or unvouched accounts, *&c. &c.*

By means of these or other clauses better imagined, but of the same intention, this undoubtedly beneficial measure of inclosing would be infinitely extended, and the interests of the community, as well as individuals, greatly secured.

Many people inclosing upon old rents, think the great advance of rent upon their farms is owing to inclosures, whereas their farms would very well have allowed of an additional rent without it.

I am not here arguing against inclosures, the advantages arising from them are certainly very extensive; I am only saying, they are not so great as they are frequently imagined to be, and they do not always indemnify the *present* possessor from the great expence he is at in obtaining them, by the absurd and extravagant manner in which they are generally conducted.

(*b*) [By a complicated series of calculations and tables, Young has shown] that the larger the farms, a very few instances excepted, the more population is encouraged. This is so very contrary to the notions most common, that it may be expected something should be offered by way of accounting for it.

Great farmers are generally rich farmers; and it requires no great skill in agriculture to know, that they who have most money in their pockets, will, upon an average, cultivate the soil in the most complete manner; *good* culture, in most cases, is but another word for *much* labour. And this state of the question opens another view of this branch of rural œconomy, which should not be slighted:–A very considerable portion of the labour of a farm is of the *extra* kind; all included in these tables is the regular yearly allowance; but *improvements*, and most articles of vigorous culture, are done by *extra* hands; witness, marling; chalking; paring and burning; turnip hoeing; walling; *&c. &c. &c.* consequently the great farmers (the richest men) use a much greater proportion of this *extra* labour, than smaller (poorer) ones: And this remark is not only consistent with reason, but is verified by common observation, in every county in *England*.

In the next place I should observe, that great farmers do not keep near the proportion of servants, maids, and boys, that smaller ones do. Their superiority in population lies totally in labourers; indeed it would be useless and impossible for them to keep the proportion of servants of small farmers; their houses would not contain them. Now it is not the employment of single hands that promotes population, but that of men who have families; and this circumstance must operate strongly, in giving so great a superiority to large farms. The variation from these rules, between, under, and over three hundred acres, is not great; nor can any remark be wholly unexceptionable.

We may draw from these tables this general corollary, which will state the case in the clearest manner:

> That the farms most advantageous to population, without exceptions, are those from five hundred acres upwards; and of such, those above a thousand acres are the superior; those under five hundred acres much inferior.

I doubt not but you will allow me to add upon this conclusion, that the vulgar ideas, of great farms depopulating the kingdom, are here proved, from facts, to be false; and not from one or two instances, but from the divisions of above seventy thousand acres of land; of all soils, in all situations, and under a vast variety of circumstances; throughout a line of country extending above two thousand five hundred miles. I will not assert that the average of such a tour must be the average of the whole kingdom; but I may surely be allowed to think, that there is a much greater probability of it, than of the truth of random assertions, general reasonings, and vulgar prejudices, all deduced from opinion, and founded upon that, and partial instances. If facts do not give me this advantage, they will yield me nothing, and I will reject them in favour of *notions*, as more satisfactory evidence.

118A–C. Arthur Young on the agrarian improvements of the age, 1770–1771

118A. Improvements in stock breeding

(Arthur Young, *The Farmer's Tour Through the East of England*, I (1771), pp. 110–114.)

Mr. *Bakewell* of *Dishley*, one of the most considerable farmers in this country, has in so many instances improved on the husbandry of his neighbours, that he merits particular notice in this journal.

His breed of cattle is famous throughout the kingdom; and he has lately sent many to *Ireland*. He has in this part of his business many ideas which I believe are perfectly new; or that have hitherto been totally neglected. This principle is to gain the beast, whether sheep or cow, that will weigh most in the most valuable joints:–there is a great difference between an ox of 50 stone, carrying 30 in roasting pieces, and 20 in coarse boiling ones–and another carrying 30 in the latter, and 20 in the former. And at the same time that he gains the shape, that is, of the greatest value in the smallest compass; he asserts, from long experience, that he gains a breed much hardier, and easier fed than any others. These ideas he applies equally to sheep and oxen.

In the breed of the latter, the old notion was, that where you had much and large bones, there was plenty of room to lay flesh on; and accordingly the graziers were eager to buy the largest boned cattle. This whole system Mr. *Bakewell* has proved to be an utter mistake. He asserts, the smaller the bones, the truer will be the make of the beast–the quicker she will fat–and her weight, we may easily conceive, will have a larger proportion of valuable meat: *flesh*, not *bone*, is the butcher's object. Mr. *Bakewell* admits that a large boned beast, may be made a large fat beast, and that he may come to a great weight; but justly observes, that this is no part of the profitable enquiry; for stating such a simple proposition, without at the same time shewing the expence of covering those bones with flesh, is offering no satisfactory argument. The only object of real importance, is the proportion of *grass* to *value*. I have 20 acres; which will pay me for those acres best, large or small boned cattle? The latter fat so much quicker, and more profitably in the joints of value; that the query is answered in their favour from long and attentive experience.

Among other breeds of cattle the *Lincolnshire* and the *Holderness* are very large, but their size lies in their bones: they may be fattened to great loss to the grazier, nor can they ever return so much for a given quantity of grass, as the small boned, long horned kind.

The breed which Mr. *Bakewell* has fixed on as the best in *England*, is the *Lancashire*, and he thinks he has improved it much, in bringing the carcass of the beast into a truer mould; and particularly by making them broader over the backs. The shape which should be the criterion of a cow, a bull, or an ox, and also of a sheep, is that of an hogshead, or a firkin; truly circular with small and as short legs as possible: upon the plain principle, that the value lies in the barrel, not in the legs. All breeds, the backs of which rise in the least ridge, are bad. I measured two or three cows, 2 feet 3 inches flat across their back from hip to hip–and their legs remarkably short.

Mr. *Bakewell* has now a bull of his own breed which he calls *Twopenny*, which leaps cows at 5*l.* 5*s.* a cow. This is carrying the breed of horned cattle to wonderful perfection. He is a very fine bull–most truly made, according to the principles laid down above. He has many others got by him, which he lets for the season, from 5 guineas to 30 guineas a season, but rarely sells any. He would not take 200*l.* for *Twopenny*. He has several cows which he keeps for breeding, that he would not sell at 30 guineas apiece.

Another particularity is the amazing gentleness in which he brings up these animals. All his bulls stand still in the field to be examined: the way of driving them from one field to another, or home, is by a little swish; he or his men walk by their side, and guide him with the stick where-ever they please; and they are accustomed to this method from being calves. A lad, with a stick three feet long, and as big as his finger, will conduct a bull away from other bulls, and his cows from one end of the farm to the other. All this gentleness is merely the effect of management, and the mischief often done by bulls, is undoubtedly owing to practices very contrary–or else to a total neglect.

The general order in which Mr. *Bakewell* keeps his cattle is pleasing; all are fat as bears; and this is a circumstance which he insists is owing to the excellence of the breed. His land is no better than his neighbours, at the same time that it carries a far greater proportion of stock; as I shall shew by and by. The small quantity, and the inferior quality of food that will keep a beast perfectly well made, in good order, is surprizing: such an animal will grow fat in the same pasture that would starve an ill made, great boned one.

118B. Improvements in arable farming

(Arthur Young, *The Farmer's Tour Through the East of England*, II (1771), pp. 150–151, 156–157, 161–162.)

As I shall present leave *Norfolk*, it will not be improper to give a slight review of the husbandry which has rendered the name of this county so famous in the farming world. Pointing out the practices which have succeeded so nobly here, may perhaps be of some use to other countries possessed of the same advantages, but unknowing in the art to use them.

From 40 to 60 years ago, all the northern and western, and a part of the eastern tracts of the county, were sheep-walks, let so low as from *6d.* to *1s. 6d.* and *2s.* an acre. Much of it was in this condition only 30 years ago. The great improvements have been made by means of the following circumstances.

FIRST. By inclosing without assistance of parliament.
SECOND. By a spirited use of marle and clay.
THIRD. By the introduction of an excellent course of crops.
FOURTH. By the culture of turnips well hand-hoed.
FIFTH. By the culture of clover and ray-grass.
SIXTH. By landlords granting long leases.
SEVENTH. By the country being divided chiefly into large farms.

In this recapitulation, I have inserted no article that is included in another. Take any one from the seven, and the improvement of *Norfolk* would never have existed....

THE COURSE OF CROPS.

After the best managed inclosure, and the most spirited conduct in marling, still the whole success of the undertaking depends on this point: No fortune will be made in *Norfolk* by farming, unless a judicious course of crops be pursued. That which has been chiefly adopted by the *Norfolk* farmers is,

1. Turnips
2. Barley
3. Clover; or clover and ray-grass
4. Wheat.

Some of them, depending on their soils being richer than their neighbours (for instance, all the way from *Holt* by *Aylsham* down through the *Flegg* hundreds) will steal a crop of pease or barley after the wheat; but it is bad husbandry, and has not been followed by those men who have made fortunes. In the above course, the turnips are (if possible) manured for; and much of the wheat the same. This is a noble system, which keeps the soil rich; only one exhausting crop is taken to a cleansing and ameliorating one. The land cannot possibly in such management be either poor or foul. . . .

LARGE FARMS.

If the preceding articles are properly reviewed, it will at once be apparent that no small farmers could effect such great things as have been done in *Norfolk*. Inclosing, marling, and keeping a stock of sheep large enough for folding, belong absolutely and exclusively to great farmers. None of them could be effected by small ones–or such as are called middling ones in other countries.–Nor should it be forgotten, that the best husbandry in *Norfolk* is that of the largest farmers. You must go to a *Curtis*, a *Mallet*, a *Barton*, a *Glover*, a *Carr*, to see *Norfolk* husbandry. You will not among them find the stolen crops that are too often met with among the little occupiers of an hundred a year in the eastern part of the county. Great farms have been the soul of the *Norfolk* culture: split them into tenures of an hundred pounds a year, you will find nothing but beggars and weeds in the whole county. The rich man keeps his land rich and clean.

These are the principles of *Norfolk* husbandry, which have advanced the agriculture of the greatest part of that county to a much greater height than is any where to be met with over an equal extent of country. . . .

118C. The contribution of Young's own writings to the improvement of agricultural methods

(*Autobiography of Arthur Young*, ed. M. Betham-Edwards (1898), pp. 53–55.)

1770. . . . It is necessary here to pause a little in order to examine the object and the effect of the three tours I made and published. They have, by the very best judges, been esteemed highly useful to practical agriculturists, and unquestionably they are equally so for the information they afford in political economy: they have accordingly, in these views, been celebrated in almost every language of Europe. When a work appears, the object and execution of which are equally novel and unexampled, it is not surprising that a certain measure of success should attend such a work. Nothing in the least similar to it had before appeared in the English language; for though there had been a tour of Great Britain, and other tours through great part of the kingdom, yet all these works agreed in one circumstance–that of the authors confining their attention absolutely to towns and seats, without paying any more thought to agriculture than if that art had no existence between the towns they visited. Indeed my work was admitted on all hands to be perfectly original. In regard to the practical husbandry of the farmers, and the experimental observations of the gentlemen I visited, the utility of these could not be doubted. When a Lord Chancellor of England, amusing himself with husbandry, read the English works on that subject for information, and burnt them as affording him nothing but contradictions, without doubt he complained that these writers did not describe the common management of the farmers, and on that management founding their propositions of improvement. But the fact was, and it must be, in the nature of things, writers confined to their closets, or, at most, to a single farm, could not describe what it was impossible for them to know; and before the appearance of my tours there was scarcely a district in the kingdom described in such a manner as to convince the reader that the authors had any practical knowledge of the art; for a man to quit his farm and his fireside in order to examine the husbandry of a kingdom by travelling above four thousand miles through a country of no greater extent than England was certainly taking means sufficiently effective for laying a sure basis for the future improvement of the soil. To understand well the present state of cultivation is surely a necessary step prior to proposals of improvement. This I effected; and in the opinion of some very able agriculturists now living, the greatest of the subsequent improvements that have been made during the last forty years have, in a great measure, originated in the defects pointed out by me in the detail of these journeys.

119. Arthur Young's average prices of provisions and labour, 1770

(Arthur Young, *A Six Months Tour through the North of England*, IV (1770), pp. 423, 433–435, 438–441, 445–446.)

Young made similar calculations after his East Anglian tour; see *The Farmer's Tour Through the East of England* (1771), vol. IV.

The multiplicity of subjects which demand a particular review in the minutes of this tour is so great, that I am in every letter fearful of swelling it to too great a length; and yet much of the utility, which attends such an undertaking, would be totally lost, if the average of every article was not stated, and compared with collateral circumstances that either do, or may probably affect it. The subject upon which I now enter, viz. the prices of provisions, is one of the most important that can engage the attention of the statesman. It ought to be known with the utmost perspicuity in every possible variation, and in every the most remote combination. Circumstances, that at first sight appear to have scarce any connection, are sometimes found, on a near inspection, to be intimately united.

The first view I shall offer of these prices, is that of butcher's meats, bread, butter, and cheese; and the average of meats, with the distance of each place from *London*. . . .

[Tables of average prices of these commodities in 85 places, adding their distances from London.]

RECAPITULATION.

	Bread.	*Butter.*	*Cheese.*	*Average of meats.*
To 50 miles	1½	6¾	4	3¾
50 to 100	1½	6	¾	3¼
100 to 200	1¼	6	3¼	3
200 to 300	1	6	2	2¾
300 upwards	—	5	2½	2½

The influence of the capital appears very strongly in this table. It is apparent even in the article bread, which one would suppose, in reason, not to be much affected. The equality of the price of butter surprizes me: But even that is dearest near *London*, and cheapest the farthest from it: But the sameness from fifty to three hundred miles contradicts so far the general tenor of the table. Cheese, near the capital, is double the price it is at a distance from it; but this circumstance requires some explanation. Scarce any cheese is made around *London*: It answers so much better to make butter, and to suckle, that the quantity of cheese made is very trifling; but the cheese of the western counties is to be had through all *England* nearly as cheap as at *London*; but the poor do not eat it as their brethren do around *London*: They consume only their own country cheese, of a much poorer sort.

The variations in the prices of butcher's meat are so regular; the fall so unbroken, in proportion to the distance from the capital, that one cannot but attribute it *to the distance*. The fall of price is regular, even in circumstances that one would apprehend sufficient totally to destroy it. The populous manufacturing counties of *Lancaster*, and the West Riding of *Yorkshire*, I expected to find as dear as *London*; but, on the contrary, the fall of price is regular throughout them. If this regularity of variation is not owing to the distance from *London*, I know not to what to attribute it; nor can any other satisfactory account be given for it.

You will next allow me to review the other particulars of the poor's house-keeping, &c. which were minuted throughout the Tour; but some of these I shall omit. Milk is, in general, of a uniform price; the variations not considerable enough to give rise to any conjectures of causes. Potatoes depend on the quantity cultivated; and as to candles and soap, the uniformity of price throughout the kingdom is surprizing. The remaining articles, to which I shall confine myself, are *House-rent*, *Firing*, and *Wear of Tools*. . . .

[After stating figures for these three items at many places he concludes that on an average]

	l.	*s.*	*d.*
House rent, ...	1	8	2
Firing, ...	1	3	11
Tools, ...	0	7	11
Total,	3	0	0

This amount will, in no part of the kingdom, be found of an unreasonable height.

The price of labour is allowed by all to be one of the most important objects in political œconomy. Agriculture, arts, manufactures, and commerce, are but so many aggregates of labour: Every circumstance that can affect the prosperity of a nation, is intimately connected, and even founded on labour. All nations subsist by labour: where trade is neglected, labour is nothing more than the measure of subsistence; but in commercial states it is the measure of riches, which include every thing else. The grand point respecting labour, is *the quantity* that is *well performed*; and it is obvious enough that the price of it must have considerable effect on the quantity: By various methods of stating, we shall be able to discover the peculiar circumstances attendant upon *high*, *low*, and *middling prices*; and, perhaps, more than conjecture the advantages or disadvantages of the present average rates throughout this tour. I shall begin with the labour of husbandry. But as the prices are seldom to be found in single sums without some other consideration besides money, such must be valued; board, ale, beer, milk, &c. I proceeded in this method in the Six Weeks Tour,[1] but as provisions in general are much cheaper in the north than in the south, all the rates I there used will not be of the same truth here.

Board in the north (including *York* and *Lancashire*) I shall call 8*d*. a day.
In the south, 10*d*.
Ale, 2*d*.
Small beer, 1*d*.
Milk, ½.
Broath, 2*d*.
A dinner, 4*d*½. in the north.
In the south 6*d*.

In respect to the periods of labour, they are minuted throughout the Tour in the divisions of harvest, hay-time, and winter; in most of the counties I travelled, the winter price does not vary for spring; but as in a few there is a price between the winter and the hay ones, we must reckon the latter somewhat longer than common.
Harvest I call five weeks.
Hay time six weeks.*
Winter forty-one weeks.

And as much work is, in many places, done by the piece, I shall, in some places where it lessens the day work greatly, allow a proportion for it. I shall likewise add the distance from *London*. . . .

[Tables for 82 places, with distances from London.]

The general average prices in proportion to the distance from *London* are as follow.

	s.	*d.*
To 50 miles, ...	7	1
From 50 to 100, ...	6	9
From 100 to 200, ...	7	2
From 200 to 300, ...	7	0
Upwards of 300, ...	5	8

This table is not, upon the whole, absolutely decisive of the influence of the capital on the prices of labour: The fall, proportioned to distance, being broken in the middle; fifty miles round *London* is not so dear a circle as one hundred to two hundred; from fifty to one hundred is much cheaper, and upwards of three hundred vastly lower still; but from one hundred to three hundred the price is equal to the *London* ones, and the occasion is what I can by no means conjecture. Within those distances are included part of two counties remarkably full of manufactures; but many reasons will hereafter prove that this is a circumstance totally without effect. . . .

[1] *A Six Weeks' Tour through the southern counties of England and Wales* (1768).
* In many parts of the north of *England* their hay time is of a surprising length.

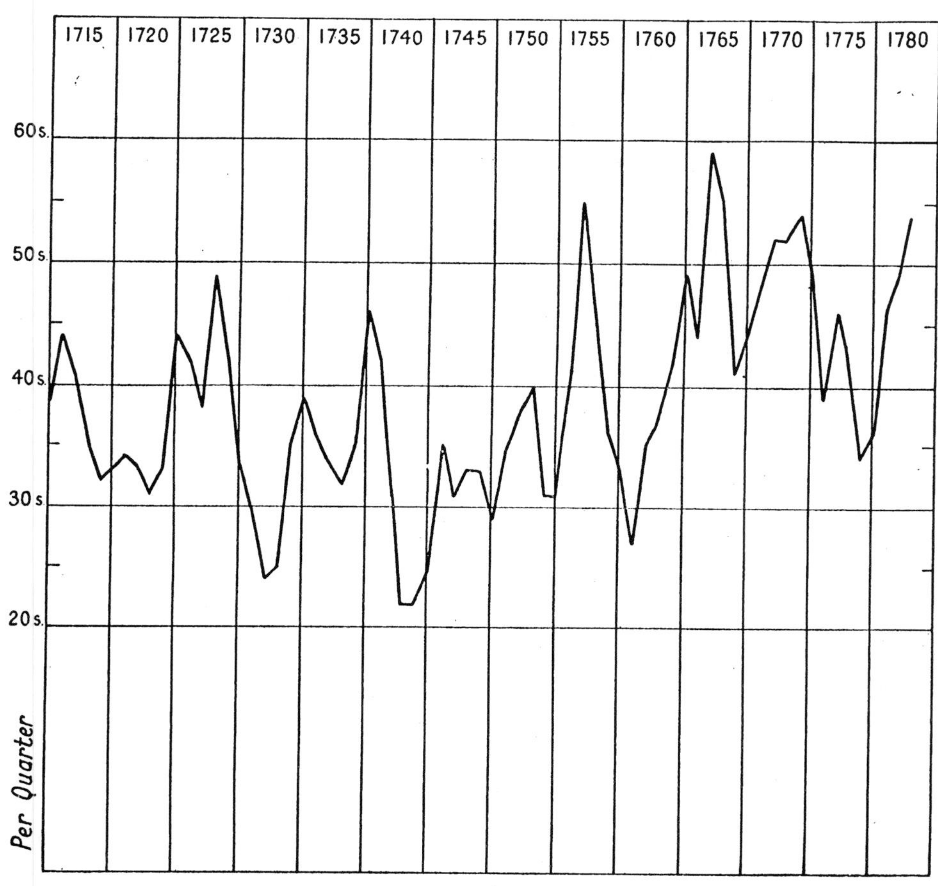

Diagram 2

WHEAT PRICES, 1715–1783

[R. E. Prothero, *English Farming Past and Present* (1936 ed.), pp. 488–9.]

B. INDUSTRY

(a). TEXTILES

120. Daniel Defoe describes the Yorkshire cloth industry, *circa* 1724

(Daniel Defoe, *A Tour Thro' the Whole Island of Great Britain*, III (1724–1727), pp. 97–102, 115, 116–121.)

From *Blackstone Edge* to *Hallifax* is eight Miles, and all the Way, except from *Sorby* to *Hallifax*, is thus up Hill and down; so that, I suppose, we mounted to the Clouds and descended to the Water level about eight times, in that little Part of the Journey.

But now I must observe to you, that after having pass'd the second Hill, and come down into the Valley again, and so still the nearer we came to *Hallifax*, we found the Houses thicker, and the Villages greater in every Bottom; and not only so, but the Sides of the Hills, which were very steep every way, were spread with Houses, and that very thick; for the Land being divided into small Enclosures, that is to say, from two Acres to six or seven Acres each, seldom more; every three or four Pieces of Land had a House belonging to it.

Then it was I began to perceive the Reason and Nature of the Thing, and found that this Division of the Land into small Pieces, and scattering of the Dwellings, was occasioned by, and done for the Convenience of the Business which the People were generally employ'd in, and that, as I said before, though we saw no People stirring without Doors, yet they were all full within; for, in short, this whole Country, however mountainous, and that no sooner we were down one Hill but we mounted another, is yet infinitely full of People; those People all full of Business; not a Beggar, not an idle Person to be seen, except here and there an Alms-House, where People antient, decrepid, and past Labour, might perhaps be found; for it is observable, that the People here, however laborious, generally live to a great Age, a certain Testimony to the goodness and wholesomness of the Country, which is, without doubt, as healthy as any Part of *England*; nor is the health of the People lessen'd, but help'd and establish'd by their being constantly employ'd, and, as we call it, their working hard; so that they find a double Advantage by their being always in Business.

This Business is the Clothing Trade, for the Convenience of which the Houses are thus scattered and spread upon the Sides of the Hills, as above, even from the Bottom to the Top; *the Reason is this*; such has been the Bounty of Nature to this otherwise frightful Country, that two Things essential to the Business, as well as to the Ease of the People are found here, and that in a Situation which I never saw the like of in any Part of *England*; and, I believe, the like is not to be seen so contrived in any Part of the World; I mean Coals and running Water upon the Tops of the highest Hills: This seems to have been directed by the wise Hand of Providence for the very Purpose which is now served by it, namely, the Manufactures, which otherwise could not be carried on; neither indeed could one fifth Part of the Inhabitants be supported without them, for the Land could not maintain them. After we had mounted the third Hill, we found the Country, in short, one continued Village, tho' mountainous every way, as before; hardly a House standing out of a speaking distance from another, and (which soon told us their Business) the Day clearing up, and the Sun shining, we could see that almost at every House there was a *Tenter*, and almost on every Tenter a Piece of *Cloth*, or *Kersie*, or *Shalloon*, for they are the three Articles of that Country's Labour; from which the Sun glancing, and, as I may say, shining (the White reflecting its Rays) to us, I thought it was the most agreeable Sight that I ever saw, for the Hills, as I say, rising and falling so thick, and the Vallies opening sometimes one way, sometimes another, so that sometimes we could see two or three Miles this Way, sometimes as far another; sometimes like the Streets near St. *Giles's*, called the *Seven Dials*; we could see through the Glades almost every Way round us, yet look which Way we would, high to the Tops, and low to the Bottoms, it was all the same; innumerable Houses and Tenters, and a white Piece upon every Tenter.

But to return to the Reason of dispersing the Houses, as above; I found, as our Road pass'd among them, for indeed no Road could do otherwise, wherever we pass'd any House we found a little Rill or Gutter of running Water, if the House was above the Road, it came from it, and cross'd the Way to run to another; if the House was below us, it cross'd us from some other distant House above it, and at every considerable House was a *Manufactury* or Work-House, and as they could not do their Business without Water, the little Streams were so parted and guided by Gutters or Pipes, and by turning and dividing the Streams, that none of those Houses were without a River, if I may call it so, running into and through their Work-Houses.

Again, as the Dying-Houses, Scouring-Shops and Places where they used this Water, emitted the Water again, ting'd with the Drugs of the Dying Fat, and with the Oil, the Soap, the Tallow, and other Ingredients used by the Clothiers in Dressing and Scouring, *&c.* which then runs away thro' the Lands to the next, the Grounds are not only universally watered, how dry soever the Season, but that Water so ting'd and so fatten'd enriches the Lands they run through, that 'tis hardly to be imagined how fertile and rich the Soil is made by it.

Then, as every Clothier must keep a Horse, perhaps two, to fetch and carry for the use of his Manufacture, (*viz.*) to fetch home his Wooll and his Provisions from the Market, to carry his Yarn to the Spinners, his Manufacture to the Fulling Mill, and, when finished, to the Market to be sold, *and the like*; so every Manufacturer generally keeps a Cow or two, or more, for his Family, and this employs the two, or three, or four Pieces of enclosed Land about his House, for they scarce sow Corn enough for their Cocks and Hens; and this feeding their Grounds still adds by the Dung of the Cattle, to enrich the Soil.

But now, to speak of the Bounty of Nature again, which I but just mentioned; it is to be observed, that these Hills are so furnished by Nature with Springs and Mines, that not only on the Sides, but even to the very Tops, there is scarce a Hill but you find, on the highest Part of it, a Spring of Water, and a Coal-Pit. I doubt not but there are both Springs and Coal-Pits lower in the Hills, 'tis enough to say they are at the top; but, as I say, the Hills are so full of Springs, so the lower Coal-Pits may perhaps be too full of Water, to work without Dreins to carry it off, and the Coals in the upper Pits being easie to come at, they may chuse to work them, because the Horses which fetch the Coals, go light up the Hill, and come loaden down.

Having thus *Fire* and *Water* at every Dwelling, there is no need to enquire why they dwell thus dispers'd upon the highest Hills, the Convenience of the Manufactures requiring it. Among the Manufacturers Houses are likewise scattered an infinite Number of Cottages or small Dwellings, in which dwell the Workmen which are employed, the Women and Children of whom, are always busy Carding, Spinning, *&c.* so that no Hands being unemploy'd, all can gain their Bread, even from the youngest to the antient; hardly any thing above four Years old, but its Hands are sufficient to it self.

This is the Reason also why we saw so few People without Doors; but if we knock'd at the Door of any of the Master Manufacturers, we presently saw a House full of lusty Fellows, some at the Dye-fat, some dressing the Cloths, some in the Loom, some one thing, some another, all hard at work, and full employed upon the Manufacture, and all seeming to have sufficient Business.

I should not have dwelt so upon this Part, if there was not abundance of Things subsequent to it, which will be explained by this one Description, and which are needful to be understood by any one that desires a full understanding of the Manner how the People of *England* are employed, and do subsist in these remoter Parts where they are so numerous; for this is one of the most populous Parts of *Britain*, *London* and the adjacent Parts excepted. . . .

And this brought me from the Villages where this Manufacture is wrought, to the Market where it is sold, which is at *Leeds*. . . .

The Market it self is worth describing, tho' no Description can come up to the Thing it self; however, take a Sketch of it with its Customs and Usages as follows:

The Street is a large, broad, fair and well-built Street, beginning, as I have said, at the Bridge, and ascending gently to the North.

Early in the Morning, there are Tressels placed in two Rows in the Street, sometimes two Rows on a Side, but always one Row at least; then there are Boards laid cross those Tressels, so that the Boards lie like long Counters on either Side, from one end of the Street to the other.

The Clothiers come early in the Morning with their Cloth; and as few Clothiers bring more than one Piece, the Market being so frequent, they go into the Inns and Publick-Houses with it, and there set it down.

At seven a Clock in the Morning, the Clothiers being supposed to be all come by that time, even in the Winter, but the Hour is varied as the Seasons advance (in the Summer earlier, in the Depth of Winter a little later) I take it, at a Medium, and as it was when I was there, at six or seven, I say, the Market Bell rings; it would surprize a Stranger to see in how few Minutes, without hurry or noise, and not the least disorder, the whole Market is fill'd; all the Boards upon the Tressels are covered with Cloth, close to one another as the Pieces can lie long ways by one another, and behind every Piece of Cloth, the Clothier standing to sell it.

This indeed is not so difficult, when we consider that the whole Quantity is brought into the Market as soon as one Piece, because as the Clothiers stand ready in the Inns and Shops just behind, and that there is a Clothier to every Piece, they have no more to do, but, like a Regiment drawn up in Line, every one takes up his Piece, and has about five Steps to march to lay it upon the first Row of Boards, and perhaps ten to the second Row; so that upon the Market Bell ringing, in half a quarter of an Hour the whole Market is fill'd, the Rows of Boards cover'd, and the Clothiers stand ready.

As soon as the Bell has done Ringing, the Merchants and Factors, and Buyers of all Sorts, come down, and coming along the Spaces between the Rows of Boards, they walk up the Rows, and down as their Occasions direct. Some of them have their foreign Letters of Orders, with Patterns seal'd on them, in Rows, in their Hands; and with those they match Colours, holding them to the Cloths as they think they agree to: when they see any Cloths to their Colours, or that suit their occasions, they reach over to the Clothier and whisper, and in the fewest Words imaginable the Price is stated; one asks, the other bids; and 'tis agree, or not agree, in a Moment.

The Merchants and Buyers generally walk down and up twice on each Side of the Rows, and in little more than an Hour all the Business is done; in less than half an Hour you will perceive the Cloths begin to move off, the Clothier taking it up upon his Shoulder to carry it to the Merchant's House; and by half an hour after eight a Clock the Market Bell rings again; immediately the Buyers disappear, the Cloth is all sold, or if here and there a Piece happens not to be bought, 'tis carried back into the Inn, and, in a quarter of an Hour, there is not a Piece of Cloth to be seen in the Market.

Thus, you see, Ten or Twenty thousand Pounds value in Cloth, and sometimes much more, bought and sold in little more than an Hour, and the Laws of the Market the most strictly observed as ever I saw done in any Market in *England*; for,

1. Before the Market Bell rings, no Man shews a Piece of Cloth, nor can the Clothiers sell any but in open Market.

2. After the Market Bell rings again, no Body stays a Moment in the Market, but carries his Cloth back if it be not sold.

3. And that which is most admirable is, 'tis all managed with the most profound Silence, and you cannot hear a Word spoken in the whole Market, I mean, by the Persons buying and selling; 'tis all done in whisper.

The reason of this Silence, is chiefly because the Clothiers stand so near to one another; and 'tis always reasonable that one should not know what another does, for that would be discovering their Business, and exposing it to one another.

If a Merchant has bidden a Clothier a Price, and he will not take it, he may go after him to his House, and tell him he has considered of it, and is willing to let him have it; but they are not to make any new Agreement for it, so as to remove the Market from the Street to the Merchant's House.

By nine a Clock the Boards are taken down, the Tressels are removed, and the Street cleared, so that you see no Market or Goods any more than if there had been nothing to do; and this is done twice a Week. By this quick Return the Clothiers are constantly supplied with Money, their Workmen are duly paid, and a prodigious Sum circulates thro' the County every Week.

If you should ask upon all this, where all these Goods, as well here as at *Wakefield*, and at *Hallifax*, are vented and disposed of? It would require a long Treatise of Commerce to enter into that Part: But that I may not bring you into the Labyrinth, and not show you the way out, I shall, in three short Heads, describe the Consumption, for there are three Channels by which it goes:

1. For the home Consumption; their Goods being, as I may say, every where made use of, for the cloathing the ordinary People, who cannot go to the Price of the fine Medley Cloths made, as I formerly gave you an Account, in the Western Counties of *England*. There are for this purpose a Set of travelling Merchants in *Leeds*, who go all over *England* with Droves of Pack Horses, and to all the Fairs and Market Towns over the whole Island, I think I may say none excepted. Here they supply not the common People by Retail, which would denominate them Pedlars indeed, but they supply the Shops by Wholesale or whole Pieces; and not only so, but give large Credit too, so that they are really travelling Merchants, and as such they sell a very great Quantity of Goods; 'tis ordinary for one of these Men to carry a thousand Pounds value of Cloth with them at a time, and having sold it at the Fairs or Towns where they go, they send their Horses back for as much more, and this very often in a Summer, for they chuse to travel in the Summer, and perhaps towards the Winter time, tho' as little in Winter as they can, because of the badness of the Roads.

2. Another Sort of Buyers are those who buy to send to *London*; either by Commissions from *London*, or they give Commissions to Factors and Warehouse-keepers in *London* to sell for them; and these drive also a very great Trade: These Factors and Warehouse-keepers not only supply all the Shop-keepers and Wholesale Men in *London*, but sell also very great Quantities to the Merchants, as well for Exportation to the *English* Colonies in *America*, which take off great Quantities of those course Goods, especially *New England*, *New York*, *Virginia*, &c. as also to the *Russia* Merchants, who send an exceeding Quantity to *Petersburgh*, *Riga*, *Dantzic*, *Narva*, and to *Sweden* and *Pomerania*.

3. The third Sort of Buyers, and who are not less considerable than the other, are truly Merchants, that is to say, such as receive Commissions from Abroad to buy Cloth for the Merchants chiefly in *Hamburgh*, and in *Holland*, and from several other Parts; and these are not only many in Number, but some of them are very considerable in their Dealings, and correspond as far as *Nuremberg*, *Frankfort*, *Leipsick*, and even to *Vienna* and *Ausburgh*, in the farthest Provinces of *Germany*.

On Account of this Trade it was, that some Years ago an Act of Parliament was obtained for making the Rivers *Aire* and *Calder* Navigable; by which a Communication by Water was opened from *Leeds* and *Wakefield* to *Hull*, and by which means all Woollen Manufactures which those Merchants now export by Commission, as above, is carried by Water to *Hull*, and there shipped for *Holland*, *Bremen*, *Hamburgh*, and the *Baltick*. And thus you have a brief Account, by what Methods this vast Manufacture is carried off, and which way they find a Vent for it.

121. Joseph Massie on the decline of the West Country cloth industry and the predominance of the Yorkshire industry, 1764

(J. Massie, *Observations on the New Cyder-Tax* (1764), pp. 2–3.)

The pamphlet attacked the Cider Tax of 1763 on the grounds that it fell chiefly on the south-western counties, which were no longer the most wealthy in the country, because of the shift of the cloth trade to the West Riding. The author, Joseph Massie (d. 1784) wrote a number of pamphlets on trade and on political economy.

. . . [The author gives, from a printed parliamentary paper in his possession, a list of fifty-one woollen manufacturers who, with their families, left Taunton and its neighbourhood about 1697 to settle in Ireland.] . . . So great a Flight of Woollen Manufacturers was there, from only the Town and Neighbourhood of Taunton! and it is easy to believe that the same Motives which induced them to forsake their Native Country, did in like Manner induce a Multitude of other English Woollen Manufacturers to follow their Example, altho' I have not met with, or there may not be, any printed Lists of their Names; and all this at a Time when the Taxes of England were only about Half what they now are, without the new Cyder-Tax. . . .

. . . I must therefore beg leave to mention a later Migration of English Woollen Manufacturers out of the South-Western Cyder-Counties into the Northern Counties where Malt Liquor is generally drank, for it so happens that the higher Taxes on Malt and Beer than on Cyder did not prevent the Inhabitants of the West-Riding of Yorkshire from quadrupling their Woollen Manufactury in less than Thirty Years.

An Account of the Numbers of Pieces of Broad Woollen Cloth *manufactured in the West-Riding of the County of York, from the Year 1726, to the Year 1750, distinguishing the Number made in each Year; extracted from the Register-Books kept in the said County.*

Years		*No. Pieces*	*Years*		*No. Pieces*
1726	—	26,671	1739	—	43,086½
1727	—	28,990	1740	—	41,441
1728	—	25,223½	1741	—	46,364
1729	—	29,643½	1742	—	44,954
1730	—	21,579½	1743	—	45,178½
1731	—	33,563	1744	—	54,627½
1732	—	35,548½	1745	—	50,453
1733	—	34,620	1746	—	56,637
1734	—	31,123	1747	—	62,480
1735	—	31,744½	1748	—	60,705½
1736	—	38,899	1749	—	60,447½
1737	—	42,256	1750	—	60,964
1738	—	42,404			

The Gentleman by whose Friendship this Account was obtained, informs me, that the *Lengths* of the *Pieces of Woollen Cloth*, manufactured in *Yorkshire*, were between *Thirty* and *Forty* Yards each *Piece*, till the Year 1733 or 1734; but that since then, the said *Lengths* have been gradually increased, and each *Piece* now manufactured is near

Seventy Yards long: So that the *Increase of these Manufacturies* is about double in Quantity to what it appears to be, by the Increase in the Number of *Pieces* of *Cloth*. . . .

While the Woollen Manufactury was so rapidly increasing in Yorkshire, it declined in the South-western Cyder Counties, the melancholy Consequences of which were not only the Loss of Multitudes of Inhabitants, who before had paid for much of the Produce of the Land, but such an Increase of poor People as so enormously raised the Poor Rates, that I do not chuse to relate what I have heard on that Head; nor is it indeed either necessary, or consistent with the Brevity of these Observations, for me to enter into a Discussion of Matters, which are not only better known to, but can be much better vouched by, those Gentlemen who represent in Parliament the Inhabitants of such Counties as were the Sufferers by that Decrease of their Woollen Manufactury, and enormous Increase of their Poor Rates. . . .

Proving that English Woollen Manufactury, in some one or more of those Cyder-Counties, hath within the Memory of People now living much increased or even doubled, amounts to nothing at all in this Case, because the Exports of English Woollen Manufactures have within that Time trebled their former Amount; and therefore, by the Rules of National Increase, the Woollen Manufactury should have nearly doubled in every Cyder-County; but when making due Inquiry into the former and present State of our Woollen Trading Towns, I believe it will be found that the Southern ones, comprehending those in the Cyder-Counties, have had a much less than proportional Share of those vast Advantages which have resulted from a Threefold Increase in the yearly Exports of English Woollen Manufactures, since the Accession of King William. . . .

122. Exports of woollen goods and prices of wool in England, 1715–1781

(Sir Joseph Banks, *The Propriety of allowing a qualified Exportation of Wool discussed Historically* (1782), Appendix, pp. 83–85.)

The value of the woollen goods exported each year are taken from the custom-house books; the prices from 1696 to 1746 from J. Smith's *Memoirs of Wool*; those from 1745 to 1781 "have been ascertained from the best manuscript documents that could be procured; comparing from five to ten different accounts, *with the candid purpose of fixing the nearest medium-price*".

A TABLE, shewing the VALUE of the WOOLEN GOODS *of every Kind*, which were entered for EXPORTATION at the CUSTOM-HOUSE from 1697 to 1781 inclusive; and also the PRICES OF WOOL in England during the same Period.

Years.	*Value of Woolen Goods exported.*	*The successive Prices of Wool in England.* £	*s.*	*d.*	[*per tod.*]			
1715	£3,359,029							
1716	3,253,652							
1717	3,706,349	1	3	0	Average Price from 1700 to 1720	0	19	10½
1718	2,673,695	1	7	0				
1719	2,730,298	1	1	0				
1720	3,059,050	1	1	6				

Years.	Value of Woolen Goods exported.	The successive Prices of Wool in England. £	s.	d.	[per tod.]			
1721	2,903,309	1	0	0				
1722	3,384,841	1	0	0				
1723	2,920,600	0	17	6				
1724	3,068,374	0	16	0				
1725	3,512,897	0	16	0				
1726	3,038,148	0	15	9				
1727	2,877,245	0	16	0				
1728	3,193,155	0	18	0				
1729	3,199,322	0	18	0				
1730	3,467,973	0	18	0				
1731	3,166,257	0	19	0				
1732	3,566,655	0	19	0				
1733	3,427,098	0	18	6				
1734	3,032,693	0	16	0				
1735	3,712,875	0	14	0				
1736	4,008,031	0	14	0				
1737	4,046,811	0	14	0	Average Price			
1738	4,158,643	0	13	6	from 1720	0	16	9½
1739	3,218,272	0	13	0	to 1740			
1740	3,056,719	0	14	0				
1741	3,669,735	0	14	0				
1742	3,358,786	0	15	0				
1743	3,541,559	0	19	6				
1744	2,762,870	1	1	0				
1745	2,947,356	0	16	6				
1746	3,646,842	0	17	0				
1747	3,554,039	0	17	3	Average Price			
1748	3,514,395	0	18	6	from 1740	0	17	7½
1749	4,477,852	0	19	0	to 1750			
1750	4,320,005	0	18	6				
1751	4,206,763	0	18	6				
1752	3,718,122	1	0	0				
1753	4,223,234	0	15	0				
1754	3,624,696	0	14	6				
1755	3,575,297	0	14	0				
1756	4,933,505	0	15	6				
1757	4,758,095	0	18	0	Average Price			
1758	4,673,462	1	0	0	from 1750	0	17	5
1759	5,352,299	1	0	0	to 1760			
1760	5,453,172	0	18	6				
1761	4,344,078	0	18	0				
1762	3,905,064	0	17	0				
1763	3,971,439	1	0	0				
1764	5,170,989	1	0	0				

Years.	Value of Woolen Goods exported.	£	s.	d.	The successive Prices of Wool in England. [per tod.]	£	s.	d.
1765	4,475,482	1	1	0				
1766	4,629,162	1	1	6				
1767	4,277,462	1	0	0	Average Price			
1768	4,358,835	0	16	0	from 1760			
1769	3,896,567	0	15	3	to 1770	0	18	3
1770	4,113,583	0	14	0				
1771	4,960,240	0	15	0				
1772	4,436,784	1	5	6	Average Price			
1773	3,773,930	0	15	6	from 1770			
1774	4,333,583	0	17	6	to 1775	0	16	2
1775	4,220,172	0	18	6				
					Prices of long combing wool.			
1776	3,868,352	0	18	6		0	18	6
1777	3,747,537	0	18	3		0	18	3
1778	3,213,331	0	17	0		0	15	0
1779	2,820,616	0	18	6		0	12	0
1780	2,589,109	0	19	6		0	11	6
1781		1	0	0		0	9	0

123. Act prohibiting the use and wear of printed calicoes, 1721

(*Statutes at Large*, XIV, pp. 318–321, 7 Geo. I, Stat. 1, cap. 7.)

This Act was passed as a result of riots by Spitalfields weavers in 1719. It was repealed in 1774.

An act to preserve and encourage the woollen and silk manufactures of this kingdom, and for more effectual employing the poor, by prohibiting the use and wear of all printed, painted, stained or dyed callicoes in apparel, houshold stuff, furniture, or otherwise, after the twenty-fifth day of December *one thousand seven hundred and twenty-two (except as therein is excepted.)*

WHEREAS *it is most evident, That the wearing and using of printed, painted, stained and dyed callicoes in apparel, houshold stuff, furniture, and otherwise, does manifestly tend to the great detriment of the woollen and silk manufactures of this kingdom, and to the excessive increase of the poor, and if not effectually prevented, may be the utter ruin and destruction of the said manufactures, and of many thousands of your Majesty's subjects and their families, whose livelihoods do intirely depend thereupon:* for remedy thereof, may it please your most excellent Majesty, That it may be enacted; and be it enacted by the King's most excellent majesty, by and with the advice and consent of the lords spiritual and temporal, and commons, in this present parliament assembled, and by the authority of the same, That from and after the twenty-fifth day of *December* which shall be in the year of our Lord one thousand seven hundred and twenty-two, it shall not be lawful for any person or persons whatsoever to use or wear in *Great Britain*, in any garment or apparel whatsoever, any printed, painted, stained or dyed callico, under the penalty of forfeiting to the informer the sum of five pounds of lawful money of *Great Britain* for every such offence, being lawfully convicted thereof by the oath or oaths of one or more credible witness or witnesses before any one or more justice or justices of the peace; . . .

II. And be it further enacted by the authority aforesaid, That if any mercer, draper, upholder, or any other person or persons or corporation whatsoever, shall at any time or times after the said twenty-fifth day of *December* one thousand seven hundred and twenty-two sell, utter or expose to sale any printed, painted, stained or dyed callico, or any bed, chair, cushion, window-curtain or other houshold stuff or furniture whatsoever, made up or mixed with any printed, painted, stained or dyed callico, unless for exportation thereof, and unless the same shall be cleared outwards accordingly, as is usual in case of sale for exportation; every such person or corporation so offending shall for every offence, being lawfully convicted thereof, forfeit and pay the sum of twenty pounds of lawful money of *Great Britain*, to be recovered as is herein after directed; and every steward or other officer of such corporation, or his deputy, offending herein, and being lawfully convicted of such offence, shall, over and besides the forfeiture or penalty aforesaid, forfeit and lose his office and employment and be incapable to hold the same.

III. And be it further enacted by the authority aforesaid, That from and after the said twenty-fifth day of *December* one thousand seven hundred and twenty-two, it shall not be lawful for any person or persons to use or wear in *Great Britain*, in or about any bed, chair, cushion, window-curtain or any other sort of houshold stuff or furniture, any printed, painted, stained or dyed callico (except as herein after is excepted) under the penalty of forfeiting (being thereof lawfully convicted) the sum of twenty pounds of lawful money of *Great Britain*, to be recovered as herein after is directed. . . .

VI. Provided always, and it is hereby further enacted by the authority aforesaid, That this act, or any thing therein contained shall not extend or be construed to extend in any wise to any callicoes which have already been, or which before the said twenty-fifth day of *December* one thousand seven hundred and twenty-two shall be made up or used in any bed, chair, cushion, window-curtain or other sort of houshold stuff or furniture: provided the same be continued to be worn and used in such houshold stuff or furniture, and not otherwise.

VII. Provided also, That nothing in this act contained shall extend or be construed to extend to repeal, make void or alter any law now in force for prohibiting callicoes printed, painted, dyed or stained in foreign parts, or for prohibiting any other goods or manufactures whatsoever. . . .

X. And be it further enacted by the authority aforesaid, That the prohibition of callicoes intended by this act, and the penalties thereby inflicted for wearing or using printed, painted, stained or dyed callico in apparel, houshold stuff or furniture, after the twenty-fifth day of *December* one thousand seven hundred and twenty-two, contrary to this act, shall respectively extend to prohibit, and shall be levied and recovered for wearing or using in apparel, houshold stuff or furniture, after the said twenty-fifth day of *December* one thousand seven hundred and twenty-two, any stuff made of cotton or mixt therewith, which shall be printed or painted with any colour or colours, or any callico chequered or striped, or any callico stitched or flowered in foreign parts with any colour or colours, or with coloured flowers made there (muslins, neckcloths and fustians excepted) in such manner as the penalties inflicted by this act for wearing or using printed, painted, stained or dyed callico in apparel, houshold stuff or furniture after the said twenty-fifth day of *December* one thousand seven hundred and twenty-two, contrary to this act, are to be levied or recovered; but under such limitations, and with such liberties, privileges and advantages as are mentioned and expressed in this act, or in any other act or acts of parliament now in force relating thereto, or relating to printed, painted, stained or dyed callicoes.

XI. Provided, That nothing in this act contained shall extend or be construed to extend to such callicoes as shall be dyed all blue.

124. An account by a former apprentice of Lombe's silk-mill at Derby

(W. Hutton, *The History of Derby* (1791), pp. 191–194, 196–200, 202–209.)

William Hutton (1723–1815) became a bookseller in Birmingham in 1750, and wrote a history of that town and other topographical works. Lombe's silk-mill is interesting as an example in the eighteenth century of a fully developed textile factory of the type generally associated with the Industrial Revolution.

All the writers, from *Gregory* to *Gough*, who have travelled through Derby, for half a century, give us a description of the *silkmill*. But it is doubtful, whether an adequate idea can be formed of that wonderful machine, when described by an Author who does not understand it himself. Some have earnestly wished to see this singular piece of mechanism; but I have sincerely wished I never had. I have lamented, that while almost every man in the world was born *out* of Derby, it should be my unhappy lot to be born *in*. To this curious, but wretched place, I was bound apprentice for seven years, which I always considered the most unhappy of my life; these I faithfully served; which was equalled by no other, in my time, except a worthy brother, then my companion in distress, and now my intelligent friend. It is therefore no wonder if I am perfectly acquainted with every movement in that superb work. My parents, through mere necessity, put me to labour before Nature had made me able. Low as the engines were, I was too short to reach them. To remedy this defect, a pair of high pattens were fabricated, and lashed to my feet, which I dragged after me till time lengthened my stature. The confinement and the labour were no burden; but the severity was intolerable, the marks of which I yet carry, and shall carry to the grave. . . . It was again my unhappy lot, at the close of this servitude, to be bound apprentice to a stocking-maker, for a second seven years; so that, like Jacob, I served two apprenticeships; but was not, like him, rewarded either with wealth or beauty. The time spent at the silk-mill is not included in the last fifty years. The erection of other mills has given a choice of place; and humanity has introduced a kinder treatment. . . .

John Lombe, a man of spirit, a good draughtsman, and an excellent mechanic, travelled into Italy, with a view of penetrating the secret. [of silk throwing] He staid some time; but as he knew admission was prohibited, he adopted the usual mode of accomplishing his end by corrupting the servants. This gained him frequent access in private. Whatever part he became master of, he committed to paper before he slept. By perseverance and bribery he acquired the whole, when the plot was discovered, and he fled, with the utmost precipitation, on board a ship, at the hazard of his life, taking with him two natives, who have favoured his interest and his life, at the risk of their own. But though he judged the danger over, he was yet to become a sacrifice.

Arriving safe with his acquired knowledge, he fixed upon Derby as a proper place for his purpose, because the town was likely to supply him with a sufficient number of hands, and the able stream with a constant supply of water. This happened about the year 1717.

He agreed with the Corporation for an island or swamp in the river, five hundred feet long, and fifty-two wide, at eight pounds *per ann.* where he erected the present works, containing eight apartments, and 468 windows, at the expence of about £30,000. This island, with another, called the Bye-flat, were part of the continent, but separated, ages past, by cutting two sluices to work four sets of mills. The ground continuing flat, farther West, would yet allow one or two sets more.

This ponderous building stands upon huge piles of oak, from sixteen to twenty feet long, driven close to each other with an engine made for that purpose. Over this solid mass of timber is laid a foundation of stone.

During three or four years, while this grand affair was constructing, he hired various rooms in Derby, and particularly the Town-hall, where he erected temporary engines, turned by hand. And although he reduced the prices so far below those of the Italians, as to enable him to monopolize the trade, yet the overflowings of profit were so very considerable, as to enable him to pay for the grand machine as the work went on.

It appears that the building was compleated, and in full employ, several years before the leases were executed, which was not done till 1724, and extended to seventy-nine years.

Being established to his wish, he procured in 1718 a patent from the Crown, to secure the profits during fourteen years. But, alas! he had not pursued this lucrative commerce more than three or four years, when the Italians, who felt the effects of the theft from their want of trade, determined *his* destruction, and hoped that of his works would follow.

An artful woman came over in the character of a friend, associated with the parties, and assisted in the business. She attempted to gain both the Italians, and succeeded with one. By these two, slow poison was supposed, and perhaps justly, to have been administered to John Lombe, who lingered two or three years in agonies, and departed. The Italian ran away to his own country; and Madam was interrogated, but nothing transpired except what strengthened suspicion. . . .

John dying a bachelor, his property fell into the hands of his brother William, who enjoyed, or rather possessed the works but a short time; for, being of a melancholy turn, he shot himself. This superb erection, therefore, became the property of his cousin, Sir Thomas Lombe. I believe this happened about the year 1726.

If the Italians destroyed the man, they miscarried in their design upon the works; for they became more successful, and continued to employ about 300 people.

In 1732 the patent expired; when Sir Thomas, a true picture of human nature, petitioned Parliament for a renewal, and pleaded, "That the works had taken so long a time in perfecting, and the people in teaching, that there had been none to acquire emolument from the patent." But he forgot to inform them that he had already accumulated more than £80,000: thus veracity flies before profit. It is, however, no wonder disguise should appear at St. Stephen's, where the heart and the tongue so often disagree.

Government, willing to spread so useful an invention, gave Sir Thomas £14,000 to suffer the trade to be open, and a model of the works taken; which was for many years deposited in the Tower, and considered the greatest curiosity there.

A mill was immediately erected at Stockport, in Cheshire, which drew many of the hands from that of Derby, and, among others, that of Nathaniel Gartrevelli, the remaining Italian, who, sixteen years before, came over with John Lombe: him I personally knew; he ended his days in poverty; the frequent reward of the man who ventures his life in a base cause, or betrays his country.–Since then eleven mills have been erected in Derby, and the silk is now the staple trade of the place: more than a thousand hands are said to be employed in the various works, but they are all upon a diminutive scale compared to this.

The describers of this elaborate work tell us mechanically, as followers of the first author, that "it contains 26,000 wheels, 97,000 movements, which work 71,000 yards of silk-thread, while the water-wheel, which is eighteen feet high, makes one revolution, and that three are performed in a minute. That one fire-engine conveys warmth to every individual part of the machine; and that one regulator governs the whole."–By these wholesale numbers, the Reader is left about as wise as before. The design of writing is to communicate the same intelligence to the understanding, as might be conveyed through the eye or the ear, upon the spot.–Had the Author made the number of his *wheels* 10,000 less, he would have been nearer the mark; or if he had paid an unremitting attendance for seven years, he might have found their number 13,384. Perhaps his *movements*, an indeterminate word, will also bear a large discount; but as I am neither in the humour to calculate nor contradict, I shall leave him in possession of his own authority. What number of *yards* are wound, every circuit of the wheel, no man can tell; nor is the number open to calculation. The wheel revolves about *twice* in a minute. Nor is the superb *fire-engine*, which blazes in description, any more than a common stove, which warmed *one corner* of that large building, and left the others to starve: but the defect is now supplied by fire-places. The *regulator* is a peg in the master-wheel, which strikes a small bell every revolution: near it is a pendulum, which vibrates about fifty times in a minute. Twenty-four returns of the pendulum is the medium velocity of the wheel.–Although there are a vast number of parts, any one of which may be stopped, and separated at pleasure; yet the whole, extending through five large rooms, is *one* regular machine, which moves and stops together. Every minute part is attended with two wheels, one of which turns the other. If you separate the two, the last stops of course, while the former moves gently on.

The raw silk is brought in hanks, or skaines, called slips, and would take five or six days in winding off, though kept moving ten hours a day. Some are the produce of Persia; others of Canton, coarse, and in small slips; some are from Piedmont, these are all of a yellowish colour; and some are from China, perfectly white. The work passes through three different engines; one to wind; the second to twist; and the third to double. Though the thread is fine, it is an accumulation of many. The workman's care is chiefly to unite, by a knot, a thread that breaks; to take out the burs and uneven parts, some of which are little bags, fabricated by the silk-worm, as a grave for itself, when Nature inspires the idea of leaving the world: the bags are neatly closed up, and hung to a thread, as the last efforts towards its own funeral. They generally moulder to a darkish dust; sometimes are totally gone: but I have frequently taken them out alive. The threads are continually breaking; and to tye them is principally the business of children whose fingers are nimble. The machine continually turns a round bobbin, or small block of wood, which draws the thread from the slip, while expanded upon a swift,[1] suspended upon a centre. The moment the thread breaks, the swift stops. One person commands from twenty to sixty threads. If many cease, at the same time, to turn, it amounts to a fault, and is succeeded by punishment. From the fineness of the materials, the ravelled state of the slips and bobbins, and the imprudence of children, much waste is made, which is another motive of correction; and when correction is often inflicted, it steels the breast of the inflictor.

125. Arthur Young on the Manchester cotton industry, 1770

(Arthur Young, *A Six Months Tour Through the North of England*, III (1770), pp. 242–250.)

A. P. Wadsworth and J. de L. Mann (*The Cotton Trade and Industrial Lancashire*, p. 402) comment on the low wages quoted by Young for dimity and counterpane weavers, and suggest that these may be errors in transcription.

The *Manchester* manufactures are divided into four branches,

The fustian
The check
The hat
The worsted small wares.

All these are subdivided into numerous branches, of distinct and separate work. In that of fustians are thirteen.

No. 1. Corded dimities
2. Velvets
3. Velverets
4. Thicksets
5. Pillaws

[1] Revolving frame for winding yarn.

6. Quilts
7. Petticoats
8. Draw-boys
9. Diapers
10. Herringbones
11. Jeans
12. Jeanets
13. Counterpanes.

These goods are worked up of cotton alone, of flax and cotton, and of *Hamborough* yarn. All sorts of cotton are used, but chiefly the *West Indian*. These branches employ men, women, and children.

In branch No. 1. Men earn from 3*s*. to 8*s*. week.
Women the same.
No children employed in it.
2. Men from 5*s*. to 10*s*.
Neither women or children.
3, and 4. Men from 5*s*. to 10*s*. average 5*s*. 6*d*.
Women as much.
Children 3*s*.
5. Men from 4*s*. to 5*s*.
Women the same.
Children 2*s*. 6*d*.
6, and 7. Men from 6*s*. to 12*s*.
Neither women or children.
8. Men, at an average, 6*s*. but a boy paid out of it.
No women.
9. Men from 4*s*. to 6*s*.
Women as much.
No children.
10. All children, 1*s*. 6*d*.
11. Men from 4*s*. to 10*s*.
No women or children.
12. Women 1*s*. 6*d*. to 3*s*. 6*d*.
Children the same.
13. Men from 3*s*. to 7*s*.
Neither women or children.

These branches of manufacture work both for exportation and home consumption: Many low priced goods they make for *North America*, and many fine ones for the *West Indies*. The whole business was exceedingly brisk during the war, and very bad after the peace; but now are pretty good again, though not equal to what they were during the war. All the revolutions of late in the *North American* affairs are felt severely by this branch. It was never known in this branch that poor people applied for work but could not get it, except in the stagnation caused by the stamp act.

I enquired the effects of high or low prices of provisions, and found that in the former the manufacturers were industrious, and their families easy and happy; but that in times of low prices the latter starved; for half the time of the father was spent at the ale-house. That both for the good of the masters, and the working people, high prices were far more advantageous than low ones: And the highest that were ever known much better than the lowest.

All in general may constantly have work that will: And the employment is very regular: The master manufacturers not staying for orders before the people are set to work, but keep, on the contrary, a great many hands in pay, in expectation of the spring orders.

The principal sub-divisions of the check branch are the following.

No. 1. Handkerchiefs.
2. Bed ticking.
3. Cotton hollands.
4. Gowns.
5. Furniture checks.
6. Silk and cotton ginghams.
7. Sousees.
8. Damascus's.
9. *African* goods, in imitation of the *East Indian.*

These branches employ both men, women, and children; their earnings as follow.

No. 1. Men 7*s.*
Women 7*s.*
Children 2*s.* to 5*s.*
2. Men 6*s.* to 10*s.*
Neither women or children.
3. Men 7*s.*
Women 7*s.*
Children a few, 2*s.* to 5*s.*
4. Men 8*s.*
Neither women or children.
5. Men 7*s.*
Women 7*s.*
No children.
6. Men 7*s.* 6*d.*
Neither women or children.
7. Men 7*s.* 6*d.*
Neither women or children.
8. Men 7*s.* 6*d.*
Neither women or children.
9. Men from 6*s.* to 9*s.*
Women the same.
No children.

Most of these articles have many preparers; among others,

Dyers at 7*s*. 6*d*.
Bleachers 6*s*. 6*d*.
Finishers 7*s*. 6*d*.

The check branch, like the fustian, works both for exportation and home consumption, but vastly more for the former than the latter. During the war the demand was extremely brisk: very dull upon the peace, but lately has arisen greatly, though not equal to the war; and the interruptions caused by the convulsions in *America*, very severely felt by every workman in this branch: None ever offered for work but they at once had it, except upon the regulations of the colonies cutting off their trade with the *Spaniards*, and the stamp act. The last advices received from *America* have had a similar effect, for many hands were paid off in consequence of them.

In the hat branch the principal sub-divisions are,

1. Preparers.
2. Makers.
3. Finishers.
4. Liners.
5. Trimmers.

They employ both men, women and children, whose earnings are somewhat various.

No. 1. No men.
Women, 3*s*. 6*d*. to 7*s*.
No children.
2. Men 7*s*. 6*d*.
No women.
Children, 2*s*. 6*d*. to 6*s*.
3. Men, 12*s*.
No women.
Children, 7*s*. 6*d*.
4. No men.
Women, 4*s*. to 7*s*. 6*d*.
Children, 2*s*. 6*d*. to 6*s*.
5. No men.
Women, 4*s*. to 7*s*. 6*d*.
Children, 2*s*. 6*d*. to 6*s*.

This branch works chiefly for exportation; during the war it was surprizingly brisk; after the peace quite low; lately it has been middling.

In the branch of small wares are numerous little articles, but the earnings in general run as follow:

Men from 5*s*. to 12*s*.
Women from 2*s*. 6*d*. to 7*s*.
Children from 1*s*. 6*d*. to 6*s*.

The number of spinners employed in and out of *Manchester* is immense; they reckon 30,000 souls in that town; and 50,000 manufacturers employed *out* of it.

Cotton spinners earn,

Women, 2*s.* to 5*s.*

Girls from six to twelve years, 1*s.* to 1*s.* 6*d.*

In general all these branches find, that their best friend is high prices of provisions: I was particular in my enquiries on this head, and found the sentiment universal: The manufacturers themselves, as well as their families, are in such times better cloathed, better fed, happier, and in easier circumstances than when prices are low; for at such times they never worked six days in a week; numbers not five, nor even four; the idle time spent at alehouses, or at receptacles of low diversion; the remainder of their time of little value; for it is a known fact, that a man who sticks to his loom regularly, will perform his work much better, and do more of it, than one who idles away half his time, and especially in drunkenness. . . .

America takes three-fourths of all the manufactures of *Manchester.*

126. The introduction of machines into the Manchester cotton industry, described by James Ogden, 1783

(James Ogden, *A Description of Manchester . . . By a Native of the Town* (1783), pp. 86–94.)

James Ogden (1718–1802) was a Manchester schoolmaster and poet, who was said to have started life as a fustian shearer.

[After describing how the printing of cotton, originally carried out in London, was largely transferred to Lancashire in the later eighteenth century, he continues–]

The acquisition of this last branch, with large exports in foreign trade, have given such employment to large capitals, that the interior business of the country is, in a great measure, given up to the middle class of manufacturers and petty chapmen: but no exertion of the manufacturers or workmen could have answered the demands of trade, without the introduction of spinning machines.

These were first used by the country people on a confined scale, twelve spindles being thought a great affair at first, and the awkward posture required to spin on them, was discouraging to grown up people, while they saw, with a degree of surprize, children, from nine to twelve years of age, manage them with dexterity, which brought plenty into families, that were before overburthened with children, and delivered many a poor endeavouring weaver out of bondage to which they were exposed, by the insolence of spinners, and abatement of their work, for which evils there was no remedy till spinning-jennies were invented. The following state of their case, will give our readers an idea of the oppression.

From the time that the original system was changed in the fustian branch, of buying pieces in the grey from the weavers, by delivering them out work, the custom of giving them the weft in cops,[1] which obtained for a while, grew into disuse, as there was no detecting the knavery of spinners till a piece came in woven; so that the practice was changed, and wool given with warps, the weaver answering for

[1] Balls of thread wound on spindles.

spinning; and the weavers, in a scarcity of spinning, have been paid less for the weft than they gave the spinner, but durst not complain, much less abate the spinner, lest their looms should stand unemployed: but when jennies were introduced, and children could work on them, the case was altered, and many who had been insolent before, were glad to be employed in carding and slubbing[1] cotton for these engines.

The plenty of weft produced by this means gave uneasiness to the country people, and the weavers were afraid lest the manufacturers should demand finer weft woven at the former prices, which occasioned some risings, and the jennies were opposed, some being demolished before those who used them could be protected, or convince others of their general utility, till *Dorning Rasbotham*, Esq.; a worthy magistrate who lived in that part of the country towards *Bolton*, where they were used, convinced the weavers, in a sensible printed address, that it was their true interest to encourage jennies, urging the former insolence of spinners, and the happiness of such as had already relieved themselves, and procured employment for their children; and appealed to their own experience of the fly shuttle, against which the like clamour had been raised, and the inventor driven to *France*, where he found encouragement, while his shuttles are yet in such estimation here, as to be used generally even on narrow goods, to the benefit of trade in general, without any bad consequence in the experience of several years, but they are rather of particular benefit to the weavers.

This seasonable address produced a general acquiescence in the use of these engines, to a certain number of spindles, but they were soon multiplied to three or four times the quantity; nor did the invention of ingenious mechanics rest here, for the demand of twist for warps was greater as weft grew plenty, therefore engines were soon constructed for this purpose: one in particular was purchased at a price which was a considerable reward for the contriver's ingenuity, and exposed at the Exchange, where he spun on it, and all that were disposed to see the operation, were admitted gratis.

The improvements kept increasing till the capital engines for twist were perfected; and it is amazing to see what thousands of spindles may be put in motion by a water wheel, and managed mostly by children, without confusion, and with less waste of cotton than the former methods: but the carding and slubbing, preparatory to twisting, required a greater range of invention than the twisting engines, and there were sufficient motives to encourage the attempt; for while carding was performed by common cards, and slubbing by the hand, these operations took half the price of spinning.

The first attempts were carding engines, which are very curious, and now brought to great perfection, though they are still improving; and an engine has now been contrived for converting the carded wool to slubbing, by drawing it to about the thickness of candle-wick, preparatory to throwing it into twist.

We suppose, and even wish that the principle of this last engine may be applied to reduce combed sheeps wool to a slubbing, for the purpose of spinning it upon the more complex machines, which would be a great acquisition to some branches of trade here. It is already spun on the common flax wheel with a fly (which has been

[1] Combing and slightly twisting wool or cotton in preparation for spinning.

adopted by these engines) the length way of the combing, which is capable of being handled and divided at pleasure, and may be prepared as a slubbing for the spinning machines, by any contrivance in the drawing out, which has a respect to the length of staple and cohesion of parts, wherein combed wool differs from carded cotton.

When the larger machines were first set to work by water, they produced such excellent twist for warps, that they soon outrivalled the makers of warps on the larger jennies, some of whom had several at work, and had reaped a good harvest of profit by them; but as the larger machines were encouraged, they suffered abatement in proportion; and one of them concerned, making his complaint to others when they were intoxicated at the ale-house, a resolution was taken to destroy the water machines, and some were demolished before the owners could be protected, or the deluded country people who joined them could reflect, that if more warps were made, there would be a greater demand for weft from their jennies, and a better price for it; which has been fully experienced in the introduction of muslins, for no contrivance in the other machines can make the thread hold when it is so slack thrown as to suit for weft, nor can it be supposed the attempt would be made, if possible, as the demand of twist for warps will fully employ them; for if cotton comes down to a reasonable price, the warps made of this twist would be as cheap as those made of yarn, and keep the money here which was sent abroad for that article, there being no comparison between yarn and cotton warps for goodness, and the advantages in that case would be greater to the workmen, the manufacturers, and the consumer, as well as to the general interest of the kingdom.

We had given in our manuscript a particular description of the principles and movements of these machines; but have suppressed it for the present, as it has been hinted that this publication might be translated into *French*, and communicated to our rivals in trade; which is giving a consequence we little expected to our description of *Manchester*, and history of its manufactures.

We are now hastening to a conclusion, and shall observe by the way, that perhaps nothing has more contributed to the improvements in trade here, than the free admission of workmen in every branch, whereby the trade has been kept open to strangers of every description, who contribute to its improvement by their ingenuity; for *Manchester* being only a market town, governed by Constables, is not subject to such regulations as are made in corporations, to favour freemen in exclusion of strangers: and, indeed, nothing could be more fatal to its trading interest, if it should be incorporated, and have representatives in Parliament. For such is the general course of popular contests, that in places where the immediate dependence of the inhabitants is not upon trade, the health and morals of the people are ruined upon these occasions. How much more fatal would the effects be in such a town as this, where, to the above evils, there would be added the interruption of trade, and perpetuation of ill-will between masters and workmen, who were independent; while those who had nothing to depend on but labour, would contract habits of idleness and drunkenness, or fly to other places, where they could be free from the tyrannical restrictions and partial usage which generally prevail in corporations.

THE END.

(b) THE MIDLAND INDUSTRIES

127. Mrs. Abiah Darby describes developments in the Darby ironworks at Coalbrookdale, 1708–1763

(Letter from Mrs. Darby, *circa.* 1775, printed in T. S. Ashton, *Iron and Steel in the Industrial Revolution* (1924), Appendix, pp. 249–252.)

Professor Ashton has pointed out (*Trans. of Newcomen Society*, v, pp. 9–14) that this letter makes it clear that it was the first Abraham Darby who first used coke in place of charcoal in the production of iron castings, not his son, as some writers have supposed. This substitution of coke for charcoal, completed by Henry Cort in 1784, freed the iron industry from its dependence on woodlands and made possible its transference to the coalfields of the Midlands, Yorkshire and Wales.

Sunniside.
[Probably about 1775.]

Esteemed Friend,

Thy very acceptable favour of the 9th ulto. claim'd my earliest acknowledgments, which I should immediately have made, had not thy kind condescension in taking notice of my late honour'd Husband, and requesting to be inform'd of any circumstance which may be interesting relating him, caused my delay–to recollect what might occur concerning his transactions or improvements in the Manufactory of Iron, so beneficial to this nation. But before I proceed further, I cannot help lamenting with thee in thy just observation, "that it has been universally observed, that the Destroyers of mankind are recorded and remembered, while the Benefactors are unnoticed and forgotten". This seems owing to the depravity of the mind, which centres in reaping the present advantages, and suffering obscurity to vail the original causes of such benefits; and even the very names of those to whom we are indebted for the important discoveries, to sink into oblivion. Whereas if they were handed down to posterity, gratitude would naturally arise in the commemoration of their ingenuity, and the great advantages injoyed from their indefatigable labours–I now make free to communicate what I have heard my Husband say, and what arises from my own knowledge; also what I am inform'd from a person now living, whose father came here as a workman at the first beginning of these Pit Coal Works.

Then to begin at the original. It was my Husband's Father, whose name he bore (Abraham Darby[1] and who was the first that set on foot the Brass Works at or near Bristol) that attempted to mould and cast Iron pots, &c., in sand instead of Loam (as they were wont to do, which made it a tedious and more expensive process) in which he succeeded. This first attempt was tryed at an Air Furnace in Bristol. About the year 1709 he came into Shropshire to Coalbrookdale, and with other partners took a lease of the works, which only consisted of an old Blast Furnace and some Forges. He here cast Iron Goods in sand out of the Blast Furnace that blow'd with wood charcoal; for it was not yet thought of to blow with Pit Coal. Sometime after he suggested the thought, that it might be practable to smelt the Iron from the ore in the blast Furnace with Pit Coal: Upon this he first try'd with raw coal as it came out of

[1] 1677–1717.

the Mines, but it did not answer. He not discouraged, had the coal coak'd into Cynder, as is done for drying Malt, and it then succeeded to his satisfaction. But he found that only one sort of pit Coal would suit best for the purpose of making good Iron.–These were beneficial discoveries, for the moulding and casting in sand instead of Loam was of great service, both in respect to expence and expedition. And if we may compare little things with great–as the invention of printing was to writing, so was the moulding and casting in Sand to that of Loam. He then erected another Blast Furnace, and enlarged the Works. This discovery soon got abroad and became of great utillity.

This Place and its environs was very barren, little money stiring amongst the Inhabitants. So that I have heard they were Obliged to exchange their small produce one to another instead of money, until he came and got the Works to bear, and made Money Circulate amongst the different parties who were employed by him. Yet notwithstanding the Service he was of to the Country, he had opposers and ill-wishers, and a remarkable circumstance of awful Memory occurs; of a person who endeavour'd to hinder the horses which carried the Iron Stone and Coal to the Furnaces, from coming through a road that he pretended had a right to Oppose: and one time when he saw the horses going alone, he in his Passion, wished he might Never Speak More if they should Ever come that way again. And instantly his Speech was stop'd, and altho' he lived Several years after yet he Never Spoke More!

My Husband's Father died early in life; a religious good man, and an Eminent Minister amongst the people call'd Quakers.

My Husband Abraham Darby[1] was but Six years old when his Father died–but he inherited his genius–enlarg'd upon his plan, and made many improvements. One of Consequence to the prosperity of these Works was as they [were] very short of water that in the Summer or dry Seasons they were obliged to blow very slow, and generally blow out the furnaces once a year, which was attended with great loss. But my Husband proposed the Erecting a Fire Engine to draw up the Water from the lower Works and convey it back into the upper pools, that by continual rotation of the Water the furnaces might be plentifully supplied; which answered Exceeding Well to these Works, and others have followed the Example.

But all this time the making of Barr Iron at Forges from Pit Coal pigs was not thought of. About 26 years ago my Husband conceived this happy thought–that it might be possible to make bar from pit coal pigs. Upon this he Sent some of our pigs to be tryed at the Forges, and that no prejudice might arise against them he did not discover from whence they came, or of what quality they were. And a good account being given of their working, he errected Blast Furnaces for Pig Iron for Forges. Edward Knight Esqr a capitol Iron Master urged my Husband to get a patent, that he might reap the benefit for years of this happy discovery: but he said he would not deprive the public of Such an Acquisition which he was Satisfyed it would be; and so it has proved, for it soon spread, and Many Furnaces both in this Neighbourhood and Several other places have been errected for this purpose.

Had not these discoveries been made the Iron trade of our own produce would

[1] 1711–1763. His son, the third Abraham Darby (1750–1791), built the first iron bridge over the Severn at Coalbrookdale in 1779.

have dwindled away, for woods for charcoal became very Scarce and landed Gentlemen rose the prices of cord wood exceeding high–indeed it would not have been to be got. But from pit coal being introduced in its stead the demand for wood charcoal is much lessen'd, and in a few years I apprehend will set the use of that article aside.

Many other improvements he was the author of. One of Service to these Works here they used to carry all their mine and coal upon horses' backs but he got roads made and laid with Sleepers and rails as they have them in the North of England for carring them to the Rivers, and brings them to the Furnaces in Waggons. And one waggon with three horses will bring as much as twenty horses used to bring on horses' backs. But this laying the roads with wood begot a Scarcity and rose the price of it. So that of late years the laying of the rails of cast Iron was substituted; which altho' expensive, answers well for Ware and Duration. We have in the different Works near twenty miles of this road which cost upwards of Eight hundred pounds a mile. That of Iron Wheels and axletrees for these waggons was I believe my Husband's Invention.

He kept himself confined to the Iron Trade and the Necessary Appendages annex'd thereto. He was just in his dealings–of universal benevolence and charity, living Strictly to the Rectitude of the Divine and Moral Law, held forth by his great Lord and Saviour, had an extraordinary command over his own spirit, which thro' the Assistance of Divine Grace enabled to bear up with fortitude above all opposition: for it may seem very strange, so valuable a man should have Antagonists, yet he had. Those called Gentlemen with an Envious Spirit could not bear to see him prosper; and others covetious; strove to make every advantage by raising their Rents of their collieries and lands in which he wanted to make roads; and endeavour'd to stop the works. But he surmounted all: and died in Peace beloved and Lamented by many.

128A–B. Two descriptions of Birmingham and its industries, 1766–1784

128A. Extracts from the Diary of Lady Shelburne, 1766

(Lord Fitzmaurice, *Life of William, Earl of Shelburne*, I (1912), pp. 274–278.)

The Shelburnes visited Birmingham in May 1766. Shelburne exaggerates the newness of Birmingham's industries.

May 14th [1766, London.]–We got into the coach for Birmingham, and arrived through rough roads at nine o'clock there. We were kindly and politely received by Mr Garbett.[1]. . .

May 15th–We breakfasted, and went soon after with Mr Garbett to see the manufactory of buttons and hardwares, which are very curious, and entertained us much till dinner-time. Mr Taylor, the principal manufacturer there, dined with us, and we went afterwards to Mr Bolden's,[2] who trades much in the same way. His house is a

[1] Samuel Garbett, a rich merchant, friend and one-time partner of John Roebuck. See No. 192.
[2] Matthew Boulton (1728–1809), who started the Soho works in 1764.

very pretty one about a mile out of the town, and his workshops newly built at the end of his garden, where they take up a large piece of ground which he has named Soho Square. There, as in the morning, we purchased some watch chains and trinkets at an amazing cheap price, and drank tea afterwards in his house, which is a very pleasant one. We returned home to supper between nine and ten, for we kept early hours. Mr Baskerville[1] supped with us.

May 16th.–This morning we went to Gimlett's, where we bought a great many toys and saw his warehouse of watches &c., one of which I bought for Master Parker. We also went to a Quaker's to see the making of guns, but neither Lady Louisa or I being much interested about that, we left Lord Shelburne and Mr Garbett and went with his son to the toyshops, where we made some purchases. At Mr Taylor's we met again, and he made and ennamel'd a landscape on the top of a box before us, which he afterwards gave me as a curiosity from my having seen it done. The method of doing it is this: a stamping instrument managed only by one woman first impresses the picture on paper, which paper is then laid even upon a piece of white enamel and rubbed hard with a knife or instrument like it, till it is marked upon the box. Then there is spread over it with a brush some metallic colour reduced to a fine powder which adheres to the moist part, and, by putting it afterwards into an oven for a few minutes, the whole is completed by fixing the colour. We came home, dined, went again to Gimlett's, and from thence to drink tea at Mr Taylor's villa. This is a very handsome house with a dairy and garden about it. His wife and daughter, a girl of about fourteen, received us, and she played on the harpsichord and sung to us. Mr Taylor and his son walked about with Lord Shelburne and Mr Garbett. After this Mr Frank Garbett went with Lady Louisa and me in the coach to Mr Baskerville's, which is also a pretty place out of the town; he showed us his garden and hot-house, Mrs Baskerville the Japan, which business she has chiefly the management of. By this time Mr Garbett and Lord Shelburne, who walked, arrived; he bought some new books printed by Mr Baskerville, and I some Japan, and it being now dark we returned home.

May 17th.–As soon as breakfast was over we went to see the making of buckles, *papier mâché* boxes, and the melting, painting, and stamping of glass. By twelve o'clock we returned to Mr Garbett's, took some chocolate, and, thanking him for our entertainment at Birmingham, got into our coach to return home. . . .

May 19th.–. . . We dined alone and in the evening Lord Shelburne was so good to write for me the following account of the place we had been so much amused at:

"Birmingham originally had no manufacture except a small one of linen thread, which continues there to this day, though now to the amount of ten or twelve thousand pounds. It is not fifty years since the hardware began to make a figure, from thence begun by people not worth above three or four hundred pounds a-piece, some of which are now worth three or four hundred thousand, particularly a Mr. Taylor, the most established manufacturer and trader; some, however, are beginning to rival him in the extent of his trade. Its great rise was owing to two things, first the discovery

[1] John Baskerville (1706–1775) the famous printer, who had also started a japanning business at Moor Street, Birmingham, in 1740.

of mixed metal so mollient or ductile as easily to suffer stamping, the consequence of which is they do buttons, buckles, toys, and everything in the hardware way by stamping machines which were before obliged to be performed by human labour. Another thing quickly followed, instead of employing the same hand to finish a button or any other thing, they subdivide it into as many different hands as possible, finding beyond doubt that the human faculties by being confined to a repetition of the same thing become more expeditious and more to be depended on than when obliged or suffered to pass from one to another. Thus a button passes through fifty hands, and each hand perhaps passes a thousand in a day; likewise, by this means, the work becomes so simple that, five times in six, children of six or eight years old do it as well as men, and earn from ten pence to eight shillings a week. There are besides an infinity of smaller improvements which each workman has and sedulously keeps secret from the rest. Upon the whole they have reduced the price so low that the small matter of gold on a button makes the chief expense of it, being as three to one including all other materials and manufacture. However, they have lately discovered a method of washing them with aquafortis, which gives them the colour of gold, and are come to stamp them so well that 'tis scarce possible at any distance to distinguish them from a thread button. There are many other manufactures here; most of the spirit of hartshorn consumed in England, and oil of a great quantity, but the greatest manufacture of that is now removed to Preston Pans in Scotland. The reason Mr. Garbett gave for it was, first, secrecy as to the method of making it (which is almost impossible to preserve in Birmingham, there is so much enterprise and sharpness); next, the cheapness of provisions; and, lastly, the obedient turn of the Scotch. Refining of gold and silver, and gun-making to a prodigious amount for exportation, are likewise another branch of their trade, of which they send annually above a hundred and fifty thousand to the coast of Africa, some of which are sold for five and sixpence a-piece, but what is shocking to humanity, above half of them, from the manner they are finished in, are sure to burst in the first hand that fires them. If an Act of Parliament was passed ordering a proof-master to be settled at the expence of the manufacturers themselves, for one shilling more the barrels might be properly bored and finished, so as to secure the buyer at least from certain danger, the trade by this means assured and confirmed in its present channel, and the moral infamy in the individuals who are thus induced to multiply gain, suppressed. This trade, great as it is, is not above twenty or twenty-five years' standing. Another thing they are in great want of is an assay-master, which is allowed both at Chester and York; but it is very hard on a manufacturer to be obliged to send every piece of plate to Chester to be marked, without which no one will purchase it, where the great object of the whole trade is to make a quantity and thus to reduce the profits as low as 'tis possible. It would be of infinite public advantage if silver plate came to be manufactured here as watches lately are, and that it should be taken out of the imposing monopoly of it in London."

128B. Faujas de Saint-Fond's impressions of Birmingham, 1784

(B. Faujas de Saint-Fond, *A Journey through England and Scotland to the Hebrides in 1784*, trans. Sir Archibald Geikie (1907), II, pp. 345–350, 356–357.)

Barthélemy Faujas de Saint-Fond (1741–1819) was a noted French geologist, who later became Professor of Geology at the Muséum d'Histoire Naturelle in Paris. His *Journey* was first published in 1797. For his account of the Newcastle coal-mines, see No. 131.

We left Derby at noon, but as the roads are all still very bad along the whole of this route, we had much difficulty in arriving on the same day at Birmingham. It was past nine in the evening when we reached the inn, after having crossed black and arid heaths, and an extremely wild country.

We had letters of recommendation to Doctor Withering,[1] the translator of the Sciagraphia of Bergmann, and a lover of both botany and chemistry: we hastened to wait on him next day to present them. He lives in a fine house, furnished with much taste and elegance. We had tea at his house in company with ladies as pleasant as they were good-looking, and to complete our good fortune, we were here introduced to Mr Watt, one of the most scientific men in England as regards mechanics, and who also possesses great knowledge in chemistry and physics.

From the activity of its manufactures and its commerce, Birmingham is one of the most curious towns in England. If any one should wish to see in one comprehensive view, the most numerous and varied industries, all combined in contributing to the arts of utility, of pleasure, and of luxury, it is hither that he must come. Here all the resources of industry, supported by the genius of invention, and by mechanical skill of every kind are directed towards the arts, and seem to be linked together to co-operate for their mutual perfection.

I know that some travellers who have not given themselves the trouble to reflect on the importance and advantage of these kinds of manufactures in such a country as England, have disapproved of most of these industrial establishments. I know that even an Englishman who has only taken a hasty, I would almost say an inconsiderate view of these magnificent establishments, William Gilpin,[2] has said that it was difficult for the eye to be long pleased in the midst of so many frivolous arts, where a hundred men may be seen, whose labours are confined to the making of a tobacco box. But besides that this statement is exaggerated and ill-considered, its author has not deigned to cast his eyes over the vast works where steam-pumps are made, these astonishing machines, the perfecting of which does so much honour to the talents and knowledge of Mr Watt; over the manufactories in constant activity making sheet-copper for sheathing ships' bottoms; over those of plate-tin and plate-iron, which make France tributary to England, nor over that varied and extensive hard-ware manufacture which employs to so much advantage more than thirty thousand hands, and compels all Europe, and a part of the New World, to supply themselves from England, because all ironmongery is made here in greater perfection, with more economy and in greater abundance, than anywhere else.

Once more, I say with pleasure, and it cannot be too often said to Frenchmen, that it is the abundance of coal which has performed this miracle and has created, in

[1] Chief physician to the Birmingham General Hospital and a noted botanist and mineralogist.
[2] Author of *A Picturesque Tour in England.*

the midst of a barren desert, a town with forty thousand inhabitants, who live in comfort, and enjoy all the conveniences of life.

Here a soil, once covered with the most barren and sombre heath, has been changed into groves of roses and lilacs, and turned into fertile and delightful gardens by Mr Boulton, associated with Mr Watt, in whose work more than a thousand hands are engaged.

The population of Birmingham has made such an advance, that during the war with the United States of America, a war which weakened the resources of England, at least three hundred new houses were added annually to the town, and this rate doubled as soon as peace was concluded. A well-informed person assured me that this was true, and he showed me, during my stay in the town, a whole street which was in process of erection with such rapidity that, all the houses being built on a given plan and at the same time, one could believe that the street would be entirely completed in less than two months.

I had much pleasure in visiting Mr Watt as often as I could, whose wide accomplishments in chemistry and the arts, inspired me with the very greatest interest. His moral qualities, and his engaging manner of expressing his thoughts, increased my respect and regard for him. He joins to the frank manners of a Scotsman the gentleness and amiability of a kind-hearted man. Surrounded with charming children, all well-informed, full of talent and having had the best education, he enjoys among them the unalloyed happiness of making them his friends and of being adored by them as their father.

I had one day a delightful dinner with this amiable family, and it was doubly interesting to me, for Doctor Priestley who is a relation and friend of Mr Watt, was there; I had the pleasure of making the acquaintance of this celebrated man, to whom the physical sciences owe such great obligations, and whose gentle and kindly manners increased our affection for his virtues. . . .

We passed several days in Birmingham in the midst of the arts and industries, and in the society of enlightened men and amiable women. Nothing can equal so peaceful a charm; the mind is fed and inspirited; the head is filled with facts, and the heart with gratitude. Such was our experience in this town which we could not leave without regret.

129. Letter from Matthew Boulton to Lord Dartmouth on the extension of the patent for Watt's steam-engine, 22 February 1775

(*Hist. MSS. Comm., Dartmouth MSS.*, III, p. 213.)

Boulton and Watt had recently become partners. Watt's original patent in 1769 had been for six years; by an Act of 1775 (15 Geo. III, cap. 61) it was extended for twenty-four years. Dartmouth was at this time President of the Board of Trade, and was personally interested in scientific matters.

Matthew Boulton to the Earl of Dartmouth.

1775, February 22. Soho.[1]

I take the liberty of writing to your lordship in favour of my friend Mr. James Watt, an engineer, who intends to petition parliament for a prolongation of a term of an exclusive privilege granted by his majesty's patent which he has already

[1] Staffs., near Birmingham.

obtained for certain very capital improvements invented by him in steam or fire engines. And I am convinced that your lordship will excuse this liberty, and will even interest yourself in the affair, when I acquaint you that the legislature's compliance with the prayer of the petition will not only be a kind of justice to an ingenious man who has spent much of his attention and fortune in the discovery of an useful invention, and who from certain circumstances, which I shall explain to your lordship, cannot reap any advantage from it, unless he obtains the indulgence requested: but will also be really a public benefit, as without that indulgence his discoveries will not probably be ever carried into execution. I need not point out to your lordship's consideration the great utility of steam or fire engines in collieries, in lead, tin, and copper mines, and in other great works where great power is required, but I shall beg leave to observe, that Mr. Watt's intentions, if carried into execution, will very much extend the utility of fire engines by rendering them one-fourth of the expense usual, and by adapting them to a great variety of purposes and manufactures to which the present engines cannot be applied. Mr. Watt has spent a great part of his life and fortune in making experiments upon steam and steam-engines, and is the first and only man that has discovered the true principles upon which they can be constructed to the best advantage and very much superior to those commonly employed.

In the year 1769, he took out a patent for the sole use of his invention, but from the many mechanical difficulties that occurred in carrying into execution his newly discovered principles, from bad health, and from his having been employed by the boards of police and other public boards in Scotland, in making surveys, superintending the execution of a navigable canal, and other public works, and from the expense attending the necessary trials, experiments and models of engines, he has not been able to finish large engines till the latter end of last year, when he completed, in my manufactory at Soho, two engines (one rotatory and the other reciprocating) which perfectly answer to his and my satisfaction.

From the difficulties Mr. Watt has met with in the execution of this invention and from those he still saw before him, he was discouraged, and would have dropped the scheme, had I not assisted him. But as a great part of the time of his patent is elapsed and his own life very precarious and as a large sum of money must yet be expended before any advantage can be gained from it, I think that his abilities and my money may be otherwise better employed, unless parliament be pleased to grant a prolongation of the term of his exclusive privilege. I have obtained the favour of Lord Guernsey to present the petition to the House of Commons, and if it has the happiness to meet with your lordship's countenance and patronage, I doubt not but a communication of your favourable sentiments to Lord North, would greatly facilitate and ensure the success of it, as that communication would effectually convince his lordship of the justice and public utility of the measure, which seem to me to be the standards by which his lordship directs his public conduct. . . .

(c) MINES

130. A visit to Tyneside, May 1725

(*Hist. MSS. Comm.*, *Portland MSS.*, VI, pp. 103–106.)

This is part of a narrative of "A Journey through Hertfordshire, Lincolnshire and Nottinghamshire to the Northern Counties and Scotland" made by Edward Harley, second earl of Oxford, accompanied by Mr. Thomas, his chaplain, who is the author of the ensuing account.

May 6. [1725]

From Chester [-le Street] we go about half a mile to the left where is a very large fire engine for draining the coal pits there.

The boiler holds eighty hogsheads.

The fire stove consumes five fothers, or sixty bushels of coals in twenty four hours.

The brass barrel or cylinder is nine feet long. Its diameter two feet four inches.

Thickness of the brass–one inch and a half. From the surface of the ground to the bottom of the water is twenty four fathoms or forty eight yards.

The water in the pit is two yards deep. From the surface of the water to the drift or level where the engine forces it out is twelve fathoms.

It discharges two hundred and fifty hogsheads in one hour; it strikes (as they term it) or makes a discharge fourteen times in one minute.

In the same place are two other engines for draining, called Bob-gins, and are moved by water turning a wheel.

They all belong to Mr. Headworth, Dean of the church, and Mr. Allan. The weekly expense of these three engines is 5*l.* paid by the owners of the colliery to Mr. Potter the undertaker of the fire engine, the owners allowing whatever coals are expended.

Coming from this engine towards Newcastle we pass over two way leaves which cross the great road. These way leaves are an artificial road made for the conveyance of coal from the Pit to the Steaths on the riverside; whereby one horse shall carry a greater burden than a whole team on a common way, and as they generally pass through the grounds of several proprietors, are very expensive to the coal owners, who pay very high prices for their trespass on that occasion. The nearest to Chester is a single one and belongs to Mr. Allan's colliery, the other about half a mile further is a double one, and belongs to Dean Headworth; the loaded cart goes upon one, and the empty one returns upon the other. The whole length of these two way leaves from the coal pits to the place from whence the coals are loaded into the lighters or keels at Sunderland, is five miles.

On a great part of this road to Newcastle we go upon the Roman Way, but as we come up the hill to Eyton, the common road is lately turned from it by Sir H. Lyddell, who has built new walls on each side of the way for the improvement of an estate edjoining, gained by him after a contention at law for it with the Bishop of Durham, about ten years ago. The Roman way went a little more to the right than the present road, and the causeway where it ran was lately dug up there.

Near this Eyton are good grindstone quarries, which Newcastle is no less famous for than its coals, insomuch that it is a common saying that–"A Scot, a rat and a Newcastle grindstone may be found all the world over."

Over the moors or fells, which have collieries upon them on each hand, we came a very bad, rough, rugged, ragged, rocky descent through Gateshead over the Tyne into Newcastle, where we had a steep ascent again to get to our inn, Mr. Plat's at the . . .

We were here in six hours and a half from Durham which if we had come directly is computed but twelve miles; as we came is sixteen. It was so late by that time we had dined that we could not look about the town this evening: but an invitation was sent to my Lord from the Corporation, by Mr. Alderman Fenwick and Alderman Ellison to do them the honour of going in the City Barge the next day, to take a view of the river and to see Shields and Tynemouth; which though it was not agreeable to the privacy his Lordship proposed to himself, he however consented to.

May 7.–At a quarter after ten this morning we took water in the City Barge at the Mayor's house which is upon the river and built on purpose by the Corporation for the use of the Mayor for the time being. The present Mayor, Mr. Carr, was absent at London; the persons that attended were the three Aldermen, Fenwick, Ridley, and Ellison: the Recorder, Mr. Douglass, a hearty old gentlemen of about eighty five years of age: Mr. White, a gentleman of the town and very likely to be one of their next aldermen: and the Rev. Mr. Bradford, the Vicar of the town. The City Music attended in another barge. There were guns fired from five different places from the shore. Several steathes, being the places where the coals are brought to in order to be shipped off from the coal pits, are on each side of the river close upon the banks; those that are covered with timber work are called trunks. From these steathes or trunks the fillers take it off in lighters (here called keels) and carry it down to the ships which lie chiefly about Shields. There were many of these keels dispersed on the river, but few or no ships at this time. Each keel contains eight chaldrons, which is equal to sixteen of the London chaldrons. There are just eight hundred of them in all upon the river, and every keel employs four men. These people have a particular manner of giving a pledge for their standing by one another upon any occasion, which is by spitting upon a stone, as they lately did upon account of an affront given to one of them by the person who kept a public house on the north side of the Tyne. The keelman that was injured went and spit upon a stone near the house, and renounced any further communication with it, and the rest that were of his mind performed the same ceremony, and they have kept so religiously to their vow that the people are obliged to quit their house for want of business. These keelmen live in that part of Newcastle which is called Sandgate, and is somewhat like the Wapping of London, and the number of people in it supposed to be above ten thousand.

On the right hand before we come to Tynemouth, the river stretches out for a great way on a large flat, which covers about a thousand acres. Mr. Shephard, the East India merchant, proposed to gain all this land from the river by running a strong wall or mound to keep it out, and building a town there; but as the town of Newcastle was jealous of suffering in its trade by such a project, and has the conservatorship of the navigation of the Tyne (which privilege they justly set a high value upon) an entire stop was put to this design. This flat of water is called Jarrowslike or Jarrowlake, and close to it is the church of St. Bede, belonging to the Dean and Chapter of Durham, to whom it is worth 1800*l.* per annum, out of which they allow a curate twenty marks.

A little farther on the same side of the river is South Shields, which is the chief place for making of salt. The houses there are poor little low hovels, and are in a perpetual thick nasty smoke. It has in all two hundred salt pans, each of which pans employs three men; and there besides, women and children are in a very extraordinary plenty. We were at Tynemouth fort, which is just upon the mouth of the river, in one hour and three quarters. The Fort is but a very poor one, I think it has about twenty-eight guns. The river just here is but very narrow, not above one hundred and twenty yards over. Here are two lighthouses, in each of which is constantly burnt in the night time a large tallow candle, for the guiding of the ships into the harbour. It happened to be a cloudy day, so that we could have no prospect into the sea, and could just see where the mouth of the river was.

The dinner was dressed in the little ale house adjoining to the Fort, we sat down to it in the Barge, where we had a very handsome and decent entertainment, and some guns from the Fort fired as we drank the King's health and the Royal Family's after dinner.

When this was over we came back again up the river, and landed at Willington Stairs on the north side to see the salt pans, which I think are called Howdon pans.

Each pan makes one tun and a quarter of salt at eight boilings, which lasts three days and a half. Each consumes fourteen chaldrons of coal in seven days; in which time it makes two tuns and a half of salt.

The whole annual produce of all these pans at Shields, &c., is about one hundred and fifty thousand pounds per annum.

The wages for Pumpers, *i.e.*, those people who pump the salt water out of the river into the pans is five pence per diem.

The Watchers, *i.e.*, Those who continually have an eye to the pans and the fire stoves have sixpence a day.

What salt is here sold for twenty-five shillings produces to the Government six pounds and six shillings.

We came from hence directly to the town, were saluted by two ships as we came along, and by guns from seven different places from the shore: which were crowded with the greatest number of people I ever saw together upon any occasion, except it be upon some very extraordinary show at London.

We landed below the Bridge at half an hour after six, and walked to see the Town Hall and the adjoining conveniences, which are altogether the best I believe of any in England; here are two good pictures of King Charles II. and King James II.

This is the most populous and busy town I have ever seen excepting London: it has but one Parish Church, a very large one, St. [Nicholas], and–clergymen, all of whom are paid by the Corporation; which expends an that account 900*l.* per annum. There are in the whole town above ten thousand communicants.

Betwixt August and Christmas here are killed weekly about three thousand sheep, besides other meat in proportion.

Its chief trade is the coal, which produces about 250,000*l.* per annum. They seem at present a little jealous of Sunderland, which has of late shared with it pretty considerably in this trade, and as I am told is likely to gain more and more upon it every day.

The whole progress of the coal trade and the terms made use of in it, as far as I can remember, are thus: the breaking of the ground to come at the coals, they call–sinking of a pit; when they have sunk it till they come at the bed of coals, they are then said to have won the colliery. That pit through which they bring up the coal and is sometimes thirty, forty, fifty, sixty etc. fathoms deep is called the shaft. The lining of it with wood in order to hinder it from falling in, is timbering of it. The baskets in which the coal is brought up to the mouth of the pit are the [ ].[1] The chief workman that stands at the mouth of the pit to overlook the other labourers above ground is the upper overman; he that is foreman below ground is the under overman.

The coal at the mouth of the pit (where it is disposed round about) is loaded into the wagons for that purpose, and brought on the wayleaves to the steathes, from whence it is taken away by the fillers who buy it at the steathes and carry it down in the keels to be laden into the ships.

131. Faujas de Saint-Fond describes the Newcastle coal-mines, 1784

(B. Faujas de Saint-Fond, *A Journey through England and Scotland to the Hebrides in 1784*, ed. Sir Archibald Geikie (1907), 1, pp. 135–142.)

For Faujas de Saint-Fond, see No. 128B.

The coal-mines in the neighbourhood of Newcastle are so numerous that they may be regarded as not only one of the immense magazines of England, but also as the source of a profitable foreign commerce.

Vessels loaded with coal, for London and different parts of Europe, sail daily from this port, and, so to say, every hour of the day. Besides this commerce, the navigation which results from working these mines, gives an incalculable advantage to the navy, by forming a great nursery of seamen. In time of war, more than a thousand coal vessels can be armed, and do considerable injury to the enemy's commerce.

In this practical school of navigation are to be found men inured to every danger. The celebrated Cook began his naval career, as a sailor, on board of a Newcastle collier; . . . The modest house in which he was born, in the neighbourhood of Newcastle, is preserved with veneration.

The coal-mines, in the neighbourhood of Newcastle, are situated in so fortunate a position that the soil which covers them yields fine pasture that supports herds of horses. Under this fertile soil there is to be found a sand-stone, of excellent quality for grind-stones. This second richness of the earth forms another extensive object of trade for the industry of the inhabitants of Newcastle: these stones have so great a reputation, that they are exported to all the ports in Europe.

The first mine I visited belongs to a private individual; it is situated about two

[1] Omission.

miles from the town, and requires one hundred men to work it; thirty for the work above ground, and seventy in the pit: twenty horses live in this profound abyss, and drag the coal through the subterranean passages to the pit-bottom; four outside work the machine which raises the coal, and some more are employed in auxiliary labours.

The following is the order of the mineral substances, as they appear in descending to the coal:

	Feet
Vegetable soil, of good quality	2
Beds of rounded pieces of limestone and sandstone	15
Grey clay, more or less pure	16
Hard quartzose sandstones, with flakes of mica	25
Very hard black clay, somewhat bituminous, intermixed with some specks of mica	26
Black clay, more bituminous, and partly inflammable; when the laminae of this clay, which separate with facility, are examined with attention, some prints of ferns appear, but they are scarcely discernible	18
Total	102

At this depth of one hundred and two feet the coal is found. The seam is five feet thick in some places, and varies in others; but in general it is easily wrought, and much of it is brought up in large blocks. This last circumstance is of considerable advantage, as such pieces are always easily transported, and are besides well suited for chamber-fires; which makes this kind of coal sell at a higher price.

When the bed of black and bituminous clay is penetrated, the coal is found adhering to it; but this is not always the case, for there are other mines in the neighbourhood where the roof is of sandstone, which in the points of contact is mixed with coal to the thickness of two or three inches; the latter imbedded in the sandstone, in the form of splinters which, when attentively examined, have the appearance of wood.

The mine has a large steam-engine for pumping out the water, and at the same time working a ventilator to purify the air.

The winding machine which raises the coal from the pit is convenient, and easily worked by two stout horses. The buckets, in which the coal is brought up, are not of wood, but of osier, strongly made, and having an iron handle. They contain at least twelve hundred pounds of coal each; and as the one ascends while the other descends, one of these baskets arrives at the mouth of the pit every four minutes. It is received by a single man who while it is yet suspended, places it upon a truck drawn by one horse. He then unhooks the basket, puts an empty one in its place, and pushes the truck to a place somewhat raised at a short distance, where he empties the basket on the latticed roof above a kind of shed; the dust passes through the open spaces and falls below, while the large pieces of coal rolling down the inclined plane, fall upon the ground in heaps on the outside of the shed. Waggons, which I am about to describe, then take it up, and carry it to wharfs on the river-side.

It might be expected that the land transport of such an immense amount of coal would require numberless horses and men, which would involve immense expense. But art has surmounted this difficulty in the following manner.

Roads which have an almost insensible inclination are formed with the greatest care, and prolonged to the place where the vessels are loaded. The length of these roads is often more than several miles.

This first operation being finished, two parallel lines are traced along the road, at the exact distance which separates the wheels of the waggons. Logs of hard wood are then laid along these two parallel lines, and firmly fixed in the earth with pins.

The upper surface of these logs is carefully cut into a kind of moulding, which is well rounded, and projects upwards. The thickness of this elevated ledge must correspond with the width of the groove in the waggon-wheels, which are made of cast-iron, and hollowed in the manner of a metal pulley.

These wheels are completely cast in one piece, in a mould from which the rim comes out hollowed. This large groove is several inches deep, and of a proportional width; so that the wheel exactly encases the projecting part of the log, from which it cannot slide in any direction. As the moulding is well greased and is also polished by continual friction, four-wheeled waggons, containing eight thousand weight of coal each, move along the inclined plane, by the laws of gravity, and proceed as it were by magic one after another, until they reach the Tyne. Arrived there, a strongly and artistically made wooden frame prolongs the road for several fathoms at such a height above the water as to permit vessels to pass below it on lowering their masts. A man stationed on the platform opens a hatch, whence a large wooden hopper descends towards the vessel, the hatches of which are open. When the waggon comes to the trap in the platform it stops, its conical bottom opens, and all the coal runs in a moment through the hopper into the vessel. The waggon being emptied, returns by a second road parallel to the first. Other waggons follow the same course after having been in this manner relieved of their contents; and in a short time the vessel is loaded. A few horses suffice to bring back the empty waggons to the pit, and they soon return with a new freight of coal. This contrivance, as expeditious as it is economical, soon repays the cost of constructing the roads.

I have here given but a rapid sketch of these extraordinary roads, which are varied in several ways. It would require me to enter into details which might prove too long, and ill-suited to the nature of this work, were I to describe all the ingenious means which art and industry have employed in working wonders of this kind. Where local circumstances have permitted, the weight of the load, and the accelerated movement have been combined in such a manner, that files of loaded waggons run down the inclined plane and at the same time cause the empty waggons to reascend without the assistance of horses, along another road parallel to the first.

The great economy produced by these ingenious contrivances, which save the employment of men and horses, enables the English to sell the coal which they export in such abundance to all our ports on the ocean and the Mediterranean, at a price lower than that of our own mines, in all cases where we have to bring it only three or four leagues by land. . . .

132. Dr. Richard Pococke describes tin-mining in Cornwall, 1750

(*Travels through England of Dr. Richard Pococke*, ed. J. J. Cartwright, Camden Society, I (1888), pp. 110–113.)

Richard Pococke (1704–1765), later bishop successively of Ossory and Meath, was a noted traveller, especially in the Middle East. Stream tin was declining at this period, and the lode mining here described was becoming the more important source of Cornish tin.

Padstow, in Cornwall,
Oct. 10th, 1750.

On the 1st of October I set forward from Truro to the west, enter'd on a wild heathy country, and came in three miles to Casewater, a country of tin and copper. I had the curiosity to see the nature of the tin works. They call a work a balle. There are to each mine two shafts or wells, which, as they are open one to another, and only some frames of wood between them, are in the working but one well; one they call the ladder-shaft, in which the perpendicular ladders are fixt by which they descend; they are about thirty feet long to a landing place, called a solear, which brings to another ladder; the other is called the wem-shaft, from the wem or windlace, turned by a horse, by the help of which they let down the tub, called a kible, to bring up the ore, another coming up at the same time. Below the ladders, when they have come to the lode or vein, they burrow down in holes which they call gunnies; and at this place the wem-shaft is an inclined plane, in which a frame is made for the kible to slide on, which is called the sliding poles. Besides these shafts there is the fire engine shaft, by which they pump up the water by means of the fire engine, which was invented about 40 or 50 year ago by Mr. Newcommen, of Dartmouth, as I mentioned, and one Captain Savory in partnership. At the bottom is a hole, about six feet deep, to receive the water which runs from all parts; this is called the prison bottom, out of which the water is pumped up 24 fathoms three feet, to the channel call'd an audit, which conveys it to a valley abroad, and this audit is about thirty fathoms from the top, the whole being about 55 fathoms, or 330 feet. The lode or vein of tin or copper may be of a different thickness to twelve feet, and they call it a big or a small lode. They commonly run near east and west, that is, about a point to the south of the east, and as much to the north of the west; but there are some which have another direction: the lode commonly dips or under lays, as they call it, to the north, and that about five feet in six; sometimes, but rarely, they are perpendicular, and very seldom horizontal. The vein has on each side of it rock or earth, that to the north they call the north wall or under laying side, the other they call the south wall. Working towards the south wall they call working towards the back; if they work to the north wall, it is called following the lode; if they work down, it is sinking the course of the lode; when they work at the end, it is called driving. The stone or earth on each side of the lode they call country; if it be a hard smooth slate, they call it keller; if it be earth or clay, they call it flechen, and there are veins of these; if it be a spar or hard stone, they call it kepel. If any of these come across the lode and alter its course, it may be ten or twenty feet, more or less, 'tis called disordering the lode; but then, tho' moved either up or down, it afterwards keeps the same direction: but a keller never alters the lode; if the wall sets in upon the vein, they call it a bulk.

The top of a lode is commonly poor, and thrown away. The parts of the mine where they have followed the lode they call bottoms, and say they are of such or such a depth; those of this mine were about thirty fathoms, that is, below the ladders. The water runs through the lode which is looser than the walls; and where there is copper or mundik it leaves a yellow slime on the walls, called a water-slime. There are also in the mines a soft black stalactites, called the droppings of the water. The tools they work with are, first, a hammer, called a pick, having commonly a driving end and a sharp end; with one they work into the lode, with the other they drive an iron wedge, called a gall, from 3 to 9 inches long and about an inch and a-half one way and an inch another, ending in a point, by which they separate the ore. They have also a bar of iron, call'd a brosier, about 2½ feet long, 2 inches broad at bottom, and sharpened as a wedge: this is used to make holes in order to blow, one holding it, and giving it a turn, after every blow given by another with a mallet or hammer, with two [*blank*] or heads, as they bore for blowing; the operation of blowing up the rock by gun-powder being well known. A succession of men are always in the mine, except on Sundays. They work eight hours, from six to two, and from two to ten, and from ten to six, and are out of the mine sixteen hours. When they come up, they call it coming to the grass. When the ore is brought up, women and children are employed in breaking it, and separating the country from the ore, and the tin from the copper. No copper is smelted here, but is bought for smelting houses at Bristol and other parts. The men are paid so much a tun for what they deliver separated from the country. In the mines in general the lord has a fifteenth, and the owner, called the bounder, has a tenth.

C. COMBINATIONS OF WORKMEN

133. **Report** from a committee of the House of Commons on combinations of workers in the West Country woollen industry, 31 March 1726

(*Journals of the House of Commons*, xx, pp. 647–648.)

This report resulted in the passing of an Act forbidding these combinations. See No. 134.

[31 March 1726.] Sir *William Yonge* reported from the Committee, to whom the Petition of the Mayor, Capital Burgesses, and Assistants, of the Town of *Tiverton*, in the County of *Devon*, being the principal Merchants and Traders in the Woollen Manufactures there; and also the Petition of the Fullers, Sergemakers, and others concerned in the Woollen Manufacture, within the City of *Exon*; and also the Petition of the principal Traders and Dealers in the several Branches of the Woollen Manufacture, in the City of *Bristol*, and Parts adjacent; and also the Petition of the Mayor, Aldermen, and Burgesses, and also of the principal Traders, of the Town of *Taunton*, in the County of *Somerset*; and also the Petition of the poor oppressed Weavers of *Taunton*; were referred; That the Committee had examined the Matter of the Four first-mentioned Petitions; and had directed him to report the same, with their Opinion thereupon, to the House; and that no Evidence was produced before the Committee, on the last-mentioned Petition; and he read the Report in his Place; and afterwards delivered it in at the Clerk's Table; Where the same was read; and the Report, and the Resolution, of the Committee, are as followeth: *viz.*

That the Committee have, pursuant to the Order of this House, of the Third of this instant *March*, examined the Matter of the said Petition; and find the same, upon the Examination of Witnesses, to be as followeth; *viz.*

Mr. *John Vowler*: Who said, That the Weavers have many Clubs in several Places in the West of *England*, particularly at *Exeter*, where they make Bye-laws; some of which he has seen; which Bye-laws are, among divers other things, to appoint Places of Meeting, fix their Officers, make Allowances to travelling Workmen, and to ascertain their Wages:

That several Weavers have brought home their Work, and durst not go on to serve their Masters, for fear of other Weavers of the Club, who have deterred them therefrom: And he believes, one of the Occasions of the late Riots, that have happened, has been, that the Masters have refused to raise the Workmen's Wages to what Price they pleased:

That he was present at a great Mob in the Town of *Crediton*, in *Devonshire*, consisting of Weavers, and others concerned in the Woollen Manufacture; who were headed by a Captain, who threatened their Masters, if they refused to raise their Wages; and carried about with them a Chain of Serge cut off from a Loom; and declaring they would do the like to the Pieces of Serge of the other Masters, who refused to comply with their Demands: That, when the Constables had seized some of the Ringleaders, and brought them before Two Justices of Peace, the Mob beset the House, insulted the Justices, threw Stones at them, and forced them to fly, and rescued the Prisoners: That at *Callington*, on another Riot, he has seen a Master carried about on a Coolstaff, for refusing to comply with their Demands; and that others have been threatened with the like Usage:

That most of the Masters do pay their Workmen in Money; but some of them do pay by way of Truck; which is not so satisfactory; however, he believes, the Masters would all willingly be obliged to pay the Whole in Money.

Mr. *William Pike* said, That he has seen the Weavers at their Clubs, where none but Weavers are admitted; and that they have their Ensigns and Flags hung out at the Door of their Meetings:

That they go about, in Parties, to Looms; and demand Twelve Pence, or some other Sum of Money, towards supporting such of their own Gangs as are now in Prison; and has seen several Looms cut within these Eight Months past, and the Work carried away for the Non-payment of the Money, and because some would work cheaper than others; and that Pieces of Serge are frequently cut on the Racks:

That the Weavers complain of paying them in Truck; but believes, that is not the Cause of their Riots; for that they generally begin in the Spring, when there is the greatest Demand for Goods, and most Plenty of Work:

That his own Weavers would willingly have worked for him at the Wages he gave; but that the Club threatened, if they did so, to pull them out of the House, and coolstaff them; upon which, he was forced to pay them the Price demanded, to save his Work from being cut; and has known several that have been coolstaffed:

That he is willing to pay his Workmen in Money; and, believes, all the other Masters would willingly be obliged to do the same.

William Blake said, That, upon the last grand Riot at *Taunton*, several Warrants were issued for apprehending the Rioters; and he, and about Thirty more, went to serve them; but a Body of about a Thousand got together, and cried, One and all; and came up into the Hall, and fell upon *William Garway* Constable, and beat and wounded him very much; and so wounded Mr. *John Coggin* with a Brickbat, that he was not well in three Months after: That Mr. Justice *Catby* seized One of the Mob; and the Mob came about him, and struck him, and took away the Man; and that several were seized, but rescued again:

That the Town Clerk read the Proclamation for dispersing the Mob; but they pulled off his Hat and Wig, and put Dirt upon his Head:

That he saw a Man carried upon a Coolstaff because he fetched Mr. *Myner*'s Work contrary to the Orders of the Club; and that he has seen several Letters, which have been dropt in Master Weavers Houses, threatning, That if they would not comply with their Workmens Demands, they would burn their Houses, kill their Horses, and cut down and deface their Orchards.

That, upon the whole Matter, the Committee, having considered the respective Petitions referred to them, relating to the said unlawful Clubs and Combinations, came to the following Resolution;

Resolved, That it is the Opinion of this Committee, That the Petitioners have made good the Allegations of their several Petitions.

Sir *William Yonge* also acquainted the House, That he was directed by the Committee to move the House, That Leave may be given to bring in a Bill to prevent unlawful Combinations of Workmen employed in the Woollen Manufactures; and for the better Payment of their Wages:

And he moved the House accordingly.

Ordered, That Leave be given to bring in a Bill to prevent unlawful Combinations of Workmen employed in the Woollen Manufactures; and for the better Payment of their Wages: And that Sir *William Yonge*, Mr. *Molyneux*, Mr. *Dean*, Mr. *Whitworth*, and Mr. *Elton*, do prepare, and bring in, the same.

134. Act to prevent unlawful combinations of workmen in the woollen industry, 1726

(*Statutes at Large*, XV, pp. 361–365, 12 Geo. I, cap. 34.)

This Act was passed after rioting for higher wages by weavers in Devon and Gloucestershire (see No. 133). It was extended to other classes of workmen by 22 Geo. II, cap. 27.

An act to prevent unlawful combinations of workmen imployed in the woollen manufactures, and for better payment of their wages.

WHEREAS *great numbers of weavers, and others concerned in the woollen manufactures in several towns and parishes in this kingdom, have lately formed themselves into unlawful clubs and societies, and have presumed, contrary to law, to enter into combinations, and to make by-laws or orders, by which they pretend to regulate the trade and the prices of their goods, and to advance their wages unreasonably, and many other things to the like purpose: and whereas the said persons so unlawfully assembling and associating themselves have committed great violences and outrages upon many of his Majesty's good subjects, and by force protected themselves and their wicked accomplices against law and justice; and it is absolutely necessary that more effectual provision should be made against such unlawful combinations, and for preventing such violences and outrages for the future, and for bringing all offenders in the premisses to more speedy and exemplary justice;* may it therefore please your most excellent Majesty that it may be enacted and be it enacted by the King's most excellent majesty, by and with the advice and consent of the lords spiritual and temporal, and commons, in this present parliament assembled, and by the authority of the same, That all contracts, covenants or agreements, and all by-laws, ordinances, rules or orders, in such unlawful clubs and societies, heretofore made or entred into, or hereafter to be made or entred into, by or between any persons brought up in or professing, using or exercising the art and mystery of a woolcomber or weaver, or journeyman woolcomber or journeyman weaver, in any parish or place within this kingdom, for regulating the said trade or mystery, or for regulating or settling the prices of goods, or for advancing their wages, or for lessening their usual hours of work, shall be and are hereby declared to be illegal, null and void to all intents and purposes; and further, that if any woolcomber or weaver, or journeyman woolcomber or journeyman weaver, or other person concerned in any of the woollen manufactures of this kingdom shall, at any time or times after the twenty-fourth day of *June* in the year of our Lord one thousand seven hundred and twenty-six, keep up, continue, act in, make, enter into, sign, seal or be knowingly concerned in any contract, covenant or agreement, by-law, ordinance, rule or order of any club, society or combination by this act declared to be illegal, null and void, or shall presume or attempt to put any such illegal agreement, by-law, ordinance, rule or order in execution, every person so offending being thereof lawfully convicted upon the oath or oaths of one or more credible witness or witnesses, before any two or more justices of the peace for the county, city, town or place where such offence shall be committed, upon any information exhibited or prosecution within three calendar months after the offence committed (which oaths the said justices are hereby impowered and required to administer) shall, by order of such justices, at their discretion be committed either to the house of correction, there to remain and be kept to hard labour for any time not exceeding three months, or to the common gaol of the county, city, town or place where such offence shall be committed, as they shall see cause, there to remain, without bail or mainprize, for any time not exceeding three months.

II. And be it further enacted by the authority aforesaid, That if any person actually retained or employed as a woolcomber or weaver, or servant in the art or mystery of a woolcomber or weaver shall, at any time or times after the twenty-fourth day of *June* in the year of our Lord one thousand seven hundred and twenty-six, depart from his service before the end of the time or term for which he is or shall be hired or retained, or shall quit or return his work before the same be finished according to agreement, unless it be for some reasonable or sufficient cause, to be allowed by two or more justices of the peace within their respective jurisdictions; then in every such case every person so offending, being thereof lawfully convicted before two or more justices of the peace as aforesaid, shall be committed to the house of correction, there to be kept to hard labour for any time not exceeding three months; and if any woolcomber, weaver, servant or person hired, retained or imployed in the art or mystery of a woolcomber or weaver shall wilfully damnify, spoil or destroy (without the consent of the owner) any of the goods, wares or work committed to his care or charge, or wherewith he shall be intrusted, every such offender, being thereof lawfully convicted as aforesaid, shall forfeit and pay to the owner or owners of such goods or wares so damnified, spoiled or destroyed, double the value thereof, to be levied by distress and sale of the offenders goods and chattels, by warrant or warrants under the hands and seals of any two or more justices of the peace within their respective jurisdictions, and for want of sufficient distress, such justices shall commit the party or parties offending to the house of correction, there to remain and be kept to hard labour for any time not exceeding three months, or until satisfaction be made to the party or parties aggrieved for the same.

III. And be it enacted by the authority aforesaid, That every clothier, sergemaker or woollen or worsted stuffmaker, or person concerned in making any woollen cloths, serges or stuffs, or any wise concerned in employing woolcombers, weavers or other labourers in the woollen manufactury, shall, and they are hereby obliged and required to pay unto all persons by them employed in the woollen manufacture, the full wages or other price agreed on in good and lawful money of this kingdom, and shall not pay the said wages or other price agreed on, or any part thereof, in goods or by way of truck, or in any other manner than in money as aforesaid, or make any deduction from such wages or price for or on account of any goods sold or delivered previous to such agreement by any person or persons whatsoever; . . .

IV. [Clothiers paying wages in goods, etc. to forfeit £10.] . . .

VI. And be it enacted by the authority aforesaid, That if any person or persons shall, after the twenty-fourth day of *June* in the year of our Lord one thousand seven hundred and twenty-six, assault or abuse any master woolcomber or master weaver, or other person concerned in any of the woollen manufactures of this kingdom, whereby any such master, or other person shall receive any bodily hurt, for not complying with, or not conforming, or not submitting to any such illegal by-laws, ordinances, rules or orders aforesaid; or if any person or persons shall write or cause to be written, or knowingly send or cause to be sent, any letter, or other writing or message, threatning any hurt or harm to any such master woolcomber or master weaver, or other person concerned in the woollen manufacture, or threatning to burn, pull down or destroy any of their houses or outhouses, or to cut down or destroy any of their trees, or to maim or kill any of their cattle, for not complying with any demands, claims or pretences of any of his or their workmen, or others employed by them in the said manufacture, or for not conforming or not submitting to any such illegal by-laws, ordinances, rules or orders as aforesaid; every person so knowingly and wilfully offending in the premisses, being thereof lawfully convicted upon any indictment, to be found within twelve calendar months next after any such offence committed, shall be adjudged guilty of felony, and shall be transported for seven years to some or one of his Majesty's colonies or plantations in *America*, by such ways, means and methods, and in such manner and under such pains and penalties, as felons in other cases are by law to be transported.

VII. And be it further enacted by the authority aforesaid, That if any person or persons shall, by day or by night, break into any house or shop, or enter by force into any house or shop, with intent to cut or destroy any serge or other woollen goods in the loom, or any tools employed in the making thereof, or shall wilfully and maliciously cut or destroy any such serges or woollen goods in the loom or on the rack, or shall burn, cut or destroy any rack on which any such serges or other woollen goods are hanged in order to dry, or shall wilfully and maliciously break or destroy any tools used in the making any such serges or other woollen goods, not having the consent of the owner so to do, every such offender, being thereof lawfully convicted, shall be adjudged guilty of felony, and shall suffer death as in case of felony, without benefit of clergy.

[Clause VIII omitted]

135. A discussion of the causes of a riot against Wiltshire clothiers, 1739

(John Smith, *Chronicon rusticum-commerciale : or Memoirs of Wool*, II (1747), pp. 301–305.)

This work gives abstracts of a number of pamphlets on wool. The two following take opposite sides over the riot, and illustrate conditions in the industry at this period.[1]

An Essay on Riots, &c.* 1739.

1. THE Riot of the poor Weavers and other Woolen Manufacturers in *Wilts*, is said to have been occasioned by Oppression, in various Shapes, practised towards them by *some Clothiers*. The Badness, or rather the Decay of the Woolen Trade, acknowledged by all, and occasioned by the Rivalship of *France* and other neighbour Nations, must needs be attended with fatal Effects to Masters as well as Workmen.

2. The Progress of our Neighbours in that Trade, is said to be owing to our *Run Wool*, and to their under-selling our Merchants at foreign Markets. Be these Things as they will, they are no Justification of the late Riot, and I could wish that a mixed Commission might be appointed, consisting of *Gentlemen* and *Clothiers* of the *best Character* that can be picked out in the Country, to examine impartially into the Causes of the late Riot, as–1. *If any Combinations have been entered into, to lower the Price of Weaving, Spinning*, &c. *and by whom?*–2. *If any Masters have forced the poor Manufacturers to take* Truck, *and at what Prices?*–3. *If any Masters have obliged their Work People to buy Bread*, &c. *at any particular Shops, and how they have been served?* – 4. *If some particular Manufacturers do not give extravagant Rents for their Tenements*, &c. *and if they are not under Compulsion from their Masters in that Article?*–5. *Who were the Heads of the late* Riot? *what Damage is done? and what Sums may be raised through the Country by the Statutes against* Truck *or* Combinations, *towards paying the Damages?*

3. I cannot conclude without wishing some Publick-spirited Person well skilled in all the different Branches of a *Clothier's Trade*, would publish a short Essay, to shew the Prices now commonly given by our *ready Money* Clothiers to their several Sorts of Work People; that so the Publick may judge what *clear Profit* a Clothier has. My Reason for it is; that as Money is sunk to three *per Cent.* Interest with many People, the Profits might appear so considerable, as would probably prevail on some to employ their Money in that. No body can think the *Mystery of Cloth-working inscrutable*, when he sees how many People practise it, who never served a regular Apprenticeship to it. And one that has Money of his own in his Pocket, may make a *better Master*, and get as much, as those who make Cloth on other Peoples Stocks.

Remarks on the Essay on the Weavers Riot, &c. 1739.

1. One Cause of these Riots is said to be, Oppression of the Poor by their rich Masters. 1. *By entering into Combinations to lower Wages.* 2. *Not paying their Wages.* 3. *Or else paying them in* Truck *by Goods at an advanced Price.* As to the *first* and *second* of these, I must declare myself an absolute Stranger to any such Methods of Practice.

2. But, that the Workmen are able in a dull Season of Trade, &c. when Work is

[1] Some of the notes are omitted.

* In the Month of *December* 1738, was a Riot in *Wiltshire*, in which the Goods of Mr. *Coulthorst* and other Clothiers, were destroyed, &c. and their Dwelling-houses attempted to be pulled down; for which Fact, three Persons, *viz.* a Weaver, a Sheerman, and a Bricklayer, were executed at *Sarum*.

scarce, *&c.* to make their Wages as comfortable, as in a quick Time of Trade, when their Hands are full, is not to be supposed; for in the Clothing Trade, as in other Employs, the Value of Labour has its Ups and Downs, according to the Demand for it. If the Necessity of the Times require it, and the Master advertises his Servants that he can give but 14*d.* instead of 15 or 16*d. per* Yard, must this be called Oppression? When at the same Time, the Workman is at full Liberty to make the most of his Labour elsewhere? Again, when the Workman has finished his Piece of Work, if the Master pays him his agreed Price, what Ground of Complaint has the Workman? If the Master refuses, the Remedy is easy, by Recourse to a Magistrate–But if on the contrary, the Workman has ill wrought that Piece, or feloniously detained from the Master any Part of his Stuff, every Master has a Right to exact Reparation, to be settled by a Magistrate, unless (as is frequently the Case) the Workman (rather than be exposed) chuses to agree the Damage with the Master at a small Allowance. But will this be called *defrauding, or oppressing the Servants*? So far from it, that I am apt to believe, the Lenity shewn to Workmen, on these Occasions, has been a great Cause of the several Riots and Insults made upon them of late Years; and that if the Clothiers, instead of this false Pity shewn, had put the Laws in Execution against Felony, we had ere now got rid of the greatest Number of those idle immoral Wretches, that generally turn out the Ring-Leaders of such Assemblies.

3. As to the honest and industrious Part of our Work People, no doubt, the Decay of Trade must affect them. And it's well known, the Impoverishment of many reputable Masters is to be ascribed to their keeping on Business, in Tenderness to the Poor, without any View but their Employment and Service. But the Clothiers are not obliged to ruin themselves, as has been the Misfortune of a great many within these few Years.

4. Some Branches of our Woolen Fabrick are quite lost; others going along with our Wool. And indeed there seem to be but two Remedies; the one is, securing our Wool from falling into our Rivals Hands; and the other, by lowering the Prices of our Workmanship. If the Clothiers apply for the former, they are answered; that will sink the Price of Wool, disable Tenants from paying Rents, *&c.* And if a Reduction in the Price of Labour is attempted, we are charged by our Author with Injustice, and are said hereby to be driving the Poor on to this riotous Method of revenging themselves upon their Masters for their Oppressions, *&c.*

5. But one Thing I am led here to observe, which must affect the Poor much more than the Penny *per* Yard abated, and contribute more to the late Disorders, *viz.* That at the Time of the rising, there was not less than 60 Looms standing still, for want of Employment, in that Neighbourhood–And without some Regard to be had for the Preservation of our *foreign* Trade, I despair of seeing our Hands better filled.

6. As to the clear Profits of the Clothier, if the Author has Courage enough to make the Purchase, I will insure him, the neat Produce on 4 Fifths of the Woolen Goods that have been made for seven Years past in the three Western Counties of *Wilts, Somerset,* and *Gloucester,* for 3 *per Cent. per Ann.* on the Stock employed in those Trades. Nay, I will go farther, and engage to deliver him several hundred thousand Pounds worth of Woolen Goods at 5 *per Cent.* less than Prime Cost.

7. As to the Article of *Trucking*, I own it to be a Practice not only illegal, but scandalous; yet it is attended with worse Consequences by far to the Fair-Trader, than to the Workman that complies with it, who as he knows before-hand the Disadvantages thereof, so he knows how to suit his Workmanship thereto. I am very glad to hear that a large Body of Clothiers are so heartily disposed and engaged to put a Stop to *Truck*, but am afraid the Work People are but too well reconciled to the Payments of their *Trucking*, or they would have accepted the Offer* made them. But were the Author to consider this in his own Light, as an Oppression, yet it's stupid to affirm it the Cause of the Riot at *Melksham*; seeing neither Mr. *Colthurst*, nor any Gentleman upon whom Depredations were committed, ever made any other Payments, that ever I could learn, than in Money; and if this was the Cause of Complaints, why was any other struck at but Delinquents?

* What that Offer was, does not appear.

D. TRADE

136. Some general maxims of Trade, from *The British Merchant*, 1721

(*The British Merchant: A Collection of Papers relating to the Trade and Commerce of Great Britain and Ireland*, first published by Mr. Charles King, 2nd ed. (1743), I, pp. 1–5.)

This work was regarded as an authority during the early part of the century. The papers, by various writers, originally appeared in 1713 in opposition to the government paper *Mercator*, started to defend the proposed treaty of commerce with France, and largely written by Defoe. The collected edition was first published by King in 1721.

THERE are general Maxims in Trade which are assented to by every body.

That a Trade may be of Benefit to the Merchant and injurious to the Body of the Nation, is one of these Maxims.

I shall confine myself to speak of Trade only as it is nationally good or bad.

I. That Trade which exports Manufactures made of the sole Product or Growth of the Country, is undoubtedly good; such is the sending abroad our *Yorkshire* Cloth, *Colchester* Bays, *Exeter* Serges, *Norwich* Stuffs, *&c.* which being purely of *British* Wool, as much as those Exports amount to, so much is the clear Gain of the Nation.

II. That Trade which helps off the Consumption of our Superfluities, is also visibly advantageous; as the exporting of Allum, Copperas, Leather, Tin, Lead, Coals, *&c.* so much as the exported Superfluities amount unto, so much also is the clear National Profit.

III. The importing of foreign Materials to be manufactured at home, especially when the Goods, after they are manufactured, are mostly sent abroad, is also, without dispute, very beneficial; as for instance *Spanish* Wool, which for that reason is exempted from paying any Duties.

IV. The Importation of foreign Materials to be manufactur'd here, altho' the manufactured Goods are chiefly consumed by us, may also be beneficial; especially when the said Materials are procur'd in exchange for our Commodities; as Raw-Silk, Grogram-Yarn, and other Goods brought from *Turkey*.

V. Foreign Materials, wrought up here into such Goods as would otherwise be imported ready manufactured, is a means of saving Money to the Nation; and if saving is getting, that Trade which procures such Materials ought to be look'd upon as profitable: Such is the Importation of Hemp, Flax, and Raw-Silk. 'Tis therefore to be wonder'd at, that these Commodities are not exempt from all Duties as well as *Spanish* Wool.

VI. A Trade may be call'd good which exchanges Manufactures for Manufactures, and Commodities for Commodities. *Germany* takes as much in Value of our Woollen and other Goods, as we do of their Linen: by this means numbers of People are employ'd on both sides, to their mutual Advantage.

VII. An Importation of Commodities, bought partly for Money and partly for Goods, may be of National Advantage; if the greatest part of the Commodities thus imported are again exported, as in the case of *East-India* Goods: and generally all Imports of Goods which are re-exported, are beneficial to a Nation.

VIII. The carrying of Goods from one foreign Country to another, is a profitable Article in Trade. Our Ships are often thus employ'd between *Portugal*, *Italy*, and the *Levant*, and sometimes in the *East-Indies*.

IX. When there is a necessity to import Goods which a Nation cannot be without, altho' such Goods are chiefly purchased with Money, it cannot be accounted a bad Trade; as our Trade to *Norway* and other Parts, from whence are imported Naval Stores, and Materials for Building.

But a Trade is disadvantageous to a Nation,

1. Which brings in things of meer Luxury and Pleasure, which are entirely, or for the most part, consumed among us; and such I reckon the Wine-Trade to be, especially when the Wine is purchased with Money, and not in exchange for our Commodities.

2. Much worse is that Trade which brings in a Commodity that is not only consumed amongst us, but hinders the consumption of the like quantity of ours; as is the importation of Brandy, which hinders the spending of our Extracts of Malt and Molasses; therefore very prudently charged with excessive Duties.

3. That Trade is eminently bad, which supplies the same Goods as we manufacture our selves, especially if we can make enough for our Consumption: and I take this to be the case of the Silk Manufacture, which with great Labour and Industry is brought to perfection in *London*, *Canterbury*, and other places.

4. The Importation upon easy Terms of such Manufactures as are already introduc'd in a Country, must be of bad consequence, and check their progress; as it would undoubtedly be the case of the Linen and Paper Manufactures in *Great Britain* (which are of late very much improved) if those Commodities were suffer'd to be brought in without paying very high Duties.

Wise Nations are so fond of encouraging Manufactures in their Infancy, that they not only burden foreign Manufactures of the like kind with high Impositions, but often totally condemn and prohibit the consumption of them.

To bring what hath been already said into a narrower compass, it may be reduced to this, *viz.*

That the Exportation of Manufactures is, in the highest degree, beneficial to a Nation.

That the Exportation of Superfluities, is so much clear Gain.

That the Importation of foreign Materials to be manufactur'd by us, instead of importing manufactur'd Goods, is the saving a great deal of Money.

That the exchanging Commodities for Commodities, is generally an Advantage.

That all Imports of Goods which are re-exported, leave a real Benefit.

That the letting Ships to Freight to other Nations, is profitable.

That the Imports of things of absolute necessity, cannot be esteemed bad.

That the importing Commodities of mere Luxury, is so much real Loss as they amount to.

That the Importation of such Goods as hinder the consumption of our own, or check the progress of any of our Manufactures, is a visible Disadvantage, and necessarily tends to the Ruin of multitudes of People.

137. R. Campbell on the importance of commerce, 1747

(R. Campbell, *The London Tradesman* (1747), pp. 284–292.)

This is a compendium of information about all the trades practised in London.

Of the MERCHANT.

HAVING gone through the several Arts and Trades, and discovered their Dependance one upon another, we come now to a larger Field, to the Life, Spring and Motion of the Trading World. The Trades we have been hitherto speaking of, are confined to one Place, one City or Country; but Commerce, the Sphere of the Merchant, extends itself to all the known World, and gives Life and Vigour to the whole Machine. Some Tradesmen we have treated of employ several different Branches, some particular Crafts dependant on them; but the Merchant employs them all, sets the whole Society at work, supplies them with Materials to fabricate their Goods, and vends their Manufactures in the most distant Corners of the Globe. Other Arts, Crafts and Mysteries live upon one another, and never add one Sixpence to the aggregate Wealth of the Kingdom; but the Merchant draws his honest Gain from the distant Poles, and every Shilling he returns more than he carried out, adds so much to the National Riches and Capital Stock of the Kingdom. Wherever he comes, wherever he lives, Wealth and Plenty follow him: The Poor is set to work, Manufactures flourish, Poverty is banished, and Public Credit increases. The Advantages of Commerce is evident to all Mankind; the wisest, the politest Nations on Earth now court her to their Dominions: The *Dutch* and us are two pregnant Proofs of the Power and Advantages of Traffic. Before we were a Trading People, we were, it is true, subsisted by the natural Produce of the Island; but we lived in a kind of Penury, a Stranger to Money or Affluence, inconsiderable in ourselves, and of no Consequence to our Neighbours: Our Manners were rude, our Knowledge of the World trifling; Politeness was a Stranger at our Courts; Ignorance and barbarous Simplicity spread their Empire over the whole Island: But we no sooner became a Trading People, than the Arts and Sciences began to revive, and polished us out of our rustic Simplicity and Ignorance; the People found out new Means of supplying their Wants, and the Nation in general accumulated Riches at Home, and commanded Respect abroad; a new Scene of Power started out of Commerce, and the wide Ocean owned the Sovereignty of Imperial *Britain*; a Dominion which some few Years ago was not purely chymerical. There was a Time when our Superiority at Sea was uncontestable, and the Influence that had upon the other Powers of *Europe* very conspicuous. The *Dutch* is another Instance of the mighty Power of Traffic; they possess a Country not much larger than *Yorkshire*, of a Soil naturally barren: The Number of People in the *United Provinces* are not one Fifth of the Number of the Inhabitants of *Great Britain*; and yet this little State, but a few Years ago a petty Province of the Crown of *Spain*, can maintain Armies and Fleets capable of checking the Power of the greatest Monarchs on Earth; they set themselves upon a Level with Crowned Heads, and many private Burgo-Masters can raise as much Money upon their own Credit, as the Amount of the Revenues of some Kingdoms in *Europe*. We have had but a few Days ago a flagrant Instance of the vast Influence of Commerce, when Six Millions Sterling was subscribed for the Use of the Government by private

Merchants in less than four Hours. Tho' *Spain* is possessed of the rich Gold and Silver Mines of *Mexico* and *Peru*, and the *French* King governs a large, populous, and rich Kingdom, yet neither the Kings of these two potent Monarchies, nor all their Subjects put together, could raise such a Sum on private Subscription. An Alderman of *London* can undertake for supplying the State with Three or Four Million Sterling, and raise it within the Circle of his own Acquaintance; a Thing unheard-of in former Ages, and would have been thought Arrogance and Folly even in the Days of Queen *Elizabeth*, to have supposed such a Thing practicable.

All States and Kingdoms have flourished, and made a Figure in proportion to the Extent of their Commerce. The *Cathaginians*, though but a Society of Merchants, were able to dispute the Empire of the World with All-conquering *Rome*; who never could be secure of Universal Sway till *Carthage* was laid in Ruins. The *Venetians*, by being possessed of the Trade of the *East*, were able to give Laws to *Italy*, and dispute Conquests with the mighty *Ottoman Port*; but as soon as they were deprived of that lucrative Branch of Commerce, by the Discovery of a Passage to the *East* by the Cape of *Good Hope*, they dwindled into their present Insignificancy.

The Trade of *England* has been much more considerable than at present, occasioned by various Accidents: The *Dutch* are our Rivals in Trade, and have run away with some of the most beneficial Branches of Commerce: The Public Expence, occasioned by two long Land Wars in the Reigns of King *William* and Queen *Anne*, has loaded Trade with many heavy Taxes, and discouraged the honest Merchant: Bad Policy, and the Peace that succeeded the *Queen*'s War, has enabled *France* to rob us of a large Share of our Trade: She has set up her *East-India* Companies, and by various Schemes has possessed herself of the Commerce of the *Spanish West-Indies*, which we formerly enjoyed. The *Danes*, *Swedes*, and *Russians* have put in for their Share of Traffic, and are making large Advances in the Knowledge and Practice of Trade and Navigation. In a word, we have but the Shadow of what we had forty Years ago. And to compleat our Trading Misfortunes, we scarce enjoy one Branch of Trade wherein the Ballance is not against us. *Portugal* is the only Kingdom we deal with upon a Par, and that is dwindling daily; and were it not for our Plantations, the Ballance against us with other Kingdoms, and the Remittance we are obliged to make to support our Armies and Alliances, would long before now have stripped us of every Ounce of Bullion.

The Trade of *Britain* may be divided into Inland and Foreign: Inland Trade is the transporting of the Commodities of one Part of the Kingdom to another, and especially to the grand Mart of Trade, the City of *London*. The chief Articles imported to *London* from other Parts of the Island are Corn, Coal, Hops, Woollen and Linen Goods. Corn and Hops are sold at *Bear-Key* by Factors, termed Corn or Hop Factors; Coals are sold at the Pool; Woollen Goods are sent up by the Clothiers, and sold by the Factors of *Blackwell-hall* Factory; and Linen Cloth from *Ireland* and *Scotland* to the Factors for that Commodity.

These Factors are a Species of Merchants, who deal by Commission and sell the Goods of other People consigned to them, for a Customary Premium; sometimes Two *per Cent.* or more, according to the Nature of the Trade they are concerned in. A Farmer in the Country has two or three Hundred Quarters of Wheat, or a Maltster as much Malt, to sell at the *London* Market; neither Maltster nor Farmer can conveniently come up to Town, therefore they ship their Goods and consign them to a Corn-Factor, who sells them to the best Advantage, receives the Money, remits it to the Farmer, with an Account of the Sales; from whence he deducts Two and a Half *per Cent.* or the ordinary Commission, for Trouble and Expence. There are Factors who deal in Foreign Commodities in the same Manner; that is, have Goods consigned them by Merchants in Foreign Countries, to be sold on their Account: These Factors are distinguished either by the Countries they deal with, or by the Goods most commonly consigned to them. Most Merchants are Factors for one another in this Shape, and reckon it the most certain, though not the most profitable Part of their Business.

The Foreign Merchant exports the Goods of the Growth or Manufacture of this Kingdom to the proper Markets, and imports the Commodities of other Countries in Exchange. The Merchants are distinguished one from another either by the Goods they traffic in, or by the Countries wherewith they have the greatest Correspondence; Thus a Merchant dealing in Tobacco is termed a Tobacco-Merchant, or a *Virginia*-Merchant: The Dealer in Wines is termed a *French* or *Portugal* Merchant, or a Wine-Merchant; and so of all others. Some Merchants deal to all the Kingdoms on Earth, and import and export Goods to and from the most distant Nations; others confine themselves to some few particular Commodities: Some import Wines, others Tobacco, other Sugars, some Timber, Iron, Copper, Flax, Hemp, *&c.* and export Goods proper for the Markets of these Countries from whence they have their particular Returns.–The best Way then to distinguish the several Classes of Merchants, is to take a View of our Imports and Exports.

We export to *Jamaica*, and the rest of the Sugar Colonies, all manner of Materials for Wearing Appearel, Houshold Furniture of all Sorts, Cutlery and Haberdashery Wares, Watches, Jewels and Toys, *East-India* Goods of all sorts, some *French* Wines, *English* Malt Liquor, Linen Cloths of the Growth of *Scotland*, *Ireland*, and *Germany*, and our Ships generally touch in *Ireland* and take in Provisions, such as Beef, Pork, and Butter. The Returns from thence are Rums, Sugars, Cotton, Indigo, some fine Woods, such as Mahogany, Lignum Vitæ, *&c*, and some Dying Woods, particularly Logwood.

We export to *New England*, *New York*, *Pensilvania*, and the rest of our Northern Colonies, the same Articles mentioned in the last Paragraph; in a word, every Article for the Use of Life, except Provisions: We have in return, Wood for Shipping, Corn and other Provisions for the Southern Colonies: Some Furs and Skins, Flax, Rice and Flax-Seed from the Provinces of *Georgia* and *Pensilvania*, and Fish from *New England*, for the *Levant* Market.

We export to *Virginia* and *Maryland* every Article mentioned before, and have in return Tobacco and Pig-Iron. From all the Colonies we have Ready Money, besides the Goods sent them, which they procure by the Illicite Trade carried on between our Island and the *Spanish* Main.

We export to *Ireland* the Growth of our Plantations, Sugar and Tobacco, *East-India* Goods of all sorts, Silks of the Manufacture of *England*, and Raw-Silk, the Product of *Italy*; Broad-Cloths, Hats and Stockings, Gold and Silver Lace, and many other Articles of the Product of this Country; for which we take nothing from them in return but Ready Money, except some Linen Cloth, and Provisions for our Southern Colonies: The Ballance paid by *Ireland* in Exchange of Goods, and the Money spent by their Gentry and Nobility in *England*, amount at least to One Million Sterling *per Annum*, which is a greater Advantage than we reap from all our other Branches of Commerce; yet we grudge these People the common Privileges of Subjects, despise their Persons, and condemn their Country, as if it was a Crime to be born in that Kingdom from whence we derive the greatest Part of our Wealth.

We export to *Holland* and *Flanders* some Woollen Goods, *Birmingham* and *Sheffield* Goods, Coals, Lead, Tin, and Lead-Oar; sometimes Corn, Butter, Cheese, and Hides from *Ireland*; some Leather, Tobacco, and Sugars. From thence we have Holland, Cambrick, Paper, Whale-Fin, and Whale-Oil, Delft and Earthen-Ware, Thread and Thread-Laces, and a monstrous Quantity of *East-India* Goods run in upon our Coast by the Smugglers. The *Dutch* have scarce any Export of Commodities peculiar to themselves; the Ground of their Commerce is *East-India* Goods and Fish catched upon the Coast of *Britain*; with these two Articles they purchase all the Product of the Earth, and are more Masters of the *American* Wealth than the proud Monarch, whose Property it is.

We send to *Germany*, some Woollen Goods; but fewer of late Years than formerly; some Lead, Leather, and Tin: And in return have Linen Cloths, for our Home Consumption, and the Use of our Plantations; and pay a large Ballance in Ready Money.

We export to *France* scarce any thing but Lead and Tin, some Tobacco to *Dunkirk*, and some Salmon from *Scotland*; but we import Wine, Brandy, Silks of various Sorts, Cambricks, Laces of Thread and of Gold and Silver, Paper, Cards, and an innumerable Quantity of trifling Jewels and Toys; for all which we pay an annual Ballance of One Million and an Half. In reckoning up the Imports from *France*, I should have mentioned Pride, Vanity, Luxury, and Corruption; but as I could make no Estimate by the Custom-House Books of the Quantity of these Goods entered, I chose to leave them out.

We export to *Sweden* and *Denmark* some Woollen Goods, Tobacco, Sugar, and a few *East-India* Goods; but this last Article is daily decaying: We send them Soap and Salt, and some Fish; but the *Dutch* monopolize that Branch. We receive in return Deal, Iron, Copper, and Oaken-Planks; and pay them a great Ballance in Ready Money.

We send to the *East* Country much the same Goods last mentioned, and receive in return Naval Stores of all sorts, some Linen Cloth, and some Goods of the Growth of *Persia*, brought through *Russia* by Land.

We used to send to *Spain* Woollen Goods of various Fabrics, and furnished their Plantations with the same Articles we send to our own; we furnished them with *Negroes* from the Coast of *Guinea*. For all which we had in return, some Wines of the Growth of *Spain*, Fruits, Oil, and Olives, and a large Remittance in Gold and Silver; but this Trade has now dwindled to nothing, the *French* have engrossed it wholly to themselves.

We send to *Portugal* Lead, Tin, Woollen Goods, Goods for their Plantations in the *Braziles*, and have our Returns in Wines, Oils, and Ready Money.

We send to *Italy*, Fish from *New England* and *Newfoundland*, Lead, Tin, some Woollen Goods, Leather, Tobacco, Sugars, and *East-India* Goods; and have, in return, some rich Wines, Currants, Silks wrought and raw, Oils, Olives and Pickles.

To the *East-Indies* we send out some Woollen Goods, Lead, Watches, Clocks, Fire-Arms, Hats; but our chief Export is Silver Bullion: For which we receive in Exchange, Gold, Diamonds, Spices, Drugs, Teas, Porcelain or China-Ware, Silk wrought and raw, Cotton-Cloths of different kinds, Salt-Petre, *&c.* A great Part of these Goods are consumed at Home and in our Plantations, and the Remainder is exported to other Countries of *Europe*; the Return of which makes Amends for the Bullion exported.

To *Guinea* we send some Woollen and Linnen Goods, Cutlery Ware, Fire-Arms, Swords, Cutlasses, Toys of Glass and Metal, *&c.* and receive in return *Negroes* for the Use of our Plantations, Gold Dust, and Elephant's Teeth.

To *Turkey* we send Woollen Goods of all sorts, Lead, Tin, *East-India* Goods, Sugars, *&c.* and receive in return, Coffee, Silks, Mohair, Carpets, *&c.* This is a beneficial Branch of Trade; the Imports and Exports being near upon a Par.

138. An account of the prevalence of smuggling in Cornwall, 16 September 1765

(*Hist. MSS. Comm., Dartmouth MSS.*, III, pp. 178–179.)

The writer of this letter was a wine merchant at St. Columb, Cornwall. His letters to Dartmouth, then President of the Board of Trade, give a vivid picture of the prevalence of smuggling in the West Country and the complete inadequacy of government machinery to prevent it.

W. Rawlings to the Earl of Dartmouth.

1765, September 16. St. Columb.–It will give me unspeakable pleasure if by any means I can serve my King and Country by giving such intelligences as from time to time come to my notice, of any illicit practices carried on in this neighbourhood. I hope your Lordship may depend on my veracity in what I relate, though in many instances without being partaker in guilt (which I am sure I durst not be) it may not be in my power to obtain proof of the facts. The generality of mankind are one way or other engaged in these under-hand practices, which are the inlets of immorality and licentiousness and sap the very vitals of the trade of the kingdom. Happy shall I think myself if any of these hints I from time to time think it my duty to give you are in the least degree instrumental to promote the public good. If smuggling in all its branches is suppressed I need not say how likely this is to alleviate our National Debt, prevent the necessity of new supplies and thereby give universal satisfaction to every honest mind. As things have been long conducted we have seen a few rise on the ruins of our trade, while many by the piracies of these few, have been oppressed and injured.

Having the peculiar happiness to have access to your Lordship, I am determined to hide nothing from you that may be of any use. My business lately called me to Falmouth, while the *Vansittart*, Indiaman, lay in the harbour. It gave me pain to see the vast concourse of people that were there for the purposes of smuggling, and I was told from very good authority that every day, Sunday not excepted, the number of people on board was like the busiest fair we have in the county. I suppose the amount of the goods sold cannot be so little as 5,000 *li.* some say double that sum. Of this I am sure, it has drained the country of cash so that it is with great difficulty we can get exchange for 100 *li.* bill. Muslins, silks, and handkerchiefs are hawked about in every part of the county, nor do I find there were any seizures made worth notice. Indeed I heard but of one in these many days the ship was there, and that but trifling. I think it is plain the officers cannot discharge their duty, for is it possible for them to be ignorant of what is a doing? Have we not reason to fear they are bribed to overlook these practices which are so very notorious?

While we were at dinner in the inn, a person came in with a large bundle of silk handkerchiefs and wanted to know if any was wanting, three of the company said they had already supplied themselves on board and added they had come off safe, a shame to the officers that they did so. But what can we expect from the wretches who by indirect methods obtain these places of trust. How valuable such as reverence conscience and who would not violate that to gain a world. Permit me my Lord to offer one hint which may be of use at such seasons when India ships are in the harbour or even at other times, suppose the public waggons were to be searched on some convenient distance on the road? I think it might prevent smuggling through that channel, especially if they were severely threatened if they took any goods not properly permitted. I also beg leave to add to my last another method of wine smuggling which I knew not till lately and I find is carried on by the salt ships between Lisbon and Falmouth. One person only, if I am not misinformed had lately no less than 72 quarter casks at once.

I find the greatest part of tea and brandy smuggling is now carried on in the south coast of this county from Plymouth to the Lands End. Quantities of both come from thence, the tea sold at 3*s.* 6*d.* a pound, the brandy at 5*s.* I fancy if we were to take the county through, 90 families in a 100 drink tea generally twice a day, perhaps not one family in a hundred buys what pays duty. I am apt to think that nearly as much brandy is drunk in the county as before the late restrictions, then we drunk our own produce, now we buy, with money, from France. A good look-out on the south side in winter and the north side in summer is much to be wished for. Suppose my Lord an order were to be obtained to burn all the ships concerned in smuggling, or found carrying brandy or tea under the limited burden. Might we not hope that this would in some measure prevent this detestable practice.

I beg leave also to recommend a strict watch to be placed over His Majesty's Stores of powder, &c. in Plymouth Dock and elsewhere, I know not from whence, if not from thence the vast quantities of cannon powder, from time to time hawked about the county and sold at 6*d.* and 8*d.* a pound, comes. How deplorable is it that such as eat our gracious Sovereign's bread should so shamefully betray his and the Nation's interest, and falsify the solemn obligations by which they are bound–how unworthy such the stipend they enjoy.

I have but one hint more to give your Lordship for the present and that is relating to the deal-board and timber trade carried on at Penryn, Truro, and Marazion in this county. I fear not one half the duty is paid of what is imported. Some of the persons concerned have landing places in the river between Falmouth and Truro, where are kept very large quantities and where the more favourable opportunity offers for carrying on this trade. There is a new quay in the river, lately built by one Daniel of Truro, who keeps several ships in the Norway Trade. The Government will do well to employ proper persons to see that not only what he imports, but every one else, pays the whole duty. The gentleman with whom Mr Daniel served as clerk in a few years amassed a fortune of upwards 150,000 *li.* part of which indeed by success in mining but how much the other way was known only to himself.

139A–D. Some contemporary trade statistics, 1782

139A. A Chronological Account of Commerce in this Island, from the Restoration to the year 1780, inclusive

(George Chalmers, *An Estimate of the Comparative Strength of Britain* (1782), p. 37.)
For Chalmers, see note to No. 85. For statistics of colonial trade, see No. 225.

Epochs		*Ships cleared outwards*			*Value of cargoes exported*			*Balance of Trade*			*Nett customs English*	*Money coined*	
		Tons English	*Do. Foreign*	*Total*	*English*	*Scotch*	*Total*	*English*	*Scotch*	*Total*			
The Restoration	1663 1669	95,266	47,634	142,900	£2,043,043	—	£2,043,043	Unfavourable	—	—	£390,000	By Charles II By James II	£7,524,105 2,737,637
The Revolution, 1688		190,533	95,267	285,800	4,086,087	—	4,086,087	Doubtful	—	—	551,141		£10,261,742
Peace of Ryswick, 1697		144,267	100,524	244,788	3,525,907	—	3,525,907	£43,320	—	43,320	694,892	By William III	£10,511,963
Last Years of William III	1700 01 02	273,693	43,635	317,328	6,045,432	—	6,045,432	1,386,832	—	1,386,832	1,474,861		
Wars of Anne	1709	243,693	45,625	289,318	5,913,357	—	5,913,357	2,116,451	—	2,116,451	1,273,587	By Anne	£2,691,626
	1712	326,620	29,115	355,725	6,868,840	—	6,868,840	3,014,175	—	3,014,175	—		
First of George I	1713 14 15	421,431	26,573	448,004	7,696,573	—	7,696,573	1,904,151	—	1,904,151	1,588,496	By George I	£8,725,921
First of George II	1726 27 28	432,832	23,651	456,483	7,951,772	—	7,951,772	3,514,768	—	3,514,768			
Peaceful Years	1736 37 38	476,941	26,627	501,673	9,993,232	—	9,993,232	4,642,502	—	4,642,502			
War of	1739 40 1741	384,191	87,260	471,451	8,869,498	—	8,869,498	2,455,313	—	2,455,313			
Peaceful Years	1749 50 51	609,798	51,386	661,184	12,599,112	—	12,599,112	6,521,964	—	6,521,964		By George II Gold, Silver,	 £11,662,216 304,360
War of	1755 56 57	451,254	73,456	524,711	11,708,515	663,401	12,371,916	4,046,465	—	4,046,465	1,855,334		£11,966,576

First of George III 1760	471,241	102,737	573,978	14,694,970	1,086,205	15,781,175	5,746,270	235,412	5,981,682	
61	508,220	117,835	626,055	14,873,191	1,165,722	16,038,913	6,822,051	417,082	7,239,133	
62	480,444	120,126	600,560	13,545,171	998,165	14,543,336	5,263,858	289,240	5,553,098	
63	561,724	87,293	649,217	14,487,507	1,091,436	15,578,943	4,495,146	187,545	4,682,691	2,076,735
64	583,934	74,800	658,734	16,512,404	1,243,927	17,756,331	6,148,096	357,575	6,505,671	
65	651,402	67,855	719,257	14,550,507	1,180,867	15,731,374	3,660,764	258,466	3,919,230	
66	684,281	61,753	746,034	14,024,964	1,163,704	15,188,668	2,549,189	182,715	2,731,904	
67	645,835	63,206	709,041	13,844,511	1,245,490	15,090,001	1,770,555	222,293	1,992,848	
68	668,786	72,734	741,520	15,117,983	1,502,150	16,620,133	3,239,322	265,501	3,504,823	
69	709,855	63,020	772,857	13,438,236	1,563,053	15,001,289	1,529,676	337,523	1,867,199	
1770	703,495	57,476	760,971	14,266,654	1,729,915	15,996,569	2,049,716	514,556	2,564,272	
71	714,835	64,680	779,515	17,161,147	1,857,334	19,018,481	4,339,151	471,005	4,810,156	
72	716,861	76,415	793,276	16,159,413	1,560,756	17,720,169	2,860,961	350,492	3,211,453	
73	752,836	55,284	808,120	14,763,253	1,612,175	16,375,428	3,356,412	496,376	3,852,788	
74	798,864	65,192	864,056	15,916,344	1,372,143	17,288,487	2,888,678	169,866	3,058,544	2,503,353
75	767,282	64,046	831,328	15,202,366	1,123,998	16,326,364	2,275,003	—	2,275,003	
76	778,878	72,188	851,066	13,729,726	1,025,973	14,755,699	2,962,424	279,292	3,242,716	
77	736,234	83,468	819,702	12,653,363	837,643	13,491,006	1,472,996	35,389	1,508,385	
78	657,238	98,113	755,351	11,551,070	702,820	12,253,890	1,379,653	—	1,379,653	
79	590,911	139,124	730,035	12,693,430	837,273	13,530,700	2,092,133	62,501	2,154,634	2,412,993
1780	619,462	134,515	753,977	11,622,333	1,002,039	12,624,372	1,688,494	99,315	1,787,809	

By George III before the 31st of Dec. 1780

Gold,	30,457,805
Silver,	7,126
	£30,464,931

139B. Growth of the export trade, 1750–1772

Ibid. p. 46.

The subjoined extract from the register of shipping, which displays the tonnage of ships, English and foreign, cleared outwards from our *five principal ports*, as representatives of the whole, will not only demonstrate *the great progress of our navigation in twenty years*, though a long war intervened, but will arrange the relative importance of each, which had not yet been distinctly done. London has always been the first in commercial greatness; Bristol, which is only the fifth, has been hitherto deemed the second; and Whitehaven, whose rank has been altogether unascertained, now claims an equality with London, in respect of the numbers of native shipping. By including the years 1773 and 1774, which were times of still greater traffic, as part of the comparative period, the later part of the twenty years had shewn a much greater superiority. But candour requires that extremes should be avoided.

A TABLE of the SHIPPING which were cleared Outwards at the FIVE FOLLOWING PORTS during the years annexed.

1750		1751		1752		
Tons English	*Do. Foreign*	*Tons English*	*Do. Foreign*	*Tons English*	*Do. Foreign*	
146,187	33,673	140,508	28,051	145,999	25,502	LONDON
100,068	710	113,092	—	123,154	210	WHITEHAVEN
33,233	9,429	32,675	2,228	31,213	6,682	LIVERPOOL
41,826	3,400	56,448	920	48,406	1,550	NEWCASTLE
24,411	3,225	25,720	2,511	25,057	3,673	BRISTOL

	1770		1771		1772	
	Tons English	*Do. Foreign*	*Tons English*	*Do. Foreign*	*Tons English*	*Do. Foreign*
LONDON	178,220	34,656	196,230	38,335	198,758	47,077
WHITEHAVEN	187,448	—	203,368	—	192,436	—
LIVERPOOL	67,043	9,535	69,868	7,968	76,036	11,284
NEWCASTLE	52,704	1,560	52,154	3,470	61,603	1,866
BRISTOL	30,063	4,776	31,482	7,333	31,529	4,185

139C. The balance of trade, 1771–1773

Ibid. pp. 54–58.

This illustrates the still generally accepted mercantilist idea of the balance of trade.

. . . Considering the balance of trade as an interesting subject to a commercial nation, it must be deemed not only of use, but of moment, to enquire minutely who of our mercantile correspondents are our debtors, and who are our creditors; to state which country remits us a favourable balance, and to which we are obliged in our turn to pay one. Nor, is it satisfactory to contrast the general balances of different periods, in order to form general conclusions, which may be either just or fallacious, as circumstances are attended to or neglected. From a particular statement it will clearly appear, that we trade with the greater number of the nations of Europe on an advantageous ground; with few of them on an unfavourable one; that some states, as Italy, Turkey, and Venice, may be considered as of a doubtful kind, because they are not in their balances either constantly favourable or unfavourable. To banish uncertainty from disquisition is always of importance. With this design, it is proposed to state an average of the balance of apparent payments, which were made during the years 1771–2–3 to England by each corresponding community, or which she made to them: and the averages of these years are taken, in order to discover the genuine balance of trade on the whole, since they seemed to be the least affected by the approaching storm. Where the scale of remittance vibrates in suspense, between the countries of doubtful payments, an average of six years is taken, deducting the adverse excesses of import and of export from each other.

Let us examine the following detail of our European commerce:

Countries of favourable balances.	
Denmark and Norway	£ 78,478
Flanders	780,088
France	190,605
Germany	695,484
Holland	1,464,149
Italy (doubtful)	43,289
Portugal }	274,132
Madeira }	9,514
Spain }	442,539
Canaries }	23,347
Streights	113,310
Ireland	663,516
Isle of Man	13,773
Alderney	1,229
Guernsey (doubtful)	6,269
Jersey (doubtful)	8,850
	£4,808,572

Countries of unfavourable balances.	
East Country (doubtful)	£ 100,230
Russia	822,607
Sweden	117,365
Turkey (doubtful)	120,497
Venice (doubtful)	11,369
	£1,172,068
Favourable balance,	3,636,504

. . . [Figures for Africa and Asia factories and for the colonies.]

Let us now recapitulate the foregoing balances:

Gained on our European commerce	£3,636,504
Deduct the loss on the trade of our factories	448,912
	£3,187,596
Gained on the balance of our colony commerce	261,291
Nett balance gained on the trade of England	£3,448,887
Nett balance gained on the trade of Scotland, according to an average of 1771–2–3	435,957
Nett gain on British commerce	£3,884,844

Of an extensive building, executed by a complicated plan, in vain we attempt to form an accurate judgment, either with regard to the proportion of the parts, or the beauty of the whole, without measuring the size of the columns, and examining the congruity of the result, by the suitableness of every dimension. Of the British commerce, so luxuriant in its shoots, and so interwoven in its branches, it is equally impossible to discover the total or relative products, without calculating the gain or loss, that ultimately results to the nation from every market. Thus, in the foregoing statement we perceive, which of our European customers pay us a balance, favourable and constant; which of them are sometimes our debtors, and at other times our creditors; which of them continually draw an unfavourable balance from us: and, by opposing the averages of the profits and losses of every annual adventure to each other, we at length discovered from the result the vast amount of our gains. The mercantile transactions at our factories in Africa and Asia, were stated against each other, because they seemed to be of a similar nature; and we have discovered in the deduction the apparent loss. But, whether we ought to consider the balance of £.448,912 as absolutely lost, must depend on the essential circumstance, whether we consume at home the merchandizes of the East, or, by exporting them for the consumption of strangers, we draw back with interest what we had only advanced: should the nation prefer the beautiful manufactures of the Indian to her own, we ought to regard her prudence as on a level with the indiscretion of the milliner, who adorns her own person with the gaudy attire which she had prepared for the ornament of the great and gay. Our colonies were stated against each other, in order to shew the relative advantage of each, as well as the real importance of the whole. Of the valuable products imported from them, which seem to form so great a balance against the nation, we ought to observe, that they are either gainful, or disadvantageous, as we apply them: we gain by the tobacco, the sugars, the spirits, the drugs, the dying-woods, which we re-export to our neighbours: we lose by what we unnecessarily consume. The moralist and the merchant are both ready to advise us, on the subject of our general commerce, to adopt, without reserve, the gainful policy of the Dutch, during the days† of Sir William Temple, who assures us "*that they furnished infinite luxury, which they never practised; and trafficked in pleasures that they never tasted.*" . . .

† It seems universally agreed among the most intelligent persons that the Dutch have gone, in the present times, into the other extreme.

139D. Estimate of annual produce of principal manufactures of Great Britain, *c.* 1783

(D. Macpherson, *Annals of Commerce*, IV (1805 ed.), p. 15.)

Macpherson states that this estimate was published *c.* 1783, and that he gives it as he finds it, "not knowing upon what principles it is founded". He comments that the authority might surely have stated the woollen manufacture as increasing and the cotton manufacture as increasing with astonishing rapidity.

Estimate of annual produce of principal manufactures of Great Britain.

Woollen	16,800,000	
Leather	10,500,000	declining.
Flax	1,750,000	rather declining.
Hemp	890,000	stationary.
Glass	630,000	rapidly increasing.
Paper	780,000	increasing.
Porcelain	1,000,000	rapidly increasing.
Silk	3,350,000	increasing.
Cotton	960,000	
Lead	1,650,000	stationary.
Tin	1,000,000	declining.
Iron	8,700,000	rapidly increasing.
Steel and plating &c.	3,400,000	
	51,410,000	
Smaller manufactures	5,250,000	
	56,660,000	

E. SOME POPULATION STATISTICS

140A–C. Dr. Heysham's calculations from the Bills of Mortality in Carlisle, 1779–1783

(William Hutchinson, *History of the County of Cumberland,* II (1794). Tables following p. 678.)

These figures are taken from Dr. Heysham's *Observations on the Bills of Mortality in Carlisle, from the Year 1779, to 1787, inclusive,* published annually between those dates. An abridgement of these *Observations* was printed, with Heysham's approval, in Hutchinson's *History of Cumberland,* and later published in pamphlet form at Carlisle in 1797. They were reprinted, with Life Tables calculated from them, by Joshua Milne in his *Treatise on the Valuation of Annuities* in 1815. As contemporary detailed calculations from the Bills of Mortality – the records of burials and baptisms kept by the Company of Parish Clerks in London and a few other towns – these Carlisle tables are almost unique. Heysham's table showing the number of annual deaths in Carlisle during these years from certain diseases (not given by Hutchinson) is printed as an Appendix to M. C. Buer, *Health, Wealth and Population in the early days of the Industrial Revolution* (1926).

140A. Deaths in each month for the following years

Deaths in	*1779*		*1780*		*1781*		*1782*		*1783*	
	Males	*Females*	*Males*	*Females*	*Males*	*Females*	*Males*	*Females*	*Males*	*Females*
January	4	7	11	6	2	7	9	10	5	5
February	6	4	10	8	5	2	7	11	10	11
March	6	6	4	8	3	4	7	15	8	8
Total in 3 months	16	17	25	22	10	13	23	36	23	24
April	6	3	14	15	8	11	7	15	6	11
May	7	10	14	20	8	9	5	20	8	7
June	5	3	8	10	13	9	5	13		10
Total in 3 months	18	16	36	45	29	29	17	48	14	28
July	7	7	7	8	8	7	8	11	7	6
August	14	5	4	12	14	9	3	3	8	6
September	20	22	11	8	9	12	10	9	10	8
Total in 3 months	41	34	22	28	31	28	21	23	25	20
October	30	23	11	14	11	15	10	2	10	10
November	18	20	6	7	14	7	6	6	8	7
December	10	15	8	1	8	9	7	7	5	7
Total in 3 months	58	58	25	22	33	31	23	15	23	24

		Males		*Females*
Total in the Years	1779	133	—	125
	1780	108	—	117
	1781	103	—	101
	1782	84	—	122
	1783	85	—	96
	Total	513	—	561

140B. Of the proportion of the deaths to the living, under different ages

	1779	*1780*	*1781*	*1782*	*1783*
Under 5 years	1 in $6\frac{9}{10}$	1 in $9\frac{9}{10}$	1 in $15\frac{1}{7}$	1 in $13\frac{2}{5}$	1 in $14\frac{1}{2}$
5—10	1 — $64\frac{6}{7}$	1 — $56\frac{3}{4}$	1 — $113\frac{1}{2}$	1 — $75\frac{2}{3}$	1 — 227
10—15	1 — $119\frac{1}{6}$	1 — $357\frac{1}{2}$	1 — $178\frac{3}{4}$	1 — 143	1 — $357\frac{1}{2}$
15—20	1 — $168\frac{3}{4}$	1 — $112\frac{1}{2}$	1 — $84\frac{3}{8}$	1 — $96\frac{4}{7}$	1 — $168\frac{3}{4}$
20—30	1 — $132\frac{4}{5}$	1 — 83	1 — $189\frac{5}{7}$	1 — $120\frac{8}{11}$	1 — $110\frac{2}{3}$
30—40	1 — $146\frac{1}{6}$	1 — $109\frac{5}{8}$	1 — $54\frac{3}{4}$	1 — $79\frac{8}{11}$	1 — $87\frac{7}{10}$
40—50	1 — $95\frac{1}{3}$	1 — $85\frac{4}{5}$	1 — $40\frac{6}{7}$	1 — 66	1 — 78
50—60	1 — $58\frac{4}{5}$	1 — $65\frac{1}{3}$	1 — $26\frac{2}{3}$	1 — 42	1 — 49
60—70	1 — $24\frac{1}{3}$	1 — $20\frac{6}{7}$	1 — $24\frac{1}{3}$	1 — $29\frac{1}{5}$	1 — 23
70—80	1 — $13\frac{3}{5}$	1 — $10\frac{5}{8}$	1 — $12\frac{4}{5}$	1 — $9\frac{1}{2}$	1 — $9\frac{1}{2}$
80—90	1 — $4\frac{5}{6}$	1 — $6\frac{4}{9}$	1 — $6\frac{4}{9}$	1 — $4\frac{1}{7}$	1 — $5\frac{1}{3}$
90—100	1 — 5	1 — $3\frac{1}{3}$	1 — $3\frac{1}{3}$	1 — 5	1 — 5
100—102				1 — 2	
Of all the inhabitants	1 — $30\frac{3}{9}$	1 — $34\frac{1}{2}$	1 — $38\frac{3}{5}$	1 — 38	1 — $43\frac{1}{7}$

N.B.—This table makes the Mortality greater than it actually is, as the Calculations for 1779–1787 inclusive, were made from the Number of Inhabitants which existed in January 1780; whereas there was an Increase of a Thousand in that Period.

140C. Of christenings and deaths in both parishes[1]

	Christenings				Deaths				
	Males	*Females*	*Total*	*Dis-senters*	*Males*	*Females*	*Total*	*Increase*	*Decrease*
1779	102	109	211	x	133	125	258		47
1780	132	120	252	x	108	117	225	27	
1781	136	130	266	x	103	101	204	62	
1782	118	139	257	38	84	122	206	51	
1783	139	123	262	35	85	96	181	81	

xxx The Christenings of Dissenters in these three years were not obtained. – The Dissenters are included in the Columns of the Males and Females.

[1] St. Mary's and St. Cuthbert's.

141. John Rickman's calculations of the population of England and Wales during the eighteenth century, 1801

(*Observations on the Results of the Population Act, 41 Geo. III*, p. 9; included in *Abstract of the Answers and Returns* . . . vol. II (1802).)

This is not a strictly contemporary document, since Rickman's calculations were based on the 1801 Census; but it is included as the only near-contemporary estimate in existence which gives some idea of population trends in the eighteenth century. Rickman's methods are explained and criticized in the General Introduction to the present volume. John Rickman (1771–1840) prepared the first Census Act of 1800, worked out the methods to be used and prepared the Census Reports of 1801, 1811, 1821 and 1831.

TABLE of POPULATION throughout the last Century.

ENGLAND AND WALES

In the Year	*Population*	*In the Year*	*Population*
1700	5,475,000	1770	7,428,000
1710	5,240,000	1780	7,953,000
1720	5,565,000	1785	8,016,000
1730	5,796,000	1790	8,675,000
1740	6,064,000	1795	9,055,000
1750	6,467,000	1801	9,168,000
1760	6,736,000		

Part VII

THE STATE OF THE NATION: SOCIAL

THE STATE OF THE NATION: SOCIAL

Introduction

DOCUMENTS of all kinds illustrating the social life of the eighteenth century abound, and a whole volume of them could easily be compiled. There are, however, many collections of all kinds of material illustrating different aspects of this subject; and the selection here has been strictly limited by considerations of space. The extracts in this section have been chosen to give some idea of the customs, habits, amusements and general background of eighteenth-century life, and to give also some impression of the variety of the materials available.

Herman Moll's *New Description of England* gives in its opening paragraphs a very fair idea of what the eighteenth-century Englishman knew about the geography, population, climate and natural resources of his own country. He goes on, in a later passage, to analyse the various classes which together made up "the Commons of England".[1] Though the barriers between classes were much more definite and difficult to surmount than in present-day England, contemporaries such as Defoe took pride in the rise of the moneyed merchant class and their gradual incorporation with the old nobility and gentry. The war profiteer or successful merchant or wealthy planter who was looked down on by the county could begin "a new race, who should be as good Gentlemen as any that went before them".[2] Some idea of the day-to-day domestic habits of ordinary middle-class people can be gathered from the impressions of the Swedish naturalist, Pehr Kalm, although his visit to England was short.[3] He was particularly impressed by the comfort and ease of the lives of country people, especially the women. He was also, on the whole, favourably impressed by English food, though he found it monotonous; but he only visited London and the home counties, and would therefore be unaware of the differences in diet in various parts of the country. The holiday pastimes of the upper and middle classes are illustrated in the young Fanny Burney's artless description of a summer visit to Teignmouth.[4]

This was one of the great periods of English domestic architecture. Wealthy peers and prosperous merchants vied with each other in building magnificent town and country houses. Many treatises on architecture were published, and it was assumed that a gentleman would have a taste for architecture and some knowledge of building, even if he did not act as his own architect. The result was usually a good compromise between "the convenience of the inhabitant and the beauty and proportion of the fabrick".[5] Much attention was also devoted to the surrounding garden, though here the results were on the whole less satisfactory.[6] Sir Thomas Robinson's description of Sir Robert Walpole's new house at Houghton[7] affords some notion of the furnishings and kind of life led in an eighteenth-century mansion as well as of the building itself.

Transport greatly improved in the course of the century, though travellers still complained bitterly of the state of the roads. The turnpike trusts for the improvement

[1] No. 142. [2] No. 143. [3] No. 144. [4] No. 145.
[5] No. 146. [6] No. 147. [7] No. 148.

and upkeep of roads in a particular area were a feature of the period. In Defoe's day they were a comparatively new feature, and he wrote about them with undue optimism.[1] As late as 1770 Arthur Young, in the course of his tour through the north of England, found much to condemn in these roads, especially in Lancashire.[2] Canal building was important in the middle and later years of the century.[3]

A new and growing spirit of humanitarianism was developing in the eighteenth century, especially in the second half, which can justly be called the Age of Benevolence. Defoe, writing in the 1720s, describes the numerous charities then existing in London and Westminster.[4] An important piece of social legislation which shows the beginning of a new attitude by the State of responsibility for the welfare of its members is the Gin Act of 1751;[5] the first effective attempt to check the excessive drinking of spirits, particularly in London, which was having disastrous effects on the health of the population, especially infants. Jonas Hanway, a philanthropist of many interests, worked tirelessly and in the end successfully for the improvement of the lot of the infant parish poor in London.[6] The work of John Howard for improving conditions in the prisons differed significantly from that of an earlier period in concerning itself with the physical as well as the moral condition of the prisoners.[7]

Mrs. Susannah Wesley's account of the way in which she brought up her family[8] can probably be taken as fairly typical of the middle classes, though one may doubt whether even this redoubtable mother was as systematic as she makes out. Probably most of the children of the upper classes were brought up not very differently. Certainly the freedom from restrictions upon which the parents of Charles James Fox prided themselves at Holland House was exceptional. As has been explained in the General Introduction, the Dissenting Academies played a prominent part amongst the educational agencies of the eighteenth century. One of the best-known of these was conducted by the Reverend Philip Doddridge.[9] An important institution in eighteenth-century education was the Grand Tour, and Lord Chesterfield's letter gives a fair idea of the benefits a young man was expected to derive from foreign travel.[10] There was as yet in England hardly any provision for specialized education for particular professions, apart from the universities, which catered for the Church, and the Inns of Court for the legal profession. A modest beginning had been made in the case of some others, such as the navy and medicine, but in the case of the latter it was still thought desirable for the young physician or surgeon to complete his training abroad. The eighteenth century was not a great period in the history of the English universities, as is made clear by the strictures of Gibbon on his own university and college.[11] Both in England and Wales and in Scotland[12] a substantial contribution to elementary education was made by charity schools of various types, and Mrs. Sarah Trimmer, in her description of these schools, expressed some sensible views about education in general.[13]

[1] No. 149. [2] No. 150. [3] No. 151. [4] No. 152. [5] No. 153.
[6] No. 154. [7] No. 155. [8] No. 156. [9] No. 157. [10] No. 158.
[11] No. 159. [12] Part ix, No. 190. [13] No. 160.

BIBLIOGRAPHY

I. CONTEMPORARY WORKS

Perhaps the best approach to the social life of the times is through the literature and art of the period. Boswell's *Life of Johnson*, the famous novels of Defoe, Richardson, Fielding and Smollett, the works of Hogarth and Zoffany, the formal portraits and carefully posed 'conversation pieces' of the great painters of the age, the innumerable political and personal caricatures for which the century is famous, taken together give an impression of the eighteenth century which remains long after the words of the historical textbook have faded from the reader's mind. The caricatures are listed in the British Museum, *Catalogue of Prints and Drawings*, and reviewed by G. Paston, *Social Caricature in the Eighteenth Century* (London, 1905).

(*a*) LETTERS AND MEMOIRS

Some of these already listed for their political importance are equally informative on social conditions, especially the works of Lady Mary Wortley Montagu, Lord Hervey, Horace Walpole, Lord Chesterfield and Sir Charles Hanbury Williams. J. H. Jesse, *George Selwyn and his Contemporaries* (4 vols., London, 1843–1844), prints a mass of letters addressed to a man about town from 1740 to 1780. The life of a country gentleman of moderate fortune and some scholarly tastes is fully illustrated in *Purefoy Letters*, edited by G. Eland (2 vols., London, 1931). *The Memoirs of William Hickey* (4 vols., 9th edition, London, 1948) is one of the most varied and valuable sources. Life in society is admirably drawn in *Correspondence of Emily, Duchess of Leinster*, edited by Brian Fitzgerald (2 vols., Dublin, 1949, 1953). The many collections of letters written by poets, dramatists, novelists, essayists, etc., such as those of Johnson, Boswell, Goldsmith, Hume, Gibbon, are all of use to the social historian. Other collections include *Verney Letters of the Eighteenth Century*, edited by Lady Verney (2 vols., London, 1930); *The Williamson Letters, 1748–1765*, edited by F. J. Manning (Bedfordshire Historical Record Society, vol. XXXIV, 1954); Gladys Scott Thomson, *Letters of a Grandmother* [the duchess of Marlborough] (London, 1943), *Letters and Journals of Lady Mary Coke*, edited by Hon. J. A. Home (4 vols., Edinburgh, 1889–1896); *Lord Hervey and his Friends 1726–38*, edited by earl of Ilchester (London, 1950), and *Memoirs of Richard Cumberland* (2nd edition, 2 vols., London, 1807). The lower-middle and lower classes are represented by such works as *Memoirs of the First 45 Years of the Life of James Lackington* (London, n.d., *c.* 1791), an eighteenth-century success story telling how a Methodist shoemaker became a leading London bookseller, and *Memoirs of an Eighteenth Century Footman*, edited by J. Beresford (London, 1927). The footman served twenty-seven masters in thirty-three years and showed no tendency to become an ancient family retainer. From the numerous collections which illustrate the lives of women of every class from high society to the *demi-monde* the following are selected for mention: *Autobiography and Correspondence of Mary Granville, Mrs. Delany*, edited by Baroness Llandover (6 vols., London, 1861–1862); *Elizabeth Montagu, Queen of the Bluestockings. Her Correspondence from 1720 to 1761*. By her great-great-niece, Emily J. Climenson (2 vols., London, 1906): *Dear Miss Heber*, edited by F. Bamford (London, 1936); Robert Halsband, *Life of Lady Mary Wortley Montagu* (London, 1956); *Memoirs of Mrs. Letitia Pilkington*, new edition by J. Isaacs (New York, 1928), recording the life in Dublin and London of an Irish adventuress; and *A Narrative of the Life of Mrs. Charlotte Charke written by Herself* (London, 1755, and later editions).

(*b*) DIARIES

Many diaries already noticed for their political value are as important for social history. Lord Ponsonby's anthologies, especially *English Diaries* (London, 1923), contain much interesting material. H. I. Longden in the *Transactions of the Royal Historical Society*, Third Series, I

(1907), pp. 181–203, summarized the diaries of Sir Justinian Isham, a country gentleman with a taste for travel. *Blundell's Diary and Letter Book*, edited by Margaret Blundell (Liverpool, 1952), provides evidence of the daily life of a Roman Catholic country gentleman, while J. Byrom, *Private Journal*, Cheetham Society (4 vols., Manchester, 1854–1857), gives useful information on the lives of the professional classes in the towns. *Yorkshire Diaries and Autobiographies*, Surtees Society (2 vols., Durham, 1877–1886), is of value for lower middle-class life in the north of England. *Sussex Archaeological Collections* (London, 1857), IX, pp. 182–207, and XI (1859), pp. 179–220, give extracts from the diaries of a village schoolmaster [Walter Gale] and small town shopkeeper [Thomas Turner] respectively. Turner's diary was later published in full by Florence M. T. Lamb (London, 1925) and used by D. K. Worcester as the basis of his *Life and Times of Thomas Turner* (New Haven, 1948). Similar material is the foundation of R. Arnold, *A Yeoman of Kent* (London, 1949). The *Early Diary of Frances Burney*, edited by Annie R. Ellis (2 vols., London, 1889), records the daily life of an unusual girl with exceptional opportunities. Boswell's diaries are included in the magnificent edition of *Private Papers of James Boswell*, edited by G. Scott and F. A. Pottle (18 vols., New York, 1928–1934. Index, 1937). A recent addition to this category is *The Diary of Sylas Neville 1767–1788*, edited by B. Cozens-Hardy (London, 1950).

(*c*) ACCOUNT BOOKS, ETC.

Shardeloes Papers, edited by G. Eland (London, 1947), gives a picture of the life of the prosperous squirearchy who could afford to spend £19,000 on building a new mansion. The Scottish History Society has published several account books relating to this period, especially *Ochtertyre House Booke of Accomps* (Edinburgh, 1907) and *Household Book of Lady Grisell Baillie* (Edinburgh, 1911).

(*d*) TRAVELS IN BRITAIN

J. Macky, *Journey Through England* [and Scotland] (3 vols., London, 1714–1729), is the first, while G. E. Fussell, *Exploration of England: a Select Bibliography of Travel and Topography* (London, 1931), conveniently lists the torrent of guide-books published in this period. Defoe, *A Tour Through the Whole Island of Great Britain* (3 vols., London, 1724–1726, and many later editions, including a two-volume one of England and Wales in Everyman's Library, London, 1928), and Young's *Tours* are outstanding examples of this class. *The Torrington Diaries*, edited by C. B. Andrews, with an introduction by John Beresford (4 vols., London, 1934–1938), contain the tours through England and Wales of the Hon. John Byng between 1781 and 1794. There is a one-volume abridged edition (London, 1954). There are interesting accounts of travels in Britain in the *Portland Manuscripts* (*Historical Manuscripts Commission*), vol. VI. Bishop Richard Pococke's *Travels Through England*, edited by J. J. Cartwright, Camden Society (2 vols., London, 1888–1889), and *Tours in Scotland*, edited by D. W. Kemp, Scottish History Society (Edinburgh, 1887), are mainly concerned with antiquarian and natural curiosities. Of more general interest are the *Tours* of Thomas Pennant, especially *Tour in Scotland 1769* (Chester, 1771, and later editions) and *Tour in Scotland and Voyage to the Hebrides, 1772* (2 vols., Chester, 1774–1776). In spite of the titles these two works cover most of the North of England: so far as Scotland is concerned Pennant was the forerunner of an endless stream of English travellers, including Dr. Johnson, whose *A Journey to the Western Islands of Scotland* (London, 1775) has been frequently reprinted. The most distinguished foreign visitor was certainly Voltaire, whose superficial but influential remarks on the English will be found in his *Letters Concerning the English Nation* (London, 1733), best read in F. A. Taylor's edition of *Lettres Philosophiques* (Oxford, 1943). Other foreign travellers who wrote about England were the Portuguese, Gonsalez; the Swedish botanist, Pehr Kalm, whose *Account of his Visit to England* appeared in translation (London, 1892); the Swiss César de Saussure, whose letters were printed in *A Foreign View of England*, edited by Madame van Muyden (London, 1902); the German scholar, Lichtenberg, some of whose letters have been translated and annotated by Margaret L. Mare and

W. H. Quarrell, *Visits to England* (Oxford, 1938); two Frenchmen who visited England in 1784, B. Faujas de Saint Fond, *A Journey through England and Scotland to the Hebrides in 1784*, translated by A. Geikie (London, 1907) and Francois de la Rochefoucauld, whose *Mélanges Sur l'Angleterre* have been translated in *A Frenchman in England, 1784*, by S. C. Roberts (Cambridge, 1933); and perhaps the most interesting of all, the German schoolmaster, C. P. Moritz, whose *Travels in England in 1782* were edited by P. E. Matheson (London, 1924). The travels of Gonsalez and several others may be read in John Pinkerton, *General Collection of Voyages and Travels* (17 vols., London, 1808–1814), vols. 2 and 3 of which relate to travel in the British Isles. H. Moll, *New Description of England and Wales* (London, 1724), fulfilled the functions of a modern gazeteer. There are many works on English inns, amongst others those listed on p. 23 of the *Local History Handlist*, published by the Historical Association, London, 1947.

(*e*) TRAVEL ABROAD

E. G. Cox, *A reference Guide to the literature of travel* (2 vols., Seattle, 1935–1938), claims to include all books on foreign travel published in Great Britain during our period. Bishop Pococke travelled extensively in the eastern Mediterranean and recorded his observations in his *Description of the East* (2 vols., London, 1743–1745). Lady Mary Wortley Montagu's accounts of her travels and residence in this area are well known. Jonas Hanway, *Historical Account of the British Trade over the Caspian Sea* (4 vols., London, 1753), recorded a journey overland to Persia in 1743 from which great commercial advantages were expected, but failed to materialize. Many Englishmen travelled extensively in northern Europe, including the historian Archdeacon Coxe, but most of them preferred to concentrate on the countries of south-western Europe, especially France and Italy, which were included in nearly every Grand Tour. Interesting details of one such tour will be found in *Elizabeth, Henry and George*, edited by Lord Herbert (London, 1939). Professor Constantia Maxwell contributes a scholarly introduction to the subject in *The English Traveller in France, 1698–1815* (London, 1932). The voyages of Anson, Cook and others are included in the bibliography on Colonial History.

II. GENERAL MODERN WORKS

A. S. Turberville, *English Men and Manners in the Eighteenth Century* (Oxford, 1926), is perhaps the best introduction, but should be supplemented by *Johnson's England*, edited by A. S. Turberville (2 vols., Oxford, 1933), which consists of essays with select bibliographies on a wide variety of social topics. Lecky's *History* is strong on social life. *Social England*, edited by H. D. Traill and J. S. Mann (6 vols., London, 1901–1904), is still useful; and G. D. H. Cole and R. Postgate, *The Common People 1746–1938* (London, 1938), may be recommended. The brief treatment by Dr. G. M. Trevelyan in his *English Social History* (London, 1944), pp. 293–415, is in a class by itself.

Gladys Scott Thomson's three books on the ducal house of Russell, *Life in a Noble Household* (London, 1937), *The Russells in Bloomsbury* (London, 1940) and *Family Background* (London, 1949), provide an admirable account of the life of a great nobleman of the period and the organization of his household. M. Dorothy George, *London Life in the Eighteenth Century* (London, 1925), is the best account of the conditions of life of the poor in the metropolis. Less specialized surveys include E. B. Chancellor, *The Eighteenth Century in London* (London, 1920); A. E. Richardson, *Georgian England* (London, 1931); E. S. Roscoe, *English Scene in the Eighteenth Century* (London, 1912); Dorothy Marshall, *English People in the Eighteenth Century* (London, 1956); two popular works by Rosamond Bayne-Powell, *English Country Life in the Eighteenth Century* (London, 1935), and *Eighteenth Century London Life* (London, 1937); G. E. Fussell, *Village Life in the Eighteenth Century* [chiefly in the Midlands] (Worcester, 1948), and G. E. and K. R. Fussell, *The English Countrywoman. A Farmhouse Social History, 1500–1900* (London, 1953).

E. Hughes, *North Country Life in the Eighteenth Century: The North East, 1700–1750* (Oxford, 1952), is a mine of information about social and economic conditions in this area. Christina Hole, *English Home Life, 1500–1800* (London, 1941), is a popular but useful compilation with a good bibliography. Marjorie Williams, *Lady Luxborough goes to Bath* (Oxford, 1946), and J. A. R. Pimlott, *The Englishman's Holiday* (London, 1947), deal with life at spas and seaside resorts.

III. SPECIAL SUBJECTS

(*a*) FOOD, DRINK AND CLOTHING

Perhaps the most helpful modern treatment of eighteenth-century cookery is J. R. Ainsworth-Davis, *Cooking Through the Centuries* (London, 1931). Sir John Drummond and Anne Wilbraham, *The Englishman's Food* (London, 1939), gives some average diets and their nutritive values, while Sir N. Curtis-Bennett, *The Food of the People* (London, 1949), also deals briefly with our period. G. E. Fussell discussed "The Change in Farm Labourers' Diet during Two Centuries" in *Economic History*, I (1926–1929), pp. 268–274. The drinking habits of the age are notorious and may be studied *ad nauseam* in such sources as Hickey's *Memoirs*. S. and B. Webb, *History of Liquor Licensing in England* (London, 1903), is a useful conspectus. There are many works on the dress of both sexes, such as J. Laver and Iris Brooke, *English Costume of the 18th century* (London, 1931), G. Clinch, *English Costume* (London, 1909), and C. Willett and Mrs. Phillis Cunnington, *Handbook of English Costume in the Eighteenth Century*, (London, 1957).

(*b*) THE POOR

Contemporaries were keenly interested in this perennial problem. H. Fielding, *Proposal for Making an Effectual Provision for the Poor* (London, 1753), and Jonas Hanway, *Letters on the Importance of the Rising Generation* (2 vols., London, 1767), may be mentioned as examples of the contemporary attitude. The classic work of Sir F. M. Eden, *State of the Poor* (3 vols., London, 1797, abridged, edited by A. G. L. Rogers, London, 1928), deals fully with conditions in our period. The standard modern works are the first volume of S. and B. Webb, *English Poor Law History* (London, 1927), and Dorothy Marshall, *English Poor in the Eighteenth Century* (London, 1926), the main conclusions in which are briefly stated in her "Old Poor Law, 1662–1795" in the *Economic History Review*, VIII (1937–1938), pp. 38–47. Betsy Rodgers, *Cloak of Charity* (London, 1949), gives a popular account of the life and work of the best-known philanthropists of the century: Coram, Hanway, Howard, Raikes, etc. Specialized studies include W. S. Lewis and R. M. Williams, *Private Charity in England 1747–57* (New Haven, 1938); Ethel M. Hampson, *Treatment of Poverty in Cambridgeshire 1597–1834* (Cambridge, 1934); and H. Levy, "Sickness and Medical Benefit since the Puritan Revolution", in the *Economic History Review*, XIV (1944–1945), pp. 135–160.

(*c*) EDUCATION

The more important contemporary works, such as Locke's *Some Thoughts Concerning Education* (London, 1693) and Richard Steele's articles in *The Spectator*, as well as many modern monographs are listed in C. L. Grose, *Select Bibliography of British History* (Chicago, 1939), Section VIII, 4. Professor J. W. Adamson's survey in the *Cambridge History of English Literature*, vol. IX (Cambridge, 1912), is still of use. N. Hans, *New Trends in Education in the Eighteenth Century* (London, 1951), gives valuable statistical and other factual information. H. McLachlan, *English Education Under the Test Acts* (Manchester, 1931), gives information on the dissenting academies and sums up their influence. M. G. Jones, *Charity School Movement* (Cambridge, 1938), deals with another important educational agency. The same author's *Hannah More* (Cambridge, 1952) is also useful. D. A. Winstanley's two works, *University of Cambridge in the Eighteenth*

Century (Cambridge, 1922) and *Unreformed Cambridge* (Cambridge, 1935), taken with A. D. Godley, *Oxford in the Eighteenth Century* (London, 1908), and Sir C. E. Mallet, *History of the University of Oxford* (3 vols., London, 1924–1927), give accounts of the universities. The lives and papers of the outstanding dons, such as Richard Bentley and Thomas Hearne, throw light on conditions in the universities and the comments of their pupils, Gibbon, Adam Smith and Bentham, are still more illuminating. C. R. Weld's classic *History of the Royal Society* (London, 1848) must now be supplemented by Sir H. Lyons, *The Royal Society* (Cambridge, 1944), and Dorothy Stimson, *Scientists and Amateurs* (London, 1949). There are also histories of all the prominent schools, and a brief account of "Public Schools in the Eighteenth Century" by G. MacGregor in *Quarterly Review* (October, 1947), pp. 580–591. General works which include references to the eighteenth century are J. Rodgers, *Old Public Schools of England* (London, 1938), and Dorothy Gardiner, *English Girlhood at School* (London, 1929). On the teaching of writing, A. Heal, *English Writing Masters and their Copy Books* (Cambridge, 1931), is authoritative and F. J. H. Darton, *Children's Books in England* (Cambridge, 1932), brings together some interesting material.

(*d*) LITERATURE

It is impossible to list here the innumerable editions of the famous literary works of the eighteenth century and the flood of modern commentaries upon them, including those published in *Essays and Studies by Members of the English Association* and in other periodicals. Oliver Elton, *Survey of English Literature 1730–80* (2 vols., London, 1928), covers our period neatly and Basil Willey, *Eighteenth Century Background* (London, 1940), is indispensable. The *Cambridge History of English Literature*, vols. 9 and 10 (Cambridge, 1912–1913), is useful and *The Cambridge Bibliography of English Literature*, vol. 2, *1660–1800* (Cambridge, 1940), provides under convenient headings exhaustive lists of literary works published in the eighteenth century. James Sutherland, *A Preface to Eighteenth Century Poetry* (London, 1948), is a readable introduction and the *Oxford Book of Eighteenth Century Verse*, chosen by D. Nichol Smith (Oxford, 1926), a representative and attractive anthology. Allardyce Nicoll, *History of Early Eighteenth Century Drama* (Cambridge, 1925), and *History of Late Eighteenth Century Drama* (Cambridge, 1927) are authoritative on the theatre. Margaret Barton, *Garrick* (London, 1948), is not only a portrait of the greatest actor of the age but a valuable study of the society background. The fullest history of the novel is E. A. Baker, *History of the English Novel* (10 vols., London, 1924–1939), but this is a poor substitute for reading the novels themselves. J. M. Longaker, *English Biography in the Eighteenth Century* (Philadelphia, 1931); D. Nichol Smith, *Shakespeare in the 18th Century* (Oxford, 1928); S. H. Monk, *The Sublime: a Study of Critical Theories in Eighteenth Century England* (New York, 1935); and A. S. Collins, *Authorship in the Days of Johnson* (London, 1927), and "The Growth of the Reading Public" in *Review of English Studies* (July–October 1926) are all helpful special studies. John Nichols, *Literary Anecdotes* (9 vols., London, 1812–1815), is an ill-digested source from which much interesting material has been drawn by later writers. H. W. Troyer, *Ned Ward of Grub Street, a Study of Sub-Literary London in the Eighteenth Century* (Cambridge, Mass., 1946), as its title indicates, is at least as important for social conditions as for literary history.

(*e*) SCHOLARSHIP

J. E. Sandys, *History of Classical Scholarship* (3 vols., Cambridge, 1906–1908), must now be supplemented by M. L. Clarke, *Greek Studies in England 1700–1830* (Cambridge, 1945). J. B. Black, *The Art of History* (London, 1926), is the best introduction to the great historians and D. M. Low, *Edward Gibbon* (London, 1937), a good account of the greatest of them. L. M. Knapp's article in *Transactions of the Bibliographical Society*, New Series, XVI (1935), pp. 295–308, dealing with Smollett has interesting information on the public demand for historical works. Sir C. H. Firth, *Modern Languages at Oxford* (London, 1929); D. C. Douglas, *English Scholars* [1660–1730] (London, 1939), and the same author's "Development of English Medieval

Scholarship between 1660 and 1730" in the *Transactions of the Royal Historical Society*, Fourth Series, XXI (1939), pp. 21–39; and A. Esdaile, *The British Museum Library* (London, 1947), are all of value. Professor Stuart Piggott's life of *William Stukeley* (Oxford, 1950) discusses the achievements and limitations of eighteenth-century archaeologists. Other works will be found in the bibliographies on Education and on The Sciences.

(*f*) PAINTING, ETC.

Horace Walpole, *Anecdotes of Painting* (4 vols., Strawberry Hill, 1762–1771), includes also a catalogue of engravers and at once became a classic. W. Hogarth in his *Analysis of Beauty* (London, 1753; new edition by Joseph Burke, 1955), and Sir Joshua Reynolds in his celebrated *Discourses delivered in the Royal Academy* (London, 1778) discuss aesthetic theories. The *Farington Diary*, edited by J. Greig (7 vols., London, 1793–1814), is invaluable for social and professional details about the artists of the closing decades of the eighteenth century. The most satisfactory modern works are W. T. Whitley, *Artists and their Friends in England 1700–99* (2 vols., London, 1928), and C. H. Collins Baker, *British Painting* (London, 1933). Professor E. K. Waterhouse's *Painting in Britain 1530–1790*, a volume in the Pelican History of Art (London, 1952), should also be consulted. Sir K. Clark, "Painting of English Landscape" in *Proceedings of the British Academy*, vol. XXI (1935); Charles Mitchell, "Benjamin West's 'Death of General Wolfe' and the Popular History Piece" in *England and the Mediterranean Tradition*, edited by The Warburg and Courtauld Institutes (London, 1945), pp. 179–192; and A. M. Hind, *Short History of Engraving and Etching* (London, 1908), and later editions, are useful special studies.

(*g*) SCULPTURE AND ARCHITECTURE

On sculpture E. B. Chancellor, *Lives of the British Sculptors* (London, 1911), and Katherine A. Esdaile, *English Monumental Sculpture* (London, 1927) and *English Church Monuments 1510 to 1840* (London, 1946), are the leading authorities. On architecture contemporary architects, notably Colin Campbell and William Adam, produced works of permanent value. *An Eighteenth Century Correspondence*, edited by Lilian Dickins and Mary Stanton (London, 1910), gives details of the architectural activities of Sanderson Miller. H. M. Colvin, *Biographical Dictionary of British Architects, 1660–1840* (London, 1954), is invaluable. The standard modern work is Sir R. Blomfield, *History of Renaissance Architecture in England* (London, 1897), and the same author briefly reviews the architecture of our period in "English Architecture in the 17th and 18th Centuries" in the *Transactions of the Royal Historical Society*, Fourth Series, XIV (1931), pp. 121–140. A. E. Richardson, *Georgian Architecture* (London, 1949), gives brief accounts of some leading architects and their work, and R. Francis, *Looking for Georgian England* (London, 1952), selects for discussion certain towns and villages of southern England which still possess Georgian buildings, but perhaps the best introduction is J. Summerson, *Georgian London* (London, 1946), and the same author's *Architecture in Britain, 1530–1830* (London, 1953) in the Pelican History of Art. There are good accounts of *Georgian Buildings of Bath* and *Georgian Buildings of Bristol*, both by W. Ison (London, 1948 and 1952), and of *Georgian Edinburgh* by I. G. Lindsay (Edinburgh, 1948). On the town and country houses which are so prominent a feature of the age R. Dutton, *The English Country House* (London, 1935); A. E. Richardson and H. D. Eberlein, *The Smaller English House of the Later Renaissance* (London, 1925); J. A. Gotch, *The English Home from Charles I to George IV* (London, 1918); and B. Oliver, *Cottages of England 16th to 18th Centuries* (London, 1929), should be consulted. J. Lees-Milne, *The Age of Adam* (London, 1948), is a useful monograph and C. H. Collins Baker and Muriel I. Baker, *Life and Circumstances of James Brydges* [duke of Chandos] (Oxford, 1949), is chiefly important for the duke's architectural activities. T. Burke, *Streets of London* (London, 1940), deals with town houses and shops while G. E. Fussell and Constance Goodman discuss "The Housing of the Rural Population in the Eighteenth Century" in *Economic History*, II (1930–1933), pp. 63–90.

(*h*) INTERIOR DECORATION

A. Stratton, *The English Interior* (London, 1920), is a brief survey; R. Dutton, *The English Interior 1500 to 1900* (London, 1949), is also rather sketchy, though it has well-chosen illustrations of eighteenth-century rooms. There are fuller treatments by F. Lenyon in *Decoration in England from 1660 to 1760* (London, 1914) and *Furniture in England from 1660 to 1760* (London, 1914). Margaret Jourdain, *English Decoration and Furniture of the later 18th century* (London, 1922), continues Lenyon's works. P. Macquoid and R. Edwards, *Dictionary of English Furniture* (3 vols., London, 1924–1928), H. Cescinsky, *English Furniture of the Eighteenth Century* (3 vols., London, 1909–1911), and Oliver Brackett, *English Furniture Illustrated* (revised edition by H. C. Smith, London, 1950), are still more elaborate. There is a good life of *Thomas Chippendale* (London, 1924) by O. Brackett, and some of the magnificent plates from his *Gentleman and Cabinetmaker's Director* are reproduced with an introductory essay by R. W. Symonds in his *Ornamental Designs of Chippendale* (London, 1948). Margaret Jourdain, *The Work of William Kent* (London, 1948), deals with Kent's activities as painter, architect, interior decorator and landscape gardener. On ceramics W. B. Honey, *English Pottery and Porcelain* (London, 1933), and F. Tilley, *English Pottery and Porcelain of the Eighteenth Century* (London, 1947), are recommended. H. C. Marillier, *English Tapestries of the Eighteenth Century* (London, 1930), is a useful guide to this subject: the more modern equivalent of tapestry is dealt with in A. V. Sugden and J. L. Edmondson, *A History of English Wallpaper* (London, 1925). There is a useful list of other works on the contents of secular buildings in the *Local History Handlist* of the Historical Association (London, 1947), Section XIII (6 and 7).

(*i*) GARDENING

Contemporaries who wrote on this subject included Horace Walpole, whose essay on "Modern Gardening" appeared in the fourth volume of his *Anecdotes of Painting*; the architects William Kent and William Chambers, whose *Dissertation on Oriental Gardening* (London, 1772) was influential; and T. Whately, whose *Observations on Modern Gardening* (Dublin, 1770) is highly commended by the leading modern authority on this subject, Mr. H. F. Clark, who has recently published *The English Landscape Garden* (London, 1949). R. Dutton, *The English Garden* (London, 1937), may also be consulted.

(*j*) MUSIC

The leading contemporary authorities were Charles Burney, *General History of Music* (4 vols., London, 1776–1789), and John Hawkins, *General History of the Science and Practice of Music* (5 vols., 1776). The first edition of *Cathedral Music*, edited by W. Boyce (London, 1760–1778), also appeared in 3 vols. Burney's *General History* was re-edited by F. Mercer in 2 vols. (London, 1935), and P. A. Scholes, *The Great Dr. Burney* (2 vols., London, 1948), is definitive. The standard modern authorities are Sir George Grove, *Dictionary of Music and Musicians*, edited by H. C. Colles (4th edition, 6 vols., London, 1940), and *The Oxford History of Music* (6 vols., especially vol. 4), *The Age of Bach and Handel* by J. A. Fuller Maitland (Oxford, 1902). L. F. Benson, *The English Hymn* (London, 1915), is a useful study.

(*k*) THE SCIENCES

Contemporary ideas on scientific subjects are to be found scattered through the *Philosophical Transactions of the Royal Society* or collected in a more accessible form in the eighteenth-century editions of E. Chambers's *Cyclopaedia*. W. Whewell, *History of the Inductive Sciences* (3 vols., London, 1837, and later editions), may still be used, but the best and most comprehensive modern authority is A. Wolf, *History of Science, Technology and Philosophy in the Eighteenth Century* (London, 1938). Since the latter work gives classified lists of books on the various branches of knowledge, it is unnecessary to mention such works here. Of the more general accounts of scientific studies, R. W. T. Gunther, *Early Science at Oxford* (14 vols., Oxford, 1921–1945), has little on our period and H. T. Pledge, *Science since 1500* (London, 1939), gives the impression that the eighteenth century was almost a blank in the history of modern science. Dr. G. N. Clark in *Science and Social Welfare in the Age of Newton* (Oxford, 1937, 2nd edition, 1949), unfortunately concludes his survey in the reign of Queen Anne, but H. Butterfield in *The Origins of Modern Science 1300–1800* (London, 1949) devotes two chapters to the study of chemistry and biology in the eighteenth century, and Professor L. T. Hogben's inaugural lecture at Aberdeen (Exeter, 1937), gives an estimate of the Scottish contributions to technological science. The technological revolution in one industry is discussed by A. and N. L. Clow, *The Chemical Revolution* (London, 1952).

Many students will find the actual publications of eighteenth-century scientists more interesting and informative than résumés of their work at second-hand. Such books include Joseph Black, *Experiments upon Magnesia Alba* (Edinburgh, reprinted 1777); B. Franklin, *Experiments and Observations on Electricity* (2 vols., London, 1751–1753); S. Hales, *Statical Essays* (London, 1727); J. Priestley, *History and Present State of Discoveries Relating to Vision, Light and Colours* (2 vols., London, 1772); and the Reverend John Lightfoot, *Flora Scotica* (2 vols., London, 1777). W. S. Scott, *White of Selborne and his Times* (London, 1946), is a useful study of the best-known naturalist of our period.

(*l*) MEDICINE

D. Guthrie, *History of Medicine* (London, 1945), F. H. Garrison, *Introduction to the History of Medicine* (London, 1913, 4th edition, 1929), and A. H. Buck, *Growth of Medicine to 1800* (New Haven, 1917), are excellent outlines. G. Parker, *Early History of Surgery in Great Britain* (London, 1920), has a brief chapter on the eighteenth century, but F. Beekman, "The Rise of British Surgery in the 18th century" in *Annals of Medical History*, IX (1937), pp. 549–566, is more informative, and there is much of interest in "The Medical Professions in the Eighteenth Century" by Bernice Hamilton in the *Economic History Review*, Second Series, IV (1951–1952), pp. 141–169. *The Diary of a West Country Physician* [Claver Morris], edited by E. Hobhouse (London, 1934), has some interesting details. There are good modern accounts of the Hunters, *e.g.* by G. C. Peachey, *Memoir of William and John Hunter* (Plymouth, 1924), and of other eminent physicians, including R. W. Johnstone, *William Smellie* (Edinburgh, 1952), as well as a number of special studies such as C. T. Mullet, *Public Baths and Health in England* [sixteenth to eighteenth centuries] (Baltimore, 1946).

A. SOCIAL LIFE

142. A general view of England, 1724

(Herman Moll, *A New Description of England and Wales* (1724), pp. 1–2, 14–15.)

Herman Moll (d. 1732), a Dutchman, settled in London about 1698, and became well known for the excellence of his maps and his many geographical compilations.

INTRODUCTION.

THAT Part of *Britain* call'd *England*, is bounded on the North by *Scotland*, from which it is separated by the Rivers *Tweed* and *Solway*, though its Limits on that Side in former Times extended as far as *Edenburgh* Frith on the East, and the Frith of *Dunbarton* on the West, but since contracted into a narrower Compass; On the East and North East by the *German* Ocean, that flows between it and *Denmark*, *Germany*, and the *Netherlands*. On the West by the *Irish* Sea; and on the South by the *English* Channel. It's environ'd with turbulent Seas, guarded in many Places with inaccessible Rocks; and where these are wanting, with some strong Fortresses, and the most powerful Navy in the World; and is very advantageously situated for Traffick into all the Parts of the Earth.

As to its Position in respect to the Heavens, many accurate Observations of later Years have been made. Mr. *Gascoigne*, who has survey'd *Cornwall*, and is a Gentleman of distinguished Ability in the Art of Surveying, has justly fix'd the *Lizard Point*, or most Southerly Parts of *England*, at forty nine Degrees, and fifty six Minutes North Latitude; as the curious *Scotch* Geographer Mr. *Adair* does *Berwick*, the most Northern Town in it, at fifty five and forty six Degrees. The Longitude heretofore was usually reckon'd Eastward, from a Meridian assign'd at any Place at Pleasure, and called the first Meridian; but of late it has been, by some ingenious Persons, judged more convenient for *Englishmen*, to fix their first Meridian at *London*, and so reckon Eastward and Westward from thence.

Now it appears from what has been said concerning the Longitude and Latitude, that *England*, where it is longest between the *Lizard* and *Berwick*, is three hundred and eighty Miles; as it is from the *Land's End* to the *North Foreland*, where it's broadest, three hundred Miles; so that it must be above one thousand three hundred and twenty Miles in Circumference. It's also manifest, that the longest Day at the *Lizard* is sixteen Hours, and at *Berwick* about seventeen Hours, because the former lies in the eighth, and the other within the eleventh Climate.

It is computed, that *England* contains thirty nine Millions, thirty eight thousand, and five hundred Acres; and about one Million, a hundred and seventy five thousand nine hundred and one and fifty Houses. We shall wave the Comparison some have made of its Bigness, in respect to *France* and other Countries, as being unaccurate, and observe concerning the Number of Inhabitants, allowing the above mention'd Number of Houses, and six Persons, one with another, to each House, that there will be found in all seven Millions, fifty five thousand, seven hundred and six Souls; and amongst them a Million of fighting Men. In the next Place, as to the yearly Rent of all the Lands in *England* and *Wales*, it appears from the Observations and Calculations of the late *Gregory King*, Esq; published by Dr. *Davenant*, that they seem to be near ten Millions a Year; and that the Houses not let with the Lands, amount to two Millions *per Annum*, and all other Hereditaments to about two Millions more; in all, fourteen Millions: So that the People and Territories of the King of *England* alone, may be valued for Wealth and Strength at above one half of those of *France*. Lastly, there are in all *England* and *Wales* together, five and twenty Cities, seven hundred and fifty great Towns, call'd Market Towns, about nine thousand nine hundred and twenty Parishes, some of forty or fifty Miles in Circumference; sixty one Forests, and about three hundred Parks.

The whole Island was anciently known by the Name of *Albion*, but afterwards better by that of *Britain*, and so continued 'till the Time of King *Ecbert*, the first *Saxon* Monarch, who called the Southern Part of it, from the Angles, the most numerons Nation of the *Saxons*, by the Name of *England*; the Air of which is so temperate, that the Natives are not usually vex'd with the Extreams either of Heat or Cold; one of these Blessings, it is presumed, they owe partly to the Climate; and the other, among many other Happinesses, to their being encompassed with the Sea. It is withal so healthy, that many of the Inhabitants live to a great Age. The Salubrity of the Air is ascribed by a learned foreign Physician, to the Windiness of our Climate, who says, *Anglia ventosa, Anglia non morbosa*: However, there are some Distempers that seem to be peculiar to us, more particularly Consumptions and Melancholy; the last of which is attended with more fatal Effects than are to be met with from it in all *Europe* besides.

The Soil here is so very fruitful, especially in Corn, that the Island was anciently call'd the Granary of the Western World; and we cannot but think that it may still in a great Degree deserve that Name, because at present some of the greatest Kingdoms in *Europe* are supply'd with that necessary Support of Life from hence. In a Word, *England*, which no other Nation can with so much Justice pretend to, produces of itself all that can really conduce either to the Necessities and Convenience, or to the Pleasures and Satisfaction of Life; most of her Plenties and Ornaments being expressed in this old Verse.

> *Anglia*, 1 *Mons*, 2 *Pons*, 3 *Fons*, 4 *Ecclesia*,
> 5 *Fœmina*, 6 *Lana*.
> For Mountains, Bridges, Rivers, Churches fair,
> Women and Wool, *England*'s past compare.

There is no need of descanting upon these Particulars, nor on the rich Treasures the Bowels of the Earth afford us, in greater Plenty and Variety than to any of our neighbouring Nations; such as Lead, Tin, Copper, Coals, *&c.* these things being taken Notice of in their proper Places in the Body of the Work. We might likewise enlarge upon the vast Quantities of most excellent Fish our Seas and Rivers afford us; concerning which some affirm, that the very single Article of Oysters bring us in yearly two hundred thousand Pounds from the *Dutch* alone; but we must wave 'em, and come to shew the Vicissitude this Part of *Britain* underwent since the first Planting of it, after the universal Deluge, but as to the Time when we are wholly in the Dark; neither can it possibly be otherwise, seeing we are assured from good Authority, that neither the *Druids*, who were the first Priests here, nor the *Bards*, who celebrated the Atchievements of their great Men, ever did, or ever would, in those Days, commit any thing of this kind to Writing. . . .

As to the Commons of *England*, none are called Noble under a Baron; even the Sons of Peers are by our Constitution reckoned among the Commons, the main Body of which consists of Baronets, Knights of several Sorts, Esquires, Gentlemen, Merchants, Yeomen, and Tradesmen. The Title of Baronet, first instituted by King *James* I. in 1611, is an hereditary Honour by Patent, descending to the Heirs Male lawfully begotten, and when their eldest Sons are at full Age they may claim Knighthood. Baronets have a Precedency before all Knights except those of the Garter, Knights of the Privy Council, Knights Bannerets, made under the King's Banner or Standard display'd in an Army Royal in open War, the King being there in Person: They are now very numerous, and no Honour is ever to be created between Baronets and Barons.

Knights anciently signified a lusty Servitor or Horseman, because they were wont to be Servants, and in our Common Law *Milites*, because they commonly held Lands by Knight-Service, to serve the King in his Wars as Soldiers. We have several Sorts of them; the chiefest are those of the Order of the Garter, esteemed the most honourable and most ancient of any Lay-Order now in *Europe*, having been instituted by *Edward* III. so far back as the Year 1350: The greatest Monarchs of Christendom have been enroll'd, and taken it for an Honour to be of this Order, though I think there are none now of it. We do not pretend here to enter upon a Detail of it, but referring the Reader to the Institution, Laws, *&c.* of it at large, wrote by Mr. *Ashmole*, we pass over the Knights-Bannerets already mentioned, an Order become obsolete, and of which there are none now in *England*, no more than there are of the Knights of the Bath, first instituted in 1399, seeing no new ones have been created since the Coronation of King *Charles* II. The next are those commonly called Knights-Batchelors, formerly rewarded with that Honour for their military Atchievements, and sparingly bestowed till after the Reign of Queen *Elizabeth*; but our Princes have been since so profuse in conferring it, that it has lost much of its ancient Repute.

The next in Degree are Esquires. Of this Title are first Viscounts and Barons eldest Sons, and all their younger Sons; and by the Common Law all the Sons of Earls, Marquesses and Dukes are Esquires, and no more. Next are the Esquires of the King's Body, ranked among the Officers of the King's Court. Next them are reckoned the eldest Sons of younger Sons of Barons, and of all Noblemen of higher Rank. There may be also Esquires created by the King by putting about their Necks a Collar of SS, and bestowing a Pair of Silver Spurs upon them. Others are reputed Esquires, or equal to them; as Sergeants of the several Offices of the King's Court, and other Officers of Rank and Quality: So are Justices of the Peace, Mayors of Corporations, Barristers, Batchelors of Divinity, Law, or Physick, though none of them are really so.

A Gentleman is properly one whose Ancestors have been reputed Free Men, and have owned no Obedience to any Man besides their natural Prince; so that no Man, properly speaking, is a Gentleman, but one that was born so: However the King, who is the Fountain of Honour, can make a Gentleman by Charter, or conferring some honourable Imployment upon him; and tho' all Noblemen are Gentlemen, yet all Gentlemen are not Noblemen.

Next to the lower Nobility, as some reckon all those to be under the Degree of Peers of the Realm, are placed the Yeomantry or Freeholders of *England*, of whom in some Cases the Law has conceived a better Opinion than of Tradesmen, Artificers, or Labourers: They are all of Use and Support to the Publick in their several Stations, and it would be invidious to make Comparisons between them; and as for Merchants, it is well known how much they contribute to the Wealth and Reputation of the Kingdom.

Having briefly stated the several Ranks of People in the Kingdom, it will be proper to add a few Lines concerning their Precedencies. It's to be observed, that after the King and Princes of the Blood, *viz.* the Sons, Grandsons, Brothers, Uncles, or Nephews of the King and no farther; and after the two Archbishops, between whom however he that has the Custody of the Great Seal, is placed; Dukes, amongst all the Nobility, have the Precedency; then Marquesses, Dukes eldest Sons, Earls, Marquesses eldest Sons, Dukes younger Sons, Viscounts, Earls eldest Sons, Marquesses younger Sons, Barons, the eldest Sons of Viscounts, the younger Sons of Earls, eldest Sons of Barons, Privy Counsellors and Judges; Viscounts younger Sons, Barons younger Sons, Baronets, Knights of the Bath, Knights-Batchelors, Sergeants at Law, Esquires, Gentlemen, Citizens, Yeomen, Husbandmen, and Labourers. Some have brought in Military Officers into the List, but they have in reality no Precedency as such allotted to them.

143. Daniel Defoe on the wealthy trading class, 1726

(Daniel Defoe, *The Complete English Tradesman, in Familiar Letters* (1726), pp. 372–378.)

As to the wealth of the nation, that undoubtedly lies chiefly among the trading part of the people; and tho' there are a great many families rais'd within few years, in the late war by great employments, and by great actions abroad, to the honour of the *English* gentry; yet how many more families among the tradesmen have been rais'd to immense estates, even during the same time, by the attending circumstances of the war? such as the cloathing, the paying, the victualling and furnishing, *&c.* both army and navy? And by whom have the prodigious taxes been paid, the loans supplied, and money advanced upon all occasions? By whom are the Banks and Companies carried on? And on whom are the Customs and Excises levied? Has not the trade and tradesmen born the burthen of the war? And do they not still pay four millions a year interest for the publick debts? On whom are the funds levied, and by whom the publick credit supported? Is not trade the inexhausted fund of all funds, and upon which all the rest depend?

As is the trade, so in proportion are the tradesmen; and how wealthy are tradesmen in almost all the several parts of *England*, as well as in *London*? How ordinary is it to see a tradesman go off of the stage, even but from mere shop-keeping, with, from ten to forty thousand pounds estate, to divide among his family? when, on the contrary, take the gentry in *England* from one end to the other, except a few here and there, what with excessive high living, which is of late grown so much into a disease, and the other ordinary circumstances of families, we find few families of the lower gentry, that is to say, from six or seven hundred a year downwards, but they are in debt and in necessitous circumstances, and a great many of greater estates also.

ON the other hand, let any one who is acquainted with *England*, look but abroad into the several counties, especially near *London*, or within fifty miles of it: How are the antient families worn out by time and family misfortunes, and the estates possess'd by a new race of tradesmen, grown up into families of gentry, and establish'd by the immense wealth, gain'd, as I may say, behind the counter; that is, in the shop, the warehouse, and the compting-house? How are the sons of tradesmen rank'd among the prime of the gentry? How are the daughters of tradesmen at this time adorn'd with the ducal coronets, and seen riding in the coaches of the best of our nobility? Nay, many of our trading gentlemen at this time refuse to be Ennobled, scorn being knighted, and content themselves with being known to be rated among the richest Commoners in the nation: And it must be acknowledg'd, that whatever they be as to court-breeding, and to manners, they, generally speaking, come behind none of the gentry in knowledge of the world.

AT this very day we see the son of Sir *Thomas Scawen* match'd into the ducal family of *Bedford*, and the son of Sir *James Bateman* into the princely house of *Marlborough*, both whose ancestors, within the memory of the writers of these sheets, were tradesmen in *London*; the first Sir *William Scawen*'s apprentice, and the later's grandfather a *P*—— upon, or near, *London-Bridge*.

How many noble seats, superior to the palaces of sovereign Princes (in some countries) do we see erected within few miles of this city by tradesmen, or the sons of tradesmen, while the seats and castles of the antient gentry, like their families, look *worn out*, and fallen into *decay*; witness the noble house of Sir *John Eyles*, himself a Merchant, at *Giddy-hall* near *Rumford*; Sir *Gregory Page* on *Black-heath*, the son of a *Brewer*; Sir *Nathanael Mead* near *Weal-green*, his father a *Linen-Draper*, with many others, too long to repeat; and to crown all, the Lord *Castlemain*'s at *Wanstead*, his father Sir *Josiah Child* originally a Tradesman.

IT was a smart, but just repartee of a *London* tradesman, when a gentleman, *who had a good estate too*, rudely reproach'd him in company, and bad him hold his tongue, for he was no Gentleman; *No, Sir*, says he, *but I can buy a Gentleman*, and therefore, I claim a liberty to speak among Gentlemen.

AGAIN, in how superior a port or figure (as we now call it) do our tradesmen live, to what the middling gentry either do or can support? An ordinary tradesman now, not in the city only, but in the country, shall spend more money by the year, than a gentleman of four or five hundred pounds a year can do; and shall encrease and lay up every year too; whereas the gentleman shall at the best stand stock still, just where he began, nay, perhaps decline; and as for the lower gentry, from an hundred pounds a year to three hundred, or thereabouts, *though they are often as proud and high in their appearance as the other*; as to them, I say, a *Shoemaker* in *London* shall keep a better house, spend more money, cloath his family better, and yet grow rich too: It is evident where the difference lies, *an Estate's a pond*, but *a Trade's a spring*; The first, if it keeps full, and the water wholesom, by the ordinary supplies and dreins from the neighbouring grounds, 'tis well, and 'tis all that is expected; but the other is an inexhausted current, which not only fills the pond, and keeps it full, but is continually running over, and fills all the lower ponds and places about it.

THIS being the case in *England*, and our trade being so vastly great, it is no wonder that the tradesmen in *England* fill the lists of our nobility and gentry; no wonder that the gentlemen of the best families marry tradesmen's daughters, and put their younger sons apprentices to tradesmen; and how often do these younger sons come to buy the elder sons estates, and restore the family, when the elder, and head of the house, proving rakish and extravagant, has wasted his patrimony, and is obliged to make out the blessing of *Israel*'s family, where the younger son bought the birth-right, and the elder was doom'd to serve him?

TRADE is so far *here* from being inconsistent with a Gentleman, that *in short* trade in *England* makes Gentlemen, and has peopled this nation with Gentlemen; for after a generation or two the tradesmen's children, or at least their grand-children, come to be as good Gentlemen, Statesmen, Parliament-men, Privy-Counsellors, Judges, Bishops, and Noblemen, as those of the highest birth and the most antient families; and nothing too high for them: Thus the late Earl of *Haversham* was originally a Merchant, the late Secretary *Craggs* was the son of a *Barber*; the present Lord *Castlemain*'s father was a Tradesman; the great grandfather of the present Duke of *Bedford* the same, and so of several others: Nor do we find any defect either in the genius or capacities of the posterity of tradesmen, arising from any remains of mechanick blood, which 'tis pretended should influence them; but all the gallantry of spirit, greatness of soul, and all the generous principles, that can be found in any of the antient families, whose blood is the most untainted, as they call it, with the low mixtures of a mechanick race, are found in these; and, as is said before, they generally go beyond them in knowledge of the world, which is the best education.

WE see the tradesmen of *England*, as they grow wealthy, coming every day to the Herald's office, to search for the Coats of Arms of their ancestors, in order to paint them upon their coaches, and engrave them upon their plate, embroider them upon their furniture, or carve them upon the pediments of their new houses; and how often do we see them trace the registers of their families up to the prime nobility, or the most antient gentry of the kingdom?

IN this search we find them often qualified to raise new families, if they do not descend from old; as was said of a certain tradesman of *London*, that if he could not find the antient race of Gentlemen, from which he came, he would begin a new race, who should be as good Gentlemen as any that went before them: They tell us a story of the old Lord *Craven*, who was afterwards created Earl of *Craven* by King *Charles* II. that being upbraided with his being of an upstart nobility, by the famous *Aubery*, Earl of *Oxford*, who was himself of the very antient family of the *Veres*, Earls of *Oxford*, the Lord *Craven* told him, he (*Craven*) would Cap pedigrees with him

(*Oxford*) for a wager; the Earl of *Oxford* laugh'd at the challenge, and began, reckoning up his famous ancestors, who had been Earls of *Oxford* for an hundred years past, and Knights for some hundreds of years more; but when my Lord *Craven* began, he read over his family thus; I am *William* Lord *Craven*, my father was *Lord* Mayor of *London*, and my grandfather was *the Lord knows who*; wherefore I think my pedigree as good as yours, my Lord, (meaning the Earl of *Oxford*:) The story was merry enough, but is to my purpose exactly; for let the grandfather be who he would, his father Sir *William Craven*, who was Lord-Mayor of *London*, was a Wholesale-*Grocer*, and rais'd the family by trade, and yet no body doubts but that the family of *Craven* is at this day, as truly noble in all the beauties which adorn noble birth and blood, as can be desir'd of any family, however antient, or antiently noble.

144. Pehr Kalm on English habits, 1748

(*Kalm's Account of his visit to England*, trans. Joseph Lucas (1892), pp. 7–8, 12–16, 326–328.)

Pehr Kalm (1716–1779), Swedish naturalist and Professor of Œconomie at Abo, visited England, on his way to America, from February till August 1748. He visited only London and its neighbourhood. The greater part of his notes are concerned with natural history.

[London. February 1748.]

Thermometrical observations were made yesterday. The room which the people lived in had a fire in it the whole day from morning till night, although most of the heat went away through the chimney, because in London they neither use a *spjäll*, nor know what a *spjäll* is, for which reason also there is no name for it in the whole of the English language. The thermometer was first set by the side of the window, when it always stood at 10° Cels. [50° Fahr.] During my visit to Norway I also made similar observations in the large hall which we lived in, which was only warmed by a little iron stove, and that seldom over twice a day. When it was warm enough in the hall, the thermometer stood at 19° or 20° Cels. [66·2° to 68° Fahr.] but when it fell to 15°, 14°, or 13° Cels. [59°, 57·2°, 55·4° Fahr.] we thought it was tolerably cold and chilly. . . . Today the thermometer hung from morning till evening in the same room in the middle of the wall between the window and the fireplace, when it ranged through the day between 8° and 5° Cels. [46·4° and 41° Fahr.] In the fireplace however nothing but coal was burned. The following day it ranged between 7° and 4° Cels. [44·6° and 39·2° Fahr.] It remained thus all the other days and never went above 10° Cels. [50° Fahr.] . . .

[March 1748.]

English women generally have the character of keeping floors, steps, and such things very clean. They are not particularly pleased if anyone comes in with dirty shoes, and soils their clean floors, but he ought first to rub his shoes and feet very clean, if he would be at peace with them in other things. Hence it is, that outside every door there stands a fixed iron, on which the men scrape the mould, and other dirt off their shoes before they step in. The women leave in the passage their *pattins*, that is, a kind of wooden shoes which stand on a high iron ring. Into these wooden shoes they thrust their ordinary leather, or stuff, shoes (when they go out) and so go by that means quite free from all dirt into the room. In the hall or passage, and afterwards at every door, though there were ever so many one within the other, there lies a mat, or something else, to still more carefully rub the soil off the shoes, so that it is never, in short sufficiently rubbed off.

Breakfast, which here in England was almost everywhere partaken of by those more comfortably off, consisted in drinking Tea, but not as we do in Sweden, when we take a quantity of hot water on an empty stomach, without anything else to it, but the English fashion was somewhat more natural, for they ate at the same time one or more slices of wheat-bread, which they had first toasted at the fire, and when it was very hot, had spread butter on it, and then placed it a little way from the fire, so that the butter might melt well into the bread. In the summer they do not toast the bread, but only spread the butter on it before they eat it. The cold rooms here in England in the winter, and because the butter is then hard from the cold, and does not so easily admit of being spread on the bread, have perhaps given them the idea to thus toast the bread, and then spread the butter on it while it is still hot. Most people pour a little cream or sweet milk into the tea cup, when they are about to drink the tea. The servants in London also commonly get such a breakfast, but in the country they have to content themselves with whatever else they can get.

Dinner did not here consist of one particular kind of food, any more than it does among other peoples: but still the English nation differed somewhat particularly from others in this; that butcher's meat formed with them the greater part of the meal, and the principal dishes. The meat is prepared in various ways; yet generally speaking it is either boiled or roasted. When I say that it was boiled, let no one imagine that it was made into soup, for what we in Sweden call *supan-mat* seems hardly ever to be in use among Englishmen. . . . Thus, it is that in England at dinner-time they hardly ever use spoons for anything but pouring the *sauce* on the "steak"; to take turnips, potatoes, carrots, etc. from the dish and lay them in abundance on their plates. It is indeed true that one sometimes gets a kind of *köttsoppa*, or *broth*, as it is called. . . . No *Ragouts*, *Fricasees*, etc. does one ever see in their houses, but the meat is cooked in large pieces. Roast meat is the Englishman's *delice* and principal dish. It is not however always roasted to the same hardness as with us in Sweden. The English roasts are particularly remarkable for two things. 1. All English meat, whether it is of Ox, Calf, Sheep, or Swine, has a fatness and a delicious taste, either because of the excellent pasture, which consist of such nourishing and sweet-scented kinds of hay as there are in this country, where the cultivation of meadows has been brought to such high perfection, or some way of fattening the cattle known to the butchers alone, or, for some other reason. 2. The Englishmen understand almost better than any other people the art of properly roasting a joint, which also is not to be wondered at; because the art of cooking as practised by most Englishmen does not extend much beyond roast beef and plum pudding. *Pudding* in the same way is much eaten by Englishmen, yet not so often as butcher's meat, for there are many meals without *pudding*. I do not believe that any Englishman, who is his own master, has ever eaten a dinner without meat. *Puddings* are prepared here in manifold ways, with or without raisins; currants, and such like things in it, but they all deserve the credit of being well prepared. *Potatoes* are now very much used together with the roast meat. They are cooked as we cook turnips, and either put on the same dish as the meat or on a special one. A cup of melted butter stands beside it, to pour on to them. When they have *boiled meat*, whole carrots are laid round the sides of the dish. Cucumbers are much used with their roast meat as before described; also several kinds of green vegetables, as lettuce, salad, sprouts, and other cabbage, prepared mostly like lettuce or spinach etc. Turnips are here used in exactly the same way as potatoes. There is also much eaten green peas when they can be had; but otherwise than green, beans and peas are very seldom eaten. *Cider* is also much drunk with roast meat. Their *pies*, which are mostly a kind of *tarts* and *pastry*, are also sometimes seen. Cheese nearly always concludes the meal. Commonly, there is set on the table, whole, a large and strong cheese, and each person cuts what he likes from it. Milk is hardly ever seen at their meals, either dinner or supper, except what is taken in puddings, and in *tea* in the mornings. Butter is seldom placed on the table. Their drinks are various. Those who can afford it mostly drink wine, others ale, cyder, "swag", or small beer, but the favourite drink of all Englishmen is *Punch*. After meal times one generally sits for an hour at the table, or at least as long as till certain toasts have been drunk by all, such as the King's health, the Prince of Wales, the Royal Family, absent friends, etc.

Supper is taken by some Englishmen, but by others, never. It is, however, with those who eat it, a very sparing meal. It seldom consists of more than one dish, which is commonly butchers' meat, for the most part roasted, and a little cheese after it. It often consists only of cold meat, and that which is over from dinner. As Englishmen eat a late breakfast and a late dinner, they do not require such a heavy supper. . . .

[Little Gaddesden. April 1748.]

When English women in the country are going out to pay their compliments to each other, they commonly wear a red cloak. They also wear their *pattens*, under their ordinary shoes when they go out, to prevent the dirt on the roads and streets from soiling their ordinary shoes. All go laced, and use for everyday a sort of *Manteau*, made commonly of brownish *Camlot*. The same head-dress as in London. Here it is not unusual to see a farmer's or another small personage's wife clad on Sundays like a lady of "quality" at other places in the world, and her every-day attire in proportion. 'Paniers' are seldom used in the country. When they go out they always wear straw hats, which they have made themselves from wheat-straw, and are pretty enough. On high days they have on ruffles. One hardly ever sees a woman here trouble herself in the least about outdoor duties, such as *tending* in the arable and meadows, etc. – The duty of the women in this district scarcely consists in anything else but preparing food, which they commonly do very well, though roast beef and *Pudding* forms nearly all an Englishman's eatables.

Besides that, they wash and scour dishes and floors, etc., for about cleanliness they are very careful, and especially in these things, to wash clothes, and to hem one thing and another minutely.

They never take the trouble to bake, because there is a baker in every parish or village, from whom they can always have new bread. Nearly the same can be said about brewing. Weaving and spinning is also in most houses a more than rare thing, because their many *manufacturers* save them from the necessity of such. For the rest, it belongs to the men to tend the cattle, milk the cows, and to perform all the work in the arable fields and meadows, and in the 'lodge' and 'lathe', etc. I confess that I at first rubbed my eyes several times to make them clear, because I could not believe I saw aright, when I first came here, out in the country, and saw the farmers' houses full of young women, while the men, on the contrary, went out both morning and evening to where the cattle were, milk-pail in hand, sat down to milk, and afterwards carried the milk home. I had found, then, that every land has its customs. In short, when one enters a house and has seen the women cooking, washing floors, plates and dishes, darning a stocking or sewing a chemise, washing and starching linen clothes, he has, in fact, seen all their household economy and all that they do the whole of God's long day, year out and year in, when to these are added some *visitors*. Nearly all the evening occupations which our women in Sweden perform are neglected by them, but, instead, here they sit round the fire without attempting in the very least degree what we call household duties. But they can never be deprived of the credit of being very handsome and very lively in society. In pleasant conversation, agreeable *repartie*, polite sallies, in a word, in all that the public calls *politesse* and *savoir vivre*, they are never wanting.

They are lucky in having turned the greater part of the burden of responsible management on to the men, so that it is very true what both Englishmen and others write, that England is a paradise for ladies and women. It is true that common servant-girls have to have somewhat more work in them, but still this also is moderate, and seldom goes beyond what has been reckoned up above. But the mistresses and their daughters are in particular those who enjoy perfect freedom from work.

145. Fanny Burney describes a sea-side holiday, July–September 1773

(*Early Diary of Frances Burney*, *1768–78*, ed. A. R. Ellis, I (1889), pp. 220–221, 223–227, 232, 234–237, 244–245.)

In the summer of 1773 Fanny Burney, then aged twenty-one, paid a visit to Teignmouth, staying with a Mr. and Mrs. Rishton. Mrs. Rishton, formerly Maria Allen, was the daughter of the second Mrs. Burney by her first marriage, and was thus Fanny's stepsister. Her marriage to Mr. Rishton the previous year had been disapproved of by Mrs. Burney. The following extracts are from Fanny's "Tingmouth Journal", written to her sister Susan.

[July 1773.]

Tingmouth is situated the most beautifully of any town I ever saw, or perhaps in England, ever can see. Mr Rishton's house is on the *Den*, which is the *Mall* here. It is a small, neat, thatched and white-washed cottage, neither more nor less. We are not a hundred yards from the sea, in which Mrs Rishton bathes every morning. There is no end to the variety of delightful walks and rides which this sweet spot affords. . . .

Mr Rishton is still more in love with retirement than his wife, if that is possible;

there are but two families he approves keeping up acquaintance with: though I find there is at present a great deal of company at Tingmouth, as this is the *season* for sea-bathing, and as the rural beauties of the place become every year more known, in so much that the price of all provisions, &c., is actually doubled within these three years. The two families honoured with Mr Rishton's preference are those of the Phips and the Hurrels, which latter consists of Mr Hurrel, a clergyman of £1500 per ann. his wife and her sister, Miss Davy, who are daughters of Sir John Davy.

In returning from Mrs Phips we were met by Mr Crispen. It seems he has interested himself very much in my father's musical plan. He is the wrong side of an elderly man, but seems to have good health and spirits. He has spent many years abroad, and is perfect master of French and Italian. He is at Tingmouth for the summer season, but I believe Bath is his usual place of residence.

I was also introduced the same morning to Miss Bowdler, a young woman, who according to Mr Rishton, bears a rather singular character. She is very sensible and clever, and possesses a great share of wit and poignancy, which spares, he says, neither friend nor foe. She reckons herself superior, he also adds, to the opinion of the world and to all common forms and customs, and therefore lives exactly as she pleases, guarding herself from all real evil, but wholly regardless and indifferent of appearances. She is about six and twenty; a rather pretty little figure, but not at all handsome, though her countenance is very spirited and expressive. She has father, mother, and sisters alive; but yet is come to Tingmouth alone; though for the moment indeed, she is with a Miss Lockwood, a rich old maid; but she will very soon be entirely *at liberty*. She and her family are old acquaintances of Mrs Rishton, and of mama; she is therefore frequently here; but Mr Rishton, who gave me most of this account of her, cannot endure even the sight of her, a woman, he says, who despises the customs and manners of the country she lives in, must, consequently, conduct herself with impropriety. For *my* part I own myself of the same sentiment, but, nevertheless, we have not any one of us the most distant shadow of doubt of Miss Bowdler's being equally innocent with those who have more worldly prudence, at the same time, that her conduct appears to me highly improper: for she finds that the company of gentlemen is more entertaining than that of ladies, and therefore, without any scruples or punctilio, indulges her fancy. She is perpetually at Mr Crispen's, notwithstanding a very young man, Mr Green, lives in the same house; not contented with a *call*, she very frequently sups with them; and though she does this in the fair face of day, and speaks of it as openly and commonly as I should of visiting my sister, yet I can by no means approve so great a contempt of public opinion. As to Mr Rishton he almost *detests* her; but his wife is really attached to her, which is an unfortunate circumstance. . . .

I find myself very happy here. I am treated with the most unbounded confidence by Mr Rishton himself as well as by his wife, and I am most comfortable in finding that every thing in the family goes on just the same as if I was away, and that I am no restraint either in their affairs or conversation.

The rest of our family consists of four dogs who are prodigious favourites. Two of them are spaniels, Vigo and Trump; the third is a Newfoundland dog, excellent for diving, who always goes with Mr Rishton to swim or bathe: he is named Tingmouth; the fourth is most particularly for Mrs Rishton, it is called Romeo and is a very faithful old dog, it is a brown Pomeranian. . . .

Mr Hurrel has an exceeding pretty boat of his own here, with which he makes frequent excursions on the river Ting, and sometimes on the sea. His wife called here on Tuesday evening, to invite us to be of their party on Wednesday, when they intended sailing to Torbay, to see a Fleet under Admiral Spry, which was just come from Portsmouth. We very gladly accepted the offer, and set off the next morning about seven o'clock, our company consisting of Mr and Mrs Hurrel, Mr Phips, a boatswain, another sailor, Mr Hurrel's servant, and ourselves.

Mr Hurrel is quite a poet's priest; he is fat as Falstaff, unable to use exercise and eke unwilling; his love of ease is surpassed by nothing, but his love of good living, which equals whatever detraction has hitherto devised for a parson's gluttony. Mrs Hurrel is an obliging, civil, tiresome woman.

Our plan was to see the fleet, and if possible, a man o'war's *inside*, and then to land on one of the safest and pleasantest rocks, to dine, as Mr Hurrel had taken special care of this particular. But when he came near the ships, the sea grew rough, and having no invitation, we were obliged to give up the thought of entering any of them. There were seven men of war in the bay, and we sailed round them. They are most noble vessels. I had reason to think myself very fortunate that I was not sea-sick, though I never before was on the ocean. We *put in* at Brixham, a most excellent fishing-town, but very dirty and disagreeable. We made but a short stay, and set sail again. Brixham is about ten miles from Tingmouth by sea.

The wind was against us, and we were hardly out of the harbour, before we found the sea terribly rough. I own I was not very easy, as our boat, though a large one for the Thames, was very small for the sea; but still I considered myself as the person of the least consequence, whatever our danger. However, it was no sport to me to be danced up and down, and to find the waves higher and rougher every instant, especially when I saw Mr Hurrel who had hitherto guided us, quit the helm to the Boatswain, and exclaim, "We shall run foul of these rocks!"

The waves foamed in little white mountains rising above the green surface of the sea; they dashed against the rocks off the coast of Brixham with monstrous fury; and really to own the truth, I felt no inclination to be boat-wrecked, however pathetic and moving a Tale our adventure might have made. Mrs H. grasped my hand, and looked very much frightened; her agreeable husband repeated several times his most comfortable exclamation of "We shall run foul of the rocks!" There followed a most terrible confusion. I don't remember or understand sea-phrases; but the hurrying, loud, violent manner in which they gave orders to one another, was really frightful. "Is there any danger," cried Mrs Hurrel; "pray, Boatswain, tell me, is there any danger?" "No; I don't think there is Ma'am."

This was the most alarming sound I had heard yet–I don't *think there is*! However, I found we were all in equal danger; for the two sailors assured us their swimming would be totally useless, as the fury of the waves would presently swallow them up. Mrs Hurrel grasped my hand harder than ever. Her husband forgot his cloth, and began to swear, but always adding, "God forgive me!"–At length, after being tosst up and down in a most terrible manner for about a quarter of an hour, the Boatswain said we should not reach Tingmouth before midnight; and just then the waves seemed to redouble their violence, and the boat scooped one fairly over us.

I gave up the ghost; Mrs Hurrel burst into tears, and cried vehemently, "For mercy's sake! Mr Hurrel, pray let us go back to Brixham,–pray do,–we shall all be drowned! Oh! pray don't let me be drowned! Set me down! Set me down!"

"But where are we to *dine*?" cried he.

"Oh! any where, Mr Hurrel, any where, so as we do but get a-shore. I don't mind, I assure-*ee*!"

"Oh! that's pretty talking," answered the priest, "but that won't serve for a meal."

However, I believe he also had no objection to prolong his days; for when the boatswain said that it blew fresher higher up, he immediately ordered, that we should *tack about*; and so we returned to Brixham.

When we landed, I was so very giddy, that I could hardly stand, and was obliged to go into the first house for a glass of water; but I am only amazed that I was not dreadfully sea-sick. . . .

[August.]

We are just going to Tingmouth Races, which, indeed, are to be held in sight of our house. We hope for very good sport,–a great deal of company are arrived on the Den. . . .

The sport began by an Ass Race. There were sixteen of the long eared tribe; some of them really ran extremely well; others were indeed truly ridiculous; but all of them diverting. Next followed a Pig Race. This was certainly cruel, for the poor animal had his tail cut to within the length of an inch, and then that inch was soaped. It was then let loose and made run. It was to be the property of the man who could catch it by the tail; which after many ridiculous attempts was found to be impossible, it was so very slippery. Therefore the candidates concluded this day's sport by running for it themselves. The great *Sweep Stakes* of the asses were half-a-guinea; the second prize a crown, and the third half-a-crown. However, the whole of it was truly laughable.

The next Race day was not till Friday, which day was also destined to a grand Cricket Match. Mr Rishton is a very good player; and there is an excellent ground on the Den. . . . The cricket players dined on the Green, where they had a boothe erected, and a dinner from the Globe, the best Inn here, to which Mrs Rishton added a *hash*, which Mr T. Mills assured her was most excellent, for Mr Hurrel himself eat three times of it! and that, he remarked, indisputably proved its goodness!

The Cricket Match was hardly over before the Tingmouth games began. All that was to be done this second day was Wrestling, a most barbarous diversion, and which I could not look on, and would not have gone to if I had not feared being thought affected. A ring was formed for the combattants by a rope railing, from which we stood to see the sport!! The wrestler was to conquer twice, one opponent immediately after another, to entitle himself to the prize. A strong labouring man came off victorious in the first battles; but while his shins were yet bleeding, he was obliged to attack another. The hat (their gauntlet) was thrown by a servant of Mr Colbourn's. He was reckoned by the judges an admirable wrestler, and he very fairly beat his adversary. . . .

The Tingmouth Games concluded the day after with a Rowing Match between the women of Shaldon, a fishing town on the other side of the Ting, and the fair ones of this place. For all the men are at Newfoundland every summer, and all laborious work is done by the women, who have a strength and hardiness which I have never seen before in our race. . . .

The women rowed with astonishing dexterity and quickness. There were five boats of them. The prizes which they won were, shifts with pink ribbands. Games such as these, Mr Crispen says, ought to make future events be dated as universally from Tingmothiads as former ones were from Olympiads. . . .

Today, for the first time, I bathed. Ever since I went to Torbay I have been tormented with a dreadful cold, till within this day or two, and Mr Rishton very much advised me to sea bathing in order to *harden* me. The women here are so poor, and this place till lately was so obscure and retired, that they wheel the bathing machine into the sea themselves, and have never heard of .[1] I was terribly frightened, and really thought I should never have recovered from the plunge. I had not breath enough to speak for a minute or two, the shock was beyond expression great; but, after I got back to the machine, I presently felt myself in a glow that was delightful–it is the finest feeling in the world, and will induce me to bathe as often as will be safe.

146. Isaac Ware's *Complete Body of Architecture*, 1756

(Isaac Ware, *A Complete Body of Architecture* (1756), pp. 293–295.)

The following extract is a chapter from one of the many eighteenth-century treatises on architecture. At the time of its publication Ware was Clerk of the Board of Works. In the Preface he says his book is intended "to serve as a library on this subject to the gentleman and the builder", and that it is meant to instruct, not amuse.

CHAP. X.

Of proportioning the several parts of a house with judgment.

THE extent of ground being determined, the materials chosen, and the weight of the roof, and thickness of the wall, settled in the builder's mind, he is next to consider the article of proportion.

Here is a space to be covered with building: and the great consideration is its division into parts, for different uses; and their distribution. In this regard is to be had to two things, the convenience of the inhabitant, and the beauty and proportion of the fabrick. Neither of these should be considered independently of the other, because if it be, the other will not fail to be sacrificed to it; and this, which would be very disagreeable, is never absolutely necessary.

If the house be for a person in trade, the first and principal attention must be

[1] Blank in text.

shewn to the article of convenience; but with this the builder should always carry in his mind the idea of beauty, proportion, and a regular distribution of the parts; that, wherever it can be done, he may favour the one, while he is absolutely consulting the service of the other: in the same manner, when the house is for a person of fashion, the beauty and proportional disposition of parts is to be principally considered; yet the great and needful article of convenience must not be disregarded.

In the building where there is to be a shop, it would be absurd to thrust the parlour into the middle of it, in order to give that room an exact proportion; but, on the other hand, a little may be retrenched from some less conspicuous parts of the shop, to enlarge that necessary apartment behind it.

The merchant's house must have warehouse-room, but that need not break in upon every apartment, because there is no necessity for any exact inch of ground in a particular spot for this use; though there must be a certain quantity upon the whole.

The parlour, in a small private house, is a very convenient room; but, as it is not the apartment of most shew, there is no necessity it should reduce the passage to an alley; and in larger houses, inhabited by persons of distinction, there must be anti-chambers, and rooms where people of business may attend the owner's leisure. These must not be ill constructed, because those of some rank may often wait in them; and beside, every thing in a great house should have an air of grandeur: but, on the other hand, the care of rendering these convenient and proper for their use, is not to extend so far as to intrench upon the rooms of state and elegance.

When convenience has been thus far considered in the plan, the next regard is to be shewn to proportion.

This is a thing of more strict concern than the other, and must be managed with the greatest accuracy. The matter of convenience falls under the direction of fancy, but proportion is established upon rule; there is no apology for an unneedful violation of the truth of the science in this article.

The proportion of the several parts of an edifice is of two kinds; for they are to be adapted, in this respect, first to the whole building, and afterwards to one another.

It is strange to see that many of our architects, who have been able to plan out a whole of a good building, have miscarried miserably in the proportion of its parts. It is in this the antient architects are found, by all that remains of them, to have been most particularly excellent: they formed at once an idea of the whole structure they designed, and of all its apartments, and it is evident they throughout kept that general idea always in remembrance. It is hence we see such a perfect harmony in all their works, and from this, as we have shewn in its place, arose those several variations in their larger parts: these, and the least, in all their works, are perfectly suited to one another. It is in this the student who would distinguish himself in architecture should principally follow them in the disposition of a house; we err greatly, and he will scarce set any modern model before himself that is not defective; whereas when he turns his eyes up to the antient, there is not any one in which he will not find perfect truth.

The first kind of proportion is that of the several parts to the whole, and in this reason is a very plain and general guide. We may divide houses under three heads, the large, the midling, and the small; and in each of these classes plain sense will dictate, that the several apartments should be of the same character with the whole; that the rooms in the large house should be large, in the midling they should be midling, and in the small they should also be small.

This is proportioning the parts of a building to the whole; and this rule, which is directed by common reason, is confirmed by all the writers on architecture: for sciences are built upon reason, and experience which supports her determinations.

The dimensions not only of every room, but of every part of a house whatsoever, should be thus laid out in a just proportion to the extent of the ground plan; for it would be absurd to see a great house divided into a multitude of closets, or a little house consisting only of a hall and dining room. . . .

The apartments being thus suited to the house in general, are next to be proportioned to one another: this, one would think, were as rational and plain a precept as the other, yet we see it continually violated. Nothing is so common as to see a house built for the sake of one room; and in that case the rest not being proportioned to that room, it seems not to belong to the house, and there wants that symmetry which is the great beauty in building.

In houses which have been some time built, and which have not an out of proportion room, the common practice is to build one to them: this always hangs from one end, or sticks to one side, of the house, and shews to the most careless eye, that, though fastened to the walls, it does not belong to the building.

The custom of routs has introduced this absurd practice. Our forefathers were pleased with seeing their friends as they chanced to come, and with entertaining them when they were there. The present custom is to see them all at once, and entertain none of them; this brings in the necessity of a *great room*, which is opened only on such occasions, and which loads and generally discredits the rest of the edifice.

This is the reigning taste of the present time in *London*, a taste which tends to the discouragement of all good and regular architecture, but which the builder will be often under a necessity to comply with, for he must follow the fancy of the proprietor, not his own judgment.

This taste for a great room is not confined to *London*; I remember to have seen in *Leicestershire* a house, the proprietor of which was so fond of a large hall, that it was only surrounded with a number of deep flat closets, and shallow galleries. This was the structure of the fabrick both above stairs and below; but in this the architect stood excused, for it was too much for any one to have been guilty of but its owner. In the same manner we see, where an ignorant fancy will not be controuled by the judgment of the architect, many a large edifice spoiled at a great expence, and rendered at once ridiculous and inconvenient.

Whatever the false taste of any particular time may adopt, the builder, though he complies with it from the orders he receives, yet he must never suppose that the caprice, or fashion, can change the nature of right and wrong. He must remember that there is such a thing as truth, though the present mode will not follow its steps; and establish it as a maxim in his own mind, that proportion and regularity are real sources of beauty, and always of convenience.

147. Sir William Chambers's *Dissertation on Oriental Gardening*, 1772

(Sir William Chambers, *A Dissertation on Oriental Gardening* (1772), Preface, pp. iii–x.)

Sir William Chambers (1726–1796) visited China as a young man, and later studied architecture in Italy and France. He was responsible for the laying out of Kew Gardens. The following extract illustrates the change which took place during the eighteenth century from the classical style of gardening to the 'natural' style fashionable in England in the second half of the century.

. . . Is it not singular then, that an Art with which a considerable part of our enjoyments is so universally connected should have no regular professors in our quarter of the world? Upon the continent it is a collateral branch of the architect's employment, who, immersed in the study and avocations of his own profession, finds no leisure for other disquisitions; and, in this island, it is abandoned to kitchen gardeners, well skilled in the culture of sallads, but little acquainted with the principles of Ornamental Gardening. It cannot be expected that men uneducated, and doomed by their condition to waste the vigor of life in hard labour, should ever go far in so refined, so difficult a pursuit.

To this unaccountable want of regular masters may, in a great measure, be ascribed the scarcity of perfect gardens. There are indeed very few in our part of the globe wherein nature has been improved to the best advantage, or art employed with the soundest judgment. The gardens of Italy, France, Germany, Spain, and of all the other countries where the antient style still prevails, are in general mere cities of verdure; the walks are like streets conducted in strait lines, regularly diverging from different large open spaces, resembling public squares; and the hedges with which they are bordered, are raised, in imitation of walls, adorned with pilasters, niches, windows and doors, or cut into colonades, arcades and porticos; all the detached trees are shaped into obelisks, pyramids and vases; and all the recesses in the thickets bear the names and forms of theatres, amphitheatres, temples, banqueting halls, ball rooms, cabinets and saloons. The streets and squares are well manned with statues of marble or lead, ranged in regular lines, like soldiers at a procession; which, to make them more natural, are sometimes painted in proper colours, and finely gilt. The lakes and rivers are confined by quais of hewn stone, and taught to flow in geometrick order; and the cascades glide from the heights by many a succession of marble steps: not a twig is suffered to grow as nature directs; nor is a form admitted but what is scientific, and determinable by line or compass.

In England, where this antient style is held in detestation, and where, in opposition to the rest of Europe, a new manner is universally adopted, in which no appearance of art is tolerated, our gardens differ very little from common fields, so closely is common nature copied in most of them; there is generally so little variety in the objects, such a poverty of imagination in the contrivance, and of art in the arrangement, that these compositions rather appear the offspring of chance than design; and a stranger is often at a loss to know whether he be walking in a meadow, or in a pleasure ground, made and kept at a very considerable expence: he sees nothing to amuse him; nothing to excite his curiosity, or keep up his attention. At his first entrance, he is treated with the sight of a large green field, scattered over with a few straggling trees, and verged with a confused border of little shrubs and flowers; on farther inspection, he finds a little serpentine path, twining in regular esses amongst the shrubs of the border, upon which he is to go round, to look on one side at what he has already seen, the large green field; and on the other side at the boundary, which is never more than a few yards from him, and always obtruding upon his sight. From time to time he perceives a little seat or temple stuck up against the wall: he rejoices at the discovery, sits down, rests his wearied limbs, and then reels on again, cursing the line of beauty; till, spent with fatigue, half roasted by the sun, for there is never any shade, and tired for want of entertainment, he resolves to see no more: vain resolution! there is but one path; he must either drag on to the end, or return by the tedious way he came.

Such is the favourite plan of all our smaller gardens: and our larger works are only a repitition of the small ones: more green fields, more shrubberies, more serpentine walks, and more seats; like the honest batchelor's feast, which consisted in nothing but a multiplication of his own dinner; three legs of mutton and turneps, three roasted geese, and three buttered apple-pies.

It is I think obvious that neither the artful nor the simple style of Gardening here mentioned, is right: the one being too extravagant a deviation from nature; the other too scrupulous an adherence to her. One manner is absurd; the other insipid and vulgar: a judicious mixture of both would certainly be more perfect than either.

But how this union can be effected, is difficult to say. The men of art, and the friends of nature, are equally violent in defence of their favourite system; and, like all other partizans, loth to give up any thing, however unreasonable.

Such a coalition is therefore now not to be expected: whoever should be bold enough to attempt it, would probably incur the censure of both sides, without reforming either; and consequently prejudice himself, without doing service to the Art.

But though it might be impertinent as well as useless to start a new system of one's own, it cannot be improper, nor totally unserviceable, to publish that of others; especially of a people whose skill in Gardening has often been the subject of praise; and whose manner has been set up amongst us as the standard of imitation, without ever having been properly defined. It is a common saying, That from the worst things some good may be extracted; and even if what I have to relate should be inferior to what is already known, yet surely some useful hints may be collected from it.

I may therefore, without danger to myself, and it is hoped without offence to others, offer the following account of the Chinese manner of Gardening; which is collected from my own observations in China, from conversations with their Artists, and remarks transmitted to me at different times by travellers. . . .

I must not enter upon my subject, without apologizing for the liberties here taken with our English Gardens: there are, indeed, several that do not come within the compass of my description; some of which were laid out by their owners, who are as eminently skilled in Gardening, as in many other branches of polite knowledge; the rest owe most of their excellence to nature, and are, upon the whole, very little improved by the interposition of art; which, though it may have heightened some of their beauties, has totally robbed them of many others.

It would be tedious to enumerate all the errors of a false taste: but the havock it has made in our old plantations, must ever be remembered with indignation: the ax has often, in one day, laid waste the growth of several ages; and thousands of venerable plants, whole woods of them, have been swept away, to make room for a little grass, and a few American weeds. Our virtuosi have scarcely left an acre of shade, nor three trees growing in a line, from the Land's-end to the Tweed; and if their humour for devastation continues to rage much longer, there will not be a forest-tree left standing in the whole kingdom.

148. Sir Thomas Robinson's description of Houghton, 1731

(*Hist. MSS. Comm.*, *Carlisle MSS.*, pp. 85–86.)

Sir Thomas Robinson (1700?–1777) of Rokeby, Yorkshire, was M.P. for Morpeth, and later Governor of Barbados. He was Lord Carlisle's son-in-law. Houghton was built for Sir Robert Walpole between 1722 and 1735 by Thomas Ripley, from Colin Campbell's designs. The gardens were laid out by Charles Bridgman, King's Gardener to George I and George II.

Sir Thomas Robinson to Lord Carlisle.

1731, Dec. 9, Albemarle Street. . . .

I was a fortnight in my tour into the eastern parts of England, and was, during that time, a week at Houghton. We were generally between 20 and 30 at two tables, and as much cheerfulness and good nature as I ever saw where the company was so numerous. Young Lady Walpole and Mrs. Hamond (Sir R[obert Walpole's] sister) were the only two ladies. Sir Robert does the honours of his house extremely well, and so as to make it perfectly agreeable to everyone who lives with him. They hunted six days in the week, three times with Lord Walpole's fox-hounds, and thrice with Sir R[obert's] harriers and indeed 'tis a very fine open country for sport.

During the Duke of Lorrain's being there the consumption both from the larder and the cellar was prodigious. They dined in the hall, which was lighted by 130 wax candles, and the saloon with 50; the whole expense in that article being computed at fifteen pounds a night.

The house is less than Mr. Duncomb's,[1] but as they make use of the ground storey, and have cellars under that, I believe it is the best house in the world for its size, capable of the greatest reception for company, and the most convenient state apartments, very noble, especially the hall and saloon. The finishing of the inside is, I think, a pattern for all great houses that may hereafter be built: the vast quantity of mahogoni, all the doors, window-shutters, best staircase, &c., being entirely of that wood; the finest chimnies of statuary and other fine marbles; the ceilings in the modern taste by Italians, painted by Mr. Kent, and finely gilt; the furniture of the richest tapestry, &c.; the pictures hung on Genoa velvet and damask; this one article is the price of a good house, for in one drawing-room there are to the value of three thousand pounds; in short, the whole expense of this place must be a prodigious sum, and, I think, all done in a fine taste. There is only one dining room to be finished which is to be lined with marble, and will be a noble work. The offices are also built of Mr. Cholmley's stone,

[1] Duncombe Park, Helmsley, Yorkshire, built by William Wakefield about 1713.

and are well disposed and suitable to the house. In one wing are the kitchens and all necessary rooms belonging to a table, servants' halls, &c., and over head are several very good lodging rooms; in the other are the brew-house and wash-house, &c., and a very magnificent hall for a chapel, and a large room which looks on the parterre, designed for a gallery, there being the same in the opposite wing for a greenhouse.

The enclosure of the Park contains seven hundred acres, very finely planted, and the ground laid out to the greatest advantage. The gardens are about 40 acres, which are only fenced from the Park by a *fossé*, and I think very prettily disposed. Sir Robert and Bridgeman showed me the large design for the plantations in the country, which is the present undertaking; they are to be plumps and avenues to go quite round the Park pale, and to make straight and oblique lines of a mile or two in length, as the situation of the country admits of. This design will be about 12 miles in circumference, and nature has disposed of the country so as these plantations will have a very noble and fine effect; and at every angle there are to be obelisks, or some other building. In short, the outworks at Houghton will be 200 years hence what those at Castle Howard are now, for he has very little full-grown timber, and not a drop of water for ornament; but take all together, it is a seat so perfectly magnificent and agreeable, that I think nothing but envy itself can find fault because there is no more of the one, and I scarce missed the entire want of the other.

The stables (which are very large and [have] been finished about 13 years ago) are to be pulled down next summer, not only as they are very ill built, but stand in the way of one of the most agreeable prospects you have from the house, and 'tis not yet quite determined whether they should be rebuilt as wings to the Park front of the house, and as part of the whole design, or only a separate building, only for use and not to appear. I own I argued strenuously for the former, but Sir Robert seems almost fixed upon having a plain structure, and to be placed out of the way and not to be seen in your approach to the house. The other wings are thrown quite backwards into the garden, and make very little ornament to this front of the house, which, being without either a portico, three-quarter columns and a pediment, or any other break, appears to me to be too naked and exposed, and rather as an end front to a very large palace, than the principal one of a modern house; and wings to be built here would greatly obviate all objections of this nature. . . .

B. TRANSPORT AND COMMUNICATIONS

149. Daniel Defoe on the turnpike roads, 1724–1726

(Daniel Defoe, *A Tour Thro' the Whole Island of Great Britain*, II (1724–1727), Appendix, pp. 179–180, 194–199.)

Defoe was over optimistic in thinking the turnpike trusts would bring about a universal improvement in English roads. For Arthur Young's description of the Lancashire roads in 1770, see No. 150.

. . . The Reason of my taking Notice of this Badness of the Roads, through all the Midland Counties, is this; that as these are Counties which drive a very great Trade with the City of *London*, and with one another, perhaps the greatest of any Counties in *England*; and that, by consequence, the Carriage is exceeding great, and also that all the Land Carriage of the *Northern* Counties necessarily goes through these Counties, so the Roads had been plow'd so deep, and Materials have been in some Places so difficult to be had for Repair of the Roads, that all the Surveyors Rates have been able to do nothing, nay, the very whole Country has not been able to repair them; that is to say, it was a Burthen too great for the poor Farmers; for in *England* it is the Tenant, not the Landlord, that pays the Surveyors of the Highways.

This necessarily brought the Country to bring these Things before the Parliament; and the Consequence has been, that Turn-pikes or Toll-bars have been set up on the several great Roads of *England*, beginning at *London*, and proceeding thro' almost all those dirty deep Roads, in the Midland Counties especially; at which Turn-pikes all Carriages, Droves of Cattle, and Travellers on Horseback, are oblig'd to pay an easy Toll; that is to say, a Horse a Penny, a Coach three Pence, a Cart four Pence, at some six Pence to eight Pence, a Waggon six Pence, in some a Shilling, and the like; Cattle pay by the Score, or by the Head, in some Places more, in some less; but in no Place is it thought a Burthen that ever I met with, the Benefit of a good Road abundently making amends for that little Charge the Travellers are put to at the Turn-pikes.

Several of these Turn-pikes and Tolls had been set up of late Years, and great Progress had been made in mending the most difficult Ways, and that with such Success as well deserves a Place in this Account: And this is one Reason for taking Notice of it in this Manner; for as the Memory of the *Romans*, which is so justly famous, is preserv'd in nothing more visible to common Observation, than in the Remains of those noble Causeways and Highways, which they made through all Parts of the Kingdom, and which were found so needful, even then, when there was not the five hundredth Part of the Commerce and Carriage that is now: How much more valuable must these new Works be, tho' nothing to compare with those of the *Romans*, for the Firmness and Duration of their Work? . . .

The Benefit of these Turn-pikes appears now to be so great, and the People in all Places begin to be so sensible of it, that it is incredible what Effect it has already had upon Trade in the Countries where it is more compleatly finish'd; even the Carriage of Goods is abated in some Places, *6d. per* hundred Weight, in some Places *12d. per* hundred, which is abundantly more advantage to Commerce, than the Charge paid amounts to, and yet at the same Time the Expence is paid by the Carriers too, who make the Abatement; so that the Benefit in abating the Rate of Carriage is wholly and simply the Tradesmens, not the Carriers.

Yet the Advantage is evident to the Carriers also another Way; for, as was observ'd before, they can bring more Weight with the same Number of Horses, nor are their Horses so hard work'd and fatigued with their Labour as they were before; in which one Particular 'tis acknowledg'd by the Carriers, they perform their Work with more Ease, and the Masters are at less Expence.

The Advantage to all other kinds of Travelling I omit here; such as the Safety and Ease to Gentlemen travelling up to *London* on all Occasions, whether to the Term, or to Parliament, to Court, or on any other necessary Occasion, which is not a small Part of the Benefit of these new Methods.

Also the Riding Post, as well for the ordinary carrying of the Mails, or for the Gentlemen riding Post, when their Occasions require Speed; I say, the Riding Post is made extreamly easy, safe, and pleasant, by this Alteration of the Roads.

I mention so often the Safety of Travelling on this Occasion, because, as I observ'd before, the Commissioners for these Repairs of the Highways have order'd, and do daily order, abundance of Bridges to be repair'd and enlarg'd, and new Ones built, where they find Occasion, which not only serve to carry the Water off, where it otherwise often spreads, and lies as it were, damm'd up upon the Road, and spoils the Way; but where it rises sometimes by sudden Rains to a dangerous Height; for it is to be observ'd, that there is more Hazard, and more Lives lost, in passing, or attempting to pass little Brooks and Streams, which are swell'd by sudden Showers of Rain, and where Passengers expect no Stoppage, than in passing great Rivers, where the Danger is known, and therefore more carefully avoided.

In many of these Places the Commissioners have built large and substantial Bridges for the Benefit of Travelling, *as is said already*, and in other Places have built Sluices to stop, and open'd Channels to carry off the Water, where they used to swell into the Highway: We have two of these Sluices near *London*, in the Road thro' *Tottenham High-Cross* and *Edmonton*, by which the Waters in those Places, which have sometimes been dangerous, are now carry'd off, and the Road clear'd; and as for Bridges, I have been told, that the several Commissioners, in the respective Districts where they are concern'd, have already built above three hundred new Ones, where there were none before, or where the former were small and insufficient to carry the Traveller safe over the Waters; many of these are within a few Miles of *London*, especially, for Example, on the great Road from *London* to *Edgeworth*, from *London* to *Enfield*, from *London* to *St. Albans*, and, as before, from *London* to *Croydon*, where they are very plain to be seen, and to which I refer.

And for farther Confirmation of what I have advanc'd above, namely, that we may expect, according to this good Beginning, that the Roads in most Parts of *England* will in a few Years be fully repair'd, and restor'd to the same good Condition, (or perhaps a better, than) they were in during the *Roman* Government, we may take Notice, that there are no less than twelve Bills, or Petitions for Bills, depending before the Parliament, at this Time sitting, for the Repair of the Roads, in several remote Parts of *England*, or for the lengthening the Time allow'd in former Acts; some of which, besides those hereafter mentioned, give us Hopes, that the Grants, when obtain'd, will be very well manag'd, and the Country People greatly encourag'd by them in their Commerce; for there is no Doubt to be made, but that the Inland Trade of *England* has been greatly obstructed by the exceeding Badness of the Roads.

A particular Example of this, I have mention'd already, *viz.* the bringing of Fat Cattle, especially Sheep to *London* in the Winter, from the remoter Counties of *Leicester* and *Lincoln*, where they are bred; by which the Country Grasiers are oblig'd to sell their Stocks off, at the latter End of the Summer, namely *September* and *October*, when they sell cheap, and the Butchers and Farmers near *London* engross them, and keeping them 'till *December* and *January*, sell them, tho' not an Ounce fatter than before, for an advanc'd Price, to the Citizens of *London*; whereas, were the Roads made good and passable, the City would be serv'd with Mutton almost as cheap in the Winter as in the Summer, or the Profit of the Advance would be to the Graziers of *Leicester* and *Lincolnshires*, who were the original Breeders.

This is evidenc'd to a Demonstration in the Counties of *Essex* and *Suffolk*, from whence they already bring their Fat Cattle, and particularly their Mutton in Droves, from Sixty, Seventy, or Eighty Miles, without fatiguing, harrassing, or sinking the Flesh of the Creatures, even in the Depth of Winter.

I might give Examples of other Branches of Inland Commerce, which would be quite alter'd for the better, by this restoring the Goodness of the Roads, and particularly that of carrying Cheese, a Species of Provision so considerable, that nothing, except that of live Cattle, can exceed it.

This is chiefly made in the three *North West* Counties of *England*, *viz. Cheshire*, *Gloucester*, and *Warwickshires*, and the Parts adjacent, from whence the Nation is very meanly supply'd, by reason of the exceeding Distance of the Country where the Cheese is made, from those Counties where it is chiefly expended.

The *Cheshire* Men indeed carry great Quantities about by long Sea, as they call it, to *London*; a terrible long, and sometimes dangerous, Voyage, being thro' the *Irish Channel*, round all *Wales*, cross the *Bristol Channel*, round the *Land's End* of *Cornwall*, and up the *English Channel* to the Mouth of the *Thames*, and so up to *London*; or else by Land to *Burton upon Trent*, and so down that River to *Gainesborough* and *Hull*, and so by Sea to *London*.

Again, the *Gloucestershire* Men carry all by Land-Carriage to *Lechlade* and *Cricklade* on the *Thames*, and so carry it down the River to *London*.

But the *Warwickshire* Men have no Water-Carriage at all, or at least not 'till they have carry'd it a long Way by Land to *Oxford*; but as their Quantity is exceeding great, and they supply not only the City of *London*, but also the Counties of *Essex*, *Suffolk*, *Norfolk*, *Cambridge*, *Hungingdon*, *Hertford*, *Bedford*, and *Northampton*, the Gross of their Carriage is by meer dead Draught, and they carry it either to *London* by Land, which is full an hundred Miles, and so the *London* Cheesmongers supply the said

Counties of *Essex*, *Suffolk*, and *Norfolk*, besides *Kent*, and *Sussex*, and *Surrey* by Sea and River Navigation: or the *Warwickshire* Men carry it by Land once a Year to *Stourbridge* Fair, whence the Shop-keepers of all the Inland Country above-named, come to buy it; in all which Cases Land-Carriage being long, and the Ways bad, makes it very dear to the Poor, who are the Consumers.

But were the Ways from *Warwickshire* made good, as I have shewn they are already in *Essex*, and some other Places; this Carriage would be perform'd for little more than half the Price that it now is, and the Poor would have their Provisions much cheaper.

I could enlarge here upon the Convenience that would follow such a restoring the Ways, for the carrying of Fish from the Sea Coasts to the Inner Parts of the Kingdom, where, by reason of the Badness of the Ways, they cannot now carry them sweet; This would greatly encrease the Consumption of Fish in its Season, which now for that very Reason, is but small, and would employ an innumerable Number of Horses and Men, as well as encrease the Shipping by that Consumption.

150. Arthur Young on the Lancashire roads, 1770

(Arthur Young, *A Six Months Tour Through the North of England*, IV (1770), pp. 580–585.)

The roads here described are not typical of Young's experiences on this tour. Though he describes others as bad in other parts of the country, he also mentions a number of very good turnpike roads.

. .

To *Lancaster*. [from Windermere.] Turnpike. Very bad, rough and cut up.

To *Preston*. Turnpike. Very bad.

To *Wigan*. Ditto. I know not, in the whole range of language, terms sufficiently expressive to describe this infernal road. To look over a map, and perceive that it is a principal one, not only to some towns, but even whole counties, one would naturally conclude it to be at least decent; but let me most seriously caution all travellers who may accidentally purpose to travel this terrible country, to avoid it as they would the devil; for a thousand to one but they break their necks or their limbs by overthrows or breakings down. They will here meet with rutts which I actually measured four feet deep, and floating with mud only from a wet summer; what therefore must it be after a winter? The only mending it in places receives, is the tumbling in some loose stones, which serve no other purpose but jolting a carriage in the most intolerable manner. These are not merely opinions, but facts, for I actually passed three carts broken down in these eighteen miles of execrable memory.

To *Warrington*. Turnpike. This a paved road, and most infamously bad. Any person would imagine the boobies of the country had made it with a view to immediate destruction; for the breadth is only sufficient for one carriage; consequently it is cut at once into rutts; and you will easily conceive what a break-down dislocating road rutts cut through a pavement must be. The pretence, of wanting materials, is but a mere pretence; for I remarked several quarries of rock, sufficient to make miles of excellent road. If they will pave, the breadth ought to be such as to admit several carriages abreast, or the inevitable consequence must be, the immediate cutting up. Tolls had better be doubled, and even quadrupled, than suffer such a nuisance to remain.

To *Liverpool*. Turnpike. This road is mostly a pavement; the first part of which is such as I have just described; tho' scarcely so bad. But towards *Liverpool* is of a good breadth, and as good as an indifferent pavement can be. It is observable this is a second work; the first narrow one being found as I have described it.

To *Altringham*. Turnpike. If possible this execrable road is worse than that from *Preston*. It is a heavy sand, which cuts into such prodigious rutts, that a carriage moves with great danger. These sands turn to floods of mud in any season the least wet.

To *Manchester*. Turnpike. Part of it the same as the last; the rest a paved causeway, and done in so execrable a manner, that it is cut into continual holes: For it is made so narrow, that only one carriage can move at a time, and that consequently in a line of rutts.

From *Dunholm* to *Knotsford*. Turnpike. It is impossible to describe these infernal roads in terms adequate to their deserts: Part of these six miles I think are worse than any of the preceding.

To *Holmes Chapel*. Turnpike. Much better.

To *Newcastle*. Turnpike. This, in general, is a paved causeway, as narrow as can be conceived, and cut into perpetual holes, some of them two feet deep measured on the level; a more dreadful road cannot be imagined; and wherever the country is the least sandy, the pavement is discontinued, and the rutts and holes most execrable. I was forced to hire two men at one place to support my chaise from overthrowing, in turning out for a cart of goods overthrown and almost buried. Let me persuade all travellers to avoid this terrible country, which must either dislocate their bones with broken pavements, or bury them in muddy sand.

To *Burslem*. Turnpike. Deep muddy rutts in clay.

Here you must let me pause; for these execrable roads continuing no further, I must in general advise all who travel on any business but absolute necessity, to avoid any journey further north than *Newcastle*. All between that place and *Preston* is a country one would suppose devoid of all those improvements and embellishments, which the riches and spirit of modern times have occasioned in other parts: It is a track of country which lays a most heavy tax upon all travellers, and upon itself. Such roads are a much heavier tax than half a crown a horse for a toll would be. Agriculture, manufactures, and commerce must suffer in such a track, as well as the traveller. The rates of carriage and hire of carts must either run enormously high, or the farmers starve by letting their teams. But it is only bad management that can occasion such very miserable roads, in a country so abounding with towns, trade, and manufactures: The tolls of the turnpikes for several paved roads do not rise higher than 3*d. per* horse, for which sum they pave wide enough for one carriage. If this was quadrupled they might certainly do it well for three, and then it would escape being cut up: But if they were five times trebled, it would be infinitely preferable to the present condition. Until better management is produced, I would advise all travellers to consider this country as sea, and as soon think of driving into the ocean as venturing into such detestable roads. I am told the *Derby* way to *Manchester* is good. But further is not penetrable. . . .

151. John Campbell on the canal building in the mid-eighteenth century, 1774

(J. Campbell, *A Political Survey of Britain*, II (1774), pp. 263–270.)[1]

John Campbell (1708–1775) contributed to a number of historical series and books on travel. The duke of Bridgewater's canal, here particularly described, was built by James Brindley, and was opened in 1761.

A NOBLEMAN of the First rank formed a Design of making a Canal from Worsley Bridge to Manchester in the County of Lancaster, for the carrying thither his Coals; which not being barely for his own, but also for the publick Benefit, an Act of Parliament passed in Anno Domini 1759, to enable him to undertake this Work, with all the proper Clauses for securing the Advantages that had been proposed to the Community. After the Canal was actually begun, it was thought practicable to carry it over the River Irwell upon Arches, and so over Trafford Moss to Longford Bridge, which made another Act necessary; and such a Law being obtained, this stupendous Work was carried into effectual Execution. The Value of this Mode of Navigation came from thence to be better understood, and the very extensive Uses to which it might be applied were more clearly comprehended. In consequence of these Discoveries it was determined to carry the Duke of Bridgewater's Canal over the Rivers Mersey and Bolland, and to continue it to that Part of the River Mersey, over-against the Hemp Stones, in the County of Chester, where that River is naturally navigable, and the Passage consequently open to Liverpool. The Powers requisite for the Performance of this made a Third Act necessary, which, upon the Petition of the Inhabitants of the Country through which the proposed Canal was to pass, and who were to be benefited by it, was likewise obtained, the Duke taking upon himself the whole Expence, and this without demanding any Augmentation of Tonage.

THIS unexpected Extension of the Canal, which, from a Thing of private Convenience, was now become a Work of so much publick Utility both to Lancashire and Cheshire, very naturally excited a Spirit of Emulation in the Inhabitants of the adjacent Counties; the trading and manufacturing Part of which especially saw the Importance of this new Water-Carriage, they felt their own Wants, and, after mature Consideration, conceived they might in the same Way be relieved. This, upon due Deliberation, produced an Application to Parliament for the Powers they judged necessary for cutting a navigable Canal from Wildon Bridge in Derbyshire, to run Westward into Staffordshire, and then proceeding North to join the Duke's Canal at Preston Bridge, and to terminate therewith by falling into the Mersey at Runcorn Gap in Cheshire. An Act accordingly passed for this Purpose Anno Domini 1766; and the very same Year, so prevalent was the Desire of promoting these Inland Navigations, that an Act likewise passed for the making another Canal from between Bewdley and Tillon Brook in Worcestershire to Haywood Mill in Staffordshire. By

[1] Numerous notes have been omitted.

these Canals a Conjunction will be effected between the Severn and the Trent, and of both with the Mersey, so that consequently a Communication will be opened between the Ports of Bristol, Liverpool, and Hull.

A Scheme that would have been thought, and perhaps would have been found impracticable in the preceding Century, and which, all its Circumstances considered, must appear astonishing to our Posterity. These prodigious Works, now in a Train of Execution, shew that we ought not to despair of Things of great national Utility, though they may long dwell in the Minds, or only float upon the Tongues of Men. It proves that a single vigorous Attempt will do much more than the most serious or even the most conclusive Arguments. For Facts speak to the Senses and to the Feelings of Mankind, as well as to their Reason. As soon therefore as it appeared, that an easy and commodious Passage could be opened between Manchester and Liverpool, all Diffidence and all Difficulties vanished. Surveys were immediately directed; and, as soon as they were perfected, Subscriptions chearfully followed, the Nobility and Gentry expressing the warmest Zeal in risquing their private Property for the publick Service. But then this Zeal was according to Knowledge; they were clearly convinced of the Utility of the Undertaking; and they saw, without suffering any Uneasiness, that Time, Labour, and Expence, must purchase them those Benefits this new Navigation was to bestow; and therefore what in Days of less Industry, less Commercial Spirit, and, let us add, less Opulence, would have been held insuperable Obstacles, did not at all deter them from pursuing so great and so glorious a Design.

WHAT the actual Advantages, that will be derived from these Canals when finished, may be, Time and Experience only can determine; but upon what reasonable Expectations they have been so steadily as well as strenuously supported, is incumbent upon me to report, in order to justify the Pains taken about them in this Work. It is a vast Tract of Country through which they are to pass, and not barely one or two, but several Counties that are to share the Benefit of them, with this remarkable Circumstance in their Favour, that in no Part of this noble Island could such a Communication be of more Use, the Number considered of large, and many of them manufacturing Towns, in its Vicinity. All Kinds of Provisions, but more especially Grain, will by their means be rendered cheaper, and kept to a more equal Price. For by furnishing Manure from great Distances at a low Rate, and giving a quick Carriage even to remote Markets, the Canal will excite an active Spirit of Cultivation, and the Certainty of obtaining a speedy Supply at a small Expence will render an unreasonable Rise of Corn, where it has been in Times past frequently and fatally experienced, for the future in a great measure impracticable. Many bulky, but at the same time very useful Commodities, such as Flint, Free, Lime, Mill, Grinding, and Paving Stones, Marl, Slate, Coals of different Kinds, Marble, Alabaster, Iron Ore, will find a much easier and cheaper Passage, and of course reach many more and those too better Markets, than they can be carried to, circumstanced as they are at present.

FREQUENT Additions will probably be made to these natural Riches from the Discoveries that must arise from the cutting through a Variety of Soils in the Progress of this great Work, some Instances of which have occurred already. Besides, the Staples of these several Counties may be carried farther, in greater Quantities, and be notwithstanding afforded at lower Rates, such as Timber from different Parts of Lancashire, the Salt and Cheese of Cheshire, Earthen-ware from Staffordshire, numerous Articles from Birmingham, and all the various Manufactures from Manchester and other Places, will be relieved from a Variety of Impediments under which they have hitherto laboured. Raw Materials of every Sort will be conveyed with much more Ease and Expedition to the several Towns where they are wrought up, and, when manufactured, will with like Facility be carried to the Ports from which they are usually shipped, either Coast-ways to different Parts of this, or into other Countries. Thus Agriculture, Manufactures, domestic Trade, foreign Commerce, and every Species of Industry subservient to all these, will be evidently and in a high Degree promoted by this Inland Navigation, to say nothing of the Numbers who will live and be comfortably subsisted by it. It must however be acknowledged, that some Objections have been made against, and some Suspicions suggested, as to Inconveniencies with which it may be attended. It is but Justice to observe, that these are in their Nature far more incertain, and at the same time of much less Consequence, than the Benefits that have been before stated, nor would it be at all impossible to find Remedies for them even if they should happen.

. . . The Dexterity shewn in adapting Machines to a Variety of Intentions, which have been introduced in many new Undertakings, that might otherwise have proved impracticable, does great Honour as well to this Country, as to the present Age.

IN nothing hath this been more conspicuous, than in the last-mentioned of our Improvements, that is, the navigable Canals, which have been chiefly conducted by one original Genius, so fertile in Resources, that hitherto no Obstacles, however formidable, have put a Stop to his Designs. He was prepared for his Operations above, by his Knowledge in conducting those under Ground, in the Coal Mines at Worsley, so that the Difficulties which occurred in the Progress of the Canal, though they appeared new, or rather were so in the Sight of others, were not beheld in the same Light by him; for his Acquaintance with the Mechanic Powers, and what Experience had taught him of their Effects, produced a Confidence which was held for Temerity till the Event shewed it was well founded. But his Works being publickly carried on, their Principles were quickly understood, his Resources became known, and he readily contributing both his Advice and his Assistance, we see them extended under his Direction with equal Spirit and Success. There is little Doubt to be made, that whenever these great Works shall be completed, and their Consequences evidently displayed, they will be imitated in many Places.

C. HUMANITARIANISM

152. Hospitals and other charities in London, *c.* 1724

(Daniel Defoe, *A Tour Thro' the Whole Island of Great Britain*, II (1724–1727), Letter II, pp. 178–182, 185, 186–187, 188–189.)

By 'Hospitals' Defoe means charitable institutions, not necessarily for the care of the sick.

The Hospitals in and about the City of *London*, deserve a little further Observation, especially those more remarkable for their Magnitude, as,

I. *Bethlem*, or *Bedlam*: This and *Bridewell*, indeed, go together, for though they are Two several Houses, yet they are Incorporated together, and have the same Governors; also the President, Treasurer, Clerk, Physician and Apothecary are the same; but the Stewards and the Revenue are different, and so are the Benefactions; but to both very great.

The Orders for the Government of the Hospital of *Bethlem* are exceeding Good, and a remarkable Instance of the good Disposition of the Gentlemen concerned in it, especially those that follow;

1. That no Person, except the proper Officers who tend them, be allowed to see the Lunaticks of a *Sunday*.

2. That no Person be allowed to give the Lunaticks strong Drink, Wine, Tobacco or Spirits, or to sell any such thing in the Hospital.

3. That no Servant of the House shall take any Money given to any of the Lunaticks to their own Use; but that it shall be carefully kept for them till they are recovered, or laid out for them in such things as the Committee approves.

4. That no Officer or Servant shall beat or abuse, or offer any Force to any Lunatick; but on absolute Necessity. The rest of the Orders are for the good Government of the House.

This Hospital was formerly in the Street now called *Old Bedlam*, and was very Ancient and Ruinous: The New Building was Erected at the Charge of the City in 1676, and is the most beautiful Structure for such a Use that is in the World, and was finished from its Foundation in Fifteen Months; it was said to be taken ill at the Court of *France*, that it was built after the Fashion of one of the King of *France's* Palaces.

The Number of People who are generally under Cure in this Hospital, is from 130 to 150 at a Time.

There are great Additions now making to this Hospital, particularly for the Relief and Subsistence of Incurables, of which no full Account can be given, because they are not yet finished, or the full Revenue ascertained: The first Benefactor and Author of this Design itself, was Sir *William Withers* late Alderman, and who had been Lord Mayor, who left 500*l*. to begin it with.

II. The hospital of *Bridewell*, as it is an Hospital, so it is also a House of Correction. The House was formerly the King's City Palace; but granted to the City to be in the Nature of what is now called a Workhouse, and has been so employed, ever since the Year 1555.

As Idle Persons, Vagrants, &c. are committed to this House for Correction, so there are every Year, several poor Lads brought up to Handicraft Trades, as Apprentices, and of these the Care is in the Governors, who maintain them out of the standing Revenues of the House. . . .

The other City Hospitals, are the *Blue-coat* Hospital for poor Freemens Orphan Children, and the Two Hospitals for Sick and Maimed People, as St. *Bartholomew's* and St. *Thomas's*: These Three are so well known by all People that have seen the City of *London*, and so universally mention'd by all who have written of it, that little can be needful to add; however I shall say something as an Abridgement.

III. *Christ's* Hospital was originally constituted by King *Edward* VI. who has the Honour of being the Founder of it, as also of *Bridewell*; but the original Design was, and is owing to the Lord Mayor and Aldermen of *London*, and the Christian Endeavours of that Glorious Martyr, Dr. *Ridley* then Bishop of *London*, who never ceased moving his Charitable Master, the King, till he brought him to join in the Foundation. The Design is for entertaining, educating, nourishing and bringing up the poor Children of the Citizens, such as, their Parents being dead, or Fathers, at least, have no way to be supported, but are reduced to Poverty.

Of these, the Hospital is now so far increased in Substance, by the Benefactions of worthy Gentlemen Contributors, they now maintain near a Thousand, who have Food, Cloathing and Instruction, useful and sufficient Learning, and exceeding good Discipline; and at the proper Times they are put out to Trades, suitable to their several Genius's and Capacities, and near Five thousand Pounds a Year are expended on this Charity.

IV. St. *Bartholomew's* Hospital adjoyns to *Christ* Church, and St. *Thomas's* is in *Southwark*, both which, however, being the same in kind, their Description may come under one Head, tho' they are, indeed, Two Foundations, and differently Incorporated: The first Founder is esteem'd to be King *Henry* VIII. whose Statue in Stone and very well done, is, for that very Reason, lately erected in the new Front, over the Entrance to the *Cloyster* in *West-Smithfield*: The King gave 500 Marks a Year, towards the Support of the House, which was then founded for an Hundred poor Sick, and the City was obliged to add 500 Marks a Year more to it.

From this small Beginning, this Hospital rose to the Greatness we now see it arrived at, of which take the following Account for one Year, *viz.* 1718;

Cur'd and discharg'd, of Sick, Maimed and Wounded from all Parts	3088
Buried at the Expence of the House	198
Remaining under Cure	513

V. St. *Thomas's* Hospital in *Southwark*, has a different Foundation, but to the same Purpose; it is under the same Government, *viz.* the Lord Mayor, Aldermen and Commonalty of the City of *London*, and had a Revenue of about 2000*l.* *per Annum*, about 100 Years ago.

This Hospital has received greater Benefactions than St. *Bartholomew's*; but then 'tis also said to have suffered greater Losses, especially by several great Fires in

Southwark and elsewhere, as by the Necessity of expensive Buildings, which, notwithstanding the charitable Gifts of divers great Benefactors, has cost the Hospital great Sums. The State of this Hospital is so advanced at this Time, that in the same Year as above, *viz.* 1718. the State of the House was as follows:

Cur'd and discharged of Sick, Wounded and Maimed from all Parts,	3608
Buried at the Expence of the House	216
Remaining under Cure	566

Adjoining to this of St. *Thomas's*, is lately laid a noble Foundation of a new Hospital, by the charitable Gift and single Endowment of one Person, and, perhaps, the greatest of its kind, next to that of *Sutton's* Hospital, that ever was founded in this Nation by one Person, whether private or publick, not excepting the Kings themselves.

This will, I suppose, be called *Guy's* Hospital, being to be Built and Endowed at the sole Charge of one Mr. *Thomas Guy*, formerly a Bookseller in *Lombard-street*, who lived to see the said Hospital not only designed, the Ground purchased and cleared, but the Building begun, and a considerable Progress made in it, and died while these Sheets were in the Press.[1]. . .

Next to these Hospitals, whose Foundations are so great and magnificent, is the Work-house, or City Work-house, properly so called, which being a late Foundation, and founded upon meer Charity, without any settled Endowment, is the more remarkable, for here are a very great Number of poor Children taken in, and supported and maintained, fed, cloath'd, taught, and put out to Trades, and that at an exceeding Expence, and all this without one Penny Revenue. . . .

There are Three considerable Charities given by private Persons in the City of *Westminster*, *viz.*

1. The *Gray-coat* Hospital, Founded by a generous Subscription or Contribution; but chiefly by the Charity of one – *Sands*, Esq; It maintains 70 Boys and 40 Girls, cloathed, fed, and taught, and in some measure provided for, by being put out into Trades.
2. The *Green-coat* Hospital, in the same Fields, founded by King *Charles* I. for poor Fatherless Children of St. *Margaret's* Parish; and next to this Hospital is the House of Correction, or the *Westminster Bridewell*.
3. The *Emanuel* Hospital, Founded by the Lady *Ann Dacres*, for Ten poor Men, and Ten poor Women, in the Forty-third Year of Queen *Elizabeth*. Near this are Seven several Setts of Alms-houses; but not of any Magnitude to be called Hospitals.

There has been, also, a very noble Hospital erected by Contribution of the *French* Refugees, for the Maintenance of their Poor: It stands near the *Pest-house*, in the Footway to *Islington* in the Parish of *Cripplegate*, and Two Ranges of new Alms-houses in *Kingsland* Road beyond *Shoreditch* Church.

The Hospital call'd the *Charter House*, or *Sutton's* Hospital, is not by this supposed to be forgot, or the Honour of it lessen'd. . . . The Revenue of Mr. *Sutton's* Hospital being, besides the Purchase of the Place, and the Building of the House, and other Expences. little less than 6000*l.* *per Annum* Revenue.

[1] Guy died in 1724.

The Royal Hospitals of *Greenwich* and *Chelsea*, are also not mentioned in this Account, as not being within the Reach of the most extended Bounds of the City of *London*. . . .

These, added to the innumerable Number of Alms-houses which are to be seen in almost every Part of the City, make it certain, that there is no City in the World can shew the like Number of Charities from private Hands, there being, as I am told, not less than Twenty thousand People maintained of Charity, besides the Charities of Schooling for Children, and besides the Collections yearly at the Annual Feasts of several Kinds, where Money is given for putting out Children Apprentices, &c. so that the *Papists* have no Reason to boast, that there were greater Benefactions and Acts of Charity to the Poor given in their Times, than in our Protestant Times; and this is indeed, one of the principal Reasons for my making mention of it in this Place; for let any particular Age be singled out, and let the Charities of this Age, that is to say, for about Fifteen or Twenty Years past, and the Sums of Money bestowed by Protestants in this Nation on meer Acts of Charity to the Poor, not reckoning Gifts to the Church, be cast up, it will appear they are greater by far, than would be found in *England* in any the like Number of Years, take the Time when we will.

153. The Gin Act, 1751

(*Statutes at Large*, XX, pp. 234–250. 24 Geo. II, c. 40.)

This important piece of social legislation was the first Act to deal effectively with the evil of excessive spirit drinking, and is a landmark in the social history of London. It was passed as the result of strong pressure on Parliament, by the College of Physicians, many London magistrates and numerous petitions. Hogarth's *Gin Lane* was part of this campaign. Besides increasing the duties on spirits to make them less cheap, the Act forbade their retail by chandlers' shops, which had been one of the biggest evils.

An act for Granting to his Majesty an additional duty upon spirituous liquors, and upon licences for retailing the same; and for repealing the act of the twentieth year of his present Majesty's reign, intituled, An act for granting a duty to his Majesty to be paid by distillers upon licences to be taken out by them for retailing spirituous liquors; *and for the more effectually restraining the retailing of distilled spirituous liquors; and for allowing a drawback upon the exportation of* British *made spirits;* . . .

WHEREAS *the immoderate drinking of distilled spirituous liquors by persons of the meanest and lowest sort, hath of late years increased, to the great detriment of the health and morals of the common people; and the same hath in great measure been owing to the number of persons who have obtained licences to retail the same, under pretence of being distillers, and of those who have presumed to retail the same without licence, most especially in the cities of* London *and* Westminster, *the borough of* Southwark, *and other places within the weekly bills of mortality, contrary to the good and wholesome laws heretofore made for preventing thereof: and whereas we your Majesty's dutiful and loyal subjects the commons of* Great Britain *in parliament assembled, ever attentive to the preservation and health of your Majesty's subjects, have taken this great evil into our serious consideration, and proposed such laws and provisions as appear to us to be most likely to put a stop to the same; but it may so happen, that in consequence of the necessary regulations for that purpose, there may accrue a failure or deficiency in the respective funds to which the duties charged upon spirituous liquors and distillers' licences, were appropriated and applicable:* now, for the more effectual restraining such abuses, and to the end that such failure or deficiency may be made good, and that the publick faith, so essential to the well-being of this kingdom, may be supported, we do most humbly beseech your Majesty that it may be enacted; and be it enacted by the King's most excellent majesty, by and with the advice and consent of the lords spiritual and temporal and commons, in this present parliament assembled, and by the authority of the same, That from and after the first day of *July*, one thousand seven hundred and fifty one, there shall be raised, levied, collected and paid unto his Majesty, his heirs and successors, for the several kinds of spirituous liquors herein after mentioned, specified and enumerated (over and above all duties, charges and impositions by any former act or acts of parliament thereupon respectively set, rated and imposed) the several rates and duties of excise herein after-mentioned and expressed; that is to say,

For every gallon of low wines, or spirits of the first extraction, made or drawn from any sort of drink or wash, brewed or made from any sort of malt or corn, or from brewers wash or tilts, or any mixture with such brewers wash or tilts, to be paid by the distillers or makers thereof, three halfpence.

For every gallon of strong waters, or *Aqua Vitae*, made for sale of the materials aforesaid, or any of them, to be paid by the distillers or makers thereof, four pence halfpenny.

For every gallon of low wines, or spirits of the first extraction, made or drawn from cyder, or any sort of kind of *British* materials, except those before-mentioned, or any mixture therewith, to be paid by the distillers or makers thereof, one penny three farthings.

For every gallon of spirits made for sale from cyder, or any sort or kind of *British* materials, except those before-mentioned, to be paid by the distillers or makers thereof, three pence halfpenny.

II [Duties to be under the management of the Commissioners of excise, monies arising from the duties to be paid into the exchequer, distinct from other branches of the revenue.]

III and IV [Repeal provision of 20 Geo. II, c. 39 for granting of licences to distillers in London, Westminster and Southwark to retail spirituous liquors, upon payment of £5 for such licence: provided that nothing in the present Act shall be construed as repealing the penalties imposed by the earlier Act.]

V [Instead of this duty of £5, an additional duty of twenty shillings *per annum* shall, from and after 25 March, 1752, be laid on licences for retailing spirituous liquors taken out by keepers of taverns, victualling-houses, inns, coffee-houses or ale-houses under 16 Geo. II, c. 8.]. . . .

VIII And for the further restriction of such licences, and the granting thereof, be it enacted by the authority aforesaid, That no licence for the selling by retail of spirituous liquors shall be granted within the limits of the head office of excise in *London*, but to such as shall occupy a tenement or tenements of the yearly value of ten pounds or upwards, and for which they shall accordingly be rated and pay in the parish rates; nor to any person in any other part of the kingdom, where there are rates to church and poor, but to such as shall be assessed and pay to the church and poor in the several parishes and places in which they shall be respectively licensed; and that no licence shall be of any avail to any person not so qualified, or for any longer time than the person so licensed shall be qualified as aforesaid, but shall be absolutely void.

IX [Penalty on unlicensed retailers for first offence–seizure of all spirituous liquors on his premises at the time and six months after his conviction; for second offence may be sent to the house of correction for not more than three months; third offence shall be deemed to be a felony, punishable by transportation for not more than seven years.] . . .

XIII And be it further enacted by the authority aforesaid, That no licence shall be granted for the retailing of spirituous liquors within any gaol, prison, house of correction, workhouse, or house of entertainment for any parish poor, and that all licences granted or to be granted, contrary to this provision shall be void and of no effect from and after the said first day of *July* one thousand seven hundred and fifty one; and if any gaoler, keeper or officer of any gaol, prison or house of correction, or any governor, master or officer of any workhouse or house for the entertainment of any parish poor, shall sell, use, lend or give away, or knowingly permit or suffer any spirituous liquors or strong waters to be sold, used, lent or given away, in any such gaols, prisons or houses of correction, or brought into the same; other than and except such spirituous liquors or strong waters as shall be prescribed or given by the prescription and direction of a regular physician, surgeon or apothecary, and to be applied in pursuance of such prescription, from the shop of some regular apothecary, every such gaoler, keeper, governor, master or other officer, shall, for every such offence, forfeit and lose the sum of one hundred pounds; one moiety thereof to his Majesty, and the other moiety thereof, with full costs of suit, to such person or persons as will sue for the same, in any of his Majesty's courts of record at *Westminster*, or in the court of *Exchequer* in *Scotland*, by action of debt, bill, plaint or information; wherein no essoin, privilege, protection, wager of law, or more than one imparlance shall be granted or allowed; and in case any such gaoler or other officer, convicted thereof as aforesaid, shall again offend in like manner, and be thereof a second time lawfully convicted, such second offence shall be deemed a forfeiture of his office.

XIV and XV [Justices of the Peace, on information, may enter and search such premises, or empower constables to do so. Any person bringing spirituous liquors into such premises may be taken before a Justice of the Peace and on conviction be fined not more than £20 and not less than £10.]

XVI [Copy of the three preceding clauses, printed or fairly and legibly written, to be kept hung up in one of the most public places in all gaols etc., under penalty of 40/- fine. Justices of the Peace may enter such premises and demand to see such notice.] . . .

XXII And be it further enacted by the authority aforesaid, That from and after the said first day of *July* one thousand seven hundred and fifty-one, no person or persons whatsoever, being a common brewer of ale or beer, or innkeeper, distiller or other seller of or dealer in any kind of spirituous liquors, or who is, or are or shall be interested in any of the said trades or businesses, shall, during such time as he or they shall be such common brewer, innkeeper, distiller or other seller of or dealer in spirituous liquors, or interested in any of the said trades or businesses, be capable or have any power to act, or shall be directly or indirectly concerned in acting as a justice of the peace, in any matter or thing whatsoever, which shall any ways concern the execution of the powers or authorities given or granted by any act or acts of parliament, in any wise relating to distillers or makers of low wines, spirits or strong waters for sale, or to the duty or duties imposed upon low wines, spirits or strong waters, or any other kind of spirituous liquors whatsoever, or to the granting licences to the retailers of spirituous liquors. . . .

XXVIII And it is further enacted by the authority aforesaid, That if any persons, to the number of five or more, shall from and after the said first day of *July* one thousand seven hundred and fifty-one, in a tumultuous and riotous manner assemble themselves to rescue any offenders against this or any other act, relating to spirituous liquors or strong waters, or for licensing the retailers thereof, or to assault, beat or wound any person or persons who shall have given or be about to give any information against, or shall have discovered or given evidence against, or shall seize or bring to justice any person or persons offending against this or any of the said former acts, or forceably to oppose the execution of any of the powers given by this act, that then, all and every person or persons so assembling, their aiders and abettors, being thereof lawfully convicted, shall be, and be adjudged to be guilty of felony; . . .

154. Jonas Hanway on the state of the infant parish poor, 1766

(Jonas Hanway, *An Earnest Appeal for Mercy to the Children of the Poor* (1766), pp. 4–9.)

Jonas Hanway (1712–1786) wrote a number of philanthropical works, but was mainly interested in the improvement of conditions for the infant poor. In 1758 he became a Governor of the Foundling Hospital, started by Thomas Coram in 1745, and set about reforming the bad conditions there which had resulted from the indiscriminate reception of infants. The *Earnest Appeal* was part of his campaign which resulted in the Act of 1766 requiring London parishes to send poor infants under six years of age into the country to be nursed.

SECTION I.

Observations on the State of the Infant Parish Poor.

. . . One may with great truth assert, that many children born of poor *idle* or *unfortunate* parents, tho' they should have the best constitutions, yet die in great numbers under 5 years old; for tho' the humanity of the legislature has been extended to them by a particular act of parliament,[1] requiring a register and authentic account, how officers proceed with them, yet some of these officers regard little more than the *form*, and *this* very imperfectly. Many children instead of being nourished with care, by the fostering hand or breast of a wholesome country nurse, are thrust into the impure air of a workhouse, into the hands of some careless, worthless young female, or decrepid old woman, and inevitably lost for want of such means as the God of nature, *their* father as well as *ours*, has appointed for *their* preservation.

It is hard to say, how many lives these cities have lost, or how many they yet lose annually, by the poverty, filth, and vice of parents, which no public institutions in this land of freedom can save; and tho' we live on as fine a spot as any of the three kingdoms can boast of, yet by being closely built, and many living in confined places, and many too much congregated, joined to the sulphureous air created by so vast a number of coal fires, we must not be surprized, that so great a proportion as 20232 in 43101, or near 47 per cent. die under 2 years of age: this appears by an account now before me of 1756, 1757, and 1758. At these times the Foundling Hospital was open for an indiscriminate reception; consequently the mortality there not being comprehended in the bills of mortality,[2] rendered those bills so much the lighter.

The calamities of human life, and the customs of mankind, keep a pretty equal pace, and accordingly we find, that

There were christened in 1764	16374
Died under 2 years of age	8073
Which is $49\frac{1}{4}$ per cent.	
Remains	8301
Died more between 2 and 5 years old	1875

Which on 16374, is $11\frac{1}{2}$ per cent. and on 8301 is $22\frac{1}{2}$ per cent. Such is the mortality within the bills of mortality; but this is happily no rule to judge of any other part of these kingdoms. . . .

With regard to the *parish infant poor*, it can hardly be expected, that the best regulated parishes will preserve a greater proportion than 47 per cent. which is the general account. But the poor, who are our present object, exhibit a much more melancholy proportion.

Let us do justice where we can, and particularly to *parish officers* who do their duty; and take power out of the hands of those who neglect it, by the utmost exertion of legal authority. Let the subject be ever so poor, humanity and religion do not therefore change their nature; the legislative authority remains the same; and we ought no more to suffer a child to die for want of the *common necessaries* of life, tho' he is born to labor, than one who is the heir to a dukedom. The extinction of those who labor, would be more fatal to the community than if the number of the highest ranks of the people were reduced.

Those who are idle, and not employed in something good, are a *burthen*; and those

[1] In 1761.

[2] The records of baptisms and burials kept by the Company of Parish Clerks. The term Bills of Mortality was also applied to the area covered by these records, *i.e.* the greater London of the seventeenth century.

who are wicked, a *bane* to society, whatever their condition be: and the more irreligious the more ungovernable.–In the meantime it seems as if the richer we grow, be our riches *real* or a great part *imaginary*, the more profligate the poor become; and that where luxury and expence most abound, there the poor soonest lose that simplicity of manner and fear of God, which the rich seem to be but ill inclined to teach, unless *they* are under circumstances of *affliction*.

With regard to the sobriety of the poor, the preservation of life, and the preservation of morals, go hand in hand: their *wickedness* is often the cause of their *mortality*.

Amidst our various follies and iniquities, we still aspire at the characteristic of humane; tho' it is evident, in certain instances, there is not a nation upon earth, which acts more savagely than ourselves; Those who can bellow out for liberty and property, and raise a tumult in a *good* cause, or a *bad* one, will be *heard*; but what can the infant do? the child not arrived to his reason, who hath no parent, or none but such as are very poor, friendless or wicked; if the arm of humanity is not extended for the support of such in their infant state, they must find a cruel grave, almost as soon as they have seen the light.

As far as I can trace out the evil, there has been such devastation within the bills of mortality, for half a century past, that at a moderate computation 1000 or 1200 children have annually perished, under the direction of parish officers. I say under their direction, not that they ordered them to be *killed*; but that they *did not order* such means to be used, as are necessary to keep them *alive*. How will this stand recorded in our annals!

Never shall I forget the evidence given at Guild-Hall, upon occasion of a master of a workhouse of a large parish, who was challenged for forcing a child from the breast of the mother, and sending it to the Foundling Hospital. He alledged this in his defence, "We send all our children to the Foundling Hospital; we have not saved one alive for *fourteen years*. We have no place fit to preserve them in; the air is too confined."

When I witnessed to the appearance of the woman at the hospital, and reported that the child was dead, of which the mother had not been acquainted, she shrieked, and fell down as dead, exhibiting to the court a scene of maternal tenderness, which at once shocked and delighted the spectators.

It is to be observed that the hospital had not then been open much above *two* years of the *fourteen*, and notwithstanding the large sums raised on the poor's rates, no provision was made by parishes for sending a single infant into the country to be nursed.

Of the same nature was another parish, some years before the Foundling Hospital was opened, wherein it appeared, that of 54 children born, and taken into their workhouse, not one out-lived the year in which it was born or taken in. This seemed to be so incredible, that I went to the workhouse to enquire into the fact, and found it true. The workhouse was airy and well situated; but *such was their nursing!*

The opening of the hospital for an indiscriminate reception, afforded a great relief to many such poor infants, but unhappily, as is well known, so many others were brought from the country, which ought not to have been brought, a great havoc of life was made, where there was very little or no mischief done before. Children were brought from places where they died at 13 and 14 in 100, under two years of age, to die at the rate of 60 or 70.

Tho' it may be difficult to extend our policy or humanity to every individual in distress, even within the bills of mortality, yet when we come to a whole parish, and see a parish register, appointed by *legislative* authority, wherein it appears that *parochial* authority hath superseded the *legislative*, by a gross neglect of the spirit of the *law*, insomuch that many infants have died under circumstances, but a small remove from *violence*; if we do not nicely inspect into such a calamity, how can we ask of heaven, that *mercy* of which we stand in so much need ourselves?

This is the light in which I see the subject before us, and I hope that when others examine into it, such measures will be pursued, be it only for *five* or *six* parishes, or an *hundred*, as the exigency of the case shall require, upon the truest principles of policy and humanity.

155. Model Prison Regulations, 1789

(*An Account of the Present State of the Prisons . . . in London and Westminster. Taken from a late Publication of John Howard, Esq. F.R.S. by Permission of the Author* (1789), pp. vii–xiv.)

The following proposals for prison reforms are taken from a pamphlet issued by the Society for enforcement of the Proclamation against vice and immorality in 1789, but they provide a summary of the reforms which Howard's work between 1774 and 1783 had shown to be needed.

I. That agreeably to the act of the 32d of Geo. II cap. 28, Rules be made by the Justices, and confirmed by the Judges, for the direction of the gaolers, and the conduct of the prisoners, and that the same be painted on a board in a legible manner, and hung up in one or more conspicuous parts of every prison.

II. That the act of the 14th of Geo. III cap. 59; and the clauses against drunkenness, in the 20, 21, 22, and 23 sections of the act of the 24th of Geo. III, cap. 54, be in like manner hung up in the prisons.

III. That until the laudable example of the county of Sussex, and some few other places, in abolishing all fees, be generally adopted, a table of fees made by the Justices, and confirmed by the Judges, be also hung up in the prisons; and that no garnish, or any other fee but what is allowed as above, be permitted to be taken of any prisoner.

IV. That every prison be white-washed at least once in every year, and that this be done twice in prisons which are much crowded.

V. That a pump and plentiful supply of water be provided, and that every part of the prison be kept as clean as possible.

VI. That every prison be supplied with a warm and cold bath, or commodious bathing tubs, and that the prisoners be indulged in the use of such baths, with a proper allowance of soap, and the use of towels.

VII. That attention be paid to the sewers, in order to render them as little offensive as possible.

VIII. That no animals of any kind which render a prison dirty, be allowed to be kept in it, either by the gaoler, or any prisoner. The only exception to this rule, should be one dog kept by the gaoler.

IX. That great care be taken, that as perfect a separation as possible be made of the following classes of prisoners, *viz.* That felons be kept entirely separate from debtors; men from women; old offenders from young beginners; and convicts from those who have not been tried.

X. That all prisoners, except debtors, be clothed on their admission with a prison uniform, and that their own clothes be returned them when they are brought to trial, or are dismissed.

XI. That care be taken that the prisoners are properly supplied with food, and their allowance not deficient, either in weight or quality.

XII. That no gaoler, or any person in trust for him, or employed by him, be permitted to sell any wine, beer, or other liquors, or permit or suffer any such to be sold in any prison; or on any pretence whatever, to suffer any tippling or gaming in the prison.

XIII. That a proper salary be given to the gaoler, in lieu of the profits which he formerly derived from the tap, from fees, and other perquisites.

XIV. That those prisoners who are committed to hard labour be not permitted to be idle, and that such other prisoners as are willing to work, be supplied with materials, and be allowed part of the profits of such work, as the act directs.

XV. That a clergyman be appointed, with a proper salary, and that divine service be regularly performed on Sundays and holydays: that on those days no persons be allowed to visit the prisoners; and that such prisoners as will not attend divine service be locked up, and not suffered to disturb others while it is performed.

XVI. That care be taken that no swearing, cursing, or profane conversation be permitted, that the keepers and turnkeys be cautioned against it, and strictly enjoined not to suffer the prisoners to be guilty of it.

XVII. That cells be provided for the refractory, and night-rooms for solitary confinement, but that no prisoner be kept in any dungeon, or room under ground.

XVIII. That a surgeon or apothecary be appointed (with a proper salary) to afford the necessary assistance to the sick, and that two rooms, one for men, and one for women, be set apart as infirmaries, and be furnished with proper bedding.

XIX. That great attention be paid to what concerns the debtors, as it is found that that part of the management of our prisons has hitherto been the most neglected.

XX. That wherever any legacies have been bequeathed, or any charitable donations given for the benefit of prisoners, an account of the same be hung up in the prison; and that care be taken that the sums of money so given, be employed to the purposes for which they were intended by the donors.

XXI. That agreeably to the act of 22 Geo. III. cap. 64, the keeper of every house of correction be obliged to deliver to the Chairman at the Quarter Sessions, a list of the prisoners in his custody, distinguishing their age and sex, and mentioning in what trade or business each person hath been employed, and is best qualified for; as also the behaviour of such person during his or her confinement.

XXII. That the prisons be frequently visited; that the visiters take notice whether the

regulations which have been established are observed or neglected; that a report from the visiters be presented to the Justices at every Sessions, and that these reports be taken into consideration, at least once a year, *viz.* at the Michaelmas Quarter Sessions.
XXIII. That attention be paid to prisoners when they are discharged, and that, if possible, some means be pointed out to them, by which they may be enabled to gain a livelihood in an honest manner.

D. EDUCATION

156. Mrs. Susannah Wesley on the education of young children, 1732

(*Journal of the Rev. John Wesley*, ed. N. Curnock, III (1938), pp. 34–39.)

The following is a letter from Susannah Wesley to her son, John Wesley.

July 24, 1732.

Dear Son,

According to your desire, I have collected the principal rules I observed in educating my family; which I now send you as they occurred to my mind, and you may (if you think they can be of use to any) dispose of them in what order you please.

The children were always put into a regular method of living, in such things as they were capable of, from their birth: as in dressing, undressing, changing their linen, &c. The first quarter commonly passes in sleep. After that they were, if possible, laid into their cradles awake, and rocked to sleep; and so they were kept rocking till it was time for them to awake. This was done to bring them to a regular course of sleeping; which at first was three hours in the morning and three in the afternoon; afterwards two hours, till they needed none at all.

When turned a year old (and some before), they were taught to fear the rod, and to cry softly; by which means they escaped abundance of correction they might otherwise have had, and that most odious noise of the crying of children was rarely heard in the house, but the family usually lived in as much quietness as if there had not been a child among them.

As soon as they were grown pretty strong, they were confined to three meals a day. At dinner their little table and chairs were set by ours, where they could be overlooked; and they were suffered to eat and drink (small beer) as much as they would; but not to call for anything. If they wanted aught they used to whisper to the maid which attended them, who came and spake to me; and as soon as they could handle a knife and fork they were set to our table. They were never suffered to choose their meat, but always made eat such things as were provided for the family.

Mornings they always had spoon-meat; sometimes on nights. But whatever they had, they were never permitted to eat at those meals of more than one thing; and of that sparingly enough. Drinking or eating between meals was never allowed, unless in case of sickness; which seldom happened. Nor were they suffered to go into the kitchen to ask anything of the servants when they were at meat; if it was known they did, they were certainly beat, and the servants severely reprimanded.

At six, as soon as family prayers were over, they had their supper; at seven the maid washed them; and, beginning at the youngest, she undressed and got them all to bed by eight; at which time she left them in their several rooms awake–for there was no such thing allowed of in our house as sitting by a child till it fell asleep.

They were so constantly used to eat and drink what was given them that, when any of them was ill, there was no difficulty in making them take the most unpleasant medicine; for they durst not refuse it, though some of them would presently throw it up. This I mention to show that a person may be taught to take anything, though it be never so much against his stomach.

In order to form the minds of children, the first thing to be done is to conquer their will, and bring them to an obedient temper. To inform the understanding is a work of time, and must with children proceed by slow degrees as they are able to bear it; but the subjecting the will is a thing that must be done at once, and the sooner the better. For, by neglecting timely correction, they will contract a stubbornness and obstinacy which is hardly ever after conquered; and never, without using such severity as would be as painful to me as to the child. In the esteem of the world they pass for kind and indulgent whom I call cruel parents, who permit their children to get habits which they know must be afterwards broken. Nay, some are so stupidly fond as in sport to teach their children to do things which in a while after they have severely beaten them for doing. Whenever a child is corrected, it must be conquered; and this will be no hard matter to do if it be not grown headstrong by too much indulgence. And when the will of a child is totally subdued, and it is brought to revere and stand in awe of the parents, then a great many childish follies and inadvertences may be passed by. Some should be overlooked and taken no notice of, and others mildly reproved; but no wilful transgression ought ever to be forgiven children without chastisement, less or more, as the nature and circumstances of the offence require.

I insist upon conquering the will of children betimes, because this is the only strong and rational foundation of a religious education, without which both precept and example will be ineffectual. But when this is thoroughly done, then a child is capable of being governed by the reason and piety of its parents, till its own understanding comes to maturity, and the principles of religion have taken root in the mind.

I cannot yet dismiss this subject. As self-will is the root of all sin and misery, so whatever cherishes this in children ensures their after-wretchedness and irreligion; whatever checks and mortifies it promotes their future happiness and piety. This is still more evident if we farther consider that religion is nothing else than the doing the will of God, and not our own; that, the one grand impediment to our temporal and eternal happiness being this self-will, no indulgences of it can be trivial, no denial unprofitable. Heaven or hell depends on this alone. So that the parent who studies to subdue it in his child works together with God in the renewing and saving a soul. The parent who indulges it does the devil's work, makes religion impracticable, salvation unattainable; and does all that in him lies to damn his child, soul and body, for ever.

The children of this family were taught, as soon as they could speak, the Lord's Prayer, which they were made to say at rising and bed-time constantly; to which, as they grew bigger, were added a short prayer for their parents, and some collects; a short catechism, and some portions of Scripture, as their memories could bear.

They were very early made to distinguish the Sabbath from other days, before they could well speak or go. They were as soon taught to be still at family prayers, and to ask a blessing immediately after, which they used to do by signs, before they could kneel or speak.

They were quickly made to understand they might have nothing they cried for, and instructed to speak handsomely for what they wanted. They were not suffered to ask even the lowest servant for aught without saying, 'Pray give me such a thing'; and the servant was chid if she ever let them omit that word. Taking God's name in vain, cursing and swearing, profaneness, obscenity, rude, ill-bred names, were never heard among them. Nor were they ever permitted to call each other by their proper names without the addition of Brother or Sister.

None of them were taught to read till five years old, except Kezzy, in whose case I was overruled; and she was more years learning than any of the rest had been months. The way of teaching was this: the day before a child began to learn, the house was set in order, every one's work appointed them, and a charge given that none should come into the room from nine till twelve, or from two till five; which, you know, were our school hours. One day was allowed the child wherein to learn its letters; and each of them did in that time know all its letters, great and small, except Molly and Nancy, who were a day and a half before they knew them perfectly; for which I then thought them very dull; but since I have observed how long many children are learning the horn-book, I have changed my opinion. But the reason why I thought them so then was because the rest learned so readily; and your brother Samuel, who was the first child I ever taught, learned the alphabet in a few hours. He was five years old on the 10th of February; the next day he began to learn; and, as soon as he knew the letters, began at the first chapter of Genesis. He was taught to spell the first verse, then to read it over and over, till he could read it off-hand without any hesitation; so on to the second, &c., till he took ten verses for a lesson, which he quickly did. Easter fell low that year; and by Whitsuntide he could read a chapter very well; for he read continually, and had such a prodigious memory that I cannot remember ever to have told him the same word twice.

What was yet stranger, any word he had learned in his lesson he knew wherever he saw it, either in his Bible or any other book; by which means he learned very soon to read an English author well.

The same method was observed with them all. As soon as they knew the letters, they were put first to spell, and read one line, then a verse; never leaving till perfect in their lesson, were it shorter or longer. So one or other continued reading at school-time, without any intermission; and before we left school each child read what he had learned that morning; and, ere we parted in the afternoon, what they had learned that day.

There was no such thing as loud talking or playing allowed of, but every one was kept close to their business, for the six hours of school: and it is almost incredible what a child may be taught in a quarter of a year, by a vigorous application, if it have but a tolerable capacity and good health. Every one of these, Kezzy excepted, could read better in that time than the most of women can do as long as they live.

Rising out of their places, or going out of the room, was not permitted unless for good cause; and running into the yard, garden, or street, without leave was always esteemed a capital offence.

For some years we went on very well. Never were children in better order.

Never were children better disposed to piety or in more subjection to their parents, till that fatal dispersion of them, after the fire, into several families. In these they were left at full liberty to converse with servants, which before they had always been restrained from; and to run abroad, and play with any children, good or bad. They soon learned to neglect a strict observation of the Sabbath, and got knowledge of several songs and bad things, which before they had no notion of. That civil behaviour which made them admired when at home by all which saw them was, in great measure, lost; and a clownish accent and many rude ways were learned, which were not reformed without some difficulty.

When the house was rebuilt, and the children all brought home, we entered upon a strict reform; and then was begun the custom of singing psalms at beginning and leaving school, morning and evening. Then also that of a general retirement at five o'clock was entered upon, when the oldest took the youngest that could speak, and the second the next, to whom they read the Psalms for the day, and a chapter in the New Testament; as, in the morning, they were directed to read the Psalms and a chapter in the Old; after which they went to their private prayers, before they got their breakfast or came into the family. And, I thank God, this custom is still preserved among us.

There were several by-laws observed among us, which slipped my memory, or else they had been inserted in their proper place; but I mention them here, because I think them useful.

1. It had been observed that cowardice and fear of punishment often led children into lying, till they get a custom of it, which they cannot leave. To prevent this a law was made, That whoever was charged with a fault, of which they were guilty, if they would ingenuously confess it, and promise to amend, should not be beaten. This rule prevented a great deal of lying, and would have done more, if one in the family would have observed it. But he could not be prevailed on, and therefore was often imposed on by false colours and equivocations; which none would have used (except one), had they been kindly dealt with. And some, in spite of all, would always speak truth plainly.

2. That no sinful action, as lying, pilfering, playing at church, or on the Lord's day, disobedience, quarrelling, &c., should ever pass unpunished.

3. That no child should ever be chid or beat twice for the same fault; and that, if they amended, they should never be upbraided with it afterwards.

4. That every signal act of obedience, especially when it crossed upon their own inclinations, should be always commended, and frequently rewarded, according to the merits of the cause.

5. That if ever any child performed an act of obedience, or did anything with an intention to please, though the performance was not well, yet the obedience and intention should be kindly accepted; and the child with sweetness directed how to do better for the future.

6. That propriety be inviolably preserved, and none suffered to invade the property of another in the smallest matter, though it were but of the value of a farthing or a pin; which they might not take from the owner without, much less against, his

consent. This rule can never be too much inculcated on the minds of children; and from the want of parents or governors doing it as they ought proceeds that shameful neglect of justice which we may observe in the world.

7. That promises be strictly observed; and a gift once bestowed, and so the right passed away from the donor, be not resumed, but left to the disposal of him to whom it was given; unless it were conditional, and the condition of the obligation not performed.

8. That no girl be taught to work till she can read very well; and then that she be kept to her work with the same application, and for the same time, that she was held to in reading. This rule also is much to be observed; for the putting children to learn sewing before they can read perfectly is the very reason why so few women can read fit to be heard, and never to be well understood.

157. Education in a dissenting academy, *c.* 1730

(*Memoirs of the Life, Character and Writings of the late Reverend Philip Doddridge* (1766), pp. 87–92.)

Philip Doddridge (1702–1751), a notable dissenting minister, theologian and writer of hymns, founded an academy at Market Harborough in 1729, later moving it to Northampton. The *Memoirs* were written by Job Orton, also a dissenting minister and his assistant at Northampton.

As the Method of Education in the Seminaries of *Protestant Dissenters* is little known, it may be proper to give some general Account of his; which bears a near Resemblance to others of the Kind. He chose to have as many of his Students in his own Family as his House would contain, that they might be more immediately under his Eye and Government. The Orders of this Seminary were such, as suited a Society of *Students*; in a due Medium between the Rigour of School-discipline, and an unlimited Indulgence. As he knew that Diligence in redeeming their Time was necessary to their Attention to Business, and Improvement of their Minds, it was an established Law, that every Student should rise at *Six o'Clock* in the Summer, and *Seven* in the Winter. A *Monitor* was weekly appointed to call them, and they were to appear in the public Room, soon after the fixed Hour. Those who did not appear were subject to a pecuniary Penalty, or, if that did not cure their Sloth, to prepare an additional academical Exercise; and the Monitor's Neglect was a double Fine. Their *Tutor* set them an Example of Diligence, being generally present with them at these early Hours. . . .

One of the first Things he expected from his *Pupils*, was to learn *Rich*'s Short-hand, which he wrote himself, and in which his Lectures were written; that they might transcribe them, make Extracts from the Books they read and consulted, with Ease and Speed, and save themselves many Hours in their future Compositions. Care was taken in the first Year of their Course, that they should retain and improve that Knowledge of *Greek* and *Latin*, which they had acquired at School, and gain such Knowledge of *Hebrew*, if they had not learned it before, that they might be able to read the *Old Testament* in its original Language: A Care very important and necessary! To this End, besides the Course of Lectures in a Morning, *classical Lectures* were read every Evening, generally by his Assistant, but sometimes by himself. If any of his Pupils were deficient in their Knowledge of *Greek*, the Seniors, who were best skilled in it, were appointed to instruct them at other Times. Those of them, who chose it, were also taught *French*. He was more and more convinced, the longer he lived, of the great Importance of a *learned*, as well as a *pious* Education for the Ministry: And finding that some who came under his Care were not competently acquainted with *classical* Knowledge, he formed a Scheme to assist Youths in their Preparations for academical Studies, who discovered a promising Genius and a serious Temper. He met with Encouragement in this Scheme from the Countenance and Contributions of many of his Friends, and had some instructed under his Eye; but as it only commenced about *two* Years before his Death, much Progress could not be made in it.– Systems of *Logic*, *Rhetoric*, *Geography* and *Metaphysics* were read during the first Year of their Course, and they were referred to particular Passages in other Authors upon these Subjects, which illustrated the Points, on which the Lectures had turned. To these were added Lectures on the Principles of *Geometry* and *Algebra*. These Studies taught them to keep their Attention fixed, to distinguish their Ideas with Accuracy and to dispose their Arguments in a clear, concise and convincing Manner.–After these Studies were finished, they were introduced to the Knowledge of *Trigonometry*, *Conic-sections* and *celestial Mechanics**. A System of natural and experimental *Philosophy*, comprehending *Mechanics*, *Statics*, *Hydrostatics*, *Optics*, *Pneumatics*, and *Astronomy*, was read to them; with References to the best Authors on these Subjects. This System was illustrated by a neat and pretty large *philosophical Apparatus*; part of which was the Gift of some of his Friends, and the Remainder purchased by a small Contribution from each of the Students at his Entrance on that Branch of Science. Some other Articles were touched upon, especially *History*, *natural* and *civil*, as the Students proceeded in their Course, in order to enlarge their Understandings and give them venerable Ideas of the Works and Providence of GOD.–A distinct View of the *Anatomy* of the human Body was given them, as it tended to promote their Veneration and Love for the great Architect of this amazing Frame, whose Wonders of providential Influence also are so apparent in its Support, Nourishment and Motion: and all concurred to render them agreeable and useful in Conversation, and to subserve their honourable Appearance in the Ministry.–A large System of *Jewish Antiquities*, which their *Tutor* had drawn up, was read to them in the latter Years of their Course, in order to illustrate numberless Passages in the Scriptures, which cannot be well understood without a Knowledge of them. In this Branch of Science likewise, they were referred to the best Writers upon the Subject. *Lampe's Epitome of ecclesiastical History* was the Ground-work of a Series of Lectures upon that Subject; as was *Buddæi Compendium Historiæ Philosophicæ* of Lectures on the Doctrines of the ancient Philosophers in their various Sects.

But the chief Object of their Attention and Study, during three Years of their Course, was his *System of Divinity*, in the largest Extent of the Word; including what is most material in *Pneumatology* and *Ethics*. . . .

* A Collection of important Propositions, taken chiefly from Sir *Isaac Newton*, and demonstrated, independent on the rest. They relate especially, tho' not only, to *centripetal* and *centrifugal* Forces.

158. Lord Chesterfield on the advantages of foreign travel as education, 1746

(*Letters of Philip Dormer Stanhope, 4th Earl of Chesterfield*, ed. Bonamy Dobrée, III (1932), pp. 773–776.)

This letter gives some idea of the advantages which young men were intended to gain from the Grand Tour.

Lord Chesterfield to his Son.

Bath, 29 *September* O.S. 1746.

Dear Boy,

I received by the last mail your letter of the 23rd N.S. from Heidelberg; and am very well pleased to find that you inform yourself of the particulars of the several places you go through. You do mighty right to see the curiosities in those several places; such as the *Golden Bull* at Frankfort, the tun at Heidelberg, etc. Other travellers see them and talk of them, it is very proper to see them too; but remember, that seeing is the least material object of travelling; hearing and knowing are the essential points. Therefore pray let your inquiries be chiefly directed to the knowledge of the constitution and particular customs of the places where you either reside at, or pass through; whom they belong to, by what right and tenure, and since when; in whom the supreme authority is lodged; and by what Magistrates, and in what manner, the civil and the criminal justice is administered. It is likewise necessary to get as much acquaintance as you can, in order to observe the characters and manners of the people; for, though human nature is in truth the same through the whole human species, yet it is so differently modified and varied, by education, habit, and different customs, that one should, upon a slight and superficial observation, almost think it different.

As I have never been in Switzerland myself, I must desire you to inform me, now and then, of the constitution of that country. As for instance: Do the Thirteen Cantons, jointly and collectively, form one government, where the supreme authority is lodged; or is each Canton sovereign in itself, and under no tie or constitutional obligation of acting in common concert with the other Cantons? Can any one Canton make war or alliances with a foreign Power, without the consent of the other twelve, or at least a majority of them? Can one Canton declare war against another? If every Canton is sovereign and independent in itself, in whom is the supreme power of that Canton lodged? Is it in one man, or in a certain number of men? If in one man, what is he called? If in a number, what are they called; Senate, Council, or what? I do not suppose that you can yet know these things yourself: but a very little inquiry, of those who do, will enable you to answer me these few questions in your next. You see, I am sure, the necessity of knowing these things thoroughly, and, consequently, the necessity of conversing much with the people of the country, who alone can inform you rightly: whereas, most of the English who travel, converse only with each other, and consequently, know no more, when they return to England, than they did when they left it. This proceeds from a *mauvaise honte*, which makes them ashamed of going into company; and frequently too from the want of the necessary language (French) to enable them to bear their part in it. As for the *mauvaise honte*, I hope you are above it. Your figure is like other people's; I suppose you will take care that your dress shall be so too, and to avoid any singularity. What then should you be ashamed of; and why not go into a mixed company, with as much ease, and as little concern, as you would go into your own room? Vice and ignorance are the only things I know which one ought to be ashamed of: keep but clear of them, and you may go anywhere, without fear or concern. I have known some people, who, from feeling the pain and inconveniences of this *mauvaise honte*, have rushed into the other extreme, and turned impudent; as cowards sometimes grow desperate from the excess of danger: but this too is carefully to be avoided; there being nothing more generally shocking than impudence. The medium, between these two extremes, marks out the well-bred man; he feels himself firm and easy in all companies; is modest without being bashful, and steady without being impudent; if he is a stranger, he observes with care, the manners and ways of the people the most esteemed at that place, and conforms to them with complaisance. Instead of finding fault with the customs of that place, and telling the people that the English ones are a thousand times better (as my countrymen are very apt to do), he commends their table, their dress, their houses, and their manners, a little more, it may be, than he really thinks they deserve. But this degree of complaisance is neither criminal nor abject; and is but a small price to pay for the good-will and affection of the people you converse with. As the generality of people are weak enough to be pleased with these little things, those who refuse to please them so cheaply are, in my mind, weaker than they. There is a very pretty little French book, written by L'Abbé de Bellegarde, entitled *L'Art de plaire dans la Conversation*; and, though I confess that it is impossible to reduce the art of pleasing to a system, yet this book is not wholly useless; I dare say you may get it at Geneva, if not at Lausanne, and I would advise you to read it. But this principle I will lay down, That the desire of pleasing is at least half the art of doing it; the rest depends only upon the manner, which attention, observation, and frequenting good company will teach. But if you are lazy, careless, and indifferent whether you please or not, depend upon it you never will please.

This letter is insensibly grown too long; but, as I always flatter myself that my experience may be of some use to your youth and inexperience, I throw out, as it occurs to me, and shall continue to do so, everything that I think may be of the least advantage to you in this important and decisive period of your life. God preserve you!

P.S. I am much better, and shall leave this place soon.

159. Edward Gibbon's account of his studies at Oxford, 1752–1753

(*Memoirs of the Life of Edward Gibbon by Himself*, ed. G. Birkbeck Hill (1900), pp. 47–49, 50–51, 56–58, 59–62, 64.)

A less bitter but very similar account of Cambridge at about the same period was given by the dramatist Richard Cumberland in his *Memoirs*.

A traveller, who visits Oxford or Cambridge, is surprised and edified by the apparent order and tranquillity that prevail in the seats of the English muses. In the most celebrated universities of Holland, Germany, and Italy, the students, who swarm from different countries, are loosely dispersed in private lodgings at the houses of the burghers: they dress according to their fancy and fortune; and in the intemperate quarrels of youth and wine, their *swords*, though less frequently than of old, are sometimes stained with each other's blood. The use of arms is banished from our English universities; the uniform habit of the academics, the square cap, and black gown, is adapted to the civil and even clerical professions; and from the doctor in divinity to the under-graduate, the degrees of learning and age are externally distinguished. Instead of being scattered in a town, the students of Oxford and Cambridge are united in colleges; their maintenance is provided at their own expense, or that of the founders; and the stated hours of the hall and chapel represent the discipline of a regular, and, as it were, a religious community. The eyes of the traveller are attracted by the size or beauty of the public edifices; and the principal colleges appear to be so many palaces, which a liberal nation has erected and endowed for the habitation of science. My own introduction to the university of Oxford forms a new æra in my life; and at the distance of forty years I still remember my first emotions of surprise and satisfaction. In my fifteenth year I felt myself suddenly raised from a boy to a man: the persons, whom I respected as my superiors in age and academical rank, entertained me with every mark of attention and civility; and my vanity was flattered by the velvet cap and silk gown, which distinguish a gentleman commoner from a plebeian student. A decent allowance, more money than a schoolboy had ever seen, was at my own disposal; and I might command, among the tradesmen of Oxford, an indefinite and dangerous latitude of credit. A key was delivered into my hands, which gave me the free use of a numerous and learned library, my apartment consisted of three elegant and well-furnished rooms in the new building, a stately pile, of Magdalen College, and the adjacent walks, had they been frequented by Plato's disciples, might have been compared to the Attic shade on the banks of the Ilissus. Such was the fair prospect of my entrance (April 3, 1752) into the university of Oxford. . . .

. . . To the university of Oxford *I* acknowledge no obligation; and she will as cheerfully renounce me for a son, as I am willing to disclaim her for a mother. I spent fourteen months at Magdalen College; they proved the fourteen months the most idle and unprofitable of my whole life: the reader will pronounce between the school and the scholar; but I cannot affect to believe that Nature had disqualified me for all literary pursuits. The specious and ready excuse of my tender age, imperfect preparation, and hasty departure, may doubtless be alleged; nor do I wish to defraud such excuses of their proper weight. Yet in my sixteenth year I was not devoid of capacity or application; even my childish reading had displayed an early though blind propensity for books; and the shallow flood might have been taught to flow in a deep channel and a clear stream. . . .

. . . Our colleges are supposed to be schools of science as well as of education; nor is it unreasonable to expect that a body of literary men, devoted to a life of celibacy, exempt from the care of their own subsistence, and amply provided with books, should devote their leisure to the prosecution of study, and that some effects of their studies should be manifested to the world. The shelves of their library groan under the weight of the Benedictine folios, of the editions of the fathers, and the collections of the middle ages, which have issued from the single abbey of St. Germain de Prez at Paris. A composition of genius must be the offspring of one mind; but such works of industry as may be divided among many hands, and must be continued during many years, are the peculiar province of a laborious community. If I inquire into the manufactures of the monks of Magdalen, if I extend the inquiry to the other colleges of Oxford and Cambridge, a silent blush, or a scornful frown, will be the only reply. The fellows or monks of my time were decent easy men, who supinely enjoyed the gifts of the founder; their days were filled by a series of uniform employments; the chapel and the hall, the coffee-house and the common room, till they retired, weary and well satisfied, to a long slumber. From the toil of reading, or thinking, or writing, they had absolved their conscience; and the first shoots of learning and ingenuity withered on the ground, without yielding any fruits to the owners or the public. As a gentleman commoner, I was admitted to the society of the fellows, and fondly expected that some questions of literature would be the amusing and instructive topics of their discourse. Their conversation stagnated in a round of college business, Tory politics, personal anecdotes, and private scandal: their dull and deep potations excused the brisk intemperance of youth; and their constitutional toasts were not expressive of the most lively loyalty for the house of Hanover. . . .

. . . The silence of the Oxford professors, which deprives the youth of public instruction, is imperfectly supplied by the tutors, as they are styled, of the several colleges. Instead of confining themselves to a single science, . . . they teach, or promise to teach, either history or mathematics, or ancient literature, or moral philosophy; and as it is possible that they may be defective in all, it is highly probable that of some they will be ignorant. They are paid, indeed, by voluntary contributions; but their appointment depends on the head of the house: their diligence is voluntary, and will consequently be languid, while the pupils themselves, or their parents, are not indulged in the liberty of choice or change. The first tutor into whose hands I was resigned appears to have been one of the best of the tribe: Dr. Waldegrave was a learned and pious man, of mild disposition, strict morals and abstemious life, who seldom mingled in the politics or the jollity of the college. But his knowledge of the world was confined to the university; his learning was of the last, rather than the present age; his temper was indolent; his faculties, which were not of the first rate, had been relaxed by the climate, and he was satisfied, like his fellows, with the slight and superficial discharge of an important trust. As soon as my tutor had sounded the insufficiency of his pupil in school-learning, he proposed that we should read every morning from ten to eleven the comedies of Terence. The sum of my improvement in the university of Oxford is confined to three or four Latin plays; and even the study of an elegant classic, which might have been illustrated by a comparison of ancient and modern theatres, was reduced to a dry and literal interpretation of the author's text. During the first weeks I constantly attended these lessons in my tutor's room; but as they appeared equally devoid of profit and pleasure I was once tempted to try the experiment of a formal apology. The apology was accepted with a smile. I repeated the offence with less ceremony; the excuse was admitted with the same indulgence: the slightest motive of laziness or indisposition, the most trifling avocation at home or abroad, was allowed as a worthy impediment; nor did my tutor appear conscious of my absence or neglect. Had the hour of lecture been constantly filled, a single hour was a small portion of my academic leisure. No plan of study was recommended for my use; no exercises were prescribed for his inspection; and, at the most precious season of youth, whole days and weeks were suffered to elapse without labour or amusement, without advice or account; I should have listened to the voice of reason and of my tutor; his mild behaviour had gained my confidence. I preferred his society to that of the younger students; and in our evening walks to the top of Heddington Hill, we freely conversed on a variety of subjects. Since the days of Pocock and Hyde, Oriental learning has always been the pride of Oxford, and I once expressed an inclination to study Arabic. His prudence discouraged this childish fancy; but he neglected the fair occasion of directing the ardour of a curious mind. During my absence in the summer vacation, Dr. Waldegrave accepted a college living at Washington in Sussex, and on my return I no longer found him at Oxford. . . .

. . . After the departure of Dr. Waldegrave, I was transferred, with his other pupils, to his academical heir, whose literary character did not command the respect of the college. Dr. – well remembered that he had a salary to receive, and only forgot that he had a duty to perform. Instead of guiding the studies, and watching over the behaviour of his disciple, I was never summoned to attend even the ceremony of a lecture; and, excepting one voluntary visit to his rooms, during the eight months of his titular office, the tutor and pupil lived in the same college as strangers to each other. . . .

160. Mrs. Sarah Trimmer on the education of children in charity schools, 1792

(Mrs. Trimmer, *Reflections upon the Education of Children in Charity Schools* (1792), pp. 4–9, 11–12, 29–31, 34–36.)

Sarah Trimmer (1741–1810), daughter of John Joshua Kirby, teacher of perspective to George III, and a friend of Hannah More, published a large number of tracts for the education of the poor and started Sunday schools at Brentford similar to the More sisters' schools in the Mendips.

. . . The important question, Whether it is consistent with sound policy to bestow education upon children in the lowest classes of life, has employed the pens of some of our best writers in the last and present centuries; and we may judge from the wonderful increase of schools supported by charitable contributions, that it is at length generally decided in the affirmative.

The objection against giving learning to the poor, lest it raise them above their situation, is completely obviated by making such learning as general as possible; for then it ceases to give pre-eminence, or to be a distinction, and must eventually qualify all better to fill their respective stations in society: and nothing could be thought of so well calculated to diffuse a moderate and useful share of learning among the lower orders of people, as these schools. To this I may add, that as literature has made such considerable advances in the kingdom, the poor seem to have a just claim to more liberal instruction than was formerly allotted to them. But there still subsist various opinions in respect to the manner in which they ought to be educated, more particularly, whether the mode of *religious instruction* adopted at the first established CHARITY SCHOOLS, in this kingdom, should be continued in them, and extend to the institutions of the present day; or whether charity children in general, but particularly those trained in *Sunday Schools*, and *Day Schools of Industry* should not be taught upon a plan limited chiefly to lessons of morality. . . .

It is much to be lamented, that institutions respectively calculated, by their reflective and united benefits, to complete the long-desired end, of educating all degrees of people in the lower ranks of life suitably to their various stations and callings, should ever be regarded in the light of rivalship and competition. *Charity Schools* hold out such superior advantages, in some respects, as to give them a decided pre-eminence over all the subsisting establishments for gratuitous instruction, as the money collected for them is usually sufficient to afford clothing to the children, as well as learning; and in many Charity Schools the children are entirely maintained in the house, and some of them afterwards apprenticed to trades and manufactures.

But *Sunday Schools* and *Schools of Industry*, though the emoluments of the children are less, are of equal importance with the above institutions, as they afford instruction to unlimited numbers of children, who could not be admitted into *Charity Schools*, on account of the expense attending them; neither could such multitudes be trained up as *Charity Children* are, without great injury to society; for, however desirable it may be to rescue the lower kinds of people from that deplorable state of ignorance in which the greatest part of them were for a long time suffered to remain, it cannot be right to train them *all* in a way which will most probably raise their ideas above the very lowest occupations of life, and disqualify them for those servile offices which must be filled by some of the members of the community, and in which they may be equally happy with the highest, if they will do their duty.

Many ill consequences are observed to arise among the higher orders of people from educating the children of persons whose opulence is the fruit of their own industry, and who have made themselves respectable without the aid of literary acquirements, together with those whose parents are of high rank and independent fortune; but this injudicious practice we cannot expect to see abolished while in the education of youth so much regard is paid to externals, and so little to the regulation of the heart and the improvement of the understanding. It will, however, readily be allowed, that the children of the poor should not be educated in such a manner to set them above the occupations of humble life, or so as to make them uncomfortable among their equals, and ambitious of associating with persons moving in a higher sphere, with whom they cannot possibly vie in expense or appearance without manifest injury to themselves.

But there are degrees of poverty as well as of opulence; and if it be improper to educate the children of the higher classes promiscuously, it surely must be equally so to place all the children of the poor upon the same footing, without any regard to the different circumstances of their parents, or their own genius or capacity. It would be thought very cruel to send the child, or orphan, of a pious clergyman, or a respectable but reduced tradesman, to be brought up among the offspring of thieves and vagabonds in the schools so happily and judiciously founded for those most wretched of all poor children, by the Philanthropic Society; and it would appear very absurd to send a boy designed for husbandry to the Marine Society, to be educated in the art of navigation.

Yet nothing is more common than to mix poor children together in *Charity*

Schools, whose separate claims to the superior advantages which these institutions hold out, are by no means equal, and whose mental abilities will bear no comparison.

It would be justly deemed very illiberal to refuse to lads of bright parts, and uncommon activity of mind, the learning which *Charity Schools* afford, and consign them to the labours of the fields; but is it not equally injurious, both to society and individuals, to condemn those who are invincibly dull and stupid to literary studies, as irksome to them as the most servile occupations are to boys of quick parts and aspiring tempers? . . .

In CHARITY SCHOOLS a comprehensive plan of tuition holds forth advantage proper for the *first degree* among the lower orders, who in these seminaries might be qualified for teachers in schools supported by charity, for apprentices to common trades, and for domestic servants in respectable families.

DAY SCHOOLS OF INDUSTRY, by mixing labour with learning, are particularly eligible for such children as are afterwards to be employed in manufactures, and other inferior offices in life, as well as for training those who are usually called *common servants*.

And SUNDAY SCHOOLS, while they hold out religious instruction suitable to all degrees of poor children, furnish a sufficient portion of learning* for such as cannot be spared on week-days from the labours of the plough, or other occupations by which they contribute to the support of families.

Sunday Schools may also serve (as was before hinted) as probationary schools to try the capacities of children previously to their admission into *Charity Schools*.

Could this distribution of learning be universally made, I am persuaded a very material objection to *Charity Schools* would be effectually done away: for by this means children endowed by nature with good capacities, would be put in the way to improve them; and others, to whom liberal instruction would be no benefit, would be prevented from losing that time over books which they might turn to more advantage by employing it in manual occupations. . . .

I shall now proceed to make some further observations upon the *religious instruction* given in *Charity Schools*.

Notwithstanding the plan is still in force which was originally concerted for the purpose of giving the children educated by charity a comprehensive knowledge of the principles of Christianity, and to exercise them betimes in the practice of piety; it must be acknowledged, that the education of children brought up in *Charity Schools* is in general very defective in these particulars. In order to discover from what cause the imperfection proceeds, it will be proper to inquire what is now the general mode of putting this plan in execution – which I conceive to be this: The children are first taught to read in a Spelling Book, the lessons of which chiefly consist of sentences collected from the scriptures, most of them in figurative language; as soon as they can read and spell a little, they are put into the New Testament, and when they have read this from beginning to end, they proceed to the Old Testament, and go through that in the same manner, without regard to any thing farther than improvement in the *art of reading*. They learn, by stated regular tasks, the columns of spelling in the Spelling

* Excepting in the articles of writing and accounts, a little of which one could wish all the poor might obtain, though the sabbath day is not the proper time for these acquirements.

Book; and in some schools they are taught English grammar, writing and arithmetic. Once or twice a week the scholars are catechised, that is, they stand up in classes and answer in rotation the questions in the Church Catechism, and explanations of it. They learn, perhaps, besides, chapters, prayers, etc. by heart, and are sometimes taught psalmody. They go to church twice every Sunday, and, where there is a weekly duty performed, they attend also on Wednesdays, Fridays and Holidays. When the scholars leave school to go out into the world as servants or apprentices, a Bible, Common Prayer Book, and *Whole Duty of Man* are given to them, and it is supposed, from the years they have been at school, that they must necessarily be furnished with a competent share of Christian knowledge to enable them to read with advantage and improvement as long as they live.

How far the original plan of education answered at the first introduction of Charity Schools, is not easy to determine at this distance of time; but, for several obvious reasons, we may suppose that it was more effectual then than it is now; for it was very natural for those whose zeal for the reformed religion led them to establish and endow these schools, to continue their zeal towards the objects of their benevolence, to give personal attendance, and to examine the children themselves, in order to see whether their design was properly executed. Add to this, that public catechising was much more generally practised in former times than it has been of late years, as a means of preserving the principles of orthodox Christianity from corruption. So that most probably, the children who were first received into Charity Schools had the benefit of more *verbal instruction* than those who now fill their places: of course they were not left, as many of the latter are, to the discretion of teachers ill qualified to explain difficult words and phrases, and illustrate points of doctrine, which frequently require to be placed in a variety of lights to be accommodated to the comprehension of children. . . .

In making these remarks, I do not mean to impute *carelessness* or *neglect* to the teachers; it is very likely they have done their duty to the best of their abilities: their scholars can read, write, and cast accounts, and have learnt every thing usually taught to Charity Children; we must therefore seek another cause to which the deficiencies here pointed out are assignable.–I do not scruple to say that they are in a great measure to be ascribed to the prevailing method of exercising the memories of the children in learning by rote lessons greatly above their capacities, and suffering them to read without reflection, instead of initiating them by such simple instructions as would gradually unfold their understandings, and render their minds capable of receiving lasting impressions concerning things of the utmost importance to their present and future happiness.

The generality of *religious books*, now used in *Charity Schools*, have been written by men of deep erudition. Such authors, accustomed to read the works of the learned, and to compose in elegant language themselves, are apt to conclude that what is familiar to their own cultivated understandings must be universally intelligible; but it is far otherwise–the totally illiterate require previous instruction to prepare their minds for those lessons, which, however good and excellent, are almost as obscure to them as if they were written in a dead language.

It requires personal experience in the employment of teaching children of the lower classes of life, to enable any person to form an accurate judgment in respect to what they are capable of understanding: of this experience I have had a considerable share, having for several years given regular attendance as a visiter in Sunday Schools; I have also had frequent opportunities of examining children brought up in Charity Schools, and am convinced that the latter, in general, do little more than store their memories with *words* and *sentences*, or at best obtain a few crude indistinct notions of the great truths of Christianity, unless they are so fortunate as to have very intelligent teachers to assist them in their studies by *verbal instructions*, suited to their tender capacities; the number of whom is proportionately very small, though sufficient to prove, by comparison, that the books in general use in *Charity Schools* are not fully adequate to the end of conveying to young minds such a thorough knowledge of the principles of religion as children ought to acquire in these schools, considering the time which is apparently devoted to the attainment of it.

Part VIII

THE ARMED FORCES

THE ARMED FORCES[1]

Introduction

IN the eighteenth century the Royal Navy was very much the senior service. While the Army was treated rather as a potential 'fifth column' in the State, the Navy was regarded as the bulwark of English liberties against continental despotism. It was on the ground that the Navy was essential to the safety of the State that impressment was reluctantly accepted by Mr. Justice Foster in 1743,[2] and by Lord Mansfield in the Court of King's Bench in 1776.[3] Unfortunately the strict limitations theoretically imposed on the exercise of this right were seldom observed in practice; nor did the undoubted popularity of the Navy with politicians lead to any improvement in the conditions of service of the ordinary seaman once he had enlisted or been impressed. Under these conditions the sailor's worst enemy was not the hostile fleet, nor even the inevitable fevers which decimated whole squadrons in tropical waters, but the ever-present scourge of scurvy. Interesting experiments in the control of this disease, leading half a century later to its virtual disappearance from the Navy, were carried out by Dr. James Lind during the Austrian Succession War,[4] and later by Captain Cook on his famous voyages of exploration.[5] The foundation of the naval hospital at Haslar also marks an epoch in naval medical history.[6]

Ships of the line were divided into six 'rates' according to size and armament. The Admiralty sought to standardize and improve the design of the various categories of warship and to reduce the cost of building them.[7] Difficulties were sometimes experienced in securing adequate supplies of suitable timber and naval stores at a reasonable price.[8] The Navy suffered from the policy of retrenchment in naval expenditure which successive governments tended to adopt in years of peace, and even more from the system of administration whereby in time of war naval strategy was largely decided by civilians. The lack of confidence often felt by serving officers in their civilian masters, and their fears that when things went wrong they would be made the scapegoats for civilian inefficiency was much increased by the famous court martial and acquittal of Admiral Keppel in 1779, and is reflected in Keppel's criticism of Lord Sandwich's administration of the navy, drawn up in 1782.[9] Sandwich made a spirited defence of his conduct against the attacks of the parliamentary opposition,[10] and his administration was in fact not as black as his enemies painted it.

In retrospect the eighteenth century appears as a great period in our naval history, but contemporaries found the actual achievements of the Royal Navy disappointing. It was suggested that this was due not to any inferiority in the spirit of English seamen but to old-fashioned tactics and fighting instructions, inferior to those of our chief naval rivals, the French.[11] Much the most important technical development during this period was the gradual introduction of an entirely new system of signalling. The

[1] The achievements of the forces in action are illustrated in Part XII, section B. *Wars.*
[2] No. 161. [3] No. 162. [4] No. 163. [5] No. 164. [6] No. 165.
[7] No. 166. [8] No 167. [9] No. 168. [10] No. 169. [11] No. 170.

Fighting Instructions of 1691, which had become stereotyped before 1714, were very inelastic; if the admiral wanted to carry out a manœuvre not foreseen in the instructions he had no means of communicating his wishes to his fleet and was to all intents and purposes dumb. During the American War of Independence, however, Kempenfelt and Howe worked out a new numerary system of signals.[1] The final adoption of this new system after 1783 made possible the naval victories of the Revolutionary and Napoleonic Wars.

Since there was no conscription for the Army, the number of men annually authorized by Parliament was raised chiefly by the promise of a substantial bounty,[2] often combined, no doubt, with sharp practice and in extreme cases kidnapping.[3] In time of war the magistrates were often given statutory powers to enlist idle or disorderly persons, and the royal bounty was often increased by donations from individuals, corporations and patriotic associations. Often these public spirited individuals recouped themselves from the profits of patronage. Commissions in the Army were to a great extent part of the general fund of political patronage available to the government, a state of affairs denounced by the duke of Argyll,[4] and later disliked by George III on grounds of military efficiency. Conditions of service varied a good deal even within England, but those revealed in Humphrey Bland's *Treatise of Military Discipline*[5] are probably typical. This book also gives some indication of tactics. Washington owned a copy of it and, in the opinion of Professor S. Pargellis, General Braddock would not have been defeated in the opening stages of the Seven Years War had he taken the precautions advised by Bland. George II made serious efforts to standardize army uniforms by issuing several Royal Clothing Warrants.[6] Here the Army was definitely in advance of the Navy though naval officers were now beginning to wear uniforms of regulation pattern. Similar to the work of Lind for the health of the Navy is that of John Pringle for the Army. The publication of his *Observations on the Diseases of the Army*, based on his experiences as an army physician in the War of the Austrian Succession, marks a real beginning of scientific study of military hygiene in this country.[7]

Although the Revolution of 1689 had in fact established a standing army as a permanent English institution, contemporaries were extremely reluctant to recognize what was to them an unpalatable fact. It was still feared that any armed forces under royal control, even the Militia, might be dangerous to English liberty, and this feeling is illustrated by the protest of a minority of the peers against the Mutiny Act of 1718.[8] The unpopularity of the Army was further increased by the fact that the troops were usually quartered upon inns, or even, in emergencies such as the Jacobite rebellion of 1745, upon private houses.[9]

The need for home defence when all available regular troops were required abroad led in the early years of the Seven Years War to a radical reorganization of the Militia. Three important Acts were passed for this purpose between 1757 and 1761, the first being usually known as Pitt's Militia Act.[10] Amended in 1760 and consolidated in 1761, it superseded the obsolete Militia Acts of Charles II and remained the basis of the militia organization for a century. Not until 1797, in spite of the protests of Scottish patriots, was a similar force permitted in Scotland.

[1] No. 171. [2] Nos. 172 & 173. [3] No. 174. [4] No. 175. [5] No. 176.
[6] No. 177. [7] No. 178. [8] No. 179. [9] Nos. 180 & 181. [10] No. 182.

BIBLIOGRAPHY

I. THE NAVY

(a) BIBLIOGRAPHICAL REFERENCES

Unlike the Army, the Navy has always had a good Press, and more attention has been paid to its history in the eighteenth century than to that of the land forces. The standard guide both to manuscript and printed sources is G. E. Manwaring, *Bibliography of British Naval History* (London, 1930), which is arranged chronologically. Geoffrey R. A. Callender's short lists of useful books on naval history, published by the Historical Association as pamphlets Nos. 58 and 61 (1924–1925), may also be consulted. Articles on all aspects of naval and maritime history will be found in the *Mariner's Mirror*, published quarterly from 1911 by the Society for Nautical Research.

(b) ORIGINAL SOURCES

Harold W. Hodges and Edward A. Hughes, *Select Naval Documents* (Cambridge, 1922), is a useful compilation which draws heavily upon the publications of the Navy Records Society, which are the main source for primary material in print. They include *Fighting Instructions 1530–1816*, edited by J. S. Corbett (1905); *Letters and Papers of Charles, Lord Barham*, edited by Sir J. K. Laughton (3 vols., 1907–1911); *Naval Ballads and Songs*, edited by C. H. Firth (1908); *Signals and Instructions 1776–1794*, edited by J. S. Corbett (1908); *Papers Relating to the Loss of Minorca*, edited by H. W. Richmond (1913); *The Byng Papers*, edited by W. B. Tunstall (3 vols., 1930–1931, 1933); *The Private Papers of the Earl of Sandwich* [1771–1782], edited by G. R. Barnes and J. H. Owen (4 vols., 1932–1938); *Barrington Papers*, edited by D. Bonner-Smith (2 vols., 1937–1941); and *Pattee Byng's Journal 1718–20*, edited by J. L. Cranmer-Byng (1950). Another volume in this series, *Recollections of J. A. Gardner*, edited by Sir R. V. Hamilton and Sir J. K. Laughton (1906), gives vivid details of naval life at the end of our period, while *Samuel Kelley: an Eighteenth Century Seaman*, edited by C. Garstin (New York, 1925), contains an original diary telling of life in the Merchant Navy and on a troop transport. C. Aspinall-Oglander, *Admiral's Wife* (London, 1940) and *Admiral's Widow* (London, 1943), have some information on naval affairs. *Augustus Hervey's Journal, 1746–59*, edited by David Erskine (London, 1953), contains accounts of Mediterranean campaigns by a strong supporter of Admiral Byng. G. Cornwallis-West, *Life and Letters of Admiral Cornwallis* (London, 1927), prints on pp. 118–127 Cornwallis's apparently contemporary criticism of Rodney's behaviour before and during the famous battle of the Saintes on 12 April 1782. The Naval History Society has published *Letter Books and order Book of George, Lord Rodney*, edited by Dorothy C. Barek (2 vols., New York, 1932). The *Du Cane Manuscripts*, published in the *Historical Manuscripts Commission Reports*, edited by Sir J. K. Laughton (1905), and to a less extent the *Delaval Manuscripts Report XIII app. 6* (1893), contain valuable source material on naval affairs in the first half of the eighteenth century, and especially on naval operations in the war of the Austrian Succession. The *Cornwallis-Wykeham-Martin Manuscripts* (*Report on Manuscripts in Various Collections*, vol. VI (1909)) are equally useful under George III. Sir J. K. Laughton also edited the *Memoirs of Lord Torrington* in the Camden Series for the Royal Historical Society (London, 1889). More recently R. R. Bellamy published, under the title *Ramblin' Jack*, the journal of Captain John Cremer, 1700–1774 (London, 1936).

Finally, reference may be made to a few contemporary naval works. On strategy and tactics the French Jesuit professor of mathematics, Paul Hoste, *L'art des armées navales* (1st edition in French, Lyons, 1697), was widely read throughout the century, and in 1762 was partially translated into English by Christopher O'Bryen. Its influence is marked on theorists such as John Clerk of Eldin as well as on serving officers. R. Walter, *A Voyage Round the World* [1740–1744] by George Anson (London, 1748), at once became a classic. It has been frequently reprinted and there is an abridged Penguin edition by S. W. C. Pack (1947). Two nearly contemporary historical works, R. Beatson, *Naval and Military Memoirs of Great Britain from 1727* (3 vols., London, 1790), and John Charnock, *History of Marine Architecture* (3 vols., London, 1800–1802), have provided later historians with much valuable material on naval affairs.

(*c*) GENERAL WORKS

Sir W. L. Clowes and others, *The Royal Navy* (7 vols., London, 1897–1903), is still the only large-scale general work. Michael Lewis, *The Navy of Britain* (London, 1948), is designed to be "not a short Naval History of Britain, but a short History of the British Navy". Within these self-imposed limitations it studies in orderly sequence the origins, ships, officers and men, management, weapons, tactics and fights of the Royal Navy. The brief, lucid account of the principal naval actions between 1739 and 1783 is particularly valuable. D. Hannay, *Short History of the Royal Navy* [1688–1815], vol. 2 (London, 1909), is still useful. Admiral A. T. Mahan's classic work, *Influence of Sea Power upon History 1660–1783* (first published at Boston, Mass., in 1890), has largely determined the subsequent investigations of naval problems.

(*d*) MONOGRAPHS AND ARTICLES

Admiral Sir H. W. Richmond briefly described "The Expedition to Sicily, 1718" in the *Journal of the Royal United Service Institution*, vol. LV (1911), and his posthumously published lectures on *Statesmen and Sea power* (Oxford, 1946) deal admirably with the basic principles of naval strategy from the Tudors to the present day. His most important work, however, is *The Navy in the War of 1739–48* (3 vols., Cambridge, 1920). The standard treatment of the naval side of the Seven Years War is Sir J. S. Corbett, *England in the Seven Years War* (2 vols., London, 1907). Chapter XVI of this work is elaborated in Marshall Smelser, *The Campaign for the Sugar Islands, 1759* (London, 1955). George A. Ballard discusses "First and Second Anglo-French Conflicts in the Indian Ocean [1740–60]" in the *Mariner's Mirror*, XIII (1927), pp. 14–37. There are also two works by G. S. Graham, "The Naval Defence of North America 1739–63" in the *Transactions of the Royal Historical Society*, Fourth Series, XXX (1948), pp. 95–110, and *The Maritime Struggle for North America* (Oxford, 1951). R. Pares has thrown light on "The Manning of the Navy in the West Indies 1702–63" in *ibid.*, XX (1937), pp. 31–60 and has also discussed the strategic problems of "American versus Continental Warfare, 1739–63" in the *English Historical Review*, LI (1936), pp. 429–465. Similar problems are examined by C. E. Fayle in two important articles on "Deflection of Strategy by Commerce in the Eighteenth Century" and "Economic Pressure in the War of 1739–48" in the *Journal of the Royal United Service Institution*, LXVIII (1923), pp. 281–290 and 434–446. Taken together these articles virtually supersede P. H. Colomb, *Naval Warfare, its Ruling Principles and Practice Historically Treated* (London, 1891), though it remains the only attempt at a complete treatment of its subject.

Several monographs have been devoted to the naval aspects of the war of American Independence, notably A. T. Mahan, *Major Operations of the Navies in the War of American Independence* (London, 1913); C. O. Paullin, *Navy of the American Revolution* (Chicago, 1906); and–the best treatment of the war–Sir W. M. James, *British Navy in Adversity* (London, 1926). The war's eastern aspects are discussed in Admiral Sir H. W. Richmond, *Navy in India 1763–1783* (London, 1931).

There are quite a number of useful biographies of prominent admirals, including those to be found in the *Dictionary of National Biography* and others referred to in a note on "Collected Naval Biography" by G. F. James in the *Bulletin of the Institute of Historical Research*, XV (1937–1938), pp. 162–175. Individual biographies include Sir John Barrow, *Life of Anson* (London,

1839), and *Life of Howe* (London, 1838); G. B. Mundy, *Life of Rodney* (2 vols., London, 1830), and D. Hannay, *Rodney* (London, 1891); Montagu Burrows, *Life of Hawke* (London, 1883); the Reverend T. Keppel, *Life of Keppel* (2 vols., London, 1842); D. Ford, *Admiral Vernon and the Navy* (London, 1907); W. V. Anson, *Life of Anson* (London, 1912); B. Tunstall, *Admiral Byng and the Loss of Minorca* (London, 1928); and Dorothy Hood, *The Admiral Hood* (London, 1942). Mary E. Matcham, *A Forgotten John Russell* (London, 1905), sketches the career of a man who was for a time a dockyard official, while Mrs. Reginald De Koven does as much for the American privateer, Paul Jones, in *The Life and Letters of John Paul Jones* (2 vols., New York, 1913).

Reference must also be made to some studies of a miscellaneous character. R. G. Albion, *Forests and Sea Power* (Cambridge, Mass., 1926), is a valuable monograph on the problem of securing adequate and suitable supplies of timber. Michael Lewis in *England's Sea Officers* (London, 1939) shows clearly how in the seventeenth and eighteenth centuries a hierarchy of carefully graded commissioned and warrant officers was organized and trained. On the uniforms they were now beginning to wear as well as on a variety of other topics, valuable information is provided by G. E. Manwaring, *The Flower of England's Garden* (London, 1936). Under the title *Britain's Sea Soldiers* there is a good history of the Royal Marines by C. Field, vol. I (Liverpool, 1924).

II. THE ARMY

(*a*) CONTEMPORARY WORKS

Much less has been written about the eighteenth-century Army than about the more popular and publicized senior service. The *Memoirs* of Donald Macleod (1791), published when he was in the hundred-and-third year of his age, give a first-hand account of life in the ranks. Macleod enlisted under William III, and his active service apparently covered the period from Blenheim to the war of American Independence. Contemporary military textbooks contain useful information, especially H. Bland, *Treatise of Military Discipline* (London, 1727), which was frequently reprinted and often appealed to; and Sir D. Dundas, *Principles of Military Movements* (London, 1788), which includes a detailed study of British campaigns in Germany during the Seven Years War. *The Jacobite Risings of 1715 and 1745*, edited by R. C. Jarvis, Cumberland Record Series (Carlisle, 1955), contains much interesting information about the organization of the local militia. The letters from Lieutenant-Colonel Russell in the *Frankland-Russell-Astley Manuscripts* (Historical Manuscripts Commission, 1900) and the letters of Captain Philip Browne, edited by Lieutenant-Colonel J. H. Leslie in the *Journal of the Society of Army Historical Research*, V (1926), pp. 49–65, 97–111 and 145–155, both belong to the period of the war of the Austrian Succession. Not unnaturally more attention was paid to the Seven Years War, both on its continental and colonial sides. J. Entick published a *General History of the Late War* (5 vols., London, 1763), Captain John Knox his *Historical Journal of the Campaigns in North America* (2 vols., London, 1769; reprinted by the Champlain Society, 1914–1916), and Thomas Mante a *History of the late war in North-America* (1772). The Order Books of the British Army in Germany (1758–1759) have been published in the "Clements Manuscripts" in the *Historical Manuscripts Commission, Report on Various Collections*, VIII (1913), pp. 418–568. The campaigns in India are described in R. O. Cambridge, *Account of the War in India* (London, 1761), and R. Orme, *History of the Military Transactions of the British Nation in Indostan from 1745* (2 vols., London, 1763–1778). After the Seven Years War the prevailing dissatisfaction with military corruption and inefficiency is well brought out in the anonymous, satirical work, *Advice to the Officers of the British Army* (London, 1782), attributed to Francis Grose in Pargellis and Medley's *Bibliography of British History, 1714–89*. A contemporary attempt by a young British officer to give a connected account of the whole War of American Independence is made in *A Journal by Thomas Hughes*, edited by

E. A. Benians (Cambridge, 1948); while Clinton's defence of his conduct in the American War against contemporary criticism is contained in *The American Rebellion. Sir Henry Clinton: Narrative of his Campaigns 1775–1782*, edited by W. B. Willcox (Yale and Oxford, 1954).

(*b*) MODERN WORKS: GENERAL

On military law and administration the two works of C. M. Clode, *Military Forces of the Crown* (2 vols., London, 1869), and *Administration of Justice under Military and Martial Law* (London, 1872) remain unsuperseded. Just because it neglects problems of organization and concentrates on campaigns and battles, the well-known work of the Hon. Sir J. W. Fortescue on the *History of the British Army* (13 vols., London, 1899–1930) is rather disappointing on the eighteenth century. C. Dalton, *George I's Army* (2 vols., London, 1910–1912), is a valuable study devoted chiefly to regimental history. E. M. Lloyd, *Review of the History of Infantry* (London, 1908), is mainly interesting for its comparison of English and Prussian methods of drill. A. Forbes, *A History of the Army Ordnance Services*, vol. I (London, 1929), is helpful on the development of the artillery. John Luard, *History of the Dress of the British Soldier* (London, 1852), is now superseded for the period down to 1760 by C. C. P. Lawson, *History of the Uniforms of the British Army* (2 vols., London, 1940–1941). On weapons H. J. Jackson and C. E. Whitelaw, *European Hand Firearms of the 16th, 17th and 18th Centuries* (London, 1923), and C. J. Ffoulkes and E. C. Hopkinson, *Sword, lance and bayonet* (Cambridge, 1938), may be consulted. J. S. Omond, *Parliament and the Army* (Cambridge, 1933), deals with an important topic. There are also numerous regimental histories such as those listed in C. L. Grose, *Select Bibliography of British History 1660–1760* (Chicago, 1939), p. 62. E. Robson's article on "Purchase and Promotion in the British Army in the Eighteenth Century" in *History*, XXXVI (1951), pp. 57–72, is a useful conspectus. There are helpful articles in the *Journal of the Royal United Service Institution* (1857)–and the *Journal of the Society of Army Historical Research* (1921)–with index volume for 1921–1932.

Few British generals have the compliment of a modern biographical study, though most of them appear briefly in the *Dictionary of National Biography*. Exceptions are W. E. Manners, *Some Account of the Marquis of Granby* (London, 1899); Sir C. V. F. Townshend, *Military Life of the 1st Marquess Townshend* (London, 1901); Hon. Evan Charteris, *William Augustus, Duke of Cumberland* (2 vols., London, 1913, 1925); B. Willson, *Life and Letters of J. Wolfe* (London, 1909); and W. T. Waugh, *James Wolfe, man and soldier* (Montreal, 1928).

(*c*) STRATEGY

Almost the only attempt to survey as a whole the problems of military strategy is an article by Major-General Sir W. E. Bird on "British Land Strategy in Four Great Wars, 1702–1802" in the *Army Quarterly*, XX (1930), pp. 30–44, 307–318, and XXI (1930–1931), pp. 44–53. J. W. Wright's article in the *American Historical Review*, XXXIX (1933–1934), pp. 629–644, on "Sieges and Customs of War at the Opening of the Eighteenth Century" deals mostly with the war of the Spanish Succession before the beginning of our period. The Hon. Sir J. W. Fortescue's *Last Post* (Edinburgh, 1934) includes essays on eighteenth-century topics. There is little on the war of the Austrian Succession except F. H. Skrine, *Fontenoy and Great Britain's Share in the War of the Austrian Succession* (Edinburgh, 1906), and the article by G. W. Forrest on "The Siege of Madras in 1746" in *Transactions of the Royal Historical Society*, Third Series, II (1908), pp. 189–234. C. T. Atkinson writes in the *Journal of the Royal United Service Institution*, LXXIX (1934), pp. 733–740, on "British Strategy and Battles in the Westphalian Campaigns of 1758–62". A. G. Doughty and G. W. Parmelee, *Siege of Quebec* (6 vols., Quebec, 1901), is exhaustive on Wolfe's campaign in Canada and is well summarized in W. C. H. Wood, *The Fight for Canada* (Westminster, 1904). *Military affairs in North America 1748–65*, edited by S. M. Pargellis (New York, 1936), contains a good selection of documents from the Cumberland Papers at Windsor

Castle, and *Lord Loudoun in North America* (New Haven, 1933), by the same author, is essential for the American side of the Seven Years War. E. M. Lloyd contributed to the *English Historical Review*, XVII (1902), pp. 466–469, a useful note on "The Raising of the Highland Regiments in 1757". On India, S. C. Hill's contribution to the *English Historical Review*, XXVIII (1913), pp. 260–291, 496–514, on "The Old Sepoy Officer" is also helpful. W. B. Willcox in the *American Historical Review*, LII (1946–1947), pp. 1–35, describes the course of events leading to the surrender of Cornwallis at Yorktown. E. Robson in the *English Historical Review*, vol. LXVI (1951), pp. 535–560, "The Expedition to the Southern Colonies 1775–6", emphasizes delays between conception and execution of military plans as a factor in British military failure, while G. S. Graham in the *Bulletin of the Institute of Historical Research*, XXII (1949), pp. 22–34, "Considerations on the War of American Independence", insists that "the dominating factor was not administrative negligence nor military ineptitude but political isolation". The best account of the war as a whole is given by J. C. Miller, *The Triumph of Freedom* (Boston, Mass., 1948). E. E. Curtis, *Organisation of the British Army in the American Revolution* (New Haven, 1926), is excellent.

A. THE NAVY

(*a*) RECRUITMENT AND GENERAL CONDITIONS

161. Mr. Justice Foster's argument in *Rex* v. *Broadfoot*, 30 August 1743

(*State Trials*, XVIII, pp. 1331–1358.)

In the trial of Alexander Broadfoot at Bristol on a charge of murder for killing an officer of the press-gang, the Recorder directed the jury to convict him of manslaughter only, as the press-gang had exceeded their authority; but upheld the right of impressing for the navy.

FOSTER, J., THE RECORDER. . . .

According to my present comprehension, (and I have taken some pains to inform myself) the right of impressing mariners for the public service is a prerogative inherent in the crown, grounded upon common law, and recognized by many acts of parliament.

A general immemorial usage not inconsistent with any statute, especially if it be the result of evident necessity, and withal tendeth to the public safety, is, I apprehend, part of the common law of England. If not, I am at a loss to know what is meant by common law, in contradistinction to statute-law. And therefore it is a great mistake in this case, as indeed it would be in any other, to conclude that there is no law, because perhaps there may be no statute that expressly and in terms impowereth the crown to press. For the rights of the crown, and the liberties of the subject too, stand principally upon the foot of common law; though both have been in many cases confirmed, explained, or ascertained by particular statutes.

As to the point of usage in the matter of pressing, I have met with a multitude of commissions and mandatory writs to that purpose conceived in various forms; and from time to time directed to different officers, as the nature of the service required. . . .

And now, when I consider these precedents, not fetched from dark, remote, and unsettled times, but running uniformly through a course of many ages, all, as I conceive, speaking to the same purpose, though in different forms of expression; some for making choice of, others, and those the much greater number and of the latest date, for making choice of and taking up, or for arresting, pressing and taking up, mariners, and putting them on board for the public service: when I consider these precedents, with the practice down to the present time, I cannot conceive otherwise of the point in question, than that the crown hath been always in possession of the prerogative of pressing mariners for the public service. Which prerogative hath been carried into execution, as well by virtue of special commissions, issued as the exigency of affairs required, as by the persons who from time to time have been intrusted with the whole admiralty-jurisdiction. . . .

I come now to the statutes which speak of this matter.

And I do admit, that I know of no statute now in force, which directly and in express terms impowereth the crown to press mariners into the service: and admitting that the prerogative is grounded on immemorial usage, I know of no necessity for any such statute; for let it be remembered, that a prerogative grounded upon general immemorial usage not inconsistent with any statute, nor repugnant to the public utility, is as much part of the law of England, as statute law. You will be pleased to carry this observation too along with you, that the statutes which mention pressing as a practice then subsisting and not disallowed, are at least an evidence of the usage, if they go no farther, I mean if they do not amount to a tacit approbation of it.

For it is hard to conceive, that the legislature should frequently mention a practice utterly illegal, and repugnant to the principles of the constitution as subsisting, without some mark of disapprobation....

For rights of every kind, which stand upon the foot of usage, gradually receive new strength in point of light and evidence from the continuance of that usage; as it implieth the tacit consent and approbation of every successive age, in which the usage hath prevailed. But when the prerogative hath not only this tacit approbation of all ages, the present as well as the former on its side, but is recognized, or evidently presupposed, by many acts of parliament, as in the present case I think it is, I see no legal objection that can be made to it.

I make no apology for the length of my argument, because I hope the importance of the question will be thought a sufficient excuse for me in that respect. For it is no more nor less than, whether the only effectual method yet found out for manning our navy in time of war, for raising that number of mariners which the legislature from time to time declare to be necessary for defending our coast and protecting our trade,–whether this method be legal or not. This I say is the question. And therefore I could not satisfy myself without entering as far into the merits of it as I could.

And I have delivered my opinion upon it without any reserve.

162. Lord Mansfield's judgment in the King's Bench in *Rex* v. *Tubbs*, 28 November 1776

(Henry Cowper, *Reports of Cases adjudged in the Court of King's Bench*, II (1800), pp. 517–519.)

John Tubbs, impressed while navigating a ship on the Thames, obtained a writ of *habeas corpus* and claimed that as a waterman of the City of London he was exempt from impressment.

[28 November, 1776.]

LORD MANSFIELD.

The power of pressing is founded upon immemorial usage, allowed for ages: If it be so founded and allowed for ages, it can have no ground to stand upon, nor can it be vindicated or justified by any reason but the safety of the state: And the practice is deduced from that trite maxim of the constitutional law of *England*, "that private mischief had better be submitted to, than that public detriment and inconvenience should ensue." To be sure, there are instances where private men must give way to the public good. In every case of pressing, every man must be very sorry for the act, and for the necessity which gives rise to it. It ought, therefore, to be exercised with the greatest moderation; and only upon the most cogent necessity. And though it be a legal power, it may like many others be abused in the exercise of it. A bailiff may execute legal process in such a manner as the court would commit him for: In like manner, the power of pressing may be abused; as by pressing the watermen of the lord-mayor whilst they are in the act of rowing him in his barge. And many other instances might be put. . . .

Persons liable, must come purely *within the description* of seamen, sea-faring men, *&c.* He therefore, who is not within the description, does not come within the usage. The commission is not to press landmen, or persons of any other description of life, but such men as are described to be sea-faring men, *&c.* Officers are not within the description. It is a very strong circumstance, therefore, that there is in fact no other exemption stated or alluded to, which rests upon the common law. There are many exemptions by statute: But they are grounded upon considerations of public policy at the particular times of their being made; and upon the circumstance of its being in fact better for the service that the objects of those acts should be exempted, than that they should be subject to be pressed; as, apprentices, landmen entering voluntarily; fishermen; all foreigners; and in respect of these last mentioned, the reason is very obvious: For, during the time of a war, the act of navigation has been dispensed with, and two thirds of the crew of merchantmen have been allowed to be *foreigners.* Harpooners and others have been exempted. A line has been drawn with respect to the age: And many other instances might be put. But the exemption of those called the watermen of the city of *London,* is to be found in no statute or common law book whatsoever. . . . Therefore to give my opinion upon the case as at present stated, and upon the mere fact whether this exemption as here claimed is, or is not, warranted by immemorial usage, I cannot say it is.

163. Dr. James Lind's cure for scurvy, *c.* 1750

(James Lind, M.D., *A Treatise of the Scurvy* (1753), pp. 191–196.)

James Lind (1716–1794) was a surgeon in the Navy, serving in the Mediterranean and the West Indies. His cure for scurvy was one of the most important events in naval history in the eighteenth century.

. . . On the 20th of May, 1747, I took twelve patients in the scurvy, on board the *Salisbury* at sea. Their cases were as similar as I could have them. They all in general had putrid gums, the spots and lassitude, with weakness of their knees. They lay together in one place, being a proper apartment for the sick in the fore-hold; and had one diet common to all, *viz.* water-gruel sweetened with sugar in the morning; fresh mutton-broth often times for dinner; at other times puddings, boiled biscuit with sugar, &c; and for supper, barley and raisins, rice and currants, sago and wine, or the like. Two of these were ordered each a quart of cyder a-day. Two others took twenty-five gutts of *elixir vitriol* three times a-day, upon an empty stomach; using a gargle strongly acidulated with it for their mouths. Two others took two spoonfuls of vinegar three times a-day, upon an empty stomach; having their gruels and their other food well acidulated with it, as also the gargle for their mouths. Two of the worst patients, with the tendons in the ham rigid, (a sympton none of the rest had), were put under a course of sea-water. Of this they drank half a pint every day, and sometimes more or less as it operated, by way of gentle physic. Two others had each two oranges and one lemon given them every day. These they eat with greediness, at different times, upon an empty stomach. They continued but six days under this course, having consumed the quantity that could be spared. The two remaining patients, took the bigness of a nutmeg three times a-day, of an electuary recommended by an hospital-surgeon, made of garlic, mustard-seed, *rad. raphan.* balsam of *Peru*, and gum myrrh; using for common drink, barley-water well acidulated with tamarinds; by a decoction of which, with the addition of *cremor tartar*, they were gently purged three or four times during the course.

The consequence was, that the most sudden and visible good effects were perceived from the use of the oranges and lemons; one of those who had taken them, being at the end of six days fit for duty. The spots were not indeed at that time quite off his body, nor his gums sound; but without any other medicine, than a gargarism of *elixir vitriol*, he became quite healthy before we came into *Plymouth*, which was on the 16th of *June*. The other was the best recovered of any in his condition; and being now deemed pretty well, was appointed nurse to the rest of the sick.

Next to the oranges I thought the cyder had the best effects. It was indeed not very sound, being inclinable to be aigre or pricked. However, those who had taken it, were in a fairer way of recovery than the others at the end of the fortnight, which was the length of time all these different courses were continued, except the oranges. The putrefaction of their gums, but especially their lassitude and weakness, were somewhat abated, and their appetite increased by it.

As to the *elixir* of *vitriol*, I observed that the mouths of those who had used it by way of gargarism, were in a much cleaner and better condition than many of the rest, especially those who used the vinegar; but perceived otherwise no good effects from its internal use upon the other symptoms. I indeed never had a great opinion of the efficacy of this medicine in the scurvy, since our longest cruise in the *Salisbury*, from the 10th of *August* to the 28th *October* 1746; when we had but one scurvy in the ship. The patient was a marine, (one *Walsh*); who, after recovering from a quotidian ague in the latter end of *September*, had taken the *elixir vitriol* by way of restorative for three weeks; and yet at length contracted the disease, while under a course of a medicine recommended for its prevention.

There was no remarkable alteration upon those who took the electuary and tamarind decoction, the sea-water, or vinegar, upon comparing their condition, at the end of the fortnight, with others who had taken nothing but a little lenitive electuary and *cremor tartar*, at times, in order to keep their belly open; or a gentle pectoral in the evening, for relief of their breast. Only one of them, while taking the vinegar, fell into a gentle flux at the end of ten days. This I attributed to the genius and course of the disease, rather than to the use of the medicine. As I shall have occasion elsewhere to take notice of the effects of other medicines in this disease, I shall here only observe, that the result of all my experiments was, that oranges and lemons were the most effectual remedies for this distemper at sea. I am apt to think oranges preferable to lemons, though perhaps both given together will be found most serviceable. . . .

164. Letter from Captain Cook to Sir John Pringle on his precautions against scurvy on his second voyage, 5 March 1776

(Sir John Pringle, Bart., *A Discourse upon Some Late Improvements of the Means for Preserving the Health of Mariners* (1776), pp. 39–44.)

Sir John Pringle (1707–1782) had been Physician-General to the forces in Flanders in 1744, and in 1774 became physician to George III. His chief work was the reform of military medicine and sanitation. Captain Cook on his first long voyage had lost 30 out of a crew of 85 from scurvy. He here describes his highly successful precautions on his second voyage of 1772–1775.

Mile-end.
March 5, 1776.

Sir,

As many gentlemen have expressed some surprize at the uncommon good state of health which the crew of the *Resolution*, under my command, experienced during her late voyage; I take the liberty to communicate to you the methods that were taken to obtain that end. Much was owing to the extraordinary attention given by the Admiralty, in causing such articles to be put on board, as either by experience or conjecture were judged to tend most to preserve the health of seamen. I shall not trespass upon your time in mentioning all those articles, but–confine myself to such as were found the most useful.

We had on board a large quantity of Malt, of which was made sweet-wort, and given (not only to those men who had manifest symptons of the scurvy, but to such also as were, from circumstances, judged to be most liable to that disorder) from one or two or three pints in the day to each man, or in such proportion as the surgeon thought necessary; which sometimes amounted to three quarts in the twenty-four hours. This is without doubt one of the best antiscorbutic sea-medicines yet found out; and if given in time will, with proper attention to other things, I am persuaded, prevent the scurvy from making any great progress for a considerable time: but I am not altogether of opinion, that it will cure it in an advanced state at sea.

Sour-Krout, of which we had also a large provision, is not only a wholesome vegetable food, but, in my judgment, highly antiscorbutic, and spoils not by keeping. A pound of it was served to each man, when at sea, twice a week, or oftener when it was thought necessary.

Portable-Soup, or broth, was another essential article, of which we had likewise a liberal supply. An ounce of this to each man, or such other proportion as was thought necessary, was boiled with their pease three days in the week; and when we were in places where fresh vegetables could be procured, it was boiled, with them and with wheat or oatmeal, every morning for breakfast, and also with dried pease and fresh vegetables for dinner. It enabled us to make several nourishing and wholesome messes, and was the means of making the people eat a greater quantity of greens than they would have done otherwise.

Further, we were provided with Rob of lemons and oranges; which the surgeon found useful in several cases.

Amongst other articles of victualling we were furnished with sugar in the room of oil, and with wheat instead of much oatmeal, and were certainly gainers by the exchange. Sugar, I imagine, is a very good antiscorbutic; whereas oil, such at least as is usually given to the navy, I apprehend has the contrary effect. But the introduction of the most salutary articles, either as provision or medicines, will generally prove unsuccessful, unless supported by certain rules of living.

On this principle, many years experience, together with some hints I had from Sir HUGH PALLISER, the Captains CAMPBELL, WALLIS, and other intelligent officers, enabled me to lay down a plan whereby all was to be conducted. The crew were at three watches, except upon some extraordinary occasions. By this means they were not so much exposed to the weather as if they had been at watch and watch; and they had generally dry cloaths to shift themselves when they happened to get wet. Care was also taken to expose them as little as possible. Proper methods were employed to keep their persons, hammocks, bedding, cloaths, &c. constantly clean and dry. Equal pains were taken to keep the ship clean and dry between decks. Once or twice a week she was aired with fires; and when this could not be done, she was smoaked with gunpowder moistened with vinegar or water. I had also frequently a fire made in an iron pot at the bottom of the well, which greatly purified the air in the lower parts of the ship. To this and cleanliness, as well in the ship as amongst the people, too great attention cannot be paid; the least neglect occasions a putrid offensive smell below, which nothing but fires will remove; and if these be not used in time, those smells will be attended with bad consequences. Proper care was taken of the ship's coppers, so that they were kept constantly clean. The fat, which boiled out of the salt beef and pork, I never suffered to be given to the people, as is customary; being of opinion that it promotes the scurvy. I never failed to take in water wherever it was to be procured, even when we did not seem to want it; because I look upon fresh water from the shore to be much more wholesome than that which has been kept some time on board. Of this essential article we were never at an allowance, but had always abundance for every necessary purpose. I am convinced that with plenty of fresh water, and a close attention to cleanliness, a ship's company will seldom be much afflicted with the scurvy, though they should not be provided with any of the antiscorbutics before mentioned. We came to few places where either the art of man or nature did not afford some sort of refreshment or other, either of the animal or vegetable kind. It was my first care to procure what could be met with of either by every means in my power, and to oblige our people to make use thereof, both by my example and authority; but the benefits arising from such refreshments soon became so obvious, that I had little occasion to employ either the one or the other.

These, SIR, were the methods, under the care of Providence, by which the *Resolution* performed a voyage of three years and eighteen days, through all the climates from 52° North to 71° South, with the loss of one man only by disease, and who died of a complicated and lingering illness, without any mixture of scurvy. Two others were unfortunately drowned, and one killed by a fall; so that of the whole number with which I set out from England I lost only four.

I have the honour to be, SIR, &c.

Extract of a Letter from Captain COOK *to Sir* JOHN PRINGLE, Bart. *dated* Plymouth Sound, July 7, 1776.

I entirely agree with you, that the dearness of the Rob of lemons and of oranges will hinder them from being furnished in large quantities, but I do not think this so necessary; for though they may assist other things, I have no great opinion of them alone. Nor have I a higher opinion of vinegar: my people had it very sparingly during the late voyage; and towards the latter part, none at all; and yet we experienced no ill effects from the want of it. The custom of washing the inside of the ship with vinegar I seldom observed, thinking, that fire and smoke answered the purpose much better.

165. Letter from James Lind to Sir Alexander Dick, Bart., describing Haslar Naval Hospital, 3 September 1758

(*Edinburgh Medical Journal* (June 1926), pp. 335–336; Professor R. Stockman, "James Lind and Scurvy".)

Haslar Hospital at Gosport, Portsmouth, was the first hospital on the naval establishment and was started on Lord Sandwich's recommendation in 1746. In 1758 Lind was physician there, and Sir Alexander Dick was President of the Edinburgh College of Physicians.

. . . Haslar Hospital is an immense pile of building & tho' of Brick will when finished have cost the Government about £100,000. It is surrounded by a high wall (to prevent desertion) containing 32 acres of ground. It will certainly be the largest hospital in Europe when finished but even then will not be able properly to receive above 2200 patients. This is owing to the Largeness of the regular wards.

The annual expence at present is £14,000 pr an but then we never have had above 1040 patients, we this winter shall open wards for 500 patients more.

The hospital is under the direction of the Physician and Council – the latter consists of the Physician who presides two master Surgeons, the Agent & Steward, & lately two new members are added to the council *viz* Dr Welch Physician to Gorton hospital (which receives the marines only about a mile distance from us) & the Surgeon of that hospital.

But this Council must act entirely by Orders from the Board of Sick & hurt.

Six upper assistant Surgeons at 5 sh pr Day & 4 under assistants at 3s 6d were allowed with an apothecary & two assistants but it is proposed to reduce the number of assistant Surgeons & increase the number of apothecaries, as these last are to be appropriated to visit with the Physician in his Wards.

We are remarkably clean. No patient is admitted into the hospital until he is stripped of all his cloths & well washed with warm water & soap in tubs always kept for the purpose, he is allowed the hospital dress during the time he continues in the hospital or until his cloths are returned him quite clean, & he is regularly shifted and kept quite neat clean & sweet at the Government's expence. None of his cloths bedding &c is ever permitted to be brought into the hospital we have large outhouses for their reception.

In cases of fevers the Patients cloths are directly fumigated with Brimstone in the smoak house & baked in an oven sprinkled with vinegar. The fever Wards are cut off from all communication with the rest & nothing but hospital dresses are used in them. We have sometimes 90 women nurses at a time their pay is £12 pr an. In our wash house we have seldom less than 24 women constantly employed. All these are under sober & discreet Matrons.

We have about 20 Labourers at 1s 6d everyday employed in the different branches of Duty in the House. And indeed no expence is spared for the regular managment of the house. . . .

Dr Sir
Your most obedient & obliged hble Servant
JAMES LIND.

Royal Hospital At Haslar,
3d Sept. 1758.

(*b*) ADMINISTRATION

166. Letter from the Admiralty Board to Sir John Norris, Commander-in-Chief, on plans for standard methods of building ships for the Navy, *c.* 1740

(John Charnock, *An History of Marine Architecture*, III (1802), pp. 123–125.)

John Charnock (1756–1807), writer on naval subjects, had served in the navy as a volunteer. Sir John Norris (1660?–1749) had distinguished himself in the War of the Spanish Succession, was knighted in 1705 and became Commander-in-Chief in 1734.

(No date. ? 1740)

SIR,

The Lords Commissioners of the Admiralty have, sometime since, taken into consideration the methods now in use for building and re-building the ships of the royal navy, and find that there has been no regular establishment made therein since that dated the 18th of November, 1719, which has been for several years discontinued. They observe that in the year 1732 there was an attempt towards making a new establishment; and, in order thereunto, the master shipwrights of all his majesty's yards, were directed to consider and propose their several opinions in relation to the building ships, and to the dimensions for a ship of each class; which they accordingly did, but no determination was made thereupon: from whence it has proceeded, that the ships of the royal navy are not new-built according to any certain or uniform standard or establishment; but every particular ship has been built, or re-built, according to different proposed dimensions. Those of the same class or denomination have been built of unequal sizes and proportions: so that the furniture and stores for one ship have not fitted another of the same rank; which has been the cause of infinite inconveniences to the service, as well as of a great increase in the expence of the navy. It has been likewise observed, that the scantling of his majesty's ships, in general, are not so large and strong as they should be, and it is also a general complaint, that the ships are crank, and heel so much in blowing weather, that they cannot open their lee-ports; at the same time that the ships of some other nations go upright, with all their batteries open, and ready for action. Their lordships esteem it, therefore, a matter of the highest importance, that the great inconvenience arising from the present loose and irregular manner of building his majesty's ships, and the complaints made of their bad qualities, should be rectified and amended; that the dimensions of the ships in the navy should be brought to a certain size and standard, according to their several classes; that in doing this the opinion and advice of the master shipwrights of his majesty's several yards, and of such others as their lordships judged qualified, should be taken, in order to come at a general fixed establishment. They conceive the same should be such as would not only enable his majesty's ships to carry the number and nature of guns, according to the present establishment; but that their lower tier should be six feet above water, with four months provisions on board, and stores for foreign service; they wish also all other considerations should be comprehended, which, it may be hoped, will give them the proper qualities of good ships of war; in point of sailing, fighting the enemy, durableness, and all other respects whatsoever.

Their lordships accordingly sent directions to Sir Jacob Acworth, surveyor of the navy; to the several master shipwrights of his majesty's yards, and to several other eminent shipbuilders, to take the present establishment of the ships of the navy into their separate consideration; so that they might propose and lay before this board such a solid and well-digested system and establishment for building a ship of each class or rate, down to a sloop, inclusive; as well with respect to their principal dimensions, as to their masts and yards, and whatsoever else might, in their opinion, contribute to make them complete ships of war. But, as the present ships of 80 guns, with three decks, are, in general, ill approved, they were directed to propose ships carrying 74 guns, with two decks and half, in their room. They were likewise directed to take into their consideration, and give their opinion, concerning such a disposition of the cabin rooms, platforms, awnings, as well as of all other parts of the ship, that may improve them for the several uses they are allotted to, by a fit placing, as well as proportioning the same; and likewise to consider whether any reasonable saving can be made in the present method of finishing his majesty's ships: or whether any superfluous or unnecessary expence might be retrenched. They have accordingly taken this important affair into their separate considerations, and severally made their report to us, their lordships, upon the several points referred to them; but their lordships thinking it necessary to have the said reports examined and considered by the flag officers of the navy, as well as by such of the senior captains as shall be thought proper, their lordships command me to signify to you their desire, that you will appoint a convenient day for your coming to town, and their lordships knowing the time you shall fix for that purpose, will order the flag officers, and some of the senior captains, who shall be in the way, to meet you at a place to be appointed for that purpose, in order to take the reports and proposals of the several persons above mentioned into your consideration; also that you may be attended by the said persons, for demonstrating and explaining to you their respective schemes; and enable you, by consulting or advising together, to form a judgment upon the best rules and methods of building the ships of the royal navy, so that you may report the same to their lordships. I am, &c.

167. Report from a Committee on the Problem of supplying the Navy with Timber, 1771

(*Reports from the committees of the House of Commons*, III (1803), pp. 15–17.)

[May 6th, 1771.]

The COMMITTEE, who were appointed to consider how His Majesty's Navy may be better supplied with Timber, have, pursuant to the Order of the House, considered the Matter to them referred, and have agreed upon the following Report:

WHEN Your Committee proceeded to the Execution of the Enquiry ordered by the House, they immediately found the Necessity of directing that Enquiry to certain Points; First, the State of Timber fit for the Supply of His Majesty's Navy, its Sufficiency or Insufficiency for that Purpose; Secondly, in case of Insufficiency, to what Causes it might be imputed; Thirdly, its Operation on the Prices; Fourthly, the Means of further Supply at Home, and by Importation; and under this Head, naturally come the Nature and Quality of the different Sorts of Timber. . . .

And First, as to the Sufficiency or Insufficiency of the Supply, Your Committee thought it necessary to examine *John Williams*, Esquire, Surveyor, *Hugh Palliser*, Esquire, Comptroller, and *Timothy Brett*, Esquire, another Commissioner of His Majesty's Navy: And they informed Your Committee, that there was a great Scarcity of Timber for Ship-building in *England*; and that, for the better Supply of Timber and Plank for the Use of His Majesty's Navy, it had been found necessary to apply to Foreign Countries: That the Timber chiefly imported, was of a large Scantling, Compass Timber, for Knees, and other Purposes: That the *New Forest*, and the Forest of *Dean*, are the only King's Forests which yield any considerable Supply for the Use of His Majesty's Navy; the first to *Portsmouth*, the other to *Plymouth*: That of 6,000 Loads worked up every Year at *Portsmouth*, the *New Forest* sends no more than 870 Loads of Oak, and 100 Beach Trees; and of 5,000 Loads worked up at *Plymouth* every Year, the Forest of *Dean* sends no more than 5 or 600 Loads: That some Years ago there was an Order for felling Trees in the Forest of *Sherwood*; but they were found to have stood so long, and were so red, that it was thought fit not to have any more of them: That, from the Information they have received from their Purveyors and the Timber Merchants, they are of Opinion, that there is not a sufficient Quantity of Timber in *England* to be purchased at any Price; and all their Purveyors and Timber Merchants agree, that the large Timber near the Sea Coast, that is to say, within such a Distance that the Land and Water Carriage does not exceed 38*s*. a Load, is nearly exhausted.

That, notwithstanding their Application to all the Timber Merchants in *England*, to know what they could be supplied with, they have received Answers from very few: One of them says, that he has a Parcel of Timber offered him, but that he will not engage for it unless he is allowed an additional Land Carriage of 40 Miles. That the Stock of Timber in the King's Yards has been lessening for these Eight or Nine Years past, so that though they used to keep Three Years Stock beforehand, they have not now enough for the Service of the current Year, and no Appearance of procuring it; but that the Purveyors had not been able to purvey the Kingdom all over, so as to know with Certainty what Quantity there is in the Kingdom. . . .

As to the Causes of the Insufficiency of the Supply, they informed Your Committee, that the Scarcity of Timber is occasioned, partly by building such a large Number of *East India* Ships, partly by the general Increase of Shipping, and in a considerable Degree by the Augmentation of the King's Ships, in their Number, their Size, and their Scantlings; that in the Year 1740 the Navy was greatly increased in Number and Size; that a great Number were built in the King's Yards, and also by Contract in the Merchants Yards; and in 1745, the several Classes in the Navy were greatly increased by a new Establishment in building Ships for the Navy; and that at the Opening of the War in 1755 the Number and Size still increased; in 1756 the Size of the Ships were very considerably increased; insomuch that Seventy Gun Ships, which formerly were about 1,300 Ton, now are increased to 74 Guns and 1,600 Ton; that during the last War there were 50 or 60 Ships of the Line built, the least of them carrying 60 Guns; and upon the Conclusion of the War, the Ships that the War began with, were most of them in Want of Re-building, or a thorough Repair, except those that were built during the War; and that the Consumption of Timber since 1762, in building and repairing Ships, has been as great as would have built 60 Ships of the Line; and that in Fact, since the Year 1762, 34 Ships of the Line have been actually built and launched.

That there has been a great Increase of Shipping in general; and Ships of all Dimensions interfere with the King's Ships of the like Dimensions, and the Price has been raised in Proportion upon all Timber; but the Increase has particularly been in the *East India* Company's Ships, which from 30 Sail, their Number 30 Years ago, are now 90 Sail, one of which Ships of 800 Ton would take the same Scantling as a Ship of War of 50 or 60 Guns: That within these 20 Years the *East India* Company have greatly increased the Tonnage of their Ships; . . .

As to the Expedients for removing the present Scarcity and procuring a sufficient Supply, the said Messieurs *Williams*, *Palliser*, and *Brett*, informed Your Committee, that one Expedient for supplying the Deficiency of Timber would be the Introduction of Foreign Timber in a larger Quantity than at present; and that the Navy Board are now actually treating for it from *Hamburgh*, *Stetin*, *Holland*, and *America*, and particularly for a certain Kind of Live Oak, for Knees, from *Carolina*; but this last in very small Quantities, by Way of Specimen only: Another Expedient the Board has used, has been, by advancing the Price of Carriage, to enable the Merchants to bring it from the Inland Parts of the Country; . . . that the Commissioners, upon finding the Scarcity of Timber, have tried to enlarge their Supplies from Abroad, by endeavouring to purchase in certain Foreign Countries, from which they had not been used to receive any Supplies before; and Offers have been made from *Sweden*; but the Person who had undertaken to bring the Supply did not perform it; that they have had some Timber and a great deal of Plank from *Silesia*, by Way of *Stetin*; that they had about 1,000 Load from *Holland* last Year, and are now under Contract for 1,000 Load more of Plank from *Silesia* for this Year; but that the Foreign Timber is inferior in Quality to the *English*, and will turn out dearer (Duty included) than their standing Contract Price; that with respect to the *American* Timber, the Board has attempted to get some Cedar and Mahogany Beams from the *Musquito* Shore, but the Undertaker failed in the Attempt; that they have likewise imported Plank from *Quebec*, some of which was good in its Quality, but its Durability cannot be ascertained, as it has been used only Two Years, and it is supposed it would answer the Purpose of, and comes cheaper than, *Dantzic* Plank, and upon that Presumption the Commissioners had engaged for 1,000 Load more, but this Undertaker likewise failed in his Attempt; and that they have had small Parcels of Plank from *New York*, but it has been found very bad in its Quality.

That in the Course of the last War, the Navy have used Fir in the Construction of Ships of 28 Guns, by Way of Experiment, and in order to gain Time; but they do not think it answers, on Account of its Want of Durability; and likewise is more expensive, as the Merchants will not undertake to build a Fir Ship at the same Price they will an Oak Ship.

168. Admiral Keppel's criticism of Lord Sandwich's administration of the Navy, 1782

(Thomas Keppel, *Life of Augustus Viscount Keppel*, II (1842), pp. 340–345.)

This extract is from a paper drawn up by Keppel for Lord Rockingham, apparently to enable him to uphold charges against Sandwich's administration of the Admiralty. It was divided into two general headings: (1) "Means employed for preserving and putting the Navy on a proper footing." (2) "Use made of the naval forces", this being divided into (*a*) Home; (*b*) American; (*c*) West Indian. The extract is taken from (*a*), with which Keppel himself was most closely concerned. Admiral Augustus Keppel (1725–1786), later first Viscount Keppel, was a member of the parliamentary opposition to Lord North's government. He had refused to serve against the American colonists and had been court martialled for failing to destroy the French fleet in the action off Ushant in 1778, and acquitted. He became First Lord of the Admiralty in the Rockingham ministry in 1782.

1780.

. . . The beginning of this campaign is distinguished by the same neglect to watch the port of Brest that has uniformly marked the administration of the First Lord of the Admiralty with ignorance and criminality. No less than three separate armaments were suffered to sail from that port before the end of April, unwatched and unmolested; two of them were known to be destined for the West Indies, yet no exertions were made to send adequate detachments with proper dispatch, either to pursue them, or to counteract their operations when arrived there.

On the 4th of February, De Guichen put to sea with seventeen sail of the line, nine frigates, and a large convoy of transports. The only attempt we heard of to counteract his designs, was the appointment of a squadron of six sail of the line, to be commanded by Commodore Walsingham. Had this force been sent out at the time it was appointed, it might, when joined by Rear-Admiral Parker's ships, have prepared a sufficient strength for Sir George Rodney, on his arrival to oppose the enemy, with a certainty of success. As Mons. De Guichen was encumbered with such a number of transports, their ships, sailing without a convoy, must have outrun him a considerable length of time; but the Admiralty, under the usual appearance of hurry and dispatch, detained Commodore Walsingham in the Channel till full six weeks after Mons. De Guichen had arrived at Martinique. On the 13th of April, he left Spithead, in complete order, with a fair wind; but he was soon stopped by the Aurora frigate, and returned to Torbay, where he remained till the 29th of May.

Towards the latter end of April, Mons. De Tourney sailed from Brest, with six or seven sail of the line, conveying 6000 French troops to America. Ministers had early notice of the equipping of this armament, and it was detained, by contrary winds, long after the French had published its destination.

A month before it sailed, Admiral Digby returned from Gibraltar, having had the good fortune to fall in with a convoy for the East Indies, unlooked-for and unexpected, and to take the Prothee man-of-war, and four or five trading ships. After his return, the only ships that were taken from the grand fleet, which before his sailing with Sir George Rodney consisted of forty-six sail, were, five under Commodore Walsingham, ready for the West Indies; two detached to the Islands, without convoy; six under Admiral Graves, fitted for America; and four employed in different services. The remaining ships, therefore, amounted to twenty-four. From this number, the First Lord of the Admiralty might have easily detached a sufficient force to prevent the sailing of Mons. de Ternay, either by reinforcing Admiral Graves, who was then detained in Cawsand Bay, which might have been done with five coppered ships, and ordering him off Brest to watch the motions of the French commander; or, by ordering a proper force under some other commander to blockade the Port of Brest, and prevent his sailing. Twelve ships would have been sufficient for this purpose, and Admiral Graves might have proceeded to reinforce Admiral Arbuthnot, and prepare him, in case of Mons. de Ternay's escaping out to sea. It will appear from the then state of the fleet, he could easily have accomplished either or both of these schemes; the neglect of which laid the foundation of all the last year's disgraces in America.

With equal neglect and inattention was Don Solano permitted to sail from Cadiz on the 28th of April, with twelve ships of the line, and a large convoy of troops for the West Indies. It may be said we could not expect to find ships sufficient for all these services. But the crime of the First Lord of the Admiralty consisted in not attending to some of them, though at this time, as the detachments under Graves and Walsingham had not sailed, he had near forty sail of the line lying idle in the ports of England.

After the detachment for foreign service, the next great object should have been to prevent the junction of the home fleets of the enemy, as the only measure from which we could hope for success. As early as the month of May, the French began to detach for Cadiz. They continued to do so with success from Toulon and the other ports during that and the following month, and in the beginning of July we find the united fleet cruising in force off the coast of Portugal. On our side, not a single attempt was made to oppose their junction or interrupt their cruise.

Sir Charles Hardy having died at Portsmouth about the middle of May, Admiral Geary was called upon to take the chief command. It was the 8th of June before he was enabled to sail with twenty-two or twenty-three sail of the line.

As the French and Spanish were ordered, as fast as they refitted, to rendezvous at Cadiz, it was evident to every one, except, perhaps, the First Lord of the Admiralty, that from thence they meant to enter on their summer service. The obvious measure, therefore, for the Admiralty to have embraced, was to have detached early to the coast of Spain, to annoy the enemy in their junction, or at least to have ordered Admiral Geary, on his first sailing, to proceed immediately to the southward for that purpose. When his cruise was nearly half over, he was, indeed, ordered to detach; but it then proved useless.

This neglect, joined to other circumstances equally marked with ignorance and criminality, led to an event at once disgraceful to our arms, and destructive to our trade. The Admiralty were possessed of the clearest and most distinct intelligence that the enemy's fleet were at Cadiz, and at times at sea in those latitudes, for the purpose of annoying the British trade. Yet they sent orders to Captain Moubray, who was to convoy the East and West India trade, to rendezvous at Madeira, the track of all others the most dangerous, and which, in that position of the enemy, could not have been marked out but by infatuation and madness. It will appear that Admiral Geary saw Captain Moubray and his convoy, and he stood as far to the westward as Moubray was ordered to stand. Yet, it seems, no orders were given him to see that valuable and important fleet so far safe; and as to his doing it himself, when he saw them, he might not have been prepared so to do from the state of his water and provisions. The obvious consequences, which were dreaded by every officer of experience, from these extraordinary and criminal arrangements actually took place. Don Cordova sailed from Cadiz with twenty-two sail of Spanish and nine of French men of war. On the 19th of August he intercepted Captain Moubray, and carried upwards of fifty of his convoy safe into port.

At the end of August, Admiral Geary returned to port for water and provisions, after a cruise, during which it does not appear that he was directed to take any one proper step, either to defend our own trade, or in any shape to annoy the enemy. Some of the ships were reported to stand in need of refitting; but their repairs, instead of being carried on with a view to the service, were made subservient to an object at this time much more essential in the eyes of the Government. Some of the largest three-deckers were sent to refit in Plymouth Sound, at an alarming risk, but evidently for the purpose of aiding the election at Plymouth, by paying the crews there. Vice-Admiral Darby was set up for that town by Government–a situation as new to him as the command of the fleet, to which he was appointed on the resignation of Admiral Geary. At the same time, the frigates from the northern stations were collected in the Downs, for the sole purpose of aiding Government in the election at Sandwich, &c. &c.

169. Lord Sandwich's defence of his administration of the Navy, 1782

(*Correspondence of King George III*, ed. Sir John Fortescue, v (1928), pp. 342–358.)

John, fourth earl of Sandwich (1718–1792), held the office of First Lord of the Admiralty on three occasions: 1748–1751, 1763–1768 and 1771–1782. The parliamentary opposition to Lord North's government strongly attacked his administration of the Navy during the last of these periods, holding him responsible for the disasters of the later stages of the American war. See No. 168.

[? January 1782.]

Though the Naval enquiry may branch out into many points, both civil and military, it is to be supposed that the principal object in view is to see whether every possible exertion has been used to increase our number of ships and to keep them in constant readiness for service; and that if it shall appear to the House that the Admiralty have done everything in their power to attain this end, and have carried their exertions infinitely further than ever was done before in any period, the prejudices that may subsist against the present Naval Administration will insensibly die away, and the enquiry be attended with applause instead of censure on that important Department.

I will therefore begin by observing what has been done since the year 1771, the time when the Earl of Sandwich first came to the Head of the Board, to the present moment. And here I must first desire that it may be recollected that he came to the management of a Fleet that had been exceedingly neglected for some years past, was greatly out of repair, that there was scarcely any timber in any of the Dockyards, and a total despondency at the Navy Office as to the means of procuring it; it being generally understood that the timber of this country was exhausted; which opinion was confirmed to Lord Sandwich by Sir John Williams, who then was and still is one of the Surveyors of the Navy. But the First Lord of the Admiralty was not of a disposition to join in with these melancholy ideas, without sifting them to the bottom; and after a very little investigation, he soon found that the scarcity arose from a combination among the Timber growers and Timber Merchants to keep up the price of their commodity, and from some other inferior causes, particularly the vast and unnecessary profusion of ship-building by the East India Company, who avowedly kept on foot upwards of 16,850 tons of shipping more than their trade required, in order to secure their Election by the votes of the people employed by them in Shipbuilding.

To remedy these inconveniences, a Bill was brought into Parliament to restrain the East India Company* from building any more ships till their tonnage should be reduced to 45,000 for the space of three years.

The Bill was warmly contested by the Opposition and a reason given (in private conversation) by a leading Admiral now in Parliament for his opposition to the Bill was that if it passed Lord Sandwich would gain the credit of repairing the Fleet. However the Bill did pass and was attended with every good consequence that was expected from it. . . .

Is the Coppering the whole Fleet of England no act of exertion? In the year 1770 there were not above one or two Frigates coppered by way of experiment, and people in general doubted whether the experiment had answered, as it was generally supposed that the corrosive faculties of copper would have such an effect upon the Iron bolts by which the frames of the Ships are kept together, that it was dangerous to carry the measure farther than to some frigates; and that it was necessary that those Frigates which were to be coppered should be fastened with copper instead of iron bolts. This measure accordingly was carried into execution for a time; but the industry and superior knowledge of the present Comptroller of the Navy adopted and recommended a Preservative, well proved and attested to have answered every purpose for the space of nine years, which effectually preserves the fastening of the ships from the corrosion of the copper sheathing; and upon that foundation the whole Fleet of England (except a very few ships that are not yet returned from foreign stations) from a first Rate to the smallest Cutter, has now a copper bottom; and as a

* The Company had then 86 ships, in tonnage 61,800.

conclusive proof of our conviction on this subject, we have returned to iron bolts, and have in a great measure laid aside copper ones. It seems highly proper in this place to mention the number of ships that have been coppered since this Regulation took place, which are as follows:

Line of Battleships	82
Of 50 Guns, ...	14
Frigates, from 44 to 20 guns, ...	115
Sloops and Cutters, ...	102

It is scarcely necessary to mention the immense advantages which in the present War have been derived from our being in possession of this invaluable discovery: it has been called (I believe in the House of Commons) by an Admiral who is often mentioned, a bold measure; so it is, but it is a wise and successful one, and one that all other nations are imitating as fast as their means of procuring the materials will allow them to do it. If anyone doubts of the efficacy of copper, let him read the intercepted letters of Mons. de Grasse, who expressly says that he should have annihilated Admiral Hood's Fleet if it had not been for his ships being coppered, which enabled him to manœuvre as he thought proper, and take any advantage that wind or weather might give him to avoid an action if he judged it advisable so to do. . . .

The next new point of exertion that I shall mention is a matter very little known in the world, but is the only very material improvement that appears likely to be made, which will enable us to build and repair a much larger number of ships than could otherwise be built or repaired; and that is the establishment of Task Work in His Majesty's Yards, which I will undertake to prove would save more than a third in dispatch, and more than double in the expense. I shall annex, as a proof of this, two articles of work to be done by the Day or Task Work, which need no comment. The Blenheim and Atlas of 98 guns each, the one building, the other undergoing a thorough repair at Chatham have been brought forwards at least eight months by means of Task work. . . .

The period in which the largest number of Line of Battle Ships have ever been employed during the late and present Reign, was in the year 1759, when it appears that 97 ships of the line were in commission. But it is to be considered that this number was in consequence of two victorious wars; and that at that period we had ten ships taken from the Enemy in our Line of Battle.

However these 97 ships were greatly inferior to what we had in commission in the beginning of the year 1780; for though the number then consisted of no more than 89, yet the size of the ships was so much increased, that the 97 was a very inferior force to the 89. To make up the list of the year 1759, you must include 29 ships of 80 guns; at present there are only five of that class of ships in commission. But the fact of our Fleet being greater now than in the year 1759 is to be proved by various other evidences; the first is, the different number of seamen now in pay from that of the year 1759; the next from the different tonnage of the shipping at those periods. The whole number of seamen in actual pay on the 30th September 1759 were 88,477; on the same day in the year 1781, there were 99,831; and the men employed in the line of battleships at the same periods were in 1759, 51,540; in 1781, 53,135. The tonnage of the line of battleships was at the former date 188,195, and in 1781 it was 250,430. Our number of line of battle ships in commission in November 1781 amounts to no more than 92, and it is very extraordinary that considering our immense losses by the late dreadful hurricanes and other misfortunes which seem to have persecuted us in every part of the globe, we should still have so many remaining. To illustrate this position I will not go further back than from the first of March 1780 to the 29th September 1781, during which time no less than six ships of the line in commission were irrecoverably lost and 17 others came home in so disabled a state that a considerable time must elapse before they can again be brought into service; many of them probably never will. The names of these ships will be found in a list hereunto annexed. Had it not been for these calamities, it is a demonstration that our Naval force of the line would have been infinitely greater in numbers as well as in size in the year 1781 than in the year 1759; and nothing is more certain than that if we are not visited by any fresh hurricanes, or other calamity, we shall far exceed the number 97 in the year 1782, as we shall launch ten new ships during that period, and most probably bring forth as many old ones thoroughly repaired.

It is to be observed that we have hitherto been talking of Line of Battle Ships only; but it is very deserving notice that our number of Frigates, which in this extensive war, are of equal importance, have increased near one fourth in number, and greatly in size. For it appears that in 1759, all the ships, great and small, in the King's pay, amounted to 305; the number now in pay is 405. From these premises, it is clearly demonstrated that our present Naval force is greater than in the preceding war. I will now proceed to consider what efforts have been used in the branch of ship-building, and whether our exertions have exceeded, or been behind those of former times. Something has already been said on this subject but Demonstration cannot be got at but by an accurate comparison. I must therefore state the number of ships of the Line that were building in December 1759, and in 1781, and it will then be easy to draw the conclusion.

It appears from the weekly Progress Dec. 28th, 1759, which was (as has already been said) the year of the highest exertion in the last war, that the number of Ships of the Line then building both in the King's and Merchant's Yards amounted to 17. At the same time in 1781 they consisted of 37; in the year 1770 the number building was only 16. The Line of Battleships building in the river by Contract on the 30th December 1759 were three; in 1781, seventeen.

By this statement it is evident that we have more than double the number of ships in hand, than we had at the height of the last war, and at the time when the present Board commenced its existence: therefore it is more than presumption that we have not been more negligent than our Predecessors in this important Article, either in time of war or peace, and that when our Administration began, whatever was done in the way of building was almost in its infancy. But I suppose I shall be told that though we have done twice as much as ever was done before, we might still have done more, and might have had more than 37 ships in hand at this moment, when the Fate of the British Empire is at stake.

The answer to this is that there is a Line beyond which the exertions of every country cannot go. We cannot, nor ever could do more than employ all the shipwrights that this country affords; the Law does not allow compulsion upon any race of men but common Sailors, and if the trade of this country is to go on, the Merchants will, and always must give more money for ship-building than the Crown. The increase of wages without the increase of work in the Dockyards would be exactly so much money thrown away, as the Merchants would rise in proportion; therefore according to my reasoning there is no possibility of alluring the men by profit, or getting them by compulsion, and it is on this account that no mode has yet been found out of extending our Naval construction but by making contracts with all responsible people, who have a capital sufficient, materials at hand, and a proper place to build in. . . .

But to return from this digression; I beg that it may be remembered that we are now engaged in a War with the House of Bourbon closely united, and their Naval force unbroken (it's being unbroken was not the fault of the Admiralty) that these Powers have no Continental struggles to draw their attention, and to exhaust their finances, so that they are enabled to point the whole of their efforts to their Naval Department; that we are also at war with Holland and America, and that our Peace with all the Northern powers hangs by a very slender thread; and yet during these two last campaigns notwithstanding our inferiority of force, we have not been brought to disgrace. We have seen all our rich Baltic fleets, and our trade from the East and West Indies arrive in safety; we have at present an established superiority in the East Indies, where we have reason to expect great successes; we have obliged the Dutch to lay aside all their Fisheries, while ours, both in Europe and elsewhere have remained unmolested. We have effectually blocked the Port of Amsterdam during all the last summer, and had it not been for the subterfuge of Neutral Colours, and from our fear of disgusting the Northern Powers, not a ship could have got in or out of the Texel. We have taken possession of St. Eustatia, Demerary, and Essequibo, and under Commodore Johnstone, we have brought off the Dutch homeward bound ships from the Bay of Saldanha; we have twice relieved Gibraltar, and the last time forced the Fleet of Spain, though equal in numbers to ours, to retreat for refuge into Cadiz. We have kept the Channel open for the ingress and egress of our trade, except in the absence of the Fleet for the relief of Gibraltar, when the St. Eustatia fleet fell into the enemy's hands; and it is very certain that if the intended arrangement of the Admiralty had been successfully executed, which would have been the case if no sinister accident had interfered, we should have had an equal if not superior force to have contended for the possession of the Chesapeak. These exertions however meet with little attention, and because we have not done more than ought to have been expected from us, if we had been by a third superior to the enemy, we are supposed to have been negligent, or as some have said *treacherous*, because we have not conquered everywhere with a decided inferiority on our side. I own I think much more has been done than could have been expected, considering our losses by the hand of God, and the unnatural combinations against us among the Powers of Europe. Whatever may be the issue of this enquiry, I can put my hand upon my heart, and say that I have done my duty, with an honest intention, and to the best of my ability, and I have no doubt but that every impartial person (if such there is) will on cool and unprejudiced consideration and after having made himself master of the subject, allow me some farther degree of merit than I think it decent to arrogate to myself.

(c) TACTICS AND FIGHTING INSTRUCTIONS

170. Extract from John Clerk of Eldin's *An Essay on Naval Tactics*, 1782

(John Clerk of Eldin, *An Essay on Naval Tactics* (1790), Part I, pp. 5–6, 16–21, 147–148.)

John Clerk of Eldin (1728–1812) was an Edinburgh merchant. The *Essay* was written in 1781 and privately printed in 1782. He had studied and been much influenced by French writers, especially the French Jesuit mathematician, Paul Hoste, whose *L'art des armées navales* had been translated into English in 1762. Clerk's study of naval tactics was entirely theoretical, and he had never seen a naval engagement, but his essay became a popular textbook on the subject.

INTRODUCTION.

Upon inquiring into the transactions of the British Navy, during the two last wars, as well as the present*, it is remarkable, That, when single ships have encountered one another, or when two, or even three, have been engaged of a side, British seamen, if not victorious on every occasion, have never failed to exhibit instances of skilful seamanship, intrepidity, and perseverance; yet, when ten, twenty, or thirty great ships have been assembled, and formed in line of battle, it is equally remarkable, That, in no one instance, has ever a proper exertion been made, any thing memorable atchieved, or even a ship lost or won on either side.†

Whoever studies the history of the times, will be convinced of the truth of both these assertions. But many, without properly attending to the first, acknowledge, and endeavour to account for, the last, by insinuating that as our seamen, whatever they were in former times, are now, in no respect, preferable to those of our rivals, it would be absurd to expect from them a greater degree of exertion; and that the ships of our enemies, being better constructed, have had it always in their power to avoid an engagement, by outsailing us. As these opinions, unhappily, have already had too much influence, even among seamen, it will be partly the business of the following Treatise to show, That they are ill founded; and that it is neither to any abatement of spirit in our men, nor even to any fault in the construction of our shipping, that the want of success in the late great sea battles ought to be attributed....

Again, while we remark the wonderful exertions, and constant success, attending the lesser conflicts; while we remark how much, and how often, our ships have been put to severe trial, by being exposed, in all weathers, during the storms of winter, the enemy not daring to set out their heads‡; when, after recollection, we

* By the present war is understood the American war; this Tract being written in October 1781, immediately after the surrender of Lord Cornwallis's army, the consequence of Admiral Greaves's unsuccessful rencounter with the French fleet off the mouth of the Chesapeak. A few copies only were printed, and at that time distributed among friends.

† Neither the gallant manœuvres off St. Christophers, nor the memorable 12th of April, took place till the spring following.

‡ Alluding to the squadron of British ships kept in the Bay of Biscay during the course of the last war, to watch over the motions of the enemy, in winter as well as in summer.

remark, that, to the numerous, bold, and successful enterprises, *coups de mains*, performed during the last 250 years, and that our enemies have only the single disgrace which befel us at Chatham to counterbalance so great an account, should we not at the same time remark, that this boasted intrepidity, this persevering courage of British seamen, has never once been brought to trial, where it would have been of the greatest importance; that is, in the greater engagements; of which, because this superiority has never had an opportunity of being displayed, the result has always been the same, namely, that, in such actions, our fleets, in the two last wars and the present, have been invariably baffled, nay worsted, without having ever lost a ship, or almost a man?

While we remark these circumstances, is it not evident, and will it not be admitted, that one of three things must be the fact, either that our enemy, the French, having acquired a superior knowledge, have adopted some new system of managing great fleets, not known, or not sufficiently attended to by us? or that, on the other hand, we have persisted in following some old method, or instructions, which, from later improvements, ought to have been rejected? Or, lastly, that these miscarriages, so often, and fatally repeated, must have proceeded from a want of spirit in our seamen?

But as, from the many instances given, both of public and private exertion, the mind must revolt at this last supposition, it follows, that these repeated miscarriages must have proceeded from one or other of the two first, or from both.

During the course of the wars with the Dutch, before mentioned, much improvement was made, particularly in the invention of signals. But the naval instructions then framed, although founded upon experience and observation, and though they might be admirably fitted for fighting in narrow seas, where these battles were fought; yet, from later experience, it will be found, that they have been but ill qualified for bringing on an action with a fleet of French ships, unwilling to stand a shock, having sea-room to range in at pleasure, and desirous to play off *manœuvres* of defence, long studied with the greatest attention.

But, if it were possible that there could have remained a doubt of the truth or force of these observations before the breaking out of the present war, will not this doubt be resolved, if they shall be confirmed by every case that has followed since; whether we consider the intrepidity and exertion so conspicuous in the lesser conflicts, or the defect of conduct and address, so palpable in most of the greater engagements, although, at the same time, our Admirals, whether by good fortune, by skillful seamanship, or by permission of the enemy, have never failed, on every occasion, to acquire their wish, *viz.* the circumstance of being to windward; excepting, indeed, on those occasions, where the FRENCH have chosen to keep such an advantage, without availing themselves of it; a circumstance which is plainly a confirmation that their system or mode is different from ours, and that they are uniformly determined never to be brought to make the attack, if it can be avoided.

From all which these three conclusions will naturally follow: 1*st*, That, in bringing a single ship to close action, and in conduct during that action, the British seamen have never been excelled: 2*dly*, That the instructions, (by which is meant the method hitherto practised of arranging great fleets, so as to give battle, or to force our enemy, the French, to give battle upon equal terms), after so many and repeated trials, having been found unsuccessful, must be wrong: And, *lastly*, that, on the other hand, the French having repeatedly and uniformly followed a *mode* which has constantly the effect intended, they therefore must have adopted some new system, which we have not discovered, or have not yet profited by the discovery.

But, it may be asked, Have the French ever effected any thing decisive against us? Have they ever, in any of these rencounters, taken any of our ships? Have they ever, presuming upon their superior skill, dared to make the attack?–No. But, confident in their superior knowledge in Naval Tactic, and relying on our want of penetration, they have constantly offered us battle to leeward, trusting that our headlong courage would hurry us on to make the customary attack, though at a disadvantage almost beyond the power of calculation; the consequences of which have always been, and always will be, the same, as long as prejudices prevent us from discerning either the improvements made by the enemy, or our own blunders.

To be completely victorious cannot always be in our power; but, to be constantly baffled, and repeatedly denied the satisfaction of retaliation, almost on every occasion, is not only shameful, but, in truth, has been the cause of all our late misfortunes.

Before concluding this part of the subject, it may be proper further to observe, That, though our apprehensions of suffering in character and importance, as a Naval Power, might have been very great at the breaking out of the war with the Colonies, from an idea that the recent increase of that importance had arisen alone from the growth of these Colonies; yet, from experience, from the great exertions made, and from the continuance of the war itself, it has been clearly proved, that that increase must have arisen from other resources, which will every day more and more be found to exist in the Mother Country herself. At the same time, from that superior exertion, so constantly and gloriously exhibited by our seamen in the lesser conflicts, as well during the course of the present as of the two last wars, we may rest satisfied that the character of the British tar is not in the least debased, but still as predominant as formerly.

Hence, if the American Colonies shall accomplish their wished for separation, Britain, by her force being more collected, and, with these resources, will yet be more powerful than ever. . . .

Conclusion, with General Observations.

In the preceding Narrative and Demonstrations, we think it is shown,

1. That British seamen, from the nature, as well as the greater extent of the navigation upon our coasts, must, of necessity, be superior, both in skill and intrepidity, as well as in number, to those of other nations.

2. That deficiency in point of sailing, upon many occasions, evidently has not been the cause of these late miscarriages; but, if it has *really* been the cause of miscarriage in others, Is it not high time to set about such reformation in our dock-yards as may recover an equality in a point so important? Even supposing this to be true, Why should we uniformly attempt getting up with the enemy's van, with a view to carry their whole fleet, instead of contenting ourselves with a certainty of cutting off a few of their dullest sailing vessels in the rear?

3. That the mode of running down the wind in a line, each ship directing her course upon her opposite, and pointing the attack upon the van, with a view of stopping it, in preference to an attack upon the rear, has proceeded from an idea of carrying every ship in the enemy's fleet; but this mode has evidently given the enemy an opportunity of disabling our ships, and preventing us from coming close alongside of them.

171. Admirals Kempenfelt and Howe's Fighting Instructions, 1781–1782

(*Signals and Instructions*, ed. Julian S. Corbett, *Navy Records Society* (1908), pp. 151–167.)

The evolution of a new system of Fighting Instructions was one of the major events of naval history in the eighteenth century. The Fighting Instructions of 1691 became stereotyped for nearly a century, and though additional instructions were issued from time to time, they had an increasingly deadening effect on naval tactics. Each article of these instructions could be signalled during an action, usually by displaying a single flag whose significance depended upon the place in which it was shown. This system was very inelastic. It had been drawn up for use in the orthodox naval tactics of the later seventeenth century, which were largely designed for engagements in narrow seas, and were quite unsuited to the engagements of the Seven Years War and American War, where the problem was often to prevent the avoidance of an engagement, in seas where there was plenty of room to manœuvre, by French fleets running the blockade of their ports in order to proceed to some other scene of operations. A new system was, therefore, gradually evolved, largely by Kempenfelt and Howe, based on a Signal Book containing a list of every conceivable order, numbered in succession. The Fighting Instructions, such as the set printed below, became little more than a statement of general principles which could be adapted quickly by signals as the tactical needs of the moment required. The method was modelled on that used by the French Navy, and made possible the British naval victories of the Revolutionary and Napoleonic wars. The engagement in Chesapeake Bay in September 1781 (see No. 273) is an example of the disastrous misunderstandings which could arise in this period of transition from one system of signalling to another.

Instructions respecting the order of battle and conduct of the fleet, preparative to and in action with the enemy.

ARTICLE I.

When the signal is made for the fleet to form in order of battle, each captain or commander is to get most speedily into his station, and keep the prescribed distance from his seconds ahead and astern upon the course steered, and under a proportion of sail suited to that carried by the Admiral.

But when the signal is made for tacking, or any similar occasion, care is to be taken to open, in succession, to a sufficient distance for performing the intended evolution. And the ships are to close back to their former distance respectively as soon as it has been executed. . . .

V.

The ships which from the inequality of their rates of sailing cannot readily keep their stations in the line, are not to obstruct the compliance with the intent of the signal in others; nor to hazard throwing the fleet into disorder by persisting too long in their endeavours to preserve their stations under such circumstances; but they are to fall astern and form in succession in the rear of the line.

The captains of such ships will not be thereby left in a situation less at liberty to distinguish themselves, as they will have an opportunity to render essential service by placing their ships to advantage when arrived up with the enemy already engaged with the other part of the fleet.

The ships next in succession in the order of battle, are to occupy in turn, on this and every other similar occasion, the vacant spaces that would be otherwise left in the line; so that it may be always kept perfect at the appointed intervals of distance. . . .

IX.

When, the ships of the fleet being more in number than the enemy, the Admiral sees proper to order any particular ships to withdraw from the line, they are to be placed in a proper situation, in readiness to be employed occasionally as circumstances may thereafter require; to windward of the fleet, if then having the weather-gage of the enemy, or towards the van and ahead if the contrary; to relieve, or to go to the assistance of any disabled ship or otherwise act as by signal directed.

The captains of ships stationed next astern of those so withdrawn are directly to close to the van, and fill up the vacant spaces thereby made in the line. . . .

XV.

When any ship in the fleet is so much disabled as to be in the utmost danger and hazard of being taken by the enemy, or destroyed, and makes the signal expressive of such extremity; the captains of the nearest ships, most at liberty, with respect to the state of their opponents in the enemy's line, are strictly enjoined to give all possible aid and protection to such disabled ship as they are best able, and the captain of any frigate (or fire-ship) happening at that time to be in a situation convenient for that purpose is equally required to use his utmost endeavour for the relief of such disabled ship, by joining in the attack of the ship of the enemy opposed to the disabled ship, if he sees opportunity to place his ship to advantage, by favouring the attempt of the fire-ship to lay the enemy on board; or by taking out any of the crew of the disabled ship, if practicable and necessary, as may be most expedient.

XVI.

No captain, though much pressed by the enemy, is to quit his station in time of battle, if possible to be avoided, without permission first obtained from the commanding officer of his division, or other nearest flag-officer, for that purpose; but when compelled thereto by extreme necessity, before any adequate assistance is furnished, or that he is ordered out of the line on that account, the nearest ships, and those on each part of the disabled ship's station, are timely to occupy the vacant space occasioned by her absence before the enemy can take advantage thereof.

And if any captain shall be wanting in the due performance of his duty in time of battle, the commander of the division, or other flag-officer nearest to him, is immediately to remove such deficient captain from his post, and appoint another commander to take the charge and conduct of the ship on that occasion.

XXIII.

As soon as the signal is made to prepare for battle, the fire-ships are to get their boarding grapnels fixed; and when in presence of an enemy, and that they perceive the fleet is likely to come to action, they are to prime, although the signal for that purpose should not have been made, being likewise to signify when they are ready to proceed on service by putting abroad the appointed signal.

They are to place themselves abreast of the ships of the line, and not in the openings between them, the better to be sheltered from the enemy's fire, keeping a watchful eye upon the Admiral, so as to be prepared to put themselves in motion the moment the signal is made, which they are to answer as soon as observed. . . .

XXIV.

Frigates have it in particular charge to frustrate the attempts of the enemy's fire-ships and to favour those of our own. When a fire-ship of the enemy therefore attempts to board a ship of the line, they are to endeavour to cut off the boats that attend her, and even to board her if necessary.

XXV.

The boats of a ship attempted by an enemy's fire-ship with those of her seconds ahead and astern are to use their utmost efforts to tow her off, the ships at the same time firing to sink her.

XXVI.

In action all the ships in the fleet are to wear red ensigns.

B. THE ARMY

(a) RECRUITMENT, DISCIPLINE AND GENERAL CONDITIONS

172. Recruiting Order and notice of bounty, July 1715

(Charles M. Clode, *The Military Forces of the Crown*, II (1869), pp. 580–581.)

The Order is signed by William Pulteney, Secretary at War.

BEATING ORDER FOR RAISING RECRUITS BY BEAT OF DRUM, AND NOTICE AS TO BOUNTY.

GEORGE R.

THESE are to authorise you by Beat of Drum or otherwise to raise Volunteers in any County or part of this Our Kingdom of Great Britain, for a Regiment of Foot under your Command for Our Service, to consist of Ten Companies, of Two Sergeants, Two Corporals, One Drummer, and Forty Private Soldiers, including the Widows' Men in each Company. And when you shall have listed twenty Men fit for Service in any of the said Companies, you are to give notice to two of Our Justices of the Peace of the Town or County wherein the same are, who are hereby authorised and required to view the said Men and certify the day of their so doing; from which day the said Twenty Men and the Commissioned and Non-Commissioned Officers of such Companies are to enter into Our pay. And you are to cause the said Volunteers to be raised and levyed as aforesaid, to march under the command of such Commanding Officers as you shall direct to

appointed for the Rendezvous of Our said Regiment.

And all Magistrates, &c.

Given at Our Court at St. James's, this 23rd day of July, 1715, in the first year of Our Reign.

By His Majesty's Command,

WM. PULTENEY.

To Our Trusty and Well-beloved Thomas Stanwix, Esq., Brigadier-General of Our Forces, and Colonel of one of Our Regiments of Foot, or to the Officer or Officers appointed by him to raise Volunteers for that Regiment.

NOTICE FOR LONDON GAZETTE.

Whitehall, 26th July, 1715.

WHEREAS, His Majesty has issued out new Commissions for the raising of several Regiments, Notice is hereby given, that every man who lists himself in any of the Regiments of Foot shall receive forty shillings levy money.

Mr. Secretary Pulteney desires the above Advertisement may be inserted in this day's 'Gazette.'

I am, &c.,

Mr. Buckley.[1] JAMES TAYLOR.

[1] Samuel Buckley, printer of the *London Gazette*.

173. A Recruiting Order, July 1782

(*Curiosities of a Scots Charta Chest 1600–1800.* With the Travels and Memoranda of Sir Alexander Dick, Bart., ed. Hon. Mrs. Atholl Forbes (1897), p. 302.)

Recruiting Order brought to Glasgow by Sir Alexander Dick's son in the Guards, July 1782.

HIS MAJESTY'S FIRST ROYAL REGIMENT
OF
FOOT GUARDS.

The greatest OPPORTUNITY *ever known for* YOUNG SCOTCHMEN *to raise themselves and Families.*

YOUR Duty is a constant Pleasure, being only to attend and Guard his MAJESTY'S Person at the Palace, and to the Theatres, Opera-Houses, Masquerades, and Reviews of different Regiments.

When off Duty, you are under no Restraint; there is no Roll-calling; you may dress as you please, go where you please any where within 10 miles round London, and follow any Profession you please; which being constantly in London, is of great consequence to you, the Wages there being about three times more than any where else.

Your Pay is 10d. *per* day, and Subsistence 4s. *per* week, and 15s. a-year of QUEEN'S Bounty, with excellent Quarters, a good Room to yourself, with a Lock and Key, with the full Use of the House, Coal and Candle, and 5 Pints of choice Beer or good Cyder every Day, which the Landlord must furnish you by Act of Parliament.

It is well known you cannot be draughted to any other Regiment.

So great an Opportunity as this cannot be supposed to last long; therefore, before it is too late, let all handsome young Men, whose Hearts beat at the Sound of the Drum, and are above mean Employments, inquire after the Party commanded by Captain DICK, where you shall have the Honour of being made one of His MAJESTY'S own First Regiment of FOOT GUARDS.

The BOUNTY *is* THREE GUINEAS *and a* CROWN.

Lads from 16 to 19 are taken 5 Feet 5 inches and an Half; from that to 25 years of Age, at 5 feet 6 Inches and an Half.

N.B. *The Bringer of a good Recruit shall receive* ONE GUINEA, *by applying to Serjeant* SMITH, *at the Sign of the Marquis of Granby's Head, Lady Milton's Dike, Canongate, Edinburgh.*

174. The Rev. Francis Welles, J.P., on the behaviour of recruiting officers, April 1727

(*Law Magazine and Law Review*, XI (1861), pp. 281–283; "Journal of a Gloucestershire Justice, A.D. 1715–56".)

This extract is from the journal of his work on the Bench kept by the Reverend Francis Welles, vicar of Prestbury, Gloucestershire.

[11 April, 1727.]

We had a contest with some young officers, who pretended to have enlisted a soldier (one Thomas Wright) at Cheltenham, the Thursday before, and brought him to Gloucester. The fellow was drunk, (at the George, I think,) and the officer and a sergeant came into him, and asked if he would serve the King. He refusing to serve him as a soldier, the officer bid the sergeant mind his business, upon which (as one of Charlton Ks.[1] swore before Mr. Delabere and me) the sergeant went to him, lifted up the skirt of his coat, and put his hand towards his pocket, and soon after told him he was listed. The man denying it, the sergeant said he was, and had taken his money, a guinea, and 'twas in such a pocket. The man said he had nothing but brass in his pocket, and pulling it out a guinea was among it; so we were well satisfied the sergeant put it in unknown to the man. The officers had employed an attorney to draw up their information, sworn to by Mr. John Wells, who was, I think, the officer who beat up at Cheltenham, and one or two more, the substance of which was to show how fairly he was enlisted, and had owned himself to be so. And Mr. Payn moved the matter for them in Court. I sent for the Act 5 & 6 W. & M. and told Mr. Payn then, and three of the officers who came to us in the evening at the King's Head, when Mr. Delabere, Mr. Cocks, the Archdeacon, and myself sent to demand the man, that we would not dispute it with him whether the guinea was put into his pocket or whether he took it and put it in himself or whether he was fairly as they called it or fowly enlisted; what I insisted upon was, he was not enlisted at all. That all their whole proceedings were illegal. That, by that Act, they were to have brought him before a Justice of the Peace of the Division, or High Constable of the Hundred where enlisted, before whom he was to declare his consent; and till then was not to be deemed a soldier, nor subject to any military punishment nor entered into the Muster Role, under penalty of false mustering (which is, I think, cashiering the officer offending, incapacity of any post civil or military, and 100 li. forfeiture). That Mr. Delabere and I were Justices of that Division, and to aggravate the crime both at Cheltenham then holding a Petty Session when this transaction happened: and yet without bringing him before us, they had taken him not only out of our Division, but out of our County into the County of the City of Gloucester: and then illegally imprisoned one of the King's subjects, kept him out of a bed from Thursday to Tuesday, and even handcuffed him. That this was such treatment as could not be endured by Englishmen, who always gloried in their liberties and in the excellency of their Constitution. So they thought fit to release the man. . . .

175. Speech by the duke of Argyll in the House of Lords on the evils of patronage in the army, 9 December 1740

(*Parl. Hist.*, XI, pp. 895–897.)

This speech was made in a debate on the state of the Army and on a resolution against augmenting it by new regiments. John, second duke of Argyll (1678–1743), was at this time one of the most violent members of the opposition to Walpole's government.

. . . Regular forces are necessary in this nation in time of peace, with a proper regard to our situation, and so long as our neighbours keep such forces. And I have not changed my opinion, that 17,000 are not too many: but never was of that opinion for the

[1] Kings.

reasons of those I voted with, as I always took care to shew. I understood that the troops were to be a military body, not kept on foot for the destruction of the liberties of this country. I do not mean by burning and ravaging: these are idle apprehensions. But an army that can assist in elections, and vote away our liberties, this is the danger. And now I will shew which is an army to do good, which to do mischief. An army should be rightly proportioned of every species of officers fitted to do service. A hundred general officers for 100,000 men would be an improper proportion. It must be under military direction. The general officers must advise in military affairs, and none but military men must advise in the military part. There must be the very strictest military subordination, on which must be founded the strictest discipline. And so long as you have officers who have seen service in time of war, which alone is service, you ought not to have recourse to others. There may be exceptions to this, and distinctions shewn to persons of the first rank. But it ought to be a general rule. The rest of the places must be filled up with people that have such talents as experience will ripen. And all these must be preferred for their military merit, and punished only for military faults, or breach of the laws. But the methods of conducting an army designed for civil purposes only must be very different. You must have no regard to military services, but take such as can assist you in elections or votes in parliament. These must be indulged in applying to nothing military, must be raised for the same services they were introduced for: there must be no subordination, for that may afflict gentlemen: they must think of paying for their preferments by their votes: if they will not assist as they are directed, they must be discouraged, others put over their heads; or, if they are very obstinate, turned out, and their bread taken from them. These being the two methods, how hath the fact been? I have been 20 years the third officer in the army, eight or 9 years the second, several years the first. Therefore I may be a good evidence as to facts. And ever since this ministry hath mounted into power, military methods have been laid aside; the chain broken between the crown and the colonel; general officers have had commissions, as a man of great wit hath said, only to intitle them to call one another names; the general hath been only colonel of his own regiment, and a much less man even there than colonels were in king William's time; no discipline hath been kept up; for reviews and exercises are not discipline, but the A B C of service, of which it is necessary to know a little and no more; the general officers have had no power of acting or advising about the placing so much as an ensign sometimes not even in their own regiments. The same methods have been pursued since the war begun. General officers have not been employed or consulted excepting the lowest; such as were not general officers in the war time: and no man hath been consulted in a proper way. It was necessary last year to augment the army, and it might have been very usefully employed: we might have ravaged the whole coast of Spain, as France will do ours if ever they break with us and are masters at sea. But this was not done by additional men to each company, which it was my opinion formerly, as well as now ought to have been done, but six regiments of marines were raised in order to erect new offices, and out of above 200 half pay officers, not above 36 were put into those regiments. I spoke well of one youth who had distinguished himself in two years Russian campaigns, and by the means of the secretary at war, the general made an ensign. Numbers paid for their commissions; tradesmen from the counter were made officers; numbers taken from school, that looked as if their cockades would tumble them over. And these may be of use, if their fathers, brothers, cousins, or cousin's cousins were members of parliament. In these six regiments when they went abroad, there did not go one member of parliament. There hath been one or two since: but one of them had voted wrong. Were there no other harm in this method of augmenting, it is too expensive.

176. Extracts from Humphrey Bland's *A Treatise of Military Discipline*, 1727

(Humphrey Bland, *A Treatise of Military Discipline* (1727), pp. 133–135, 189–190.)

Humphrey Bland (1686–1763), General and military writer, served in Marlborough's campaigns and at Culloden and was Governor of Gibraltar in 1749. His *Treatise* had reached its ninth edition in 1762.

. . .

ARTICLE II.

In Marching up to attack the Enemy, the Line should move very slow, that the Battalions may be in Order, and the Men not out of Breath when they come to engage.

The Commanding Officer of every Battalion should march up close to the Enemy, before he suffers his Men to give their Fire; and if the Enemy have not given theirs, he should prevent their doing it, by falling upon them, with the Bayonets on the Muzzles the Instant he has fired, which may be done under the cover of the Smoke, before they can perceive it: So that by the Shock they will receive from your Fire, by being close, and attacking them immediately with your Bayonets, they may, in all Probability, be beat with a very inconsiderable Loss: But if you don't follow your Fire that Moment, but give them time to recover from the Disorder yours may have put them into, the Scene may change to your Disadvantage. I therefore don't recommend this way of Proceeding, but when the Enemy are Obstinate and Persevere in not giving theirs first; it being a receiv'd Maxim, that those who preserve their Fire the longest, will be sure to Conquer: But if the Method here propos'd is duly executed, that Maxim, I believe, will be found Fallible. However, it should only be pursued in the Case spoken of, as a proper Expedient when you can't draw the Enemy's Fire from them 'till you come up close; but if you can draw away their Fire at some Distance without giving yours, and that the Execution has not disorder'd the Battalion so much but that it keeps moving on towards them, you may be sure of Success; it being certain, that when Troops see others Advance, and going to pour in their Fire amongst them, when theirs is gone, they will immediately give way, or at least it happens seldom otherwise. The Point then to be aimed at is, that of receiving the Enemy's Fire first; but when both Sides pursue the same Maxim, in preserving their Fire last, I don't know a more proper Expedient than the one already mention'd: For when the Fire is given near, there won't be only a great many kill'd and wounded, but those who remain unhurt will be put into such Disorder and Confusion by it, that it will contribute to their being beat without much Difficulty, if the Blow is follow'd.

When it is apprehended that the Enemy will persist in Reserving their Fire, the Commanding Officers should prepare their Men for it before they go on, and direct them how they are to give their Fire, and in what manner they are to proceed afterwards, with the Advantages that will be gain'd by the following of it, and that their own Safety, as well as the Destruction of the Enemy, depends on the due Execution.

ARTICLE III.

When any of the Battalions have forced those they attack'd to give way, great Care must be taken by the Officers to prevent their Men from Breaking after them; neither must they pursue them faster than the Line advances: For if a Battalion advances out of the Line, it may be attack'd on the Flanks by the Enemy's Horse, who are frequently posted between the first and second Lines for that Purpose. The Commanding Officers must therefore remain satisfied with the Advantage of having obliged the Enemy to give way, and not break the Line by advancing before it in the Pursuit; but in order to keep up the Terrour of the Enemy, and to prevent their Rallying, the Granadiers may be order'd to Advance 20 or 30 Paces before the Line, to fire upon them from time to time: And while the Granadiers are thus employ'd, the Commanding Officers should take great care to keep their Regiments in good Order, that they may be ready to engage the second Line of the Enemy, which they may reasonably expect will come up to sustain those they had routed.

The Granadiers being detach'd in the Front only to prevent those who were routed from Rallying, they must by no means advance too far from the Line, lest they should be cut off from it by the Enemy. They must therefore act with Precaution; and as soon as they perceive the Second Line of the Enemy, or a Body of their Troops, marching towards them, they are to quit the Pursuit and return to their Regiments, or halt 'till their own Line comes up, if the Enemy don't advance too fast upon them.

Unless these Directions are punctually observed by every Battalion in the Line, the Advantage so gain'd may be snatch'd from them in a Moment: For by pursuing the Enemy too far, they may be surrounded by fresh Troops, and cut to Pieces before the Line can come up to their Assistance. It is therefore the Duty of every Commanding Officer, to regulate his March according to the Motions of the Line, and not suffer themselves to be too much elated on the first Success, lest it hurries them on too fast without reflecting on the Danger that may attend it: For which Reason the whole Line must act like one Battalion, both in Advancing, Attacking and Pursuing the Enemy together. While they keep in a Body, they can mutually assist one another; but if they should separate in Pursuing those they beat, the Enemy may destroy them one after another, with such an inconsiderable Number of Troops, that were they in a Body, would fly at their Appearance. The Consequence therefore of Separating during the Action, is of such Weight and Moment, that by doing it, the Enemy may not only re-establish their Affairs in such a manner as to renew the Action, but in all Probability likewise gain a compleat Victory, if they make a proper Use of the

Advantage so given; which we are always to suppose they will, and for that Reason we ought not to give them an Opportunity by which they may have it in their Power. . . .

DUTIES OF ORDERLY N.C.O.'S

They [the Orderly Serjeants and Corporals] are likewise to see that the Men keep the Caserns or Barracks very clean and in good Order, and that the Utensils belonging to them are neither spoil'd nor lost. They are to make the Men sweep their Rooms very clean every Morning, and make their Beds; and afterwards to wash themselves very clean, and dress in a Soldier-like way, by having their Shoes well-black'd, their Stockings and Cravats well roll'd, their Hats cock'd, and their Hair tuck'd under them, and their Cloaths brush'd and put on to the best Advantage; but 'till these things are done, they are not to suffer them to leave their Quarters, that they may not appear slovenly in the Streets.

They are to call over the Roll of their Companies as often as it shall be order'd, and make a Report of the absent Men to their own Officers and the Adjutant, that they may be punish'd for it.

They must go through every Room immediately after Tat-too, and oblige the Men to put out their Fire and Candle, and go to Bed.

The Men of each Company should be divided into Messes, each Mess consisting of four or six Men, or according to the Number in each Room; and every Pay-Day, each Man should be oblig'd to appropriate such a Part of his Pay to buy Provisions, which Money should be lodg'd in the Hands of one of them, in order to be laid out to the best Advantage, which the Orderly Serjeants and Corporals are to see duly executed, and make each Mess boil the Pot every Day. Without this is carefully look'd into, the Soldiers will be apt to spend their Pay on Liquor, which will not only occasion their Neglect of Duty, but, in all Probability, the Loss of a great many Men by Sickness for want of proper Victuals to support them. It is therefore a Duty incumbent on every Officer, to be more than ordinary careful in this Particular, and not to think themselves above the looking into these Things, since the Preservation of their Men depends so much on it: For in those Regiments where this Method is duly observ'd, the Men are generally Healthful; but when it is neglected, great Numbers fall sick and die.

The Captains should visit their Men's Quarters at least once a Week, and the Subalterns twice, to see that they are kept clean and in good Order; as also to inspect into the several Messes of their Companies, and to see whether their Provisions are good, and the Money laid justly out.

In some Regiments there is an Officer appointed daily to visit the Caserns or Barracks of the Regiment, to see that they are kept clean, and that the Men dress their Victuals, and to make a Report of the whole to the Colonel: However, that should not prevent the other Officers from looking into it also.

The Major should visit the Whole very often, that he may know whether the other Officers do their Duty, and reprimand those who neglect it; it being his immediate Business and Duty, to see all Orders punctually obey'd.

177. Royal Clothing Warrant of 1751

(Daniel MacKinnon, *Origins and Services of the Coldstream Guards*, II (1833), pp. 346, 352–353.)

Under George II efforts were made to standardize Army uniforms. *A Representation of the Cloathing of . . . all the Forces upon the Establishments of Great Britain and Ireland*, a kind of illustrated Dress Regulations, was published under official authority in 1742.

Warrant regulating the Standards, Colours, Clothing, &c^a^. and Rank or Number of Regiments of Cavalry and Infantry. Dated 1st July, 1751.

George R.–Our will and pleasure is, that the following regulations for the colours, cloathing, &c^a^, of our marching regiments of Foot, and for the uniform cloathing of our cavalry, their standards, guidons, banners, &c^a^, be duly observed and put in execution, at such times as these particulars are or shall be furnished, *vizt*:

Regulation for the colours, cloathing, &c^a^, of the marching regiments of Foot.

No colonel to put his arms, crest, device, or livery, on any part of the appointments of the regiment under his command.

No part of the cloathing or ornaments of the regiments to be altered after the following regulations are put in execution, but by us, or our Captain-General's permission. . . .

The coats of the Dragoon Guards to be lapelled to the waist with the colour of the regiment, and lined with the same colour; slit sleeves, turned up with the colour of the lapell.

The coats of the Horse to be lapelled to the bottom with the colour of the regiment, and lined with the same colour (except the fourth regiment of Horse, whose facings are black, and the lining buff colour); small square cuffs of the colour of the lapell.

The coats of the Dragoons to be without lapells, double-breasted; slit sleeves, turned up with the colour of the facings of the regiments, the lining of the same colour.

The whole to have long pockets; the button-holes to be of a very narrow yellow or white lace, as hereafter specified, and set on two and two, or three and three, for distinction sake: the shoulder-knots of the dragoon regiments to be of yellow or white worsted, and worn on the right shoulder. The waistcoats and breeches to be of the colour of the facings, except those of the fourth regiment of Horse, which are buff colour.

The serjeants of the Dragoon Guards and Dragoons to be distinguished by a narrow gold or silver lace on the lapells, turn-up of the sleeves and pockets, and to have gold or silver shoulder-knots: the corporals of Horse, by a narrow gold or silver lace on the lapells, cuffs, pockets, and shoulder-straps; the corporals of Dragoon Guards and Dragoons by a narrow silver or gold lace on the turn-up of the sleeves and shoulder-strap, and to have yellow or white silk shoulder-knots.

The kettle drummers, trumpetters, drummers and hautbois coats to be of the colour of the facing of the regiment, lined and turned up with red, (except the royal regiments, which are allowed to wear the royal livery, *viz.* red, lined, and turned up with blue, blue waistcoats and breeches,) and laced with the same coloured lace as that on the housings and holster caps, red waistcoats and breeches. The drummers and hautbois of the Dragoon Guards, and the kettle drummers, and trumpetters of the Horse to have long hanging sleeves, fastened at the waist.

The caps of the drummers to be such as those of the Infantry, with the tassel hanging behind; the front to be of the colour of their facing, with the particular badge of the regiment embroidered on it, or a trophy of guidons and drums; the little flap to be red, with the White Horse and motto over it–'Nec aspera terrent;' the back part of the cap to be red likewise; the turn-up to be the colour of the front; and in the middle part of it behind, a drum, and the rank of the regiment.

HATS AND CAPS OF THE CAVALRY.

The hats to be laced with gold or silver lace, and to have black cockades.

The Royal North British Dragoons only, to wear caps instead of hats, which caps are to be of the same form as those of the Horse Grenadier Guards; the front blue, with the same badge as on the second guidon of the regiment; the flap red, with the White Horse and motto over it–'Nec aspera terrent;' the back part to be red, and the turn-up blue, with a Thistle embroidered between the letters II. D., being the rank of the regiment. The watering or forage-caps of the Cavalry to be red, turned up with the colour of the facing, and the rank of the regiment on the little flap.

CLOAKS.

The cloaks to be red, lined as the coats, and the buttons set on at top, in the same manner, upon frogs, or loops of the same colours as the lace on the housings, the capes to be the colour of the facings.

HOUSINGS AND HOLSTER CAPS.

The housings and holster caps to be of the colour of the facing of the regiment, (except the First Regiment or King's Dragoon Guards, and the Royal Dragoons, whose housings are red, and the Fourth regiment of Horse, whose housings are buff colour,) laced with one broad white or yellow worsted, or mohair lace, with a stripe in the middle of one-third of the whole breadth, as hereafter specified. The rank of the regiment to be embroidered on the housings upon a red ground, within a wreath of roses and thistles, or the particular badge of the regiment, as on the second guidon or standard: the King's cypher with the Crown over it to be embroidered on the holster caps, and under the cypher the number or rank of the regiment.

UNIFORM OF THE OFFICERS, &c[a].

The clothing or uniform of the officers, to be made up in the same manner as those of the men, laced, lapelled, and turned up with the colour of the facing, and a narrow gold or silver lace or embroidery to the binding and button-holes, the buttons being set on in the same manner as on the men's coats; the waistcoats and breeches being likewise of the same colour as those of the men.

The housings and (holster) caps of the officers to be of the colour of the facing of the regiment, laced with one gold or silver lace, and a stripe of velvet in the middle, of the colour of that on the men's.

The standard belts to be the colour of the facing of the regiment, and laced as the housings.

Their sashes to be of crimson silk, and worn over the left shoulder.

Their sword-knots to be crimson and gold in stripes, as those of the Infantry.

QUARTER-MASTERS.

The Quarter-Masters to wear crimson sashes round their waists.

SERJEANTS.

The Serjeants to wear pouches as the men do, and a worsted sash about their waist, of the colour of the facing of the regiment and of the stripes on the lace of the housings.

178. Sir John Pringle on the Diseases of the Army, 1752

(John Pringle, *Observations on the Diseases of the Army*, 2nd ed. (1753), Preface, pp. vi–x.)

For Pringle, see note to No. 164. His *Observations* were first published in 1752.

. . . I have divided the work into three parts. In the first, after a short account of the air and endemic diseases of the Low Countries (so often the seat of our wars), I proceed to give an abridgment of the medical journal, which I had kept of all the campaigns. In this I mention the epidemics and more frequent diseases of our troops, in the order they occurred, the embarkations, encampments, cantonements, quarters, marches, fixed camps, the changes of the weather, and, in a word, all the circumstances of the army, that seemed to me likely to affect the health, or to afford materials for others to reason differently upon. In this part I have entered little into the description of diseases, much less have I touched upon their cure; reserving both those heads to be considered in a subsequent part of the work. My chief intention here was to collect materials for tracing the remoter causes of military distempers, in order that whatever depended upon those in command, and was consistent with the service, might be fairly stated, so as to suggest proper measures either for preventing, or palliating such causes in any future campaign. And I have been the more studious of exactness in these observations, as I foresaw that in whatever manner the whole was to be received, this part, at least, would be acceptable; as it was chiefly a narration of facts, by one who was present, and employed all the time. My inferences are few and short, as a full discussion of those points would have too much interrupted the series of incidents, that were to be presented at one view.

I have, therefore, thrown most of the reasoning, that results from the first part, into the second; in which, after dividing and classing the diseases common to a military life, I enquire into the more remote or general causes of them: namely, such as depend upon the air, diet, and other circumstances, usually comprehended under the head of the *non-naturals*. And here I have ventured to assign some sources of diseases, very different from the sentiments of other writers upon this subject; and I have also shewn how little instrumental some other causes are in producing sickness, which yet have been thought of all the most frequent. Nor will this liberty, I hope, be condemned, when it is considered what greater opportunities I have had beyond others to make such remarks; and that, as natural knowledge is daily improving, those authors, who write last on subjects connected therewith, are most likely to be in the right.

Among the chief causes of sickness and death in an army, the reader will little expect that I should rank, what is intended for its health and preservation, the *Hospitals* themselves, and that on account of the bad air and other inconveniencies attending them. During the late war, [War of the Austrian Succession], one considerable step was made for their improvement. Till then it had been usual to remove the sick a great way from the army, whereby many were in a manner lost before they came under the care of the physicians; or, which was attended with equally bad consequences, if the hospitals were nigh, they were for the greater security to be frequently shifted, according to the changes of the camp. But the Earl of *Stair*, my late illustrious patron, being sensible of this hardship, when the army was encamped at Aschaffenburg, proposed to the Duke *de Noailles*, of whose humanity he was well assured, that the hospitals on both sides should be considered as sanctuaries for the sick, and mutually protected. This was readily agreed to by the French General, who took the first opportunity to shew a particular regard to his engagement. For, when our hospital was at Feckenheim, a village upon the Maine, at a distance from the camp, the Duke *de Noailles* having occasion to send a detachment to another village, upon the opposite bank, and apprehending this might alarm the sick, he sent over to acquaint them, that as he knew the British hospital was there, he meant them no harm, and had given express orders to his troops not to disturb them. This agreement was strictly observed on both sides all that campaign; and tho' it has been since neglected, yet we may hope, that on future occasions, the contending parties will make it a precedent.

After explaining the general causes of the sickness, in armies, I proceed to point out the means of removing some, and rendering others less dangerous. Without this addition, the former considerations could have been of little use. But it is easy to conceive, that the prevention of diseases cannot consist in the use of medicines, or depend upon anything a soldier shall have it in his power to neglect; but upon such orders as shall not appear unreasonable to him, and such as he must necessarily obey.

I conclude the second part with comparing the numbers of the sick at different seasons, in order that the Commander may know, nearly, what force he can, at any time, rely upon for service; the effects of short or long campaigns upon the health; the difference between taking the field early, and going late into winter quarters; with other calculations, founded upon such materials as were furnished by the late war. The *data* are, perhaps, too few to deduce certain consequences from them; but as I have not found any other I could depend upon, I was obliged to use these only; which at least will serve for a specimen of what may be done in this way, upon farther experience.

Hitherto, as I have written for the information of officers as well as physicians,

I have endeavoured to relate the facts and propose my arguments in as plain a manner, and with as few scientific terms, as was consistent with the nature of the subject; and I hope with as much perspicuity as to be understood by any reader, not unacquainted with the common principles of natural knowledge.

But the third part, containing the practice, is intended for those of my own profession only; as it could neither be rightly explained, nor prove instructive to others. . . .

(*b*) UNPOPULARITY OF A STANDING ARMY

179. Protest of a minority of the House of Lords against the Mutiny Act, 24 February 1718

(*Journals of the House of Lords*, xx, pp. 623–624.)

This illustrates the various grounds of objection to a standing army: its possible use for tyrannical purposes; the burden of supporting it; and the undesirability of martial law. For the original Mutiny Act of 1689, see vol. VIII of these *Documents*, No. 311. The Act had to be passed annually to provide the means of maintaining discipline in the army, and thus afforded annual opportunity for these protests.

1st, Because the Number of Sixteen Thousand Three Hundred and Forty-seven Men is declared necessary by this Bill: But it is not therein declared, nor are we able, any Way, to satisfy ourselves, from whence that Necessity should arise; the Kingdom being now (GOD be praised) in full Peace, without any just Apprehension, either of Insurrections at Home, or Invasions from Abroad.

2d, Because so numerous a Force is near double to what hath ever been allowed within this Kingdom, by Authority of Parliament, in Times of public Tranquillity; and being, as we conceive, no Ways necessary to support, may, we fear, endanger our Constitution, which hath never yet been intirely subverted but by a Standing Army.

3d, Because the Charge of keeping up so great a Force ought not unnecessarily to be laid on the Nation, already overburthened with heavy Debts: And this Charge we conceive to be still more unnecessarily increased, by the great Number of Officers now kept on the Establishment, in Time of Peace; a Number far greater (in Proportion to that of the Soldiers commanded by them) than hath ever yet been thought requisite in Times of actual War.

4th, Because such a Number of Soldiers, dispersed in Quarters throughout the Kingdom, may occasion great Hardships, and become very grievous to the People, and thereby cause or increase their Disaffection; and will probably ruin many of His Majesty's good Subjects on whom they shall be quartered, and who have been already by that Means greatly impoverished.

5th, Because such a standing Force, dangerous in itself to a free People in Time of Peace, is, in our Opinion, rendered yet more dangerous, by their being made subject to Martial Law; a Law unknown to our Constitution, destructive of our Liberties, not endured by our Ancestors, and never mentioned in any of our Statutes but in order to condemn it.

6th, Because the Officers and Soldiers themselves, thus subjected to Martial Law, are thereby, upon their Trials, divested of all those Rights and Privileges which render the People of this Realm the Envy of other Nations, and become liable to such Hardships and Punishments as the Lenity and Mercy of our known Laws utterly disallow: And we cannot but think those Persons best prepared, and most easily tempted, to strip others of their Rights, who have already lost their own.

7th, Because a much larger Jurisdiction is given to Courts Martial, by this Bill, than to us seems necessary for maintaining Discipline in the Army; such Jurisdiction extending not only to Mutiny, Desertion, Breach of Duty, and Disobedience to Military Commands, but also to all Immoralities, and every Instance of Misbehaviour, which may be committed by any Officer or Soldier towards any of his Fellow subjects: By which Means, the Law of the Land, in Cases proper to be judged by that alone, may, by the summary Methods of Proceedings in Courts Martial, be obstructed or superseded, and many grievous Offences may remain unpunished.

8th, Because the Officers, constituting a Court Martial, do at once supply the Place of Judges and Jurymen; and ought therefore, as we conceive, to be sworn, upon their trying any Offence whatsoever: And yet it is provided by this Bill, "That such Officers shall be sworn, upon their trying such Offences only as are punishable by Death:" Which Provision we apprehend to be defective, and unwarranted by any Precedent; there being no Instance, within our Knowledge, wherein the Judges of any Court, having Cognizance of Capital and lesser Crimes, are under the Obligation of an Oath in respect of the one, and not of the other.

9th, Because the Articles of War, thought necessary to secure the Discipline of the Army in Cases unprovided for by this Bill, ought, in our Opinion, to have been inserted therein, in like Manner as the Articles and Orders for regulating and governing the Navy were enacted, in the Thirteenth Year of King *Charles* the Second; to the End that due Consideration might have been had, by Parliament, of the Duty enjoined by each Article to the Soldiers, and of the Measure of their Punishment; whereas the Sanction of Parliament is now given, by this Bill, to what they have had no Opportunity to consider.

10th, Because the Clause in the Bill, enabling His Majesty to establish Articles of War and erect Courts Martial, with Power to try and determine any Offences to be specified in such Articles, and to inflict Punishments for the same, within this Kingdom, in Time of Peace, doth, as we conceive, in all those Instances, vest a sole Legislative Power in the Crown; which Power, how safely soever it may be lodged with His present Majesty, and how tenderly soever it may be exercised by Him, may yet prove of dangerous Consequence, should it be drawn into Precedent in future Reigns.

11th, Because the Clause in the Bill, alledged to be made for enabling honest Creditors to recover their just Debts from Soldiers, seems to us rather to give a Protection to the Soldier, than any real Advantage to his Creditor, or other Person having just Cause of Action against him. It protects the Person of a Soldier from Executions, as well as Mesne Process, for any Debt under Ten Pounds; and it protects the Estate and Effects, as well as the Person, of every Soldier, from all other Suits but for Debt, where the Cause of Action doth not amount to the Like Sum. And in other

Cases, where the Cause of Action exceeds that Value, Plaintiffs are, in many Instances, put under such unreasonable Difficulties, as, we conceive, before they can be allowed even to commence their Suit, that their bare Compliance therewith may become more grievous to them than the Loss of their Debt, or a quiet Submission to the Wrong sustained; by which Means, His Majesty's good Subjects may be highly injured in their Properties, and insulted in their Persons, by the Soldiery; and yet be deprived of the legal Remedies appointed for the Redress of such Grievances.

W. EBOR. NORTHAMPTON.
STRAFFORD.
FRAN. CESTRIENS.
SCARSDALE.
BRISTOL.
GOWER. GREENWICH.
BOYLE.
COMPTON. POULETT.
LITCHFIELD.
TADCASTER.
BUTE.
GUILDFORD.
HARCOURT.
BINGLEY.
NORTH & GREY. FOLEY. I'LAY.
DARTMOUTH. MANSEL.
MONTJOY.
BATHURST. WESTON.
P. HEREFORD. TREVOR.
OXFORD.
FR. ROFFEN. ABINGDON.

180. Petition from Manchester and Salford against billeting of soldiers in private houses, 1746

(*Hist. MSS. Comm., 14th Report, Part IV, Kenyon MSS.*, pp. 487–490.)

The next two documents illustrate the unsatisfactory methods of housing the Army. The only barracks in England were at the Tower and the Savoy, and at Hull. The building of more was discouraged because it was held that the English people rightly associated barracks with slavery. Billeting was extremely unpopular with innkeepers (see No. 181). The billeting of soldiers in private houses was an emergency measure, due, in the case complained of here, to the 1745 rising.

PETITION to the MEMBERS OF PARLIAMENT for the County of LANCASTER.

[1746.]–We hope it will not be thought improper nor unbecoming to apply ourselves to you, the representatives of our county in the sitting of a Parliament, and in a matter of grievance and heavy oppression we labour under, and therefore, without apology, we presume to lay the case of our hardships before you.

There have been quartered within the towns of Manchester and Salford, from near the time of the action at Preston, which is now four months since, one regiment of foot and one of dragoons, making nine hundred men in both the towns, for they lie contiguous and appear but as one town, but have indeed distinct constables and are differently taxed. There are not above six inns that can entertain any number of horses, nor more than twenty public houses of any sort that can receive more than two horses apiece, the town being no throughfare, nor upon any public road for travellers, nor place of public resort other than for their own trade only, so that one single regiment of dragoons quartered upon the public houses would fill them all, so as not to leave one bed for a guest in their houses, nor room for one traveller's horse in any public stable in the two towns.

The officers therefore have forced the Constables, though against law, to billet both themselves and their soldiers upon the private houses, and not only so, but have compelled them to follow their directions therein upon what persons to billet and whom to excuse, and this by threats of commitment, of stabbing and beating, and one of the officers upon this occasion drew his sword upon one of the constables and struck him therewith, in the presence of his wife, who was then great with child. Some officers likewise have demanded more billets than they have had soldiers, and by taking the billets into their own hands, have excused such houses as they pleased from quartering soldiers, and have made private advantage to themselves thereby.

At their first coming to town, there were not more than three or four officers that were quartered at any public house, nor would they suffer the Constables to quarter them there, and five parts in six of the officers and above six hundred private soldiers are still quartered upon the private houses. Besides the soldiers, there are near two hundred and fifty women and children belonging to them in the two towns. For a considerable time after their coming to town, besides the regimental horses, there were belonging to the officers of dragoons and of the foot, and to several private soldiers, other horses not regimental, equal at least in number to the horses of the regiment, and great numbers are still continued, many officers having two or three apiece, some five, six, or more, and some near twenty horses, that are not regimental.

The women and children and most of the horses are likewise forced upon private houses, the women and children entirely upon free quarter, and the greatest part of these horses the same, though, by law, all horses not regimental ought to pay sixpence a night for hay. The better to colour their illegal billeting upon private houses, and to make it specious as if done by consent of the people themselves, they have provided the Constables with a form of a billet, which is thus:–By consent, upon A. B. so many men and so many horses, from thence insisting that the Constable does not force any person, for he only draws his billet in case the party consent; and the officer or soldier, they say, forces nobody, for he comes there by their consent, as is plain from their receiving him. Notwithstanding this pretence of consent, yet when the people seemed averse to it, they demanded the names of all such as refused; they gave out they would be committed to the gaol or taken prisoner to the guard, and that they had a commission to do so at discretion; others that refused they threatned to be sent for to London by messengers and others, to be plundered.

There fell out two very flagrant instances of plundering in the neighbourhood, both yet unpunished, and one with circumstances very suspicious upon some of the officers. There happened likewise, many instances of persons committed to the guard, and one of very severe usage there to a tradesman of substance in the town, who, without any offence charged upon him, was tyed neck and heels till blood sprung out of his eares. The apprehensions of these things, therefore, have made the billeting generally complied with, except only some dissenters who have stood upon the privilege of the subject, and have found favour beyond their neighbours.

But to take off all pretence to this implied consent, such as it was, whether for fear or for peace sake, we beg leave to give an instance or two of their dealing with those that withstood them. One was an attorney, who, being a young man, a bachelor, and haveing only two lodging rooms fitted up, one for himself, the other for his sister, and a stable for his own horse, had a dragoon and two horses billeted upon him, and he refuseing to admit them, an officer of the dragoons ordered the soldier to break open the stable and to make his quarters good, which he did, put in the two dragoon horses and turned out the attorney's, for the stable would but very inconveniently hold two horses, and hath compelled the attorney to fit up a lodging for him and to entertain him. Another is of a tradesman, who having no stable, and having two dragoons and their horses billeted upon him, offered to entertain the dragoons, provided he might be freed from the horses, as having no stable; whereupon the dragoons, as they were ordered, took the horses into his parlour, and kept them there two days, till such time as he otherwise provided them a stable.

It was expected, where they quartered upon houses not compellable by law to receive them, they would be the more punctual in the payment of those quarters. Yet for some time after their coming to town, neither officers nor soldiers in general paid anything at all. A great many officers and several soldiers have paid nothing to this day. Methods have been taken that some have had not only their hay but their corn provided. The dragoons who do pay, yet pay only eight pence a night for themselves and their horse; the foot soldiers who pay highest, pay two shillings a week, some twenty pence, some eighteen pence, some less, and some nothing at all. Though the pay of the dragoons, by Act of Parliament, is nine pence a night, and for the foot soldiers two shillings and four pence *per* week, and by law expresly, the quarters ought to be paid before any subsistance is given either to officer or soldier, if any of the quarters dare to insist upon nine pence *per* night they are threatned to be made much more losers in their hay than that comes to, and yet they are forced to give receipts in full for the subsistance.

A further hardship the Constables of the town suffer under is by being compelled to provide and pay rent for guard rooms, for a hospital for the sick rooms, for the tents and baggage of the soldiers, and likewise to provide coals and candles for the guard rooms and hospital, and bedding, linnen, washing and other necessaries for the hospital, which at the first, and for the cold season, cost three pounds a week, besides ten or fifteen pounds in fitting and preparing them, and does yet and is like still to continue to be thirty shillings a week, a charge which, as it cannot be assessed upon the town in a tax, by law, so, considering the other sufferings the inhabitants have undergone by quartering soldiers, is not likely to be voluntarily contributed to by the town, and if it must fall upon the Constables, will unavoidably ruin them. Now to estimate the damages, though far short of the truth, the penny a day for nine hundred soldiers, if all was paid to it, is three pounds fifteen shillings a day, and one thousand three hundred and sixty-eight pounds fifteen shillings a year short of the allowance of the Government; the women and children, at four pence *per* day, is four pounds three shillings and four pence *per* day, and one thousand five hundred and twenty pounds thirteen shillings and four pence a year. The charge of the non-regimental horses, we conceive should be six pence a night, but where there has been anything at all paid for them, it has not exceeded four pence by the highest officers.

We will not compute, nor can we state, what the free quarter of the officers and soldiers will amount unto, because they may allege that though they have not yet paid, yet they do design to pay at last, but we beleive these two articles do much exceed all the other.

By these hardships the town hath already suffered very much, and in a short time must be entirely ruined, several having already given up their houses, and a great many more families preparing to break up and leave the town; the revenue of excise– though by the addition of nine hundred soldiers it might be expected to be exceedingly advanced–does hardly keep up to its former rate, and the returns by the trade in the town, by computation, are already found to have sunk a thousand pounds a week.

We will not presume to judge of a reason for quartering so great a body of men upon us, when there are near half a score considerable market towns in our county and in Cheshire, within twelve or fourteen miles of us, that have not a soldier amongst them, but we humbly hope we may enjoy the benefit of the laws of England, and if there be any necessity for keeping so great a body of men together, either upon us or in any one place, more than there is convenient quarters for by law, that barracks or other conveniences may be provided at the charge of the Government; that we may be maintained in our rights and properties, so long as the law continues them to us.

We applied to Mr. Wills, whilst in town, and more especially concerning the women, children, and non-regimental horses, and were promised to be freed therein. We have applied to the commanding officers since, and likewise to the civil magistrates, for releif, but can obtain none, nor any hopes thereof, nor can we hear of any time the burden is likely to be removed. The people's patience is tired out thereby, the Constables are in danger to be torne to peices by actions on that account, the inhabitants are leaving the place, and the trade does visibly decline every day, and this without the least charge of crime or disaffection to be fixed upon any one person of substance in the town, after the most strict and diligent inquiry.

We therefore humbly beg your direction and assistance for redress, in the most proper legal and dutiful method, that the towns may not be burthened with more soldiers than they are able to quarter, and that those may be placed in the public houses, with reasonable convenience to them; that the officers and soldiers may be removed from the private houses or from such as are not willing longer to continue them; that we may be freed from the quartering of women, children, and non-regimental horses; that the officers and soldiers may be obliged to pay their quarters and to the full subsistence, as allowed by law, and that the extraordinary expenses and rent for guard rooms, hospital, and the other charges above mentioned, may be repaid and, for the future, discharged by the Government. We will make good in proof every allegation charged, with much more if it be insisted on, as shall be directed by you, and will, with all thankfulness, pursue your orders herein. *Draft.*

181. Petition of Winchester inn-keepers against the quartering of soldiers in public-houses, 30 May 1759

(*Journals of the House of Commons*, XXVIII, p. 600.)

[30 May, 1759.]

A Petition of the Innkeepers and Public-house Keepers within the City of *Winchester*, and Suburbs of the said City, was presented to the House, and read; complaining of the several Hardships, which the Petitioners allege they have laboured under ever since the *French* Prisoners came there; and alleging, that not less than Twenty-six Public Houses, in the said City and Suburbs, have lately given off, on Account of having so great a Number of Soldiers quartered in the said City and Suburbs as have been necessary to guard the said Prisoners, which has reduced the Number of Public Houses to Four Inns and Thirty-two small Public Houses; and further alleging, that the Petitioners, if not speedily redressed, must be obliged to give up their Houses, or be totally ruined; and that the Petitioners apprehend, that, if the Soldiers necessary to guard the said *French* Prisoners were put into Barracks in the Palace there, where the Petitioners are informed there is sufficient Room for that Purpose, it would be, as they are advised, the most speedy and effectual Method to remedy their great Grievances: And therefore the Petitioners implore the House to take their hard Case under Consideration, and give them such Relief in the Premises as the House shall think meet.

Ordered, That the said Petition do lie upon the Table.

C. THE MILITIA

182. Pitt's Militia Act, 1757

(*Statutes at Large*, xxii, pp. 129–130. 30 Geo. II, c. 25.)

This Act superseded the Militia Acts of Charles II (see vol. viii of these *Documents*, Nos. 302 and 303), and remained the basis of the organization of the militia until its remodelling in the second half of the nineteenth century. The most important new principle introduced by Pitt's Act was the raising of the force by ballot, thus for the first time applying coercion to men other than paupers. It defined the quota to be provided by each county, placed the militia when in training under the Mutiny Act and articles of war, though not to the extent of "loss of life or limb", and gave power to the Crown to call out the militia in case of invasion or rebellion. The aim was to make the militia an effective second line of defence in time of war.

An act for the better ordering of the militia forces in the several counties of that part of Great Britain *called* England.

Whereas *a well-ordered and well-disciplined militia is essentially necessary to the safety, peace and prosperity of this kingdom: and whereas the laws now in being for the regulation of the militia are defective and ineffectual;* be it enacted by the King's most excellent majesty, by and with the advice and consent of the lords spiritual and temporal, and commons, in parliament assembled, That from and after the first day of *May* one thousand seven hundred and fifty-seven, his Majesty, his heirs and successors may and shall issue forth commissions of lieutenancy for the respective counties, ridings and places herein after mentioned; and the respective lieutenants thereby appointed shall have full power and authority to call together all such persons, and to arm and array them at such times and in such manner as is herein after expressed; and such respective lieutenants shall from time to time constitute and appoint such persons as they shall think fit, qualified as is herein after directed, and living within their respective counties, ridings and places, to be their deputy lieutenants; the names of such persons having been first presented to and approved by his Majesty, his heirs or successors; and shall give commissions to a proper number of colonels, lieutenant colonels, majors and other officers, also qualified as is herein after directed, to train and discipline the persons so to be armed and arrayed, according to the rules, orders and directions herein after provided; and shall certify to his Majesty, his heirs and successors, the names of such commission officers, within one month after they shall be so appointed, and shall have accepted their respective commissions.

II. Provided always, and be it enacted, That nothing herein contained shall be construed to vacate any commission of lieutenancy already granted by his Majesty, nor any deputations granted to deputy lieutenants; but that the same shall continue in full force and vigour for the purposes of this act, so as the said deputy lieutenants be qualified as is herein after directed.

III. And be it enacted, That his Majesty's lieutenant of every county, riding or place shall have the chief command of the militia thereof, which shall be raised by virtue of this act; and in every county, riding or place in *England* and *Wales*, (except as is herein after excepted) there shall be appointed twenty or more deputy lieutenants, if so many persons, qualified as is herein before and after expressed, can be therein found; and if twenty persons so qualified cannot be therein found, then there shall be appointed so many persons as can be therein found; and each person so to be appointed a deputy lieutenant or colonel, shall be seised or possessed, either in law or equity, for his own use and benefit, in possession of a freehold, copyhold or customary estate for life, or for some greater estate, or of an estate for some long term of years, determinable on one or more life or lives, in manors, messuages, lands, tenements or hereditaments in *England*, *Wales* or the town of *Berwick* upon *Tweed*, of the yearly value of four hundred pounds, or shall be heir apparent of some person who shall be in like manner seised or possessed of a like estate as aforesaid, of the yearly value of eight hundred pounds; and each person so to be appointed a lieutenant colonel or major, shall be in like manner, seised or possessed of a like estate as aforesaid, of the yearly value of three hundred pounds, or shall be heir apparent of some person who shall be, in like manner, seised or possessed of a like estate as aforesaid, of the yearly value of six hundred pounds; and each person so to be appointed a captain, shall be in like manner, seised or possessed of a like estate as aforesaid, of the yearly value of two hundred pounds, or shall be heir apparent of some person who shall be, in like manner, seised or possessed of a like estate as aforesaid, of the yearly value of four hundred pounds, or shall be a younger son of some person who shall be, or at the time of his death was in like manner seised or possessed of a like estate as aforesaid, of the yearly value of six hundred pounds; and that each person so to be appointed a lieutenant, shall be, in like manner, seised or possessed of a like estate as aforesaid, of the yearly value of one hundred pounds, or shall be son of some person who shall be, or at the time of his death was, in like manner, seised or possessed of a like estate as aforesaid, of the yearly value of two hundred pounds; and each person so to be appointed an ensign, shall be, in like manner, seised or possessed of a like estate as aforesaid, of the yearly value of fifty pounds, or shall be son of some person who shall be, or at the time of his death was, in like manner, seised or possessed of a like estate as aforesaid, of the yearly value of one hundred pounds; one moiety of which said estates, required as qualifications for each deputy lieutenant, colonel, lieutenant colonel, major, captain, lieutenant and ensign respectively, shall be situate or arising within such respective county or riding in which he shall be so appointed to serve. . . .

V. Provided always, and be it enacted, That any officer may be promoted on account of merit in the said militia, when called out and assembled, in case of actual invasion, or upon imminent danger thereof, or in case of rebellion, by the lieutenant of any county, riding or place, from a lower to an higher commission, inclusive of that of lieutenant colonel, notwithstanding he should not have the qualifications requisite for his first admittance into such higher rank of the militia.

VI. Provided, That no person, not having the qualification herein before directed for a captain, shall be promoted to an higher rank than that of captain. . . .

XII. Provided always, and be it enacted, That the acceptance of a commission in the militia shall not vacate the seat of any member returned to serve in parliament. . . .

XIV and XV. [Adjutant from the King's forces to be appointed to each regiment; serjeants to be appointed out of the army.]

XVI. And be it enacted, That the number of private men to be raised by virtue of this act, in that part of *Great Britain* called *England*, the dominion of *Wales* and town of *Berwick* upon *Tweed* (exclusive of the places herein after excepted) shall be

For the county of *Bedford*, four hundred. . . . [In all 31,800]. . . .

XIX. [All men between 17 and 50 years of age to be registered and the numbers required to be chosen by lot. Fit substitutes may be provided by those selected by lot.]

XXXIII. Provided always, and be it enacted, That his Majesty's lieutenant of any county, riding or place, or the colonel of any regiment of militia, is hereby authorized, by warrant under his hand and seal, to employ such person or persons as he shall think fit, to seize and remove the arms, clothes and accoutrements, belonging to the militia, whenever his Majesty's said lieutenant, or the said colonel, shall judge it necessary to the peace of the kingdom, and to deliver the said arms, clothes and accoutrements, into the custody of such person or persons as his Majesty's said lieutenant, or the said colonel, shall appoint to receive the same, for the purposes of this act. . . .

XXXVI. [Authorizes justices of the peace to fine militia men who are absent from exercise, drunk, disobedient or who neglect to return their arms in good order. If these fines are not paid, militia men are to be set in the stocks or committed to the house of correction.] . . .

XLV. And be it enacted, That in case of actual invasion, or upon imminent danger thereof, or in case of rebellion, it may and shall be lawful for his Majesty, his heirs and successors (the occasion being first communicated to parliament, if the parliament shall be then sitting, or declared in council, and notified by proclamation, if no parliament shall be then sitting or in being) to order and direct his lieutenants, and on their death or removal, or in their absence from their respective counties, ridings or places, any three or more deputy lieutenants, with all convenient speed, to draw out and embody all the regiments and battalions of militia of their respective counties, ridings or places, herein appointed to be raised and trained, or so many of them as his Majesty, his heirs and successors, shall in his or their great wisdom judge necessary, in such manner as shall be best adapted to the circumstances of the danger; and to put the said forces under the command of such general officers as his Majesty, his heirs and successors, shall be pleased to appoint over them; and to direct them to be led by their respective officers into any parts of this kingdom, for the suppression of such invasions and rebellions: and the said officers of the militia, and private militia men, shall from the time of their being drawn out and embodied as aforesaid, and until they shall be returned again, by order of their commanding officers, to their respective parishes or places of abode, remain under the command of such general officers, and shall be intitled to the same pay as the officers and private men in his Majesty's other regiments of foot receive, and no other; and the officers of the militia shall, during such time as aforesaid, rank with the officers of his Majesty's other forces of equal degree with them as the youngest of their rank; and the officers of the militia, and private militia men, shall be hereby, during such time as aforesaid, subjected and made liable to all such articles of war, rules and regulations, as shall be then by act of parliament in force, for the discipline and good government of any of his Majesty's forces in *Great Britain*; any thing herein contained to the contrary notwithstanding; and when they shall be returned again to their respective parishes or places of abode, they shall be under the same orders and directions only, as they were before they were drawn out and embodied as aforesaid: and if any non-commission officer of the militia, or private militia man, shall be maimed or wounded in actual service, he shall be equally intitled to the benefit of *Chelsea Hospital*, with any non-commission officer, or private soldier, belonging to his Majesty's other forces: and if any militia man so ordered to be drawn out and embodied as aforesaid (not labouring under any infirmity incapacitating him to serve as a militia man) shall not appear and march in pursuance of such order, every such militia man, being convicted thereof upon oath, before two or more justices of the peace, shall forfeit and pay the sum of forty pounds; and if such militia man shall refuse immediately to pay such penalty, the justices of the peace before whom such militia man shall be so convicted, shall by warrant commit such militia man to the common gaol of the county, riding or place where he shall have been so convicted, there to remain without bail or mainprize for the space of twelve months, or until he shall have paid the penalty aforesaid.

XLVI. [In case of invasion, or rebellion, parliament may by royal proclamation be summoned to meet.] . . .

XLVIII. [Officers and private men, when called out to their annual exercise, are to be quartered on public-houses.] . . .

LI. Provided always, and be it enacted, That neither this act, nor any matter or thing herein contained, shall be deemed or construed to extend to the giving or declaring any power for the transporting any of the militia of this realm, or any way compelling them to march out of this kingdom. . . .

LXX. [Repeal of all former acts for raising the militia.] . . .

LXXIII. [Act to be in force for five years.]

Part IX

SCOTLAND

SCOTLAND

Introduction

THE eighteenth century, though a time of political stagnation in Scotland, was nevertheless the period in which modern Scotland was born. This period may be divided at about the year 1745, not only for the obvious reason that the failure of the rising of that year really marked the end of effective Jacobitism in Scotland, but also for other reasons. The Union of 1707 had been accepted by the Scots largely on account of the economic advantages which it was hoped would flow from it. These advantages necessarily did not accrue at once, and in the years following the Union there was much bitter dissatisfaction with it. By the middle of the century, however, Scotland was beginning to reap the benefits for which she had hoped, and economic prosperity was further increased by greater political stability after the failure of the '45.

The Church had remained, in the years following the Union, the most important institution in Scotland. A description by an English clergyman of a Presbyterian service[1] shows the rather condescending contempt felt by the English for the Scottish Church, and throws light on at least one reason for lack of sympathy between the two countries. Dissensions arose in this period within the Scottish Church, which are illustrated in the debate in the General Assembly on the Schism Overture in 1766.[2] By the later part of the century 'Moderatism' had triumphed over the more extreme and militant type of Calvinism. The Lowland Scot, especially in the early years of the period, was a churchman first and foremost, and politics took second place in his thoughts and actions. The refusal of 'James III' to dissimulate about his religion meant, therefore, that Jacobitism could never become a genuinely national movement.[3]

The situation was, however, very different in the Highlands. Once across the Highland line Englishman and Lowland Scot alike found a state of affairs that was completely incomprehensible to them and out of which developed the rising in favour of Prince Charles Edward in 1745.[4] The description by Flora MacDonald of the Prince's voyage from the Outer Islands to Skye after his defeat at Culloden[5] illustrates the devoted loyalty of the Highlanders to the House of Stuart. The measures taken by the Hanoverian Government for the pacification of the Highlands after the suppression of the rebellion[6] transformed the Highlands and had important repercussions on the Lowlands. It should be noted that they were not limited to the restrictions on wearing Highland dress and the abolition of heritable jurisdictions.

As time went on, religion and education also played their part in the pacification of the Highlands.[7] There was extensive emigration from the Highlands, and to a less extent from the Lowlands, in the mid-eighteenth century;[8] but by the turn of the century the opening to Scotland, by the Union, of colonial trade had led to a great increase in wealth, and industry and agriculture both developed rapidly. With the

[1] No. 183. [2] No. 184. [3] No. 185. [4] No. 186.
[5] No. 187. [6] No. 188 and 189. [7] No. 190. [8] No. 191.

founding of the Carron Iron Works[1] the heavy industries were securely established for good or evil as the basis of Scottish industrial development. Agriculture was revolutionized, mainly, as in England, by the efforts of big landowners with an interest in agricultural improvements,[2] and the Lothians became one of the most advanced farming areas in the world. Edinburgh, having lost its effective position as a capital city, nevertheless adopted and in the main carried out a grandiose plan for the building of its new town.[3] Glasgow, though as late as 1769 it was described by Pennant as "the best built of any modern second-rate city I ever saw", had benefited most from the opening of the trade with the American colonies, and laid the foundations of its greatness in the years immediately following the '45.[4] The literary and artistic renaissance which took place in Scotland in the eighteenth century is less clearly the result of the Union than these advances in economic prosperity. It is an important feature of Scottish history in this period, and was appreciated by continental writers.[5]

[1] No. 192. [2] No. 193. [3] No. 195. [4] No. 194. [5] No. 196.

BIBLIOGRAPHY

I. BIBLIOGRAPHIES, ETC.

For the non-specialist reader the best list of books is *A Brief Bibliography of Scottish History* by Dr. H. W. Meikle, Historical Association Pamphlet No. 109 (London, 1937). The same editor has prepared a more comprehensive bibliography of Scotland–a select bibliography published by the National Book League for the British Council. More advanced students should use C. S. Terry, *Catalogue of the Publications of Scottish Historical and Kindred Clubs and Societies and of the Volumes relating to Scottish History, issued by His Majesty's Stationery Office* (Glasgow, 1909), continued by C. Matheson to 1927, including *Historical Manuscripts Reports* (Aberdeen, 1928). On economic history W. H. Marwick, "Bibliography of Scottish Economic History" in *Economic History Review*, III (1931–1932), pp. 117–137, and the supplementary article in *ibid.*, Second Series, IV (1951–1952), pp. 376–382, should be consulted. On local history and topography reference should be made to Sir A. Mitchell and C. G. Cash, *A Contribution to the Bibliography of Scottish Topography*, Scottish History Society (2 vols., Edinburgh, 1917), and to the volumes of the *Proceedings of the Society of Antiquaries of Scotland* with general indexes for vols. 1–48 (Edinburgh, 1892 and 1936), and especially to Sir A. Mitchell's list of travellers in Scotland in vol. 35 (1901), pp. 431–638, of this series (Edinburgh, 1901), continued in vol. 39 (1905), pp. 500–527. On family history there are two invaluable works, *The Scots Peerage*, edited by Sir. J. Balfour Paul (9 vols., Edinburgh, 1904–1914), and *Scottish Family History: A Guide to Works of Reference on the History and Genealogy of Scottish Families* by Margaret Stuart and Sir J. Balfour Paul (Edinburgh, 1930). Hew Scott, *Fasti Ecclesiae Scoticanae* (new edition, 7 vols., Edinburgh, 1915–1928), gives brief biographies of the ministers of the Church of Scotland and useful bibliographies of the local divisions of the Church. G. E. C[ockayne], *The Complete Peerage* and the *Dictionary of National Biography*, should also be used for lives of eminent eighteenth-century Scotsmen. The Royal Scottish Geographical Society has published *Early Maps of Scotland* (Edinburgh, 2nd edition, 1936), some of which relate to this period. M. E. Craig, *The Scottish Periodical Press* [1750–1789] (Edinburgh, 1931), is useful. Many valuable articles on all branches of Scottish history are to be found in *Scottish Historical Review* (Glasgow, 1903–1928), including the two index volumes. After a gap of twenty years the *Review* has now been revived and is published twice a year by Nelson (Edinburgh, 1947 onwards). The *Juridical Review* (Edinburgh, 1889–with index volume for vols. 1–46, Edinburgh, 1934) contains occasionally articles of historical interest.

II. ORIGINAL SOURCES

Comparatively little of the official material preserved in the Public Record Office or H.M. Register House has been published. Several volumes of the Historical Manuscripts Commission's publications are, however, useful on this period, notably *Athole Manuscripts*, Report 12, part 8 (1891); *Laing Manuscripts* (2 vols., 1914 and 1925); *Graham Manuscripts* in Various Collections, V (1909), and *Polwarth Manuscripts* (4 vols., 1911–1942). Some indication of the richness of the unofficial material may be obtained from the selections published by J. G. Fyfe in *Scottish Diaries and Memoirs* (Stirling, 1928 *et seq.*). As outstanding classics may be mentioned, *The Autobiography of the Reverend Dr. [Jupiter] Carlyle*, edited by J. H. Burton (Edinburgh, 1860, new edition, Edinburgh, 1910); J. Ramsay of Ochtertyre, *Scotland and Scotsmen in the 18th century*, edited by A. Allardyce (2 vols., Edinburgh, 1888); the Reverend Thomas Somerville, *My Own Life and Times, 1741–1814* (Edinburgh, 1861), and, at the very end of the period Lord Cockburn, *Memorials of His Time 1779–1850* (Edinburgh, new edition, 1909). Another important section consists of selections published from family archives by the historical clubs and more recent works such as Dr. I. F. Grant, *Everyday Life on an old Highland Farm 1769–82* (London, 1924), Professor H. Hamilton, *Selections from the Monymusk Papers 1713–55*, Scottish History Society (Edinburgh, 1945), and James Fergusson, *John Fergusson 1727–1750* (London, 1948) and *Lowland Lairds* (London, 1949).

III. MODERN WORKS: GENERAL

P. Hume Brown, *History of Scotland*, vol. III (Cambridge, 1909), still holds the field as a general introduction. Agnes Mure Mackenzie, *Scotland in Modern Times 1720–1939* (London, 1942, new edition, 1947), is the best of more recent treatments. W. C. Mackenzie, *The Highlands and Isles of Scotland: A Historical Study* (Edinburgh, 1937), justifies its title. The works of the older Scottish historians are still worth reading, and this also applies to the third volume of H. T. Buckle, *History of Civilisation in England* (London, 1857–1861, and later editions), which in spite of its title is devoted to Scotland. Two works by W. L. Mathieson between them cover the political and religious aspects of the eighteenth century: *Scotland and the Union* (Glasgow, 1905) and *The Awakening of Scotland* (Glasgow, 1910). A. V. Dicey and R. S. Rait, *Thoughts on the Union between England and Scotland* (London, 1920), and G. S. Pryde, *Treaty of Union of Scotland and England* (London, 1950), are excellent commentaries on the Union. E. and A. G. Porritt, *The Unreformed House of Commons*, vol. II, gives a full account of the Scottish parliamentary system. John Galt, *Annals of the Parish* (Edinburgh, 1821, and frequently reprinted), can hardly be improved upon as an introduction to the problems of transition from rural life to industrialism, but H. Hamilton, *The Industrial Revolution in Scotland* (Oxford, 1932), is the standard work on the subject. James Handley, *Scottish Farming in the Eighteenth Century* (London, 1953), has a good bibliography. Smollett's *Humphry Clinker* (numerous editions) and some of Sir Walter Scott's novels, especially *Waverley* and *Rob Roy*, are also valuable. R. S. Rait and G. S. Pryde, *Scotland* in Benn's Modern World Series (London, 1934 new edition, largely rewritten by G. S. Pryde), is a good general history, useful for the eighteenth century. H. G. Graham, *Social Life of Scotland in the Eighteenth Century* (2 vols., London, 1899, and later editions), is still useful, and G. M. Trevelyan, *English Social History* (London, 1944), makes a masterly comparison of Scotland's social life at the beginning and end of the eighteenth century. Marjorie Plant, *The Domestic Life of Scotland in the 18th century* (Edinburgh, 1952), is a useful compilation. On emigration I. C. G. Graham, *Colonists from Scotland* (Cornell, 1955), should be consulted.

G. W. T. Omond, *The Lord Advocates of Scotland* (2 vols., Edinburgh, 1883), throws light on Scottish politics and administration. G. Menary, *Life and Letters of Duncan Forbes of Culloden* (London, 1936), is an admirable study of the career of the best-remembered Scottish lawyer of the early eighteenth century. There are also two good studies of the career of Henry Dundas, one by C. Matheson, the other by H. Furber (London, 1933 and 1931 respectively), both with the title *Henry Dundas, 1st Viscount Melville*. J. B. Salmond, *Wade in Scotland* (Edinburgh, 1934), gives an excellent account of Wade's road-making work. Less scholarly but useful is Marion Lochhead, *The Scots Household in the 18th century* (Edinburgh, 1948).

IV. WORKS ON JACOBITISM

The specialized bibliography on Jacobitism in the *Journal of Modern History*, XI (1939), pp. 49–60, should be consulted. From the publication of Sir Walter Scott's *Tales of a Grandfather* and R. Chambers, *History of the Rebellion*, Jacobitism has attracted an amount of attention out of proportion to its significance. The Scottish History Society has published a great mass of original materials notably the three volumes of *The Lyon in Mourning*, edited by H. Paton, relating to Prince Charles Edward (Edinburgh, 1895–1896); Dr. W. K. Dickson's volume based on Ormonde's letters, *The Jacobite Attempt of 1719* (Edinburgh, 1891);

W. B. Blaikie's scholarly *Itinerary of Prince Charles Edward* (Edinburgh, 1897), and a number of more recent but less important volumes on the '45 and its aftermath. *Intercepted Post*, edited by Donald Nicholas (London, 1956), is an interesting collection of about a hundred letters from ordinary people in Scotland written during the course of the '45. The Stuart Papers at Windsor have provided historians with a rich quarry utilized by Andrew Lang in his *Prince Charles Edward* (London, 1900) and other works, and more recently by A. and H. Tayler in a series of studies, the most important of which are *1715: The Story of the Rising* (London, 1936) and *1745 and After* (London, 1938). Other useful works are Audrey Cunningham, *The Loyal Clans* (Cambridge, 1932), and Winifred Duke, *Lord George Murray and the Forty-Five* (Aberdeen, 1927). G. H. Jones, *The Main Stream of Jacobitism* (London, 1954) is a good account of the various Jacobite plots. C. S. Terry published a composite narrative of the '45, *The Forty-five* (Cambridge, 1922), using the *ipsissima verba* of the original authorities, and a similar volume on the earlier risings, *The Jacobites and the Union* (Cambridge, 1922). The second volume of Sir Charles Petrie's history of Jacobitism, *The Jacobite Movement The Last Phase 1716–1807* (London, 1950), is a convenient conspectus, if its manifest bias is discounted.

V. CULTURAL HISTORY

J. H. Millar, *A Literary History of Scotland* (London, 1903), is strong on the eighteenth century, and H. G. Graham, in *Scottish Men of Letters in the Eighteenth Century* (London, 1901), made a special study of the period. The most useful of several recently published works by American historians on Scottish cultural development in the eighteenth century are Gladys Bryson, *Man and Society: the Scottish Inquiry of the 18th century* (Princeton, 1945), and H. W. Thompson, *A Scottish Man of Feeling* (London, 1931), with valuable bibliography. The standard works on painting are Sir J. L. Caw, *Scottish Painting 1620–1908* (Edinburgh, 1908), and S. Cursiter, *Scottish Painting* (London, 1949). Mr. Cursiter has also published a general conspectus of Scotland's artistic development, *Scottish Art to the 19th Century* (London, 1949). D. MacGibbon and T. Ross, *Castellated and Domestic Architecture of Scotland* (5 vols., Edinburgh, 1887–1892) remains the authoritative work on eighteenth-century architecture. The *Reports of the Royal Commission on the Ancient and Historical Monuments and Constructions of Scotland* (London, 1909 onwards) now include surveys of many of the most important counties. There are numerous popular accounts of Scottish architecture but none is really adequate on the eighteenth century. I. G. Lindsay, *Georgian Edinburgh* (Edinburgh, 1948), and Ian Finlay, *Scottish Crafts*, including architecture (London, 1948), may, however, be recommended. A. Morgan, *Rise and Progress of Scottish Education* (London, 1927), is the best account of its subject. On Scots law the student will find the Stair Society's volume, *The Sources and Literature of Scots Law* (Edinburgh, 1936, with index, 1939), invaluable. John Macinnes, *The Evangelical Movement in the Highlands of Scotland* (Aberdeen, 1951), is instructive and well balanced.

A. THE CHURCH

183. An English visitor's account of a Presbyterian service in 1725

(*Hist. MSS. Comm.*, *Portland MSS.*, VI, pp. 122–124.)

From a narrative of a tour made by the second earl of Oxford, written by his chaplain. See also No. 130.

May 23. [1725.] Our being at this place[1] this Sunday morning afforded us an opportunity of a sight which was curious enough for a stranger. It was that Meeting or Assembly of the members of the Presbyterian Kirk, which is by them termed an Occasion: and perhaps may be so called because the Celebration of the Sacrament is the occasion of such assembling together. There is notice given some time before hand when and where this Occasion is to be held, at which time and place (which is generally one of the Kirks most commodious for its largeness) the ministers of the several "Parochs", to the number of ten, twenty, or perhaps thirty sometimes, are desired to attend and give their assistance, according as their several parts are allotted to them of praying or preaching, which is to continue without any intermission both within the kirk and without it in some field adjoining for this whole day from morning to night. St. Ringins was the place appointed for this day's solemnity, and about ten o'clock we went forth to observe it; both the church and the field they were met in being within a bowshot of our inn. We first walked into that part of the open ground where they met to the number of many hundreds, and disposed themselves on a shelving ground facing their preacher, who held forth at the lower part of it, from a tent erected for that purpose. This part of the occasional assembly seemed altogether made up of the very meanest sort of people that this country could show. It was a rainy day, but they sat or stood it out with great patience and attention to what the twentieth part of them could not possibly hear one word of, or rather indeed I should say one sentence: for the preacher every now and then took care to lift up his voice at some particular, insignificant word which might reach the ears of the greatest part of the congregation: the present preacher seemed an elderly and weakly man, but had a special knack at this elevation of tone when he saw convenient. I pressed on through the crowd, till I came so near that I could hear him distinctly, he soon satisfied my curiosity with a confused medley and jargon of words, uttered with great emotion; and I could not tell which to compassionate the most, the preacher or the spectators; for I cannot properly call them the hearers.

The field exercise seems to be contrived only as an entertainment and amusement to keep those poor people together, who cannot get into the church till room be made for them, by the retirement of some of those who crowd within it, so that they make a continual succession, whilst those who are tired of their entertainment within doors are glad of getting forth into the fresh air and a fresh amusement, and those of the field are ready to succeed and take their places.

After seeing their disposition in the open air, we got into the body of the church by the favour of a porter who kept the door constantly shut, but when people had

[1] St. Ninians, near Stirling.

occasion to come out, or enter in. It was exceedingly thronged both in the body of the church and in the lofts or galleries; however, we pressed forward through the crowd till we came pretty near the pulpit where Master Loggin, the parish minister, was just upon the conclusion of his sermon, which was the first that day, and called the Earnest sermon: after which, having sung a psalm, he gave the discharge, that is, he generally pronounced the several sort of sinners whom he discharged or forbid from partaking of the Sacrament. After which a psalm was again sung, and then he came down from the pulpit into the body of the church (another immediately mounting up in his room) where some boards were laid for the whole length of it from west to east about two feet wide and the height of a table, and covered over with an ordinary linen cloth. The persons who were first to communicate, about fifty or more, sat on each side (but to the best of my remembrance were all uncovered). The minister stood about the middle of it, and after some short preface signifying to what purpose they were met on that occasion, he read to them that part of the chapter to the Corinthians from whence the Church of England takes the Form of the Consecration Prayer. When this was done the persons thereunto appointed went down on each side of the long table I before mentioned, and received the tickets from every person, that was sat down in order to communicate: for without producing such a ticket (as described on the other side), no person was admitted. When these officers were returned with the tickets to the Minister who stood at the side of the table about the centre of the kirk, he proceeded to send the bread to the Communicants on each hand of him, it was shoved along the table on platters which held each of them several large pieces of wheaten bread, which the people took out thence, and divided every man with his neighbours that sat near him on the same side or over against him. After this followed the flagons with the wine, which every one took and drank according to his discretion. We did not stay within the kirk until this set of communicants were removed and the next sermon begun: for indeed the crowd was great and very troublesome to stand in for so long a time; though some people of a better sort who were placed in pews near the place where I stood very civilly invited me to come in and sit down with them, which could I have afforded to have stayed much longer, I should gladly have accepted: but my curiosity was by this time pretty well satisfied, and I was very willing to retire both on account of the various offensiveness met with in the common throng, and the disagreeable and shocking appearance their celebration of this duty carried in it, especially to those who thought they had great reason upon this sight to bless God for having been used to a behaviour very different both as to decency and reverence of it.

I am told there are frequent disorders amongst the poor people on these occasions, who being to make a whole day of it at the place where they meet, cannot be supposed wholly to abstain from meat and drink, and sometimes to go to excess in the latter. But as I saw nothing of this kind, I cannot charge them with it. It was now about eleven o'clock in the morning, and if there ever are any excesses of this kind committed it most probably must happen towards the evening; and indeed no wonder it should fall out so, where there are so many thousands of ordinary people got together, as generally attend these occasions, there being already at this place three thousand at least, besides great numbers that were continually coming on their way, and very probably there might be double the number before the close of the evening.

184. An account of the debate in the General Assembly of the Church of Scotland on the Schism Overture, May 1766

(*Scots Magazine* (1766), pp. 338, 339–340, 395–397.)

In the eighteenth century a 'Moderate' party grew up in the Scottish Church, comparable with the Latitudinarian party in England, stressing good works and the ethical teaching of the Bible in contrast to the traditional Calvinist party's emphasis upon faith. The two parties also took opposite sides over the question of patronage, the Moderates favouring the implementation of the Patronage Act of 1712, which had caused the first secession from the Scottish Church in 1740; the traditionalists upholding the rights of congregations to choose their own ministers. In the General Assembly of 1766, the traditionalists proposed an inquiry into the causes of schism and the evils of patronage, which was only defeated by 99 votes to 85.

The overture itself . . . consists of a short narrative as to the increase of secession, and these propositions: 1. *That the assembly should appoint an inquiry into the fact.* 2. *That as the abuse of patronage has been one great cause of schism they would consider what methods may be employed to remedy so great an evil.* 3. *That they would appoint a committee to correspond with presbyteries, and gentlemen of property and influence; and to report.*

The debate was opened by the moderator of the preceding assembly,[1] who spoke, as he always does, with great strength and propriety, and with very much dignity. He stated the fact as to the numbers who had separated from the church of Scotland of different denominations,–the proportion they bore to the whole,–the continuance and increase of separation every year,–the unhappy consequences of it both in a spiritual and temporal view,–the obligation upon the general assembly to endeavour at least in some degree to remedy it.–He then took notice of the abuse of the law of patronage; shewed how it might be, and had been, abused, by patrons; but particularly insisted, that he did not understand the abuse of patronage meant in the overture to be confined to patrons, but that it had been abused by the church-courts in many respects; and that if they desired reformation, they ought to begin at home, and do every thing within their own sphere in a legal and constitutional manner to promote it. He complained of the unjust and slanderous representations which had been made without doors of the designs of the friends of the overture, as if they were mad unreasonable men, of furious tempers, and enthusiastic principles, who intended to bring every thing into confusion both in church and state; he declared, that he knew none but who desired to be determined in their judgment by cool and rational principles, to conduct their designs according to law and good order, and to attempt nothing towards an alteration of the statutes now in force immediately, nor at all, unless they could convince gentlemen of rank and property, that it was their own interest, and that of their country. He then concluded in favour of the overture in all its parts. . . .

[Arguments against the overture.]

5. It was observed, That there was only one cause of schism mentioned in the overture, *viz.* the abuse of the patronage-act; but that it was no way certain, that this was either the only or the chief cause of it. One great cause of it was mentioned,

[1] Dr. Oswald of Methven.

and laid to the charge of the opposite party, *viz.* instilling into the minds of the people, that they had a divine right, purchased to them by Christ, to chuse their own pastors; which imaginary right had taken such possession of them as had made them quite untractable; so that they refused submission to the pastors settled among them in an orderly manner. Here occasion was taken to inveigh severely against the unreasonable prejudices and obstinacy of the common people. Instances were mentioned of their opposition to persons of the greatest ability, and most unexceptionable character, merely because they had accepted of presentations. To this also it was alledged they were generally stirred up by the conduct of presbyteries, or by the artful insinuations of particular ministers.[1]

6. There were some who scrupled not to give it as their opinion, That patronage was the best way of settling churches: That the nobility and gentry, in whom the right of presenting was usually vested, must be presumed the best judges of the qualifications of ministers, and were naturally intitled to that distinction by the eminence of their station: That if the election were in the common people, they would be easily carried away by men of superficial rather than solid talents, one candidate would be set up against another, and the animosity of the contending parties would occasion infinite tumult and confusion. On the contrary, it was observed, that the law of patronage, when supported by uniformity in the decisions of the church, always produced peace and good order, as in our neighbour church, where no body thinks of making any opposition to the person presented.

This being indeed the hinge of the cause, was most laboured by the speakers on both sides. The eminent doctor formerly hinted at,[2] favoured us with a sketch of the history of patronage in the church of Scotland, with a particular view to shew its happy influence on the characters of ministers. He told us, That at the revolution, and for a considerable time after it, the ministers of the church of Scotland were sober and pious men, but of mean abilities, and little acquaintance with the world: That about the end of Q. Anne's reign, patronage was re-established in a manner well enough known, and after that young gentlemen intended for the ministry endeavoured to accomplish themselves by a more free and liberal education, and such qualifications as might render them acceptable to the politer part of mankind: That if, in attempting this, some of them had fallen into a few faults on the side of levity, it was natural, and very pardonable: That in his opinion nothing of this kind had ever happened worth mentioning, or being laid in the balance with the opposite conduct of others: That no character whatever was more contemptible in a minister, than a mean and low desire of popularity among the vulgar: and upon the whole, That the church of Scotland never was in higher reputation for the characters of her ministers than at present; which ought in justice to be imputed to the way in which public measures had been carried on for some time past. . . .

[Arguments for the overture.]

5. It was agreed by the friends of the overture, That there might be other causes of schism besides what is mainly pointed at; and that accordingly they had not called

[1] Note omitted. [2] Dr. Robertson, the historian and leader of the 'Moderate' party (see No. 196).

this the *only*, but one *great cause*, of the disorders that had happened. They mentioned particularly relaxation of discipline, as what might be justly complained of, and what they hoped the assembly would take into their serious consideration, and set an example to future assemblies by the vigorous exercise of it in some cases that were to come before them; but that as they could not help thinking that the relaxation itself was in a good measure owing to what they had pointed out, so it was a thing manifest, and beyond all question, that patronage, in the manner in which it had been exercised, was the chief and immediate cause of the erection of all or most part of the meeting-houses that had been built in Scotland: That this was not a matter of conjecture, but the reason openly professed for the building of such houses, by those who were concerned in them. And who has not seen many examples of whole parishes going off at once upon a disagreeable settlement's taking place?

It was denied, that any minister now alive could be justly charged with instilling false principles into the minds of the people as to their right in calling their pastors: That the meaning of this phrase deserved well to be a little attended to; for it was capable of two senses: That it might seem to relate to the natural right which every man has to chuse or judge for himself in religion, and every thing belonging to it; and therefore, in particular,–to chuse his own pastor, to whom he was to commit the care of his soul, and on whom he was to depend for daily instruction and comfort: Or, 2. It might relate to the question, Who had a right in fact, or who ought in justice to have the right, of calling a parochial minister upon an establishment? That in the first sense it belongs to every individual, no consistent Protestant will perhaps be hardy enough to deny. And in the second, perhaps it will be as difficult to find any body who ever asserted it. Who has the power at present among us, being a matter of fact, and not of right, depends upon the statutes now in force. Nay, though a new law were to be made upon the subject, probably no body would plead for every adult inhabitant having an equal share, because such a seeming equality would be a real inequality. But at the same time it is certain, that where any power of judging is left to us, such regard ought to be had to the general principle, as to promote the end of settling a gospel-ministry; which undoubtedly is the edification of the people within a certain district. When this end is not answered, men say or think of it what they please, but it is just so much of the public money entirely thrown away.

As to the prejudices of the people, it was said, that though neither they nor their betters are without prejudices of different kinds, yet the time was long passed in which they excepted against any man merely for his getting a presentation. When a man is presented with whose doctrine and life they are well satisfied, the presentation giving him a right to the benefice is never quarrelled. How many instances might be given, and those very recent, of whole parishes uniting to supplicate their patron for a presentation in favour of a minister of whom they had a high esteem? So that if ever there were any such childish prejudice as to be offended at the very name, it is plain that it has not at this time any existence.

As to the stale complaint, of opposition being raised or fomented by presbyteries or ministers, nothing could be more easily refuted by experience. Many instances might be given of the most uncomfortable settlements, where all possible pains had been taken by the presbyteries of the bounds to reconcile the people, and where every body knew it was both their interest and inclination to do it effectually if it had been in their power. But however innocent they were in this matter, it was said they despaired of being free from the false accusation; for it was abundantly sufficient in the eye of many, to accuse a minister of fomenting an opposition, unless he would fairly give up all his own professed principles, and openly embrace theirs.

6. As to the expediency of settling churches by presentations, it was said, That both the reason of the thing, and daily experience, shewed the unhappy consequences of enforcing them in the rigorous and tyrannical manner they had been of late: That it was natural for patrons to look upon the right as merely a piece of civil property, and accordingly to dispose of them so as they might best promote their private interest: In former periods, indeed, considerable regard was paid to the inclinations of gentlemen of rank and influence in the parish; but now this was entirely laid aside: That there had been discovered some very scandalous ways of obtaining presentations, and many more were strongly suspected: And if things went on in the present channel, the same practices would prevail to a degree still more open, more offensive, and more hurtful.

Could it be denied, that when a presentation absolutely secured a man's settlement, whatever was his character among the people, it would make students and probationers much less watchful and circumspect in their behaviour? This was the more to be regarded in our church, which, wanting the splendor of dignities and revenues, could only obtain or preserve respect by the purity and regularity of the clergy: That there were too many instances of our falling short of our fathers in these particulars; and as the effect was manifest, the cause was not hard to discover.

That we need but open our eyes to see the bad effects of the present measures: Whole parishes scattered, the ministers hated or despised, and rendered utterly useless either in a civil or religious capacity. What instruction can a minister give to those who will not hear him? What authority can he have over those who despise him? What comfort among those that hate him; unless he become wholly indifferent about his work, and warming himself with the fleece, give up all care of or attention to the flock? How far this is the case with too many already, the world is at liberty to judge. . . .

As mention had been made of our neighbour church of England, it was observed, this was no way favourable to the cause of presentations. There, whoever is presented, be he of ever so immoral a character, is indeed ordained without opposition; but the consequence is, that the parishes are shamefully neglected; and the common people in England of the church-persuasion, are perhaps more ignorant and profane than the members of any Protestant church in the world. Can any man desire to reduce us to a similarity with them in this particular? Surely not: and yet patronage continuing on its present footing is the high road to lead us to it. It is in vain to hope to make men indifferent about their ministers till they are indifferent about religion itself. The last may be sometimes without the first, but the first never was, nor ever will be, without the last. . . .

The history given of patronage, and its effects, did not pass unnoticed. It was observed, That from the reformation downwards, the friends of the Presbyterian establishment always considered patronage as unfavourable to, or rather inconsistent with, that form of government. As there was a constant struggle before the revolution between Presbytery and Episcopacy, so it might be said, almost without any exception, that when Presbytery prevailed, patronage was either wholly abolished, or greatly restrained. At the revolution, in particular, it was taken away by the act of parliament 1690: and the restitution of it in 1712 is well known to have been brought about by the inveterate enemies of our constitution, and to have been intended as a thrust at its very vitals, though it did not come to have much influence in the settlement of parishes till many years after, and that by slow degrees.

The preference in point of character given by the learned Doctor to the ministers of the present, in comparison with those of former generations, was not only doubted, but denied. For though just at the revolution, from the penury of ministers, some of but indifferent abilities might find admission; yet it was well known, that in the following years there appeared in the church of Scotland a set of men, who, for learning, piety, usefulness, and every truly ministerial qualification, have been equalled by few, and exceeded by none of the present boasted period. It was also thought, that magnifying the reputation of the present ministers of the church of Scotland savoured a little of vanity, as being supposed to contain a tacit reference to some late successful publications, which, whatever evidence they might be of the ability of the particular authors, must be a very slender proof, if any at all, of the clerical merit of the whole body.

B. THE HIGHLANDS AND THE RISINGS OF 1715 AND 1745

185. Refusal of 'James III' to compromise over his religion, 1716

(*Hist. MSS. Comm. Stuart MSS.*, IV, pp. 11–13.)

Prince James Francis Edward reached Scotland in December 1715, by which time, in spite of the partial success of Mar at the battle of Sheriffmuir, the defeat of the Jacobite army at Preston and the fall of Inverness had really ended all hope of Jacobite success. He remained in Scotland till early February 1716, when he returned to France. His stiff and reserved manner was a disillusionment to his most ardent supporters, and his refusal to compromise or try to deceive people over his religion lost him all hope of support in the Lowlands.

1716, January. Reasons for not assisting at the *Te Deum* at Perth.

I cannot well understand why some people have laid so much stress on my assisting once at a *Te Deum* joined to the daily service of the Church of England, except they think by it that the people will be imposed on and conclude that I am either a Protestant or in a fair way towards it, and in that case it cannot be wondered I should decline that step, in which, conscience apart, there would be so manifest a dissimulation, and which would at the same time only serve to excite people's expectation, and to make the disappointment of my not changing my religion at last the greater. For it is not to be supposed that men of sense or honour could believe me to play the hypocrite so notoriously as to be a Protestant in exterior and a Catholic in my heart, or to think on t'other hand that once going to church and that alone could quiet people's minds in relation to religion, when they would see by my future conduct that I was not less a Catholic for that. All this being, it is very manifest to me that the point aimed at is an absolute change, at least according to reason it ought to be so, and that I should no sooner have yielded one thing but another would be pressed, the same arguments would be used for one as for t'other, and to think that less than an absolute change would entirely satisfy, I believe, nobody doth believe, all the rest, as I may well call it, is but chicane, much unbecoming both my character and dignity and that reputation of sincerity my interest as well as honour engages me to maintain, and, if I were well known, people would not be so mealy mouthed but speak plain, which, I am sure, I should neither wonder at nor take ill, there being nothing so natural as for all men to desire others should be of the same religion as they, nor more becoming a loyal Protestant than to wish I should condescend to what is so manifestly my interest. But, as my resolution in that respect may be easily concluded, and that except that one main point I have given sufficient proofs of my moderation, of my kindness for my Protestant subjects, and of the happiness they may enjoy under me, the whole of the question must come to this dilemma, either they have and will receive me as a Catholic, or they will not. If the first, why speak more of the matter? if the last, why not tell me so plainly and send me back, since, though I have and am yet willing to venture my life to relieve them, yet I cannot betray my conscience on any account whatsoever? It was not, I am sure, either ambition or the prospect of future greatness and happiness that determined me to this undertaking, reputation was the only private view I had in it, and their delivery was my principal object, towards the effecting of which, if they will not join with me, it will be their misfortune more than mine and more sensible to me than my own, but can never be my fault. After this I must appeal to any reasonable man, if I have not on this head done all that was possible for me towards quieting people's minds, or if my conduct can be said to have anything of harshness or bigotry in it. The bare re-presentation of the Jesuits being disagreeable in England made me part with them as a thing indifferent in itself to religion and what might be pleasing to the generality of my friends. Did not I promise to hear what the Protestants had to say for themselves in due time and place? Did not I send for Mr. Leslie out of England to assist my Protestant servants abroad? I gave them a place to pray in and assemble in my own house, and that they did with less mystery than I have Mass here; I had all my Protestant servants with me at Bar, and all favour and distinction was shown them. As to myself, since my coming here everybody knows I had not so much as a priest with me nor have not now any living constantly at this place. I hear not Mass so much as every day, and, when I do, it is in so private a manner that the last Catholic subject I have could not do it with more caution; and what are the returns I receive for all this, when even that liberty, which in a king would be looked upon as tyranny to refuse to his subjects, is grudged by them to me, who give me in my own person but a sad example of that leniency and moderation in religious matters they preach so much and practise so ill, but which they shall never make me desist from showing to them.

If, therefore, people would but think seriously of the matter, I am persuaded they would let that matter fall, and in my present unfortunate circumstance not increase my mortifications by pressing upon me what I cannot comply with, and what it is, therefore, for my interest more than my ease should not be mentioned, at least at this time, nay, I may say more, that my affairs being as uncertain as they now are, were I even resolved to change, it would be against my interest to do so now, as must be visible to all thinking men.

186. A description of the Highlands on the eve of the rising of 1745

(John Home, *The History of the Rebellion in the Year 1745* (1802), pp. 3–12.)

John Home (1722–1808), author of *Douglas* and other plays, took part in the defence of Edinburgh against the Jacobites in 1745.

Scotland is divided into Highlands and Lowlands: these countries, whose inhabitants speak a different language, and wear a different garb, are not separated by friths or rivers, nor distinguished by northern and southern latitude: the same shire, the same parish at this day, contains parts of both; so that a Highlander and Lowlander (each of them standing at the door of the cottage where he was born) hear their neighbours speak a language which they do not understand.

That the extent and limits of the country called the Highlands, (at the time of which I write,[1]) may be seen at one glance, a map of Scotland is prefixed to this

[1] 1745.

volume, where a winding line from Dunbarton upon the river Clyde, to Duninstra, upon the frith of Dornoch, separates the Highlands from the Lowlands.

This line, beginning at Dunbarton, goes on by Crief and Dunkeld to Blairgowrie in Perthshire, from which it runs directly north to the forest of Morven, in the heights of Aberdeenshire: at Morven it proceeds still northwards to Carron in Banff-shire; from Carron it takes its course due west, by Tarnoway, in the shire of Murray, to the town of Nairne (in the small shire of that name); from Nairne, the line is continued by Inverness to Conton, a few miles to the west of Dingwall in Rossshire: at Conton, it turns again to the north-east, and goes on to Duninstra, upon the south-side of the frith of Dornoch, where the line of separation ends, for the country to the north of the frith of Dornoch (that runs up between Rossshire and Sutherland,) is altogether Highland, except a narrow stripe of land, between the hills and the German Ocean, which washes the east coast of Sutherland and Caithness. To the west of this line lie the Highlands and Islands, which make nearly one half of Scotland, but do not contain one eighth part of the inhabitants of that kingdom. The face of the country is wild, rugged, and desolate, as is well expressed by the epithets given to the mountains, which are called the grey, the red, the black, and the yellow mountains, from the colour of the stones of which in some places they seem to be wholly composed, or from the colour of the moss, which, in other places, covers them like a mantle.

In almost every strath, valley, glen, or bottom, glitters a stream or a lake; and numberless friths, or arms of the sea, indent themselves into the land.

There are also many tracts of no small extent, (which cannot properly be called either mountains or valleys,) where the soil is extremely poor and barren, producing short heath, or coarse sour grass, which grows among the stones that abound every where in this rough country. Nor is the climate more benign than the soil: for the Highlands in general lying to the west, the humid atmosphere of that side of the island, and the height of the hills in such a northern latitude, occasion excessive rains, with fierce and frequent storms, which render the Highlands for a great part of the year a disagreeable abode to any man, unless it be his native country. In the Highlands, there are no cities nor populous towns,* no trade or commerce, no manufactures but for home consumption; and very little agriculture. The only commodity of the country that fetches money is cattle; and the chief employment of the inhabitants is to take care of the herds of their black cattle, and to wander after them among the mountains.

From this account of the Highlands, it is manifest, that the common people, earning little, must have fared accordingly, and lived upon very little: but it is not easy to conceive, how they really did live, and how they endured the want of *those things which* other people call the conveniencies, and even the necessaries of life. Their houses scattered in a glen or strath,† were usually built of sod or turf, sometimes of clay and stone, without lime. In such habitations, without household stuff or utensils

* There are several Royal Boroughs in the Highlands, that make a part of the different districts (each of which districts sends a representative to parliament). Some of these boroughs lie near the line of separation, and are inhabited by a mixed race of people, Highlanders and Lowlanders. In the borough of Nairne, at the time of the rebellion, the inhabitants of one side of the town spake English, and their neighbours on the other side spake Gaelic.

† A glen is a narrow vale with a rivulet, and hills on each side. A strath is a valley with its hills, and a river.

wrought by an artificer, the common people lived during the winter,* lying upon boards with heath or straw under them, and covered with their plaids and blankets. For a great part of the year, they subsisted chiefly upon whey, butter, cheese, and other preparations of milk, sometimes upon the blood† of their cattle, without much grain or animal food, except what of the latter they could procure by fishing or hunting, which, before the late rebellion, were free to people of all ranks, in a country where the rivers and lakes swarmed with fish, and the hills were covered with game. Making a virtue of necessity, the Highlanders valued themselves upon being able to live in this manner, and to endure cold and hunger, to a degree almost incredible. In those days, the chieftains and gentlemen who were, many of them, stock farmers and graziers, though much better accommodated than their inferiors, occasionally lived like the common people,‡ and contended with them in hardiness, maintaining that it was unworthy of a Highlander to stand in need even of oat-meal, to discharge the prime duty of a man, and fight for his chief.

In these words, which are their own,§ the Highlanders expressed their opinion of themselves, and their enthusiasm for clanship. As that singular institution formed and stamped the peculiar character of the Highlanders, I shall endeavour to explain the principle of the domination of chiefs, which now exists no more.

The Highlands are divided into a number of territories or districts, separated by rivers, lakes, or mountains, sometimes by ideal and arbitrary boundaries. Each of these districts, called by the natives a country, was the residence of a clan or kindred, who paid implicit obedience to the Cean Cinne or head of the kindred. This person (known in the English language by the name of Chief) was the hereditary magistrate, judge, and general of the clan: he determined all disputes that arose amongst his people, and regulated their affairs at his discretion. From his judgment there was no appeal: to decline the tribunal of the chief, and apply to any of the king's courts for redress against one of the same kindred, was considered as highly criminal, a kind of treason against the constitution of clanship, and the majesty of the chief. The sirname of the chief, was the name of the clan, and the title which he bore constantly reminded the Highlanders of the *kindly* origin of his power; for the Cean Cinne was the kinsman of his people, the source and fountain of their blood. His habitation was the place of general resort, the scene of martial and manly exercises: a number of the clan constantly attended him both at home and abroad: the sons of the most respectable persons of the name lived a great part of the year at his house, and were bred up with his children. To bind the kindred faster together, the cord of interest (in the most

* The winter town, as it was called, consisted of a number of such houses, and sometimes a better one belonging to a gentleman or farmer. In summer the Highlanders left the winter town with their cattle and servants, and went to the hills (for to each of the winter towns belonged a considerable tract of land in the adjacent hills). There they built temporary huts in the shylings, or best spots of pasture, removing from one shyling to another, when the grass failed. About the end of August they left the hill and returned to the winter town.

† The first thing the Highlanders did when they went to the hills, was to bleed all their black cattle; and, boiling the blood in kettles, with a great quantity of salt, as soon as the mass became cold and solid, they cut it in pieces, and laid it up for food.

‡ The Highland gentlemen used to make hunting parties, and go to the hills in time of frost and snow, where they remained several days. They carried with them no provisions, but bread and cheese with some bottles of whiskey, and slept upon the ground, wherever night overtook them, wrapped up in their plaids.

§ The words of Sir Ewen Cameron, often quoted by his countrymen.

ordinary sense of the word) was drawn strait between them: the lands of the chief were let to his nearest relations upon very easy terms; and, by them, parcelled out to their friends and relations, in the same manner. That consanguinity, the great principle of clanship, might not lose its force by being diffused amongst a multitude of men, many of whom were far removed from the chief, there were intermediate persons called the chieftains, through whom the inferiors looked up to their chief. Every clan consisted of several tribes; and the head of each tribe was the representative of a family descended from that of the chief. His patronimick (which marked his descent) denominated the tribe of which he was chieftain, and his lands (for every chieftain had some estate in land) were let to his friends and relations in the same manner that the lands of the chief were let to his friends: each chieftain had a rank in the clan regiment according to his birth; and his tribe was his company. The chief was colonel, the eldest* cadet was lieutenant-colonel, and the next cadet was major. In this state of subordination, civil and military, every clan was settled upon their own territories, like a separate nation, subject to the authority of their chief alone. To his counsels, prowess and fortune, (to his auspices,) they ascribed all their success in war. The most sacred oath to a Highlander, was to swear by the hand of his chief. The constant exclamation, upon any sudden accident, was, may God be with the chief, or, may the chief be uppermost. Ready at all times to die for the head of the kindred, Highlanders have been known to interpose their bodies between the pointed musket, and their chief,† and to receive the shot which was aimed for him.

In such communities, the king's peace and the law‡ of the land were not much regarded: beyond the territories of each clan, the sword was the arbiter of all disputes: several of the clans had inveterate quarrels, and deadly feuds; they went to war and fought battles. Rapine was often practised, under pretext of reprisal, and revenge; and, in those parts of the low country that bordered upon the Highlands, depredation and rapine were often committed, without any pretence at all: hence, fierceness of heart, prompt to attack or defend, at all times and places, became the characteristic of the Highlanders. Proud of this prime quality, they always appeared like warriors; as if their arms had been limbs and members of their bodies, they were never seen without them: they travelled, they attended fairs and markets,§ nay they went to church with their broad swords and dirks; and in latter times, with their muskets and pistols. Before the introduction of fire arms, the bow, the broad sword and target,

* In settling the rank of their officers, the same rule was not observed by every clan that took arms in the year 1745. In some regiments, the eldest cadet was lieutenant-colonel, and in the others the youngest cadet. The Highlanders say, that, according to the original customs of clanship, the eldest cadet ought to be next in command to the chief, and that the appointment of the youngest cadet to be lieutenant-colonel, was an innovation introduced by those chiefs who had great land estates.

† Examples of this sort of enthusiasm are handed down by tradition and preserved in the memoirs and manuscript histories of the Highland families. A low country man, not many years ago, expressing his admiration of one of those commoners who sacrificed himself to save the life of his chief, a Highland gentleman said that he saw no reason to admire the action so much, that the man did his duty, and no more; for he was a villain and a coward who, in the same circumstances, would not do the same.

‡ The chiefs sometimes went to law with one another, but the decisions of the court of session, and the judgments of the privy council, were not of much avail, unless the party who had obtained judgment in his favour was more powerful than his antagonist, or better supported by his neighbouring chiefs. Locheil and Mackintosh were at law and at war for 360 years.

§ In those days, that is, about 170 years ago, a clergyman in the Isle of Skye went to church with a broad sword at his side, and his servant walked behind him with his bow and quiver full of arrows.

with the dirk, were the weapons offensive and defensive of the Highlanders. When the use of fire arms became common in the kingdom, they assumed the musket instead of the bow, and, under the smoke of their fire, advanced to close with the enemy. As to their dress, or Highland garb (for so they call it at this day), which, like every thing unusual in war, had an effect of terror in the last rebellion, it is needless now, when so many battalions of the king's troops wear it as their uniform, to describe a dress which is to be seen every day in the streets of London and Edinburgh; but it seems necessary to mention, that the target was no part of a Highlander's accoutrements, except on the day of battle; and in those battles that were fought during the rebellion, most of the men in the front rank of every Clan regiment, besides his other arms, had a pistol; though in the present times, neither the 42d regiment, renowned for valour, nor any other Highland regiment, has any arms but the musket and bayonet.

Such were the arms and accoutrements of the Highlanders when they went to war. Order and regularity, acquired by discipline, they had little or none; but the spirit of clanship, in some measure, supplied the want of discipline, and brought them on together; for when a Clan advanced to charge an enemy, the head of the kindred, the chief, was in his place, and every officer at his post, supported by his nearest relations, and most immediate dependants. The private men were also marshalled according to consanguinity: the father, the son, and the brother, stood next each other. This order of nature was the sum of their tactic, the whole of their art of war.

187. Journal taken from the mouth of Miss Flora MacDonald by Dr. Burton of York, when in Edinburgh, 1746

(R. Forbes, *The Lyon in Mourning*, ed. H. Paton, I; *Scottish History Society*, XX (1895), pp. 299–301, 303–305.)

Dr. Burton came to Scotland in 1746 to inquire into the affairs of Prince Charles Edward. Forbes (later bishop of Ross) visited him in Edinburgh in 1747 and received this account from him. After the battle of Culloden on 16 April, Prince Charles Edward was a fugitive in Scotland for five months, before escaping to France.

. . .

28 June [1746].

At eight o'clock, June 28th, Saturday, 1746, the Prince, Miss Flora MacDonald, Neil MacKechan, etc., set sail in a very clear evening from Benbecula to the Isle of Sky. It is worth observing here that Benbecula is commonly reckoned a part of South Uist, they being divided from one another by the sea only at high water, which then makes a short ferry betwixt the two; but at low water people walk over upon the sand from the one to the other.

They had not rowed from the shore above a league till the sea became rough, and at last tempestuous, and to entertain the company the Prince sung several songs and seemed to be in good spirits.

In the passage Miss MacDonald fell asleep, and then the Prince carefully guarded her, lest in the darkness any of the men should chance to step upon her. She awaked in a surprize with some little bustle in the boat, and wondered what was the matter, etc.

29 June

Next morning, Sunday, June 29th, the boatmen knew not where they were, having no compass and the wind varying several times, it being then again calm. However, at last they made to the point of Waternish, in the west corner of Sky, where they thought to have landed, but found the place possessed by a body of forces who had three boats or yawls near the shore. One on board one of the boats fired at them to make them bring-to; but they rowed away as fast as they could, being all the chance they had to escape, because there were several ships of war within sight. They got into a creek, or rather clift of a rock, and there remained some short time to rest the men, who had been all night at work, and to get their dinners of what provisions they had along with them. As soon as they could they set forwards again, because as the militia could not bring them to, they had sent up to alarm a little town not far off. It was very lucky for them that it was a calm then, for otherwise they must inevitably have perished or have been taken.

From thence they rowed on and landed at Kilbride, in Troternish, in the Isle of Sky, about twelve miles north from the above-mentioned point. There were also several parties of militia in the neighbourhood of Kilbride. Miss left the Prince in the boat and went with her servant, Neil MacKechan, to Mougstot, Sir Alexander MacDonald's house, and desired one of the servants to let Lady Margaret MacDonald know she was come to see her ladyship in her way to her mother's house. Lady Margaret knew her errand well enough by one Mrs MacDonald, who had gone a little before to apprize her of it.

As Mr. Alexander MacDonald of Kingsburgh was accidentally there, Lady Margaret desired him to conduct the Prince to his house; for it is to be remarked that Lady Margaret did not see the Prince in any shape. Kingsburgh sent a boy down to the boat with instructions whither to conduct the Prince about a mile, and he (Kingsburgh) would be there ready to conduct him.* Then Kingsburgh took some wine, etc., to refresh the Prince with, and set forwards for the place of rendezvous, leaving Miss MacDonald with Lady Margaret at Mougstot, where the commanding officer of the parties in search of the Prince was, and who asked Miss whence she came, whither she was going, what news? etc., all which Miss answered as she thought most proper, and so as to prevent any discovery of what she had been engaged in.

Lady Margaret pressed Miss very much in presence of the officer to stay, telling her that she had promised to make some stay the first time she should happen to come there. But Miss desired to be excused at that time, because she wanted to see her mother, and to be at home in these troublesome times. Lady Margaret at last let her go, and she and Mrs MacDonald above mentioned set forwards with Neil MacKechan and said Mrs MacDonald's maid and her manservant. They overtook the Prince and Kingsburgh. Mrs. MacDonald was very desirous to see the Prince's countenance; but

* Here is a mistake; for Mr. MacDonald of Kingsburgh declared to me more than once that he sought for the Prince some time to no purpose, and had almost despaired to find him, when at last the accidental running of a flock of sheep proved the occasion of finding him out.–ROBERT FORBES, A.M.

as he went along he always turned away his face from Mrs MacDonald to the opposite side whenever he perceived her endeavouring to stare him in the countenance. But yet she got several opportunities of seeing his face, though in disguise, which the maid could not help taking notice of, and said she had never seen such an impudent-looked woman, and durst say she was either an Irish woman or else a man in a woman's dress. Miss MacDonald replied she was an Irish woman, for she had seen her before. The maid also took notice of the Prince's awkward way of managing the petticoats, and what long strides he took in walking along, etc., which obliged Miss MacDonald to desire Mrs. MacDonald (they being both on horseback), to step a little faster and leave those on foot, because, as there were many parties of militia in the great roads, it was necessary for the Prince to cross the country, and it was not proper to let Mrs. MacDonald's man or maid servant see it. So on they went, and the Prince and Kingsburgh went over the hills and travelled south-south-east till they arrived at Kingsburgh's house, which was about twelve o'clock at night, and they were very wet. But Miss MacDonald, who had parted with her companions and her man-servant on the road, arrived some short time before the Prince. . . .

1747. 23 Nov.

N.B.–The above I[1] transcribed from Dr. Burton's own hand-writ. Happening to mention several questions that were fit to be proposed to Miss MacDonald, the Doctor desired me to give him them in writing, for that he would endeavour to procure direct answers to them. Accordingly, I gave them to him in writing, and he performed what he had promised. Here follows an exact copy of the questions and their answers. . . .

4.–Ask what particular songs he chaunted in crossing from the Long Isle to Sky? if she can give the names of them?

ANSWER.–He sung 'The King shall enjoy his own again,' and 'The twenty-ninth of May,' etc.

5.–Ask whether or not Lady Clanronald furnished the Prince and Miss MacDonald with some bottles full of milk as part of their provisions on board the boat in the passage to Sky? And whether or not the Prince did put the bottle to his head, and drink in common with those on board?

ANSWER.–Lady Clanronald did furnish them with some bottles of milk, and the Prince (in the passage) putting the bottle to his head, drank in common with those on board *Jock-fellow-like*. Lady Clanronald had put one half-bottle of wine (there being so many demands upon her, particularly from parties of the military) which she likewise caused to be put on board the boat. The Prince in the passage would not allow any person to share in this small allowance of wine, but kept it altogether for Miss MacDonald's use, lest she should faint with the cold and other inconveniences of a night passage.

[1] Reverend Robert Forbes.

188. The Disarming Act, 1746

(*Statutes at Large*, XVIII, pp. 519–531. 19 Geo. II, c. 39.)

This Act, passed as a result of the 1745 rising, forbade the bearing of arms or the wearing of the kilt and tartans, and was described by Duncan Forbes, Lord President of the Court of Session, as "the most important medicine" for disaffection in the Highlands. It also provided for the registration of all private schools and the taking the oaths prescribed for office-holders by all teachers.

An act for the more effectual disarming the highlands in Scotland; *and for the more effectually securing the peace of the said highlands; and for restraining the use of the highland dress; and for further indemnifying such persons as have acted in defence of his Majesty's person and government, during the unnatural rebellion; and for indemnifying the judges and other officers of the court of justiciary in* Scotland, *for not performing the northern circuit in* May *one thousand seven hundred and forty-six; and for obliging the masters and teachers of private schools in* Scotland, *and chaplains, tutors and governors of children or youth, to take the oaths to his Majesty, his heirs and successors, and to register the same.*

WHEREAS *by an act made in the first year of the reign of his late majesty King* George *the First, of glorious memory, intituled,* An act for the more effectual securing the peace of the highlands in *Scotland, it was enacted, That from and after the first day of* November, *which was in the year of our Lord one thousand seven hundred and sixteen, it should not be lawful for any person or persons (except such persons as are therein mentioned and described) within the shire of* Dunbartain, *on the north side of the water of* Levin, Stirling *on the north side of the river of* Forth, Perth, Kincardin, Aberdeen, Inverness, Nairn, Cromarty, Argyle, Forfar, Banff, Sutherland, Caithness, Elgine, *and* Ross *to have in his or their custody, use, or bear, broad sword or target, poignard, whinger, or durk, side pistol, gun, or other warlike weapon, otherwise than in the said act was directed, under certain penalties appointed by the said act; which act having by experience been found not sufficient to attain the ends therein proposed, was further enforced by an act made in the eleventh year of the reign of his late Majesty, intituled,* An act for more effectual disarming the highlands in that part of *Great Britain* called *Scotland;* and for the better securing the peace and quiet of that part of the kingdom: *and whereas the said act of the eleventh year of his late Majesty being, so far as it related to the disarming the highlands, to continue in force only during the term of seven years, and from thence to the end of the next session of parliament, is now expired: and whereas many persons within the said bounds and shires still continue possessed of great quantities of arms, and there, with a great number of such persons, have lately raised and carried on a most audacious and wicked rebellion against his Majesty, in favour of a popish pretender, and in prosecution thereof did, in a traiterous and hostile manner, march into the southern parts of this kingdom, took possession of several towns, raised contributions upon the country, and committed many other disorders, to the terror and great loss of his Majesty's faithful subjects, until, by the blessing of God on his Majesty's arms, they were subdued:* now, for preventing rebellion, and traiterous attempts in time to come, and the other mischiefs arising from the possession or use of arms, by lawless, wicked, and disaffected persons inhabiting within the said several shires and bounds; be it enacted by the King's most excellent majesty, by and with the advice and consent of the lords spiritual and temporal, and commons, in this present parliament assembled, and by the authority of the same, That from and after the first day of *August* one thousand seven hundred and forty-six, it shall be lawful for the respective lords lieutenants of the several shires above recited, and for such other person or persons as his Majesty, his heirs or successors shall, by his or their sign manual, from time to time, think fit to authorize and appoint, in that behalf, to issue, or cause to be issued out, letters of summons in his Majesty's name, and under his or their respective hands and seals, directed to such persons within the said several shires and bounds, as he or they, from time to time, shall think fit, thereby commanding and requiring all and every person and persons therein named, or inhabiting within the particular limits therein described, to bring in and deliver up, at a certain day, in such summons to be prefixed, and at a certain place therein to be mentioned, all and singular his and their arms and warlike weapons, unto such lord lieutenant, or other person or persons appointed by his Majesty, his heirs or successors, in that behalf, as aforesaid, for the use of his Majesty, his heirs or successors, and to be disposed of in such manner as his Majesty, his heirs or successors shall appoint; and if any person or persons, in such summons mentioned by name, or inhabiting within the limits therein described, shall, by the oaths of one or more credible witness or witnesses, be convicted of having or bearing any arms, or warlike weapons, after the day prefixed in such summons, before any one or more of his Majesty's justices of the peace for the shire or stewartry where such offender or offenders shall reside, or be apprehended, or before the judge ordinary, or such other person or persons as his Majesty, his heirs or successors shall appoint, in manner herein after directed, every such person or persons so convicted, shall forfeit the sum of fifteen pounds sterling, and shall be committed to prison until payment of the said sum; and if any person or persons, convicted as aforesaid, shall refuse or neglect to make payment of the foresaid sum of fifteen pounds sterling, within the space of one calendar month from the date of such conviction, it shall and may be lawful to any one or more of his Majesty's justices of the peace, or to the judge ordinary of the place where such offender or offenders is or are imprisoned, in case he or they shall judge such offender or offenders fit to serve his Majesty as a soldier or soldiers, to cause him or them to be delivered over (as they are hereby impowered and required to do) to such officer or officers belonging to the forces of his Majesty, his heirs or successors, who shall be appointed from time to time to receive such men, to serve as soldiers in any of his Majesty's forces in *America*; for which purpose the respective officers, who shall receive such men, shall then cause the articles of war against mutiny and desertion to be read to him or them in the presence of such justices of the peace, or judge ordinary, who shall so deliver over such men, who shall cause an entry of memorial thereof to be made, together with the names of the persons so delivered over, with a certificate thereof in writing, under his or their hands, to be delivered to the officers appointed to receive such men; and from and after reading of the said articles of war, every person so delivered over to such officer, to serve as a soldier as aforesaid, shall be deemed a listed soldier to all intents and purposes, and shall be subject to the discipline of war; and in case of desertion, shall be punished as a deserter; and in case such offender or offenders shall not be judged fit to serve his Majesty as aforesaid, then he or they shall be imprisoned for the space of six calendar months, and also until he or they shall give sufficient security for his or their good behaviour for the space of two years from the giving thereof.

II. And be it further enacted by the authority aforesaid, That all persons summoned to deliver up their arms as aforesaid, who shall, from and after the time in such summons prefixed, hide or conceal any arms, or other warlike weapons, in any dwelling-house, barn, out-house, office, or any other house, or in the fields, or any other place whatsoever, and all persons who shall be accessary or privy to the hiding or concealing of such arms, and shall be thereof convicted by the oaths of one or more credible witness or witnesses, before any one or more of his Majesty's justices of the peace, judge ordinary, or other person or persons authorized by his Majesty in manner above mentioned, shall be liable to be fined by the said justices of the peace, judge ordinary, or other person authorized by his Majesty, before whom he or they shall be convicted, according to their discretion, in any sum not exceeding one hundred pounds sterling, nor under the sum of fifteen pounds sterling, of lawful money of *Great Britain*, and shall be committed to prison until payment; and if the person so convicted, being a man, shall refuse or neglect to pay the fine so imposed, within the space of one calendar month from the date of the said conviction, he shall, in case he be judged by any one or more justice of justices of the peace, or the judge ordinary of the place where such offender is imprisoned, fit to serve his Majesty as a soldier, be delivered over to serve as a soldier in his Majesty's forces in *America*, in the manner before directed, with respect to persons convicted of having or bearing of arms; and in case such offender shall not be judged fit to serve his Majesty as aforesaid, then he shall be imprisoned for the space of six calendar months, and also until he shall give sufficient security for his good behaviour, for the space of two years from the giving thereof; and if the person convicted shall be a woman, she shall, over and above the foresaid fine, and imprisonment till payment, suffer imprisonment for the space of six calendar months within the *Tolbooth* of the head burgh of the shire or stewartry within which she is convicted. . . .

X. And be it further enacted by the authority aforesaid, That it shall and may be lawful to and for his Majesty, his heirs and successors, by warrant under his or their royal sign manual, and also to and for the lord lieutenant of any of the shires aforesaid, or the person or persons authorized by his Majesty to summon the person or persons aforesaid to deliver up their arms, or any one or more justices of the peace, by warrant under his or their hands, to authorize and appoint any person or persons to enter into any house or houses, within the limits aforesaid, either by day or by night, and there to search for, and to seize all such arms as shall be found contrary to the direction of this act. . . .

XVII. And be it further enacted by the authority aforesaid, That from and after the first day of *August* one thousand seven hundred and forty-seven, no man or boy, within that part of *Great Britain* called *Scotland*, other than such as shall be employed as officers and soldiers in his Majesty's forces, shall, on any pretence whatsoever, wear or put on the clothes commonly called *Highland Clothes* (that is to say) the plaid, philebeg or little kilt, trowse, shoulder belts, or any part whatsoever of what peculiarly belongs to the highland garb; and that no tartan or party-coloured plaid or stuff shall be used for great coats, or for upper coats; and if any such person shall presume, after the said first day of *August*, to wear or put on the aforesaid garments, or any part of them, every such person so offending, being convicted thereof by the oath of one or more credible witness or witnesses before any court of justiciary, or any one or more justices of the peace for the shire or stewartry, or judge ordinary of the place where such offence shall be committed, shall suffer imprisonment, without bail, during the space of six months, and no longer; and being convicted for a second offence before a court of justiciary, or at the circuits, shall be liable to be transported to any of his Majesty's plantations beyond the seas, there to remain for the space of seven years.

XVIII. *And whereas by an act made in this session of parliament, intituled,* An act to indemnify such persons as have acted in defence of his Majesty's person and government, and for the preservation of the publick peace of this kingdom, during the time of the present unnatural rebellion, and sheriffs and others who have suffered escapes, occasioned thereby, from vexatious suits and prosecutions, *it is enacted, That all personal actions and suits, indictments, informations and all molestations, prosecutions and proceedings whatsoever, and judgments thereupon, if any be, for or by reason of any matter or thing advised, commanded, appointed or done during the rebellion, until the thirteenth day of* April *in the year of our lord one thousand seven hundred and forty-six, in order to suppress the said unnatural rebellion, or for the preservation of the publick peace, or for the service or safety of the government, shall be discharged and made void: and whereas it is also reasonable, that acts done for the public service, since the said thirtieth day of* April, *though not justifiable by the strict forms of law, should be justified by act of parliament:* be it enacted by the authority aforesaid, That all personal actions and suits, indictments and informations, which have been or shall be commenced or prosecuted, and all molestations, prosecutions and proceedings whatsoever, and judgments thereupon, if any be, for or by reason of any act, matter or thing advised, commanded, appointed or done before the twenty-fifth day of *July* in the year of our Lord one thousand seven hundred and forty-six, in order to suppress the said unnatural rebellion, or for the preservation of the publick peace, or for the safety or service of the government, shall be discharged and made void; and that every person, by whom any such act, matter or thing shall have been so advised, commanded, appointed or done for the purposes aforesaid, or any of them, before the said five and twentieth day of *July*, shall be freed, acquitted and indemnified, as well against the King's majesty, his heirs and successors, as against all and every other person and persons; and that if any action or suit hath been or shall be commenced or prosecuted, within that part of *Great Britain*, called *England*, against any person for any such act, matter or thing so advised, commanded, appointed or done for the purposes aforesaid, or any of them, before the said twenty-fifth day of *July*, he or she may plead the general issue, and give this act and the special matter in evidence; and if the plaintiff or plaintiffs shall become non-suit, or forbear further prosecution, or suffer discontinuance; or if a verdict pass against such plaintiff or plaintiffs, the defendant or defendants shall recover his, her or their double costs, for which he, she, or they shall have the like remedy, as in cases where costs by law are given to defendants; and if such action or suit hath been or shall be commenced or prosecuted in that part of *Great Britain*, called *Scotland*, the court, before whom such action or suit hath been or shall be commenced or prosecuted, shall allow to the defender the benefit of the discharge and indemnity above provided, and shall further decern the pursuer to pay to the defender the full and real expences that he or she shall be put to by such action or suit. . . .

XXI. *And whereas it is of great importance to prevent the rising generation being educated in disaffected or rebellious principles, and although sufficient provision is already made by law for the due regulation of the teachers in the four universities, and in the publick schools authorized by law in the royal burghs and country parishes in* Scotland, *it is further necessary, that all persons who take upon them to officiate as masters or teachers in private schools, in that part of* Great Britain *called* Scotland, *should give evidence of their good affection to his Majesty's person and government;* be it therefore enacted by the authority aforesaid, That from and after the first day of *November* in the year of our Lord one thousand seven hundred and forty-six, it shall not be lawful for any person in *Scotland* to keep a private school for teaching *English*, *Latin*, *Greek* or any part of literature, or to officiate as a master or teacher in such school, or any school for literature, other than those in the universities, or established in the respective royal burghs by public authority, or the parochial schools settled according to law, or the schools maintained by the society in *Scotland* for propagating christian knowledge, or by the general assemblies of the church of *Scotland*, or committees thereof, upon the bounty granted by his Majesty, until the situation and description of such private school be first entered and registered in a book, which shall be provided and kept for that purpose by the clerks of the several shires, stewartries and burghs in *Scotland*, together with a certificate from the proper officer, of every such master and teacher having qualified himself, by taking the oaths appointed by law to be taken by persons in offices of publick trust in *Scotland*; and every such master and teacher of a private school shall be obliged, and is hereby required, as often as prayers shall be said in such school, to pray, or cause to be prayed for, in express words, his Majesty, his heirs and successors, by name, and for all the royal family; and if any person shall, from and after the said first day of *November*, presume to enter upon, or exercise the function or office of a master or teacher of any such private school as shall not have been registered in manner herein directed, or without having first qualified himself, and caused the certificate to be registered as above-mentioned; or in case he shall neglect to pray for his Majesty by name, and all the royal family, or to cause them to be prayed for as herein directed; or in case he shall resort to, or attend divine worship in any episcopal meeting-house not allowed by the law; every person so offending in any of the premisses, being thereof lawfully convicted before any two or more of the justices of peace, or before any other judge competent of the place summarily, shall, for the first offence, suffer imprisonment for the space of six months; and for the second, or any subsequent offence, being thereof lawfully convicted before the court of justiciary, or in any of the circuit courts, shall be adjudged to be transported, and accordingly shall be transported to some of his Majesty's plantations in *America* for life; and in case any person adjudged to be so transported shall return into, or be found in *Great Britain*, then every such person shall suffer imprisonment for life. . . .

XXIII. *And whereas by an act passed in the parliament of* Scotland, *in the year of our Lord one thousand six hundred and ninety-three, all chaplains in families, and governors and teachers of children and youth, were obliged to take the oaths of allegiance and assurance therein directed; and there may be some doubt, whether by the laws, as they stand at present, they are obliged to take all the oaths appointed to be taken by persons in offices of publick trust in* Scotland: therefore be it enacted by the authority aforesaid, That from and after the first day of *November* in the year of our Lord one thousand seven hundred and forty-six, no person shall exercise the employment, function, or service of a chaplain, in any family in that part of *Great Britain* called *Scotland,* or of a governor, tutor, or teacher of any child, children or youth, residing in *Scotland,* or in parts beyond the seas, without first qualifying himself, by taking the oaths appointed by law to be taken by persons in offices of publick trust, and causing a certificate of his having done so to be entered or registered in a book to be kept for that purpose by the clerks of the shires, stewartries or burghs in *Scotland,* where such person shall reside; or in case of any such governor, tutor or teacher of any such child, children or youth, acting in parts beyond the seas, then in a book to be kept for that purpose by the clerk of the shire, stewartry or burgh where the parent or guardian of such child, children, or youth shall reside. And if any person, from and after the said first day of *November,* shall presume to exercise the employment, function, or service of chaplain, in any family in *Scotland,* or of a governor or teacher of children or youth as aforesaid, without having taken the said oaths, and caused the certificate of his having duly taken the same, to be registered, as is above directed; every person so offending, being thereof lawfully convicted before any two or more justices of peace, or before any other judge competent of the place summarily, shall, for the first offence, suffer imprisonment by the space of six months; and for the second or any subsequent offence, being thereof lawfully convicted before the court of justiciary, or in any of the circuit courts, shall be adjudged to be banished from *Great Britain* for the space of seven years.

XXIV. Provided always, That it shall be lawful for every chaplain, schoolmaster, governor, tutor, or teacher of youth, who is of the communion of the church of *Scotland,* instead of the oath of abjuration appointed by law to be taken by persons in offices civil or military, to take the oath directed to be taken by preachers and expectants in divinity of the established church of *Scotland,* by an act passed in the fifth year of the reign of King *George* the First, intituled, *An act for making more effectual the laws appointing the oaths for security of the government to be taken by ministers and preachers in churches and meeting-houses in* Scotland; and a certificate of his having taken that oath, shall, to all intents and purposes, be as valid and effectual as the certificate of his having taken the oath of abjuration above-mentioned; and he shall be as much deemed to have qualified himself according to law as if he had taken the abjuration appointed to be taken by persons in civil offices. . . .

189. Act for the abolition of heritable jurisdictions in Scotland, 1747

(*Statutes at Large*, XIX, pp. 127–143. 20 Geo. II, c. 43.)

A further Act for the pacification of the Highlands after the 1745 rising. It substituted sheriffs and circuits of the king's judges for the old feudal jurisdictions, with compensation to the chiefs.

An act for taking away and abolishing the heretable jurisdictions in that part of Great Britain *called* Scotland; *and for making satisfaction to the proprietors thereof; and for restoring such jurisdictions to the crown; and for making more effectual provision for the administration of justice throughout that part of the united kingdom, by the King's courts and judges there; and for obliging all persons acting as procurators, writers or agents in the law in* Scotland *to take the oaths; and for rendering the union of the two kingdoms more complete.*

For remedying the inconveniencies that have arisen and may arise from the multiplicity and extent of heretable jurisdictions in the part of *Great Britain* called *Scotland*, for making satisfaction to the proprietors thereof, for restoring to the crown the powers of jurisdiction originally and properly belonging thereto, according to the constitution, and for extending the influence, benefit and protection of the King's laws and courts of justice to all his Majesty's subjects in *Scotland*, and for rendering the union more complete; be it enacted by the King's most excellent majesty, by and with the advice and consent of the lords spiritual and temporal, and commons, in this present parliament assembled, and by the authority of the same, That all heretable jurisdictions of justiciary, and all regalities and heretable baillieries, and all heretable constabularies, other than the office of high constable of *Scotland*, and all stewartries, being parts only of shires or counties, and all sheriffships and deputy sheriffships of districts, being parts only of shires or counties within that part of *Great Britain* called *Scotland*, belonging unto, or possessed or claimed by any subject or subjects, and all jurisdictions, powers, authorities and privileges thereunto appurtenant or annexed or dependant thereupon, shall be, and they are hereby from and after the twenty-fifth day of *March* in the year of our Lord one thousand seven hundred and forty-eight, abrogated, taken away, and totally dissolved and extinguished.

II. Provided always, That all lands annexed or belonging to the said heretable baillieries, stewartries and constabularies hereby intended to be dissolved and extinguished, and the rents and duties, consisting in money, victual, cattle or other goods, payable to the possessors of the said heretable baillieries, stewartries or constabularies, shall remain with and belong to them, their heirs and successors, and continue to be enjoyed by and paid to them, their heirs and successors, notwithstanding the extinction of the said offices.

III. And be it further enacted by the authority aforesaid, That all jurisdictions, powers and authorities legally vested in or belonging to any such justiciary, regalities, baillieries, constabularies, stewartries, sheriffships and deputy sheriffships, or any of them, shall, from and after the said twenty-fifth day of *March* be vested in and exercised by the court of session, court of justiciary at *Edinburgh*, the judges in the several circuits, and the courts of the sheriffs and stewarts of shires or counties, and other of the King's courts in *Scotland* respectively, to which such jurisdictions, powers and authorities would now by law have belonged, in case such justiciary, baillierie, constabulary, regality, stewartry, sheriffship or deputy sheriffship had never been granted or erected; and that the several towns, villages, places, districts and bounds which lie within or were subject to such justiciary, regalities, baillieries, constabularies, stewartries, sheriffships or deputy sheriffships hereby taken away and dissolved respectively, and the inhabitants and residenters within the same, from and after the said twenty-fifth day of *March*, shall be subject to the jurisdiction and authority of the said court of session, court of justiciary at *Edinburgh*, the judges in their circuits, the sheriffs and the courts of the sheriffs or stewarts of counties or shires, and such other of the King's courts as aforesaid respectively, in the same manner as such towns, villages, places, districts and bounds, and the inhabitants and residenters within the same would have been in case such justiciary, regalities, baillieries, constabularies, stewartries, sheriffships or deputy sheriffships had never existed.

IV. And it is hereby further enacted by the authority aforesaid, That from and after the said twenty-fifth day of *March*, all sheriffships of any county or shire, and all stewartries not hereby before taken away and extinguished, within that part of *Great Britain* called *Scotland*, granted unto or possessed by any subject or subjects, either heretably or for life, and all jurisdictions, authorities or privileges thereunto belonging or annexed, or dependant thereupon, shall be, and they are hereby resumed and annexed to the crown; and that the sheriffs and stewarts of such counties, shires and stewartries respectively, shall, from thenceforth be nominated and appointed by his Majesty, his heirs and successors. . . .

VI. And be it further enacted by the authority aforesaid, That reasonable and just compensation and satisfaction shall be made out of the next aids to be granted in parliament, for and in respect of every such justiciary, regality, sheriffship, deputy sheriffship, stewartry, constabulary and baillierie hereby taken away and dissolved, or resumed and annexed to the crown, to all and every person and persons respectively, who shall appear to be lawfully possessed of any such justiciary, regality, sheriffship, deputy sheriffship, stewartry, constabulary or baillierie, and to every clerk thereof, who was on the eleventh day of *November* one thousand seven hundred and forty-six, lawfully possessed for life of his clerkship, in case such office shall be necessarily extinguished in consequence of this act. . . .

XVII. *And whereas the jurisdiction in capital cases, that was heretofore granted to many heretors or proprietors of lands within that part of* Great Britain *called* Scotland, *whose lands were erected by the crown into baronies, or granted* cum fossa et furca, *or with power of pit and gallows, or with the like words, importing such capital jurisdiction, hath been long discontinued or fallen into disuse, as to the exercise thereof, and it is now unnecessary and improper that the right or title of such jurisdiction in barons should be any longer retained: and whereas it is also reasonable that some further regulation should be made relating to the jurisdictions of such barons, or of other heretors of lands, who are infeofft* cum curiis, *or intitled to the jurisdictions of barons, or other lower jurisdiction;* be it enacted by the authority aforesaid, That from and after the said twenty-fifth day of *March* in the year of our Lord one thousand seven hundred and forty-eight, [the barons etc. are to have no jurisdiction in capital cases nor in criminal causes except assaults, etc., nor in civil causes where the sum shall exceed forty shillings, except in recovering rents and duties.]

[Clauses XVIII–XXV regulate the management of the prisons and procedure of the private courts left by the Act.]

XXVI. [Jurisdictions vested in Royal Burghs not to be affected.]

XXVII. [Cumulative jurisdictions vested in Burghs of Regality etc. also reserved, except any power or privilege of re-pledging from the Sheriffs or Stewart's Court or any other of the King's Courts.]

[XXVIII–XLIV lay down the procedure and organization of the Courts to which are assigned the jurisdiction of the abolished Courts.]

C. SCOTLAND AFTER 1745

190. Religion and education in the western Highlands and Islands, 1765

(*Calendar of Home Office Papers of the reign of George III*, 1760–1765, pp. 560–563.)

The writer of this letter encloses a report made by a Dr. Walker to the General Assembly of the Church of Scotland. Lord Sandwich, to whom the letter is addressed, was at that time Secretary of State for the Northern Department.

13 June [1765.] Mr. Wishart "Cls. Eccl. Scot." to the Earl of Sandwich.

Dr. Walker states that he visited 52 Gaelic parishes in the Western Highlands and Islands, which had not fallen under the examination of the visitors appointed by the Assembly in 1760. He gives an account of the extent and number of inhabitants of eight of these parishes; *viz.*, six included in the promontory of Cantire, two in the Island of Ila,[1] the parish of Jura comprehending Jura, Colonsay, and a number of lesser adjacent islands. Their extent was very large, and the ministers' residences in some at a distance of 10 or 15 miles from places of worship, which were often also difficult of access. To Colonsay, distant above 20 miles of sea from Jura, the minister was only able to go twice a year; and in Scarba he preached once a quarter to its own inhabitants, and those of several smaller adjacent islands. In this parish (Jura) the Sacrament of the Supper had never been dispensed but once in the century.

In character the people were acute and sensible, extremely desirous of instruction, and capable of great attainments, both in knowledge and industry; the ignorance and idleness that too much prevailed amongst them being by no means their fault, but the misfortune of their situation. Wherever they had access to schools, to public worship, and to the ordinances of religion, there they were more regular in their morals, more civilized in their manners, and in their way of life more active and industrious than their countrymen who were strangers to these advantages. A considerable part of the Royal Bounty was employed in supporting missionary ministers. In the countries which Dr. Walker visited, there were 10 of these ministers whom he found, without exception, well qualified, and every way worthy of the station they filled, and some of them men whose learning, abilities, and behaviour were far superior to the small salary of 25*l*. or 30*l*. a year they received. Another part of the bounty was employed in supporting catechists, who had generally from 5*l*. to 15*l*. a year; their business being to catechise the people who had not access to public worship, to meet with them on the Sabbath, to read the Scriptures, and to join with them in psalms and prayer. He examined 18 of them in the course of his journey. Some were as well qualified and as useful as could be expected, though others were rather inadequate to the task to which they were appointed. He thought the well qualified amongst them might be most usefully stationed in the Popish countries. The bursaries established by the Committee on the Royal Bounty in 1756 for students in

[1] Islay.

Divinity, with a salary of 10*l*. or 15*l*. a year, had been followed with all the success that had been expected. As the people could not be taught to read in their native tongue, and as they could only attain to a knowledge of the Scriptures or of any other books by learning English, the progress both of Divine and human knowledge among the inhabitants depended in a great measure on the progress of the English tongue. He thought the utility of promoting this design by the ministers preaching some part of every Sabbath in English, as they had been ordered, rather doubtful; for unless the people were previously instructed, it was not to be expected that they could make any proficiency by sermons, and sometimes this course rather irritated than conciliated the people, and gave them a prejudice against the language. He thought the spread of English was to be gained most effectually by schools. None of the children, when they came to the parochial or charity schools, were able to speak a word of English; yet in three years, or four at most, they learnt both to read and to speak it perfectly. Wherever there were schools planted, English made a visible and considerable progress; but there was scarce a vestige of it to be found where they were wanting. The Island of Icolmkill, though for several centuries the principal seat of religion and learning in Britain, yet, for want of a school, there was not a person amongst its 200 inhabitants who could speak English or read the Bible. The same state of ignorance prevailed in many large tracts in the Highlands, all from the want of schools, which were the most effectual means to spread the English language, and to diffuse the knowledge of the Gospel, and the useful arts of life. To accomplish these valuable purposes the laudable and well directed endeavours of the Society for Propagating Christian Knowledge had been highly conducive. They supported in the North 170 charity schools, containing about 7,000 scholars; yet these were but few compared to the whole number of children that required to be taught. In consideration of all this, Dr. Walker suggested that the catechists would be employed to greater advantage as schoolmasters, particularly where no schools existed, with a small addition to their salaries, the latter being the more laborious occupation. He also suggested that a legal school should be established in every parish. The Society did not grant a charity school, except where a legal school existed; but still the country in general was ill supplied. Of the parishes he visited, 23 had no legal parochial school. There was a practice, that was likely to prevail, which would render the erection of charity schools more and more necessary; *viz*., where two or three parishes, which had each of them a legal salary for a schoolmaster, united them in order to obtain a master who would be able to teach Latin and the other parts of education generally taught in a grammar school, the legal salary being only sufficient to procure a schoolmaster capable of teaching English, and a little writing and arithmetic. This had an excellent effect in the education of the gentlemen's children, and of such of the tenants as were able to board their children at school; but as it left one or two parishes without any school at all, children of the poorer sort were left destitute of any instruction. Dr. Walker considered that all reformation from ignorance and superstition, and all improvement of the country, must begin with the instruction of the inhabitants in their early years. Everywhere in the Highlands where he travelled the Popish religion was visibly on the increase, chiefly owing to the immoderate extent of the parishes, the ignorance of the people in the Sacred Scriptures and the Protestant principles, and the assiduity of the Romish priests. He instances the Islands of Barra, in the parish of Harris, 50 miles away from the residence of the minister, who visited them only once a year. In the reign of Charles I. the inhabitants were to a man Protestant. When he visited them, 1,300 were Papists, and only 50 Protestants, and there was a priest established amongst them. Above 20 persons had been converted to Popery within four or five years. . . . Dr. Walker, in concluding, remarks that in general the people of the Highlands were perfectly well disposed towards the reformation and improvement of their country, anxious to get free from ignorance and dependence, fond of having their children well-educated, and of acquiring knowledge of every kind, and full of affection to their ministers, who were in general men who highly deserved the esteem and confidence of their people. People of all ranks had also a sincere and hearty affection for the present Government of His Majesty. The wise measure adopted during the late war of putting confidence in the inhabitants by calling them into the field, and rewarding them for their gallant behaviour, had been followed with high returns of gratitude and fidelity, and with the most desirable and happy effects.

191. Emigration to America from the Highlands, 1774

(*Calendar of Home Office Papers of the reign of George III*, 1773–1775, pp. 204–206.)

Emigration from the Highlands had increased after the 1745 rising.

[25 April, 1774.]

LORD JUSTICE CLERK[1] to the EARL OF SUFFOLK.

Relative to the emigration to America from the Highlands of Scotland. Explains the methods he had adopted for obtaining lists of the persons who sailed in 1772 and 1773, application having been made for this purpose to the ministers of the different parishes through the channel of the sheriffs of the counties. Has not been able to obtain complete returns, but incloses such as have come to hand. The letter from Arch[i]bald Campbell, sheriff of Argyll and Bute, also transmitted, will show what difficulties have attended this inquiry, and the reasons why he has carried his return back to 1769, 1770, and 1771, and points out the causes of these emigrations. Thought it improper to alarm the whole country as if this spirit of emigration had already become general, and therefore limited his correspondence upon the subject to the sheriffs of Argyll and Bute, Inverness, Ross, Sutherland and Caithness, and Moray and Nairn, whence these emigrations had been most considerable. Has no information from the sheriff of Inverness, though he understands the emigrations from there have been considerable, and particularly from the Island of Sky; nor from the sheriff of Sutherland and Caithness; but from a list transmitted by the steward of the Countess of Sutherland, it appears that the number of emigrants from her estate there in 1772 and 1773 is no less than 735 persons,–men, women, and children. The lists

[1] Thomas Miller, Lord Glenlee (1717–1789). Suffolk was at this time Secretary of State.

enclosed are from the sheriffs of Argyll and Bute, Ross, and Moray and Nairn. This spirit of emigration to America, which first began in the Highlands, begins to spread itself in the Low Country, and in the manufacturing towns and villages; and, what is more alarming, affects not only the lower class of people, but some of the better sort of farmers and mechanics, who are in good circumstances, and can live very comfortably at home. Various associations have been formed for purchasing lands in the Colonies upon a joint stock, to be afterwards divided amongst the contributors upon their arrival in America. And if this idea of acquiring land property, so natural to man, and of improving that property in a better climate, shall seize the minds of such of our people as can carry over money to purchase and clear the lands in America, it may in time as effectually depopulate this country as the mines of Peru and Mexico have depopulated Spain. While individuals think and act for themselves, there is no great danger that many will go; but when they enter into associations, and go off in bodies from the same place, with their wives, children, and kindred, this removes the natural tie to their country. The *studium rerum novarum* begins to operate; they fortify one another in the resolution, and nothing can convince them of their mistake until it is too late. The causes of the emigration are the successive bad crops of several years past, the want of employment occasioned by the decay of our manufactures, and the rise in the rents of lands. The first two causes are, it is to be hoped, temporary, and the landlords will soon find it necessary to obviate the complaints arising from the last. But the great danger is that when these causes cease, the spirit of emigration may still continue, not from the motive of getting bread, but from the motive of attaining a better situation in America. And when so many emissaries from America are employed in seducing our people and flattering them with such high hopes, it is no wonder they yield to the temptation. Those who carry out a little money may improve their situation; but many of the lower class of people, who had not wherewithal to pay their passage outwards, are certainly in a worse situation than they were in at home, and, according to his information, would willingly return if they could pay their passage. A few hundreds of such emigrants returning to different parts of the country would more effectually open the eyes of the people, and cure them of their passion for America, than all that can be said or written on the subject.

192. The founding of the Carron Iron Works, 1759

(H. M. Cadell, *The Story of the Forth* (1913), pp. 151–152.)

The first ironworks in Scotland were started by the partnership of Dr. John Roebuck, the inventor, and friend of James Watt; Samuel Garbett, a rich Birmingham merchant; and William Cadell, a Scottish shipowner in the iron and timber trade. For Garbett, see also No. 128.

LETTER FROM MR. GARBETT TO MR. WM. CADELL, dated Birmingham, 16 June, 1759.

. . . Doctor Roebuck and I think Carron Water is a situation infinitely preferable to all others, because if the Works prove prosperous as We expect, some places in the Neighbourhood of the Firth of Forth will become one of the principal Seats of Iron works in Britain, not only for making Iron from the Ore into Barrs and Slit Iron, but into Nails and many other Manufactures; in all human probability this will be the Case. Under this Conviction it's undoubtedly right to begin our Works in a Situation that looks the most favourable for the Seat of such Manufactures and where our Works may be enlarged to a great Extent and notwithstanding continue Contiguous to one another, and in the Country that seems the most convenient for Manufacturers to settle, on account of its nearness to the Firth of Forth and its not being remote from Glasgow, and where exceeding fine Coal from Acton Boughey, Toryburn or Limekiln can be had always at a moderate expence, and not only Charcoal be delivered Cheap from the Highlands as well as from Woods that are now near it, but the Land in the Neighbourhood of Carron might be rented on such Terms as to make it advisable to plant large Woods for the Supply of our Works.

1 Furnace, 3 Forges, and a slitting Mill, would be a compleat Set of Works, and the Water of Carron is not only sufficient to supply such a Sett but is capable of supplying double that quantity, and it appeared to me that at a small expence we might be able to carry all our Iron &c from one Mill to another with Boats which is a very material consideration.

We shall however chearfully join You in beginning a Furnace in your own Neighbourhood, but we shall not be willing to leave the Water of Carron open for others to engage in, but shall probably soon make a beginning there, it would be Inconsistent with the sincere Affection and Esteem we bear you not to let You know Explicitly with the utmost frankness the true State of our Minds on the Subject for your Government, that you may consider whether it is not more prudent to make our first beginning upon the Spot where the Works will in all probability be Ultimately settled.

193. Lord Kames on improved methods in agriculture, 1776

(Lord Kames, *The Gentleman Farmer* (1776), pp. 124, 128–129, 130, 132–133.)

Henry Home, Lord Kames (1696–1782), a Scottish judge, also wrote a number of legal and historical works.

No branch of husbandry requires more skill and sagacity than a proper rotation of crops, so as to keep the ground always in heart, and yet to draw out of it the greatest profit possible. A horse is purchased for labour; and it is the purchaser's intention to make the most of him. He is well fed, and wrought according to his strength: to overwork him, is to render him useless. Precisely similar is land. Profit is the farmer's object; but he knows, that to run out his farm by indiscreet cropping, is not the way to make profit. Some plants rob the soil, others are gentle to it: some bind, others loosen. The nice point is, to intermix crops, so as to make the greatest profit consistently with keeping the ground in trim. In that view, the nature of the plants employed in husbandry, must be accurately examined. . . .

. . . Culmiferous plants[1] are robbers; some more, some less: they at the same time

[1] Wheat, rye, barley, oats and ryegrass.

bind the soil; some more, some less. Leguminous plants[1] in both respects are opposite: if any of them rob the soil, it is in a very slight degree; and all of them without exception loosen the soil. A culmiferous crop, however, is generally the more profitable: but few soils can long bear the burden of such crops, unless relieved by interjected leguminous crops. These, on the other hand, without a mixture of culmiferous crops, would soon render the soil too loose. . . .

Having discussed the nature of plants, as far as rotation of crops is concerned, the nature of the soil comes next under consideration. It is scarce necessary to be mentioned, being known to every farmer, that clay answers best for wheat, moist clay for beans, loam for barley and pease, light soil for turnip, sandy soil for rye and buck wheat; and that oats thrive better in coarse soil than any other grain. Now, in directing a rotation, it is not sufficient that a culmiferous crop be always succeeded by a leguminous: attention must be also given, that no crop be introduced that is unfit for the soil. Wheat, being a great binder, requires more than any other crop a leguminous crop to follow. But every such crop is not proper: potatoes are the greatest openers of soil; but they are improper in a wheat-soil. Neither will turnip answer, because it requires a light soil. A very loose soil, after a crop of rye requires ryegrass to bind it, or the treading of cattle in pasturing: but to bind the soil wheat must not be ventured; for it succeeds ill in loose soil.

Another consideration of moment in directing the rotation, is to avoid crops that encourage weeds. . . .

For illustrating the foregoing rules, a few instances of exceptionable rotations, will not be thought amiss. The following is an usual rotation in Norfolk. First, wheat after red clover. Second, barley. Third, turnip. Fourth, barley with red clover. Fifth, clover cut for hay. Sixth, a second year's crop of clover commonly pastured. Dung is given to the wheat and turnip. Against this rotation several objections lie. Barley after wheat is improper. The two crops of barley are too near together. The second crop of clover must be very bad, if pasturing be the best way of consuming it; and if bad, it is a great encourager of weeds. But the strongest objection is, that red clover repeated so frequently in the same field cannot fail to degenerate; and of this the Norfolk farmers begin to be sensible. Salton in East Lothian is a clay soil; and the rotation there is, wheat after fallow and dung. Second, barley after two ploughings; the one before winter, the other immediately before the seed is sown. Third, oats. Fourth, pease. Fifth, barley. Sixth, oats: and then fallow. This rotation consists chiefly of robbing crops. Pease are the only leguminous crop, which even with the fallow is not sufficient to loosen a stiff soil. But the soil is good, which in some measure hides the badness of the rotation. About Seaton, and all the way from Preston to Gossford, the ground is still more severely handled: wheat after fallow and dung, barley, oats, pease, wheat, barley, oats, and then another fallow. The soil is excellent; and it ought indeed to be so, to support many rounds of such cropping.

[1] Pease, beans, clover, cabbage, etc.

194. Life in Glasgow in the 1740's

(*Autobiography of the Rev. Dr. Alexander Carlyle*, ed. J. H. Burton, 2nd ed. (1860), pp. 72–73, 74–75.)

Alexander Carlyle (1722–1805) was minister of Inveresk, a leader of the Scottish 'Broad Church' party, and a friend of Hume and Adam Smith.

The city of Glasgow at this time, though very industrious, wealthy, and commercial, was far inferior to what it afterwards became, both before and after the failure of the Virginia trade. The modes of life, too, and manners, were different from what they are at present. Their chief branches were the tobacco trade with the American colonies, and sugar and rum with the West India. There were not manufacturers sufficient, either there or at Paisley, to supply an outward-bound cargo for Virginia. For this purpose they were obliged to have rècourse to Manchester. Manufactures were in their infancy. About this time the inkle manufactory was first begun by Ingram & Glasford, and was shown to strangers as a great curiosity. But the merchants had industry and stock, and the habits of business, and were ready to seize with eagerness, and prosecute with vigour, every new object in commerce or manufactures that promised success.

. . . It must be confessed that at this time they were far behind in Glasgow, not only in their manner of living, but in those accomplishments and that taste that belong to people of opulence, much more to persons of education. There were only a few families of ancient citizens who pretended to be gentlemen; and a few others, who were recent settlers there, who had obtained wealth and consideration in trade. The rest were shopkeepers and mechanics, or successful pedlars, who occupied large warerooms full of manufactures of all sorts, to furnish a cargo to Virginia. It was usual for the sons of merchants to attend the College for one or two years, and a few of them completed their academical education. In this respect the females were still worse off, for at that period there was neither a teacher of French nor of music in the town. The consequence of this was twofold; first, the young ladies were entirely without accomplishments, and in general had nothing to recommend them but good looks and fine clothes, for their manners were ungainly. Secondly, the few who were distinguished drew all the young men of sense and taste about them; for being void of frivolous accomplishments, which in some respects make all women equal, they trusted only to superior understanding and wit, to natural elegance and unaffected manners.

There never was but one concert during the two winters I was at Glasgow, and that was given by Walter Scott, Esq. of Harden, who was himself an eminent performer on the violin; and his band of assistants consisted of two dancing-school fiddlers and the town-waits.

The manner of living, too, at this time, was but coarse and vulgar. Very few of the wealthiest gave dinners to anybody but English riders, or their own relations at Christmas holidays. There were not half-a-dozen families in town who had men-servants; some of those were kept by the professors who had boarders. There were neither post-chaises nor hackney-coaches in the town, and only three or four sedan-chairs for carrying midwives about in the night, and old ladies to church, or to the dancing assemblies once a-fortnight.

195. The Town Council of Edinburgh approves James Craig's plan for the New Town, 29 July 1767

(*Book of the Old Edinburgh Club*, XXIII (1940), pp. 11–12.)

The bridge over the Nor'loch, leading to the site for the New Town, was begun in 1763, and the first stage of the building of the New Town took place between 1767 and 1793.

Act anent settling the plan of the new buildings and for feuing[1] *the grounds on the north of the city*. [29 July 1767.]

. . . Reported, that the Committee, after many meetings and consulting with Lord Kaims, Lord Alemour, Commissioner Clerk, and Mr. Adams, and other persons of skill in these matters, had reviewed all the former plans with the greatest care and attention, and considered several amendments proposed by Mr. Craig; and that Mr. Craig, by their direction, had made out a new plan, which plan, signed by the Lord Provost of this date was produced. . . . That they were of opinion (1) that the Council should immediately form the principal street of the plot now to be feued in the manner of a turnpike road; and so proceed in the same way with the other plots, as they come to be feued, for the conveniency of the feuars. (2) That the pavement upon each side of the street should be ten feet broad, not to rise higher than a foot above the level of the street, and that there should be no posts erected betwixt the street and the pavement. (3) That the pavement ought to be laid and repaired at the expense of the proprietors of houses, in the same way as is practised in the Old Town. (4) That all the houses should be built in a line, eight feet from the foot pavement, excepting as is after mentioned. (5) That those who incline to feu three lots upon the principal street, should be allowed to carry their houses farther back than eight feet, . . . such three lots being in the centre of one of the plots; which the Committee were of opinion would not hurt the plan, but rather be an additional beauty to it. (6) As it is not intended at present to feu out the ground betwixt the South Street and the North Loch, the feuars upon that street should have an obligation in their favour, that if houses were afterwards built there, they should not be nearer to their houses than ninety-six feet. (7) That no sign posts should be erected, so as to project from the walls of the respective buildings. (8) That the Council should execute a common sewer in the middle of the street, to be kept up at the expence of the city; and that the feuars should have liberty to make a communication or sewer from their respective houses to the said common sewer, to be kept up at their expence. (9) That the areas or lots lying betwixt the back street and the meuse, should not be feued, until the areas lying in parallel lines betwixt the meuse and the principal street are feued out, that it may be optional for the purchasers on the principal street to take both. [Clauses 10 and 11 refer to water supply and the granting of feu charters.]

[1] A 'feu' is a perpetual lease at a fixed rent, or a piece of land so held. [O.E.D.]

196. An Italian view of the progress of learning in Scotland, 1763

(*Scottish Historical Review*, VII (1910), pp. 291–293; "Extract from an Essay on the Progress of Learning among the Scots, annexed to an Essay on the State of Learning in Italy, . . . by Carlo Denina, a Piedmontese. . . . Printed in the year MDCCLXIII.")

This essay, with a Preface by SCOTUS, was published as a pamphlet in 1763. Carlo Denina was an Italian historian, author of *Revoluzioni d'Italia*. It illustrates the literary revival in Scotland in the second half of the eighteenth century.

[After speaking of the state of learning in Scotland, for two hundred years after the revival of letters, he adds,]

In a word, two entire ages had elapsed from the time of the general revival of letters, before any one could have imagined that this kingdom should have become so distinguished by science and erudition. A learned Irishman, by his zeal and talents, and a noble and generous duke, were raised up by heaven as the distinguished instruments of causing to spring and flourish in those cold and northern regions what it was once foolishly thought could only shoot with vigour in the warm climates of the Lesser Asia, of Greece or Italy. Francis Hutchinson[1] having come into Scotland to profess philosophy and the studies of humanity in the University of Glasgow, diffused throughout the whole country, by his lectures and discourses, as well as by his excellent printed works, a lively taste for the studies of philosophy and learning.

Without enumerating one by one those sublime geniuses who by new discoveries have illustrated the mathematics or natural philosophy, or have treated them in their books with greater clearness, precision and elegance, such as Simpson, Maclaurin, Ferguson and Cullen, history hath been cultivated amongst them with wonderful and unexpected success, and poetry of all kinds hath flourished greatly.

The name of Thompson, a poet no less eminent in tragic than didactic compositions, will be one day no less known and celebrated than that of Pope. His *four seasons of the year* are already universally read with infinite pleasure by the lovers of good poetry, and his tragedies seem to obscure the glory that Addison had acquired by his Cato.

The Epigoniad of Mr. Wilkie[2] would have been a most estimable production if it had come to light in other times: But, at present, that Homer is so well known in England, both by the study of the Greek language which prevails there, and by the celebrated version of Mr. Pope, it is no wonder that Mr. Wilkie finds not a greater number of readers.

Blacklock[3] will be to future times a fable, as he is a prodigy of the present; and it will seem a story contrived to puzzle and astonish, that a man wholly blind from three years of age, besides having acquired the knowledge of various languages, Greek, Latin, Italian and French, should at the same time be a great poet in his own.

The great Theatres of London have more than once given their applause to the dramas of Mr. Mallet[4] and of Mr. John Hume.[5] Poetry, however, is not that branch

[1] Francis Hutcheson (1694–1746), Professor of Moral Philosophy at Glasgow, 1729–1746.

[2] William Wilkie (1721–1772), Professor of Natural Philosophy at St. Andrews, 1759, and known as 'the Scottish Homer'.

[3] Thomas Blacklock (1721–1791), poet and translater.

[4] David Mallett (1705?–1765), friend and collaborator of James Thomson.

[5] John Home (1722–1808). See No. 186.

of literature which the Scots have cultivated with a glory proper and peculiar to themselves. England, although abundantly rich and well provided of all kinds of excellent books, could scarce reckon among these, as was before observed, a good historian. It was reserved to Scotland to compleat in so remarkable a branch the English library. Who among the Literati of Europe knows not, and does not celebrate the works of Mr. Hume? Who in particular does not read and admire his histories? Mr. Smollet might perhaps have produced to his country a great work of the historic kind, if he had preferred, as is peculiar to great geniuses, [perpetual glory to present gain and] an honourable name to the pay of the bookseller.

But Mr. Robertson[1] hath justly merited unstained and immortal praise, who, having applied himself with extraordinary labour to illustrate the antient Scottish history, together with the most striking passages of the modern, hath by his judgment and accurate discernment signalized himself amongst the noblest writers of that class, and at the same time surpast in elegance of stile not only his compatriot authors, but even the most celebrated native English writers.

The fact is altogether indisputable that the principal authors who for some years past have done honour to the English literature, and those who do so at present, have been born and educated in Scotland.

[1] William Robertson (1721–1793), historiographer for Scotland, 1763.

Part X

IRELAND

IRELAND

Introduction

WHILE the eighteenth century saw a marked improvement in the relations between England and Scotland and the beginning of the process of assimilation of the two countries, an exactly opposite tendency is visible in Ireland. At the beginning of the Hanoverian period an attempt by the Irish House of Lords to assert its claim to be the final court of appeal for Ireland led to the passing of the Declaratory Act (Ireland) by the British Parliament in 1719.[1] This measure formally asserted the legislative dependence of Ireland upon the Parliament of Great Britain. From time to time protests were made in Ireland against the complete control of Irish affairs by the English Government. The granting in 1722 of a patent to William Wood for the issue of a new copper coinage in Ireland led to addresses of protest from both Houses of the Irish Parliament,[2] and to the well-known protest by Swift in the *Drapier's Letters*.[3] A more serious conflict arose in the years 1753–1756 over the disposal of the Irish revenues, and from this time a party independent of the Crown and enjoying a measure of popular support may be discerned in the Irish Parliament, which now began to vote large sums for objects of national importance and party advantage, outside the fixed establishments. Another indication of the growing restlessness of the Irish Parliament may be seen in the passing of the Octennial Act of 1767.[4] Until then an Irish Parliament was only necessarily terminated by the demise of the sovereign.

The outbreak of the war of American Independence brought matters to a crisis, especially as it became clear that the war was going against Britain, and a French invasion threatened. The American war had also increased economic distress by adding fresh restrictions on trade to the existing mercantilist regulations from which Ireland had suffered since the reign of William III.[5] The result was the general adoption of non-importation agreements[6] and the organization of bodies of volunteers against the threat of a French invasion. As a result, some of the commercial restrictions were removed by Lord North's government in 1780.[7] The volunteers soon turned from their ostensible object of resisting a French invasion to demand the repeal of Poynings' law and the recognition of the Irish Parliament as the sovereign legislature for Ireland.[8]

The basis of the constitutional settlement reached in 1782–1783 was the renunciation by the British Parliament of any claim to legislate for Ireland and the retention by the British Government of its control over the Irish executive. The English Parliament repealed the Declaratory Act of 1719;[9] and simultaneously the Irish Parliament passed a whole series of measures intended to carry out this general principle. Yelverton's Act regulated the manner of passing Bills;[10] a second Act confirmed the validity of certain laws passed by the English Parliament;[11] a third restored the

[1] No. 197. [2] No. 198. [3] No. 199. [4] No. 200. [5] No. 201. [6] No. 204.
[7] Nos. 202 and 203. [8] No. 205. [9] No. 206. [10] No. 207. [11] No. 208.

appellate jurisdiction of the Irish House of Lords;[1] and a fourth secured the independence of the Irish judges.[2] The simple repeal of the Declaratory Act failed to satisfy a section of Irish opinion, led by Henry Flood, who pressed for specific renunciation by the English Parliament of its right to legislate for Ireland. This was opposed by Grattan,[3] but the English Government felt it politic to pass the Renunciation Act of 1783, whereby England abandoned for ever the claim to legislate for Ireland.[4]

Political problems in Ireland were always complicated by the religious problem inevitably involved in the domination of a predominantly Catholic population by a Protestant minority. An eighteenth-century writer estimated that in 1731 the Catholic population numbered some 1,309,768, as against a Protestant population of 700,451, which would presumably include Presbyterians, themselves a religious group dissenting from the established Anglican Church.[5] The revenues of that Church were considerable, and the financial position of Irish bishops and deans often compared very favourably with their brethren in England.[6] Some measures were passed in 1771 and 1774 to reduce the stringency of the penal laws against Catholics. The political crisis of 1778 and the invasion scare of that year led some, like the bishop of Derry, to urge a measure of religious toleration upon the English Government,[7] and further Catholic Relief Acts were passed in 1778[8] and 1782. The combined effect of these Acts, however, was quite insufficient to satisfy the Irish Catholics.

The documents in the next group have been chosen to illustrate the general social and economic state of Ireland in this period. The sufferings of the Irish people under English domination were a source of burning indignation to Swift, who expatiated upon them–unavailingly–to Walpole in 1726.[9] The particular grievance of the draining away of Irish wealth by absentee landlords led to the publication by Thomas Prior of his *List of the Absentees of Ireland* in 1729.[10] Figures compiled by Thomas Newenham, later an opponent of the Union of 1801, show the state of the linen industry, Ireland's most important industry, throughout our period.[11] Agriculture and the social condition of the Irish peasantry were discussed with his usual thoroughness by Arthur Young in his *Tour in Ireland*.[12]

[1] No. 209. [2] No. 210. [3] No. 211. [4] No. 212. [5] No. 213. [6] Nos. 214 and 217.
[7] No. 215. [8] No. 216. [9] No. 218. [10] No. 219. [11] No. 220. [12] No. 221.

BIBLIOGRAPHY

I. BIBLIOGRAPHIES, ETC.

Much the most practical of these is included by Professor C. L. Grose as Section XIV of his *Select Bibliography of British History 1660–1760* (Chicago, 1939). Constantia E. Maxwell, *Short Bibliography of Irish History*, Historical Association Pamphlet No. 23 (new edition, London, 1921), lists practically all the books dealing with eighteenth-century Ireland and published before 1921 which the ordinary reader is likely to wish to consult. This may be supplemented by R. H. Murray's bibliography on Ireland (1714–1829), which forms No. 35 in the series *Helps for Students of History* (S.P.C.K., 1920). There is an extensive bibliography of older books for our period compiled by R. Dunlop in the *Cambridge Modern History*, VI (Cambridge, 1909), pp. 913–924. John Lodge, *Peerage of Ireland* (2nd revised edition, Dublin, 7 vols., 1789), is now superseded by G. E. C[ockayne], *Complete Peerage*. The *Dictionary of National Biography* and J. S. Crone, *Concise Dictionary of Irish Biography* (Dublin, 1928, revised edition, 1937), give biographies of the eminent Irishmen of the eighteenth century. There is an excellent "Select Bibliography of Irish Economic History, Part 2, 17th and 18th Centuries" by P. L. Prendeville in the *Economic History Review*, III (1931–1932), pp. 402–416. E. Curtis and R. B. McDowell, *Irish Historical Documents* (London, 1943), contains a section on the eighteenth century, but it is virtually limited to constitutional and political documents. Much wider is the scope of J. Carty, *Ireland from the Flight of the Earls to Grattan's Parliament* (Dublin, 1949). The recently published periodical *Irish Historical Studies* (Dublin, 1938 onwards) has already published valuable contributions to the history of eighteenth-century Ireland, especially the annual lists of *Writings on Irish History* from 1936 onwards.

II. ORIGINAL SOURCES

Many official documents have been published in *The [Irish] Statutes at Large* (20 vols., Dublin, 1765–1801); *Journals of the [Irish] House of Lords* (8 vols., Dublin, 1779–1800); *Journals of the [Irish] House of Commons* (19 vols., with appendix and index, Dublin, 1796–1800); and the *Parliamentary Register [of Ireland]* [1781–1800] (20 vols., Dublin, 1784–1800), *The Shapland Carew Papers*, edited by A. K. Longfield (Dublin, 1946), includes many documents of value on social and economic conditions. The Historical Manuscripts Commission has published several collections of outstanding value for the eighteenth century, notably the *Charlemont Manuscripts* (Report 12, part 10) (1891), being the correspondence of James, first earl of Charlemont, 1745–1783, and also Report 13, part 8; the *Stopford Sackville Manuscripts*, enlarged edition in 2 vols. (1904–1910); and the *Egmont Manuscripts* (3 vols., 1920–1923), being the Diary of Viscount Percival, later first earl of Egmont. The *Clements Manuscripts*, *Donoughmore Manuscripts*, *Lothian Manuscripts*, *O'Connor Manuscripts* (Report 8, Appendix 441–492), relating to the penal laws, *Eyre Matcham Manuscripts* [1725–1762], *Emly Manuscripts* [1771–1783], *Howard Manuscripts* [1715–1773], *Carlisle Manuscripts*, *Fortescue Manuscripts*, *Kenyon Manuscripts*, *Knox Manuscripts* and the *Lansdowne Manuscripts* also all have some bearing on the eighteenth-century history of Ireland. For the first few years of Hanoverian Ireland, *Letters Written by Hugh Boulter [1724–38]* (2 vols., Oxford, 1769–1770), and *Letters to and from William Nicolson [1683–1726/7]*, edited by J. Nichols (2 vols., 1809), are still important. Swift's numerous pamphlets on Irish affairs and especially the *Drapier's Letters* will be found in the various editions of his works. C. L. Falkiner published in the *English Historical Review*, XX (1905), pp. 508–542 and 735–763, valuable extracts from "The Correspondence of Archbishop Stone and the Duke of Newcastle on Irish Affairs between 1752 and 1758". *The Autobiography and Correspondence of Mrs. Delany* (6 vols., London, 1861–1862), covering the period 1737–1788, throws much light on Dublin Society. The best accounts of Ireland by contemporary travellers are those by Bishop Pococke, edited by G. T. Stokes under the title *Pocock's Tour in Ireland in 1752* (Dublin, 1891); by Arthur Young in his *A Tour in Ireland* (2 vols., Dublin, 1780); and by T. Campbell, author of *Philosophical Survey of the South of Ireland* (London, 1777).

III. GENERAL HISTORIES

Two large-scale works on eighteenth-century Ireland by eminent Victorians are still used. W. E. H. Lecky is seen at his best in his *History of Ireland in the Eighteenth Century* (5 vols., London, new edition, 1892), which at once superseded J. A. Froude, *The English in Ireland in the Eighteenth Century* (3 vols., 1872–1874). E. A. Dalton, *History of Ireland*, vol. 2 (London, 1912), takes a strong anti-English line; and there are short histories by R. Dunlop, *Ireland: from the Earliest Times to the Present Day* (London, 1922), and Edmund Curtis, *A History of Ireland* (London, 1936). The only general work on constitutional history is J. G. S. MacNeill, *Constitutional and Parliamentary History of Ireland till the Union* (London, 1917).

IV. MONOGRAPHS AND ARTICLES

R. H. Murray, *Revolutionary Ireland and its Settlement* (London, 1911), is a useful introduction to our period, while M. J. Bonn, *Die Englische Kolonisation in Irland* (2 vols., Stuttgart and Berlin, 1906), studies in its concluding chapter the character and methods of the English administration. There is an interesting review of the latter work in the *English Historical Review*, XXI (1906), pp. 772–778. J. C. Beckett's article in *Irish Historical Studies*, II (1940–1941), pp. 280–302, on "The Government and the Church of Ireland under William III and Anne" explains the outlines of the system which remained intact until the closing years of our period, while he has surveyed the whole century from one point of view in his *Protestant Dissent in Ireland 1687–1780* (London, 1948). W. A. Phillips edited a *History of the Church of Ireland* (3 vols., London, 1933–1934). R. Quintana, *The Mind and Art of Jonathan Swift* (New York, 1936), comments helpfully on Swift as an Irish patriot. The best account of the Drapier controversy will, however, be found in A. Goodwin's article on "Wood's Halfpence" in the *English Historical Review*, LI (1936), pp. 647–674. C. L. Falkiner's *Essays Relating to Ireland* (London, 1909), includes one on Archbishop Stone. Grattan has attracted numerous biographers, including R. Dunlop, *Life of Henry Grattan* (London, 1889), R. J. McHugh, *Henry Grattan* (Dublin, 1936), and S. Gwynn, *Henry Grattan and his Times* (London, 1939). All these draw largely on the *Memoirs of the Life and Times of the Rt. Hon. Henry Grattan*, edited by his son, Henry Grattan (5 vols., London, 1839–1846). On Grattan's older contemporary, Henry Flood, there is little except the unsatisfactory *Memoirs of the Life and Correspondence of Rt. Hon. Henry Flood* by Warden Flood (Dublin, 1838). Francis Hardy, *Memoirs of James Earl of Charlemont* (London, 1810, 2nd edition in 2 vols., 1812), is still useful, though there is a more recent life of Lord Charlemont by M. J. Craig under the title *The Volunteer Earl* (London, 1948). R. B. McDowell, *Irish Public Opinion 1750–1800* (London, 1944), brings together much interesting material. E. and A. G. Porritt, *The Unreformed House of Commons*, vol. II (Cambridge, 1903), gives a full account of the Irish parliamentary system. The article by J. L. McCracken on "Irish Parliamentary Elections 1727–68" in *Irish Historical Studies*, V (1946–1947), pp. 209–230, is a valuable summary, while the crisis of 1753–1756 has been studied afresh by the same author in his essay on "The Conflict between the Irish Administration and Parliament 1753–56" in *Irish Historical Studies*, III (1942–1943), pp. 159–179. The greater crisis of 1778–1782 is examined in H. Butterfield's work on *George III, Lord North and the People*, included in the sectional bibliography on Parliament. The accuracy of reports of "Debates in the Irish House of Commons 1776–1789" is discussed by M. W. Jernegan in the *English Historical Review*, XXIV (1909), pp. 104–106. *Essays in British and Irish History* [in honour of J. E. Todd], edited by H. A. Cronne, T. W. Moody and D. B. Quinn (London, 1949), has several contributions of importance to eighteenth-century Irish history.

V. ECONOMIC HISTORY

The standard textbook is still G. O'Brien, *Economic History of Ireland in the Eighteenth Century* (London, 1918). Dr. O'Brien has also contributed a useful article on "The Irish Free Trade Agitation of 1779" to the *English Historical Review*, XXXVIII (1923), pp. 564–581, and XXXIX (1924), pp. 95–109. There is a discussion of Anglo-Irish economic relations by Alice E. Murray (Mrs. Radice) entitled *History of the Commercial and Financial Relations between England and Ireland* (London, 1903). The best book on the land question is W. F. T. Butler, *Confiscation in Irish History* (Dublin, 1917). On finance, T. J. Kiernan, *History of the Financial Administration of Ireland to 1817* (London, 1930), may be consulted. C. Gill, *Rise of the Irish Linen Industry* (Oxford, 1925), is a model monograph on the most important Irish industry. Recently K. H. Connell has studied "The Population of Ireland in the Eighteenth Century" in the *Economic History Review*, XVI (1946), pp. 111–124. *The Population of Ireland 1750–1845*, by the same author (Oxford, 1950), is mainly devoted to the period after 1783.

VI. SOCIAL HISTORY

Constantia E. Maxwell, *Country and Town in Ireland under the Four Georges* (new edition, Dundalk, 1949), is a good introduction to social history. *Dublin under the Georges 1714–1830* (London, 1936) by the same author gives an excellent survey of life in the capital, the architecture of which has been elaborately studied in The Georgian Society of Dublin's publications, *Records of Eighteenth Century Domestic Architecture in Dublin* (5 vols., Dublin, 1909–1913). On education, M. G. Jones, *The Charity School Movement* (Cambridge, 1938), chapter VII, and P. J. Dowling, *Hedge Schools of Ireland* (London, 1935), and on literature D. Hyde, *Literary History of Ireland* (London, 1899), seem to be the best of the available books.

A. RELATIONS WITH ENGLAND

197. The Declaratory Act (Ireland), 1719

(*Statutes at Large*, XIV, pp. 204–205. 6 Geo. I, c. 5.)

This Act was occasioned by the Irish House of Lords reversing a decision of the Court of Exchequer and committing the Barons of the Exchequer for obeying the English House of Lords. It was repealed in 1782 (No. 206).

An act for the better securing the dependency of the kingdom of Ireland *upon the crown of* Great Britain.

I. WHEREAS *the house of lords of* Ireland *have of late, against law, assumed to themselves a power and jurisdiction to examine, correct and amend the judgments and decrees of the courts of justice in the kingdom of* Ireland; therefore for the better securing of the dependency of *Ireland* upon the crown of *Great Britain*, may it please your most excellent Majesty that it may be declared, and be it declared by the King's most excellent majesty, by and with the advice and consent of the lords spiritual and temporal, and commons, in this present parliament assembled, and by the authority of the same, That the said kingdom of *Ireland* hath been, is, and of right ought to be subordinate unto and dependent upon the imperial crown of *Great Britain*, as being inseparably united and annexed thereunto; and that the King's majesty, by and with the advice and consent of the lords spiritual and temporal, and commons of *Great Britain* in parliament assembled, had, hath, and of right ought to have full power and authority to make laws and statutes of sufficient force and validity, to bind the kingdom and people of *Ireland*.

II. And be it further declared and enacted by the authority aforesaid, That the house of lords of *Ireland* have not, nor of right ought to have any jurisdiction to judge of, affirm or reverse any judgment, sentence or decree, given or made in any court within the said kingdom, and that all proceedings before the said house of lords upon any such judgment, sentence or decree, are, and are hereby declared to be utterly null and void to all intents and purposes whatsoever.

198. Address to the King from the Irish House of Commons on "Wood's Ha'pence", 27 September 1723

(*Journals of the Irish House of Commons*, V (1753), p. 36.)

The purchase by William Wood of a patent granted in 1722 to the duchess of Kendal for the issue of a new copper coinage in Ireland, without previous consultation with the Irish Parliament, caused much indignation. Addresses against it were also presented by the Irish House of Lords and by the City of Dublin.

[27 September 1723.]

To the King's most excellent Majesty,
The humble address of the Knights, Citizens and Burgesses, in Parliament assembled.

Most gracious Sovereign,

It is with the utmost concern, that we, your Majesty's most dutiful and loyal Subjects, the Commons of *Ireland* in Parliament assembled, find ourselves indispensably obliged humbly to represent to your Majesty our unanimous opinion, that the importing and uttering of copper farthings and half-pence, by vertue of the patent lately granted to *William Wood*, Esq; under the great seal of *Great-Britain*, will be highly prejudicial to your Majesty's revenue, destructive of the trade and commerce of this Nation, and of the most dangerous consequence to the properties of the Subject.

We are fully convinced, from the tender regard your Majesty has always expressed for our welfare and prosperity, that this patent could not have been obtained, had not *William Wood* and his accomplices greatly misrepresented the state of this Nation to your Majesty, it having appeared to us by examinations taken in the most solemn manner, that, though the terms thereof had been strictly complied with, there would have been a loss to this Nation of at least one hundred and fifty pounds *per cent.* by means of the said coinage, and a much greater in the manner the said half-pence have been coined.

We likewise beg leave to inform your Majesty, that the said *William Wood* has been guilty of a most notorious fraud and deceit in coining the said half-pence, having, under colour of the powers granted unto him, imported, and endeavoured to utter great quantities of different impressions, and of much less weight, than was required by the said patent.

Your faithful Commons having found by experience, that the granting of the power or privilege of coining money, or tokens to pass for money, to private persons, has been highly detrimental to your loyal Subjects; and being apprehensive, that the vesting of such power in any body politick, or corporate, or any private person, or persons whatsoever, will be always of dangerous consequence to this Kingdom, are encouraged by the repeated assurances your Majesty hath given us of your royal favour and protection, humbly to entreat your Majesty, that whenever you shall hereafter think it necessary to coin any farthings or half-pence, the same may be made as near the intrinsick value as possible, and that whatever profit shall accrue thereby may be applied to the publick service.

And we do further humbly beseech your Majesty, that you will be graciously pleased to give such directions, as you in your great wisdom shall think proper, to prevent the fatal effects of uttering any farthings or half-pence, pursuant to the said patent.

As this enquiry has proceeded entirely from our love to our Country, so we cannot omit this opportunity of repeating our unanimous resolution, to stand by and support your Majesty, to the utmost of our power, against all your enemies both at home and abroad, and of assuring your Majesty, that we will, upon every occasion, give your Majesty and the world all possible demonstration of our zeal and inviolable duty and affection to your Majesty's most sacred Person and government, and to the Succession, as established in your Royal House.

199. The Drapier's Letters: No. IV, "To the Whole People of Ireland", 13 October 1724

(Jonathan Swift, *The Drapier's Letters; Prose Works*, ed. Herbert Davis, x (1941), pp. 61–63.)

The printer of the letter from which this extract is taken was unsuccessfully prosecuted by the government, which also offered a £300 reward for the discovery of the author, but without success.

. . . ANOTHER Slander spread by *Wood* and his Emissaries is, that by opposing him, we discover an Inclination to *shake off our Dependance upon the Crown of* England. Pray observe how Important a Person is this same *William Wood*, and how the publick Weal of two Kingdoms is involved in his private Interest. First, all those who refuse to take his Coin *are Papists*; for he tells us that *none but Papists are associated against him*; Secondly, they *dispute the King's Prerogative;* Thirdly *they are Ripe for Rebellion*, and Fourthly, They are going to *shake off their Dependance upon the Crown of* England; That is to say, *they are going to chuse another King*: For there can be no other Meaning in this Expression, however some may pretend to strain it.

And this gives me an Opportunity of explaining, to those who are ignorant, another Point, which hath often *swelled in my Breast*. Those who come over hither to us from *England*, and some *weak* People among ourselves, whenever in Discourse we make mention of *Liberty* and *Property*, shake their Heads, and tell us, that *Ireland* is a *depending Kingdom*, as if they would seem, by this Phrase, to intend that the People of *Ireland* is in some State of Slavery or Dependance different from those of *England*: Whereas a *depending Kingdom* is a *modern Term of Art*, unknown, as I have heard, to all antient *Civilians*, and *Writers upon Government*; and *Ireland* is on the contrary called in some Statutes an *Imperial Crown*, as held only from God; which is as high a Style as any Kingdom is capable of receiving. Therefore by this Expression, a *depending Kingdom*, there is no more understood than that by a Statute made here in the 33d year of *Henry VIII. The King and his Successors are to be Kings Imperial of this Realm as united and knit to the Imperial Crown of* England. I have looked over all the *English* and *Irish* Statutes without finding any Law that makes *Ireland depend* upon *England*, any more than *England* doth upon *Ireland*. We have indeed obliged ourselves to have the *same King with them*, and consequently they are obliged to have *the same King with us*. For the Law was made by *our own Parliament*, and our Ancestors then were not such Fools (*whatever they were in the preceding Reign*) to bring themselves under I know not what *Dependance*, which is now talked of without any Ground of *Law*, *Reason* or *common Sense*.

LET whoever think otherwise, I *M. B. Drapier*, desire to be excepted, For I declare, next under God, I *depend* only on the King my Sovereign, and on the Laws of my own Country; And I am so far from *depending* upon the People of *England*, that if they should ever *Rebel* against my Sovereign (which GOD forbid) I would be ready at the first Command from his Majesty to take Arms against them, as some of *my* Country-men did against *theirs* at *Preston*. And if such a Rebellion should prove so successful as to fix the *Pretender* on the Throne of *England*, I would venture to transgress that *Statute* so far as to lose every Drop of my Blood to hinder him from being *King* of *Ireland*.

It is true indeed, that within the Memory of Man, the Parliaments of *England* have *Sometimes* assumed the Power of binding this Kingdom by Laws enacted there, wherein they were at first openly opposed (as far as *Truth*, *Reason* and *Justice* are capable of *Opposing*) by the Famous Mr. *Molineaux*,[1] an *English* Gentleman born here, as well as by several of the greatest Patriots, and *best Whigs* in *England*; but the *Love and Torrent* of Power prevailed. Indeed the Arguments on both Sides were invincible. For in *Reason*, all *Government* without the Consent of the *Governed* is the *very Definition of Slavery*: But in *Fact*, *Eleven Men well armed will certainly subdue one single Man in his Shirt*. But I have done. For those who have used *Power* to cramp *Liberty* have gone so far as to Resent even the *Liberty* of *Complaining*, although a Man upon the Rack was never known to be refused the Liberty of *roaring* as loud as he thought fit.

And as we are apt to *sink* too *much* under *unreasonable* Fears, so we are too soon inclined to be *Raised* by groundless Hopes (according to the Nature of all *consumptive* Bodies like ours). Thus, it hath been given about for several Days past, that *Some body in England* empowered a second *Some body* to write to a third *Some body* here to assure us, that we *should no more be troubled with those Half-pence*. And this is reported to have been done by the **same Person*, who was said to have Sworn some Months ago, that he would *ram them down our Throats* (though I doubt they would *stick in our Stomachs*). But which ever of these Reports is true or false, it is no Concern of ours. For *in this Point* we have nothing to do with *English Ministers*, and I should be sorry it leave in their Power to *redress* this Grievance or to *enforce* it: For the *Report of the Committee* hath given me a *Surfeit*. The Remedy is wholly in your own Hands, and therefore I have digressed a little in order to refresh and continue that *Spirit* so seasonably raised amongst you, and to let you see that by the Laws of GOD, of NATURE, of NATIONS, and of your own *Country*, you ARE and OUGHT to be as FREE a People as your Brethren in *England*. . . .

200. The Octennial Act, 1767

(*Statutes at Large, passed in the Parliaments held in Ireland*, IX (1769), p. 504. 7 Geo. III, c. 3.)

Prior to the passing of this Act, only the death of the king necessarily ended an Irish Parliament.

An act for limiting the duration of parliaments.

That whereas a limitation of the duration of parliaments may tend to strengthen the harmony and good agreement subsisting between his Majesty and his people of Ireland, and may be productive of other good effects to his Majesty's subjects there: we, your Majesty's most dutiful and loyal subjects, the commons of Ireland in parliament assembled, do most humbly beseech your Majesty, that it may be declared and enacted in this present parliament, and be it declared and enacted by the King's most

[1] Sir William Molyneux (1656–1698), author of *The Case of Ireland's being bound by Acts of Parliament in England stated* (1698), which was censured by the House of Commons as "of dangerous consequence to the Crown and Parliament of England".

* *Mr.* Walpole, *now* Sir Robert. [Swift's note to the 1735 edition.]

excellent Majesty by and with the advice and consent of the lords spiritual and temporal and commons in this present parliament assembled, and by the authority of the same, that from henceforth no parliament, which shall at any time hereafter be called, assembled, or held, shall have any longer continuance than for eight years, to be accounted from the day on which by the writs of summons the said parliament shall be appointed to meet.

II. And be it further enacted by the authority aforesaid, that this present parliament shall cease and determine on the twenty fourth day of June, which shall be in the year of our Lord one thousand seven hundred and sixty eight, unless his Majesty shall think fit sooner to dissolve the same.

201. Edmond Sexton Pery, Speaker of the Irish House of Commons, on the commercial regulations, June 1779

(George O'Brien, "Documents on the Irish Free Trade Agitation", *English Historical Review*, XXXVIII (1923), pp. 570–573.)

The war with America had caused much economic distress in Ireland and had much increased discontent with the commercial regulations, which, it was felt, made Ireland unable to withstand a crisis of this sort. Attempts at concession by Lord North in 1778 had been prevented by the opposition of English merchants, but in May 1779, Lord Weymouth, Secretary of State, asked the Lord Lieutenant to obtain opinions on the situation from leading Irishmen, of whom Pery was one.

Opinion of Edmond Sexton Pery.

June 12th 1779.

It is not necessary for me to say much to your Excellency relative to the State of the People of this Kingdom; that it is such, as described in the Addresses, the deficiency in the Revenue, the decrease of Rents and of the value of Estates, the accumulation of public and private Debts, and the Accounts received from all Parts of the Kingdom corresponding with what has passed immediately under your Excellency's own observation in the Metropolis, leave no room for doubt. It is true the Distresses of the lower classes of the Manufacturers, particularly in the City of Dublin have been of late in some measure alleviated by Associations for the Consumption of Home Manufactures[1] which have sett those at Work who were before unemployed; but it is to be apprehended that these Associations, however innocent and perhaps necessary at present to prevent the effects of Despair in the People, will not continue long so unless the progress of them be stopped by cutting off the source of the Evil.

It is equally unnecessary for me to point out to your Excellency more than one general Cause of this Distress, for tho' many others certainly concurr, yet they are either of a Nature not to be redressed by Parliament, such as the great and constant flux of Wealth from this Kingdom to supply absentee Proprietors and Creditors whose numbers increase in proportion to its distress, or they are such as require no remedy but a due and vigorous execution of the Laws, and a few internal Regulations.

The general Cause of Distress is undoubtedly the restraint upon the Trade, and

[1] Non-importation associations on the same lines as those formed in the American colonies. For an example, see No. 204.

consequently upon the Industry of the Kingdom. If the extent and operation of the Laws, which limit the Trade of Ireland are considered, it will appear that her Complaints upon that Head are not without foundation.

Ireland is excluded from all direct Commerce with the British Colonies in Asia, Africa and America, except for Victuals and white and brown Linens, and except for a few trifling not enumerated Articles in return, which are of little, if any, advantage to it, and in some Instances perhaps of prejudice. It is true, some alteration has been lately made with respect to certain Articles of Export; but they are so few and subject to such limitations restrictions and duties, especially as nothing can be brought back in return, that the Law has not yet had, and probably never will have, any operation. Ireland is likewise prevented from carrying on any Trade with the Colonies of other Nations, for the principal Articles of their produce can only be imported from Great Britain.

Ireland is also restrained under the severest Penalties, from sending to any Part of the World any Manufacture made of or mixed with Wool.

Thus is Ireland in effect cut off from all Trade, at least what deserves the name of Trade, with the rest of the World, for it is well known that Commerce cannot be carryed on to advantage without assortments of the different kinds of Goods which are in demand in the Country traded with, and without permission to bring back in return the produce of such Country or of its Colonies; the only two Articles then of Trade from which Ireland can derive any advantage, are Linens and Provisions; with respect to the former, there are many powerful Rivals to contend with, who get the Materials upon much cheaper terms, and, She is restrained from sending the most profitable branch of that Manufacture to the only Markets where there is a demand for it; with respect to the latter, the trade is frequently stopped at the most critical Seasons, it must be presumed upon Reasons of State, by Embargoes, the last of which continued for three Years. The situation of a Nation which depends upon one single Manufacture is precarious, it must sensibly feel every revolution and uncertainty, to which every particular Manufacture is exposed, upon the least Check the Poor are thrown out of Employment, and of consequence become idle and miserable; Such is the Case of Ireland, and such it must remain, as long as those Laws which I have mentioned subsist. It would not become me to question the Justice of those Laws, but the Policy of them may be examined without offence. That Ireland must continue in a State of Poverty, frequently of Misery, under those Laws, appears evident not only from Reason but Experience; it seems to be equally obvious, that it is not the Interest of Great Britain to keep her in that State; in the view of Commerce only, Great Britain must be a loser by it, little is to be got by trading with a poor Country, much by trading with a rich one; the Profits of Great Britain upon its Trade with Ireland must be in proportion to the Wealth of the latter; the Benefit of one Nation constitutes that of the other; in every other point of view the Interest of Great Britain in the Prosperity of Ireland seems equally evident; Great Britain being the center of Power, all the Riches of Ireland must ultimately flow to it, if the Trade of Ireland increases, the Revenue of it must increase in proportion, and may in Time become a Fund not only sufficient to maintain its own Establishments, but to assist Great

Britain in Time of War; on the other hand if the Revenue of Ireland by the depression of it's Trade proves insufficient for the support of it's Military Establishment, the Deficiency must either be made up by Great Britain, of which there has been a recent instance, or the Army must be disbanded to the manifest hazard of both Kingdoms.

But tho' it is obvious, that the general State of Great Britain must necessarily derive many advantages from the increase of Manufactures and Trades in Ireland, yet several Bodies of Manufacturing People in the former Kingdom more attentive to their own private Interest than to that of the Public, look upon the progress of Improvement in the latter with a jealous Eye, and suppose it impossible that it's Trade should flourish but at their expence, not reflecting that the Objects of Industry are not to be exhausted, and that there are Markets for more Manufactures than both Countries can possibly supply, provided they sell cheaper than other Nations, without which Circumstance neither can succeed. But it is supposed that Food being cheaper in Ireland than in England, the Manufacturers in the former Kingdom can undersell the latter; It is true that the Food of the Manufacturers in the former Kingdom is at present cheaper than in the latter, principally because it is of an inferior quality, being Potatoes and Milk, but if they were to feed upon Bread and Butcher's Meat, as no doubt they would if they could, the difference would be very inconsiderable, and would daily become less as Ireland increased in Industry and Population; But let the difference be what it may, the advantages of superior Skill, Ingenuity, Stocks and established Correspondence, are much more than an equivalent for it, of which Scotland affords a strong Example, for tho' Provisions are as cheap there, as in Ireland, yet the Commerce of that Kingdom has not in the least injured that of England.

The Woolen Manufacture, the great Subject of jealousy, requires some particular Notice. It is asserted by the Drapiers and Clothiers in Ireland, that all the Wool produced in Ireland is not sufficient to cloath its Inhabitants; the Price of Wool in Ireland being so much higher than in England seems to countenance the Assertion, unless it be raised by a great Demand for it in France, and the consequent temptation to Smugglers to transport it into that Kingdom; of this Fact I am by no means certain; it is asserted on the one side, and denyed on the other with equal confidence, and by People who may be supposed to know the truth; but on which soever side the truth lies, it shews that England has nothing to fear from the competition of Ireland in the Woolen Trade, tho' it were laid open; the opening of that Trade could not lower the Price of Wool in Ireland, on the contrary it would probably raise it, and as England at present undersells Ireland, even in it's own Market, in all Branches of the Woolen Manufacture, tho' subject to considerable Duties and charged with Freight, Commission and Insurance, it would probably continue to do so after the Trade was left open. If England should be excluded from the Irish Market, the Woolen Manufacture would suffer more by the loss of that Market than it can by any competition in a Foreign Market.

Thus upon the enlarged and generous principles of Commerce, as well as of Policy and Justice, it seems to be the Interest of Great Britain to permit the People of Ireland to exert their own Talents and to reap the Profits of their own Industry in common with their fellow Subjects of Great Britain; Nothing more is asked by them, and Your Excellency may be assured, I say it with confidence, nothing less will content them. Expedients may, and I believe will be tried, but I am persuaded they will prove not only fruitless, but tend to exasperate, instead of mollifying the Minds of the People. I have heard it asked, what will Ireland give in return for such Benefits? To Bargain is not suitable to the Dignity of the Crown or of either Nation, it would be a Subject of distrust and jealousy, and disappoint the very end of it. The Parliament of Ireland has ever considered the Interest of Great Britain as its own, even when it resented most the State in which it was held, and granted Supplies to the extent of its Abilities and the demands of the Crown. What reason to suspect that it would be less liberal for being gratified? Ingratitude is not the growth of Ireland. The Parliament of Ireland as well as that of Great Britain may be trusted with providing for the exigencies of the State, when it considers itself as a part of it. At present the People of Ireland are taught by those partial Laws to consider themselves as separated from the Inhabitants of Great Britain: were that fatal Obstacle removed, they would be united as much in Affection, as they certainly are in Interest; and it would not then be in the power of Malice to disturb their Harmony. But the Seeds of Discord are sown, and if suffered to take root, it is to be feared will soon overspread the Land.

If I have treated this Subject with too much freedom, I am persuaded your Excellency's candour will impute it to my Zeal for the Prosperity of both Nations equally dear to me.

202. Act removing restraints on the export of Irish woollen and glass manufactures, 1780

(*Statutes at Large*, XXXIII, p. 4. 20 Geo. III, c. 6.)

This and the following Act (No. 203) were passed by Lord North's government as a result of the Irish free-trade agitation of 1778–1779. The Acts were greeted with much joy in Ireland, but did not prove as beneficial as had been hoped, as Ireland's lack of capital and of shipping still left her at a great disadvantage in the colonial trade.

An act to repeal certain acts made in Great Britain *which restrain the trade and commerce of* Ireland *with foreign parts.*

WHEREAS, *in order to promote and advance the welfare and prosperity of his Majesty's kingdom of* Ireland, *it is expedient that certain acts of parliament, formerly made in* Great Britain, *which lay restraints upon the trade and commerce of* Ireland, *respecting the articles herein-after mentioned, should be repealed: may it therefore please your Majesty that it may be enacted*; and be it enacted by the King's most excellent majesty, by and with the advice and consent of the lords spiritual and temporal, and commons, in this present parliament assembled, and by the authority of the same, That, from and after the passing of this act, so much of an act of parliament, made in the tenth and eleventh years of the reign of King *William* the Third, (intituled, *An act to prevent the exportation of wool out of the kingdoms of* Ireland *and* England *into foreign parts; and for the encouragement of the woollen manufactures in the kingdom of* England;) and so much of any other act or acts of parliament made in *Great Britain*, which prohibit or in any manner restrain the exportation of cloth, serge, bays, kerseys, says, frizes, druggets, cloth-serges, shalloons, or any other drapery stuffs, or woollen manufactures whatsoever, made up or mixed with wool or wool flocks, from the kingdom of *Ireland* into foreign parts, shall be, and the same is and are hereby repealed and made void.

II. And it is hereby further enacted by the authority aforesaid, That, from and after the passing of this act, so much of an act, made in the nineteenth year of the reign of his late majesty King *George* the Second (intituled, *An act for granting to his Majesty several rates and duties upon glass and upon spirituous liquors; and for raising a certain sum of money by annuities, and a lottery, to be charged on the said rates and duties; and for obviating some doubts about making out orders as the exchequer for the monies advanced upon the credit of the salt duties, granted and continued to his Majesty by an act of the last session of parliament;*) as relates to the exportation of glass, glass bottles, or glass of any kind or denomination whatsoever, from or out of the kingdom of *Ireland*, shall be, and the same is hereby repealed and made void.

203. Act to allow trade between Ireland and the British Colonies, 1780

(*Statutes at Large*, XXXIII, pp. 12–16. 20 Geo. III, c. 10.)

An act to allow trade between Ireland *and the* British *colonies and plantations in* America *and the* West Indies, *and the* British *settlements on the coast of* Africa, *to be carried on in like manner as it is now carried on between* Great Britain *and the said colonies and settlements.*

[Preamble recites the various Acts regulating Irish trade with the colonies.]

. . . be it enacted by the King's most excellent Majesty, by and with the advice and consent of the lords spiritual and temporal, and commons, in this present parliament assembled, and by the authority of the the same, That any goods, wares, or merchandize, of the growth, product, or manufacture of the *British* colonies or plantations in *America*, or the *West Indies*, or of any settlement belonging to *Great Britain* on the coast of *Africa*, and which by any act or acts of parliament are required to be imported from such colonies, plantations, or settlement into *Great Britain*; and also any other goods, which, having been in any way legally imported into the said colonies, plantations, or settlements, may now or hereafter be legally exported from thence for *Great Britain*, shall and may be laden in, and exported from such colonies, plantations, and settlements, respectively and in like manner imported directly from thence into the kingdom of *Ireland*; and that any goods or commodities of the growth, production, or manufacture of *Ireland*, or of the growth, production, or manufacture of *Great Britain*, legally exported from thence into *Ireland*, or of the growth, production, or manufacture of any other part of *Europe*; and any goods or commodities of the growth, product, or manufacture, of the *East Indies*, or other places beyond the *Cape of Good Hope*, which are now required by any act of parliament to be shipped or laden in *Great Britain*, to be carried directly from thence to any *British* colony or plantation in *Africa* or *America*; as also any other goods, wares, or merchandize, which now or hereafter may be legally shipped or laden in *Great Britain*, to be carried directly from thence, and imported into any colony or plantation in *America* or the *West Indies*, or into any *British* settlement on the coast of *Africa*; shall and may be shipped and laden at any port or place in the kingdom of *Ireland*, and exported directly from thence, and in like manner imported into any *British* colony or plantation in *America* or the *West Indies*, or into any *British* settlement on the coast of *Africa*; anything in the said herein-before recited acts, or either of them, or any other act or acts of parliament made in *Great Britain*, or any usage or custom, to the contrary notwithstanding: subject nevertheless to the conditions herein-after expressed.

II. Provided always, and it is hereby further enacted by the authority aforesaid, That the importation and exportation allowed by this act, shall commence from and as soon, and shall have continuance so long, and in such respective cases only, as the goods, or any of them, which are hereby allowed to be imported from the said colonies, plantations, or settlements into *Ireland*, or to be exported from *Ireland* into the said colonies, plantations, or settlements, shall be liable, by some act or acts of parliament to be made in the kingdom of *Ireland*, to equal duties and drawbacks, and shall be made subject to the same securities, regulations, and restrictions, in all other respects, as the like goods now are, or thereafter may be, liable and subject to upon being imported from the said colonies, plantations, or settlements, into *Great Britain*, or exported from thence to such colonies, plantations, or settlements respectively; in the consideration of which equal duties and drawbacks, due attention may be given to an allowance made for, any duty or imposition, or any part of the same, which shall be retained in *Great Britain*, or not drawn back, or not compensated by bounty in *Great Britain*, upon the export of any such goods, wares, or merchandize from thence to *Ireland*, as also for any duty paid on importation of such goods, wares, or merchandize into *Ireland*, so as the said goods, wares, or merchandize respectively be not exported from *Ireland* with less incumbrance of duties or impositions than now do, or hereafter shall, remain upon the like goods when legally exported from *Great Britain*.

III. And it is hereby further enacted by the authority aforesaid, That during the continuance of this act, so much of the herein-before recited act, made in the twenty-second and twenty-third years of the reign of King *Charles* the Second, as directs or requires the word *Ireland* to be left out of any bond taken for any ship or vessel that shall load any enumerated commodities in any *British* plantation in *America*, *Asia*, or *Africa*, shall be, and the same is hereby repealed and made void; anything in the said recited act, or any other act or acts of parliament, to the contrary notwithstanding.

IV. And it is further enacted by the authority aforesaid, That so much of an act of the fourth year of his present Majesty's reign, as is herein-before recited, shall not extend, or be construed to extend, to subject to seizure and forfeiture, any goods, wares, or merchandize, which by this act, or by any other act or acts of parliament may now or hereafter, be legally imported from *Ireland* into any of the *British* colonies or plantations in *America*, or any *British* settlement on the coast of *Africa*; provided the master, or other person taking the charge of the ship or vessel carrying such goods, shall produce a cocquet or cocquets, clearance or clearances, from the proper officer, or officers, of his Majesty's customs, certifying that the said goods were laden on board the said ship or vessel in some port of *Great Britain*, or in some port of *Ireland*, respectively.

V. Provided also, and it is hereby further enacted by the authority aforesaid, That if it shall so happen that any additional duty shall be imposed, or any alteration shall be made in the drawbacks, or otherwise, upon any goods so as aforesaid imported into, or exported from *Great Britain*, by any act of parliament that may hereafter be made in this kingdom at any time when the parliament of *Ireland* shall not be sitting; that then and in such case the liberty of importation and exportation, granted by this act, shall have continuance, and remain in full force, with respect to such goods, until the end of four calendar months after the meeting of the then next session of parliament in *Ireland*; but if the parliament of *Ireland* shall be sitting at the time that any such additional duty shall be imposed, or any such alteration shall be made in *Great Britain*, then, and in such case, the liberty of importation and exportation granted by this act shall have continuance, and remain in full force, upon such goods as aforesaid, until the end of four calendar months from the time that such additional duty shall be laid, or such alteration made, in case the parliament of *Ireland* shall so long continue to sit without prorogation or dissolution; and in case it shall within that time be prorogued or dissolved, then the liberty of importation and exportation aforesaid shall have continuance, and remain in full force, until the end of four calendar months next after the meeting of the then next session of parliament in *Ireland*.

VI. Provided always, and be it declared and enacted by the authority aforesaid, That nothing herein-before contained shall extend to, or be construed to extend to, the imposing any condition or restriction upon or in respect of any goods, wares, or merchandize, which by an act passed in the eighteenth year of his present Majesty's reign, intituled, *An act to permit the exportation of certain goods directly from* Ireland *into any* British *plantation in* America, *or any* British *settlement on the coast of* Africa; *and for further encouraging the fisheries and navigation of* Ireland; or which by any other act or acts of parliament may now be legally exported from *Ireland* to any of the *British* colonies or plantations in *America* and the *West Indies*, or to the *British* settlements on the coast of *Africa*, or which may now be legally imported into *Ireland* from any of the colonies, plantations, or settlements aforesaid; anything herein-before contained to the contrary notwithstanding.

VII. Provided also, and it is hereby further enacted by the authority aforesaid, That this act shall not extend, or be construed to extend, to allow any person or persons to trade from, or in, any colony or plantation in *America*, during such time, and in such manner, as the trade or intercourse of *Great Britain* with such colony or plantation is or shall be prohibited or restrained by any act or acts of parliament made, or hereafter to be made, in this kingdom; but whenever trade and intercourse shall be permitted between *Great Britain* and such colony or colonies, the same trade and intercourse shall in like manner be permitted and allowed between *Ireland* and the said colony or colonies.

204. Dublin non-importation agreement, 5 September 1780

(*Memoirs . . . of the Rt. Hon. Henry Grattan*, by his son, Henry Grattan, II (1829), pp. 135–137.)

The immediate occasion of this agreement was the rejection by the English Privy Council of the Irish Parliament's proposed protective duty on sugar imported into Ireland.

Tholsel, Dublin, Sept. 5th, 1780.

At a most numerous and respectable meeting of the freemen and freeholders of the City of Dublin, held pursuant to public notice,

William James and John Exshaw, Esqrs. High Sheriffs,
in the chair:–

Resolved, that we are convinced it is now necessary to have recourse to a Non-Importation Agreement, as being pregnant with greater benefits to the country than a partial and an imperfect grant of a nominal Free Trade–a trade (as now regulated) unsubstantial and unproductive, to our wishes delusive, to our wants inadequate. And we trust that the spirit and patriotism of our countrymen will effectually relieve this kingdom from the many disadvantages to which it has been so long subjected.

Resolved, That we will not, from the date hereof, until the grievances of this country shall be removed, directly or indirectly, import or consume any of the manufactures of Great Britain; nor will we deal with any merchant or shopkeeper who shall import such manufactures; and that we recommend an adoption of a similar agreement to all our countrymen who not only regard the commerce and constitution of this country, but wish to preserve that valuable part of the community (our poor manufacturers) from a return of those calamities out of which they were so recently extricated by the spirit of the nation.

Resolved unanimously, That we highly applaud the manly and patriotic sentiments of the several corps of Merchants', Independent Dublin, Liberty, and Goldsmiths' Volunteers, and heartily thank them for their early demonstration of zeal and ardour in the cause of their country, and that we shall ever be ready to join with them in defending our rights and constitution, and gladly and cheerfully contribute to protect them from prosecution or persecution.

205. Resolutions of the Ulster Volunteers at the convention of Dungannon, 15 February 1782

(C. H. Wilson, *A compleat Collection of the Resolutions of the Volunteers, Grand Juries, &c. of Ireland* (1782), pp. 1–4.)

Similar resolutions were carried by many other corps and county meetings. Compare with the Yorkshire Association and its imitators in England (No. 53).

At a Meeting of the Representatives of ONE HUNDRED and FORTY THREE CORPS of VOLUNTEERS *of the Province of* ULSTER, *held at* DUNGANNON *on Friday the* 15*th Day of February*, 1782.

Colonel WILLIAM IRVINE in the Chair.

WHEREAS it has been asserted, "That Volunteers, as such, cannot with propriety, debate or publish their opinions on political subjects, or on the conduct of parliament, or public men."

Resolved unanimously, That a citizen, by learning the use of arms, does not abandon any of his civil rights.

Resolved unanimously, That a claim of any body of men, other than the King, Lords, and Commons of Ireland, to make laws to bind this kingdom, is unconstitutional, illegal, and a *grievance.*

Resolved (with one dissenting voice only) That the powers exercised by the Privy Council of both kingdoms, under, or under colour or pretence of the Law of Poyning's, are unconstitutional, and a *grievance.*

Resolved unanimously, That the ports of this country are, by right, open to all foreign countries, not at war with the king, and that any burthen thereupon, or obstruction thereto, save only by the parliament of Ireland, are unconstitutional, illegal, and a *grievance.*

Resolved (with one dissenting voice only) That a Mutiny Bill, not limited in point of duration, from session to session, is unconstitutional, and a *grievance.*

Resolved unanimously, That the independence of judges is equally essential to the impartial administration of justice in Ireland, as in England, and that the refusal or delay of this right to Ireland, makes a distinction where there should be no distinction, may excite jealousy where perfect union should prevail, and is, in itself, unconstitutional, and a *grievance.*

Resolved (with eleven dissenting voices only) That it is our decided and unalterable determination, to seek a redress of those grievances; and we pledge ourselves to each other, and to our country, as freeholders, fellow-citizens, and men of honour, that we will, at every ensuing election, support those only, who have supported, and will support us therein, and that we will use all constitutional means to make such pursuit of redress speedy and effectual.

Resolved (with one dissenting voice only) That the right honourable and honourable minority in parliament, who have supported these our constitutional rights, are entitled to our most grateful thanks, and that the annexed address be signed by the chairman, and published with these resolutions.

Resolved unanimously, That four members from each county of the province of Ulster, eleven to be a quorum, be and hereby are appointed a committee till next general meeting, to act for the Volunteer Corps here represented, and as occasion shall require, to call general meetings of the province, *viz.*
[32 names.]

Resolved unanimously, That the said committee do appoint nine of their members to be a committee in Dublin, in order to communicate with such other Volunteer associations in the other provinces, as may think proper to come to similar resolutions and to deliberate with them on the most constitutional means of carrying them into effect. In consequence of the above resolution, the committee have appointed the following gentlemen for said committee, three to be a quorum, *viz.*
[9 names.]

Resolved unanimously, That the Committee be, and are hereby instructed to call a general meeting of the province, within twelve months from this day, or in fourteen days after the dissolution of the present Parliament, should such an event sooner take place.

Resolved unanimously, That the Court of Portugal have acted towards this kingdom (being a part of the British empire) in such a manner as to call upon us to declare and pledge ourselves to each other, that we will not consume any wine of the growth of Portugal, and that we will, to the extent of our influence, prevent the use of said wine, save and except the wine at present in this kingdom, until such time as our exports shall be received in the kingdom of Portugal, as the manufactures of part of the British Empire.[1]

Resolved (with two dissenting voices only, to this and the following resolution) That we hold the right of private judgment, in matters of religion, to be equally sacred in others as in ourselves.

Resolved therefore, That as Men and as Irishmen, as Christians and as protestants, we rejoice in the relaxation of the *Penal Laws* against our *Roman Catholic fellow-subjects*, and that we conceive the measure to be fraught with the happiest consequences to the union and prosperity of the inhabitants of Ireland.

Resolved unanimously, That the Dundalk Independent Troop of Light Dragoons, commanded by Captain Thomas Read, having joined a regiment of this province (the first Newry regiment or Newry Legion) and petitioning to be received as part of this body, and under its protection, is accordingly hereby received.

Whereas a letter has been received by the chairman of this meeting from the united corps of the county of Cavan, Colonel Ennery in the chair, declaring their readiness to co-operate with their brother Volunteers in every constitutional support of their rights;

Resolved unanimously, That the thanks of this meeting be presented to the said united corps of the said county of Cavan for their spirited resolution, and that a copy of the proceedings of this meeting be inclosed by the chairman to Colonel Ennery, to be by him communicated to the said united corps, and that they shall have a right, if they choose, to associate with the corps represented at this meeting, to nominate four members to act with those already appointed as a committee by the delegates at this meeting.

Resolved unanimously, That the thanks of this meeting be presented to Captain Richardson and the Dungannon Light Company, for their politeness in mounting guard this day.

Resolved unanimously, That the thanks of this meeting be presented to the Southern Battalion of the First Ulster Regiment, commanded by the Earl of Charlemont, for that patriotic zeal which we are convinced induced them to call this meeting.

Resolved unanimously, That the thanks of this meeting be presented to Colonel William Irvine, for his particular propriety and politeness of conduct in the chair.

Resolved unanimously, That the thanks of this meeting be presented to Captain

[1] After the trade concessions of 1779, the Irish attempted to export wool to Portugal, which was refused admittance because the Methuen Treaty of 1703 bound the Portuguese to admit only British wool. Portugal held that as in 1703 Irish wool was not allowed to be exported at all, it could not be covered by the treaty.

James Dawson, for his readiness in undertaking the office of Secretary to this meeting, and for his particular attention and ability in the laborious duty thereof.

Resolved unanimously, That these resolutions be published.

To the Right Honourable and Honourable the Minority in both Houses of Parliament.

My Lords and Gentlemen,

We thank you for your noble and spirited, though hitherto ineffectual efforts in defence of the great constitutional and commercial rights of your country. Go on–the almost unanimous voice of the people is with you; and, in a free country, the voice of the people *must* prevail. We know our duty to our Sovereign, and are loyal.–We know our duty to ourselves, and are resolved to be free. We seek for our rights, and no more than our rights, and, in so just a pursuit, we should doubt the being of a Providence, if we doubted of success.

Signed by order,

WM IRVINE.

206. Repeal of the Declaratory Act of 1719 in 1782

(*Statutes at Large*, XXXIV, p. 78. 22 Geo. III, c. 53.)

This Act, the four following Acts of the Irish Parliament (Nos. 207–210) and the Renunciation Act passed by the English Parliament (No. 212) form the Constitution of 1782, giving complete legislative independence to the Irish Parliament. For the Declaratory Act of 1719, see No. 197.

An act to repeal an act, made in the sixth year of the reign of his late majesty King George *the First, intituled,* An act for the better securing the dependency of the kingdom of *Ireland* upon the crown of *Great Britain.*

WHEREAS *an act was passed in the sixth year of the reign of his late majesty King* George *the First, intituled,* An act for the better securing the dependency of the kingdom of *Ireland* upon the crown of *Great Britain*; may it please your most excellent Majesty that it may be enacted; and be it enacted by the King's most excellent majesty, by and with the advice and consent of the lords spiritual and temporal, and commons, in this present parliament assembled, and by the authority of the same, That from and after the passing of this act, the above mentioned act, and the several matters and things therein contained, shall be, and is and are hereby repealed.

207. Yelverton's Act, 1782

(*Statutes at Large passed in the Parliaments held in Ireland*, XII, p. 356; 21 and 22 Geo. III, c. 47.)

This Act abrogated the relevant provisions of Poynings Act, passed by the Irish Parliament in 1495, whereby all Bills to be introduced into the Irish Parliament had first to be approved in England. Yelverton (1736–1805) was M.P. for Carrickfergus and Attorney-General of Ireland, 1782, and created Baron Avonmore, 1795.

An Act to regulate the Manner of passing Bills, and to prevent Delays in summoning of Parliaments.

WHEREAS it is expedient to regulate the manner of passing bills in this kingdom, be it enacted by the King's most excellent Majesty, by and with the advice and consent of the lords spiritual and temporal and commons in this present Parliament assembled, and by the authority of the same, That the lord lieutenant, or other chief governor or governors and council of this kingdom, for the time being, do and shall certify all such bills, and none other, as both houses of Parliament shall judge expedient to be enacted in this kingdom, to his Majesty, his heirs and successors, under the great seal of this kingdom, without addition, diminution, or alteration.

II. And be it further enacted by the authority aforesaid, That all such bills as shall be so certified to his Majesty, his heirs and successors, under the great seal of this kingdom, and returned into the same under the great seal of Great Britain, without addition, diminution, or alteration, and none other shall pass in the Parliament of this kingdom; any former law, statute, or usage to the contrary thereof in any wise notwithstanding.

III. And be it further enacted, That no bill shall be certified into Great Britain, as a cause or consideration for holding a Parliament in this kingdom, but that Parliaments may be holden in this kingdom, although no such bill shall have been certified previous to the meeting thereof.

IV. Provided always, That no Parliament shall be holden in this kingdom until a licence for that purpose shall be first had and obtained from his Majesty, his heirs and successors, under the great seal of Great Britain.

208. Act confirming certain English Statues applying to Ireland, 1782

(*Statutes at Large passed in the Parliaments held in Ireland*, XII, pp. 357–358; 21 and 22 Geo. III, c. 48.)

This confirmed existing Acts of the English Parliament which concerned titles to land, and commercial regulations which also bound England.

An Act for extending certain of the Provisions, contained in an Act, intituled, *An Act confirming all the Statutes made in England.*

WHEREAS by an act of Parliament made in this kingdom in the tenth year of the reign of his late Majesty King Henry the seventh, intituled, *An Act for confirming all the statutes made in England*, all such statutes therefore made in England, as concerned the common weal of the realm were confirmed in this kingdom: and whereas after that time, and particularly upon occasion of the rebellions which subsisted in this kingdom in the years one thousand six hundred and forty one, and one thousand six hundred and eighty eight, divers statutes were made in the Parliament of England, and since the union in the Parliament of Great Britain, for settling and assuring the forfeited and other estates in this kingdom, and for the regulation of trade, and other purposes: and whereas it is at all times expedient to give every assurance, and to remove every apprehension concerning the title of lands: and whereas it is the earnest and affectionate desire, as well as the true interest of your Majesty's subjects of this kingdom to promote, as far as in them lies, the navigation, trade, and commercial interests of Great Britain as well as Ireland; and whereas a similarity of laws, manners, and customs, must naturally conduce to strengthen and perpetuate that affection and harmony which do, and at all times ought to subsist between the people of Great Britain and Ireland: be it enacted by the King's most excellent Majesty, by and with the advice and consent of the lords spiritual and temporal and commons, in this present Parliament assembled, and by the authority of the same, That all statutes heretofore made in England or Great Britain, for the settling and assuring the forfeited estates in this kingdom, and also all private statutes made in England or Great Britain, under which any lands, tenements, or hereditaments in this kingdom, or any estate or interest therein; are, or is holden or claimed, or which any way concern the title thereto, or any evidence respecting the same; and also all such clauses and provisions contained in any statutes made in England or Great Britain, concerning commerce, as import to impose equal restraints on the subjects of England and Ireland, or of Great Britain and Ireland, and to entitle them to equal benefits; and also all such clauses and provisions contained in any statutes made as aforesaid, as equally concerning the seamen of England and Ireland, or of Great Britain and Ireland, save so far as the same have been altered or repealed, shall be accepted, used, and executed in this kingdom, according to the present tenor thereof respectively.

II. Provided always, That all such statutes, so far as aforesaid, concerning commerce, shall bind the subjects of Ireland only, so long as they continue to bind the subjects of Great Britain.

III. And be it further enacted by the authority aforesaid, That all such statutes made in England or Great Britain, as concern the stile or calendar and also all such clauses and provisions contained in any statutes made as aforesaid, as relate to the taking any oath or oaths, or making or subscribing any declaration or affirmation in this kingdom, or any penalty or disability for omitting the same, or relate to the continuance of any office, civil or military or of any commission, or of any writ, process, or proceeding at law or in equity, or in any court of delegacy or review, in case of a demise of the crown, shall be accepted, used, and executed in this kingdom, according to the present tenor of the same respectively.

209. Act for the Redress of Erroneous Judgments, 1782

(*Statutes at Large passed in the Parliaments held in Ireland*, XII, pp. 358–359; 21 and 22 Geo. III, c. 49.)

This Act established the supreme appellate jurisdiction of the Irish House of Lords.

An Act for Redress of erroneous Judgments, Orders, and Decrees.

WHEREAS erroneous judgments, orders, and decrees, ought only to be reformed finally in the high court of Parliament in this kingdom; be it declared and enacted by the King's most excellent Majesty, by and with the advice and consent of the lords spiritual and temporal and commons, in this present Parliament assembled, and by the authority of the same, That from henceforth all such judgments, orders, and decrees, shall be finally examined and reformed in the high court of Parliament in this kingdom only; any law, statute, or practice to the contrary thereof, in any wise notwithstanding.

II. Provided always, and be it enacted by the authority aforesaid, That nothing herein contained shall invalidate or affect any judgment, order, or decree which has been given or made in Great Britain, previous to the first day of June, one thousand seven hundred and eighty two, but that the same shall remain in full force; any thing herein contained to the contrary thereof in any wise notwithstanding.

III. And be it enacted by the authority aforesaid, That it shall and may be lawful to and for the lord lieutenant or other chief governor or chief governors of this kingdom for the time being, to grant warrants for sealing writs of error returnable into Parliament, and that the sum of three pounds shall be paid to the cursitor for every such writ of error by the party applying for the same, to be distributed in such manner as the lord high chancellor shall direct.

210. Act for securing the independence of the judiciary, 1782

(*Statutes at Large passed in the Parliaments held in Ireland*, XII, p. 359; 21 and 22 Geo. III, c. 50.)

This Act placed the Irish judges on the same footing as the English.

An Act for securing the Independency of Judges, and the impartial Administration of Justice.

WHEREAS the independency of the judges of the land is essential to the impartial administration of justice, and highly conductive to the support of the honour of the crown, and the security of the rights and liberties of the people; be it enacted by the King's most excellent Majesty, by and with the advice and consent of the lords spiritual and temporal and commons in this present Parliament assembled, and by the authority of the same, That from and after the passing of this act, the present, and all future commissions of judges for the time being, shall continue and remain in full force during their good behaviour; and that the same shall continue and remain in full force during the term aforesaid, notwithstanding the demise of the King (whom God long preserve) or of any of his heirs or successors; any law, usage, or practice to the contrary thereof in any wise notwithstanding.

II. And be it enacted by the authority aforesaid, That all such salaries and appointments as have been or shall be granted by his Majesty, his heirs and successors, to any judge or judges, shall in all times coming be paid and payable to every such judge and judges for the time being, so long as the patents or commissions of them, or any of them respectively, shall continue and remain in force.

III. Provided always, and be it enacted by the authority aforesaid, That it shall and may be lawful to and for his Majesty, his heirs and successors, to remove any judge or judges upon the address of both houses of Parliament; any thing herein to the contrary thereof in any wise notwithstanding.

211. Speech by Henry Grattan in the Irish House of Commons on the simple repeal of the Declaratory Act, 14 June 1782

(*Speeches of the Right Honourable Henry Grattan*, edited by his son, I (1822), pp. 144–145.)

This speech was made on a motion by Flood, "That the opinion of all the judges be desired on the following question: 'Does the repeal of the declaratory act amount, in legal construction, to a repeal or renunciation of the legal principle on which the declaratory act grounded itself?'"

MR. GRATTAN said, If the security that the honourable gentleman desires be a British statute, I reject it: I would reject Magna Charta under a British statute. We have not come to England for a charter, but with a charter; and we have asked her to cancel all her declarations made in opposition to it. This is the true idea of the situation of Ireland:–no man will be content with less than a free constitution; and I trust no man will be frantic enough to hazard that, in attempting to gain more. I should have been pleased if the renunciation of the claim had been made, but as it is, I think the repeal of the 6th of George the First, to every ingenuous, rational, and honest man, must show that England is sincere, and by giving up the final jurisdiction, she has scarcely left a possibility of renewing her claim. There are certain rights inherent in parliaments which they cannot relinquish or give up. Now, though the present Parliament of Great Britain has renounced all claims to bind Ireland, yet a man who has a mind to argue with impossibilities, may say, We are not secure, because a future English parliament may think themselves entitled to exercise a power which their predecessors could not relinquish. Thus we may go on with a spirit of insatiety, supposing ideal dangers, and finding food for perpetual discontent, if, when matters are brought to a final adjustment, gentlemen choose to break new ground, and go into further discussion. Our address went to obtain from England a renunciation; and she has yielded that, in the late repeal, which is, in fact, a repeal of the principle itself. Our own act expressly cut off the English from the power of making any future laws to bind this kingdom. We asked but a repeal of the act, and the act was repealed; and yet, after all this, the matter is now to be opened afresh. Can any thing be more dangerous, after the treaty is concluded, than to think of such a measure? After the faith of England has been pledged, with a full recantation of her assumed power! The two principles by which I guided myself in this business are accomplished; the first, to obtain liberty for Ireland; and the second, to obtain that liberty with as little chance of danger as possible. But, from the very emphatic manner in which the right honourable gentleman has spoken, and the very strong figures in which he has conveyed his language, it would seem as if the nation was called on to believe that the country had been betrayed, and that the right honourable gentleman was the only man who could be found to stand up for the constitution.

212. The Renunciation Act, 1783

(*Statutes at Large*, XXXIV, p. 256. 23 Geo. III, c. 28.)

Passed to satisfy Flood and his followers, who held that by the repeal of the Declaratory Act (No. 206) England had not renounced her powers, but only ceased to affirm them, and might therefore reaffirm them later.

An act for removing and preventing all doubts which have arisen, or might arise, concerning the exclusive rights of the parliament and courts of Ireland, *in matters of legislation and judicature; and for preventing any writ of error or appeal from any of his Majesty's courts in that kingdom from being received, heard, and adjudged, in any of his Majesty's courts in the kingdom of* Great Britain.

WHEREAS, *by an act of the last session of this present parliament (intituled,* An act to repeal an act, made in the sixth year of the reign of his late Majesty King *George* the *First*, intituled, *An act for the better securing the dependency of the kingdom of* Ireland *upon the crown of* Great Britain,) *it was enacted, That the said last-mentioned act, and all matters and things therein contained, should be repealed: and whereas doubts have arisen whether the provisions of the said act are sufficient to secure to the people of* Ireland *the rights claimed by them to be bound only by laws enacted by his Majesty and the parliament of that kingdom, in all cases whatever, and to have all actions and suits at law or in equity, which may be instituted in that kingdom, decided in his Majesty's courts therein finally, and without appeal from thence:* therefore, for removing all doubts respecting the same, may it please your Majesty that it may be declared and enacted; and be it declared and enacted by the King's most excellent majesty, by and with the advice and consent of the lords spiritual and temporal, and commons, in this present parliament assembled, and by the authority of the same, That the said right claimed by the people of *Ireland* to be bound only by laws enacted by his Majesty and the parliament of that kingdom, in all cases whatever, and to have all actions and suits at law or in equity, which may be instituted in that kingdom, decided in his Majesty's courts therein finally, and without appeal from thence, shall be, and it is hereby declared to be established and ascertained for ever, and shall, at no time hereafter, be questioned or questionable.

II. And be it further enacted by the authority aforesaid, That no writ of error or appeal shall be received or adjudged, or any other proceeding be had by or in any of his Majesty's courts in this kingdom, in any action or suit at law or in equity, instituted in any of his Majesty's courts in the kingdom of *Ireland*; and that all such writs, appeals, or proceedings, shall be, and they are hereby declared null and void to all intents and purposes; and that all records, transcripts of records or proceedings, which have been transmitted from *Ireland* to *Great Britain*, by virtue of any writ of error or appeal, and upon which no judgment has been given or decree pronounced before the first day of *June*, one thousand seven hundred and eighty-two, shall, upon application made by or in behalf of the party in whose favour judgment was given, or decree pronounced, in *Ireland*, be delivered to such party, or any person by him authorized to apply for and receive the same.

B. RELIGION

213. Proportions of Protestants and Roman Catholics in the population, 1731

(Thomas Newenham, *A View of the Natural, Political and Commercial Circumstances of Ireland* (1809), Appendix, p. 19.)

Thomas Newenham (1762–1831) was M.P. for Clonmel, 1798. He opposed the Union in 1801.

POPULATION of IRELAND, as returned to Parliament, in 1731.

	Protestants	*Protestants*	*Both*
Ulster	360,630		
Leinster	203,087		
Munster	115,130	700,451	
Connaught	21,604		
	Roman Catholics	*Roman Catholics*	2,010,219
Ulster	158,028		
Leinster	447,916		
Munster	482,044	1,309,768	
Connaught	221,780		

214. Arthur Young on the revenues of the Irish Church, 1776

(Arthur Young, *A Tour in Ireland*, Part II (1780), pp. 56–57, 166.)

The *Tour* covers the years 1776–1778. See also No. 221.

The revenues of the clergy in Ireland are very considerable. Here is a list of the bishopricks with the annual value, which I have had corrected so often in the neighbourhood of each, that I believe it will be found nearly exact.

	£		£
The Primacy per annum	8,000	Brought over	45,500
Dublin	5,000	Clonfert	2,400
Tuam	4,000	Clogher	4,000
Cashel	4,000	Kilmore	2,600
Derry	7,000	Elphin	3,700
Limerick	3,500	Killala	2,900
Corke	2,700	Kildare	2,600
Cloyne	2,500	Raphoe	2,600
Ossory	2,000	Meath	3,400
Waterford	2,500	Kilaloo	2,300
Down	2,300	Leighlin and Ferns	2,200
Dromore	2,000		
Carried over	£45,500		£74,200

This total does not, however, mark the extent or value of the land which yields it. I was informed in conversation that the lands of the primacy would, if lett as a private estate, be worth near one hundred thousand a year. Those of Derry half as much, and those of Cashel near thirty thousand a year. These circumstances taken into account will shew that seventy-four thousand pounds a year include no inconsiderable portion of the kingdom. I have been also informed, but not on any certain authority, that these sees have the patronage of an ecclestical revenue of above one hundred and fifty thousand pounds a year more. . . .

Deaneries of Ireland.

	£		£
Raphoe	1,600	Elphin	250
Derry	1,600	Ross	20
Ardfert	60	Killala	150
Connor	200	Cloyne	220
Clonmacnoise	50	Kilfenora	210
Corke	400	Dromore	400
St. Patrick's	800	Clonfert	20
Down	1,700	Leighlin	80
Kildare	120	Armagh	150
Achonry	100	Waterford	400
Killaloe	140	Christ Church	2,000
Ossory	600	Limerick	600
Kilmacdaugh	120	Cashel	200
Lismore	306	Clogher	800
Ardagh	200	Tuam	300
Emly	100	Fens	300
Kilmore	600	Archdeaconry of Kells	1,200

215. The bishop of Derry on the necessity of religious toleration, 1778

(*Hist. MSS. Comm.*, *Stopford-Sackville MSS.*, I, pp. 249–250.)

The writer is Frederick Augustus Hervey (1730–1803), later earl of Bristol. He writes at the time of the French invasion scare which produced the Volunteer Movement. The bishop became chaplain to the Volunteers in 1782. His violent opposition to the Union of 1801 seems to have been due to a desire for popularity as much as to conviction.

The Bishop of Derry to Lord G. Germain.[1]

[1778, Before July?] I cannot omit so safe an opportunity as the present of renewing my assurance to your Lordship that the great armament is levell'd against Ireland, tho' a ridiculous feint will be made on the Isle of Wight. The coast of Galway is the place of landing, as the bearer can inform you, who knows much of the detail. The manifesto intended to be dispers'd exhibits *Independence*, *Liberty of religion* to all sects, and *a free trade*. The man who gave the plan is son to a late minister, well acquainted

[1] Secretary of State for the Colonies.

with England, and therefore dissuaded them from their first intentions. They are encourag'd likewise to fix on Ireland by letters and emissaries from both ends of the kingdom.

Your Lordship will please to remember that nothing has yet been done for the Romish clergy or for the people of that persuasion, who hold everything cheap in comparison of their religion; that the Romish gentlemen are few, and of course have little interest either over the clergy or peasantry; that to my knowledge they think the gentlemen sacrific'd the liberty of religion to the security of their property, which idea has considerably lessen'd the little influence they had. If something therefore be not speedily affected to pacify both the Papists and the Presbyterians, we risque a general insurrection even upon the appearance of the French.

With all the regard I have for the Presbyterians, many of whom I know to be excellent men, yet I deem them much more dangerous at this crisis than the Papist. Their principles are truly republican, and the profer of independency, which will be instantly exhibited by the French, cannot fail of success among them. The bearer can tell you this idea is only the revival of a scheme under *Conflans*, and tho' it will not now be back'd by the Popish gentlemen, yet it will be greedily swallowed by almost all the Presbyterians.

For God's sake, then, my Lord, let us not be sacrific'd either to ind[olence?] or incredulity, and much less to the fear of disgusting a venal faction in Ireland. The rights of humanity demand a general and unlimited toleration at all times. Policy peculiarly requires it at present. A seasonable indulgence to the Presbyterian and Papist may save the kingdom. The Presbyterians cannot believe that the K[ing] loves them–let his Attorney General, or rather his eloquent Prime Sergeant, move a repeal of the Test Act. It can disgust only a few ignorant High Churchmen among ourselves, and will reclame some thousands of ill dispos'd subjects among those sectaries.

Place us all, my Lord, on the same footing, and we shall all be equally good subjects; but whilst Benjamin's mess is distributed only to a few Episcopalians you cannot wonder that the rest of the brethren should do something more than murmur. 'Tis unreasonable to expect equal loyalty where there has not been shown equal favor; the crop will ever correspond to the culture, and woe must betide that farm where one spot is cherish'd and the rest neglected. One happy, masterly stroke may save Ireland for ages; its ruin shall not lie at my door.

216. Catholic Relief Act, 1778

(*Statutes at Large passed in the Parliaments held in Ireland*, XI (1782), pp. 298–301. 17 and 18 Geo. III, c. 49.)

This Act relieved Catholics prepared to take an oath of allegiance from disabilities connected with the holding and inheriting of land.

An act for the relief of his Majesty's subjects of this kingdom professing the popish religion.

WHEREAS by an act made in this kingdom in the second year of her late Majesty queen Anne, entitled, *An act to prevent the further growth of popery*, and also by another act made in the eighth year of her said reign for explaining and amending the said act, the Roman Catholicks of Ireland are made subject to several disabilities and incapacities therein particularly mentioned: and whereas from their uniform peaceable behaviour for a long series of years it appears reasonable and expedient to relax the same, and it must tend not only to the cultivation and improvement of this kingdom, but to the prosperity and strength of all his Majesty's dominions, that his subjects of all denominations should enjoy the blessings of our free constitution, and should be bound to each other by mutual interest and mutual affection: therefore be it enacted by the king's most excellent Majesty by and with the advice and consent of the lords spiritual and temporal and commons in this present parliament assembled, and by the authority of the same, that from and after the first day of August one thousand seven hundred and seventy eight it shall and may be lawful to and for any papist, or person professing the popish religion, subject to the provisoe hereinafter contained as to the taking and subscribing the oath and declaration therein mentioned, to take, hold, and enjoy any lease or leases for any term or terms of years, not exceeding nine hundred and ninety nine years certain, or for any term of years determinable upon any number of lives, not exceeding five, provided always, that upon every such lease a rent *bona fide* to be paid in money shall be reserved and made payable during such terms with or without liberty of committing waste as fully and beneficially to all intents and purposes, as any other his Majesty's subjects in this kingdom, and the same to dispose of by will or otherwise as he shall think fit; and all lands, tenements, and hereditaments, whereof any papist or person professing the popish religion is now seized or shall be seized by virtue of a title legally derived by, from, or under such person or persons, now seized in fee simple or fee tail, whether at law or in equity, shall from and after the time aforesaid be descendable, deviseable, and transferable, as fully, beneficially, and effectually, as if the same were in the seizin of any other of his Majesty's subjects in this kingdom.

II. And be it further enacted by the authority aforesaid, that all papists or persons professing the popish religion shall and may from and after the time aforesaid be to all intents and purposes capable to take, hold, and enjoy all or any such estate or estates, which shall descend, or be devised, or transferred as aforesaid, any thing contained in the said acts of the second or eighth of queen Anne, or in any other statute or law, to the contrary in any wise notwithstanding.

III. Provided, that no papist or person professing the popish religion shall take any benefit by this act, unless he or she shall on or before the first day of January one thousand seven hundred and seventy nine, or some time previous to any such lease made to or in trust for him, if he or she shall be in this kingdom, or within six months after any devise, descent, or limitation shall take effect in possession, if at that time within this kingdom, or if then abroad beyond the seas, or under the age of twenty one years, or in prison, or of unsound mind, or under coverture, then within six months after his or her return from abroad, or attaining the age of twenty one years, or discharge from prison, or becoming of sound mind, or after she shall become a *feme sole*, take and subscribe the oath of allegiance and the declaration prescribed by an act passed in this kingdom in the thirteenth and fourteenth years of his present Majesty's reign, entitled, *An act to enable his Majesty's subjects of whatever persuasion to testify their allegiance to him in some one of his Majesty's four courts in Dublin, or at the quarter sessions of the peace for the county of Dublin, or before the going judges of assize in open court;* which oath the judges presiding in the said court, the chairman of the said sessions, and the said judges of assize, are hereby empowered and required to administer. . . .

VI. And whereas by an act made in this kingdom in the second year of the reign of her late Majesty queen Anne, entitled, *An act to prevent the further growth of popery,* it is amongst other things enacted to the effect following; in case the eldest son and heir of a popish parent shall be a protestant, that from the time of the enrolment in the chancery of a certificate of the bishop of the diocese, testifying his being a protestant and conforming himself to the church of Ireland as by law established, such papist parent shall become and be only tenant for life of all the real estate, whereof such popish parent shall be then seized in fee tail or fee simple, and the reversion in fee shall be vested in such eldest son, being a protestant subject, as in the said act is mentioned: and whereas it is found inexpedient to continue any longer that part of the said recited act: be it enacted by the authority aforesaid, that from and after the first day of November one thousand seven hundred and seventy eight the conformity of the eldest son, and the filing of the bishop's certificate, and performing the requisites by that act or any other act required in that respect, shall not affect or alter the estate of any popish parent by making such popish parent become tenant for life, or by vesting a reversion or estate in such eldest son; but such popish parent shall remain seized and possessed of the same estate and interest in all and every his or her real estate, as he or she would have been, if such eldest son had not conformed, or the said act of the second of queen Anne had not been made. . . .

X. Provided also, that no person shall take benefit by this act who having been converted from the popish to the protestant religion shall afterwards relapse to popery, nor any person being a protestant who shall at any time become a papist, or shall educate, or suffer to be educated, any of his children under the age of fourteen years in the popish religion. . . .

217. The bishop of Clogher on the amenities of his see, 1782

(*Hist. MSS. Comm., Stopford-Sackville MSS.*, I, pp. 279–280.)

The writer is Dr. John Hotham (1734–1795), later Sir John Hotham, Bart. He was bishop of Ossory, 1779–1782, when he was translated to Clogher. He owed both these appointments largely to the patronage of Lord Sackville, formerly Lord George Germain.

The Bishop of Clogher to Viscount Sackville.

1782, July 9. Dublin. . . .–In the beginning of this letter I mentioned my having been lately on an expedition. It was to Clogher. I took advantage of our present parliamentary recess to run down and see what sort of a thing I had gotten. Since your Lordship was at Clogher things are greatly changed. My cathedral is now no longer a miserable but very neat and respectable parish church. It was rebuilt by Bishop Sterne and substantially repaired and beautified by the late bishop. Bishop Sterne also built the present palace, which though not so well contrived as it might have been, is far from a despicable place of residence, especially as my predecessor added two wings, the one an eating room of thirty feet by twenty, the other a library of thirty-two feet by twenty-two, exclusive of the bow window in each. The demesne is sufficiently planted, and from that circumstance, and the uncommon irregularity of the ground, in my opinion extremely beautiful. It measures 560 English acres, and the whole is surrounded by a stone wall, without a road or even a pathway through any part of the ground except for my own servants, such as parkkeeper, shepherd, &c. My beef, mutton, veal, and lamb are all as good in their kinds as can be, the farm is to produce pigs, poultry, cream and butter, hay, oats, and straw. The decoy gives me teal and wild ducks. The warren supplies me with as excellent rabbits as I ever tasted; the pidgeon house with pidgeons; the water furnishes carp, tench, trout, eels, perch and pike, the venison in the park is remarkably good, and a most extensive range of mountain, of which I have absolute dominion, yields in the proper seasons an astonishing profusion of partridge, hares, and grouse. The city of Clogher stands on my ground, and the citizens are all of course my tenants. The borough is at present secure and likely to continue so till the present or some future furiously patriotic and vehemently virtuous House of Commons do me the honour to inform me (as I expect will be the case next session if not sooner) that it will be better in the hands of the volunteers than in mine. The country is healthy and fine and the roads about me very good. The diocese is in the highest order of any in Ireland, the clergy are a most respectable body of men, many of them very learned, all of them conscientious and exemplary, and except two or three for whom I must get houses to be built, strictly resident on their respective benefices. Finally, the income of the see is not less, as I am informed, than 4,000*l.* per annum, which in my judgement is no trifling emolument.

Such, my Lord, is now my situation, and with unfeigned gratitude to the Supreme Disposer of all events, and those steady and active friends with whose assistance He has blessed me in my pursuits, I may now I think sit quietly down in my retreat and enjoy in my own way for the rest of my life the very great prize I have had the good fortune to draw in the lottery of the world. These are not times in which a person of my disposition can delight. So long as reason is attended to, a man in my line of life may hope to be of some little publick use by the exertion of that degree of common sense which God has given him. But when infatuation shall evidently appear to prevail, when solid argument and sound doctrine shall be drowned in clamor and confusion, and everything tend fast to anarchy and oppression, what is left for the man of moderation but to withdraw in time, and in silence lament the evils which all his endeavors could not prevent? . . .

C. ECONOMIC AND SOCIAL CONDITIONS

218. Swift on the state of Ireland, 1726

(*Correspondence of Jonathan Swift*, ed. F. Elrington Ball, III (1912), pp. 308–311.)

Swift's pamphlet, *The Present Miserable State of Ireland*, was written soon after the interview with Walpole described in this letter, and makes many of the same points as the letter.

Swift to the Earl of Peterborough.

April 28th, 1726.

MY LORD,

Your Lordship having, at my request, obtained for me an hour from Sir Robert Walpole, I accordingly attended him yesterday at eight o'clock in the morning, and had somewhat more than an hour's conversation with him. Your Lordship was this day pleased to inquire what passed between that great Minister and me, to which I gave you some general answers, from whence you said you could comprehend little or nothing.

I had no other design in desiring to see Sir Robert Walpole, than to represent the affairs of Ireland to him in a true light, not only without any view to myself, but to any party whatsoever: and, because I understood the affairs of that kingdom tolerably well, and observed the representations he had received were such as I could not agree to; my principal design was to set him right, not only for the service of Ireland, but likewise of England, and of his own administration.

I failed very much in my design; for I saw he had conceived opinions, from the example and practices of the present, and some former governors, which I could not reconcile to the notions I had of liberty, a possession alway understood by the British nation to be the inheritance of a human creature.

Sir Robert Walpole was pleased to enlarge very much upon the subject of Ireland, in a manner so alien from what I conceived to be the rights and privileges of a subject of England, that I did not think proper to debate the matter with him so much as I otherwise might, because I found it would be in vain. I shall, therefore, without entering into dispute, make bold to mention to your Lordship some few grievances of that kingdom, as it consists of a people, who, besides a natural right of enjoying the privileges of subjects, have also a claim of merit from their extraordinary loyalty to the present king and his family.

First, that all persons born in Ireland are called and treated as Irishmen, although their fathers and grandfathers were born in England; and their predecessors having been conquerors of Ireland, it is humbly conceived they ought to be on as good a foot as any subjects of Britain, according to the practice of all other nations, and particularly of the Greeks and Romans.

Secondly, that they are denied the natural liberty of exporting their manufactures to any country which is not engaged in a war with England.

Thirdly, that whereas there is a University in Ireland, founded by Queen Elizabeth, where youth are instructed with a much stricter discipline than either in Oxford or

Cambridge, it lies under the greatest discouragements, by filling all the principal employments, civil and ecclesiastical, with persons from England, who have neither interest, property, acquaintance, nor alliance, in that kingdom; contrary to the practice of all other States in Europe which are governed by viceroys, at least what hath never been used without the utmost discontents of the people.

Fourthly, that several of the bishops sent over to Ireland, having been clergymen of obscure condition, and without other distinction than that of chaplains to the governors, do frequently invite over their old acquaintances or kindred, to whom they bestow the best preferment in their gift. The like may be said of the judges, who take with them one or two dependents, to whom they give their countenance; and who, consequently, without other merit, grow immediately into the chief business of their courts. The same practice is followed by all others in civil employments, if they have a cousin, a valet, or a footman in their family, born in England.

Fifthly, that all civil employments, grantable in reversion, are given to persons who reside in England.

The people of Ireland, who are certainly the most loyal subjects in the world, cannot but conceive that most of these hardships have been the consequence of some unfortunate representations, at least, in former times; and the whole body of the gentry feel the effects in a very sensible part, being utterly destitute of all means to make provision for their younger sons, either in the Church, the law, the revenue, or, of late, in the army; and, in the desperate condition of trade, it is equally vain to think of making them merchants. All they have left is, at the expiration of leases, to rack their tenants, which they have done to such a degree, that there is not one farmer in a hundred through the kingdom who can afford shoes or stockings to his children, or to eat flesh, or drink anything better than sour milk or water, twice in a year; so that the whole country, except the Scottish plantation in the north, is a scene of misery and desolation hardly to be matched on this side of Lapland.

The rents of Ireland are computed to be about a million and a half, whereof one half million at least is spent by lords and gentlemen residing in England, and by some other articles too long to mention. About three hundred thousand pounds more are returned thither on other accounts; and, upon the whole, those who are the best versed in that kind of knowledge agree, that England gains annually by Ireland a million at least, which even I could make appear beyond all doubt. But, as this mighty profit would probably increase, with tolerable treatment, to half a million more, so it must of necessity sink, under the hardships that kingdom lies at present.

And whereas Sir Robert Walpole was pleased to take notice, how little the King gets by Ireland, it ought, perhaps to be considered, that the revenues and taxes, I think, amount to above four hundred thousand pounds a-year; and reckoning the riches of Ireland, compared with England, to be as one to twelve, the King's revenues there would be equal to more than five millions here; which, considering the bad payment of rents, from such miserable creatures as most of the tenants in Ireland are, will be allowed to be as much as such a kingdom can bear. The current coin of Ireland is reckoned, at most, but five hundred thousand pounds; so that above four-fifths are paid every year into the exchequer.

I think it manifest, that whatever circumstances can possibly contribute to make a country poor and despicable, are all united with respect to Ireland. The nation controlled by laws to which they do not consent, disowned by their brethren and countrymen, refused the liberty not only of trading with their own manufactures, but even their native commodities, forced to seek for justice many hundred miles by sea and land, rendered in a manner incapable of serving their king and country in any employment of honour, trust, or profit; and all this without the least demerit; while the governors sent over thither can possibly have no affection to the people, further than what is instilled into them by their own justice and love of mankind, which do not always operate; and whatever they please to represent hither is never called in question.

Whether the representatives of such a people, thus distressed and laid in the dust, when they meet in a Parliament, can do the public business with that cheerfulness which might be expected from free-born subjects, would be a question in any other country except that unfortunate island; the English inhabitants whereof have given more and greater examples of their loyalty and dutifulness, than can be shown in any other part of the world.

What part of these grievances may be thought proper to be redressed by so wise and great a minister as Sir Robert Walpole, he perhaps will please to consider; especially because they have been all brought upon that kingdom since the Revolution; which, however, is a blessing annually celebrated there with the greatest zeal and sincerity. I most humbly entreat your Lordship to give this paper to Sir Robert Walpole, and desire him to read it, which he may do in a few minutes.

I am, with the greatest respect, my Lord,
Your lordship's
most obedient and humble servant,
JON. SWIFT.

219. Extracts from Thomas Prior's *List of the Absentees of Ireland*, 1729

(Thomas Prior, *A List of the Absentees of Ireland and the Yearly Value of their Estates*, 3rd ed. (1730), pp. 1, 14–16.)

Thomas Prior (1679–1751) was one of the founders and the first Secretary of the Royal Dublin Society for promoting agriculture, founded in 1731. The *List of Absentees* first appeared in 1729.

A LIST OF LORDS, GENTLEMEN, and OTHERS, *Who having* ESTATES, EMPLOYMENTS, *and* PENSIONS *in* Ireland, *spend the same abroad. Together with an Estimate of the Yearly Value of the Same, as taken in the Months of* May *and* June 1729.

The Lords and Gentlemen of Estate, are divided into Three Classes.

FIRST CLASS comprehends those, who live constantly abroad, and are seldom, or never seen in *Ireland*.

SECOND CLASS comprehends those, who live generally abroad, and visit *Ireland* now and then, for a Month or two.

THIRD CLASS takes in those, who live generally in *Ireland*, but were occasionally absent at the time the said List was taken, either for Health, Pleasure, or Business;

but their Number is commonly the same: for, if some come home, others go abroad, and supply their Places. . . .

A GENERAL ABSTRACT of the Quantity of Money drawn out of the Kingdom yearly, *viz.*

	Yearly value spent abroad		
	£	s.	d.
By those of the First Class	199100	00	0
By those of the Second Class	91200	00	0
By those of the Third Class	53400	00	0
By those whose Income is under 400L. per *ann.*	40000	00	0
By those, who have Employments in *Ireland*,	31510	00	0
For the Education of Youth, Lawsuits, Attendance, and by Dealers	33000	00	0
By the Pensioners on the Civil List,	23070	13	01
By those on the Military Establishment,	67658	10	0
By *French* Pensioners,	2560	00	0
By Remittances to *Gibraltar*	30000	00	0
By Adventurers to *America*,	30000	00	0
On Account of the several Articles mentioned in the last Paragraph[1]	20000	00	0
	621499	03	1[2]

SUPPLEMENT.

I shall, by way of Supplement, take Notice of some additional Articles, which ought to be taken into Consideration, whenever we come to compute the Quantity of Money yearly drawn out of the Kingdom, and which could not so properly be brought under any of the Heads mention'd in the preceding List.

1st, WE are to observe, that a great many Estates, and Woods, have of late, been sold in *Ireland* and all the Purchase-Money at once carry'd into *England*. And, which is farther remarkable, some Estates have, in the Compass of a few Years, been sold again, and all the Purchase-Money sent away a second Time.

2d, THAT great Sums of Money are yearly sent abroad, to discharge old Debts, contracted by Persons now residing in *Ireland*.

3d, THO' some of the aforesaid Persons, may spend less abroad than here rated, yet many of them spend much more than their yearly Income; which Debts must be paid in *England*, after they come to reside in *Ireland*.

4th, THAT several Estates of *Irish* landlords who live abroad, have, of late, been much rais'd, and large Fines taken and remitted to them; and, many more Estates will not fail to be rais'd to the Heighth, as the old Leases expire, and thereby encrease their yearly Draughts upon us.

5th, THAT several Persons, who live abroad, have large Mortgages on Estates in *Ireland*; the Interest-Money whereof is constantly return'd to them in *England*.

[1] *e.g.* Insurance, newspapers from England, watches, 'rich toys', etc.
[2] In the 6th edition, published in 1783, this total had risen to £2,085,394.

6th, MANY of our young Lords and Gentlemen, in a few Years after they come to Age, squander, in other Countries, all the ready Money which had been saved for them, by their Guardians, in their Minorities.

7th, GREAT Numbers live abroad, whose Names or Estates, for want of due Information, are here omitted.

8th, THERE is, yearly, carried out of this Kingdom, about 60,000L. by the Colliers of *England* and *Scotland*, who take very little else, but ready Money, in Return for their Coals.

220. The linen industry, 1720–1782

(Thomas Newenham, *A View of the Natural, Political and Commercial Circumstances of Ireland* (1809), Appendix, p. 10.)

For Newenham, see note to No. 213.

TABLE, Shewing the Quantity of Plain and Coloured LINEN, CAMBRICK and LINEN YARN, exported from Ireland, in different Periods, since the Year 1698: also the Quantity of FLAX SEED imported, in different Periods, since the Year 1770.

Years Ending 25 Mar.	*Plain Linen*	*Coloured Linen*	*Ann. av. of both*	*Cambrick*	*Linen yarn*	*Ann. av.*	*Flax seed*	*Ann. av.*
	Pieces	*Yards*	*Pieces*	*Yards*	*Cwts.*	*Cwts.*	*Hogsheads*	*Hogsheads*
1720	2,637,984				15,002			
1721	2,520,781		2,859,556		14,696	14,817		
1722	3,419,904				14,754			
1730	4,136,203				10,088			
1731	3,775,830		3,901,528		13,746	13,059		
1732	3,792,551				15,343			
1740	6,627,771				18,542			
1741	7,207,741		6,969,893		21,656	18,842		
1742	7,074,168				16,330			
1750	11,200,460			72	22,373			
1751	12,891,318		11,580,493	1,493	23,743	23,141		
1752	10,649,703				23,407			
1760	13,375,456				31,042			
1761	12,048,881		13,661,337	9,183	39,699	35,563		
1762	15,559,676				35,950			
1770	20,560,754				33,471		19,432	
1771	25,376,808		22,178,913	1,163	34,166	33,359	45,089	29,583
1772	20,599,178				32,441		24,230	
1780	18,746,902	7,319		21	42,369		19,567	
1781	14,947,265	111,295	19,619,168	404	37,202	35,919	23,640	22,939
1782	24,970,303	74,422			28,187		25,611	

221. Arthur Young on Irish agriculture and the conditions of life of the Irish peasants, 1776

(Arthur Young, *A Tour in Ireland*, Part II (1780), pp. 12–13, 18–19, 23–26, 29.)

Young's *Tour* covers the years 1776–1778. See also No. 214.

Tillage in Ireland is very little understood. In the greatest corn counties, such as Louth, Kildare, Carlow and Kilkenny, where are to be seen many very fine crops of wheat, all is under the old system, exploded by good farmers in England, of sowing wheat upon a fallow, and succeeding it with as many crops of spring corn as the soil will bear. Where they do best by their land, it is only two of barley or oats before the fallow returns again, which is something worse than the open field management in England, of 1. fallow; 2. wheat; 3. oats; to which, while the fields are open and common, the farmers are by cruel necessity tied down. The bounty on the inland carriage of corn to Dublin has increased tillage very considerably, but it has no where introduced any other system. And to this extreme bad management, of adopting the exploded practice of a century ago, instead of turneps and clover, it is owing that Ireland, with a soil, acre for acre, much better than England, has its products inferior.

But keeping cattle of every sort, is a business so much more adapted to the laziness of the farmer, that it is no wonder the tillage is so bad. It is every where left to the cottars, or to the very poorest of the farmers, who are all utterly unable to make those exertions, upon which alone a vigorous culture of the earth can be founded; and were it not for potatoes, which necessarily prepare for corn, there would not be half of what we see at present. While it is in such hands, no wonder tillage is reckoned so unprofitable; profit in all undertakings depends on capital; and is it any wonder that the profit should be small when the capital is nothing at all? Every man that has one gets into cattle, which will give him an idle, lazy superintendence, instead of an active attentive one.

That the *system* of tillage has improved very little, much as it has been extended in the last fourteen years, there is great reason to believe, from the very small increase in the import of clover seed, which would have doubled and trebled, had tillage got into the train it ought. . . .

Of the Labouring Poor.

Such is the weight of the lower classes in the great scale of national importance, that a traveller can never give too much attention to every circumstance that concerns them; their welfare forms the broad basis of public prosperity; it is they that feed, cloath, enrich and fight the battles of all the other ranks of a community; it is their being able to support these various burthens without oppression, which constitutes the general felicity; in proportion to their ease is the strength and wealth of nations, as public debility will be the certain attendant on their misery. Convinced that to be ignorant of their state and situation, in different countries, is to be deficient in the first rudiments of political knowledge, I have upon every occasion, made the necessary enquiries, to get the best information circumstances would allow me. . . .

FOOD.

The food of the common Irish, potatoes and milk, have been produced more than once as an instance of the extreme poverty of the country, but this I believe is an opinion embraced with more alacrity than reflection. I have heard it stigmatized as being unhealthy, and not sufficiently nourishing for the support of hard labour, but this opinion is very amazing in a country, many of whose poor people are as athletic in their form, as robust, and as capable of enduring labour as any upon earth. The idleness seen among many when working for those who oppress them is a very contrast to the vigour and activity with which the same people work when themselves alone reap the benefit of their labour. To what country must we have recourse for a stronger instance than lime carried by little miserable mountaineers thirty miles on horses backs to the foot of their hills, and up the steeps on their own. When I see the people of a country in spite of political oppression with well formed vigorous bodies, and their cottages swarming with children; when I see their men athletic, and their women beautiful, I know not how to believe them subsisting on an unwholesome food.

At the same time, however, that both reason and observation convince me of the justice of these remarks, I will candidly allow that I have seen such an excess in the laziness of great numbers, even when working for themselves, and such an apparent weakness in their exertions when encouraged to work, that I have had my doubts of the heartiness of their food. But here arise fresh difficulties, were their food ever so nourishing I can easily conceive an habitual inactivity of exertion would give them an air of debility compared with a more industrious people. . . . Granting their food to be the cause, it decides very little against potatoes, unless they were tried with good nourishing beer instead of their vile potations of whisky. When they are encouraged, or animate themselves to work hard, it is all by whisky, which though it has a notable effect in giving a perpetual motion to their tongues, can have but little of that invigorating substance which is found in strong beer or porter, probably it has an effect as pernicious, as the other is beneficial. . . .

But of this food there is one circumstance which must ever recommend it, they have a belly full, and that let me add is more than the superfluities of an Englishman leaves to his family: let any person examine minutely into the receipt and expenditure of an English cottage, and he will find that tea, sugar and strong liquors, can come only from pinched bellies. I will not assert that potatoes are a better food than bread and cheese; but I have no doubt of a bellyfull of the one being much better than half a bellyfull of the other; still less have I that the milk of the Irishman is incomparably better than the small beer, gin, or tea of the Englishman; and this even for the father, how much better must it be for the poor infants; milk to them is nourishment, is health, is life.

If any one doubts the comparative plenty, which attends the board of a poor native of England and Ireland, let him attend to their meals: the sparingness with which our labourer eats his bread and cheese is well known; mark the Irishman's potatoe bowl placed on the floor, the whole family upon their hams around it, devouring a quantity almost incredible, the beggar seating himself to it with a hearty welcome, the pig taking his share as readily as the wife, the cocks, hens, turkies, geese, the cur, the cat, and perhaps the cow–and all partaking of the same dish. No man can often have been a witness of it without being convinced of the plenty, and I will add the chearfulness, that attends it. . . .

CLOATHING.

The common Irish are in general cloathed so very indifferently, that it impresses every stranger with a strong idea of universal poverty. Shoes and stockings are scarcely ever found on the feet of children of either sex; and great numbers of men and women are without them: a change however, in this respect as in most others, is coming in, for there are many more of them with those articles of cloathing now than ten years ago.

An Irishman and his wife are much more solicitous to feed than to cloath their children: whereas in England it is surprizing to see the expence they put themselves to, to deck out children whose principal subsistence is tea. Very many of them in Ireland are so ragged that their nakedness is scarcely covered; yet are they in health and active. As to the want of shoes and stockings I consider it as no evil, but a much more cleanly custom than the beastiality of stockings and feet that are washed no oftener than those of our own poor. Women are oftener without shoes than men; and by washing their cloaths no where but in rivers and streams, the cold, especially as they roast their legs in their cabbins till they are *fire* spotted, must swell them to a wonderful size and horrid black and blue colour always met with both in young and old. They stand in rivers and beat the linen against the great stones found there with a beetle.

I remarked generally, that they were not ill dressed of sundays and holidays, and that black or dark blue was almost the universal hue.

HABITATIONS.

The cottages of the Irish, which are all called cabbins, are the most miserable looking hovels that can well be conceived: they generally consist of only one room: mud kneaded with straw is the common material of the walls; these are rarely above seven feet high, and not always above five or six; they are about two feet thick, and have only a door, which lets in light instead of a window, and should let the smoak out instead of a chimney, but they had rather keep it in: these two conveniencies they hold so cheap, that I have seen them both stopped up in stone cottages, built by improving landlords; the smoak warms them, but certainly is as injurious to their eyes as it is to the complexions of the women, which in general in the cabbins of Ireland has a near resemblance to that of a smoaked ham. The number of the blind poor I think greater there than in England, which is probably owing to this cause.

The roofs of the cabbins are rafters, raised from the tops of the mud walls, and the covering varies; some are thatched with straw, potatoe stalks, or with heath, others only covered with sods of turf cut from a grass field; and I have seen several that were partly composed of all three; the bad repair these roofs are kept in, a hole in the thatch being often mended with turf, and weeds sprouting from every part, gives them the appearance of a weedy dunghill, especially when the cabbin is not built with regular walls, but supported on one, or perhaps on both sides by the banks of a broad dry ditch, the roof then seems a hillock, upon which perhaps the pig grazes. Some of these cabbins are much less and more miserable habitations than I had ever seen in England. . . . The furniture of the cabbins is as bad as the architecture; in very many, consisting only of a pot for boiling their potatoes, a bit of a table, and one or two broken stools; beds are not found universally, the family lying on straw, equally partook of by cows, calves and pigs, though the luxury of sties is coming in in Ireland, which excludes the poor pigs from the warmth of the bodies of their master and mistress: I remarked little hovels of earth thrown up near the cabbins, and in some places they build their turf stacks hollow, in order to afford shelter to the hogs. This is a general description, but the exceptions are very numerous. I have been in a multitude of cabbins that had much useful furniture, and some even superfluous; chairs, tables, boxes, chest of drawers, earthen ware, and in short most of the articles found in a middling English cottage; but upon enquiry, I very generally found that these acquisitions were all made within the last ten years, a sure sign of a rising national prosperity. . . . In England a man's cottage will be filled with superfluities before he possesses a cow. I think the comparison much in favour of the Irishman; a hog is a much more valuable piece of goods than a set of tea things; and though his snout in a crock* of potatoes is an idea not so poetical as

Broken tea cups, wisely kept for shew,
Rang'd o'er the chimney, glisten'd in a row.

Yet will the cotter and his family, at Christmas, find the solidity of it an ample recompence for the ornament of the other. . . .

OPPRESSION.

. . . a long series of oppressions, aided by many very ill judged laws, have brought landlords into a habit of exerting a very lofty superiority, and their vassals into that of an almost unlimited submission: speaking a language that is despised, professing a religion that is abhorred, and being disarmed, the poor find themselves in many cases slaves even in the bosom of *written* liberty. Landlords that have resided much abroad, are usually humane in their ideas, but the habit of tyranny naturally contracts the mind, so that even in this polished age, there are instances of a severe carriage towards the poor, which is quite unknown in England.

A landlord in Ireland can scarcely invent an order which a servant, labourer, or cottar dares to refuse to execute. Nothing satisfies him but an unlimited submission. Disrespect or any thing tending towards sauciness he may punish with his cane or his horsewhip with the most perfect security, a poor man would have his bones broke if he offered to lift his hand in his own defence. Knocking down is spoken of in the

* The iron pot of an Irish cabbin.

country in a manner that makes an English man stare. Landlords of consequence have assured me that many of their cottars would think themselves honoured by having their wives and daughters sent for to the bed of their master; a mark of slavery that proves the oppression under which such people must live. Nay, I have heard anecdotes of the lives of people being made free with without any apprehension of the justice of a jury. But let it not be imagined that this is common; formerly it happened every day, but law gains ground. It must strike the most careless traveller to see whole strings of cars whipt into a ditch by a gentleman's footman to make way for his carriage; if they are overturned or broken in pieces, no matter, it is taken in patience, were they to complain they would perhaps be horsewhipped. . . .

Part XI
THE COLONIES

THE COLONIES

Introduction

THE documents in this section have been selected to illustrate the history of the colonies in their relationship to England. It has not been possible in the limited space available to include documents concerned with the domestic history of the individual colonies.

In the eighteenth century the sole *raison d'être* of colonies was their economic usefulness to the mother country.[1] Almost the only exceptions to this rule were the strategic posts maintained by the government in the Mediterranean at Gibraltar and Minorca; and even they were valued almost as much for economic as for political reasons. Towards the end of the century, Adam Smith attacked this mercantilist view of colonies,[2] in his general criticism of the mercantile system, and other writers, such as Josiah Tucker, were also propounding free trade views. The protracted difficulties with the Thirteen Colonies and the long and expensive war began to arouse doubts of the value of colonies in the minds of some merchants, and the loss of the American colonies led to the beginning of the formulation of a new colonial system,[3] though Shelburne was perhaps the only statesman to see the need for this. During this period the colonies were, by almost everybody, regarded as valuable in proportion to the contribution each made to the wealth of the mother country. Some idea of the relative value of the different colonies from this point of view can be gathered from the statistics of colonial trade with Great Britain collected from the customs records by Sir Charles Whitworth and David Macpherson.[4]

Colonial affairs at the beginning of this period were the responsibility of the Secretary of State for the Southern Department, though their actual direction was in the hands of the Lords Commissioners for Trade and Plantations, generally known as the Board of Trade. This division of functions did not make for efficient administration, and when Halifax became President of the Board of Trade in 1748 he set about trying to co-ordinate colonial administration. The Order in Council of 1752, conferring real responsibility and the control of colonial patronage on the Board of Trade, was the result. The Board lost its control of patronage and much of its prestige by the Order in Council of 1761, and the Order of 1752 was completely revoked by that of 1766.[5] A third Secretaryship for the colonies was created in 1768, but its status was not recognized as equal to that of the other two secretaryships till the appointment of Lord George Germain in 1775.[6] It was abolished in the Rockingham ministry's economical reforms in 1782.

The case of *Campbell* v. *Hall*, in which Lord Mansfield gave judgment in 1774, established the general principle that once the Crown had set up a legislative assembly in a conquered territory its prerogative power of levying taxation there could not be revived.[7]

The most important colonies were those in America, both the mainland colonies

[1] No. 222. [2] No. 223 [3] No. 224. [4] No. 225. [5] No. 226. [6] No. 227. [7] No. 228.

and the West Indies. The Thirteen Colonies are the subject of vol. IX of these *Documents*; but a few documents are included here to illustrate the English attitude to the clash between these colonies and the mother country. The colonial resistance to the Stamp Act and its repeal by the first Rockingham ministry in 1766 led to long debates in the House of Commons,[1] in which the ministry took the line that Parliament had the right to tax the colonies, but it was not at present expedient to enforce it; Pitt held that the right of taxation was not included in Parliament's undoubted sovereignty over the colonies; while Grenville, the originator of the Stamp Act, was strongly in favour of its enforcement. In the House of Lords, Lord Mansfield upheld the right of taxation,[2] in opposition to Lord Camden, whose view was much the same as Pitt's. Newspaper comment followed much the same lines as the discussion in Parliament.[3] On the eve of hostilities Burke in his famous speech on American taxation urged the wisdom of not insisting upon rights which were offensive to the colonists' sense of liberty, and the impossibility of ruling them by force.[4] But by this time public opinion was probably behind the government's firm attitude, though newspaper comment immediately after the outbreak of hostilities showed that even now opinion was divided.[5]

After the Thirteen Colonies, the colonies regarded by contemporaries as the most important on account of their wealth were the West Indies.[6] Constitutionally, these islands presented, in a lesser degree, the same sort of problems as the mainland colonies. Here, as for the mainland colonies, government by representative assemblies was regarded as the general rule to be followed; and the only islands which had not obtained such a government by the end of the seventeenth century–the Bahamas–were given an assembly in 1728.[7] The West Indian assemblies were jealous of their privileges, and the friction between the governors and assemblies in the Thirteen Colonies at this time find their counterparts in the West Indies, perhaps the most outstanding example being the dispute between the governor and assembly of Jamaica over Olyphant's case in 1764.[8] Again, like the mainland colonies, the West Indian islands had nearly all adopted the practice of appointing agents in London to take care of their interests, and the duties of these agents can be gathered from the Act of Appointment of agents for Jamaica in 1731.[9] In addition to these agents, who represented the resident planters, by the mid-eighteenth century a society of the West Indian merchants in London had been formed to take care of their special interests; and a formidable political interest had also been built up by the absentee planters residing in England. The planters scored notable successes with the passing of the Molasses Act of 1733, and the Sugar Act of 1739,[10] which allowed West Indian sugar to be shipped direct to Europe, provided it went in British ships. The decision of the government to retain Canada at the peace in 1763, and give up the captured French West Indian islands of Guadeloupe and Martinique, in fact marks a turning-point in British colonial interest in America, but it was not generally so regarded at the time. The arguments for and against Canada and Guadeloupe were discussed in many pamphlets,[11] and the decision to keep Canada was a further success for the West Indian planters, who feared the competition of Guadeloupe in the sugar trade. The interests of planters and merchants did not always coincide; but over the crisis between the government and the American colonies and its effect upon the prosperity of the West Indies, merchant and planter were united, and their method of going to work in

[1] No. 229. [2] No. 230. [3] No. 231. [4] No. 232. [5] No. 233. [6] No. 234.
[7] No. 235. [8] No. 237. [9] No. 236. [10] No. 238. [11] No. 239.

defence of their interests is illustrated by accounts of their proceedings published in the newspapers in 1775.[1]

There were, however, those who were alive to the potential value of Canada as a part of the empire. As early as 1745 William Shirley, at that time Governor of Massachusetts, had written to Newcastle on this subject;[2] and it is interesting to see that in 1782, at the end of the American war, the same kind of strategic and commercial arguments for the keeping of Canada at the peace were being put forward by Thomas Pownall, another former Governor of Massachusetts.[3] At the same time it must be admitted that those who, in 1763, had prophesied that the expulsion of the French and the incorporation of Canada in the empire would have an unsettling effect upon the Thirteen Colonies had seen their prophesies fulfilled. In particular, the Quebec Act of 1774,[4] granting to a Catholic Canada religious freedom and a constitution in which French laws and customs were established, greatly embittered feeling in New England, while securing French Canadian loyalty to the home government.

Nova Scotia and Newfoundland had been acquired from France at the Peace of Utrecht. In 1749 measures for the settlement of Nova Scotia were taken on the initiative of Lord Halifax, then President of the Board of Trade. An advertisement setting out the terms upon which ex-soldiers and sailors and their families were invited to emigrate appeared in the *London Gazette*,[5] and a number of settlers sailed. During the Seven Years War anxiety was felt about possible attacks on Nova Scotia by the French, and it was thought politic to allay the discontent of its inhabitants by giving them a representative assembly on the same model as the other American colonies.[6] Newfoundland was also liable to be attacked by the French, and a pamphlet written in 1768 by a captain of artillery serving there, urged the building of fortifications and the increase of the garrisons as a first step towards settlement and the increasing of the value of the fisheries.[7]

While the centre of gravity of the first British empire undoubtedly lay in North America, the eighteenth century witnessed a remarkable expansion of British interest in India. As late as the middle of the century, the French came within measurable distance of completely excluding their British competitors from the riches of India. This danger was averted by the victories of Clive and Coote in the Seven Years War, but as Clive himself clearly realized, these triumphs raised new problems. The East India Company was ceasing to be a mere company of traders; it was becoming the political ruler of large tracts of India. Clive at first tried to tempt Pitt with the idea of securing the sovereignty of Bengal for the Crown, but Pitt gave him little encouragement.[8] Both men later changed their minds; Clive when he saw that the arrangement he had proposed would lead to interference by the government in the Company's affairs in India; Pitt in 1767 when, in common with other politicians of the time, he was tempted by the potential value to the government of the East India Company's vastly increased wealth. The Company was able on this occasion to avoid any government control, other than a limitation of its power to increase its dividends;[9] but parliamentary criticism of the Company's servants continued. Clive's speech in defence of his administration in Bengal included a general defence of the Company's servants which provides a vivid picture of the temptations to which they were exposed.[10] The Regulating Act of 1773[11] was the first real attempt to deal with the new problems. Warren Hastings became the first Governor-General in Bengal, with

[1] No. 240. [2] No. 241. [3] No. 243. [4] No. 242. [5] No. 244. [6] No. 245.
[7] No. 246. [8] No. 247. [9] No. 248. [10] No. 249. [11] No. 250.

powers over the governors of the other two presidencies, and in this period is laid the foundation of civilian rule of British India. The Act, however, had grave weaknesses in practice, as Hastings pointed out in a pamphlet written on his return to England in 1786.[1] It was only a matter of time before the government assumed greater control over Indian administration. To military and financial considerations there was now being added an increasing pressure of public opinion that England had a responsibility towards the Indian population and a duty to see that a just and efficient administration was established. This is illustrated by Burke's impassioned indictment of the whole system of the Company's rule in India, and his advocacy of the more direct government control which would have been provided by Fox's India Bill,[2] and was in fact provided, though by a different method, in Pitt's India Act of 1784.

The British settlements on the west coast of Africa were in the eighteenth century chiefly valued for the lucrative slave trade. During the early years of the century the Royal African Company was declining, in face of competition from other countries, especially France. This, and the consequent decay of the African trade, on which, it was held, the wealth of the West Indies depended, was lamented in a number of pamphlets,[3] and was the subject of petitions to Parliament. In 1747 the Royal African Company petitioned Parliament for relief,[4] and in 1750 an Act was passed setting up a new Company of Merchants trading to Africa, a regulated company of a different type from the Royal African Company. The constitution of the new company was described and criticized by Adam Smith in the *Wealth of Nations*.[5]

[1] No. 251. [2] No. 252. [3] No. 253. [4] No. 254. [5] No. 255.

BIBLIOGRAPHY

Works wholly or mainly concerned with the Thirteen Colonies have generally been omitted, as there are full bibliographies in vol. IX of these *Documents*.

I. BIBLIOGRAPHIES, ETC.

E. Lewin, *Subject Catalogue of the Library of the Royal Empire Society* (4 vols., London, 1930–1937), and W. F. Craven's bibliographical article on "Historical Study of the British Empire" in the *Journal of Modern History*, VI (1934), pp. 40–69, are helpful. The bibliographies at the end of each volume of the *Cambridge History of the British Empire* are full and readily accessible. For more recent works L. B. Frewer, *Bibliography of Historical Writings* [1940–1945] (Oxford, 1947) and the sections on colonial history in the *Annual Bulletins* of the Historical Association must be consulted. *Writings on American History*, edited by Grace G. Griffin and others, published annually for each year from 1906 at Washington (1908 onwards), includes works on Canada and the British West Indies.

II. ORIGINAL SOURCES

There are three sets of official publications: (1) *Acts of the Privy Council of England, Colonial Series*, edited by W. L. Grant and J. Munro, vols. 2–6 [1680–1783] (Hereford and London, 1910–1912); (2) *Calendar of State Papers Colonial* [1714–1733], edited by C. Headlam and A. P. Newton (13 vols., London, 1928–1939); and (3) *Journals of the Board of Trade and Plantations* [1704–1782] (14 vols., London, 1920–1938). L. F. Stock, *Proceedings and Debates of the British Parliaments respecting North America* (5 vols., to 1754, Washington, 1924–1942, and still being published), is essential. V. Harlow and F. Madden, *British Colonial Developments, 1774–1834: Select Documents* (Oxford, 1953), is also useful, though mainly concerned with the period after 1783.

III. GENERAL HISTORIES OF THE EMPIRE

Sir John Seeley, *Expansion of England* (London, 1883), for long the most influential textbook, is superseded by J. A. Williamson, *A Short History of British Expansion* (revised edition, 2 vols., London, 1943–1945). *The Cambridge History of the British Empire*, edited by J. H. Rose and others (7 vols., Cambridge, 1929–1940), is elaborate and authoritative. L. H. Gipson, *British Empire before the American Revolution* (7 vols., Caldwell, Idaho, 1936–1949), is the only work on this scale. G. B. Hertz, *The Old Colonial System* (Manchester, 1905), and *British Imperialism in the eighteenth century* (London, 1908) are still useful. For the period it covers, V. T. Harlow, *Founding of the Second British Empire, 1763–1793*, vol. I (London, 1952), is the standard treatment. K. E. Knorr, *British Colonial Theories, 1570–1850* (Toronto, 1944), is a valuable survey. On constitutional development A. B. Keith, *Constitutional History of the First British Empire* (Oxford, 1930), is generally used. R. Coupland, *The American Revolution and the British Empire* (London, 1930), is useful. On the economic aspects the works of G. L. Beer, *Old Colonial System* (2 vols., New York, 1912, new edition, 1933), *British Colonial Policy, 1754–65* (New York, 1907, new edition, 1933), and *Commercial Policy of England toward the American Colonies* (reprinted New York, 1948), continued by R. L. Schuyler, *The Fall of the Old Colonial System* (New York, 1945), are still useful, but Professor Beer's views have been challenged in certain respects in C. P. Nettels, *The Roots of American Civilisation* (London, 1938), and O. M. Dickerson, *The Navigation Acts and the American Revolution* (Philadelphia, 1951). R. Pares, "Economic factors in the history of the Empire" in the *Economic History Review*, vol. VII (1936–1937), pp. 119–144, deals at some length with the eighteenth century. Works on mercantilism and on the economic aspects of British colonial policy during this period generally deal mainly with the Thirteen Colonies and are discussed in vol. IX of these *Documents*, p. 315.

IV. MONOGRAPHS

O. M. Dickerson studied the problems arising between the Board of Trade and the American Colonies in *American Colonial Government 1696–1765* (Cleveland, 1912). L. W. Labaree concentrated on the actual colonial administration in his *Royal Government in America* (New Haven, 1930) and later edited *Royal Instructions to British Colonial Governors, 1670–1776* (2 vols., New York, 1935). M. Wight, *The Development of the Legislative Council, 1606–1945* (London, 1946), is also valuable. E. B. Russell, *Review of American Colonial Legislation by the King in Council* (New York, 1915), is typical of the numerous studies of more specialized character. On the slave trade, Elizabeth Donnan, *Documents Illustrative of the History of the Slave Trade to America* (4 vols., Washington, 1930–1935), E. Williams, *Capitalism and Slavery* (Chapel Hill, 1944), and C. M. Macinnes, *England and Slavery* (Bristol, 1934) and *A Gateway of Empire* (Bristol, 1939) are useful. For the Seven Years War period Kate Hotblack, *Chatham's Colonial Policy* (London, 1917), and Gertrude S. Kimball, *Correspondence of William Pitt with Colonial Governors* (2 vols., New York, 1906), are essential. C. W. Alvord, *The Mississippi Valley in British Politics* (2 vols., Cleveland, 1917), and T. P. Abernethy, *Western Lands and the American Revolution* (New York, 1937), study British policy in connexion with the settlement of the west, and the article by R. A. Humphrys, "Lord Shelburne and British Colonial Policy, 1766–68" in *English Historical Review*, L (1935), pp. 257–277, should also be consulted on this subject. Reference may be made to W. Odham, "The administration of the system of transportation of British convicts 1763–93" in the *Bulletin of the Institute of Historical Research*, XI (1933–1934), pp. 126–127.

V. CANADA

There are two standard collections of documents which cover this period: *Documents relating to the Constitutional History of Canada, 1759–1791*, edited by A. Shortt and A. G. Doughty (2 vols., Ottawa, 2nd edition, 1918); and *Statutes, Treaties and Documents of the Canadian Constitution*, edited by W. P. M. Kennedy (Toronto and Oxford, 1930). R. Coupland, *The Quebec Act* (Oxford, 1925), is a valuable commentary, though the view taken of the statesmanship of the Act is not shared by all historians. G. M. Wrong, *Rise and Fall of New France* (2 vols., New York, 1928) and *Canada and the American Revolution* (New York, 1935) are essential. The critical period of the Seven Years War has been exhaustively studied in F. Parkman, *Montcalm and Wolfe* (2 vols., Boston, Mass., 1884, and later editions); A. G. Doughty and G. W. Parmalee, *Siege of Quebec* (6 vols., Quebec, 1901); and W. C. H. Wood, *The Fight for Canada* (Westminster, 1904). G. S. Graham, *British Policy in Canada 1774–91* (London, 1930), studies British trade policy, and A. G. Bradley, *The United Empire Loyalists* (London, 1932), traces the establishment of British colonists in Canada. F. Mason Wade, *The French Canadians, 1760–1945* (London, 1955), is also useful. Harold A. Innis, *The Fur Trade in Canada* (New York, 1930), is the standard work on the subject. Three works on Anglo-Canadian-American relations may be added: Max Savelle, *The Diplomatic History of the Canadian boundary, 1749–63* (New Haven, 1940); J. B. Brebner, *North Atlantic Triangle* (New Haven, 1945); and A. L. Burt, *The United States, Great Britain and British North America* [1776–1812] (New Haven, 1940). Reference should also be made to the *Canadian Historical Review* (Toronto, 1920 onwards), where many important articles have appeared.

On the outposts there are studies of varying value, including J. B. Brebner, *New England's Outpost: Acadia before the Conquest of Canada* (New York, 1927); G. G. Campbell, *History of Nova Scotia* (Toronto, 1948); A. B. Warburton, *History of Prince Edward Island* (St. John, 1923); D. W. Prowse, *History of Newfoundland* (London, 1895); and R. G. Lounsbury, *British Fishery at Newfoundland* (New Haven, 1934). There are summaries of unpublished theses by Janet Paterson, "History of Newfoundland 1713–63", and G. O. Rothney, "History of Newfoundland and Labrador 1754–83", in *Bulletin of the Institute of Historical Research*, XI (1933–1934), pp. 45–48, and XIII (1935–1936), pp. 110–112 respectively. *Newfoundland: Economic, Diplomatic and Strategic Studies*, edited by R. A. Mackay (London, 1946), includes some valuable work, mainly on the economic aspect of the colony's history. On Hudson's Bay the evidence given to a Committee of the House of Commons and published in *Reports from Committees of the House of Commons*, II (London, 1773), pp. 215–286, and a few other contemporary accounts, especially Joseph Robson, *Account of Six Years' Residence in Hudson's Bay* (London, 1759), are of great service. Three volumes of the Hudson's Bay Record Society are concerned with the eighteenth century: *James Isham's Observations on Hudson's Bay, 1743*, and *Notes and observations on a Book entitled 'A Voyage to Hudson's Bay in the Dobbs Galley, 1749'*, edited by E. E. Rich (Champlain Society, Toronto and London, 1949); and *Cumberland and Hudson House Journals*, edited by E. E. Rich, First Series, 1775–1779 (London, 1951), Second Series, 1779–1782 (London, 1952). The best popular narratives will be found in B. Willson, *The Great Company* (2 vols., Toronto, 1900), and D. Mackay, *The Honourable Company* (New York, 1936).

VI. THE WEST INDIES

L. J. Ragatz, *Guide to the Study of British Caribbean History, 1763–1834* (Washington, 1932), and R. Pares, "Public Records in British West India Islands", in *Bulletin of the Institute of Historical Research*, VII (1929–1930), pp. 149–157, are helpful. A. P. Newton discussed in broad outline the place of "The West Indies in International Politics 1550–1850" in *History*, XIX (1934–1935), pp. 193–207 and 302–310. There is a useful short history by W. L. Burn, *The British West Indies* (London, 1951). Useful on administration is Lillian M. Penson, *Colonial Agents of the British West Indies* (London, 1924), and J. H. Parry, "The Patent Offices in the British West Indies", in *English Historical Review*, LXIX (1954), pp. 200–225. Professor Penson also contributed to the *English Historical Review*, XXXVI (1921), pp. 373–392, a study of "The London West India Interest in the Eighteenth century". C. G. S. Higham discusses the problem of reorganizing the British colonial empire after the Seven Years War in "The General Assembly of the Leeward Islands, Part II" in *English Historical Review*, XLI (1926), pp. 366–388. Though their importance transcends the local history of the West Indies, the two monographs of R. Pares, *War and Trade in the West Indies* (Oxford, 1936), and *Colonial Blockade and Neutral Rights, 1739–63* (Oxford, 1938) must be mentioned here. The same author's *A West India Fortune* (London, 1950) is based on the papers of the Pinney family, of Bristol and Nevis, while his essay, "A London West-India Merchant House, 1740–1769", in *Essays presented to Sir Lewis Namier* (London, 1956), is a similar study of the Lascelles family, with interests in Barbados. His *Yankees and Creoles* (London, 1956) is concerned with the trade between the West Indies and the Thirteen Colonies before the American Revolution. The article by H. C. Bell on "The West India Trade before the American Revolution" in the *American Historical Review*, XXII (1916–1917), pp. 272–287, is a useful summary; Frances Armytage, *The Free Port System in the British West Indies, 1766–1822* (London, 1953), is a useful study of this aspect of West Indian trade. F. W. Pitman, *Development of the British West Indies 1700–1763* (New Haven, 1917), is less general in scope than its title suggests, being largely concerned with the sugar industry. There is a good account by the same writer of "The settlement and financing of British West India Plantations" in *Essays presented to C. M. Andrews* (New Haven, 1931), and an article on "A Jamaica Slave Plantation" by U. B. Phillips in *American Historical Review*, XIX (1913–1914), pp. 543–558. L. J. Ragatz, *The Fall of the Planter Class in the British Caribbean 1763–1833* (New York, 1928), is an important monograph.

It is impossible to list here works dealing with individual islands, such as Agnes M. Whitson, *Constitutional development of Jamaica 1660–1729* (Manchester, 1929), and H. C. Wilkinson, *Bermuda in the Old Empire* (London, 1950). Space must, however, be found for Edward Long's classic work, *The History of Jamaica* (3 vols., London, 1774).

VII. CENTRAL AND SOUTH AMERICAN COLONIES

There is a *History of British Guiana* (3 vols., Georgetown, 1891–1894) by J. Rodway; and G. C. Edmundson discussed "The Relations of Great Britain with Guiana" in the *Transactions of the Royal Historical Society*, Fourth Series, VI (1923), pp. 1–21. On Central America, A. R. Gibbs, *British Honduras* (London, 1883); Sir J. A. Burdon, *Archives of British Honduras*, vol. I (London, 1931); and E. O. Wimserling, *The Beginning of British Honduras* (New York, 1946), should be consulted. The *Bulletin of the Institute of Historical Research*, IV (1926–1927), pp. 180–181, summarizes an unpublished thesis by J. McLeish on "British activities in Yucatan and on the Moskito Shore in the eighteenth century"; and A. M. Wilson contributed a study of "The Logwood Trade in the Seventeenth and Eighteenth Centuries" to *Essays in the History of Modern Europe*, edited by D. McKay (New York, 1936). L. H. Gipson's article on "British Diplomacy in the light of Anglo-Spanish New World Issues, 1750–57" in the *American Historical Review*, LI (1945–1946), pp. 627–648, is also devoted mainly to the logwood trade.

VIII. INDIA

Sir W. Foster, *Guide to the India Office Records* (London, 1919), describes the various classes of records which have been preserved there, but unfortunately there are no calendars relating to the eighteenth century. S. C. Sutton, *A Guide to the India Office Library* (London, 1952), gives a general account of the printed books, manuscripts and other source material preserved in the library. The India Records Series includes some sources for the eighteenth century, such as H. D. Love, *Vestiges of Old Madras 1640–1800* (4 vols., London, 1913). A new start has now been made with this series of publications under the control of the director of the National Archives of India. *Fort William-India House Correspondence and other Contemporary Papers relating thereto (Public Series)*, 1767–1769, edited by N. K. Sinha (Delhi, 1949), covers an interesting period in the administration of Bengal. V. G. Dighe, *Descriptive Catalogue of the Secret and Political Department Series 1755–1820* (Bombay, 1954), catalogues documents relating to the former Bombay Presidency and is particularly useful on the French threat to British power after 1763. H. B. Morse, *Chronicles of the East India Company Trading to China*, vols. I and V (Oxford, 1926–1929), prints extensive excerpts from the records of trade with China.

There is a good chapter on India by Sir A. C. Lyall and P. E. Roberts in the *Cambridge Modern History*, vol. VI (Cambridge, 1909). The *Cambridge History of India*, vol. V (Cambridge, 1929), covers our period much more fully. Sir William Hunter, *History of British India* (2 vols., London, 1899–1900), may still be recommended. H. Furber, *John Company at Work* (Cambridge, Mass., 1948), provides a useful account of the commercial side of the East India Company's activities in the second half of the eighteenth century, and T. G. P. Spear, *The Nabobs* (London, 1932), describes the daily lives of English men and women in India during our period. E. Thompson and G. T. Garratt, *Rise and Fulfilment of British rule in India* (London, 1934), is brief but suggestive. A. B. Keith, *Constitutional History of India* (London, 1936), may be recommended. On the economic side reference may be made to S. Bhattacharaya, *The East India Company and the Economy of Bengal, 1704–1740* (London, 1954); F. P. Robinson, *Trade of the East India Company from 1709 to 1813* (Cambridge, 1912); B. Krishna, *Commercial Relations between*

India and England 1601–1757 (London, 1924); and I. D. Parshad, "Some Aspects of Indian Foreign Trade 1757–1893" in the *Bulletin of the Institute of Historical Research*, VII (1929–1930), pp. 183–184. The *Journal of Indian History* (Allahabad, 1920 onwards) contains articles of varying quality on the history of India in the eighteenth century.

Monographs include W. F. Irvine, *Later Mughals*, edited by Sir J. Sarkar (2 vols., Calcutta, 1921–1922), which tells the story of the decline and fall of the Mogul empire. G. B. Malleson, *History of the French in India* (London, 1868), and F. C. Danvers, *The Portuguese in India* (2 vols., London, 1894), remain unsuperseded. Biographies of Clive and Dupleix abound. The official *Life of Clive* (3 vols., London, 1835) by Sir J. Malcolm must be supplemented by Sir G. Forrest, *Life of Lord Clive* (2 vols., London, 1918). H. H. Dodwell, *Dupleix and Clive* (London, 1920), and Virginia M. Thompson, *Dupleix and his Letters* (New York, 1933), are interesting. A. C. Roy, *The Career of Mir Jafar Khan 1757–1765* (Calcutta, 1953), takes a favourable view of Clive's conduct. P. Moon, *Warren Hastings and British India* (London, 1947), is a slight introduction to the career of the first governor-general, which has been fully studied by Reverend G. R. Gleig in *Memoirs of the Life of the Rt. Hon. Warren Hastings, compiled from the Original Documents* (Calcutta, 1892, and later edition, Oxford and London, 1910); and by C. C. Davies in *Warren Hastings and Oudh* (London, 1939) and his edition of *The Benares Diary of Warren Hastings*, Camden Miscellany, vol. XVIII (London, 1948). Keith Feiling's *Warren Hastings* (London, 1954) is the latest biography. M. E. Monckton Jones, *Warren Hastings in Bengal* (Oxford, 1918), is a scholarly treatment of his administration from 1772 to 1774, and S. Weitzman, *Warren Hastings and Philip Francis* (Manchester, 1929) studies the famous quarrel. J. H. Rose discussed "The Influence of Sea Power on Indian History 1746–1802" in the *Journal of Indian History*, III (1924–1926), pp. 188–204. Lucy S. Sutherland, *The East India Company in Eighteenth Century Politics* (Oxford, 1950), must be mentioned here, though its scope is wider than other monographs included in this section. It is indispensable for the relations between the Company and the Government at this period. C. H. Phillips's paper on "The East India Company's 'Interest' and the English Government" in the *Transactions of the Royal Historical Society*, Fourth Series, XX (1937), pp. 83–101, is devoted mainly to a discussion of Fox's India Bill.

IX. BURMA AND FARTHER EAST

D. G. E. Hall, *Europe and Burma* (London, 1945), and the same author's *Early English Intercourse with Burma 1587–1743* (London, 1928) provide some useful information. The *Bulletin of the Institute of Historical Research*, XV (1937–1938), pp. 40–1, refers to an unpublished thesis by T. C. P. Edgell on "British Policy and Trade in Borneo and the Adjacent Islands 1667–1786". J. B. Eames, *The English in China* (London, 1909), may be supplemented by two works by E. H. Pritchard, *Anglo-Chinese Relations* [in the 17th and 18th centuries] (Urbana, 1929) and *Crucial Years of Early Anglo-Chinese Relations* [1750–1800] (Pullman, Washington, 1936).

X. AFRICA

Bibliography of the Negro in Africa and America (New York, 1928) is the standard reference book. The preparatory volume of an *Encylopaedia of the Negro* (New York, 1945) outlines the scope and content of what promises to be an important work.

W. E. F. Ward, *A History of the Gold Coast* (London, 1949), supplements but does not supersede W. W. Claridge, *History of the Gold Coast and Ashanti* (2 vols., London, 1915). Sir R. Coupland, *East Africa and its Invaders* (Oxford, 1938), and Sir A. C. Burns, *History of Nigeria* (4th edition, London, 1948), contain little on the eighteenth century, which is more fully treated in J. M. Gray, *History of the Gambia* (Cambridge, 1940). Eveline C. Martin, *British West African Settlements 1750–1821* (London, 1927), and the article on "English Establishments on the Gold Coast" by the same author in the *Transactions of the Royal Historical Society*, Fourth Series, v (1922), pp. 167–189, which emphasizes the problems raised by joint control by the crown and a trading company, should be consulted. Dr. Martin has also edited the *Journal of a Slave-Dealer* [Nicholas Owen], who settled in Guinea (London, 1930). *Letters of a West African Trader, Edward Grace*, edited by T. S. Ashton (Council for the Preservation of Business Archives, 1950), illustrates the triangular trade–Europe–West Africa–West Indies–of a London merchant engaged in the slave trade. C. H. Hoskins, *British Routes to India* (New York, 1928), is also useful for West Africa.

XI. MARITIME EXPLORATION AND IMPERIAL EXPANSION

Many of the original sources, including the official accounts of Cook's three voyages, were published in the eighteenth century and often reprinted in collections such as the *General Collection of Voyages and Travels*, edited by J. Pinkerton (17 vols., London, 1808–1814). Others were first published after 1847 by the Hakluyt Society. New editions of the classic voyages of Dampier, Woodes Rogers and Shelvocke appeared from time to time, and Anson's famous *Voyage round the World* [1740–1744], edited by R. Walter (London, 1748), at once became a best seller. Even more important were the epoch-making voyages of Captain Cook, the significance of which is admirably brought out by Dr. J. A. Williamson in his *Cook and the Opening of the Pacific* (London, 1946), with a select list of earlier works on Cook. Official accounts of each of Cook's voyages were published in several volumes shortly after its completion and abbreviated unofficial editions, testifying to the contemporary interest in travel books, soon appeared.

A. EIGHTEENTH-CENTURY VIEWS ON COLONIES

222. Sir William Keith on the relationship between the mother country and its colonies, 1738

(Sir William Keith, Bart., *History of the British Plantations in America* (1738), pp. 10–14.)

Sir William Keith (*c.* 1669–1749), fourth baronet of Ludquhairn, was Governor of Pennsylvania, 1712–1726.

. . . When either by the Deficiency of a sufficient Quantity of our own Product to be exported, and given in Exchange to other Nations, or (which is sometimes the Case) when by a greater Share of Industry we are outdone by Foreign States, in the Improvement of the same Manufactures and Merchandize, whereby the Balance of Trade is turn'd against us, and our artificers and labouring People thereby driven from us to seek for Employment elsewhere; then the Wisdom of the State has sometimes thought fit to send such of their People as could be spared, to settle themselves in various Climates, where some new Species of Product might be raised, and sent home to revive Commerce, and to assist the Public by restoring to it again the lost Balance of National Trade.

AND this being the original Intention of, and the only justifiable Reason that can be given for the Practice within these last Two Centuries, of making Settlements and planting Colonies on the uninhabited vacant Lands of *America*, whose People are protected by, but made subservient to, and dependent on their respective Mother States in *Europe*; it may be of Service towards completing the Design of the following History of the *British* Plantations, to make some particular Observations in this Place, on that mutual Interest which unites these Colonies to *Great Britain*, and on the reciprocal Obligations which always subsist between them.

IN all the Royal Patents and Deeds of Gift which have been made to particular Persons, of Lands for planting Colonies in *America*, Care has been taken not only to preserve the Sovereignty and Allegiance due to the Crown of *Britain*, but likewise to restrain the People of the respective Colonies, from enacting amongst themselves any By-Laws or Ordinances whatsoever, repugnant to, or any ways inconsistent with, the Fundamental Laws and Constitution of the Mother State, to whose Legislative and Supreme Authority they most certainly are, and ought always to be subjected.

AND as by the Design of those Settlements to raise new and different kinds of Merchandize for the *European* Market, it was both reasonable and necessary that they should be protected, and their Inhabitants encouraged, in the Produce of such Commodities, as being exchanged for *British* Manufactures, would furnish Cloathing, and other Necessaries, to themselves, and at the same time assist *Great Britain* in the Balance of National Trade with other Countries; especially by providing large Quantities of such Goods out of the Labour of their own Subjects in *America*, and in Exchange for *British* Manufacture, as before the Settlement of the Colonies they were obliged to purchase with ready Money from other Nations; so the Inhabitants of the Colonies, on the other hand, not only enjoyed the Advantage of the same Laws, and the sweet Comforts of *English* Liberty in all respects, but they were also sure of being protected from the Insults and Attacks of any foreign Enemy, by the Naval Force, and at the Public Expence of *Great Britain.*

MOREOVER, in tolerable good Seasons it depends on the Frugality and Industry of the Planter in *America,* when he acts uprightly, and is fairly dealt with, to secure a Balance in his *British* Factor's Hands, over and above providing himself with all that he wants from *Europe*: And as such Overplus or Balance is commonly placed in some of the Public Funds, or laid out on Land-Security in *Great Britain,* it seldom or never returns again to *America,* but remains a Part of the National Wealth or Stock.

IN like Manner the Profits arising to *British* Subjects in *America,* from their exchanging Lumber, *&c.* with the Product of foreign Plantations, either to be used in *America,* or returned to *Europe* for *British* Account, must terminate in the Advantage of *Great Britain*; who thereby reaps a certain Gain from the Labour of Foreigners, as well as from that of her own Subjects, besides engrossing a larger Share of such Commodities as the better enables her to govern the *European* Market. . . .

IT is easy to talk of Penal Laws, Prohibitions, and such-like Severities, to be executed by the Force of Power; but the most effectual and profitable Way of restraining the Subjects in the Plantations from interfering with *Great Britain* in her Home-Trade and Manufactures, will be, to take due Care that the Colonies be always plentifully supply'd with *British* Cloths, and other *European* Commodities, at a much cheaper Rate than it is possible for them to raise and manufacture such Things within themselves: And likewise, that the Importation of all such Product and Manufacture from the Colonies, as are fit to supply the Wants of *Great Britain,* and to assist the Public in the Balance of National Trade with other Countries, be properly encouraged.

WE find by daily Experience, that Mens Minds are no other ways to be subdued under a just and free Government, than by making them feel, that it is their Interest to submit themselves to, and chearfully comply with the Laws and Ordinances of the State; for as long as the Generality of a People are truly sensible, that their Rulers and Governors have nothing so much at Heart as the public Good of the Society, and the Honour and Prosperity of the Commonwealth, there will be no Occasion to apprehend either Discontent, Insurrection or Rebellion.

223. Adam Smith on Colonies, 1776

(*An Inquiry into the Nature and Causes of the Wealth of Nations,* 1904 ed., II, pp. 125–127.)

In the *Wealth of Nations,* first published in 1776, Adam Smith attacked the prevalent 'mercantilist' view of colonies.

. . . The discovery of America, and that of a passage to the East Indies by the Cape of Good Hope, are the two greatest and most important events recorded in the history of mankind. Their consequences have already been very great; but, in the short period of between two and three centuries which has elapsed since these discoveries were made, it is impossible that the whole extent of their consequences can have been seen. What benefits or what misfortunes to mankind may hereafter result from those great events, no human wisdom can forsee. By uniting, in some measure, the most distant parts of the world, by enabling them to relieve one another's wants, to increase one another's enjoyments, and to encourage one another's industry, their general tendency would seem to be beneficial. To the natives, however, both of the East and West Indies, all the commercial benefits which can have resulted from those events have been sunk and lost in the dreadful misfortunes which they have occasioned. These misfortunes, however, seem to have arisen rather from accident than from anything in the nature of those events themselves. At the particular time when these discoveries were made, the superiority of force happened to be so great on the side of the Europeans that they were enabled to commit with impunity every sort of injustice in those remote countries. Hereafter, perhaps, the natives of those countries may grow stronger, or those of Europe may grow weaker, and the inhabitants of all the different quarters of the world may arrive at that equality of courage and force which, by inspiring mutual fear, can alone overawe the injustice of independent nations into some sort of respect for the rights of one another. But nothing seems more likely to establish this equality of force than that mutual communication of knowledge and of all sorts of improvements which an extensive commerce from all countries to all countries naturally, or rather necessarily, carries along with it.

In the meantime one of the principal effects of those discoveries has been to raise the mercantile system to a degree of splendour and glory which it could never otherwise have attained to. It is the object of that system to enrich a great nation rather by trade and manufactures than by the improvement and cultivation of land, rather by the industry of the towns than by that of the country. But, in consequence of those discoveries, the commercial towns of Europe, instead of being the manufacturers and carriers for but a very small part of the world (that part of Europe which is washed by the Atlantic Ocean, and the countries which lie around the Baltic and Mediterranean seas), have now become the manufacturers for the numerous and thriving cultivators of America, and the carriers, and in some respects the manufacturers too, for almost all the different nations of Asia, Africa, and America. Two new worlds have been opened to their industry, each of them much greater and more extensive than the old one, and the market of one of them growing still greater and greater every day.

The countries which possess the colonies of America, and which trade directly to the East Indies, enjoy, indeed, the whole show and splendour of this great commerce. Other countries, however, notwithstanding all the invidious restraints by which it is meant to exclude them, frequently enjoy a greater share of the real benefit of it. The colonies of Spain and Portugal, for example, give more real encouragement to the industry of other countries than to that of Spain and Portugal. In the single article of linen alone the consumption of those colonies amounts, it is said, but I do not pretend to warrant the quantity, to more than three millions sterling a year. But this great consumption is almost entirely supplied by France, Flanders, Holland, and Germany. Spain and Portugal furnish but a small part of it. The capital which supplies the colonies with this great quantity of linen is annually distributed among, and furnishes a revenue to the inhabitants of, those other countries. The profits of it only are spent in Spain and Portugal, where they help to support the sumptuous profusion of the merchants of Cadiz and Lisbon.

Even the regulations by which each nation endeavours to secure to itself the exclusive trade of its own colonies are frequently more hurtful to the countries in favour of which they are established than to those against which they are established. The unjust oppression of the industry of other countries falls back, if I may say so, upon the heads of the oppressors, and crushes their industry more than it does that of those other countries. By those regulations, for example, the merchant of Hamburgh must send the linen which he destines for the American market to London, and he must bring back from thence the tobacco which he destines for the German market, because he can neither send the one directly to America nor bring back the other directly from thence. By this restraint he is probably obliged to sell the one somewhat cheaper, and to buy the other somewhat dearer than he otherwise might have done; and his profits are probably somewhat abridged by means of it. In this trade, however, between Hamburgh and London, he certainly receives the returns of his capital much more quickly than he could possibly have done in the direct trade to America, even though we should suppose, what is by no means the case, that the payments of America were as punctual as those of London. In the trade, therefore, to which those regulations confine the merchant of Hamburgh, his capital can keep in constant employment a much greater quantity of German industry than it possibly could have done in the trade from which he is excluded. Though the one employment, therefore, may to him perhaps be less profitable than the other, it cannot be less advantageous to his country. It is quite otherwise with the employment into which the monopoly naturally attracts, if I may say so, the capital of the London merchant. That employment may, perhaps, be more profitable to him than the greater part of other employments, but, on account of the slowness of the returns, it cannot be more advantageous to his country.

After all the unjust attempts, therefore, of every country in Europe to engross to itself the whole advantage of the trade of its own colonies, no country has yet been able to engross to itself anything but the expense of supporting in time of peace and of defending in time of war the oppressive authority which it assumes over them. The inconveniencies resulting from the possession of its colonies, every country has engrossed to itself completely. The advantages resulting from their trade it has been obliged to share with many other countries.

At first sight, no doubt, the monopoly of the great commerce of America, naturally seems to be an acquisition of the highest value. To the undiscerning eye of giddy ambition, it naturally presents itself amidst the confused scramble of politics and war as a very dazzling object to fight for. The dazzling splendour of the object, however, the immense greatness of the commerce, is the very quality which renders the monopoly of it hurtful, or which makes one employment, in its own nature necessarily less advantageous to the country than the greater part of other employments, absorb a much greater proportion of the capital of the country than what would otherwise have gone to it.

224. Extract from a pamphlet on the Peace Preliminaries of 1783

(*Considerations on the Provisional Treaty with America, and the Preliminary Articles of Peace with France and Spain* (1783), pp. 32–33, 42–44, 144–145.)

This pamphlet was probably written by Andrew Kippis (1725–1795), a nonconformist minister and part editor of the *Biographia Britannica*. It was said to have been written at Shelburne's direction and to represent his point of view. It considers the need for a new colonial system after the loss of the Thirteen Colonies.

. . . BUT since the Independence of America hath been reasonably and unavoidably acknowledged, it is our business to make the best use of an event which can never be recalled. By a wise conduct, it may not prove so unfortunate for this kingdom as might at first view be apprehended; and at any rate, it was better to submit to it than pursue a destructive and hopeless contest. Whilst we are delivered from the vast expence of maintaining and protecting the Colonies, our commercial intercourse with them will still be productive of many advantages. Perhaps, with proper management, the advantages may not be much inferior to what they were in former times; and possibly, if America, as may rationally be expected, should rapidly increase in populousness and cultivation, the benefits of our trade with her may be greater than ever. There can, at least, be no doubt but that the superiority we possess, in point of capital, of industry, and the suitableness of our manufactures to the wants of the United States, will secure to us a large share of their commerce. It will much contribute to so happy an event, for us to treat the Americans in a liberal manner, and to do whatever lies in our power, to promote the return of harmony and affection. . . .

UPON the whole question concerning the Canada boundaries, it may be observed, that government, in consenting to them, had two views, the one political, the other commercial. In a political light, if we could have gotten back to the state we were in in 1763, it would have been a very desirable circumstance. But since that was become no longer practicable, what was it which sound wisdom prescribed in such a situation? It certainly prescribed that we should lay the foundation of another large and liberal system, the first object of which should be permanent peace. To the attainment of this end, it was necessary to prevent every ground of future jealousies and quarrels. If any harsh or galling conditions had been insisted upon, the negotiation would either have entirely broken off, or if the Americans had submitted to them, their prejudices against England would have acquired fresh strength and occasions have been afforded for those dissensions which might have plunged us again into the horrors of war. It was the part of true policy to pursue the measures that tended to restore a cordial friendship, and which, perhaps, might, at length, be productive of a federal union between the two countries.

IF the matter be considered in a commercial view, it will appear, that it was necessary to proceed upon the establishment of a new principle; a principle which hath already notoriously taken place in the instance of Ireland, and which is avowed by America, not only to England, but to all the powers of Europe. The system of monopolies and little restrictions in trade, begins to be exploded in the world, and will justly every day grow more and more out of fashion. It is for the real honour and interest of Great Britain to prosecute an enlarged plan of commerce: and to have contended about a few furs, would have been incompatible with a design of such magnitude and importance. . . .

. . . Since the old edifice is necessarily destroyed, by the unavoidable separation of Great Britain and America, we should exert ourselves to the utmost of our power, that the new one may be founded in justice, in union, and in general conviction. Its superstructure depends upon it, and the inhabitants of the kingdom will be more or less active, in proportion to the confidence they have in its wisdom and stability. It behoves those who made it, to recommend themselves to the public by promoting the principles of it, whether in or out of Government. These are a cordial intercourse with North America; a well-grounded hope, first of returning affection, and then of returning union; and an universal freedom of commerce. It becomes those who objected to the peace equally to adhere to these principles. If we are so happy as to recover the confidence of our American brethren, the trade is sure to follow. If we are so wise as to profit by experience, and to send liberal laws to our remaining Colonies, instead of troops, bad Governors, and machiavelian systems, we shall be freed from the burthen of transmitting large sums thither, which we can no longer afford, and shall receive considerably from thence in return, by the necessary balance of our commerce. If we have resolution enough to open our ports at home, and to make Great Britain and Ireland, what Nature and Providence intended them for, a magazine between the old and new world, between the north and south of Europe; and if strict economical regulations be adopted, without loss of time, in every department, we may still find a substitute for all that we have given up, and be more at our command, by being within ourselves. . . .

B. COLONIAL TRADE

225. Statistics of Colonial Trade with Great Britain 1714–1783

(Sir Charles Whitworth, *The State of the Trade of Great Britain* (1776), pp. 19, 43, 64; David Macpherson, *Annals of Commerce*, III (1805), pp. 599; IV, p. 40.)

In the following tables, the figures for the Colonies and Plantations (omitting those for the American Colonies) have been extracted from the annual tables of official values of the total imports and exports of Great Britain. Table 1 is taken from Whitworth's *State of Trade*, which covers the years 1697–1773. Table 2 is taken from Macpherson's *Annals of Commerce*. For statistics of the trade of the American Colonies and of trade between those colonies and the British West Indies, see vol. IX of these *Documents*, No. 55.

TABLE 1

The IMPORTS and EXPORTS compared with the EXCESS of each Country

Countries	*From Christmas 1714, to Christmas 1715. 2 Geo. I*			
	Imports £ *s d*	*Exports* £ *s d*	*Import Excess* £ *s d*	*Export Excess* £ *s d*
Africa	30,096 12 6	51,912 6 2		21,815 13 8
East India	579,944 4 2	36,997 12 6	542,946 11 8	
Antigua	162,503 17 9	27,032 5 9	135,471 12 0	
Barbadoes	386,787 7 3	144,649 3 10	242,138 3 5	
Bermudas	523 7 10	1,809 17 10		1,286 10 1
Cape Breton				
Guadaloupe				
Hudson's Bay		1,402 18 8		1,402 18 8
Jamaica	273,747 3 6	110,870 7 4	162,876 16 2	
Montserrat	30,675 8 9	4,476 11 6	26,198 17 3	
Nevis	88,161 17 1	9,498 14 0	78,663 3 1	
Newfoundland	11,288 2 2	8,120 1 10	3,168 0 4	
New Providence				
Nova Scotia				
Quebec				
St. Croix				
St. Christopher's	57,536 3 0	4,077 3 9	53,458 19 3	
Tortola				

TABLE 1—*continued*

Countries	Imports £ s d	Exports £ s d	Import Excess £ s d	Export Excess £ s d
	From Christmas 1738, to Christmas 1739. 13 Geo. II.			
Africa	43,035 19 2	219,813 15 0		176,837 15 10
East India	1,278,859 11 1	217,395 6 0	1,061,464 5 1	
Antigua	291,988 4 6	45,757 4 7	246,230 19 11	
Barbadoes	197,838 1 3	56,354 17 0	141,483 4 3	
Bermudas	215 5 2	197 18 0	17 7 2	
Cape Breton				
Guadaloupe				
Hudson's Bay	13,659 10 5	3,984 4 4	9,675 6 1	
Jamaica	705,675 13 6	126,745 17 3	578,929 16 3	
Montserrat	39,382 12 4	1,509 19 5	37,872 12 11	
Nevis	68,431 4 3	1,156 6 4	67,274 17 11	
Newfoundland	46,753 18 8	31,746 19 1	15,006 19 7	
New Providence				
Nova Scotia				
Quebec				
St. Croix				
St. Christopher's	263,324 19 8	14,000 4 8	249,324 15 0	
Tortola				
	From Christmas 1759, to Christmas 1760. 1 Geo. III.			
Africa	39,410 14 0	345,546 0 1		306,135 6 1
East India	1,785,679 11 1	1,161,670 6 0	624,009 5 1	
Antigua	159,162 19 0	191,117 13 2		31,954 14 2
Barbadoes	223,716 12 11	269,449 6 2		45,732 13 3
Bermudas	70 12 7	16,115 14 8		16,045 2 1
Cape Breton	5 8 3	11,048 14 5		11,043 6 2
Guadaloupe	424,366 18 4	118,569 5 10	305,797 12 6	
Hudson's Bay	9,142 12 5	4,959 15 10	4,182 16 7	
Jamaica	1,034,283 3 8	585,771 13 2	448,511 10 6	
Montserrat	75,936 12 4	23,143 13 4	52,792 19 0	
Nevis	45,750 11 0	20,390 9 8	25,360 1 4	
Newfoundland	26,360 2 4	56,643 1 6		30,282 19 2
New Providence	1,730 0 7		1,730 0 7	
Nova Scotia	701 7 4	52,767 2 2		52,065 14 10
Quebec	2,154 18 5	51,629 18 5		49,475 0 0
St. Croix		1,657 3 7		1,657 3 7
St. Christopher's	292,470 19 2	149,142 4 10	143,328 14 4	
Tortola	30,351 19 0	397 18 7	29,954 0 5	

TABLE 2

THE OFFICIAL VALUE OF THE IMPORTS AND EXPORTS OF GREAT BRITAIN. [Figures for Scotland omitted]

Countries etc.	*From Christmas 1775 to Christmas 1776*						*From Christmas 1782 to Christmas 1783*					
	Imports			*Exports*			*Imports*			*Exports*		
	£	*s*	*d*	£	*s*	*d*	£	*s*	*d*	£	*s*	*d*
Africa	99,674	13	11	470,779	1	1	47,860	12	9	787,563	8	0
East India	1,468,077	13	7	726,398	8	5	1,301,495	13	3	701,473	18	8
Hudson's Bay	6,634	12	3	5,778	2	5	7,554	19	1	7,098	18	0
Newfoundland	50,442	3	1	130,280	4	1	58,377	9	7	149,563	3	2
Cape Breton				164	11	0						
Quebec	54,925	13	4	446,928	2	11	81,136	6	10	370,319	15	6
Nova Scotia	6,529	15	2	245,036	10	10	2,904	19	5	205,330	5	0
Florida	30,628	15	4	174,175	3	1	25,638	10	8	25,356	16	4
Anguilla							10,680	16	3			
Antigua	297,535	14	9	169,436	10	9	77,022	6	1	120,334	3	5
Barbados	191,531	19	1	142,134	11	6	106,766	5	10	151,464	14	11
Bermuda	238	11	4	11,413	3	11	7,446	6	9	86,019	15	0
Dominica	257,775	15	3	64,697	18	6	80,701	7	5	42,830	12	3
Grenada	370,884	9	0	163,366	11	6	217,743	10	6	49,355	17	9
Jamaica	1,359,033	2	1	632,315	5	9	1,578,881	3	10	950,075	16	10
Montserrat	64,521	19	5	22,938	12	8	39,166	15	6	13,686	11	10
Nevis	93,231	11	5	23,836	14	5	35,564	13	1	11,913	16	1
New Providence	2,950	15	2	5,422	16	8	1,356	7	2	2,527	17	8
St. Croix	16,869	1	3	406	3	0						
St. Eustathius	709	13	6	1,656	9	2						
St. Christopher's	293,482	0	7	160,635	2	10	211,849	4	0	65,079	4	2
St. Lucia							173,152	8	3	44,442	13	7
St. Martins							1,071	14	9	31	15	0
St. Thomas	1,675	17	8	2,388	8	7	8,713	19	8	57,526	1	5
St. Vincents	135,919	14	2	45,993	11	6	74,077	3	7	20,404	10	8
Tobago	83,066	19	0	21,913	13	7	114,925	0	2	13,386	15	2
Tortola	44,451	10	5	28,841	18	5	112,772	5	6	41,149	8	0

C. GENERAL ORGANIZATION

226A–C. Orders in Council regulating the powers of the Board of Trade 1752, 1761 and 1766

(*Acts of the Privy Council, Colonial Series*, IV, pp. 154–156, 157; V, pp. 3–4.)

226A. Order in Council of 11 March 1752

This was the result of the vigorous policy of Halifax, President of the Board of Trade, 1748–1761, who sought to end the confusion caused by dual management of colonial affairs by the Board and the Secretary of State for the Southern Department, and to create an American department. It gave the Board power to nominate to all colonial offices and to control all correspondence with the colonial governors; though in practice any correspondence concerning foreign policy had to be sent to the Secretary of State for his opinion before it was answered. The Board thus became a really effective body under its President, who, though not a member of the Cabinet, attended all Cabinet meetings when colonial affairs were being discussed.

[1752]

11 Mar. [The following Order drafted by the Committee on 24 Feb. is issued:] His Majesty having taken into His Consideration the flourishing State and Condition of the Manufactures Trade and Commerce of these Kingdoms and also the State and Condition of His Colonys and Plantations in America and elsewhere with respect as well to their Trade and Commerce as to their Civil Policy and Government; And Whereas it doth Appear to His Majesty that the said Colonys and Plantations have of late Years been greatly improved the Wealth of his Subjects much increased and the Navigation of these Kingdoms extended by the Mutual Intercourse between them and the said Colonys and Plantations by the Trade and Commerce arising therefrom. And His Majesty being sensible of how great Importance it is to his Crown and Government and how much it will contribute to the Satisfaction Convenience and Advantage of His Subjects that all due care be taken and proper and necessary Regulations made for the further Improvement and Extension of the Manufactures and commerce of these Kingdoms and for the Encouragement Protection and Security of the said Colonys and Plantations His Majesty [orders that the Board of Trade] do with all Diligence care and Concern Apply themselves to a faithfull and vigorous Execution and Discharge of all the Trusts and Powers vested in them by their Commission under the Great Seal; And Whereas nothing can more effectually tend to the Peace Welfare and good Government of the said Colonys and Plantations than the appointment of able Discreet and Prudent persons to be Governors Lieutenant Governors and other Officers and Magistrates It is therefore hereby further Ordered that the said Lords Commissioners for Trade and Plantations do from time to time as Vacancys shall happen by Deaths or Removals present unto His Majesty in Council for his Approbation the Names of such persons as the said Commissioners from the best of their Judgment and Information shall think duly qualified to be Governors or Deputy Governors or to be of His Majestys Council or of His Counsel at Law or Secretarys in the respective Plantations and likewise to present to His Majesty for his Approbation the names of all other Officers which have been or may

be found necessary for the Administration of Justice and the Execution of Government there excepting only such as are or may be under the Direction and Regulation of His Majestys Customs and Revenues and such as are or may be under the Directions and Authority of the Lords Commissioners of the Admiralty; And when any persons shall have been Approved by His Majesty in Council for any of the above-mentioned Offices The said Lords Commissioners shall (unless His Majesty shall otherwise Direct) prepare and make out proper Draughts of such Commissions Warrants or Instructions as may be thought necessary to be given to such Officers in Order to be laid before His Majesty in Council for His Royal Approbation And when any persons shall be presented to His Majesty for any of the other Offices of an Inferior nature not judged necessary to be laid before his Majesty in Council and yet shall have otherwise received His Majestys Approbation The said Lords Commissioners shall in those Cases (unless His Majesty shall otherwise Direct) prepare and make out proper Draughts of Commissions or Warrants necessary to be given to such Officers in Order to be laid before His Majesty for His Royal Authority accordingly. And it is hereby further Ordered that the said Lords Commissioners for Trade and Plantations do Execute and perform all other things necessary or proper for answering the Intention of the said Commission. And whereas the Governors of all His Majestys Colonys and Plantations in America more immediately under His Majestys Government are in particular Cases as well as in general directed by His Majestys Instructions to transmit unto His Majesty by One of His Principal Secretarys of State and to the Commissioners for Trade and Plantations Accounts from time to time of all their proceedings and of the Condition of Affairs within their respective Governments. And Whereas it will tend to the Benefit of the said Colonys the ease and convenience of His Majestys Subjects and the greater regularity and Dispatch of Business if the Correspondence be confined and pass through but One Channel. It is therefore further Ordered that the said Lords Commissioners do prepare the Draught of an Additional Instruction to be sent to the Governors of all His Majestys said Colonys and Plantations respectively signifying His Majestys pleasure that in all Cases wherein by His Majestys Instructions they are directed to transmit any particular or General Accounts of their Proceedings or of matters relative to their Governments they do for the future transmit the same to the Lords Commissioners for Trade and Plantations only in Order that they may be laid before His Majesty Provided nevertheless that whenever any Occurrencys shall happen within their respective Governments of such a Nature and Importance as may require His Majestys more immediate Directions by One of His principal Secretarys of State and also upon all Occasions and in all Affairs whereon they may receive His Majestys Orders by One of His Principal Secretarys of State the said Governors shall in all such Cases transmit to the Secretary of State only an Account of all such Occurrencys and of their Proceedings relative to such Orders and it is hereby further Ordered that a Copy of this Order be transmitted to the said Lords Commissioners for Trade and Plantations to be entered upon the Books of the Plantation Office and that the said Commissioners do likewise transmit Copys thereof to the Governors of His Majestys Colonys and plantations respectively to the End that all persons concerned may Govern themselves accordingly.

226B. Order in Council of 15 May 1761

This revoked the Order of 1752, except the provision that the Board of Trade should carry on the correspondence with the colonial governors. Colonial patronage was returned to the Southern Secretaryship, now held by Pitt. The Order made no changes in the internal organization of the Board, but the Board's prestige was much lowered, especially as the vigorous Halifax was replaced as President by Samuel Sandys, an old man of no great political reputation.

[1761]
15 May. [On consideration of the order of 11 March, 1752, his Majesty] is hereby pleased with the Advice of the Privy Council, to revoke and repeal the same in every part, except that which Relates to the Correspondence to be carried on between the Lords Commissioners for Trade and Plantations and the Governors of his Majestys Colonies, which is still to be carried on in the same manner prescribed by the additional Instruction which was directed by the above Order of Council of his late Majesty of 11th March 1752 to be prepared and sent to the Governors of all His Majestys Colonies and Plantations respectively. And his Majesty doth hereby signify his further Pleasure, that the Lords Commissioners for Trade and Plantations do Cause a Copy of this Order to be Entered upon the Books of the Plantation Office; And that one of his Majestys Principal Secretarys of State do cause Copys thereof to be sent to the Governors of his Majestys Colonies and Plantations in America to the End that all Persons concerned may govern themselves accordingly.

226C. Order in Council of 8 August 1766

The increasing difficulties with the American colonies made the necessity to co-ordinate control of colonial affairs obvious. The Rockingham ministry considered the possibility of creating an American Secretary, but nothing was done. When Pitt came into office in 1766 he adopted the other alternative of placing control entirely in the hands of the Southern Secretary and making the Board of Trade no more than a source of information and a Board of report. The Order of 1766 completely revoked that of 1752.

[1766]
8 Aug. Whereas there was this Day laid before His Majesty at the Board an Order made by His late Majesty in Council on the 11th Day of March 1752 containing several Rules and Regulations relating to His Majestys Colonies and plantations in America particularly with respect to the Correspondence to be carried on between the Lords Commissioners for Trade and plantations and the Governors of the said Colonies and plantations respectively; His Majesty taking the afore-mentioned Order into His Consideration; Is hereby pleased with the Advice of His Privy Council, to revoke and repeal the same and every Clause, Article and thing therein contained; and His Majesty doth hereby Signify His further pleasure that the Lords Commissioners for Trade and plantations do Cause a Copy of this Order to be entered upon the Books of the plantation-office, and that one of His Majestys principal Secretaries of State do Cause Copies thereof to be sent to the Governors of His Majestys Colonies and Plantations in America to the End that all persons concerned may govern themselves accordingly. And His Majesty doth hereby further Order that the said Lords Commissioners for Trade and plantations do prepare the Draft of an Additional Instruction to be sent to the Governors and Commanders in Chief of all His Majestys said Colonies and plantations respectively as well in America as Elsewhere revoking

and annulling all and every such part and parts of the General Instructions to them as do direct the said Governors to Correspond in matters relative to their said Governments respectively with the said Lords Commissioners for Trade and plantations only, and signifying His Majestys Pleasure, that in all Cases where the said Governors are directed and required to transmit any particular or General Accounts of their proceedings or of Matters relative to their Government they do for the future transmit the same to His Majesty by one of his Majestys principal Secretaries of State; and also transmit Duplicates thereof to the Lords Commissioners for Trade and Plantations, for their Information, Except in Cases of a Secret Nature.

227. William Knox on the status of the American Secretary, 1775

(*Hist. MSS. Comm. Various Collections*, VI, *Knox MSS.*, pp. 256–257.)

By 1768 it had become clear that American affairs required a separate Secretary, and Lord Hillsborough was appointed American Secretary. This did not cause any immediate change in the procedure of the Board of Trade, which continued to function under the Order in Council of 1766, the American Secretary simply taking the place of the Secretary of State for the Southern Department. Neither Hillsborough nor his successor, Lord Dartmouth, seem to have been regarded as full Secretaries of State by their colleagues, and their commissions of appointment limited their activities to American affairs. The commission of appointment of Lord George Germain in 1775 was, however, the same as that of the other secretaries, and he was accepted by them as of equal status. Hillsborough, Dartmouth and Germain till 1779 also held the office of President of the Board of Trade.

The writer of the following memorandum was William Knox (1732–1810), Under-Secretary for the American Colonies, 1770–1782.

Memoranda by William Knox, November, 1775

. . . [He describes various difficulties over appointments in 1775.]

Lord Weymouth accepting the Southern Department made all easy. Lord Dartmouth then got the Privy Seal, and Lord George Germain became the American Secretary. A difficulty had formerly been made by Lord Weymouth of considering the American Secretary as a Secretary of State. Lord Hillsborough had never been so considered by the other Secretaries; he was only held to be first Lord of Trade with Seals and Cabinet; his commission confined his efficiency to the Colonies. Lord Dartmouth's commission was the same, and Lord Weymouth had refused the Department when Lord Dartmouth got it on that very account. Lord George Germain being a commoner, it became necessary to make some alteration in his commission, for the former commissions made it a new office, and consequently excluded him from the House of Commons.[1] A commission in the terms of those of the other Secretaries obviated this difficulty, for there were precedents of three persons being at the same time Secretaries of State. A difficulty in giving Lord George Germain such a commission 'twas apprehended, would be made by Lord Weymouth and Lord Suffolk. Lord Suffolk, however, we supposed, would acquiesce for the sake of his own plan,[2] and with him the Solicitor-General[3] would concur. The Attorney-General[4] and Lord Weymouth were supposed to object together.

[1] Under the Regency Act of 1707. See vol. VIII of these *Documents*, No. 45.

[2] Lord Suffolk was the other Secretary of State. He wanted Germain in the Cabinet to increase his own strength there.

[3] Alexander Wedderburn (1733–1805), later Lord Loughborough.

[4] Edward Thurlow (1731–1806), later Lord Thurlow, like Weymouth, a supporter of the Bedford party.

The King, by one of those minute strokes for which he is so eminent, removed all difficulty. When the Council was met to swear in the new officers, Lord Gower, being Lord President, moved the King, of course, that Lord Weymouth might be sworn Secretary of State. The King replied, "there are two Secretaries of State to be sworn; let them both be sworn together," which was done accordingly. Lord Weymouth perfectly understood the King, and finding his Majesty would have Lord George considered as a Secretary made the best of it by taking Lord George Germain aside, and telling him he understood there was some difficulty about his commission, but to him there appeared to be none, for if this commission was in the same terms as the others, there could be no objection to his sitting in the House of Commons. . . .

228. Lord Mansfield's judgment in *Campbell* v. *Hall*, 1774

(*State Trials*, XX, pp. 322–323, 328–330.)

Alexander Campbell had bought land in the island of Grenada, after its cession to Great Britain by France at the Peace of Paris in 1763. In July 1764 a duty of 4½ per cent on goods exported from the island was imposed by letters patent, thus bringing Grenada into line with the other British West Indies, and in 1765 this duty was collected from Campbell on sugar exported by him, the collector being William Hall. Campbell subsequently sued Hall for the recovery of the money, on the grounds that the duty was not legal because it was imposed by letters patent and not by the Assembly of Grenada, now established as promised to all the ceded territories by the Proclamation of 1763. (See vol. IX of these *Documents*, No. 98.) The case established the principle that once the Crown had set up a legislative assembly in a conquered territory its prerogative power of levying taxation in that territory lapsed.

November 28. Judgment of the Court [of King's Bench] was this day given by lord Mansfield, as follows:

Lord *Mansfield*. . . . Upon the whole of the case this general question arises, being the substance of what is submitted to the Court by the verdict: "Whether these letters patent of the 20th of July 1764, are good and valid to abrogate the French duties, and in lieu thereof to impose this duty of four and a half per cent." which is paid by all the Leeward islands subject to his majesty.

That the letters are void has been contended at the bar, upon two points.

1st, That although they had been made before the proclamation, the king by his prerogative could not have imposed them.

2dly, That, although the king had sufficient authority before the 20th of July 1764, he had divested himself of that authority by the proclamation.

A great deal has been said and authorities cited–relative to propositions in which both sides exactly agree, or which are too clear to be denied. The stating of these will lead us to the solution of the first point.

1st, A country conquered by the British arms becomes a dominion of the king in right of his crown, and therefore necessarily subject to the legislative power of the parliament of Great Britain.

2dly, The conquered inhabitants once received into the conqueror's protection become subjects; and are universally to be considered in that light, not as enemies or aliens.

3dly, Articles of capitulation upon which the conquest is surrendered, and treaties of peace by which it is ceded, are sacred and inviolable, according to their true intent.
4thly, The law and legislation of every dominion equally affects all persons and property within the limits thereof, and is the true rule for the decision of all questions which arise there: whoever purchases, sues or lives there, puts himself under the laws of the place, and in the situation of its inhabitants. An Englishman in Minorca or the isle of Man, or the plantations, has no distinct right from the natives while he continues there.
5thly, Laws of a conquered country continue until they are altered by the conqueror. The justice and antiquity of this maxim is unconvertible; and the absurd exception as to pagans, in Calvin's case, shews the universality of the maxim. The exception could not exist before the Christian aera, and in all probability arose from the mad enthusiasm of the crusades.–In the present case the capitulation expressly provides and agrees, that they shall continue to be governed by their present laws, until his majesty's pleasure be further known.
6thly, If the king has power (and, when I say the king, I mean in this case to be understood "without concurrence of parliament") to make new laws for a conquered country, this being a power subordinate to his own authority, as a part of the supreme legislature in parliament, he can make none which are contrary to fundamental principles; none excepting from the laws of trade or authority of parliament, or privileges exclusive of his other subjects.

The present proclamation is an act of this subordinate legislative power: . . .

. . . But upon full consideration we are all of opinion that before the 20th of July, 1764, the king had precluded himself from an exercise of the legislative authority by virtue of his prerogative, which he had before over the island of Grenada.

The first material instrument is the proclamation of the 7th of October 1763. See what it is that the king says, and with what view he says it; how and to what he engages himself and pledges his word. "Whereas it will greatly contribute to the speedy settling our said new governments, that our loving subjects should be informed of our paternal care for the security of the liberties and properties of those who are and shall become inhabitants thereof; we have thought fit to publish and declare by this our proclamation, that we have in the letters patent under our great seal of Great Britain, by which the said governments are constituted, given express power and direction to our governors of our said colonies respectively, that, so soon as the state and circumstances of our said colonies will admit thereof, they shall, with the advice and consent of the members of our council, summon and call general assemblies" (and then follow the directions for that purpose.) And to what end? "To make, constitute and ordain laws, statutes, and ordinances, for the public peace, welfare and good of our said colonies (of which this of Grenada is one) and of the people and inhabitants thereof, as near as may be agreeable to the laws of England."

With what view is the promise reciting the commission actually given? To invite settlers; to invite subjects. Why? The reason is given. They may think their liberties and properties more secure when they have a legislative assembly. The governor and council depending on the king he can recall them at pleasure, and give a new frame to the constitution; but not so of the other which has a negative on those parts of the legislature which depend on the king.

Therefore that assurance is given them for the security of their liberties and properties, and with a view to invite them to go and settle there after this proclamation that assured them of the constitution under which they were to live.

The next act is of the 26th of March 1764, which, the constitution having been established by proclamation, invites further, such as shall be disposed to come and purchase, to live under the constitution. It states certain terms and conditions on which the allotments were to be taken, established with a view to permanent colonization and the encrease and cultivation of the new settlement.

In farther confirmation, on the 29th of April 1764, three months before the impost in question was imposed, there is an actual commission to governor Melville, to call an assembly as soon as the state and circumstances of the island should admit.–You will observe in the proclamation there is no legislature reserved to be exercised by the king, or by the governor and council under his authority, or in any other method or manner until the assembly should be called: the promise imports the contrary; for whatever construction is to be put upon it, (which perhaps it may be somewhat difficult to pursue through all the cases to which it may be applied) it apparently considers laws then in being in the island, and to be administered by courts of justice; not an interposition of legislative authority between the time of the promise and of calling the assembly.

It does not appear from the special verdict when the first assembly was called; it must have been in about a year at farthest from the governor's arrival, for the jury find he arrived in December 1764, and that an assembly was held about the latter end of the year 1765. So that there appears to have been nothing in the state and circumstances of the island to prevent calling an assembly.

We therefore think by the two proclamations and the commission to governor Melville, the king had immediately and irrevocably granted to all who did or should inhabit, or who had or should have property in the island of Grenada–in general to all whom it should concern–that the subordinate legislation over the island should be exercised by the assembly with the governor and council, in like manner as in the other provinces under the king.

And therefore, though the right of the king to have levied taxes on a conquered country, subject to him in right of his crown, was good, and the duty reasonable, equitable and expedient, and according to the finding of the verdict paid in Barbadoes, and all the other Leeward islands; yet by the inadvertency of the king's servants in the order in which the several instruments passed the office, (for the patent of the 20th of July 1764, for raising the impost stated, should have been first) the order is inverted, and the last we think contrary to and a violation of the first; and therefore void.

How proper soever the thing may be respecting the object of these letters patent, it can only now be done (to use the words of sir Philip Yorke and sir Clement Wearg) "by an act of assembly of the island, or by the parliament of Great Britain."

D. AMERICA

(a) THE THIRTEEN COLONIES

[The history of these colonies to 1776 is the subject of vol. IX of these *Documents*. The extracts given below are chosen to illustrate English opinion on the issue between the American colonies and the mother country.]

229. Debates in the House of Commons on the repeal of the Stamp Act, January–February 1766[1]

(Horace Walpole, *Memoirs of the Reign of George III*, ed. G. F. Russell Barker, II, pp. 184–188, 191–193, 210–212.)

Walpole was himself a member of Parliament at this time, and his accounts of debates are perhaps the most valuable part of his *Memoirs*. In these debates on America, all upheld the sovereignty of Parliament over the colonies, but Pitt held that it did not include the right of taxation. The Rockingham ministry held that it did, but that it was not expedient to insist upon that right. The attitudes adopted by individuals and groups over the Stamp Act remained substantially their attitudes throughout the American crisis.

On the 14th of January the Houses met. Lord Villiers[2] and Mr. Thomas Townshend[3] moved the Addresses. Seymour[4] and Bamber Gascoyne,[5] Nugent[6] and Stanley,[7] attacked the Ministers for their want of spirit against the Americans, and for suffering the authority of Parliament to be called in question by the rebellious Colonies. "The tax," said Stanley, "was not a twentieth part of what they could afford to pay; but that was not the point: he had rather have a peppercorn to acknowledge our sovereignty, than millions paid into the Treasury without it." As he was speaking, Mr. Pitt appeared in the House, and took the first opportunity of opening his mind, not only on the Stamp Act, but on the general situation of affairs. Though he had on other occasions, perhaps, exerted more powers of eloquence (though he was much admired now even in that light), yet the novelty and boldness of his doctrines, the offence he gave by them at home, and the delirium which they excited in America, made his speech rank in celebrity with his most famous orations. For these reasons, and as the repeal of the Stamp Act was the last great question on which he figured in the House of Commons, I shall be more particular in the detail of it, having received authentic notes from one that was present at the delivery, and therefore more to be depended on than the printed copy.

He had come to town that morning, he said, *unconcerted* and unconnected, and not having arrived early enough, desired to hear the proposed Address read, which being

[1] For the Stamp Act and an account of the debate upon it on 11 January 1765, see vol. IX of these *Documents*, No. 101; for the repeal and the Declaratory Act of 1766, see Nos. 112 and 113 in that volume.

[2] (1735–1805), later fourth earl of Jersey.

[3] (1733–1800), later first Viscount Sydney, a Lord of the Treasury.

[4] Henry Seymour (1729–1805), M.P. for Totnes.

[5] (1725–1791), M.P. for Midhurst.

[6] Robert Nugent (1702–1788), later Earl Nugent, M.P. for Bristol; President of the Board of Trade as Lord Clare, 1766–1768.

[7] Hans Stanley (1720?–1780), M.P. for Southampton.

done, he thought it, he said, a very proper one, though he should wish to separate from it the unhappy measure of the Stamp Act. No day had been so important since the time, a little above a century ago, when it had been debated whether we should be bond or free. More than ordinary circumspection was requisite on that nice, difficult, and hardly debateable question. Truth did extort from him that the compliment of *early* applied to the present meeting of Parliament did *not* belong to the American part of the question. *He* would have called Parliament sooner. He then pronounced that *the House of Commons did not represent North America*. It had, as the Legislature, not as representatives, taxed North America. For him, the question was too hard; but popular, or unpopular, he would do as he thought right. Was there a set of men in this country by whom he had not been sacrificed? He saw before him a set of gentlemen whom he respected–some of them his old acquaintance; these were part of the Administration: but were there not other parts? One day one man was uppermost, another day, another man. Was there not an invisible influence from more quarters than one. No matter whence they came, if they did mischief–God knew whither this country was going! Had we not seen one Ministry changed after another, and passing away like shadows? All that could be done for this country was to place it in a safe situation. When he served his Majesty, he had mentioned it as his advice that he wished to have that part of the Act of Settlement enforced, which directs that every Minister should sign his opinion. Liberty formerly was not made use of as a horse to ride into employment upon; they rode into the field upon it, and left their bones there. As he might be deprived by ill health from attending his duty in the House when this question should come on, he begged leave to deliver his opinion then. He would repeal the Stamp Act immediately, and accompany it with a bill declaratory of their own high rights and privileges over that country, which should be done upon the most extensive plan. But he would repeat it, *That House had no right to lay an internal tax upon America, that country not being represented. . . .*

Mr. Grenville said, the Stamp Act had been thoroughly considered, not hurried at the end of a Session. It had passed through the different stages in full Houses with, he thought, only one division on it. "Look," said he, "into Magna Charta; you will see we have a right to tax America; and that all laws are enacted by Commune Consilium Regni: and will the honourable gentleman then say we have not a right – " He was interrupted by Pitt; and, after some squabbling and explanation, Grenville continued: "Why then I understand the gentleman's opinion to be, that you have a right, on every other occasion except to lay an internal tax – " Being again interrupted, Mr. Pitt begged to be indulged in a few words by way of reply, and then, as was common with him, launched out into a new harangue: "Though the gentleman," said he, "is armed at all points with Acts of Parliament, yet I will venture to say that if he was to take the three first words he might find in a dictionary, they would be full as much to the purpose as his Commune Consilium Regni. Does he consider that, at the time he speaks of, the barons had all the land–though indeed the Church, God bless it! had then a third, when the bishops, mitred abbots, and such things, had influence? I laugh, sir, I laugh, when it is said this country cannot coerce America; but will you do it upon a point that is intricate, and in a matter of right

NORTH AMERICA
SHOWING THE PRINCIPAL PLACES MENTIONED IN THE DOCUMENTS

that is disputed? Will you, after the Peace you have made, and the small pittance of the fishery that is left you, will you sheathe your sword in the bowels of your brothers, the Americans? You may coerce and conquer, but when they fall, they will fall like the strong man embracing the pillars of this Constitution, and bury it in ruin with them. Gentlemen may double down Acts of Parliament till they are dog'seared, it will have no effect upon me. I am past the time of life to be turning to books to know whether I love liberty or not. There are two or three lines of Prior applicable to the present question, supposing America in the situation of a wife: they are these, where he says:–

"Be to her faults a little blind,
Be to her virtues very kind,
And clap the padlock on her mind."

. . . On the 27th of January, Mr. Cooke, of Middlesex, presented a petition from some of the North-American provinces assembled in Congress, against the Stamp Act. Jenkinson and Dyson,[1] placemen, but creatures of Lord Bute, opposed receiving it; as did Nugent and Ellis[2] who called it a dangerous federal union. Dowdswell,[3] the new Chancellor of the Exchequer, agreed with them, as there was nothing, he said, in the petition, but what had been already received in others from the separate provinces, and therefore he wished Cooke to withdraw what he had offered. Mr. Pitt warmly undertook the protection of the petition, which he affirmed was innocent, dutiful, and respectful. He did not know the time, he said, when he had been counsellor to timid councils; but on this occasion should have thought it happy to have made this the first act of harmony. He painted the Americans as people who, in an ill-fated hour, had left this country to fly from the Star-chamber and High Commission Courts. The desert smiled upon them in comparison of this country. It was the evil genius of this country that had riveted amongst them this union, now called *dangerous and federal*. He did not see but honest Wildman's[4] or Newmarket might be talked of in the same strain. This country upon occasion has its meetings, and nobody objects to them; but the names of six or eight Americans are to be big with danger. He could not guess by the turn of the debate, whether the Administration intended lenity or not. To him lenity was recommended by every argument. He would emphatically hear the Colonies upon this their petition. The right of representation and taxation always went together, and should never be separated. Except for the principles of Government, records were out of the question. "*You have broken*," continued he, "*the original compact if you have not a right of taxation.*" The repeal of the Stamp Act was an inferior consideration to receiving this petition.

Sir Fletcher Norton[5] rose with great heat, and said, He could hardly keep his temper at some words that had fallen from the right honourable gentleman. He had said, that the original compact had been broken between us and America, if the

[1] Charles Jenkinson (1727–1808), later first earl of Liverpool, Secretary to the Treasury; Jermiah Dyson (1722–1776), Commissioner of the Board of Trade.

[2] Welbore Ellis (1713–1802), later first Baron Mendip.

[3] William Dowdeswell (1721–1775), M.P. for Worcester.

[4] A club in Albemarle Street.

[5] (1716–1789), later first Baron Grantley; Attorney-General in the Grenville ministry; Speaker, 1770.

House had not the right of taxation. Pitt rose to explain–Norton continued; "The gentleman now says, I mistook his words; I do not now understand them." Pitt interrupted him angrily, and said, "I did say the Colony-compact would be broken–and what then"? Norton replied, "The gentleman speaks out now, and I understand him; and if the House go along with me the gentleman will go to another place."[1] Pitt at this looked with the utmost contempt, tossed up his chin, and cried "Oh! oh!–oh! oh!" "I will bear that from no man," said Norton: "changing their place, did not make Englishmen change their allegiance. I say the gentleman sounds the trumpet to rebellion; or would he have the strangers in the gallery go away with these his opinions? He has chilled my blood at the idea." "The gentleman," rejoined Pitt, "says I have chilled his blood: I shall be glad to meet him in any place with the same opinions, when his blood is warmer." . . .

On the 21st of February the House of Commons came at last to the great question of the repeal of the Stamp Act. The Opposition endeavoured to fight it off by pretending fresh accounts were that very morning arrived of a disposition in some of the Colonies, particularly New York, to submit to the Act; from whence was inferred the inutility of repealing it. But this was properly treated as the lie of the day; and had no effect. General Conway[2] moved for leave to bring in a bill to repeal that Act; and drew an affecting and alarming picture of the mischiefs it had occasioned and threatened. All orders for goods from this country were stopped: the North Americans would neither take any more, nor pay for what they had had. Eight merchants, who had received orders to the amount of 400,000l., had received counter-orders. The debt to those merchants amounted to 950,000l. Antigua was near ruined by famine. The tax fell chiefly on the poor, particularly on the poor of Georgia. At home, the situation of our manufacturers was most calamitous. Nottingham had dismissed a thousand hands: Leicester, Leeds, and other towns in proportion. Three in ten of the labourers of Manchester were discharged. The trade of England was not only stopped, but in danger of being lost. If trade suffered, land would suffer in its turn. Petitions would have been sent from every trading town in England, but that they apprehended that the very hearing of their petitions would delay the repeal. Every part of the Act breathed oppression. It annihilated juries; and the Admiralty courts might drag a man three hundred miles from his habitation. The fisheries were in equal danger. The right of taxation he did not doubt would be given for us in Westminster Hall; but the conflict would ruin both countries. We had but five thousand men in three thousand miles of territory: the Americans an hundred and fifty thousand fighting men. If we did not repeal the Act, he did not doubt but France and Spain would declare war, and protect the Americans. As the Colonies would not take our manufactures, they would set up of their own. He had a piece of cloth, he said, in his pocket, made at Philadelphia, as cheap as in England. Would the House risk the whole for so trifling an object as this Act modified?

I will not detail the rest of the debate, the essence of which had been so much

[1] *i.e.* to the Bar of the House for breach of privilege.

[2] Henry Seymour Conway (1721–1795), Walpole's cousin; Secretary of State for the Southern Department, which included the American colonies.

anticipated. The great, and no trifling argument on the other side, was the danger from being beaten out of an Act of Parliament, because disagreeable to those on whom it fell; and the high probability that the Americans would not stop there; but, presuming on their own strength, and the timidity of the English Government, would proceed to extort a repeal of the Act of Navigation. Grenville particularly exposed the futility of declaring a right which the Government would not dare to exert: and he pushed the Ministers home with giving up the brightest jewel of the Crown, the right of taxation. How would they justify it to his Majesty?–how to future Administrations? Mr. Pitt, who acknowledged his perplexity in making an option between two such ineligible alternatives, pronounced, however, for the repeal, as due to the liberty of unrepresented subjects, and in gratitude to their having supported England through three wars. He begged to stand a feeble isthmus between English partiality and American violence. He would give the latter satisfaction in this point only. If America afterwards should dare to resist, he would second a resolution of the most vigorous nature to compel her with every man and every ship in this country.

At half an hour past one in the morning the committee divided, and the motion was carried by 275 to 167. This majority, though the question was but a prelude to the repeal, decided the fate of that great political contest. And though Lord Rockingham with childish arrogance and indiscretion vaunted in the palace itself that he had carried the repeal against the King, Queen, Princess-dowager, Duke of York, Lord Bute, the Tories, the Scotch, and the Opposition, (and it was true he had,) yet in reality it was the clamour of trade, of the merchants, and of the manufacturing towns, that had borne down all opposition.[1] A general insurrection was apprehended as the immediate consequence of upholding the bill; the revolt of America, and the destruction of trade was the prospect in future. A nod from the Ministers would have let loose all the manufacturers of Bristol, Liverpool, Manchester, and such populous and discontented towns, who threatened to send hosts to Westminster to back their demand of repeal. As it was, the lobby of the House, the Court of Requests, and the avenues were beset with American merchants. As Mr. Conway went away they huzzaed him thrice, stopped him to thank and compliment him, and made a lane for his passage. When Mr. Pitt appeared, the whole crowd pulled off their hats, huzzaed, and many followed his chair home with shouts and benedictions. The scene changed on the sight of Grenville. The crown pressed on him with scorn and hisses. He, swelling with rage and mortification, seized the nearest man to him by the collar. Providentally the fellow had more humour than spleen–"Well, if I may not hiss," said he, "at least I may laugh,"–and laughed in his face. The jest caught–had the fellow been surly and resisted, a tragedy had probably ensued.

[1] For documents illustrating the opposition of the merchants to the Stamp Act, see vol. IX of these *Documents*, Nos. 111 and 112A.

230. Speech by Lord Mansfield in the House of Lords on the right of Parliament to tax the colonies, 10 February 1766

(*Parl. Hist.*, XVI, pp. 172–176.)

This speech was made on a resolution by the duke of Grafton that Parliament had authority to make laws binding the American colonies "in all cases whatever". In the course of the debate Lord Camden had argued, on the same lines as Pitt in the House of Commons, that Parliament had no right to tax the colonies, since they were not represented.

Lord Mansfield. I stand up to bring your lordships to the question before you, which is, whether the proposition made by the noble duke is, from what appears from our law and history, true or not true.

What has been wrote by those who have treated on the law of nature, or of other nations, in my opinion, is not at all applicable to the present question.

It is out of this question too, whether it is or is not expedient to repeal this act: out of this question too are the rules which are to guide the legislature in making a law. The law is made, and the question is, whether you had a right to make it.

I deny the proposition that parliament takes no man's property without his consent: it frequently takes private property without making what the owner thinks a compensation. If any lord makes objection to any part of the proposition, he ought to confine himself in his argument to the part he objects to, and not run into matters which do not relate to such objection.

I have, during the course of the debate on this great question, always wished to preserve unanimity among your lordships on every measure relating to America, and do verily believe that if every member of parliament had concurred in sentiments for the benefit of the whole, this great evil, as it now is, would have turned out for the advantage of the whole, and that the Americans, if they had time given them to cool, would have obeyed the law.

Your lordships must remember, upon the passing the Militia Act, how it was misrepresented, as a plot to send our subjects to America and Germany, and that the consequence of this was, that riots arose in several parts of the kingdom. A few of the rioters suffered death, but when people came to their cool senses, the act was obeyed.

I do not look upon Otis's pamphlet[1] in the light other lords may–that it is to be totally disregarded. It may be called silly and mad, but mad people, or persons who have entertained silly and mad ideas, have led the people to rebellion, and over-turned empires.

The proposition before your lordships has unhappily been attended with a difference of opinion in England. I shall therefore use my endeavours, in what I have to offer your lordships on this occasion, to quiet men's minds upon this subject.

In order to do this, I shall first lay down two propositions:

1st, That the British legislature, as to the power of making laws, represents the whole British empire, and has authority to bind every part and every subject without the least distinction, whether such subjects have a right to vote or not, or whether the law binds places within the realm or without.

[1] James Otis, *Right of the British Colonies asserted and proved* (1764).

2nd, That the colonists, by the condition on which they migrated, settled, and now exist, are more emphatically subjects of Great Britain than those within the realm; and that the British legislature have in every instance exercised their right of legislation over them without any dispute or question till the 14th of January last.

As to the 1st proposition:

In every government the legislative power must be lodged somewhere, and the executive must likewise be lodged somewhere.

In Great Britain the legislative is in parliament, the executive in the crown.

The parliament first depended upon tenures. How did representation by election first arise? Why, by favour of the crown. And the notion now taken up, that every subject must be represented by deputy, if he does not vote in parliament himself, is merely ideal.

At this day all the great companies here–the Bank, East India Company, and South Sea Company, have no representatives.

As to what has been said about the clergy–the fact is, that a demand made by them of right to tax themselves was supported by the Pope, and the king and parliament of those times were weak enough to admit of it; but this admission is no proof of the right.

No distinction ought to be taken between the authority of parliament, over parts within or without the realm; but it is an established rule of construction, that no parts without the realm are bound unless named in the act. And this rule establishes the right of parliament; for unless they had a right to bind parts out of the realm, this distinction would never have been made. . . .

As to the second proposition I laid out,

It must be granted that they migrated with leave as colonies, and therefore from the very meaning of the word were, are, and must be subjects, and owe allegiance and subjection to their mother country. . . .

I find in the Journals of the House of Commons that, upon a Bill for a free fishery being brought into that House, 19 James I, a doubt was thrown out, whether parliament had any thing to do in America. This doubt was immediately answered, I believe by Coke. The province is held of the manor of East Greenwich, and granted by charter under the great seal. This was thought a sufficient answer, and the Bill passed that House.

In the year 1650, during the Commonwealth, an act passed, avowing the subjection of the colonies to England.

The Act of Settlement is of England &c. and all the dominions thereto belonging. If Americans are not subject to English statutes, the Act of Settlement does not bind them.

But there are many statutes laying taxes in America; I know no difference between laying internal and external taxes; but if such difference should be taken, are not the acts giving duties, customs, and erecting a post office, to be considered as laying an internal tax?

In 1724, the assembly of Jamaica refused to raise taxes for their necessary support.

Application was made to the council by their agent here, and a reference to sir Clement Worge and lord Hardwicke, to know whether the king could not lay a tax. They gave their opinion, that if Jamaica was to be considered a conquered country, the king could lay taxes; if otherwise, the assembly must lay it, or it must be raised by act of parliament.

But this notion, my lords, is of a very modern date.

In December last the authority of parliament was not disputed; even on the 14th of Jan. no hint was given in this House, which was then very full, against that authority. This day is the first time we have heard of it in this House.

Before I conclude I will take the liberty of laying down one proposition, *viz.*

When the supreme power abdicates, the government is dissolved.

Take care, my lords, you do not abdicate your authority. In such an event, your lordships would leave the worthy and innocent, as well as the unworthy and guilty, to the same confusion and ruin.

231. Newspaper comment on the Stamp Act, January–February 1766

The following extracts are typical examples of newspaper comment at the time when American resistance to the Stamp Act, and the possible repeal of the Act were being discussed in Parliament. The American question was the chief political topic in the newspapers in the early months of 1766.

Against repeal.

(*Lloyd's Evening Post* (22 and 24 January 1766).)

The following appeared in the column headed POLITICAL CONTROVERSY, containing four or five letters in each number.

OUR American Colonists in vain attempt to justify their behaviour from the nature, manner, or form of their original constitution or charters. But as they are our relations and fellow-subjects, it is to be hoped and wished that they will endeavour, by their future good behaviour, to endear themselves to their mother country, instead of incurring her displeasure, contempt, or resentment, by an obstinate, despicable, and pitiful with-holding of a small contribution towards the public support, and carrying on an illicit trade in prejudice of the mother country, though lately at a very great charge and trouble in defending them against the French and Indians.

PHILOPOLITES M'ULADER.

THE trade of this kingdom with America produces annually about two millions of money; from which circumstance, I overheard a Gentleman at the Coffeehouse defend a repeal of the Stamp Act; because, as he alledged, one hundred thousand pounds a year (the greatest supposed produce of the tax) was not an object, when two millions were in danger. But this way of arguing is to the last degree absurd and fallacious. It is not for the paltry sum of one hundred thousand pounds a year that we are contending; but for the credit and welfare of the nation, together with the very essence of our excellent constitution. These are great and inestimable treasures, which no man, who loves his country, would be afraid to defend with the last drop of blood that he could drain from his heart.

ANTI-SEJANUS.[1]

MAGNA CHARTA says, "That the King engages not to raise any money on his subjects, but with the concurrence of the *states* of the realm." But it does not say, that every Englishman is to be exempted from taxation, who has not a right to vote for one of those states. In *counties*, for instance, the number of inhabitants is infinitely greater than those of the freeholders, who only have a right of voting for a Representative in Parliament; and yet ALL, without distinction, pay taxes. If the colonies are sufficiently represented to be liable to one kind of taxation, they are liable to the other. And this, I doubt not, will be considered as a clear and fundamental proposition, unless the colonists can show, that a *greater* or *different* authority is requisite to impose an internal than an external tax. That the Stamp-Act is the *first* internal tax, is not true; for the whole Post-office establishment is *internal*, and requires the payment of internal duties.

O.P.

In favour of repeal.

(*St. James's Chronicle*, 30 January and 11 February 1766.)

QUERY I

HOW many People may be reckoned employed in manufacturing and navigating the Two Millions Worth of Goods that we export to North America?

2. How much in Taxes may that Number of People be supposed to pay to Government in a Year?
3. How much per Annum will it cost the Nation to support those People when they are become entirely out of Employ?
4. Must not the Burthen of maintaining them chiefly fall on those of the landed Interest?
5. Must not the Deficiencies of Taxes, occasioned by their Ruin, be principally made good by the landed Gentlemen?
6. In what Degree will landed Property become affected, by such a Diminution of People as from the Loss of that Trade will be occasioned?
7. How far will all Kinds of Property, publick Credit, and Circulation, become injured by the Loss of annual Returns to the Amount of Two Millions?
8. How much will it cost the Nation to establish the Stamp-Act in North-America by Force of Arms?
9. How long a Time may it take effectually to do it, especially if other Nations should secretly, or openly, support them in their Resistance?

[1] Reverend James Scott, chaplain to Lord Sandwich.

10. Is it, or is it not, the Interest of France, Spain, Holland, and every other Country of Europe, at all Hazards, to support the Americans in a Revolt?
11. If the Revolts of the United Provinces of the Netherlands, Portugal and Corsica, could rationally have been foreseen to prove so successful as they have been?
12. If such in the Struggle, from unforeseen Causes, should be the Case with the Americans, what will be likely to prove the Effects thereof to Great Britain?

To the Printer of The S. J. CHRONICLE.

SIR,

IF the American Britons, in the Mis-apprehension of the Act of Taxation's being an Encroachment on their Rights, have withstood its Execution, in, most undoubtedly, an indefensible Manner, they are however, on their Principle of Liberty, rather wrong in the Form, than in the Spirit. One of the most despotic Princes in Asia, Antiochus the IIId. could write to certain Cities of his Dominions, exhorting them not to obey any Orders from him that should be contrary to their Privileges. Did this Condescension weaken or annul his Authority? Most certainly not. And this Fact is recorded by Plutarch, with great Propriety, as an Instance of a truly Royal Spirit. In the Light of Injustice then, false as that Light incontestably was, in which our Fellow-Subjects in America considered this Taxation, they were surely less to blame for their Resistance, than for those outrageous Lengths to which their Populace carried it, and which were not improbably instigated and fomented by such as had some sinister private Ends in throwing Things into Confusion, and in continuing that Confusion.

But how egregiously will such Incendaries, either in that Part of our Nation, or in this, be disappointed, if the Legislature should be of Opinion that there is infinitely the most Dignity and the most Consciousness of its just Power, in the tenderest Treatment of the Colonies, rather as of People under a momentary Delusion, than obnoxious to legal Vindictiveness! If the American Britons should obstinately persevere in the Opinions of their being in the right, as to the Cause at Bottom of their Resistance, what Way so efficacious as that of such a Lenity to bring them back at least to a Sense of their Wrong in the Excesses to which their Warmth of Spirit has betrayed them? . . .

232. Extract from Edmund Burke's speech on American Taxation, 19 April 1774

(*Works and Correspondence of Edmund Burke*, III (1852), pp. 177–178, 219–223.)

This famous speech was made in the House of Commons during the debates on the Tea Act of 1773 and the four Coercive Acts passed in 1774 as a result of the 'Boston Tea Party'. The Tea Act had reimposed the threepenny duty on tea originally imposed by Townshend's Revenue Act of 1767, and not repealed with the other Townshend duties in 1770; and also allowed the East India Company to export tea directly to the colonies. See vol. IX of these *Documents*, No. 115, for the Revenue Act of 1767, and No. 138 for the 'Intolerable Acts' of 1774. The following extract gives Burke's opening sentences and his peroration, and is taken from the published version of his speech.

SIR,

I agree, with the honourable gentleman who spoke last,[1] that this subject is not new in this House. Very disagreeably to this House, very unfortunately to this nation, and to the peace and prosperity of this whole empire, no topic has been more

[1] Charles Wolfran Cornwall, one of the Lords of the Treasury.

familiar to us. For nine long years, session after session, we have been lashed round and round this miserable circle of occasional arguments and temporary expedients. I am sure our heads must turn, and our stomachs nauseate with them. We have had them in every shape; we have looked at them in every point of view. Invention is exhausted; reason is fatigued; experience has given judgment; but obstinacy is not yet conquered. . . .

Let us, sir, embrace some system or other before we end this session. Do you mean to tax America, and to draw a productive revenue from thence? If you do, speak out; name, fix, ascertain, this revenue; settle its quantity; define its objects; provide for its collection; and then fight when you have something to fight for. If you murder–rob; if you kill, take possession; and do not appear in the character of madmen, as well as assassins, violent, vindictive, bloody, and tyrannical, without an object. But may better counsels guide you!

Again, and again, revert to your old principles–seek peace and ensue it–leave America, if she has taxable matter in her, to tax herself. I am not here going into the distinctions of rights, not attempting to mark their boundaries. I do not enter into these metaphysical distinctions; I hate the very sound of them. Leave the Americans as they anciently stood, and these distinctions, born of our unhappy contest, will die along with it. They and we, and their and our ancestors, have been happy under that system. Let the memory of all actions, in contradiction to that good old mode, on both sides, be extinguished for ever. Be content to bind America by laws of trade; you have always done it. Let this be your reason for binding their trade. Do not burden them by taxes; you were not used to do so from the beginning. Let this be your reason for not taxing. These are the arguments of states and kingdoms. Leave the rest to the schools; for there only they may be discussed with safety. But if, intemperately, unwisely, fatally, you sophisticate and poison the very source of government, by urging subtle deductions, and consequences odious to those you govern, from the unlimited and illimitable nature of supreme sovereignty, you will teach them by these means to call that sovereignty itself in question. When you drive him hard, the boar will surely turn upon the hunters. If that sovereignty and their freedom cannot be reconciled, which will they take? They will cast your sovereignty in your face. No body will be argued into slavery. Sir, let the gentlemen on the other side call forth all their ability; let the best of them get up, and tell me, what one character of liberty the Americans have, and what one brand of slavery they are free from, if they are bound in their property and industry, by all the restraints you can imagine on commerce, and at the same time are made pack-horses of every tax you choose to impose, without the least share in granting them. When they bear the burdens of unlimited monopoly, will you bring them to bear the burdens of unlimited revenue too? The Englishman in America will feel that this is slavery–that it is *legal* slavery, will be no compensation, either to his feelings or his understanding.

A noble lord,[1] who spoke some time ago, is full of the fire of ingenuous youth; and when he has modelled the ideas of a lively imagination by further experience, he will be an ornament to his country in either House. He has said, that the Americans

[1] Lord Carmarthen.

are our children, and how can they revolt against their parent? He says, that if they are not free in their present state, England is not free; because Manchester, and other considerable places, are not represented. So then, because some towns in England are not represented, America is to have no representative at all. They are "our children"; but when children ask for bread we are not to give a stone. Is it because the natural resistance of things, and the various mutations of time, hinders our government, or any scheme of government, from being any more than a sort of approximation to the right, is it therefore that the colonies are to recede from it infinitely? When this child of ours wishes to assimilate to its parent, and to reflect with a true filial resemblance the beauteous countenance of British liberty; are we to turn to them the shameful parts of our constitution? are we to give them our weakness for their strength? our opprobrium for their glory; and the slough of slavery, which we are not able to work off, to serve them for their freedom?

If this be the case, ask yourselves this question, Will they be content in such a state of slavery? If not, look to the consequences. Reflect how you are to govern a people, who think they ought to be free, and think they are not. Your scheme yields no revenue; it yields nothing but discontent, disorder, disobedience; and such is the state of America, that after wading up to your eyes in blood, you could only end just where you begun; that is, to tax where no revenue is to be found, to–my voice fails me; my inclination indeed carries me no farther–all is confusion beyond it.

Well, sir, I have recovered a little, and before I sit down I must say something to another point with which gentlemen urge us. What is to become of the Declaratory Act asserting the entireness of British legislative authority, if we abandon the practice of taxation?

For my part I look upon the rights stated in that act, exactly in the manner in which I viewed them on its very first proposition, and which I have often taken the liberty, with great humility, to lay before you. I look, I say, on the imperial rights of Great Britain, and the privileges which the colonists ought to enjoy under these rights, to be just the most reconcilable things in the world. The parliament of Great Britain sits at the head of her extensive empire in two capacities: one as the local legislature of this island, providing for all things at home, immediately, and by no other instrument than the executive power. The other, and I think her nobler capacity, is what I call her *imperial character*; in which, as from the throne of heaven, she superintends all the several inferior legislatures, and guides and controls them all, without annihilating any. As all these provincial legislatures are only co-ordinate with each other, they ought all to be subordinate to her; else they can neither preserve mutual peace, nor hope for mutual justice, nor effectually afford mutual assistance. It is necessary to coerce the negligent, to restrain the violent, and to aid the weak and deficient, by the overruling plenitude of her power. She is never to intrude into the place of the others, whilst they are equal to the common ends of their institution. But in order to enable parliament to answer all these ends of provident and beneficient superintendence, her powers must be boundless. The gentlemen who think the powers of parliament limited, may please themselves to talk of requisitions. But suppose the requisitions are not obeyed? What! Shall there be no reserved power in the empire, to supply a deficiency which may weaken, divide, and dissipate the whole? We are engaged in war–the secretary of state calls upon the colonies to contribute–some would do it, I think most would cheerfully furnish whatever is demanded–one or two, suppose, hang back, and, easing themselves, let the stress of the draft lie on the others–surely it is proper, that some authority might legally say–"Tax yourselves for the common supply, or parliament will do it for you." This backwardness was, as I am told, actually the case of Pennsylvania for some short time towards the beginning of the last war, owing to some internal dissensions in the colony. But whether the fact were so or otherwise, the case is equally to be provided for by a competent sovereign power. But then this ought to be no ordinary power; nor ever used in the first instance. This is what I meant, when I have said at various times, that I consider the power of taxing in parliament as an instrument of empire, and not as a means of supply.

Such, sir, is my idea of the constitution of the British empire, as distinguished from the constitution of Britain; and on these grounds I think subordination and liberty may be sufficiently reconciled through the whole; whether to serve a refining speculatist, or a factious demagogue, I know not; but enough surely for the ease and happiness of man.

Sir, whilst we held this happy course, we drew more from the colonies than all the impotent violence of despotism ever could extort from them. We did this abundantly in the last war. It has never been once denied–and what reason have we to imagine that the colonies would not have proceeded in supplying government as liberally, if you had not stepped in and hindered them from contributing, by interrupting the channel in which their liberality flowed with so strong a course; by attempting to take, instead of being satisfied to receive? Sir William Temple says, that Holland has loaded itself with ten times the impositions which it revolted from Spain rather than submit to. He says true. Tyranny is a poor provider. It knows neither how to accumulate, nor how to extract.

I charge therefore to this new and unfortunate system the loss not only of peace, of union, and of commerce, but even of revenue, which its friends are contending for. It is morally certain, that we have lost at least a million of free grants since the peace. I think we have lost a great deal more; and that those, who look for a revenue from the provinces, never could have pursued, even in that light, a course more directly repugnant to their purposes.

Now, sir, I trust I have shown, first on that narrow ground which the honourable gentleman measured, that you are likely to lose nothing by complying with the motion, except what you have lost already. I have shown afterwards, that in time of peace you flourished in commerce, and, when war required it, had sufficient aid from the colonies, while you pursued your ancient policy; that you threw every thing into confusion when you made the Stamp Act; and that you restored every thing to peace and order when you repealed it. I have shown that the revival of the system of taxation has produced the very worst effects; and that the partial repeal has produced, not partial good, but universal evil. Let these considerations, founded on facts, not one of which can be denied, bring us back to our reason by the road of our experience.

I cannot, as I have said, answer for mixed measures: but surely this mixture of lenity would give the whole a better chance of success. When you once regain confidence, the way will be clear before you. Then you may enforce the act of navigation when it ought to be enforced. You will yourselves open it where it ought still further to be opened. Proceed in what you do, whatever you do, from policy, and not from rancour. Let us act like men, let us act like statesmen. Let us hold some sort of consistent conduct.–It is agreed that a revenue is not to be had in America. If we lose the profit, let us get rid of the odium.

On this business of America, I confess I am serious, even to sadness. I have had but one opinion, concerning it since I sat, and before I sat, in parliament . . . I honestly and solemnly declare, I have in all seasons adhered to the system of 1766, for no other reason, than that I think it laid deep in your truest interests–and that, by limiting the exercise, it fixes, on the firmest foundations, a real, consistent, well-grounded authority in parliament. Until you come back to that system, there will be no peace for England.

233. Newspaper comment on the outbreak of hostilities, July 1775

News of the fighting at Lexington and Concord was first published in English newspapers at the end of May 1775. Comment continued to be varied. Many newspapers now took a strongly patriotic line, but others continued to criticize the government's policy and to sympathize with the Americans. An example of each of these points of view is given below.

Anti-American.

(*Morning Chronicle*, 1 July 1775.)

To the Printer of the MORNING CHRONICLE.

SIR,

THE American Rebels are constantly boasting of the prodigious services which they rendered *us*, in the course of the last war, when it is notoriously known, that the last war was entered into for their *own* immediate protection; and therefore, whatever efforts they made, were entirely made from motives of *private interest*, and not from a generous principle of *attachment* to their Mother Country: while a foreign enemy, indeed, was at their backs, they affected a prodigious deal of loyalty to the present state; but the moment their fears on that head were removed by the cession of all Canada to Great Britain, that moment the dutiful colonies began to change their tone; America was no longer *ours*, but *theirs*; the champions for *Constitutional Rights* would no longer obey the voice of the *Constitution*; from petitions which we could not grant, they proceeded to acts of outrage which we could not overlook; and, finding at last that we are not to be intimidated by the apprehension of losing their trade, these miracles of political fidelity, these paragons of patience under oppression, fly heroically to their tents, and endeavour (pretty souls) to persuade us, that they are only fighting against a wicked Ministry. The insult offered in this argument, to our national understanding, will, however, be punished as properly as the violence offered to our national honour, in their daring commencement of hostilities. 'Tis neither the cloud of manufactured perjury from the other side of the Atlantick, nor the stupid fabrications of newspaper treachery on this, which can have weight with a thinking Englishman. Every dispassionate mind must see, that be the *ostensible* object of American resistance what it may, the *British nation* must be the sufferer, if the rebel provinces should triumph; and it would be hard, after the millions of money as well as the oceans of blood which we lavished to concur [*sic*] America, if we should now pitifully suffer it to be torn from our hands.

Poor Old England.

Criticism of the government's policy.

(*Gentleman's Magazine* (July 1775), pp. 324–325.)

A FRIENDLY ADDRESS *to Lord* NORTH.

The 8th of the 7th month, 1775.

Friend N—,

THERE was a time when I entertained a tolerable opinion of thy head, and a favourable one of thy heart. There was a time when I thought that the life, liberty, and property of the subject would remain inviolate, and that thy whole study would be to encourage commerce, to redress grievances, and to promote the welfare of the mother-country and the colonies. How far thy measures have confirmed or disappointed my expectations, let the present fatal period proclaim, and an astonished world declare! Turn over the pages of antiquity, peruse the history of thy own country, and tell me whether the bloody transactions of a Nero, or a Mary, can furnish any thing that wears a worse complection than the American expedition. I tell thee plainly, I do not believe they can; and that, if thou wilt persevere, the worst consequences will follow. In vain did a certain pensioned scribbler lately ask the cause of this unhappy difference, that he might misrepresent it, by answering the question himself. In vain does a second, under the signature of *A Lawyer*, and *Matter of Fact*,[1] reflect upon that great and good man Lord Chatham, upon the present worthy Lord Mayor, and upon the faithful and virtuous city of London. Arts like these are too stale for deception, and too bare-faced not to meet with contempt. Ask thy own heart, or rather ask thy S[overeign], whether the colonists have not a right to expect and to insist upon the enjoyment of their inherent constitutional privileges? Are not their wives and children as dear to them as thine are to thee or his own to himself? Most certainly they are! Why, then, are they treated with such unexampled cruelty? Why are they put under military government? Why are thousands of them shut up in Boston to starve, or live upon salt provisions with a licentious soldiery? Why is their charter violated, and their trade removed? Why are their once happy and peaceable regions to be desolated with fire and sword, and, oh! horrible to relate! a Roman Catholic army proposed to be let loose upon them?[2]

[1] Both in *Lloyd's Evening Post*, 3 July 1775.

[2] It was widely believed in the American colonies that the object of the Quebec Act of 1774 was to use Catholic Canada against them.

Thou wilt say, perhaps, in thy justification, that the colonists are in a state of actual rebellion, and that nothing but desperate measures will avail. I answer, the more culpable thou, as the odium of it (if true) belongs to thee and to the junto only, who have taken more pains to make them rebels, than is necessary to make rebels good subjects. Did not the Americans before they took up arms in defence of their liberties, present the most humble petition that injured subjects could offer? Did they ask for any thing more than to be put in the same situation they were in at the close of the last war? They did not: yet even that request was refused them. And what is the consequence? Exactly what was predicted by those illustrious worthies, who protested against and reprobated the measure. Our friends and fellow-subjects, to the inexpressible grief of every good man, are now made desperate with injuries and wrongs; the flame of civil war rages throughout the vast continent of America; and an impolitic junto are sacrificing the flower of our troops, and exhausting the wealth of the nation, to remedy evils their own misconduct have occasioned, and which nothing but friendship and good offices can remove. Ask the merchant or the manufacturer, what he thinks of thy arbitrary proceedings? He will tell thee that they are big with ruin, and that bankruptcy stares him in the face. Enquire of innumerable journeymen weavers, and their industrious dependents what their sentiments are? Their answer will be, that their families are starving, and that they are deprived of their daily bread. In short, there is no rank nor degree of people that are not, in some measure, affected by it. But, thanks to Heaven, the British lion is at length roused; the sons of Britannia feel for their brethren in distress. Let me then entreat thee, if thou hast any regard for trade, for the peace of thy own mind, and for the prosperity of Great Britain and the colonies, immediately to repeal all the oppressive acts that have been passed, and to make such overtures as will secure a speedy accommodation. God knows, this is no time to quarrel with our best friends, and give up three millions a year by suspending their trade, and contending for an unjust tax; for, however pacific France and Spain may affect to appear at present, be assured, that, when we have enervated ourselves by the unnatural contest, we shall be attacked with the united force of both.

Once more, then, I conjure thee to desist from purposes which have no other tendency than to promote an effusion of our own and our friends blood, and to expose every thing to danger. Besides, thou wouldst do well to consider, that the national grievances so loudly complained of not long since by the city of London, are still fresh upon most peoples minds; and that the elegant marble statue, erected in Guildhall by its faithful citizens, in honour of the immortal Beckford,[1] is a constant and powerful monitor to Englishmen to be upon their guard.

Humbly recommending what I have here offered to thy serious consideration, and fervently beseeching Him, in whose hands the hearts of all men are, to soften thine, and to endue thy Master with a spirit that is gentle and easy to be entreated,

I remain, thy assured friend, B.

[1] William Beckford (1709–1770), M.P. for the City of London, 1754–1770, and Lord Mayor, 1762 and 1769, a strong supporter of Chatham.

(*b*) THE WEST INDIES

234. A pamphlet on the value of the West Indian Islands, 1731

(*The Importance of the British Plantations in America to this Kingdom* [by Fayer Hall] (1731), pp. 25–29, 31–32, 40–41, 55–56, 112–114.)

In the Preface, the author says that he has lived many years in America, traded with most of the places he describes, and visited nearly all of them. The pamphlet also deals with the American colonies, and is dedicated to Sir Robert Walpole.

. . . Hence may be perceived the Excellence of our Oeconomy and Government, that in Climes less temperate and kind, [than the Spanish Indies] on Lands less luxurious and fruitful, unacquainted with Mines of Gold or Silver, our own People enjoy Happiness and Pleasures, are comparatively more wealthy, are justly esteemed more considerable, their Productions from their Labour infinitely more valuable, and their Trade more beneficial to their Native Kingdom, as well as themselves.

In pursuance of my Design, I shall consider the Advantages we receive from our Sugar Islands: and first I shall begin with *Barbadoes*.

OF what Consequence the Island of *Barbadoes* is to this Kingdom, might in a great measure be estimated from the Amount of the 4½ *per cent* on their Sugars only, which Sum hath amounted many Years to upwards of 10,000£ a Year, as I have been informed. And the vast Advantage it is of to this Kingdom will farther appear, when we consider the numbers of People which are constantly employed for the supplying of that Island with almost all sorts of our own Manufactures: And if it be farther considered and allowed that not less than 1000 of our own Seamen are constantly employed, on account of that Island only; at a Time too when 200 Tons of Craft, or Shipping, do not require above 20 Men; so that there is not less than 10,000 Tons of Shipping constantly employ'd: which Shipping, or at least three fourths of the whole, if not built in *England* are always repaired, refitted, victualled and constantly paid here; and it never yet was suggested that one Penny of Money or Bullion was ever carried there from *England*.

Upon this Head we may also allow (what is near the Truth) that what we call the Outsett of every Ship clear for Sea for this Voyage, stands the Owners in 10*l.* per Ton, and then the Value of the Shipping employed in this Trade will be 100,000*l.* Now if after all Charges of Insurance, foreign Port Charges, and the Allowance made for the Wear of the Ship, there is gained but 10 *per Cent.* and supposing (what also may be near the Truth) that upon our own Accounts, we send of our own Manufactures and *East India* Goods, to the Value of 200,000*l.* *per Ann.* and that we gain thereby but 10 *per Cent.* then, upon these two Articles, we gain 30,000*l.* *per Ann.*

But these are not the only Ways we gain from that Island. A Governor there will find Ways to remit to *England* at the rate of 5,000*l.* *per Ann.* and if the Factors there remit but half their Commissions on the above Sum of 200,000*l.* that will be 10,000*l.* *per Ann.* Those Gentlemen in Publick Offices, and others there, who expect to return Home, we will only say remit 5,000*l.* *per Ann.* and we will suppose that there constantly are here in *England* at least a hundred Gentlemen of that Island, some for

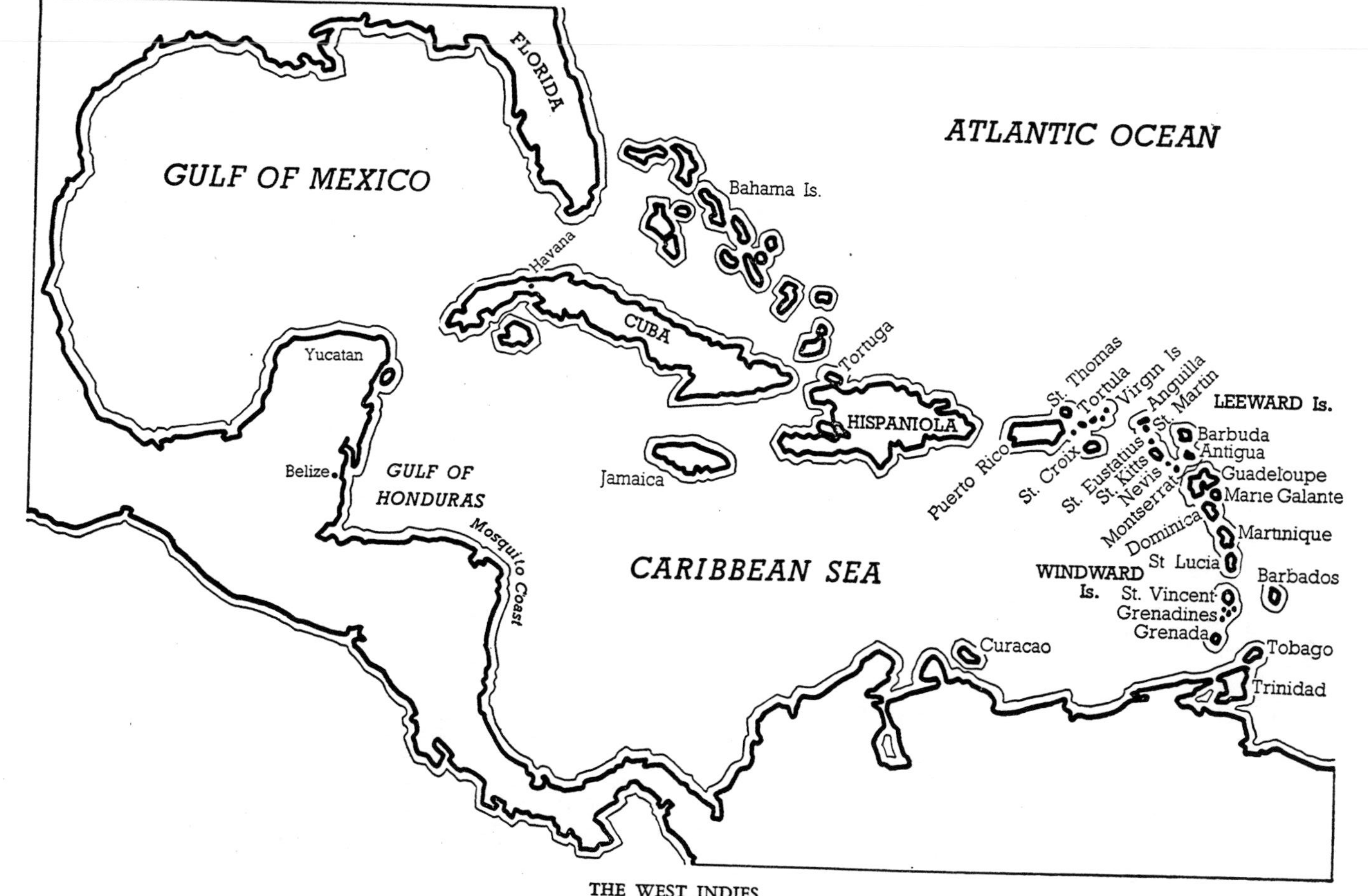

THE WEST INDIES
SHOWING THE PRINCIPAL PLACES MENTIONED IN THE DOCUMENTS

their Pleasure, and others for Education, who do not live at less Expence than 200*l.* *per Ann.* each, which is clear Gain to us 20,000*l.* *per Ann.* And if it be allowed that they are in Debt to us the Sum of 100,000*l.* for which they pay eight *per Cent. per Ann.* Interest, that is clear Gain of 8,000*l.* more; and if we reckon what we reasonably may, *viz.* The Freight of all Sugars which are again exported, and which are the Produce of this Island only, this will be 7,000*l.* more. The whole will amount to 95,000*l.* *per Ann.* A prodigious Sum to be gained annually from an Island but very little bigger than the Isle of *Wight.* But these are not the only Advantages; which will appear when we treat of the Trade of the Northern Colonies. And if we consider the *African* Trade, much more might be brought to Account of this Island, but as I design to keep within bounds in all my Computations, I will leave it as above at 95,000*l.* Sterling *per Annum*, over and above the Employment of so many Sailors and Shipping, and the vast number of all sorts of Artificers employed at Home in fitting, repairing and building those Ships, &c. besides those for the Manufactures.

If the Island of *Tobago* belongs to this Kingdom, as I have been credibly informed it does, it will appear as surprizing as any ill Management we have been hitherto guilty of, that it hath not been settled by us. An Island which, tho' not quite so large as *Barbadoes*, yet for good Roads, convenient Rivers, and Richness of Soil, is superior to it; and if the Settlement were once accomplished, there is no doubt but the Advantage arising from that small Island for many Years to come, would be very near, if not quite, as considerable to us as the Island of *Barbadoes* now is; because as it is fresh and strong Land, one Acre would produce much more than is now produced by two of old, worn out, poor Land, such as some (and indeed no small Part) of *Barbadoes* now is; and it is allowed by all, that upon good new Land the Labour of fifty Slaves will produce as much Sugar as a hundred will, or can, in *Barbadoes*; tho' the Sugar perhaps will not be so fine.

This Island is in the Latitude of 11^{d} 5^{m} North, and lies from *Barbadoes* South by West half West, near forty Leagues: Nor is it the worse to be esteemed for lying within twelve Leagues of *Trinidado*, a *Spanish* Island. . . .

The *Leeward* Islands (so called with Respect to *Barbadoes*, which is the Easternmost and Windwardmost of all the *West-India* Islands) are numerous, and inhabited by *English*, *French*, *Dutch*, and *Danes*. The most considerable of these are *Antegoa*, *St. Christophers*, *Nevis* and *Montserat*, all settled by the *English*. And tho' these four Islands, with Regard to their Bigness and Extent, are equal to three such Islands as *Barbadoes*; And tho' it is well known these Lands in general turn out better Crops than those of *Barbadoes* do, yet because I would not be thought to exaggerate, I shall consider them all, with the Islands of *Burbuda*, *Anguilla*, *Tortola* and *Spanish Town*, which are all settled by the *English*, to be all together only of equal Consequence to this Kingdom at present, as the Island of *Barbadoes*, tho' they are capable of vast Improvements. . . .

About thirty Leagues to the Westward of this delightful Island, [Hispaniola] lies the Island of *Jamaica*, in Length a Hundred and fifty Miles, in Breadth about fifty Miles. We shall be able to form some Judgment of the Importance of this Island, by the Quantity of its own Produce annually shipped off to us; namely, in Sugar 10000

Tons, in Cotton, Indigo, Ginger, Piemento, Rum, Lime-juice, Cocoa, Mahogony Wood, &c. 2000 more. By this it will appear, that there is not less than 12000 Tons of our own Shipping constantly employed in that Service only, over and above what is employed between that Island and the Northern Plantations; all which, excepting that they do not fit and repair here, are of the same Benefit and Advantage to this Kingdom in all other Respects. But of this more particularly, when I treat of the Northern Colonies. And because I would not be suspected of favouring or flattering my self in my Design, which is to shew the great Benefit and Advantage arising to this Kingdom from our own Plantations, I will only consider this Island, as a Sugar Plantation, to be of the same Advantage to us as *Barbadoes*, tho' very capable of being improved to ten, if not twenty Times that Value. . . .

The *Bahama* Islands, which are very numerous, and capable of producing all things necessary for Life, are all owned by the *English*, and some few of them are inhabited, *viz. Providence, Illethera, Harbour-Island*, and *Green Turtle Key*. The most considerable for Extent and Richness of Soil is the Island of *Abaco*; but it hath not yet been settled, nor indeed do I apprehend that any great Advantages could accrue to this Kingdom by those Islands were they all inhabited; yet I think it not improper to keep up the Government already there, only as it prevents their becoming a Nest of Pyrates.

Those Islands produce Brazilletta Wood, Lignum Vitae, Cortex Winteriana, Salt, and on the Shores have been frequently found the Sperma-Ceti Whales and Ambergris; which last I have been credibly informed is the Excrement of that Whale: A whole Sloop's Company agreed in the Relation of that Fact to me in South Carolina, where they brought many Barrels of Sperma-Ceti (I saw at least thirty) and above five hundred Pounds of Amber-gris, all which they assured me came from one Whale. The Sperma-Ceti undoubtedly did, the Amber-gris they had Reason to think did so too, because they found it near the Place where they found the Whale, and they all agreed that the Excrement of that very Whale, which was found in the Gut near the *Anus*, was really Amber-gris, tho' not quite so good as that which was found on the Shore and floating in the Water. This I believed when I was told it, for I saw no Interest or Pleasure they had or proposed in deceiving me, or many others, which I often heard them tell it to. Here too are found the prettiest and greatest variety of Shells that any Part of the World produces. Upon the whole, except for keeping out of Pyrates, I don't think these Islands worth inhabiting, while we have so much of as fine a Countrey as any in the World uninhabited, I mean the Province of South Carolina. . . .

Bermudas, though a small Island, or rather a great many small Islands, lies in the Latitude of 32^d^ 30^m^ North; Longitude from *London* 64^d^ West; and about two hundred Leagues distant from the Continent of America. In Queen *Ann's* War there was upwards of a hundred Sail of Brigantines and Sloops belonging to this Island; but at present I am assured that there is not above half that Number. This Island, which was formerly one of the most fruitful, is now near worn out: And such is and will be the Fate of all small Islands, where People increase so fast, and so constantly keep their Lands tilled. Such in part is the Case of the Island of *Barbadoes* already, yet the Planters there are not willing to remove to Places where twice the Quantity of Sugars may be made by the same Labour as there. The People of *Bermudas* too are not easily to be persuaded to remove to a better Country, where the same Degree of Industry and Frugality, which these People are remarkable for, would soon enrich them. These People are extremely civil and kind to Strangers; and when they have a good Governor, as it is universally allowed they had by Governor *Bennet*, no People are more happy. They have very few Priests, very few Physicians, and fewer Lawyers. All the Necessaries which they want, such as Apparel and Household Goods, they are furnished with from hence; for which they send us Money, and fine Plait for making Womens Hats, &c. together with whatever they can spare, of any Commodities which bear a Price here. The *Bermudians* in general are excellent Hands on board of Sloops, and the best Fishermen that I ever knew. They navigate their Vessels at less Expence than any other People, and consequently can get by Smaller Freights.

To conclude, I am of Opinion that this Kingdom gains clear Profit by our *American* Colonies yearly, the Sum of one million Sterling, exclusive of what we get by any Trades for Negroes or dry Goods by the Spaniards; and that in and by our Colonies only we maintain and employ at least eighteen thousand Seamen and Fishermen.

235. Grant of a representative Assembly to the Bahama Islands, 1728

(*Acts of the Privy Council, Colonial Series*, III (1720–1745), pp. 194, 196, 204–205.)

The representative principle had been generally accepted for the government of the American colonies and plantations by the end of the seventeenth century. The last of the West Indian islands to receive a representative Assembly (other than the islands ceded in 1763) were the Bahamas, which were acquired by the Crown in 1728 from the Carolina Proprietors, who, since 1670, had exercised nominal authority, but had been unable to defend the islands from Spanish attacks. Directions for summoning representative Assemblies were inserted in the Instructions issued by the Privy Council to governors with their commissions of appointment, and amended as required.

[1728.]

20 July. [The Committee for Plantation Appeals and for the Affairs of Jersey and Guernsey report their agreement with the recommendations of the Board of Trade, whose representation is as follows:] Having received Severall Letters from Captain Phenny Your Majestys Governor of the Bahama Islands in relation to the Nature and Consequence of those Islands to the Plantation Trade, and to the advantage they would be of were they effectually Settled, and proposing as the first means to encourage People to go and Settle there, that an Assembly may be appointed, that they may as in other Colonies pass Laws for the good Government of the whole, We have had the said Letters under Consideration, and as We find that without an Assembly, it is impossible for them to raise a Revenue Sufficient to answer the common Expences of the Government, or to put their Islands in any tolerable posture of Defence, We humbly take leave to propose that Your Majesty may be graciously pleased to Give the Governor Power to call an Assembly consisting of twenty four Members to be chosed by a Majority of the Inhabitants in the following Places respectively, Vizt. Eight Members to be chosen for the Town of Nassau which is the

chief Town of the Bahama and the Seat of Government, four for the Eastern District, Four for the Western, Four for the Island of Eleutheria and Four for the Harbour Island. . . .

25 July. [Orders accordingly. A clause to be inserted in the Governor's commission directing the calling of an Assembly.] . . .

[1729.]
14 May. [The Committee approve[1] as the only additions and alterations are found to be] that as Your Majesty hath been pleased to allow Captain Rogers to call an Assembly of Freeholders and Planters in those Islands, and to Establish a Civil Judicature so the said Lords Commissioners have added to the Draught of Generall Instructions such others, as were necessary upon this Occasion, and which Your Majesty hath already been pleased to approve in the Instruction to Your Majesty's other Governors in America–But in regard they may not be at present a Sufficient Number of Freeholders and Planters in those Places empowered to return Members, The said Lords Commissioners have inserted the 11th Instruction Empowering the Governor to admitt of the most Substantial Inhabitants being returned in the room of such Freeholders and Planters, untill there shall be a Sufficient Number of Freeholders and Planters to serve in such Generall Assembly.

236. Act of Appointment by the Jamaica Assembly of Agents for Jamaica, 11 February 1731

(Printed in Lillian M. Penson, *The Colonial Agents of the British West Indies* (1924), pp. 269–271.)

The practice of the American and West Indian colonies of appointing agents to take care of their interests in England developed in the last years of the seventeenth century and had been adopted by nearly all these colonies by the mid-eighteenth century. The following document is an example of the Acts of the Colonial Assemblies appointing these agents, who were often merchants or planters living in England; sometimes M.P.s, lawyers or minor civil servants, such as Charles Delafaye, appointed by this Act.

AN ACT for appointing an Agent or Agents in Great Britain to sollicite the Passing of Laws and other publick Affairs of this Island, And Impowering certain Members of the Council and Assembly, during the Intervals of Assembly from time to time, as Occasion shall be, to give Instructions for such his Management.

WHEREAS it is absolutely necessary that the Inhabitants of this Island should have One or more Persons fitly Qualifyed in Great Britain fully Impowered to Sollicite the Passing such Laws and to Transact such other Publick matters as shall be from time to time Committed to his or their care for the good of the said Island Be it therefore enacted by His Majesty's Governor Council and Assembly And it is hereby enacted by the Authority of the same That Charles Delaffaye Esqr. and the Honourable John Gregory Esquire be and are hereby nominated and Appointed Agents in Great Britain for this Island for the purpose aforesaid And that the Honble Richard Mill and Edward Charlton Esquires two of the Members of His Majesty's Council

[1] Instructions to Captain Woodes Rogers as Governor.

of this Island and John Stewart Esqr. Speaker of the present Assembly or the Speaker of the Assembly for the time being Dennis Kelly, Alger Pestell, Andrew Arcedeckne and George Ellis Esquires five of the Members of the present Assembly shall be and are hereby Impowered and Appointed to be Commissioners for Instructing and directing the said Agent in his Sollicitations pursuant to such Powers and Authoritys as the said Commissioners shall from time to time receive from the Council and Assembly when sitting Provided Nevertheless that the Commissioners before mentioned or the Major part of them, whereof One of the Council shall be one, may from time to time in the Interval of Assemblys or upon any emergent Occasions give to the said Agents in Great Britain such further Instructions as they shall think fitt for the Publick Service of this Island And in case of the death Absence or refusal of any of the Commissioners before mentioned That then if a Councillor, the Council or the Major part of them shall chuse out of their body or if an Assembly man such person or persons of the Assembly or the Major part of them shall think fitt to chuse in the room of him or them which shall remove dye or refuse And that the Person or Persons so chosen shall be Impowered to Act to all Intents and purposes as if he or they had been mentioned or appointed by name in this Act And in case it shall be thought fitt to alter the said Agent or Agents or to continue them or either of them for longer time the said Commissioners or the Major part of them (whereof One of the Council shall be one) are hereby Impowered to remove them or either of them And in such case or in case of their or either of their deaths to Nominate and Appoint another Agent in Great Britain who shall and is hereby Authorized to Act as if herein named And be it further enacted by the Authority aforesaid That the Commissioners hereby Appointed shall Enter Copies of all and every their proceedings in pursuance of this Act in a fair Book to be bought and kept for that purpose Which proceedings or any of them shall and are hereby directed to be laid before the Governor Council and Assembly for the time being when sitting, as often as the same shall be required And the said Commissioners shall have no manner of ffee or Reward or any Allowance for their Trouble and Care in their Transactions pursuant to this Act (the Charges of a Clerk and Books Excepted) And be it further Enacted by the Authority aforesaid That the said Agents shall be paid at the rate of Three hundred pounds sterling money of Great Britain per Annum for such time as they shall continue Agents for their Care and trouble in and about the Affairs of this Island in Great Britain And that the same shall be remitted to them by William Crosse Esquire His Majesty's Receiver General from time to time when and as often as he shall be required so to do by the Commissioners herein before named or the Major part of them (Whereof One to be of the Council) together with such Charges as they shall find he or they may have expended in or about the Publick business of this Island And this Act to continue and be in force for Twelve Months from the Passing thereof and no longer.

237. Disagreement between the Governor and Assembly of Jamaica over *Olyphant's Case*, 1764–1766

(*Acts of the Privy Council, Colonial Series*, IV (1745–1766), pp. 704–713.)

The following extract illustrates the difficulties which arose frequently between the governors and the colonial assemblies in the West Indies as well as in the Thirteen Colonies, as a result of the increasingly independent attitude of the assemblies and their jealous regard for their privileges. The Governor of Jamaica on this occasion was William Henry Lyttelton (1724–1808), later Baron Lyttelton of Frankley, Governor of South Carolina, 1755–1762, and of Jamaica, 1762–1766. He was recalled in 1766, largely as a result of this case, and became Envoy to Portugal, 1767–1771. It will be seen that the revised Instructions to the Governor in 1766 substantially allowed the assembly's claims.

[1765.]

4 Mar. [Reference to the Committee of a Board of Trade representation of 1 March, transmitting several papers from the Governor of Jamaica relative to a dispute with the Assembly concerning privileges claimed by them, whereby it appears that he has judged it necessary for preserving the peace and tranquillity of the island to dissolve the Assembly and issue writs for a new one. No supply bills had been passed, and the Governor,] being apprehensive in case the New Assembly should revive the said Disputes and adopt the Doctrines and Resolutions of the former, that no Supply Bills will be passed by them, whereby His Majestys Troops will be left destitute of the Additional Pay usually granted by the Assembly, requests to be enabled upon such an Emergency to subsist the Forces, and suggests some expedients for that purpose.

15 Mar. [The Committee consider Governor Lyttelton's letter of 24 Dec., 1764, and other papers,] wherein it is set forth, That upon the 8th of December last, the House of Assembly of Jamaica ordered one Richard Thomas Wilson, an Officer of the Provost Marshall to be taken into the Custody of their Messenger for what they termed a Breach of their Priviledge with such other Persons as were concerned with him in executing a Writ of Venditioni exponas on the Coach Horses of John Olyphant Esq. one of their Members at the suit of Mr. Pierce Cook, who had obtained a Judgment for a considerable Sum of Money; And that two Days after the House came to a Resolution, That as it appeared from the Examination of Richard Thomas Wilson, that Mr. Pierce Cook, and Lachlan McNeill, had been concerned with him in executing the Writ of Venditioni exponas, they should be taken into Custody which was done accordingly; whereupon the said Pierce Cook and Lachlan McNeill made immediate Application to the Governor as Chancellor, praying for Writs of Habeas Corpus, who ordered the same to be issued; That the Governor did, as an expedient to preserve the publick Tranquillity, with the unanimous Advice of the Council, prorogue the Assembly for one day, in consequence of which the Persons in Custody were of course set free without having been brought before the Governor or any Decision given whether the Commitment of them was legal or not; But that the said Assembly did, upon their Meeting after the said Prorogation, upon the 19th of December come to several Resolutions in Support of certain pretended Priviledges, among which were [orders that Wilson, Cooke, and McNeill be again] taken into the Custody of the Messenger; And that Mr. Speaker sign Warrants for that purpose.

That Mr. Pierce Cook and Lachlan McNeill, being thereupon again taken into Custody of Edward Bolt the Messenger, did Petition the Governor as Chancellor a second time for Writs of Habeas Corpus, and having obtained them, were carried before him on the 21st December in the Court of Chancery, and upon full hearing of what was alledged by Counsel, the Governor, as Chancellor, Declared, That it did not appear to him, from the Words of any Act of Parliament, or of any Act of the Governor, Council and Assembly of the said Island, or of Your Majestys Commission and Instructions to him, as Governor of the said Island, or by any other Means whatsoever, that the Commitment of the said Pierce Cook, and Lachlan McNeill, into the Custody of the said Edward Bolt, was legal, the said Governor as Chancellor therefore Ordered, adjudged and Decreed, that the said Pierce Cook and Lachlan McNeill should be, by the Authority of the said Court released and discharged from the Custody of the said Edward Bolt. That the said House of Assembly, being informed thereof, did, on the said 21st December come to several Resolutions among which were the following Vizt.

"That his Excellency William Henry Lyttelton Esqr. in taking upon himself, as Chancellor, to determine against the Priviledge of this House, and to discharge Pierce Cook and Lachlan McNeill who were committed to the Custody of the Messenger of this House for a Contempt and Breach of the Priviledge of this House has acted in an unjustifiable Manner, and has been guilty of a flagrant Breach, Contempt and Violation of the Priviledges of this House, and the Liberties of the People" – And "That this House cannot with any Dignity to itself, or Justice to the People, proceed to any other Business until it should be righted in its Priviledges, and has received ample Reparation for the Indignity that has been offered to this House; And also that the said Mr. Pierce Cook and Lachlan McNeill be severally taken into and kept close in the Custody of the Messenger of this House for a Contempt and Breach of the Priviledges of this House." – And that Mr. Speaker do sign Warrants for that purpose.

That the said Governor being made acquainted with the Resolutions of the said House of Assembly judged it necessary to put the said Assembly under an immediate prorogation, and did, on the 24th of the said December, with the Unanimous Advice of the Council, Dissolve them, and ordered Writs to be issued for the Election of a New Assembly returnable on the 5th day of this Instant March.

[The Committee reported] That the Governor has in every respect acted in conformity to the Oath and Duty of his Office; And that the said House of Assembly has passed several Resolutions unjustly reflecting upon the Conduct of the said Governor, affecting Your Majestys Authority, the liberty of Your Majestys Subjects, and tending to throw the Affairs of Your Majestys said Island into the greatest Confusion, and that by means of that of the 21st December, wherein it is resolved not to proceed to any Business till that House should be righted in its Priviledges, The Supply Bills for the Support of Government were not passed and in case the future Assembly should not pass them Your Majestys Troops stationed there will be left destitute of the necessary Supplies annually granted by the said Assembly – And the Lords of the Committee having upon this Occasion taken into their Consideration Your Majesty's Instructions to the Governor of Jamaica find, That with respect to the Priviledge of the Members of the Assembly, it is by the 13th Article ordered in the Words following–Vizt.

"And Whereas the Members of several of the Assemblies in the Plantations have frequently assumed to themselves the Priviledge of being protected from Suits at Law, during the Term they remain of the Assembly, to the great prejudice of their Creditors, and the Obstruction of Justice; And Whereas it was declared by Her Majesty Queen Anne in Council, on the 31st of May 1713, upon a full Examination of the Matter, That there was no ground for the claiming such pretended Priviledge, nor have You Our Governor any Authority by Our Commission to You to allow the same; It is therefore Our Will and Pleasure, that no such pretended Priviledge be allowed to any Member of the Assembly, or of Our Council, otherwise than in their Persons, which You are to signify to them, that all Officers and other Persons, whom it may concern, may take Notice thereof and pay due Obedience hereunto."

And their Lordships are of opinion, That it may be adviseable for Your Majesty to signify to the said Governor Your Majestys Royal Approbation of his Conduct and that Your Majesty is highly displeased with the several Resolutions passed by the late House of Assembly in Support of certain pretended Priviledges; And that Your Majesty is perswaded, that the new Assembly will not adopt the Doctrines and Principles of the former Assembly, but that they will in every respect proceed with Temper and Moderation in carrying on the Business of the Publick, and expects to hear that the new House of Assembly has passed the necessary supply Bills for the Support of Government, and for the payment of Your Majestys Troops stationed in the said Island in the manner hitherto constantly practiced; otherwise Your Majesty will find Yourself obliged to lay the whole of the matter before the Parliament of Great Britain in order that they may take such Measures for raising the usual Supplies within the said Island, and for providing for the Publick Service, and the Security of Your Majestys Subjects there, as so unbecoming a Proceeding in the Assembly will render unavoidably necessary. . . .

21 June. [Reference to the Committee of a Board of Trade representation of 17 June that they had received a letter from Governor Lyttelton,] by which it appeared, that the New Assembly of that Island, which met on the 19th of March last had not only adopted the same Sentiments expressed in the Resolutions of the former Assembly in respect of their Privileges upon which His Majesty was pleased to signify His pleasure to the Governor in March last but had also pursued other extraordinary measures and come to several Resolutions which the said Lords Commissioners conceive to be unconstitutional and of a very dangerous tendency.

22 Nov. [Reference to the Committee of a Board of Trade representation of 8 Nov. with a letter from the Governor of Jamaica containing a particular account of the proceedings of the Assembly summoned by him for 13 Aug. in consequence of the letter from the Council of 19 March.]

29 Nov. [Order in accordance with the Committee report of 26 Nov., which shows that the Governor's letters give an account] of the proceedings of the two last

Assemblies in that Island whereby it appears, that the first of the said Assemblies had claimed and demanded Privileges of a very extraordinary nature, and had come to several resolutions thereupon which had obliged the Governor to prorogue, and afterwards dissolve the said Assembly; And that upon the Meeting of the subsequent Assembly, when the Speaker was presented to the Governor and approved of, he refused to make application to the Governor for the usual Privileges (though the same had been constantly applyed for by the Speakers of all former Assemblies) under a notion, as the Governor had been afterwards informed, that the Privileges of the Assembly did not flow from the Grace of the King, but are Rights inherent in themselves; The Governor therefore in order to preserve the just Orders of the proceedings of the Assembly and to maintain their usual privileges, and to prevent Your Majesty's Prerogative from suffering any violation, did judge it necessary to dissolve that Assembly likewise; That it further appeared by the Governor's Letter of 24th August that a project had been devised and adopted by a Majority of the Members of the last Assembly to apply to the House of Commons for redress concerning the violation of their Privileges and that a Petition for this purpose, had been actually subscribed by a Majority of the said last Assembly. [As it appears] that the Governor had caused the aforementioned Letter from the Lords of the Council to be communicated to the respective Members of the last Assembly by the Attorney General of the said Island without producing any good effect–The Committee do therefore agree humbly to report as their Opinion, that it may be adviseable for Your Majesty to cause Copies of the aforementioned Letters, Order of Council, and other Papers relative to this matter, to be laid before Parliament. And in case your Majesty shall be pleased to approve thereof, the Committee think it would be proper, that the Lords Commissioners for Trade and Plantations should be directed to notify the same to the Governor of Jamaica for his information, and at the same time to apprise the Governor, that as to the calling another New Assembly or not, previous to his being informed of the Sentiments of Parliament upon this affair it is left entirely to his own discretion. . . .

[1766.]
7 May. [Various letters, reports and orders in relation to this affair were read.] Mr. Secretary Conway[1] then acquainted the Board that he had (soon after he received His Majesty's Order in Council dated 29 November 1765 for laying before Parliament the Letters and other Papers relative to the extraordinary Proceedings of some of the late Assemblies in the Island of Jamaica respecting their Priviledges) applied to His Majesty for his Pleasure with respect to the time and manner of laying the said Papers before Parliament, and at the same time acquainted His Majesty, that application had been made to him by the Agent for the Island of Jamaica, and some of the Principal Inhabitants and Planters of the said Island, in which they had represented their desire, that if possible some Accommodation might be made of the several Matters in dispute between the Governor, and House of Assembly of Jamaica wishing the Affair might take that Course, and not be brought before Parliament–In consequence of which he

[1] Secretary of State for the Southern Department, in whose province the West Indies were.

received His Majesty's Commands to delay laying the several papers afore-mentioned before Parliament, until it should be known whether any such accommodation could be effected; And His Majesty commanded Mr. Secretary Conway to communicate this to the Board.

Mr. Conway further acquainted this Board, that the Great Attention necessarily given to the American Affairs before Parliament had prevented any thing being done upon this Subject in the first part of the Session, that his Illness for Six weeks past had further prevented his laying this matter before their Lordships, and that the several Persons above-mentioned have lately signified to Mr. Conway their Desire of attending this Board, in order to lay before the Committee their Sentiments and Propositions upon the Subject Matter of their Application.

The Lords of the Council are pleased to order that this Affair be taken into Consideration on Tuesday next the 13th Instant at one o'Clock, and that Mr. Alderman Beckford, Rose Fuller Esq.[1] and Stephen Fuller Esq. Agent for the Island of Jamaica, be summoned to attend at that time and that Mr. Attorney General and Mr. Sollicitor General be also summoned to attend at the same time. . . .

28 May. [Order for preparing an additional instruction for the Governor in accordance with a representation of "the Lords of the Council", dated 13 May, which recapitulates the proceedings, and declares their opinion, upon further hearing several of the parties,] that it may be adviseable for Your Majesty to suspend (during the present Session) signifying Your Royal pleasure for laying before Parliament the several Papers mentioned in Your Majesty's said Order in Council of the 29th of November last; And humbly propose as an Expedient for restoring Peace and Tranquillity to the said Island, and preventing for the future any Disputes between the Governor and Assembly, respecting Matters of Privilege; that by an Additional Instruction to the Governor of the said Island, Your Majesty would be pleased to signify Your Royal Will and Pleasure, That there be allowed to every Member of the Council, and House of Assembly respectively, during the sitting of the General Assembly, and for Six Days before the Meeting of such Assembly, and for the like Number of Days after an Adjournment Prorogation or Dissolution of such Assembly (in Addition to the Privilege already allowed to the said Members respectively in their Persons by Your Majesty's Royal Instruction to Your Governor) a further Privilege from Arrests in all Civil Suits for such Servants and Equipage only as are absolutely necessary for the personal Accommodation of the said Members in attending their respective Duties in general Assembly.

And if Your Majesty shall be pleased to approve of what is above proposed, Their Lordships submit, That Your Majestys Governor should be instructed to recommend to the Council and House of Assembly, as a Means for securing, as far as may be, such Additional Privilege from being violated, That every Member of the Council and House of Assembly respectively, do cause to be set down in Writing the Names of the several Servants, with a Description of the Equipage, and other particulars for which such Additional Privilege is to be allowed to the Extent above proposed, and

[1] Rose Fuller (d. 1777), M.P. for Maidstone, a West Indian planter and brother of Stephen Fuller.

having subscribed his Name thereto, deliver, or cause such Writing so subscribed to be delivered to the Provost Marshall General of the said Island, or his Deputy, or left at the Office of the said Provost Marshall, to the Intent that He or his Deputy, and all other Officers and Persons whom it may concern, may take Notice of the same. and govern themselves agreeably thereunto.

18 June. [On a Board of Trade report of 3 June, the Instruction is approved.]

238. The Sugar Act, 1739

(*Statutes at Large*, XVII, pp. 329–332. 12 Geo. II, c. 30.)

This Act, allowing the direct shipment of sugar from the British West Indies to Europe in ships built and owned in England (extended in 1742 by 15 Geo. II, c. 33, to colonial ships), was an important breach in the colonial policy of the Navigation Acts and a considerable triumph for the West Indian interest. Although its alleged object was the recovery of European markets, its chief effect was to raise the price of sugar in the English market. For the Navigation Acts and the Molasses Act of 1733, see vol. IX of these *Documents*, Nos. 51A, B, C and D.

An act for granting a liberty to carry sugars, of the growth, produce or manufacture of any of his Majesty's sugar colonies in America, *from the said colonies directly to foreign parts, in ships built in* Great Britain, *and navigated according to law.*

WHEREAS *by an act made in the twelfth year of the reign of the late King* Charles *the Second, intituled,* An act for encouraging and increasing of shipping and navigation, *and another act made in the fifteenth year of the said King, intituled,* An act for the encouragement of trade, *and another act made in the five and twentieth year of the reign of the said King, intituled,* An act for the encouragement of the *Greenland* and *Eastland* trade, and for the better securing the plantation trade; *which acts have been by subsequent acts since continued, and are now in force, all sugars of the growth or production of the* English *plantations in* America, Asia *or* Africa, *are obliged to be imported into* England, Wales *or* Berwick upon Tweed, *or to some other of the* British *plantations in* America *under such securities and penalties as other enumerated goods and commodities of the growth, production or manufacture of the said plantations, are subjected to by the said acts, some or one of them: and whereas his Majesty's sugar colonies in* America *are of great importance to the trade, navigation and strength of this kingdom: and whereas the planters of the said sugar colonies are unable to improve or carry on the sugar trade on an equal footing with foreign sugar colonies, without some advantages and relief be given them from* Great Britain: *and whereas it is reasonable to expect, that not only the produce of the said commodity in the said colonies, but also the exportation thereof, would be greatly increased, for the mutual benefit of this kingdom and the said colonies if (notwithstanding the laws relating to navigation and trade to and from the plantations) liberty or licence were granted for ships built in and sailing from* Great Britain, *and chiefly owned by the subjects of his Majesty residing in* Great Britain, *to load sugars in the said colonies, and to carry the same directly to any foreign ports in* Europe, *first touching at some port or ports in* Great Britain (*except where such ship goes to the southward of* Cape Finisterre) *whereby the said sugars will arrive at such ports sooner, with less charge, and in better condition for the consumption thereof:* for this end, and to encourage his Majesty's subjects in the *British* sugar colonies in *America* to improve and extend their settlements there, and to prevent any prejudice or damage to this nation, which might happen thereby from any unlawful commerce between the plantations and any foreign countries, and to secure the navigation, shipping, intercourse and dependence on *Great Britain*; may it therefore please your most excellent Majesty that it may be enacted: and be it enacted by the King's most excellent Majesty, by and with the advice and consent of the lords spiritual and temporal, and commons in this present parliament assembled and by the authority of the same, That the said three acts passed in the twelfth, fifteenth, and five and twentieth years of the reign of the late King *Charles* the Second, so far as the same extend to sugar of the growth and produce of his Majesty's plantations in *America*, being one of the commodities enumerated in the said acts, shall be and are hereby ratified and confirmed, as to all persons, ships, vessels, or places, in all respects whatsoever; except only as to such sugars as by this act shall be permitted or allowed to be exported from his Majesty's said sugar colonies in *America*, by such persons, and in such ships and vessels, and to such foreign countries and places and under such entries, securities, restrictions, regulations, limitations, penalties and forfeitures, as are herein after particularly described, appointed, limited and enacted for that purpose.

II. And be it enacted by the authority aforesaid, That from and after the twenty ninth day of *September*, one thousand seven hundred and thirty nine, it shall and may be lawful, notwithstanding any of the acts aforesaid, or any other act of parliament, for any of his Majesty's subjects, in any ship or vessel built in *Great Britain*, and navigated according to law, and belonging to any of his Majesty's subjects, of which the major part shall be residing in *Great Britain*, and the residue shall be residing either in *Great Britain* or in some of his Majesty's sugar colonies in *America*, and not elsewhere, that shall clear outwards in any port of *Great Britain* for any of the said colonies, to ship or load in the said colonies, or any of them, any sugars of the growth, produce and manufacture of the said colonies, or any of them, and to carry the same from thence to any foreign part of *Europe*; provided a licence be first taken out for that purpose under the hands of the commissioners of his Majesty's customs at *London* or *Edinburgh*, or any three or more of them respectively, subject to the regulations, and on the conditions hereafter mentioned, that is to say . . .

[Notice to be given in writing to the customs collector at the port where the ship is, of proposed voyage to the sugar colonies to load sugar to be carried to Europe: the master or owner of the ship shall enter into bond, with one or more sufficient securities, for £1,000 if ship is less than 100 tons, for £2,000 if over 100 tons: no tobacco, molasses, ginger, cotton, wool, indigo, fustick or other dyeing-wood, tar, pitch, turpentine, hemp, masts, yards, bowsprits, copper ore, beaver skins, or other furs of the growth, production or manufacture of any of the British plantations in America, may be taken on board, except as necessary provisions for the voyage; the ship, before proceeding to any foreign port, must touch at a British port and the master must give an exact account, on oath, of the whole cargo: after discharging cargo at a foreign port, the ship must return to Great Britain within 8 months, and before returning to any of the plantations.]

III. [The master must also take an oath, or, if a Quaker, affirm, that the ship belongs to British subjects, before a licence is granted.] . . .

The Oath. A.B. (maketh oath or solemnly declares & affirms) *that the* (ship or vessel) *called the* (name) *whereof he this* (deponent or affirmant) *is master, and hath charge and command for this present voyage to* (place bound to) *being* (describe the build) (ship or vessel) *of the burthen of* (number) *tons was built at* (place) *in the year* (time when) *and that the said* (ship or vessel) *is wholly owned by the* (person or persons) *whose* (name or names) *and usual* (place or places) *of abode* (is or are) *under-mentioned and subscribed by this deponent or affirmant, that such* (owner or owners) (is or are) *his Majesty's British* (subject or subjects) *and that no foreigner directly or indirectly hath any share, part or interest in the said* (ship or vessel) *to the best of this* (deponents or affirmants) *knowledge or belief; and that he this* (deponent or affirmant) *and three fourths of the mariners navigating the said* (ship or vessel) *are his Majesty's* British *subjects.*

IV. And be it further enacted, That in case any ship or vessel, licensed by virtue of this act shall take on board in any of the sugar islands, or in her voyage thence, any sugars, or other goods, being the property of any other person than some of his Majesty's subjects, and such as shall be shipped and laden on their proper risque and account, to be carried to foreign parts; then all such sugars or other goods so laden on such ship shall be forfeited and lost. . . .

239. Reasons for keeping Guadaloupe at a Peace, preferable to Canada, 1760

(J. Almon, *Anecdotes of the Life of the Right Hon. William Pitt, Earl of Chatham,* III (1793 ed.), pp. 208–215; "Copy of a Letter from a Gentleman in Guadaloupe to his Friend in London, August, 1760.")

The following pamphlet is the first of five such letters, reprinted in 1761 as *Reasons for keeping Guadaloupe at a Peace, preferable to Canada.* The decision to keep Canada was a further triumph for the West Indian interest, which feared the competition of Guadaloupe in the sugar trade.

THE different opinions of the people concerning the value of Canada and the value of Guadaloupe to Great Britain, have occasioned many disputes in private and public, in which private views have too often influenced the debate.

Those who are for acquiring all Canada, and giving up Guadaloupe, and everything else, argue in this manner: That no terms with the French can be secure or lasting; at the very time they are making a peace, they are contriving how to break it, and will do so as soon as any opportunity occurs to do it to advantage: That we entered into the war only upon account of America: That the French invaded our properties there, and were long contriving to do it; now that we have beaten them out of all that country, what we did never claim, as well as what we did claim, therefore we ought to keep all America, as the greatest acquisition we can make, or ever was made; for if we allow them the smallest footing even in Canada itself, we can never be secure they will not drive us out of that country: That the trade of North America is the great fountain of all the British wealth and power; that of late years it furnishes and employs so many ships and so many sailors, makes so great a consumption of the produce of Great Britain, sends so much of its produce to the sugar islands, and pours in such a tide of wealth from the West Indies upon Britain, as enables her to make the figure she now does to the rest of the world: That if all North America were her own, she could be drawn into no more wars on that account; our trade there would rise to the highest pitch, and that country so extensive, so rich, and full of so many lakes and rivers fit for navigation would soon raise the power and naval strength of Great Britain to a degree beyond any power on earth. That the fur trade might be entirely our own; that one ship of the Hudson Bay Company is often so rich as to bring home more value than ten sugar ships: That we have sufficiency of the sugar islands already: That Jamaica alone, if it were properly cultivated, can afford more sugar than England wants; it sends home near 40,000 hogsheads every year, when the third part is not cultivated: That Guadaloupe is a place of no significancy compared with Jamaica, and could add very little strength or wealth to Great Britain: That the French have long outdone us in the hats; a trade that we may have entirely to ourselves by acquiring Canada; and that if we leave the French the smallest footing or possession there, we never can be secure or safe in the rest, we have done nothing, but must be always liable to repeat the same expence.

Those who wish the keeping of Guadaloupe answer as follows; That Guadaloupe we certainly have, and that Canada we have not; the fate of it is still dubious: That all the reasoning before mentioned is sophistical and unsolid: That the advantages of North America to Britain, exclusive of Canada, are very great: why join them all to Canada, of itself worth little or nothing, but to give it weight, which it has not of itself? If our barrier in America shall be fixed by treaty to the certain limits we insist upon, and Cape Breton retained or demolished, we are in a much better situation there than ever; which would render America of much more advantage to us than it was in former times, and more secure; nay, as secure as the instability of human affairs can admit: the benefit of North America to Britain does not depend upon Canada at all; it is a frothy and false argument, Canada can add nothing; but first, a little improvement of the fur trade, which might be in very great perfection without it. Secondly, preventing the French from disturbing us in that quarter of the world for some time; and even that argument is equally strong for taking the Mississippi, otherwise it is not conclusive.

But as it is argued, that the French will never be at peace with us, it must follow, that when they cannot make war in America they must disturb us in Europe; now let those gentlemen answer, Whether we have more advantage over the French by a war in America, or a war in Flanders, when they have Ostend, &c. in their hands. The present war compared with those of King William, Queen Anne, and the war in 1744, soon solves that question. The sugar trade is far preferable to the fur trade.

What does a few hats signify, compared with that article of luxury, sugar; the consumption of sugar is daily increasing both in America and Europe, and become one of the necessities of life. Jamaica has not encreased in sugars these thirty years past, and never can encrease much, as the greatest part of it is so mountainous that it is not capable of culture, and cannot answer the expence in many places of carrying the sugars over the mountains to be shipt; though they have made a monopoly for themselves of that commodity of a long time past, they must now be the more reluctant to part with it.

It is our sugar islands that raise the value of North America, and pours in such wealth upon the mother country. The more we have of those islands, America becomes from that cause the more important and valuable, and England the richer. In America we have more than enough; in the sugar islands a great deal too little: the nearer they can be proportioned to one another the better for both, and the more trade and wealth for England. The fur trade does not employ the hundredth part of the shipping and seamen, that the sugar trade does.

The having all North America to ourselves by acquiring Canada dazzles the eyes, and blinds the understanding of the giddy and unthinking people, and it is natural for the human mind to grasp at every appearance of wealth and grandeur: yet it is easy to discover that such a peace might soon ruin Britain. I say the acquisition of Canada would be destructive; because such a country as North America, ten times larger in extent than Britain, richer soil in most places, all the different climates you can fancy, all the lakes and rivers for navigation one could wish, plenty of wood for shipping, and as much iron, hemp, and naval stores as any part of the world, such a country, at such a distance, could never remain long subject to Britain: you have taught them the art of war, and put arms in their hands, and they can furnish themselves with every thing in a few years without the assistance of Britain. They are always grumbling and complaining against Britain, even while they have the French to dread; what may they not be supposed to do, if the French are no longer a check upon them? You must keep a most numerous standing army to overawe them; these troops will soon get wives and possessions, and become Americans. Thus, from these measures, you lay the surest foundation of unpeopling Britain, and strengthening America to revolt: a people who must become more licentious from their liberty, and more factious and turbulent from the distance of the power that rules them: One must be very little conversant in history, and totally unacquainted with the passions and the operations of the human mind, who cannot foresee those events as clearly as any thing can be discovered that lies concealed in the womb of time. It is no gift of prophecy: it is only the natural and unavoidable consequences of such and such measures: and must appear so to every man whose head is not too much affected with popular madness, or political enthusiasm.

But without dipping too deep into futurity, pray what can Canada yield to Britain, in this or any subsequent age, but a little extension of the fur trade? Whereas Guadaloupe can furnish as much sugar, cotton, rum, and coffee, as all the islands we have put together, and consume a vast quantity of the British and American produce, from which trade the shipping and naval strength of Britain must greatly increase:

without any allowance for the cinnamon trade, which of itself may bring a good deal of wealth to the mother country, as we have the wild cinnamon in common with the other islands, so we have also the true genuine cinnamon tree, and have sent home to England samples of it, as good as any the Dutch have.

The consumption of sugar is daily increasing both in Europe and America, and we cannot at this day serve ourselves with that article; but are we not to endeavour to serve foreign markets if we can? Did ever the French bring half so much wealth to their country from hats, as from their sugar islands? To say we have sugar enough, is to say we have trade enough, a new doctrine truly; and if so, what use have we for Canada? In a word, it is most obvious to every impartial eye, that the increase of the sugar islands is particularly the interest of Britain: she is there too weak, and as those islands bring most wealth both to Britain and America, so from their weakness they can never be in any danger of revolting; and that every person, as soon as he can make a fortune there, comes home to the mother country and enjoys it; witness the number of the proprietors of the sugar islands that reside at London, and many of them sit in Parliament. If they dread Guadaloupe as a rival to their private interest, they must at the same time own, it is a great acquisition to the public wealth and strength. Thus Guadaloupe, one of the greatest acquisitions ever Britain made, acquires many powerful enemies from private views, and has nothing to plead but her public utility and advantage, often found too feeble an opponent to the private interest of a few.

But to conclude, nothing can secure Britain so much against the revolting of North America, as the French keeping some footing there to be a check upon them. If the peace be made with any tolerable attention to our barrier in America, as we may be most certain it will, France must ever after be an enemy too feeble to be dreaded in that corner of the world. But if we were to acquire all Canada, we should soon find North America itself too powerful and too populous to be long governed by us at this distance. We have often, too often, wasted our blood and treasure to raise up other powers to wealth and strength; who have too often become our enemies; and it were much to be wished that we could take warning, and do so no more.

Guadaloupe is supposed to be capable of producing at least 100,000 hogsheads of sugar every year. Whereas all the British islands are not upon an average supposed to exceed the following calculation:

Barbadoes	14,000
Antigua	16,000
Mountserrat	3,000
Nevis	3,500
St. Kitt's	17,000
Anguilla	50
Tortola	2,500
Jamaica	50,000
	105,050

240. The West Indian 'Interest' in London, 1775

The following extracts from a contemporary newspaper illustrate the organization of the West Indian 'interest' which was so powerful in London in the eighteenth century. In addition to the Colonial Agents, who represented the resident planters in the various islands, there was by the 1760's a Society of West India Merchants in London; and in the crisis caused by events in America, this society worked in co-operation with the planters in London and became the executive of the West India 'interest' as a whole.

(a) *Gazetteer and New Daily Advertiser*, 5 Jan. 1775.

London Tavern, Bishopsgate-street, Jan. 3, 1775.

At a General Meeting of the West-India Merchants, the Chairman produced a letter which he received, signed by several gentlemen of the West-India Islands. of which the following is a copy.

London, Jan. 1, 1775.

"Sir,

"The very alarming situation in which the West-India Islands are placed by the late American proceedings, induces us to apply to you, as Chairman of the Society of West-India Merchants, to request that they will not come to any resolution as a separate body at their next meeting, but that they will join with us in calling a General Meeting of the whole body of Planters and West-India Merchants, to deliberate on the steps necessary to be taken by us jointly on the present important crisis.

(Signed)

John Pennant,
Charles Spooner,
Thomas Storer,
Peeke Fuller,
Samuel Vaughan,
George Chandler,
Michael M'Nemara,
John Trent,
B. Edwards,
Montague James,
Sam. Torr. James,
Nathaniel Phillips,
John Davis,
Charles Fuller,
Rose Fuller,
Flo. Vassell,
John Ellis,
J. Kennion,
Neill Malcolm,
Philip Gibbes,
Thomas Walker,
William Gunthorp."

In consequence of which it was

Resolved, That this Society do very chearfully concur in opinion with the Gentlemen Planters, that we ought not to come to any resolution as a separate body at this meeting; and do also readily join in calling a General Meeting of the whole body of Planters and West-India Merchants. And having been informed that the 18th of the present month is a day recommended by the Subscribers to the above letter, as proper for such a meeting, it is further

Resolved, That immediate notice be given in the public papers, that such General Meeting be called and holden on the day aforesaid, at the hour of twelve, at the London Tavern, in Bishopsgate-street, then and there to deliberate on the measures necessary to be taken for the preservation of the general interest of the West-India Islands in the present important crisis.

JAMES ALLEN, Secretary.

(b) *Gazetteer and New Daily Advertiser*, 16 Feb. 1775.

MINUTES of the General Meetings of the WEST-INDIA PLANTERS and MERCHANTS, at the London Tavern, in Bishopsgate-street,

January 18, 1775.

Resolved,

THAT it is the opinion of this Meeting, that an humble Petition be presented to the House of Commons, representing the alarming situation in which the West-India Islands are placed by the resolutions of the Congress, held at the city of Philadelphia in North-America, on the 5th of September, 1774, and praying their interposition,

Resolved, That the Petition do set forth, That the planters and merchants are exceedingly alarmed at an agreement and association entered into by a Congress held at the city of Phildelphia, in North-America, on the 5th day of September, 1774, whereby the members thereof agreed and associated for themselves, and the inhabitants of the several provinces lying between Nova Scotia and Georgia, that from and after the first day of December, 1774, they would not import into British America any melasses, syrups, paneles, coffee, or pimento, from the British plantations; and that after the 10th day of September, 1775, if the acts, or parts of acts, of the British parliament therein mentioned are not repealed, they would not, directly or indirectly, export any merchandize or commodity whatsoever to the West-Indies.

And most humbly to represent, That the British property and stocks invested in the West India islands amounts to upwards of thirty millions sterling. That a farther property of many millions is employed in the commerce, created by the said islands; a commerce comprehending Africa, the East-Indies, and Europe. That the whole profits and produce of these capitals ultimately center in Great-Britain, and add to the national wealth; while the navigation, necessary to all its branches, establishes a strength which wealth can neither purchase nor balance.

That the sugar plantations in the West-Indies are subject to a greater variety of contingencies than many other species of property from their necessary dependence on external support; and that therefore should any interruption happen in the general system of their commerce, the great national stock, thus vested and employed must become unprofitable and precarious.

That the profits arising from the present state of the said islands, and that are likely to arise from their future improvement, in a great measure depend on a free and reciprocal intercourse between them, and the several provinces of North-America, from whence they are furnished with provisions, and other supplies, absolutely necessary for their support, and the maintenance of their plantations.

That the scarcity and high price in Great-Britain, and other parts of Europe, of those articles of indispensable necessity, which they now derive from the middle colonies of America, and the adequate population in some parts of that continent, with the distance, danger and uncertainty of the navigation from others, forbid the planters and merchants to hope for a supply in any degree proportionate to their wants.

That if the first part of the said agreement and association, for a non-importation, hath taken place, and shall be continued, the same will be highly detrimental to the sugar colonies; and if the second part of the said agreement and association for a non-exportation, shall be carried into execution, which the planters and merchants do firmly believe will happen, unless the harmony that subsisted a few years ago between this kingdom and the provinces of America, to the infinite advantage of both, be restored, the islands which are supplied with most of their subsistence from thence, will be reduced to the utmost distress, and the trade between all the islands and this kingdom, will of course be obstructed, to the diminution of the public revenue, to the extreme injury of a great number of the planters, and to the great prejudice of the merchants, not only by the said obstruction, but also by the delay of payment of the principal and interest of an immense debt due from the former to the latter.

And to pray, that the Honourable House will be pleased to take into their most serious consideration that great political system of the colonies heretofore so very beneficial to the mother country and her dependencies, and adopt such measures as to them, in their great wisdom, shall seem meet to prevent the evils with which the planters and merchants are threatened, and to preserve the intercourse between the West India islands and the Northern colonies, to the general harmony and lasting benefit of the whole British empire, and that they may be heard by themselves, their agents, or counsel, in support of their petition.

Resolved, That a Committee be appointed to prepare a petition agreeably to the above instructions.

Resolved, That the Committee do make their report to the next General Meeting, to be held at the London Tavern, on Wednesday the 25th instant, at twelve o'clock.

Ordered, That the thanks of this meeting be given to Beeston Long, Esq; the Chairman.

January 25, 1775.

Sir Philip Gibbes, Bart. Chairman of the Committee, to whom it was referred to prepare the petition to the House of Commons, reported the General Meeting held this day the petition prepared.

Resolved, that the petition be engrossed, and left at the London Tavern tomorrow, to be signed from the hours of one to three o'clock in the afternoon; and so from day to day (Sunday excepted) to the 30th instant; and at the St. Alban's Tavern, Pall-mall, the same hours, on Wednesday following; and that the clerk of the meeting do attend the signing thereof.

Resolved, That Mr. Alderman Oliver[1] be requested to present the petition to the

[1] M.P. for the City of London; born in Antigua, where he had estates. See also No. 25.

House of Commons, and that Mr. Rose Fuller,[1] and all other members of parliament, interested in, and immediately connected with the sugar colonies, be requested to support it.

Resolved, That the Committee appointed to draw up the petition, do prepare and manage the evidence to be offered in support of the same.

Resolved, That all who have signed the petition shall have voices in the Committee.

Resolved, That the Committee have a power to appoint agents to prepare the evidence to be laid before the House.

Resolved, That it be referred to the Committee to consider the propriety of a petition to the House of Lords.

January 31, 1775.

Resolved, That the petition to the House of Commons be presented on Thursday next, unless Mr. Alderman Oliver shall see cause to postpone it.[2]

Resolved, That Mr. Oliver be instructed, when he presents the said petition, to represent to the House, that the petitioners request that evidence may be heard in support of their petition, before the House proceed to any determination that affects the petitioners.

Resolved, That the present Committee, being an open one, do meet from day to day.

Resolved, That the Committee be at liberty to adjourn as they see fit, from place to place, and to call a General Meeting when they think proper.

February 7, 1775.

Sir Philip Gibbes (at a General Meeting) reported the petition to the House of Lords, as settled by the Committee; which being read, it was

Resolved, That the said petition be forthwith signed, and that the Gentlemen of the Committee be impowered by this meeting, humbly to request some Peer to present the same this day.

Resolved, That the Committee continue to sit from day to day, by their own adjournments, until they shall think proper to report to a general meeting to be called by them.

JAMES ALLEN, Secretary.

[1] See No. 237.

[2] The petition was presented on 2 February, 1775. For a similar petition from the London Merchants interested in the American trade, presented on 23 January, see vol. IX of these *Documents*, No. 160.

(c) CANADA

241. William Shirley on the potential value of Canada, October 1745

(*Correspondence of William Shirley, Governor of Massachusetts and Military Commander in America, 1731–60*, ed. Charles Henry Lincoln, I (1912), pp. 284–285.)

William Shirley (1694–1771) was Governor of Massachusetts, 1741–1756, and of the Bahamas, 1759–1770. His views on the importance of Canada to Great Britain should be compared with those expressed by Thomas Pownall in 1782 (No. 243).

William Shirley to the Duke of Newcastle

Louisbourg, October 29, 1745.

. . . I took the Liberty to mention in a former Letter to your Grace, that I thought, if the Expedition against Cape Breton should succeed, a Spirit would be immediately rais'd in the Colonies for pushing that success as far as Canada; which observation I find was not ill grounded; And I trouble your Grace with the Repetition of it now, because the Reduction of that Country to the Obedience of his Majesty seems to be the most effectual means of securing to the Crown of Great Britain not only Nova Scotia, and this Acquisition, but the whole Northern Continent as far back as the French Settlements on the River of Mississippi, which are about 2000 miles distance from Canada, by making all the Indians inhabiting within that Tract, (who are now chiefly, almost wholly indeed in the French Interest) dependent upon the English; the immediate consequence of which would be throwing the whole furr Trade, except such part of it as the French Settlements at Mississippi might keep, into the hands of His Majesty's Subjects; breaking up all the French Fishing Settlements in the Gulph and river of St. Lawrence, and even on the bank of Newfoundland, and Securing the whole Codfishery to the English; which besides the Profits arising from that part which the French lately had of it amounting to near one Million Sterl as computed in the account of it, which I lately inclos'd to your Grace would be farther Beneficial to the British Subjects by the great Consumption of Rum, and Cloathing necessary for the Men in carrying on the Fishery, and the great Quantity of Shipping, small Craft and Fishing Gear of all Sorts necessarily employed in it, which would in such Case be all British. To what I also mention'd concerning the Nursery of Seamen, which that Fishery would maintain for the Royal Navy, I may add, that from the Healthfulness of the Climates on this Continent and the Surprizing Growth of it's Inhabitants within the last Century it may be expected that in one or two more centuries there will be such an addition from hence to the Subjects of the Crown of Great Britain, as may make 'em vye for numbers with the subjects of France, and lay a foundation for a superiority of British Power upon the Continent of Europe at the same time that it secures that which the Royal Navy of Great Britain has already at Sea; and this is a remarkable Difference between the other acquisitions in America belonging to the several Crowns in Europe and this Continent, that the others diminish the Mother Country's Inhabitants, as Jamaica, Barbadoes, and the other Southern Collonies belonging to Great Britain have done, and the Spanish West Indies have done even to the exhausting of Old Spain.

In the mean while the Vent of the Woollen Manufacture and other European Commodities from Great Britain to these Colonies must be Increasing in proportion to the Increase of their Inhabitants; and the Mother Country will be independent of all foreign States for Naval Stores, which she will purchase from thence, with her own produce, and at moderate rates; she will supply all the Roman Catholick States with their Baccaleau; The profits of the whole Trade of these Colonies will all finally center in her, her Navigation will be greatly Increas'd, and the Ballance of her growing Trade to North America will for ever be in her favour: And what seems to make these Advantages still the more valuable is, that they weaken the Power of France whilst they add to that of Great Britain. . . .

242. The Quebec Act, 1774

(*Statutes at Large*, XXX, pp. 549–554, 14 Geo. III, c. 83.)

This Act, largely the work of Sir Guy Carleton, Governor of Quebec, was an attempt, by restoring French civil law and custom in Canada, to conciliate the French Canadians in face of the expected attempt by the French to reconquer the territory. It was, however, widely regarded by the American colonists as an attempt by the mother country to use a Catholic Canada against them. It represented a reversal both of the policy of complete subordination implied by the Proclamation of 1763 (the official 'constitution' of Canada since its cession by France), and of the policy of compromise between English and French law adopted in practice between 1763 and 1774. For the Proclamation of 1763, see vol. IX of these *Documents*, No. 98.

An act for making more effectual provision for the government of the province of Quebec *in* North America.

WHEREAS *his Majesty, by his royal proclamation, bearing date the seventh day of* October, *in the third year of his reign, thought fit to declare the provisions which had been made in respect to certain countries, territories, and islands in* America, *ceded to his Majesty by the definitive treaty of peace, concluded at* Paris *on the tenth day of* February, *one thousand seven hundred and sixty-three; and whereas, by the arrangements made by the said royal proclamation, a very large extent of country, within which there were several colonies and settlements of the subjects of* France, *who claimed to remain therein under the faith of the said treaty, was left, without any provision being made for the administration of civil government therein; and certain parts of the territory of* Canada, *where sedentary fisheries had been established and carried on by the subjects of* France, *inhabitants of the said province of* Canada, *under grants and concessions from the government thereof, were annexed to the government of* Newfoundland, *and thereby subjected to regulations inconsistent with the nature of such fisheries:* may it therefore please your most excellent Majesty that it may be enacted; and be it enacted by the King's most excellent Majesty, by and with the advice and consent of the lords spiritual and temporal, and commons, in this present parliament assembled, and by the authority of the same, That all the territories, islands, and countries in *North America*, belonging to the crown of *Great Britain*, bounded on the south by a line from the bay of *Chaleurs*, along the high lands which divide the rivers that empty themselves into the river *Saint Lawrence* from those which fall into the sea, to a point in forty-five degrees of northern latitude, on the eastern bank of the river *Connecticut*, keeping the same latitude directly west, through the lake *Champlain*, until, in the same latitude, it meets the river *Saint Lawrence*; from thence up the eastern bank of the said river to the lake *Ontario*; thence through the lake *Ontario*, and the river commonly called *Niagara*; and thence along by the eastern and south-eastern bank of lake *Erie*, following the said bank, until the same shall be intersected by the northern boundary, granted by the charter of the province of *Pensylvania*, in case the same shall be so intersected; and from thence along the said northern and western boundaries of the said province, until the said western boundary strike the *Ohio*; but in case the said bank of the said lake shall not be found to be so intersected, then following the said bank until it shall arrive at that point of the said bank which shall be nearest to the north-western angle of the said province of *Pensylvania*, and thence by a right line, to the said north-western angle of the said province; and thence along the western boundary of the said province, until it strike the river *Ohio*; and along the bank of the said river, westward, to the banks of the *Mississippi*, and northward to the southern boundary of the territory granted to the merchants adventurers of *England*, trading to *Hudson's Bay*; and also all such territories, islands, and countries, which have, since the tenth of *February*, one thousand seven hundred and sixty-three, been made part of the government of *Newfoundland*, be, and they are hereby, during his Majesty's pleasure, annexed to, and made part and parcel of, the province of *Quebec*, as created and established by the said royal proclamation of the seventh of *October*, one thousand seven hundred and sixty-three.

II. Provided always, That nothing herein contained, relative to the boundary of the province of *Quebec*, shall in anywise affect the boundaries of any other colony.

III. Provided always, and be it enacted, That nothing in this act contained shall extend, or be construed to extend, to make void, or to vary or alter any right, title or possession, derived under any grant, conveyance, or otherwise howsoever, of or to any lands within the said province, or the provinces thereto adjoining; but that the same shall remain and be in force, and have effect, as if this act had never been made.

IV. *And whereas the provisions, made by the said proclamation, in respect to the civil government of the said province of* Quebec, *and the powers and authorities given to the governor and other civil officers of the said province, by the grants and commissions issued in consequence thereof, have been found, upon experience, to be inapplicable to the state and circumstances of the said province, the inhabitants whereof amounted, at the conquest, to above sixty-five thousand persons professing the religion of the church of* Rome, *and enjoying an established form of constitution and system of laws, by which their persons and property had been protected, governed, and ordered, for a long series of years, from the first establishment of the said province of* Canada; be it therefore further enacted by the authority aforesaid, That the said proclamation, so far as the same relates to the said province of *Quebec*, and the commission under the authority whereof the government of the said province is at present administered, and all and every the ordinance and ordinances made by the governor and council of *Quebec* for the time being, relative to the civil government and administration of justice in the said province, and all commissions to judges and other officers thereof, be, and the same are hereby revoked, annulled, and made void, from and after the first day of *May*, one thousand seven hundred and seventy-five.

V. *And, for the more perfect security and ease of the minds of the inhabitants of the said province*, it is hereby declared, That his Majesty's subjects, professing the religion of the church of *Rome* of and in the said province of *Quebec*, may have, hold, and enjoy, the free exercise of the religion of the church of *Rome*, subject to the King's supremacy, declared and established by an act, made in the first year of the reign of Queen *Elizabeth*, over all the dominions and countries which then did, or thereafter should belong, to the imperial crown of this realm; and that the clergy of the said church, may hold, receive, and enjoy, their accustomed dues and rights, with respect to such persons only as shall profess the said religion.

VI. Provided nevertheless, That it shall be lawful for his Majesty, his heirs or successors, to make such provision out of the rest of the said accustomed dues and rights, for the encouragement of the protestant religion, and for the maintenance and support of a protestant clergy within the said province, as he or they shall, from time to time, think necessary and expedient.

VII. Provided always, and be it enacted, That no person, professing the religion of the church of *Rome*, and residing in the said province, shall be obliged to take the oath required by the said statute passed in the first year of the reign of Queen *Elizabeth*, or any other oaths substituted by any other act in the place thereof; but that every such person who, by the said statute, is required to take the oath therein mentioned, shall be obliged, and is hereby required, to take and subscribe the following oath before the governor, or such other person in such court of record as his Majesty shall appoint, who are hereby authorised to administer the same; *videlicet*,

I A.B. *do sincerely promise and swear, That I will be faithful, and bear true allegiance to his majesty King* George, *and him will defend to the utmost of my power, against all traitorous conspiracies, and attempts whatsoever, which shall be made against his person, crown, and dignity; and I will do my utmost endeavour to disclose and make known to his majesty, his heirs and successors, all treasons, and traitorous conspiracies, and attempts, which I shall know to be against him, or any of them; and all this I do swear without any equivocation, mental evasion, or secret reservation, and renouncing all pardons and dispensations from any power or person whomsoever to the contrary.*

So help me GOD.

And every such person, who shall neglect or refuse to take the said oath before mentioned, shall incur and be liable to the same penalties, forfeitures, disabillities, and incapacities, as he would have incurred and been liable to for neglecting or refusing to take the oath required by the said statute passed in the first year of the reign of Queen *Elizabeth*.

VIII. And be it further enacted by the authority aforesaid, That all his Majesty's *Canadian* subjects within the province of *Quebec*, the religious orders and communities only excepted, may also hold and enjoy their property and possessions, together with all customs and usages relative thereto, and all other their civil rights, in as large, ample, and beneficial manner, as if the said proclamation, commissions, ordinances, and other acts and instruments, had not been made, and as may consist with their allegiance to his Majesty, and subjection to the crown and parliament of *Great Britain*; and that in all matters of controversy, relative to property and civil rights, resort shall be had to the laws of *Canada*, as the rule for the decision of the same; and all causes that shall hereafter be instituted in any of the courts of justice, to be appointed within and for the said province by his Majesty, his heirs and successors, shall, with respect to such property and rights, be determined agreeably to the said laws and customs of *Canada*, until they shall be varied or altered by any ordinances that shall, from time to time, be passed in the said province by the governor, lieutenant governor, or commander in chief, for the time being, by and with the advice and consent of the legislative council of the same, to be appointed in manner herein-after mentioned.

IX. Provided always, That nothing in this act contained shall extend, or be construed to extend, to any lands that have been granted by his Majesty, or shall hereafter be granted by his Majesty, his heirs and successors, to be holden in free and common soccage.

X. Provided also, That it shall and may be lawful to and for every person that is owner of any lands, goods, or credits, in the said province, and that has a right to alienate the said lands, goods, or credits, in his or her life-time, by deed of sale, gift, or otherwise, to devise or bequeath the same at his or her death, by his or her last will and testament; any law, usage, or custom, heretofore or now prevailing in the province, to the contrary hereof in any-wise notwithstanding; such will being executed either according to the laws of *Canada*, or according to the forms prescribed by the laws of *England*.

XI. *And whereas the certainty and lenity of the criminal law of* England, *and the benefits and advantages resulting from the use of it, have been sensibly felt by the inhabitants, from an experience of more than nine years, during which it has been uniformly administered;* be it therefore further enacted by the authority aforesaid, That the same shall continue to be administered, and shall be observed as law in the province of *Quebec*, as well in the description and quality of the offence as in the method of prosecution and trial; and the punishments and forfeitures thereby inflicted to the exclusion of every other rule of criminal law, or mode of proceeding thereon, which did or might prevail in the said province before the year of our Lord one thousand seven hundred and sixty-four; any thing in this act to the contrary thereof in any respect notwithstanding; subject nevertheless to such alterations and amendments as the governor, lieutenant-governor, or commander in chief for the time being, by and with the advice and consent of the legislative council of the said province, hereafter to be appointed, shall, from time to time, cause to be made therein, in manner herein-after directed.

XII. *And whereas it may be necessary to ordain many regulations for the future welfare and good government of the province of* Quebec, *the occasions of which cannot now be foreseen, nor, without much delay and inconvenience, be provided for, without intrusting that authority, for a certain time, and under proper restrictions, to persons resident there: and whereas it is at present inexpedient to call an assembly;* be it therefore enacted by the authority aforesaid, That it shall and may be lawful for his Majesty, his heirs and successors, by warrant under his or their signet or sign manual, and with the advice of the privy council, to constitute and appoint a council for the affairs of the province of *Quebec*, to consist of such persons resident there, not exceeding twenty-three, nor less than seventeen, as his Majesty, his heirs and successors, shall be pleased to appoint; and, upon the death, removal, or absence of any of the members of the said council, in like manner to constitute and appoint such and so many other person or persons as shall be necessary to supply the vacancy or vacancies; which council, so appointed and nominated, or the major part thereof, shall have power and authority to make ordinances for the peace, welfare, and good government of the said province, with the consent of his Majesty's governor, or, in his absence, of the lieutenant-governor, or commander in chief for the time being.

XIII. Provided always, That nothing in this act contained shall extend to authorise or impower the said legislative council to lay taxes or duties within the said province, such rates and taxes only excepted as the inhabitants of any town or district within the said province may be authorised by the said council to assess, levy, and apply, within the said town or district, for the purpose of making roads, erecting and repairing publick buildings, or for any other purpose respecting the local convenience and oeconomy of such town or district.

XIV. Provided also, and be it enacted by the authority aforesaid, That every ordinance so to be made, shall, within six months, be transmitted by the governor, or, in his absence, by the lieutenant-governor, or commander in chief for the time being, and laid before his Majesty for his royal approbation; and if his Majesty shall think fit to disallow thereof, the same shall cease and be void from the time that his Majesty's order in council thereupon shall be promulgated at *Quebec*.

XV. Provided also, That no ordinance touching religion, or by which any punishment may be inflicted greater than fine or imprisonment for three months, shall be of any force or effect, until the same shall have received his Majesty's approbation.

XVI. Provided also, That no ordinance shall be passed at any meeting of the council where less than a majority of the whole council is present, or at any time except between the first day of *January* and the first day of *May*, unless upon some urgent occasion, in which case every member thereof resident at *Quebec*, or within fifty miles thereof, shall be personally summoned by the governor, or, in his absence, by the lieutenant-governor, or commander in chief for the time being, to attend the same.

XVII. And be it further enacted by the authority aforesaid, That nothing herein contained shall extend, or be construed to extend, to prevent or hinder his Majesty, his heirs and successors, by his or their letters patent under the great seal of *Great Britain*, from erecting, constituting, and appointing, such courts of criminal, civil, and ecclesiastical jurisdiction within and for the said province of *Quebec*, and appointing, from time to time, the judges and officers thereof, as his Majesty, his heirs and successors, shall think necessary and proper for the circumstances of the said province.

XVIII. Provided always, and it is hereby enacted, That nothing in this act contained shall extend, or be construed to extend, to repeal or make void, within the said province of *Quebec*, any act or acts of the parliament of *Great Britain* heretofore made, for prohibiting, restraining, or regulating, the trade or commerce of his Majesty's colonies and plantations in *America*; but that all and every the said acts, and also all acts of parliament heretofore made concerning or respecting the said colonies and plantations, shall be, and are hereby declared to be, in force, within the said province of *Quebec*, and every part thereof.

243. Thomas Pownall on the importance of retaining Canada, 1782

(*Two Memorials, not originally intended for publication, now published;* with an Explanatory Preface; by Governor Pownall (1782), pp. 34–37, 38–40, 42.)

Thomas Pownall (1722–1805) was Governor of Massachusetts, 1757–1759, and a sympathetic supporter of the American colonists in Parliament before the Declaration of Independence. For extracts from his book, *The Administration of the Colonies* (1764), see vol. IX of these *Documents*, No. 36. The *Two Memorials*, urging the opening of negotiations for peace with the Americans by acknowledging their independence, were written in 1781 and given to Lord George Germain for presentation to the king. On Germain's resignation they were returned to Pownall, who published them in 1782. His views on Canada were broadly those of Shelburne and the negotiators of the Peace of Paris. Compare with the views of Shirley, No. 241.

. . . The possession of the provinces of Quebec and Nova Scotia, is necessary to Great Britain so long as she retains her plantations in the islands of the West Indies: they are the sources from whence (at a certainty under all events) these islands can draw their necessary supply of lumber, fish, and live stock. The memorialist does not here take notice of the supply of flour, corn, and grain, nor of salt-provisions, which may in future be drawn from thence, as he conceives that these may be more beneficially at present drawn, the first from England, the last from Ireland.

The possession of these provinces is necessary to Great Britain as a naval power: without them, she can have no naval station, command, or protection in the American seas: with them, she may have all these, although they may not be able to supply at present her navy with all the naval stores that she may want. They will, however, supply sufficient quantity to ward off the monopoly which some of the northern Powers of Europe have formerly endeavoured, and may again endeavour, to establish against Britain; and have, and may again, as far as such could be established, use it hostilely against her.

The province of Quebec, occupied to the extent that the variety of its natural products and capabilities go to, will become a much greater source of trade, in all events, than may appear openly at first sight. This province, by the command which it hath of water-carriage (if the maintaining of that command shall be duly attended to and continued) will be the market to, and have the supply of, not only the Indians, but of all the inhabitants of the back countries, as they shall become settled, be they settled by whomsoever they may; for the merchants of this province, by advantage of their water-carriage, and by their ease of communication, will be able to supply the distant market cheaper than any other can, and will of course have the custom.

To defend and to maintain command in this province, the Memorialist ventures to say it will be necessary to maintain such a naval establishment on the great lakes, and on Lake Champlain particularly, as shall hold command in them. This measure this Memorialist first had the honour to suggest and recommend at a congress held at Albany in the year 1754; this measure was then adopted, was for the first time in 1755 put into efficient execution, and proved a decisive measure in the events of last war.

Such a naval power is necessary for the defence of Montreal and Quebec; such is necessary to the maintaining of authority with the Indians, and to the keeping open the courses of trade and commerce; it is necessary to cover the advancing settlements of the province, as in time it shall be enlarged in population and habitancy.

The possession of the province Nova Scotia, by the command that a naval station at Halifax may give, is necessary to the protection of the northern fisheries in America, at least to such share as this country may hereafter have in them.

The sort of interest and power which may arise from a right occupying of these provinces, will always retain some hold on the *thirteen tribes which have gone off from Israel*; and when war shall end, will make it their interest to seek the alliance of Great Britain: as, on the other hand, Great Britain will always find it her interest to maintain a maternal alliance with the Americans, her descendants. . . .

The settling such of the loyalists, refugees from the Americans, as choose to live under British Government, in a way not to ruin but to preserve them, is not only a measure which honour, justice, and humanity require; but the settling of them in these provinces (if that be done as it ought to be) will in time become one of the principal means of defence and strength to them. The giving to these unfortunate and ruined people lands, in the common idea of that measure, would be cruelty under the cloak of benevolence; but the purchasing for such of them, who had been farmers, farms, in part brought forward into culture (called by the Americans improvements) and the settling them where they will be of the greatest use to the civil government, as also to the military defence, as a militia, would be an act wherein true wisdom and real benevolence would unite. To those who had not been used to farming, but were merchants, houses should be given, with the means of commencing again, in some degree, their business. Those who were merely tradesmen and mechanics will be more easily settled and reinstated. Those who in their original homes, from whence they have been driven, were advanced, or were advancing, to honours, and a share in the government of their country, will of course become subjects for trust and employment with your Majesty. . . .

This Memorialist would betray his duty, if he did not here mention the necessity which will arise of establishing a Free Colonial Constitution of Government in these provinces; but he does not now enter into it, as that is an important matter of consideration separate from the present. It will however mix itself essentially in the consequences. . . .

(*d*) NOVA SCOTIA AND NEWFOUNDLAND

244. The settlement of Nova Scotia, 1749

(*Selections from the Public Documents of the Province of Nova Scotia*, ed. Thomas B. Akins, I (1869), pp. 495–496.)

The plan for the settlement of Nova Scotia, which had been ceded by France at the Peace of Utrecht, was largely the work of Halifax, President of the Board of Trade, 1748–1761, after whom the town of Halifax, Nova Scotia, was named. The response to the advertisement was good, and in June 1749 the new Governor, Edward Cornwallis, went out with over 2,300 settlers.

Advertisement published in the *London Gazette*, March 1749.

WHITEHALL, 7th March, 1749.

A proposal having been presented unto His Majesty for the establishing a civil government in the Province of Nova Scotia, in North America, as also for the better peopling and settling the said Province, and extending and improving the

Fishery thereof, by granting lands within the same, and giving other encouragement to such of the officers and private men lately dismissed His Majesty's land and sea service, as shall be willing to settle in the said Province. And His Majesty having signed his royal approbation of the report of the said proposals, the Right Honourable the Lords Commissioners for Trade and Plantations, do by His Majesty's command, give notice that proper encouragement will be given to such of the officers and private men lately dismissed His Majesty's Land and Sea service, as are willing to accept grants of land, and to settle with or without families in Nova Scotia. That 50 acres of land will be granted in fee simple to every private soldier or seaman, free from the payment of any quit rents or taxes for the term of ten years, at the expiration whereof no person to pay more than one shilling per annum, for every 50 acres so granted.

That a grant of 10 acres, over and above the 50, will be made to each private soldier or seaman having a family, for every person including women and children of which his family shall consist, and further grants made to them on the like conditions as their families shall increase, or in proportion to their abilities to cultivate the same.

That eighty acres on like conditions will be granted to every officer under the rank of Ensign in the land service, and that of Lieutenant in the sea service, and to such as have families, fifteen acres over and above the said eighty acres, for every person of which their family shall consist.

That two hundred acres on like conditions will be granted to every Ensign, three hundred to every Lieutenant, four hundred to every Captain, and six hundred to every officer above the rank of Captain. And to such of the above mentioned officers as have families, a further grant of thirty acres will be made over and above their respective quotas for every person of which their family shall consist.

That the lands will be parcelled out to the settlers as soon as possible after their arrival, and a civil government established, whereby they will enjoy all the liberties, privileges and immunities enjoyed by His Majesty's subjects in any other of the Colonies and Plantations in America, under His Majesty's Government, and proper measures will also be taken for their security and protection.

That all such as are willing to accept of the above proposals shall, with their families, be subsisted during the passage, also for the space of twelve months after their arrival.

That they shall be furnished with arms and ammunition as far as will be judged necessary for their defence, with a proper quantity of materials and utensils for husbandry, clearing and cultivating the lands, erecting habitations, carrying on the fishery, and such other purposes as shall be deemed necessary for their support.

That all such persons as are desirous of engaging in the above settlement, do transmit by letter, or personally give in their names, signifying in what regiment or company, or on board what ship they last served, and if they have families they intend to carry with them, distinguishing the age and quality of each person to any of the following officers appointed to receive and enter the same in the books opened for that purpose, *viz*:–John Pownell, Esq., Solicitor and Clerk of the Repts. of the Lords Comrs. of Trade and Plantations, at their office at Whitehall; John Russell, Esq.,

Comr. of His Majesty's Navy at Portsmouth; Philip Vanburgh, Esq., Comr. of His Majesty's Navy at Plymouth.

And the proper notice will be given of the said Books being closed, as soon as the intended number shall be completed, or at least on the 7th day of April.

It is proposed that the Transports shall be ready to receive such persons on board on the 10th April, and be ready to sail on the 20th, and that timely notice will be given of the place or places to which such persons are to repair in order to embark.

That for the benefit of the settlement, the same conditions which are proposed to private soldiers and seamen shall likewise be granted to Carpenters, Shipwrights, Smiths, Masons, Joiners, Brickmakers, Bricklayers and all other artificers necessary in building or husbandry, not being private soldiers or seamen.

That the same conditions as are proposed to those who have served in the capacity of Ensign shall extend to all Surgeons, whether they have been in His Majesty's service or not, upon their producing proper certificates of their being duly qualified.

By order of the Right Hon. the Lords Comrs. of Trade and Plantations.

THOMAS HILL, Secretary.

245A–B. Grant of a representative assembly to Nova Scotia, 1758

(*Selections from the Public Documents of the Province of Nova Scotia*, ed. Thomas B. Akins, I (1869), pp. 718–719, 725–726.)

Representative government on the same lines as that enjoyed by the other American colonies had been promised to Nova Scotia at the time of the settlement, and by 1758 the settlers were growing restive at the delay in implementing this promise. The plan for an assembly drawn up by the Governor's Council was forwarded to the Board of Trade by the Governor, Charles Lawrence, who was himself against the grant of an assembly at that time, with all the uncertainties of the war with the French in America and his own military preoccupations, and he told the Board of Trade that all substantial and responsible people in the province agreed with him. The Board of Trade, however, felt that the grant of an assembly could no longer be delayed.

245A. Minutes of the Council of Nova Scotia, 3 January 1757

At a Council holden at the Governors House in Halifax on Monday the 3rd Jany. 1757.

PRESENT—

The Lieutenant Governor

Jonn. Belcher, Jno. Collier, Chas. Morris,	Councs.	Benj. Green, Robt. Grant

His Excellency the Governor together with His Majestys Council having had under mature consideration the necessary and most expedient measures for carrying into Execution those parts of His Majesty's Commission and Instructions which relate to the calling General Assemblies within the Province, came to the following Resolutions thereon, *viz.*

That a House of Representatives of the inhabitants of this Province, be the Civil Legislature thereof, in Conjunction with His Majesty's Governor or Commander in Chief for the Time being, and His Majesty's Council of the said Province, the first

House to be Elected and Convened in the following manner, and to be stiled the General Assembly, vizt.

That there shall be Elected for the Province at large until the same shall be divided

into Counties	12 members
For the Township of Halifax	4 "
For the Township of Lunenburg	2 "
For the Township of Dartmouth	1 "
For the Township of Lawrence Town	1 "
For the Township of Annapolis Royal	1 "
For the Township of Cumberland	1 "
	22

[Limits of the Townships described.]

That when Twenty five Qualified Electors shall be settled at Pisiquid, Minas, Cobequid, or any other Townships which may hereafter be erected, each of the said Townships so settled, shall for their encouragement be entitled to send one Representative of the General Assembly, and shall likewise have a Right of voting in the Election of Representatives for the Province at large.

That the House shall always consist of at least Sixteen members present, besides the Speaker, before they enter upon Business.

[Franchise to be in freeholders over twenty-one years of age, Popish Recusants being excluded.

Procedure for elections laid down.]

245B. Extract from a letter of the Board of Trade to Governor Lawrence, 7 February 1758

WHITEHALL, Feby. 7, 1758.

We have fully considered that part of your Letter, which relates to the calling an Assembly, and also the Plan for that purpose, contained in the minutes of the Council transmitted with it, and having so often and so fully repeated to you our sense and opinion of the Propriety & Necessity of this measure taking place, it only now remains for Us to direct its being carried into immediate execution, that His Majesty's Subjects (great part of whom are alleged to have quitted the Province on account of the great discontent prevailing for want of an Assembly) may no longer be deprived of that privilege, which was promised to them by His Majesty, when the Settlement of this Colony was first undertaken, and was one of the Conditions upon which they accepted the Proposals then made.

We are sensible that the Execution of this measure may in the present situation of the Colony be attended with many difficulties, and possibly may in its consequences, in some respects interfere with, and probably embarrass His Majesty's Service; but without regard to these Considerations, or to what may be the opinion of individuals with respect to this measure, We think it of indispensable necessity that it should be immediately carried into execution.

We approve in general that part of your Plan which establishes Townships and ascertains their Limits as corresponding with the Plan laid down in the Instructions given to Mr. Cornwallis at the first Settlement of the Colony; but We do not think it advisable, that any of those Townships, which has not fifty settled families, should be allowed to send Representatives to the Assembly; and therefore we would propose that for the present, those only, which have that number of Settled Families, should have that Privilege, & that the rest of the members, computing the whole at twenty two, should be elected for the Province at large, considered as one County, according to the Plan agreed upon, but that whenever any of those Townships, which are now established, or any others which may hereafter be established, shall contain Fifty Settled Families, they shall be entitled to a Writ for electing two Representatives, and the number of members for the whole Province at large, considered as one County, shall be diminished in proportion.

As to the other parts of your Plan, they do not appear to us liable to objection, excepting only that part which establishes the Quorum of the Assembly, and fixes it at Seventeen, which We apprehend to be too great a proportion of the whole; and that it ought not at the most to exceed one half of the whole number, which is more agreeable to what has been judged to be proper in cases of other American Assemblies, whose great Inconveniencies have been found to result from the Quorum of the Assembly being too great a proportion of the whole. . . .

246. A contemporary account of Newfoundland, 1765

(Captain Griffith Williams, *An Account of the Island of Newfoundland*. . . (1765), pp. 1–4, 10–18, 22–23.)

The author describes himself as "of the Royal Regiment of Artillery, who resided in the Island Fourteen Years when a Lieutenant, and now has a Command there".

The Island of *Newfoundland* is not inhabited any-where, but along the Sea Shore; and there are but very few People that know any Thing of the interior Part: Almost all the Country, for several Miles from the Sea, is covered with Woods of different Kinds, very useful for Ship and Boat-building; also; for erecting Stages and Flakes for curing and drying Fish.

I have been between Twenty and Thirty Miles into the Country, where I found the Land clear of Woods, which produced very rich Pasturage. I saw great Numbers of Deer, of a prodigious Size, and vast Quantities of Partridges, Wolves, and Foxes; and in the Lakes and Rivers (which are numerous) there are Bever, Otter, Trout, Wild Ducks and Geese, in great Quantities.

It is very surprising, that, for so many Years past, no Care has been taken to improve so valuable a Branch of Commerce as the *Newfoundland* Fishery might be to *Great Britain*! This Trade, to my certain Knowledge, for many Years, remitted, in Specie, near a Million Sterling, to the Mother Country: And at this Time, I dare say, it does not remit One Sixth Part of that Sum.

The Lords of the Admiralty, and of Trade and Plantations, did, I suppose, and do still, think, the Commodores or Governors of *Newfoundland* always send them a just State of the Fishery, I believe they have wished to have done it; and, dare say, they thought it exact. The Methods they take are as follow.

The Commodore or Governor generally arrives at *St. John's* some time in *June*, and sails again in *September*, or the Beginning of *October*, for *Europe*: Therefore, suppose him to be on that coast three Months, and, conformable to his Instructions, he is obliged to have a State of the Fishery made out, in order to be sent to the Board of Trade, etc. in Consequence of this, his Clerk goes to one of the Magistrates on Shore, and desires him to send to each of the Harbours, one of those States, ruled and worded, ready to be filled up (for Example). The Magistrate sends one of them to a Merchant at Harbour *Grace* (which is one of the Harbours in *Conception* Bay), who, in the Hurry of Business, fills it up at Random, thinking it mere Matter of Form, and of little Consequence; for had he been ever so desirous of being exact, he could not have been so without a vast deal of Trouble, as the Bay is, at least, seventy Miles round, and Boats kept in every Creek and Cove of it. This State is returned to the Governor, and he sends it Home to *England*, taking it for granted to be right; by which Method the Commodore, who is Governor during his Command there, can know very little more of the Matter than if he had remained at *Portsmouth*, or *Plymouth*.

I remember one of the above Kind of Returns being sent to the Governor, with an Account of the Number of Boats kept, the Quantity of Fish and Oil caught, etc, etc. Having a Boat and Men of my own, I had the Curiosity to know how near they came to the Truth, and therefore began at Bay *Verds* in *Conception* Bay, and went into every Creek and Cove quite round to *Portugal* Cove, which is the other Extremity of the Bay, and found they had not got within a Third Part in any one Account. . . .

The Fisheries of *Newfoundland* were originally carried on by the Ships only, and none allowed to Fish but such as cleared out of some Port in *Great Britain*: But, in Time, those concerned in that Trade found much greater Advantage by fishing in Boats along the Shore; in consequence of which, they found it necessary for Numbers to remain in the Island during the Winter, in order to build Boats for the Service of the ensuing Season, as also to get Materials out of the Woods, for their Fishing Rooms, etc.

This is a Brand of the Fishery that should be taken most particular Notice of, as it is found to be, by far, the most advantageous: Therefore great Amendments should be made in the Act of Parliament, relative to the Fishery of *Newfoundland*; the greatest Encouragement should be given to those that would reside there in the Winter, as they are not only useful in preparing every Thing necessary for the Voyage, but also often begin fishing a Month before the Ships are come from *Europe*.

A great deal has been said concerning the *Newfoundland* Fishery, by many of the News Writers, and others; but I have not found that any of them have the least Notion of it. Some would have it, that the best Part of it was given away when the Islands of St. *Peter* and *Miquelon* were ceded to the *French*;[1] others thought, when you had drove them from Cape *Breton*, the Fishery was secured to us; some, again,

[1] At the Peace of Paris, 1763.

would have *Canso* to be the best Part of the Fishery; others preferred *Halifax*; and even some went so far as to think *Boston* in *New England* a very convenient Place to carry on the Fish Trade: But I will take upon me to say, that you need not be jealous of all the Cod Fisheries in the World, had you all to the Northward of Cape *Race* in *Newfoundland*. But I am sorry to say, that the *French* have, by far, the best part of it. . . .

The great Staple for Fish, is from Cape *Race*, all along the Eastern Coast of *Newfoundland* to the Streights of *Bellisle*, and from thence to Point *Riche* (the Part inhabited by the *English*), which begins in *Placentia* Bay, and continues all along the Shore to *Trapassee*, *Fermoves*, *Feriland*, and as far Northward as Cape *Bonavista*.

The *French*, at the Time they were in Possession of Cape *Breton*, had a small Fishery carried on at *Louisburg*, and at several Creeks and Coves opposite to the said Island on the Coast of *Newfoundland*, and some within the Gulph of St. *Lawrence*; but their greatest Resource, was from Cape *Bonavista* to Point *Riche*.

This was the Fishery we had then Cause to lament the Loss of; and, indeed, so we have to this Day; the Fish in those Parts being in greater Abundance, and the Fishery carried on at Half the Expence, the Weather being much better for curing because the Fogs don't go any farther Northward than the Great Bank of *Newfoundland* (the Northward Point of which runs to Latitude 48 or 49 Deg.), which is something to the Northward of *Bonavista*.

It may be asked, Why don't our Fishermen extend their Fisheries Northward? The Reason is very clear: The Expence of building Storehouses, clearing of Plantations, and building Fishing Rooms, Stages, etc. etc. are very expensive; therefore none would embark in it, without a Certainty of Protection, both in Time of Peace and War; as it takes some Years to be properly fixed to carry on the said Trade. There is not any Thing so advantageous and necessary, as to have Numbers of People remain in the Country the whole Winter.

It is very clear, that not a Foot of the Country from Cape *Sable*, in the Bay of *Fundy*, to Cape *Race*, in *Newfoundland*, is worth One Shilling to *England*, otherwise than the Troops you keep there, are a Check upon the *French* and *Indians*.

We have now an Opportunity of establishing that most valuable Branch of the Fish Trade; and there is nothing wanting but our falling on a proper Method to make the Returns double to what they ever have been.

I would therefore propose, that a Governor for the whole Island should reside at St. *John's*, which should be the Capital, as it is the most convenient Place to make up a Convoy; and it is likewise the nearest Place that can be for the Center of Trade, and also the most Eastern Part of the Island; by which Means, Ships cannot be imbayed; but, in Half an Hour after they are out of the Harbour, they have Sea Room enough, and can stand North or South with great Safety.

St. *John's*, *Feriland*, *Carboniere*, and *Trinity* Harbours, should be put on the same Footing, they were intended in 1745; and such other Forts and Batteries, should be erected at such Harbours, as should be found useful and advantageous for carrying on the Fishery to the Northward. . . .

Had those Places remained on the before-mentioned Footing, I am convinced, that France could not have sent an Armament against it at the Time they did, to meet with any success, and indeed the success they met with at the Time they took it, was chiefly owing to the Irish Roman Catholics.

I am of opinion, that none but the Inhabitants of *Great Britain*, *Newfoundland*, with *Jersey* and *Guernsey*, (being *Protestants*) should have the Privilege of being possessed of any Fish Rooms, or Plantations in the Island of *Newfoundland*. The *Irish Roman Catholics* are useful as Servants, but very dangerous in that Part of the World, when in Power.

I would propose, that all Manner of Necessaries for the support of the Fishermen, should be made as cheap as possible, provided you don't hurt the Mother Country. Every Thing for the carrying on this immense Branch of Trade, is the Product of *England*, except Beef, Pork, and Butter, from *Ireland*; Rum, Sugar, and Melasses, from the *West-Indies* and *New-England*; as also a good deal of Bread and Flour, from *New-York*, *Philadelphia*, *Boston*, etc.

We have from *Portugal* and *Spain*, Salt and Olive Oil, and a mere Trifle of Port and *Lisbon* Wines; Oil is what the Fishermen cannot do without, to eat with Salt Fish, both Winter and Summer; and as the Oil must first be brought to *England*, and then re-shipped for *Newfoundland*, notwithstanding it leaves but the meerest Trifle at the Custom House, yet the double Freight, and many other Expences, make it come exceeding dear to the Fishermen; therefore was it allowed to be taken on Board the Ships that are constantly returning from *Lisbon*, and other Ports, with Salt to *Newfoundland*, the Fishermen would be able to purchase it at 75 per cent. cheaper, than its coming by Way of *England*. . . .

I cannot help again observing the Absurdity of a Captain of a Man of War's being Governor of so extensive a Branch of Trade. It is not in the Nature of Things, from their short Residence there, that they can ever arrive to any Degree of Knowledge of it. I have known them give Grants to particular People, that would have ruined the whole Trade, and could mention the Names of those Governors, but rather chuse to avoid it, as they did it from want of a true Knowledge of the Trade, and therefore were liable to be imposed upon by designing People. Sir *George Rodney*, when he was Governor, invalidated several of them, and one, in particular, which was a Patent for a Man to have the sole Privilege of drawing Baite at a certain Beech; which, had it remained in Force, would have ruined the remaining Part of the Inhabitants for Forty Leagues along the Coast.

E. INDIA

247A–B. Robert Clive's proposals for the government of India, 1759

247A. Letter from Robert Clive to William Pitt, 7 January 1759

(*Correspondence of William Pitt, Earl of Chatham*, ed. W. S. Taylor and J. H. Pringle, I (1838), pp. 387–392.)

Clive later changed his mind about the arrangement proposed in this letter, when he saw it would lead to the interference by the government in the East India Company's affairs. He shows himself well aware of the new problems created for the Company by the vast increase of territory and wealth resulting from the successes of the Seven Years War.

Calcutta, January 7, 1759.

Sir,

Suffer an admirer of yours at this distance to congratulate himself on the glory and advantage which are likely to accrue to the nation by your being at its head, and at the same time to return his most grateful thanks for the distinguished manner you have been pleased to speak of his successes in these parts, far indeed beyond his deservings.

The close attention you bestow on the affairs of the British nation in general has induced me to trouble you with a few particulars relative to India, and to lay before you an exact account of the revenues of this country; the genuineness whereof you may depend upon, as it has been faithfully copied from the minister's books.

The great revolution that has been effected here by the success of the English arms, and the vast advantages gained to the Company by a treaty concluded in consequence thereof, have, I observe, in some measure engaged the public attention; but much more may yet in time be done, if the Company will exert themselves in the manner the importance of their present possessions and future prospects deserves. I have represented to them in the strongest terms the expediency of sending out and keeping up constantly such a force as will enable them to embrace the first opportunity of further aggrandizing themselves; and I dare pronounce, from a thorough knowledge of this country's government, and of the genius of the people, acquired by two years' application and experience, that such an opportunity will soon offer. The reigning Subah, whom the victory at Plassey invested with the sovereignty of these provinces, still, it is true, retains his attachment to us, and probably, while he has no other support, will continue to do so; but Mussulmans are so little influenced by gratitude, that should he ever think it his interest to break with us, the obligations he owes us would prove no restraint: and this is very evident from his having very lately removed his prime minister, and cut off two or three of his principal officers, all attached to our interest, and who had a share in his elevation. Moreover, he is advanced in years; and his son is so cruel and worthless a young fellow, and so apparently an enemy to the English, that it will be almost useless trusting him with the succession. So small a body as two thousand Europeans will secure us against any apprehensions from either the one or the other, and in case of their daring to be troublesome, enable the Company to take the sovereignty upon themselves.

There will be the less difficulty in bringing about such an event, as the natives themselves have no attachment whatever to particular princes; and as, under the present government, they have no security for their lives or properties, they would rejoice in so happy an exchange as that of a mild for a despotic government; and there is little room to doubt our easily obtaining the mogul's sannud (or grant) in confirmation thereof, provided we agree to pay him the stipulated allotment out of the revenues. That this would be agreeable to him can hardly be questioned, as it would be so much to his interest to have these countries under the dominion of a nation famed for their good faith, rather than in the hands of people who, a long experience has convinced him, never will pay him his proportion of the revenues, unless awed into it by the fear of the imperial army marching to force them thereto.

But so large a sovereignty may possibly be an object too extensive for a mercantile company; and it is to be feared they are not of themselves able, without the nation's assistance, to maintain so wide a dominion. I have therefore presumed, Sir, to represent this matter to you, and submit it to your consideration, whether the execution of a design, that may hereafter be still carried to greater lengths, be worthy of the government's taking it into hand.

I flatter myself I have made it pretty clear to you, that there will be little or no difficulty in obtaining the absolute possession of these rich kingdoms; and that with the mogul's own consent, on condition of paying him less then a fifth of the revenues thereof. Now I leave you to judge, whether an income yearly of upwards of two millions sterling, with the possession of three provinces abounding in the most valuable productions of nature and of art, be an object deserving the public attention; and whether it be worth the nation's while to take the proper measures to secure such an acquisition,—an acquisition which, under the management of so able and disinterested a minister, would prove a source of immense wealth to the kingdom, and might in time be appropriated in part as a fund towards diminishing the heavy load of debt under which we at present labour.

Add to these advantages the influence we shall thereby acquire over the several European nations engaged in the commerce here, which these could no longer carry on but through our indulgence, and under such limitations as we should think fit to prescribe. It is well worthy consideration, that this project may be brought about without draining the mother country, as has been too much the case with our possessions in America. A small force from home will be sufficient, as we always make sure of any number we please of black troops, who, being both much better paid and treated by us than by the country powers, will very readily enter into our service.

Mr. Walsh, who will have the honour of delivering you this, having been my secretary during the late fortunate expedition, is a thorough master of the subject, and will be able to explain to you the whole design, and the facility with which it may be executed, much more to your satisfaction, and with greater perspicuity, than can possibly be done in a letter. I shall therefore only further remark, that I have communicated it to no other person but yourself; nor should I have troubled you, Sir, but from a conviction that you will give a favourable reception to any proposal intended for the public good.

The greatest part of the troops belonging to this establishment are now employed in an expedition against the French in the Deccan; and, by the accounts lately received from thence, I have great hopes we shall succeed in extirpating them from the province of Golconda, where they have reigned lords paramount so long, and from whence they have drawn their principal resources during the troubles upon the coast.

Notwithstanding the extraordinary efforts made by the French in sending out M. Lally with a considerable force the last year, I am confident, before the end of this, they will be near their last gasp in the Carnatic, unless some very unforeseen event interpose in their favour. The superiority of our squadron, and the plenty of money and supplies of all kinds which our friends on the coast will be furnished with from this province, while the enemy are in total want of every thing, without any visible means of redress, are such advantages as, if properly attended to, cannot fail of wholly effecting their ruin in that as well as in every part of India.

May your zeal, and the vigorous measures projected for the service of the nation, which have so eminently distinguished your ministry, be crowned with all the success they deserve, is the most fervent wish of him who is, with the greatest respect, Sir,

Your most devoted humble servant,

ROB. CLIVE.

247B. Extract from a letter from John Walsh to Robert Clive, 26 November 1759

(Sir John Malcolm, *Life of Robert, Lord Clive*, I (1836), pp. 126–128.)

This contains Pitt's oral reply to Clive's letter of 7 January. Pitt also changed his mind later. In 1767 he took the line that the Company's conquered territories belonged to the Crown, or at least to the Crown and Company jointly. John Walsh (1725?–1795) was Clive's private secretary and paymaster of the troops in Madras.

. . . It was not till six days ago that I had admittance to Mr. Pitt. He had made one or two appointments, but was obliged by business to postpone them, for certainly he has an infinite deal on his hands. He received me with the utmest [*sic*] politeness, and we had a *tête-à-tête* for an hour and a quarter, of which I will endeavour to sum up the particulars. He began by mentioning how much he was obliged to you, for the marks you have given him of your friendship; and then began on the subject of your letter. I said I was apprehensive, from my not having had the honour to speak with him before, that he looked upon the affair as chimerical: he assured me, not at all, but very practicable; but that it was of a very nice nature. He mentioned the Company's charter not expiring these twenty years; that upon some late transactions it had been inquired into, whether the Company's conquests and acquisitions belonged to them or the Crown, and the Judges seemed to think to the Company. He spoke this matter a little darkly, and I cannot write upon it with precision: he said the Company were not proper to have it, nor the Crown, for such a revenue would endanger our liberties; and that you had shown your good sense by the application of it to the public. He said the difficulty of effecting the affair was not great, under such a genius as Colonel Clive; but the sustaining it was the point: it was not probable he would be succeeded by persons equal to the task. He asked how long you proposed continuing there; that by your letter he might conclude you intended to carry the business into execution. I answered that no one's zeal for the public service was greater than yours; but that I believed your ill health would oblige you to return shortly. I then mentioned Van [sittart]'s abilities, and that he was upon the point of being made Governor of Bengal. I observed to him that it was necessary for him to determine whether it was an object for the Company or the State; for I was persuaded, that, if the State neglected it, the Company, in process of time, would secure it; that they would even find themselves under a necessity to do it for their greater quiet and safety, exclusive of gain. He seemed to weigh that; but, as far as I could judge by what passed then, it will be left to the Company to do what they please.

I took an opportunity of mentioning that the French seemed to direct their views greatly towards India; spoke of Dupleix's designs, Bussy's letter, and Lally's armament, which, happily for us, had melted away to nothing, but that in time of peace, if not somehow restrained, they would certainly pour men into India, and be formidable in after times. He asked me about Mauritius; whether the reduction of that would not be laying the axe to the root, and how far it was practicable. . . .

248A–B. Proceedings in Parliament on the East India Company's affairs, May–June 1767

(*Parl. Hist.*, XVI, pp. 343–346, 351–353.)

The Company's greatly increased wealth and territories after the Seven Years War created new problems of administration and in their relations with the government. The Chatham ministry brought the whole question of the Company's affairs before Parliament in 1766, but Chatham's illness and retirement from public affairs, and the fact that the ministers were divided over the method to be pursued, enabled the Company to make terms with the government whereby they kept control over all their territories in India, while paying the government a yearly sum of £400,000. In 1767 the Company, which had already in 1766 raised its dividend from 6 to 10 per cent, declared a dividend of 12½ per cent. The government then passed a Bill to prohibit the Company from raising the dividend above 10 per cent. The following extracts show the terms of the agreement between the Company and the government; and the grounds on which the Dividend Bill was opposed. The Rockingham Whigs were the strongest opponents of the Bill, and their views in 1767 may be compared with those of Burke in 1783 (No. 252).

248A. Proceedings in the House of Commons, May 1767

After the House had several times, resolved itself into this Committee of enquiry, and had called for papers, and accounts relating to this affair, at last on the 20th of May, there was presented to the House, and read, a Petition of the united company of merchants of England, trading to the East Indies, setting forth:

"That the petitioners, being duly sensible of the great obligation they lie under to government, and that their interests are, and must ever be, inseparable from those of the state, are most earnestly desirous that the public, and the East India Company should mutually reap the benefits arising from the acquisitions and revenues, lately obtained in India; and the petitioners conceiving, that in the present state of things, a temporary agreement, for the space of three years, may be conducive to the advantage of both, do submit to the consideration of parliament the following Proposition, in order to the carrying such agreement into execution.

1. "They beg leave humbly to suggest, that it will be not only expedient but necessary to the extending their commerce, and enabling them to invest those revenues

in India in the produce of the country, that this House will take under their consideration the inland duties upon teas, in order to prevent the pernicious practice of smuggling, and encourage the consumption of that commodity, by such an alteration in the duties as to the House shall seem fitting, and by granting a drawback on such teas as may be exported to Ireland, or to any of his Majesty's colonies, and also by such alterations, as may conduce to the same salutary purposes, in regard to the duties on callicoes, muslins, and raw silk.

2. "That in order to render the advantages expectant from the revenues before mentioned certain and permanent, the House will provide effectual methods, as well for recruiting the forces necessary in India, as for regulating the Company's civil and military servants there, for preventing the exportation of military stores thither, except for the Company's service, and for preventing illicit trade.

3. "That from the said revenues, there shall be deducted, the expences attending the collection thereof, together with the civil, military, and marine establishments, and also the charges incurred for fortifications, buildings, and repairs, the same to be adjudged by annual accounts transmitted from, and properly authenticated by, the several presidencies, in which the same shall be incurred.

4. "That an account of the Company, including the residue of the said revenues, and the produce of their exports, shall be annually made up, and that of the sums arising from the general sales, the sum of 400,000l. shall be deducted, in lieu of profits, which the petitioners have hitherto enjoyed.

5. "That the net surplus shall be equally divided between the public and the company.

6. "That the Company's share of the said surplus shall be duly and solely appropriated to the payment of their present debts, until they shall be reduced to the sum due to the Company from the public.

7. "That this agreement shall commence from the 1st of February, 1767, upon all goods to be imported from India, and shall continue for three years, provided the Dewannee of Bengal, Bahar, and Orixa,[1] shall remain in the Company's hands.

8. "But if it should be the opinion of the House, that it will be the more beneficial for the public to enjoy a specific sum, instead of the proportion of the revenues and trade above mentioned, then the petitioners proposed to pay, in lieu thereof, 400,000l. per annum for three years, by half yearly payments; the first payment to commence March 25, 1768; and they are also willing to indemnify the public in respect of such draw-back on teas exported, as shall be granted by parliament, taking the same in a medium of the duties on the quantity of teas exported for five years past; and that such indemnification shall also extend to the inland duty of one shilling in the pound on the quantities of all black and singlo teas, consumed in Great Britain, upon a like medium of five years, in case it shall also appear a fit measure to parliament to take off the said duty; and provided the duties on the increased consumption shall not be sufficient to replace or supply the aforesaid duty of one shilling in the pound: and the petitioners hope, that what is hereby proposed, either in the mode of participation, or by a certain yearly payment, will appear reasonable and equitable to the House,

[1] The control of the finances of these provinces granted to the Company by Clive's treaty with the Mogul Emperor in 1765.

more especially considering that the public revenue during this interval, must continually increase in the same proportion with the commerce of the Company, and the petitioners entreat the House to recollect the imminent dangers to which, in many critical conjunctures, their properties have been often exposed, the very large sums they have expended since the commencement of the wars in India, in which they were never the aggressors, the low dividends, which notwithstanding their few losses at sea, they have received during a course of years, whilst the public remained in the uninterrupted participation of an annual revenue, arising from the Company's trade, of the full value of one third of their capital; circumstances, which, the proprietors flatter themselves, will procure them the favour and protection of this honourable House, and entitle them to that candour and justice, which have ever been the characteristics of the British senate."

This Petition was referred to a committee, who came to the following Resolutions, *viz.* "That it is the opinion of this committee,

1. That it would be for the mutual benefit of the public, and the East India Company, that a temporary agreement be made, in regard to the territorial acquisitions and revenues lately obtained in India.
2. That it is expedient, for the purposes of the said agreement, that it should continue for a term, not exceeding three years, to commence from the 1st of February, 1767.
3. That the said acquisitions and revenues do remain in the possession of the Company, during the continuance of such agreement: and that the Company do pay the public, annually, during the said term, the sum of 400,000l., by half yearly payments, each payment to be made within six months after the same shall have become due.
4. That it will be necessary and proper, for the better carrying on and extending the trade of the said Company, that provision be made for granting a drawback on teas exported to Ireland, and the British dominions in America; and for taking off the inland duty of one shilling per pound weight on black and singlo teas, consumed in Great Britain; upon such indemnification to be made by the Company to the public, in respect to such duty and drawback, as is mentioned in the Petition of the said Company."

The three first of these Resolutions were agreed to by the House *nem. con.* and a Bill ordered to be brought in upon them. And the fourth Resolution was referred to the Committee of Ways and Means.

248B. Proceedings in the House of Lords upon the Dividend Bill, 26 June 1767

June 26. The Bill was read a third time and passed. The following is the substance of the arguments made use of for and against the said Bill:

The advocates of the Bill seemed to ground their motives on the following principles. To prevent the payment of a higher dividend than the circumstances of the Company could afford, without endangering their credit. To regulate the dividend in such a manner, as to put an end to the fluctuation of that stock, which if allowed to go on, was not only likely to introduce a pernicious spirit of gaming, but would also tend to keep down the other stocks, the rise of which is a great means of reducing the interest of the national debt. That no encroachment might be made by any dividend of the Company, upon the revenue of its late territorial acquisitions, so that the claim of the public may suffer no loss, till that affair was finally decided.

On the other side, the opposers to the Bill shewed, that by the state of the Company's affairs, which were laid before the parliament, it was evident that they were in circumstances able to make a much greater increase of dividend, without in any degree affecting their credit; as it appeared that they had effects not only amply sufficient to discharge every just demand, but that, after even repaying their capital, a prodigious surplus would still remain; and that a doubt of their being able to divide 80,000l. among themselves, when they were allowed to be in circumstances to pay the government 400,000l. a year, could scarcely deserve a serious consideration.

It was said, that if a Bill for restraining the future dividend of the Company were proper, upon the ideas of fixing and preventing a fluctuation in the price of its stock, that end required only that the dividend should be fixed, without any regard to the quantum of it, and may be as well attained by a dividend of 12½ as of 10 per cent. That this is so far from being any part of the real purpose of the present Bill, that the short period to which the restriction is confined, cannot but increase instead of preventing that fluctuation; and encourage instead of checking the infamous practices of the Alley. For that the passions of men would be warmly agitated during the summer, in speculating on the probability of this restriction being suffered to expire on the opening of the next session, or of its being farther continued. That the proposal made by the Company, of submitting to a restriction of dividend of 12½ per cent, during the temporary agreement, would have obviated all those mischiefs, and secured every good end which might have been proposed, but cannot be attained by the present Bill; with this additional advantage, that as it would have been done with their consent, it would have been liable to no objection of injustice or violence.

That the arguments which had been made use of, on a supposition that the right to the territorial acquisitions in the East Indies was not lodged in the Company, but in the public, if admitted as one of the grounds of the Bill, was a precedent of the most dangerous nature; for the Company being in possession, and no claim against them being as much as made, much less established, it would be highly dangerous to the property of the subject, and extremely unbecoming the justice and dignity of parliament, by extrajudicial opinions, to call into question the legality of such a possession.

Many other objections were made as well to the form of this Bill, as to the principles on which it was founded; and the probable consequences that might attend it, were placed in a strong point of view. Among the rest it was observed, that a legislative interposition controuling the dividend of a trading company, which had been legally voted and declared by those to whom the power of doing it was intrusted, and to whom there was no ground to impute an abuse of that power, who had lent their money to the public upon the express stipulation that they might exercise their discretion with regard to the dividends provided that their effects, undivided, were sufficient to answer their debts, was altogether without example. That, as it tended to lessen the idea of that security and independence of the power of the state, which had induced all Europe to deposit their money in the funds of Great Britain, the precedent may be attended with the most fatal consequences to public credit.

All these reasons, and many others which were given, proved entirely ineffectual; the Bill was carried through a great opposition in both Houses; in the upper House 59 Lords voted for it, and 44 against it; and a strong and nervous protest was entered against it, signed by 19 lords.

249. Speech by Lord Clive in the House of Commons in defence of his conduct and that of the Company's servants in Bengal, 30 March 1772

(*Parl. Hist.*, XVII, pp. 328–331, 354–357.)

The speech from which the following extracts are taken was made during the debate on the East India Judicature Bill, introduced into the House of Commons by Laurence Sulivan, deputy chairman of the East India Company and leader of the group in the Company that was opposed to Clive. The object of the Bill was to give the Company greater control over its servants in India, to extend the judicature at Calcutta to the whole province of Bengal and to prohibit the Governor and Council from engaging in trade, measures provoked by abuses of his powers as Governor alleged to have been committed by Clive. The Bill was dropped after the second reading, and a select committe under General Burgoyne set up to inquire into Indian affairs. This was followed by the Regulating Act of 1773 (No. 250).

Lord *Clive*[1] rose and said:

Sir; it is with great diffidence that I attempt to speak to this House, but I find myself so particularly called upon, that I must make the attempt, though I should expose myself in so doing. With what confidence can I venture to give my sentiments upon a subject of such national consequence, who myself stand charged with having been the cause of the present melancholy situation of the Company's affairs in Bengal? This House can have no reliance on my opinion, whilst such an impression remains unremoved. The House will therefore give me leave to remove this impression, and to endeavour to restore myself to that favourable opinion, which, I flatter myself, they entertained of my conduct before these charges were exhibited against me. Nor do I wish to lay my conduct before the members of this House only;–I speak likewise to my country in general, upon whom I put myself, not only without reluctance, but with alacrity.

It is well known that I was called upon, in the year 1764, by a general court, to undertake the management of the Company's affairs in Bengal, when they were in a very critical and dangerous situation. It is well known, that my circumstances were independent and affluent. Happy in the sense of my past conduct and services, happy in my family, happy in my connections, happy in every thing but my health, which I lost in the Company's service, never to be regained. This situation, this happiness, I relinquished at the call of the Company, to go to a far distant, unhealthy climate, to undertake the envious task of reformation.–My enemies will suppose, that I was actuated by mercenary motives. But this House, and my country at large, will, I hope, think more liberally. They will conceive that I undertook this expedition from a principle of gratitude, from a point of honour, and from a desire of doing essential service to that Company, under whose auspices I had acquired my fortune and my fame.

[1] Clive had been created an Irish Peer in 1762.

My prospects on going abroad were by no means pleasing or encouraging; for after a violent contest, thirteen directors only were chosen, who thought favourably of my endeavours to serve the Company; the other eleven, however well they might wish to the Company, were not willing that their good purposes should be accomplished by me. They first gave all possible obstruction to my acceptance of the government, and afterwards declined investing me with those powers, without which I could not have acted effectually, for the benefit of the Company. Upon my arrival in Bengal, I found the powers given were so loosely and jesuitically worded, that they were immediately contested by the council. I was determined, however, to put the most extensive construction upon them, because I was determined to do my duty to my country.

Three paths were before me. One was strewed with abundance of fair advantages. I might have put myself at the head of the government as I found it. I might have encouraged the resolution which the gentlemen had taken, not to execute the new covenants, which prohibited the receipt of presents: and although I had executed the covenants myself, I might have contrived to return to England with an immense fortune, infamously added to the one before honourably obtained. Such an increase of wealth might have added to my weight in this country, but it would not have added to my peace of mind; because all men of honour and sentiment would have justly condemned me.

Finding my powers thus disputed, I might in despair have given up the commonwealth, and have left Bengal, without making an effort to save it. Such a conduct would have been deemed the effect of folly and cowardice.

The third path was intricate. Dangers and difficulties were on every side. But I resolved to pursue it. In short, I was determined to do my duty to the public, although I should incur the odium of the whole settlement. The welfare of the Company required a vigorous exertion, and I took the resolution of cleansing the Augean stable. . . .

But before I proceed, I must beg leave to deviate a little into a digression, on behalf of the Company's servants in general. It is dictated by humanity, by justice, and by truth.

Indostan was always an absolute despotic government. The inhabitants, especially of Bengal, in inferior stations, are servile, mean, submissive, and humble. In superior stations, they are luxurious, effeminate, tyrannical, treacherous, venal, cruel. The country of Bengal is called, by way of distinction, the paradise of the earth. It not only abounds with the necessaries of life to such a degree, as to furnish a great part of India with its superfluity, but it abounds in very curious and valuable manufactures, sufficient not only for its own use, but for the use of the whole globe. The silver of the west and the gold of the east have for many years been pouring into that country, and goods only have been sent out in return. This has added to the luxury and extravagance of Bengal.

From time immemorial it has been the custom of that country, for an inferior never to come into the presence of a superior without a present. It begins at the nabob, and ends at the lowest man that has an inferior. The nabob has told me, that the small presents he received amounted to 300,000l. a year; and I can believe him; because I know that I might have received as much during my last government. The Company's servants have ever been accustomed to receive presents. Even before we took part in the country troubles, when our possessions were very confined and limited, the governor and others used to receive presents; and I will take upon me to assert, that there has not been an officer commanding his Majesty's fleet; nor an officer commanding his Majesty's army; not a governor, not a member of council, not any other person, civil or military, in such a station as to have connection with the country government, who has not received presents. With regard to Bengal, there they flow in abundance indeed. Let the House figure to itself a country consisting of 15 millions of inhabitants, a revenue of four millions sterling, and a trade in proportion. By progressive steps the Company have become sovereigns of that empire. Can it be supposed that their servants will refrain from advantages so obviously resulting from their situation? The Company's servants, however, have not been the authors of those acts of violence and oppression, of which it is the fashion to accuse them. Such crimes are committed by the natives of the country acting as their agents, and for the most part without their knowledge. Those agents, and the banyans,[1] never desist, till, according to the ministerial phrase, they have dragged their masters into the kennel; and then the acts of violence begin. The passion for gain is as strong as the passion of love. I will suppose, that two intimate friends have lived long together; that one of them has married a beautiful woman; that the friend still continues to live in the house, and that this beautiful woman, forgetting her duty to her husband, attempts to seduce the friend; who, though in the vigour of youth, may, from high principles of honour, at first, resist the temptation, and even rebuke the lady. But if he still continues to live under the same roof, and she still continues to throw out her allurements, he must be seduced at last or fly. Now the banyan is the fair lady to the Company's servant. He lays his bags of silver before him to-day; gold to-morrow; jewels the next day; and if these fail, he then tempts him in the way of his profession, which is trade. He assures him that goods may be had cheap, and sold to great advantage up the country. In this manner is the attack carried on; and the Company's servant had no resource, for he cannot fly. In short, flesh and blood cannot bear it. Let us for a moment consider the nature of the education of a young man who goes to India. The advantages arising from the Company's service are now very generally known; and the great object of every man is to get his son appointed a writer to Bengal; which is usually at the age of 16. His parents and relations represent to him how certain he is of making a fortune; that my lord such a one, and my lord such a one, acquired so much money in such a time; and Mr. such a one, and Mr. such a one, so much in such a time. Thus are their principles corrupted at their very setting out, and as they generally go a good many together, they inflame one another's expectations to such a degree, in the course of the voyage, that they fix upon a period for their return before their arrival.

Let us now take a view of one of these writers arrived in Bengal, and not worth a groat. As soon as he lands, a banyan, worth perhaps 100,000l. desires he may have

[1] Hindu traders or brokers.

the honour of serving this young gentleman, at 4s. 6d. per month. The Company has provided chambers for him, but they are not good enough;–the banyan finds better. The young man takes a walk about the town, he observes that other writers, arrived only a year before him, live in splendid apartments or have houses of their own, ride upon fine prancing Arabian horses, and in palanqueens and chaises; that they keep seraglios, make entertainments, and treat with champaigne and claret. When he returns, he tells the banyan what he has observed. The banyan assures him he may soon arrive at the same good fortune; he furnishes him with money; he is then at his mercy. The advantages of the banyan advance with the rank of his master, who in acquiring one fortune generally spends three. But this is not the worst of it: he is in a state of dependence under the banyan, who commits acts of violence and oppression, as his interest prompts him to, under the pretended sanction and authority of the Company's servant. Hence, Sir, arises the clamour against the English gentlemen in India. But look at them in a retired situation, when returned to England, when they are no longer nabobs and sovereigns of the east: see if there be any thing tyrannical in their disposition towards their inferiors: see if they are not good and humane masters: Are they not charitable? Are they not benevolent? Are they not generous? Are they not hospitable? If they are, thus far, not contemptible members of society, and if in all their dealings between man and man, their conduct is strictly honourable: if, in short, there has not yet been one character found amongst them sufficiently flagitious for Mr. Foote to exhibit on the theatre in the Haymarket, may we not conclude, that if they have erred, it has been because they were men, placed in situations subject to little or no controul?

But if the servants of the Company are to be loaded with the demerit of every misfortune in India, let them also have the merit they are entitled to. The court of directors surely will not claim to themselves the merit of those advantages which the nation and Company are at present in possession of. The officers of the navy and army have had great share in the execution; but the Company's servants were the cabinet council, who planned every thing; and to them also may be ascribed some part of the merit of our great acquisitions. . . .

250. Lord North's Regulating Act, 1773

(*Statutes at Large*, XXX, pp. 124–143. 13 Geo. III, c. 63.)

This Act was intended to be a temporary measure, to be replaced by a permanent one when the Company's charter expired in 1780. It set up at Calcutta a Governor-General and Council (nominated partly by the Company and partly by the government), controlling the other two Presidencies, and being themselves controlled by the Court of Directors, supervised by the Treasury and Secretary of State, who had access to all relevant papers. Ineffective as it proved in operation, the Act was of great importance as the first participation of the English Government in the administration of India.

An act for establishing certain regulations for the better management of the affairs of the East India Company, *as well in* India *as in* Europe.

WHEREAS *the several powers and authorities granted by charters to the united company of merchants in* England *trading to the* East Indies *have been found, by experience, not to have sufficient force and efficacy to prevent various abuses which have prevailed in the government and administration of the affairs of the said united company, as well at home as in* India, *to the manifest injury of the publick credit, and of the commercial interests of the said company; and it is therefore become highly expedient that certain further regulations, better adapted to their present circumstances and condition, should be provided and established:* . . .

[The Act then lays down provisions governing the election of Directors.]

. . .

VII. *And, for the better management of the said united company's affairs in* India, be it further enacted by the authority aforesaid, That, for the government of the presidency of *Fort William* in *Bengal*, there shall be appointed a governor-general, and four counsellors; and that the whole civil and military government of the said presidency, and also the ordering, management and government of all the territorial acquisitions and revenues in the kingdoms of *Bengal, Bahar*, and *Orissa*, shall, during such time as the territorial acquisitions and revenues shall remain in the possession of the said united company, be, and are hereby vested in the said governor-general and council of the said presidency of *Fort William* in *Bengal*, in like manner, to all intents and purposes whatsoever, as the same now are, or at any time heretofore might have been exercised by the president and council, or select committee, in the said kingdoms.

VIII. And be it enacted by the authority aforesaid, That in all cases whatsoever wherein any difference of opinion shall arise upon any question proposed in any consultation, the said governor-general and council shall be bound and concluded by the opinion and decision of the major part of those present: and if it shall happen that, by the death or removal, or by the absence, of any of the members of the said council, such governor-general and council shall happen to be equally divided; then, and in every such case, the said governor-general, or in his absence, the eldest counsellor present, shall have a casting voice, and his opinion shall be decisive and conclusive.

IX. And be it further enacted by the authority aforesaid, That the said governor-general and council, or the major part of them, shall have, and they are hereby authorised to have, power of superintending and countrouling the government and management of the presidencies of *Madras, Bombay*, and *Bencoolen* respectively, so far and in so much as that it shall not be lawful for any president and council of *Madras, Bombay*, or *Bencoolen*, for the time being, to make any orders for commencing hostilities, or declaring or making war, against any *Indian* princes or powers, or for negotiating or concluding any treaty of peace, or other treaty, with any such *Indian* princes or powers, without the consent and approbation of the said governor-general and council first had and obtained, except in such cases of imminent necessity as would render it dangerous to postpone such hostilities or treaties until the orders from the governor-general and council might arrive; and except in such cases where the said presidents and councils respectively shall have received special orders from the said united company, and any president and council of *Madras, Bombay*, or *Bencoolen*, who shall offend in any of the cases aforesaid, shall be liable to be suspended from his or their office by the order of the said governor-general and council; and every president and council of *Madras, Bombay*, and *Bencoolen*, for the time being, shall, and they are hereby respectively directed and required to pay due obedience to such orders as they shall receive, touching the premises, from the said governor-general and council for the time being, and constantly and diligently to transmit to the said governor-general and council advice and intelligence of all transactions and matters whatsoever that shall come to their knowledge, relating to the government, revenues, or interest, of the said united company; and the said governor-general and council for the time being shall, and they are hereby directed and required to pay due obedience to all such orders as they shall receive from the court of directors of the said united company, and to correspond, from time to time, and constantly and diligently transmit to the said court an exact particular of all advices or intelligence, and of all transactions and matters whatsoever, that shall come to their knowledge, relating to the government, commerce, revenues, or interest, of the said united company; and the court of directors of the said company, or their successors, shall, and they are hereby directed and required, from time to time, before the expiration of fourteen days after the receiving any such letters or advices, to give in and deliver unto the high treasurer, or commissioners of his Majesty's treasury for the time being, a true and exact copy of such parts of the said letters or advices as shall any way relate to the management of the revenues of the said company; and in like manner to give in and deliver to one of his Majesty's principal secretaries of state for the time being, a true and exact copy of all such parts of the said letters or advices as shall any way relate to the civil or military affairs and government of the said company; all which copies shall be fairly written, and shall be signed by two or more of the directors of the said company.

X. And it is hereby further enacted, That *Warren Hastings* esquire shall be the First governor-general; and that lieutenant-general *John Clavering*, the Honourable *George Monson*, *Richard Barwell* esquire, and *Philip Francis* esquire, shall be the four first counsellors; and they, and each of them, shall hold and continue in his and their respective offices for and during the term of five years from the time of their arrival at *Fort William* in *Bengal*, and taken upon them the government of the said presidency, and shall not be removeable, in the mean time, except by his Majesty, his heirs and successors, upon representation made by the court of directors of the said united company for the time being: and in case of the avoidance of the office of such governor-general by death, resignation, or removal, his place shall, during the remainder of the term aforesaid, as often as the case shall happen, be supplied by the person of the council who stands next in rank to such governor-general; and, in case of the death, removal, resignation, or promotion, of any of the said council, the directors of the said united company are hereby impowered, for and during the remainder of the said term of five years, to nominate and appoint, by and with the consent of his Majesty, his heirs and successors, to be signified under his or their sign manual, a person to succeed to the office so become vacant in the said council; and, until such appointment shall be made, all the powers and authorities vested in the governor-general and council shall rest and continue in, and be exercised and executed by, the governor-general and council remaining and surviving; and from and after the expiration of the said term of five years, the power of nominating and removing the succeeding governor-general and council shall be vested in the directors of the said united company. . . .

XII. Provided always, That nothing in this act shall extend, or be construed to extend, to prevent, controul, or restrain the said united company from constituting and appointing such officers, factors, or agents, as they shall think proper and necessary, by virtue or in pursuance of any powers, rights, or privileges, granted to them by any former act or acts of parliament, or by any charter of charters, for managing, conducting, and transacting the trade and commerce of the said company, at and within the said presidency of *Fort William* in *Bengal*.

XIII. *And whereas his late majesty King* George *the Second did, by his letters patent, bearing date at* Westminster *the eighth day of* January, *in the twenty-sixth year of his reign, grant unto the said united company of merchants of* England *trading to the* East Indies *his royal charter, thereby, amongst other things, constituting and establishing courts of civil, criminal, and ecclesiastical jurisdiction, at the said united company's respective settlements at* Madras-patnam, Bombay *on the island of* Bombay, *and* Fort William *in* Bengal; *which said charter does not sufficiently provide for the due administration of justice in such manner as the state and condition of the company's presidency of* Fort William *in* Bengal, *so long as the said company shall continue in the possession of the territorial acquisitions before mentioned, do and must require:* be it therefore enacted by the authority aforesaid, That it shall and may be lawful for his Majesty, by charter, or letters patent under the great seal of *Great Britain*, to erect and establish a supreme court of judicature at *Fort William* aforesaid, to consist of a chief justice and three other judges, being barristers in *England* or *Ireland*, of not less than five years standing, to be named from time to time by his Majesty, his heirs and successors; which said supreme court of judicature shall have, and the same court is hereby declared to have, full power and authority to exercise and perform all civil, criminal, admiralty, and ecclesiastical jurisdiction, and to appoint such clerks, and other ministerial officers of the said court, with such reasonable salaries, as shall be approved of by the said governor-general and council; and to form and establish such rules of practice, and such rules for the process of the said court, and to do all such other things as shall be found necessary for the administration of justice, and the due execution of all or any of the powers which, by the said charter, shall or may be granted and committed to the said court; and also shall be at all times, a court of record, and shall be a court of oyer and terminer, and gaol delivery, in and for the said town of *Calcutta*, and factory of *Fort William* in *Bengal* aforesaid, and the limits thereof, and the factories subordinate thereto. . . .

XV. Provided also, That the said court shall not be competent to hear, try, or determine, any indictment or information against the said governor-general, or any of the said council for the time being, for any offence, (not being treason or felony) which such governor-general, or any of the said council, shall or may be charged with having committed in *Bengal*, *Bahar*, and *Orissa*. . . .

XVIII. And be it further enacted by the authority aforesaid, That it shall and may be directed, in and by the said new charter which his Majesty is herein-before impowered to grant, that in case any person or persons whatsoever shall think himself, herself, or themselves aggrieved by any judgement or determination of the said supreme court of judicature, to be established as aforesaid, he, she, or they, shall and may appeal from such judgement or determination of his Majesty in council, his heirs or successors, within such time, in such manner, and in such cases, and on such security, as his Majesty, in his said charter, shall judge proper and reasonable to be appointed and prescribed. . . .

XXIII. And be it further enacted by the authority aforesaid, That no governor-general, or any of the council of the said united company's presidency of *Fort William* in *Bengal*, or any chief justice, or any of the judges of the supreme court of judicature at *Fort William* aforesaid, shall, directly, or indirectly, by themselves, or by any other person or persons for his or their use, or on his or their behalf accept, receive, or take, of or from any person or persons, in any manner, or on any account whatsoever, any present, gift, donation, gratuity, or reward, pecuniary or otherwise, or any promise or engagement for any present, gift, donation, gratuity, or reward; and that no governor-general, or any of the said council, or any chief justice or judge of the said court, shall carry on, be concerned in, or have any dealing or transactions, by way of traffick or commerce of any kind whatsoever, either for his or their use or benefit, profit or advantage, or for the benefit or advantage of any other person or persons whatsoever, (the trade and commerce of the said united company only excepted); any usage or custom to the contrary thereof in anywise notwithstanding.

XXIV. And be it further enacted by the authority aforesaid, That from and after the first day of *August*, one thousand seven hundred and seventy-four, no person holding or exercising any civil or military office under the crown, or the said united company in the *East Indies*, shall accept, receive, or take, directly or indirectly, by himself, or any other person or persons on his behalf, or for his use or benefit, of and from any of the *Indian* princes or powers, or their ministers or agents, (or any of the natives of *Asia*), any present, gift, donation, gratuity, or reward, pecuniary or otherwise, upon any account, or on any pretence whatsoever; . . .

XXVII. And be it further enacted by the authority aforesaid, That from and after the first day of *August*, one thousand seven hundred and seventy-four, it shall not be lawful for any collector, supervisor, or any other of his Majesty's subjects, employed or concerned in the collection of the revenues, or the administration of justice, in the provinces of *Bengal*, *Bahar*, or *Orissa*, or their agents or servants, or any person or persons in trust for them, to buy any goods, wares, merchandise, or other commodities whatsoever, by way of traffick or trade, at any place within the provinces of *Bengal*, *Bahar*, or *Orissa*, and to sell the same again, or any part thereof, at the place where he or they bought the same, or at any other place within the said provinces respectively; and it shall not be lawful for any of his Majesty's subjects in the said provinces, to engage, intermeddle, or be any way concerned, directly or indirectly, in the inland trade, in salt, beetlenut, tobacco, or rice, except on the account of the said united company, on pain of forfeiting all such goods or commodities which he shall so buy and sell again, by way of traffick, or in which he shall so trade; and also treble the value thereof; one moiety to the said united company, and the other moiety to him or them who will sue for the same, in the said supreme court; and every such person, on conviction, shall, moreover, be liable to be sent to *England*, by such order as aforesaid, unless he or they shall give sufficient security to remove him or themselves within twelve months after such conviction. . . .

XXXIV. And be it further enacted by the authority aforesaid, That all offences and misdemeanours which shall be laid, tried, and enquired of in the said supreme court, shall be tried by a jury of *British* subjects resident in the town of *Calcutta*, and not otherwise. . . .

XXXVI. [Governor-general and Council may make such Regulations as may appear just; which shall not be valid until duly registered in the Supreme Court. Appeals may be made to the King in Council, who may repeal such Rules; and a Copy of all Regulations to be affixed in the India House.]

XXXVII. [Governor-general and Council to transmit Copies of their Rules to One of the Secretaries of State; which if His Majesty does not signify His Disallowance of, shall have full Force.] . . .

XXXIX. [If the Governor-general, President, &c. commit Offences, the same may be tried and determined in the Court of King's Bench.] . . .

251. Warren Hastings on the state of India, 1772–1785

(Warren Hastings, *Memoirs relative to the State of India* (1786), pp. 105–111, 124, 153–158.)

Hastings became Governor of Bengal in 1772, to implement reforms in administration planned by the East India Company, and Governor-General under the Regulating Act in 1773. In the Preface to the pamphlet from which the following extract is taken, Hastings says he wrote it at sea on his voyage back to England in 1785 and did not at first intend it for publication. In stressing the inadequate authority given to the Governor-General, *i.e.* the man on the spot, as the root of all India's troubles, he was putting his finger on the chief weakness of the Regulating Act.

. . . The first acts of the government of Bengal, when I presided over it, were well known at the time to have been of my formation, or formed on principles which I was allowed to dictate. These consisted of a variety of regulations, which included every department of the service, and composed a system as complete as a mind incompetent like my own, though possessed of very superior aids, could form, of military, political, productive, œconomical, and judicial connection. I found the Treasury empty, the revenue declining, the expences unchecked, and the whole nation yet languishing under the recent effects of a mortal famine. Neither was this a season for war, nor, occupied as I was in it, would candor impute to me even a possible disposition to war. The land required years of quiet to restore its population and culture; and all my acts were acts of peace. I was busied in raising a great and weighty fabric, of which all the parts were yet loose and destitute of the superior weight which was to give them their mutual support; and (if I may so express myself) their collateral strength. A tempest, or an earthquake, could not be more fatal to a builder whose walls were uncovered, and his unfinished columns trembling in the breeze, than the ravages or terrors of war would have been to me and to all my hopes.

I LAID my plans before the Court of Directors, and called upon them to give me the powers which were requisite for their accomplishment and duration. These were silently denied me, and those which I before possessed, feeble as they were, were taken from me. Had I been allowed the means which I required, I will inform my readers of the use to which I intended to apply them. I should have sought no accession of territory. I should have rejected the offer of any which would have enlarged our line of defence, without a more than proportionate augmentation of defensive strength and revenue. I should have encouraged, but not solicited, new alliances; and should have rendered that of our government an object of solicitation, by the example of those which already existed. To these I should have observed, as my religion, every principle of good faith; and where they were deficient in the conditions of mutual and equal dependance, I should have endeavoured to render them complete; and this rule I did actually apply to practice in the treaty which I formed with the Nabob *Shujah o'Dowlah* in the year 1773.

WITH respect to the provinces of the Company's dominion under my government, I should have studied to augment both their value and strength by an augmentation of their inhabitants and cultivation. This is not a mere phantásy of speculation. The means were most easy, if the power and trust were allowed to use them. Every region of Indostan, even at that time, groaned under different degrees of oppression, desolation, and insecurity. The famine which had wasted the provinces of Bengal, had raged with equal severity in other parts, and in some with greater, and the remembrance of it yet dwelt on the minds of the inhabitants with every impression of horror and apprehension. I would have afforded an asylum in Bengal, with lands and stock, to all the emigrants of other countries: I would have employed emissaries for their first encouragement; and I would have provided a perpetual and proclaimed incentive to them in the security of the community from foreign molestation, and of the individual members from mutual wrong; to which purpose, the regulations already established were sufficient, with a power only competent to enforce them. And for the same purpose, and with a professed view to it, I early recommended, even so early as the year 1773, the erection of public granaries on the plan since happily commenced.

THOSE who have been in the long habits of familiar communication with me, whether by letter or by discourse, will know that the sentiments which I have been describing are of as old a date as that of my late office in the first appointment and state of it. And to every candid reader I appeal for his conviction of their effect, if I had been permitted to follow their direction: for what man is there so immovably attached to his native soil, as to prefer it, under the scourge of oppression, the miseries of want, and the desolation of war, embittering or destroying every natural affection, and ultimately invading the source of life itself, to a state of peace, of external tranquillity and internal protection, of assured plenty, and all the blessings of domestic increase?

THOSE who have seen, as I did, in a time of profound peace, the wretched inhabitants of the Carnatic, of every age, sex, and condition, tumultuously thronging round the walls of Fort St. George, and lying for many successive days and nights on the burning soil, without covering or food, on a casual rumor falsely excited of an approaching enemy, will feelingly attest the truth of the contrast which I have exhibited in one part of it, and will readily draw the conclusion which I have drawn from it, even without attending to the rest. That such a state as I have described would have been attained without imperfection or alloy, I do not pretend to suppose; but I confidently maintain, that under an equal, vigorous, and fixed administration, determined on the execution of such a plan to its accomplishment, it would have been attainable, even with common talents prosecuting it, to a degree as nearly approaching to perfection as human life is capable of receiving. The submissive character of the people; the fewness of their wants; the facility with which the soil and climate, unaided by exertions of labour, can supply them; the abundant resources of subsistence and trafficable wealth which may be drawn from the natural productions, and from the manufactures, both of established usage and of new introduction, to which no men upon earth can bend their minds with a readier accomodation; and above all, the defences with which nature has armed the land, in its mountainous and hilly borders, its bay, its innumerable intersections of rivers, and inoffensive or unpowerful neighbours; are advantages which no united state upon earth possesses in an equal degree; and which leave little to the duty of the magistrate; in effect, nothing but attention, protection, and forbearance. . . .

. . . If the same act of the legislature which confirmed me in my station of President over the Company's settlements in Bengal, had invested me with a controul as extensive as the new denomination I received by it indicated; if it had compelled the assistance of my associates in power, instead of giving me opponents;[1] if, instead of creating new expectations which were to be accomplished by my dismission from office, it had imposed silence on the interested clamours of faction, and taught the servants of the Company to place their dependance upon me, where it constitutionally rested; if, when it transferred the real controul over the company's affairs from the Direction to the Ministers, instead of extending, it had limited the claims of patronage, which every man possessing influence himself, or connected with those who possessed it, thought he had a right to exert; and if it had made my continuance in office to depend upon the rectitude of my intentions, and the vigour with which they were exerted, instead of annexing it to a compliance with those claims, I should have had little occasion, at this period, to claim the public indulgence for an avowal of duties undischarged. But the reverse took place in every instance. . . .

. . . FROM the vehemence and perseverance with which my immediate superiors laboured during the course of ten years to weaken my authority, to destroy my influence, and to embarrass all my measures, at a time when their affairs required the most powerful exertions to sustain them, which I alone by my office could direct; and from the great importance which they have ascribed to points, some of which had no relation to their interests, and others were even repugnant to them; I much fear, that it is not understood as it ought to be, how near the Company's existence has on many occasions vibrated to the edge of perdition, and that it has been at all times suspended by a thread so fine, that the touch of chance might break, or the breath of opinion dissolve it: and instantaneous will be its fall whenever it shall happen. May GOD in his mercy long avert it!

TO say why a dominion held by a delegated and fettered power over a region

[1] The three government-appointed members of the Governor-General's Council under the Regulating Act were General Clavering, Colonel Monson and Philip Francis, who combined together to oppose Hastings.

exceeding the dimensions of the parent state, and removed from it a distance equal in its circuit to two-thirds of the earth's circumference, is at all times liable to be wrested from it, would be a waste of argument, nor would it be prudent to aggravate the portrait by displaying all the artificial evils by which a fabric, so irregular even in its best construction, is loosened and debilitated.

IT is true, that it has hitherto stood unimpaired, because it has met with no domestic stroke of fortune to agitate and try its texture, one late instance perhaps excepted, which was too suddenly repelled to produce the effect which might have attended a long duration of it. And it may yet stand for some years to come, though still liable to the same insecurity. The remedy is easy and simple; but I fear it will be vain to propose it; because, if it is not (as I believe it is not) contrary to the principles of our national constitution, it will at least meet with very formidable obstacles in the prejudices which arise out of it.

I AFFIRM, as a point incontestable, that the administration of the British Government in Bengal, distant as it is from the reach of more than general instruction from the source of its authority, and liable to daily contingencies, which require both instant decision, and a consistency of system, cannot be ruled by a body of men variable in their succession, discordant in opinion, each jealous of his colleagues, and all united in common interest against their ostensible leader. Its powers are such, that if directed by a firm and steady hand, they may be rendered equal to any given plan of operation; but may prove the very instruments of its destruction, if they are left in the loose charge of unconnected individuals, whose interests, passions, or caprices, may employ them in mutual contests, and a scramble for superiority.

IT has been my lot to derive, from long possession and casual influence, advantages which have overcome the worst effects of my own deficiencies; and it has been one maxim of my conduct (may I be pardoned for the apparent boast, but necessary allusion) to do what I knew was requisite to the public safety, though I should doom my life to legal forfeiture, or my name to infamy. I could verify this by instances in which by an implicit submission to positive duty and express orders, the Company's possessions might have been devoted to desolation, and even its existence annihilated. I hazarded an opposite conduct; and whatever may have been its effects, I have at least had the happiness to see one portion of the British dominion in India rise from the lowest state of degradation; another rescued from imminent subjection; and that which gives life to the whole, enjoying the blessings of peace and internal security, while every other part of the general empire was oppressed by war, or the calamities of intestine discord.

I MAY not expatiate on such a discussion. I mention it only to shew, that if the British power in India yet holds a reprieve from ruin, it derives its preservation from causes which are independant of its constitution; and that it might have been lost if left to that alone for its protection.

THE inference to be drawn from these premises is, that whatever form of government may yet be established for those provinces, whether its controul be extended to the other presidencies, or confined to its own demesnes; it is necessary that the Governor, or first executive member, should possess a power absolute and complete within himself, and independant of actual controul. His character, which requires little more than two qualifications, an inflexible integrity, and a judgment unsusceptible of the bias of foreign suggestion, should be previously ascertained, and its consistency assured by the pledge of his life for the faithful discharge of so great a trust. . . .

252. Speech by Edmund Burke in the House of Commons on Fox's India Bill, 1 December 1783

(*Works and Correspondence of Edmund Burke*, III (1852), pp. 454–455, 467–469, 508–510, 511.)

Fox's India Bill, of which Burke himself was probably to a large extent the author, would have placed the administration of India in the hands of seven commissioners, named in the Bill, to hold office for at least four years. Their successors would have been appointed by the Crown. An awkward situation might well have arisen if there had been a change of government during the commissioners' four years of office; but it was in fact to provide continuity in Indian administration that this arrangement was made. The commercial affairs of the East India Company would have been administered by nine sub-commissioners, chosen by the Court of Directors. For the method by which this Bill was defeated in the House of Lords, see No. 18. Burke's views on the evils of British rule in India are forcibly expressed in his speech on the Bill.

. . . This bill, and those connected with it, are intended to form the *Magna Charta* of Hindostan. Whatever the treaty of Westphalia is to the liberty of the princes and free cities of the empire, and to the three religions there professed–Whatever the Great Charter, the statute of tallege, the petition of right, and the declaration of right, are to Great Britain, these bills are to the people of India. Of this benefit, I am certain, their condition is capable; and when I know that they are capable of more, my vote shall most assuredly be for our giving to the full extent of their capacity of receiving; and no charter of dominion shall stand as a bar in my way to their charter of safety and protection.

The strong admission I have made of the Company's rights (I am conscious of it) binds me to do a great deal. I do not presume to condemn those who argue *a priori*, against the propriety of leaving such extensive political powers in the hands of a company of merchants. I know much is, and much more may be, said against such a system. But, with my particular ideas and sentiments, I cannot go that way to work. I feel an insuperable reluctance in giving my hand to destroy any established institution of government, upon a theory, however plausible it may be. My experience in life teaches me nothing clear upon the subject. I have known merchants with the sentiments and the abilities of great statesmen; and I have seen persons in the rank of statesmen, with the conceptions and characters of pedlers. Indeed, my observation has furnished me with nothing that is to be found in any habit of life or education, which tends wholly to disqualify men for the functions of government, but that by which the power of exercising those functions is very frequently obtained, I mean a spirit and habits of low cabal and intrigue; which I have never, in one instance, seen united with a capacity for sound and manly policy.

To justify us in taking the administration of their affairs out of the hands of the East-India Company, on my principles, I must see several conditions. 1st. The object affected by the abuse should be great and important. 2nd. The abuse affecting this great object ought to be a great abuse. 3rd. It ought to be habitual, and not accidental. 4th. It ought to be utterly incurable in the body as it now stands constituted. All this ought to be made as visible to me as the light of the sun, before I should strike off an atom of their charter.

. . . Our conquest there, after twenty years, is as crude as it was the first day. The natives scarcely know what it is to see the grey head of an Englishman. Young men (boys almost) govern there, without society, and without sympathy with the natives. They have no more social habits with the people, than if they still resided in England; nor, indeed, any species of intercourse but that which is necessary to making a sudden fortune, with a view to a remote settlement. Animated with all the avarice of age, and all the impetuosity of youth, they roll in one after another; wave after wave; and there is nothing before the eyes of the natives but an endless, hopeless prospect of new flights of birds of prey and passage, with appetites continually renewing for a food that is continually wasting. Every rupee of profit made by an Englishman is lost for ever to India. With us are no retributory superstitions, by which a foundation of charity compensates, through ages, to the poor, for the rapine and injustice of a day. With us no pride erects stately monuments which repair the mischiefs which pride had produced, and which adorn a country out of its own spoils. England has erected no churches, no hospitals,* no palaces, no schools; England has built no bridges, made no high roads, cut no navigations, dug out no reservoirs. Every other conqueror of every other description has left some monument, either of state or beneficence, behind him. Were we to be driven out of India this day, nothing would remain, to tell that it had been possessed, during the inglorious period of our dominion, by any thing better than the ourang-outang or the tiger.

There is nothing in the boys we send to India worse, than in the boys whom we are whipping at school, or that we see trailing a pike, or bending over a desk at home. But as English youth in India drink the intoxicating draught of authority and dominion before their heads are able to bear it, and as they are full grown in fortune long before they are ripe in principle, neither nature nor reason have any opportunity to exert themselves for remedy of the excesses of their premature power. The consequences of their conduct, which in good minds, (and many of theirs are probably such,) might produce penitence or amendment, are unable to pursue the rapidity of their flight. Their prey is lodged in England; and the cries of India are given to seas and winds, to be blown about, in every breaking up of the monsoon, over a remote and unhearing ocean. In India all the vices operate by which sudden fortune is acquired; in England are often displayed by the same persons, the virtues which dispense hereditary wealth. Arrived in England, the destroyers of the nobility and gentry of a whole kingdom will find the best company in this nation, at a board of elegance and hospitality. Here the manufacturer and husbandman will bless the just and punctual hand that in India has torn the cloth from the loom, or wrested the scanty portion of rice and salt from the peasant of Bengal, or wrung from him the very opium in which he forgot his oppressions and his oppressor. They marry into your

* The paltry foundation at Calcutta is scarcely worth naming as an exception.

families; they enter into your senate; they ease your estates by loans; they raise their value by demand; they cherish and protect your relations which lie heavy on your patronage; and there is scarcely a house in the kingdom that does not feel some concern and interest, that makes all reform of our eastern government appear officious and disgusting; and, on the whole, a most discouraging attempt. In such an attempt you hurt those who are able to return kindness, or to resent injury. If you succeed, you save those who cannot so much as give you thanks. All these things show the difficulty of the work we have on hand; but they show its necessity too. Our Indian government is in its best state a grievance. It is necessary that the corrective should be uncommonly vigorous; and the work of men, sanguine, warm, and even impassioned in the cause. But it is an arduous thing to plead against abuses of a power which originates from your own country, and affects those whom we are used to consider as strangers. . . .

For my part, Sir, in this business I put all indirect considerations wholly out of mind. My sole question, on each clause of the bill, amounts to this:–Is the measure proposed required by the necessities of India? I cannot consent totally to lose sight of the real wants of the people who are the objects of it, and to hunt after every matter of party squabble that may be started on the several provisions. On the question of the duration of the commission I am clear and decided. Can I, can any one who has taken the smallest trouble to be informed concerning the affairs of India, amuse himself with so strange an imagination, as that the habitual despotism and oppression, that the monopolies, the peculations, the universal destruction of all the legal authority of this kingdom, which have been for twenty years maturing to their present enormity, combined with the distance of the scene, the boldness and artifice of delinquents, their combination, their excessive wealth, and the faction they have made in England, can be fully corrected in a shorter term than four years? None has hazarded such an assertion–none, who has a regard for his reputation, will hazard it.

Sir, the gentlemen, whoever they are, who shall be appointed to this commission, have an undertaking of magnitude on their hands, and their stability must not only be, but it must be thought, real;–and who is it will believe, that anything short of an establishment made, supported, and fixed in its duration, with all the authority of parliament, can be thought secure of a reasonable stability? The plan of my honourable friend is the reverse of that of reforming by the authors of the abuse. The best we could expect from them is, that they should not continue their ancient, pernicious activity. To those we could think of nothing but applying *control*; as we are sure that even a regard to their reputation (if any such thing exists in them) would oblige them to cover, to conceal, to suppress, and consequently to prevent, all cure of the grievances of India. For what can be discovered, which is not to their disgrace? Every attempt to correct an abuse would be a satire on their former administration. Every man they should pretend to call to an account would be found their instrument, or their accomplice. They can never see a beneficial regulation, but with a view to defeat it. The shorter the tenure of such persons, the better would be the chance of some amendment.

But the system of the bill is different. It calls in persons in nowise concerned with any act censured by parliament; persons generated with, and for, the reform, of which they are themselves the most essential part. To these the chief regulations in the bill are helps, not fetters; they are authorities to support, not regulations to restrain them. From these we look for much more than innocence. From these we expect zeal, firmness, and unremitted activity. Their duty, their character, binds them to proceedings of vigour; and they ought to have a tenure in their office which precludes all fear, whilst they are acting up to the purposes of their trust; a tenure without which none will undertake plans that require a series and system of acts. When they know that they cannot be whispered out of their duty, that their public conduct cannot be censured without a public discussion, that the schemes which they have begun will not be committed to those who will have an interest and credit in defeating and disgracing them, then we may entertain hopes. The tenure is for four years, or during their good behaviour. That good behaviour is as long as they are true to the principles of the bill; and the judgment is in either house of parliament. This is the tenure of your judges; and the valuable principle of the bill is to make a judicial administration for India. It is to give confidence in the execution of a duty, which requires as much perseverance and fortitude, as can fall to the lot of any that is born of woman. . . .

It has been said, if you violate this charter,' what security has the charter of the Bank, in which public credit is so deeply concerned, and even the charter of London, in which the rights of so many subjects are involved? I answer, in the like case they have no security at all.–No–no security at all. If the Bank should, by every species of mismanagement, fall into a state similar to that of the East-India Company; if it should be oppressed with demands it could not answer, engagements which it could not perform, and with bills for which it could not procure payment; no charter should protect the mismanagement from correction, and such public grievances from redress. If the city of London had the means and will of destroying an empire, and of cruelly oppressing and tyrannizing over millions of men as good as themselves, the charter of the city of London should prove no sanction to such tyranny and such oppression. Charters are kept, when their purposes are maintained: they are violated, when the privilege is supported against its end and its object.

Now, Sir, I have finished all I proposed to say, as my reasons for giving my vote to this bill. If I am wrong, it is not for want of pains to know what is right. This pledge, at least, of my rectitude I have given to my country. . . .

F. AFRICA

253. A pamphlet on the importance of the African trade, 1745

(*The African Trade the Great Pillar and Support of the British Plantation Trade in America*, by a British merchant (1745), pp. 3–4, 5–7, 13–15, 17–18.)

This anonymous pamphlet, possibly by Malachy Postlethwayt, author of the *Universal Dictionary of Trade and Commerce*, published in 1751, is typical of a number of pamphlets on the African Trade. It deplored the decay of the Royal African Company and regarded the African slave trade as the foundation of British commerce.

. . . Had not too long Experience proved the contrary, one would think it impossible, that the obvious Connection and Dependency subsisting between our *Plantation* and *Guinea Trades* should be so notoriously disregarded; and remain as much unobserved as if there really were no such Relation between those Branches of our Commerce. Yet this has been the Case; we have suffered our *African Company*, the sole Guardian of our *Guinea Trade*, to moulder and dwindle away almost to Nothing; and then vainly have expected that our *Plantation Commerce*, not only first founded on that Trade, but still daily upheld thereby, should stand alone without its fundamental Prop and Support!

The Policy of our dangerous Rivals has been quite otherwise. *France* has long seen the essential Dependency between those Trades, and that the *one* cannot subsist or prosper without giving all due Encouragement to the *other*. Wherefore, while this Nation has accountably suffered our *African Company* to labour under every Difficulty and Discouragement, (as will appear) *France* has wisely cherished and encouraged *Theirs*; Is it to be wondered therefore, that our Enemies should raise a magnificent Superstructure of *American Commerce* and *Naval Power* on an *African Foundation*, while ours has been for many Years past–neglected, and suffered to decline. . . .

Whoever will take upon him to suggest that the same reciprocal Connection, the same mutual Dependency does not subsist in as essential a Manner between the *British Plantation* and *British Guinea Trades*, as between these Trades belonging to *France*, let him discriminate, and shew wherein the Difference consists.

But is it not notorious to the whole World, that the Business of *Planting* in our *British Colonies*, as well as in the *French*, is carried on by the Labour of *Negroes*, imported thither from *Africa*? Are we not indebted to that valuable People, the *Africans*, for our *Sugars*, *Tobaccoes*, *Rice*, *Rum*, and all other *Plantation Produce*? And the greater the Number of *Negroes* imported into our *Colonies*, from *Africa*, will not the Exportation of *British* Manufactures among the *Africans* be in Proportion; they being paid for in such Commodities only? The more likewise our Plantations abound in *Negroes*, will not more Land become cultivated, and both *better* and greater *Variety* of *Plantation Commodities* be produced? As those Trades are subservient to the Well Being and Prosperity of each other; so the more either flourishes or declines, the other must be necessarily affected; and the general Trade and Navigation of their *Mother Country*, will be proportionably benefited or injured. May we not therefore say, with equal Truth, as the *French* do . . . that the general NAVIGATION of *Great Britain* owes all its

Encrease and *Splendor* to the Commerce of its *American* and *African Colonies*; and that it cannot be maintained and enlarged otherwise than from the constant Prosperity of both those Branches, *whose Interests are mutual and inseparable*?

Whatever *other* Causes may have conspired to enable the *French* to beat us out of all the Markets in Europe in the *Sugar* and *Indigo Trades*, etc. the great and extraordinary Care they have taken to cherish and encourage their *African Company*, to the End that their *Plantations* might be cheaply and plentifully stocked with Negroe Husbandmen, is amply sufficient of itself to account for the Effect; for this Policy, they wisely judged, would enable them to produce those Commodities cheaper than we, who have suffered the *British* Interest to decline in *Africa*, as that of the *French* has advanced; and when they could produce the Commodities cheaper, is it at all to be admired that they have undersold us at all the foreign Markets in *Europe*, and hereby got that most beneficial Part of our Trade into their own Hands?

As their great Care and our great Neglect of the *African Trade*, has for many Years past given *France* the Advantage over us in *Planting*; so while the same *Cause* continues, Is it not impossible, in the Nature of Things that the *Effect* should cease, and our Trade return to its former flourishing State? All other Measures as they hitherto have, so always will prove only *temporary Expedients*, not *effectual Restoratives*: They have none of them struck at the Root of the Evil; nor is it possible to work a thorough Cure any other way, but by enabling the *African Company* effectually to maintain and support *British* Rights and Privileges on the Coast of *Africa* against the Encroachments of the *French*, and all other Rivals; and in Consequence thereof, by stocking our own Plantations with greater Plenty of *Negroes*, and at *cheaper Rates* than our Rivals would, in such Case, be able to do. . . .

As *Negroe Labour* hitherto has, so that only can support our *British* Colonies, as it has done those of other Nations. It is *that* also will keep them in due Subserviency to the Interest of their *Mother Country*; for while our Plantations depend only on Planting by *Negroes*, and that of such Produce as interferes only with the Interests of our Rivals not of their *Mother-Country*, our Colonies can never prove injurious to *British* Manufactures, never become independent of these Kingdoms, but remain a perpetual Support to our *European* Interest, by preserving to us a Superiority of Trade and Naval Power.

But if the whole *Negroe Trade* be thrown into the Hands of our Rivals, and our Colonies are to depend on the Labour of *White Men* to supply their Place, they will either soon be undone, or shake off their Dependency on the Crown of *England*. For *White Men* cannot be obtained near so cheap, or the Labour of a sufficient Number be had for the Expence of their Maintenance only, as we have of the *Africans*. Has not long Experience also shewn that *White Men* are not constitutionally qualified to sustain the Toil of Planting in the Climates of our *Island Colonies* like the Blacks?

Were it possible however, for *White Men* to answer the End of *Negroes* in Planting, must we not drain our own Country of *Husbandmen*, *Mechanicks* and *Manufacturers* too? Might not the latter be the Cause of our Colonies interfering with the Manufactures of these Kingdoms, as the *Palatines* attempted in *Pensilvania*?[1] In such Case

[1] Note omitted.

indeed, we might have just Reason to dread the Prosperity of our Colonies; but while we can be well supplied with *Negroes*, we can be under no such Apprehensions; their Labour will confine the Plantations to *Planting* only; which will render our *Colonies* more beneficial to these Kingdoms than the *Mines* of *Peru* and *Mexico* are to the *Spaniards*.

Doctor Davenant tells us, that in the Time of King CHARLES II. our *Merchants*, interested in the *American Trade*, made a Representation to that King, setting forth, that by a just Medium, they made it appear, that the Labour of an hundred *Negroes* was, at that Time of Day, 1600l. *per Annum* Profit to this Nation, deducting therefrom the Amount of the Value of what we consume in Plantation Produce. It was then estimated there were no more than 100,000 *Negroes* in *America*; but the most experienced Judges now do not rate them at less than 300,000: So that if we reckon them of no more Worth to *Great Britain* now than at that Time, and estimate the Value of our Home Consumption of Plantation Commodities at the highest Rate, the annual Gain of the Nation by *Negroe Labour* will fall little short of Three Million *per Annum*: And it is to be hoped we shall not sacrifice such an Annuity rather than give all just and reasonable Encouragement for the due Support of our *African Company*, which has been the FOUNDATION of such Profit to these Kingdoms! . . .

Our *African* Trade had its Being before we had any Plantations in the *West Indies*: From the Reign of *Queen Elizabeth* our Merchants separately, or in joint Stocks, prosecuted this Trade till the Commencement of the present Company. Nor have the Struggles, Difficulties, Hazards, and Expences of this present Corporation, first to establish their Trade on a good Footing, and since, to preserve and maintain it to Posterity, been any way inferior to the first Adventurers in our *American Settlements*: But to put this Matter in its true Light, would take a Volume by itself. . . .

254. Petition of the Royal African Company, 16 February 1748

(*Journals of the House of Commons*, XXV, p. 526.)

The Royal African Company had for some years been unable to maintain its forts and settlements on the West Coast of Africa without financial help from Parliament, and the following petition is one of several presented to the House of Commons at this time. Petitions were also presented in 1748 and 1749 by London merchants concerned in the African and West Indian trade, stressing the value of the African trade and urging Parliament to take steps to prevent its further decay.

[16 February 1747/8.]

A Petition of the Royal *African* Company of *England* being offered to be presented to the House;

Mr. Chancellor of the Exchequer, by his Majesty's Command, acquainted the House, That his Majesty, having been informed of the Contents of the said Petition, recommended it to the Consideration of the House:

Then the said Petition was brought up, and read; setting forth, That the Trade to *Africa* is known and acknowledged to be highly beneficial to this Nation, as well on account of the many valuable Commodities which it naturally produces, as of the Supply of Negro Servants, seasoned to such Climates, with which it yearly furnishes the *British* Colonies and Plantations in *America*; and that the Forts and Settlements belonging to the Petitioners in *Africa* should be kept up, for the Protection and Benefit of all his Majesty's Subjects trading to *Africa*, or interested in the Preservation of the same; and that the Petitioners having been at great Expence in erecting, enlarging, and maintaining, the said Forts and Settlements, former Parliaments have likewise granted sundry Sums of Money for better enabling the Petitioners to maintain and keep their said Forts and Settlements; but that the Petitioners have found by Experience, that such Aids have not proved sufficient for that Service; and that, according to the best Information the Petitioners can procure, our most formidable Rivals in this beneficial Trade have granted such Privileges and Immunities, and established such large Funds, for the Support of their Forts and Settlements in *Africa*, and by that means have acquired such Influence and Power with the Natives, and such Advantages over the Petitioners, that it is become impracticable for the Petitioners to support and maintain their said Forts and Settlements, for the Protection and Benefit of all his Majesty's Subjects trading to, and interested in the Preservation of the Trade to, *Africa*, without further Aid and Encouragement from Parliament: And therefore, in Consideration of the Premises, praying, That the House will be pleased to take the Case of the Petitioners into Consideration, and to enable them to keep up and maintain the said Forts and Settlements for the Protection of all his Majesty's Subjects trading to the Coast of *Africa*; or to grant the Petitioners such other Relief as to the House shall seem meet.

255. Adam Smith on the African Company of 1750

(*An Inquiry into the Nature and Causes of the Wealth of Nations*, 1904 ed., II, pp. 229–231.)

As a result of the decline of the Royal African Company and its petitions to Parliament for relief, an "Act for extending and improving the trade to Africa" was passed in 1750, setting up the "Company of Merchants trading to Africa", a regulated company. The Royal African Company was finally divested of its charter in 1752. Adam Smith here describes and criticizes the constitution of the new company.

Long after the time of Sir Josiah Child, however, in 1750, a regulated company was established, the present company of merchants trading to Africa, which was expressly charged at first with the maintenance of all the British forts and garrisons that lie between Cape Blanc and the Cape of Good Hope, and afterwards with that of those only which lie between Cape Rouge and the Cape of Good Hope. The act which establishes this company (the 23rd of George II, c. 31) seems to have had two distinct objects in view; first, to restrain effectually the oppressive and monopolising spirit which is natural to the directors of a regulated company; and secondly, to force them, as much as possible, to give an attention, which is not natural to them, towards the maintenance of forts and garrisons.

For the first of these purposes the fine for admission is limited to forty shillings. The company is prohibited from trading in their corporate capacity, or upon a joint stock; from borrowing money upon common seal, or from laying any restraints upon the trade which may be carried on freely from all places, and by all persons being British subjects, and paying the fine. The government is in a committee of nine persons who meet at London, but who are chosen annually by the freemen of the company at London, Bristol, and Liverpool; three from each place. No committee-man can be continued in office for more than three years together. Any committee-man might be removed by the Board of Trade and Plantations, now by a committee of council, after being heard in his own defence. The committee are forbid to export negroes from Africa, or to import any African goods into Great Britain. But as they are charged with the maintenance of forts and garrisons, they may, for that purpose, export from Great Britain to Africa goods and stores of different kinds. Out of the monies which they shall receive from the company, they are allowed a sum not exceeding eight hundred pounds for the salaries of their clerks and agents at London, Bristol, and Liverpool, the house rent of their office at London, and all other expences of management, commission, and agency in England. What remains of this sum, after defraying these different expences, they may divide among themselves, as compensation for their trouble, in what manner they think proper. By this constitution, it might have been expected that the spirit of monopoly would have been effectually restrained, and the first of these purposes sufficiently answered. It would seem, however, that it had not. Though by the 4th of George III, c. 20, the fort of Senegal, with all its dependencies, had been vested in the company of merchants trading to Africa, yet in the year following (by the 5th of George III, c. 44) not only Senegal and its dependencies, but the whole coast from the port of Sallee, in south Barbary, to Cape Rouge, was exempted from the jurisdiction of that company, was vested in the crown, and the trade to it declared free to all his Majesty's subjects. The company had been suspected of restraining the trade, and of establishing some sort of improper monopoly. It is not, however, very easy to conceive how, under the regulations of the 23rd George II., they could do so. In the printed debates of the House of Commons, not always the most authentic records of truth, I observe, however, that they have been accused of this. The members of the committee of nine, being all merchants, and the governors and factors, in their different forts and settlements, being all dependent upon them, it is not unlikely that the latter might have given peculiar attention to the consignments and commissions of the former which would establish a real monopoly.

For the second of these purposes, the maintenance of the forts and garrisons, an annual sum has been allotted to them by parliament, generally about £13,000. For the proper application of this sum, the committee is obliged to account annually to the Cursitor Baron of Exchequer; which account is afterwards to be laid before parliament. But parliament, which gives so little attention to the application of millions, is not likely to give much to that of £13,000 a year; and the Cursitor Baron of Exchequer, from his profession and education, is not likely to be profoundly skilled in the proper expense of forts and garrisons. The captains of his Majesty's navy, indeed, or any other commissioned officers appointed by the Board of Admiralty, may inquire into the condition of the forts and garrisons, and report their observations to that board. But that board seems to have no direct jurisdiction over the committee, nor any authority to correct those whose conduct it may thus inquire into; and the captains of his Majesty's navy, besides, are not supposed to be always deeply learned in the science of fortification. Removal from an office which can be enjoyed only for the term of three years, and of which the lawful emoluments, even during that term, are so very small, seems to be the utmost punishment to which any committee-man is liable for any fault, except direct malversation, or embezzlement, either of the public money, or of that of the company; and the fear of that punishment can never be a motive of sufficient weight to force a continual and careful attention to a business to which he has no other interest to attend. The committee are accused of having sent out bricks and stones from England for the reparation of Cape Coast Castle on the coast of Guinea, a business for which parliament had several times granted an extraordinary sum of money. These bricks and stones too, which had thus been sent upon so long a voyage, were said to have been of so bad a quality that it is necessary to rebuild from the foundation the walls which had been repaired with them. The forts and garrisons which lie north of Cape Rouge are not only maintained at the expence of the state, but are under the immediate government of the executive power; and why those which lie south of that Cape, and which too are, in part at least, maintained at the expence of the state, should be under a different government, it seems not very easy even to imagine a good reason. The protection of the Mediterranean trade was the original purpose or pretence of the garrisons of Gibraltar and Minorca, and the maintenance and government of those garrisons has always been, very properly, committed, not to the Turkey Company, but to the executive power. In the extent of its dominion consists, in a great measure, the pride and dignity of that power; and it is not very likely to fail in attention to what is necessary for the defence of that dominion. The garrisons at Gibraltar and Minorca, accordingly, have never been neglected; though Minorca has been twice taken, and is now probably lost for ever that disaster was never even imputed to any neglect in the executive power. . . .

Part XII

FOREIGN POLICY AND WARS

FOREIGN POLICY AND WARS

Introduction

FOREIGN policy is a subject which it is peculiarly difficult to illustrate from original documents in a limited space. Diplomatic negotiations clearly cannot be included, and the policy adopted in this section has been to include only treaties, preceded by four extracts illustrating some general principles of British foreign policy during this period. The eighteenth century was a time of intense activity in foreign policy. Her successes in the Spanish Succession War had firmly established Britain as a European Great Power and the accession of the House of Hanover involved her more closely than ever before in the politics of Central Europe. At the same time, the Treaty of Utrecht[1] had made her, potentially at least, "a World Venice with the Seas for streets", but much had still to be done before this potentiality could be fully realized and consolidated.

Hence throughout the period there is a continual dualism in British foreign policy between continental interests, which were paramount under Stanhope and Carteret, and colonial development, which came first with Pitt and Shelburne. The fundamental problem was to establish such a balance between the leading continental powers that Britain, freed from any danger of attack at home, could devote her resources to extending and developing her commerce and colonial empire.[2]

On their return to power in 1714 the Whigs naturally reverted to the policy of restoring the 'old system' of alliances between Great Britain, the United Provinces and the House of Hapsburg. Differences had arisen between the three former allies over the Netherlands. The signature of the Barrier Treaty of 1715,[3] which gave the Netherlands to Austria subject to safeguards for the commercial and strategic interests of the Maritime Powers, was intended as a step in that direction. But the death of Louis XIV brought into power in France the Regent Orléans. Louis XV was a sickly boy, and Orléans was next in the succession to the French throne, provided the exclusion of Philip V of Spain by the Treaty of Utrecht was maintained. The French Regent and the Hanoverian king of Great Britain had, therefore, a common dynastic interest in upholding the Utrecht settlement. This was the basis of the Triple Alliance treaty of 1717[4] between Great Britain, France and the United Provinces. It had the curious result that the Whigs who had violently denounced the Utrecht settlement in 1713–1714 now made its maintenance the basis of their foreign policy.

For the next twenty years Britain co-operated with France much more closely than with Austria. At times she was definitely hostile to Austria, as for example during the crisis of 1725–1727, caused by the Austro-Spanish alliance. With the birth of the Dauphin in 1729, the conditions which had brought about the Franco-British alliance passed away, the alliance began to weaken, and the Second Treaty of Vienna in 1731[5] marks the beginning of a return to the traditional Whig policy of alliance with the Emperor and the United Provinces. But even after the first family compact

[1] For the Treaty of Utrecht, see vol. VIII of these *Documents*, No. 348.
[2] No. 259.
[3] No. 277.
[4] No. 278.
[5] No. 279.

of 1733 between France and Spain, Walpole firmly refused to support the Emperor against Bourbon aggression in the War of the Polish Succession. Consequently the party line between Whig and Tory on foreign policy became somewhat blurred. This becomes clear if Walpole's review of foreign policy from 1714 to 1739[1] is compared with Bolingbroke's statement of the principles on which it ought, in his opinion, to be based.[2]

This first period ended with the British declaration of war against Spain in 1739[3] and the restoration of the old system of alliances when the War of the Austrian Succession broke out in the following year.[4] This ended with the Treaty of Aix-la-Chapelle in 1748,[5] which did nothing to remove the fundamental causes of the war, either on the Continent or in the colonies and was negotiated in a way that did permanent injury to the restored 'old system'.

By the summer of 1755 it was clear that Britain and France were on the point of war, and that Austria was no longer prepared to play on the Continent the role for which British statesmen believed she had been designed by Providence. In the opinion of some contemporaries this was in itself a positive advantage, but it was counterbalanced by the fact that without Austria no adequate measures could be taken for the protection of Hanover. George II and his chief minister, the duke of Newcastle, then concluded with Russia the Treaty of St. Petersburg,[6] with the double intention of encouraging Austria to join once again with Britain, and overawing the king of Prussia and preventing him from attacking Hanover. This second object seemed to be secured when Frederick II hastily signed the Convention of Westminster in 1756.[7]

Quite unintentionally the British Government by its feverish activity had brought about the diplomatic revolution. France and Austria concluded the first Treaty of Versailles, abandoned their venerable tradition of hostility and remained allies until the end of our period. The British Government's continental sheet anchor disappeared overnight, and there seemed nothing to put in its place. It was not even certain that Prussia would abide by the stipulations of the Convention of Westminster. At the same time the military and naval inadequacy of the British Government's preparations was shown by defeats in America and the sensational loss of Minorca to a French attack.[8] Newcastle hurriedly resigned in the hope of escaping impeachment and Pitt took office.

From 1756 onwards, British foreign policy is in effect British colonial policy. Pitt saw France as the great rival and enemy of Britain in the maritime and colonial fields, and his planning of the war aimed at striking at France in every part of the globe, either directly or indirectly. Thus Clive's victory at Plassey in June 1757[9]–a victory not over the French but over a hostile Indian prince–by giving the British East India Company control over Bengal greatly strengthened them in their rivalry with France in the Carnatic, and could be regarded as a blow struck in the world-wide contest between the two countries.

In the winter of 1757 Pitt planned the campaign of 1758. In America, two expeditions were planned with the idea of a subsequent attack on Quebec: the combined military and naval expedition to Louisbourg, and the invasion of Canada by way of Crown Point, with the assistance of contingents from the North American colonies.[10] This plan was only partially successful, as Abercromby failed to take Ticonderoga, and although Louisbourg fell in July, it was not possible to attack Quebec this year.

[1] No. 256. [2] No. 257. [3] No .258. [4] No. 260. [5] No. 280.
[6] No. 281. [7] No. 282. [8] No. 261. [9] No. 262. [10] No. 263.

Pitt had previously criticized continental campaigns, but he now saw continental war as a means to a colonial end–the policy of 'containment' by which French troops and resources could be kept locked up in Europe. Help in men and money was therefore sent to Frederick the Great, and raids on the French coast planned to distract the French still further.[1] In the autumn of 1758 operations were extended to the West Indies, an expedition being sent against the French island of Martinique,[2] and later diverted to the second most important of the French sugar islands, Guadeloupe, which was captured in 1759. In the same year the triple invasion of Canada planned in the winter of 1758,[3] resulted in the capture of Quebec in September;[4] and the policy of naval blockade of the French ports to prevent the sailing of their fleets either against England or to North America and the West Indies, resulted in the spectacular victories of Boscawen at Lagos in August and of Hawke at Quiberon Bay in November.[5]

The change of king in 1760 soon brought about a change of foreign policy. The young George III and his mentor, Lord Bute, were both determined to bring to an end a war which they considered bloody and unnecessary. Unlike his grandfather, George III was not interested in Hanover, and particularly disliked a continental war. Peace negotiations were opened between Pitt and Choiseul, the French foreign minister, in 1761, but Pitt haughtily rejected the French proposals as insufficient. Rumours of the Third Family Compact between France and Spain now reached England, confirming Pitt's view that Choiseul was not sincere in the negotiations, and Pitt was in favour of an immediate declaration of war against Spain, while she was still unprepared. He failed to carry the Cabinet with him and resigned on 2 October. The publication of the Family Compact in January 1762, however, made war with Spain inevitable, and an expedition was dispatched against Havana, the most important port in the Spanish West Indies, which surrendered on 12 August after great loss of life.[6] The Bute Government had already reopened peace negotiations, and the definitive Treaty of Paris was signed in February 1763.[7] Though violently attacked by Pitt as inadequate, it was widely approved in England.

As long as France and Austria remained allies, Britain's only hope of restoring her influence in continental politics after 1763 lay in the recovery of the Prussian alliance, which she had forfeited by her conduct in the closing stages of the war. This in fact, and not the inadequacy of the colonial gains, is the most serious criticism of the Treaty of Paris. Just as the Whigs in the early part of the century had differed in their attitude to the French alliance, so did they now take opposing views of the Prussian alliance. While Pitt continued to believe in it and tried to bring it about during his period of office, Grenville advocated a policy of non-intervention and Newcastle said frankly he did not know what to advise. They all would have agreed, however, with Pitt on "the impossibility for this country to contend with the united power of the House of Bourbon, merely on the strength of its own resources". From 1763 to the outbreak of the War of American Independence, Britain can hardly be said to have had a foreign policy at all. She remained completely isolated in Europe and the danger of this situation speedily became apparent. When the war with America broke out Britain also had to face a great continental coalition, without any assistance whatever.

Foreign intervention did not, however, take place at once, and a vigorous and efficient prosecution of the war at the outset might well have resulted in the defeat of

[1] No. 264. [2] No. 265. [3] No. 266. [4] Nos. 267 and 268.
[5] No. 269. [6] No. 270. [7] No. 283

the colonies before such intervention occurred. England had complete command of the sea; a loyal Canada to the north of the New England colonies, and strong loyalist support in the southern colonies. Plans for the isolation of the New England colonies were not, however, made till 1777 and then most inefficiently pursued. Muddled instructions–largely due to the carelessness of the American Secretary of State, Lord George Germain[1]–resulted in the disaster of Burgoyne's surrender at Saratoga in October 1777.[2] In 1778 France entered the war, Spain in 1779 and the Dutch in 1780. The question of sea power now became vital. The policy of blockading the French ports was less successful than in the Seven Years War, and the French fleet under de Grasse got to the West Indies, where several indecisive actions took place, that in Chesapeake Bay on 5 September 1781[3] resulting in the fall of Yorktown in October,[4] loss of the command of the sea at a vital moment making it impossible to relieve Cornwallis and his garrison. In 1782 the tide began to turn a little, Rodney defeating de Grasse at the battle of the Saintes in the West Indies,[5] and Gibraltar, which had stood a siege of three years, being at last relieved after a final desperate assault.[6] The war–and our period–ends with a batch of peace treaties; the Treaty of Versailles with France,[7] and the Treaty of Versailles with Spain; the Treaty of Paris with the United States,[8] and the Treaty of Paris with the United Provinces.

[1] No. 271. [2] No. 272. [3] No. 273. [4] No. 274.
[5] No. 275. [6] No. 276. [7] No. 285. [8] No. 284.

BIBLIOGRAPHY

I. ORIGINAL SOURCES

Reference should be made to the section on Manuscript Sources in the General Bibliography, and particularly to Frances G. Davenport, *Materials for English Diplomatic History 1509–1783* [in British Museum and Historical Manuscripts Commission Reports], published in the 18th Report, part 2, 1917, pp. 357–402. Some of the more important collections of documents calendared or published by the Historical Manuscripts Commission dealing with eighteenth-century foreign policy are indicated in the General Bibliography, Section II (*e*). The Royal Historical Society has published *British Diplomatic Instructions 1689–1789* (7 vols., London, 1922–1934), which contains not merely the official instructions, which became so stereotyped in this period as to be almost useless, but also additional instructions and excerpts from the correspondence between the secretaries of state and the diplomatic agents abroad. Four of these volumes, edited by L. G. Wickham Legg, deal with France. The other three, edited by J. F. Chance, are devoted to Sweden (2 vols.) and Denmark (1 vol.). Owing to the practice of the secretaries of state in the eighteenth century, there are few instructions or dispatches which give anything like a comprehensive review of our relations with a particular foreign power at a definite time such as are to be found in every volume of the *Recueil des Instructions Données aux Ambassadeurs et Ministres de France* [1648–1789] (Paris, 1884–1936). In default of these the editors have sometimes allowed themselves to become bogged in the minor issues of diplomacy. The Society has also published *British Diplomatic Representatives 1689–1789*, edited by D. B. Horn (London, 1932), which provides a complete list of diplomatic agents accredited by the British Government to other courts, along with references to original sources on their respective missions. These lists were used to compile skeleton lists for Great Britain, without bibliographical material, in *Repertorium der diplomatischen Vertreter aller Länder*, edited by L. Bittner and L. Gross of which vols. I and II, 1648–1763 (Oldenburg, 1936, and Zürich, 1950) have been published. Unfortunately the volumes devoted to Great Britain in the *Recueil des Instructions* stop at 1690; but other volumes in the series cover the relations between France and all the leading and many of the less important European countries in the eighteenth century. They are essential to any serious study of British foreign policy. So far as the last forty years of our period are concerned, this is equally true of the monumental publication in 46 volumes–still incomplete –*Politische Correspondenz Friedrichs des Grossen* (Berlin, 1879–1939). Amongst other such collections the specialist will refer frequently to *Archives ou Correspondance inédite de la Maison d'Orange-Nassau* [1552–1789] (27 vols., Leyden, 1835–1917) on Anglo-Dutch relations: to *Sbornik Imperatorskago Russkago Istoriceskago Obscestva* (148 vols., St. Petersburg, 1867–1916), which includes the official correspondence (in English) of several British diplomatists accredited to the Russian Government and with some gaps covers the years 1714–1719, 1728–1762 and 1764–1778.

Publication of other original sources has been quite accidental and unsystematic. It had not yet become customary for diplomatists to publish accounts either of their missions or of their views on our relations with the court to which they were accredited, though one or two did so, as Onslow Burrish, *Batavia Illustrata*, dedicated to Walpole (2 vols., London, 1728); C. Cole, *Historical and Political Memoirs* (London, 1735); and Sir George Macartney, *Account of Russia, 1767* (London, 1768). Usually publication of such material was left to pious members of their families, who, long after the death of their ancestor, published selections from his letters and papers. Less frequently, historians have been so impressed by the value of such a collection of papers that they have felt impelled to edit them for publication. Among the most useful works of this kind may be mentioned A. Bisset, *Memoirs and Papers of Sir Andrew Mitchell* (2 vols., London, 1850) [Anglo-Prussian relations, 1756–1771]; *Diaries and Correspondence of James Harris,*

First Earl of Malmesbury [edited by his grandson], vols. 1 and 2 (London, 1844) [chiefly relations with Prussia, 1772–1776, and Russia, 1778–1783]; R. Lodge, *Private Correspondence of Benjamin Keene* (Cambridge, 1933) [Spain and Portugal, 1730–1757]; Adelaide D'A. Collyer, *Despatches and Correspondence of John, Second Earl of Buckinghamshire, Ambassador to . . . Russia 1762–65* (2 vols., Camden Society, London, 1900–1902); *Correspondence of John, Fourth Duke of Bedford*, edited by Lord John Russell (3 vols., London, 1842–1846), for negotiations leading to the Treaty of Paris of 1763; *Memorials and Correspondence of Charles James Fox*, edited by Lord John Russell, vol. 4 (London, 1857), for negotiations at the end of the war of American Independence; Mrs. Gillespie Smyth, *Memoirs and Correspondence of Sir Robert Murray Keith* (2 vols., London, 1849) [chiefly relations with Austria, 1772–1792]; Lady Minto, *Memoir of the Right Honourable Hugh Elliot* (Edinburgh, 1868) [various courts, 1772–1783]; J. Doran, *"Mann" and Manners at the Court of Florence, 1740–86* (London, 1876), based on Horace Mann's letters to Horace Walpole; *Journal and Correspondence of William Eden, Baron Auckland from 1771 to 1814* (4 vols., London, 1861–1862); Sir George Larpent, *Turkey, its History and Progress from the Journals and Correspondence of Sir James Porter* (2 vols., London, 1854 [ambassador at Constantinople, 1746–1762]; W. Coxe, *Memoirs of Horatio, Lord Walpole* (2 vols., London, 1802, 2nd edition, 2 vols., 1808) [useful on British foreign policy generally from 1720 to 1757]; *Correspondance de Catherine Alexéievna, Grande-Duchesse de Russie et de Sir Charles H. Williams*, edited by S. Goriaïanow (Moscow, 1909, translated by the earl of Ilchester and Mrs. Langford-Brooke, London, 1928).

The Historical Manuscripts Commission has published much valuable material of this sort, including the *Townshend Manuscripts* (1887) (papers of the second earl, while secretary of state); the *Polwarth Manuscripts* (4 vols., 1911–1942) (papers of the British diplomatic representative at Copenhagen and the Congress of Cambrai, 1716–1725, on the editing of which Sir Richard Lodge's article in the *Transactions of the Royal Historical Society*, Fourth Series, xv, pp. 243–269, should be read); the *Clements Manuscripts, Report on Manuscripts in Various Collections*, vol. VIII (1913) [letters to and from the Honourable John Molesworth, envoy at Turin]; the *Trevor Manuscripts* (1895) [chiefly correspondence of Robert Trevor, envoy to the United Provinces during the Austrian Succession War], included in the *Manuscripts of the Earl of Buckinghamshire Report XIV App. 9*; the *Lothian Manuscripts* (1905) [including the earl of Buckinghamshire's papers as ambassador to Russia, 1762–1765]; and the *Leeds Manuscripts* (1888) [relating to the earl of Holdernesse, as secretary of state].

II. TREATIES

D. P. Myers, *Manual of Collections of Treaties* (Cambridge, Mass., 1922), provides a complete list of the collections. These include J. Rousset de Missy, *Supplément au Corps Universel du Droit des Gens* (2 vols., Amsterdam, 1739), which gives the text of various treaties between 1714 and 1738, and the same author's *Recueil Historique d'Actes, Négociations, Mémoires et Traitez* [1713–1748] (The Hague, 21 vols., 1728–1755), which provides a running commentary on the principal diplomatic transactions of these years. F. A. W. Wenck, *Codex Juris Gentium Recentissimi* (3 vols., Leipsiz, 1781–1795), prints the texts of the principal treaties concluded between 1735 and 1772. G. F. von Martens, *Recueil des Principaux Traités depuis 1761* (7 vols., Göttingen, 1791–1801) and *Supplément au Recueil des Principaux Traités . . . depuis 1761 . . . précedé de Traités du 18e Siècle antérieurs à cet Epoque* (4 vols., Göttingen, 1802–1808), are standard collections. C. G. de Koch and M. S. F. Schoell, *Abrégé de l'Histoire des Traités de Paix* [1648–1815] (15 vols., Paris, 1817–1818, and later editions), fills up some of the gaps. Two eighteenth-century collections give English texts, based on the official translations made for the use of Parliament and the civil service, of nearly all the important treaties of the century. These are C. Jenkinson, *Collection of all the Treaties of Peace, Alliance, and Commerce between Great Britain and other Powers* [1648–1784] (3 vols., London, 1785), and G. Chalmers, *Collection of Treaties between Great Britain and other Powers* (2 vols., London, 1790).

There are also some useful collections of treaties relating to particular countries. F. de Martens, *Recueil des Traités et Conventions Conclus par la Russie*, vol. IX (X) *avec l'Angleterre* (St. Petersburg, 1892), attempts to link the treaties with accounts of Anglo-Russian negotiations. L. Bittner, *Chronologisches Verzeichnis der Österreichischen Staatsverträge*, vol. I [1526–1763] (Vienna, 1903), and vol. II [1763–1847], lists and A. F. Pribram, *Österreichische Staatsverträge*: England (2 vols., Innsbruck, 1907, and Vienna, 1913), prints the treaties between Austria and Britain. C. O. Paullin, *European Treaties bearing on the History of the United States*, vol. IV, 1716–1815 (Washington, 1937), extracts from many of the treaties clauses which affected the North American continent.

III. WORKS ON DIPLOMACY AND INTERNATIONAL RELATIONS

A. van Wicquefort, *L'Ambassadeur et ses Fonctions* (2 vols., The Hague, 1681–1680), was widely used and was translated into English by J. Digby (London, 1716). Also useful are F. de Callières, *De La Manière de Négocier avec les Souverains* (Paris, 1716), translated into English by Sir A. Frederick Whyte (Boston and New York, 1919), and A. Pecquet, *Discours sur l'Art de Négocier* (Paris, 1737). J. A. A. J. Jusserand's address to the American Historical Association reprinted in the *American Historical Review*, XXVII (1921–1922), pp. 426–464, "School for Ambassadors" discusses these and other works. The most useful modern historical work on this subject is D. P. Heatley, *Diplomacy and the Study of International Relations* (Oxford, 1919). Sir E. Satow, *A Guide to Diplomatic Practice* (2 vols., London, 1917, 3rd edition, revised H. Ritchie, 1932), refers occasionally to our period. Some account of the British diplomatic service in the eighteenth century will be found in D. B. Horn, *Scottish Diplomatists 1689–1789*, Historical Association Publications, No. 132 (London, 1944).

IV. GENERAL ACCOUNTS OF BRITISH FOREIGN POLICY

A. H. L. Heeren, "Historical Development of the Rise and Growth of the Continental Interests of Great Britain", in his *Historical Treatises* (Oxford, 1836), pp. 199–422, is of interest to the historiographer rather than to the historian. M. Burrows, *History of the Foreign Policy of Great Britain* (London, 1895), and H. E. Egerton, *British Foreign Policy in Europe* (London, 1917), are slight and long out of date. Sir A. W. Ward, who contributed a long opening essay to the *Cambridge History of British Foreign Policy 1783–1919*, edited by himself and G. P. Gooch (3 vols., Cambridge, 1922–1923), failed to make the best use of his opportunity. E. Malcolm Smith's brief essay, *British Diplomacy in the Eighteenth Century 1700–89* (London, 1937), is therefore the best introduction for the general reader, though it does not carry him far. Some of the chapters in the *Cambridge Modern History*, vol. VI (Cambridge, 1909), are still valuable. More up-to-date accounts of the European background of British foreign policy are provided by P. Roberts, *The Quest for Security 1715–40* (New York, 1947), W. L. Dorn, *Competition for Empire, 1740–63* (New York, 1940), and L. Gershoy, *From Despotism to Revolution, 1763–89* (New York, 1944), all in the series edited by W. L. Langer, "The Rise of Modern Europe". These volumes vary considerably in quality. All three, however, have extensive, annotated bibliographies. The French volume in the series "Peuples et Civilizations", P. Muret, *La Prépondérance Anglaise* (Paris, 1937), and P. Sagnac, *La Fin de l'Ancien Régime et la Révolution Américaine* (Paris, 1941), may also be consulted. *A Select List of Works on Europe and Europe Overseas 1715–1815*, edited by J. S. Bromley and A. Goodwin (Oxford, 1956), is useful.

V. MONOGRAPHS

Monographs dealing with short periods or particular countries are legion. The reign of George I and the early years of George II are admirably covered by Basil Williams, *Stanhope* (Oxford, 1932), and the same author's five articles on the "Foreign Policy of England under

Walpole" in the *English Historical Review*, xv (1900), pp. 251–276, 479–494 and 665–698, and xvi (1901), pp. 67–83, 308–327 and 439–451. J. F. Chance's two works, based on long research in the archives, *George I and the Northern War* (London, 1909) and *Alliance of Hanover* (London, 1923), also deal with the principal problems of British foreign policy in this period, including the conflicts between British and Hanoverian interests and intentions. J. C. Walker's article on "The Duke of Newcastle and the British envoys at the Congress of Cambrai" in the *English Historical Review*, L (1935), pp. 113–119, and J. J. Murray's articles on "Scania and the end of the Northern Alliance" and "Robert Jackson's Mission to Sweden (1709–1717)," both in the *Journal of Modern History*, xvi (1944), pp. 81–92, and xxi (1949), pp. 1–16, add to our knowledge. The early years of George II's reign are best studied in the works of Professor Vaucher, *Robert Walpole et la Politique de Fleury 1731–42* and *La Crise du Ministère Walpole en 1733–4* (Paris, 1924), and in A. M. Wilson, *French Foreign Policy of Cardinal Fleury 1726–43* (Cambridge, Mass., 1936), which is largely concerned with Fleury's relations with Walpole. Almost the only account since Carlyle's *Frederick the Great* (London, 1868) of the diplomacy of the War of the Austrian Succession is by Sir Richard Lodge in his *Studies in Eighteenth Century Diplomacy* (London, 1930). The two monographs by Professor R. Pares, cited in the section on Colonies, are essential to the study of foreign policy in the middle years of the century. D. B. Horn, *Sir Charles Hanbury Williams and European Diplomacy 1747–58* (London, 1930), and the same author's article in the *English Historical Review*, XLII (1927), pp. 361–370, on "The origins of the proposed election of a King of the Romans", discuss the main problems of British foreign policy in these years from the standpoint of the origins of the diplomatic revolution. This is not the place to list the enormous number of controversial works on that revolution in French, German and other languages. The outstanding contribution, however, is undoubtedly R. Waddington, *Louis XV et le Renversement des Alliances* (Paris, 1896). The same author's *La Guerre de Sept Ans* (5 vols., Paris, 1899–1914) is equally the leading work on the European aspects of the Seven Years War. British policy and activities during this war are adequately explained in the various biographies of Pitt (see sectional bibliography on The Monarchy). Sir J. S. Corbett in his *England in the Seven Years War* (2 vols., London, 1907, 2nd edition, 1918) concentrates on the naval and colonial side, while R. Pares in "American *versus* Continental Warfare 1739–63" in the *English Historical Review*, LI (1936), pp. 429–465, illustrates and criticizes the contemporary attitudes to matters of high policy. C. W. Eldon, *England's Subsidy Policy* (Philadelphia, 1938), and B. Tunstall, *Admiral Byng and the Loss of Minorca* (London, 1928), deal exhaustively with these special topics. H. Butterfield, *The Reconstruction of an Historical Episode: the History of the Enquiry into the Origins of the Seven Years War* (Glasgow, 1951), is an interesting and controversial study in historiography. Many historians have studied the complicated negotiations which ended the war. H. W. V. Temperley in the *Cambridge History of the British Empire*, vol. I (Cambridge, 1929), surveys them briefly: Z. E. Rashed, *The Peace of Paris* (Liverpool, 1951), is fuller but less inspiring. Two eminent authorities, J. H. Rose in "Frederick the Great and England 1756–63" in the *English Historical Review*, XXIX (1914), pp. 79–93 and 257–275, and W. L. Dorn in "Frederic the Great and Lord Bute" in the *Journal of Modern History*, I (1929), pp. 529–560, have examined the breach in our alliance with Prussia, which was largely to determine our foreign policy for the next generation. W. L. Grant's two articles, one on "Mission de M. de Bussy à Londres en 1761" in *Revue d'Histoire Diplomatique*, XX (1906), pp. 351–366, and the other on "Canada versus Guadeloupe" in the *American Historical Review*, XVII (1911–1912), pp. 735–743, are useful contributions, as are Kate Hotblack's "Peace of Paris 1763" in the *Transactions of the Royal Historical Society*, Third Series, II (1908), pp. 235–267; A. S. Aiton's "The Diplomacy of the Louisiana Purchase" in the *American Historical Review*, XXXVI (1930–1931), pp. 701–720; T. C. Pease's "The Mississippi Boundary of 1763" in the *American Historical Review*, XL (1934–1935), pp. 278–286; and L. S. Sutherland's "The East India Company and the Peace of Paris" in the *English Historical Review*, LXII (1947), pp. 179–190. Much less attention has been paid to British foreign policy between 1763 and the outbreak of the American War of Independence than to its manifestations in the earlier years of the century.

The Falkland Islands crisis of 1770–1774 has been studied primarily from the standpoint of an international lawyer in Julius Goebel, *The Struggle for the Falkland Islands* (New Haven, 1927). J. Brown Scott, *The Armed Neutralities of 1780 and 1800* (New York, 1918), brings together a vast collection of documents on this important question. On the peace negotiations of 1782–1783 S. F. Bemis, *The Hussey-Cumberland Mission and American Independence* (Princeton, New Jersey, 1931) and the same author's *Diplomacy of the American Revolution* (New York, 1935) should be consulted.

VI. WORKS DEALING WITH RELATIONS BETWEEN BRITAIN AND PARTICULAR COUNTRIES

(*a*) THE BOURBON POWERS

Since relations with France, usually hostile, were the central theme of British foreign policy in the eighteenth century, most works on Franco-British relations have been included in the previous section. Sir Richard Lodge's essay on "The Anglo-French Alliance 1716–1731" in *Studies in Anglo-French History* (edited by A. Coville and H. Temperley, Cambridge, 1935), and J. F. Ramsey, *Anglo-French Relations 1763–70* (Berkeley, California, 1939), and W. F. Lord, *England and France in the Mediterranean* (London, 1901), must, however, be included here. W. Coxe, *Memoirs of the Kings of Spain* (2nd edition, 5 vols., London, 1815), being based largely on the correspondence of British diplomatic agents at Madrid, and E. Armstrong's biography of "the termagant of Europe", *Elizabeth Farnese* (London, 1892), are still useful for Anglo-Spanish relations. They must, however, be supplemented by the works of R. Pares mentioned in the bibliography to the section on the Colonies; by Jean O. McLachlan, *Trade and Peace with Old Spain 1667–1750* (Cambridge, 1940), and the same author's article on "The Seven Years Peace and the West Indian Policy of Carvajal and Wall" in the *English Historical Review*, LIII (1938), pp. 457–477; and by Vera L. Brown, *Studies in the History of Spain in the second half of the 18th century* (Northampton, Mass., 1929). Articles by H. W. V. Temperley on "Causes of the War of Jenkins' Ear, 1739" in the *Transactions of the Royal Historical Society*, Third Series, III (1909), pp. 197–236, by E. G. Hildner on "Role of South Sea Company in the Diplomacy leading to the War of Jenkins' Ear, 1729–39" in the *Hispanic American Historical Review*, XVIII (1938), pp. 322–341, and by G. H. Nelson on "Contraband Trade under the Assiento 1730–39" in the *American Historical Review*, LI (1945–1946), pp. 55–67, are useful on relations in the thirties, while the "Economic Background of the Anglo-Spanish War of 1762" has been examined by A. Christelow in the *Journal of Modern History*, XVIII (1946), pp. 22–36, and "Anglo-Spanish Relations in America in the Closing Years of the Colonial Era" by Vera L. Brown in the *Hispanic American Historical Review*, V (1922), pp. 325–483. Stetson Conn, *Gibraltar in British Diplomacy* (New Haven, 1942), at times widens its scope to survey Anglo-Spanish relations in general from 1714 to 1783; G. T. Garratt, *Gibraltar and the Mediterranean* (London, 1939), has three chapters on the eighteenth century. M. S. Anderson, "Great Britain and the Barbary States in the Eighteenth Century", in *Bulletin of the Institute of Historical Research*, XXIX (1956), pp. 87–107, is also useful.

(*b*) THE NETHERLANDS

A good deal of attention has been given to British relations with the Low Countries, but most of the literature is in Dutch or French, and there are very few translations of these works. R. Geikie and Isabel A. Montgomery in *The Dutch Barrier 1705–19* (Cambridge, 1930) explained the origins of a problem which worried British diplomatists throughout the century. S. T. Bindoff, *The Scheldt Question to 1839* (London, 1945), is valuable. H. Pirenne, *Histoire de Belgique*, vol. 5 (Brussels, 1921), is excellent on our relations with the Low Countries generally. Ragnhild Hatton, *Diplomatic Relations between Great Britain and the Dutch Republic 1714–1721* (London,

1950), and *An Honest Diplomat at The Hague*, edited by J. J. Murray (Indiana University Publication, 1955), are useful. One of the leading Dutch historians, Professor P. Geyl, contributed an article on "William IV of Orange and his English Marriage" to the *Transactions of the Royal Historical Society*, Fourth Series, VIII (1925), pp. 14–37, and wrote briefly on "Holland and England during the War of the Austrian Succession" in *History*, x (1925–1926), pp. 47–51. Sir Richard Lodge edited *The Private Correspondence of Chesterfield and Newcastle 1744–46* for the Royal Historical Society (London, 1930), and wrote on "The Maritime Powers in the Eighteenth Century" in *History*, XV (1930–1931), pp. 246–251. Alice M. C. Le Mesurier's unpublished thesis on "The Anglo-French Struggle for Control of Dutch Policy 1755–63" is referred to in *Bulletin of the Institute of Historical Research*, XII (1934–1935), pp. 122–125. On the commercial side, there is C. H. Wilson, *Anglo-Dutch Commerce and Finance in the Eighteenth Century* (Cambridge, 1941); and G. B. Hertz wrote in the *English Historical Review*, XXII (1907), pp. 255–279, on "England and the Ostend Company". A. Cobban, *Ambassadors and Secret Agents* (London, 1954), deals mainly with the period after 1783.

(*c*) THE GERMAN POWERS

Some of the problems involved in the personal union between Great Britain and Hanover were dealt with by Sir A. W. Ward in *Electress Sophia and the Hanoverian Succession* (enlarged edition, London, 1909) and *Great Britain and Hanover* (Oxford, 1899). In default of any modern survey of our relations with Austria, W. Coxe, *History of the House of Austria* (3 vols., 3rd edition (Bohn), London, 1847–1853, or, new impression in 4 vols., London, 1893–1895), must be supplemented by much useful material in the classic work (in German) of A. von Arneth, *Geschichte Maria Theresia's* (10 vols., Vienna, 1863–1879). On Prussia there is the authoritative work of Sir Richard Lodge, *Great Britain and Prussia in the Eighteenth Century* (Oxford, 1923), and an elaborate monograph by Sir E. Satow, *The Silesian Loan and Frederick the Great* (Oxford, 1915). Other works already listed, especially Bisset's *Andrew Mitchell* and the *Malmesbury Diaries*, are also essential.

(*d*) SCANDINAVIA

There is little to record here apart from the volumes of *British Diplomatic Instructions* for Sweden and Denmark, and J. F. Chance's two monographs already mentioned. The general histories in English of the Scandinavian countries such as C. Hallendorff and A. Schueck, *History of Sweden* (London, 1939), have only a few pages to devote to the eighteenth century, and the student is thrown back on the chapters in the volumes of the *Cambridge Modern History*. There is, however, a useful article by J. J. Murray on "Baltic Commerce and Power Politics in the Early Eighteenth Century" in the *Huntington Library Quarterly*, VI (1942–1943), pp. 293–312; and C. E. Hill, *The Danish Sound Dues and the Command of the Baltic* (Duke University Press, 1926).

(*e*) RUSSIA AND POLAND

Some information may be gleaned from the standard histories, especially V. O. Klyuchevsky, *History of Russia* (5 vols., London, 1911–1931); G. Vernadsky, *A History of Russia* (New Haven, 1929); and W. F. Reddaway and others, *The Cambridge History of Poland from Augustus II to Pilsudski* (Cambridge, 1941). The dispatches of many British diplomatic agents to Russia have been printed, as well as most of the treaties they concluded with the Russian Government. (See earlier sections of this bibliography.) M. S. Anderson deals with "English Views of Russia in the Age of Peter the Great" in *American Slavic and East European Review* (1954), pp. 200–214. D. K. Reading, *The Anglo-Russian Commercial Treaty of 1734* (New Haven, 1938), is excellent on the diplomatic as well as on the economic aspect of our relations with Russia in the early part of the century. Adelaide D. Collyer's "Notes on the Diplomatic Correspondence between England and Russia in the First Half of the Eighteenth Century" in the *Transactions of the Royal Historical Society*, New Series, XIV (1900), pp. 143–173, is useful, and Sir Richard Lodge examined in some detail Anglo-Russian diplomatic relations from 1739 to 1749 in a series of articles in the *English Historical Review*, XLIII (1928), pp. 354–375, 540–571; XLV (1930), pp. 579–611; and XLVI (1931), pp. 48–76 and 389–422. But the best work on Anglo-Russian relations is W. Mediger, *Moskavs Weg Nach Europa* (Brunswick, 1952). On the second half of the eighteenth century there is a solid study by D. Gerhard, *England und der Aufstieg Russlands* (Munich and Berlin, 1933), which is not by any means limited to diplomacy. On Anglo-Polish relations there is useful information from Polish and Swedish archives in Przezdziecki, *Diplomatic Ventures and Adventures* (London, 1953). On the first partition of Poland there is a good introductory chapter in R. H. Lord, *The Second Partition of Poland* (Cambridge, Mass., 1915); D. B. Horn, *British Public Opinion and the First Partition* (Edinburgh, 1945), gives some indication of the contemporary British attitude towards it. The same subject is approached from a different angle by W. Konopezynski in "England and the 1st Partition of Poland" in *Journal of Central European Affairs*, VIII (1948–1949), pp. 1–23. W. F. Reddaway contributed two valuable articles to the *Cambridge Historical Journal*, III (1929–1931), pp. 260–294, and *ibid.*, IV (1932–1934), No. 3, pp. 223–262, on "Macartney in Russia" and "Great Britain and Poland 1762–72" respectively; and M. S. Anderson articles on "Great Britain and the Russo-Turkish War of 1768–74" in the *English Historical Review*, LXIX (1954), pp. 39–58, and on "Great Britain and the Russian Fleet, 1769–70" in *Slavonic and East European Review*, XXXI (1952), pp. 148–163.

(*f*) EASTERN QUESTION

Direct British interest in the Eastern Question is only beginning at the very end of our period. A. Sorel, *The Eastern Question in the Eighteenth Century* (English translation, London, 1898), is still the best introduction, and A. C. Wood, *History of the Levant Company* (London, 1935), is almost as much a diplomatic as a commercial study.

A. POLICY

256. Sir Robert Walpole's review of Whig foreign policy, 1714–1739, in a speech in the House of Commons, 21 November 1739

(*Parl. Hist.*, XI, pp. 229–233.)

Walpole was answering Sir William Windham's speech in support of a resolution for addressing the king not to make peace with Spain till the right of British ships to navigate in the American seas is acknowledged by the Spaniards.

. . . Has this nation ever since seemed to be divided from her best and most natural allies? The treaty of Utrecht laid the foundation of these differences. It was this treaty, Sir, that gave rise to those dissensions which the makers and abbetters of it have since endeavoured to improve to the ruin of this nation. If France has attained such a degree of power as puts her again in a condition to disturb the peace of Europe, is it not to be imputed to that treaty? Thus, Sir, gentlemen who once were ministers, and who, by a series of blunders, have laid their successors under a necessity of retrieving them by measures which perhaps they would willingly avoid, did not the misconduct of their predecessors lay constraints upon them, are the first to call out for justice upon the succeeding ministry, though they cannot be ignorant that every step that these gentlemen have taken was in order to rectify the errors which the former had committed.

The hon. gentleman says that we have been outwitted by the powers with whom we have negotiated. There is nothing so easy, Sir, as general charges; nothing so true, Sir, as the old maxim, "Throw out your calumnies with assurance, and some of them will find credit." I could say twenty times as much, Sir, were I to run into general terms in favour of the ministry, or, if the hon. gentleman will have it so, in favour of myself; I could then be as lavish of panegyric as the hon. gentleman is of censure. Outwitted, Sir! give me leave to ask, how or when we have been outwitted? Have we given up any one branch of our commerce to our neighbours? Have we made any one treaty that so much as seems to take away the smallest advantage we enjoyed by former stipulations? I will venture to say, that the trade of Great Britain is at this instant more flourishing, her ships more numerous, and her navigation better protected, than ever was known in former ages. Are these, Sir, symptoms of a weak administration? Are these proofs that we have been outwitted?

And here, Sir, I will once for all join issue with the hon. gentleman who, with his friends, are perpetually expatiating upon that exhausted subject of inconsistent negotiations, and dishonourable treaties. What treaties, Sir, or what negotiations have either been dishonourable or inconsistent for these 20 years past? I know the hon. gentleman and his friends are ready to answer, the treaty of Hanover.[1] By that treaty, says he, you deserted your natural allies; you aggrandized the power of France, and you rendered all the rest of Europe jealous of you. No, Sir, our allies deserted us; the German court formed alliances, and entered into schemes that must have been

[1] 1725, between England, France and Prussia.

fatal not only to the trade, but to the liberties of this country. Such schemes as I tremble at the remembrance of; which, if not timely discovered by the vigilance of his late majesty and the administration, must have forced the pretender upon us. But, Sir, if our natural allies treated us in this perfidious manner, what were we to do? Were we not to preserve ourselves in the best manner we could? Accordingly, a favourable opportunity offered, and we seized it; a disgust given to the court of Spain by the French, threw her into the arms of the emperor of Germany. Thus, Sir, the interests of France and Spain were divided; those of Spain and Germany were connected. Were we, Sir, to stand single? Were we to suffer France to enter into the alliance, and then to make it triple, exclusive of us? No, we joined with France, and we did wisely; because we were sure that while this system that was formed by the German and Spanish courts continued, it was the interest of France to be faithful to us; for she, Sir, had a great deal more to apprehend from the first treaty of Vienna[1] than we had. Thus, Sir, the treaty of Hanover was the best and wisest step that could be taken at that juncture and the vigorous preparations which we made in order to support it, broke all the destructive schemes of the German and Spanish courts. But it is asked, Why did we not support the emperor of Germany when he was so distressed by France?[2] Why did we not lay hold on that opportunity to reduce the French power? Sir, I think we acted very wisely in not interposing in that quarrel at all. In the first place the balance of Europe was not in danger, whatever the event of that war had been. If there were any grounds for the least apprehension, Sir, it was not from the French, but from the German greatness. In the next place, the emperor of Germany had been very ungrateful to this nation. It is well known, Sir, what treatment we received from him, even in that noble isle Sicily which our arms conquered for him. It is well known how strenuously he persisted in the scheme of the Ostend trade, which must have given a fatal blow to the most valuable branches of our commerce. These, Sir, are so many proofs of German gratitude for all the benefits which this country has conferred upon that. And, Sir, in the last place, by our neutrality at that juncture, we reaped the sweets of an unrivalled, uninterrupted commerce for several years; a consideration, Sir, that, of all others, ought most to influence the conduct of a trading people; a consideration, Sir, that, give me leave to say it, was singly sufficient to justify our conduct.

But say the hon. gentlemen on the other side, why did we enter into so many negotiations, preliminaries, and conventions afterwards? I answer, Sir, in one word, that we did not enter into any by which the nation suffered, and those we did enter into, were in order to preserve the benefits of a flourishing commerce. With this view, Sir, it was that his majesty thought fit to conclude the treaty of Seville; a treaty which, though it was not attended with all the good effects that we could desire, yet was still infinitely preferable to a war, notwithstanding the clamours raised about this treaty, as if the interests of our merchants had been entirely given up by it, and as if it had laid the foundation for all the disputes that have since happened with Spain.

As to the conduct of Spain with regard to our merchants, I own it will admit of no defence; but nothing is more unreasonable than to impute it, or any neglect of

[1] 1725, between Spain and the Emperor.

[2] In the War of the Polish Succession, 1733.

their interests, to the ministry, whose care in this treaty was very evident; for it contained a foundation not for further disputes, but for putting an end to our differences. If the Spaniards hindered the good effects of it by breach of faith, I am afraid they were too much encouraged by the dispositions which they observed to prevail among a certain party here. It was with a view of avoiding, if possible, a ruinous war, that the negotiations of the commissaries on both sides, in consequence of this treaty of Seville, were continued so long. And give me leave to say, Sir, that however some private persons might suffer, with whatever reason they might call out for justice upon Spain, yet our pacific forbearance was the safest and the wisest conduct for the general interest of a trading people.

I have lived, Sir, long enough in the world to see the effects of war on this nation; I have seen how destructive the effects, even of a successful war, have been; and shall I, who have seen this, when I am admitted to the honour to bear a share in his majesty's councils, advise him to enter upon a war while peace may be had? No, Sir, I am proud to own it, that I always have been, and always shall be, an advocate for peace. I would act the same part over again that I have already acted. I would give the same advice to his majesty, I would make the same opposition in this House that I have ever done, to those who delight in bloodshed and confusion, and who can be happy only in the misery of their country.

But, Sir, when it was found that our commerce was no longer to be preserved but by a war, when the Spaniards by a flagrant breach of faith refused to fulfil the stipulations they had entered into, the same considerations, which had hitherto dictated to me, that peace if possible was to be preserved, then determined me in my acquiescence to the advice of a vigorous war.

257. Lord Bolingbroke's view of foreign policy, 1738

(*Works . . . of Viscount Bolingbroke*, IV (1809), pp. 310–313. From "The Idea of a Patriot King".)

This represents the traditional Tory view of foreign policy. Comparison of this with No. 256 illustrates the blurring of the opposition between the Tory and Whig theories of foreign policy at this time.

. . . Great Britain is an island: and while nations on the continent are at immense charge in maintaining their barriers, and perpetually on their guard, and frequently embroiled, to extend or strengthen them, Great Britain may, if her governors please, accumulate wealth in maintaining hers; make herself secure from invasions, and be ready to invade others when her own immediate interest, or the general interest of Europe, requires it. Of all which queen Elizabeth's reign is a memorable example, and undeniable proof. I said the general interest of Europe; because it seems to me that this, alone, should call our councils off from an almost entire application to their domestick and proper business. Other nations must watch over every motion of their neighbours: penetrate, if they can, every design; foresee every minute event; and take part by some engagement or other in almost every conjuncture that arises. But as we cannot be easily nor suddenly attacked, and as we ought not to aim at any acquisition of territory on the continent, it may be our interest to watch the secret workings of the several councils abroad; to advise, and warn; to abet, and oppose; but it never can be our true interest easily and officiously to enter into action, much less into engagements that imply action and expense. Other nations, like the velites or light-armed troops, stand foremost in the field, and skirmish perpetually. When a great war begins, we ought to look on the powers of the continent, to whom we incline, like the two first lines, the principes and hastati of a Roman army: and on ourselves like the triarii, that are not to charge with these legions on every occasion, but to be ready for the conflict whenever the fortune of the day, be it sooner or later, calls us to it, and the sum of things, or the general interest, makes it necessary.

This is that post of advantage and honour, which our singular situation among the powers of Europe determines us, or should determine us, to take, in all disputes that happen on the continent. If we neglect it, and dissipate our strength on occasions that touch us remotely or indirectly, we are governed by men who do not know the true interest of this island, or who have some other interest more at heart. If we adhere to it, so at least as to deviate little and seldom from it, as we shall do whenever we are wisely and honestly governed, then will this nation make her proper figure: and a great one it will be. By a continual attention to improve her natural, that is her maritime strength, by collecting all her forces within herself, and reserving them to be laid out on great occasions, such as regard her immediate interests and her honour, or such as are truly important to the general system of power in Europe; she may be the arbitrator of differences, the guardian of liberty, and the preserver of that balance, which has been so much talked of, and is so little understood.

"Are we never to be soldiers?" it will be said. Yes, constantly, in such proportion as is necessary for the defence of good government. To establish such a military force as none but bad governors can want, is to establish tyrannical power in the king or in the ministers; and may be wanted by the latter, when the former would be secure without his army, if he broke his minister. Occasionally too we must be soldiers, and for offence as well as defence; but in proportion to the nature of the conjuncture, considered always relatively to the difference here insisted upon between our situation, our interest, and the nature of our strength, compared with those of the other powers of Europe; and not in proportion to the desires, or even to the wants, of the nations with whom we are confederated. Like other amphibious animals, we must come occasionally on shore: but the water is more properly our element, and in it, like them, as we find our greatest security, so we exert our greatest force.

What I touch upon here, very shortly, deserves to be considered, and reconsidered, by every man who has, or may have, any share in the government of Great Britain. For we have not only departed too much from our true national interest in this respect; but we have done so with the general applause even of well-meaning men, who did not discern that we wasted ourselves by an improper application of our strength in conjunctures, when we might have served the common cause far more usefully, nay with entire effect, by a proper application of our natural strength. There was something more than this. Armies grew so much into fashion, in time of war, among men who meant well to their country, that they who mean ill to it have kept and keep them still up in the profoundest peace; and the number of our soldiers, in this island alone, is almost double to that of our seamen. That they are kept up against foreign enemies, cannot be said with any colour. If they are kept for show, they are ridiculous; if they are kept for any other purpose whatever, they are too dangerous to be suffered. A Patriot King, seconded by ministers attached to the true interest of their country, would soon reform this abuse, and save a great part of this expense; or apply it, in a manner preferable even to the saving it, to the maintenance of a body of marine foot, and to the charge of a register of thirty or forty thousand seamen. . . .

258. The Declaration of War against Spain, 19 October 1739

(*Parl. Hist.*, XI, pp. 3–6.)

Horace Walpole the Elder thought this Declaration "seem'd to favour and support the notions of some favourite lords to his grace (*i.e.* Newcastle) that are in opposition, rather than to justify the advice and proceedings of those with whom he is tyed in the ministry, and with whom he has concurr'd in the concill and management of affairs".[1] It marks the triumph of the more vigorous foreign policy advocated by the opposition, and especially by Pitt.

George *R.*

Whereas many unjust seizures have been made, and depredations carried on, for several years, in the West-Indies, by Spanish guarda costas, and other ships, acting under the commission of the king of Spain, or his governors, contrary to the treaties subsisting between us and the crown of Spain, and to the law of nations, to the great prejudice of the lawful trade and commerce of our subjects; and great cruelties and barbarities have been exercised on the persons of divers of our subjects, whose vessels have been so seized; and the British colours have been insulted in the most ignominious manner; and whereas we have caused frequent complaints to be made to the king of Spain of these violent and unjust proceedings, but no satisfaction or redress has been given for the same, notwithstanding the many promises made, and cedulas issued, signed by the said king, or by his order, for that purpose; and whereas the evils above mentioned have been principally occasioned by an unwarrantable claim, and pretension, set up, on the part of Spain, that the guarda costas, and other ships, authorized by the king of Spain, may stop, detain, and search the ships and vessels of our subjects navigating in the American seas, contrary to the liberty of navigation, to which our subjects have not only an equal right with those of the king of Spain, by the law of nations, but which is moreover expressly acknowledged and declared to belong to them by the most solemn treaties, and particularly by that concluded in the year 1670; and whereas the said groundless claim and pretension, and the unjust practice of stopping, detaining, and searching ships and vessels, navigating in the seas of America, is not only of the most dangerous and destructive consequence to the lawful commerce of our subjects, but also tends to interrupt and obstruct the free intercourse and correspondence between our dominions in Europe, and our colonies and plantations in America, and by means thereof, to deprive us, and our subjects, of the benefits of those colonies and plantations; a consideration of the highest importance to us, and our kingdoms; and a practice,

[1] W. Coxe, *Life of Walpole*, III, p. 548.

which must affect, in its consequence, all other princes and states of Europe, possessed of settlements in the West Indies, or whose subjects carry on any trade thither; and whereas besides the notorious grounds of complaint above mentioned, many other infractions have been made on the part of Spain, of the several treaties and conventions subsisting between us and that crown, and particularly of that concluded in the year 1667, as well by the exorbitant duties and impositions laid upon the trade and commerce of our subjects, as by the breach of ancient and established privileges, stipulated for them by the said treaties; for the redress of which grievances, the strongest instances have been, from time to time, made by our several ministers residing in Spain, without any effect; and whereas a convention, for making reparation to our subjects for the losses sustained by them, on account of the unjust seizures and depredations committed by the Spaniards in America, and in order to prevent for the future all the grievances and causes of complaint therein taken notice of, and to remove absolutely, and for ever, everything which might give occasion thereto, was concluded between us, and the king of Spain, on the 14th day of January last, N.S. by which convention it was stipulated, That a certain sum of money should be paid at London, within a term therein specified, as a balance admitted to be due, on the part of Spain, to the crown and subjects of Great Britain, which term expired on the 25th day of May last, and the payment of the said sum was not made, according to the stipulation for that purpose; by which means the convention above mentioned was manifestly violated and broken by the king of Spain, and our subjects remained without any satisfaction or reparation for the many grievous losses sustained by them; and the methods, agreed upon by the said convention, in order to the obtaining future security for the trade and navigation of our subjects, are, contrary to good faith, frustrated and defeated: in consequence of which, we found ourselves obliged, for vindicating the honour of our crown, and for procuring reparation and satisfaction for our injured subjects, to order that general reprisals should be granted against the said king of Spain, his vassals and subjects, and their ships, goods, and effects: and whereas the court of Spain has been induced to colour the open violation of the convention aforesaid, by reasons and pretensions, which are void of all foundation: and, at the same time, has not only published an order, signed by the said king, for seizing the ships, goods, and effects belonging to us and our subjects, where-ever they shall be met with, but has caused seizures to be actually made of the goods and effects of our subjects, residing in his dominions, and has also ordered our said subjects to depart out of the Spanish dominions, within a short limited time, contrary to the express stipulations of the treaties between the two crowns, even in case of a war actually declared: we have taken into our royal and most serious consideration these injuries, which have been offered to us and our subjects, and the manifest violation of the several treaties subsisting between the two crowns; all which have been, in many particulars, eluded, or evaded, by the unwarrantable behaviour of the court of Spain, and their officers, notwithstanding the repeated instances we have given of our desire to cultivate a good understanding with the king of Spain, and the essential proofs of our friendship and regard for him and his family, which we have demonstrated to all the world: and being fully satisfied, that the honour of our crown, the interest of our subjects, and that regard, which ought to be had to the most solemn treaties, call upon us to make use of the power, which God has given us, for vindicating our undoubted rights, and securing to our loving subjects the privileges of navigation and commerce to which they are justly entitled: we, therefore, relying on the help of Almighty God, who knows the uprightness of our intentions, have thought fit to declare, and do hereby declare war against the said king of Spain; and we will, in pursuance of such declaration, vigorously prosecute the said war, being assured of the ready concurrence and assistance of all our loving subjects in so just a cause, wherein the honour of our crown, the maintenance of our solemn treaties, and the trade and navigation of our subjects, (which are so essential to the welfare and prosperity of this nation, and which we are determined, at all times, with our utmost power to preserve and support) are so greatly concerned: and we do hereby will, and require, our generals and commanders of our forces, our commissioners for executing the office of high admiral of Great Britain, our lieutenants of our several counties, governors of our forts and garrisons, and all other officers, and soldiers under them, by sea and land to do and execute all acts of hostility in the prosecution of this war against the king of Spain, his vassals, and subjects, and to oppose their attempts: and we do hereby command as well our own subjects, as advertise all other persons of what nation soever, not to transport, or carry any soldiers, arms, powder, ammunition, or other contraband goods, to any of the territories, lands, plantations, or countries of the said king of Spain; declaring, that whatsoever ship or vessel shall be met withal, transporting, or carrying any soldiers, arms, powder, ammunition, or other contraband goods, to any of the territories, lands, plantations, or countries of the said king of Spain, the same, being taken, shall be condemned as good and lawful prize. Given at our court at Kensington the 19th day of October, 1739, in the 13th year of our reign.

God save the King.

259. John Campbell[1] on the principles which should guide British foreign policy, 1750

(John Campbell, *The Present State of Europe* (1750), pp. 504–505.)

There is a Distinction often made, chiefly by Foreigners, between the Interest and the Commerce of *Great Britain*; but in reality this is a Distinction without a Difference; for the Interest and the Commerce of the *British* Empire are so inseparably united, that they may be very well considered as one and the same. For Commerce is that tie, by which the several, and even the most distant Parts of this Empire, are connected and kept together, so as to be rendred [*sic*] Parts of the same whole, and to receive not only Countenance and Protection, but Warmth and Nourishment from the vital Parts of our Government of which, if I may be indulged so figurative an Expression, our Monarchy is the Head, and our Liberty the Soul. Whatever therefore assists, promotes, and extends our Commerce, is consistent with our

[1] For Campbell, see note to No. 151.

Interest, and whatever weakens, impairs, or circumscribes it, is repugnant thereto. We may easily, considering things in this light, (and if we consider them in any other, we shall deceive ourselves) derive from thence a true Notion of the Interest of *Great Britain*, with respect to the other Powers of *Europe*; and be able to judge when that Interest is really pursued, and when it is either neglected or abandoned.

The first Point dictated by our Interest, is the maintaining others in their Rights, or to make use of a more known Term, to support the Independency of the Powers of *Europe*; because the engrossing, subjecting, or subduing several Countries under one Potentate, naturally and even necessarily contributes to lessen the Number of Inhabitants, to extinguish Industry amongst them, and consequently to enfeeble and impoverish them, which must be detrimental to us, if we correspond or trade with them. Another Point is, the stipulating with foreign Nations proper Terms of Security, Indulgence, and Respect for our Subjects, and for the Effects which from time to time they shall carry into those Countries, in return for which we must covenant on our Parts, to do and perform what shall be thought reasonable. When these kind of Alliances are made with due Deliberation, they become sacred Ties with respect to us, and we are bound to fulfil them punctually, so that whatever different Form Appearances may wear, the true Interest of *Great Britain* is always to comply exactly with her Treaties.

A third Rule is, to resent Wrongs done us, vigorously and without delay, more especially where it is in our Power to do it, by employing our maritime Force, since in this Case it answers a double End; first, it redresses the Mischief, whatever it is, for the present; and next, it raises our Reputation for the future. We ought likewise to be ready to assist any Nation that is unjustly attacked, or in any Danger of being oppressed, that it may be seen we are true Lovers of Freedom, and are as unwilling to behold the Necks of others put under a Yoke, as to submit our own. These Rules constantly attended to, are sufficient to keep us upon good Terms with all the World, and to make it the Interest of every Potentate and State in *Europe*, to court as well as to respect our Friendship; which ought to be freely bestowed, and not either purchased or prostituted. It may sometimes happen, that a strict Compliance with these Rules will interfere with some Branch or other of our Commerce; neither in such a Case must that be regarded, for it is not this or that particular Branch of Commerce, which coincides with the general Interest of this Nation, but the whole Circle of our Commerce; and therefore there is nothing absurd or contradictory in affirming, that the Whole must take place of a Part, any more than it is ridiculous to affirm, that whatever respects the Interest of a Nation, becomes worthy the Concern of a Monarch, let its Nature be what it will. And therefore they are in an Error, who think the Royal Character any way lessened, by being obliged to attend to Trade, a Thing already acknowledged in many Parts of *Europe*, and which by Degrees will be found true in all; to which let me add another Truth, that Trade is a mean and inconsiderable Thing, in those Countries only where this Error still prevails.

B. WARS

(a) WAR OF THE AUSTRIAN SUCCESSION

260. A contemporary account of the battle of Dettingen, 16 June 1743

(*Hist. MSS. Comm., Frankland-Russell-Astley MSS.*, pp. 252–254.)

The War of the Austrian Succession was, from the English point of view, almost totally devoid of results, the real issues between England and France remaining to be settled in the Seven Years War. It is, therefore, only represented here by this account of the battle of Dettingen, fought between the 'Pragmatic Army' supporting the claims of Maria Theresa, and the French, and notable as the last battle in which an English army in the field was commanded by the reigning sovereign. The writer is a lieutenant-colonel in the Coldstream Guards, son of John Russell, Governor of Fort William for the East India Company.

Lieut.-Col. Charles Russell to his Wife.

1743, June 19. From the Camp near Hanau upon the Main.

Though I wrote to you but yesterday, lest that should miscarry, I'm resolved to tell you once more that I am well; believe you will hear a great deal and may see the particulars in the Gazette relating to the engagement we have so lately had with the French, yet I persuade myself you will be better pleased to see it under my hand; that when I wrote to you from our camp near Aschaffenburg last Wednesday, I little thought what was so soon to happen, but immediately after, we received orders to strike our tents, lie upon our arms that night and marched the next morning at four o'clock, being Thursday the 16th instant, O.S. As we, the brigade of Guards, were on the left of all, we were appointed as a rear guard to the whole army, and when we had marched about a mile and a half we were joined with the Hanoverian Guards and part of their horse, which was about six in the morning, at which time his Majesty rode up to us and received us. He then left us under the command of General Ilton, an Hanoverian General, and so rode away with a proper escort to the right of the army.

No sooner had we marched above half a mile further, but a battery of cannon played upon us to intercept us from the main army, upon which General Ilton had orders sent him to wheel to the right to be covered from the fire of the cannon, so that we marched up a hill on the top of which we halted and was separated by this means from our army about two miles, and nothing but woods between us. From thence we could see what I am now faintly going to describe, that about twelve o'clock the French begun playing several batteries of cannon at our forces from the other side of the water, which annoyed us a little; upon our marching a little forward our forces perceived the French army had passed the Main near a little village called Dittingen, and was advancing up to us through a wood, cannonading us all the time, upon which a very smart engagement ensued. Lord Carteret was in a coach and six not far from the field, and in no small anxiety, you may imagine. The French, by the best accounts we can learn, was come over with the greatest part of their army, and was not far short of being double in number to what we had in the field, had in short all their *mason du roy* and all their best infantry, leaving nothing but their militia (which they had lately raised) on the other side of the water to guard their camp. Their scheme was so well laid, and so sure were they of success, that they had sent the Emperor[1] to Francfort the day before the battle; but however, by the blessing of God and the great bravery of our English infantry, which is hardly to be paralleled, we made them retreat, and at last so precipitately that great numbers were drowned. His Majesty was in the field of battle the whole time and behaved very gallantly, went himself and placed a battery of Hanoverian cannon, which was of utmost service and did great execution. The Duke[2] also charged with General Clayton[3] in the first line in the warmest part of the action, riding about animating the men with great bravery and resolution, at which time he received a wound in his leg, but is likely to do very well. The whole cry was, "where were the Guards, what shall we do without 'em, why are they not sent for"; in short we came, but had it been one hour sooner, before they had begun to retire, we must have made a complete victory, by pushing 'em with our fresh troops, which must have [so] added to their panic that scarce any of their men could have escaped; must have been forced into the river, or made prisoners of war. As it is, the advantage we have reaped is so great that the flower of their army is certainly destroyed; scarce any of their *mason du roy* has escaped being cut to pieces or made prisoners of war; and the number of their drowned is so great, that with the wounded, killed and drowned, it is said it amounts to between six and seven thousand, and the most we've lost don't exceed fifteen hundred, the wounded included. The Dragoons had great share in the action, particularly late Honeywoods, there not being above one squadron left of the regiment out of three. The Horse Guards and Grenadiers also behaved well, but our other corps of horse have not acquired so much fame in this engagement. The officers in general are greatly applauded, I mean of the English. The Hannoverian had scarce any share at all in it, but some of the Austrians behaved well, only one of their battalions made an unfortunate mistake, by firing upon our troops several times. Both the King and the Duke are thoroughly sensible of all the honour of the day being owing to the English. His Grace of Marl[boroug]h,[4] who commanded our brigade, but was commanded, wont in haste forgive the Han[overia]n general, for the moment we came into the field of battle, expecting to be of some service, the enemy was all flown; such a sight I never saw as the number of dead bodies all round us, among which we lay all that night without our tents. Many prisoners of distinction we saw that were wounded and taken, and carried 'em water and other necessaries, for which they expressed great gratitude. I fear I wrote you a strange account yesterday, was then in a great hurry, being just ordered to remove our ground to where we now are; could not write before, for it rained without ceasing from the end of the battle twenty four hours, which was all Thursday night and all Friday, nor was I under cover the whole time but in a soldier's tent at night, and eighteen hours a horse back all Friday till ten at night, but a good rest all last night in my own bed has quite

[1] Charles VII.
[2] Of Cumberland (1721–1765), third son of George II.
[3] General Jasper Clayton, killed in this battle.
[4] Charles, third duke of Marlborough (1706–1758).

refreshed me, and many more I find I'm likely to have. Major Brereton is alive and well, who I mentioned dead yesterday. I can't help pitying poor Mrs. Swan.

Postscript. Duke of Richmond and Lord Har[cour]t[1] were with the King the whole time: the latter with his Grace of Marl[borou]gh. Mr. Carteret and George Stanhope has been sitting in our tent with us from dinner all this evening.

(*b*) SEVEN YEARS WAR

261. Captain Augustus Hervey's account of the failure to relieve Minorca, May 1756

(*Journal of Augustus Hervey, 1746–59*, ed. David Erskine (1953), pp. 204–213, 214–217.)

Admiral John Byng (1704–1757) was ordered to the Mediterranean in April 1756 to relieve Minorca, where a French army under the Duc de Richelieu was besieging Fort St. Philip. Byng was by nature inclined to magnify difficulties. After an indecisive engagement with the French fleet, he decided he could do no more for Minorca and returned to Gibraltar without trying to land reinforcements for the besieged garrison, or, by cruising off Toulon, to cut the communications of the besieging force. For this negligence he was court martialled and shot. Futile as Byng's conduct had been, the Newcastle government was chiefly to blame, since the sending of a larger force sooner would have prevented the French ever getting to Minorca at all. News of concentrations of troops and ships in the French western ports, as well as at Toulon, and pressure from merchants for the protection of their shipping, had led the government to keep too many ships in the English Channel.

Captain Augustus Hervey (1724–1779), later third earl of Bristol, had served under Byng before and was a devoted friend and supporter of the Admiral all through his trial. He is unfair to Anson, the First Lord of the Admiralty, who in fact often stood up to Newcastle about naval appointments and insisted that efficiency must not be entirely sacrificed to the needs of political patronage. The *Journal* was probably written between 1767 and 1770.

[May 1756]

The morning early the 18th I went on board of Admiral Byng and did lament his not having more force, when he told me that Lord Anson sent all the best ships cruising with his favourites, and, all he could do, he could not obtain two or three more, tho' he might with ease have brought them. He ordered the next day the *Chesterfield* and *Dolphin* under my orders, and I was to endeavour to get a letter into St. Philip's if possible at daylight. Therefore I was within pistol-shot of the Lare of Mahon, when it fell calm, and I got my boats to tow. The English colours were still flying on the castle of St. Philip's, which the enemy were firing upon from all parts, and French colours on Cape Mola, and many other parts of the island. But soon after, the signal being made for the enemy's fleet, my signal was made on board the Admiral to return, which I obeyed, and found the fleet preparing for action. I then went and offered my service to the Admiral as a fireship, as my ship was old and that he had ne'er a one, and I had material on board with which I could make her one. He consented, and I prepared her accordingly. I put several men on board the *Revenge*, and several on board the *Deptford*. I fixed graplings everywhere, made a great quantity of shavings, picked oakum, dipped them in rosin, pitch, brimstone and gunpowder mixed, and twisted rope with these combustables all about my rigging and decks,

[1] Charles, second duke of Richmond (1701–1750); Simon, first Earl Harcourt (1714–1777), Lord Lieutenant of Ireland, 1772–1777.

which were scuttled. It came on foggy in the afternoon and scarce any wind, that we lost sight of the French, but in the night took some tartanes[1] that were carrying out some piquets of soldiers to the French fleet.

The 20th we saw the French fleet about 7 in the morning, and a signal was made for all cruisers. About 10 a signal was made for the fleet to tack, which was to gain the wind of the enemy, and soon after a signal for the line of battle ahead. I then went on board the Admiral to wish him good success, receive my orders, and fix on the signal to be made from him for scuttling my decks and priming, and sent all my things and useless people on board a tender prepared for me. About 11 of our fleet was all formed and standing towards the enemy, which were then sixteen sail, twelve appeared large and of the line, which then formed, and as they saw we had gained the wind they waited for us. Their evolutions were pretty and regular. Our fleet stretched out to the westward till the van was the length of their rear, then the Admiral made the signal for the fleet to tack together, which was performed at once by every ship except the *Portland*, who missed stays. Our line was then much to windward of the enemy, about four miles I believe. The Admiral then made the signal for the ships that led the van to bear away, intending all should go down close to the French line slanting and regular, but the *Portland* and *Defiance* that led did not go down as the signal directed, tho' I repeated it three different times. The Admiral perceiving this, found as he himself edged away that he had nothing for it but making the general signal to engage, as they were then about 2¾ miles from the French, and that everyone then would bear down on the ships of the enemy's that fell to him. A few minutes after 2 this signal was made. The Rear-Admiral[2] and his second, Mr. Edgcumbe[3] in the *Lancaster*, bore down upon their ships and engaged, tho' I thought at too great a distance. The ships in the van bore down but slowly to close the enemy. The Admiral in the centre was then going down and made the *Deptford*'s signal to quit the line and lay by for a reserve, as we had twelve and twelve without her, but the *Kingston* (Parry)[4] instead of closing the line left this vacancy and lay sometime with his main topsail to the mast. The *Culloden* also appeared to me a great way from the Admiral, and that the *Ramillies* was exposed to much fire when they began.

A little time after the Admiral began to engage I saw the *Intrepid* had lost her fore-topmast, and very unfortunately was driving down upon the other ships astern, as they had no command of her head sails. But this accident making the *Revenge* and others back to avoid the *Intrepid*, this divided the Rear-Admiral's division and the Admiral for some minutes. The ships ahead of the Admiral laid all aback, which obliged the Admiral to do the same for fear of being on board of them. The *Trident* also threw all into confusion by not bearing down with the Admiral at first, tho' often called to. This unlucky accident I look upon as the cause of this day's disgrace, if one may call it so, for the French, tho' superior, certainly avoided a close action. The Admiral made the signal for closing the line, and threw out all the sail he could

[1] Single-masted vessels used in the Mediterranean.
[2] Rear-Admiral Temple West (1713–1757), Byng's second-in-command.
[3] George, later first earl of Mount-Edgcumbe (1721–1795).
[4] Captain William Parry (d. 1778), Rear-Admiral, 1762.

as soon as the *Intrepid* was clear of him, and ordered the *Deptford* to supply the *Intrepid*'s place, and the *Chesterfield* to lay by the *Intrepid*, but 'twas now easily perceived that the French ships wronged ours much in sailing, and kept edging away the whole time. I saw the French Admiral fire several shot at one of his own men-of-war which Mr. Byng had drove out of the line, and boats sent after her. By the time our van and rear were closed, the French had got a great way to leeward and ahead withall, and then the French put before the wind. Our two leaders, the *Portland* and *Lancaster*, stood on with all their sail and was greatly separated from Mr. West, so much so that I was going to send to acquaint the Admiral with it, lest in the smoke he should not see it. The French body kept bearing away to join their ships to leeward and endeavour to rally them, for I think they had flown. But our ships in the van soon were disabled in their rigging and masts, tho' they kept a constant fire on the enemy. The Admiral kept all his sail out going after the enemy, but they outsailed him much, and he was then obliged to make the signal for his van to tack, that they might close him, or he would run a risk of losing them as night drew on. The Admiral saw that the French might soon tack and gain the wind of him, made the signal to tack himself, which closed the action, the French being then so far ahead. The disabled ships were by this manœuvre covered from the enemy, and by this may be said to have kept the field of battle and gained the victory, for the French might have continued and fought on if they pleased. The Admiral immediately brought to about 8 o'clock in the evening.

I went to the Admiral immediately and found he was very sensible of the many errors of some of his captains. He sent on board to Mr. West to know how he did, and Mr. West came on board of him late as it was. Then it was these two admirals saw the effect of having been sent with the worst ships in England. However an account was to be had immediately of our situation, and the fleet got ready as well as they could for action next morning, for this I know was Mr. Byng's determination when I left him with the Rear-Admiral, for he then told me Lord Anson had sold him, but by God he would fight till every ship sunk before he would give this up, if the council of war did not think his instructions bound him otherwise. I saw the consequence of this early battle in a different light. I told the Admiral the day before I thought the best thing would have been to have landed all the officers and troops for the garrison if possible before any action, as that was the material object now the French were landed, and then, if he thought proper, come to an engagement and try them, because if we were beat, (having thrown in what succours we could) it was of no great consequence, there must soon come up other ships; whereas if the enemy by their superiority obliged us to retire without throwing in any succours, then the consequence would be fatal to the island; but now the event proved what I said to be true, for the fleet had been disabled and lost so many men and had so many sick, and ne'er an hospital-ship for them, nor no storeship, and no port nearer than Gibraltar, that it was giving up all to think of retiring thither. In short I left the two Admirals together to consider what was to be done in this very critical affair.

The next morning it was very thick weather, the *Intrepid* and *Chesterfield* not in sight, and we were all laying-to. The *Dolphin* and *Phoenix* were sent to look for the

Intrepid and *Chesterfield* whilst the rest of the fleet were refitting and many of them appeared like racks. The next morning, the 22nd, the Admiral sent for me and told me as Captain Andrews of the *Defiance* of 60 guns was killed he would give me that ship, which I accepted of, altho' a perfect rack and the worst manned ship in the service now, and I was obliged to borrow men to fit her, but had her in order that evening, when the *Intrepid* and *Chesterfield* joined us. The next day we lay to refitting the ships. The Rear-Admiral found great fault with Captain Ward[1] and Captain Parry for not closing the Admiral in action, as also with Captain Cornwall[2] of the *Revenge*, and was for bringing them to a court-martial, which would have been better if the Admiral had listened to.

A council of war was called the 24th of all the land and sea officers. To this council the Admiral shewed his instructions first, which were to endeavour to relieve the island of Minorca, but to take care to secure Gibraltar, and in case the French fleet should be passed the Straits (in that case) to send a number of ships after them. The Admiral made no comment on these absurd instructions, tho' others did. The present state of the shattered fleet was taken into consideration next, and which proved how unfit they were to engage again if they were to protect Gibraltar, as they found they could not relieve Mahon, already so closely besieged. The Admiral told them his instructions were peremptory with regard to Gibraltar, and desired the opinion of the council of war relative to the situation. They all agreed, first, that the fleet was in no condition to attack the enemy's again, which was so superior, without risking every part of the instructions, as the French might then go down to Gibraltar and attack that place also. I was of this opinion with the rest. Mr. West particularly said we ought on no account to risk another engagement, on which the Admiral said if there was any officer that thought we ought he would attack them to-morrow. The next question was whether we ought not immediately to proceed to Gibraltar to cover that place. This was agreed to by all but myself. I said I thought we should send an express there, but keep off here till joined by some other ships, and endeavour at some opportunity to throw in succours to Minorca, and be ready to re-attack the enemy as soon as re-inforcements arrived, which would keep up the spirits of those in the castle, and be doing, I thought, the best service to publick. Mr. West particularly exclaimed against this, and said it would be risking both places, and acting directly contrary to the Admiral's instruction. I answered that I did not pretend to contend or debate it, but I had done my duty as one called there and given my sincere opinion. Then Mr. West and Lord Robert Bertie[3] were for inserting resolutions and reasons for those resolutions, which were only reflections on government for sending such a force. This was opposed.

Mr. West at first refused sitting at this council with Captain Ward and Captain Parry, and said their behaviour in action, as well as Captain Cornwall's, was such that he could not submit to sit with them. The Admiral, who had no inclination to bring a slur on the action, replied to that, that if he, Mr. West, would accuse them, he would confine and try them. But Mr. West could not do that, and there it ended,

[1] Henry Ward (d. 1766), placed on half-pay, 1757.

[2] Frederic Cornwall (d. *c.* 1786), badly wounded in 1744, and retired after Byng's trial, at which he gave evidence.

[3] In command of the troops on board.

with only bad blood among them. The council broke up after a resolution to proceed to Gibraltar, cover that place, and land our sick and wounded.

. . . .

The 12th [June] I was ordered to make the best of my way to Gibraltar and get the hospital ready, and stores etc.: to fit the fleet with all dispatch. I spoke to a Dutch man-or-war from Cadiz who told me the French had sent expresses everywhere that we were beat and they had gained a complete victory, and the Admiral killed. I arrived the 16th at Gibraltar where I found Commodore Broderick[1] and five sail of the line arrived yesterday from England with a regiment on board. Alas, had these been sent out with Mr. Byng Minorca had been saved, the French fleet destroyed and the Duke de Richelieu's army obliged to lay down their arms. Such was the inexcusable error of our wicked Ministers, that detested wretch Lord Holland, and that poor contemptible one Lord Anson. Among these five sail the *Hampton Court* of 64 guns was sent out for me, commanded by Captain Knight who was to have the *Phoenix*. I went on shore and dined with the General, gave a faithful account of the engagement, and told them the French were too strong and too good sailors, our fleet in too shattered a condition to re-engage, and the instruction too peremptory to leave Gibraltar exposed, as they could not hope to relieve Minorca. We had a council of war next day on board the Commodore, when a ship was proposed to be sent out to look for the Admiral, and I proposed the whole squadron going out to join him, but it was carried against me.

The 20th the fleet came in in a very sickly and shattered condition. I pressed the Admiral much to sail the next day with all and take some troops on board and press every seaman in the bay, but tho' he determined to go as soon as he said he could, yet I was very uneasy. I attended poor Captain Noel's[2] funeral.

The next day I found Captain Cornwall of the *Revenge* had asked for a court-martial on himself about the battle, which the Admiral was too averse to, I thought, but his reasons were that it would delay us. However Cornwall insisted so much that one was ordered. Admiral West was President; Captain Amherst,[3] Captain Lloyd[4] and myself declined sitting, as by our situation we must be evidences as to the *Revenge*'s conduct. This made a bustle. On my getting up and protesting to my sitting they were for sending for more Captains. In short here was a confusion, and they adjourned the court to Monday. After this was over Admiral West desired every one to be attentive to him, and then threw out that he had been told that it was reported he was the promoter of these enquiries, which he absolutely denied; that he knew court-martials were always a disgrace to a fleet, tho' sometimes necessary; that all he had said was that five of our van beat five of the enemy's, and that our van was not supported –he did not know the cause; that he accused no one, nor ever had; that it was true he had refused to sit at a council of war with some Captains but he had accused none.

[1] Thomas Brodrick (d. 1769), Rear-Admiral, 1756.
[2] Thomas Noel, died of wounds received in the battle on 20 May.
[3] John Amherst (1718?–1778), younger brother of General Jeffrey Amherst.
[4] John Lloyd (d. 1778), gave evidence at Byng's trial. Rear-Admiral, 1775.

In short he dwelt a long time on all this, with very artful insinuations that I thought reflected on Admiral Byng. On which I got up and said I knew the Commander-in-chief was very averse to court-martials for the same reason Mr. West was, and wished to have postponed this, but not to have suppressed it. But that I did not see what Admiral West meant by not accusing when he says five of our van beat five of the enemy's and that the van was not supported; that, indirect as this is, I insisted it carried an accusation on the rear of the fleet, and therefore ought to be cleared up; that, had I have been of that line of battle, I should have thought myself engaged in honour to have asked Admiral West when he objected to sit with some Captains at a council of war whether I was one and I therefore should think it the duty of every officer there to know who and why he objected to them, but as I was not, let those sit still who may, for my part I rise only to justify the Commander-in-chief, to whose conduct I was so situated as to be a judge of that day, and I could with truth and honour, and would, justify to the last, but that I knew Mr. West had said Captain Cornwall might have passed the *Intrepid* as well as the *Buckingham* passed another ship, (the *Defiance*). Mr. West then took this up, and acknowledged it, and said he thought so still. However this occasioned two or three sharp replies between Mr. West and me; but I cared not, I saw what he was at. In the evening General Fowke[1] sent to me and wished me to endeavour to reconcile the two Admirals, but I begged to be excused interfering with anything more than pressing the Admirals to sail.

I was all day the 26th employed with the Admiral to assist in writing his letters. The 28th a signal for a court-martial was made on board the Rear-Admiral. Captain Cornwall appeared, and there being no accuser, the Judge-Advocate making proclamation three times for it, it was agreed that Captain Cornwall's letter desiring a court-martial, being founded on reports heard, were not grounds sufficient (as no one appeared to those reports) to proceed on, and so adjourned the court.

The 31st the Admiral and Mr. West went on shore together, which pleased me very much, as I was in hopes they would be well together. I kept pressing their sailing immediately to endeavour to find the enemy, and wish my advice had been followed for the next day Admiral West had a letter overland that himself and Mr. Byng were recalled. And sure enough the 2nd July at 10 in the morning the *Antelope* of 50 guns in thirteen days from England arrived with Sir Edward Hawke and Rear-Admiral Saunders[2] to relieve Mr. Byng and West, Lord Tyrawly[3] to relieve General Fowke, Lord Panmure[4] to relieve General Stuart,[5] Captain Batten and several other officers; the gentlemen relieved were all to proceed to England immediately, Mr. Byng as a prisoner. Mr. Broderick was made a flag and to go home also. The land officers were superceded for their council of war at Gibraltar before they went up, and not complying with the King's orders,[6] and here the whole garrison were astonished to

[1] Major-General Thomas Fowke (d. 1765), Governor of Gibraltar since 1754. He was court martialled and cashiered in 1756 for his part in the Minorca disaster, but restored to his rank by George III in 1761.

[2] Sir Charles Saunders (1713 ?–1775), Commander-in-Chief of the fleet at the siege of Quebec, 1759.

[3] James, second baron (1690–1773), wounded at Almanza and Malplaquet.

[4] William, first earl (1700–1782).

[5] Second-in-command at Gibraltar.

[6] At a council of war at Gibraltar on Byng's first arrival in the Mediterranean, it had been decided that it would be useless to send a reinforcement to St. Philip's from Gibraltar, as ordered. In fact, this reinforcement, though small, might just have saved the situation for the besieged garrison.

find a set of gentlemen stigmatised only on the accounts of the French admiral, which were the only ones received when these sailed. They did not give time for the arrival of Admiral Byng's express, such was their determination to sacrifice that officer to screen their own wicked heads. Even Sir Edward Hawke, whom I went to see, condemned the hasty manner in which it was done, and much more so the unprecedented infamous reports Lord Holland, Lord Anson and the Duke of Newcastle encouraged everywhere against Mr. Byng's character in order to raise the mob against him and turn all the resentment and just indignation of the people from themselves to Admiral Byng.

262. Robert Orme's account of the battle of Plassey, 23 June 1757

(Robert Orme, *History of the Military Transactions of the British Nation in Indostan*, II (1803 ed.), pp. 172–178.)

Robert Orme (1728–1801) entered the service of the East India Company in 1743 and later became the Company's historiographer. He was a member of the Madras Council, 1754–1758, and recommended the appointment of Clive to command against Surajah Dowlah, Nabob of Bengal, in 1756. The battle of Plassey followed the secret treaty made by Clive with Meer Jaffier, the Nabob's commander-in-chief, for which Clive was subsequently much criticized in Parliament. Surajah Dowlah was murdered shortly after the battle and Meer Jaffier became Nabob of Bengal in his place.

1757.
June.

The grove of Plassy[1] extended north and south about 800 yards in length, and 300 in breadth, and was planted with mango-trees, in regular rows. It was inclosed by a slight bank and ditch, but the ditch was choaked with coarse weeds and brambles. The angle to the south-west was 200 yards from the river, but that to the north-west not more than 50. A little to the north of the grove, and on the bank of the river, stood a hunting-house of the Nabob's, encompassed by a garden-wall. The river, a mile before it reaches this house, curves to the south-west nearly in the shape of a horse-shoe, including a peninsula about three miles in circumference, of which the neck, from the stream to the stream again, is not more than a quarter of a mile across. About 300 yards to the south of the peninsula, began an entrenchment, which Roydoolub had thrown up to secure his camp: the southern face, fronting the grove of Plassy, extended nearly in a straight line, about 200 yards inland from the bank of the river; and then turning to the north-east by an obtuse angle, continued nearly in this direction about three miles. Within this entrenchment encamped the whole army,[2] of which a part likewise occupied the peninsula. In the angle was raised a redoubt, on which cannon were mounted. About 300 yards to the east of this redoubt, but without the camp, was a hillock covered with trees; and 800 yards to the south of this hillock and the redoubt, was a small tank or pond; and 100 yards farther to the south was another, but much larger tank: both, as all such public reservoirs of water in Bengal, were surrounded by a large mound of earth at the distance of some yards from the margin of the water.

At day-break, the enemy's army issuing from many different openings of the camp, began to advance towards the grove; 50,000 foot, 18,000 horse, and 50 pieces

[1] Where Clive's army was encamped. [2] Of Surajah Dowlah.

of cannon. The greatest part of the foot were armed with matchlocks, the rest with various arms, pikes, swords, arrows, rockets. The cavalry, both men and horses, drawn from the northern regions, were much stouter than any which serve in the armies of Coromandel. The cannon were mostly of the largest calibres, 24 and 32 pounders; and these were mounted on the middle of a large stage, raised six feet from the ground, carrying besides the cannon, all the ammunition belonging to it, and the gunners themselves who managed the cannon, on the stage itself. These machines were drawn by 40 or 50 yoke of white oxen, of the largest size, bred in the country of Purnea; and behind each cannon walked an elephant, trained to assist at difficult tugs, by shoving with his forehead against the hinder part of the carriage. The infantry and cavalry marched in many separate and compact bodies. Forty vagabond Frenchmen under the command of one Sinfray, appeared at the larger tank, that nearest the grove, with four pieces of light cannon. Two larger pieces advanced and halted on a line with this tank, close to the bank of the river. Behind these posts 5000 horse and 7000 foot took their station under the command of Meer Murdeen, and the son of Moonlol. The rest of the army in large columns of horse and foot extended in a curve from the left of the hillock near their camp, to the ground about 800 yards east of the southern angle of the grove of Plassy; and in this part were the troops of Meer Jaffier, Roydoolub, and Latty. In all the openings between the columns were interspersed the artillery, two, three, and four pieces together.

Colonel Clive, viewing the enemy's army from the top of the hunting-house, was surprized at their numbers, as well as the splendor and confidence of their array: but judging, that if his own troops remained in the grove, the enemy would impute the caution to fear, and grow bolder, he drew them up in a line with the hunting-house, and facing to the nearest tank. They were 900 Europeans, of whom 100 were artillery-men, and 50 were sailors; 100 Topasses, and 2100 Sepoys; the artillery were eight field-pieces, all six pounders, and two howitz: the Topasses were blended in the battalion with the Europeans, the sailors assisted the artillery-men. The battalion with three field-pieces on the right, and the same number on their left, were in the centre; on the right and left of which extended the Sepoys in two equal divisions. The other two field-pieces and the howitzes were advanced 200 yards in front of the left division of Sepoys, and posted behind two brick-kilns. This line extended 600 yards beyond the right of the grove; but the distance of the enemy in this quarter, prevented any danger of their falling upon the flank before whatsoever troops were ordered could fall back, and range along the east side of the grove. The first shot was fired by the enemy, at eight o'clock, from the tank; it killed one, and wounded another of the grenadier company, which was posted on the right of the battalion. This, as a signal, was followed by the continual fire of the rest of the Nabob's artillery on the plain. But most of their shot flew too high. The two advanced field-pieces answered the fire from the tank, and those with the battalion acted against the different divisions of heavy artillery on the plain; but firing out of the reach of point-blank shot, hit none of the enemy's guns; nevertheless, every shot took place, either in one or other of the bodies of infantry or cavalry. But ten for one killed, was no advantage in such a disparity of numbers, and in half an hour the English lost 10 Europeans and 20

Sepoys; on which Colonel Clive ordered the whole army to retire into the grove. The enemy elated by this retreat, advanced their heavy artillery nearer, and fired with greater vivacity than before; but their shot only struck the trees; for the troops were ordered to sit down, whilst the field-pieces alone answered the enemy's cannon from behind the bank. Explosions of powder were frequently observed amongst their artillery. At eleven o'clock Colonel Clive consulted his officers at the drum head; and it was resolved to maintain the cannonade during the day, but at midnight to attack the Nabob's camp. About noon a very heavy shower covered the plain, and very soon damaged the enemy's powder so much, that their fire slackened continually; but the English ammunition served on. The Nabob had remained in his tent out of the reach of danger, continually flattered by his attendants and officers, of whom one half were traitors, with assurances of victory; but about noon he was informed, that Meer Murdeen, the best and most faithful of his generals, was mortally wounded by a cannon-ball. The misfortune disturbed him to excess; he immediately sent for Meer Jaffier; and as soon as he entered the tent, flung his turban on the ground, saying, "Jaffier, that turban you must defend." The other bowed, and with his hands on his breast, promised his utmost services; and returning to his troops and associates, immediately dispatched a letter to Colonel Clive, informing him of what had passed, and advising him either to push forward in the instant, or at all events, to attack the Nabob's camp at three the next morning; but the messenger was afraid to proceed whilst the firing continued. In the mean time, the terrors of the Nabob increased continually: Roydoolub taking advantage of them, counselled him to return to his capital: his advice prevailed, and the Nabob ordered the army to retreat into the intrenchments.

Accordingly, about two o'clock, the enemy ceased the cannonade, and were perceived yoking their trains of oxen to their artillery, and as soon as these were in motion, their whole army turned and proceeded slowly towards the camp. But Sinfray with his party and field-pieces still maintained his post at the tank. This was a good station to cannonade the enemy from, during their retreat; and Major Kilpatrick impatient to seize the opportunity, advanced from the grove with two companies of the battalion, and two field-pieces, marching fast towards the tank, and sent information of his intention, and the reason of it, to his commander, who chanced at this time to be lying down in the hunting-house. Some say he was asleep; which is not improbable, considering how little rest he had had for so many hours before; but this is no imputation either against his courage or conduct. Starting up, he ran immediately to the detachment, reprimanded Kilpatrick sharply for making such a motion without his orders, commanded him to return to the grove, and bring up the rest of the army; and then proceeded himself with the detachment to the tank which Sinfray, seeing his party left without support, abandoned; and retreated to the redoubt of the intrenchment, where he planted his field-pieces ready to act again.

As the main body of the English troops were advancing to the tank, that part of the Nabob's army, which in the beginning of the action had formed opposite to the south-east angle of the grove of Plassy, lingered in the retreat behind the rest, and when they had passed the parallel of the grove, halted, faced, and advanced towards the north-east angle. These were the troops of Meer Jaffier; but their signals not being understood, it was supposed that they intended to fall upon the baggage and boats at the grove, whilst the English army were engaged at the tank. Three platoons of the line, whilst in march, and a field-piece, were detached to oppose them, under the command of Captain Grant and Lieutenant Rumbold;[1] and Mr. John Johnstone, a volunteer, managed the field-piece, the fire of which soon stopped the approach of the supposed enemy. Meanwhile the army being arrived at the tank, got all their field-pieces upon the mound, and from thence began to cannonade into the Nabob's camp; on which many of the troops came again out of the intrenchment, and several pieces of their artillery were likewise preparing to return; on this, Colonel Clive advanced nearer, and posted half his troops and artillery at the lesser tank, and the other half at a rising ground about 200 yards to the left of it. From these stations the cannonade was renewed with more efficacy than before, and killed many of the oxen which were drawing the artillery, which threw all the trains that were approaching into disorder. On the other hand, the Frenchmen with Sinfray plyed their field-pieces from the redoubt; and matchlocks from the intrenchments, from ditches, hollows, and every hole or shelter, as also from the bushes on the hillock east of the redoubt, kept up a constant although irregular fire, whilst the cavalry advanced several times threatening to charge sword in hand, but were always stopped and repulsed by the quick firing of the English field-pieces. Nevertheless, the English suffered as much in this, as they had during all the former operations of the day. At length the troops of Meer Jaffier appeared moving away from the field of battle, without joining the rest of the Nabob's army; which convincing Colonel Clive who they were, he determined to make one vigorous effort for victory by attacking at once Sinfray's redoubt, and the eminence to the eastward of it, in the cover of which an ambuscade was suspected. Two divisions of the army were appointed to the two attacks, and the main body advanced in the centre ready to support both, and to act, as occasion should offer, of itself. The division on the right gained the eminence without firing or receiving a single shot. At the same time the left marched up to the redoubt, which Sinfray, finding himself again deserted by his allies, quitted without farther resistance, and without carrying off his field-pieces. Thus the whole of the English army entered the camp at five o'clock, without other obstacle than what they met from tents, artillery, baggage, and stores, dispersed around them, and abandoned by an army which out-numbered them ten to one, and were flying before them on all sides in the utmost confusion.

The cause of this sudden panic was the flight of the Nabob, who hearing that Meer Jaffier remained inactive on the plain, and that the English were advancing to storm his camp, mounted a camel, and fled at the utmost pace of the animal, accompanied by about 2000 horsemen. The victory was decided, and was confirmed by the arrival of the messenger with the letter sent by Meer Jaffier at noon; soon after came another, whom Colonel Clive immediately returned with a note, requesting Meer Jaffier to meet him next morning at Daudpore.

[1] Later Sir Thomas Rumbold, Bart. (1736–1791), Governor of Madras, 1777–1780; dismissed from the Company's service as responsible for the invasion of the Carnatic, but acquitted on a parliamentary inquiry.

263. Letter from William Pitt to colonial governors on the proposed invasion of Canada, 30 December 1757

(*Correspondence of William Pitt . . . with Colonial Governors*, ed. G. S. Kimball, I (1906), pp. 136–140.)

The campaign of 1756–1757 in America, under the command of Lord Loudoun, had proved disastrous, and Loudoun was recalled and replaced as commander-in-chief by General James Abercromby. An invasion of Canada by way of Crown Point was planned for 1758, and also an expedition against Louisbourg. This year's campaign was only partially successful. Abercromby failed to take Ticonderoga; and although Louisbourg fell in July 1758, the stubborn defence by the French prevented operations against Quebec this year. Pitt greatly valued the loyal co-operation of the colonial governors, and was always at pains to keep them fully informed.

Pitt to the Governors of Massachusetts Bay, New Hampshire, Connecticut, Rhode Island, New York, New Jersey.

WHITEHALL, Decr. 30th. 1757.

Sir,

His Majesty having nothing more at Heart, than to repair the Losses and Disappointments, of the last inactive, and unhappy Campaign; and by the most vigorous and extensive Efforts, to avert, by the Blessing of God on His Arms, the Dangers impending in North America; And not doubting, that all His faithful and brave Subjects there, will chearfully co-operate with, and second to the utmost, the large Expence, and extraordinary Succours supplied by this Kingdom for their Preservation and Defence; And His Majesty considering, that the several Provinces, in particular, from Proximity and accessibility of Situation, more immediately obnoxious to the main Irruptions of the Enemy from Canada, are, of themselves, well able to furnish, at least, Twenty Thousand Men, and to join a Body of The King's Forces for Invading Canada, by the way of Crown Point*, and carrying the War into the Heart of the Enemy's possessions; And His Majesty not judging it expedient to limit the zeal and Ardor of any of His Provinces, by making a Repartition of the Force to be raised by Each respectively, for this most important Service; I am commanded to signify The King's Pleasure, that you do forthwith use your utmost Endeavours, and Influence with the Council and Assembly of your Province, to induce Them to raise, with all possible Dispatch, as large a Body of Men within your Government, as the Number of Its Inhabitants may allow; and, forming the same into Regiments, as far as shall be found convenient, That you do direct them to hold Themselves in Readiness, as early as may be, to march to the Rendezvous at Albany, or such other Place, as His Majesty's Commander in Chief in America, shall appoint, in order to proceed, from thence, in Conjunction with a Body of The King's British Forces, and under the supreme Command of His Ma'ty's said Commander in Chief in America, so as to be in a Situation to begin the Operations of the Campaign, by the First of May, if possible, or as soon after, as shall be in any way practicable, by attempting to make an Irruption into Canada, as above, by the Way of Crown Point, and, if found

* A point on the western shore of the southern end of Lake Champlain, where the lake suddenly narrows so that a few cannon would stop the passage. The French, in 1731, established a garrison there, and called the place Fort Frédéric. It was a halfway station between Albany and Montreal, and a basis for forays against the surrounding country. [Note by Editor of the *Correspondence.*]

practicable, to attack either Montreal or Quebec, or Both of the said Places successively, with the whole Force in one Body, or at one and the same Time, by a Division of the Troops, into separate and distinct Operations, according as His Majesty's said Commander in Chief shall, from His Knowledge of the Countries, thro' which the War is to be carried, and from emergent Circumstances, not to be known here, judge any of the said Attempts to be practicable. And the better to facilitate this important Service, The King is pleased to leave it to you to issue Commissions to such Gentlemen of your Province as you shall judge, from their Weight and Credit with the People, and their zeal for the publick Service, may be best disposed and enabled to quicken and effectuate the speedy Levying of the greatest Number of Men; In the Disposition of which Commissions, I am persuaded, you will have nothing in View but the Good of the King's Service, and a due Subordination of the Whole, when join'd, to His Majesty's Commander in Chief; And all Officers of the Provincial Forces, as high as Colonels inclusive, are to have Rank, according to their several respective Commissions, in like Manner, as is already given, by His Majesty's Regulations, to the Captains of Provincial Troops in America.

The King is further pleased to furnish all the Men, so raised as above, with Arms, Ammunition, and Tents, as well as to order Provisions to be issued to the same, by His Ma'ty's Commissaries, in the same Proportion and Manner as is done to the rest of the King's Forces: A sufficient Train of Artillery will also be provided, at His Majesty's Expence, for the Operations of the Campaign; And the Ship that conveys this, carries Orders for timely providing, at The King's Charge, with the utmost Diligence, and in an ample Manner, Boats & Vessels, necessary for the Transportation of the Army on this Expedition.

The Whole, therefore, that His Majesty expects and requires from the several Provinces, is, the Levying, Cloathing, and Pay of the Men; And, on these Heads also, that no Encouragement may be wanting to this great and salutary Attempt, The King is farther most Graciously pleased to permit me to acquaint You, that strong Recommendations will be made to Parliament in their Session next Year, to grant a proper Compensation for such Expences as above, according as the active Vigour and strenuous Efforts of the respective Provinces shall justly appear to merit.*

Altho' several Thousand Stands of Arms will be forthwith sent from England, to be distributed to the Troops, now directed to be raised, in the Northern and Southern Provinces; Yet, as it is hoped, that the Numbers of Men, levyed in all Parts of America, may greatly exceed the Quantity of Arms that can at present, be supplied from England; It is His Majesty's Pleasure, that you do, with particular Diligence, immediately collect, and put into the best Condition, all the serviceable Arms that can be found within your Government, in order that the Same may be employed, as far as They will go, in this Exigency.

I am further to inform You, that similar Orders are sent, by this Conveyance to Rhode Island, New Hampshire, Connecticut, New York and New Jersey.

The Southern Governments are also directed to raise Men in the same Manner, to be employed in such offensive Operations, as the Circumstances and Situation of

* £200,000 was voted in April 1759. 32 George II, c. 36. [Note by Editor of the *Correspondence*.]

the Enemy's Posts, in those Parts, may point out; which, it is hoped, will oblige them so to divide their Attention and Forces, as will render the several Attempts more easy and successful.

It is unnecessary to add any thing to animate your zeal, in the Execution of His Majesty's Orders on this great Occasion, where the Safety and Preservation of America and of your own Province in particular, (N.B. To be omitted to Connecticut & Rhode Is[d].) are at Stake; And the King doubts not, from your known Fidelity and Attachment, that you will employ Yourself, with the utmost Application and Dispatch, in this urgent and dangerous Crisis.

Altho' the Knowledge of an Intention to invade Canada is apprehended to be not only unattended with any Inconvenience, but necessary to be propagated in the Provinces, in order to give Success to the Levies; Yet, as Secresy, in all Enterprizes on particular Places, is of the greatest Importance, The King is persuaded, that you will use all proper Discretion in communicating, by Name, any of the immediate Objects before pointed out, further than to such Persons, to whom it may be necessary, for the Good of the Service, confidentially to entrust the same. I am, Gentlemen,

Your most obedient humble Servant,

W. PITT.

264. Letter from William Pitt to General Amherst announcing successes in Europe, 10 June 1758

(*Correspondence of William Pitt . . . with Colonial Governors*, ed. G. S. Kimball, I (1906), p. 266.)

This letter illustrates the policy of 'containment' in both its aspects; the assisting of Frederick the Great in the continental campaign, and the raids on the French coast, planned to relieve pressure on Frederick. The expedition to St. Malo in 1758 in fact inflicted little real damage on the French, and Pitt was criticized, both at the time and by later writers, for these raids, which Henry Fox described as "breaking windows with guineas".

Pitt to General Amherst.[1]

WHITEHALL, June 10th. 1758.

Sir,

His Majesty having thought proper to employ a considerable Body of His Land Forces, amounting to 14,000 Men, under the Command of the Duke of Marlborough, with a Number of Ships of War, under that of the Honble Captain Howe, on an Expedition to the Coasts of France, I have the Satisfaction to acquaint You, that, on Thursday Night, an Officer arrived with an Account, that, on the 5th and 6th Instant, His Majesty's Troops had been so fortunate as to make good a Landing, with little or no Opposition in Cancalle Bay, about seven miles from St. Malo. And the inclosed Extraordinary Gazette will give you a full Account, that His Majesty's Forces, under the Command of Prince Ferdinand of Brunswick, had, by the best concerted Plan, executed with the greatest Ability, happily passed the Rhine on the 2d. Inst. There is the greatest reason to hope, that this fortunate Coincidence of Events will not fail

[1] In the margin, "A like letter was sent to Adml. Boscawen". General Jeffrey Amherst (1717–1797), later first Baron Amherst, and Admiral Edward Boscawen (1711–1761) were in command respectively of the land and naval forces in the expedition against Louisbourg.

to have the best Effects in Disconcerting, and Distracting the Views of the Enemy, and Distressing the French in such distant Parts.

I flatter myself this Letter will find you safely arrived in North America, and tho' I had no new Orders to send you from His Majesty, I would not omit the first Opportunity of communicating to You this agreeable News, which, I am persuaded, will not only give you the greatest Pleasure, but may also have its Use in adding fresh Spirit, & Vigor to the Operations of the Troops under your Command.

I am etc.

W. PITT.

265. Instructions for the expedition against Martinique, 16 October 1758

(*Correspondence of William Pitt . . . with Colonial Governors*, ed. G. S. Kimball, I (1906), pp. 366–368.)

Pitt's plan for the extension of operations against France to the West Indies at the end of 1758 was mainly due to his wish to secure a French island of value to be exchanged for Minorca when peace negotiations began. The attack on Martinique was subsequently abandoned, but the expedition captured Guadeloupe, the second most important of the French sugar islands.

Pitt to General Hopson.[1]

WHITEHALL, Octr 16th. 1758.

Sir,

I inclose herewith the Secret Instructions, which the King has been pleased to sign for your Guidance and Direction, in addition to which, I am to inform you, that Captain Hughes[2] is directed, immediately on His Arrival at Portsmouth, if all the Transport Vessels shall, as it is hoped, be then ready or as soon after as possible, to dispatch, in Concert with you, under proper Convoy, to Plymouth, such Part thereof, as shall be sufficient to receive the Two Regiments to be embarked at that Place, and It is His Majesty's Pleasure that you do give the necessary Directions for the said Two Regiments to be put on Board with all possible Expedition, in order that the same may be, in every Respect ready, on any signal or order from Captain Hughes, to join Him, without Loss of Time, on His arrival, with the rest of the Fleet, off Plymouth.

I am also to inform You, that Captain Hughes is directed, when you shall have made such Progress in your Voyage as shall be judged expedient, to Dispatch, in Concert with you, a Ship to Captain Moore,[3] or the Commander in Chief of His Majesty's Ships at the Leeward Islands, (who has been ordered to repair to Carlisle Bay in Barbados) with a Duplicate of the King's Instructions; And you will, by that Opportunity, give Captain Moore any Information, that you shall think fit for the Good of His Majesty's Service.

I inclose herewith a Letter for the Governor of Barbados, and also one for the Governor of the Leeward Islands, which you will, respectively, send to them, when

[1] Major-General Thomas Hopson, died at Guadeloupe, 27 February 1759.

[2] Edward Hughes (1720–1794) served at Louisbourg and Quebec, Rear-Admiral and knighted, 1778.

[3] John Moore (1718–1779), commander-in-chief on the Leeward Islands station since 1756. Took part in the capture of Guadeloupe. Rear-Admiral, 1762; created baronet, 1766.

you shall dispatch the Applications for Assistance, as directed by your Instructions; and I add, for your Information, a Copy of the said Letters.

Colonel Haldane, Governor of Jamaica, being appointed to serve under you, as a Brigadier General, on the Expedition against Martinico; I am to acquaint you, that It is His Majesty's Pleasure, that, as soon as That Service shall be finished, Colonel Haldane do proceed to His Government in Jamaica.

I heartily wish you a good Voyage, and Success in the Important Command, with which the King has been pleased to honor you.

I am etc.

W. PITT.

Pitt to the Governor of Barbados[1] *and of the Leeward Islands.*[2]

WHITEHALL, Oct[r] 16th. 1758.

Govr. of Barbados and
Govr. of Leeward Islands. *Sir,*

You will receive this Letter from Major Gen[l] Hopson, whom the King has appointed Commander in Chief of a Body of His Land Forces to make an Attack upon the Island of Martinico; and I am to signify to you His Majesty's Pleasure, that you do give all the Assistance and Succour in your Power to Major General Hopson, whenever He shall apply to you; and particularly, in case It shall, as it is hoped, be found practicable to employ, in any Operations for Annoying and distressing the Enemy in the said Island, a number of the Natives, or Inhabitants of the Island under your Government, that you do exert all your Influence, and use all legal Methods to procure such a Number thereof, as General Hopson shall judge expedient. And you cannot render a more essential or acceptable Service to the King, than by Employing your utmost Endeavours to supply His Majesty's Forces, appointed for this important Expedition, with all sorts of Aid, Provisions and Refreshments, that the Island under your Command, shall afford, or That you shall be able to procure from other Parts.

To the Governor of the Leeward Islands, only.

I am further to acquaint you, that Major General Hopson is directed to order a Detachment from the 38th. Regiment of Foot, now on Duty in the Leeward Islands, to join Him in Case It shall be judged, that the same can, consistent with the Safety and Defence of the said Islands, be spared; It is, therefore, the King's Pleasure, that you do, if necessary, give any Orders, that may depend upon You, for making, as speedily as possible, such Detachment from the said Regiment, as Major General Hopson shall think proper to direct.

I am etc.

W. PITT.

P.S. *to Govr. of Barbados.* If Gen[l] Hopson should require any Assistance of Horses, or Beasts of Draught, you will exert all possible Diligence, in supplying Him with the same, in the most speedy and ample manner, that shall be practicable.

[1] Charles Pilford.

[2] George Thomas, planter of Antigua; Lieutenant-Governor of Pennsylvania, 1738–1747.

266. Instructions to General Amherst for the campaign of 1759, 28 December 1758

(*Correspondence of William Pitt . . . with Colonial Governors*, ed. G. S. Kimball, I (1906), pp. 432–434, 438–441.)

After his failure to take Ticonderoga in 1758 Abercromby was recalled and Amherst became commander-in-chief in America. A triple attack on Canada was planned for 1759; (i) up the St. Lawrence, under General Wolfe and Admiral Saunders; (ii) by way of Crown Point and Ticonderoga (as in the previous year), under Amherst himself; (iii) by way of Oswego, under General John Prideaux, who was killed during the siege of Fort Niagara. Amherst's and Prideaux's operations forced Montcalm to detach troops for the defence of Montreal, and greatly helped Wolfe and Saunders in the main operations against Quebec.

Pitt to General Amherst.

Sir WHITEHALL Dec: 29th 1758

His Majesty having nothing so much at heart as to improve the great and important advantages gained the last Campaign as well as to repair the Disappointment at Ticonderoge, and, by the most vigorous & decisive Efforts, to establish, by the Blessing of God on his Arms, His Majesty's just and indubitable Rights, and to avert all future Dangers to His Majesty's Subjects in No. America, I am now to acquaint you that the King has come to a Resolution to allot an adequate Proportion of His Forces in No. America amounting (as you will see by the inclosed Paper containing the Destination of the Troops) to 12,005–Men, to make an attack upon Quebeck, by the River St. Lawrence against which place they are to proceed from Louisburg, as early in the Year, as on or about, the 7th. of May, if the season shall happen to permit, under the Direction of Brigadier Genl. Wolfe, whom the King has appointed for the Command of that Operation, and who will have the rank of Major General, for that Expedition only;–And I am to signify to you His Majesty's Pleasure that you do cause the several Regiments appointed by the said List, to be employed accordingly on that Service, without making any change therein, unless some alteration should be found absolutely necessary, from extraordinary Inconvenience, that might otherwise arise to the Service, from the unforseen Circumstances or Situation, of any particular Regt. or Regimts., in the Allotment, herewith transmitted, of the Forces destined for the above operation; and, in case it should be found absolutely necessary to change any Regt. or Regiments in the said Allotment, you are to take especial care, that notwithstanding any such Change of particular Corps, the Total of Regular Forces prescribed & fixed for this Service, do amount to the full Number, allotted in the inclosed Paper, for the same.–It is also the King's Pleasure, that you do forthwith cause such Part of the Troops above mentioned, except Genl. Brag's Regt., which is already at Louisburg, to be so disposed, that they may be ready, and embarked, at New York, Boston, Halifax or such other place, as shall be most convenient, on board the Transports, which shall be provided for that purpose, in such time, as that all the Troops abovenamed for this Service, may be rendezvoused at Cape Breton, as nearly as may be, on, or about, the 20th. of April if the Season shall happen to permit, and you will without Loss of time,–dispatch all necessary Orders and in particular to the Governor, or Commander in Chief at Halifax, to the Govr. of Louisburg, with regard to any Troops in their respective Departments, destined for this Expedition, as by the inclosed State of the

Troops, in order that no Disappointment may happen, in proceeding from Louisburg, in case the Season permits, by the River St Lawrence to Quebeck, on, or about, the 7th of May, as directed in the former Part of this letter; And you will not fail to order forthwith, all proper Provision (and particularly fresh Provision as far as may be) to be immediately procured for the Subsistence and Refreshment of the Troops, during the Stay they may happen to make at Cape Breton, the Place appointed for their Rendezvous, and that all the Preparations there and Elsewhere, for this Service, be quicken'd and pressed, with the utmost Diligence–

[Detailed instructions follow for the equipping of Wolfe's force.]

. . . .

I come now to that Part of the Operations for the ensuing Campaign, in N^o^ America, which are to be under your own immediate Direction, and which, from their Importance Difficulty and Extent, as well as from the Correspondence and Intercourse that they will constantly demand with the several Governors, throughout the whole of North America, must necessarily require the Presence of the Officer, on the Continent of America, vested with the Command in Chief of the King's Forces there, by his Commission under the Great Seal; and His Majesty hopes from your distinguished Zeal for the Honor of his Arms and your known Abilities & Experience, that the Execution of a Plan of Operations of such Weight, and formed at such Expence–for an Irruption into Canada: will be attended with a happier & more honorable Event than heretofore.

I am therefore to signify to you the King's Pleasure that you do immediately concert the properest Measures for pushing the Operations of the Campaign, with the utmost Vigour, early in the Year, by an Invasion of Canada, with such Part, as you shall judge proper of his Majesty's Troops (not allotted as above for the Expedition against Quebec) in Conjunction with such a numerous Body of the Forces of the Northern Provinces as you will have seen by the copy of my letter of the 9th inst. to the Governors thereof, it is hoped, will, in consequence of those pressing Orders to that Effect, which are renewed and enforced in the strongest manner by my Letter of this Date (Copy of which I now enclose) be ready to join in this most important service, and to this great End, it is His Majesty's Pleasure that you do attempt an invasion of Canada, by the Way of Crown Point or La Galette, or both, according as you shall judge practicable, and proceed, if practicable, and attack Montreal or Quebec, or both of the said places successively, with such of the Forces as shall remain under your own immediate Direction, in one Body, or at one and the same time, by a Division of the s^d^ Forces into separate & distinct Operations, according as you shall, from your Knowledge of the Countries, thro' which the War is to be carried, & from emergent Circumstances, not to be known here, judge all or any of the said attempts to be practicable.

It is also the King's Pleasure that you should give a due Attention to the Lake Ontario and facilitate, as far as possible, consistent with other main Operations of the Campaign, the Re-establishment of the important Port of Oswego, a Place so highly essential to His Majesty's Possessions in North America in time of Peace as well as

War; and you will accordingly not fail to concert with the Lieutenant Governor of New York, within whose Province Oswego is situated, all necessary and effectual Measures for re-establishing that Post in the Course of the ensuing Year, and for building a sufficient & proper Fort for the security and Defence thereof, and the inclosed Copy of my Letter to M^{r} De Lancey, will show you that he has similar Orders to concert with, and assist you in the Execution of this very important Service.

It were as much to be wished that any Operations on the side of Lake Ontario could be pushed on as far as Niagara, and that you may find it practicable to set on foot some Enterprize against the Fort there, the Success of which would so greatly contribute to establish the uninterrupted Dominion of that Lake, and, at the same time, effectually cut off the Communication between Canada, and the French Settlements to the South; and the Utility and Importance of such an Enterprize against Niagara, is, of itself, so apparent, that I am persuaded, it is unnecessary to add anything to enforce your giving all proper Attention to the same, as far as the great and main Objects of the Campaign shall permit.

You are already by my letter of the 9th Ins^{t} directed to exert your utmost Endeavours to incite & encourage the several Provinces to the full & due Execution of the King's Commands; and the Success of the ensuing decisive Campaign, depends so much on commencing the several Operations as early as shall be practicable, and thereby preventing the last Efforts, there is Reason to suppose the Enemy is preparing to make, to save their Possessions in N^{o} America, from total Ruin, that you cannot be too urgent with the Provinces to quicken and expedite the Levies, so as that the said Provincial Troops may be assembled at the Rendezvous, and be, in every respect, ready, in Conjunction with the regular Forces, to open the Campaign by the 1st of May, as nothing can contribute so much to the Success of the Operations to be undertaken in different Parts of N^{o} America, and particularly of the Attempt in Quebeck, as putting the Forces early in Motion, on the other Frontiers of Canada, and thereby distracting the Enemy, and obliging them to divide their Strength.

With regard to the Southern Operations, I am to signify to you His Majesty's Pleasure that you do continue Brigadier Genl Forbes[1] in that Command, or, if his Health shall not permit him to undertake that Service, that you do appoint such other Officer as you shall think proper to command such Forces as you shall judge proper to leave in the Southern Provinces, and that Brig^{r} Forbes, or such other Officer do proceed, without Loss of time, to Pensylvania, or such other of the Southern Provinces, as shall be thought most expedient in order to concert any Operations, to be undertaken by the said Troops, who, in Conjunction with the Forces, directed by my Letter of the 9th Inst, to the Southern Governors, to be raised in those Provinces, are to be employed under the Command of Brig^{r} Forbes, or such Officer whom you shall appoint as above, on any such offensive Operations as you shall judge most expedient for annoying the Enemy, and most efficacious towards removing all future Dangers from the Frontiers of any of the Southern Colonies on the Continent of America. . . .

[1] John Forbes (1710–1759) had led the expedition to Fort Duquesne in 1758.

267. General Wolfe describes the difficulties of the expedition against Quebec, 9 September 1759

(*Correspondence of William Pitt, Earl of Chatham*, ed. W. S. Taylor and J. H. Pringle, I (1838), pp. 425–430.)

The English fleet, under Admiral Saunders, had by 26 June sailed up the St. Lawrence as far as the Island of Orleans, opposite Quebec. An attack on the French defences at Beauport on 31 July had failed, and the town seemed impregnable. On 8 September it was decided to transport troops, under cover of darkness, past the town to the upper St. Lawrence, to land on the north bank and proceed up the steep track to the Heights of Abraham, and so, by taking him in the rear, to force Montcalm to come out and fight in the open.

Major-General Wolfe to the Earl of Holdernesse.[1]

On board the *Sutherland*, at anchor off Cape Rouge,
September 9, 1759.

My Lord,

If the Marquis de Montcalm had shut himself up in the town of Quebec, it would have been long since in our possession, because the defences are inconsiderable and our artillery very formidable; but he has a numerous body of armed men (I cannot call it an army) and the strongest country, perhaps, in the world to rest the defence of the town and colony upon. The ten battalions, and the grenadiers of Louisbourg, are a chosen body of troops, and able to fight the united force of Canada upon even terms. Our field artillery, brought into use, would terrify the militia and the savages; and our battalions are in every respect superior to those commanded by the Marquis, who acts a circumspect, prudent part, and entirely defensive; except, in one extraordinary instance, he sent sixteen hundred men over the river to attack our batteries upon the Point of Levy, defended by four battalions. Bad intelligence, no doubt, of our strength, induced him to this measure: however, the detachment judged better than their general, and retired. They dispute the water with the boats of the fleet, by the means of floating batteries, suited to the nature of the river, and innumerable battoes. They have a great artillery upon the ramparts towards the sea, and so placed that shipping cannot affect it.

I meant to attack the left of their entrenchments, favoured by our artillery, the 31st July. A multitude of traverses prevented, in some measure, its effect, which was nevertheless very considerable: accidents hindered the attack, and the enemy's care to strengthen that post has made it since too hazardous. The town is totally demolished, and the country in a great measure ruined; particularly the lower Canada. Our fleet blocks up the river, both above and below the town, but can give no manner of assistance in an attack upon the Canadian army. We have continual skirmishes; old people, seventy years of age, and boys of fifteen, fire at our detachments, and kill or wound our men from the edges of the woods. Every man able to bear arms, both above and below Quebec, is in the camp of Beauport. The old men, women, and children are retired into the woods. The Canadians are extremely dissatisfied; but, curbed by the force of this government, and terrified by the savages that are posted

[1] Robert D'Arcy, fourth earl of Holdernesse (1718–1778), Secretary of State for the Northern Department, Pitt being Secretary for the Southern Department.

round about them, they are obliged to keep together, to work and to man the entrenchments. Upwards of twenty sail of ships got in before our squadron, and brought succours of all sorts; which were exceedingly wanted in the colony. The sailors of these ships help to work the guns, and others conduct the floating batteries; their ships are lightened and carried up the river out of our reach, at least out of the reach of the men of war. These ships serve a double purpose: they are magazines for their provisions, and at the same time cut off all communication between General Amherst's army[1] and the corps under my command; so that we are not able to make any detachment to attack Montreal, or favour the junction, or, by attacking the fort of Chambly, or Bourlemaqui's corps behind, open the general's way into Canada; all which might have been easily done with ten floating batteries carrying each a gun, and twenty flat-bottomed boats, if there had been no ships in the river. Our poor soldiery have worked without ceasing and without murmuring; and as often as the enemy have attempted upon us, they have been repulsed by the valour of the men. A woody country so well known to the enemy, and an enemy so vigilant and hardy as the Indians and Canadians are, make entrenchments everywhere necessary; and by this precaution we have saved a number of lives, for scarce a night passes that they are not close in upon our posts, watching an opportunity to surprise and murder. There is very little quarter given on either side.

We have seven hours, and sometimes (above the town, after rain) near eight hours of the most violent ebb tide that can be imagined, which loses us an infinite deal of time, in every operation on the water; and the stream is so strong, particularly here, that the ships often drag their anchors by the mere force of the current. The bottom is a bed of rock; so that a ship, unless it hooks a ragged rock, holds by the weight only of the anchor. Doubtless, if the equinoctial gale has any force, a number of ships must necessarily run ashore and be lost.

The day after the troops landed upon the Isle of Orleans, a violent storm had nigh ruined the expedition altogether. Numbers of boats were lost; all the whale boats and most of the cutters were stove; some flat-bottomed boats destroyed, and others damaged. We never had half as many of the latter as are necessary for this extraordinary and very important service. The enemy is able to fight us upon the water, whenever we are out of the reach of the cannon of the fleet.

The extreme heat of the weather in August, and a good deal of fatigue, threw me into a fever; but that the business might go on, I begged the generals to consider amongst themselves what was fittest to be done. Their sentiments were unanimous, that (as the easterly winds begin to blow, and ships can pass the town in the night with provisions, artillery, &c.) we should endeavour, by conveying a considerable corps into the upper river, to draw them from their inaccessible situation, and bring them to an action. I agreed to the proposal; and we are now here, with about three thousand six hundred men, waiting an opportunity to attack them, when and wherever they can best be got at. The weather has been extremely unfavourable for a day or two, so that we have been inactive. I am so far recovered as to do business; but my constitution is entirely ruined, without the consolation of having done any

[1] On the shores of Lake Champlain.

considerable service to the state; or without any prospect of it. I have the honour to be, with great respect, my Lord,

Your Lordship's most obedient
and most humble servant,
JAM. WOLFE.

268. Captain John Knox's account of the battle of Quebec, 13 September 1759

(Captain John Knox, *An Historical Journal of the Campaigns in North America*, II (1769), pp. 67–73.)

Knox was the son of a Sligo merchant, and retired on half-pay in 1763. His *Journal* has been reprinted by the Champlain Society (1914–1916), edited by A. G. Doughty. He here describes the scaling of the Heights of Abraham and the battle in which Wolfe was killed. Quebec surrendered on 18 September.

Thursday, September 13, 1759.

Before day-break this morning we made a descent upon the north shore, about half a quarter of a mile to the eastward of Sillery; and the light troops were fortunately, by the rapidity of the current, carried lower down, between us and Cape Diamond; we had, in this debarkation, thirty flat-bottomed boats, containing about sixteen hundred men. This was a great surprise on the enemy, who, from the natural strength of the place, did not suspect, and consequently were not prepared against, so bold an attempt. The chain of centries, which they had posted along the summit of the heights, galled us a little, and picked off several men*, and some Officers, before our light infantry got up to dislodge them†. This grand enterprise was conducted, and executed with great good order and discretion; as fast as we landed, the boats put off for reinforcements, and the troops formed with much regularity: the General, with Brigadiers Monckton[1] and Murray,[2] were a-shore with the first division. We lost no time here, but clambered up one of the steepest precipices that can be conceived, being almost a perpendicular, and of an incredible height. As soon as we gained the summit, all was quiet, and not a shot was heard, owing to the excellent conduct of the light infantry under Colonel Howe;[3] it was by this time clear day-light. Here we formed again, the river and the south country in our rear, our right extending to the town, our left to Sillery, and halted a few minutes‡. The General then detached the light troops to our left to route the enemy from their battery, and to disable their guns,

* In the boat where I was, one man was killed; one seaman, with four soldiers, were slightly, and two mortally wounded.

† Captain Donald M'Donald, a very gallant Officer, of Fraser's Highlanders, commanded the advanced-guard of the light infantry, and was, consequently, among the foremost on shore; as soon as he and his men gained the height, he was challenged by a centry, and, with great presence of mind, from his knowledge of the French service, answered him according to their manner: it being yet dark, he came up to him, told him he was sent there, with a large command, to take post, and desired him to go with all speed to his guard, and to call off all the other men of his party who were ranged along the hill, for that he would take care to give a good account of the B— Anglois, if they should persist; this *finesse* had the desired effect and saved us many lives, &c.

‡ *The hill they climb'd, and halted at its top, of more than mortal size:*
Tow'ring they seem'd, an host angelic, clad in burning arms!

[1] Robert Monckton (1726–1782), Wolfe's second-in-command.

[2] James Murray (1719?–1794), left in command of Quebec after its capture.

[3] Later General Sir William Howe (see No. 271).

except they could be rendered serviceable to the party who were to remain there; and this service was soon performed. We then faced to the right, and marched towards the town by files, till we came to the plains of Abraham; an even piece of ground which Mr. Wolfe had made choice of, while we stood forming upon the hill. Weather showery: about six o'clock the enemy first made their appearance upon the heights, between us and the town; whereupon we halted, and wheeled to the right, thereby forming the line of battle.* The first disposition then was: "Grenadiers of Louisbourg on the right, forty-seventh regiment on the left, twenty-eighth on the right, and the forty-third on the left;" part of the light infantry took post in the houses at Sillery, and the remainder occupied a chain of houses which were opportunely situated for that purpose, and covered our left flank, inclining towards our rear; the General then advanced some platoons from the grenadiers and twenty-eighth regiment below the height on our right, to annoy the enemy, and prevent their getting round the declivity between us and the main river, which they had attempted. By this time the fifteenth and thirty-fifth regiments joined us, who formed a second line, and were soon after followed by the forty-eighth and fifty-eighth, two battalions of the sixtieth and seventy-eighth regiments, (Highlanders) by which a new disposition was made of the whole; *viz.* "first line, thirty-fifth to the right, in a circular form on the slope of the hill; fifty-eighth, left; grenadiers, right; seventy-eighth, left; twenty-eighth, right; forty-seventh, left; forty-third, in the center." General Wolfe, Brigadiers Monckton and Murray, to our front line; and the second was composed of the fifteenth, and two battalions of the sixtieth regiment, under Brigadier Townshend, with a reserve of the forty-eighth regiment, under Colonel Burton, drawn up in four grand divisions, with large intervals. The enemy had now likewise formed the line of battle, and got some cannon to play on us, with round and canister-shot; but what galled us most was a body of Indians and other marksmen they had concealed in the corn opposite to the front of our right wing, and a coppice that stood opposite to our center, inclining towards our left; but the Colonel Hale, by Brigadier Monckton's orders, advanced some platoons, alternately, from the forty-seventh regiment, which, after a few rounds, obliged these sculkers to retire: we were now ordered to lie down, and remained some time in this position. About eight o'clock we had two pieces of short brass six-pounders playing on the enemy, which threw them into some confusion, and obliged them to alter their disposition, and Montcalm formed them into three large columns; about nine the two armies moved a little nearer each other. The light cavalry made a faint attempt upon our parties at the battery of Sillery, but were soon beat off, and Monsieur de Bougainville, with his troops from Cape Rouge, came down to attack the flank of our second line, hoping to penetrate there; but, by a masterly disposition of Brigadier Townshend, they were forced to desist, and the third battalion of Royal Americans was then detached to the first ground we had formed on after we gained the heights, to preserve the communication with the beach

* Quebec was then to the eastward of us in front, with the enemy under its walls. Our right was flanked by the declivity and the main river to the southward, and what is called the lower road leading (westward) from the town, with the river Charles and the north country, were on our left. If the reader will attend to this description, observing the cardinal points, he may thereby form as lively an idea of the field of battle as if a plan were laid before him; and, though our first disposition was afterwards altered, yet our situation, with that of the enemy, and the scene of action, could not vary.

and our boats. About ten o'clock the enemy began to advance briskly in three columns, with loud shouts and recovered arms, two of them inclining to the left of our army, and the third towards our right, firing obliquely at the two extremities of our line, from the distance of one hundred and thirty ——, until they came within forty yards; which our troops withstood with the greatest intrepidity and firmness, still reserving their fire, and paying the strictest obedience to their Officers: this uncommon steadiness, together with the havoc which the grape-shot from our field-pieces made among them, threw them into some disorder, and was most critically maintained by a well-timed, regular, and heavy discharge of our small arms, such as they could no longer oppose*; hereupon they gave way, and fled with precipitation, so that, by the time the cloud of smoke was vanished, our men were again loaded, and, profiting by the advantage we had over them, pursued them almost to the gates of the town, and the bridge over the little river, redoubling our fire with great eagerness, making many Officers and men prisoners. The weather cleared up, with a comfortably warm sun-shine: the Highlanders chaced them vigorously towards Charles's river, and the fifty-eighth to the suburb close to John's gate, until they were checked by the cannon from the two hulks; at the same time a gun, which the town had brought to bear upon us with grape-shot, galled the progress of the regiments to the right, who were likewise pursuing with equal ardour, while Colonel Hunt Walsh, by a very judicious movement, wheeled the battalions of Bragg and Kennedy to the left, and flanked the coppice where a body of the enemy made a stand, as if willing to renew the action; but a few platoons from these corps completed our victory. Then it was that Brigadier Townshend[1] came up, called off the pursuers, ordered the whole line to dress, and recover their former ground. Our joy at this success is inexpressibly damped by the loss we sustained of one of the greatest heroes which this or any other age can boast of,–GENERAL JAMES WOLFE, who received his mortal wound, as he was exerting himself at the head of the grenadiers of Louisbourg; and Brigadier Monckton was unfortunately wounded upon the left of the forty-third, and right of the forty-seventh regiment, at much the same time; whereby the command devolved on Brigadier Townshend, who, with Brigadier Murray, went to the head of every regiment, and returned thanks for their extraordinary good behaviour, congratulating the Officers on our success. There is one incident very remarkable, and which I can affirm from my own personal knowledge,–that the enemy were extremely apprehensive of being rigorously treated; for, conscious of their inhuman behaviour to our troops upon a former occasion, the Officers who fell into our hands most piteously (with hats off) sued for quarter, repeatedly declaring they were not at Fort William Henry (called by them Fort St. George) in the year 1757. A soldier of the Royal Americans, who deserted from us this campaign, and

* When the General formed the line of battle, he ordered the regiments to load with an additional ball. The forty-third and forty-seventh regiments, in the center, being little affected by the oblique fire of the enemy, gave them, with great calmness, as remarkable a close and heavy discharge, as I ever saw performed at a private field of exercise, insomuch that better troops than we encountered could not possibly withstand it: and, indeed, well might the French Officers say, that they never opposed such a shock as they received from the center of our line, for that they believed every ball took place, and such regularity and discipline they had not experienced before; our troops in general, and particularly the central corps, having levelled and fired,–*comme une coup de canon.*

[1] George, later fourth viscount and first Marquis Townshend (1724–1807).

fought against us to-day, was found wounded on the field of battle; he was immediately tried by a general court-martial, and was shot to death, pursuant to his sentence. While the two armies were engaged this morning, there was an incessant firing between the town and our south batteries. By the time that our troops had taken a little refreshment, a quantity of intrenching tools were brought a-shore, and the regiments were employed in redoubting our ground, and landing some cannon and ammunition. The Officers who are prisoners say, that Quebec will surrender in a few days: some deserters, who came out to us in the evening, agree in that opinion, and inform us, that the Sieur de Montcalm is dying, in great agony, of a wound he received to-day in their retreat. Thus has our late renowned Commander, by his superior eminence in the art of war, and a most judicious *coup d'etat*, made a conquest of this fertile, healthy, and hitherto formidable country, with a handful of troops only, in spite of the political schemes, and most vigorous efforts, of the famous Montcalm, and many other Officers of rank and experience, at the head of an army considerably more numerous. My pen is too feeble to draw the character of this *British Achilles*; but the same may, with justice, be said of him as was said of Henry IV of France: *He was possessed of courage, humanity, clemency, generosity, affability and politeness.* And though the former of these happy ingredients, how essential soever it may be in the composition of a soldier, is not alone sufficient to distinguish an expert Officer; yet, I may, with strict truth, advance, that Major General James Wolfe, by his great talents, and martial disposition, which he discovered early in life, was greatly superior to his experience in generalship, and was by no means inferior to a Frederic, a Henry, or a Ferdinand.

"When the matter match'd his mighty mind,
Up rose the Hero: on his piercing eye
Sat observation, on each glance of thought
Decision follow'd, as the thunderbolt
Pursues the flash."

269. Admiral Hawke's dispatch to the Admiralty on the battle of Quiberon Bay, 24 November 1759

(Montagu Burrows, *Life of Edward Lord Hawke* (1883), pp. 394–397.)

Hawke had blockaded Brest from May to November 1759, to prevent the Brest fleet coming out to join that of Toulon. On 19 August the Toulon fleet was defeated by Admiral Boscawen in Lagos Bay. In November, bad weather drove Hawke's fleet temporarily into Torbay, and the Brest fleet under Admiral Conflans put to sea. Hawke pursued them, and on 20 November won the battle of Quiberon Bay.

ROYAL GEORGE, off Penris Point,
November 24th, 1759.

SIR

In my letter of the 17th by express, I desired you would acquaint their Lordships with my having received intelligence of 18 sail of the line, and three frigates of the Brest squadron being discovered about 24 leagues to the north-west of Belleisle, steering to the eastward. All the prisoners, however, agree that on the day we chased them, their squadron consisted, according to the accompanying list, of four ships of 80, six of 74, three of 70, eight of 64, one frigate of 36, one of 34, and one of 16 guns, with a small vessel to look out. They sailed from Brest the 14th instant, the same day I sailed from Torbay. Concluding that their first rendezvous would be Quiberon, the instant I received the intelligence I directed my course thither with a pressed sail. At first the wind blowing hard at S.b.E. & S. drove us considerably to the Westward. But on the 18th and 19th, though variable, it proved more favourable. In the mean-time having been joined by the *Maidstone* and *Coventry* frigates, I directed their commanders to keep ahead of the squadron, one on the starboard and the other on the larboard bow.

At ½ past 8 o'clock on the morning of the 20th, Belleisle, by our reckoning, bearing E.b.N. ¼ N. about 13 leagues, the *Maidstone* made the signal for seeing a fleet. I immediately spread abroad the signal for the line abreast, in order to draw all ships of the squadron up with me. I had before sent the *Magnanime* ahead to make the land. Observing, on my discovering them, that they made off, I threw out the signal for the seven ships nearest them to chase, and draw into a line of battle ahead of me, and endeavour to stop them till the rest of the squadron should come up, who were also to form as they chased, that no time might be lost in the pursuit. That morning they were in chase of the *Rochester*, *Chatham*, *Portland*, *Falkland*, *Minerva*, *Vengeance*, and *Venus*, all which joined me about 11 o'clock, and in the evening the *Sapphire* from Quiberon Bay. All the day we had very fresh gales at N.W. and W.N.W. with heavy squalls. Monsieur Conflans kept going off under such sail as all his squadron could carry, and at the same time keep together; while we crowded after him with every sail our ships could bear. At ½ past 2 P.M., the fire beginning ahead, I made the signal for engaging. We were then to the southward of Belleisle, and the French Admiral headmost, soon after led round the Cardinals, while his rear was in action. About 4 o'clock the *Formidable* struck, and a little after, the *Thesèe* and *Superbe* were sunk.

About 5, the *Hèros* struck, and came to an anchor; but, it blowing hard, no boat could be sent on board her. Night was now come; and, being on a part of the coast among islands and shoals, of which we were totally ignorant, without a pilot, as was the greatest part of the squadron, and blowing hard on a lee shore, I made the signal to anchor, and came-to in 15 fathom water, the Island of Dumet bearing E.b.N. between 2 and 3 miles, the Cardinals W. ½ s., and the steeples of Crozie S.E., as we found next morning.

In the night we heard many guns of distress fired, but, blowing hard, want of knowledge of the coast, and whether they were fired by a friend or an enemy, prevented all means of relief.

By day-break of the 21st, we discovered one of our ships[1] dismasted, ashore on the Four. The French *Hèros* also, and the *Soleil Royal*, which under cover of the night had anchored among us, cut and run ashore to the westward of Crozie. On the latter's moving, I made the *Essex*'s signal to slip and pursue her; but she unfortunately got upon the Four, and both she and the *Resolution* are irrevocably lost, notwithstanding

[1] The *Resolution*.

we sent them all the assistance that the weather would permit. About fourscore of the *Resolution*'s company, in spite of the strongest remonstrances of their Captain, made rafts, and with several French prisoners belonging to the *Formidable*, put off, and I am afraid drove out to sea. All the *Essex*'s are safe, with as many of the stores as possible, except one Lieutenant and a boat's crew, who were drove on the French shore, and have not since been heard of. The remains of both ships are set on fire. We found the *Dorsetshire*, *Revenge*, and *Defiance*, in the night of the 20th, put out to sea, as I hope the *Swiftsure* did, for she is still missing. The *Dorsetshire* and *Defiance* returned next day and the latter saw the *Revenge* without. Thus what loss we have sustained has been owing to the weather, not the enemy, seven or eight of whose line of battle ships got to sea, I believe, the night of the action.

As soon as it was broad daylight, in the morning of the 21st, I discovered seven or eight of the enemy's line of battle ships at anchor, between Point Penris and the river Vilaine, on which I made the signal to weigh in order to work up and attack them. But it blowed so hard from the N.W. that instead of daring to cast the squadron loose, I was obliged to strike topgallant masts. Most of those ships appeared to be aground at low water. But on the flood, by lightening them, and the advantage of the wind under the land, all, except two, got that night into the river Vilaine.

The weather being moderate on the 22nd, I sent the *Portland*, *Chatham*, and *Vengeance*, to destroy the *Soleil Royal* and *Hèros*. The French, on the approach of our ships, set the first on fire; and soon after, the latter met the same fate from our people. In the meantime I got under way, and worked up within Penris Point, as well for the sake of its being a safer road as to destroy, if possible, the two ships of the enemy, which still lay without the river Vilaine. But before the ships I sent a-head for that purpose could get near them, being quite light, and with the tide of flood, they got in.

All the 23rd we were occupied in reconnoitring the entrance of that river, which is very narrow, and only 12 foot water on the bar at low water. We discovered 7 if not 8 line of battle ships, about half a mile within, quite light, and two large frigates moored across to defend the mouth of the river. Only the frigates appeared to have guns in. By evening I had twelve long boats fitted as fire-ships ready to attempt burning them under cover of the *Sapphire* and *Coventry*. But the weather being bad, and the wind contrary, obliged me to defer it, till at least the latter should be favourable. If they can by any means be destroyed it shall be done.

In attacking a flying enemy, it was impossible in the space of a short winter's day, that all our ships should be able to get into action, or all those of the enemy brought to it. The Commanders and companies of such as did come up with the rear of the French on the 20th behaved with the greatest intrepidity, and gave the strongest proofs of a true British spirit. In the same manner I am satisfied would those have acquitted themselves, whose bad-going ships, or the distance they were at in the morning, prevented them from getting up.

Our loss by the enemy is not considerable. For in the ships which are now with me, I find only one Lieutenant and fifty seamen and marines killed, and about two hundred and twenty wounded.

When I consider the season of the year, the hard gales on the day of action, a flying enemy, the shortness of the day, and the coast they were on, I can boldly affirm that all that could possibly be done has been done. As to the loss we have sustained, let it be placed to the account of the necessity I was under of running all risks to break this strong force of the enemy. Had we had but two hours more daylight, the whole had been totally destroyed or taken; for we were almost up with their van when night overtook us.

Yesterday came in here the *Pallas*, *Fortune* sloop, and the *Proserpine* fireship. On the 16th I had despatched the *Fortune* to Quiberon with directions to Captain Duff[1] to keep strictly on his guard. In her way thither she fell in with the *Hebe*, a French frigate of 40 guns, under jury masts, and fought her several hours. During the engagement Lieutenant Stuart, 2nd of the *Ramilies*, whom I had appointed to command her was unfortunately killed. The surviving officers, on consulting together, resolved to leave her, as she proved too strong for them. I have detached Captain Young[2] to Quiberon Bay, with five ships, and am making up a flying squadron to scour the coast to the southward, as far as the Isle of Aix; and if practicable, to attempt any of the enemy's ships that may be there.

I am etc.

EDWARD HAWKE.

270. Thomas Mante's account of the capture of Havana, 1762

(Thomas Mante, *History of the late War in North America* (1772), pp. 397–400, 460–462, 464.)

Rumours of the third Family Compact between France and Spain reached England in the autumn of 1761. Pitt wished to declare war at once on Spain, but only Temple supported him in the Cabinet, and he resigned. When the Compact became known, war was declared on Spain, and an expedition against Havana dispatched, though peace negotiations with France were resumed shortly afterwards. Pitt's views on the terms to be demanded were still to some extent represented in the Cabinet, against the 'peace at any price' policy of Bute, by Grenville and Egremont, and their hands were much strengthened by the news of the capture of Havana. Thomas Mante was, according to his own account, assistant engineer at the siege, though his name does not appear in army lists of the period, and little is known about him. He wrote a number of military treatises.

We have already mentioned the declaration of war made by the English against the Spaniards, and are now to give an account of the hostilities which followed it. The most effectual method that the former could take to annoy the latter, and at the same time counteract the formidable accession of strength which France, by this time almost subdued, must otherwise receive from the acquisition of such an ally, was vigorously to attack some of the Spanish settlements in America, before they could be put into a proper posture of defence: For, should this plan be attended with success, it would not only obstruct the channels through which the Spaniards received all their wealth from that quarter of the globe, but possibly deprive them of the very sources which furnished it. The Havanna, on the Island of Cuba, was therefore the object singled out by the British ministry, as the most proper to accomplish these ends.

This city is situated exactly under the tropic of Cancer, 83° west of London, and is by far the most considerable place in the West-Indies as well on account of its trade,

[1] Robert Duff (d. 1787), Vice-Admiral, 1778. [2] James Young (d. 1789), Rear-Admiral, 1762.

as of its harbour and docks, in which ships of war of the first magnitude are built. But what rendered it of yet far greater consequence, was its being also the key of the riches of Mexico, and the usual repository till their final embarkation for Old Spain. The harbour lies to the east of the town, and is spacious enough to receive an hundred ships of the line. The entrance into it is defended by the Moro, a fort built upon a narrow point of land to the north of the town, and which is large enough to hold a garrison of one thousand men, with all the necessary provisions to resist a long and vigorous siege. It contains very good casements, and two cisterns which afford plenty of water. As it stands on steep rocks, it is inaccessible from the sea, which lashes its foundations. It is fortified to the east with two bastions, a courtin and good covered way, with a dry ditch, half of which is cut out of the solid rock. It commands the Fort de la Punta on the opposite side of the harbour's mouth, part of the town, and its three bastions to the north. A little more within the entrance into the harbour, and on the Moro side, is a battery built of stone, called the Twelve Apostles; and a little higher up, another called the Shepherds battery; above these a chain of hills called the Cavannos, extend themselves from the Moro to the plains of Guanamacoa. These hills command the town and docks, and can always be protected by the ships in the port, the very bottom of the harbour affording anchorage for men of war of the first rate, and being withal defended by a steep hill called Gonzales.

A chain of ten bastions and nine curtines, with an indifferent covered way, and some counterguards before the fronts of the bastions, form the ceinture of the town to the west. The ground in front is, in some places, marshy, the rest is nothing but bare rock, the earth that formerly covered it having been taken away to construct the ramparts of the town. It is no uncommon thing, however, to meet upon such rocks, with morasses two or three feet deep, formed by the rain-water collected in the hollows, and producing, in the course of its stagnation, herbs and slime, the general materials of morasses on all bottoms.

All the eastern coast is covered with wood, the rest of the environs of the town is entirely cleared, and well cultivated; and besides embellished with several small villages, and a prodigious number of country houses.

The operations against this capital object, by the possession of which England might be sure to intercept the treasures that were to give vigour to the united efforts of the house of Bourbon, were to be conducted by the Right Honourable the Earl of Albemarle,[1] as Commander-in-chief of the land forces, and by Admiral Sir George Pococke,[2] who was to command the fleet. . . .

[Explains the difficulties of co-ordination, as only a small part of the force was sent from England, the rest being supplied from America and the West Indies. Then follows a long and detailed account of the whole operation, from the arrival off Havana on 6th June to the capitulation on 13 August.]

THUS did this conquest prove the heaviest blow, in itself, and in its consequences the most decisive, of any that had been given since the commencement of the present

[1] George Keppel, third earl of Albemarle (1724–1772), brother to Admiral Keppel.
[2] Sir George Pocock (1706–1792), promoted Admiral, 1761.

hostilities between so many great powers. In the acquisition of the Havanna were combined all the advantages that could be procured in war. It was a military victory of the first magnitude; it was equal to the greatest naval victory by its effects on the whole marine of the Spaniards, who lost on that occasion a whole fleet. The vast quantity of tobacco and sugar, collected at the Havanna on the Spanish monarch's account, sold on the spot, exclusive of the ships and merchandize sent to, and sold in England, for seven hundred thousand pounds, which was divided amongst the conquerors in the proportion settled for the division of the plunder on the expedition of Lord Cathcart and Admiral Vernon, if they had succeeded, when they went against Carthagena.

From their first landing to the 13th of August, this important conquest cost the English, in killed, wounded, and prisoners, including those who died, two thousand seven hundred and sixty-four men. History, perhaps, does not record a siege with such a variety of difficulties to retard the approaches, as what attended the assailants of the Moro-castle. Not only there was scarce a spit of earth near any of the intended batteries, as we have already taken notice; but the cutting down, binding up, and carrying the vast quantities of fascines, which it was necessary to substitute, proved a work of infinite labour; nay, the earth necessary to give stability and resistance to the fascines, was not to be obtained but by scratching it from between the crevices of rocks, at a great distance from the spot where it was to be used.

Though a great part of the provisions brought from England had been spoiled by the heat of the climate, the most distressing circumstance of the campaign was the scarcity of water. Of the vast catalogue of human ills, thirst is the most intolerable. On this occasion, it soon caused the tongue to swell, extend itself without the lips, and become black as in a state of mortification; then the whole frame became a prey to the most excruciating agonies, till death at length intervened, and gave the unhappy sufferer relief. In this way, hundreds resigned themselves to eternity. A greater number fell victims to a putrid fever. From the appearance of perfect health, three or four short hours robbed them of existence. Many there were, who endured a loathsome disease for days, nay weeks together, living in a state of putrefaction, their bodies full of vermin, and almost eaten away before the spark of life was extinguished. The carrion crows of the country kept constantly hovering over the graves, which rather hid than buried the dead, and frequently scratched away the scanty earth, leaving in every mangled corpse a spectacle of unspeakable loathsomeness and terror to those, who, by being engaged in the same enterprise, were exposed to the same fate. Hundreds of carcases were seen floating on the ocean. Yet all these accumulated horrors damped not the ardour of the survivors. Used to conquest, and to brave every kind of danger, every one exerted himself with such a particular aim to victory, as if the whole enterprise depended on his single arm.

Having said thus much in praise of the bravery and patience of the English, candour requires we should add, that the Spaniards were far from being deficient in point of valour; and had their conduct been equal, it is more than probable, that the English had never obtained the noblest wreath of victory, that ever graced the brow of a conqueror in this quarter of the world. . . .

If we have not given as minute a detail of the operations of this important siege, as that which was transmitted to the British ministers, signed by the chief Engineer; but which, we have the greatest reason to believe the General never saw, till he arrived in England, it is to avoid the confusion which every where occurs in that account. But though we have aimed at clearness in the relation of this glorious achievement, we hope we shall not be found to have omitted any circumstance which might the least have contributed to the brilliant success of the English arms. After all, it will scarce be credited by future ages, that an army of Europeans persisted, for two months and eight days together, in the siege of a fortress situated in the hottest climate of the torrid zone, and during the hottest season of that climate. Be posterity therefore farther informed, that during the whole of this siege, there subsisted such a perfect harmony between the land and sea-services, with such an extraordinary degree of good-will in the inferior officers and common men, to execute the orders of their Admiral and General, that both owed their success to such patriotic endeavours.

(c) WAR OF AMERICAN INDEPENDENCE

271A–B. Instructions for the campaign of 1777

271A. Instructions for General Burgoyne, 26 March 1777

(*Hist. MSS. Comm. Stopford-Sackville MSS.*, II, pp. 60–63.)

An elaborate plan for the isolation of the New England colonies was worked out for the summer of 1777. General John Burgoyne (1722–1792) was to bring an army, including both English troops and the German troops hired by the government for use in America, from Canada along the Lakes to the Hudson River; General Sir William Howe (1729–1814), brother of Admiral Howe, and commander-in-chief of the forces in the American colonies, was meanwhile to contain the enemy and prevent interruption of Burgoyne's march, and the two armies were to meet at Albany and proceed thence to cut off the New England colonies from the rest of the colonies. Howe never received sufficiently precise official instructions and was left under the impression that his meeting with Burgoyne was left to his own discretion. In fact, he embarked on the capture of Philadelphia instead. Burgoyne's army became surrounded and had to surrender at Saratoga in October 1777 (see No. 272). As a result of this disaster, the northern colonies were virtually lost. Burgoyne had friends among the parliamentary opposition, who vigorously defended him against the government's attempt to make him a scapegoat for the carelessness of Lord George Germain (later Lord Sackville), Secretary of State for the American colonies and thus responsible for the organization of the war.

Lord George Germain to Sir Guy Carleton.[1]

1777, March 26. Whitehall.–

. . . [Explains that an earlier letter containing these instructions failed to arrive, as the aide-de-camp was unable to reach Quebec; he therefore now sends them.]

You will be informed by the contents thereof that as soon as you should have driven the rebel forces from the frontiers of Canada, it was his Majesty's pleasure that you should return to Quebec, and take with you such part of your army as in your judgment and discretion appeared sufficient for the defence of the province. That you should detach Lieut.-General Burgoyne, or such other officer as you should think most proper with the remainder of the troops, and direct the officer so detached

[1] Governor of Quebec.

to proceed with all possible expedition to join General Howe and to put himself under his command.

. . . [Reviews the events since the earlier letter was written, and the unexpected reinforcement of the rebel forces in New York and New Jersey.]

Upon these accounts, and with a view of quelling the rebellion as soon as possible, it is become highly necessary that the most speedy junction of the two armies should be effected, and therefore as the security and good government of Canada absolutely require your presence there, it is the King's determination to leave about 3,000 men under your command for the defence and duties of the province, and to employ the remainder of your army upon two expeditions–the one under the command of Lieut.-General Burgoyne, who is to force his way to Albany, and the other under the command of Lieut.-Colonel St. Leger, who is to make a diversion on the Mohawk River.

As this plan cannot advantageously be executed without the assistance of Canadians and Indians, his Majesty strongly recommends it to your care to furnish both expeditions with good and sufficient bodies of those men. And I am happy in knowing that your influence amongst them is so great that there can be no room to apprehend you will find it difficult to fulfil his Majesty's expectations.

In order that no time may be lost in entering upon these important undertakings, General Burgoyne has received orders to sail forthwith for Quebec, and that the intended operations may be maturely considered, and afterwards carried on in such a manner as is most likely to be followed by success, he is directed to consult with you upon the subject, and to form and adjust the plan, as you both shall think most conducive to his Majesty's service.

. . . [Particulars of the troops to remain in Canada.]

It is likewise his Majesty's pleasure that you put under the command of Lieut. General Burgoyne:–

The Grenadiers and Light Infantry of the Army (except of the 8th Regiment) and the 24th Regt. as the advanced corps under the command of Brigadier General Fraser	1,568
1st Brigade, battalion companies of the 9th, 21st and 47th Regiments, deducting a detachment of 50 from each corps to remain in Canada	1,194
2nd Brigade, battalion companies of the 20th, 53rd, and 62nd Regiments, deducting 50 from each corps as above	1,941
All the German troops except Hanau chasseurs and a detachment of 650	3,217
The Artillery excepting such parts as shall be necessary for the defence of Canada.	
	7,920

Together with as many Canadians and Indians as may be thought necessary for this service. And after having furnished him, in the fullest and completest manner, with artillery, stores, provisions, and every other article necessary for his expedition, and secured to him every assistance which it is in your power to afford and procure, you are to give him orders to pass Lake Champlain, and from thence, by the most vigorous exertion of the force under his command, to proceed with all expedition to Albany and put himself under the command of Sir William Howe.

From the King's knowledge of the great preparation made by you last year to secure the command of the lakes, and your attention to this part of the service during the winter his Majesty is led to expect that everything will be ready for General Burgoyne's passing the Lake by the time you and he shall have adjusted the plan of the expedition.

. . . [Particulars of troops for St. Leger's expedition.]

I shall write to Sir William Howe from hence by the first packet. But you will nevertheless endeavour to give him the earliest intelligence of this measure, and also direct Lieut.-General Burgoyne and Lieut.-Colonel St. Leger to neglect no opportunity of doing the same, that they may receive instructions from Sir William Howe. You will at the same time inform them that until they shall have received orders from Sir William Howe, it is his Majesty's pleasure that they act as exigencies may require and in such manner as they shall judge most proper for making an impression on the rebels, and bringing them to obedience, but that in so doing they must never lose view of their intended junctions with Sir William Howe as their principal objects. . . . *Copy. Endorsed.* "No. 6. Copy of this letter was sent to Sir William Howe in a letter from Mr. D'Oyley, by the *Somerset* man-of-war, which arrived at New York the 24th May. Sir Wm. Howe acknowledged the receipt of it in his letter, of the 5th July, No. 9."

271B. William Knox on the failure to send proper instructions to General Howe in 1777

(*Hist. MSS. Comm. Various Collections*, VI, *Knox MSS.*, p. 277.)

The following passage occurs in an account written some years later by William Knox, Colonial Under-Secretary, 1770–1782.

. . . There certainly was a weak place in Lord Sackville's defence, which was the want of an official communication to Howe of the plan and Burgoyne's Instructions, with orders for his co-operation; of which I was not only innocent, but it was owing to my interference that Howe had any knowledge of the business. Mr. D'Oyley, my then colleague, having been some time Deputy-Secretary at War, and the particular friend of Howe, had the entire conduct of the military business; and Burgoyne and he had settled the force and Instructions, and Burgoyne had gone in to the King and obtained his consent for having the command and everything in his own way; even the specific detachments and corps were all named and not left to Carleton to select.

When all was prepared, and I had them to compare and make up, Lord Sackville came down to the office to sign the letters on his way to Stoneland,[1] when I observed to him that there was no letter to Howe to acquaint him with the plan or what was

[1] His country house.

expected of him in consequence of it. His Lordship started, and D'Oyley stared, but said he would in a moment write a few lines. "So," says Lord Sackville, "my poor horses must stand in the street all the time, and I shan't be to my time anywhere." D'Oyley then said he had better go, and he would write from himself to Howe and inclose copies of Burgoyne's Instructions, which would tell him all that he would want to know; and with this his Lordship was satisfied, as it enabled him to keep his time, for he could never bear delay or disappointment; and D'Oyley sat down and writ a letter to Howe, but he neither shew'd it to me or gave a copy of it for the office, and if Howe had not acknowledged the receipt of it, with the copy of the Instructions to Burgoyne, we could not have proved that he ever saw them.

272. A German account of the Surrender at Saratoga, 17 October 1777

(Frederike, Baroness Riedesel, *Letters and Journals relating to the American Revolution*, trans. W. L. Stone (1867), pp. 125–128, 133–134.)

The writer was the wife of General Riedesel, in command of the Brunswick troops hired by the English Government for use in America. She accompanied her husband, and wrote these *Journals* for her mother and intimate friends in Germany.

[9 October 1777.]

Toward evening we at last came to Saratoga, which was only half an hour's march from the place where we had spent the whole day. I was wet through and through by the frequent rains, and was obliged to remain in the condition the entire night, as I had no place whatever where I could change my linen. I, therefore, seated myself before a good fire, and undressed my children; after which, we laid ourselves down together upon some straw. I asked General Phillips,[1] who came up to where we were, why we did not continue our retreat while there was yet time, as my husband had pledged himself to cover it, and bring the army through? "Poor woman," answered he, "I am amazed at you! Completely wet through, have you still the courage to wish to go further in this weather! Would that you were only our commanding general! He halts because he is tired, and intends to spend the night here and give us a supper." In this latter achievement, especially, General Burgoyne was very fond of indulging. He spent half the nights in singing and drinking, and amusing himself with the wife of a commissary, who was his mistress, and who, as well as he, loved champagne.

On the 10th, at seven o'clock in the morning, I drank some tea by way of refreshment; and we now hoped from one moment to another, that at last we would again get under way. General Burgoyne, in order to cover our retreat, caused the beautiful houses and mills at Saratoga, belonging to General Schuyler, to be burned. An English officer brought some excellent broth, which he shared with me, as I was not able to refuse his urgent entreaties. Thereupon we set out upon our march, but only as far as another place not far from where we had started. The greatest misery and the utmost

[1] Major-General William Phillips (1731?–1781) had served with General Riedesel under Prince Ferdinand of Brunswick in the Seven Years War. He was exchanged in 1781 and died during the campaign in Virginia that year.

disorder prevailed in the army. The commissaries had forgotten to distribute provisions among the troops. There were cattle enough, but not one had been killed. More than thirty officers came to me, who could endure hunger no longer. I had coffee and tea made for them, and divided among them all the provisions with which my carriage was constantly filled; for we had a cook who, although an arrant knave, was fruitful in all expedients, and often in the night crossed small rivers, in order to steal from the country people, sheep, poultry and pigs. He would then charge us a high price for them—a circumstance, however, that we only learned a long time afterward. At last my provisions were exhausted, and in despair at not being able to be of any farther help, I called to me Adjutant General Patterson,[1] who happened at that moment to be passing by, and said to him passionately: "Come and see for yourself these officers, who have been wounded in the common cause, and who now are in want of every thing, because they do not receive that which is due to them. It is, therefore, your duty to make a representation of this to the General." At this he was deeply moved, and the result was, that, a quarter of an hour afterward, General Burgoyne came to me himself and thanked me very pathetically for having reminded him of his duty. He added, moreover, that a general was much to be pitied when he was not properly served nor his commands obeyed. I replied, that I begged his pardon for having meddled in things which, I well knew, a woman had no business with, but that it was impossible to keep silent, when I saw so many brave men in want of every thing; and had nothing more to give them. Thereupon he thanked me once more (although I believe that in his heart he has never forgiven me this lashing), and went from me to the officers, and said to them, that he was very sorry for what had happened, but he had now through an order remedied every thing, but why had they not come to him as his cook stood always at their service. They answered that English officers were not accustomed to visit the kitchen of their general, and that they had received any morsel from me with pleasure, as they were convinced I had given it to them directly from my heart. He then gave the most express orders that the provisions should be properly distributed. This only hindered us anew, besides not in the least bettering our situation. The general seated himself at table, and the horses were harnessed to our calashes ready for departure. The whole army clamoured for a retreat, and my husband promised to make it possible, provided only that no time was lost. But General Burgoyne, to whom an order had been promised if he brought about a junction with the army of General Howe, could not determine upon this course, and lost every thing by his loitering. About two o'clock in the afternoon, the firing of cannon and small arms was again heard, and all was alarm and confusion. My husband sent me a message telling me to betake myself forthwith into a house which was not far from there. I seated myself in the calash with my children, and had scarcely driven up to the house, when I saw on the opposite side of the Hudson river, five or six men with guns, which were aimed at us. Almost involuntarily I threw the children on the bottom of the calash and myself over them. At the same instant the churls fired, and shattered the arm of a poor English soldier behind us, who was already wounded and was also on the point of retreating into the house. Immediately after our arrival a

[1] Probably Lord Petersham, one of Burgoyne's aides-de-camp.

frightful cannonade began, principally directed against the house in which we had sought shelter, probably because the enemy believed, from seeing so many people flocking around it, that all the generals made it their head-quarters. Alas! it harbored none but wounded soldiers, or women! We were finally obliged to take refuge in a cellar, in which I laid myself down in a corner not far from the door. My children laid down on the earth with their heads upon my lap, and in this manner we passed the entire night. A horrible stench, the cries of the children, and yet more than all this, my own anguish, prevented me from closing my eyes. . . .

In this horrible situation we remained six days. Finally, they spoke of capitulating, as by temporizing for so long a time, our retreat had been cut off. A cessation of hostilities took place, and my husband, who was thoroughly worn out, was able, for the first time in a long while, to lie down upon a bed. In order that his rest might not be in the least disturbed, I had a good bed made up for him in a little room; while I, with my children and both my maids laid down in a little parlor close by. But about one o'clock in the night, some one came and asked to speak to him. It was with the greatest reluctance that I found myself obliged to awaken him. I observed that the message did not please him, as he immediately sent the man back to head-quarters, and laid himself down again considerably out of humor. Soon after this, General Burgoyne requested the presence of all the generals and staff officers at a council-of-war, which was to be held early the next morning; in which he proposed to break the capitulation, already made with the enemy, in consequence of some false information just received. It was, however, finally decided, that this was neither practicable nor advisable; and this was fortunate for us, as the Americans said to us afterwards, that had the capitulation been broken we all would have been masacred; which they could have done the more easily, as we were not over four or five thousand men strong, and had given them time to bring together more than twenty thousand.

On the morning of the 16th of October, my husband was again obliged to go to his post, and I once more into my cellar.

On this day, a large amount of fresh meat was distributed among the officers, who, up to this time, had received only salted provisions, which had exceedingly aggravated the wounds of the men. The good woman who constantly supplied us with water, made us capital soup from the fresh meat. I had lost all appetite, and had the whole time taken nothing but crusts of bread dipped in wine. The wounded officers, my companions in misfortune, cut off the best piece of the beef and presented it to me, with a plate of soup. I said to them that I was not able to eat any thing, but as they saw it was absolutely necessary I should take some nourishment, they declared that they themselves would not touch a morsel until I had given them the satisfaction of taking some. I could no longer withstand their friendly entreaties, upon which they assured me that it made them very happy to be able to offer me the first good thing which they themselves enjoyed.

On the 17th of October the capitulation was consummated. The generals waited upon the American general-in-chief, Gates, and the troops laid down their arms, and surrendered themselves prisoners of war.

273A–B. Letters describing the engagement in Chesapeake Bay, 5 September 1781

After the disaster at Saratoga the northern colonies were lost, and the situation for the English Government was further gravely complicated by the entry of France into the war on the side of the Americans in 1778. The war became a struggle for the southern colonies, in which command of the sea was vital. The indecisive action in Chesapeake Bay, as a result of which the English fleet was obliged to return to New York to refit, leaving the French fleet undefeated, resulted in the surrender of Yorktown the following month (see No. 274). It is also interesting as illustrating the transition which was gradually taking place from the old, stereotyped system of signalling to a more elastic system (see No. 171). Dr. Julian Corbett has pointed out that Graves had served in the Channel fleet, where, under the influence of Kempenfelt and Howe, the more elastic system was already being used, whereas Hood had long served in North America and the West Indies, and was accustomed only to the orthodox system.

273A. Letter from Admiral Graves to Lord Sandwich, 14 September 1781

(*Sandwich Papers, 1771–82*, ed. G. R. Barnes and J. H. Owen, *Navy Records Society*, IV (1933), pp. 181–183.)

The writer is Rear-Admiral Thomas Graves (1725–1802), later first Baron Graves. His official dispatch on this engagement is in *Letters of Sir Samuel Hood, Navy Records Society* (1895), p. 40.

London at sea off the Chesapeake, 14 Sept. 1781.

My Lord–As I have done myself the honour of writing your Lordship more fully in a private letter than the official intercourse conveyed upon less important occasions, I will now in a matter of far greater moment follow the same method.

My last mentioned the arrival of Sir Samuel Hood[1] with fourteen sail of the line and four frigates, as well as of my sailing with five sail from the Hook, upon 30th August, proceeding without anchoring with the whole to the Chesapeake, as that place seemed to be the object of contention. The Rhode Island fleet were gone and had probably joined M. de Grasse.

The 5th September we discovered the whole at anchor from Cape Henry to the Middle Ground. They got under sail and stood out to meet us as we run down before the wind. The enclosed paper of Minutes will show the disposition and signals for that day.

My aim was to get close, to form parallel, extend with them, and attack all together; to this end I kept on until the van drew so near a shoal called the Middle Ground as to be in danger. I therefore wore the fleet all together and came to the same tack with the enemy, and lay with the main topsail to the mast dressing the line and pressing toward the enemy, until I thought the enemy's van were so much advanced as to offer the moment for successful attack; and I then gave the signal for close action–the enemy's centre and rear at this time were too far behind to succour their own van.

Your Lordship will perceive my constant attention by the Minutes was to press the enemy close. And to prevent the signal for the line becoming an impediment to the rear, I took in the signal for the line before any firing began and urged the close action, and only resumed the signal for the line for about five or seven minutes to push the ships ahead of me forward, and who were some of them upon my off beam. Unfortunately, the signal for the line was thought to be kept up until half after five, when the rear division bore down; but the fair occasion was gone.

[1] Sir Samuel Hood, Bart. (1724–1816), later first Viscount Hood, Graves's second-in-command (see also No. 275B).

The French centre and rear had pushed forward, until they approached our centre, kept away at long shot, and enabled their shattered van to take shelter by veering before the wind until they closed with their centre. This brought sunset; and soon after I discontinued the action, and sent a frigate to the van and rear, which brought me such a state of damages that we could only think of preserving the best appearance.

The French line was twenty-four heavy ships, ours nineteen; yet I think that had our efforts been made together, some of their van, four or five sail, must have been cut to pieces. The signal was not understood. I do not mean to blame anyone, my Lord. I hope we all did our best. . . .

The mutilated state of the squadron prevented my keeping the wind of the enemy, as well as several shifts of wind in their favour. The state of the *Terrible* and several of the West India ships, being in want of bread as well as of water, contribute to this misfortune. The *Shrewsbury*, *Intrepid*, *Ajax*, and *Montagu* full of complaints; and the *Terrible* had made the signal of distress in full view of the enemy. Several of the West India squadron were the shadow of ships more than the substance.

For my own particular, my Lord, I know not how to do more. If I err, it is from want of knowledge, not disinclination.

I believe the French have suffered much; their ships were cut from the van to the *Ville de Paris* in the centre.

Captain Molloy[1] behaved most gallantly and saved the *Shrewsbury*.

I fear much for our ships in York River in the Chesapeake, as well as for the Earl of Cornwallis. His post is a good one, and I understand he has 7000 veteran troops. We cannot succour him, nor venture to keep the sea any longer. I have &c.

273B. Letter from Admiral Hood to George Jackson, second Secretary to the Admiralty, 16 September 1781

(*Letters written by Sir Samuel Hood, in 1781–3*, ed. David Hannay, *Navy Records Society* (1895), pp. 28–31.)

Private. *Barfleur*, off the Delaware, 16th of September, 1781.
Going to New York.

My dear Jackson:–On the 5th instant, about 10 a.m., one of the look-out frigates made the signal for a fleet, and at eleven we plainly discovered twenty-four sail of French ships of the line and two frigates at anchor about Cape Henry, with their topsail yards hoisted aloft as a signal for getting under sail. Soon after they began to come out in a line of battle ahead, but by no means regular and connected, which afforded the British fleet a most glorious opening for making a close attack to manifest advantage, but it was not embraced; and as the French fleet was close hauled and the English line steered large, the two vans got pretty near, at four, when the signal for battle was hoisted–that part of the enemy's fleet being to windward of their centre, and the centre to windward of their rear. Our centre then upon a wind began to engage at the same time, but at a most *improper* distance (and the *London* had the signal for close action flying, as well as the signal for the line ahead at *half a cable* was under

[1] Anthony James Pye Molloy, nephew of Admiral Pye.

her topsails, with the main topsail to the mast, though the enemy's ships were pushing on), and our rear being barely within random shot did not fire while the signal for the line was flying. No. 1[1] contains my sentiments upon the truly unfortunate day, as committed to writing the next morning and which I mentioned to Mr. Graves when I attended his first summons on board the *London*. On the 6th it was calm the whole day, and in the evening Mr. Drake[2] and I were sent for, when Mr. Graves communicated to us intelligence he had received from the captains of the *Medea* and *Iris*, who had reconnoitered the Chesapeake, which was as follows: That a ship of the line, a 40-gun ship, and a frigate, were at anchor between the Horse Shoe Shoal and York Rivers, and that they saw three large ships coming down the bay, which they thought were of the line. Mr. Graves also made known to us a letter from Sir H. Clinton to General Earl Cornwallis, which he was desired to convey to his Lordship, if possible. The *Richmond* and *Iris* were detached upon that service, I fear to be cut off, and think the whole squadron should have gone; they might then not only most effectually have succoured Lord Cornwallis, but have destroyed the enemy's ships there. On the 7th and 8th, the enemy being to windward, had an opportunity of attacking us if they pleased, but showed no sort of inclination for it. On the 9th, the French fleet carried a press of sail, which proved to me beyond a doubt that De Grasse had other views than fighting, and I was distressed that Mr. Graves did not carry all the sail he could also, and endeavour to get off the Chesapeake before him; it appeared to me to be a measure of the utmost importance to keep the French out, and if they did get in they should first beat us. Instead of that, Mr. Graves put his Majesty's squadron on a contrary course just at dark, and at 8 o'clock made the signal to lay to. At daylight next morning nothing was to be seen of the French fleet from the *Barfleur*. This alarmed me exceedingly, and I debated with myself some little time whether I should venture to write Mr. Graves a few lines or not, as it is rather an awkward and unpleasant business to *send* advice to a senior officer. However, I at last took courage to do it, and having made the signal for my repeating frigate to come under the *Barfleur*'s stern, sent her with the letter of which No. 2 is a copy. This occasioned another summons to Mr. Drake and me on board the *London*, when I found, to my very great astonishment, Mr. Graves was as ignorant as myself where the French fleet was, and that no frigates were particularly ordered (for we had several with us) to watch and bring an account of the enemy's motions. The question was put to me, what was most proper to be done? to which I replied that I thought the letter I had taken the liberty to send had fully and clearly explained what my sentiments were, but if it was wished I should say more, it could only be that we should get into the Chesapeake to the succour of Lord Cornwallis and his brave troops if possible, but that I was afraid the opportunity of doing it was passed by, as doubtless De Grasse had most effectually barred the entrance against us, which was what human prudence suggested we *ought* to have done against him. On the 13th, early in the morning, I received the note No. 3 from Mr. Graves, and No. 4 is my answer to it, which again called Mr. Drake and me on board the *London*.

[1] The letter contained five enclosures.

[2] Rear-Admiral Francis Samuel Drake (d. 1789). Served at Quiberon Bay and at the battle of the Saintes (see No. 275A). Created baronet, 1782.

When the resolution contained in the paper No. 5 was taken,[1] there was nothing else left to be done, irksome and much to be lamented as the alternative was. I unbosom myself to you in great confidence that you will not show what I write to a single soul. With every affectionate wish for health and happiness, to you and yours,

I am, my dear Jackson,

Your most faithful and sincere

S.H.

274. Lord Cornwallis's account of the siege of Yorktown, 29 September–19 October 1781

(*Correspondence of Charles, first Marquis of Cornwallis*, ed. Charles Ross, I (1859), pp. 510–513.)

In March 1781 Cornwallis defeated General Greene at Guildford Court-house in North Carolina and advanced into Virginia, but this was disapproved of by Sir Henry Clinton, the commander-in-chief, who feared a combined French-American attack upon his headquarters at New York, and he ordered Cornwallis to go to Yorktown, where he would have access to the sea. Washington, eluding Clinton, joined Lafayette in Virginia, blockading Yorktown on the land side; and the French fleet under de Grasse, having driven the English fleet back to New York in September, had at this critical moment the command of the sea. Cornwallis was therefore obliged to surrender on 19 October.

Earl Cornwallis to Sir Henry Clinton.

Yorktown, Virginia, Oct. 20, 1781.

SIR,

I have the mortification to inform your Excellency that I have been forced to give up the posts of York and Gloucester, and to surrender the troops under my command, by capitulation, on the 19th instant, as prisoners of war to the combined forces of America and France.

I never saw this post in a very favourable light, but when I found I was to be attacked in it in so unprepared a state, by so powerful an army and artillery, nothing but the hopes of relief would have induced me to attempt its defence, for I would either have endeavoured to escape to New York by rapid marches from the Gloucester side, immediately on the arrival of General Washington's troops at Williamsburg, or I would, notwithstanding the disparity of numbers, have attacked them in the open field, where it might have been just possible that fortune would have favoured the gallantry of the handful of troops under my command, but being assured by your Excellency's letters that every possible means would be tried by the navy and army to relieve us, I could not think myself at liberty to venture upon either of those desperate attempts; therefore, after remaining for two days in a strong position in front of this place in hopes of being attacked, upon observing that the enemy were taking measures which could not fail of turning my left flank in a short time, and receiving on the second evening your letter of the 24th of September, informing me that the relief would sail about the 5th of October, I withdrew within the works on the night of the 29th of September, hoping by the labour and firmness of the soldiers to protract the defence until you could arrive. Everything was to be expected from

[1] That the squadron should return to New York to refit.

the spirit of the troops, but every disadvantage attended their labour, as the works were to be continued under the enemy's fire, and our stock of intrenching tools, which did not much exceed 400 when we began to work in the latter end of August, was now much diminished.

The enemy broke ground on the night of the 30th, and constructed on that night, and the two following days and nights, two redoubts, which, with some works that had belonged to our outward position, occupied a gorge between two creeks or ravines, which come from the river on each side of the town. On the night of the 6th of October they made their first parallel, extending from its right on the river, to a deep ravine on the left, nearly opposite to the centre of this place, and embracing our whole left at a distance of 600 yards. Having perfected this parallel, their batteries opened on the evening of the 9th against our left, and other batteries fired at the same time against a redoubt advanced over the creek upon our right, and defended by about 120 men of the 23rd Regiment and marines, who maintained that post with uncommon gallantry. The fire continued incessant from the heavy cannon, and from mortars and howitzers throwing shells from 8 to 16 inches, until all our guns on the left were silenced, our work much damaged, and our loss of men considerable. On the night of the 11th they began their second parallel, about 300 yards nearer to us. The troops being much weakened by sickness, as well as by the fire of the besiegers, and observing that the enemy had not only secured their flanks, but proceeded in every respect with the utmost regularity and caution, I could not venture so large sorties as to hope from them any considerable effect, but otherwise, I did everything in my power to interrupt this work by opening new embrasures for guns and keeping up a constant fire from all the howitzers and small mortars that we could man. On the evening of the 14th they assaulted and carried two redoubts that had been advanced about 300 yards for the purpose of delaying their approaches, and covering our left flank, and during the night included them in their second parallel, on which they continued to work with the utmost exertion. Being perfectly sensible that our works could not stand many hours after the opening of the batteries of that parallel, we not only continued a constant fire with all our mortars and every gun that could be brought to bear upon it, but a little before daybreak on the morning of the 16th, I ordered a sortie of about 350 men, under the direction of Lieut-Colonel Abercrombie,[1] to attack two batteries which appeared to be in the greatest forwardness, and to spike the guns. A detachment of Guards with the 80th company of Grenadiers, under the command of Lieut-Colonel Lake,[2] attacked the one, and one of light infantry, under the command of Major Armstrong, attacked the other, and both succeeded in forcing the redoubts that covered them, spiking 11 guns, and killing or wounding about 100 of the French troops, who had the guard of that part of the trenches, and with little loss on our side. This action, though extremely honourable to the officers and soldiers who executed it, proved of little public advantage, for the cannon having been spiked in a hurry, were soon rendered fit for service again, and before dark the whole parallel and batteries appeared to be nearly complete. At this time we knew that

[1] Robert Abercromby (1740–1827), later commander-in-chief in India, 1793.
[2] Gerard Lake (1744–1808), later first Viscount Lake. Commander-in-chief in India, 1800.

there was no part of the whole front attacked on which we could show a single gun, and our shells were nearly expended. I, therefore, had only to choose between preparing to surrender next day, or endeavouring to get off with the greatest part of the troops, and I determined to attempt the latter, reflecting that, though it should prove unsuccessful in its immediate object, it might at least delay the enemy in the prosecution of further enterprises. Sixteen large boats were prepared, and upon other pretexts were ordered to be in readiness to receive troops precisely at 10 o'clock. With these I hoped to pass the infantry during the night, abandoning our baggage, and leaving a detachment to capitulate for the townspeople, and the sick and wounded, on which subject a letter was ready to be delivered to General Washington. After making my arrangements with the utmost secrecy; the light infantry, greatest part of the Guards, and part of the 23rd Regiment, landed at Gloucester; but at this critical moment the weather, from being moderate and calm, changed to a most violent storm of wind and rain, and drove all the boats, some of which had troops on board, down the river. It was soon evident that the intended passage was impracticable, and the absence of the boats rendered it equally impossible to bring back the troops that had passed, which I had ordered about two in the morning. In this situation, with my little force divided, the enemy's batteries opened at daybreak. The passage between this place and Gloucester was much exposed, but the boats having now returned, they were ordered to bring back the troops that had passed during the night, and they joined us in the forenoon without much loss. Our works, in the mean time, were going to ruin, and not having been able to strengthen them by an abattis, nor in any other manner but by a slight fraizing, which the enemy's artillery were demolishing wherever they fired, my opinion entirely coincided with that of the engineer and principal officers of the army, that they were in many places assailable in the forenoon, and that by the continuance of the same fire for a few hours longer, they would be in such a state as to render it desperate, with our numbers, to attempt to maintain them. We at that time could not fire a single gun; only one 8-inch and little more than 100 Cohorn shells remained. A diversion by the French ships of war that lay at the mouth of the York River was to be expected. Our numbers had been diminished by the enemy's fire, but particularly by sickness, and the strength and spirits of those in the works were much exhausted, by the fatigue of constant watching and unremitting duty. Under all these circumstances, I thought it would have been wanton and inhuman to the last degree to sacrifice the lives of this small body of gallant soldiers, who had ever behaved with so much fidelity and courage, by exposing them to an assault which, from the numbers and precautions of the enemy, could not fail to succeed. I therefore proposed to capitulate; and I have the honour to enclose to your Excellency the copy of the correspondence between General Washington and me on that subject, and the terms of capitulation agreed upon. I sincerely lament that better could not be obtained, but I have neglected nothing in my power to alleviate the misfortune and distress of both officers and soldiers. The men are well clothed and provided with necessaries, and I trust will be regularly supplied by the means of the officers that are permitted to remain with them. The treatment, in general, that we have received from the enemy since our surrender has been perfectly good and proper, but the kindness and attention that has been shown us by the French officers in particular–their delicate sensibility of our situation–their generous and pressing offer of money, both public and private, to any amount–has really gone beyond what I can possibly describe, and will, I hope, make an impression on the breast of every British officer, whenever the fortune of war should put any of them into our power.

Although the event has been so unfortunate, the patience of the soldiers in bearing the greatest fatigues, and their firmness and intrepidity under a persevering fire of shot and shells that, I believe, has not often been exceeded, deserved the highest admiration and praise. A successful defence, however, in our situation was, perhaps, impossible, for the place could only be reckoned an intrenched camp subject in most places to enfilade, and the ground in general so disadvantageous that nothing but the necessity of fortifying it as a post to protect the navy, could have induced any person to erect works upon it. Our force diminished daily by sickness and other losses, and was reduced, when we offered to capitulate, on this side to little more than 3200 rank and file fit for duty, including officers, servants, and artificers; and at Gloucester about 600, including cavalry. The enemy's army consisted of upwards of 8000 French, nearly as many continentals, and 5000 militia. They brought an immense train of heavy artillery, most amply furnished with ammunition, and perfectly well manned.

The constant and universal cheerfulness and spirit of the officers in all hardships and danger deserve my warmest acknowledgments; and I have been particularly indebted to Brigadier-General O'Hara[1] and to Lieut.-Colonel Abercrombie, the former commanding on the right and the latter on the left, for their attention and exertion on every occasion. The detachment of the 23rd Regiment and of marines in the redoubt on the right, commanded by Captain Apthorpe, and the subsequent detachments, commanded by Lieut.-Colonel Johnson, deserve particular commendation. Captain Rochfort, who commanded the artillery, and indeed, every officer and soldier of that distinguished corps, and Lieutenant Sutherland, the commanding engineer, have merited in every respect my highest approbation; and I cannot sufficiently acknowledge my obligations to Captain Symonds,[2] who commanded His Majesty's ships, and to the other officers and seamen of the navy for their active and zealous co-operation.

I transmit returns of our killed and wounded. The loss of seamen and townspeople was likewise considerable.

I trust that your Excellency will please to hasten the return of the *Bonetta*[3] after landing her passengers, in compliance with the article of capitulation.

Lieut.-Colonel Abercrombie will have the honour to deliver this despatch, and is well qualified to explain to your Excellency every particular relating to our past and present situation.

I have the honour to be, &c.

CORNWALLIS.

[1] Charles O'Hara (1740?–1802), friend of Horace Walpole; Governor of Gibraltar, 1795–1802.

[2] Thomas Symonds (d. 1793). His ship was blown up in York River and he became a prisoner with Cornwallis's army.

[3] The sloop-of-war left at Cornwallis's disposal to carry an aide-de-camp with dispatches to Clinton.

275A–C. Documents illustrating the battle of the Saintes, 12 April 1782

In this battle the British fleet in the West Indies, under Admiral Rodney, with Admiral Hood as his second-in-command, defeated the French fleet under de Grasse and prevented the capture of Jamaica. Rodney was criticized for not following up the attack, as Hood wished, and destroying the French fleet.

275A. Letter from Admiral Rodney to Philip Stephens, Secretary to the Admiralty, describing the battle

(G. B. Mundy, *Life and Correspondence of Admiral Lord Rodney*, II (1830), pp. 255–258.)

Formidable, at sea,
April 14th, 1782.

It has pleased God, out of his Divine Providence, to grant to his Majesty's arms a most complete victory over the fleet of his enemy, commanded by Count de Grasse, who is himself captured, with the *Ville de Paris*, and four other ships of his fleet, besides one sunk in the action.

This important victory was obtained on the 12th instant, after a battle which lasted with unremitting fury, from seven in the morning till half-past six in the evening, when the setting sun put an end to the contest.

Both fleets have greatly suffered; but it is with the highest satisfaction I can assure their Lordships, that though the masts, sails, rigging, and hulls of the British fleet are damaged, yet the loss of men has been but small, considering the length of the battle, and the close action they so long sustained, in which both fleets looked upon the honour of their King and country to be most essentially concerned.

The great supply of naval stores lately arrived in the West Indies, will, I flatter myself, soon repair all the damages his Majesty's fleet has sustained.

The gallant behaviour of the officers and men of the fleet I have the honour to command, has been such as must for ever endear them to all lovers of their King and country.

The noble conduct of my second in command, Sir Samuel Hood, who in both actions most conspicuously exerted himself, demands my earnest encomiums. My third in command, Rear-Admiral Drake,[1] who with his division led the battle of the 12th, deserves the highest praise; nor can less be given to Commodore Affleck,[2] for his gallant behaviour in leading the centre division.

My own captain, Sir Charles Douglas,[3] merits every thing I can possibly say. His unremitted diligence and activity greatly eased me in the unavoidable fatigue of the day.

In short, I want words to express how sensible I am of the meritorious conduct of all the captains, officers, and men who had a share in this glorious victory obtained by their gallant exertions.

The enemy's whole army, consisting of 5500 men, were on board their ships of

[1] See No. 273B.
[2] Philip Affleck (1726–1799), served under Boscawen at Louisbourg, 1758.
[3] Sir Charles Douglas, Bart. (d. 1789), inventor of improvements in naval gunnery.

war. The destruction among them must be prodigious, as, for the greatest part of the action, every gun told; and their Lordships may judge what havoc must have been made, when the *Formidable* fired near eighty broadsides.

Inclosed I have the honour to send for their inspection, the British and French lines of battle, with an account of the killed and wounded, and damages sustained by his Majesty's fleet.

Lord Cranstoun, who acted as one of the captains of the *Formidable* during both actions, will have the honour of delivering these despatches. To him I must refer their Lordships for every minute particular they may wish to know, he being perfectly master of the whole transaction.

That the British flag may ever flourish in every quarter of the globe, is the most ardent wish of him, who has the honour of being, with great regard,

&c. &c. &c.

275B. Letter from Admiral Hood to George Jackson, second Secretary to the Admiralty, describing the battle

(*Letters written by Sir Samuel Hood*, ed. D. Hannay, *Navy Records Society* (1895), pp. 101–104.)

Barfleur, off Guadaloupe, 16th of April, 1782.
Private and Confidential.

My dear Sir.–I wished to have told you by the *Andromache*, but it was not in my power, that his Majesty's fleet had given such a beating to the *one* of France as no great fleet ever received before; and I was the less concerned at not being able to indulge my inclinations, as one of my gallant seconds (Goodall) promised me to write to you; my other second was Reynolds,[1] and I hold myself greatly indebted to both, as well as to every captain of my division, which on the 9th sustained two attacks at a short space of time one from the other, from the whole of the enemy's van and centre, between the islands of Guadaloupe and Dominica, while the *greatest part* of our centre and every ship of the rear were becalmed under the latter; and had De Grasse known his duty, he might have cut us up by pouring a succession of fresh ships upon us as long as he pleased, but we handled them very roughly, and they being to windward hauled off, and our fleet joined in the evening. Here Sir George did [not] exhibit much judgment in separating his fleet. The next morning the French ships were very far to windward. Sir George carried a stiff sail all day, neared them very much by sunset, and intended to have carried a plain sail all night, but by a strange blunder in Sir Charles Douglas, by making the signal for the *leading* ship to *shorten* sail, which was then under her topsails *only*, with her mizen topsails *aback*, the fleet lay to all night; at least, the centre and rear did so. Captain Byron can best tell what the van did, as he was employed the whole night in carrying messages between the *chief* and *third* in command. At daylight only a few of the leewardmost part of the

[1] John Reynolds (1713 ?–1788), Governor of Georgia, 1754–1759; Admiral, 1787.

French fleet could be seen from the masthead. We again worked to windward, and next morning by a lucky shift of wind we could look up three or four of the enemy's ships; this brought the whole down to succour them, and they formed on a contrary tack to our fleet. Every ship on both sides was engaged. Sir George Rodney cut through the rear of the French line so soon as my division (which was then the rear one) had passed the sternmost of the enemy's ships, which it was a long while in doing, it being almost a calm. I perceived the signal for the line of battle was down, upon which I got my boats out and towed the ship round towards the enemy, made all the sail I could (for we had soon after a little breeze), and threw out the signal for every ship of my division to do the same; and we took the *Caesar*, *Ardent*, and *Ville de Paris*. Observing the *Ville de Paris* to edge towards the *Barfleur* (for every ship of the enemy was then *flying* before the wind), I concluded the Count de Grasse had a mind to be my prisoner, as an old acquaintance, and therefore met his wishes, by *looking towards him*. As soon as I got within random shot he began to fire upon me, which I totally disregarded till I had *proved* by firing a single gun from the quarter-deck that I was *well* within *point blank*, when I opened so heavy a fire against him that in ten minutes he *struck*; this was just at sunset, and my boat had scarcely got on board when Sir George Rodney made the signal and brought to, and to my very great astonishment continued to lie to the *whole night*. After the truly glorious business of the 12th, I was most exceedingly disappointed in and mortified at the commander-in-chief. In the first instance, for not making the signal for a general chase the moment he hauled *that* down for the line of battle, which was about one o'clock: had he so done (as I *did* with my division in the *only mode* I *could*) I am very confident we should have had twenty sail of the enemy's ships of the line before dark. Instead of that he pursued only under his topsails (sometimes his foresail was set, and at others his mizen topsail a-back) the greatest part of the afternoon, though the *flying* enemy had all the sail set their very shattered state would allow. In the *next*, that he did not pursue under that easy sail, so as never to have lost sight of the enemy in the night, which would clearly and most undoubtedly have enabled him to have taken almost every ship the next day. But why he should bring the fleet to because the *Ville de Paris* was taken, I cannot reconcile. At sunrise next morning I went on board the *Formidable* to pay my compliments, and to try if it was possible to recover the mistake that had unfortunately been made, and so far prevailed upon Sir George to leave the ships of his own fleet, which were most disabled, to take care of the prizes and carry them to Jamaica, and to push on in search of the enemy with the rest. Though the *Barfleur* and other ships of my division had a topsail yard shot in two, and in other respects much maimed, not one but chased in the afternoon with steering sails below and aloft.

Had I, my dear friend, have had the honour of commanding his Majesty's noble fleet on the 12th, I may, without the imputation of much vanity, say the flag of England should now have graced the sterns of *upwards* of twenty sail of the enemy's ships of the line.

I herewith send you copies of a few letters between Sir George Rodney and me, and had he been my father, brother, or dearest and best friend I had, I could not have *proved* myself a *better second*, or have been more open, candid, and sincere in all I have suggested to him, from my zeal and ardour for our royal and most gracious master's service, and my extreme veneration and love for his sacred person, in competition with which no consideration in this world can ever stand.

I lamented to Sir George on the 13th that the signal for a general chase was not made when *that* for the line was hauled down, and that he did not continue to pursue, so as to keep sight of the enemy all night, to which he only answered, 'Come, we have done very handsomely as it is.' . . .

275C. Admiral Rodney's reasons for not pursuing the enemy after the victory

(G. B. Mundy, *Life and Correspondence of Admiral Lord Rodney*, II (1830), pp. 248–250.)

[No date.]

Reasons for not pursuing the Enemy after the victory.

1st. The length of the battle was such as to cripple the greatest part of the van and centre, and some ships of the rear, that to have pursued all night would have been highly improper, as the prisoners on board the prizes could not have been shifted, and those, with the much-crippled ships of the British fleet, might have been exposed to a recapture, as the night was extremely dark, and the enemy going off in a close connected body, might have defeated, by rotation, the ships that had come up with them, and thereby exposed the British fleet, after a victory, to a defeat; more especially as some of the British fleet were dispersed, and at a very considerable distance from each other; and I had reason to conclude that they would have done more damage to each other than to the enemy, during a night action, and considering the very great fatigue they had undergone during the battle of a whole day.

If I had inconsiderately bore away in the night, and left the two ninety-gun ships, the *Prince George* and *Duke*, and several others greatly damaged, with the *Ville de Paris*, and the captured ships, without shifting the prisoners, the enemy, who went off in a body of twenty-six ships of the line, might, by ordering two or three of their best-sailing ships or frigates to have shown lights at times, and by changing their course, have induced the British fleet to have followed them, while the main of their fleet, by hiding their lights, might have hauled their wind, and have been far to windward before day-light, and intercepted the captured ships, and the most crippled ships of the English; as likewise have had it in their power, while the British fleet had during the night gone far to leeward, and thereby rendered themselves incapable of gaining their station to windward, to have anchored in their own ports, and from thence have conquered the British islands of Antigua, Barbadoes, and St. Lucie, while the British fleet must, from the damages they had received, have repaired to Jamaica, as the condition of all their masts would not have permitted their return to Ste. Lucie; and though Jamaica might have been saved, the Windward Islands might have been lost.

276. A contemporary account of the defence of Gibraltar, 13–14 September 1782

(*Lives of the Lindsays*, ed. Lord Lindsay, III (1849), pp. 359–367.)

The investment of Gibraltar by the Spaniards was the immediate result of Spain's entry into the war on the American side in 1779, and the garrison under Sir George Eliott, later Baron Heathfield, withstood a siege of three years. Following the capture of Minorca by the French in 1781, the French and Spanish fleets made a final assault upon Gibraltar in September 1782. This combined military and naval operation is described in a letter from the Honourable Colin Lindsay, of the 73rd Highlanders, to the earl of Balcarres.

ASSAULT ON GIBRALTAR.

Gibraltar, Sept. 14, 1782.
Parole, King George and Victory.

I sit down with no small satisfaction to inform you, that last night and this morning we have defeated the attack of France and Spain, and that their Armada, so long in preparing, is totally destroyed before the eyes of their whole combined fleet and army.

We have experienced various sensations during the last four-and-twenty hours, and I seize the very first moment of leisure to relate to you the events as they happened, in as plain and concise a manner as my imagination will allow in speaking of the grandest and most awful objects which perhaps were ever exhibited.

In my two last letters I gave you a full detail of their immense preparations; they had nearly forty thousand men before the place, and piles of ammunition, which, to appearance, could never be all expended, even by their innumerable and heavy ordnance; I also described, as they appeared to us across the bay, their long labours upon ten large ships, mounting nearly two hundred pieces of heavy cannon. On these, by our information from various quarters, they had tried numberless experiments, and had clearly demonstrated to their people that they were impenetrable to cannon-ball and shells, that it was impossible to burn them, and that they could not be sunk. The truth of these assertions we found to be incontestable for many hours. Such was the situation of our affairs on the 11th instant, when my last letter to you was sent. On the 12th a large fleet appeared in the Straits from the west, but, the morning being hazy, it was not till they approached very near that we discovered them to be the combined fleets of France and Spain, consisting of forty-four sail of the line, including those that were here before, with three fifties and several frigates and fire-ships.

It must not now be denied that their arrival, which was totally unexpected, had some effect upon the spirits of the garrison. The numerous assaults which the enemy would now be enabled to make, on every side at once, could not fail, as was almost generally thought, to divide and distract our very inferior numbers; consisting, on the 1st of September, of five thousand seven hundred and one men, including seventy-two Corsicans, to which must be added near eight hundred seamen. Or, if this should not be the mode of attack, still it appeared to many that their repeated efforts could not fail to wear down the garrison with fatigue, when no man could ever quit his alarm-post, or, if he did, could obtain rest in his tent, exposed on every quarter to the cannon of the enemy.

In short, a degree of uneasiness existed until the hour of action was at hand; and those who had beheld the Duc de Crillon's formidable force by land, and frequently had stood his cannonade and bombardment, from nearly two hundred guns and mortars, with firmness of mind, were startled at the addition of a force greater than had been ever brought against any place in the history of the world; and at inventions which, though new, promised to be of a most extraordinary nature, and had inspired the enemy with the most unbounded confidence.

But, on the memorable 13th of September, at eight in the morning (the anniversary of the day when General Wolfe fell and Quebec was won), they appeared in motion on the other side, and all ideas of doubt or apprehension instantly gave way to others of a very different nature. The wind was strong at North-west, and their vessels had been so stationed that it was now directly in their stern.

Our artillery and additional gunners instantly repaired to their alarm-posts, till it should be seen at what and how many points of the garrison the efforts were to be directed. We then saw, what we could not have believed, that these unwieldy-looking machines sailed and steered with as much quickness and precision as the lightest ships, so that before nine o'clock, they were at their station. Their admiral, Don Buenaventura Moreno, did not bring up till his vessel had brushed the ground; they then all followed his example, and were anchored and moored almost instantaneously, without the least confusion; their right extending a little beyond the King's Bastion, their left nearly opposite to Waterport. Our batteries could not open upon them more than about ten minutes before they began their fire, seconded with all Monsieur de Crillon's artillery. The regiments remained undisturbed spectators on their respective parades to the South, except such officers as chose from curiosity to risk reprehension, and to be eye-witnesses of the gallantry of the artillery, or to animate by their presence, if necessary, the men of their respective corps employed on the batteries, or on duty in the ruins of the town.

But no man stood in need of encouragement; and yet it may be affirmed, that such a shower of shot and shells, in various directions, would have prevented any soldiers from doing their duty with effect, but such as had been in the daily habit of being exposed to danger for near two years.

Yet, after many hours of this trying situation, their efforts still appeared to be unsuccessful; they had long found the range of the battering ships of war, but now, when it was near sunset, their fire, and that from the enemy by land, continued still incessant, unabating, and well directed; penetrating through the merlons of the old thin wall between the bastions, killing and wounding numbers there, and, most probably, shaking the foundations in places which we did not see.

Our well-directed fire appeared, even at that hour, to have no effect; our balls seemed to rebound into the sea, and even such shells from the thirteen-inch mortars as struck glanced off the shelving roofs, composed of logs, and did them not the least apparent injury; yet shells of this nature, when loaded, weigh above two hundred pounds upon the ground, and where they fall from their elevation, as that weight increases every instant of the fall, we might suppose the shock to be irresistible; accordingly, wherever they fall on our most solid fortifications, they never fail to make such havock as requires time and prodigious labour to repair. Of what sort of materials, it was then naturally asked, can these formidable engines be made, to possess a repelling and elastic power to so very wonderful a degree?

It occurred to many that our artillery-men must soon be exhausted with mere bodily fatigue; and now, that the wind had subsided to a breeze, and the sea was smooth, their whole train of gun and mortar boats and all their ships of war were every hour expected; they however never appeared, and the men declared that, had they but a short refreshment, they could stand to the guns for eight-and-forty hours, whatever might be apprehended. One hundred sailors now arrived to their assistance, and their refreshment was a draught of water from the fountain and such salt provisions as could be brought. After this short abatement, their fire was renewed with redoubled vigour, and red-hot shot continued to be wheeled from the furnaces, and were put into the guns with the same speed and dexterity as if they had been cold. A little before dark the enemy hoisted a chequered flag, which inspired some hopes that all might not be quite so well with them on board; some lucky shot, entering their embrasures, were heard to ring against their cannon, and several ten-inch shells, sent with a fortunate horizontal direction from our howitzers, were seen to enter in the same manner, and some at last to stick in their sides, and afterwards explode; a considerable and increasing smoke was seen to issue from the vessel of their admiral, but was soon extinguished. To what purpose then was all our fire? It was directed against masses composed of cork, of wool stuffed hard, of the largest cables laid the one above the other, and of earth rammed in to fill up every chink. The very wood, it was said, was soaked in alum piece by piece, and, wherever it was exposed, was covered with strong plates of tin,–as to the effect of alum upon wood, we were entirely ignorant; but the other materials were such as every one knew could scarcely be made to catch the flames; and the same truth, it was feared, was but too applicable to the solid mass which they composed, six feet in thickness.

With these unflattering ideas in the mind of almost every person in the garrison, the night came on; the regiments and their officers retired to take repose, not knowing how soon they might be called upon to withstand the enemy's assault; and the Duc de Crillon had often publicly declared that one-half of his army should be sacrificed, were it necessary, in order that the other might obtain his point; and that, in such case, no quarter should be given to the garrison. The Marquis de Santa Cruz, from whose book all these operations have received almost implicit directions, strongly inculcates the same principle–that only the chief officers should be spared. Such declarations would have served our purpose well, and could not have failed, if the trial had been made, to have produced the most desperate resistance from every individual, when the principle of self-preservation was so intimately connected with their duty to their king and country; they were not lost for want of industry on the part of the officers in spreading them amongst the people.

It soon appeared, however, that ours was not a situation in which we could expect repose; and events, very different from what we expected, soon occurred to interrupt every disposition of that nature.

First, about eleven at night a boat was seen approaching to the shore, which, on its coming near, was discovered to be floating on its side, with twelve French soldiers and a Spanish officer upon it. The assistance they implored was sent to them, and they were received into the garrison. We learnt that the slaughter of the enemy on board had been so great, that a reinforcement had been necessary; that they had been volunteers for that purpose, and had almost reached the vessel they were destined for, which was manned entirely by the French, when a shot from the garrison overset the boat, which had fourscore men on board; that they had floated above four hours in the water, between both the fires; that the tide had driven them in beneath our walls, where they every instant expected destruction; but being received in a different manner, and treated with great humanity, they seemed thankful for their preservation; and, on being asked, they shook their heads and said, "that, if we thought to destroy the battering-ships by our artillery or by fire, we might spare ourselves the trouble of making the attempt; that whatever numbers we might kill on board could be of no avail, for their whole army and their fleet would eagerly crowd to supply the places of the slain, well knowing that it could not require any great length of time to make a sufficient breach." Nor were these opinions given with an air of gasconade; they appeared nothing more than the creed with which the enemy were universally inspired.

But the hour was at hand when these their sanguine expectations were to be as universally disappointed; for the admiral's ship burst out in flames a little after twelve,* and the cannonade from all of them began to slacken, while ours increased. Another soon, and then a third, took fire, not in the same manner as the admiral's, but slowly, and with a progress hardly visible for nearly two hours, till the flames gradually insinuated, and, established to a certain pitch, then rapidly increased in fury.

Then were heard the shrieks of horror, of agony, and despair, rendered more striking from the perfect stillness of the night, the scene illuminated to a distance and at hand as bright as day, closed in the background with the rugged declivity of Gibraltar, towering to the sky, and projecting upon every side defiance to two haughty nations.

The dawn was now approaching fast, and, our twelve-gun boats being manned, Captain Curtis,[1] of the navy, sallied forth with them, directing their fire against the approach of boats which might attempt to carry off the people from the ships; but nearly all of them had already retreated, and daylight increasing discovered only three boats just putting off from them, and several already at a distance. One of these three immediately was taken, one escaped, the third attempted to row off, but was struck by a ball from our boats, which wounded five men and pierced her sides.

But the attention of Captain Curtis was soon called to objects of a far more interesting nature to humanity, the entreating cries and gestures of the people that were still on board,–and every ship was now on fire but one; he listened only to the dictates of his feelings, and not to the suggestion that the gunpowder in the ships would soon catch fire. He was already in the midst of them, when one of them did actually blow up with a prodigious explosion, totally enveloping our boats, and involving the

* The fire previously kindled not having been sufficiently extinguished.

[1] Roger Curtis (1746–1816), knighted 1782; Rear-Admiral and created baronet, 1794.

whole garrison in a state of prodigious anxiety and suspense on their account,–this was not without cause, for one of them immediately was sunk; the people in her were saved, though not unhurt. Captain Curtis's helmsman was killed; fortunately he himself received no injury, and still persevered in his design of saving the lives of the enemy. He sent his boats on board of every ship, and nearly four hundred were rescued from destruction. He even ransacked the holds of several, and removed the wounded. Some infatuated wretches were employed in drinking spirits, and in search of plunder, losing thereby the opportunity of being saved. Of these there were in number three, who afterwards appeared upon the decks, cured of their intoxication by the terrors of approaching death in the various choice of horrible appearances, whether by the flames, by drowning, or explosion of the powder. In vain they stretched their supplicating hands, falling on their knees, entreating our assistance, uttering the yells of despair, and at length of madness. No boat durst venture to approach them; the most positive orders had been given that no one should attempt it, and the boats had been hauled on shore. Captain Curtis had well nigh been destroyed a second time, another vessel having blown up the moment after he had taken out the prisoners, some of whom were up to the neck in water to relieve themselves from the scorching heat; and, strange to say, the enemy directed every mortar they could bring to bear upon our boats while they were thus laudably employed. On these three wretches then the eyes of thousands were engaged for nearly an hour, forming a thousand fruitless wishes for their preservation, till two of them were seen at length to throw themselves reluctantly into the sea, and one remained the only victim. He retreated from the fire to various quarters of the vessel. He appeared repeatedly as if he was preparing some materials to float upon, and as often laid the enterprise aside. At length he was obliged to take refuge on the bow, still followed by the flames. He was at last compelled by them to quit his hold, which he contrived however to regain, after floundering in the water like a drowning man; he hardly was replaced when the wreck blew up, and he was seen no more. The other two were saved; one, though it appeared he could not swim, yet gained a piece of wood and paddled with his hands, assisted by the tide, till he gained the Spanish shore, none of our sentries offering to fire upon him. The other, by being a remarkably good swimmer, had well nigh lost his life; he at first depended too much upon himself, and, being soon hurried out of the reach of the floating materials, swam half way to Spain; he most likely would have gained his point, one deserter having swum into the garrison during the siege, the distance being about two miles, but the tide turned and hurried him back among the burning ships. Having fortunately gained a barrel, he was taken up by our boats after being above six hours in the water. His joy at being saved, and indeed that of all the prisoners, was next to being frantic.

When they were saved there then remained nothing to interrupt our attention to the vessels burning on the water, and the prodigious explosions which they formed; particularly one which contained their magazine. After it had burnt almost an hour, we felt everything near us tremble; there was a thunder from it which was dreadful; but the cloud which it formed was beyond all description, rolling its prodigious volumes one over another, mixed with fire, with earth, with smoke, and heavy bodies innumerable, on which the fancy formed various conjectures while they rose and fell, till, the whole arriving at its height in a gradual progress of near ten minutes, the top rolled downwards, forming the capital of a column of prodigious architecture, which a first-rate painter must have been eager, though perhaps unequal, to have imitated. Thus perished seven of their vessels before twelve at noon, and two were burnt down, the enemy having themselves drowned the powder. One remained entire, and we flattered ourselves that we should possess her as a trophy; but, for reasons unknown, a boat was sent on board of her by the governor's command, with an officer of the navy on board of her, and she was set on fire, blazing out in a far more sudden manner than any of those which had been burnt by the red shot.

The governor took his place on the King's Bastion during almost the whole of the attack, the lieutenant-governor on the South Bastion.

Such is hitherto the event of the long and immense preparations against Gibraltar, towards which, we flatter ourselves, the eyes of all Europe have been turned for some time past; a glorious recompense to the garrison for three years of a situation irksome and disagreeable from many causes which shall now be nameless.

C. TREATIES

277. The Barrier Treaty of 1715

(C. Jenkinson, *A Collection of all the Treaties of peace, alliance and commerce between Great-Britain and other Powers*, II (1785), pp. 148–173.)

This treaty marks the reversion by the Whigs, on coming to power in 1714, to the system of alliances between Britain, the United Provinces and the Emperor.

Treaty between Charles VI. *Emperor of the* Romans, *and Catholic King of* Spain, *on the one Part, and* George, *King of* Great Britain, *and the Lords the States General of the United Provinces of the* Netherlands, *on the other Part, for the entire Restitution of the* Spanish Netherlands, *to his Imperial and Catholic Majesty; with the Reserve of a strong and solid Barrier to the said* Netherlands, *in Favour of their High Mightinesses; as also of the yearly Payment of several great Sums, as well for the Maintenance of the said Barrier, as for the Reimbursement of those which were due to them before. Made at* Antwerp *the 15th of* November, 1715; *together with a separate Article relating to Mortgages of the same Date, and Forms of the Oaths to be taken by the Governors of Places, full Powers and Ratifications.*

Forasmuch as it pleased the Almighty to restore peace some time ago to Europe, and as nothing is more desirable and necessary, than as far as possible to re-establish and secure the common and public safety and tranquillity; and whereas the Lords the States General of the United Provinces have engaged to remit the Netherlands to his Imperial and Catholic Majesty Charles VI. as it was stipulated and agreed by the treaty made at the Hague the 7th of September, 1701, between his Imperial Majesty Leopold, of glorious memory, his Britannic Majesty William III. also of glorious memory, and the said States General, that the said potentates should agree upon what related to their reciprocal interests; particularly with respect to the manner of establishing the security of the Netherlands, to serve as a Barrier to Great Britain and the United Provinces, and with respect to the commerce of the inhabitants of Great Britain and the United Provinces. And whereas at present, his Imperial and Catholic Majesty, Charles VI. to whom the said Netherlands shall be remitted by this treaty, his Britannic Majesty King George, both at this time reigning and the lawful heirs and successors of the said Emperor, and King and the States General of the United Provinces, acting therein by the same principles of friendship, and with the same intention to procure and establish the same mutual security, and the more to confirm a strict union, have for that end named, commissioned, and appointed for the Ministers Plenipotentiaries, *viz.* [names and styles of plenipotentiaries follow]. Who being assembled in the city of Antwerp, which by common consent had been named for the place of congress, and having exchanged their full powers, copies whereof are inserted at the end of this treaty, after many conferences, have agreed for, and in the name of his Imperial and Catholic Majesty, his Britannic Majesty, and the Lords the States General, in the manner as follows:

I. The States General of the United Provinces, immediately after the exchange of the ratifications of the present treaty, shall, by virtue of the grand alliance in 1701, and of the engagements they have entered into since, remit to his Imperial and Catholic Majesty all the provinces and towns of the Netherlands, with their dependencies, as well those which were possessed by the late King of Spain, Charles II. of glorious memory, as those which were lately given up by his late Majesty the most Christian King, also of glorious memory; which provinces and towns together, as well those that are remitted by this present treaty, as those which were remitted before, shall hereafter be and compose in the whole or in part but one undividable, unalienable, and unchangeable domain, which shall be inseparable from the estates of the house of Austria in Germany, to be enjoyed by his Imperial and Catholic Majesty, his heirs and successors, in the full and irrevokable sovereignty and propriety; that is to say, with respect to the former, as they were enjoyed, or ought to have been enjoyed by the late King Charles II. of glorious memory, pursuant to the treaty of Ryswick; and with respect to the latter, in the same manner, and upon the same conditions as they were surrendered up, and remitted to the Lords the States General, by the late most Christian King, of glorious memory in favour of the most august house of Austria, and without any other charges, mortgages or engagements, which may have been constituted on the part of the States General, and to their profit.

II. His Imperial and Catholic Majesty promises and engages, that no province, city, place, fortress or territory of the said Netherlands, shall be surrendered, transferred, granted, or descended to the crown of France, nor to any prince or princes of the house and line of France, nor to any other who shall not be the successor, heir and possessor of the dominions of the house of Austria in Germany, either by donation, sale, exchange, marriage-contract, inheritance, testamentary succession, or *ab intestato*, or upon any other title or pretext whatsoever. So that not any province, city, place, fortress or territory of the said Netherlands, shall ever be subject to any other prince, than the successors of the said house of Austria; only excepting what was formerly yielded to the King of Prussia, and what shall be given up by the present treaty to the said Lords the States General.

III. Whereas the safety of the Austrian Netherlands will chiefly depend upon the number of troops that may be kept in the said Netherlands, and places that are to form the barrier which has been promised to the Lords the States General by the grand alliance, his Imperial and Catholic Majesty, and their high Mightinesses, have agreed constantly to maintain therein, at their own expence, a body of from 30 to 35000, whereof his Imperial and Catholic Majesty shall provide three fifths, and the States General two fifths. Provided always, that if his Imperial and Catholic Majesty shall diminish his quota, it shall be in the power of the said States General, to lessen theirs in proportion: and when there is any appearance of war or attack, the said body shall be augmented to 40,000 men, according to the same proportion; and, in case of actual war, a farther force shall be agreed upon, according as shall be found necessary. The repartition of the said troops in time of peace, for as much as concerns the places committed to the guard of the troops of their High Mightinesses, shall be made by them only, and the repartition of the rest by the governor of the Netherlands, by imparting reciprocally to each other the dispositions they shall have made.

IV. His Imperial and Catholic Majesty grants to the States General, a privative or separate garrison of their own troops, in the towns and castles of Namur and Tournay, and in the towns of Menin, Furnes, Warneton, Ypres, and Fort Knoque; and the States General engage themselves, not to employ any troops in the said places, which although in their own pay, belong to any prince or nation that may be at war with, or suspected to be in engagements contrary to the interests of his Imperial and Catholic Majesty.

V. It is agreed, that in the town of Dendermonde there shall be a common garrison, which shall be composed, for the present, of one battalion of Imperial troops, and one batallion of the troops of the States General; and that if hereafter it should be necessary to augment the said garrison, such augmentation shall be made equally by the troops of both parties, and by mutual concert. The governor shall be put in by his Imperial and Catholic Majesty, and, together with the subaltern officers, shall take an oath to the States General, never to do, or suffer any thing to be done in the said town, which may be prejudicial to their service, with respect to the preservation of the town and garrison: and he shall be obliged, by the said oath, to grant free passage to their troops always, and as often as they shall desire; provided it be demanded before-hand, and that it be for a moderate number at a time.

VI. His Imperial and Catholic Majesty consents also, that in the places hereby granted to the States General, to hold their separate garrisons in, they may place such governors, commanders, and other officers that compose the state major as they shall think fit, on condition that they shall be no charge to his Imperial and Catholic Majesty nor to the provinces and towns, unless it be for convenient lodging, and the emoluments accruing from the fortifications, and that they be not persons who may be disagreeable or suspected to his Majesty, for particular reasons that may be given.

VII. Which governors, commanders and officers, shall be entirely and separately dependent on, and subject to the sole orders and jurisdiction of the States General, for all that concerns the defence, guard, security, and all other military affairs of their places. But the said governors, as well as their subalterns, shall be obliged to take [a]n oath to his Imperial and Catholic Majesty, to keep the said places true to the sovereignty of the house of Austria, and not to intermeddle in any other affairs, according to the form that is agreed upon and inserted at the end of this treaty. . . .

IX. His Imperial Catholic Majesty grants to the troops of the States General, wherever they are in garrison, the free exercise of their religion, so as to be in particular places convenient and proportionable to the number of the garrison, which the magistrates shall assign and maintain in every town and place where there has been none assigned already, and to which places no external mark of a church shall be given: and it shall be strictly enjoined by both parties, to the civil and military officers, as also to ecclesiastics, and all others concerned, to hinder all occasion of scandal and controversies that may arise upon the subject of religion; and when any dispute or difficulty shall happen, both parties shall amicably accommodate it. And as for religion, with regard to the inhabitants of the Austrian Netherlands, all things shall continue and remain on the same foot they were during the reign of Charles II. of glorious memory.

X. All the ammunition, artillery, and arms of the States General, as also materials for the fortifications, corn in time of scarcity, provisions to put into the magazines, when there is an appearance of war; and moreover, the cloth and furniture for cloathing the soldiers, which shall be certified to be designed for that use, shall pass freely, and without paying any customs or tolls, by virtue of passports which shall be demanded and granted, upon the specification signed; on condition nevertheless, that at the first custom-house of his Imperial and Catholic Majesty, where the said provisions, materials, arms and mountings shall enter, and at the place where they are to be unladen, the boats and other carriages may be duly visited, to hinder the mixture of other merchandize therewith, and to prevent fraud and abuse, against which it shall be always lawful to take such precautions, as length of time and experience shall shew to be necessary; and the governors and their subalterns shall not be permitted in any manner whatsoever, to hinder the effect of this article.

XI. The States General may change their garrisons, and the disposition of the troops in the towns and places committed to their particular guard, according as they shall judge proper, . . .

XIII. The States General may, at their own cost and expence, cause the said towns and places to be fortified, either by new works, or by causing the old to be repaired, and maintain them, and generally provide all that they shall find necessary for the security and defence of the said towns and places, excepting that they shall not cause new fortifications to be built, without giving notice of it before-hand, to the governor-general of the Netherlands, and having his opinion and advice thereupon, nor bring the charges thereof to the account of his Imperial and Catholic Majesty, or the country, without his said Majesty's consent. . . .

XVII. As it appears by the experience of the last war, that for securing the frontiers of the States General in Flanders, it was necessary to leave so many considerable bodies of troops there, that the army was thereby very much weakened: to prevent this inconvenience, and the better to secure the said frontiers for the future, his Imperial and Catholic Majesty yields to the States General such forts, and as much of the territory of the Austrian Flanders bordering upon the said frontiers, as they shall want to make the necessary inundations, and for covering them from the Schelde to the sea, in places where they are not already sufficiently secured, and where they cannot be secured by making inundations upon those lands only that already belong to the States General.

For this purpose his Imperial and Catholic Majesty agrees and approves, that the limits of the States General in Flanders, [delimitation of frontiers of Flanders follows].
. . .

And the Roman-catholic religion shall be preserved and maintained in the places given up as above, on the same footing as it is now, and was exercised in the reign of King Charles II. of glorious memory; and all the privileges of the inhabitants shall be preserved and maintained in like manner. . . .

XVIII. His Imperial and Catholic Majesty yields to their High Mightinesses the States General for ever, in full sovereignty and propriety, the town of Venlo in the upper part of Guelderland, [and other territories].

Provided, and be it understood, that this surrender is made with this express clause, that the statutes, antient customs, and in general, all privileges civil and ecclesiastical, as well with regard to the magistrates and private persons, as to the churches, convents, monasteries, schools, seminaries, hospitals, and other public places, with all their appurtenancies and dependencies, as also the diocesan right of bishop of the Ruremonde, and in general every thing that concerns the rights, liberties, immunities, functions, usages, ceremonies, and the exercise of the Catholic religion, shall be preserved and subsist without any charge [change?] or innovation, either directly or indirectly, in all the places yielded as above, in the same manner as in the time of King Charles II. of glorious memory, and as it shall be explained on both sides more fully, in case any dispute happens on that account; and the officers of the magistracy and the police, shall be given to none but persons of the Catholic religion. . . .

XIX. In consideration of the great charge and extraordinary expence which the States General are unavoidably obliged to be at, as well for maintaining the great number of troops which they are engaged by the present treaty to keep in the towns above named, as for supplying the great sums absolutely necessary for the maintenance and repair of the fortifications of the said places, and for furnishing them with ammunition and provisions, his Imperial and Catholic Majesty engages and promises to cause to be annually paid to the States General, the Sum of 500,000 crowns, or 1,250,000 florins Dutch money over and above the revenue of the part of the upper quarter of Guelderland, given up by his Imperial and Catholic Majesty in propriety to the States General, by the 18th article of the present treaty, as also over and above the cost of lodging the troops, according to the regulation made in the year 1698, in the manner as shall be particularly agreed upon: which sum of 500,000 crowns, or 1,250,000 florins Dutch money, shall be secured and mortgaged, as it is by this article secured and mortgaged upon all the revenues of the Austrian Netherlands in general, including therein the countries yielded up by France; and in particular, upon the clear neat revenues of the provinces of Brabant and Flanders, and of the countries, towns, chatellanies and dependencies yielded up by France, according as it is more particularly specified by a separate article, as well for the said mortgage, as for the means and terms of receiving the said sums. . . .

XX. His Imperial and Catholic Majesty, by this article, confirms and ratifies the capitulations granted to the provinces and towns of the Netherlands, heretofore called Spanish, at the time of their reduction to the obedience of his said Majesty, together with the general administration of the said country therein, exercised by Great Britain, and the States General of the United Provinces, the lawful sovereign having been represented by their ministers who resided at Brussels, and by the council of state commissioned to the general government of the said Netherlands, in pursuance of the power and instructions that were given them, and of the requests that were made on the part of the two powers, as well in matters of regale, justice and police, as of the finances; as also the particular administration of the states, provinces, colleges, towns and communities in the open country, as also in the sovereign courts of justice, and the other subaltern courts and judges.

Which acts of police, regale, justice, and the finances, shall subsist and have their full and entire effect, according to the tenor of the said acts and sentences passed: the whole in the same manner, as if they had been done by the lawful sovereign of the country, and under his government. . . .

[XXII, XXIII and XXIV regulate in detail payment of the principal and interest on the existing public debts of the Netherlands, for which Charles VI made himself responsible.] . . .

XXVI. As to commerce, it is agreed, that the ships, merchandize and commodities coming from Great-Britain and the United Provinces, and entering into the Austrian Netherlands, and also the ships, merchandize, and commodities going from the said Netherlands to Great Britain and the United Provinces, shall pay no other duties of importation or exportation, than what are paid upon the present foot, and particularly such as were regulated before the signing of the present treaty, according to the request made to the council of state at Brussels, by the ministers of the two powers, dated the 6th of November: and so every thing shall remain, continue, and subsist generally upon the same foot, without any alteration, innovation, diminution, or augmentation, under any pretence whatsoever, till his Imperial and Catholic Majesty, his Britannic Majesty, and the Lords the States General shall otherwise appoint by a treaty of commerce to be made as soon as possible. In the mean time, the commerce, and all that depends on it between the subjects of his Imperial and Catholic Majesty in the Austrian Netherlands, and those of the United Provinces, in the whole and in part, shall remain upon the foot established, and in the manner appointed by the articles of the treaty concerning commerce, made at Munster, the 30th of January, 1648, between his Majesty King Philip IV. of glorious memory, and the said Lords the States General of the United Provinces; which articles are now confirmed by the present treaty. . . .

XXVIII. And for the further security and performance of the present treaty, his Britannic Majesty promises and engages to confirm and guarantee it, in all its points and articles, as he does by these presents accordingly confirm and enter into a guaranty of it.

XXIX. The present treaty shall be ratified and approved by his Imperial and Catholic Majesty, by his Britannic Majesty, and by the Lords the States General of the United Provinces; and the ratifications shall be delivered within six weeks, or sooner, if possible, to be computed from the day of signing. In witness whereof, we the Ministers Plenipotentiary of his Imperial and Catholic Majesty, his Britannic Majesty, and the Lords the States General, by virtue of our respective full powers, have in their names signed these presents, and thereto affixed the seal of our arms. Done at Antwerp, Nov. 15, 1715.

(L.S.) *J.L.C. a Konigsegg.*
(L.S.) *W. Cadogan.*
(L.S.) *B. v. Dussen.*
(L.S.) *The Count de Rechteren.*
(L.S.) *S. L. Gockinga.*
(L.S.) *Adr. v. Borssele Sig. v. Geldermalsen.*

[Separate article makes detailed arrangements for payment of the subsidy due to United Provinces.]

278. The Triple Alliance Treaty, 4 January 1717

(C. Jenkinson, *Collection of Treaties . . .*, II, pp. 185–194.)

The Triple Alliance marks the overthrow of the traditional Whig foreign policy of regarding France as Britain's natural enemy. After the death of Louis XIV Britain and France had a joint interest in maintaining the Utrecht settlement, both because they needed a period of peace and because the exclusion of Philip V from the succession to the French crown suited the Regent Orleans as next heir to Louis XV.

A Treaty of Alliance between Lewis XV. *King of* France *and* Navarre, George *King of* Great Britain, *and the Lords the States General of the* United Provinces, *for the Maintenance and Guarantee of the Treaties of Peace made at* Utrecht *in* 1713, *and particularly for maintaining the Order of the Succession to the Crowns of* France *and* England, *as established by the said Treaties, and for the Demolition of the Port of* Mardyke. *Concluded at the* Hague, Jan. 4, 1717.

LEWIS by the Grace of God King of France and Navarre, to all who shall see these presents, greeting. Whereas our trusty and well-beloved the Abbot du Bois, Counsellor in ordinary in our Council of State; and our trusty and well-beloved the Sieur de Chateauneuf, Marquis de Castagnere, Honorary Counsellor of our Court of Parliament at Paris, our Ambassadors Extraordinary and Plenipotentiary, have by virtue of the full powers which we gave them, agreed to conclude and sign the following treaty of defensive alliance, on the 4th of this present month of January with William Lord Cadogan, Baron of Reading, Knight of the order of St. Andrew, Master of the Robes to our most dearly beloved brother the King of Great Britain, Lieutenant General of his armies, Colonel of the second regiment of his Guards, Governor of the Isle of Wight, and his Ambassador Extraordinary and Plenipotentiary, who was also furnished with full powers; and with the Sieur John Van Essen, Burgomaster of Zutphen, Curator of the University of Harderwick; [and others] in quality of Plenipotentiaries from their High Mightinesses, our very dear and great friends the States General of the United Provinces of the Netherlands, likewise furnished with full powers.

Forasmuch as the most serene and most mighty Prince Lewis XV. by the grace of God, most Christian King of France and Navarre, the most serene and most mighty Prince George, by the grace of God King of Great Britain, Duke of Brunswick and Lunenberg, Elector of the Holy Roman Empire, &c. and the high and mighty Lords the States General of the United Provinces of the Netherlands, being desirous to corroborate more and more the peace that is established between their kingdoms and states respectively to remove entirely on every side, all cause of jealousy, which might in any manner whatsoever disturb the tranquillity of their dominions, and to bind yet more strongly by new ties, that friendship which is between them, in order to attain so salutary an end, they have thought it necessary to come to an agreement between themselves: and to that purpose their Majesties aforesaid, and the said Lords the States General have named, *viz.*

[Plenipotentiaries are named by the three contracting parties.]

Who after having communicated their full powers to one another, and after having exchanged the same according to custom, agreed upon a treaty of defensive alliance, between the most Christian King, the King of Great Britain, and the lords the States General of the United Provinces, their kingdoms, dominions, and subjects on the following conditions.

I. That from this day forth and for ever, there shall be a true, firm, and inviolable peace, a most sincere and intimate friendship, and a most strict alliance and union between the said most serene Kings, their heirs and successors, and the lords the States General, their lands, countries, and towns respectively, and their subjects and inhabitants, as well within as out of Europe: and that the same be preserved and cultivated in such manner, that the contracting parties may faithfully and reciprocally reap their profit and advantage thereby; and that by the most convenient measures all losses and damages which might befal them, may be averted and prevented.

II. And forasmuch as it is known by experience, that the near abode of the person, who in the life-time of King James II. did take upon him the title of Prince of Wales, and since the death of the said King has taken the title of King of Great Britain, may excite commotions and troubles in Great Britain, and the dominions depending thereon, it is agreed upon and determined, that his most serene Majesty the most Christian King do oblige himself, by the present treaty, to engage the said person to depart out of the country of Avignon, and to go and take up his residence on the other side of the Alps, immediately after the signing of the treaty, and before the exchange of the ratifications. And the most Christian King, yet farther to testify his sincere desire, not only to observe all the engagements which the crown of France has formerly entered into concerning the said person, religiously and inviolably, but also to prevent all manner of suspicion and diffidence for the future; does again promise and engage for himself, his heirs and successors, not to give, or furnish at any time whatever, directly or indirectly, either by sea or by land, any advice, aid, or assistance, by money, arms, ammunition, military stores, ships, soldiers, seamen, or any other manner of help whatsoever, to the said person, who takes upon himself the title before mentioned, or to any other persons whatever, who having commission from him may in consequence thereof disturb the tranquillity of Great Britain by open war, or by secret conspiracies, or insurrections and rebellions, and make opposition to the government of his Britannic Majesty.

Moreover, the most Christian King promises and engages, not to permit the person above designed to return at any time hereafter to Avignon or to pass through the lands depending on the crown of France; on pretence of returning either to Avignon or to Lorrain, or so much as to set foot on any part of his most Christian Majesty's dominions, much less to reside there under any name or appearance whatsoever.

III. The said most serene Kings and the said Lords the States General do also promise and engage themselves, reciprocally to refuse all kind of refuge and protection to the subjects of either of them, who have been, or shall be declared rebels, whenever it shall be requested by the contracting party, whose subjects those rebels shall be known to be, and likewise to compel the said rebels to depart out of the dominions under their obedience, in a week's time after the minister of the said ally shall have required, it in his master's name.

IV. And the most Christian King being sincerely desirous, that every thing heretofore agreed on with the crown of France, concerning the town of Dunkirk, may be fully executed, and that nothing be omitted which the King of Great Britain may think necessary for the entire destruction of the port of Dunkirk, and to prevent all manner of suspicion that there is an intention to make a new port at the canal at Mardyke, and to put it to some other use than draining off the waters which might drown the country, and carrying on the commerce necessary for the subsistence and maintenance of the people on that part of the Netherlands, which is only to be carried on by small boats, that are not allowed to be above 16 feet wide; his most Christian Majesty doth engage, and promise to cause every thing to be executed, which the Sieur d'Ibberville, his most Christian Majesty's envoy, having full power for that purpose, did agree to, at Hampton-Court, as is contained in a memorial of the $\frac{19}{30}$ of November, 1716, signed by the Sieur d'Ibberville, and by the Lord Viscount Townshend, and Mr. Methuen, secretaries of state for Great Britain, which is as follows: [detailed arrangements for destruction of canals and fortifications at Mardyke and Dunkirk.]

V. It being the true end and purpose of this alliance, between the said most serene Kings, and the Lords the States General, to preserve and maintain reciprocally the peace and tranquillity of their kingdoms, dominions, and provinces, established by the late treaties of peace, concluded and signed at Utrecht the 11th of April, 1713, between their most serene Majesties the most Christian King, the Queen of Great Britain, and the said high and mighty Lords the States General of the United Provinces: it is agreed upon and concluded, that all and singular the articles of the said treaties of peace, as far as they relate to the interest of the said three powers respectively, and of each of them in particular, and likewise the successions to the crown of Great Britain in the Protestant line, and to the crown of France, according to the said treaties, shall remain in their full force and vigour; and that the said most serene Kings and the said Lords the States General do promise their reciprocal guarantee for the execution of all the conventions contained in the said articles, so far as they regard the successions and interests of the said kingdoms and states as above said, and likewise for the maintaining and defending of all the kingdoms, provinces, states, rights, immunities, and advantages, which each of the said allies respectively shall really be possessed of, at the time of the signing of this alliance. And for this end the said most serene Kings, and the Lords the States General, have agreed and concluded between themselves, that if any one of the said allies be attacked by the arms of any prince or state whatever, the other allies shall interpose their good offices with the aggressor, to procure satisfaction to the party offended, and to engage the aggressor to abstain entirely from all kinds of hostility.

VI. But if such good offices have not the expected effect, to reconcile the two parties, and to obtain a satisfaction and reparation of damages within two months, then those of the allies who have not been attacked shall be obliged without delay to assist their ally, and to furnish him the succours hereafter mentioned, *viz.*

The most Christian King, 8,000 foot and 2,000 horse.

The King of Great Britain, 8,000 foot and 2,000 horse.

The States General, 4,000 foot and 1,000 horse.

But if the ally who shall be engaged in a war, as aforesaid, chuse rather to have succours by sea, or even prefers money to either sea or land forces, the same shall be left to his discretion, provided a proportion be always observed between the sums given, and the number of troops above specified.

And to the end that there may be no dispute about this point, it is stipulated, that 1000 foot soldiers shall be valued at the sum of 10,000 livres per month, and 1000 horse at the sum of 30,000 livres per month, Dutch money, reckoning 12 months in the year; and succours by sea shall be valued at the same proportion.

VII. It is likewise stipulated and agreed upon, that if the kingdoms, countries or provinces, of any of the allies are disturbed by intestine quarrels, or by rebellions on account of the said successions, or under any other pretext whatever, the ally thus in trouble shall have full right to demand of his allies the succours abovementioned, or such part thereof as he shall judge necessary, at the cost and expence of the allies that are obliged to furnish these succours, which shall be sent within the space of two months after they are demanded; saving, however, as is aforesaid, to the party that requires them, his free choice to demand succours either by land or sea: and the allies shall be reimbursed of what charges they shall be at for the succours given, by virtue of this article, within the space of a year after those troubles are pacified and appeased. But in case the said succours be not sufficient, the said allies shall agree in concert to furnish a greater number, and also if the case require it, they shall declare war against the aggressors, and assist one another with all their forces.

VIII. The present treaty shall be ratified by their most Christian and Britannic Majesties, and the Lords the States General, and the letters of ratification shall be delivered in due form on all sides, within the space of four weeks, or sooner if possible, counting from the day of signing these presents.

In witness whereof we the underwritten, being vested with full powers from their most Christian and Britannic Majesties, and the Lords the States General of the United Provinces, have in their names signed this present treaty, and caused the seals of our arms to be thereto affixed. Done at the Hague, Jan. 4, 1717.

Signed by the plenipotentiaries above named in the preamble to the treaty.

The separate Article, signed and ratified between France *and* Holland.

[Limits reciprocal guarantees to European territories of France and the States General.]

279. The second Treaty of Vienna, 16 March 1731

(C. Jenkinson, *Collection of Treaties . . .*, II, pp. 318–325.)

This treaty marked the triumph of the policy of Walpole and Newcastle over that of Townshend, whose policy of supporting Spain over the Italian duchies had produced the Treaty of Seville in 1729. Britain gained the suppression of the Ostend Company, but had to guarantee the Pragmatic Sanction, committing her to the support of Maria Theresa on the death of the Emperor.

Treaty of Peace and Alliance, between the Emperor Charles VI. *and* George II. *King of* Great Britain, *in which the States of the* United Provinces *of the* Netherlands *are included. Made at* Vienna, *the 16th of* March, 1731.

In the Name of the most Holy and Undivided Trinity, Amen.

To all to whom it does or may any way appertain. Be it known, that the most serene and most potent Prince and Lord, Charles VI, Emperor of the Romans, &c. and the most serene and most potent Prince and Lord, George II. King of Great Britain, France and Ireland, together with the High and Mighty Lords the States General of the United Provinces of the Netherlands, having taken into consideration the present unsettled and perplexed state of affairs in Europe, seriously bethought themselves of finding proper methods, not only to prevent those evils which must naturally arise from the cavils and divisions that were daily increasing, but also to establish the public tranquillity upon a sure and lasting foundation, and in as easy and speedy a manner as possible: For this end their said Majesties and the said States General, being fully animated with a sincere desire to promote so wholesome a work, and to bring it to perfection, judged it expedient to agree among themselves upon certain general conditions, which might serve as the basis for reconciling the animosities, and settling the differences of the chief Princes of Europe, which as they are heightened among themselves, do greatly endanger the public tranquillity.

For which purpose, the most high Prince and Lord, Eugene Prince of Savoy and Piedmont, &c., and also the most illustrious Lord, Philip Lewis, Hereditary Treasurer of the Holy Roman Empire, count of Zinzendorf, &c., and also the most illustrious Lord, Gundacker Thomas, count of the holy Roman Empire, &c., on the part of his Sacred Imperial and Catholic Majesty; and Thomas Robinson, Esq., minister of his Majesty of Great Britain to his said Imperial and Catholic Majesty, on the part of his Majesty of Great Britain; and on the part of the High and Mighty States of the United Provinces of the Netherlands; being all furnished with full powers, after they had held conferences together, and exchanged their credential letter and full powers, agreed upon the following articles and conditions.

I. That there shall be from this time forward, between his sacred Imperial Catholic Majesty, his sacred royal Majesty of Great Britain, the heirs and successors of both, and the High and Mighty Lords the States General of the United Provinces of the Netherlands, a firm, sincere, and inviolable friendship, for the mutual advantage of the Provinces and subjects belonging to each of the contracting powers; and that this peace be so established, that each of the contractors shall be obliged to defend the territories and subjects of the others; to maintain the peace, and promote the advantages of the other contractors as much as their own; and to prevent and avert all damages and injuries of every kind whatsoever, which might be done to them. For this end, all the former treaties or conventions of peace, friendship and alliance, shall have their full effect, and shall preserve in all and every part their full force and virtue, and shall even be looked upon as renewed and confirmed by virtue of the present treaty, except only such articles, clauses, and conditions, from which it has been thought fit to derogate by the present Treaty. And moreover, the said contracting parties have expressly obliged themselves, by virtue of this present article, to a mutual defence, or as it is called guaranty of all the kingdoms, states, and territories which each of them possesses, and even of the rights and immunities each of them enjoys, or ought to enjoy, in such manner, that they have mutually declared and promised to one another, that they will, with all their forces oppose the enterprises of all and every one who shall (perhaps contrary to expectation) undertake to disturb any of the contractors, or their heirs and successors, in the peaceable possession of their kingdoms, states, provinces, lands, rights, and immunities, which each of the contracting parties doth or ought to enjoy, at the time of the conclusion of the present treaty.

II. Moreover, as it has been frequently remonstrated on the part of his Imperial and Catholic Majesty, that the public tranquillity could not reign and last long, and that no other sure way could be found out for maintaining the balance of Europe, than a general defence, engagement, and eviction, or as they call it, a guaranty for the order of his succession, as it is settled by the imperial declaration of 1713, and received in the most serene House of Austria, his sacred Royal Majesty of Great Britain and the High and Mighty Lords the States of the United Provinces of the Netherlands, moved thereto by their ardent desire to secure the public tranquillity, and to preserve the balance of Europe, as also by a view of the terms agreed upon in the following articles, which are exceedingly well adapted to answer both purposes, do, by virtue of the present article, take upon them the general guaranty of the said order of succession, and oblige themselves to maintain it as often as there shall be occasion, against all persons whatsoever; and consequently they promise, in the most authentic and strongest manner that can be, to defend, maintain, and (as it is called) to guaranty, with all their forces, that order of succession which his Imperial Majesty has declared and established by a solemn act of the 19th April, 1713, in manner of a perpetual, indivisible, and inseparable feoffment of trust, in favour of primogeniture, for all his Majesty's heirs of both sexes; of which act there is a copy annexed at the end of this treaty: which said act was readily and unanimously received by the orders and estates of all the kingdoms, archduchies, principalities, provinces and domains, belonging by right of inheritance to the most serene House of Austria; all which have humbly and thankfully acknowledged it, and transcribed it into their public registers, as having the force of a law and pragmatic sanction, which is to subsist for ever in full force. And whereas according to this rule and order of succession, if it should please God of his mercy to give his Imperial and Catholic Majesty issue male, then the eldest of his sons, or, he being dead before, the eldest son's eldest son; and in case there be no male issue, on his Imperial and Catholic Majesty's demise, the eldest of his daughters, the most serene Archduchesses of Austria, by the order and right of seniority, which has always been indivisibly preserved, is to succeed his Imperial Majesty in all his kingdoms, provinces, and domains, in the same manner as he now possesses them; nor shall they at any time, upon any account, or for any reason whatever, be divided or separated in favour of him, or her, or them, who may be of the second, the third, or more distant branch. And this same order and indivisible right of seniority is to be preserved in all events, and to be observed in all ages; as well in his Imperial Majesty's male issue, if God grants him any, as in his Imperial Majesty's female issue, after extinction of the male heirs; or, in short, in all cases wherein the succession of the kingdoms, provinces, and hereditary dominions of the most serene House of Austria shall be called in question. For this purpose, his Majesty of Great Britain, and the High and Mighty Lords the States General of the United Provinces of the Netherlands, promise and engage to maintain him, or her, who ought to succeed according to the rule and order above set forth in the kingdoms, provinces, or domains of which his Imperial Majesty is now actually in possession; and they engage to defend the same for ever against all such as shall perhaps presume to disturb that possession in any manner whatsoever.

III. And forasmuch as it hath been often represented to his Imperial and Catholic Majesty, in terms full of friendship, on the part of his sacred royal Majesty of Great Britain, and the High and Mighty Lords the States General of the United Provinces, that there was no surer nor more speedy method for establishing the public tranquillity so long desired, than by rendering the succession of the Duchies of Tuscany, Parma, and Placentia, designed for the most serene the Infante Don Carlos, yet more secure by the immediate introduction of 6000 Spanish soldiers into the strong places of those duchies, his said Imperial and Catholic Majesty, desiring to promote the pacific views and intentions of his Britannick Majesty and the High and Mighty States General of the United Netherlands, will by no means oppose the peaceable introduction of the said 6000 Spaniards into the strong places of the Duchies of Tuscany, Parma, and Placentia, in pursuance of the abovementioned engagements entered into by his said Britannick Majesty, and by the States General. And whereas to this end, his imperial and Catholic Majesty judges the consent of the empire necessary, he promises at the same time that he will use his utmost endeavours to obtain the said consent, within the space of two months, or sooner if possible. And to obviate as readily as may be the evils which threaten the public peace, his Imperial and Catholic Majesty moreover promises, that immediately after the mutual exchange of the ratifications, he will notify the consent which he, as Head of the empire, has given to the said peaceable introduction, to the minister of the Great Duke of Tuscany, and to the minister of Parma residing at his court, or wherever else it shall be thought proper. His said Imperial and Catholic Majesty likewise promises and affirms, that he is so far from any thought of raising, or causing any hinderance, directly or indirectly, to the Spanish garrisons being admitted into the places aforesaid, that on the contrary he will interpose his good offices and authority, for removing any unexpected obstruction or difficulty that may oppose the said introduction and consequently that the 6000 Spanish soldiers may be introduced quietly, and without any delay in the manner aforesaid, into the strong places as well of the Great Duchy of Tuscany, as of the Duchies of Parma and Placentia.

IV. That therefore all the articles thus agreed to, with the irrevocable consent of the contracting parties, be so firmly and reciprocally established, and so entirely decided, that it shall not be lawful for the contracting parties to deviate from them in any wise; meaning as well those which are to be put in execution without delay, and immediately after the exchange of the ratifications, as those which ought to remain for ever inviolable.

V. Whereas for attaining to the end which the contracting parties in this treaty propose to themselves, it has been found necessary to pluck up every root of division and dissention, and therefore that the antient friendship which united the said contracting parties, may not only be renewed, but knit closer and closer every day, his Imperial Catholic Majesty promises, and, by virtue of the present article, binds himself to cause all commerce and navigation to the East-Indies to cease immediately and for ever in the Austrian Netherlands, and in all the other countries which in the time of Charles II. Catholic King of Spain, were under the dominion of Spain; and that he will, *bona fide*, act in such manner, that neither the Ostend Company, nor any other, either in the Austrian Netherlands, or in the countries which, as is abovesaid, were under the dominion of Spain in the time of the late Catholic King Charles II. shall at any time directly or indirectly contravene this rule established forever. Excepting that the Ostend Company may send, for once only, two ships, which shall sail from the said port to the East Indies, and from thence return to Ostend, where the said Company may, when they think fit, expose the merchandizes so brought from the Indies to sale. And his sacred royal Majesty of Great Britain, and the High and Mighty States General of the United Provinces, do likewise promise on their part, and oblige themselves, to make a new treaty with his Imperial Majesty without delay, concerning commerce and the rule of imposts, commonly call'd a Tariff, as far as relates to the Austrian Netherlands, and agreeable to the intention of the 26th article of the treaty, commonly called (by reason of the limits therein settled) the Barrier. And for this purpose the contracting parties shall immediately name commissioners, who shall meet at Antwerp within the space of two months, to be computed from the day of signing the present treaty, to agree together upon every thing that regards the entire execution of the said Barrier treaty, which was concluded at Antwerp the 17/7th day of November, Anno 1715, and of the convention since signed at the Hague the 11/22 day of December, 1718; and particularly to conclude a new treaty there, as has been said, concerning commerce, and the rate of imposts, as far as relates to the Austrian Netherlands, and according to the intention of the aforesaid 26th article. 'Tis moreover agreed, and solemnly stipulated, that every thing which it hath been thought fit to leave to the commissioners who are to meet at Antwerp, shall be brought to a final issue, with all the justice and integrity, as soon as possible, and in such manner that the last hand may be put to that work, at least within the space of two years.

VI. As the examination and discussion of the other points which remain to be discussed, either between the contracting parties, or any of their confederates, require much more time than can be spared in this critical situation of affairs, therefore to avoid all delays which might be too prejudicial to the common welfare, 'tis covenanted and agreed to declare mutually, that all the treaties and conventions which any of the said contracting powers have made with other princes and states, shall subsist as they now are, excepting only so far as they may be contrary to any the points regulated by the present treaty; and moreover, that all the disputes which are actually between the said contracting parties, or any of their allies, shall be amicably adjusted as soon as possible; and in the mean time the contracting parties shall mutually endeavour to prevent any of those who have differences, from having resource to arms to support their pretensions.

VII. To take away all manner of doubt from the subjects of the King of Great Britain, and the Lords the States General, touching their commerce in the kingdom of Sicily, his Imperial and Catholic Majesty has been pleased to declare, that from this time forward, they shall be treated in the same manner, and upon the same foot as they were or ought to have been treated in the time of Charles II. King of Spain of glorious memory, and as any nation in the strictest friendship has been usually treated.

VIII. There shall be included in this treaty of peace, all those who within the space of six months, after its ratifications are exchanged, shall be proposed by either party, and by common consent.

IX. This present treaty shall be approved and ratified by his Imperial and Catholic Majesty, by his sacred royal Majesty of Great Britain, and by the High and Mighty Lords the States General of the United Netherlands, and the ratifications shall be given and exchanged at Vienna, within six weeks, to be computed from the day of signing.

In witness and confirmation whereof, as well the Imperial commissioners, in quality of ambassadors extraordinary and plenipotentiaries, as the Minister of the King of Great Britain, equally furnished with full powers have signed this treaty with their own hands, and sealed it with their seals. Done at Vienna in Austria, the 16th day of March, in the year of our Lord, 1731.

(L.S.) *Eugene of Savoy.*
(L.S.) *Philip Lewis* of *Zinzendorf.*
(L.S.) *Gundacker Thomas* of *Staremberg.*
(L.S.) *Thomas Robinson.*

[Separate Articles and Declarations follow.

The guarantees in Article I shall not extend to an attack on the Emperor's domains by the Turk.

Article III in no way implies withdrawal of the guarantees of the Emperor's Italian territories contained in Article V of the Quadruple Alliance of 1718.

The succession to Parma and Placentia shall not be affected by the death of the Duke just before the conclusion of the treaty.

Great Britain and the United Provinces guarantee immediate withdrawal of the Spanish troops from the Duchies as soon as Don Carlos is secure in their peaceful possession.

A secret declaration provides that the treaty shall be signed by the government of the United Provinces within three months, their minister at Vienna not having received full powers in time to sign it on their behalf.

The Emperor will examine the grievances of the province of East Friesland and take care of the repayment of the sum borrowed by that province from the United Provinces.]

280. The Treaty of Aix-la-Chapelle, 18 October 1748

(C. Jenkinson, *Collection of Treaties* . . ., II, pp. 370–387.)

This treaty ended the War of the Austrian Succession. Its general effect was mutual restoration of conquests, leaving unsettled most of the causes for which the war had been fought.

The Definitive Treaty of Peace and Friendship, between his Britannick Majesty, *the most* Christian King, *and the* States General *of the United Provinces. Concluded at* Aix la Chapelle *the 18th Day of* October *N.S.* 1748.

In the Name of the most holy and undivided Trinity, the Father, Son, and Holy Ghost.

BE it known to all those, whom it shall or may concern, in any manner whatsoever. Europe sees the day, which Divine Providence had pointed out for the re-establishment of its repose. A general peace succeeds to the long and bloody war, which had arose between the most serene and most potent Prince George II. by the Grace of God, King of Great-Britain, France, and Ireland, Duke of Brunswick and Lunenbourg, Arch-Treasurer and Elector of the Holy Roman Empire, &c. and the most serene and most potent Princess Mary Theresia, by the Grace of God, Queen of Hungary and Bohemia, &c. Empress of the Romans, on the one part, and the most serene and most potent Prince Lewis XV. by the Grace of God, the most Christian King, on the other; as also between the King of Great-Britain, the Empress Queen of Hungary and Bohemia, and the most serene and most potent Prince Charles Emanuel III. by the Grace of God, King of Sardinia, on the one part, and the most serene and most potent Prince Philip V. by the Grace of God, King of Spain and the Indies, (of glorious memory) and after his decease, the most serene and most potent Prince Ferdinand VI. by the Grace of God, King of Spain and the Indies, on the other; in which war the high and mighty Lords the States General of the United Provinces of the Low Countries had taken part, as auxiliaries to the King of Great-Britain; and the Empress Queen of Hungary and Bohemia: and the most serene Duke of Modena, and the most serene republic of Genoa, as auxiliaries to the King of Spain. God, in his mercy, made known to all these powers, at the same time, the way which he had decreed for their reconciliation, and for the restoration of tranquility to the people, whom he had subjected to their government. They sent their ministers to Aix la Chapelle, where those of the King of Great-Britain, his most Christian Majesty, and of the States General of the United Provinces, having agreed upon preliminary conditions for a general pacification; and those of the Empress Queen of Hungary and Bohemia, of his Catholic Majesty, of the King of Sardinia, of the Duke of Modena, and of the republic of Genoa, having acceded thereunto, a general cessation of hostilities, by sea and land, happily ensued. In order to compleat, at Aix la Chapelle, the great work of a peace, equally stable and convenient for all parties, the high contracting powers have nominated, appointed, and provided with their full powers, the most illustrious and most excellent Lords their ambassadors extraordinary, and ministers plenipotentiary, *viz.*

[Here follow the names and designations of the plenipotentiaries.]

Who, after having communicated their full powers to each other, in due form, copies whereof are annexed at the end of this present treaty; and having conferred on the several objects, which their sovereigns have judged proper to be inserted, in this instrument of general pacification, have agreed to the several articles, which are as follows.

Article I.

There shall be a Christian, universal and perpetual peace, as well by sea as land, and a sincere and lasting friendship between the eight powers above-mentioned, and between their heirs and successors, kingdoms, states, provinces, countries, subjects and vassals, of what rank and condition soever they may be, without exception of places or persons. So that the high contracting powers may have the greatest attention to maintain between them and their said states and subjects, this reciprocal friendship and correspondence, not permitting any sort of hostilities to be committed, on one side or the other, on any cause, or under any pretence whatsoever; and avoiding every thing that may, for the future, disturb the union happily re-established between them; and, on the contrary, endeavouring to procure, on all occasions, whatever may contribute to their mutual glory, interests and advantage, without giving any assistance or protection, directly or indirectly, to those who would injure or prejudice any of the contracting parties.

II. There shall be a general oblivion of whatever may have been done or committed during the war, now ended. And all persons, upon the day of the exchange of the ratifications of all the parties, shall be maintained or re-established in the possession of all the effects, dignities, ecclesiastical benefices, honours, revenues, which they enjoyed, or ought to have enjoyed, at the commencement of the war, notwithstanding all dispossessions, seizures, or confiscations, occasioned by the said war.

III. The treaties of Westphalia of 1648; those of Madrid between the crowns of England and Spain, of 1667, and 1670; the treaties of peace of Nimegen of 1678, and 1679; of Ryswick of 1697; of Utrecht of 1713; of Baden of 1714; the treaty of the Triple Alliance of the Hague of 1717; that of the Quadruple alliance of London of 1718; and the treaty of peace of Vienna of 1738, serve as a basis and foundation to the general peace, and to the present treaty; and, for this purpose, they are renewed and confirmed in the best form, and as if they were herein inserted, word for word; so that they shall be punctually observed for the future in all their tenor, and religiously executed on the one side and the other; such points however, as have been derogated from in the present treaty, excepted.

IV. All the prisoners made on the one side and the other, as well by sea as by land, and the hostages required or given during the war, and to this day, shall be restored, without ransom in six weeks at latest, to be reckoned from the exchange of the ratifications of the present treaty; and it shall be immediately proceeded upon after that exchange: and all the ships of war, as well as merchant vessels, that shall have been taken since the expiration of the terms agreed upon for the cessation of hostilities at sea, shall be, in like manner, faithfully restored, with all their equipages and cargoes; and sureties shall be given on all sides for payment of the debts, which the prisoners or hostages may have contracted in the states, where they have been detained, until their full discharge.

V. All the conquests, that have been made since the commencement of the war, or which, since the conclusion of the preliminary articles, signed the 30th of April last, may have been or shall be made, either in Europe, or the East or West Indies, or in any other part of the world whatsoever, being to be restored without exception, in conformity to what was stipulated by the said preliminary articles, and by the declarations since signed; the high contracting parties engage to give orders immediately for proceeding to that restitution, as well as to the putting the most serene Infant Don Philip in possession of the states, which are to be yielded to him by virtue of the said preliminaries, the said parties solemnly renouncing, as well for themselves as for their heirs and successors, all rights and claims, by what title or pretence soever, to all the states, countries and places, that they respectively engage to restore or yield; saving, however, the reversion stipulated of the states yielded to the most serene Infant Don Philip.

VI. It is settled and agreed, that all the respective restitutions and cessions in Europe shall be entirely made and executed on all sides in the space of six weeks, or sooner if possible, to be reckoned from the day of the exchange of the ratifications of the present treaty of all the eight parties above mentioned; so that, within the same term of six weeks, the most Christian King shall restore, as well to the Empress Queen of Hungary and Bohemia, as to the States General of the United Provinces, all the conquests which he has made upon them during this war.

The Empress Queen of Hungary and Bohemia shall be put, in consequence hereof, in full and peaceable possession of all that she possessed before the present war in the Low Countries, and elsewhere, except what is otherwise regulated by the present treaty.

In the same time the Lords the States General of the United Provinces shall be put in full and peaceable possession, and such as they had before the present war, of the places of Bergen-op-Zoom and Maestricht, and of all they possessed before the said present war in Dutch Flanders, Dutch Brabant, and elsewhere:

And the towns and places in the Low Countries, the sovereignty of which belongs to the Empress Queen of Hungary and Bohemia, in which their High Mightinesses have the right of garrison, shall be evacuated to the troops of the republic, within the same space of time.

The King of Sardinia shall be in like manner, and within the same time, entirely re-established and maintained in the Duchy of Savoy, and in the county of Nice, as well as in all the states, countries, places and forts conquered, and taken from him on occasion of the present war.

The most serene Duke of Modena, and the most serene republic of Genoa, shall be also, within the same time, entirely re-established and maintained in the states, countries, places, and forts conquered and taken from them during the present war, conformably to the tenor of the 13th and 14th articles of this treaty, which relate to them.

All the restitutions and cessions of the said towns, forts and places, shall be made, with all the artillery and warlike stores, that were found there on the day of their surrender, during the course of the war, by the powers who are to make the said cessions and restitutions, and this according to the inventories which have been made of them, or which shall be delivered *bona fide*, on each side. Provided that, as to the pieces of artillery, that have been removed elsewhere to be new cast, or for other uses, they shall be replaced by the same number of the same bore, or weight in metal. Provided also, that the places of Charleroy, Mons, Athe, Oudenarde, and Menin, the outworks of which have been demolished, shall be restored without artillery. Nothing shall be demanded for the charges and expences employed in the fortifications of all the other places; nor for other public or private works, which have been done in the countries that are to be restored.

VII. In consideration of the restitutions that his most Christian Majesty, and his Catholic Majesty make, by the present treaty, either to her Majesty the Queen of Hungary and Bohemia, or to his Majesty the King of Sardinia, the duchies of Parma Placentia, and Guastalla shall, for the future, belong to the most serene Infante Don Philip, to be possessed by him and his male descendants, born in lawful marriage, in the same manner, and in the same extent, as they have been, or ought to be, possessed by the present possessors; and the said most serene Infante, or his male descendants, shall enjoy the said three duchies, conformably and under the conditions expressed in the acts of cession of the Empress Queen of Hungary and Bohemia, and of the King of Sardinia.

These acts of cession of the Empress Queen of Hungary and Bohemia, and of the King of Sardinia, shall be delivered, together with their ratifications of the present treaty, to the ambassador extraordinary and plenipotentiary of the Catholic King, in like manner as the ambassadors extraordinary and plenipotentiaries of the most Christian King and Catholic King, shall deliver, with the ratifications of their Majesties to the ambassador extraordinary and plenipotentiary of the King of Sardinia, the orders to the generals of the French and Spanish troops to restore Savoy and the county of Nice to the persons appointed by that Prince to receive them; so that the restitution of the said states, and the taking possession of the duchies of Parma, Placentia, and Guastalla, by or in the name of the most serene Infante Don Philip, may be effected within the same time, conformably to the acts of cession, the tenor whereof follows.

[The acts of cession make clear that in default of male heirs to Don Philip or in the event of his elder brother, Don Carlos, succeeding to the crown of Spain and Don Philip or one of his descendants succeeding to the throne of the Two Sicilies, the three duchies are to revert to their previous owners.]

VIII. In order to secure and effectuate the said restitutions and cessions, it is agreed, that they shall be entirely executed and accomplished on all sides, in Europe, within the term of six weeks, or sooner, if possible, to be reckoned from the day of the exchange of the ratifications of all the eight powers; it being provided, that in fifteen days after the signing of the present treaty, the Generals, or other persons, whom the high contracting parties shall think proper to appoint for that purpose, shall meet at Brussels and at Nice, to concert and agree on the method of proceeding to the restitutions, and of putting the parties in possession, in a manner equally convenient for the good of the troops, the inhabitants, and the respective countries; but so that all and each of the high contracting powers may be agreeable to their intentions, and to the engagements contracted by the present treaty, in full and peaceable possession, without any exception, of all that is to be acquired to them, either by restitution, or cession, within the said term of six weeks, or sooner if possible, after the exchange of the ratifications of the present treaty by all the said eight powers.

IX. In consideration that, notwithstanding the reciprocal engagement taken by the 18th article of the preliminaries, importing, that all the restitutions and cessions should be carried on equally, and should be executed at the same time, his most Christian Majesty engages, by the 6th article of the present treaty, to restore, within the space of six weeks, or sooner if possible, to be reckoned from the day of exchange of the ratifications of the present treaty, all the conquests which he has made in the Low Countries; whereas it is not possible, considering the distance of the countries, that what relates to America should be effected within the same time, or even to fix the time of its entire execution; his Britannick Majesty likewise engages on his part to send to his most Christian Majesty immediately after the exchange of the ratifications of the present treaty, two persons of rank and consideration, who shall remain there as hostages, till there shall be received a certain and authentic account of the restitution of Isle Royal, called Cape Breton, and of all the conquests which the arms or subjects of his Britannick Majesty may have made before, or after the signing of the preliminaries, in the East and West Indies.

Their Britannick and most Christian Majesties oblige themselves likewise to cause to be delivered, upon the exchange of the ratifications of the present treaty, the duplicates of the orders addressed to the commissaries appointed to restore, and receive, respectively whatever may have been conquered, on either side, in the said East and West Indies, agreeably to the 2d article of the preliminaries, and to the declarations of the 21st and 31st of May, and the 8th of July last, in regard to what concerns the said conquests in the East and West Indies. Provided nevertheless, that Isle Royal, called Cape Breton, shall be restored with all the artillery and warlike stores, which shall have been found therein on the day of its surrender, conformably to the inventories, which have been made thereof, and in the condition that the said place was in, on the said day of its surrender. As to the other restitutions, they shall take place conformably to the meaning of the second article of the preliminaries, and of the declarations and convention of the 21st and 31st of May, and the 8th of July last, in the condition in which things were on the 11th of June, N.S. in the West Indies, and on the 31st of October, also N.S. in the East Indies. And every thing besides shall be re-established on the foot that they were or ought to be before the present war.

The said respective commissaries, as well those for the West, as those for the East Indies, shall be ready to set out on the first advice that their Britannick and most Christian Majesties shall receive of the exchange of the ratifications, furnished with all the necessary instructions, commissions, powers, and orders, for the most expeditious accomplishment of their said Majesties intentions, and of the engagements taken by the present treaty.

X. The ordinary revenues of the countries that are to be respectively restored or yielded, and the impositions laid upon those countries for the entertainment and winter quarters of the troops, shall belong to the powers that are in possession of them, till the day of the exchange of the ratifications of the present treaty, without, however, its being permitted to proceed to any kind of execution, provided sufficient security has been given for the payment; it being always to be understood, that the forage and utensils for the troops shall be furnished till the evacuations; in consequence of which, all the powers promise and engage not to demand or exact impositions and contributions which they may have laid upon the countries, towns, and places that they have possessed during the course of the war, and which had not been paid at the time that the events of the said war had obliged them to abandon the said countries, towns, and places; all pretensions of this nature being made void by the present treaty.

XI. All the papers, letters, documents, and archives, which were in the countries, estates, towns and places which are restored, and those belonging to the countries yielded, shall be respectively, and *bona fide*, delivered or given up at the same time, if possible, as possession shall be taken, or at fartherst two months after the exchange of the ratifications of the present treaty of all the eight parties, in whatever places the said papers or documents may be, namely, those which may have been removed from the archive of the great council of Mechlin.

XII. His Majesty the King of Sardinia shall remain in possession of all that he antiently and newly enjoyed, and particularly of the acquisition which he made in the year 1743, of the Vigevanasque, a part of the Pavesan, and the county of Anghiera, in the manner as this prince now possesses them, by virtue of the cessions that have been made of them to him.

XIII. The most serene Duke of Modena, by virtue as well of the present treaty, as of his rights, prerogatives, and dignities, shall take possession six weeks, or sooner if possible, after the exchange of the ratifications of the said treaty, of all his states, places, forts, countries, effects, and revenues, and in general of all that he enjoyed before the war.

At the same time shall be likewise restored to him, his archives, documents, writings, and moveables of what nature soever they may be, as also the artillery, and warlike stores, which shall have been found in his countries, at the time of their being seized. As to what shall be wanting, or shall have been converted into another form, the just value of the things so taken away, and which are to be restored, shall be paid in ready money; which money, as well as the equivalent for the fiefs, which the most serene Duke of Modena possessed in Hungary, if they are not restored to him, shall be settled and adjusted by the respective generals or commissaries, who, according to the 8th article of the present treaty, are to assemble at Nice in fifteen days after the signature, in order to agree upon the means for executing the reciprocal restitutions and putting in possession, so that at the same time, and on the same day as the most serene Duke of Modena shall take possession of all his states, he may likewise enter into the enjoyment either of his fiefs in Hungary, or of the said equivalent, and receive the value of such things as cannot be restored to him. Justice shall also be done him, within the same time of six weeks after the exchange of the ratifications, with respect to the allodial effects of the House of Guastalla.

XIV. The most serene Republic of Genoa, as well by virtue of the present treaty, as of its rights, prerogatives, and dignities, shall re-enter into the possession, six weeks, or sooner if possible, after the exchange of the ratifications of the said treaty, of all the states, forts, places, countries, effects, of what nature soever they be, rents and revenues, that it enjoyed before the war; particularly, all and every one of the members and subjects of the said republic shall, within the aforesaid term, after the exchange of the ratifications of the present treaty, re-enter into the possession, enjoyment, and liberty of disposing of all the funds which they had in the bank of Vienna in Austria, in Bohemia, or in any other part whatsoever of the states of the Empress Queen of Hungary and Bohemia, and of those of the King of Sardinia; and the interest shall be exactly and regularly paid them, to be reckoned from the said day of the exchange of the ratifications of the present treaty.

XV. It has been settled and agreed upon between the eight high contracting parties, that for the advantage and maintenance of the peace in general, and for the tranquillity of Italy in particular, all things shall remain there in the condition they were in before the war; saving, and after, the execution of the disposi[ti]ons made by the present treaty.

XVI. The treaty of the Assiento for the trade of negroes, signed at Madrid on the 26th of March, 1713, and the article of the annual ship making part of the said treaty, are particularly confirmed by the present treaty, for the four years during which the enjoyment thereof has been interrupted, since the commencement of the present war, and shall be executed on the same footing, and under the same conditions, as they have or ought to have been executed before the said war.

XVII. Dunkirk shall remain fortified on the side of the land, in the same condition as it is at present; and as to the side of the sea, it shall remain on the footing of former treaties.

XVIII. The demands of money that his Britannick Majesty has, as Elector of Hanover, upon the crown of Spain; the differences relating to the Abb[e]y of St. Hubert; the enclaves of Hainault, and the bureaux newly established in the Low Countries; the pretensions of the Elector Palatine; and the other articles, which could not be regulated, so as to enter into the present treaty, shall be amicably adjusted immediately by the commissaries appointed for that purpose, on both sides, or otherwise, as shall be agreed on by the powers concerned.

XIX. The 5th article of the treaty of the Quadruple Alliance, concluded at London the 2d of August, 1718; containing the guaranty of the succession to the kingdom of Great Britain in the house of his Britannick Majesty now reigning, and by which every thing has been provided for, that can relate to the person who has taken the title of King of Great Britain, and to his descendents of both sexes, is expressly confirmed and renewed by the present article, as if it were here inserted in its full extent.

XX. His Britannick Majesty, as Elector of Brunswick Lunenbourg, as well for himself, as for his heirs and successors, and all the states and possessions of his said Majesty in Germany, are included and guarantied by the present treaty of peace.

XXI. All the powers interested in the present treaty, who have guarantied the Pragmatick Sanction of the 19th of April 1713, for the whole inheritance of the late Emperor Charles VI. in favour of his daughter the Empress Queen of Hungary and Bohemia, now reigning, and of her descendents for ever, according to the order established by the said Pragmatick Sanction, renew it in the best manner possible; except, however, the cessions already made, either by the said Emperor, or the said Princess, and those stipulated by the present treaty.

XXII. The dutchy of Silesia, and the county of Glatz, as his Prussian Majesty now possesses them, are guarantied to that Prince by all the powers, parties and contractors, of the present treaty.

XXIII. All the powers contracting and interested in the present treaty, reciprocally and respectively guarantee the execution thereof.

XXIV. The solemn ratifications of the present treaty, expedited in good and due form, shall be exchanged in this city of Aix la Chapelle, between all the eight parties, within the space of one month, or sooner if possible, to be reckoned from the day of its signature.

In witness whereof, we the underwritten their Ambassadors Extraordinary and Ministers Plenipotentiaries, have signed with our hands, in their name, and by virtue of our full powers, the present treaty of peace, and have caused the seals of our arms to be put thereto.

Done at Aix la Chapelle, the 18th of October, 1748.

(*Signed*)

(L.S.) *Sandwich* (L.S.) *St. Severin d'Aragon.*
(L.S.) *T. Robinson* (L.S.) *La Porte du Theil.*
(L.S.) *W. Bentinck.*
(L.S.) *G. A. Hassalaer.*
(L.S.) *J. V. Borssele.*
(L.S.) *O. Z. Van Haren.*

Separate Articles.

I. SOME of the titles made use of by the contracting powers, either in the full powers, and other acts during the course of the negociation, or in the preamble of the present treaty, not being generally acknowledged, it has been agreed, that no prejudice shall at any time result therefrom to any of the said contracting parties; and that the titles taken or omitted on either side, on account of the said negociation and of the present treaty, shall not be cited, or any consequence drawn therefrom.

II. It has been agreed and determined, that the French language made use of in all the copies of the present treaty, and which may be used in the acts of accession, shall not be made a precedent that may be alledged, or drawn into consequence, or in any manner prejudice any of the contracting powers; and that they conform themselves for the future to what has been and ought to be observed with regard to, and on the part of powers, who are used and have a right to give and receive copies of like treaties and acts in another language than the French.

The present treaty, and the accessions, which shall intervene, having still the same force and effect, as if the aforesaid practice had been therein observed: and the present separate articles shall have likewise the same force, as if they were inserted in the treaty.

In witness whereof, we the under-written ambassadors extraordinary and ministers plenipotentiaries of his Britannick Majesty, of his most Christian Majesty, and of the Lords the States General of the United Provinces, have signed the present separate articles, and caused the seals of our arms to be put thereto.

Done at Aix la Chapelle, the 18th of October, 1748. [The same signatures as on p. 929 follow.]

281. The Treaty of St. Petersburg, 30 September 1755

(*Journals of the House of Commons*, XXVII, pp. 308–310. "Translation of the Treaty, and of the Two separate and secret Articles belonging thereto, between his Majesty and the Empress of *Russia*.")

Hostilities with France were about to break out. This treaty aimed *inter alia* at the protection of Hanover from possible attack by Frederick the Great, then France's ally.

In the Name of the Holy and Undivided Trinity.

Whereas the sincere and intimate Friendship which unites his *Britannic* Majesty and her Imperial Majesty of all the *Russias*, as well as the Engagements which they contracted by the Treaty of Defensive Alliance of the Year 1742, oblige them at all times to be watchful of the public Tranquillity and their reciprocal Security: And whereas, in the present Conjuncture of Affairs, the Preservation of the General Peace, and the Defence of their respective Dominions, Rights, and Subjects, have appeared to them necessarily to require that they should be guarded against the Attacks with which they may be threatened on the Part of any Power whatever, by securing a Body of Troops capable of making a powerful Diversion in case of such Attacks: And whereas, considering the present Situation, the Contingents of the Succours stipulated by the above-mentioned Treaty, would not be sufficient for all the aforesaid Objects, his *Britannic* Majesty and her Imperial Majesty of all the *Russias* have thought proper to concert, before-hand, the farther Measures of Precaution which the general Tranquillity, and their common Interests and Security seem to demand; and, for this Purpose, they have authorized their respective Ministers; . . . who having communicated their respective full Powers, and having conferred together, have agreed on the following Articles.

Article 1.

The High Contracting Parties renew expressly, by this Convention, the Treaty of defensive Alliance concluded between them, the 11th *December* 1742, at *Moscow*, in all its Articles, and confirm the Stipulation of the Succours to be given reciprocally, as they are contained in the 4th Article of the said Treaty; which Succours shall be furnished on each Side in the Manner and on the Conditions therein expressed.[1]

Article 2.

Whereas it is declared by the 17th Article of the before-mentioned Alliance, "That if the Succours therein stipulated should not be sufficient, the Contracting Parties

[1] The 4th Article of the 1742 treaty fixed the succours at 10,000 infantry and 2,000 cavalry on the Russian and 12 ships of war of the line carrying 700 guns and 4,560 men on the British side. By the 5th Article the party attacked might demand in place of armed assistance an annual payment of 500,000 roubles from its ally.

shall then agree, without Delay, on the farther Succours to be given;" and as that would not answer the Ends proposed, and there may happen Cases which may not allow them Time to agree thereupon:

In order to obviate the Inconveniencies which would necessarily result from such a Delay, they have agreed to settle, from henceforth, and at all Events, the Means of their Defence: With this View, her Imperial Majesty of all the *Russias* has not only caused to march towards the Frontiers of *Livonia*, adjoining to *Lithuania*, but engages also to hold there as long as this Convention shall subsist, as near to those Frontiers as the Quarters will permit, a Body of her Troops, amounting to 55,000 Men; that is to say, 40,000 Infantry of her regular Troops, furnished with the necessary Artillery, and 15,000 Cavalry, composed of Three Regiments of Cuirassiers, of Twenty Companies of Horse Grenadiers, of Two Regiments of Hussars, and the Remainder of light Troops, to wit, of *Cossacks* and of *Calmucks*, each with Two Horses, as many as shall be wanting to complete these 15,000 Cavalry; so that the whole Infantry and Cavalry shall form a complete Body of 55,000 Men.

Article 3.

Her Imperial Majesty engages, moreover, to cause to be held in Readiness, during the time above specified, on the Coasts of the above-mentioned Province, Forty or Fifty Galleys, with the necessary Crews, in Condition to act on the First Order.

Article 4.

The Body of Troops and the Galleys, mentioned in the Two preceding Articles, shall not be put in Activity, but in case his *Britannic* Majesty, or any of his Allies should be attacked; and, in that Case, the General Commander in Chief of the said Corps, who, for this Purpose, shall be furnished before-hand with the Orders of her Imperial Majesty of all the *Russias*, shall march, as soon as he shall receive the Requisition on the Part of his *Britannic* Majesty, and shall make, as soon as possible, a Diversion with a Body of 30,000 Infantry, provided with the necessary Artillery, and with all the 15,000 Cavalry above-mentioned, and shall embark at the same time the other 10,000 Infantry on board the 40 or 50 Galleys, in order to make a Descent, according to the Exigence of the Case, and the Utility of the Service.

Article 5.

In case the Dominions of his *Britannic* Majesty in *Germany* should be invaded, on account of Interests which regard his Kingdoms, her Imperial Majesty declares, that she will look upon such an Invasion as a Case of the abovesaid Alliance of 1742; and that the said Dominions shall be therein comprised in this respect.

Article 6.

In Consideration of so important an Augmentation of the Succour stipulated by the Treaty of defensive Alliance above-mentioned, as also of all the other extraordinary Expences which the March and Maintenance of Troops in *Livonia*, with the Artillery and its Appurtenances, as well as the Preparations of the Galleys, may have cost, or shall still cost, his *Britannic* Majesty promises and engages to cause to be paid to her Imperial Majesty of all the *Russias* the Sum of 500,000 Pounds Sterling *per Annum*, to be reckoned from the Day when the Body of her Troops shall have passed the Frontiers of her Dominions, in Consequence of the Requisition made by his Majesty the King of *Great Britain*. This Sum shall be paid by Baron *Wolff*, Resident of *Great Britain*, in the Place where it shall be demanded, at the Rate of Ten Florins and Fifteen Stivers, current Money of *Holland*, for every Pound Sterling, and always Four Months in Advance; and the First Payment thereof shall be made the Day that this Body shall go out of the Dominions of her Imperial Majesty.

Article 7.

Whereas her Imperial Majesty of all the *Russias* is particularly interested in the Preservation of the Tranquillity of the North, and that no Innovation should happen in the Neighbourhood of her Dominions; considering also the Proximity of the Countries wherein the Diversion in question will probably be made, and the Facility her Troops will have of subsisting immediately in an Enemy's Country, she takes upon herself alone, during such a Diversion, the Subsistence and Treatment of the said Troops by Sea and Land; as also the heavy Artillery which they may have Occasion for, and of the Requisites thereto belonging.

Article 8.

Her Imperial Majesty engages to continue the Diversion to be made, and not to recall her Troops, even though she should be attacked by any other Power. On the other hand, his *Britannic* Majesty promises, that, in case her Majesty the Empress should be disturbed in the said Diversion, or should be attacked herself, his *Britannic* Majesty will furnish immediately the Succour stipulated by the Treaty of 1742.

Article 9.

In case that, contrary to all Expectation, a War should break out, his *Britannic* Majesty engages to send into the *Baltic* Sea a Squadron of his Ships of Force, suitable to the Circumstances; and the Admiral of this Squadron shall act in Concert with the Imperial *Russian* Army, as long as they shall be within Reach of each other.

Article 10.

For the Conveniency and Readiness of Correspondence, his *Britannic* Majesty shall keep with the auxiliary Body (which shall be commanded solely by the General whom her Majesty the Empress shall put at their Head, to whom also the Person who shall command the Galleys is to be subject), a Commissary, who, as well as the Admiral of the *British* Squadron, in case there should be one, shall always be invited and admitted to the General Councils of War; and shall have, moreover, Communication of every thing which may concern the common Service.

Article 11.

All the Plunder which the *Russian* Troops shall gain from the Enemy, of what Nature and Quality soever, shall be for the Advantage of those same Troops.

Article 12.

In case these auxiliary Troops should be obliged to pass, in their March, the Territories of the Republic of *Poland*, his *Britannic* Majesty takes upon himself the Care of obtaining from his *Polish* Majesty, and the Republic of *Poland*, free Passage through the said Territories.

Article 13.

This Convention shall subsist for the Space of Four Years, to be reckoned from the Day when the Ratifications of it shall be exchanged.

Article 14.

In case Peace should be made, or the Object of the Diversion to be made should cease to exist, before the Expiration of the Four Years above-mentioned, the above-said auxiliary Body shall return also before that time into the Dominions of her Imperial Majesty; and his *Britannic* Majesty consents, that, after the Return, the said Body shall enjoy Three Months of the Succour agreed on; but in case Peace should not be made before that Term, then the contracting Parties shall agree farther upon the Prolongation of this Convention.

Article 15.

The present Convention shall be ratified, and the Letters of Ratification shall be exchanged, at *St. Petersburgh*, within the Term of Two Months, or sooner, if that can be done.

In Witness whereof, we, the under-written Ministers, have made two Copies of this Convention of the same Tenor; the which, by virtue of our full Powers, we have signed, and thereto put the Seals of our Arms. Done at *St. Petersburgh* this $\frac{\text{NINETEENTH}}{\text{THIRTIETH}}$ of *September*, in the Year 1755.

C. Hanbury Williams, (L.S.)
Alexij Comte de Bestoucheff Rumin, (L.S.)
Michel Comte de Woronzow, (L.S.)

First separate and secret Article.

Whereas her Imperial Majesty of all the *Russias* has caused to be represented to his *Britannic* Majesty, that the March of the Troops, as well Infantry as Cavalry, stipulated in the Treaty signed this Day, towards the Frontiers of *Livonia*, as also the Artillery, with what belongs thereto, with which her Imperial Majesty has charged herself, and the Expence required to maintain them there during Four Years, as well as the necessary Preparations for keeping in Readiness the Galleys during the said Term, have already cost, and must still cost, great Sums of Money, over and above what would otherwise have been necessary for the ordinary Service of these Troops; in Consideration of what is above, and of the great Utility which the remaining of such a Body of Troops in the above-mentioned Province, during the Term of Four Years, will be of, and the better to enable her Imperial Majesty to supply the Expence thereof, his *Britannic* Majesty has been pleased to engage himself, and engages himself by this

Article, to furnish a Succour, at the Rate of 100,000 Pounds Sterling *per Annum*, payable each Year before-hand, to be reckoned from the Day of the Exchange of the Ratifications to the Day that, on the Requisition of his *Britannic* Majesty, this Body of *Russian* Troops shall go out of her Imperial Majesty's Dominions; for, from that Day, the abovesaid Succour of 100,000 Pounds Sterling is intirely to cease; . . .

Second separate and secret Article.

Whereas her Imperial Majesty of all the *Russias* has engaged herself, by the Treaty signed this Day, to furnish to his Majesty the King of *Great Britain* so considerable a Succour, and will consequently take a great Share in the War, if one should happen, the Two High Contracting Parties engage themselves mutually to communicate to each other, confidentially, every thing that may relate to any Negotiation with the common Enemy, and shall employ, in Concert, all their Efforts to procure themselves a Peace on honourable and advantageous Conditions, for their reciprocal Interests. . . .

282. The Convention of Westminster, 16 January 1756

(C. Jenkinson, *Collection of Treaties . . .*, III, pp. 55–60)

The motives of the British Government in signing this Convention included, as with the Treaty of St. Petersburg (No. 281), the wish to protect Hanover if war broke out with France. Frederick feared a European coalition against him. The Convention precipitated the 'diplomatic revolution'.

As the differences which have arisen in America between the King of Great Britain and the most Christian King, and the consequences of which become every day more alarming, give room to fear for the publick tranquillity of Europe; his Majesty the King of Great Britain, Elector of Brunswick Lunenbourg, &c. and his Majesty the King of Prussia, Elector of Brandenburgh, attentive to an object so very interesting, and equally desirous of preserving the peace of Europe in general, and that of Germany in particular, have resolved to enter into such measures, as may the most effectually contribute to so desirable an end; and for this purpose, they have respectively authorised their Ministers Plenipotentiary, viz. In the name and on the part of his Britannick Majesty, his Privy Counsellors, Philip Earl of Hardwicke, Chancellor of Great Britain; John Earl of Granville, President of the Council; Thomas Holles Duke of Newcastle, first Commissioner of the Treasury; Robert Earl of Holdernesse, one of the principal Secretaries of State; and Henry Fox, another of the principal Secretaries of State; and in the name, and on the part of his Prussian Majesty, the Sieur Lewis Michell his *chargé d'affaires* at the court of his Britannick Majesty; who after having mutually communicated their full powers, have agreed upon the following articles.

I. There shall be, between the said most Serene Kings, a perfect peace and mutual amity, notwithstanding the troubles that may arise in Europe, in consequence of the above-mentioned differences; so that neither of the contracting parties shall attack, or invade, directly or indirectly, the territories of the other; but, on the contrary, shall exert their utmost efforts to prevent their respective allies from undertaking any thing against the said territories in any manner whatever.

II. If, contrary to all expectation, and in violation of the peace which the high contracting parties propose to maintain by this treaty in Germany, any foreign power should cause troops to enter into the said Germany, under any pretext whatsoever; the two contracting parties shall unite their forces to punish this infraction of the peace, and maintain the tranquillity of Germany, according to the purport of the present treaty.

III. The high contracting parties renew expressly all the treaties of alliance and guaranty which actually subsist between them, and particularly the defensive alliance and mutual guaranty concluded at Westminster between their Britannick and Prussian Majesties, the 18th of November, 1742, the convention entered into between their said Majesties at Hanover the 26th of August, 1745, and the act of acceptation of his Prussian Majesty of the guaranty of his Britannick Majesty, of the 13th of October, 1746.

IV. The present treaty shall be ratified by his Majesty the King of Great Britain, and his Majesty the King of Prussia; and the letters of ratification in due form shall be delivered on both sides within the space of one month, or sooner, if possible, reckoning from the day of signing the present treaty.

In witness whereof, we the under-signed, furnished with the full powers of their Majesties the Kings of Great Britain and Prussia, have, in their names, signed the present treaty, and thereto set our seals. Done at Westminster, the sixteenth day of January, in the year of our Lord 1756.

(L.S.) HARDWICKE, C.
(L.S.) GRANVILLE, P.
(L.S.) HOLLES NEWCASTLE.
(L.S.) HOLDERNESSE.
(L.S.) H. FOX.

Secret and separate Article.

AS the convention of neutrality of the date of this day, signed by the Ministers of his Majesty the King of Great Britain, and of his Majesty the King of Prussia, furnished with the full powers necessary for that purpose, relates only to Germany; this convention must not be understood to extend to the Austrian Low Countries and their dependencies, which ought not to be considered as comprised in the present convention of neutrality, under any pretext whatsoever: the rather, as his Majesty the King of Prussia hath not, in the eighth article of the peace of Dresden, guarantied to her Majesty the Empress Queen of Hungary and Bohemia, any thing but the dominions which she possesses in Germany.

This secret and separate article shall have the same force as if it had been inserted, word for word, in the present convention of neutrality signed this day; and the ratifications of it shall be exchanged at the same time with those of the said convention.

In witness whereof, we the under-signed, furnished with the full powers of their Majesties the Kings of Great Britain and Prussia, have, in their names, signed the present secret and separate article, and thereto set our seals.

Done at Westminster, the sixteenth day of January, in the year of our Lord 1756

(L.S.) HARDWICKE, C.
(L.S.) GRANVILLE, P.
(L.S.) HOLLES NEWCASTLE.
(L.S.) HOLDERNESSE.
(L.S.) H. FOX.

DECLARATION.

IN order to prevent any disputes that might arise between their Prussian and Britannick Majesties, it is hereby declared, that as soon as his Prussian Majesty shall have taken off the attachment laid upon the Silesia debt, and caused to be paid to his Britannick Majesty's subjects what remains due to them of that debt, as well interest as principal, according to the original contract; his Britannick Majesty promises and engages, on his part, to cause to be paid to his Prussian Majesty the sum of twenty thousand pounds sterling, in full satisfaction of every claim which his said Majesty or his subjects may have against his Britannick Majesty, under any pretext whatsoever.

Done at Westminster, the sixteenth day of January, in the year of our Lord 1756.

(L.S.) LOUIS MICHELL.

283. The Treaty of Paris, 10 February 1763

(C. Jenkinson, *Collection of Treaties . . .*, III, pp. 177–191.)

George III and Bute disliked the war which they inherited and were anxious for peace at almost any price. The weakness of Bute's policy was to some extent mitigated by the resistance in the Cabinet of Grenville and Egremont. Pitt violently attacked the treaty.

In the Name of the Most Holy and Undivided Trinity, Father, Son, and Holy Ghost. So be it.

Be it known to all those whom it shall, or may, in any manner, belong,

It has pleased the Most High to diffuse the spirit of union and concord among the Princes, whose divisions had spread troubles in the four parts of the world, and to inspire them with the inclination to cause the comforts of peace to succeed to the misfortunes of a long and bloody war, which having arisen between England and France during the reign of the Most Serene and Most Potent Prince, George the Second, by the grace of God, King of Great Britain, of glorious memory, continued under the reign of the Most Serene and Most Potent Prince, George the Third, his successor, and, in its progress, communicated itself to Spain and Portugal; Consequently, the Most Serene and Most Potent Prince, George the Third, by the grace of God, King of Great Britain, France, and Ireland, Duke of Brunswick and Lunenbourg, Arch Treasurer and Elector of the Holy Roman Empire; the Most Serene and Most Potent Prince, Lewis the Fifteenth, by the grace of God, Most Christian King; and the Most Serene and Most Potent Prince, Charles the Third, by the grace of God, King of Spain and of the Indies, after having laid the foundations of peace in the preliminaries signed at Fontainbleau the third of November last; and the Most Serene and Most Potent Prince, Don Joseph the First, by the grace of God, King of Portugal and of the Algarves, after having acceded thereto, determined to compleat, without delay, this great and important work. For this purpose, the high contracting parties have named and appointed their respective Ambassadors Extraordinary and Ministers Plenipotentiary, [names and titles follow].

Who, after having duly communicated to each other their full powers, in good form, copies whereof are transcribed at the end of the present treaty of peace, have agreed upon the articles, the tenor of which is as follows:

Article I. There shall be a Christian, universal, and perpetual peace, as well by sea as by land, and a sincere and constant friendship shall be re-established between their Britannick, Most Christian, Catholick, and Most Faithful Majesties, and between their heirs and successors, kingdoms, dominions, provinces, countries, subjects, and vassals, of what quality or condition soever they be, without exception of places or of persons: So that the high contracting parties shall give the greatest attention to maintain between themselves and their said dominions and subjects this reciprocal friendship and correspondence, without permitting, on either side, any kind of hostilities, by sea or by land, to be committed from henceforth, for any cause, or under any pretence whatsoever, and every thing shall be carefully avoided which might hereafter prejudice the union happily re-established, applying themselves, on the contrary, on every occasion, to procure for each other whatever may contribute to their mutual glory, interests, and advantages, without giving any assistance or protection, directly or indirectly, to those who would cause any prejudice to either of the high contracting parties: there shall be a general oblivion of every thing that may have been done or committed before or since the commencement of the war which is just ended.

[II. Confirmation of previous treaties.]

III. All the prisoners made, on all sides, as well by land as by sea, and the hostages carried away or given during the war, and to this day, shall be restored, without ransom, six weeks, at least, to be computed from the day of the exchange of the ratifications of the present treaty, each crown respectively paying the advances which shall have been made for the subsistance and maintenance of their prisoners by the Sovereign of the country where they shall have been detained, according to the attested receipts and estimates and other authentic vouchers which shall be furnished on one side and the other. And securities shall be reciprocally given for the payment of the debts which the prisoners shall have contracted in the countries where they have been detained until their entire liberty. And all the ships of war and merchant vessels which shall have been taken since the expiration of the terms agreed upon for the cessation of hostilities by sea shall likewise be restored, *bonâ fide*, with all their crews and cargoes: and the execution of this article shall be proceeded upon immediately after the exchange of the ratifications of this treaty.

IV. His Most Christian Majesty renounces all pretensions which he has heretofore formed or might have formed to Nova Scotia or Acadia in all its parts, and guaranties the whole of it, and with all its dependencies, to the King of Great Britain: Moreover, his Most Christian Majesty cedes and guaranties to his said Britannick Majesty, in full right, Canada, with all its dependencies, as well as the island of Cape Breton, and all the other islands and coasts in the gulph and river of St. Lawrence, and in general, every thing that depends on the said countries, lands, islands, and coasts, with the sovereignty, property, possession, and all rights acquired by treaty, or otherwise, which the Most Christian King and the Crown of France have had till now over the said countries, lands, islands, places, coasts, and their inhabitants, so that the Most Christian King cedes and makes over the whole to the said King, and to the Crown of Great Britain, and that in the most ample manner and form, without restriction, and without any liberty to depart from the said cession and guaranty under any pretence, or to disturb Great Britain in the possessions above mentioned. His Britannick Majesty, on his side, agrees to grant the liberty of the Catholick religion to the inhabitants of Canada: he will, in consequence, give the most precise and most effectual orders, that his new Roman Catholick subjects may profess the worship of their religion according to the rites of the Romish church, as far as the laws of Great Britain permit. His Britannick Majesty farther agrees, that the French inhabitants, or others who had been subjects of the Most Christian King in Canada, may retire with all safety and freedom wherever they shall think proper, and may sell their estates, provided it be to the subjects of his Britannick Majesty, and bring away their effects as well as their persons, without being restrained in their emigration, under any pretence whatsoever, except that of debts or of criminal prosecutions: The term limited for this emigration shall be fixed to the space of eighteen months, to be computed from the day of the exchange of the ratifications of the present treaty.

V. The subjects of France shall have the liberty of fishing and drying on a part of the coasts of the island of Newfoundland, such as it is specified in the XIIIth article of the treaty of Utrecht; which article is renewed and confirmed by the present treaty (except what relates to the island of Cape Breton, as well as to the other islands and coasts in the mouth and in the gulph of St. Lawrence:) And his Britannick Majesty consents to leave to the subjects of the Most Christian King the liberty of fishing in the gulph of St. Lawrence, on condition that the subjects of France do not exercise the said fishery but at the distance of three leagues from all the coasts belonging to Great Britain, as well those of the continent as those of the islands situated in the said gulph of St. Lawrence. And as to what relates to the fishery on the coasts of the island of Cape Breton, out of the said gulph, the subjects of the Most Christian King shall not be permitted to exercise the said fishery but at the distance of fifteen leagues from the coasts of the island of Cape Breton; and the fishery on the coasts of Nova Scotia or Acadia, and every where else out of the said gulph, shall remain on the foot of former treaties.

VI. The King of Great Britain cedes the islands of St. Pierre and Macquelon, in full right, to his Most Christian Majesty, to serve as a shelter to the French fishermen; and his said Most Christian Majesty engages not to fortify the said islands; to erect no buildings upon them but merely for the conveniency of the fishery; and to keep upon them a guard of fifty men only for the police.

VII. In order to re-establish peace on solid and durable foundations, and to remove for ever all subject of dispute with regard to the limits of the British and French territories on the continent of America; it is agreed, that, for the future, the confines between the dominions of his Britannick Majesty and those of his Most Christian Majesty, in that part of the world, shall be fixed irrevocably by a line drawn along the middle of the River Mississippi, from its source to the river Iberville, and from thence, by a line drawn along the middle of this river, and the lakes Maurepas and Potchartrain to the sea; and for this purpose, the Most Christian King cedes in full right, and guaranties to his Britannick Majesty the river and port of the Mobile, and every thing which he possesses, or ought to possess, on the left side of the river Mississippi, except the town of New Orleans and the island in which it is situated, which shall remain to France, provided that the navigation of the river Mississippi shall be equally free, as well to the subjects of Great Britain as to those of France, in its whole breadth and length, from its source to the sea, and expressly that part which is between the said island of New Orleans and the right bank of that river, as well as the passage both in and out of its mouth: It is farther stipulated, that the vessels belonging to the subjects of either nation shall not be stopped, visited, or subjected to the payment of any duty whatsoever. The stipulations inserted in the IVth article, in favour of the inhabitants of Canada shall also take place with regard to the inhabitants of the countries ceded by this article.

VIII. The King of Great Britain shall restore to France the islands of Guadaloupe, of Mariegalante, of Desirade, of Martinico, and of Belleisle; and the fortresses of these islands shall be restored in the same condition they were in when they were conquered by the British arms, provided that his Britannick Majesty's subjects, who shall have settled in the said islands, or those who shall have any commercial affairs to settle there or in other places restored to France by the present treaty, shall have liberty to sell their lands and their estates, to settle their affairs, to recover their debts, and to bring away their effects as well as their persons, on board vessels, which they shall be permitted to send to the said islands and other places restored as above, and which shall serve for this use only, without being restrained on account of their religion, or under any other pretence whatsoever, except that of debts or of criminal prosecutions: and for this purpose, the term of eighteen months is allowed to his Britannick Majesty's subjects, to be computed from the day of the exchange of the ratifications of the present treaty; [restrictions are imposed to prevent abuse of the foregoing privilege]. . . .

IX. The Most Christian King cedes and guaranties to his Britannick Majesty, in full right, the islands of Grenada, and the Grenadines, with the same stipulations in favour of the inhabitants of this colony, inserted in the IVth article for those of Canada: And the partition of the islands called neutral, is agreed and fixed, so that those of St. Vincent, Dominico, and Tobago, shall remain in full right to Great Britain, and that of St. Lucia shall be delivered to France, to enjoy the same likewise in full right, and the high contracting parties guaranty the partition so stipulated.

X. His Britannick Majesty shall restore to France the island of Goree in the condition it was in when conquered: and his Most Christian Majesty cedes, in full right, and guaranties to the King of Great Britain the river Senegal, with the forts and factories of St. Lewis, Podor, and Galam, and with all the rights and dependencies of the said river Senegal.

XI. In the East Indies Great Britain shall restore to France, in the condition they are now in, the different factories which that Crown possessed, as well as on the coast of Coromandel and Orixa as on that of Malabar, as also in Bengal, at the beginning of the year 1749. And his Most Christian Majesty renounces all pretension to the acquisitions which he has made on the coast of Coromandel and Orixa since the said beginning of the year 1749. His Most Christian Majesty shall restore, on his side, all that he may have conquered from Great Britain in the East Indies during the present war; and will expressly cause Nattal and Tapanoully, in the island of Sumatra, to be restored; he engages farther, not to erect fortifications, or to keep troops in any part of the dominions of the Subah of Bengal. And in order to preserve future peace on the coast of Coromandel and Orixa, the English and French shall acknowledge Mahomet Ally Khan for lawful Nabob of the Carnatick, and Salabat Jing for lawful Subah of the Decan; and both parties shall renounce all demands and pretensions of satisfaction with which they might charge each other, or their Indian allies, for the depredations or pillage committed on the one side or on the other during the war.

XII. The island of Minorca shall be restored to his Britannick Majesty, as well as Fort St. Philip, in the same condition they were in when conquered by the arms of the Most Christian King; and with the artillery which was there when the said island and the said fort were taken.

XIII. The town and port of Dunkirk shall be put into the state fixed by the last treaty of Aix la Chapelle, and by former treaties. The Cunette shall be destroyed immediately after the exchange of the ratifications of the present treaty, as well as the forts and batteries which defend the entrance on the side of the sea; and provision shall be made at the same time for the wholesomeness of the air, and for the health of the inhabitants, by some other means, to the satisfaction of the King of Great Britain.

XIV. France shall restore all the countries belonging to the Electorate of Hanover, to the Landgrave of Hesse, to the Duke of Brunswick, and to the Count of La Lippe Buckebourg, which are or shall be occupied by his Most Christian Majesty's arms: the fortresses of these different countries shall be restored in the same condition they were in when conquered by the French arms; and the pieces of artillery, which shall have been carried elsewhere, shall be replaced by the same number, of the same bore, weight and metal.

XV. In case the stipulations contained in the XIIIth article of the preliminaries should not be compleated at the time of the signature of the present treaty, as well with regard to the evacuations to be made by the armies of France of the fortresses of Cleves, Wezel, Guelders, and of all the countries belonging to the King of Prussia, as with regard to the evacuations to be made by the British and French armies of the countries which they occupy in Westphalia, Lower Saxony, on the Lower Rhine, the Upper Rhine, and in all the empire; and to the retreat of the troops into the dominions of their respective Sovereigns: their Britannick and Most Christian Majesties promise to proceed, *bonâ fide*, with all the dispatch the case will permit of to the said evacuations, the entire completion whereof they stipulate before the 15th of March next, or sooner if it can be done; and their Britannick and Most Christian

Majesties farther engage and promise to each other, not to furnish any succours of any kind to their respective allies who shall continue engaged in the war in Germany.

XVI. The decision of the prizes made in time of peace by the subjects of Great Britain, on the Spaniards, shall be referred to the Courts of Justice of the Admiralty of Great Britain, conformably to the rules established among all nations, so that the validity of the said prizes, between the British and Spanish nations, shall be decided and judged, according to the law of nations, and according to treaties, in the Courts of Justice of the nation who shall have made the capture.

XVII. His Britannick Majesty shall cause to be demolished all the fortifications which his subjects shall have erected in the bay of Honduras, and other places of the territory of Spain in that part of the world, four months after the ratification of the present treaty: and his Catholick Majesty shall not permit his Britannick Majesty's subjects, or their workmen, to be disturbed or molested under any pretence whatsoever in the said places, in their occupation of cutting, loading, and carrying away logwood; and for this purpose, they may build, without hindrance, and occupy, without interruption, the houses and magazines necessary for them, for their families, and for their effects: and his Catholick Majesty assures to them, by this article, the full enjoyment of those advantages and powers on the Spanish coasts and territories as above stipulated, immediately after the ratification of the present treaty.

XVIII. His Catholick Majesty desists, as well for himself as for his successors, from all pretension which he may have formed in favour of the Guipuscoans, and other his subjects, to the right of fishing in the neighbourhood of the island of Newfoundland.

XIX. The King of Great Britain shall restore to Spain all the territory which he has conquered in the island of Cuba, with the fortress of the Havannah; and this fortress, as well as all the other fortresses of the said island, shall be restored in the same condition they were in when conquered by his Britannick Majesty's arms, provided that his Britannick Majesty's subjects who shall have settled in the said island, restored to Spain by the present treaty, or those who shall have any commercial affairs to settle there, shall have liberty to sell their lands [etc. as in article VIII].

XX. In consequence of the restitution stipulated in the preceding article, his Catholick Majesty cedes and guaranties, in full right, to his Britannick Majesty, Florida, with Fort St. Augustin, and the Bay of Pensacola, as well as all that Spain possesses on the continent of North America, to the East or to the South East of the river Mississippi. And, in general, everything that depends on the said countries and lands, with the sovereignty, property, possession, and all rights, acquired by treaties or otherwise, which the Catholick King and the Crown of Spain have had till now over the said countries, lands, places, and their inhabitants; so that the Catholick King cedes and makes over the whole to the said King and to the Crown of Great Britain, and that in the most ample manner and form. His Britannick Majesty agrees, on his side, to grant to the inhabitants of the countries above ceded, the liberty of the Catholick religion: [etc. as in article IV *mutatis mutandis*]. It is moreover stipulated, that his Catholick Majesty shall have power to cause all the effects that may belong to him, to be brought away, whether it be artillery or other things.

XXI. The French and Spanish troops shall evacuate all the territories, lands, towns, places, and castles, of his Most faithful Majesty, in Europe, without any reserve, which shall have been conquered by the armies of France and Spain, and shall restore them in the same condition they were in when conquered, with the same artillery and ammunition, which were found there: And with regard to the Portuguese Colonies in America, Africa, or in the East Indies, if any change shall have happened there, all things shall be restored on the same footing they were in, and conformably to the preceding treaties which subsisted between the Courts of France, Spain, and Portugal, before the present war.

XXII. All the papers, letters, documents, and archives, which were found in the countries, territories, towns and places that are restored, and those belonging to the countries ceded, shall be, respectively and *bonâ fide*, delivered, or furnished at the same time, if possible, that possession is taken, or, at latest, four months after the exchange of the ratifications of the present treaty, in whatever places the said papers or documents may be found.

XXIII. All the countries and territories, which may have been conquered, in whatsoever part of the world, by the arms of their Britannick and Most Faithful Majesties, as well as by those of their Most Christian and Catholick Majesties, which are not included in the present treaty, either under the title of cessions, or under the title of restitutions, shall be restored without difficulty, and without requiring any compensations.

[XXIV fixes time limits for restitutions and evacuations.]

XXV. His Britannick Majesty, as Elector of Brunswick Lunenbourg, as well for himself as for his heirs and successors, and all the dominions and possessions of his said Majesty in Germany, are included and guarantied by the present treaty of peace.

XXVI. Their sacred Britannick, Most Christian, Catholick, and Most Faithful Majesties, promise to observe sincerely and *bonâ fide*, all the articles contained and settled in the present treaty; and they will not suffer the same to be infringed, directly or indirectly, by their respective subjects; and the said high contracting parties, generally and reciprocally, guaranty to each other all the stipulations of the present treaty.

XXVII. The solemn ratifications of the present treaty, expedited in good and due form, shall be exchanged in this city of Paris, between the high contracting parties, in the space of a month, or sooner if possible, to be computed from the day of the signature of the present treaty.

In witness whereof, we the underwritten their Ambassadors Extraordinary, and Ministers Plenipotentiary, have signed with our hand, in their name, and in virtue of our full powers, the present definitive treaty, and have caused the seal of our arms to be put thereto. Done at Paris the tenth day of February, 1763.

Bedford, C.P.S.	*Choiseul, Duc*	*El Marq. de*
(L.S.)	*de Praslin.*	*Grimaldi.*
	(L.S.)	(L.S.)

[Three separate articles of a formal kind, the first two of them being printed as separate articles I and II to Anglo-French Treaty of Versailles, and several declarations are annexed to the Treaty.]

284. The Treaty of Paris, 3 September 1783, with the United States of America

(George Chalmers, *A Collection of Treaties between Great Britain and other Powers*, II (1790), pp. 528–534.)

The preliminary articles of peace with the Americans had been signed on 30 November 1782, but the Americans were pledged not to make peace without their allies. The definitive treaties were all signed on 3 September 1783. (See No. 285 for the treaty with France.)

The Definitive Treaty of Peace and Friendship, between his Britannic *Majesty, and the United States of* America. *Signed at* Paris, *the 3d of September*, 1783.

In the name of the most Holy and Undivided Trinity.

IT having pleased the Divine Providence to dispose the hearts of the most Serene and most Potent Prince George the Third, by the grace of God, King of Great Britain, France, and Ireland, Defender of the faith, Duke of Brunswic and Lunenburgh, Arch-treasurer and Prince Elector of the Holy Roman Empire, &c. and of the United States of America, to forget all past misunderstandings and differences that have unhappily interrupted the good correspondence and friendship which they mutually wish to restore; and to establish such a beneficial and satisfactory intercourse between the two countries, upon the ground of reciprocal advantages and mutual convenience, as may promote and secure to both perpetual peace and harmony; and having for this desirable end already laid the foundation of peace and reconciliation, by the provisional articles signed at Paris, on the 30th of November, 1782, by the commissioners empowered on each part; which articles were agreed to be inserted in, and to constitute, the treaty of peace, proposed to be concluded between the Crown of Great Britain and the said United States, but which treaty was not to be concluded until terms of peace should be agreed upon between Great Britain and France, and his Britannic Majesty should be ready to conclude such treaty accordingly; and the treaty between Great Britain and France having since been concluded, his Britannic Majesty and the United States of America, in order to carry into full effect the provisional articles above-mentioned, according to the tenor thereof, have constituted and appointed, that is to say, his Britannic Majesty, on his part, David Hartley, Esq: member of the parliament of Great Britain; and the said United States, on their part, John Adams, Esq; late a commissioner of the United States of America at the court of Versailles, late delegate in Congress from the state of Massachusets, and chief justice of the said state, and minister plenipotentiary of the said United States to their High Mightinesses the States General of the United Netherlands; Benjamin Franklin, Esq; late delegate in Congress from the state of Pennsylvania, president of the convention of the said state, and minister plenipotentiary from the United States of America at the court of Versailles; John Jay, Esq; late president of Congress, and chief justice of the state of New York, and minister plenipotentiary from the said United States at the court of Madrid; to be the plenipotentiaries for the concluding and signing the present definitive treaty: who, after having reciprocally communicated their respective full powers, have agreed upon and confirmed the following articles:

I. His Britannic Majesty acknowledges the said United States, *viz*. New Hampshire, Massachusets Bay, Rhode Island and Providence Plantations, Connecticut, New York, New Jersey, Pennsylvania, Delaware, Maryland, Virginia, North Carolina,

South Carolina, and Georgia, to be free, sovereign, and independent states; that he treats with them as such; and for himself, his heirs and successors, relinquishes all claims to the government, propriety, and territorial rights of the same, and every part thereof.

II. And that all disputes which might arise in future on the subject of the boundaries of the said United States may be prevented, it is hereby agreed and declared, that the following are and shall be their boundaries, *viz.* from the north-west angle of Nova Scotia, *viz.* that angle which is formed by a line drawn due north, from the source of Saint Croix river to the Highlands, along the said Highlands which divide those rivers that empty themselves into the river St. Lawrence, from those which fall into the Atlantic ocean, to the north-westernmost head of Connecticut river; thence down along the middle of that river to the forty-fifth degree of north latitude; from thence by a line due west on said latitude until it strikes the river Iroquois or Cataraquy; thence along the middle of said river into lake Ontario; through the middle of said lake, until it strikes the communication by water between that lake and lake Erie; thence along the middle of said communication into lake Erie; through the middle of said lake, until it arrives at the water-communication between that lake and lake Huron; thence along the middle of said water-communication into the lake Huron; thence through the middle of said lake to the water-communication between that lake and lake Superior; thence through lake Superior, northward of the isles Royal and Phelipeaux, to the Long Lake; thence through the middle of said Long Lake, and the water-communication between it and the Lake of the Woods, to the said Lake of the Woods; thence through the said lake to the most north-western point thereof, and from thence on a due west course to the river Mississippi; thence by a line to be drawn along the middle of the said river Mississippi, until it shall intersect the northernmost part of the thirty-first degree of north latitude:–South, by a line to be drawn due east from the determination of the line last-mentioned, in the latitude of thirty-one degrees north of the equator, to the middle of the river Apalachicola or Catahouche; thence along the middle thereof to its junction with the Flint river; thence strait to the head of St. Mary's river, and thence down along the middle of St. Mary's river to the Atlantic ocean:–East, by a line to be drawn along the middle of the river St. Croix, from its mouth in the bay of Fundy to its source; and from its source directly north to the aforesaid Highlands, which divide the rivers that fall into the Atlantic ocean from those which fall into the river St. Lawrence: comprehending all islands within twenty leagues of any part of the shores of the United States, and lying between lines to be drawn due east from the points where the aforesaid boundaries between Nova Scotia on the one part, and East Florida on the other, shall respectively touch the bay of Fundy, and the Atlantic ocean; excepting such islands as now are, or heretofore have been, within the limits of the said province of Nova Scotia.

III. It is agreed, that the people of the United States shall continue to enjoy unmolested the right to take fish of every kind on the Grand Bank and on all the other banks of Newfoundland: also in the gulph of St. Lawrence, and at all other places in the sea, where the inhabitants of both countries used at any time heretofore to fish.

And also that the inhabitants of the United States shall have liberty to take fish of every kind on such part of the coast of Newfoundland, as British fishermen shall use (but not to dry or cure the same on that island) and also on the coasts, bays, and creeks of all other of his Britannic Majesty's dominions in America; and that the American fishermen shall have liberty to dry and cure fish in any of the unsettled bays, harbours, and creeks of Nova Scotia, Magdalen islands, and Labrador, so long as the same shall remain unsettled; but so soon as the same, or either of them, shall be settled, it shall not be lawful for the said fishermen to dry or cure fish at such settlement, without a previous agreement for that purpose with the inhabitants, proprietors, or possessors of the ground.

IV. It is agreed, that creditors on either side shall meet with no lawful impediment to the recovery of the full value in sterling money of all *bonâ fide* debts heretofore contracted.

V. It is agreed, that the Congress shall earnestly recommend it to the legislatures of the respective states, to provide for the restitution of all estates, rights, and properties which have been confiscated, belonging to real British subjects: and also of the estates, rights, and properties of persons resident in districts in the possession of his Majesty's arms, and who have not borne arms against the said United States: and that persons of any other description shall have free liberty to go to any part or parts of any of the Thirteen United States, and therein to remain twelve months unmolested in their endeavours to obtain the restitution of such of their estates, rights, and properties, as may have been confiscated: and that Congress shall also earnestly recommend to the several states a re-consideration and revision of all acts or laws regarding the premises, so as to render the said laws or acts perfectly consistent, not only with justice and equity, but with that spirit of conciliation, which, on the return of the blessings of peace, should universally prevail. And that Congress shall also earnestly recommend to the several states, that the estates, rights, and properties of such last-mentioned persons shall be restored to them, they refunding to any persons who may be now in possession the *bonâ fide* price (where any has been given) which such persons may have paid on purchasing any of the said lands, rights, or properties, since the confiscation.

And it is agreed, that all persons who have any interest in confiscated lands, either by debts, marriage settlements, or otherwise, shall meet with no lawful impediment in the prosecution of their just rights.

VI. That there shall be no future confiscations made, nor any prosecutions commenced against any person or persons, for or by reason of the part which he or they may have taken in the present war; and that no person shall on that account suffer any future loss or damage either in his person, liberty, or property; and that those who may be in confinement on such charges at the time of the ratification of the treaty in America, shall be immediately set at liberty, and the prosecutions so commenced be discontinued.

VII. There shall be a firm and perpetual peace between his Britannic Majesty and the said States, and between the subjects of the one and the citizens of the other, wherefore all hostilities, both by sea and land, shall from henceforth cease: all prisoners on both sides shall be set at liberty; and his Britannic Majesty shall with all convenient speed, and without causing any destruction, or carrying away any negroes, or other property of the American inhabitants, withdraw all his armies, garrisons, and fleets from the said United States, and from every port, place, and harbour within the same; leaving in all fortifications the American artillery that may be therein: and shall also order and cause all archives, records, deeds, and papers belonging to any of the said States, or their citizens, which in the course of the war may have fallen into the hands of his officers, to be forthwith restored and delivered to the proper states and persons to whom they belong.

VIII. The navigation of the river Mississippi, from its source to the ocean, shall for ever remain free and open to the subjects of Great Britain, and the citizens of the United States.

IX. In case it should so happen that any place or territory belonging to Great Britain, or to the United States, should have been conquered by the arms of either, from the other, before the arrival of the said provisional articles in America, it is agreed that the same shall be restored without difficulty, and without requiring any compensation.

X. The solemn ratifications of the present treaty, expedited in good and due form, shall be exchanged between the contracting parties in the space of six months, or sooner, if possible, to be computed from the day of the signature of the present treaty.

In witness whereof, we, the undersigned, their ministers plenipotentiary, have in their name, and in virtue of our full powers, signed with our hands the present definitive treaty, and caused the seals of our arms to be affixed thereto.

Done at Paris, this third day of September, in the year of our Lord one thousand seven hundred and eighty-three.

(L.S.) *D. Hartley*. (L.S.) *John Adams*.
(L.S.) *B. Franklin*.
(L.S.) *John Jay*.

285. The Treaty of Versailles, 3 September 1783, with France

(George Chalmers, *A Collection of Treaties between Great Britain and other Powers*, I (1790), pp. 495–510.)

Similar treaties were concluded on the same date with Spain (at Versailles) and the United Provinces (at Paris), all these states having taken part in the War of American Independence.

The Definitive Treaty of Peace and Friendship, between his Britannic *Majesty, and the most* Christian *King; signed at* Versailles, *the 3d of* September, 1783.

In the name of the most Holy and Undivided Trinity, Father, Son, and Holy Ghost. So be it.

BE it known to all those whom it shall or may in any manner concern. The most Serene and most Potent Prince, George the Third, by the grace of God, King of Great Britain, France, and Ireland, Duke of Brunswic and Lunenburg, Arch-treasurer and Elector of the Holy Roman Empire, &c. and the most Serene and most Potent Prince, Lewis the Sixteenth, by the grace of God, most Christian King, being equally desirous to put an end to the war which for several years past afflicted their respective dominions, accepted the offer which their Majesties the Emperor of the Romans, and the Empress of all the Russias, made to them of their interposition, and of their mediation: but their Britannic and most Christian Majesties, animated with a mutual desire of accelerating the re-establishment of peace, communicated to each other their laudable intention; which Heaven so far blessed, that they proceeded to lay the foundations of peace, by signing preliminary articles at Versailles, the 20th of January, in the present year. Their said Majesties the King of Great Britain, and the most Christian King, thinking it incumbent upon them to give their Imperial Majesties a signal proof of their gratitude for the generous offer of their mediation, invited them, in concert, to concur in the completion of the great and salutary work of peace, by taking part, as mediators, in the definitive treaty to be concluded between their Britannic and most Christian Majesties. Their said Imperial Majesties having readily accepted that invitation, they have named as their representatives, . . . In consequence, their said Majesties the King of Great Britain, and the most Christian King, have named and constituted for their Plenipotentiaries, charged with the concluding and signing of the definitive treaty of peace, *viz.* the King of Great Britain, the most illustrious and most excellent Lord, George Duke and Earl of Manchester, . . .; and the most Christian King, the most illustrious and most excellent Lord, Charles Gravier, Count de Vergennes, . . .: who, after having exchanged their respective full powers, have agreed upon the following articles:

I. There shall be a Christian, universal, and perpetual peace, as well by sea as by land, and a sincere and constant friendship shall be re-established between their Britannic and most Christian Majesties, and between their heirs and successors, kingdoms, dominions, provinces, countries, subjects, and vassals, of what quality or condition soever they be, without exception either of places or persons; so that the high contracting parties shall give the greatest attention to the maintaining between themselves, and their said dominions and subjects, this reciprocal friendship and intercourse, without permitting hereafter, on either part, any kind of hostilities to be committed, either by sea or by land, for any cause, or under any pretence whatsoever; and they shall carefully avoid, for the future, every thing which might prejudice the union happily re-established, endeavouring, on the contrary, to procure reciprocally for each other, on every occasion, whatever may contribute to their mutual glory, interests, and advantage, without giving any assistance or protection, directly or indirectly, to those who would do any injury to either of the high contracting parties. There shall be a general oblivion and amnesty of every thing which may have been done or committed before or since the commencement of the war which is just ended.

II. [Confirmation of previous treaties.]

III. All the prisoners taken on either side, as well by land as by sea, and the hostages carried away or given during the war, and to this day, shall be restored, without ransom, in six weeks at latest, to be computed from the day of the exchange of the ratifications of the present treaty; each crown respectively discharging the advances which shall have been made for the subsistence and maintenance of their prisoners by the Sovereign of the country where they shall have been detained, according to the receipts and attested accounts, and other authentic vouchers, which shall be furnished on each side: and sureties shall be reciprocally given for the payment of the debts which the prisoners may have contracted in the countries where they may have been detained, until their entire release. And all ships, as well men of war as merchant-ships, which may have been taken since the expiration of the terms agreed upon for the cessation of hostilities by sea, shall likewise be restored, *bonâ fide*, with all their crews and cargoes. And the execution of this article shall be proceeded upon immediately after the exchange of the ratifications of this treaty.

IV. His Majesty the King of Great Britain is maintained in his right to the island of Newfoundland, and to the adjacent islands, as the whole were assured to him by the thirteenth article of the treaty of Utrecht; excepting the islands of St. Pierre and Miquelon, which are ceded in full right, by the present treaty, to his most Christian Majesty.

V. His Majesty the most Christian King, in order to prevent the quarrels which have hitherto arisen between the two nations of England and France, consents to renounce the right of fishing, which belongs to him in virtue of the aforesaid article of the treaty of Utrecht, from Cape Bonavista to Cape St. John, situated on the eastern coast of Newfoundland, in fifty degrees north latitude; and his Majesty the King of Great Britain consents on his part, that the fishery assigned to the subjects of his most Christian Majesty, beginning at the said Cape St. John, passing to the north, and descending by the western coast of the island of Newfoundland, shall extend to the place called Cape Raye, situated in forty-seven degrees fifty minutes latitude. The French fishermen shall enjoy the fishery which is assigned to them by the present article, as they had the right to enjoy that which was assigned to them by the treaty of Utrecht.

VI. With regard to the fishery in the gulph of St. Laurence, the French shall continue to exercise it conformably to the fifth article of the treaty of Paris.

VII. The King of Great Britain restores to France the island of St. Lucia, in the condition it was in when it was conquered by the British arms: and his Britannic Majesty cedes and guaranties to his most Christian Majesty the island of Tobago. The Protestant inhabitants of the said island, as well as those of the same religion who shall have settled in St. Lucia, whilst that island was occupied by the British arms, shall not be molested in the exercise of their worship: and the British inhabitants, or others who may have been subjects of the King of Great Britain in the aforesaid islands, shall retain their possessions upon the same titles and conditions by which they have acquired them; or else they may retire in full security and liberty, where they shall think fit, and shall have the power of selling their estates, provided it be to subjects of his most Christian Majesty, and of removing their effects, as well as their persons, without being restrained in their emigration under any pretence whatsoever, except on account of debts, or of criminal prosecutions. The term limited for this emigration is fixed to the space of eighteen months, to be computed from the day of the exchange of the ratifications of the present treaty. And for the better securing the possessions of the inhabitants of the aforesaid island of Tobago, the most Christian King shall issue letters patent, containing an abolition of the *droit d'aubaine* in the said island.

VIII. The most Christian King restores to Great Britain the islands of Grenada, and the Grenadines, St. Vincent's, Dominica, St. Christopher's, Nevis, and Montserrat; and the fortresses of these islands shall be delivered up in the condition they were in when the conquest of them was made. The same stipulations inserted in the preceding article shall take place in favour of the French subjects, with respect to the islands enumerated in the present article.

IX. The King of Great Britain cedes, in full right, and guaranties to his most Christian Majesty, the river Senegal, and its dependencies, with the forts of St. Louis, Podor, Galam, Arguin, and Portendic; and his Britannic Majesty restores to France the island of Gorée, which shall be delivered up in the condition it was in when the conquest of it was made.

X. The most Christian King, on his part, guaranties to the King of Great Britain the possession of fort James, and of the river Gambia.

XI. For preventing all discussion in that part of the world, the two high contracting parties shall, within three months after the exchange of the ratifications of the present treaty, name commissaries, who shall be charged with the settling and fixing of the boundaries of the respective possessions. As to the gum trade, the English shall have the liberty of carrying it on, from the mouth of the river St. John, to the bay and fort of Portendic inclusively. Provided that they shall not form any permanent settlement, of what nature soever, in the said river St. John, upon the coast, or in the bay of Portendic.

XII. As to the residue of the coast of Africa, the English and French subjects shall continue to resort thereto, according to the usage which has hitherto prevailed.

XIII. The King of Great Britain restores to his most Christian Majesty all the settlements which belonged to him at the beginning of the present war, upon the coast of Orixa, and in Bengal, with liberty to surround Chandernagore with a ditch for carrying off the waters: and his Britannic Majesty engages to take such measures as shall be in his power for securing to the subjects of France in that part of India, as well as on the coasts of Orixa, Coromandel, and Malabar, a safe, free, and independent trade, such as was carried on by the French East India Company, whether they exercise it individually, or united in a company.

XIV. Pondicherry shall be in like manner delivered up and guarantied to France, as also Karikal; and his Britannic Majesty shall procure, for an additional dependency to Pondicherry, the two districts of Valanour and Bahour; and to Karikal, the four Magans bordering thereupon.

XV. France shall re-enter into the possession of Mahé, as well as of its factory at Surat; and the French shall carry on their trade in this part of India conformably to the principles established in the thirteenth article of this treaty.

XVI. Orders having been sent to India by the high contracting parties, in pursuance of the sixteenth article of the preliminaries, it is further agreed, that if, within the term of four months, the respective allies of their Britannic and most Christian Majesties shall not have acceded to the present pacification, or concluded a separate accomodation, their said Majesties shall not give them any assistance, directly or indirectly, against the British or French possessions, or against the ancient possessions of their respective allies, such as they were in the year 1776.

XVII. The King of Great Britain, being desirous to give to his most Christian Majesty a sincere proof of reconciliation and friendship, and to contribute to render solid the peace re-established between their said Majesties, consents to the abrogation and suppression of all the articles relative to Dunkirk, from the treaty of peace concluded at Utrecht in 1713, inclusive, to this day.

XVIII. Immediately after the exchange of the ratifications, the two high contracting parties shall name commissaries to treat concerning new arrangements of commerce between the two nations, on the basis of reciprocity and mutual convenience; which arrangements shall be settled and concluded within the space of two years, to be computed from the first of January, in the year 1784.

XIX. All the countries and territories which may have been, or which may be conquered, in any part of the world whatsoever, by the arms of his Britannic Majesty, as well as by those of his most Christian Majesty, which are not included in the present treaty, neither under the head of Cessions, nor under the head of Restitutions, shall be restored without difficulty, and without requiring any compensation.

XX. [Fixes time limit for restitutions and evacuations.]

XXI. The decision of the prizes and seizures made prior to the hostilities shall be referred to the respective courts of justice; so that the legality of the said prizes and seizures shall be decided according to the law of nations, and to treaties, in the courts of justice of the nation which shall have made the capture, or ordered the seizures.

XXII. For preventing the revival of the law-suits which have been ended in the islands conquered by either of the high contracting parties, it is agreed, that the judgments pronounced in the last resort, and which have acquired the force of matters determined, shall be confirmed and executed according to their form and tenor.

XXIII. Their Britannic and most Christian Majesties promise to observe sincerely, and *bonâ fide*, all the articles contained and established in the present treaty; and they will not suffer the same to be infringed, directly or indirectly, by their respective subjects: and the said high contracting parties guaranty to each other, generally and reciprocally, all the stipulations of the present treaty.

XXIV. The solemn ratifications of the present treaty, prepared in good and due form, shall be exchanged in this city of Versailles, between the high contracting parties, in the space of a month, or sooner if possible, to be computed from the day of the signature of the present treaty.

In witness whereof, we the under-written Ambassador Extraordinary and Ministers Plenipotentiary have signed with our hands, in their names, and in virtue of our respective full powers, the present definitive treaty, and have caused the seals of our arms to be affixed thereto.

Done at Versailles, the third day of September, one thousand seven hundred and eighty-three.

Manchester. (L.S.) *Gravier de Vergennes.* (L.S.)

Separate Articles.

I. SOME of the titles made use of by the contracting parties, whether in the full powers, and other instruments, during the course of the negotiation, or in the preamble of the present treaty, not being generally acknowledged, it has been agreed, that no prejudice should ever result therefrom to either of the said contracting parties; and that the titles taken or omitted on either side, upon occasion of the said negotiation, and of the present treaty, shall not be cited, or quoted as a precedent.

II. It has been agreed and determined, that the French language, made use of in all the copies of the present treaty, shall not form an example which may be alledged or quoted as a precedent, or in any manner prejudice either of the contracting Powers; and that they shall conform for the future to what has been observed, and ought to be observed, with regard to, and on the part of Powers, who are in the practice and possession of giving and receiving copies of like treaties in a different language from the French; the present treaty having, nevertheless, the same force and virtue as if the aforesaid practice had been therein observed.

In witness whereof, we the under-written Ambassador Extraordinary and Ministers Plenipotentiary of their Britannic and most Christian Majesties, have signed the present separate articles, and have caused the seals of our arms to be affixed thereto.

Done at Versailles, the third of September, one thousand seven hundred and eighty-three.

Manchester. (L.S.) *Gravier de Vergennes.* (L.S.)

Declaration.

THE King having entirely agreed with his most Christian Majesty upon the articles of the definitive treaty, will seek every means which shall not only insure the execution thereof, with his accustomed good faith and punctuality, but will besides give, on his part, all possible efficacy to the principles which shall prevent even the least foundation of dispute for the future.

To this end, and in order that the fishermen of the two nations may not give cause for daily quarrels, his Britannic Majesty will take the most positive measures for preventing his subjects from interrupting, in any manner, by their competition, the fishery of the French, during the temporary exercise of it which is granted to them upon the coasts of the island of Newfoundland; and he will, for this purpose, cause the fixed settlements, which shall be formed there, to be removed. His Britannic Majesty will give orders that the French fishermen be not incommoded, in cutting the wood necessary for the repair of their scaffolds, huts, and fishing-vessels.

The thirteenth article of the treaty of Utrecht, and the method of carrying on the fishery, which has at all times been acknowledged, shall be the plan upon which the fishery shall be carried on there; it shall not be deviated from by either party; the French fishermen building only their scaffolds, confining themselves to the repair of their fishing-vessels, and not wintering there; the subjects of his Britannic Majesty, on their part, not molesting in any manner the French fishermen during their fishing, nor injuring their scaffolds during their absence.

The King of Great Britain, in ceding the islands of St. Pierre and Miquelon to France, regards them as ceded for the purpose of serving as a real shelter to the French fishermen, and in full confidence that these possessions will not become an object of jealousy between the two nations; and that the fishery between the said islands and that of Newfoundland shall be limited to the middle of the channel.

With regard to India, Great Britain having granted to France every thing that can ascertain and confirm the trade which the latter requires to carry on there, his Majesty relies with confidence on the repeated assurances of the court of Versailles, that the power of surrounding Chandernagore with a ditch for carrying off the waters, shall not be exercised in such a manner as to make it become an object of umbrage.

The new state in which commerce may perhaps be found in all parts of the world, will demand revisions and explanations of the subsisting treaties; but an entire abrogation of those treaties, in whatever period it might be, would throw commerce into such confusion as would be of infinite prejudice to it.

In some of the treaties of this sort, there are not only articles which relate merely to commerce, but many others which insure reciprocally to the respective subjects, privileges, facilities for conducting their affairs, personal protections, and other advantages, which are not, and which ought not to be of a changeable nature, such as the regulations relating merely to the value of goods and merchandize, variable from circumstances of every kind.

When therefore the state of the trade between the two nations shall be treated upon, it is requisite to be understood, that the alterations which may be made in the subsisting treaties are to extend only to arrangements merely commercial; and that the privileges and advantages, mutual and particular, be not only preserved on each side, but even augmented, if it can be done.

In this view, his Majesty has consented to the appointment of commissaries on each side, who shall treat solely upon this object.

In witness whereof, we his Britannic Majesty's Ambassador Extraordinary and Minister Plenipotentiary, being thereto duly authorized, have signed the present declaration, and caused the seal of our arms to be set thereto.

Given at Versailles, the third of September, one thousand seven hundred and eighty-three.

(L.S.) *Manchester.*

Counter-Declaration

THE principles which have guided the King in the whole course of the negotiations which preceded the re-establishment of peace, must have convinced the King of Great Britain, that his Majesty has had no other design than to render it solid and lasting, by preventing, as much as possible, in the four quarters of the world, every subject of discussion and quarrel. The King of Great Britain undoubtedly places too much confidence in the uprightness of his Majesty's intentions, not to rely upon his constant attention to prevent the islands of St. Pierre and Miquelon from becoming an object of jealousy between the two nations.

As to the fishery on the coasts of Newfoundland, which has been the object of the new arrangements settled by the two Sovereigns upon this matter it is sufficiently ascertained by the fifth article of the treaty of peace signed this day, and by the declaration likewise delivered to-day, by his Britannic Majesty's Ambassador

Extraordinary and Plenipotentiary; and his Majesty declares that he is fully satisfied on this head.

In regard to the fishery between the island of Newfoundland, and those of St. Pierre and Miquelon, it is not to be carried on, by either party, but to the middle of the channel; and his Majesty will give the most positive orders, that the French fishermen shall not go beyond this line. His Majesty is firmly persuaded that the King of Great Britain will give like orders to the English fishermen.

The King's desire to maintain the peace comprehends India as well as the other parts of the world; his Britannic Majesty may therefore be assured, that his Majesty will never permit that an object so inoffensive and so harmless as the ditch with which Chandernagore is to be surrounded, should give any umbrage to the court of London.

The King, in proposing new arrangements of commerce, had no other design than to remedy, by the rules of reciprocity and mutual convenience, whatever may be defective in the treaty of commerce signed at Utrecht, in one thousand seven hundred and thirteen. The King of Great Britain may judge from thence, that his Majesty's intention is not in any wise to cancel all the stipulations in the above-mentioned treaty; he declares, on the contrary, from henceforth, that he is disposed to maintain all the privileges, facilities, and advantages expressed in that treaty, as far as they shall be reciprocal, or compensated by equivalent advantages. It is to attain this end, desired on each side, that commissaries are to be appointed to treat upon the state of the trade between the two nations, and that a considerable space of time is to be allowed for compleating their work. His Majesty hopes that this object will be pursued with the same good faith, and the same spirit of conciliation, which presided over the discussion of all the other points comprized in the definitive treaty; and his said Majesty is firmly persuaded that the respective commissaries will employ the utmost diligence for the completion of this important work.

In witness whereof, we the under-written Minister Plenipotentiary of his most Christian Majesty, being thereto duly authorized, have signed the present counter-declaration, and have caused the seal of our arms to be affixed thereto.

Given at Versailles, the third of September, one thousand seven hundred and eighty-three.

(L.S.) *Gravier de Vergennes.*

WE, Ambassador Plenipotentiary of his Imperial and Royal Apostolic Majesty, having acted as mediator in the work of pacification, declare that the treaty of peace signed this day at Versailles, between his Britannic Majesty and his most Christian Majesty, with the two separate articles thereto annexed, and of which they form a part, as also with all the clauses, conditions, and stipulations, which are therein contained, was concluded by the mediation of his Imperial and Royal Apostolic Majesty. In witness whereof, we have signed these presents with our hand, and have caused the seal of our arms to be affixed thereto. Done at Versailles, the third of September, one thousand seven hundred and eighty-three.

(L.S.) *Le Comte de Mercy Argenteau.*

[A similar declaration by the Russian mediators follows.]

Appendices

Appendix I

PRINCIPAL OFFICIALS, 1715–1783

Archbishops of Canterbury

1715 (Since 1695) Thomas Tenison
1716 William Wake
1737 John Potter
1747 Thomas Herring
1757 Matthew Hutton
1758 Thomas Secker
1768 Frederick Cornwallis
1783 John Moore (till 1805)

Archbishops of York

1714 William Dawes
1724 Lancelot Blackburne
1743 Thomas Herring
1747 Matthew Hutton
1757 John Gilbert
1761 Robert Hay Drummond
1777 William Markham (till 1807)

Bishops of London

1714 John Robinson
1723 Edmund Gibson
1748 Thomas Sherlock
1761 Thomas Hayter
1762 Richard Osbaldeston
1764 Richard Terrick
1777 Robert Lowth (till 1787)

Lord Chancellors, Lord Keeper, and Commissioners of the Great Seal

Sept. 1714 Lord Cowper
April 1718 Sir Robert Tracey, Sir John Pratt, Sir James Montague, Commissioners
May 1718 Lord Macclesfield
Jan. 1725 Sir Joseph Jekyll, Sir Geoffrey Gilbert, Sir Robert Raymond, Commissioners
June 1725 Lord King
Nov. 1733 Lord Talbot
Feb. 1737 Lord Hardwicke
Nov. 1756 Sir John Willes, Sir S. Smythe, Sir J. Eardley Wilmot, Commissioners
June 1757 Sir Robert Henley (Lord Henley, 1760), Lord Keeper
Jan. 1761 Lord Henley (earl of Northington, 1764), Lord Chancellor
July 1766 Lord Camden
Jan. 1770 Hon. Charles Yorke (died 20 Jan.)
Jan. 1770 Sir S. Stafford Smith, Hon. Henry Bathurst, Sir Richard Aston, Commissioners
Jan. 1771 Lord Apsley (formerly Hon. Henry Bathurst)
June 1778 Lord Thurlow
April 1783 Lord Loughborough, Sir William Ashurst, Sir Beaumont Hotham, Commissioners
Dec. 1783 Lord Thurlow

First Commissioners of the Treasury

Oct. 1714	Earl of Halifax
May 1715	Earl of Carlisle
Oct. 1715	Robert Walpole
April 1717	Viscount Stanhope
Mar. 1718	Earl of Sunderland
April 1721	Sir Robert Walpole
Feb. 1742	Earl of Wilmington
Aug. 1743	Hon. Henry Pelham
10–12 Feb. 1746	Earl of Bath
Feb. 1746	Hon. Henry Pelham
Mar. 1754	Duke of Newcastle
Nov. 1756	4th duke of Devonshire
8–12 June 1757	Earl Waldegrave
June 1757	Duke of Newcastle
May 1762	Earl of Bute
April 1763	George Grenville
July 1765	Marquess of Rockingham
July 1766	Earl of Chatham
Oct. 1768	3rd duke of Grafton
Jan. 1770	Lord North
Mar. 1782	Marquess of Rockingham
July 1782	Earl of Shelburne
April 1783	Duke of Portland
Dec. 1783	William Pitt

Chancellors of the Exchequer

Oct. 1714	Sir Richard Onslow
Oct. 1715	Robert Walpole
April 1717	Viscount Stanhope
Mar. 1718	John Aislabie
Jan. 1721	Sir John Pratt, C.J.K.B.
April 1721	Sir Robert Walpole
Feb. 1742	Samuel Sandys
Aug. 1743	Hon. Henry Pelham
Mar. 1754	Sir William Lee
April 1754	Hon. Henry Bilson Legge
Nov. 1755	Sir George Lyttelton
Nov. 1756	Hon. H. B. Legge
April 1757	Lord Mansfield, C.J.K.B.
July 1757	Hon. H. B. Legge
Mar. 1761	Viscount Barrington
May 1762	Sir Francis Dashwood
April 1763	George Grenville
July 1765	William Dowdeswell
Aug. 1766	Charles Townshend
Sept. 1767	Lord Mansfield, C.J.K.B.
Oct. 1767	Lord North
April 1782	Lord John Cavendish
July 1782	William Pitt
April 1783	Lord John Cavendish
Dec. 1783	William Pitt

Lords President of the Council

Sept. 1714	Earl of Nottingham (Earl of Winchilsea and Nottingham, 1730)
July 1716	2nd duke of Devonshire
April 1717	Earl of Sunderland
Feb. 1719	Duke of Kingston
June 1720	Viscount Townshend
April 1721	Lord Carleton
Mar. 1725	2nd duke of Devonshire
May 1730	Lord Trevor
Dec. 1730	Earl of Wilmington
Feb. 1742	Lord Harrington
Jan. 1745	Duke of Dorset
June 1751	Earl Granville
Sept. 1763	Duke of Bedford
July 1765	Earl of Winchilsea and Nottingham
July 1766	Earl of Northington
Dec. 1767	Earl Gower
Nov. 1779	Lord Bathurst
Mar. 1782	Lord Camden
April 1783	Viscount Stormont
Dec. 1783	Earl Gower

Lords Privy Seal

Sept. 1714	Marquess of Wharton
April 1715	Edward Southwell Christopher Musgrave Andrew Charlton Commissioners
Sept. 1715	Earl of Sunderland
Dec. 1716	Duke of Kingston
Feb. 1719	Duke of Kent
June 1720	Duke of Kingston
Mar. 1726	Lord Trevor
May 1730	Earl of Wilmington
Jan. 1731	Abraham Stanyan Robert Jackson 3rd duke of Devonshire Commissioners
June 1731	3rd duke of Devonshire
May 1733	Viscount Lonsdale
May 1735	Earl of Godolphin
April 1740	Lord Hervey
July 1742	Lord Gower
Dec. 1743	Earl of Cholmondeley
Dec. 1744	Lord Gower
10–12 Feb. 1746	Earl of Carlisle
13 Feb. 1746	Lord Gower (1st earl, July 1746)
Jan. 1755	Duke of Marlborough
Dec. 1755	2nd Earl Gower
June 1757	Earl Temple
Oct. 1761	William Sharpe Jeremiah Dyson Commissioners
Nov. 1761	Duke of Bedford
April 1763	Duke of Marlborough
July 1765	Duke of Newcastle
July 1766	Earl of Chatham. In commission for a short time in Feb. 1768, Chatham taking office again in Mar. 1768.
Nov. 1768	Earl of Bristol
Feb. 1770	Earl of Halifax
Jan. 1771	12th earl of Suffolk
June 1771	Duke of Grafton
Nov. 1775	Earl of Dartmouth
Mar. 1782	Duke of Grafton
April 1783	Earl of Carlisle
Dec. 1783	Duke of Rutland

Secretaries of State

Southern Department		*Northern Department*	
Sept. 1714	James Stanhope	Sept. 1714	Viscount Townshend
Dec. 1716	Paul Methuen	Dec. 1716	James Stanhope
April 1717	Joseph Addison	April 1717	Earl of Sunderland
Mar. 1718	James Craggs	Mar. 1718	(James) Viscount Stanhope
Mar. 1721	Lord Carteret	Feb. 1721	Viscount Townshend
April 1724	Duke of Newcastle		
		June 1730	Lord Harrington
		Feb. 1742	Earl Granville (Carteret)
		Nov. 1744	Earl of Harrington
10 Feb. 1746	Earl Granville	10 Feb. 1746	Earl Granville
12 Feb. 1746	Duke of Newcastle	12 Feb. 1746	Earl of Harrington
		Oct. 1746	Earl of Chesterfield
Feb. 1748	Duke of Bedford	Feb. 1748	Duke of Newcastle
June 1751	Earl of Holderness		
Mar. 1754	Sir Thomas Robinson	Mar. 1754	Earl of Holderness (resigned 9, reappointed 27 June 1757)
Nov. 1754	Henry Fox		
Dec. 1756	William Pitt (to 6 April 1757)		
June 1757	William Pitt		

Southern Department

Oct. 1761 Earl of Egremont
Sept. 1763 Earl of Halifax
July 1765 Henry Seymour Conway
May 1766 Duke of Richmond
July 1766 Earl of Shelburne
Oct. 1768 Viscount Weymouth
Dec. 1770 Earl of Rochford
Nov. 1775 Viscount Weymouth
Nov. 1779 Viscount Hillsborough

Northern Department

Mar. 1761 Earl of Bute
May 1762 George Grenville
Oct. 1762 Earl of Halifax
Sept. 1763 Earl of Sandwich
July 1765 Duke of Grafton
May 1766 H. S. Conway
Jan. 1768 Viscount Weymouth
Oct. 1768 Earl of Rochford
Dec. 1770 Earl of Sandwich
Jan. 1771 Earl of Halifax
June 1771 12th earl of Suffolk
Oct. 1779 Viscount Stormont

In 1782 the Secretariat was reorganized.

Secretary of State for Home Affairs

Mar. 1782 Earl of Shelburne
July 1782 Thomas Townshend
April 1783 Lord North
19 Dec. 1783 Earl Temple
23 Dec. 1783 Lord Sydney (Thomas Townshend)

Secretary of State for Foreign Affairs

Mar. 1782 Charles James Fox
July 1782 Lord Grantham
April 1783 Charles James Fox
19 Dec. 1783 Earl Temple
23 Dec. 1783 Marquess of Carmarthen

First Lords of the Admiralty

1714 Earl of Orford
1717 Earl of Berkeley
1727 Viscount Torrington
1733 Sir Charles Wager
1742 Earl of Winchilsea and Nottingham
1744 Duke of Bedford
1748 Earl of Sandwich
1751 Lord Anson
1756 Earl Temple
1757 (April–July) Earl of Winchilsea and Nottingham
1757 Lord Anson
1762 Earl of Halifax
1763 (Jan.) George Grenville
1763 (April) Earl of Sandwich
1763 (Sept.) Earl of Egmont
1766 (Sept.) Sir Charles Saunders
1766 (Dec.) Sir Edward Hawke
1771 Earl of Sandwich
1782 Hon. Augustus Keppel (1st Viscount Keppel, 1782)
1783 (Jan.) Viscount Howe
1783 (April) Viscount Keppel
1783 (Dec.) Viscount Howe

First Lords of Trade and Plantations

1714 Lord Berkeley of Stratton
1715 6th earl of Suffolk
1718 Earl of Holderness
1719 Earl of Westmorland
1735 Earl Fitzwalter
1737 Lord Monson
1748 Earl of Halifax
1761 Samuel Sandys
1763 (Mar.) Hon. Charles Townshend
1763 (April) Earl of Shelburne
1763 (Sept.) Earl of Hillsborough

1765 Earl of Dartmouth
1766 (Aug.) Earl of Hillsborough
1766 (Dec.) Robert Nugent
1768 Earl of Hillsborough
1772 Earl of Dartmouth
1775 Lord George Germain
1779 Earl of Carlisle
1780 Lord Grantham

(The office was suppressed by Burke's Act, 1782; revived in 1784.)

Secretary of State for American Colonies

1768 Earl of Hillsborough
1772 Earl of Dartmouth
1775 Lord George Germain
1782 Welbore Ellis

(The office was suppressed by Burke's Act, 1782.)

Paymasters-General of the Forces

1714 Robert Walpole
1715 Earl of Lincoln
1720 Robert Walpole
1721 Lord Cornwallis
1722 Hon. Spencer Compton
1730 Hon. Henry Pelham
1743 Sir Thomas Winnington
1746 William Pitt
1755 Earl of Darlington
Viscount Dupplin
1757 Henry Fox
1765 Hon. Charles Townshend
1766 Lord North, George Cooke
1767 George Cooke, Thomas Townshend
1768 Richard Rigby
1782 (Mar.) Edmund Burke
1782 (July) Isaac Barré
1783 Edmund Burke

Secretaries at War

1714 William Pulteney
1717 James Craggs, Jun.
1718 (Mar.) Lord Castlecomer
1718 (May) Robert Pringle
1724 Hon. Henry Pelham
1730 Sir William Strickland
1735 Sir William Yonge
1746 Henry Fox
1755 Viscount Barrington
1761 Hon. Charles Townshend
1762 Welbore Ellis
1765 Viscount Barrington
1778 Charles Jenkinson
1782 (Mar.) Thomas Townshend
1782 (July) Sir George Yonge
1783 (April) Col. Hon. Richard Fitzpatrick
1783 (Dec.) Sir George Yonge

Treasurers of the Navy

1714 John Aislabie
1718 Richard Hampden
1720 Sir George Byng
(Viscount Torrington, 1721)
1724 Hon. Pattee Byng
1734 Arthur Onslow
1742 (May) Hon. Thomas Clutterbuck
1742 (Dec.) Sir Charles Wager
1743 Sir John Rushout
1744 George Bubb Dodington
1749 Hon. Henry Bilson Legge
1754 George Grenville
1756 George Bubb Dodington
1762 Viscount Barrington
1765 Viscount Howe
1770 Sir Gilbert Elliot
1777 Welbore Ellis
1782 (April) Isaac Barré
1782 (Aug.) Henry Dundas
1783 Charles Townshend

Chief Justices

King's Bench

1714 (Since 1710) Lord Macclesfield
1718 Sir John Pratt
1725 Sir Robert Raymond (Lord Raymond, 1731)
1733 Sir Philip Yorke (Lord Hardwicke, 1754)
1737 Sir William Lee
1754 Sir Dudley Ryder (Lord Ryder, 1754)
1756 Lord Mansfield (till 1788)

Common Pleas

1714 Sir Peter King
1725 Sir Robert Eyre
1736 Sir Thomas Reeve
1737 Sir John Willes
1762 Sir Charles Pratt (Lord Camden, 1765)
1766 Sir John Eardley-Wilmot
1771 Sir William De Grey
1780 Alexander Wedderburne (till 1793) (Lord Loughborough, 1780)

Chief Barons of the Exchequer

1714 Sir Samuel Dodd
1716 Sir Thomas Bury
1722 Sir James Montague
1723 Sir Robert Eyre
1725 Sir Geoffrey Gilbert
1726 Sir Thomas Pengelly
1730 Sir James Reynolds
1738 Sir John Comyns
1740 Sir Edmund Probyn
1742 Sir Thomas Parker
1772 Sir Sydney Stafford Smythe
1777 Sir John Skynner (till 1786)

Masters of the Rolls

1714 (Since 1693) Sir John Trevor
1717 Sir Joseph Jekyll, M.P.
1738 Hon. John Verney
1741 William Fortescue
1750 Sir John Strange, M.P.
1754 Sir Thomas Clarke, M.P.
1764 Sir Thomas Sewell (till 1784)

Attorneys-General

1714 (Since 1710) Sir Edward Northey
1718 Sir Nicholas Lechmere
1720 Sir Robert Raymond
1724 Sir Philip Yorke
1734 Sir John Willes
1737 Sir Dudley Ryder
1754 Hon. William Murray (Lord Mansfield, 1756)
1756 Sir Robert Henley
1757 Sir Charles Pratt (Later Lord Camden)
1762 Hon. Charles Yorke
1763 Sir Fletcher Norton
1765 Hon. Charles Yorke
1766 William De Grey
1771 Edward Thurlow
1778 Alexander Wedderburne
1780 James Wallace
1782 (April) Lloyd Kenyon (Lord Kenyon, 1788)
1783 James Wallace (died Nov.)
1783 (Nov.) John Lee
1783 (Dec.) Lloyd Kenyon

Speakers of the House of Commons

1713 Sir Thomas Hanmer
1715 Hon. Spencer Compton
1728 Arthur Onslow
1761 Sir John Cust
1770 Sir Fletcher Norton
1780 Charles Wolfran Cornewall

SCOTLAND

Secretaries of State for Scotland

Sept. 1714 Duke of Montrose (dismissed Aug. 1715)
Dec. 1716 Duke of Roxburgh (dismissed Aug. 1725)
Feb. 1742 Marquess of Tweeddale (resigned Jan. 1746)

(Office discontinued till the nineteenth century.)

Lords President of the Court of Session

1714 (Since 1707) Sir Henry Dalrymple
1737 Duncan Forbes of Culloden
1748 Robert Dundas of Arniston
1754 Robert Craigie of Glendoich
1760 Robert Dundas of Arniston (the 2nd) (till 1787)

Lords Advocate

1714 (Since 1709) Sir David Dalrymple
1720 Robert Dundas of Arniston (the 1st)
1725 Duncan Forbes of Culloden
1737 Charles Erskine of Tinwald
1742 Robert Craigie of Glendoich
1746 William Grant of Prestongrange
1754 Robert Dundas of Arniston (the 2nd)
1760 Thomas Miller of Glenlee
1766 James Montgomery
1775 Henry Dundas
1783 Hon. Henry Erskine

IRELAND

Lords Lieutenant of Ireland

Oct. 1714 Earl of Sunderland
Feb. 1717 Viscount Townshend
April 1717 Duke of Bolton
Aug. 1720 2nd duke of Grafton
Oct. 1724 Lord Carteret
June 1730 Duke of Dorset
Sept. 1737 3rd duke of Devonshire
Jan. 1745 Earl of Chesterfield
Nov. 1746 Earl of Harrington
Sept. 1751 Duke of Dorset
May 1755 Marquess of Hartington (4th duke of Devonshire, 1755)
Sept. 1757 Duke of Bedford
April 1761 Earl of Halifax
April 1763 Earl of Northumberland
June 1765 Viscount Weymouth
Aug. 1765 Earl of Hertford
Oct. 1766 Earl of Bristol
Aug. 1767 Viscount Townshend
Oct. 1772 Earl of Harcourt
Dec. 1776 Earl of Buckinghamshire
Nov. 1780 Earl of Carlisle
April 1782 Duke of Portland
Aug. 1782 Earl Temple
May 1783 Earl of Northington

Lord Chancellors

1714 Alan Brodrick (Viscount Midleton)
1725 Richard West
1726 Thomas Wyndham
1739 Robert Jocelyn
1757 John Bowes
1767 James Hewitt (till 1789)

Archbishops of Armagh

1714 Thomas Lindsay
1724 Hugh Boulter
1742 John Hoadly
1747 George Stone
1765 Richard Robinson (till 1795) (Lord Rokeby)

Archbishops of Dublin

1714 (Since 1703) William King
1729 John Hoadly
1742 Charles Cobb
1765 Hon. William Carmichael
1766 Arthur Smythe
1772 John Craddock
1778 Robert Fowler (till 1801)

Speakers of the Irish House of Commons

1715 William Conolly
1729 Sir Ralph Gore
1733 Henry Boyle (Earl of Shannon)
1756 John Ponsonby
1769 Edmund Sexton Pery (till 1784)

Appendix

TABLE I. THE EN

Possible claimants by descent at t

(Taken from *Cambridge Modern History*. XIII. Ta

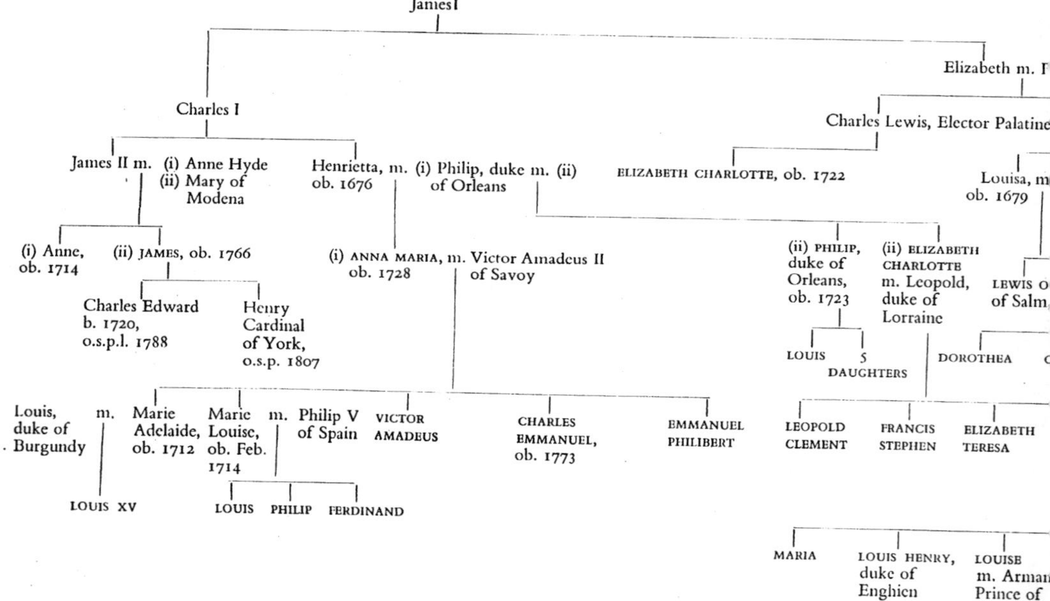

ogical Tables

SUCCESSION 1714.

Queen Anne's death are in capitals

and H. Tayler, *The Old Chevalier*, Table p. 179.)

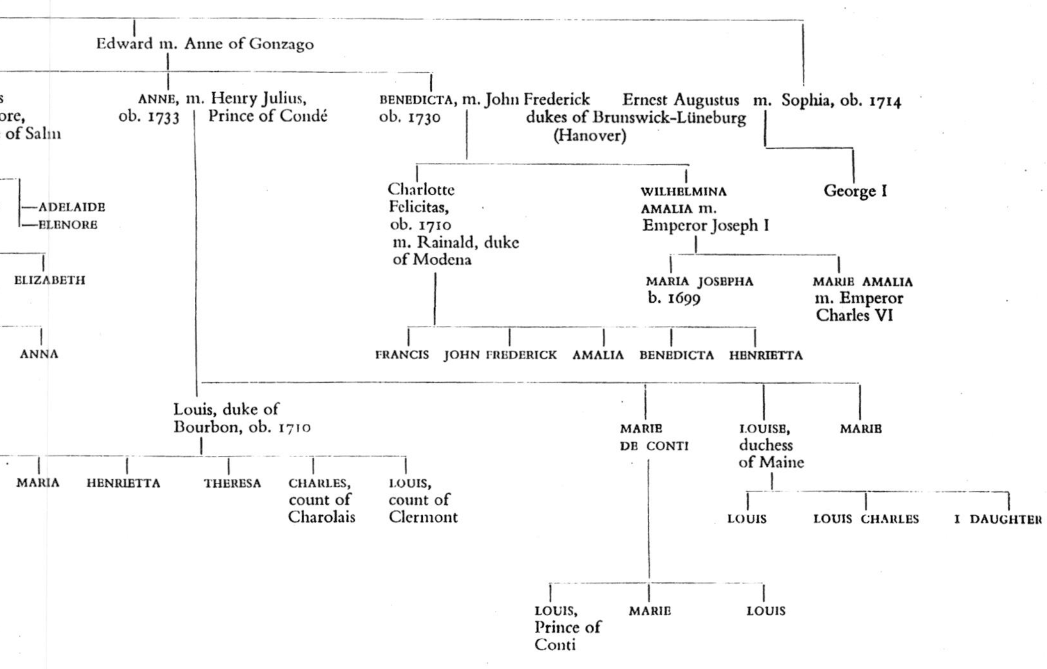

TABLE II. THE HOUSE OF HANOVER, 1714–1783.

Showing its connexions with the Protestant dynasties of Western Europe.

(Constructed with some minor modifications and additions from H. B. George, *Genealogical Tables illustrative of Modern History*, ed. J. R. H. Weaver, 1930, Table IX.)

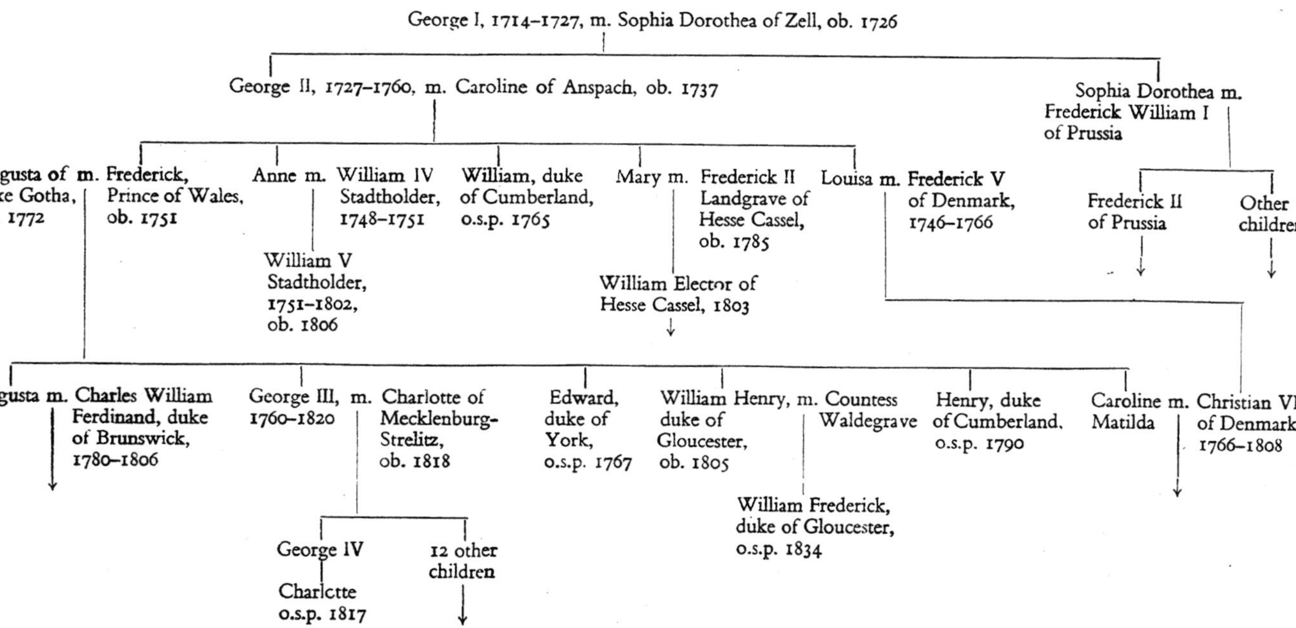

INDEX TO TEXTS

The figures refer to the numbered documents, not to the pages. Anonymous pamphlets are listed under their titles, and also under the heading 'Anonymous': newspapers and periodicals are grouped under the heading 'Newspapers'; Acts of Parliament under 'Statutes', and legal cases under 'Cases'.